W9-CJW-526

Burt Franklin: Research & Source Works Series #168

TEUFFEL'S

HISTORY OF ROMAN LITERATURE.

VOL. I.

THE REPUBLICAN PERIOD.

TEUFFEL'S

HISTORY OF ROMAN LITERATURE.

REVISED AND ENLARGED

BY

LUDWIG SCHWABE.

AUTHORISED TRANSLATION FROM THE FIFTH GERMAN EDITION,

BY

GEORGE C. W. WARR, M.A.,

VOL. I.

THE REPUBLICAN PERIOD.

Burt Franklin: Research & Source Works Series #168

Burt Franklin
New York, N. Y.

Published By
BURT FRANKLIN
235 East 44th St.
New York, N.Y. 10017

ORIGINALLY PUBLISHED
LONDON: 1892

Reprinted 1967

This work has been reprinted on
long-life paper.

Printed in U.S.A.

PREFACE.

THE *Geschichte der römischen Literatur*, the principal work of the late Wilhelm Sigmund Teuffel, differed from previous histories in its wider range and scope. It was carried from the earliest period down to, and beyond, the sixth century A.D., the literary history of that century being exhaustively treated, with such notice of the minor writers as was needed to present the greater in their true light. Jurisprudence, natural philosophy, and the other technical subjects were included, and its proper literary place was assigned to the Christian as an integral part of the Roman literature. Another special aim of the writer, as explained in his preface, was to make the most of all the fragmentary remains, and to estimate each constituent of the whole by its intrinsic worth and weight apart from the accidents of tradition. And, finally, he claimed to have maintained an unprejudiced and thoroughly impartial stand-point in his criticism—the justice of which claim his readers well understand.

The book was published in 1870. It was considerably enlarged by the author in two subsequent editions (1872 and 1874), in the prefaces to which he acknowledges the assistance of M. Hertz, F. A. Eckstein, L. Müller, E. Wölfflin, H. Nolte, W. Weissbrodt, and of Dr. L. Schwabe, his colleague in the University of Tübingen.

Prof. Teuffel, who died in 1878, left his work in the hands of the last-named scholar. Dr. Schwabe, in discharge of that trust, republished it in 1882, revised throughout in accordance with the latest researches, and much augmented. The additions and alterations were too important to be thrown into separate notes. The Editor preferred to incorporate his own work in the text, which he modified as he deemed necessary, here and there cancelling the author's statements. This method of editing (he explains in his first preface) was facilitated by what he regards as a characteristic merit of Teuffel's writing, its perfect definiteness and objectivity of view—the reverse of the vague rhetoric which pervades most books concerned with the history of literature.

In his new edition (1890) Dr. Schwabe has further expanded and still more freely recast the original History. In so doing, however, he has continually adhered to the strict chronological plan laid down by the author, though in his own opinion it is not necessarily the best for elucidating the general movement of literature and the interdependence of its different branches. He records in the preface the continued assistance which has been rendered by Prof. Hertz. In the preparation of the previous edition he was aided by F. H. Reusch (in the sections on the Patristic literature) and A. v. Gutschmid (who revised the sections on the historians of the Imperial period); in the preparation of the present edition, by R. Förster, L. Havet, O. Keller, W. Meyer, and especially by his colleague O. Crusius.

An English translation was made, with the author's sanction, by the late Dr. Wilhelm Wagner, from the first German edition —with addenda (incomplete) from the second—and published by Messrs. Bell in 1873. This is retained throughout as the basis of the present translation. But in incorporating the author's additions, together with the larger additions and improvements which the work has acquired under Dr. Schwabe's able editorship, I have likewise revised the translation itself, with so much alteration as appeared requisite to make it more completely accurate, and (I hope) more uniformly idiomatic and readable.

In the bibliographical sections I have occasionally added to the list of editions and treatises, chiefly English.

As regards orthography, I have retained the usual Romanized spelling for Greek names of localities, while I have followed the German edition in writing Greek personal names without exception as in Greek (keeping *y* as the proper representative of *upsilon*). It is particularly convenient in a history of Roman literature that the Greek writers should be thus kept distinct from the Roman.

I have adopted the spelling "Vergil" instead of "Virgil," whereas Dr. Schwabe retains the latter side by side with "Vergilius." The juxtaposition of the true and false spelling is obviously awkward, and the latter appears to be fast retreating, at any rate from scholastic literature, in England and America.

With these few exceptions the translation, as it now stands, corresponds in all points with the latest German edition. The typographical improvements, which distinguish that edition from the fourth, have also been reproduced, *e.g.* the printing of the quotations in italics.

G. C. W. WARR.

KING'S COLLEGE, LONDON, *December*, 1890.

CONTENTS OF VOL. I.

Part I.—*GENERAL VIEW OF THE SUBJECT.*

Part II.—*SPECIAL AND PERSONAL.*

I.—THE EARLY HISTORY OF ROMAN LITERATURE, to the Year u.c. 514–b.c. 240.

II.—HISTORY OF ROMAN LITERATURE.

Part I.—The Time of the Republic and of Augustus.

First Period: *from Andronicus to the time of Sulla, A.* 514/240–670/84.

A. The Sixth Century u.c.

ABBREVIATIONS.

Ber. MBer. SBer. = Berichte, Monatsberichte, Sitzungsberichte (reports, monthly reports, sessional reports) of the philosophical and historical Faculties of the Academies at Berlin, Munich, Vienna and of the sächs. Gesellschaft der Wissenschaften at Leipzig. BerlphWschr. = Berliner philologische Wochenschrift. BlfdbayrG. = Blätter für das bayerische Gymnasialschulwesen. Herm. = Hermes, Zeitschrift für klassische Philologie. JB. = Jahresbericht über die Fortschritte der klass. Altertumswissenschaft. JJ. = Neue Jahrbücher f. Philol. u. Pädagogik (the [old] Jahrbücher f. Philol. u. Pädag. are distinguished by the addition of the year). JJ. Arch. = Archiv für Philologie (edited by JChrJahn and others). JJ. Suppl. = Supplementbände zu den Jahrbb. für Philol. u. Pädag. (edited by AFleckeisen). NArchfädG. = Neues Archiv der Gesellschaft für ältere deutsche Geschichtskunde. Phil. = Philologus, Zeitschrift für das klassische Altertum. RhM. = Rheinisches Museum für Philologie, new series (the [old] Rhein. Mus. is distinguished by the addition of the year). WschrfklPh. = Wochenschrift für klassische Philologie. ZfAW. = Zeitschrift für die Altertumswissenschaft. ZfGW. = [Berliner] Zeitschrift für das Gymnasialwesen. ZföG. = Zeitschr. für die österreichischen Gymnasien. ZfRG. = Zeitschrift für Rechtsgeschichte, Zeitschrift d. Savigny-Stiftung für Rechtsgeschichte, Romanistiche Abteilung.

AL. = Anthologia Latina, rec. ARiese, see § 31, 4. Chatelain = EChatelain, paléographie des classiques Latins. CIL. = Corpus inscriptionum latinarum, see § 40, 1. DIE. = Dialectorum italicarum exempla selecta ed. ESchneider I, Lpz. 1886. AEbert, LdMA. = his Allgem. Gesch. der Literatur des Mittelalters im Abendlande. FPR. = Fragmenta poetarum Romanorum, coll. et em. EBährens, see § 19, 4. GL. = Grammatici latini ex recensione HKeilii, see § 41, 6. Migne = his Cursus patrologiae (latinae) completus. Orelli (Or.-Henzen) = his Collection of inscriptions, see § 40, 2. PLM. = Poetae latini minores, rec. et emend. EBährens, Lpz. 1879–83 V (the numbers are those of the volume and page. Wernsdorf's PLM. distinguished by the addition of the name). PM. = Priscae latinitatis monumenta, ed. Ritschl, see § 40, 1 l. 5. PRE. = Pauly's Realencyclopädie der klass. Alterthumswissenschaft. Wilm. = GWillmanns' Collection of inscriptions, see § 40, 2. Wordsw. EL. = JWordsworth, Fragments and specimens of early Latin, see § 61, 2.

Numbers to which § is prefixed refer to the Sections of the book.

PART I:

GENERAL VIEW OF THE SUBJECT.

1. The Romans lacked the versatility, manysidedness and imaginative power of the Greeks; their eminent qualities are sober and acute thought, and firmness and perseverance of will. Their intellect was directed to the practical, and sometimes degenerated into egotism and cunning, just as their perseverance often turned into obstinacy and pedantry. In the domain of state and law these qualities accomplished great and enduring results, while they were decidedly unfavourable to art and literature.

1. Cic. Tusc. 1, 2 *quae tanta gravitas, quae tanta constantia, magnitudo animi, probitas, fides, quae tam excellens in omni genere virtus in ullis fuit, ut sit cum maioribus nostris comparanda?* (3) *doctrina Graecia nos et omni litterarum genere superabat* etc. De imp. Pomp. 60 *maiores nostros semper in pace consuetudini, in bello utilitati paruisse.* Cf. Plin. NH. 25, 4. Tac. dial. 5 *si ad utilitatem vitae omnia consilia factaque nostra dirigenda sunt.* Quintil. 12, 2, 7 *ego illum quem instituo romanum quendam velim esse sapientem, qui non secretis disceptationibus, sed rerum experimentis atque operibus vere civilem virum exhibeat.*

2. Varro RR. 1, 2, 2 *vetus proverbium: Romanus sedendo vincit.* Liv. 23, 14, 1 *insita (Romanorum) animis industria.* Liv. 42, 62 *romana constantia*, cf. 30, 7 and Polyb. 3, 75 extr. 27, 8 *ἴδιον τοῦτο πάντῃ παρὰ Ῥωμαίοις ἔθος καὶ πάτριόν ἐστι, τὸ κατὰ μὲν τὰς ἐλαττώσεις αὐθαδεστάτους καὶ βαρυτάτους φαίνεσθαι, κατὰ δὲ τὰς ἐπιτυχίας ὡς μετριωτάτους.* ib. 1, 39 *ὄντες ἐν παντὶ φιλότιμοι διαφερόντως.*

3. Fronto epist. p. 135 Nab. *putem, quia reapse nemo est Romae φιλόστοργος, ne nomen quidem huic virtuti esse romanum.* The *romana simplicitas* (e.g. in Martial. 11, 20, 10 and Symmach. epist. 7, 123; cf. Hor. S. 1, 3, 52) is frequently much less plainness than coarseness. Of the Romana fides also (Liv. 5, 27, 11; cf. *more romano* in Cic. ad fam. 7, 5, 3. 16, 3. 18, 3) the other nations formed a peculiar opinion. Liv. 9, 11, 7 *semper aliquam fraudi speciem iuris imponitis.* Plut. Crass. 31.

4. The younger Africanus ap. Macr. sat. 3, 14, 7 *eunt in ludum histrionum, discunt cantare, quae maiores nostri ingenuis probro ducier voluerunt.* ib. 10 *Cato,*

cui . . . etiam cantare non serii hominis videtur. SEN. contr. 1, praef. 8 *cantandi saltandique obscena studia.* TAC. dial. 10 *in Graecia, ubi ludicras quoque artes exercere honestum est.* All occupations without immediate practical tendency are *artes leviores* (CIC. Brut. 3) and *mediocres* (CIC. de or. 1, 6), *studia leviora* (CIC. de or. 1, 212. Cat. 50) and *minora* (CIC. Brut. 70). It is only when the practical occupations are no longer possible that the others also become *optimae artes* (CIC. fam. 7, 3, 4).

2. As long as the peculiar character of the Roman nation remained unaltered, literary occupation was thought admissible only so far as it was of practical value. It is true that the importance of eloquence as a means of political influence, the value of information in regard to events that had taken place, and the importance of jurisprudence were recognised at an early time; but the oldest historians shrank from the difficulty of moulding their still unschooled native tongue into a literary language, and wrote in Greek. All other fields of knowledge were all the more neglected; poetry was tolerated only for the purposes of worship, and during a long time limited to a single species. The earliest poets were foreigners, little respected in their inferior position, and thus doubly hindered in their influence. Only in the course of the 6th century U.C. the increased acquaintance with Greek life and literature produced new ideas, interests, and requirements.

1. CIC. Planc. 66 *M. Catonis illud . . . clarorum hominum atque magnorum non minus otii quam negotii rationem exstare oportere.* The same Cato ap. GELL. 11, 2, 5 says in praise of ancient Rome: *poeticae artis honos non erat.* FESTUS 333 *scribas proprio nomine antiqui et librarios et poetas vocabant.* The literary activity of the elder Cato sufficiently shows what branches of literature were held admissible. He feared ὡς ἀποβαλοῦσι Ῥωμαῖοι τὰ πράγματα γραμμάτων ἑλληνικῶν ἀναπλησθέντες (PLUT. Cato mai. 23). CIC. Tusc. 1, 1–6 gives a sketch of the part taken by the Romans in literature.

2. MHERTZ, Schriftsteller u. Publikum in Rom, Berl. 1853. LFRIEDLÄNDER, Sittengesch. Roms 3[5], 329.—Concerning the Roman book-trade, which took a considerable start only in the time of Cicero, and flourished specially during the first centuries of the Empire, see THBIRT, antikes Buchwesen 357. LHÄNNY, Schriftsteller u. Buchhändler in Rom, Zürich 1884. Cf. § 172, 1. 219, 21.

3. A significant result of the conservative and practical tendency of that part of the literature which may be called typically Roman is found in the great number and importance of the works intended to form introductions to the various departments of public life. In this isagogic literature the works of the elder Cato and many of those of Varro are specially prominent. But Q. Cicero's treatise de petitione consulatus and Frontinus de aquis also belong to this class. LMERCKLIN, d. isagogischen Schriften d. Röm., Philol. 4, 413. OJAHN, on Roman encyclopaedias, Ber. d. sächs. Ges. d. W. 1850, 263.

4. General works on the history of Roman literature: IAFABRICIUS, Bibliotheca Latina, Hamb. 1697 (best edited by IAERNESTI, Lps. 1773. 74 III); bibl.

Lat. mediae et infimae aetatis, Hamb. 1734–46 VI (last ed. Flor. 1858 VI). IN Funccius, de origine et pueritia, de adolescentia, de virili aetate, de imminente senectute, de vegeta senectute, de inerti ac decrepita senectute linguae Lat., Giessen etc. 1720 sqq. VI.—GBernhardy, Grundriss d. röm. Literatur, Halle[5] 1872. JCh FBähr, Gesch. d. röm. Literatur, Carlsruhe[4] 1868–70 III; with 3 suppl. I: die christl. Dichter u. Geschichtschreiber, Carlsr.[2] 1872; II: d. Theologie u.d. Rechtsquellen, Carlsr. 1837; III: d. röm. Lit. im karoling. Zeitalter, Carlsr. 1840. Cf. § 345, 1. For the literature of the Republic see also the sections relating thereto in ThMommsen's röm. Geschichte.—EHübner, Grundriss zu Vorless. üb. d. röm. Lit.-Gesch. Berl.[4] 1878.—EMunk-OSeyffert, Gesch. d. röm. Lit. für Gymn. usw., Berlin 1875. 77 II.—GASimcox, History of Latin Literature from Ennius to Boethius, London, 1883 II.

3. Of the various kinds of poetry, dramatic poetry seems after all to be most in conformity with the character of the Roman people. Like all Italians, the Romans possessed a quick eye for all peculiarities of outward appearance, the talent of close observation, lively imitation and quick repartee. Hence it comes that improvisation and songs of a jocular and abusive character, poetical dialogues and amoebaean ditties are found in Italy at a very remote date.

1. Histories of Latin poetry: ORibbeck, Gesch. der röm. Dichtung I Dichtung der Republik, Stuttg. 1887. MPatin, études sur la poésie lat. Par.[2] 1875. II. WYSellar, the Roman poets of the Republic,[2] Lond. 1881.

2. Specimens of *italum acetum* (Hor. S. 1, 7, 32; cf. *maledica civitas*, Cic. Cael. 38; *Romanorum facetiae*, Trebell. Gallien. 9) are furnished by the numerous surnames which were originally nicknames taken from corporal peculiarities; see Quint. 1, 4, 25. EHübner in IwMüller's Handb. d. Altertumswiss. 1, 515. This quality was further developed by the political and legal quarrels of subsequent times. Cf. Cic. de or. 2, 216. Quint. 6, 3, 1.

3. The *occentationes* were prohibited in the XII tables on punishment of flogging.—Plaut. Aul. 3, 2, 31 *te iam . . . pipulo hic differam ante aedes.*—For the satirical songs on the triumphator, see § 84.—The custom is described by Suet. Vesp. 19 *in funere Favor archimimus personam eius* (i.e. Vespasiani) *ferens imitansque, ut est mos, facta ac dicta vivi.*—The amoebaean form prevails in the songs of the fratres arvales, the Fescennine songs, the songs used in the triumphs, songs of beggars (Schol. Hor. E. 1, 17, 48), shepherds' songs (Verg. ecl. 3, 59; as at the present day: cf. AHolm, Gesch. Sicil. 2, 306). A certain liking for dialogue long prevails in Roman literature, e.g. in the instance of the jurist Junius Brutus (§ 132, 2), and C. Curio (§ 153, 6). Its popularity appears e.g. from the inscription of Aesernia (colloquy between a hostess and guest), CIL 9, 2689.

4. On festive occasions merry performances of this kind took place even in public to the accompaniment of a tibia and with dancing. The actors were disguised, in accordance with the fondness of Southern nations for mummery, their faces being painted or masked. There was only a small step from the

farcical representation of an actual event to exhibiting a fictitious action, in which the plot was invented and set down, but the detail of the execution left to the performers. Popular performances of this kind were the Fescennine songs, the Saturae, the Mimi, and later on the Atellanae.

1. VERG. G. 2, 385 *Ausonii . . . coloni versibus incomptis ludunt risuque soluto oraque corticibus sumunt horrenda cavatis*, etc. (TIBULL. 2, 1, 55 *agricola . . . minio suffusus . . . rubenti primus inexperta duxit ab arte choros* of a Greek character.) Cf. MOMMSEN, RG. 1[6], 222.

5. The name of the Fescenninae is derived from the Faliscan town of Fescennium in the South of Etruria, though they belong in general to central Italy. They made part of rustic merrymakings, being performed on occasions of rejoicing, the performers indulging in mutual abuse and coarse jokes etc. Though this custom was originally also practised on rustic festivals (e.g. at harvest-time, and the festivals of Tellus and Silvanus), it was gradually confined to narrower limits and restricted to weddings. When, after the downfall of the Republic, the Fescenninae were drawn into the domain of artistic poetry, they retained their scoptic character and continued to be used at weddings.

1. KZELL, Ferienschrr. 2, 121. OMÜLLER, Etrusker 2[2], 296. RKLOTZ, lat. Lit.-Gesch. 1, 292. WCORSSEN, Origines poes. 124. ATHBROMAN, de versibus fesc., Upsala 1852. AROSSBACH, röm. Ehe (1853) 340.—FESTUS in PAUL. 85 *Fescennini versus, qui canebantur in nuptiis, ex urbe Fescennina dicuntur allati, sive ideo dicti quia fascinum putabantur arcere.* The immediate connection of the name with the name of the town should not be denied, witness the grammatical formation of the word and the analogy of the Atellanae. Cf. *acies Fescennina* VERG. Aen. 7, 695 and from the neighbourhood of *Fescennium* e.g. *Arretium -tini*, *Clusium -sini*, *Crustumium -mini*, *Sutrium -trini.* The derivation from *fascinum* (which reappears in RIBBECK, Gesch. d. röm. Dicht. 1, 9) is upset by the linguistic difficulties.

2. HOR. E. 2, 1, 139 *agricolae prisci . . . condita post frumenta levantes tempore festo corpus et ipsum animum . . . Tellurem porco, Silvanum lacte piabant, floribus et vino Genium . . .* (145) *Fescennina per hunc inventa licentia morem versibus alternis* (cf. SEN. Med. 108) *opprobria rustica fudit, libertasque recurrentes accepta per annos lusit amabiliter, donec iam saevus apertam in rabiem coepit verti iocus* etc. LIV. 7, 2, 7 *non . . . fescennino versu similem incompositum temere ac rudem alternis iaciebant.* LUCAN. 2, 368 *non soliti lusere sales nec more sabino excepit tristis convicia festa maritus.* MACR. sat. 3, 14, 9 *M. Cato senatorem non ignobilem Caecilium . . . Fescenninum vocat*, probably on account of his habit of *ridicularia fundere, iocos dicere* (ib.) Cf. FEST. 344 v. spatiator.

3. CATULL. 61, 122 *ne diu taceat* (at a wedding) *procax fescennina locutio.* SEN. Med. 107 *concesso iuvenes ludite iurgio. hinc illinc iuvenes mittite carmina. rara est in dominos iusta licentia.* ib. 113 *festa dicax fundat convicia fescenninus, solvat turba*

iocos. SEN. contr. 7, 21, 12 *inter nuptiales fescenninos* (so PLIN. NH. 15, 86; cf. SERV. Aen. 7, 695 *Fescennium oppidum est, ubi nuptialia inventa sunt carmina*) *in crucem generi nostri iocabantnr.* AUSON. opusc. 28 (cento nupt.) p. 145 Sch. *fescenninos amat celebritas nuptialis verborumque petulantiam notus vetere instituto ludus admittit.* SYMMACH. or. pro patre 13, p. 335 S. CLAUDIAN. Fescenn. 4, 29 *ducant pervigiles carmina tibiae permissisque iocis turba licentior exsultet tetricis libera legibus.* APOLL. SID. ep. 1, 5 in fin. (of Ricimer's wedding) *cum per omnia theatra. . . . Talasio fescenninus explicaretur.* DRACONT. 6, 71. 8, 644. 10, 288.

4. Catullus' first epithalamium (61) is an imitation (v. 122 sqq.) of the national custom. For the Fescenninae of Annianus the Faliscan see § 353, 3. Of Claudianus we possess de nuptiis Honorii Aug. et Mariae fescennina (4 poems in different metres). On the other hand see MACR. sat. 2. 4, 21 *temporibus triumviralibus Pollio, cum fescenninos* (satirical poems) *in eum Augustus scripsisset, ait: at ego taceo. non est enim facile in eum scribere qui potest proscribere.*

5. The original metre of the Fescenninae, as far as they may have been at all metrical, was no doubt the Saturnian line. The Fescenninae never made their way to the stage. The passage in DIOMED. GL. 1. 479, 13, where Fescenninus appears to be mentioned as another name for the creticus (– ⏑ –) is corrupt.

6. In the Saturae the dramatic element seems to have prevailed from the beginning. Most likely they were merry performances of the country clowns of Latium, separate songs or comic stories, recited with gesticulation and dancing to the accompaniment of a tibia, more varied in their occasions and subjects than the Fescenninae. They belonged to the popular festivities, and when in the year 390/364 a public stage was erected at Rome, they were also enacted on it by wandering mountebanks. Later on, when regular dramas in the Greek fashion were established among the public entertainments, they were joined to them and thus gradually came to be looked upon as farces or after-plays (exodia), though this place was afterwards occupied by the Atellanae.

1. With regard to the saturae all is obscure and uncertain. Something may be gathered from the expression *saturas agere* (LIV. 7. 2, 7 *impletas modis saturas descripto iam ad tibicinem cantu motuque congruenti peragebant*), the adaptation to the stage and transition to the sense of exodia; see LIV. 7. 2, 11 *iuventus histrionibus fabellarum actu relicto ipsa inter se more antiquo ridicula intexta versibus iactitare coepit; quae exodia postea appellata . . . sunt.*

2. Derivation of the name. DIOMED. GL. 1, 485 *satira dicta sive a Satyris, quod similiter in hoc carmine ridiculae res pudendaeque dicuntur, quae velut a Satyris proferuntur et fiunt; sive satura a lance, quae referta variis multisque primitiis in sacro apud priscos dis inferebatur et a copia ac saturitate rei satura vocabatur . . .; sive a quodam genere farciminis, quod multis rebus refertum saturam dicit Varro vocitatum . . . alii autem dictam putant a lege satura, quae uno rogatu multa simul conprehendat, quod scilicet et satura carmine multa simul poemata conprehenduntur.* Most probably the term passed from a ritualistic use (*lanx satura*) to the legislative sphere (*imperium per saturam dare, aliquid in* [*per*] *saturam ferre, aedilem per*

saturam facere, sententias per saturam exquirere) and was transferred thence to the literary sphere. With *satura* (from *satur*) a substantive has to be supplied in every case (*lanx*, *lex*), *fabula* of course with the literary *satura*. Cf. also the Ital. farsa, prop. stuffing, mixture.—For attempts to connect *satura* with the Greek Σάτυροι see DIOMEDES l.l., MOMMSEN RG 1[6], 28. 222. 457, recently OKELLER, Phil. 45, 390 and RIBBECK, röm. Dicht. 1, 9. The last-named supposes the sense of 'the well-filled' to have been derived, but at a very early time, from *satura* 'the goat-play' of the *saturi* 'goats,' because the latter were filled with meat and drink: this is improbable, regard being had to the antiquity, meaning and use of the words *satur* (found even in the chant of the Arvales), *saturare*, *saturitas*, *saturio; satis*, *satietas*, *satias* etc. See also § 28.—*Satura* as a designation of comedies by Naevius (see however § 95, 7), Quinctius Atta, Pomponius.

3. The principal reference for the development of the drama among the Romans: LIV. 7, 2 (evidently full of arbitrary conclusions, see OJAHN, Herm. 2, 224.)—A wooden stage (scena, σκηνή) was erected in the Circus for performances for the amusement of the people (by Etruscan dancers to the flute, etc.) in the year 390/364. This new arrangement was no doubt connected with the remodelling and prolongation of the chief Roman festival (the *Ludi Romani*), which had been carried out shortly before (388/366); MOMMSEN RG. 1[6], 457. FEST. 326 *scenicos* (*ludos*) *primum fecisse C.* ⟨*Ati-?*⟩ *lium*, *M. Popilium M. f.* (*cos.* 395/359) ⟨*curules*⟩ *aediles memoriae* ⟨*prodiderunt*⟩ *historici*. A starting-point was thus given for a regular theatre, such as was commenced by Andronicus 120 years later. After the introduction of a regular book for the play, adopted from the Greek, the old songs to a tibia may have still been used for filling up the intervals, while the farcical performances, in like manner as the Greek Satyr-drama, were added after the serious performances which were in accordance with the rules of art.

4. Exodium denotes the conclusion of a performance (compare VARRO in Nonius 27 *Socrates . . . in exodio vitae; vitae cursum . . . ab origine ad exodium adductae; ut ad exodium ducas*), especially a merry farce acted after a serious play; cf. PLUT. Crass. 33 εἰς τοιοῦτό φασιν ἐξόδιον τὴν Κράσσου στρατηγίαν, ὥσπερ τραγῳδίαν, τελευτῆσαι. Cf. Pelopid. 34 τὴν ταφὴν, οἷον τραγῳδίας μεγάλης, τῆς τυραννίδος ἐξόδιον θεατρικὸν γενομένην. SCHOL. Iuv. 3, 175 *exodiarius apud veteres in fine ludorum intrabat, qui ridiculus foret, ut quidquid lacrimarum atque tristitiae, quae exissent ex tragicis affectibus, huius spectaculi risus detergeret. exodiarius* AMM. MARC. 28, 4, 33. In an inscription, CIL. 6, 1064 WILM. 1501[a]: *Asinius Ingenuus exodiarius*. See also WILM. 574. After the disappearance of the old *saturae*, the *Atellanae* and *mimi* (§ 7, 4) were especially used for this purpose; hence *Atellanicum exodium* (SUET. Tib. 45), *exodium Atellanae* (IUV. 6, 71) and LYD. de mag. 1, 40 Ἀτελλάνη ἐστὶν ἡ τῶν λεγομένων ἐξοδιαρίων. Erroneously LIVY 7, 2, 11 *quae exodia postea appellata consertaque fabellis potissimum Atellanis sunt*.

7. The mimus came from Magna Graecia; as a farcical representation on the stage of persons and actions, it is in all probability at Rome of about the same age as the stage itself. Originally these mimi may have been acted on the stage by themselves (as they were still later at the Floralia), but when performances of a serious nature had gained the ascendency, they were employed as after-plays, though for a long time they were less popular than the newly accepted Atellanic farces; until in

Cicero's time the mimus also obtained a place in literature and then maintained itself on the stage all the longer, at first as an after-play, but also in the Imperial period by itself.

1. Diomed. GL. 1, 491 *mimus est sermonis cuiuslibet motus* (*sermonem movere*, like *iocum movere* in Sall. Cat. 95) *sine reverentia, vel factorum et* (*etiam*) *turpium cum lascivia imitatio; a Graecis ita definitus: μῖμός ἐστι μίμησις βίου τά τε συγκεχωρημένα καὶ ἀσυγχώρητα περιέχων.* In the same manner Euanthius p. 7 Reiffersch. states that the *mimi* were named so *ab diuturna imitatione vilium rerum et levium personarum*, and Isid. orig. 18, 49 *mimi sunt dicti graeca appellatione quod rerum humanarum* (rather *humilium*, see Donat. note 3 below, and Teuffel JJ. 113, 880) *sint imitationes.* CIGrysar, der römische Mimus, Wien 1854 (=SBer. der Wiener Akad. 12, 237). LFriedländer in JMarquardt's röm. Staatsverwaltung 3^2, 549 and in his Sittengesch. 2^5, 392.

2. As long as the mimus was not fixed in writing, not being strictly separated from the mountebank representations in every-day life, it was left unnoticed. The traces of its existence in the time before Sulla have been collected by MHertz, JJ. 93, 581. The oldest trace occurs in Festus 326, where the writer, after mentioning the erection of a stage and the introduction of performances (*ludi scenici, saltationes*) on it, thus proceeds: *solebant* ⟨*his prodire mimi*⟩ *in orchestra, dum* ⟨*in scena actus fa*⟩*bulae componeren*⟨*tur, cum gestibus ob*⟩*scaenis.* Then follows a mention of *ludi* (*Apollinares*) *C. Sulpicio C. Fulvio cos.* (rather *P. Sulp. Cn. Fulvio* =543/211), at which appeared a *libertinus mimus magno natu qui ad tibicinem saltaret*, and of the deviating opinion of Sinnius Capito, who placed the event *Claudio et Fulvio cos.* (542/212). In the 7th century u.c. are mentioned excesses of the mimi by *nominatim compellare in scena* (Cornif. ad Her. 1, 14, 24. 2. 13, 19), and in the year 639/115 Cassiodorus states that the censors *artem ludicram ex urbe removerunt.* To the same period belongs the *mimus vetus oppido ridiculus* called *Tutor* in Cic. de or. 2, 259 (the time a. 663/91), and the *suavis mimus Protogenes* '*Plourima que*(*i*)*fecit populo soueis gaudia nuge*(*i*)*s*' (CIL., 1, 1297. 9, 4463.)—Mimes were performed especially at the *Floralia* (first celebrated 516/238, regularly from 581/173) on a stage erected expressly for this purpose in front of the temple of Flora (Aug. civ. d. 2, 26. Merkel on Ov. Fasti. p. CLXIII); the final effect: *exuuntur vestibus populo flagitante meretrices quae tunc mimarum funguntur officio* (Lact. inst. 1, 20, 6). Val. Max. 2, 10, 8 notices the *nudatio mimarum* on the stage as a *priscus mos iocorum.*

3. Diomed. GL. 1, 490 *quarta species* (fabularum latinarum) *est planipedis, qui graece dicitur μῖμος. ideo autem latine planipes dictus quod actores pedibus planis, i.e. nudis, proscenium introirent, non ut tragici actores cum cothurnis neque ut comici cum soccis . . . cuius planipedis Atta . . ita . . meminit: 'daturin estis aurum? exsultat planipes.'* Festus 277 *mimi planipedes.* Auson. epist. 11 *de mimo planipedem.* Iuv. 8, 191 *planipedes audit* (populus) *Fabios* (cf. Suet. Ner. 4. Tac. hist. 3, 62). Donat. de com. p. 9 Reiffersch.: *planipedia dicta ob humilitatem argumenti eius ac vilitatem actorum, qui non cothurno aut socco nituntur in scaena aut pulpito sed plano pede.* Gell. 1, 11, 12 *si ut planipedi saltanti . . . numeros et modos . . . tibicen incineret.* Macr. sat. 2, 1, 9 *planipedis et fabulonis* (sannionis?) *impudica . . . verba iacientis.* Cf. also Sen. ep. 8, 8 *excalceati* in contrast to *cothurnati* (see also the passage of Seneca just below). According to this the popular *planipes* designates the actor of the *mimus* in opposition to those of the higher drama. *mimus* signifies, like *μῖμος*, the actor as well as the farce itself.—The mimus as an after-play was given on the front part of the stage divided from the back by a

drop-scene (*siparium.*) DONAT. de com. p. 12 Reiffersch. *mimicum velum quod populo obsistit, dum fabularum actus commutantur* (see above, n. 2, l. 7). SEN. tranq. 11, 8 *Publilius* (§ 212, 3) . . . *inter multa alia cothurno, non tantum sipario, fortiora et hoc ait.* IUV. 8, 105 *vocem . . . locasti sipario, clamosum ageres ut Phasma Catulli.*

4. CIC. fam. 9, 16, 7 *secundum Oenomaum Accii non, ut olim solebat, Atellanam, sed, ut nunc fit, mimum introduxisti.* Cf. § 6, 4. § 10, 1. The dying Augustus, however, in his question (SUET. Aug. 99) *ecquid amicis videretur mimum vitae commode transegisse* did not use the word *mimus* of the 'after-play' of life, as OHIRSCHFELD, Wiener Stud. 5, 116 assumes; he compared life, in Stoical fashion, to a stage-play; cf. SEN. epist. 80, 7 *hic humanae vitae mimus, qui nobis partes quas male agamus adsignat;* UvWILAMOWITZ, Herm. 21, 626.—The phrase *scenicum exodium* in SUET. Dom. 10 (cf. § 324, 5) also no doubt means a mimus.

8. At the end of the Republic the mimus, or farce, was introduced into literature by D. Laberius, Publilius Syrus and perhaps L. Valerius. At the same time its form was assimilated to that of the other species of drama, and the scope of its materials was enlarged, so that it gradually absorbed all the earlier kinds of comedy, the Attic-Roman palliata, the togata with its domestic and Roman subject-matter, the Atellanae with their roughness and indelicacy. Under the Empire, when the higher branches of the drama barely maintained their position with the old stock pieces, the mimus independently performed and the pantomimus acted in dumb-show were in the ascendant; new mimi continued to be composed in response to the daily demand till the latest period of the Empire, although the higher literature, as in the case of our modern farces etc., took no particular notice of them. As writers of mimi are mentioned a certain Catullus and Lentulus, also Atticus, Helvidius, Vergilius Romanus, Hostilius, Marullus, Aemilius Severianus and Aesopus.

1. On the mimiambi of Cn. Matius § 150, 2; on the σατυρικαὶ κωμῳδίαι supposed to have been written by Sulla τῇ πατρίῳ φωνῇ see § 157, 3. On Philistion § 254, 6 and L. Crassicius § 263, 2. On Lucilius § 307, 2.—The fragments of the mimi belonging to the Empire in RIBBECK com.[2] p. 392.

2. CIC. de or. 2, 242 *mimorum est ethologorum, si nimia est imitatio* (caricatures), *sicut obscenitas.* Cf. ib. 239. orat. 88 *ridiculo sic usurum oratorem ut . . nec subobsceno* (*utatur*), *ne mimicum* (*sit*). OVID. trist. 2, 497 (*obscena iocantes*) and 515 (*imitantes turpia*). QUINTIL. 6, 1, 47. Cf. n. 5.—The principal purpose was to provoke laughter: HOR. S. 1, 10, 6; APULEI. flor. 1, 5 *si mimus est riseris, . . si comoedia est faveris.* CASSIOD. Var. IV. fin.: *mimus, qui nunc tantummodo derisui habetur.* This was also done by means of making faces (QUINTIL. 6, 3, 29), imitating the noises of animals, etc. Performance by a trained dog, PLUT. de sollert. animal. 10 (mor. p. 973 ad fin.).

3. Plan and general scheme. CIC. Phil. 2, 65 *persona de mimo, modo egens, repente dives.* Cael. 65 *mimi est iam exitus, non fabulae: in quo cum clausula non invenitur*

fugit aliquis ex manibus, deinde scabilla concrepant, aulaeum tollitur. Later on, greater accuracy was used. QUINT. 4, 2, 53 *est quidam et ductus rei credibilis, qualis in comoediis etiam et in mimis.* PLUT. de sollert. anim. 19 (of the time of Vespasian) *μίμῳ πλοκὴν ἔχοντι δραματικὴν καὶ πολυπρόσωπον.*—Specimens of dialogue in CIC. de or. 2, 274, e.g.: *quid est tibi Ista mulier?* '*Uxor.*' *Similis, me dius fidius.*—Laberius' prologue in MACR. sat. 2, 7, 2. Cf. ISID. orig. 18, 49 *habebant* (mimi) *suum actorem qui antequam mimum ageret fabulam pronuntiaret.* On the cantica, see below n. 11.

4. Being a scurrilous representation of low life, the mimus is to a certain extent like the togata and both have many titles in common, e.g. *Aquae caldae*, *Augur*, *Compitalia*, *Fullo*, *Virgo*, the latter two occurring also among the artistic Atellanae, with which the mimus shares also the titles *Gemini*, *Hetaera*, *Nuptiae*, *Piscator*. The principal difference may be found in the prevalence of the mimic element in the mimus (n. 2), and the existence of the *oscae personae* in the Atellanae. With the palliata the mimus shares the titles *Colax*, *Hetaera*, and *Phasma*, and besides we find the following originally Greek titles of mimi: *Alexandrea*, *Belonistria*, *Cacomnemon*, *Cophinus*, *Ephebus*, *Necyomantia*, and *Scylax*.

5. The plots were in general of an obscene character (n. 2), esp. seductions, scenes of adultery, cheating of husbands or fathers or persons easily imposed upon. Cf. CIC. Rab. Post. 35 *illinc omnes praestigiae, . . . omnes fallaciae, omnia denique ab iis mimorum argumenta nata sunt.* OVID. trist. 2. 497. IUV. 6, 44. 8, 197. CAPITOL. M. Anton. 29, 2. LAMPRID. Heliog. 25, 4 (*mimica adulteria*). DONAT. on Aen. 5. 64 *mimi solis inhonestis et adulteris placent.* LACTANT. inst. 6. 20 (*mimi*) *docent adulteria dum fingunt.* MINUC. FEL. Oct. 37, 12 *in scenicis* (*ludis*) . . *turpitudo prolixior, nunc enim mimus vel exponit adulteria vel monstrat, nunc enervis histrio amorem dum fingit infigit.* With the same tendency mythological subjects were selected and treated, and this most frequently under the Emperors (by Laberius: Lacus Avernus, Necyomantia). ARNOB. adv. gent. 4, 35 *etiam mimis et scurrilibus ludicris sanctissimorum personae interponuntur deorum, et ut spectatoribus vacuis risus possit atque hilaritas excitari, iocularibus feriuntur cavillationibus numina.* Cf. 7, 33. TERTULL. apolog. 15 (here are mentioned as mimi Anubis moechus, Luna mascula, Diana flagellata, Iovis mortui testamentum recitatum, tres Hercules famelici; cf. § 363, 7). Similar subjects are Kinyras and Myrrha (IOSEPH. ant. 19, 1, 13), Paris and Oenone (SUET. Dom. 10), Priapus (AUGUSTIN. civ. dei 6, 7). In this way, the mimi were both a symptom and an important vehicle of the most horrible immorality.

6. This scurrility and corruption are seemingly contrasted (SEN. ep. 8, 8) by the wise and moral sayings with which especially Syrus' mimi abounded, perhaps owing to the influence of Greek comedy (comp. PLAUT. Rud. 4, 7, 23). But this combination of scurrility and wisdom is quite in keeping with the popular character (see WHERTZBERG on Juvenal 15, 16), and in the Imperial period the second feature may have been less conspicuous. On the other hand, personal allusions, which had been made in the mimi even before (CORNIFICIUS above § 7, 2. LABERIUS v. 7), were then sometimes indulged in by the mimi against the very highest persons. CAPIT. M. Ant. 8, 1 (cf. § 363, 7), ib. 29, 1. Maximin. 9, 3 sqq. LAMPRID. Comm. 3, 4. Cf. VOPISC. Aurel. 42, 5. MINUC. FEL. Oct. 34, 7 *non philosophi studio, sed mimi convicio* (cf. CIC. Mur. 13) *digna ista sententia est.*

7. The mimi were performed by one principal actor (cf. MACR. sat. 2, 7, 7 below § 212, 3), who was at the same time the director of the troupe of mimi (*archimimus*). Such are often mentioned: e.g. ἀρχιμῖμος Σῶριξ, the friend of Sulla (PLUT. Sull. 36).

Others: SUET. Vesp. 19. IUV. 8, 187. MAR. Max. in SCHOL. Iuv. 4, 53. PORPH. on Hor. S. 2, 6, 72. AUGUSTIN. civ. d. 6, 10. VICT. VIT. de persec. Vand. 1, 47. CIL. 3, 6113 (cf. Herm. 17, 495). 6, 1063. 1064. 4649. OR. 2625 = WILM. 2624; cf. below n. 9 and above § 7, 2. On the *archimimae* n. 8. Besides this first actor were also *actores secundarum* (SUET. Cal. 37), inferior to the first (Hor. E. 1, 18, 13. S. 1, 9, 46), who imitated him throughout (SUET, l.l.) and received blows from him (IUV. 5, 171. 8, 192. MARTIAL. 2, 79, 3. 5, 61, 11. ARNOB. adv. g. 7, 33). Sorix, named above as archimimus, appears also in secondary parts CIL. 10, 814 (*C. Norbani Soricis secundarum* etc.). Among these we find in a prominent place the customary part of the *stupidus* (OR. 2645. WILM. 2635 *Aurelius Eutyches, stupidus gregis urbani*, cf. OR. 2608 and below n. 9. IUV. 8, 197. CAPITOL. M. Ant. 29, 2), who appeared *capite raso* (HEINRICH on Iuv. 5, 171. NON. MARC. 6 *calvitur = frustratur, tractum a calvis mimis, quod sint omnibus frustratui.* ARNOB. l.l. *delectantur dii stupidorum capitibus rasis, salpittarum sonitu ac plausu, factis et dictis turpibus, fascinorum ingentium rubore*, cf. SCHOL. Iuv. 6, 66 *penem ut habent in mimo.* FESTUS 326 s. v. salva res (erroneously bringing in the palliata): *secundarum partium fuit, qui fere omnibus mimis parasitus inducitur.*—CIL. 6, 10104 *P. Cornelius P. l. Esq. Nig. tertiarum.* Qu. in place here?

8. Peculiar to the mimus, and a principal source of dissoluteness, was the representation of female parts by women. Cf. § 7, 2. AMMIAN. 23, 5, 3 *cum Antiochiae . . . scenicis ludis mimus cum uxore immissus e medio sumpta quaedam imitaretur.* Many mimae attained a kind of celebrity, *e.g.* Arbuscula, Dionysia, Cytheris, Origo, Quintilia, Thymele (in Juv. and Martial), Basilla (CIG. 3, p. 1023); *Claudia Hermione, archimima*, CIL. 6, 10106 OR. 4760; *Fabia M. et C. lib. Arete archimima* CIL. 6, 10107. *Sociarum mimarum* CIL. 6, 10109.

9. In the Imperial period we find no longer the number of performers restricted to certain limits, but an attempt is made to cast the parts systematically. Cf. PETRON. 80 *grex agit in scena mimum, pater ille vocatur, filius hic, nomen divitis* (cf. SEN. ep. 114, 6 *in mimo divites fugitivi*) *ille tenet.* PLUT. de sol. an. 19 μίμῳ πλοκὴν ἔχοντι . . . πολυπρόσωπον. Thus the Laureolus (§ 285, 1) must have required a large company. Seven scenici, amongst them besides *archimimi* and *stupidi* (i.e. *stupidi Graeci* and ordinary *stupidi*) a *pec*(*uniosus*) and a *mul*(*ier*), are mentioned in two inscriptions of the beginning of the 3rd cent. CIL. 6, 1063–1064 = WILM. 1501 a and b, cf. MOMMSEN, Herm. 5, 303.

10. The costume of the mimi was a many-coloured harlequin's jacket, *centunculus* (APULEI. apol. 13); without calcei (*excalceati*, SEN. ep. 8, 8), whence the name planipedes, § 7, 3. In keeping with their character the mimae were gaily dressed leaving the person almost nude; peculiar to them seems to have been the recinium or ricinium. FESTUS 274 *recinium . . . esse dixerunt vir⟨ilis⟩ toga⟨e simile vestimentum quo⟩ mulieres utebantur, praetextum clavo purpureo, unde reciniati mimi planipedes.* Cf. VARRO LL. 5, 132. NON. 542 *ricinium . . . palliolum femineum breve.* SERV. Aen. 1, 282 *togas etiam feminas habuisse cycladum et recini usus ostendit. recinus autem dicitur ab eo quod post tergum reicitur.* Masks were necessarily excluded by the conditions of mimicry. Elaborate painting of the face; cf. HIERONYM. ep. 60, 29 *eas quae rubore frontis addito parasitos* (cf. n. 7 ad fin.) *vincunt mimorum.* With respect to the estimation in which the mimi were held, see e. g. VOPISC. Carin. 16, 7 *mimis, meretricibus, pantomimis, cantoribus, lenonibus.* TREBELL. Gallien. 21, 6. trig. tyr. 9, 1.

11. The diction of the popular mimi was plebeian, that of the written ones less so, partly because of their metrical form; regarding Laberius see GELL. 16, 7. For

the metres we find in the fragments iambic senarii and trochaic tetrameters. Cf. § 192, 7. Before and after Laberius and Syrus, metrical form was probably restricted to cantica. That such were in existence is clear from Petron. 35 (*de Laserpiciario mimo canticum;* cf. μιμῳδοί Plut. Sull. 2.) The *obscena cantica* with which *omne convivium strepit* (Quint. 1, 2, 8) were probably taken chiefly from mimi. *Versus cantare* in Capitol. Maximin. 9, 5. Also *salva res est dum cantat senex,* Fest. 326. The accompaniment of the tibia appears to have belonged principally to the saltatio; Festus 326ᵇ, 13 *ad tibicinem saltare;* Gell. 1, 11, 12 *si ut planipedi saltanti . . . numeros et modos . . . tibicen incineret.* See the graceful epitaph of the mimus Vitalis AL. 683 PLM. 3, 245.

12. Interesting evidence of the survival of the mimus, and its diffusion in the Eastern Roman Empire, is the Apology for the mimi written, under Justinian, by the rhetor Chorikios, published by ChGraux, Rev. de philol. 1, 209. Cf. also Joh.Lydus magistr. 1, 40 ἡ μιμική, ἡ νῦν δῆθεν μόνη σωζομένη, τεχνικὸν μὲν ἔχουσα οὐδὲν λόγῳ, μόνον τὸ πλῆθος ἐπάγουσα γελῶτι. On the mediaeval mimi cf. Grysar l.l. 331 and Krahner, ZfAW. 1852, 388: the last pagan priests were at the same time the last mimi and joculatores (see the description of a person of this kind by Maximus Taurinensis, Muratori Anecd. 4, 99), and the earliest notices with regard to the drama at the beginning of the Middle Ages represent it as ecclesiastical, and as retaining the same joculatores in its service.

13. The pantomimus, being a kind of ballet, hardly belongs to literature. It was evolved from the drama (which had already in the *canticum* (§ 16, 3) introduced the separation between actor and singer) in consequence of the ever-increasing taste for dancing and dumb-show, and quite superseded dialogue. Under Augustus (732/22 see Hieron. ad chron. Eus. for that year) this species of play was given an independent form by the Cilician Pylades and the Alexandrine Bathyllos: the former founded tragic pantomime, which remained by far the more popular, the latter comic pantomime. A pantomimus (*lusor mutus* CIL. 6, 4886 Or. 6118), appearing in different parts (male or female) and costumes, according as the story required, represented in a succession of solos the chief incidents of a plot (*canticum saltare; in mimis saltantibus* = in pantomimes CIL. 6, 10118; see however n. 11, l. 11), while a choir sang the words during and between the dances of the pantomimus. This connecting text was of course very subordinate: it is only rarely that we hear of poets of note undertaking to supply such librettos. Lucan, however, wrote *fabulae salticae* (§ 303, 4), and likewise Statius (§ 321, 1) and Arbronius Silo (§ 252, 14). Cf. LFriedländer, Sittengesch. 2^5, 406, and in Marquardt's röm. Staatsverwalt. 3^2, 551. The pantomimus was acted by a single soloist: *pantomimae* are quite detached: Sen. ad Helv. 12, 6. AL. 310 = PLM. 4, 464 and on a tessera CIL. 6, 10128 *Sophe Theorobathylliana arbitrix imboliarum* is named as a pupil of Bathyllos and of Theoros, who was also very celebrated as a pantomimus (CIL. 6, 10115). Concerning the *embolia* (interludes) cf. *embolium* (Cic. Sest. 116), *emboliarius* (CIL. 4, 1949), *emboliaria* (Plin. NH. 7, 158. CIL. 6, 10127 = Or. 2613).

9. The Atellanae (fabulae A.) are so called from Atella, a small town in Campania, in a country originally Oscan. Atellan plays originally denoted comic descriptions of the life in small towns, in which the principal persons gradually assumed a fixed character. After the Romans (543/211) had annihilated the independence of Campania, and latinized the district, both the

thing and its name migrated to Rome, and soon Maccus, Bucco, Pappus and Dossennus were well-known and favourite figures with the Roman people also, who joined to them similar ones, such as Manducus, Mania, Lamia, Pytho. The youth of Rome most probably liked the new performances as an improved kind of saturae, and they themselves played in them masked and speaking in Latin. Only the general plot was then arranged, the rest being left to improvisation. The scheme of the plays was all the simpler. Their form may be presumed to have been, in most cases, a simple dialogue, songs in saturnian metre being perhaps interspersed; the jokes were coarse, accompanied by lively gesticulation, which was also obscene; the diction bore a plebeian character.

1. The fragments in Ribbeck's Com. 225[2]: ibid. 503 a list of the recorded titles of Atellanae. EMunk, de fabulis Atellanis, Bresl. 1840. Mommsen RG. 2[6], 437. Teuffel, PRE. 1[2], 1957. LFriedländer, Sittengesch. 2[5], 391; in Marquardt's röm. Staatsverwalt. 3[2], 548.

2. Diomedes GL. 1, 490 *tertia species est fabularum latinarum quae a civitate Oscorum Atella, in qua primum coeptae* (more probably in Capua) *appellatae sunt Atellanae, argumentis dictisque iocularibus similes satyricis fabulis graecis.* They resemble the Greek Satyr-drama (n. 8) more in their use as after-plays. (Hence the confusion of the two Porph. on Hor. AP. 221.) Mommsen l.l. considers the Atellan plays as having been originally from the earliest times Latin, and the Oscan country (latinized since 543/211) as their poetical scene only. This would be at variance with the general designation of the Atellanae as *osci ludi* (Cic. fam. 7, 1, 3), *oscum ludicrum* (Tac. A. 4, 14), the principal persons as *oscae personae* (Diomed. l.l. 490, 20). Moreover, it is easy to understand how in Capua 'provincials' came to be called Atellani, but not why this should have been so in Rome. Besides, there is no doubt that this Oscan play was influenced to some extent by the farces of Magna Graecia (cf. n. 3).

3. Maccus (cf. Μακκώ, μακκοᾶν) is stupid, voracious and wanton, Bucco grimaces with his *bucca*, gobbling and chattering. Pappus (πάππος) is a vain, deluded old man, who is constantly outwitted, the pantaloon. Dossennus (*dorsum;* cf. Vel. Long. GL. 7, 79, 4) is a cunning sharper, the dottore. See on this Munk l.l. 28. Mommsen, unterital. Dial. 118. A maccus in CIL. 6, 10105 *L. Annaeus M. f. Esq. Longinus maccus* (cf. Apul. apol. 81). For maccus and Maccius see § 96, 1.—It is also the same typical Dossennus, not a comic poet of the name, who is intended by Horace E. 2, 1, 173, a passage which has not yet however been certainly explained. Cf. Ritschl. parerg. p. xiii, opusc. 2, 544. FRitter, RhM. 5, 216. HDüntzer, ib. 6, 283. ChrCron. JJ. 129, 63. Also Sen. ep. 89, 7 probably quotes from a scene in an Atellana: *hoc verbo* (σοφίᾳ) *Romani quoque utebantur sicut philosophia nunc quoque utuntur. quod et togatae tibi antiquae probabunt et inscriptus Dossenni monumento titulus 'Hospes resiste et sophian Dossenni lege.'* Dossennus indeed occurs also as a real cognomen: L. Rubrius Dossennus CIL. 1, 430. C. Petronius Dossennus CIL. 5, 2256 and Fabius Dossennus, a Roman author of unknown date and profession (jurist or grammarian ?), mentioned by Plin. NH. among his authorities for b. 14 and 15 (fruit-trees) and quoted 14, 92.

4. Liv. 7, 2, 12 *quod genus ludorum (At.) ab Oscis acceptum tenuit iuventus nec ab histrionibus pollui passa est. eo institutum manet ut actores Atellanarum nec tribu moveantur et stipendia tamquam expertes artis ludicrae faciant.* This is repeated in his peculiar manner by Val. Max. 2, 4, 4. Fest. v. personata 217 *per Atellanos, qui proprie vocantur personati, quia ius est iis non cogi in scena ponere personam, quod ceteris histrionibus pati necesse est.* Cf. OJahn, Herm. 2, 225.

5. Non. 8, 29 *Varro Gerontodidascalo: putas eos non citius tricas Atellanas quam id extricaturos?* Cf. Tertull. spect. 17 *Atellanus gesticulator.* Quint. 6, 3, 47 *amphibolia, neque illa obscena quae Atellani e more captant.*

6. Incorrectly Strabo 5, p. 233 C *τῶν Ὄσκων ἐκλελοιπότων ἡ διάλεκτος μένει παρὰ τοῖς Ῥωμαίοις, ὥστε καὶ ποιήματα σκηνοβατεῖσθαι κατά τινα ἀγῶνα πάτριον καὶ μιμολογεῖσθαι.* The Oscan language was not understood at Rome; cf. Liv. 10, 20, 8. Titin. v. 104. Gell. 17, 17, 1. Macr. sat. 6, 4, 23. Perhaps the rustic language in the Atellanae (Varro LL. 7, 84, 96) appeared so strange to Strabo that he thought it was a different dialect, a mistake perhaps also facilitated by the name osci ludi.—But what are the *ludi* given by Caesar to the people *regionatim urbe tota per omnium linguarum histriones* in Suet. Iul. 39? No doubt, besides Latin and Greek pieces, popular plays written in the Italic languages and dialects.

7. When 639/115 the Censors *artem ludicram ex urbe removerunt*, they only excepted the *latinum tibicinem et ludum talanum.* Cassiod. (chron. ad a. p. 620 M.). MHertz (de ludo talario, Bresl. 1873) writes (with Mommsen) *talarium*, and understands by it a rude national and popular play, consisting of song with instrumental accompaniment, like the *μαγῳδοί*, and so called from the vestis talaris of the players. Cic. Att. 1, 16, 3. off. 1, 150. Quint. 11, 3, 58. Fronto p. 160 Nab. Lyd. magistr. 1, 40 (*καταστολαρία*; cf. A. Reifferscheid, JB. 1880 3, 267).

8. It does not appear that satyr-dramas ever belonged to Roman literature; cf. in Diomedes (n. 2) *graecis* and *satyrica est apud graecos fabula;* Mar. Victor. GL. 6, 82 (*haec apud graecos metri species*). Welcker, griech. Trag. 1361. Ribbeck, röm. Trag. 623, see below § 190, 2. But it is possible that Horace in his full discussion of the Satyr-drama (AP. 290) tacitly purposed to induce some one to transplant this kind of drama to Roman soil, and thereby assist in dislodging the coarse Atellana from its place as after-piece. Cf. Teuffel, RhM. 28, 493 and above § 8, 1.

10. In the time of Sulla, the Atellan plays, which previously had been only popular farces, received literary treatment at the hands of Pomponius of Bononia and Novius, they being the first to write complete texts of their plays. By means of a well-laid plot, consistent characters and metrical form, the Atellan plays were then raised to the same level with the other kinds of comedy, though they preserved more the character of burlesques. Besides the description of popular life and the personal allusions, we now find also mythological titles (cf. § 18). Henceforth the Atellan plays were used in Rome as after-plays, and performed by professional actors. Even under the first Emperors these plays were still in vogue and cultivated by Mummius, but owing to the character of the period their voice was gradually silenced and they were merged in the pantomimes.

1. CIC. fam. 7, 1, 3 (performance of osci ludi by Pompeius a. 699/55). 9, 16, 7 (a. 708/46) *secundum Oenomaum Accii, non, ut olim solebat, Atellanam, sed, ut nunc fit, mimum introduxisti.* Cf. MAR. VICT. GL. 6, 82 and § 6, 4. In small country-towns Atellan plays were occasionally performed by themselves, IUV. 3, 175.

2. SUET. Nero 39 *Datus Atellanarum histrio in cantico* etc. cf. Galb. 13 *Atellanis notissimum canticum exorsis.* IUV. 6, 71 *Urbicus exodio risum movet Atellanae gestibus Autonoes.* CIL. 4, 2457 (from Pompeii):—*Methe Cominiaes Atellana.* TAC. A. 4, 14 *Caesar* (Tiberius) *de immodestia histrionum rettulit . . . oscum quondam ludicrum, levissimae apud volgum oblectationis, eo flagitiorum et virium venisse ut auctoritate patrum coercendum sit.* Cf. SUET. Tib. 45. Calig. 27 *Atellanae poetam* (perhaps Mummius?) *ob ambigui ioci versiculum media amphitheatri arena igni cremavit.*—MACR. sat. 1, 10, 3 *Mummius, qui post Novium et Pomponium diu iacentem artem Atellaniam suscitavit.*—SPARTIAN. Hadr. 26, 4 *in convivio tragoedias, comoedias, Atellanas . . . semper exhibuit* (Hadrian). TERTULL. spectac. 17. Arnob. adv. gent. 7, 33. Concerning the relation of the Atellan plays to the mimi, see § 8, 4.

11. Under the head of the popular poetry of the Romans may be classed all they possessed in a metrical form (i.e. in the saturnian metre) before the introduction of art-poetry, i.e. before Andronicus and the year 514/240. Some productions handed down from later and literary periods belong to an older time, both in tendency and character. In the Imperial period we meet especially with lampoons, mural inscriptions, and similar occasional pieces, chiefly in trochaic seven-foot metre, with a tendency to accented rhythm and indifferent treatment of hiatus. This accounts for the fact of the early Christian hymns, intended as they were for the use and understanding of the people, being composed in the same manner.

1. A list of poetical productions in the time before Andronicus will be found below, § 61 sqq.

2. The custom of singing at work. VARRO ap. Non. 56 *homines rusticos in vindemia incondita cantare, sarcinatrices in machinis.* VICTORIN. GL. 6, 122 *metrum . . . usurpatum a pastoribus Calabris qui decantare res rusticus his versibus solent.* Singing of sailors while rowing: A rowing song from a cod. Berol. s. VIII/IX. PLM. 3, 167, RPEIPER, RhM. 32, 523. In the literary period we may assume an earlier origin for the following: a) popular love-songs, one of which is alluded to by HOR. S. 1, 5, 15. But the serenades in PLAUT. Curc. 1, 2, 60 (in cretic metre), HOR. C. 3. 10 and OVID. amor. 1, 6 are not popular.—b) Nursery songs; see SCHOL. Pers. 3, 16 *quae infantibus, ut dormiant, solent dicere saepe: lalla lalla, lalla aut dormi aut lacta* (FPR. 34; cf. RhM. 24, 619); cf. lallare in PERS. 3, 18 and AUSON. epist. 16, 90 *nutricis inter lemmata Lallique somniferos modos.*—c) Songs used in the games of boys, HOR. E. 1, 1, 59. 2, 3, 417 (with the Schol.), from which (FPR. 56; see LMÜLLER, JJ. 89, 484) the lines should most probably be arranged as follows: *Hábeat scabiem quisquis ad me vénerit novissimus. Réx erit qui récte faciet; quí non faciet, nón erit.* Such probably was the song of Caesar's army at his Triumph (708/46): *Plécteris si récte facies, si non facies réx eris* (cf. DIO. 43, 23). Trochaic also is *V́bi non sis qui fúeris non est cúr velis ⟨tu⟩ vivere* (CIC. fam. 7, 3, 4;

cf. RIBBECK's com. p. 127, TEUFFEL JJ. 111, 432). Moreover such sentences might pass from literature into popular usage and become proverbial.—d) Soldiers' songs in praise and in mockery of the triumphator, see § 84, lampoons on belated husbandmen (HOR. S. 1, 7, 28 with AUSON. Mosell. 116 *navita labens . . . probra canit seris cultoribus;* on this see MANNHARDT, mythol. Forsch. 53), on misers (PLAUT. Trin. 350 '*Quód habes ne habeás et illuc quod nón habes habeás: malum, Quándo equidem nec tíbi bene esse póte pati neque álteri*'). The death of L. Crassus (§ 152) gave occasion to the following verse: *Póstquam Crassus cárbo factust, Cárbo* (§ 153, 4) *crassus fáctus est* (SACERDOS GL. 6, 461. MHAUPT opusc. 3, 325). The inscriptions in trochaic septenarii have been collected by FBÜCHELER, anthol. lat. epigr. lat. spec. 3 (Bonn 1876), 11.

3. In the popular effusions of the Imperial period we also find a predilection for the trochaic tetrameter, which is well suited to the Latin language. In this metre we have e.g. CIL. 3, 293, OR.-HENZEN 6674 (epitaph of the soldier T. Cissonius: *dúm vixi bibí libenter; bíbite vos qui vívitis*), and the lampoons of this period in SUETON. Iul. 80 (cf. 49, 51), SCHOL. Iuv. 5, 3. Cf. SUET. Calig. 6. Galb. 6. VOPISC. Aurel. 6, 5. 7, 2. Cf. § 31, 2. The refrain of which Festus (285) says *retiario adversus mirmillonem pugnanti cantatur* appears to be in sotadic metre: '*Nón té peto, piscém peto quíd mé fugi*', *Gállé?*' An *epigrammatarius* in VOPISC. Florian. 16, 3. Cf. GHBERNSTEIN, versus ludicri in Roman. Caesares priores. Halle 1810. ZELL, Ferienschr. 2, 165.—For Church-hymns cf. e.g. *Ápparebit répentina Dies magna dómini*, etc. More below under Commodianus, Damasus, Ambrosius, Venantius Fortunatus and others. Rhyme (assonance) soon began to assert itself; it is to be found not infrequently in Plautus in the first half of the trochaic tetrameters; see HUSENER, JJ. 107, 174; L. BUCHHOLD, paromoeosis 74; also the two popular poems of the 6th cent. A.D. in GREGOROVIUS, Gesch. d. St. Rom. 1, 372. WGRIMM, zur Gesch. d. Reims, Abh. d. Berl. Akad. 1851.

4. ZELL, Ferienschr. 2, 97. EDÉLÉSTAND DU MÉRIL, poésies populaires latines antérieures au douzième siècle, Paris 1843. TEUFFEL, PRE. 6, 2736. LMÜLLER, de re metr. poett. latt. (Lps. 1861) 445 (de poesi rhythmica). WESTPHAL, griech. Metrik 2^2 (Lps. 1868), 58.

12. The regular drama was the first of the various kinds of art-poetry imported at Rome at the beginning of the 6th century, and was soon diligently cultivated both in its serious and its comic side, with more or less originality. But the entertaining kinds prevailed greatly, the palliata, togata (including the trabeata and tabernaria); the mimus (or the planipedia, § 7, 3), to which the Atellan plays in their later form and the Rhinthonica may be added. Of serious plays we have besides tragedy only the praetexta to name.

1. DONAT. de com. p. 9, 23 Reiffersch.: *Fabula generale nomen est; eius duae primae partes sunt tragoedia et comoedia.* CAESIUS BASSUS GL. 6, 312 (cf. ib. 247) enumerates: *tragoedia, praetextata, comoedia, tabernaria, Atellana, Rhinthonica, mimi.* DONATUS l.l. p. 10 R.: *comoediarum formae sunt tres: palliatae, graecum habitum referentes, togatae, iuxta formam personarum habitum togarum desiderantes, . . . Atellanae* etc. and p. 9 R.: *comoedia multas* (ἑπτά LYD. de mag. 1, 40) *species habet: aut enim palliata est aut togata aut tabernaria aut Atellana aut mimus aut Rhin-*

thonica aut planipedia (πλανιπεδαρία LYD. l.l.), EUANTH. de com. p. 7 R.: *post* νέαν κωμῳδίαν (therefore after the palliata) *Latinos multa fabularum genera protulisse, ut togatas, ab scaenicis* (?*scaenis*) *atque argumentis latinis; praetextas* . . .; *Atellanas* . . .; *Rhinthonicas, ab auctoris nomine; tabernarias, ab humilitate argumenti et stili; mimos, ab diuturna imitatione vilium rerum et levium personarum.* Valuable notices on the various kinds (though mixed with errors) are found in DIOMEDES, GL. 1, 487–492, as also in EUANTHIUS and DONATUS de comoedia. Cf. § 405, 6.

2. After 514/240 there were legitimate dramatic performances at the *ludi Romani*, § 94, 2. As early as 540/214 *ludi scaenici* were given yearly at the *ludi Romani, plebeii* and *Apollinares;* likewise after 560/194 at the *Megalesia.* Theatrical performances also took place from an early date at *ludi votivi* (see PvBOLTENSTERN, de rebus scaenicis Rom., Greifsw. 1875). In the year 600/154, by a decree of the Senate, the demolition of a stone theatre which had been already begun was ordered, and at the same time the people were forbidden to sit during the games. More brilliant productions (*ludi curatius editi* TAC. A. 14, 21) after LMummius 609/145. From this time complete theatres were erected each year in the Greek fashion, with rows of raised seats, although still of wood, and so constructed that the theatre was pulled down on each occasion after being used; it was only after the year 699/55 that the first stone theatre in Rome was built by Pompey; this was followed 741/13 by the stone theatres of Cornelius Balbus and Marcellus; these three permanent theatres,—the only ones which Rome possessed—accommodated altogether about 50,000 persons.—The manager (*dominus gregis*), who probably as a rule sustained the chief character as well, bought the piece from the author on his own account (cf. § 110, 2, 2; also § 223, 2), concluded, at his own risk, the contract for the representation with the *curatores ludorum*, selected the company, costumes etc. (*vestis, ornamenta = apparatus scaenicus*) and rehearsed the parts under the direction of the author. The practical management of theatrical troupes was no doubt conducted in imitation of the Greek σύνοδοι τῶν περὶ τὸν Διόνυσον τεχνιτῶν, of which we also find traces in Syracuse, Rhegium and Naples: at a later time there were Greek theatrical companies in Rome itself: AMÜLLER, griech. Bühnenaltert. Freib. 1886, 394. 410.—See in gen. RITSCHL, Parerga 227, sq. RIBBECK, röm. Trag. 647. LFRIEDLÄNDER in Marquardt's röm. Staatsverw. 3², 528. BARNOLD, das altröm. Theatergebäude, Wurzb. 1873. Cf. above § 6, 3.

13. In tragedy the Romans were throughout dependent upon the Greeks. It is true that there were points in the character, the institutions and history of the Romans which would have been favourable to the creation of an independent tragic literature; but the poetical power necessary for shaping these subjects was not possessed by them, least of all when tragedies were first presented to them. They were translations from the Greek, of rude execution in the case of Andronicus, but steadily improved and made more original by Naevius, Ennius, Pacuvius and Accius. The taste of the mass for spectacles, unable as they were to derive much pleasure from the subject-matter and form of the foreign plays, was gratified by brilliant *mise en scène.* All these tragic writers of the Republican time possessed great

gravity in their characters, sentiments and style, though they fell occasionally into bombast or triviality, and made their verses somewhat awkwardly. The same may be assumed of the tragedies of Atilius, C. Titius, C. Julius Caesar Strabo, Varro, Q. Cicero, Cassius of Parma, and also probably of those of Santra and Asinius Pollio, though the last of them seems to have been original in his subjects. The early Imperial period, during which the attention of educated men was again turned to the ancient Roman tragic writers, produced also new plays, of course with more technical finish. Here we may mention L. Varius' Thyestes, Ovid's Medea, Pupius and also Gracchus, Turranius, Mam. Scaurus, Pomponius Secundus and, above all, the tragedies of Seneca. But these compositions were, doubtless, for the most part book-dramas, which did not pretend to popular effect, and only courted the applause of the poet's friends at recitations. Among the later tragic writers only Curiatius Maternus is of any consequence.

1. Tragicorum latin. reliquiae, rec. ORibbeck, Lps.[2] 1871. Textual criticism in EBährens (JJ. 105, 621), Bergk (op. 1, 319, and against this Ribbeck, RhM. 29, 209). FGWelcker, die griech. Tragödien (Rhein. Mus. Suppl. 2, 3), Bonn 1841, p. 1332–1484 and ORibbeck, die röm. Tragödie d. Republ., Lpz. 1875; cf. likewise AReifferscheid JB. 1880 3, 265. It is open to question whether, as Ribbeck supposes (röm. Trag. 24, 204), ancient Roman tragedies, such as Livius' Ino and Ennius' Athamas were modernised in the first century A.D.—CHorstmann, de vett. tragg. rom. lingua, Münst. 1870. LBrunel, de tragoedia ap. Rom. circa princip. Aug. corrupta, Par. 1884.

2. The number of tragic poets known to us by more or less explicit mention amounts at the utmost to 36; that of their plays to 150 at most (lists in Ribbeck trag.[2] p. 363; röm. Trag. 634); only those of Seneca have been preserved. The subjects of the Trojan cycle were especially popular. A general criticism in Quint. 10, 1, 97.

3. Tragedy also consisted of portions of sedate and of more excited character, of dialogue and of lyric parts which were sung—*diverbium* (*deverbium*) and *cantica*. The dialogue was principally in iambic trimeters, admitting, however, in the Republican period, of spondees (and so also anapaests and dactyls) in all places except the last, and was only treated with more purity after the time of Augustus. The *cantica* show little variety in their metres, anapaests and cretics being the most frequent, besides which we have also trochaic and iambic tetrameters, and dactylic lines. They were accompanied by a *tibia* (Cic. or. 184. de or. 1, 254. Tusc. 1, 107. Hor. AP. 215), and habitués were skilled enough to know the piece about to be performed from the prelude of the tibicen (Cic. Acad. pr. 2, 20, cf. de or. 3, 196. Donat. de com. p. 12, 11 R).—Regarding the splendid mounting: Cic. fam. 7, 1. Hor. E. 2, 1, 203. Ribbeck, röm. Trag. 664.—For *crepidata* (from *crepida*, κρηπίς, equivalent to *cothurnus*) denoting Roman tragedy with Greek subject-matter, see § 14, 2.

4. In Cicero's time the eminent actor Aesopus (see Ribbeck, röm. Trag. 674) brought tragedies (espec. those of Pacuvius and Accius) very much into vogue:

see e.g. Cic. Sest. 120, fin. 5, 63. Tusc. 1, 106. Lael. 24. Other *tragoediarum actores* are Rupilius (Cic. off. 1, 114), Catienus and Fufius (Hor. S. 2, 3, 60), Apelles (Suet. Calig. 33), Glyko (Pers. 5, 9), Apollinaris (Suet. Vesp. 19).—In Cicero's time tragedies were written in three acts: see Cic. ad Q. fr. 1, 1, 46. Ribbeck, röm. Trag. 641.

5. A chorus in the Greek manner was impossible for the Romans for the simple reason of the Senate occupying the *orchestra.* Choric dancing (cf. also § 1, 4) being thus excluded, we find now and then a number of performers simultaneously on the stage, which was wider for this reason (A. Müller, Bühnenaltert. 19), and singing together (*catervae atque concentus,* Cic. de or. 3, 196; cf. Columella 12, 2; cf. § 16, 5). In the ancient Roman tragedians a certain imitation of the Greek choric songs is not improbable, because they were mere translators; this is supported by such titles as *Bacchae, Eumenides* (cf. Cic. Rosc. Am. 66, Pis. 46), *Hellenes, Myrmidones, Phinidae, Phoenissae, Stasiastae, Troades,* as well as by numerous details. The account of Lucullus, e.g. in Hor. E. 1, 6, 40 (cf. Plut. Lucull. 39) presupposes a chorus (§ 16, 4). Cf. Polyb. 30, 13. In Andronicus' Ino (§ 94, 5) the *chorus* sang *hymnum Triviae* (Ter. Maur. 1934=GL. 6, 383); in Naevius' Lycurgus we find a chorus of bacchanals, in Ennius' Iphigenia (Gell. 19, 10, 12) and Medea (fr. 14=Eur. Med. 1251) there is a *chorus;* in Pacuvius is a *stasimum* (Mar. Vict. GL. 6, 77), and in Antiopa, Chryses, Niptra there are also parts resembling a chorus. A *chorus Proserpinae* is mentioned by Varro LL. 6, 94. Traces of choruses are more scarce in Accius, though evident in the Bacchae and Philocteta. Pomponius Secundus (§ 284, 7) and Seneca would not, it may be supposed, have composed choric songs (to mark the acts) without the example of the ancient poets, and Horace (AP. 193) would not have discussed so fully the arrangement of the Greek chorus, if it had not existed in the Roman drama. Cf. concerning a *dexter actor* Manil. astr. 5, 485 *aequabit choros gestu.* Phaedr. 5, 7, 25 *tunc chorus ignotum modo reducto canticum insonuit, cuius haec fuit sententia: Laetare, incolumis Roma, salvo Principe.* Grysar, d. Canticum u. d. Chor in der röm. Trag., Wien 1855=SBer. d. Wien. Ak. 15, 365. OJahn, Herm. 2, 227. Ribbeck, röm. Trag. 637.

6. In the Imperial period the tragic representations resolved themselves into their component parts, and degenerated into soli by virtuosi (singers and pantomimists). For the pantomimi see above § 8, 13. Just as these reproduced tragic scenes by gesticulation, so the singers executed tragic arias in a costume corresponding to their rôle. Regarding Nero's passion for such performances § 286, 9. Cf. LFriedländer, Sittengesch. 2^5, 404. GBoissier, de la signification des mots *cantare* et *saltare tragoediam,* Rev. archéolog. N.S. 4 (1861), 333.

14. The (fabula) praetexta is the Roman tragedy of a national character; in the absence of indigenous heroic legends, historic subjects were adopted and, as a rule, by poets who also wrote tragedies (on Greek subjects and after Greek originals). Thus Naevius (Clastidium, Romulus), Ennius (Ambracia, Sabinae), Pacuvius (Paullus), Accius (Aeneadae s. Decius, Brutus), and Balbus Iter ad Lentulum; as dramas for reading Pomponius Secundus composed an Aeneas, Persius a play of which the subject is unknown, Curiatius Maternus a Domitius and a Cato, an unknown poet a Marcellus (?) The tragedy of Octavia claims to be

a praetexta. In form and character these plays were made after tragic models, they were even more elaborately furnished, as the themes were of national interest, and perhaps it was only their style which, in agreement with the subjects, was less sublime.

1. The form *praetexta* is used by Asinius Pollio (in Cic. fam. 10, 32, 3. 5). Horace (AP. 288), Probus (vita Persii, p. 237 Jahn), Festus (223; cf. 352); the designation *praetextata* prevails in the later grammarians.

2. Diomedes GL. 1, 489 *prima species est togatarum* (national dramas) *quae praetextatae dicuntur, in quibus imperatorum negotia agebantur et publica et reges romani vel duces inducuntur, personarum dignitate et sublimitate tragoediis similes. praetextatae autem dicuntur quia fere regum vel magistratuum qui praetexta utuntur in eiusmodi fabulis acta comprehenduntur.* (Cf. *praetextati in magistratibus, in sacerdotiis,* Liv. 34, 7. Also Non. 541.) Diomed. l.l. 490 *togata praetextata a tragoedia differt quod in tragoedia heroes inducuntur, . . . in praetextata autem . . Brutus vel Decius, item Marcellus* (§ 94, 6) ⟨*vel Africanus et his similia,* is added by Rhabanus Maurus, Opera 1, 47 ed. Colon. 1627: is this credible?? See Ribbeck, com.[2] p. cxviii⟩. Manil. 5, 483 (*dexter actor*) *magnos heroas aget civisque togatos.* Donat. de com. p. 9 R. *tragoedia, si latina argumentatio sit, praetexta dicitur.* Euanth. de com. p. 7 R. *praetextatas, a dignitate personarum tragicarum ex latina historia.* Lydus de mag. 1, 40 (tragedy) τέμνεται εἰς κρηπιδάταν (§ 13, 3. Donat. Ter. Ad. prol. 7) καὶ πραιτεξτάταν· ὧν ἡ μὲν κρηπιδάτα ἑλληνικὰς ἔχει ὑποθέσεις, ἡ δὲ πραιτεξτάτα ῥωμαϊκάς. Tacitus dial. 2, inaccurately, designates Curiatius Maternus' Cato as *tragoedia* (cf. Plaut. Amphitr. prol. 41. 93. Capt. 62). Sen. ep. 1, 8, 8 means praetextae in speaking of togatae; see § 17, 1. Performance of the *praetextae* perhaps at *ludi triumphales* (GRöper). We may fairly conclude that separate portions of Greek tragedies were utilised, just as in the togatae (below, § 17) use was made of individual details in the new Attic comedy. Traces of the utilising of praetextae in Livy? e.g. in the siege of Veii 5, 21 (cf. in the same chapter § 8 *haec ad ostentationem scaenae gaudentis miraculis aptiora,* see Ribbeck, RhM. 36, 321). Perhaps we may also refer to a praetexta the beautiful Pompeian wall-painting (copied in the Mus. Borbon. 1, 34. Visconti, iconogr. rom. 3, 56), which among all those found there stands alone as historical, and represents the dying Sophoniba attended by Scipio and Masinissa; see OJahn, der Tod der Sophoniba, Bonn 1859. AReifferscheid, JB. 1880 3, 265.—Collection of the remains of the praetextae in Ribbeck, trag.[2] 277. Cf. FGWelcker, die griech. Trag. (1841) 1344. 1388. 1402.

15. The earliest of the different kinds of comedy (cf. § 12) is the palliata, on Greek subjects and imitated from Greek originals, especially the New Attic Comedy. Its period extends over the whole 6th century u.c. To this belong Andronicus, Naevius, Plautus, Ennius, Trabea, Atilius, Licinius Imbrex, Juventius, Statius Caecilius, Luscius Lanuvinus, Terence, Plautius, Turpilius: a series of names on the one hand representing a scale of increasing refinement in style, but on the other hand also of decreasing originality with regard to the treatment of the Greek originals. The first composers of palliatae endeavoured to assimilate their pieces to the popular taste by various additions of a local or temporal character, or by making them more coarse;

the later ones, Terence e.g., despised attractions of this kind, but in so doing lost the popular sympathies, which were turned to the more amusing style of the togatae, Atellanae and mimi. The consequence was that the production of new palliatae ceased, and if plays of this class were wanted, the stage had to fall back upon older literature. The plays of Plautus and Terence subsisted on the stage after the establishment of the Empire (cf. § 99. 109). The original productions during this latter period, e.g. by Vergilius Romanus and M. Pomponius Bassulus, were confined to small circles and remained without effect.

1. DIOMED. GL. 1, 489 *graecas fabulas ab habitu palliatas Varro ait nominari.* PLAUT. Curc. 2, 3, 9 *isti Graeci palliati* etc. *Pallium graecanicum* (SUET. Dom. 4)= ἱμάτιον ἑλληνικόν (LUCIAN. merc. cond. 25). SEN. controv. 9, 26, 13 *cum latine declamaverunt, toga posita, sumpto pallio, . . . graece declamabant.* The palliata was also briefly styled *comoedia* and the poets belonging to it *comici* (RITSCHL, Parerga 189). Hence DIOMED. GL. 1, 490 *togata tabernaria a comoedia differt, quod in comoedia graeci ritus inducuntur personaeque graecae . . ., in illa vero latinae . . . Terentius et Caecilius comoedias scripserunt.* In this way QUINT. 11, 3, 178 mentions Demetrius and Stratokles as *maximos actores comoediarum* of his time, the following description and ib. 182 showing that palliatae are understood. So also FRONTO ep. p. 54 and 211 Nab. (*comoedias, Atellanas*). 106 (*sententias comes ex comoedis*) etc.

2. The Old Attic Comedy was too much connected with its own period to be fit for imitation by another nation and in a different period (on Vergilius Romanus, the imitator of Old Attic Comedy, see § 332, 7). On the other hand, the New Comedy, the nearest in time, in the 6th century U.C. held the stage, and was by its typical delineation of character and general human bearing especially fitted to be transplanted to foreign soil. In it we notice especially Menander, next to him Diphilos and Philemon. Others are mentioned by GELL. 2, 23, 1 *comoedias lectitamus nostrorum poetarum sumptas ac versas de Graecis, Menandro aut Posidippo aut Apollodoro aut Alexide et quibusdam item aliis comicis.* BUGGE, de causis neglectae ap. Rom. comoediae Graecorum veteris et mediae, Christiania 1823.

3. On the dying out of the pall. (?) in the Imperial period, see M. AUREL. comm. 11, 6 ἡ νέα κωμῳδία πρὸς τί ποτε παρείληπται, ἣ κατ' ὀλίγον ἐπὶ τὴν ἐκ μιμήσεως φιλοτεχνίαν ὑπερρύη. A mere exercise of the pen was the experiment of *Surdinus, ingeniosus adulescens* (in the Augustan period, § 268, 6), *a quo graecae fabulae eleganter in sermonem latinum conversae sunt* (SEN. suas. 7, 12). *Comoedias audio* in PLIN. ep. 5, 3, 2 should be understood of recitation (as in the case of Vergilius Romanus). On the traces of the acting of comedies in late Imperial times, see LFRIEDLÄNDER, Sittengesch. Roms 2^5, 566.

4. A curious classification of the poets of palliatae (Caecilius Statius, Plautus, Naevius, Licinius, Atilius, Terentius, Turpilius, Trabea, Luscius, Ennius) by Volcacius Sedigitus, in GELL. 15, 24, see § 147, 3.

5. The fragments of the written palliatae (except Plautus and Terence) especially in ORIBBECK, Comicorum rom. . . . fragm., Lps.[2] 1873. For textual criticism cf. THBERGK op. 1, 379. HAKOCH JJ. 109, 137. FBÜCHELER RhM. 29, 195. KDZIATZKO ib. 31, 376. ASPENGEL, die lat. Komödie (address), München 1878 (Bayr. Akad.).

16. From the New Comedy the palliata borrowed the general spirit of the later over-refined Hellenism with its moral inertia and levity, and in particular the plots, characters, construction and outward form, even in details, e.g. the prologue and epilogue. The palliata being without a chorus like the New Comedy, each piece is divided into portions of dialogue (diverbia) and monodies (cantica). In the first the poets of the palliatae curtailed, for their audiences, the loquacity of their originals, while they introduced more action, especially by means of the so-called 'contamination,' being moreover less limited in the number of their performers than their originals. The dialogue is generally in iambic senarii; in the cantica we have, besides septenarii, a frequent use of cretics and bacchics, the latter proportionately strict, the prosody of the senarii with numerous and large concessions to the popular pronunciation. The delivery, in imitation of the Greek custom, consisted partly of declamation (without musical accompaniment) partly of recitative and song; these two last were accompanied by a tibia. The performers were not masked until after the time of Terence.

1. Description of the palliata esp. in Ribbeck, röm. Dicht. 1, 57. The chief characters in both are miserly fathers, spendthrift sons, cunning slaves, greedy and amorous hetaerae, low panders, coarse and boastful soldiers, starved parasites. Manil. 5, 472 *ardentis iuvenes raptasque in amore puellas elusosque senes agilesque per omnia servos.* Apul. flor. 16, 64 *et leno perfidus* (thus AArlt reads for *periurus*) *et amator fervidus et servulus callidus et amica inludens et uxor inhibens* (? *inprudens* OCrusius) *et mater indulgens et patruus obiurgator et sodalis opitulator et miles gloriator* (thus LTraube, RhM. 39, 630 reads for *proeliator*), *sed et parasiti edaces et parentes tenaces et meretrices procaces.* Isidor. orig. 18, 46 *comoedi sunt qui privatorum hominum acta dictis ac gestu canebant atque stupra virginum et amores meretricum in suis fabulis exprimebant.* On the personal names in comedy see Donat. ad Ter. Ad. 1, 1, 1 and Andr. 1, 3, 21 and Ritschl. op. 3, 303. 333. 350.

2. Euanth. de com. p. 7 R. *comoediae motoriae sunt aut statariae aut mixtae. motoriae turbulentae, statariae quietiores, mixtae ex utroque actu consistentes.* According to this the Plautine plays are nearly all *motoriae*, (but e.g. Capt. and Trin. are *statariae*), the Terentian mostly *mixtae*, Phormio is a *motoria*, Heautontim. a *stataria* (Heaut. prol. 36). In agreement with this the actors (cf. Donat. ad Ter. Ad. prol. 24 and Quintil. 11, 3, 178) and then also the orators (Cic. Brut. 116. 239) were divided into *statarii* and *motorii*. According to their contents the pieces are either character-plays (*e.g.* Plautus' Aul., and likewise e.g. Mil. Truc.) or strictly intrigues (*e.g.* Bacch. Pseud. Pers. Poen.) with a variety of by-plots and episodes: the dramatic expedients are also tolerably uniform, as e.g. the surprises, modes of duping, disguises, confusions, recognitions, etc.

3. Diomedes GL. 1, 491 *latinae comoediae chorum non habent, sed duobus membris tantum constant, diverbio et cantico* (cf. Ritschl, op. 3, 34). *primis autem temporibus, sicuti adserit Tranquillus* (§ 347), *omnia quae in scena versantur in comoedia age-*

bantur. Nam et pantomimus et pythaules et choraules in comoedia canebant (the *pantomimus* perhaps after the separation of singing and acting; cf. Liv. 7, 2, 10 *inde ad manum cantari histrionibus coeptum diverbiaque tantum ipsorum voci relicta*). Gradually, he states, the *histriones* (*actores comoediarum*) were separated from the *mimi* and *tibicines*. The notice in the *glossae Salomonis* is exaggerated (RhM. 22, 446. 28, 418): *aput Romanos quoque Plautus comoediae choros exemplo Graecorum inseruit* (so in Rudens 290–305 chorus of fishermen). Cf. n. 5.

4. The Old Attic Comedy seldom employed more than three actors; see AMüller, gr. Bühnenaltertümer 176. But in the later comedy, after the chorus was abolished, it would appear that this number was often exceeded; cf. Euanthius de com. p. 4 R.: *ad ultimum qui primarum partium, qui secundarum et tertiarum, qui quarti loci atque quinti actores essent distributum et divisa quinquepartito actu tota est fabula.* In Rome the poets were still less restricted in the number of their personages. Diomed. l.l. 491 *in graeco dramate fere tres personae solae agunt . . ., quarta semper muta: at latini scriptores complures personas in fabulas introduxerunt, ut speciosiores frequentia facerent.* But the *centum chlamydes* which in Hor. E. 1, 6, 41 (*chlamydes Lucullus . . . centum scenae praebere rogatus*) are borrowed for the stage, are certainly only for the chorus or supers. Cf. § 13, 5. Ps.-Ascon. on Cic. div. in Caec. 48 (p. 119 Or.) *latinae fabulae per pauciores agebantur personas* (than the palliatae), *ut Atellanae, togatae et huiusmodi aliae.* Martial alludes to the ancient Greek rule, 6, 6: *comoedi tres sunt, sed amat tua Paula, Luperce, quattuor: et κωφὸν Paula πρόσωπον amat.* Only in two of the plays of Plautus (Cist. and Stich., both of which are however incomplete) would three actors suffice, four of them (Capt., Epid., Merc., Pseud.) require at least four, and ten at least five performers, while the Poenulus and Rudens need six. Ritschl p.² lv conjectures seven in the Trinummus. Of the plays of Terence the Heaut. and Hec. require five, the Ad. and Phorm. six actors; the Andr. and Eun. require even more. The writers of the palliatae did not even restrict themselves in the narrower sense in which Horace (AP. 192; cf. Diomed. GL. 1, 491, 23), taking the Greek tragedy as his starting-point, warns them, for the sake of simplicity, against scenes for more than three speaking characters; see the enumeration in FSchmidt p. 4. In this subject there are several details which cannot easily be determined, e.g., in regard to the number of actors, whether there was a fixed maximum (Steffen l.l. concludes that it was seven), how the actors were cast for a number of parts, and whether one part was given to several performers in different acts so as to bring on the best actors more frequently; this theory is employed to explain e.g. why the part of Laches in Ter. Hec. in Bemb. and Vict. is marked with two Greek letters. See however n. 8. FSchmidt, d. Zahl. der Schauspieler bei Plaut. u. Ter., Erl. 1870. CSteffen, de actorum in fabulis Terent. numero et distributione, in Ritschl's Acta soc. philol. Lips. 2, 109. HBosse, quaest. Terent. (c. II), Lips. 1874. FSchöll, JJ. 119, 41. GHSchmitt, qua ratione vett. et quot inter actores Terentii fabularum in scenam edendarum partes distribuerint in the Festschr. z. Karlsruher Philol. Vers. 1882, 24. Cf. n. 8.

5. GHermann, de canticis in Rom. fabb., opusc. 1, 290. GABWolff de canticis etc., Halle 1824. Grysar (see above § 13, 5 ad fin.). There are, however, comedies without *cantica* properly so-called, as Plaut. mil. glor., and others in which they occur rarely, e.g. Asin. Curc. Merc. Frequently (as in Plautus As. Bacch. Capt. Cist. Epid.) the whole company which had taken part in the play came on at the end as a *caterva*, with a concluding address (in trochaic septenarii) to the *spectatores* (Fleckeisen, JJ. 111, 547). Cf. n. 3 and § 17, 5. In the MSS. of Plautus, not only lyric scenes in irregular or mixed metres, but others which are confined to trochaic

septenarii are designated as C (*canticum* or *cantio*) and accordingly accompanied by music, while the declamatory scenes in iambic senarii, which were simply recited, are DV as *diverbia*. Perhaps more correctly *deverbia*? see Dziatzko and Ribbeck l.l. On the other side Bücheler, JJ. 103, 273. Ritschl, op. 3, 25. Of these *cantica* the lyric parts were regularly sung (singing with musical accompaniment), while the scenes in trochaic septenarii were given in recitative (recitativo accompagnato, παρακαταλογή, chanted declamation with musical accompaniment). Ritschl, opusc. 3, 1, ed. Trin.[2] p. lvi. Götz-Löwe on Pl. Asin. p. xiii. KDziatzko, RhM. 26, 97 and JJ. 103, 819. ThBergk, op. 1, 192. WChrist, die Parakataloge im gr. u. röm. Drama, Münch. 1875 (Abh. d. Bayr. Ak. 13, 3, 153) p. 29. 48; Metrik[2] 676. Ribbeck, röm. Trag. 632. See likewise AMüller, gr Bühnenaltertümer 190. Zielinski, Gliederung d. att. Kom., Lpz. 1885, 288. 313.

6. A musician supplied the accompaniment (*modos fecit*), e.g. for Plautus Marcipor Oppi; for Terence, Flaccus Claudi. The didascaliae to Terence (§ 109, 4) are the chief authority for the nature of the music; the following accompaniment is there mentioned, but cannot be understood in detail: *tibiis paribus* or *tibiis imparibus* or *tibiis duabus dextris* or *tibiis sarranis* (Tyrian, Sarra =Tyre). Varr. RR. 1, 2, 15 *dextera tibia alia quam sinistra, ita ut tamen sit quodam modo coniuncta, quod est altera eiusdem carminis modorum incentiva* (first voice), *altera succentiva* (second voice). Diomed. l.l. p. 492, 9. Donat. praef. Eun. p. 10, 11 R. and praef. Adelph. p. 7, 11 R.: *modulata est tibiis dextris*, i.e. *Lydiis ob seriam gravitatem, qua fere in omnibus comoediis utitur hic poeta* (Ter.), *saepe tamen mutatis per scenam modis cantata, quod significat titulus scaenae habens subiectas personis litteras* M.M.C. (*mutatis modis cantici* or *mutantur modi cantici;* cf. Ritschl, op. 3, 39). Thus we read in the didascalia of Ter. Heauton.: *acta primum tibiis imparibus, deinde duabus dextris.* Donat. de com. p. 12, 13 *agebantur tibiis paribus et imparibus, id est dextris aut sinistris* ⟨Reifferscheid inserts *aut dextra et sinistra*⟩. *Dextrae autem tibiae sua gravitate seriam comoediae dictionem praenuntiabant, sinistrae serranae* [Reifferscheid rightly erases *serr.*] *acuminis levitate iocum in comoedia ostendebant: ubi autem dextra et sinistra acta fabula inscribebatur, mixtim ioci et gravitates denuntiabantur.* Cf. KDziatzko, RhM. 20, 594. Cf. Grysar l.l. 376. EBrunér, quaest. terent. (Helsingf. 1868) p. 1 (de canticis et tibiis fabul. Ter.). KvJan, JJ. 119, 591, 21.

7. In the Old Attic Comedy the intervals in the action were marked and filled up by choric songs, but these were given up at an early time (AMüller, Bühnenaltertümer 342), in the later comedy the αὐλητής probably as a rule took their place. Cf. Plaut. Ps. 573. But we hear nothing of a division into acts in the later comedy, nor of any fixed number of these, and Aristotle moreover is silent on the subject. In the Roman comedy too the poet left it to the manager to insert the necessary or desirable pauses. Consequently the original MSS. of Plautus and Terence showed no division into acts, nor is there any trace of such in the manuscripts which have come down to us. In the prologue of L. Ambivius (§ 16, 14) to Ter. Hec. 39 *primo actu placeo* may be equivalent to *in prima fabula.* Naturally the practice in relation to these intervals became gradually fixed, and hence acts are also spoken of in a figurative sense; cf. Varro (RR. 1, 26 *quartus actus;* 2, 5, 2 *secundus actus;* 3, 17, 1 *tertius actus*) and Cic. ad Qu. fr. 1, 1, 46 (see § 13, 4), cf. Apul. flor. 16, 64 *cum iam in tertio actu, quod genus in comoedia fieri amat, iucundiores affectus moveret.* Horace AP. 189 is the first to speak directly of the five acts, which subsequently came to be regarded as the regular number: *neve minor neu sit quinto productior actu.* Donatus complains repeatedly of the difficulty of division into acts. Cf. Euanth. de com. p. 5, 25 R *postquam otioso tempore fasti-*

diosior spectator effectus esset et tum cum ad cantores ab actoribus fabula transibat consurgere et abire coepisset, admonuit poetas ut primo quidem choros tollerent locum eis relinquentes, ut Menander fecit . . .: postremo ne locum quidem reliquerunt, quod Latini fecerunt comici, unde apud illos dirimere actus quinquepartitos difficile est. The fact that the division into acts as transmitted to us is frequently impracticable proves its late origin. Cf. STEFFEN (n. 4 ad fin.) p 147. For a general view see DONAT. arg. Andr. p. 7, 11 R.: *est attente animadvertendum ubi et quando scena vacua sit ab omnibus personis, ut in ea chorus* (in the tragedy) *vel tibicen* (in the comedy) *obaudiri possint; quod cum viderimus, ibi actum esse finitum debemus agnoscere.* Five acts as the rule are also presupposed by DONAT. for the Ad. p. 7, 1 R.: *haec quoque, ut cetera huiusmodi poemata, quinque actus habeat necesse est*, and for the Hec. p. 12, 16 R.: *divisa est ut ceterae quinque actibus legitimis.* The first act generally contains the explanation of the plot (πρότασις), in acts II to IV the knot is entangled and the intrigue brought about (ἐπίτασις), in the fifth is the dénouement (καταστροφή). Cf. EUANTH. p. 7, 21 R. DONAT. de com. 10, 9 R. VICTORIN. GL. 6, 78, 29 *haec per medios actus varie, rursus in exitu fabularum* etc. RITSCHL, opusc. 2, 354. KFHERMANN, de Ter. Adelphis in Jahn's Jahrbb. Suppl. 6, 71. WSCHMITZ, de actuum in Plaut. fab. discriptione, Bonn 1852. EBRUNÉR, quaest. terent. (1868) 20. On the metrical and musical composition of the several acts ASPENGEL, d. Akteinleitung d. Kom. d. Plaut., Münch. 1877.

8. The division into scenes is regularly found in all MSS. of Plautus and Terence, the names of the characters speaking in each being indispensable as headings. The interlocutors are generally in the MSS. marked within the scenes, with the initial letter of their names; but sometimes, for the sake of abbreviation, with single Greek letters; the key to this system is given in the heading of the scenes, where the names are inscribed with the letters which correspond to them. So in some places in the cod. vet. (B) of Plautus (§ 99, 7, most completely in the Trin.) and most thoroughly carried out in the Bembinus and Victorianus codd. of Terence (§ 109, 2). RITSCHL, op. 2, 294. 365; ed. Trin.[2] p. LV. and others (TEUFFEL, JJ. 105, 108. CSTEFFEN [n. 4] 116. 150. WWAGNER, JB. 1873, 446) have wrongly assumed that these letters had a dramaturgic meaning and referred to the distribution of the parts among the actors, and to their comparative importance as leading and secondary parts, etc.: see FLEO on Sen. trag. 1, p. 85.—ASPENGEL, Szenentitel u. Szenenabteilung in d. lat. Kom., Münch. SBer. 1883, 257.

9. As a compensation for their curtailing of the originals and in order to increase the attraction of a play, Naevius, Plautus (cf. GGÖTZ, act. soc. Lips. 6, 310. 315), Ennius and, following their example, Terence also (Andr. prol. 18) took single scenes out of a Greek play of similar plot, and transferred them into the one adopted by them, which proceeding Luscius (§ 107, 5) by way of censure called *contaminare* (see Andr. prol. 16, Heaut. prol. 16). This clumsy proceeding, while it gained for the play a few effective incidents, no doubt often injured the composition as a whole and caused all sorts of irreconcilable discrepancies.

10. The prologue commonly contained a summary of the subject of the play (TER. Andr. prol. 5), but, like the parabasis of the old comedy, was also used for the exposition of the poet's personal wishes. DONATUS de com. p. 10, 11 R. accordingly distinguishes four varieties: *συστατικός, commendaticius; ἐπιτιμητικός * *, relativus; δραματικός, argumentativus; μικτός, mixtus.* The prologue was recited without any theatrical costume (*sine ornamentis*, PLAUT. Poen. prol. 123,=*ornatu prologi*, TER. Hec. prol. B, 1) by an actor who had not to appear at the very beginning of the first act (change of dress, Poen. prol. 126; exceptions in RITSCHL

Parerg. 19) or by the *dominus gregis* (as frequently in Terence). But it does not always precede the first act (PLAUT. mil. 2, 1. Cist. 1, 3; cf. DONAT. praef. to Ter. Phorm. p. 14, 24 R.) and may even be omitted altogether (PLAUT. Curc.). For new performances of a play, even after the poet's death, new prologues used to be composed; those prefixed to plays of Plautus, which have been preserved, are chiefly of this kind, and for the most part insufferably diffuse and insipid; see RITSCHL, Parerga 209. 225. 233, and below § 99, 1.

11. The πρόσωπα προτατικά chiefly serve to facilitate the exposition, on which great care was bestowed, there being no play-bill to assist the intelligence of the spectator. DONAT. arg. Andr. p. 4, 4 R: *persona protatica intellegitur quae semel inducta in principio fabulae in nullis deinceps fabulae partibus adhibetur.* EUANTH. de com. p. 6, 7 R. προτατικὰ πρόσωπα, i.e. *personas extra argumentum arcessitas, non facile ceteri habent* (Plautus however employs as such Artotrogus in the Miles and Grumio in the Most.), *quibus Terentius saepe* (in Andr. Phorm. and Hec.) *utitur, ut per harum inductiones facile pateat argumentum.*

12. The customary form of the epilogue is: *plaudite.* Cf. MENAND. fr. 831 ἐξάραντες ἐπικροτήσατε with PLAUT. Truc. conclusion: *plaudite atque exsurgite.* See besides QUINTIL. 6, 1, 52 *illud quo veteres tragoediae comoediaeque cluduntur 'Plodite.'* HOR. AP. 155, etc.

13. Masks. DIOMED. GL. 1, 489 *antea galearibus* (besides paint etc.), *non personis, utebantur, ut qualitas coloris indicium faceret aetatis, cum essent aut albi* (old men; cf. *albicapillus*, PLAUT. Mil. 631. Bacch. 1101. Trin. 873; also long beard and staff, Plaut. Men. 854. 856) *aut nigri* (youths; gallants with curled hair, *cincinnati*, cf. PLAUT. Mil. 923) *aut rufi* (slaves). *personis vero uti primus coepit Roscius Gallus, praecipuus histrio, quod oculis perversis erat* (cf. CIC. nat. deor. 1, 79, see concerning him RIBBECK, röm. Trag. 671) *nec satis decorus sine personis nisi parasitus pronuntiabat.* This evidently professional account, which probably comes from Suet. and Varro, is contradicted by DONAT. de comoed. p. 10, 1 R. *personati primi egisse dicuntur comoediam Cincius Faliscus, tragoediam Minucius Prothymus.* Cf. DONAT. praef. to Ter. Eun. p. 10 R. *acta est . . . etiam (iam?) tum personatis L. Minucio Prothymo, L. Ambivio Turpione* and praef. Ad. p. 7 *haec acta est* (594/160) *agentibus L. Ambivio et L. * * qui cum suis gregibus etiam tum personati agebant.* If this account were correct with regard to Ambivius Turpio, the use of masks would go back to the time of Terence, but his plays themselves disprove it (see e.g. Phorm. 210). For an attempt to assign a later date to Minucius Prothymus and to connect him with Roscius (supposing Roscius to have introduced masks into Minucius' troupe) see DZIATZKO, RhM. 21, 68 and RIBBECK, röm. Trag. 661. From CIC. de or. 3, 221 *in ore sunt omnia . . . personatum ne Roscium quidem magnopere laudabant nostri illi senes* we may assume that about 630/124 actors were still without masks, but that they came in shortly after that time, and probably in response to the universal tendency of the later Roman drama, to assimilate the performances as much as possible to the Greek custom. About 640/114 Roscius might already have appeared in masks. Having once been introduced, the wearing of masks long remained the rule; at least we may gather this from the *cogi in scena ponere personam* (FEST. 217; see above § 9, 4); and after this, when *actores comoediarum* (as distinguished from the *mimi = artifices scenici*, in SEN. ep. 1, 11, 7, who alone played without masks) are mentioned, stress is laid only on the voice, the diction and the action as characteristic, as in QUINTIL. 3, 8, 51. 11, 3, 178. It was afterwards sought to lessen the inconveniences of masks: as by large openings for the eyes and mouth, so that the facial expression (CIC. de or. 2, 193. 3, 221) should not be entirely wasted. See CROBERT, ann. 1880, 206. Finally the masks

were got rid of, most likely under the influence of the Mimus. Donat. Ter. Andr. 4, 3 *sive haec* (*femina* = Mysis) *personatis viris agitur, ut apud veteres, sive per mulierem, ut nunc videmus.* Cf. CSteffen 154. ChHoffer, de personarum usu in Terentii comoediis, Halle 1877.—Ancient representations of actors: FWieseler, Denkm. d. Bühnenwesens, Gött. 1851. ThSchreiber, kulturhist. Bilderatlas T. 1–6. AMüller's Bühnenaltert. 227 sqq.; concerning these in the MSS. of Terence, see § 109, 2.

14. As *actores comoediarum* are known to us, in the time of Plautus, a certain (*T. Publilius*) *Pellio* (§ 97, 8 n. 1. Ritschl, Parerga 250. 392. WStudemund, comment. Mommsen. 801), in the time of Terence (cf. n. 13) especially: *L. Ambivius Turpio*, the most famous manager and actor of the period before Cicero (cf. Cic. sen. 48. Tac. dial. 20. Symm. ep. 1, 31, 3. 10, 2, 1), further *L. Atilius* of Praeneste (cf. § 107, 2). Belonging to the Republican period (probably the 7th century) *M. Ofilius Hilarus* (Plin. N.H. 7, 184); to the time of Quintilian (11, 3, 178) *Stratokles* and *Demetrius* (§ 15, 1).

17. Togata is the name given, in contradistinction to palliata, to comedies with Roman (Italian) subject-matter. Later on this comedy was called also tabernaria. It represented the life of the lower classes in Rome; thus it was coarser in tone than the palliata, but at the same time had greater freshness and vitality. But it surpasses the palliata especially in its conception of family life, the female sex being far more prominent in it, and the slaves holding comparatively insignificant parts. The chronology of the togata is defined on the one hand by the over-refined palliata of Terence, and on the other by the artificial Atellana and the Mimus. Its principal poets are Titinius, Quinctius Atta and L. Afranius, all between 589/169 and 675/79. Afranius raised the togata into higher circles of society, introduced the arrangement and tone of the palliata into it, sometimes even used Greek plays for his purposes, and in this way created a kind of mixed species, which, however, died out with him. Even in the Imperial period Afranius' togatae were performed.

1. In the broadest sense of the word *togata* may designate any *fabula* (serious or light), with Roman subject-matter. Diomedes GL. 1, 489 enumerates as *togatae* a) *praetextatae*, b) *togatae* = *tabernariae*, c) *Atellanae*, d) *planipedes*, and defines them: *quae scriptae sunt secundum ritus et habitum hominum togatorum* i.e. *Romanorum.* In this sense *togata* comprises also the *trabeata* which Diomedes omits, though this was merely a transient and unimportant species, devoted especially to the equites, whose peculiar habit was the *trabea* (Pers. 3, 29. Dio 56, 31), and a species merely represented by C. Melissus its originator (§ 244, 2). In the same general sense, and especially of *praetextae*, Sen. ep. 1, 8, 8 uses the term *togatae: non attingam tragicos nec togatas nostras. habent enim hae quoque aliquid severitatis et sunt inter comoedias ac tragoedias mediae.*

2. Diomed. l. l.: *secunda species est togatarum quae tabernariae dicuntur et humilitate personarum et argumentorum similitudine comoediis* (= *palliatis*) *pares.*

The name *tabernariae* was taken from the *tabernae*, the booths of the artisans and of the industrial class in general. Festus 352 v. *togatarum* enumerates among the characters of the *tabernariae* besides others *plagiarii*, *servi denique*, in general such as *ex tabernis honeste prodeant.* Cf. also such titles of togatae as *Augur*, *Cinerarius*, *Fullonia*, *Libertus*, *Psaltria*, *Tibicina*. *Togatae* is the name given to plays of this kind espec. in Cic. Sest. 118. Hor. AP. 288. Vellei. 2, 9, 3. Sen. ep. 14, 1 (=89), 7 (cf. Afran. v. 299). Suet. Ner. 11. Quint. 10, 1, 100. Gell. 10, 11, 8. 13, 8, 3.

3. The plots of the togatae are generally laid at Rome, though not unfrequently also in a provincial town, in order to ridicule either the life of a small town or satirise Rome in a disguised manner, or to describe the impression produced by Rome on a man from the country; cf. the titles *Brundisinae*, *Ferentinatis*, *Setina*, *Veliterna*, *Ulubrana*. From the mere titles appears the large admixture of the female sex (even of virgins), and this is still more shown by the fragments. Cf. also Serv. Aen. 11, 160 *in togatis victrices appellantur quae viros extulerunt.* Donatus on Ter. Eun. 12 is very significant: *concessum est in palliata poetis comicis servos dominis sapientiores fingere, quod item in togata non fere licet.*

4. Diomed. GL. 1, 490 *togatas tabernarias in scenam dataverunt praecipue duo, L. Afranius et G. Quintius.* Ps.-Acro (from Suet.? see AKiessling, de personis horat. 8) on Hor. AP. 288 following an absurd explanation of the terms *praetexta* (=comedy with Roman subject-matter) and *togata* (=comedy with Greek subject-matter): *praetextas et togatas scripserunt Aelius Lamia, Antonius Rufus* (these two otherwise unknown, cf. also § 254, 3), *Cn. Melissus* (§ 244, 2), *Afranius*, *Pomponius* (284, 7). A performance of Afranius' Incendium under Nero, Suet. Ner. 11. Togatae publicly recited: Iuv. 1, 3.—A certain *togatarius Stephanio* (*cui in puerilem habitum circumtonsam matronam ministrasse compererat Augustus* and whom he therefore *per trina theatra virgis caesum relegavit*) occurs in Suet. Aug. 45; cf. Plin. NH. 7, 159 *minus miror Stephanionem, qui primus togatus* (more correctly *togatas*, cf. *tragoediam saltare*, § 13, 6) *saltare instituit, utrisque saecularibus ludis* (a. 737/17 and 800/47) *saltavisse* etc. Thus the Pantomimus appropriated the subject-matter of the togatae, as it had that of the tragedies and palliatae (§ 8, 13).

5. In imitation of the arrangement of the *palliata* Afranius has prologues (v. 25–30. Macr. S. 6, 5, 6 *Afranium . . . qui in prologo ex persona Priapi ait*, just as, in his *Sella*, *Sophia* appeared as a speaker) and *cantica* (even synodic ones). Cic. Sest. 118 *cum ageretur togata—Simulans, ut opinor—caterva tota clarissima concentione . . . contionata est.* The adoption of the parasites belongs to the same features, though the Roman clientship and the *scurrae* offered analogies. The fragments of togatae are collected in Ribbeck, com.[2] 131.—JHNeukirch, de fab. togata, Lps. 1833; Ladewig PRE. 6, 3024; Mommsen RG. 1^6, 904. 2^6, 436.

18. The Roman writers on literature specify the **Rhinthonica** as a separate variety of Roman comedy; it was named after the farce-writer (φλυακογράφος) Rhinthon of Tarentum, whose ἱλαροτραγῳδίαι were travesties of tragic subjects, but none of the names of the Roman adapters nor any titles or remains of Roman Rhinthonicae have come down to us. Some of these however may be incorporated among the Atellanae on mythological subjects.

1. For the authorities on the Roman Rhinthonica see § 12, 1. Lyd. de mag. 1, 40 Ῥινθωνικὴ (ἐστὶν) ἡ ἐξωτική (cf. Plaut. Men. 2, 1, 11 *Graeciamque exoticam* of southern Italy). For Rhinthon, who flourished under Ptolemaios I Soter (a. 320–285 B.C. = 437/469 U.C.), see esp. Suid. s.v. Ῥίνθων. Steph. Byz. v. Τάρας. The κωμῳδοτραγῳδία of Alkaios, Deinolochos and Anaxandrides (Meineke, hist. crit. com. gr. 247) is older than the ἱλαροτραγῳδία, of which Rhinthon was the ἀρχηγὸς (see Suid. s.v.), and is therefore not identical with it. Perhaps the κωμῳδοτραγῳδία was more like a comedy compared with the farcical ἱλαροτραγῳδία, possibly like Plaut. Amphitr., which in the prologue v. 59 and 63 is called a *tragi*[*co*]*comoedia*. (Tragicocomoedia in Lutat. on Stat. Theb. 5, 160.) Cf. also Varro's Pseudotragoediae (§ 165, 2). Plautus' Amphitruo is certainly not a Rhinthonica; see Vahlen, RhM. 16, 472.

2. The separation of the Rhinthonica from the Atellana is probably only founded on a quibble of the theorists. Titles of Atellanae which indicate farcical travesties of mytho-tragical subjects are *Agamemno suppositus*, *Ariadne*, *Armorum iudicium* (?), *Atalante*, *Sisyphus* by Pomponius, *Phoenissae* by Novius, *Autonoe* (Iuv. 6, 71).—In general cf. Neukirch, de fab. tog. 15. EMunk, de fabb. Atell. 84. Vahlen, RhM. 15, 472. E. Sommerbrodt, de phlyacogr. graec. (Bresl. 1875) p. 43.

19. The Romans possessed a tendency to preserve and cherish the recollection of past events; and as they perceived that metre facilitated both recollection and tradition, we find here a field favourable to the development of epic poetry. Hence we have at an early age ancestral songs and inscriptions of various kinds somewhat like the epic in style. The saturnian measure employed in them was also used by the most ancient epic poets, Andronicus and Naevius, the first a mere translator in his Latin Odyssey, the latter in his bellum punicum boldly plunging into the life of his nation and time. Like him, his successor Ennius chose, in his Annals, a national subject, which he expanded to a complete Roman history down to his own time, and treated in dactylic hexameters. His example became the type for later poets, both as to subject-matter and form. During the next century no other poet attempted an epic poem; but then Hostius, plainly following Ennius, wrote a bellum istricum, and similarly L. Accius and A. Furius and later on Tanusius wrote epics entitled Annales. Cicero himself wrote poems in hexameters on his consulship and exile (de suo consulatu, de temporibus meis), while Varro Atacinus treated of Caesar's bellum sequanicum. In the Augustan period Anser eulogised M. Antony, and others treated subjects of the history of the period in the manner of the Alexandrine poets and partly with panegyric tendencies, as L. Varius (de morte, sc. Caesaris; Panegyricus Augusti), Tibullus (?Panegyricus Messalae), Octavianus himself (Sicilia); important epic fragments remain to us by Cornelius Severus (res

romanae), Rabirius (bellum actiacum ?), Albinovanus Pedo (de navigatione Germanici per oceanum septentrionalem). In the Imperial period epic poetry was chiefly devoted to the past: Lucan's Pharsalia, the epic poem de bello civili (in Petronius sat. 119), and Silius Italicus' Punica). About the middle of the 3rd century of our era such subjects still found favour, and Alfius Avitus treated them even in iambic dimeters. But when contemporary history furnished the material, as under Trajan authors selected a bellum dacicum and parthicum, such subjects could only be treated in courtly fashion. To this class belong Gordian's Antoninias, Claudian with his numerous eulogistic epics on Stilicho, and the bellum gildonicum and pollentinum; lastly Corippus' Johannis and laudes Iustini.

1. The interest of the epic subject-matter remained always predominant and decisive. Cic. de imp. Pomp. 25 *sinite hoc loco, sicut poetae solent qui res romanas scribunt, praeterire me nostram calamitatem.* The Roman magnates longed to be glorified in poetry, e.g. Cic. Arch. 26. 27.. Augustus systematically favoured and promoted epic compositions, and to abstain from them almost required an excuse, as in the case of Horace. A large number of real or pretended epic poets enumerated by Ovid. Pont. 4, 16. In the time of Nero epic composition was fashionable, see Persius 1, 69. Cf. Petron. 118. Martial. 4, 14. 10, 64. Stat. silv. 2, 7, 48. HSchiller, Nero 611. In Priscian. GL. 2, 237 are three hexameters taken from the epic poem, in at least three books, of a certain *Gannius* (*G. Annius* ? cf. § 209, 12). Phrases (in prose) taken from a certain (orator, cf. § 137, 4) Gannius, Paul. Festi 369 v. *veteratores.* A certain Canius as author of an iambic verse in Varro LL. 6, 81.

2. Köne, in his Sprachgebrauch der röm. Epiker, Münst. 1840, argues that the dactylic hexameter is greatly at variance with the phonetic constituents of the Latin tongue, and that the exigencies of this metre imposed many restrictions on the Roman poets. Cf. FCHultgren, d. Technik der röm. Dicht. im ep. u. eleg. Versmass, JJ. 107, 745. ThBirt, ad hist. hexam. lat. symb., Bonn 1876. MW Humphreys, de accentus momento in versu heroico, Lps. 1874. HHelbig, de synaloephae ap. epicos lat. primi p. Chr. saeculi ratione, Bautzen 1878. KP Schulze, Hochton u. Vershebung in den 2 letzten Füssen des lat. Hex. ZfGW. 29, 590 etc.

3. FWinkelmann, d. epischen Dicht. d. Röm. bis auf Virgil, in Jahn's Arch. 2, 558. OHaube, de carminibus epicis saec. Augusti, Bresl. 1870; die Epen des silb. Zeitalters d. röm. Lit., Fraustadt 1886. On the introduction of similes among the epic and elegiac writers see JWalser, ZfdöG. 29, 595.

4. Collection of the works of the Latin poets (excluding the scenici) by WE Weber (corpus poett. lat., Frankf. 1831); of the lesser Latin poems preserved in manuscript by JChrWernsdorf (poetae lat. minores, Altenb. u. Helmst. 1780–99 VI) and EBährens (poetae lat. min., Lps. 1879–83 V). As a supplement fragmenta poett. roman. coll. et emend. EBährens, Lps. 1886 (containing the passages from poets scattered in various authors, besides the fragments of the scenici and the satura Menippea). On the editions of the so-called Anthologia latina and the collections of the Lat. poems preserved in inscriptions see § 31, 4.

20. An heroic epic was impossible at Rome in its original state, the Italian gods being mere abstractions, and godlike heroes unknown to the people. When, therefore, towards the end of the Republic the influence of the Alexandrine poets caused this class of epic poetry to be cultivated, it was necessary to choose foreign subjects for mythological tales. Thus Varro Atacinus (Argonautae), Catullus (Epithalamium Pelei et Thetidos), Helvius Cinna (Smyrna), Licinius Calvus (Io), Pedo (Theseis), as well as (in respect of its subject-matter) Ovid's Metamorphoses, later on (the Culex and) the Ciris, and Valerius Flaccus (Argonautica). Others translated the Iliad, e.g. C. Matius, at a later time Gaurus and, as appears probable, the young Silius Italicus as the author of the so-called Homerus latinus; aspirants of a higher order reverted to the Epic Cycle, as Ninnius Crassus (the Cyprian Iliad), Furius Bibaculus (Aethiopis ?), Pompeius Macer (Antehomerica and Posthomerica), Julius Antonius (Diomedea), Domitius Marsus (Amazonis), Camerinus (Excidium Troiae), Lupus and Largus; at a later time Nero's Troica, Lucan's Iliaca, Statius' Thebais and Achilleis etc. At the end of the fourth century Claudian wrote his mythological epics Raptus Proserpinae and Gigantomachia. At the end of the fifth the African Dracontius adapted the rape of Helen, the legend of Medea and parts of the myth of Herakles (Hylas and Hydra); he is in all probability also the author of the Orestis tragoedia. Between the historic or national and the Alexandrine or mythological classes stands Vergil's Aeneid, in which an indigenous legend is told in a historic and psychological manner, but with a mythological background; and this became the pattern of poetical composition to the subsequent poets.

1. Influence of rhetoric, especially in the style of description, e.g. SEN. Apoc. 2, 3 *omnes poetae, non contenti ortus et occasus describere* (like Julius Montanus, SEN. ep. v. 122, 11–13), *etiam medium diem inquietant.* A pathetic style was required: *heroici carminis sonus*, TAC. dial. 10. The style of the heroic epic was also transferred to the historic class, as in Silius: cf. PETRON. 118 *non enim res gestae versibus comprehendendae sunt, quod longe melius historici faciunt, sed per ambages deorumque ministeria et fabulosum sententiarum tormentum praecipitandus est liber spiritus, ut potius furentis animi vaticinatio appareat quam religiosae orationis sub testibus fides.*

2. Influence of Vergil see § 231.—The *Troiae halosis* in senarii (in PETRON. 89) given as a speech to Eumolpus already diverges from the traditional model. In the same metre Avienus at a later time paraphrased Vergil and Livy (§ 420, 6). Similar Greek paraphrases in trimeter were produced in large numbers (e.g. of Theokritos, Apollonios, Kallimachos and other Alexandrine poetry) by the Hellenised Roman Marianus about the year 500 A.D.; see SUID. s. v.—LACTANT.

inst. div. 1, 11 (FPR. 405) *non insulse quidam poeta triumphum Cupidinis scripsit* (list of contents follow): qu. whether an Epyllion or in elegiac metre? whether Greek (ERohde, gr. Rom. 108. 544) or Latin perhaps in the style of Reposianus (§ 398, 2)?

21. After the victory of Christianity the epic poets who belonged to the new faith treated subjects from the biblical history of the Old and New Testaments, instead of Roman history or Greek mythology. Thus Proba Faltonia in her cento; subjects from the Old Testament were treated by Avitus, by Claudius Victor (Genesis) and by Victorinus (the Maccabees), also by the author of the metrical paraphrases of the subject-matter of the Pentateuch, the book of Joshua etc (see § 403, 5); New Testament subjects by Juvencus, Sedulius (carmen paschale) and Arator (history of the Apostles). Side by side with panegyrics on Emperors as still composed by Claudian, Apollinaris Sidonius (on Avitus, Maiorianus and Anthemius), Merobaudes (on Aëtius), Corippus (on Anastasius) and Venantius Fortunatus (on Frankish nobles), were produced eulogistic poems (epic hymns) on God, Christ, Christian martyrs and saints, and on bishops and popes. On Christ, e.g. by Mamertus Claudianus (? see § 468, 5), on martyrs especially by Damasus, Prudentius (περὶ στεφάνων) and Paulinus of Nola (Felix). Martin of Tours was made the object of laudatory epics by Paulinus of Perigueux and Venantius Fortunatus, who also eulogised other bishops. On the other hand, under the influence of the school of rhetoric, panegyrics continued also to be composed in epic metre on subjects, both light and serious, taken from Paganism.

1. Enumeration of Christian epic writers ap. Venant. Fort. vita Mart. 1, 14–25. Collections: GFabricius, poetarum vett. ecclesiasticorum opera christiana et operum reliq. ac fragm., Bas. 1564. PLeyser, hist. poetarum et poematum medii aevi decem post annum a Chr. n. 400 saeculorum, Halle 1721. Henry, hist. de la poésie chrétienne, Paris 1856. Cf. § 30, 2.

2. The less sacred character of the Old Testament permitted even Christian poets a freer treatment of their subjects. Christian poems by unknown authors were in the MSS. appended to the works of particular patristic writers, especially Tertullian, Cyprian and Lactantius, and for a long time were accepted as the work of those writers. Thus the original Epyllia *Sodoma* (166 hex.) and *De Iona* (actually rather *de Ninive*, preserved in an incomplete state, 105 hex.)—both by one author, probably written in the first half of the 4th century, attributed sometimes to Cyprian (in Hartel's Cyprian 3, 289. 227), sometimes to Tertullian. LMüller, RhM. 22, 329. 464. 27, 486. AEbert., Lit. des MA. 1, 116. In MSS of Cyprian, and therefore in Hartel 3, 283, we find besides 85 hexameters addressed to a Consular who had apostatised from Christianity to the worship of Isis; *de pascha* 69 hex.; *ad Flavium Felicem de resurrectione mortuorum* 406 hex., and a fragment of a versifi-

cation of Genesis (165 hex.), belonging to a very voluminous poem on the Old Testament (Pentateuch, Joshua, Judges, etc.), by an unknown author, see § 403, 5.

3. *Laus Herculis* in 137 graceful hexameters by an anonymous author (Merobaudes? see § 439, 7. 464, 2), AL. 881, in Jeep's Claudian 2, p. 203, cf. 186. Cf. EBährens, JJ. 105, 52. 503; JB. 1873, 219. LJeep in the Begrüssungschrift d. Leipz. Philologenvers. (Lps. 1872) 46; Rivista di filol. 1, 405.—Hymnus Claudii ad Lunam (=Isis, Cybebe, etc.) AL. 723 PLM. 3, 163. Similar invocations to Mars, Juno, Liber for a safe return: AL. 749–751 PLM 3, 303–304. *In laudem Solis* AL. 389 PLM. 4, 543; cf. below § 475, 5 ad fin. Parodic hymn to Pan AL. 682 PLM. 3, 170.

22. The Epithalamium gradually became a laudatory poem on the occasion of a wedding, but retained from its original relation to erotic poetry a certain wantonness and coarseness. Of the earlier period we possess three epithalamia by Catullus, and the names of Calvus and Ticidas as authors of similar productions; of the Imperial period are preserved epithalamia by Statius, Ausonius, Claudianus, Paulinus of Nola, Apollinaris Sidonius, Dracontius, Ennodius, Luxorius, Venantius Fortunatus (on Sigibert) and the Epithalamium Laurentii.

1. The epithalamium in honour of a young couple, their parents and ancestors, is generally composed in epic metre. One by Gallienus is also mentioned, see § 385, 2. The epithalamia of Ausonius (§ 421, 2 k) and of Luxorius (§ 476, 3) are at the same time Vergilian centos (§ 26, 2).

2. The *epithalamium Laurentii* (87 hex., AL. 742 PLM. 3, 293) written by an unknown author in the MSS. of Claudian (in Jeep's ed. 2 p. 194) shows an admixture of sentimentality; if we may judge by its structure and the prominence given to Pagan customs (dedication of the beard, nuptial ceremonies, undisguised descriptions) it is as early as cent. IV/V. Cf. also Jeep l.l. 164. The bridegroom (Laurentius) is commended for his ability as a legal orator, the bride (Florida?) for her accomplishments and the lanificium. Wernsdorf, PLM. 4, 2, 462. LMüller, RhM. 22, 83. 89. 24, 126. ARiese, JJ. 97, 706. MHaupt, op. 3, 372. EBährens, JJ. 105, 501.—It was known in England in the 7th century, see Haupt l.l.

23. Didactic poetry, being in keeping with the sober mind of the Romans, was taken up at an early period. The precepts of a peasant to his son are very ancient (cf. below § 85, 1), and Appius Claudius as well as Cato wrote in a similar spirit. The subjects of Ennius' didactic poems were more varied. Lucilius' Satires likewise pursued didactic purposes and even treated of orthography. Literary history was illustrated in the didactic poems of L. Accius (Didascalica), Q. Valerius of Sora, Volcacius Sedigitus, Porcius Licinus. Only a few of these didactic poems were written in the Greek epic metre, which gained an ascendancy only towards the end of the Republic under the influence of

Greek literature. This we have in Varro Atacinus' chorographia and ephemeris, Cicero's translation of Aratus, Lucretius' system of Epicurean philosophy (de rerum natura), and subsequently in Vergil, who, in his Georgics, treated a well-chosen subject with sympathy and perfect art. Ovid, following the Hellenistic precedent, employed the elegiac metre in his explanation of the calendar by indigenous legends (Fasti), as well as in the playful didactic treatment of erotic subjects (Ars amatoria, Remedia amoris, Medicamina faciei); in epic metre he treated the Metamorphoses. Some of Ovid's contemporaries with less taste, and in blind imitation of the Alexandrine poets, treated utterly prosaic subjects in their didactic poems. Thus Valgius Rufus wrote a didactic poem on herbs, Aemilius Macer Theriaca and Ornithogonia, Grattius (Faliscus) Cynegetica, Manilius Astronomica. Likewise in the first century of our era Germanicus produced a new version of Aratus, Columella wrote on horticulture; the descriptive epic, entitled Aetna, belongs to this series, as well as in the third century the patristic Lactantius' poem de ave phoenice in distichs; in the fourth century Palladius' didactic poem de re rustica, the various works of Ausonius, especially his Mosella, Avienus' Descriptio orbis terrae and Aratea, and his Ora maritima (in iambics), and the Christian and dogmatic poems of Prudentius; in the fifth century Rutilius Namatianus' Itinerarium in elegiacs. This metre is also used in Orientius' Commonitorium, while the epic metre is used in Dracontius' didactic poems on God and the Creation, and Avitus' on the Trinity. In most of these works the metrical form is merely accessory to the subject-matter, but all semblance of poetry disappears in the didactic poems of grammarians for school-use, such as not only the versus memoriales (largely represented in Ausonius), but especially the metrical manuals of rhetoric, metre, prosody and metrology, the carmina de figuris vel schematibus (by Marbod and unknown authors), Terentianus Maurus' undeniably skilful metrical treatises de litteris, syllabis, metris, the probably similar one by Albinus, the verses de metris oratorum by Rufinus of Antioch, the carmina de ponderibus et mensuris etc. Similar works are the medical systems in epic metre by Serenus Sammonicus, Flavius and Vindicianus. The Middle Ages were very fertile in productions of this kind.

1. EBrunér, de carm. didascalico Rom., Helsingf. 1840. RKnobloch, d. röm. Lehrgedicht bis z. Ende d. Rep., Rossleben 1881. On the didactic poems by

Egnatius and others, see § 192. Rhetorical school verses by Dracontius and others (§ 45, 9). On the poems of the XII Sapientes see § 427, 1.—On the didactic poem adversus Marcionem § 436, 8.

2. Memorial verses on the names of the Muses AL. 664 PLM. 3, 243; on the names of the winds in Greek and Latin AL. 484 PLM. 5, 383 (cf. besides § 347, 3 below), the latter from Isidor. de rer. nat. 37 and composed about his time, already preserved in MSS. s. VII/VIII.—Hexameters on the constellations, seasons etc. AL. 676 sqq. PLM. 5, 349 sqq., not earlier than s. VI.—Description of a map of the heavens (*de sphaera coeli*) after Hyginus, dry and clumsy in style, in 76 hex. from MSS. s. XI AL. 761 PLM. 5, 380. Perhaps not ancient.

3. Several metrical enumerations of expressions for the voices of various animals (cf. WWackernagel, Voces variae animantium, Bas. 1869; see also GLöwe, RhM. 34, 493) of quite a late period, but in substance going back indirectly to Suetonius (see Reifferscheid's Suet. 247): e.g. AL. 733 PLM. 5, 367 in MSS. s. X/XI, further esp. AL. 762 PLM. 5, 363 ('*de philomela*,' rather on the voices of birds and quadrupeds in 70 elegiac lines) in MSS. s. XI; at the close (as in the poem to be mentioned presently) is an edifying turn, probably composed in some German convent (see v. 11 *dulce per ora sonat, dicunt quam nomine droscam*: cf. ohG. *drosca*, *droscila* = Drossel). Goldast (catal. Ovid. 71) pretends that Albius Ovidius Juventinus is named as the author in a St. Gallen MS.; see also GScherrer, St. Galler Hss.-Verzeichnis 72. In like manner he invented a certain Julius Speratus as the author of a poem of about the same date as the abovementioned, addressed to the nightingale, AL 658 PLM. 5, 368, preserved in MSS. s. X/XI, and imitated already in the s. IX by Alvarus of Cordova (AEbert, LdMA. 2, 310): the same is also attributed to Eugenius of Toledo, see § 495, 4.

24. The proverbial poems are didactic poems on a small scale, which were in the Imperial period partly selected from larger, complete works and compiled, partly independently produced (no doubt chiefly for pedagogic use). The so-called disticha Catonis are a collection of the latter kind.

1. The proverbial poem stands in the same relation to the didactic as the Epigram to the Elegy. For the proverbial literature in iambic senarii connected with Syrus see § 212, 4. On the disticha Catonis see § 398.

25. The poetical Epistle and the Fable have also a didactic tendency. Any poem may become a poetical Epistle by being addressed to a certain person, and thus didactic poems addressed e.g. to a son are at the same time Epistles. In a limited sense poems are called so in which the direction to individuals influences the whole contents and the treatment from beginning to end. In this manner Sp. Mummius addressed, from his camp before Corinth (608/146), jocular letters in verse to his friends at Rome; Lucilius also composed several of his satires in the form of letters to friends, and Catullus' poem to Manlius (68^a) is also an Epistle. In the Augustan period Horace dedicated several

satires to Maecenas, many lyric poems to individual friends, and in his later years treated with mature wisdom and perfect felicity questions concerning practical life and literature in real Epistles in epic metre. Ovid wrote in elegiacs fictitious love-letters of mythical ladies (Heroides), and also real letters of complaint and entreaty from his exile (Tristia and ex Ponto). The other elegiac poets as well as the satirists Persius and Juvenal, too, several times address individuals by name, without, however, really preserving the epistolary style. But Ausonius' 25 Epistles and many by Statius are real letters in various metres and partly on jocular subjects, as also those of Claudian and of Apollinaris Sidonius.

1. On Mummius see § 131, 8. A book or satire of Lucilius (27, 1 MÜLL.) commenced in this manner: *salutem fictis versibus Lucilius quibus potest impertit, totumque hoc studiose et sedulo* etc.

2. TIB. (LYGD.) 3, 5 for instance is also a letter; here also actually belong many epodes of Horace, esp. 1. 11 and 14; letter from a wife to her husband far away with the army in the East, in PROP. 5, 3. Both the names and circumstances are probably imaginary. Dido Aeneae AL. 83 PLM. 4, 271 with a refrain; cf. WERNSDORF PLM. 4, p. 55. 439. Real letters, e.g. STAT. Silv. 4, 4 (to Victorius Marcellus) and 4, 8 (a congratulatory letter), together with. that of Licentius to Augustine. For the letters of Claudian see § 439, 6.

26. Trifles current at table and at school were also usually written in epic metre. Riddles were connected with Greek literature; having become more popular only in the last centuries of Rome, this kind of literature continued to flourish more and more luxuriantly till late in the Middle Ages. On the other hand, from scholarly circles proceeded the numerous variations on old (especially Vergilian) themes, and the patchwork poems (centones) in which a new work was created out of verses and parts of verses selected arbitrarily from older poets. Other artificial productions in epic and elegiac metres (Acrosticha and their varieties), versus serpentini, recurrentes, reciproci and others, were very popular at a late period.

1. Among the Greeks γρῖφοι were an entertainment at the symposium (cf. ATHENAEUS b. 10). Accordingly the Roman writer of riddles Symphosius also makes use of this poetical form. For the most ancient Latin *aenigma* (*perantiquum, perquam lepidum, tribus versibus senaris compositum*, with the solution in M. Varronis de sermone lat. ad Marcellum libro II) see GELL. 12, 6. Three popular comic riddles, in PETRON. 58 (on these BÜCHELER p. 129³ and ESCHWARZ, RhM. 42, 310). Solving riddles, regarded as a proof of wisdom, Hist. Apollonii 42, cf. 4. At a later time Latin riddles became a favourite amusement in the monasteries, and accordingly, besides the riddles of Aldhelmus and Tatvinus (§ 500, 2, 4), much literature

of this kind by unnamed authors is preserved; in great part still unprinted. Sixty (62) six-line riddles of s. VII/VIII (earliest MS. Bern. 611 s. VIII) in rhythmical hexameters (of 14 syllables each, 6 falling before and 8 after the penthemimer) published AL. 481 (cf. 2, LXVI), PBRANDT in the Tirocin. philol. semin. Bonn. (Berl. 1883) 101, WMEYER, Anf. u. Urspr. d. lat. u. griech. rhythm. Dicht. (Abh. d. bayr. Akad. 17, 2) 1885, 412. Other medieval riddles (in MSS. s. IX/X) e.g. AL. 656–657c. 770. 771. AL. 685 PLM. 3, 170. AL. 727 PLM. 5, 370 (this last was composed by a certain Berno, according to Paris. 7899 s. IX; see WFRÖHNER, Phil. Suppl. 5. 69). Cf. also RIESE on AL. 2, XLII. LMÜLLER, JJ. 93, 266. 566. 95, 497; RhM. 22, 151. JKLEIN, ib. 23, 662. HHAGEN, antike u. mittelalterliche Rätselpoesie; in which use is made of the MSS. at Bern and Einsiedeln (Biel 1869). EWÖLFFLIN, Ioca monachorum, Beitr. z. mittelalterl. Rätsellit., Berl. SBer. 1872, 106.

2. HIERON. epist. 103, 7 *legimus Homerocentones et Vergiliocentones.* TERTULL. de praescr. haeret. 39 (see § 370, 5). ISIDOR. or. 1, 39, 25 *centones apud grammaticos vocari solent qui de carminibus Homeri vel Vergilii ad propria opera more centonario in unum sarciuntur corpus, ad facultatem cuiusque materiae. denique Proba, uxor Adelphi* (§ 436, 7), *centonem ex Vergilio de fabrica mundi et euangeliis plenissime expressit, materia composita secundum versus et versibus secundum materiam concinnatis. sic quoque quidam Pomponius ex eodem poeta inter cetera stili sui otia Tityrum in Christi honorem composuit*; *similiter* (as from the Vergilian Bucolica) *et de Aeneidos* (*versibus*). This *Tityrus* of Pomponius is preserved in cod. Vat. Palat. 1753 and published by CBURSIAN, SBer. d. Münch. Ak. 1878 2, 29. Other efforts were made to adapt the Pagan wording to Christian subjects, and thereby ennoble it: *Maronem mutatum in melius*, AL. 735, 4. See the centos *de incarnatione verbi* (§ 473, 5) and *de ecclesia* (§ 477, 3).—Centos for playful purposes, e.g. Ausonius' cento nuptialis (§ 421, 2, k), or for instruction, in schools etc. Twelve Vergilian centos AL. 7–18 PLM. 4, 191–240, amongst them *de alea, Narcissus, Hippodamia, Medea* (in dialogue, by Hosidius Geta, see § 370, 5), etc., also *iudicium Paridis* by Mavortius (§ 477, 3) and *epithalamium Fridi* by Luxorius (§ 22, 1. 476, 3). On a small scale as early as PETR. 132. See also BÄHRENS, RhM. 31, 91. In joining together two halves of a verse liberties were often taken with the metre at a later time: e.g. Medea (AL. 17) 93 *nunc scio quid sit amor. hospitio prohibemur harenae*, and ib. 64 sq. 87. 172. 196. 211 sq. 226. 250. 269. 315. 320. 357. 377. 387. 391 sq. 430. 435. 446 (out of 461 lines). LUXORIUS (ib. 18) 33 *nomen inest virtutis et nota maior imago.* AL. 719, 20. 25. 78 and elsewhere.—ODELEPIERRE, ouvrages écrits en centons depuis les temps anciens jusqu'au XIXe siècle, Lond. 1868; tableau de la littérature du Centon chez les anciens et les modernes, Lond. 1875 II. BBORGEN, de centonibus homer. et vergil., Kopenh. 1828. FHASENBALG, de centon. vergil., Putbus 1846. LMÜLLER, metr. lat. 465.

3. Acrosticha, esp. those concealing a name, e.g. that of the author or founder (AL. 120 PLM. 4, 298 *Condentis monstrant uersus primordia nomen*), were borrowed from Greek literature, and were not unknown to the earlier Roman; even Ennius composed one (CIC. de div. 2, 111) and subsequently Aurelius Opilius (SUET. gramm. 6. RITSCHL, Parerg. p. XVI). At a later period inscriptional acrostics, e.g. in WILMANNS 592. 593 (with the direction *Inspicies, lector, primordia versiculorum;* cf. CIL. 5, 6731 and RFABRETTI, Inscr. ant. p. 272 *qui legis revertere per capita versorum et invenies pium nomen*). 594, and CIL. 3, 6306. 5, 6723. 6725; DE ROSSI, Inscr. christ. nr. 425 (a. 395). 753. 831. In the scholiast on the Ibis (§ 250, 3) is the acrostic epigram (*Enniani*) of a supposed *Bacchus* or *Battus* poeta. Poem on Antoninus Pius in an inscription in MEYER'S AL. 812 after the acrostic by

Julius Faustinus, see LMüller, RhM. 20, 457. cf. 20, 634. MHaupt op. 1, 289. Combination of acrostic and telestic CIL. 5, 1693, AL. 669 (*Nicholao Euantius*), in Belisarius, AL. 492. 493 (*Sedulius antistes*, cf. § 473, 6), and (from a cod. s. VI/VII) AL. 2, lvi (*Laurentius vivat senio*). RhM. 23, 94. By Flavius Felix (§ 476, 1) combination of acrostic, mesostic, and telestic. For other productions of this kind see § 99, 2. 384, 3. 403, 2. 474, 2. 476, 1. 491, 8. 500, 2, 4.

4. A variety of pedagogic and monkish trifles: poems in the form of a cross etc., such as those by Porfirius Optatianus and Venantius Fortunatus, with a fixed number of letters (as by Flavius Felix and others) or without a fixed letter (found even in prose § 480, 8) etc. *Versus echoici* or *serpentini* (epanaleptic), in which the first words of the hexameter (as far as the penthemimer) are repeated as the second half of the pentameter, such as Pentadius (§ 398, 5) especially composed. Other examples in Apoll. Sid. (ep. 8, 11), Sedulius, Venantius Fortunatus (§ 491, 4), and a collection of such *serpentini* AL. 38–80 PLM. 4, 260–267.—Sidon. ep. 9, 14 *versus recurrentes . . . qui metro stante . . . sic ut ab exordio ad terminum sic a fine releguntur ad summum. sic est illud antiquum 'Roma tibi subito motibus ibit amor'* (cf. AL. 325, 3 PLM. 4, 404 *Nemo te cedis, murorum si decet omen;* CIG. 4, 2400 Kaibel's epigr. gr. 1124 ἤδη μοι Διὸς ἄρ' ἀπάτα παρὰ σοὶ Διομήδη). *nec non habentur pro recurrentibus qui pedum lege servata . . . per singula verba repetuntur . . . qualia equidem legi multa multorum*, e.g. '*praecipiti modo quod decurrit tramite flumen tempore consumptum iam cito deficiet*'. Such verses were also called *anacyclici* and *reciproci*, of which we have examples especially by Porfirius, cf. AL. 81 PLM. 4, 268. Also *carmen supinum* in Mart. 2, 86 (cf. Friedländer), who there disparages these artifices, as for instance the construction of hexameters which, read backwards, produce sotadics (cf. Quint. 9, 4, 90). Finally rhyme was made to serve as an embellishment for the hexameter, see FZarncke, Leipz. SBer. 1871, 34. WMeyer, Münch. SBer. 1873, 49. JHuemer, Wien. Stud. 4, 599. 5, 144. 6, 287.

27. The fable, in which paraenetic subjects are dressed in tales especially relating to animal-life (beast-fable), appears in Roman literature at first in the saturae of Ennius, Lucilius and Horace, but becomes an independent species in Phaedrus (in senarii) in the time of Tiberius and Claudius. In the third century Titianus made a prose translation of the fables of Babrios. Symmachus seems to have written similar works, most probably in metre, and about a century after him Avianus composed in elegiacs 42 fables on subjects taken from Babrios. Greek fables with Latin translations are to be found in the school-book of the so-called Dositheus. The prose version of the fables of Phaedrus by the so-called Romulus, dating at latest from the tenth century, formed in the Middle Ages the nucleus for a number of other collections.

1. The Aesopian fable of the crested lark in Ennius (*in satiris . . . versibus quadratis*), Gell. 2, 29. Cf. § 103, 1. The fable of the sick lion (Hor. E. 1, 1, 73 sqq.) appears already in Lucilius (Non. 303). Others in Horace, S. 2, 6, 79. E. 1, 7, 29. 1, 10, 34. Allusions to fables in Hor. S. 2, 3, 299. 2, 5, 56. E. 1, 3, 19. 1, 16, 45.

2. Seneca Cons. ad Polyb. 8, 27 *non audeo te usque eo producere ut fabellas quoque*

et Aesopeos logos, intemptatum romanis ingeniis opus, solita tibi venustate conectas. As he was then living in exile, Seneca could not yet be acquainted with Phaedrus. AVIANUS praef.: *has pro exemplo fabulas . . . poemati suo Flaccus aptavit, quod in se sub iocorum communium specie vitae argumenta contineant, quas Graecis iambis Babrius repetens in duo volumina coartavit. Phaedrus etiam partem aliquam quinque in libellos resolvit.* AUSON. epist. 16, 74 *apologos . . . Aesopiam trimetriam, quam vertit exili stilo, pedestre concinnans opus, fandi Titianus artifex.* ib. 17 he praises Symmachus: *quis ita ad Aesopi venustatem . . . accedat?*

3. QUINTIL. 1, 9, 2 *Aesopi fabellas, quae fabulis nutricularum proxime succedunt, narrare sermone puro et nihil se supra modum extollente, deinde eandem gracilitatem stilo exigere condiscant (pueri aetatis nondum rhetorem capientis).* PHAEDR. 1, prol.: *duplex libelli dos est: quod risum movet et quod prudenti vitam consilio monet.* Cf. ib. 2, prol.; 3, prol. 33; 4, 2, 1. Append. epil.: *hoc . . . Musa quod ludit mea nequitia pariter laudat et frugalitas.*

4. On the mediaeval collections of fables KROTH, Phil. 1, 523. HOESTERLEY, Romulus, die Paraphrasen des Phaedrus und die äsopische Fabel im Mittelalter, Berl. 1870. LHERVIEUX, les fabulistes latins depuis le siècle d'Auguste jusqu'à la fin du moyen-âge, Paris 1884 II.

28. Satire was introduced into literature through Ennius, who gave the title of Saturae to a collection of his miscellaneous poems. This example was followed perhaps by his nephew Pacuvius, certainly by the Roman knight C. Lucilius. Criticism of the public affairs of his time, which preponderated in the latter, henceforth became a principal feature in the conception of the satire; after a few imitators of less note, Horace, endowed with brilliant gifts, continued in the method of Lucilius, energetically pursuing the same aims. But he softened the acrimony of the personal attacks, and directed his criticism chiefly to social and literary life. Horace employed without exception the hexameter, for which Lucilius had shown a decided preference. The Saturae Menippeae of the polyhistor Varro, composed in a free interchange of prose and verse, found in Nero's time imitators in Seneca (Ἀποκολοκύντωσις) and Petronius. On the other hand Horace had an imitator in the youthful Stoic Persius. After the death of Domitian, the rhetorician Juvenal wrote his gloomy moral lectures and portraits. Besides these chief representatives of this branch, a few of less importance are named. A satirical spirit appears also in L. Apuleius' prose-novel (the Metamorphoses) and in several apologetic and polemic works of Tertullian. In the fifth century, Claudian wrote his invectives against Rufinus and Eutropius in epic metre.

1. DIOMED. GL. 1, 435 *satira dicitur carmen apud Romanos nunc quidem maledicum et ad carpenda hominum vitia archaeae comoediae charactere* (QUINT. 10, 1, 93

says more justly *satira quidem tota nostra est) compositum, quale scripserunt Lucilius et Horatius et Persius. at olim carmen quod ex variis poematibus constabat satira vocabatur, quale scripserunt Pacuvius et Ennius* (on Naevius as an author of satires see § 95, 9). Lyd. de mag. 1, 41 μεθ' ὃν (Lucilius) καὶ τοὺς μετ' αὐτόν, οὓς καλοῦσι Ῥωμαῖοι σατυρικούς, οἱ νεώτεροι . . τὴν σατυρικὴν ἐκράτυναν κωμῳδίαν, Ὁράτιος μὲν οὐκ ἔξω τῆς τέχνης χωρῶν, Πέρσιος δὲ τὸν ποιητὴν Σώφρονα μιμήσασθαι θέλων τὸ Λυκόφρονος παρῆλθεν ἀμαυρόν· Τοῦρνος (§ 323, 2) δὲ καὶ Ἰουβενάλιος καὶ Πετρώνιος αὐτόθεν ταῖς λοιδορίαις ἐπεξελθόντες τὸν σατυρικὸν νόμον παρέτρωσαν. On the original meaning of the word *satura* see § 6, 2. Cf. also § 103, 1.

2. Hor. S. 1, 10, 54 (46) *hoc erat, experto frustra Varrone Atacino* (§ 212, 2 ad fin.) *atque quibusdam aliis, melius quod scribere possem.* To these *quidam alii* most probably belonged the polyhistor Varro with his four books of Saturae, then L. Abuccius (§ 192, 1), C. Trebonius (§ 210, 9) and the freedmen Sevius Nicanor (§ 159, 3) and Lenaeus (§ 211, 3).—Other satirists are Julius Florus (§ 242, 3), Silius (§ 332, 9), Manlius Vopiscus (§ 324, 2), Julius Rufus (? § 324, 5), and subsequently Tetradius (§ 421, 2 m). On Lucillus see § 448, 5; the letter from Victor to the abbot Salomo § 464, 6; on Secundinus § 466, 10; a satire from Arelate in Ap. Sidon. 1, 11. On those of Sulpicia § 323, 7.

3. The curious mixture of prose and verse peculiar to the saturae Menippeae is shown in Martianus Capella, Boethius de consol. philos., Julius Valerius (§ 399) and the Historia Apollonii regis Tyri. But notwithstanding these cannot well be ranked as menippeae, as in them the admixture of verse only serves to give variety to the whole, but the satirical element is wanting.—The pamphlet against the Emperor Claudius, which appeared anonymously, μωρῶν ἐπανάστασις (Suet. Claud. 38) was perhaps a satura like the ἀποκολοκύντωσις; see Bücheler's Petr. ed. min.^{3} 244.—Satire in the form of a will by Fabricius Veiento (§ 297, 7); in the third to fourth cents. the will of a pig already mentioned by Jerome (cf. § 47, 1), a parody on the juridical testamentary forms, taken from MSS. s. IX sqq. last edited by Haupt, op. 2, 175 and Bücheler, Petron. ed. min.^{3} p. 241. Cf. § 47, 1. 49, 1.

4. ICasaubonus de satyrica Graecorum poesi et Roman. satira, Par. 1605. Halle 1774. CLRoth, kl. Schrr. 2 (Stuttg. 1857), 384. 411; zur Theorie und innern Gesch. d. röm. Sat., Stuttg. 1848. Teuffel PRE. 6, 819. Scheibe, de sat. Rom. orig. et progressu, Zittau 1849. FHaase, d. röm. Satire, in Prutz' Deutsch. Mus. 1851, 858. ARMacEwen, origin and growth of the Rom. Satir. poetry, Oxf. 1876. HNettleship, the Rom. satura, its original form etc., Oxf. 1878.—ESzelinski, de nominibus personarum . . . ap. poett. satir. Rom., Königsb. 1862. JSchultz, de prosodia satiricorum rom. capp. II (de muta cum liquida et de synaloephe), Königsb. 1864.

29. The Idyl was on the whole foreign to the Romans. Tibullus possesses the greatest share of idyllic spirit, after him Vergil and, in his peculiar fashion, also Horace. But on the whole the Romans were too well acquainted with country-life to idealise it. Vergil, who had grown up in the country, in his youth at first chanced upon this species and imitated Theokritos without coming up to him, even spoiling this kind of poetry by giving it an allegorical character. But the Moretum is a proof of the humour of its author. The supposed Valerius Cato's Dirae are midway between Idyl and Satire, though more akin to the

first, especially by their amoebaean composition. In the beginning of Nero's reign we have the seven Eclogues of Calpurnius Siculus, imitated by Nemesianus at the end of the third century. Perhaps to the same time belong Septimius Serenus' Opuscula ruralia, in various lyric metres, but Idyls as to their subjects. Further several portions of Ausonius' Mosella are of a rural character, and at the end of the fourth century we have the poem de mortibus boum by the Christian rhetorician Severus Sanctus Endelechius.

1. DIOMED. GL. 1, 486 *bucolica dicuntur poemata secundum carmen pastorale composita*. On the name idyl see WCHRIST, Verhandl. d. Würzb. Philologenvers. (Lpz. 1869) 49. *Ecloga* (selected piece) designated in the Imperial period any lesser poem = *idyllium*, *poematium*, see PLIN. ep. 4, 14, 9 *sive epigrammata sive idyllia sive eclogas sive . . . poematia . . . vocare malueris*. *Eclogae* is the name given in the MSS. to the pastoral songs of Vergil, Calpurnius, Nemesianus, and to a collection of lesser poems by Ausonius.

2. In VERGIL's Georg. see esp. 2, 458 sqq. HORACE (S. 2, 6. E. 1, 10) cherishes and praises rustic life as healthful and independent.—On the idyllic poet Sueius § 150, 7; on Fontanus § 254, 1; on Messala's idyls in Greek § 222, 3.

3. On the two hermitical poems (imitations of the Vergilian eclogues, converted into eulogies on Nero) see § 306, 4. On Boethius' *carmen bucolicum* see HUSENER, anecd. Holder. (1877) 42 (see § 478, 3).—The contention between Spring and Winter AL. 687 belongs to the Middle Ages, see DÜMMLER's poetae aevi Carolini 1, 270.

4. The poems, not on bucolic subjects, which in the earlier editions of Ausonius and Claudian are entitled *Eidyllia*, do not bear this name in the MSS. Cf. § 421, 2 k; § 439, 6.—HUNGER, de poesi Rom. bucolica, Halle 1841. RUNGER, Valg. Ruf. 285. TEUFFEL, PRE. 1², 2528.

30. Lyric poetry, or the poetry of the individual in its widest sense, did not greatly harmonise with the practical Roman mind, and was thus cultivated only late and to a limited extent. At a comparatively early time occur only those kinds which had a certain bearing upon actual life, e.g. religious songs (of the Salii, fratres arvales, the hymn of Andronicus etc.), songs in honour of the departed, laments, enchantments, and other things which became carmina by the employment of the saturnian metre. Besides these, the national bent for sharp criticism led at an early time to abusive ditties, such as the Fescenninae, the soldiers' songs on the triumphator, and probably many cantica were interspersed in the popular farces. Christian Latin lyric poetry developed in a remarkable manner especially in hymn-composition, in which Ambrosius particularly became the model for later times.

1. SEN. ep. 49, 5 *indignor aliquos ex hoc tempore quod sufficere ne ad necessaria quidem potest . . . in supervacua maiorem partem erogare. negat Cicero, si duplicetur sibi aetas, habiturum se tempus quo legat lyricos . . . illi ex professo lasciviunt.*—Official lyrics of Livius Andronicus (LIV. 27, 37. FEST. 333), P. Licinius Tegula (LIV. 31, 12 see § 114, 3), subsequently those of Catullus (c. 34 to Diana) and of Horace (c. saec.).—Contemporaneously with Ennius a certain Memmia (?) is supposed to have written hymns to Apollo and the Muses (ISID. orig. 1, 39, 17)!

2. ISID. offic. eccl. 1, 6 (cf. besides § 433, 4) *Hilarius Gallus, episcopus Pictaviensis* (§ 418), *hymnorum carmine floruit primus. post quem Ambrosius Mediolanensis episcopus . . . copiosius in huius modi carmine claruisse cognoscitur atque inde hymni ex eius nomine Ambrosiani vocantur, quia eius tempore primum in ecclesia Mediolanensi celebrari coeperunt, cuius celebritatis devotio dehinc per totius occidentis ecclesias observatur. carmina autem quaecumque in laudem Dei dicuntur hymni vocantur.*—HADANIEL, thesaurus hymnologicus, Halle 1841–56 V. AEBERT, Lit. d. MAlters 1, 164 and elsewhere. THIERFELDER, de Christianorum psalmis et hymnis usque ad Ambrosii tempp., Lps. 1868. JBKAYSER, Beitr. z. Gesch. u. Erkl. d. Kirchenhymnen, Paderb. [2] 1881. 1886 II. GPIMONT, les hymnes du bréviaire romain, Par. 1874. FJMONE, lat. Hymnen des MAlters, Freiburg 1853–55 III.—The Christian hymns are chiefly in trochaic and iambic metre, with particular preference for the iambic dimeter, in strophes which are frequently embellished with rhyme and alliteration. The verses are at first constructed according to quantity, increasing gradually in freedom, until at last they become entirely rhythmical. The chief representatives of hymn-composition after Ambrosius are Prudentius, Sedulius, Ennodius, Venantius Fortunatus, Gregory the Great. Cf. JHUEMER, der iamb. Dim. bei den christl.-lat. Hymnendichtern der vorkaroling. Zeit, Wien 1876; die ältesten lat.-christl. Rhythmen, Wien 1879.

31. Among the literary forms of lyric poetry, the most elegant, the Epigram, was first cultivated, partly for inscriptions, partly for allegory and occasional verses, in part too for light erotic trifles. In the first application it was used after Ennius more and more frequently on sepulchral monuments, buildings, utensils, works of art etc.; sometimes in hexameters (e.g. in the dedication by Mummius to Hercules Victor a. 608/146, CIL. 1, 542), sometimes in distichs (as in the sepulchral inscription of Cn. Cornelius Scipio Hispanus, praetor 615/139, CIL. 1, 38), most systematically in Varro's Imagines. In the first half of the seventh century U. C. we have as representatives of the two other uses of the epigram Pompilius, Valerius Aedituus, Porcius Licinus, Q. Lutatius Catulus, Quinctius Atta; in the second half Varro Atacinus, Licinius Calvus and Catullus and probably Q. Hortensius, C. Memmius, Q. Scaevola and others to whom erotic poems are ascribed. In the Augustan age Augustus himself, Domitius Marsus, Pedo, Cornificia, Sulpicia, Gaetulicus. Then under Domitian, the epigram in various forms was treated in a masterly manner by Martial; Ausonius also has several examples, and for a long time such trifles continued to be produced,

especially to serve for sepulchral inscriptions. Even in the sixth century after Christ we find a collection of epigrams by Luxorius. At the same period originated the collection of smaller poems preserved to us in the codex Salmasianus; this formed the nucleus for the collections of short poems, either detached or unappropriated, which have been made in more recent times and which bear the name of Anthologia Latina.

1. Many epigrams used as real superscriptions are preserved in inscriptions; cf. e.g. the epigram in hexameter near the paintings of the temple of Juno at Ardea, written *antiquis litteris latinis*, see PLIN. NH. 35, 115.—GELL. 19, 9, 7 *Ecquis nostrorum poetarum tam fluentes carminum delicias fecisset* (like Anacreon)? *nisi Catullus forte pauca et Calvus itidem pauca. nam Laevius implicata et Hortensius invenusta et Cinna inlepida et Memmius dura, ac deinceps omnes rudia fecerunt atque absona;* ib. 10 seq. are quoted *versus Valerii Aeditui, . . item Porcii Licini et Q. Catuli . . . quibus mundius, venustius, limatius, tersius graecum latinumve nihil quidquam reperiri puto.* MARTIAL. 1 praef.: *lascivam verborum veritatem, i.e. epigrammaton linguam, excusarem si meum esset exemplum: sic scribit Catullus, sic Marsus, sic Pedo, sic Gaetulicus, sic quicumque perlegitur.* PLIN. ep. 5, 3, 5 enumerates as erotic poets, *M. Tullium, C. Calvum, Asinium Pollionem, M. Messalam, Q. Hortensium, M. Brutum, L. Sullam, Q. Catulum, Q. Scaevolam, Ser. Sulpicium, M. Varronem, Torquatum, immo Torquatos, C. Memmium, Lentulum Gaetulicum, Annaeum Senecam, Annaeum Lucanum, . . Verginium Rufum, . . d. Iulium, d. Augustum, d. Nervam, Tiberium Caesarem;* also *Neronem*, and (ib. 6) *P. Vergilius, Cornelius Nepos et prius Accius Enniusque.* By the Torquati Pliny probably means the L. Torquati, of whom the father was cons. 689/65, and the son praetor 705/49,† a. 707/47 in Africa (cf. CIC. Brut. 239, 265. It is probably to the marriage of the son that Catullus 61 alludes, see LSCHWABE, quaestt. catull. 340).—There seems to have been an erotic anthology at an early period, from which perhaps Pliny (l.l.), Gellius (l.l.) and Apuleius (apol. 9) derived their special knowledge in this field. AL. 23–25. 29. 427–435. 446. 448–453. 458–460 are probably taken from some such source.—H. PALDAMUS, röm. Erotik., Greifsw. 1833.

2. On the so-called sepulchral inscriptions of Naevius, Plautus, Ennius, Pacuvius see § 115, 2.—On the epigrams of M. Tullius Laurea see § 191, 6. Towards the end of the Republic numerous epigrams on persons and events of the day. So on Bibulus cons. a. 695/59 (SUET. Iul. 20); on the gourmet Rufus (*ciconiarum conditor*, PORPH. Hor. S. 2, 2, 50); on a scandalous marriage (PORPH. Hor. S. 1, 7, 19); again AL. 419–426 in honour of Caesar, 426 sq. formal poems on the death of the hostile brothers Mevius (§ 309, 1). In the early Imperial period such subjects as the death of Cato Uticensis, the tomb of Pompeius and his sons, were chosen by preference; see AL. 392 sqq. 413 sq. The Emperors especially were not spared, see SUET. Aug. 70. Tib. 59. Cal. 8, Nero 39. Dom. 14, 23 etc. On later Emperors see FPR. 378. In relation to the subject see § 11, 2, 3.

3. MARTIAL. 1, praef. (see n. 1), 8, praef.: *quamvis epigrammata a severissimis quoque et summae fortunae viris ita scripta sint ut mimicam verborum licentiam affectasse videantur.* Following his precedent a certain degree of coarseness appeared even to Ennodius and Luxorius to be inseparable from this kind of writing. Fronto p. 212 *novissimos in epigrammatis versus habere oportet aliquid luminis.* The elegiac distich is the regular metre for epigram: six pentameters following one

another in an epigram on Commodus, originally Greek, but translated *a malo poeta* (LAMPRID. Diad. 7, 3).

4. On the cod. Salmasianus § 476.—Anthologia vett. lat. epigrammatum et poematum sive catalecta poett. lat. ex marmor. et monum. inscr. et codd. msc. eruta. cura PBURMANNI, Amsterd. 1759. 73 II. From this Anthol. lat. ed. HMEYER, Lps. 1835 II.—Then Anthologia latina sive poesis latinae supplementum, P. I: carmina in codicibus scripta, rec. ARIESE, Lpz. 1869. 70 (P. II: PBUECHELERI anthologia epigraphica lat. has not yet appeared. Of this we have so far three instalments: the iambic inscriptions in Greifsw. ind. schol. 1870 and in the RhM. 27, 127, the saturnian and trochaic inscriptions in the Bonn. ind. schol. 1876). The Poetae latini minores by EBÄHRENS, Lps. 1879–83 V, esp. B. 4, contains besides other matter the portions preserved in MS. of the so-called Anthol. lat.; see § 19, 4.—Numerous contributions to Latin anthology (new discoveries, textual research, criticism, etc.) see *e.g.* ENGELMANN-PREUSS, bibl. scriptt. class. 2, 56. We have in MS. (besides a few with the authors' names, *e.g.* Modestus AL. 900 PLM. 5, 95, C. Aurelius Romulus AL. 904 PLM. 5, 97) numerous anonymous epigrams, preserved sometimes in smaller groups sometimes in longer series, earlier or more recent (dating from the Middle Ages, from the early Renaissance). Such are to be found e.g. in the supplement to SCHNEIDEWIN'S Martial, and from the Oxford MSS. in RELLIS, Anecd. Oxon. 1 (1885), 1; from Austrian MSS. see JHUEMER, Wien. Stud. 9, 51.

32. Through the influence of the Alexandrine poets the Elegy, at the close of the Republic, gained ground at Rome, and in it the disciples far surpassed their Greek originals in truth and warmth of sentiment as well as in formal finish. Catullus, it is true, handles it generally with a certain awkwardness; Cornelius Gallus (Lycoris) appears to have succeeded better. Tibullus produced masterpieces, Propertius passionate pictures, and Ovid was quite at home in the Elegy. In the first century of the Christian era this kind was long fashionable, and was employed even in the schools for practice in style. But the intrinsic worth of these productions decreased in proportion. Later on, this metre shared the fate of epic verse, being employed in all kinds of subjects; and when the break-up began and the ancient prosody which was based on quantity began to decay before modern European forms of poetry had been developed, those two metres, being the most popular and widely used, were the first to suffer. Yet it is to the commencement of the sixth century that the remarkable elegiac writer Maximian of Etruria belongs.

1. DIOMED. GL. 1, 484 *elegia est carmen compositum hexametro versu pentametroque . . . quod genus carminis praecipue scripserunt apud Romanos Propertius et Tibullus et Gallus, imitati Graecos Callimachum et Euphoriona.* CIC. Tusc. 3, 45 on *Ennius: o poetam egregium, quamquam ab his cantoribus Euphorionis* (Calvus, Catullus, Gallus etc.) *contemnitur.* QUINTIL. 10, 1, 93 *elegia quoque Graecos provocamus. cuius mihi tersus atque elegans maxime videtur auctor Tibullus. sunt qui Propertium malint.*

Ovidius utroque lascivior, sicut durior Gallus. Cf. MHaupt, op. 3, 205. For their chronological succession see Ovid. trist. 4, 10, 53 *successor fuit hic* (Tibullus) *tibi, Galle, Propertius illi; quartus ab his serie temporis ipse fui.* Varro Atacinus, the earliest poet in this style, is omitted in these enumerations, as of less importance. On Cassius of Parma see § 210, 7. In the Augustan period we have the author of the third book of Tibullus (Lygdamus). Suetonius considered *elegi* attributed to Horace as spurious; see § 240, 2. Elegiac ἀδέσποτα on Maecenas and Messala § 229, 3. 230, 5. n.1.

2. Pers. 1, 51 *si qua elegidia* (epigrams?) *crudi dictarunt proceres.* Iuv. 1, 3 *impune . . . mihi recitaverit ille togatas, hic elegos?* In the reign of Domitian Arruntius Stella composed elegies, in the time of the younger Pliny that writer himself (ep. 7, 4, 3. 7) and Passennus Paullus, municeps and descendant of Propertius. The rhetorical elegy to Spes AL. 415 PLM. 4, 65 is probably as early as the first century A.D. Of a similar character AL. 440 PLM. 4, 76.

3. The Roman erotic poets shrouded the women whom they celebrated in song in a becoming chiaroscuro, partly by leaving out their individual traits, partly by the custom of mentioning them under altered names, which however were generally in prosodical agreement (cf. Acr. Hor. S. 1, 2, 64). Apul. apol. 10 *accusent C. Catullum quod Lesbiam pro Clodia nominarit, et Ticidam similiter quod quae Metella erat Perillam scripserit, et Propertium qui Cynthiam dicat, Hostiam dissimulet, et Tibullum quod ei sit Plania in animo, Delia in versu.* LSchwabe, quaest. Catull. 231. SKleemann, de Tib. III, p. 21. Enumeration of the lady-loves of poets in Martial. 8, 73, 5 sqq. and Apoll. Sidon. ep. 2, 10. Cf. § 226, 2. 232, 1.

4. For the technical laws of the elegiac distich, its grouping, the symmetry of its periods, etc., see under the several poets. In general WGebhardi, de Tib. Prop. Ovidii distichis, Königsb. 1870. FCHultgren, obss. metr. in poet. eleg. gr. et lat. I. II., Lps. 1871 and Ber. d. sächs. Ges. d. Wiss. 1872, 3 (see § 19, 2), Drobisch, Classific. der Formen des Distichon, Ber. d. sachs. Ges. d. Wiss. 1871, 1. 1872, 1. 27. BHEngbers, de metricis inter Tib. Propertiumque differentiis, Münst. 1873. EEichner, de poett. lat. usque ad Aug. distichis, Bresl. 1866; metr. u. rhythm. Bau u. Homoeoteleuta in d. Distt., Gnesen 1875. SKleemann de l. III Tib. (Strssb. 1876) p. 24. CPrien, d. Symmetrie u. Responsion der röm. Elegie, Lüb. 1867. GHBubendey, d. Symmetrie der röm. Elegie, Hamb. 1876. Madvig, adv. 2, 110.—Indebtedness of the Roman elegiac writers (e.g. Tib. 1, 7. 2, 1. 2. 5. 3, 7. Prop. 5, 6) to the nomos-like hymns of Kallimachos: OCrusius, WschrfklPh. 1885, 1298.

5. OFGruppe, die röm. Elegie; krit. Untersuchungen usw., Lpz. 1838 II—Auswahlen f. d. Schulgebr. by PKSchulze, Berl.[2] 1884. BVolz, Lpz.[2] 1876.—FTeufel, d. Cat. Tib. Prop. vocibus singularibus, Freib. in Br. 1872. FKoldewey, die fig. ἀπὸ κοινοῦ bei Cat. Tib. Prop. Hor. ZfdGW. 31, 337. OAken, de fig. ἀπὸ κοινοῦ usu ap. Cat. Tib. Prop. I, Schwerin 1884. AMansfeld, de enuntiatis conditional. ap. eleg. poett. latt., Halle 1879. OWolff, de enuntiatis interrog. ap. Cat. Tib. Prop., Halle 1883. JSenger, d. Infinitive bei Cat. Tib. Prop., Speier 1886. CSchneemann, de verbb. cum praepp. compositorum ap. Cat. Tib. Prop. constructione, Halle 1881.

6. The epitaphia and epicedia also show the close connection between epigram and elegy. Thus the epitaphs of the mimus Vitalis (AL. 683 PLM. 3, 245) and of Nymphius (AL. 722 PLM. 3, 270) by their magnitude approximate to elegies; while epitaphs characterising authors, such as those of Seneca and Lucan (AL. 667. 668 PLM. 5, 386) are epigrams on them (cf. § 31, 2).

7. Didactic poems in elegiac metre, like Ovid's Fasti, the Phoenix (§ 397, 8)

and de rosis nascentibus, AL. 646. Cf. § 229, 2 and above § 23. On riddles, centones and eccentricities in this metre see § 26.

33. Iambics, familiar from the drama, were at an early time employed for other purposes (e.g. for epitaphs). For the carmen maledicum the iambic metre seems to have been first employed among the Romans by Furius Bibaculus, after him by Catullus, Calvus, and the younger Cato, and by Horace (epodes) and Bassus. The mimiambi of Cn. Matius were a variety of this. The Imperial period was not favourable to this species, and iambics were then mostly employed without special purpose. But part of the poems of Martial are in this metre, and at a later period Ausonius endeavoured to revive iambics in their original application.

1. DIOMED. GL. 1, 485 *iambus est carmen maledicum . . . cuius carminis praecipui scriptores . . . apud Romanos Lucilius et Catullus et Horatius et Bibaculus.* QUINT. 10, 1, 96 *iambus non sane a Romanis celebratus est ut proprium opus, ⟨sed aliis⟩ quibusdam interpositus. cuius acerbitas in Catullo, Bibaculo, Horatio, quamquam illi epodos intervenit, reperietur* (cf. ib. 9, 4, 141. 10, 1, 9). OVID. rem. am. 377 *liber in adversos hostes stringatur iambus, seu celer extremum seu trahat ille pedem* (choliambics). CATULL. 36, 5 and 40, 2 uses *iambus* of *maledica carmina* in general, without regard to metre, also of hendecasyllabics, as he himself (and Martial after him) employed them by preference.

2. Lenaeus' satire (§ 211, 3) and Ovid's Ibis were iambic in their subjects. Choliambics and iambics in Catullus and in the Vergilian Catalepta; Matius' mimiambi were also choliambic, likewise Petron. sat. 5, Persius' prologue and part of the poems of Martial. Among the Priapeia the iambus is also represented. The verses of a supposed 'Iambograph' Flaccus (PAUL. Festi 263) are not iambics.—Antistius Sosianus § 304, 4, Aurelius Apollinaris § 385, 3. An epigram (alleged to be by the consul Ablabius 331 A.D.) on the domestic murder charged against Constantine in AP. SIDON. epist. 5, 8. Jocular epigrams in hendecasyllabics on contemporary events in LAMPRID. Alex. sev. 38. By AUSONIUS see esp. epigr. 44. 46. 47 against the rhetor Rufus. Cf. RIESE's AL. 2, p. 372.

3. Inscriptions in iambics are not rare. In BÜCHELER's coll. (see § 31, 4) nos. 1–101 are senarii, 102–105 chol., 106–108 dimeters.

34. At the end of the Republic, when the knowledge of Greek literature at Rome had become more extensive and life more exciting, nearly every well-educated Roman would occasionally attempt some kind or other of small poems; even the more talented poets, e.g. Varro Atacinus, Laevius, Calvus and Catullus roamed undecidedly through various kinds and metrical forms; Catullus alone became the first real lyric poet among the Romans on account of the love and hatred embodied in his poems. Horace continued in his track with inferior poetical power and less personal pathos, but with refined critical taste. His return to the style of Alkaios and Sappho was not imitated. Others in

his time did not get beyond mere playing and first attempts. In the first century of the Christian era formal elegance was very common, and as a consequence there was much dallying with poetry; but not one of the numerous lyric poets of this or the next succeeding period gained eminence and lasting influence: e.g. Caesius Bassus, Saleius Bassus, Gaetulicus, Arruntius Stella, Vestricius Spurinna, the younger Pliny, P. Annius Florus, Voconius, Hadrian, Serius Augurinus, Pompeius Saturninus, Annianus. This mastery over form, which incited many poets—e.g. Septimius Serenus and Terentianus Maurus—to write verses merely to give examples of the various metres,—is very brilliantly represented by Statius and subsequently Ausonius, and even by Apollinaris Sidonius and Boëthius; nor is the Pervigilium Veneris a despicable specimen of the lyric art of the second and third centuries. Among the Christian poets of the fourth century Prudentius is remarkable for the variety of the melic metres employed by him. Hendecasyllabics, trochaic tetrameters and iambic dimeters were in fashion for longer or shorter periods.

1. The oldest melic poets, under the influence of Roman notions and on account of their playful character, style their works *nugae*, *ineptiae*, (*Eroto-*) *paegnia*, *opuscula* etc. Many of the poets enumerated by Pliny ep. 5, 3, 5 (see § 31, 1) belong to this class, perhaps also Cassius of Parma. In the Augustan period perhaps Titius (Hor. E. 1, 3, 9), Julius Antonius (cf. Hor. C. 4, 2) and Rufus (Ovid. Pont. 4, 16, 28); besides Maecenas' attempts. On Melissus' Ineptiae § 244, 2.—The Priapeia also (see § 254, 5) date chiefly from the Augustan period.

2. Quint. 10, 1, 96 *lyricorum Horatius fere solus legi dignus . . . si quem adicere velis, is erit Caesius Bassus, quem nuper vidimus: sed eum longe praecedunt ingenia viventium* (perhaps he has in his mind especially Arruntius Stella, Vestricius Spurinna, probably even Statius, which would also give us a corrective for his judgment on Bassus). These late lyric poets lacked less the form than the subjects. *Versiculi* of Pliny, on erotic subjects, esp. hendecasyllabics, ep. 5, 3, 1. 7, 4, 1. 7 sqq. His contemporary is Passennus Paullus, an imitator of Horace (ib. 9, 22, 2). *Voconius poeta* (§ 346, 5) under Hadrian, who also wrote verses of a similar kind. There was at that time a preference for the popular (see § 11, 3) trochaic septenarius (Annius Florus); afterwards for the iambic dim. (e.g. Annianus). In the fifth cent. hendecasyllabics were again the fashion (Sidonius and others). At the same time there were various rarities, e.g. the Anacreontics in Symmach. ep. 1, 8. Intentional or involuntary over-estimation of contemporaries e.g. in reference to Numerianus (Caesar a. 284) see § 385, 3. Votive inscription of Alfenus Fortunatus in ionics, Renier Inscr. de l'Alg. 157 Wilm. 149. Cf. Ritschl, op. 4, 309. Epitaph on a lap-dog in hendecasyllabics with Catulline assonances (2d cent.), Wilm. 684. Christian hendecasyllabics AL. 768. Oracles (sortes), partly in paroemiac verse, in the SGallen MS. of Merobaudes, see Bücheler, Bonner ind. schol. 1877, 14.

3. Were the melic poems, those of Horace especially, intended to be sung to an instrumental accompaniment? He says C. 4, 9, 4 *verba loquor socianda chordis*,

and often speaks of his *lyra*, *cithara*, *testudo*, *barbitos*, of *plectrum* and of *fides*, of *canere*, *cantare*, *dicere*. See OJAHN, Herm. 2, 418, who rightly answers this question in the affirmative. Cf. besides LFRIEDLÄNDER, Sittengesch. 3[5], 294. ARIESE, JJ. 94, 480. WFÖRSTER, quaestt. Hor. 2 (Brünn 1870), 11. FSÜSS, ZföG. 30, 881. Much of course is to be traced to the language of the Greek originals; it must also be observed that H. addresses himself to Hellenising circles, and to those who mingled with the musical demi-monde. The early Roman aversion for singing (§ 1, 4) need hardly be taken into consideration, for singing and writing poems to be sung are different things. *Cantus inter convivia dulcis*, MANIL. astr. 5, 333. Ov. AA. 3, 345 *composita cantetur epistula* (an heroid) *voce*. The younger Pliny's hendecasyllabics were sung by Romans and even by Greeks (§ 340, 4). He boasts of his wife: *versus meos cantat etiam formatque cithara, . . . docente amore* (see ep. 4, 19, 4, cf. 7, 17, 3). ANN. FLOR. p. 106 H.: *urbem illam ubi versus tui a lectoribus concinuntur*. Ap. GELL. 19, 9, 10 (*Iulianus rhetor*) *voce admodum quam suavi versus cecinit Valeri Aeditui, Porcii Licini et Q. Catuli*. Again APOLL. SIDON. ep. 8, 4 *iambos, elegos, hendecasyllabos et cetera carmina . . . Narbonensibus cantitanda*.

35. As was the case in Greek literature, the Romans did not form and develop a literary prose-style until a comparatively late period. The first step towards prose-composition was taken by Appius Claudius (475/279) in publishing one of his speeches. But as the succeeding writers employed the Greek language, the history of prose does not begin, properly speaking, before Cato Major. For a long time, however, the written speech remained insignificant by the side of the oral, and became its equal only in the time of Cicero, when prose attained to its climax and became the adequate expression of the author's individuality. It always retained a rhetorical colour in accordance with the Roman character. In the first century of the Imperial period it begins already to decay, by being mixed with poetical diction and becoming estranged from natural expression. The decay of accidence and syntax begins also about this time. Later on, the plebeian element found admission. And when the influence of provincial writers, who were not guided by a native sense of language and who mingled popular and literary language and mixed up the diction and style of all periods, became prevalent in literature, the confusion became still greater. In Italy itself the language of literature became more and more different from the living language, and became entirely dependent upon the culture attained by each writer, which continually fell to a lower level. The more provincial Latin (the Romance language) developed, the more did literary Latin become a foreign tongue, familiar only to the learned.

1. ISIDOR. orig. 1, 37, 2 *praeterea* (ait Varro? aiunt?) *tam apud Graecos quam apud Latinos longe antiquiorem curam fuisse carminum quam prosae. omnia enim*

prius versibus condebantur (§ 61), *prosae autem studium sero viguit. primus apud Graecos Pherecydes Syrius soluta oratione scripsit, apud Romanos Appius Caecus adversus Pyrrhum* (§ 90) *solutam orationem primus exercuit. iam exhinc ceteri prosae eloquentiam condiderunt.*

2. Distinction between cultivated (i.e. literary or high-Latin) and vulgar (i.e. popular) Latin; the latter esp. in comic, satiric and technical writers, and in letters. Donat. on Ter. Ad. 375 *Sic loquitur populus* (see § 385, 4). African Latinity: see WMeyer's short history and grammar of popular Latin in G Gröber's Grundriss der roman. Philol. (Strassb. 1887) 355.

36. For history, as a storehouse of the glorious deeds of their ancestors, to be imitated by present and future generations, the Romans possessed a very ready mind. To the very oldest time belongs the custom of ex officio chronicles by the Pontifices, annual and monthly registers, the fasti and annales, libri pontificii, commentarii regum, magistratuum, and from the beginning of the Republic the yearly change of the magistrates was an additional stimulus to keep registers of this kind. But the families also had sufficient opportunities of preserving the memory of past events in the custom of keeping family chronicles, in the imagines, later on in the pedigrees, in the laudationes funebres, the ancestral songs during meals. On the other hand the writing of history with the Romans (as generally in antiquity) differed materially in aim and method from modern historical writing. The desire of finding out historical truth and perpetuating it as such is foreign to the Romans. Individuals were guided by some practical object, generally the desire of placing their nation, family, party or person in a favourable light. The Romans had hardly a conception of the investigation of original records, and very few concerned themselves with historical criticism; historical art was for a long period no less foreign to the Romans. The fact that the task of the historian was at an early period regarded as a rhetorical one, caused indifference, if not unscrupulousness, with regard to dates and other matters of fact, and a greater inclination to arbitrary colouring. Sallust is the first cultivated historian of the Romans; all previous productions are either mere registers or the materials are undigested, and there is a want of historical style. The oldest historians even preferred writing in Greek, because Latin had not been sufficiently cultivated for historical composition.

1. Latest collections of fragments of the Roman historians by HPeter, historicorum rom. reliquiae; Vol. I, Lps. 1870, and historicorum rom. fragmenta (till the time of Constantine the Great), Lps. 1883.

2. GJVossius, de historicis latinis, Leiden 1627. [2] 1651. HUlrici, Char-

akteristik d. antiken Historiographie, Berl. 1833. CNIPPERDEY, opusc. (Berl. 1877) 399. 411. FDGERLACH, die Geschichtschreiber d. Römer, Stuttg. 1855. ASCHÄFER, Quellenkunde d. gr. u. röm. Gesch.: 2. Abt.: röm. Gesch. 2. Aufl. v. HNISSEN, Lpz. 1885. The introductions to the history of Rome by NIEBUHR, WACHSMUTH, BLUM, SCHWEGLER, MOMMSEN (1^6, 459). Untersuchungen über die Glaubwürdigkeit der altröm. Geschichte von LOBRÖCKER (Bas. 1855), GCLEWIS (transl. by FLIEBRECHT, Hann. 1858), HPETER hist. rom. rell. 1, XLIII–LIX, KW NITZSCH (§ 37, 6), CPETER (§ 37, 6), MZOELLER, Latium u. Rom, Lpz. 1878, 1–60 etc.

3. *Pontifices, penes quos scribendae historiae potestas fuit*, VOPISC. Tac. 1, 1 (see § 76). For a long time no man of unfree birth could undertake the writing of history: *L. Voltacilius* (153, 3) *primus omnium libertinorum . . . scribere historiam exorsus, non nisi ab honestissimo quoque scribi solitam ad id tempus*, SUET. rhet. 3. Rose-coloured picture TAC. Agr. 1 *apud priores . . . celeberrimus quisque ingenio ad prodendam virtutis memoriam sine gratia aut ambitione bonae tantum conscientiae pretio ducebatur.* The ordinary view, that the oldest historians wrote in Greek in order to keep the information within the narrower Patrician circle, is contradicted by the fact that one of the oldest of them, Cincius Alimentus (§ 117), is a Plebeian; cf. Phil. Anz. 15, 161. They wrote in Greek just as the oldest German chroniclers wrote in Latin, and in the 17–18 cent. many German writers in French. How far was regard had to the foreign public? see WÖLFFLIN on Liv. XXI, p. VI.—For town-chronicles out of Rome: LIV. 5, 34. 8, 10. 10, 2. Later on the records of the city of Rome were fused with the Latin and Italic.—The historians only made superficial use of the great fund of public records in Rome. National archives in the tabularium in the Capitol, from its rebuilding (finished 685/69) by Q. Lutatius Catulus after the burning of the Capitol 671/83. Restored by Vespasian (SUET. Vesp. 8) after its destruction in A.D. 69. Imperial court-archives on the Palatine (Cass. D. ep. 72, 24, 2).

4. Practical objects: reference to precedents e.g. LIV. 8, 18, 12. Pedagogic purposes: PLUT. Cato mai. 20. Already LUCILIUS mentions a Roman who wrote Roman history for his children (26, 58 *veterem historiam inductus studio scribis ad amores tuos*).

5. QUINT. 2, 18, 5 *historiis, quod ipsum opus in parte oratoria merito ponimus.* By reason of their predilection for rhetoric, the Roman historians gladly adopted the Greek custom of interweaving speeches in their accounts of events. Cato the Elder used his own speeches thus to an exaggerated extent; so did Antipater. The artistic historians use speeches to gain variety, and to characterise both actors and situations. They are rare in Caesar, but frequent in Sallust (§ 206, 4) and Livy (§ 257, 12). These two last are rightly blamed from the point of view of the historian by Pompeius Trogus (IUSTIN. 38, 3, 11) *quod contiones directas pro sua oratione operi suo inserendo historiae modum excesserint.* At an early period the speeches and letters from Sallust (§ 205, 4 cf. 206, 4) and Livy (SUET. Domit. 10) were collected for rhetorical use in schools. ARÜDIGER, de orationibus in rerum scriptoribus gr. et lat., Schleiz 1875.

6. The reports of battles by rhetorical historians (in contradistinction to those of experts such as Xenophon, Polybios and Caesar) are either fanciful pictures, or composed in imitation of celebrated models, and are in parts rather monotonous. Verhandl. d. Würzb. Philol. Vers. (Lpz. 1869), 190. THSTADE, die Schlachtenschilderungen in Liv. 1. Dekade, Jena 1873. THZIELINSKI, zweiter pun. Krieg, Lpz. 1880, 149.

7. History and romance were actually confounded by many Roman historical writers. QUINTILIAN indeed (10, 1, 31) theorises thus: *historia est proxima poesis*

et quodammodo carmen solutum, et scribitur ad narrandum, non ad probandum. More correctly PLIN. 5, 8, 9 *habet quidem oratio et historia multa communia, sed plura diversa in his ipsis quae communia videntur*, etc. Cf. ib. 4 *orationi et carmini parva gratia, nisi eloquentia est summa: historia quoquo modo scripta delectat. sunt enim homines natura curiosi et quamlibet nuda rerum cognitione capiuntur.* For the other view see CIC. Brut. 42 *quoniam concessum est rhetoribus ementiri in historiis, ut aliquid dicere possint argutius.* de leg. 1, 5 *cum sit* (historia) *opus, ut tibi quidem videri solet, unum hoc oratorium maxime* (doubtless esp. concerning style). Cf. § 39, 2. HNISSEN, RhM. 26, 500. 515. 41, 494. Cf. § 37, 3. 6. On the difference between ancient and modern historical writing CNIPPERDEY, opusc. 411.

37. Until the end of the second Punic war Rome produced only history and sources of history. When history came to be narrated, its form was naturally like the old annals. Hence the oldest Roman historians are Annalists. There were two generations of these. The older one reaches into the 7th century U.C., consisting chiefly of men who had themselves played a part in the State and afterwards registered in a meagre chronicle-like form, yet with a certain reliability, the events in their annual succession. At their head stands Q. Fabius Pictor, who was succeeded by L. Cincius Alimentus, C. Acilius and A. Postumius Albinus. All of them dealt summarily with the oldest period and at greater length with contemporary history, all wrote in Greek, as did also the son of the older Africanus. With Pictor and Acilius, however, Latin compositions soon followed. The first who wrote in Latin was Cato (Origines), who at the same time extended the subject to a history of Italy. His example was followed with regard to the language by L. Cassius Hemina and perhaps also Ser. Fabius Pictor; then by L. Scribonius Libo, Fabius Maximus Servilianus (cos. 612/142), L. Calpurnius Piso Frugi (cos. 621/133), C. Sempronius Tuditanus (cos. 625/129). After the contests of the Gracchi begins the later generation of Annalists, who wrote under the influence of partisan motives and with increasing diffuseness; among the first of these are Vennonius and Cn. Gellius. The influence of the Greek style appears in C. Fannius and even more in L. Coelius Antipater, his younger contemporary; Polybios' pragmatical method clearly influenced Sempronius Asellio. In the middle of the 7th century U.C. and in the time of Sulla, we meet with several writers of memoirs and autobiographies, viz. M. Aemilius Scaurus, P. Rutilius Rufus, Q. Lutatius Catulus, Sulla himself, and in Greek L. Licinius Lucullus; later on M. Varro, Caesar, Augustus, Agrippa and others. In the time of Sulla Voltacilius is the first

historian who was not free-born, and Cn. Aufidius again wrote in Greek. In the same time the later style of annals is prominently represented in Q. Claudius Quadrigarius and the exaggerating Valerius Antias. More respectable was C. Licinius Macer, the last real Annalist, inasmuch as L. Cornelius Sisenna (praetor 676/78) adopted in his contemporary history an arrangement more in accordance with the subject-matter than with chronology. But even Tacitus hardly dares to free himself from the annalistic shackles, and even many biographies of Emperors were in the form of annals.

1. The older Annalists shunned deliberate falsehood; yet they sought to hush up unpleasant facts, such as the subjugation of Rome by Porsena, the ransom of the town from the Gauls, the Caudine Forks, and the ensuing rupture of the peace. Nor did they hesitate to misrepresent facts. The later Annalists abound in patriotic falsifications. The nearer to the Augustan period, the greater is the range of the annals, and so much the less on the average is their credibility. See HNissen, RhM. 25, 1. Cf. ELübbert, de Liv. l. IV fontibus, Giessen 1872, p. 3. Antipater is the first to turn to account even antagonistic authorities. Entire ignorance about foreign countries is common to all Annalists. For the unhistorical exaggeration of numbers (in accounts of battles etc.) by Annalists see e.g. CPeter, zur Kritik der Quellen d. ält. röm. Gesch. 53. Cf. § 155, 3. BNiese, de annalibus rom. obss., Marb. 1886.

2. Wherever, after the middle of the 7th century, annals are mentioned, histories in the form of annals are meant; a literary continuation of the annales maximi (§ 76). Cf. Schwegler, RG. 1, 11 seq.

3. In contradistinction from *annales* as chronicles *historia* (ἱστορία investigation) properly designates a subjective, rather pragmatical presentation of the subject-matter: but this distinction was not maintained in usage. The older grammarians partly defined *historia* as a description of personal experiences (*unde Livius ex annalibus et historia constat*, Serv. l.l.), which already Verrius Flaccus ap. Gell. l. l. rightly questioned. Cf. Gell. 5, 18. Serv. Aen. 1, 373. Isid. orig. 1, 40, 1. Niebuhr, kl. Schr. 2, 229 makes too sharp a distinction between the terms. Cf. HNissen. krit. Unters. 87. FThiersch, Münchner Gel. Anz. 1848, Nr. 131. HPeter, hist. rell. 1, xlviii. Sempronius Asellio in Gell. 5, 18, 8 *inter eos qui annales relinquere voluissent et eos qui res gestas a Romanis perscribere conati essent omnium rerum hoc interfuit. annales libri tantummodo quod factum quoque anno gestum sit, ea demonstrabant ita quasi qui diarium scribunt, quam Graeci ἐφημερίδα vocant. nobis non modo satis esse video quod factum esset, id pronuntiare, sed etiam quo consilio quaque ratione gesta essent demonstrare*: . . . (to state only the external facts, not their causes) *id fabulas pueris est narrare, non historias scribere.* Chronological sequence was naturally adhered to in the main in the *historiae* (Plin. ep. 1, 1 *non servato temporis ordine, neque enim historiam componebam*), and historical writing was always considered by the Romans to be chronological (Cic. fam. 5, 12, 5 *ordo ipse annalium mediocriter nos retinet quasi enumeratione factorum*).

4. There was great liberty allowed in using previous writers; subsequent writers copied the works of their predecessors with more or less additional matter

and changes, with or without express mention of the name. The source is generally only given for the purpose of deciding a moot point by the weight of a name or by the majority of the authorities, to find fault with the authority, or to explain why the point cannot be decided. Quotations from the principal authority are often thrown in; quotations indicating the authority as responsible are much less common. Frequently a writer would found his work on one principal source, changing this according to other sources or individual pleasure. CPeter, das Verhältn. des Liv. etc., Anclam 1853; zur Kritik der älteren röm. Gesch. (Halle 1879) 4. 6. HNissen, krit. Unters. 77. 90. HPeter, hist. rell. 1, liv. EWölfflin, on Liv. XXI, p. xxii.

5. Cic. de or. 2, 12, 52 *erat historia nihil aliud nisi annalium confectio.* Tac. dial. 22 *nulli sensus tarda et inerti structura in morem aunnalium componantur.* Dionys. 1, 7 εἰσὶ δὲ (the πραγματεῖαι of the Annalists) ταῖς ἑλληνικαῖς χρονογραφίαις ἐοικυῖαι. Judging according to the laws of rhetorical style Cic. leg. 1, 6 *post annales pontificum maximorum . . . si aut ad Fabium aut ad . . . Catonem aut ad Pisonem aut ad Fannium aut ad Vennonium venias, quamquam ex his alius alio plus habet virium, tamen quid tam exile quam isti omnes? Fanni autem aetati coniunctus Antipater paulo inflavit vehementius, . . . sed tamen admonere reliquos potuit ut accuratius scriberent. ecce autem successere huic belli* (fine historians? Guilelmus conjectures rightly: *Gellii*, see § 137, 1 and Vahlen ad loc. and GFUnger Philol. Suppl. 3, 2, 9) *Clodius, Asellio: nihil ad Coelium, sed potius ad antiquorum languorem et inscitiam.* Fronto ep. p. 114 *historiam scripsere Sallustius structe, Pictor incondite, Claudius lepide, Antias invenuste, Seisenna longinque, verbis Cato multiiugis, Coelius singulis.* Dionys. Ant. 1, 7 ἐκ τῶν ἱστοριῶν . . . ἃς οἱ πρὸς αὐτῶν ἐπαινούμενοι Ῥωμαίων συνέγραψαν, Πόρκιός τε Κάτων καὶ Φάβιος Μάξιμος καὶ Οὐαλέριος ὁ Ἀντιεὺς καὶ Λικίννιος Μάκερ, Αἴλιοί τε καὶ Γέλλιοι καὶ Καλπούρνιοι, καὶ ἕτεροι συχνοὶ πρὸς τούτοις ἄνδρες οὐκ ἀφανεῖς. The oldest Annalists (Q. Fabius and L. Cincius) are previously mentioned by Dionys. 1, 6.

6. Mommsen, RG. 2^6, 452. LKieserling, de rer. rom. scriptoribus quibus T. Livius usus est, Berl. 1858. HvdBergh, de antiquiss. annalium scriptor. rom., Greifsw. 1859. Teuffel, PRE. 1^2, 1018. KWNitzsch, röm. und deutsche Annalistik u. Geschichtschr., Sybel's hist. Zeitschr. 11, 1; die röm. Annalistik von ihren ersten Anfängen bis auf Valerias Antias, Berl. 1873; die antike Geschichtschreibung in his Gesch. d. röm. Rep. 1 (1883), 5. HKlimke, Diodor u. d. röm. Annalistik, Königshütte 1881. CPeter, zur Kritik d. Quellen d. älteren röm. Gesch., Halle 1879. LOBröcker, moderne Quellenforscher u. antike Geschichtschreiber, Innsbr. 1882.

7. Cic. fam. 5, 12, 8 *scribam ipse de me, multorum tamen exemplo et clarorum virorum.* Tac. Agr. 1 *apud priores . . . plerique suam ipsi vitam narrare fiduciam potius morum quam adrogantiam arbitrati sunt, nec id Rutilio et Scauro citra fidem aut obtrectationi fuit.* LWiese, de vitarum scriptoribus romanis, Berl. 1840. WHDSuringar, de rom. autobiographis, Leyden 1846. AFrigell, om de rom. sjelfbiograferna, Ups. 1877. Köchly and Rüstow, Einl. zu Caes. gall. Krieg. (Gotha 1857) p. 3. The apologetic tendency of these memoirs was so pronounced that Cic. Brut. 112 actually calls a work of this kind *laudes.* What others did not do themselves, was done for them by officious clients, and later on by starving Greek literati.

38. In the Ciceronian period the rich materials furnished by contemporary history, together with the spread of a certain

literary facility, led many to compose historical narratives. Thus besides Atticus, Cicero and Cornelius Nepos, there were also Hortensius, Varro, Procilius, Lucceius, Libo, and others. Among these Atticus and Cornelius Nepos were distinguished by the range of their subject-matter, but were surpassed in interest as well as in style by the performances of Caesar and Sallust. Caesar provided also materials for future historians by establishing (a. 695/59) an official journal. The Civil War produced, besides Caesar's own writings, many other party histories. On Caesar's side wrote Hirtius, Oppius and Cornelius Balbus, Pompeius was vindicated by Voltacilius and T. Ampius Balbus, and Cicero by his faithful Tiro. M. Antony's Parthian war was related by Dellius. Among the opposite party M. Brutus wrote also memoirs, and his step-son Bibulus and friend Volumnius historical treatises in his praise. Contemporary history was also treated in the Annals of Tanusius Geminus and partly by Q. Tubero, the Civil War itself by Asinius Pollio and M. Valerius Messala. The Augustan period produced, in Livy's Roman History, a work of formal perfection, and the first Universal History (an idea only timidly approached by Varro, Atticus and Cornelius Nepos) was written by Pompeius Trogus. Varro's tentative effort towards a history of culture found in Fenestella a praiseworthy imitator.

1. At the end of the Republic, historians summed up the works of their predecessors. This summary we have in Livy, in Dionysius of Halicarnassus and in the revision of the Capitoline Fasti. Nissen, RhM. 25, 65.

39. In the course of the Imperial period the due appreciation of the affairs of old Rome disappeared rapidly; so did the possibility of a courageous and truthful relation of contemporary or recent events. Servile flattery and dependence gained ground. In the reign of Tiberius, Velleius Paterculus and Valerius Maximus wrote in this spirit (at least in respect to their contemporaries); for candour Labienus suffered under Augustus, and Cremutius Cordus under Tiberius. Accordingly the historical works of members of the reigning family passed uncriticised, e.g. those of Augustus, Tiberius, Agrippina, later on those of the copious writer Claudius and still later Trajan (Dacica) and Septimius Severus. Curtius chose a neutral territory. Yet through the whole of the 1st century the historic sense was only smouldering under the ashes: a fact proved not only by

the large number of historical works of this period of which we have traditions more or less dim, e.g. those by Aufidius Bassus and his successor Pliny the Elder, by Seneca the Elder, Servilius Nonianus, Lentulus Gaetulicus, Fabius Rusticus, Cluvius Rufus, Tuscus, but also by the appearance of a writer like Tacitus in one of the first intervals in despotic rule. With rhetoric, however, history always remained in a dangerously close connection; the more this degenerated, especially by the influence of Fronto's school, the deeper sank history in estimation and merit. The historical works of the Imperial period are also characterised by a concentration upon the mere personal element, to which are due both a number of biographies of private persons, and the kind of historical composition begun by Suetonius and his successors. Historians of this class, i.e. of court-events, and biographers of Emperors, were especially Marius Maximus, Junius Cordus, Aemilius Parthenianus, Aelius Maurus, and others, from whose works the six so-called Scriptores historiae augustae, Aelius Lampridius, Julius Capitolinus, Vulcacius Gallicanus, Aelius Spartianus, Trebellius Pollio, and Flavius Vopiscus, derived their compositions, without judgment or taste. For the history of the 4th century we have an excellent authority in Ammianus Marcellinus. With regard to the history of the Republican time in this period of decay, Livy became the exclusive authority, so much so that even those old sketches of Republican history, which are by no means mere extracts from Livy, e.g. Florus and Victor's viri illustres, were still considered as such by later readers. Livy himself was thought too prolix, and his work was (at the latest in the 3rd century) reduced to a kind of abstract in the shape of tables, used by Obsequens and Cassiodorus, as well as Vopiscus, Eutropius, Rufius Festus, Orosius and Pseudo-Idacius. Licinianus founds himself especially on Livy, and so, to a less extent, does L. Ampelius; Julius Exuperantius abridged Sallust. At a later time Eutropius took the place of Livy; his successor Paulus Diaconus was in his turn continued and elaborated by Landolfus Sagax (historia miscella). After the 4th century the influence of Christianity was felt here also. The chronographer of the year 354 gives, in addition to consular Fasti, an Easter-table and, with a list of the praefecti urbis, also one of the Roman Bishops and Martyrs. Sulpicius Severus' chronicles (c. 400) contain a summary of biblical and post-biblical history; Orosius' work has a Christian and apologetic purpose; the chronicles begin with the Creation. In the 5th and 6th century it was a common custom to copy from one another: thus St. Jerome copied Eusebius, Prosper (A.D. 455) St. Jerome, Victorius (Paschale, A.D. 457) Prosper, Cassiodorus (A.D. 519) Victorius, Jordanis (A.D. 551) Cassiodorus, and all so as to continue their predecessors to their own time. The chronicle of Prosper was also carried on by Marcellinus and Victor of Tunnuna. We possess also important special histories by Jordanis (Goths) and Gregory of Tours (Franks).

1. TAC. hist. 1, 1 *postquam bellatum apud Actium . . . magna ingenia cessere; simul veritas pluribus modis infracta, primum inscitia reip. ut alienae, mox libidine adsentandi aut rursus odio adversus dominantes.* A. 1, 1 *temporibus Augusti dicendis non defuere decora ingenia, donec gliscente adulatione deterrerentur. Tiberii Gaique et Claudii ac Neronis res florentibus ipsis ob metum falsae, postquam occiderant, recentibus odiis compositae sunt.* An instance of the latter kind is probably C. Fannius (PLIN. ep. 5, 5, 3). IOSEPH. ant. 20, 8, 3 πολλοὶ τὴν περὶ Νέρωνα συντετάχασιν ἱστορίαν, ὧν οἱ μὲν διὰ χάριν, εὖ πεπονθότες ὑπ' αὐτοῦ, τῆς ἀληθείας ἠμέλησαν, οἱ δὲ διὰ μῖσος . . . ἀναιδῶς ἐνεπαρῴνησαν τοῖς ψεύσμασιν . . . μηδὲ τῶν πρὸ αὐτοῦ γενομένων γράφοντες τὴν ἀλήθειαν τῆς ἱστορίας τετηρήκασιν, καίτοι πρὸς ἐκείνους αὐτοῖς οὐδὲν μῖσος ἦν, ἅτε μετ' αὐτοὺς πολλῷ χρόνῳ γενομένοις.

2. PLIN. ep. 5, 5, 3 of C. Fannius: *tres libros absolverat subtiles . . . atque inter sermonem historiamque medios.* According to the ideas of the period (see QUINTILIAN, above § 36, 7) an *historia* required more élan, imagination, *eloquentia.* TAC. Agr. 10 *quae priores nondum comperta* (on *Britanniae situm populosque*) *eloquentia percoluere rerum fide tradentur* (cf. dial. 23). Hence the alternative, to resign either *eloquentia* (rhetorical style) or *veritas* and *fides.* VOPISC. Prob. 2, 7 *mihi id animi fuit ut non Sallustios, Livios, Tacitos, Trogos atque omnes disertissimos imitarer viros in vita principum et temporibus disserendis, sed Marium Maximum, Suetonium Tranquillum, Fabium Marcellinum, Gargilium Martialem, ceterosque qui haec et talia non tam diserte quam vere memoriae tradiderunt.* Licinianus writes from a similar point of view concerning Sallust, see § 206, 4. Hence also such judgments as SENECA's N. Q. 7, 16, 1 *nec magna molitione detrahenda est auctoritas Ephoro: historicus est . . . haec in commune de tota natione* (of the *historici*), *quae adprobari opus suum et fieri populare non putet posse nisi illud mendacio adsperserit.* On the historical compositions of the Frontoniani see Lucian's πῶς δεῖ συγγράφειν τὴν ἱστορίαν.

3. In the Imperial period we have, besides the ordinary historical sources (e.g. the *acta*), also the *ephemerides* (diaries), e.g. Aureliani (VOPISC. Aurel. 1, 6), Turduli Gallicani (VOPISC. Prob. 2, 2. cf. 3, 4. 5, 1). Hence may have been derived the small personal details chronicled by these writers, because *etiam minora plerique desiderant* (CAPIT. Max. et Balb. 6, 1). In the earlier parts of the Imperial period biographies of private persons were written by Pliny the Elder of his friend Pomponius Secundus (PLIN. ep. 3, 5, 3), by Julius Secundus of Julius Asiaticus (TAC. dial. 14), by Tacitus of Agricola, by Claudius Pollio of his friend Annius (PLIN. ep. 7, 31, 5). Of a similar character were the *laudes* of Paetus Thrasea and Helvidius Priscus by Herennius Senecio and Arulenus Rusticus (SUET. Dom. 10. PLIN. ep. 7, 19, 5); in the Christian period the *vitae sanctorum*: see EBERT, Lit. des MA. 1, 429.

4. On the mutual copying see Mommsen, Cassiodorus p. 565 sq. On the extension of previous writings e.g. Ausonius, epigr. 2 *de fastis suis* (p. 120 Sch.), and Procop. aedif. 6, 7.

5. The historia Romana of Paulus Diaconus (§ 500, 6) in 16 books was about the year 1000 enlarged by Landolfus Sagax, otherwise entirely unknown, who made considerable additions to it out of Orosius, the origo gentis Rom., Hieronymus, Nepotianus (§ 279, 10), Victor's epit. etc., continued down to Leo the Armenian, and increased to the number of 26 books by dividing two books of the hist. rom. and adding 8 new ones. The original MS. of the author of this confused compilation, which goes by the name of historia miscella, is extant in the Vaticano-Palatinus 909. See HDroysen, Herm. 12, 387. Editions by LAMuratori, scriptt. rer. ital. 1, 100 and FEyssenhardt, Berl. 1869. The books I–XVIII in Droysen's Eutrop. (ed. mai.) 1879 (see § 415, 7). Cf. ib. p. lxi.

6. As the earliest writing of Roman history began with entries in the fasti (calendar), so also the earliest monastic history began with marginal notes on the Paschale. In the same way in the annals of the monasteries, the records of the earlier times were copied out from predecessors, the copyist adding to them notices concerning his own time. From Italy this custom was introduced in the 6th cent. into the Frankish kingdom and towards the end of the 7th into Belgium and Germany, as also into England (Baeda venerabilis). Wattenbach, deutsche Geschichtsquellen p. 40. 85.

7. Malalas p. 187, 11 *ἥντινα ἔκθεσιν*—concerning the revenge of Manlius Capitolinus on the Senator Februarius—*ηὗρον ἐν Θεσσαλονίκῃ πόλει· καὶ ἀναγνοὺς ηὗρον ἐπιγεγραμμένην τὴν βίβλιον* Ἔκθεσις Βρουνιχίου (perhaps Φρυνίχιος in disguise?) Ῥωμαίου *χρονογράφου.*—Forgeries of the 15th cent. are Fenestella (§ 259, 5), Messala Corvinus (§ 222, 5), the historia Papirii (Mommsen, Herm. 1, 135) etc.

40. An important source of history are the inscriptions, of which isolated examples are extant as early as the 6th century B.C. In the 2nd century B.C. they become numerous, and belonging to the Imperial period a superabundance has been found in all the provinces of the Roman Empire.

1. Principal work: Corpus inscriptionum latinarum consilio et auctoritate academiae litterarum Borussicae editum, Berl. 1862 sqq. The portions which have not yet appeared are marked.* Vol. I: Inscriptiones antiquissimae ad C. Caesaris mortem, ed. ThMommsen. 1863. Also voluminis primi tabulae lithographae, ed. FRitschl (likewise under the title Priscae latinitatis monumenta epigraphica ad archetyporum fidem exemplis lithographis repraesentata) 1862.—II: Inscr. Hispaniae, ed. EHübner. 1869.—III: Inscr. Asiae, provinciarum Europae graecarum, Illyrici, ed. Mommsen. 1873.—IV: Inscr. parietariae Pompeianae, Hercul., Stab., ed. CZangemeister. Acced. vasorum fictilium inscr., ed. RSchöne. 1871.—V: Inscr. Galliae cisalpinae, ed. Mommsen. 1877.—VI: Inscr. urbis Romae, ed. EBormann, HDressel, WHenzen, ChrHülsen: pars 1, 1876. 2, 1882. 3, 1886. *4. 5 (falsae) 1885. *6. *7 (indices).—VII: Inscr. Britanniae, ed. EHübner. 1873.—VIII: Inscr. Africae, ed. GWilmanns. 1881.—IX: Inscr. Calabriae, Apuliae, Samnii, Sabinorum, Piceni, ed. Mommsen. 1883.—X: Inscr. Bruttiorum, Lucaniae, Campaniae, Siciliae, Sardiniae, ed. Mommsen. 1883.—*XI: Inscr. Aemiliae, Umbriae, Etruriae, ed. EBormann.—*XII: Inscr. Galliae Narbonensis, ed. OHirschfeld.—*XIII: Inscr. trium Galliarum et duarum Germaniarum, ed. OHirschfeld et

CZangemeister.—*XIV: Inscr. Latii, ed. HDessau.—As Corporis I. L. auctarium has appeared: Exempla scripturae epigraphicae lat. a Caes. dict. morte ad aetatem Iustiniani, ed. EHübner, Berl. 1885.—The inscriptions discovered since the publication of the respective volumes of the CIL. are published in the Ephemeris epigraphica corporis inscr. lat. supplementum, Berl. 1872 sqq.

2. EHübner, Röm. Epigraphik in IwMüller's Handb. d. klass. Altert.-Wiss. 1, 475.—Selections for ordinary use: JCOrelli (inscriptionum lat. selectarum amplissima collectio, Zür. 1828 II; Vol. 3 by WHenzen 1856) and GWilmanns (Exempla inscript. latt., Berl. 1873 II.)—ESchneider, dialectorum ital. aevi vetustioris exempla: I, dialecti lat. priscae et faliscae inscriptt., Lps. 1886.—On the metrical inscriptions see § 31, 4.

3. Collections of the early Christian inscriptions of the city of Rome by JBdeRossi (I Rome 1861), of Spain and of England by EHübner (Berl. 1871 and 1876), of France by ELeBlant (Par. 1857, 65 II).

41. From the same motives as historiography and in connection with it, antiquarian learning arose and prospered among the Romans, dealing both with institutions and language. The study of the latter was due to the practical necessity of fixing in writing the developing sounds of the language. But the most distinguished authors and the majority of writers turned their attention to the mos maiorum i.e. the investigation of the customs and institutions of olden times. Such are Cincius Alimentus, Cato, M. Fulvius Nobilior, Cassius Hemina, C. Sempronius Tuditanus, M. Junius Gracchanus. To these studies were added after the 7th century u.c. essays on the older literature and especially elucidations of the poets, partly historical, partly linguistic (glossographic). Representatives of this tendency are, besides L. Accius and Lucilius, Porcius Licinus, Q. Valerius of Sora, Volcatius Sedigitus, Octavius Lampadio, Sisenna, Sevius Nicanor, Aurelius Opilius, M. Antonius Gnipho, Q. Cosconius, Santra, Octavius Hersennus, and above all L. Aelius Stilo and his son-in-law Ser. Clodius. Crates the Pergamene grammarian, who in the year 595/159 came as ambassador to Rome, excited a lasting interest in linguistic studies. Etymology was attempted by two methods, some always resorting to Greek (Hypsikrates), others endeavouring to explain everything on the basis of Latin (M. Varro and Nigidius Figulus). In the Ciceronian time, when Rome was recognised as the centre of the whole intellectual life of the Empire and contained all helps to research, these studies reached their highest stage of development in Varro, and besides him Nigidius Figulus, Valerius Cato, Ateius Philologus and others. Among the statesmen Caesar

himself wrote de analogia, Appius Claudius (cos. 700/54) and L. Caesar wrote on the augural system. In the Augustan time antiquarian investigation was once more zealously cultivated by Julius Hyginus, Verrius Flaccus, M. Valerius Messala, Sinnius Capito, Scribonius Aphrodisius, L. Crassicius, succeeded by Julius Modestus, Pomponius Marcellus, A. Cornelius Celsus and Asconius Pedianus. Celsus' versatility was even surpassed by that of Pliny the Elder, and even in the 2nd century A.D. Suetonius, Sulpicius Apollinaris, Fronto and Apuleius, exhibit a varied culture and literary activity. But on the whole it may be said that, from the first century of our era, a school-system with its comparatively limited views gained ascendancy, and in this department the grammarians became the most important, while erudition became more and more restricted to one class. Thus we have Q. Remmius Palaemo, M. Valerius Probus of Berytus, Annaeus Cornutus, Caesius Bassus, Aemilius Asper, Flavius Caper, Caesellius Vindex, Urbanus, Velius Longus; in Hadrian's reign, Terentius Scaurus; under M. Aurelius A. Gellius and probably Festus. The later authors subsisted on these earlier productions. Thus in the 3rd century Arruntius Celsus, Helenius Acro, Julius Romanus, Censorinus, Sacerdos, lastly perhaps the lexicographer Nonius Marcellus and Pomponius Porphyrio. After a long interval about the middle of the 4th century we meet again grammarians of more distinction, most of them authors of manuals (artes), such as Cominianus, Marius Victorinus, Aelius Donatus, Charisius, Diomedes; the same Aelius Donatus elucidated Terence, Servius and Claudius Donatus Vergil. In the 5th century we have Macrobius and Agroecius, and at the commencement of the 6th Priscian. In this department, too, the semblance of variety and stir surpasses the reality, since here also preceding labours were copied to a great extent, and often with very little discrimination.

1. SUET. gramm. 1 *grammatica Romae ne in usu quidem olim, nedum in honore ullo erat, rudi scilicet ac bellicosa etiamtum civitate necdum magnopere liberalibus disciplinis vacante. initium quoque eius mediocre extitit, si quidem antiquissimi doctorum, qui iidem et poetae et semigraeci erant* (as Livy and Ennius), . . . *nihil amplius quam Graecos interpretabantur.* . . ib. 2 *primus* . . . *studium grammaticae in urbem intulit Crates Mallotes, Aristarchi aequalis, qui missus ad senatum ab Attalo rege inter secundum ac tertium bellum punicum, sub ipsam Enni mortem,* . . . *nostris exemplo fuit ad imitandum.* On the influence of the Pergamenes on Roman literature—exaggerated of late—AREIFFERSCHEID, ind. lect., Bresl. 1881/82. UvWILAMOWITZ, Antig. v. Karystos 161. 176. IBRZOSKA, de canone decem oratt.

Attic., Bresl. 1883, 75 and esp. ERohde, RhM. 41, 175; see § 44, 10); *hactenus tamen ut carmina parum adhuc divolgata vel defunctorum amicorum, vel si quorum aliorum probassent, diligentius retractarent ac legendo commentandoque et ceteris nota facerent; ut C. Octavius Lampadio, . . . ut postea Q. Vargunteius : . . . instruxerunt auxeruntque ab omni parte grammaticam L. Aelius Lanuvinus generque Aeli Ser. Clodius* . . . ib. 3 *posthac magis ac magis et gratia et cura artis increvit, ut ne clarissimi quidem viri abstinuerint quo minus et ipsi aliquid de ea scriberent utque temporibus quibusdam super viginti celebres scholae fuisse in urbe tradantur*, also *grammatici* were sold at a high price (as slaves), as *Lutatius Daphnis* (§ 134, 1. 142, 4. 244, 2. Cf. HPeter, JJ. 115, 750) and *L. Apuleius. iam in provincias quoque grammatica penetraverat, ac nonnulli de notissimis doctoribus peregre docuerunt, maxime in Gallia togata, inter quos Octavius Teucer et Sescennius* (*Fesc.* the MS., *Pescennius* Osann) *Iacchus* (mentioned as the authority for Plin. NH. b. 32 and 37, and quoted 37, 148) *et Oppius Chares* (cf. 54, 5).

2. The critical activity of the *grammatici* comprehended, after the example of their Greek predecessors, *emendare, distinguere, adnotare* (*notas adicere*, which *notae* consisted sometimes in mere signs, sometimes in short notes). Sueton. in the Anecd. Paris. (from Paris. 7350 s. VIII first edited by Bergk, ZfAW. 1845, 85= opusc. 1, 580; and in Reifferscheid's Sueton. 137, Keil's GL. 7, 533 and elsewhere), *Notae* XXI *quae versibus apponi consuerunt : — obelus.* ⁘ *asteriscus.* ⁘— *asteriscus cum obelo.* ⟶ *simplex ductus.* > *diple.* ⩥ *diple periestigmene.* Ɔ *antisigma.* Ɔ̇ *antisigma cum puncto.* ⸦ *coronis.* >— *diple obelismene.* ⩽ *aversa obelismene.* ⚹ *ceraunion.* ÷ *obelus adpunctus.* —< *obelus cum aversa.* ⩾ *diple superne obelata.* ⩾⩽ *recta et aversa superne obelatae.* ☧ *chi et rho.* ɸ *fi et ro.* Ͳ *ancora superior.* ⫝̸ *ancora inferior.* (ʖ) *alogus. his solis in adnotationibus Ennii, Lucilii et historicorum* (?) *usi sunt Vargunteius* (Bergk: *Varrus* the MS.), *Ennius* (§ 159, 13), *Aelius* (Stilo) *aeque et postremo Probus* (see § 300). Here follows the explanation of the use of the several signs, where it is repeatedly remarked, in accordance with the account of their employment among the Greeks: *item Probus et antiqui nostri, similiter* (*sic et*) *in nostris auctoribus* etc. Cf. Isid. orig. 1, 20. JSteup, de Probis 17. According to the explanation these 21 *notae*, with few exceptions, refer to the *emendatio* (διόρθωσις), but Suetonius knew of other *notae* as well (cf. in the Anecd. Paris. *his solis*), and some which were employed from the point of view of rhetorical and aesthetic criticism (κρίσις) are to be found enumerated in the supplement to these Anecd. GL. 7, 536, 16 as *notae simplices.* An Anecd. Cavense (ap. Reifferscheid, RhM. 23, 127) quotes some such e.g. ÷ *lemniscus in acutis.* ⁘ *asteriscus in sententiis.* ρω *oraeon in invincibilibus. oraeon cum palma in invincibilibus acutis* etc. This list of notes in La Cava is preceded by two epigrams which refer to it, one by Patricius Olybrius (cf. § 436, 7) who belonged to the school of Symmachus, which was occupied with the preservation, careful multiplication and estimation of the early Latin authors. Similar *notae* were made use of in Christian literature, e.g. by Cassiodorus (see § 483, 12).—To the above-mentioned efforts of Symmachus and his school (§ 425, 9) on behalf of early literature was due the production of a series of copies of authors. These last representatives of the ancient religion, in their struggle with Christianity, sought to make allies of the old authors, for whose multiplication in good texts they were therefore concerned (§ 425, 9). We learn of these undertakings from the so-called subscriptions in MSS. which were customary both in secular and Christian MSS. and, as a rule, appear to prove merely a revision of the copy after the original, but not a scientific and critical examination of the text. These subscriptions begin with an *emendavi* (*legi, recognovi, contuli*, etc.) and the name of the reviser, and then at discretion

are mentioned the place, time, circumstances and perhaps the assistance given by some reader. For details see the several authors: e.g. § 196, 2 (Caes.). 231, 9 (Verg.). 240, 6 (Hor.). 256, 11 (Liv.). 279, 9 (Jul. Paris). 296, 3 (Mela.). 302, 5 (Pers.). 322, 8 (Mart.). 325, 12 (Quintil.). 331, 8 (Juv.). 367, 8 (Apul.). 374, 5 (Cic.). 390, 5 (Non.). 432, 6 (Veget.). 436, 5 (Prudent.). 444, 8 (Macr.). 452, 6 (Mart. Cap.). OJahn, d. Subscriptionen in den Hss. röm. Klass., Lpz. SBer. 1851, 327. FHaase, de lat. codd. mss. subscriptionibus, Bresl. 1860. AReifferscheid, de lat. codd. subscriptionibus (in patristic MSS.), Bresl. 1872.

3. The Latin grammatical literature is almost entirely founded on the Greek, hardly possesses any scientific independence, and is chiefly practical in its purpose.—The grammarians, like the early writers in general (see § 37, 4), have no idea of literary property; quite unconcernedly Verrius Flaccus copies out Varro, Probus Verrius, Pliny Probus, Caper Pliny, Julius Romanus Caper, Charisius Julius Romanus, Aphthonius Juba, Marius Victorinus Aphthonius, etc., and this indeed is generally done with but little care. An earlier text-book is altered and recast at discretion, a more detailed one is abbreviated, one for more advanced students is toned down to suit the requirements of beginners, and then brought out as an original work. Sometimes too the first part of a text-book is adapted from one writer, and the second from another, and then possibly the name of the first author is transferred to the whole work, especially if the name was a famous one, such as Probus. Thus in quotations things are attributed to Probus, which elsewhere appear as the property of Sacerdos or Diomedes. The confusion was increased by the text-books of different authors being combined in one MS. and by the old names being left attached to such revisions, in which but little of the original work remained. During the last centuries of antiquity it even became the custom to fill in blank pages in the MSS. of grammatical school-books with other (older) works of similar contents. At the same time the authors often endeavour, even if they have only copied from one or two predecessors, to produce the impression that they have made use of a large number of authorities.

4. Arnob. adv. nat. 1, 59 *quamvis Epicados omnes, Caesellios, Verrios, Scauros teneatis et Nisos.* Hieronym. apol. c. Rufin. 1, 16 (2, 472 Vall.): *puto quod puer legeris Aspri in Vergilium et Sallustium commentarios, Vulcacii in orationes Ciceronis* (§ 381, 7), *Victorini in dialogos eius et in Terentii comoedias praeceptoris mei Donati, aeque in Vergilium et aliorum in alios, Plautum videlicet, Lucretium, Flaccum, Persium atque Lucanum.*

5. In a cod. Bonon. s. XI (HKeil, de gramm. inf. aet., Erl. 1868, 27. HHagen, anecd. Helv. p. cl) are the following notices, incorrect in many respects: *In Roma fuerunt Donatus, Priscianus, Victorinus* (as the author of the ars. gramm.), *Fothicius* (i.e. Euticius, § 482, 1), *Flavianus et Cominianus. in Spania Caper et Ogretius* (Agroecius). *in Carthagine Pompeius, Hisidorus, Sergius tractator* (expl. in Donat.) *et Augustinus. in Sicilia Honoratus et alter Sergius* (de litt. syll. etc.) *Maximus* (lib. de rat. metr.) *et Metrorius* (de final. syll.). HKeil, quaest. gramm. 2, viii. More correctly at the end of the cod. Bern. 243 the marginal note by PDaniel (from an early MS.): *De Roma, de Sicilia, de Italia, de Africa, de Ispania venerunt ad nos libri grammatici: de Roma quatuor libri Donati* (cf. Hagen l.l.). *de Sicilia IIII discipulorum eius, i.e. Honorati et Sergii et Maximi et Metrorii. de Italia duo libri Consentii de nomine et verbo et de barbarismo, et libri Prisciani XX, et Eutitii duo, et Sergii novem de littera et de barbarismo, et Asperi et Flaviani libri IIII. de Africa vero Cominiani et Pompeii. de Ispania Isodori et Capri et Agroeci et analogia* (Orthography) *Papperini et Victorini.* HHagen, anecd. Helvet. p. cxlix.—Petri grammatici (s. VIII/IX) excerpta in HHagen's anecd. Helvet. 159.

6. Best edition of the grammatici latini by HKEIL, Lps. 1856–79 VII. As a supplement to this by HHAGEN, anecdota helvetica quae ad grammaticam latinam spectant, Lps. 1870.—EICHENFELD and ENDLICHER, analecta grammatica, Wien 1837.

7. SURINGAR, historia crit. scholiastaram latt., Leid. 1834 sq. III. LLERSCH, d. Sprachphilos. der Alten, Bonn 1838–41 III. VAN HEUSDE, de L. Aelio Stilone (1839) p. 17. GRÄFENHAN, Gesch. d. klass. Philologie im Altertum, Bonn 1843 sqq. (esp. b. 4). HSTEINTHAL, Gesch. d. Sprachwissensch. bei d. Gr. u. R., Berl. 1863. EJULLIEN, les professeurs de littérature dans l'ancienne Rome, jusqu'à la mort d'Auguste, Par. 1886.

42. The same deterioration is noticeable in the separate departments. Whereas in Republican times historical research had made progress, especially in subjects of political interest such as the sacred antiquities, in the Imperial period these were left to the jurists, and study was restricted to grammar, including orthography, synonymy, and lexicography, and to prosody; this was chiefly compilation, and rarely done with any systematic thoroughness. The writers on prosody, among whom the most important are Caesius Bassus and Juba, are entirely dependent on their Greek predecessors. After grammatical studies had ceased for more than a hundred years, an effort was made, in the 4th century, to produce comprehensive abridgments, which gradually became more and more meagre, limited and wanting in independence. The old mythology is almost the only subject of technical study. At the end of the 5th century the barbarian element begins to mingle with scholarship.

1. Writers on the augural system, haruspicia and cognate subjects: Varro, Nigidius Figulus, Ap. Claudius Pulcher (cos. 100, 54), L. Caesar, Tarquitius Priscus, Caecina, Caesius, Veranius, Granius Flaccus, Aufustius, Clodius Tuscus, Umbricius Melior, Julius Aquila, the grammarian Ennius (§ 159, 13), Cornelius Labeo. RMERKEL's Prolegg. to Ovid's Fasti (1841). OMÜLLER, Etrusk. 2^2, 19. GSCHMEISSER, de etrusca disciplina, Bresl. 1872; die etr. Disziplin vom Bundesgenossenkrieg bis z. Untergang des Heidentums, Liegn. 1881; Beiträge sur Kenntn. der Techn. der Haruspices, Schwerin a/W. 1884. Cf. below § 77. On Vicellius and Fonteius see § 170, 9.

2. Scriptores latini rei metricae; ed. THGAISFORD, Oxon. 1837, now specially in the sixth volume of KEIL's Grammatici. Division of writers on prosody into two classes, according as, like Varro, they consider the hexameter and iambic trimeter as metra principalia, from which all other metres are to be derived (merely metra derivata, παραγωγά), or divide the metres by the πρωτότυπα. A few others (as in the fragm. bobiense and the centrimetrum) began with the iambus and trochaeus, but the majority (no doubt for practical reasons) with the dactylus. Cf. esp. RWESTPHAL, griech. Metrik 1^2, 105. 138. 203. 214. HWENTZEL, symb. crit. ad hist. scriptorum rei metr. lat., Bresl. 1858. HKEIL, quaest. grammaticae, Lps. 1860. JCAESAR, de nonnullis metricorum latt. locis, Marb. 1874. OHENSE, de Iuba artigrapho in Ritschl's acta Lips. 4 (1875), 37.

3. Cassiod. divin. lect. 30 *orthographos antiquos legant Velium Longum Curtium Valerianum, Papirianum, Adamantium Martyrium de* v *et b*, etc. Cassiod. de orthogr. mentions in addition Annaeus Cornutus, Caesellius Vindex, Eutyches, and Priscianus. Also Flavius Caper and Terentius Scaurus, as well as Auctores anonymi de orthographia IV in Hagen's anecd. Helvet. 291, cf. p. cxxxv. WBrambach, lat. Orthogr. (1868), 27.

4. Synonymy (differentia sermonum), which had already been treated of incidentally by Varro, Verrius Flaccus, and others, became in the later Imperial period (Charis. GL. 1, 205, 16 *illi qui de differentiis scribunt*) a favourite subject for book-making, and the writings concerning it were attributed to Probus, Suetonius, Fronto, and in the Middle Ages even to Cato, Cicero and Vergil. The collections of this kind, which have been preserved to us, much resemble each other, and are only to a small extent derived from good sources. They may be traced back to an original collection, which was compiled probably in the 5th–6th centuries A.D. from the separate collections then extant. The most important collection of extracts from the Roman synonymic remains is Montepess. H. 306 s. IX; in this, besides smaller collections, such as that of Arevalo in his Isidor. 7, 426, Hagen, anecd. Helvet. 275 (cf. JWBeck, de Sulpic. Apollin. p. 51) and FHand, published in Jena 1848, and also the differentiae of Probus (§ 300, 8, b), Suetonius (§ 347, 3), and Isidorus' diff. spiritales (Montepess. does not give Isidorus' greater profane synonymy, § 496, 1), there is a very voluminous collection ('differentiae similium orationis partium a Cicerone et ab aliis sapientibus viris in sensu et litteratura per alphabetum'); published by Beck, diff. scr. 28. Cicero's name is of course unauthorised and probably borrowed from the collection, otherwise differing entirely as to its contents, which bears the name of Cicero (§ 188, 9). Fragments of a collection of diff. serm. JJ. 127, 649 (on this see JWBeck, JJ. 131, 639. JWBeck, de differentiarum scriptoribus lat., Groningen 1883.

5. Fest. 166b, 8 *glossematorum scriptores.* Charis. GL. 1, 229, 31 *glossae antiquitatum* (old Latin). 242 . . . . *ut esse in sacris Anagninorum vocum veterum interpretes scribunt.* Gell. 18, 7, 3 *glosaria namque conligitis et lexidia, res taetras et inanes et frivolas.* The sound erudition of the earlier glossographers (e.g. of Aurelius Opilius, below § 159, 4, of Aelius Stilo, § 148, 2, and others) was preserved in a ruinously shattered condition in the glossaria, which have been preserved in great numbers, partly in very old MSS., and contain, besides a preponderating quantity of rubbish, very valuable linguistic material (taken from authorities now lost) especially for old and popular Latin. The glossaria explain rare Latin words (*glossae*) by comparing with them those in common use, frequently adding quotations and examples.—The explanation is generally in Latin likewise, but sometimes in Greek as well: more rarely the lemma is in Greek, and the explanation in Latin (see n. 7). The significance of these Gr.-Lat. glosses is contained in the Latin portion. The arrangement is generally more or less alphabetical (sometimes displaying wonderful subtlety: see Loewe's prodr. 129), more rarely according to the subjects.

6. Purely Latin glossaria: the most important is that of Placidus (on this see § 472, 7) especially rich in data for ancient Latin (Plautus). Special glossaria on Plautus (§ 99, 6), Terence (§ 109, 3), Vergil (§ 231, 7), Sidonius (? § 467, 9) etc. Numerous independent and general glossaria, e.g. the Gl. Affatim, so called from the word with which it begins (drawn from good sources, see HUsener, RhM. 23, 677), Gl. Asbestos (in the Vat. 1469 s. X with curious glosses on Lucilius, see GGoetz, RhM. 40, 324), Gl. Ab.: absens, Gl. Abavus minor, etc.—The independent glossaria, sometimes abridged, sometimes enlarged by the addition of new material,

were gathered into collections: thus in the gl. Abavus maior (ed. GFHildebrand, Gött. 1854; cf. HRönsch, RhM. 30, 449. GLoewe, gl. nom. 158; Mélanges Graux =gl. nom. 101). On other collections see n. 8. 9.—Very important MSS. for the purely Latin glossaria are SGallen, 912, s. VII/VIII (published by MWarren, transact. of the Americ. philol. assoc. 1884, Cambr. 1885) and Vat. 3321 s. VII (from this and seven other MSS. AMai, class. auct. 6, 501 compiled his glossarium vetus, AWilmanns, RhM. 24, 381).—The so-called glossae Isidori (7, 443 Arev.) first published by Vulcanius, Thes. utriusque ling. (Leid. 1600) p. 667, are (like the excerpta Pithoeana in Gothofredi auctores ling. lat., S. Gervasii 1602) not independent collections of glossae, but represent a compilation prepared by JScaliger ex variis glossariis: see Loewe, prodr. 23.—On the so-called glossae Petronii see § 305, 2.

7. The Latin-Greek glosses of Par. 7651 s. VIII/IX, attributed without foundation to Flavius Theodorus Philoxenus cos. a. 525 (see also Mommsen CIL. 5, 8120, 4), rank above all glossae on account of their high value. On the information concerning authorities contained in them see FOsann, gloss. lat. spec. Giss. 1826. JKlein, RhM. 24, 289. Traces of a similar collection in Martyrius (§ 472, 6): FBücheler, RhM. 35, 69. The collection quite groundlessly called glossae Cyrilli (in the Laudun. s. IX, Harl. 5792 s. VII/VIII) is Graeco-Latin; in this there are many originally Lat.-Gr. glosses (see Loewe, prodr. 216).—Cyrilli Philoxeni aliorumque vett. glossaria latinogr. et graecolat. a CLabbaeo collecta, Par. 1679 (to be used with caution: see RhM. 17, 159. 18, 253; particularly because the Onomasticon vocum latino-graecarum, which JSpiegel prefixed to his edition of Calepini lexicon (Strassb. 1537), is here regarded as ancient, and incorporated among the early glosses; see Loewe, prodr. 194).—New critical edition of the Philox. and Cyrill. gl. in the Corp. glossar. lat. vol. 2, Lpz. 1887. AFRudorff, d. Gl. d. Philox. u. Cyr., Abh. d. Berl. Akad. 1865, 182.—To the bilingual glossaria belong also the so-called glossae Servii (§ 431, 4 in fin.) and the Latin glossae nominum, which were translated (about the 8th century) from biligual ones (published from Erfurt and other MSS. by GLoewe, Lpz. 1884, see n. 9 ad fin.) and others. On the Pseudo-Dositheana see § 431, 8.—Graeco-Latin are also the medico-botanical glossaria, which are of material, though not of linguistic importance: such are to be found at Siena (MS. s. X/XI published by JSchmidt, Herm. 18, 521) and in the Vatic. Reg. 1260 s. X: to these belong also the sinonima Bartholomei and Gl. Alphita (in Oxford, published by JLGMowat, anecd. Oxon. 1, 1. 2). Cf. § 487, 4 ad fin.

8. A series of lesser glossaria, together with other material, was collected in the 7./8. cent. (perhaps by the still enigmatical Ansileubus? see n. 9 and OMüller, praef. Festi p. xxxiii. Loewe, prodr. 224. EBährens, JenLZ. 1877, 155), together with a statement of the sources of the several glosses (e.g. Placidi, de glosis, that is, out of anonymous collections such as Affatim, see n. 6), into a sort of Encyclopaedia, the once much used liber glossarum (e.g. in the cod. Paris. 11529. 30. s. VIII). See on this Wilmanns RhM. 24, 364. Usener ib. 24, 382. Examples in Mai, class. auct. 7, 550. 589. 6, 554. 576. Also in GThomas, SBer. d. Münch. Ak. 1868 2, 370 (cf. CHalm and CHofmann, ib. 1869 2, 1. AMiller, Bl. f. d. Bayr. Gymn. 6, 295). Fickert, Naumb. 1843. CPeter, Zeitz. 1850. SBerger (n. 9) 6.

9. From the liber glossarum were derived, with the addition of other materials, the glossae Salomonis (Bishop of Constance † 919), printed at Augsb. 1483 (cf. Usener, RhM. 24, 389), Papiae elementarium doctrinae rudimentum about 1050 (often reprinted), also Osberni (a monk at Gloucester about 1150),

Panormia (ed. AMai, class auct. vol. 8. See WMeyer, RhM. 29, 179), Hugotionis liber derivationum about 1190, the so-called breviloquus Benthemianus (s. XV; on this see KHamann, Hamb. 1879–80 II; weitere Mitteil. aus d. brevil. Benth. nebst Anhang: Abschnitte aus dem lib. derivat. des Ugutio, Hamb. 1882). Here belongs the Phillipps glossary 4626 in Cheltenham (see MWarren, Amer. journ. of philol. 6, 451. REllis, journ. of phil. 1885, 81). A Turin glossary in Pflugk-Harttung's Iter italicum 341 (on this GLoewe's commentary ib. 821) etc. SBerger, de glossariis . . . quibusdam medii aevi sive de libris Ansileubi, Papiae, Hugotionis etc., Par. 1879.

Chief work on Lat. gl.: GLoewe, prodromus corporis glossariorum lat., Lps. 1876. In addition: glossae nominum, ed. GLoewe; accedunt eius opuscula glossographica, Lps. 1884. In preparation: Corpus glossariorum latin. editum auctoritate soc. litt. reg. Saxon., Lps. 1887 sqq. (published in accordance with Loewe's preparatory work by GGoetz and others); see n. 7.

10. Among the scriptores mythographi latini are comprehended Hyginus (§ 262), Fulgentius (§ 480), Lutatius Placidus (? cf. § 249, 2), Albericus philosophus (see below), published together by ThMuncker (Amst. 1681, subsequently by AvStaveren, Leid. 1742). Cf. CLange, de nexu Hyg. fabb. 11. Three new mythographi vaticani, first published by AMai, class. auct. Vol. 3 (Rome 1831), subsequently by GHBode, scriptt. rerum myth. lat. tres (Celle 1834 II). The first of these (mythographus vaticanus I) is the earliest; it makes great use of Servius' commentary on Vergil and other scholia on poets (e.g. on Statius) and of Fulgentius, Orosius, Isidorus and others. Correspondences with Ps.-Acro: AKiessling, de person. horat. 7. This mythol. I is preserved in Vatic. Reg. 1401, s. X./XI. In it the subscriptio: *expl. liber secundus centum hñf* (=*habens*) *fabulas sicut et primus*. Cf. ORossbach, JJ. 131, 408. AMai misread the subscription (*hñf* =*hñi*, etc.) and hence gave as the title of the work *C. Hygini libri fabularum*. The mythogr. vat. II borrows much word for word from the first; lastly mythogr. vat. III (de diis gentium et illorum allegoriis), in which are quoted e.g. Johannes Scotus († about 875) and Remigius of Auxerre († a. 908), belongs according to the cod. Goth. (*poetarium Alberici*) to Albericus (living s. XIII), the same who composed the work de deorum imaginibus, included in the corp. mythogr. (see above). Cf. EKlussmann, de Alberici mythogr. cod. Goth. II (s. XIII), Rudolst. 1868. Schneider, de mythographis lat., Bresl. 1834. FOsann, Haller Lit.-Ztg. 1834. Erg. Bl. 12. FJacobs, ZfAW. 1834, 1057. Suringar, de mythographo astronomico, Lugd. 1842. MZink, der Mytholog Fulgentius (1867) 13. RFörster, d. Raub der Persephone (Stuttg. 1874), 291.

43. The Romans were naturally well qualified for oratory by their acute intellect, their love of order and their Italian vivacity, tempered with Roman gravity. The influence of habit and rule, the publicity of all transactions, the numerous occasions where good speaking was required, before the people, the senate, a jury or magistrates, the army, or at a funeral, made fluent speaking an indispensable requirement in the state and the possession of eloquence a means to the attainment of political distinction, especially when the privileges of rank disappeared one after the other, and political party-strife became more frequent

and ardent. In consequence of this oratory took from the beginning a practical direction, and practice in public speaking became an essential part of the education of a young Roman, so much so that Cato the Elder already composed a manual of it, and in several families, as in that of the Scribonii, eloquence became hereditary through several generations. To this must be attributed the large number of orators among the Romans, the early commencement of oratory and the great perfection to which it attained, its rise and decay with the various phases of the political constitution.

1. Cic. off. 2, 66 *eloquentiae a maioribus nostris est in toga dignitatis principatus datus.* Cf. or. 141. Brut. 182 . . . *in tanta et tam vetere republica maximis praemiis eloquentiae propositis omnes cupisse dicere, non plurumos ausos esse, potuisse paucos.* Liv. 39, 40 *ad summos honores alios scientia iuris, alios eloquentia, alios gloria militaris provexit.* Quint. 2, 16, 8 *pop. rom., apud quem summa semper oratoribus dignitas fuit;* see also Tac. dial. 37.

2. Cic. de or. 2, 55 *nemo studet eloquentiae nostrorum hominum nisi ut in causis atque in foro eluceat: apud Graecos* etc. (eloquence was an end in itself). Morality even suffered by the regard paid to the practical side: the forensic orator was scarcely expected to adhere to truth. Cicero's words about M. Antonius (Brut. 207), that he was *facilis in causis recipiendis*, apply also to himself, and in more than one passage he teaches that for an orator not the *verum* is the aim, but the *verisimile;* see de or. 2, 241. off. 2, 51. In a similar manner Quint. 2, 15, 32. 3, 8, 13. 12, 1, 33 sqq. 6, 2, 5 *ubi animis iudicum vis afferenda est et ab ipsa veri contemplatione abducenda mens, ibi proprium oratoris opus est.* On the other hand 12, 7, 7 *non convenit ei quem oratorem esse volumus iniusta tueri scientem;* cf. 4, 2, 93.

3. They commenced in early youth. Africanus minor says, at the age of eighteen, in Polyb. 32, 9 δοκῶ εἶναι πᾶσιν ἡσύχιός τις . . . καὶ πολὺ κεχωρισμένος τῆς ῥωμαϊκῆς αἱρέσεως καὶ πράξεως ὅτι κρίσεις οὐχ αἱροῦμαι λέγειν. Plin. ep. 5, 8, 8 *undevicesimo aetatis anno dicere in foro coepi.* Very frequently their début was a speech in praise of a recently departed relative. Again, Tiberius *novem natus annos defunctum patrem pro rostris laudavit* (Suet. Tib. 6). The youthful character of such laudationes funebres was, therefore, perhaps a reason for their rarely being published, EHübner, Hermes 1, 441. It was also very common to commence the career of orator by prosecutions; see Polyb. 32, 15 in fin. Cic. off. 2, 49. Suet. Iul. 4. Val. Max. 5, 4, 4. Quint. 12, 6, 1. Tac. dial. 34 in f. Apulei. apol. 66.

4. The speeches attributed by later historians to the regal period do not, of course, prove anything as to the oratory of that time; but even then the constitution necessitated a certain amount of political speaking. Meyer's collection from Appius Claudius to Symmachus (n. 5) amounts to 158 orators, without counting those whose speeches were never written down or of whose speeches, if written, we have no record. Cf. § 44, 12.

5. The principal sources are Cicero's Brutus, Seneca the rhetor, Tacitus' dialogus, Suetonius' viri ill., Quintilian 10, 1, 105–122 and 12, 10, 10–12, also Pliny's letters. Oratorum romanorum fragmenta coll. HMeyer, Zür. 1832. (Paris reprint 1837.) [2]1842.—AWestermann, Gesch. d. röm. Beredsamk. Lpz. 1835. FEllendt, brevis eloquentiae rom. ad Caesares hist. in his edition of Brutus 1844. FBlass

die gr. Beredsamk. von Alex. bis Aug., Berl. 1865, p. 104. JFABerger and VCucheval, hist. de l'éloquence lat. jusqu'à Cicéron, Par. 1872 II. JPoiret, l'éloquence judiciaire à Rome, Par. 1887.

44. The eloquence of the oldest period was thoroughly natural, the artless expression of an individual stimulated by a certain situation and certain purposes, possessing political importance and able to speak. But as early as the close of the 5th century Appius Claudius published a speech after it was delivered, and of the funeral orations mentioned in the 6th century it is possible that they were written down from the very beginning. The undoubtedly greatest orator of the 6th century, Cato the Elder, must generally have written down and published his speeches as political pamphlets, though perhaps only after they were delivered. On the whole, in the 6th century u.c., the spoken word was as yet the most important; writing down and publishing speeches was resorted to for political purposes. Besides those of Cato, we hear in this time of published speeches esp. by the elder Africanus, L. Papirius and C. Titius. In the beginning of the 7th century Roman oratory was already so far advanced that the acquaintance with Greek rhetoric only raised it and made it more conscious of its worth, without depriving it of its national character. The first to attempt an artistic disposition in his speeches was Ser. Sulpicius Galba (cos. 610/144), and Gracchus the Younger was a perfect orator in virtue of his combination of talent and study. It was the exception, even in the first half of that century, if an orator published none of his speeches, and there were already writers who composed speeches afterwards delivered by others. In the epoch of the Gracchi, practical political speaking had attained to its highest perfection, and maintained this level during 30 or 40 years. But by and by, when the orator no longer addressed the sovereign People, but a plebeian mob, studied perfection was regarded as less important in a spoken speech. The political purpose then became of minor importance in published speeches: speeches were composed and published as mere specimens of eloquence. The most eminent orators of this time were M. Antonius (cos. 655/99) and L. Crassus (cos. 659/95); but besides them we find a large number of orators remarkable in their way, e.g. Q. Mucius Scaevola (cos. 659/95), L. Marcius Philippus (cos. 663/91), L. Apuleius Saturninus (tr. pl. 654/100), M. Livius Drusus (tr. pl. 663/91), C. Caesar Strabo (aedilis 664/90), P. Sulpicius Rufus (tr. pl.

666/88), C. Aurelius Cotta (cos. 679/75). Without ever losing sight of their practical purposes, the orators and theorists of the Roman school (compare in Sulla's time the Rhetoric addressed to Herennius) kept aloof from the crotchets of the Greek rhetoricians, though they also knew how to appreciate the instruction derived from the Greeks. In the second half of the 7th century men of Roman birth commenced to give rhetorical instruction in Latin. Through the medium of the Greeks, the exaggerated style then prevailing in Asia was introduced in Rome, and found a representative especially in Hortensius. But his younger contemporary, Cicero, again deserted this style, and joined a mediating school, the Rhodian; by a happy combination of talents, exercised and ennobled by indefatigable industry, he was lifted to the highest place in the artistic oratory of the Romans. He did service also by making the principal doctrines of rhetoric popular among his countrymen. In the later years of his life there arose in Greece a retrograde school, which found even him too Asiatic and which soon prevailed in Rome. A number of the younger men, to whom Caesar seems to have belonged, made it their principle to revert to the genuine old Attic orators, and the majority even chose as their pattern the simplest writer among them, viz. Lysias. To this school belong M. Calidius, M. Brutus, Licinius Calvus, Caelius Rufus, Q. Cornificius and later Asinius Pollio, who admired especially Thukydides. Frequently as speeches were published, it was even then very rare that the spoken and the published speech agreed throughout, since the orators would prepare their speeches before delivering them, but remained free as to the general tenor.

1. Cato: *orator est, Marce fili, vir bonus dicendi peritus;* see Sen. controv. praef. 9. Cf. Quint. 12, 1, 1 sqq. Plin. ep. 4, 7, 5.

2. To the most ancient orators belong P. Licinius Crassus (cos. 549/205) and M. Cornelius Cethegus (cos. 550/204). Funeral orations especially were published already in the first half of the 6th century u.c., most often probably for political purposes. Cf. § 43, 3.

3. Quint. 3, 1, 19 *Romanorum primus, quantum ego quidem sciam, condidit aliqua in hanc materiam* (the theory of eloquence) *M. Cato ille Censorius* (in his praecepta). *post M. Antonius incohavit.* But for a long time afterwards self-taught orators are mentioned, such as Curio (cos. 678/76; see Cic. Brut. 214). But cases of this kind were then only exceptional, and it is wrong when Aper (in Tac. dial. 19) says of the orators of the period of Cicero: *paucissimi praecepta rhetorum aut philosophorum placita* (the latter might rather be right) *cognoverant.*

4. Cic. de or. 2, 92 *nostri oratores . . . scripta ex quibus iudicium fieri posset*

non multa sane reliquerunt. orat. 132 *Crassi perpauca sunt, nec ea iudiciorum, nihil Antoni, nihil Cottae, nihil Sulpici.* p. Cluent. 140 *M. Antonium aiunt solitum esse dicere idcirco se nullam umquam orationem scripsisse ut, si quid aliquando non opus esset ab se esse dictum, posset negare dixisse.* Cic., on the other hand, mentions written speeches of the two Gracchi (Brut. 104. 117), M. Aemilius Scaurus (ib. 112), P. Rutilius Rufus (114), the son of the younger Africanus (77), Q. Tubero (117), Curio (122) and his son (220), Sulpicius Galba (127), Flavius Fimbria (129), T. Albucius (131), Q. Lutatius Catulus (132), Q. Scaevola (163), Caesar (262); in addition Livy mentions a speech by the elder Africanus (569/185), others by C. Titius (593/161), Quint. 10, 1, 116 speeches of Ser. Sulpicius Rufus, Suetonius Iul. 55 of Caesar Strabo, Asconius Cornel. p. 62 Or. of P. Cominius. *Extra urbem,* too, *apud socios et Latinos,* existed orators and speeches published by them (Cic. Brut. 169 sq.), e.g. L. Papirius of Fregellae and T. Betutius of Asculum.

5. Cato the Elder and even (C.) Gracchus commenced all their speeches with a prayer to or at least some mention of the gods, Serv. Verg. Aen. 7, 259. 11, 301. Symmach. ep. 3, 44. Gell. 13, 23 (22), 1 (*in plerisque antiquis orationibus*). Cf. Val. Max. 1 praef.; Plin. paneg. 1. The general manner in which this is related of Cato's speeches leads to the supposition that the same holds good of those also which he made in civil causes (causae privatae), the only ones of the kind before the time of Cicero of which we know that they were published, just as in Cicero's own time only a few such speeches delivered before the tribunal of the centum-viri are known to us. HJordan, Caton. quae extant, p. lxxxvii.

6. *L. Aelius Stilo . . . scriptitavit orationes multis, orator ipse numquam fuit,* Cic. Brut. 169, cf. 205 sq. *M. Bibulus scriptitavit accurate, cum praesertim non esset orator,* ib. 267. So C. Laelius wrote speeches for Tubero and for Fabius Maximus, Plotius Gallus for Sempronius Atratinus (Suet. rhet. 2), Caesar for Metellus (Suet. Iul. 55). Cicero himself composed in like manner speeches for Cn. Pompeius and T. Ampius (Quint. 3, 8, 50) and (a. 700) for a father the funeral speech on his son Serranus (ad Q. fr. 3, 8, 5 *laudavit pater scripto meo*). Fronto p. 123 *Ventidius ille, postquam Parthos fudit fugavitque, ad victoriam suam praedicandam orationem a G. Sallustio mutuatus est.*

7. Cic. Brut. 328 *id declarat totidem quot dixit . . . scripta verbis oratio.* This was not, however, the usual thing: see ib. 91 *videmus alios oratores inertia nihil scripsisse, ne domesticus etiam labor accederet ad forensem; pleraeque enim scribuntur orationes habitae iam, non ut habeantur.* Cf. ib. 93. Plin. ep. 4, 9, 23. Sen. suas. 15 *huic actioni* (of Asinius Pollio) *qui interfuerunt negant eum haec dixisse, . . . sed postea composuisse.* Plin. ep. 1, 20, 7. . . *Ciceronis pro Murena* (57), *pro Vareno* (also p. Quinctio), *in quibus brevis et nuda quasi subscriptio quorundam criminum solis titulis indicatur. ex his apparet illum permulta dixisse, cum ederet omisisse.* So likewise did C. Galba (Cic. Brut. 127) and L. Crassus (ib. 160. 164). But as a rule Cicero appears to have published his speeches complete and as they were spoken. Thus the Corneliana was *iisdem paene verbis quibus edita est . . . perorata* (Cornel. Nep. fr. 45 H.). This does not exclude slight alterations and additions with a view to the impression to be produced in delivering the speech. The younger Pliny (ep. 9, 28, 5) and Fronto (ep. p. 184 Nab.) generally published their speeches in a revised and enlarged form.

8. Quintil. 10, 7, 30 *plerumque multa agentibus accidit ut maxime necessaria et utique initia* (of speeches) *scribant, cetera quae domo afferunt cogitatione complectantur, subitis ex tempore occurrant. quod fecisse M. Tullium commentariis ipsius apparet.* Sen. contr. 3, praef. 6 of Cassius Severus: *sine commentario numquam dixit, nec hoc commentario contentus erat in quo nudae res ponuntur, sed maxima parte*

perscribebatur actio: illa quoque quae salse dici poterant adnotabantur, sed cum procedere nollet nisi instructus libenter ab instrumentis recedebat. In the time of Cicero spoken speeches were taken down (like the one pro Milone). SUET. Iul. 55 of Caesar's speech pro Q. Metello: *non immerito Augustus existimat magis ab actuariis exceptam male subsequentibus verba dicentis quam ab ipso editam.* Quintilian too complains (7, 2, 24) that speculating booksellers have published speeches of his carelessly taken down. Unspoken speeches also were published by Cato and by Cicero (Verrin. actio II, Miloniana, Philipp. II). M. Brutus wrote merely *exercitationis gratia* a defence for Milo (QUINTIL. 3, 6, 93; cf. 10, 1, 23), Cestius Pius in Milonem (SEN. contr. 3, praef. 16), Lucan even in Octavium Sagittam et pro eo. Spurious speeches existed also at an early time. *Sulpici* (§ 153, 5) *orationes quae feruntur, eas post mortem eius scripsisse P. Canutius putatur: . . . ipsius Sulpici nulla oratio est,* CIC. Brut. 205. In the post-Ciceronian period occur speeches against Cicero under the names of Catiline and M. Antonius, ASCON. p. 95 Or. QUINTIL. 9, 3, 94.

9. SUET. gramm. 25 (= rhet. 1) *rhetorica quoque apud nos perinde atque grammatica* (above § 41, 1) *sero recepta est, paulo etiam difficilius, quippe quam constet nonnumquam etiam prohibitam exerceri . . . paulatim et ipsa utilis honestaque apparuit, multique* (as M. Antonius, Cicero, Cn. Pompeius, Augustus) *eam et praesidii causa et gloriae appetiverunt . . . plerique autem oratorum etiam declamationes ediderunt. quare magno studio hominibus iniecto magna etiam professorum ac doctorum profluxit copia, adeoque floruit ut nonnulli ex infima fortuna in ordinem senatorium atque ad summos honores processerint.* HIERONYM. ad Euseb. Chr. a. 1929=666/88 *Plotius Gallus primus Romae latinam rhetoricam docuit.* Cf. SUET. rhet. 2. SEN. contr. 2, 8, 5. QUINTIL. 2, 4, 42. The expulsion of the latini rhetores decreed by the Censors (amongst whom was L. Crassus) in a. 662/92 was without effect, as it had been already in 593/161 (GELL. 15, 11). HIERON. l.l. 1936=673/81 *Vultacilius Plotus* (§ 158, 3) *latinus rhetor, Cn. Pompei libertus et doctor, scholam Romae aperuit.* The first book on rhetoric in general written in Latin is that ad Herennium, see 4, 7, 10 *nomina rerum* (figures and such like) *graeca convertimus . . . quae enim res apud nostros non erant, earum rerum nomina non poterant esse usitata.* RVOLKMANN, die Rhetorik der Griech. u. Röm. in system. Übersicht, Lpz. [2]1885. RKRÖHNERT, d. Anfänge der Rhet. bei den Röm., Memel 1877.

10. Greek masters of oratory in the time of Cicero were Hermagoras the Elder (OHARNECKER, JJ. 131, 69), Molon, Apollodoros of Pergamon. Their pupils: *Apollodori praecepta magis ex discipulis cognoscas, quorum diligentissimus in tradendo fuit latine C. Valgius* (§ 241, 3), *graece Atticus,* QUINTIL. 3, 1, 18. Cf. HIERONYM. l. l. 1953=690/64: *Apollodorus Pergamenus, graecus orator, praeceptor Calidii et Augusti, clarus habetur.* WILAMOWITZ, Herm. 12, 333 looks upon Apollodoros as the 'founder' of classicism, i.e. of the Atticist reaction: see against this view EROHDE, RhM. 41, 176; see § 41, 1. CIC. Brut. 263 *C. Sicinius, ex disciplina Hermagorae*; so also T. Accius of Pisaurum, ib. 271. A pupil of Molon was also T. Torquatus, Brut. 245.

11. For the characterisation of Attic and Asiatic oratory cf. CIC. e.g. Brut. 51. 325. or. 27. QUINTIL. 12, 10, 16 *antiqua diviso inter Atticos atque Asianos fuit, cum hi pressi et integri, contra inflati illi et inanes haberentur, in his nihil superfuerit, illis iudicium maxime ac modus deesset.*

12. FRONTO p. 127 *omnes universos quicumque post Romam conditam oratores extiterunt . . . si numerare velis vix trecentorum numerum complebis.* Characterisation of the principal orators in VELLEI. 2, 36, 2. TAC. dial. 18 (Cato, C. Gracchus,

Crassus, Cicero, Corvinus). Fronto p. 114 *contionatur Cato infeste, Gracchus turbulente, Tullius copiose. iam in iudiciis saevit idem Cato, triumphat Cicero, tumultuatur Gracchus, Calvus rixatur.* Apulei. apol. 95 *neque Cato gravitatem requirat, neque Laelius lenitatem neque Gracchus impetum, nec Caesar calorem, nec Hortensius distributionem, nec Calvus argutias, nec parsimoniam Sallustius, nec opulentiam Cicero.* In the Ciceronian period Quintil. 12, 10, 11 *vim Caesaris, indolem Caelii, subtilitatem Calidii, diligentiam Pollionis, dignitatem Messalae, sanctitatem Calvi, gravitatem Bruti, acumen Sulpicii, acerbitatem Cassii reperiemus.*

45. The Augustan age possesses in Asinius Pollio and M. Messala late representatives of Republican oratory, and Augustus himself as well as Agrippa and Maecenas show themselves, whenever occasion requires, men of oratorical training. But in this period, in connection with the downfall of the old constitution, the opportunities and subjects of eloquence disappear, while the impediments and barriers increase in proportion. Mere theory daily encroaches in the room of practice, rhetors supplant the orators, declaiming supersedes speaking. In Augustus' own time appear, therefore, the earliest representatives of Imperial oratory: the orator Cassius Severus, the rhetors Porcius Latro, Albucius Silus, Arellius Fuscus, Junius Gallio, Cestius Pius, Fulvius Sparsus, Argentarius, Blandus, Q. Haterius, Julius Bassus, Pompeius Silo, Varius Geminus, and others, to whom may be added Rutilius Lupus and the rhetor Seneca in the last years of Augustus. The main features of this new oratory are the exclusive cultivation of style and an intentional renunciation of serious subjects and practical purposes. The rhetor's school becomes now an end in itself and a centre of intellectual life, where a world of fictions grows up. From the genus deliberativum its suasoriae are taken, from the genus iudiciale its controversiae ; in the class of epideictic compositions the laudationes and vituperationes are in favour. The methods of the rhetorical lecture-rooms are then also transferred to the few occasions of practical display, employed as they were for the exhibition of theatrical declamation. Legal knowledge was very scarce. The most eminent orators of this kind in the post-Augustan age are Votienus Montanus, Romanius Hispo, Crispus Passienus, Domitius Afer, Vibius Crispus, Galerius Trachalus, Julius Africanus, Julius Secundus, and finally Tacitus and Pliny. It is in vain that Quintilian and Tacitus (in the dialogue) point to the genuine classical authorities and struggle against the fashion of their time, though they themselves are unwittingly under its influence. In Fronto's time, the style became besides

turgid and inelegantly decked out with archaisms. Apuleius has the same mannerism, but more talent. The more manysided and intricate the Roman Law became, esp. in the 3rd century, A.D., the more inaccessible did it become to these phraseologists, who in this way also lost the last remnant of practical utility and were henceforth limited to epideictic speeches, to servile panegyrics, declamations on fictitious subjects, and to epistolary composition. Gaul was more fertile in these than the other parts of the Empire. The most distinguished representative of this school is Symmachus, and after him Ausonius; the panegyric orators extend from the time of Diocletian (Eumenius, Nazarius) to that of Julian (Claudius Mamertinus) and Theodosius I (Drepanius Pacatus), and in the sixth century we have Ennodius' eulogy on Theodoric. The African rhetors were richer in thought but less careful in style; among them Christianity found, in the 3rd and 4th centuries, its most ingenious defenders (Tertullian, Arnobius, Cyprian, St. Augustine). The rhetoricians of these centuries devoted their attention to the study of the old masters and endeavoured to make them palatable to their contemporaries by diluting them in their fashion.

1. TAC. dial. 38 extr.: (*orationes*) *mediis d. Augusti temporibus habitae, postquam longa temporum quies et continuum populi otium et assidua senatus tranquillitas et maxime principis disciplina ipsam quoque eloquentiam, sicut omnia, pacaverat.* Rhetoric was in that period taught at Rome by the Greeks Theodorus of Gadara and Caecilius of Kale Acte, and by the Roman knight Blandus (§ 268, 1). SEN. Contr. 2, praef. 5 *ante illum* (Blandum) *intra libertinos praeceptores pulcherrimae disciplinae continebantur et . . . turpe erat docere* (for payment) and *honestum erat discere.* This too shows the increased importance of rhetoric.—EAMIEL, hist. de l'éloquence sous les Césars, Par.[1] 1882 II.

2. TAC. dial. 14 extr.: *novi rhetores, veteres oratores.* At least 100 such *novi* are mentioned by Seneca the Elder: few written works by them were extant. SEN. contr. 1, praef. 11. Later ones also in IUV. 7, 143 sqq. 214. Nero was the first Emperor of the Julian dynasty who was in need *alienae facundiae*, TAC. A. 13, 3. The principal orators of his own time are thus characterised by QUINT. 12, 10, 11 *copiam Senecae, vires Africani, maturitatem Afri, iucunditatem Crispi, sonum Trachali, elegantiam Secundi.*

3. Latin writers on rhetoric in the first century (besides Seneca and Quintilian) are Celsus, Laenas, Luranius (?) Stertinius, Gallio, Porcius Latro, Cestius Pius, Pliny the Elder, Verginius, Tutilius, Vettius. Cf. QUINT. 3, 1, 19–21. Quintilian was the first professor of eloquence appointed by the State (by Vespasian). In this time already IUV. 7, 147 says *accipiat te Gallia, vel potius nutricula causidicorum Africa, si placuit mercedem ponere linguae.*

4. SEN. contr. 1, praef. 6 *ut possitis aestimare in quantum cotidie ingenia decrescant et . . . eloquentia se retro tulerit . . . in deterius . . . data res est sive luxu temporum . . . sive cum praemium pulcherrimae rei cecidisset.* The *causae corruptae eloquentiae,*

which Tacitus (dial.) and Quintilian (see 5, 12, 23. 6, prooem. 3. 8, 6, 76) attempted to point out in special treatises, consisted not only in the *licentia atque inscitia declamantium* (Quint. 2, 10, 3), for this was only one of the symptoms, and the real causes are to be found in the state of the time (cf. Sen. ep. 114): since *eloquentia saeculo servit* (Lactant. inst. div. 5, 1). The public were not better than their orators and required always something new and startling; Petron. sat. 3 seq. Tac. dial. 19. Quint. 4, 1, 57. 72. 4, 5, 10. 4, 8, 1. Nor were those who *vividam et incorruptam eloquentiam tuendis civibus exercebant* (Tac. A. 13, 42), i.e. the judicial speakers, *causidici* (Martial. 2, 64), any better than the rhetoricians; rather *in ipsa capitis aut fortunarum pericula irrupit voluptas* (Quint. 4, 2, 122. 127. 4, 3, 2. Sen. controv. 9, praef. 2. Pers. 1, 83. Martial. 6, 19). Thus the custom of applause (even by paid claqueurs) was transferred from the schools (Quint. 2, 2, 9 sqq.) to the Centumviral tribunal (Plin. ep. 2, 14, 4 sqq,), and in Gaul at a later time to the Church (Ap. Sidon. ep. 9, 3). As to legal technicalities, most of these pleaders, not having any knowledge of their own, were obliged to consult pragmatici as monitores, Quint. 12, 3, 2 sqq. Iuv. 7, 123.

5. The instruction of the rhetorician succeeds that of the grammaticus (Suet. gramm. 4). On the practices of the rhetorical schools cf. Körber, Rhetor Seneca 39. Friedländer, Sittengesch. 3[5], 343. A beginning was made with the genus demonstrativum (ἐπιδεικτικόν; cf. Quint. 2, 1, 8), then by theses for practice (declamationes) the student advanced to the deliberativum (συμβουλευτικόν) or the suasoriae and from this to the iudiciale (δικανικόν) or the controversiae. These last were divided into three portions: the sententiae (opinions on the application of the law to a particular case), divisio (division into separate questions) and colores (methods of palliating a criminal act). Quint. 10, 3, 21 *obstant fere turba discipulorum et consuetudo classium certis diebus audiendarum, nonnihil etiam persuasio patrum numerantium potius declamationes quam aestimantium.* Cf. § 44, 9.

6. Plin. ep. 2, 4, 5 *schola et auditorium et ficta causa res innoxia est.* Petron. 1. *declamatores . . . clamant: haec vulnera pro libertate publica excepi* etc. . . . *rerum tumore et sententiarum vanissimo strepitu hoc tantum proficiunt ut cum in forum venerint putent se in alium orbem terrarum delatos. et ideo ego adulescentulos existumo in scholis stultissimos fieri quia nihil ex his quae in usu habemus aut audiunt aut vident, sed piratas cum catenis in litore stantes, sed tyrannos edicta scribentes, . . . sed responsa in pestilentiam data ut virgines tres aut plures immolentur* etc. Tac. dial. 35 *tyrannicidarum praemia aut quidquid in schola quotidie agitur, in foro vel raro vel numquam, ingentibus verbis persequuntur.* The *abdicati* also belonged to these unreal themes; cf. Iuv. 7, 168. Quint. 2, 10, 5. 8, 3, 23. On the fulminations against tyrants see also Iuv. 7, 151. Favourite materials from history were e.g. Sulla (ib. 1, 16), Hannibal (7, 161); from literature esp. Vergil and Ovid (particularly for exercises in metrical form). Cf. n. 9. Sketches and elaborations of such school themes are to be found in the Quintilian declamations (§ 325, 12) and in those of Calpurnius Flaccus (§ 351, 5); especially important are the elder Seneca, and Philostratos' vitae sophistarum. Cf. also n. 9. The delivery was exaggerated, lively and redundant in gesticulation. Quint. 2, 12, 9. 4, 2, 37. 39. 11, 3, 184. The custom of applauding, see n. 4.

7. In the 3rd century Lamprid. Diad. 4, 2 *solent pueri pileo insigniri naturali* (a 'caul'), *quod obstetrices rapiunt et advocatis credulis vendunt, siquidem causidici hoc iuvari dicuntur.* Alex. Sev. 35 *oratores et poetas non sibi panegyricos dicentes, quod . . . stultum ducebat, sed aut orationes recitantes aut facta veterum canentes libenter audivit . . . ad Athenaeum audiendorum et graecorum et latinorum rhetorum vel poetarum causa frequenter processit. audivit etiam forenses oratores causas recitantes*

quas vel apud ipsum vel apud praefectos urbis egerant. ib. 44, 4. 68, 1 (see § 375, 1). Cf. CAPITOL. Maximin. 29 (iun. 3), 4 *Messalam ex familia nobili, oratorem potentissimum eundemque doctissimum.* The younger Maximinus' teacher was *orator Titianus*, ib. 27 (iun. 1), 5. In the reign of Gordianus III *Misitheus* (§ 375, 2), *quem causa eloquentiae dignum parentela sua putavit* (CAPIT. Gord. 23, 6). From the senate Numerianus received a statue with the legend: *Numeriano Caesari, oratori temporibus suis potentissimo* (ib. 11, 3). The younger Postumus was, according to TREBELL. POLL. XXX tyr. 4, 2 *ita in declamationibus disertus ut eius controversiae Quintiliano dicantur insertae.*

8. In the fourth century we may name Ausonius' masters, Ti. Victor Minervius, his son Alethius Minervius, then Latinus Alcimus Alethius, the Emperor Julian's master, Aemilius Magnus Arborius, rhetor Tolosae, AUSON. Profess. Burdig. 1. 6. 2. 16. Subjects: *panegyrici* and *fictae ludorum* (schools) *lites*, AUSON. l.l. 1, 13 sqq. SYMMACH. ep. 3, 5 *mitto decantatas iudicialium meditationum fictiones et inania simulacra causarum.* AUGUSTIN. confess. 5, 8, 14 *audiebam quietius* (than in Carthage) *ibi* (in Rome) *studere adolescentes et ordinatiore disciplinae coercitione sedari, ne in eius scholam quo magistro non utuntur passim et proterve irruant, nec eos admitti omnino nisi ille permiserit. contra apud Carthaginem foeda est et intemperans licentia scholasticorum. irrumpunt impudenter et prope furiosa fronte perturbant ordinem quem quisque discipulis ad proficiendum instituerit. multa iniuriosa faciunt . . . et punienda legibus, nisi consuetudo patrona sit.*

9. As late as the 6th century Ennodius (§ 479) uses the same materials in his school speeches, e.g. *in novercam quae cum marito privigni odia suadere non posset utrisque venena porrexit; in eum qui praemii nomine Vestalis virginis nuptias postulavit; in eum qui in lupanari statuam Minervae locavit;* and as ethicae: *verba Thetidis cum Achillem videret extinctum, verba Menelai cum Troiam videret exustam* etc. Such subjects were also treated in verse, e.g. *verba Achillis in parthenone cum tubam Diomedis audisset*, AL. 198 PLM. 4, 322; deliberation of Augustus as to whether he should burn the Aeneis (AL. 672 PLM. 4, 179); c. 4 of Dracontius (*verba Herculis cum videret Hydrae capita pullulare*), and 9 (*deliberativa Achillis an corpus Hectoris vendat*).

10. On the collection of the Panegyrici: see § 391, 1; cf. also § 483, 2. Best collection of the later works, down to Baeda: Rhetores latini minores, ex. codd. maximam partem primum adhibitis emendavit CHALM, Lps. 1863.

46. Letters, official as well as personal, are early enrolled as literature among the Romans, both independently and in historical works; those of notable men soon began to be collected. E.g. the letters of Cato the Elder to his son, of Cornelia to her son C. Gracchus, subsequently those of Caesar, M. Brutus, and especially the correspondence of Cicero which, even as it now exists, is an important authority on the history of the time. The letters which are preserved to us are, however, but rarely familiar effusions reflecting the mood of the moment, such as are most of those of Cicero; they usually serve some personal or political object, and are written in the first instance with an eye to publication. Rhetoric soon takes possession of this form of literature also, and produces suasoriae in epistolary form, like

those of Seneca; or any subject is chosen at discretion—sometimes a learned one—and is treated in a free and popular manner in this dress. Those of .Pliny have for their scope to discuss questions and events in motley variety, and above all to place their author in a favourable light. After the 2nd century A.D. the epistle develops into a special style, in which the substance is often quite subordinate. Of this sort are the letters of Fronto, Symmachus, Sidonius, and in the 5th and 6th centuries those of Salvianus, Ruricius and Ennodius. The letters of Cyprian, Lactantius, Ambrose, Jerome, Augustine, Paulinus of Nola and others, rely much on unctuous redundancy of language for some of their pastoral efficacy; those of Jerome contain most substance. Those of Cassiodorus are of a practical character, being in part official decrees on secular matters, like the Papal epistles on matters ecclesiastical. Among the latter those of Leo and Gregory the Great are of importance in a literary sense. The finished style aimed at in these pronouncements led to enormous prolixity when the Byzantine style had become paramount.

1. Real private letters, addressed to intimate friends and written without any thought of publication, are indifferent both as regards substance and style. Cic. Phil. 2, 7 *quam multa ioca solent esse in epistulis quae, prolata si sint, inepta videantur! quam multa seria neque tamen ullo modo divolganda!* (cf. Plin. ep. 6, 16, 22). Cic. fam. 9, 21, 1 *quid simile habet epistula aut iudicio aut contioni? . . . epistulas quotidianis verbis texere solemus.* 15, 21, 4 *ego illas Calvo litteras misi non plus quam has quas nunc legis existimans exituras. aliter enim scribimus quod eos solos quibus mittimus, aliter quod multos lecturos putamus.* Cf. n. 9.

2. Letters with a didactic tendency, and starting from a personal motive (as in the poetical epistle), are those from Cato to his son, and those of T. Livius addressed likewise to his son; with a political tendency those of Cornelia. On the other hand the epistolary form was of secondary importance in the letter concerning his services addressed to King Philip by the elder Africanus (§ 56, 1); in that of Scipio Nasica on the campaign against Perseus in which he took part (Plut. Aemil. Paul. 15), and probably also in that of C. Gracchus to M. Pomponius and of Q. Catulus to A. Furius. *Epistula voluminis instar* (Schol. Bob. on Cic. Planc. 85, p. 270 Or.) from Cicero to Pompeius. Similarly Q. Cicero de petitione.

3. Examples of letters in historical works are those in Antipater, Quadrigarius, Macer and especially Sallust, some original documents, others worked up. Fronto p. 126 *extant epistulae . . in serie partim scriptae historiarum vel a scriptoribus* (?) *compositae, ut illa Thucydidi* (7, 11) *nobilissima Niciae ducis epistula ex Sicilia missa, item apud C. Sallustium ad Arsacen regem Mithridatis . . . et Cn. Pompei ad senatum* (§ 205, 4) *. . . et Adherbalis apud Cirtam obsessi* (Iug. 24) *. . . breves nec ullam rerum gestarum expeditionem continentes. latae autem . . . extant Catuli litterae.* Ignorance also accepted fictitious letters in the historians and rhetoricians as historical documents; most of the compositions of this kind which we find in the scriptores hist. aug. are probably the production of earlier

rhetoricians; see CCzwalina, de epistularum actorumque quae a script. h. a. proferuntur fide et auct. P. I., Bonn 1870. Cf. n. 7.

4. The epistolary form is frequent in the writings of jurists, such as Antistius Labeo, Ateius Capito, Proculus, Neratius, Juventius, Javolenus, Africanus; this originated probably in the written decisions (responsa) returned to questions on matters of law (§ 48, 5). From these the custom was transferred to other subjects, such as history and grammar, and later on to medicine, etc. Gellius 13, 18, 2 *Erucius clarus . . . ad Sulpicium Apollinarem scripsit, . . . quaerere sese et petere uti sibi rescriberet quaenam esset eorum verborum* (Cato's) *sententia.* Cf. n. 5.

5. Learned discussions in epistolary form in Varro's Epistolae and Epistolicae quaestiones, in Cicero's correspondence, e.g. with Brutus and Calvus on questions of oratorical style (§ 210, 2), in Valgius Rufus, Valerius Messala, Sinnius Capito, Verrius Flaccus, Pomponius Secundus, M. Valerius Probus, Sulpicius Apollinaris, Lactantius.

6. Epistulae medicinales, partly apocryphal (e.g. Hippocratis ad Maecenatem), are to be found compiled in MSS. (such as that in Brussels 3701 s. X), as well as in the medical treatise of Marcellus (Empiricus). Epistulae Oribasii medici ad Eustathium filium suum, ad Eunapium nepotem suum.

7. In the rhetorical schools of the Imperial period a favourite exercise was the composition of letters, which were by preference connected with some celebrated name. In this way originated many spurious letters such as Horace's *epistola prosa oratione* (see § 240, 2), the letter *ad Caesarem senem de rep.* in the Sallustian style (see § 205, 5), and subsequently the letters of Seneca to Paul the Apostle (see § 289, 9).

8. Apollin. Sidon. epist. 1, 1 (collection of my letters) *Q. Symmachi rotunditatem, C. Plinii disciplinam maturitatemque vestigiis praesumptiosis insecuturus. nam de M. Tullio silere me in stilo epistolari melius puto, quem nec Iulius Titianus totum sub nominibus illustrium feminarum digna similitudine expressit.*

9. Quint. 9, 4, 19 *est . . . oratio alia vincta atque contexta, soluta alia, qualis in sermone et epistulis, nisi cum aliquid supra naturam suam tractant, ut de philosophia, rep. similibusque.* Plin. ep. 7, 9, 8 *epistulam diligentius scribas. nam . . . pressus sermo purusque ex epistulis petitur.* Symmach. ep. 7, 9 *ingeniorum varietas in familiaribus scriptis neglegentiam quandam debet imitari.* Apoll. Sidon. ep. 7, 18 *ita mens patet in libro* (Epp.) *veluti vultus in speculo. dictavi enim quaepiam hortando* etc. 8, 16 *in hoc stilo, cui non urbanus lepos inest, sed pagana simplicitas. . . . nos opuscula sermone edidimus arido, exili, certe maxima ex parte vulgato.* Cf. ib. 9, 3. Statements concerning the epistolary style of Greek rhetoricians in RHercher's Epistolographi graeci (Paris 1873) p. 1–16; of Latin in Halm's Rhett. latt. 447 sq. 589. Cf. EWölfflin, Phil. 34, 139.

10. Symmach. ep. 2, 35 *olim parentes etiam patriae negotia, quae nunc angusta vel nulla sunt, in familiares paginas conferebant. id quia versis ad otium rebus omisimus, captanda sunt nobis plerumque intemptata scribendi semina, quae fastidium tergeant generalium litterarum.* But the more meagre was the substance, the more pompous became the form after the 4th cent. A.D. The formal style natural to the ancient Romans had, under the influence of despotism, degenerated into false ornament, which is already strongly marked in the letters of Symmachus. It becomes the rule to begin a letter with a sententious phrase. The simple address *Tu* is superseded and overlaid with all sorts of ceremonious turns. The Emperor is addressed by Symmachus as *tua* (*vestra*) *aeternitas, perennitas, clementia,*

mansuetudo, serenitas, tranquillitas, maiestas or *tuum numen;* for others, according to their rank, the forms *tua sanctitas, religio, reverentia, praestantia, celsitudo, sublimitas, excellentia, magnificentia, laudabilitas, eximietas* are in common use, and Symmachus addresses the Nichomachi filii who were connected with him as, at least, *tua (vestra) unanimitas.* The epithet *sanctus* likewise is excessively cheapened (e.g. Symm. ep. 5, 16. 21. 31. 41). Moreover the habit of designating acquaintances, friends and colleagues, according to their age as *parens, frater* or *filius* generally in combination with *dominus* (e.g. *dominus et filius meus*), gives a sort of fulsomeness to the forms of address. Thus Honorius in official communications addresses Symmachus: *Symmache parens carissime (atque amantissime).* In the letters of Christian writers we have, in addition, *frater in Christo dilectissime*, etc. In these the beginning and end are generally practical, while the body of the letter is an overflowing pastoral effusion, intermixed with numerous biblical allusions.

11. Eight unpublished letters by Africans s. VI (esp. Ferrandus) in REIFFERSCHEID, Anecd. Casin., Bresl. 1871 (see § 494, 5).

12. Earlier collections of the Papal epistles by ACARAFA (1591), HOLSTENIUS (1662), in the collections of decrees of Councils, canones, bullaria (the most recent is that in Turin, with an appendix 1867) and others. The best by the Benedictine PCOUSTANT: Epistolae romanorum pontificum et quae ad eos scriptae sunt a s. Clemente usque ad Innocentium III quotquot reperiri potuerunt; T. I ab a. Chr. 67 ad a. 440, Paris 1721. Continued (but not published) by SMOPINOT and UDURAND. From their papers, adhibitis praestantiss. codd. Ital. et Germ. rec. et ed. (the letters a s. Hilario ad Pelagium II) ATHIEL; vol. I, Braunsb. 1868. Cf. also FMAASSEN, Gesch. d. Quellen d. kanon. Rechts (Graz 1870) 1, 226.

47. The most popular kind of entertaining literature is the romance, that is, a fictitious amusing narrative (love-stories in particular). Among the Romans it is nearly as old as was ennui among their nobility, and it affects from the first a certain strong seasoning; Sisenna's translation of the Μιλησιακά of Aristides. Hence the name milesia (fabula) for romance in general. Petronius adds to obscenity a satirical element. Apuleius (Metamorph.) translates a magical romance and mingles with it other stories, as well as pagan mysticism. At a later time the romance prefers to group its fantastic inventions round historic subjects and personages, such as the destruction of Troy (Dictys and Dares), Alexander the Great (Julius Valerius), Antiochus (Historia Apollonii, regis Tyri). Most of the productions in the way of curiosities of literature and descriptions of travel also serve the purpose of entertainment.

1. APUL. met. 4, 32 *propter milesiae conditorem.* TERT. de anima 23. Cf. § 370, 4. HIERON. c. Rufin. 1, 17 (2, 473 Vall.): *quasi non cirratorum turba milesiarum in scholis figmenta decantet et testamentum suis* (above § 28, 3) *Bessorum cachinno membra concutiat atque inter scurrarum epulas nugae istiusmodi frequententur.* Comment. in Isa. XII in. (4, 493 Vall.) *multo pars maior est milesias revolventium quam Platonis libros . . testamentum Grunnii Corocottae porcelli decantant in scholis*

puerorum agmina cachinnantium. MARTIAN. CAP. 2, 100 *mythos poeticae diversitatis, delicias milesias historiasque mortalium . . se amissuram . . formidabat.* For the part of Antiochus in the Hist. Apoll. cf. besides ERohde, gr. Roman 417.

2. Book of marvels by the senator L. Manlius. Descriptions of travel by Trebius Niger, Sebosus and others, subsequently by Licinius Mucianus.

3. The popular fairy-tale, which the Romans also possessed, does not venture into literature. There are only occasional suggestions of it. Apuleius' (met. 4, 28) story of Cupid and Psyche is a fairy-tale remodelled (see LFriedländer, Sittengesch. Roms 1^5, 468), as is shown by the opening: *Erant in quadam civitate rex et regina.* Allusions to stock incidents in fairy-tales in Persius 2, 37. 38. Cf. MHaupt, opusc. 3, 570.

48. Jurisprudence is the only part of literature the development of which among the Romans was national from first to last. An inflexible and unwavering adherence to their rights was always peculiar to the Romans, and this favoured the growth and consolidation of a system of laws, for the production of which their eminent qualities of acute intellect, practical dexterity and love of order were perfectly sufficient, and which was also favoured by the combination of conservatism and progress peculiar to the Roman Law. There were fixed rules at a very early date, at first of a religious character and in the possession of the patrician Pontifices, whence also their interpretation, application and development lay in the hands of the patricians. But when (c. 450/304) the various forms of accusations and a list of judgment-days had been made public, the law became generally accessible and was almost immediately represented by the plebeians P. Sempronius Sophus and Tib. Coruncanius. The law being of a very positive character, literary activity could at first manifest itself only in collecting and interpreting the sources; so it was in the first juridical writer, Sex. Aelius Catus (c. 550/204). The more varied life became, the more important grew the knowledge of the law, and the auctoritas prudentum, as laid down in their decisions (responsa), gradually became an acknowledged source of law. Since the beginning of the 7th century U.C. we find the responsa written down and published in collections, as e.g. by the son of Cato Censorius, by M. Junius Brutus and P. Mucius Scaevola (cos. 621/133), while M'. Manilius published a collection of formulas. As early as the middle of the 7th century U.C., most probably under the influence of the Stoic philosophy, the Roman Law was reduced to a system by Q. Mucius Scaevola (pont. max., cos. 659/95). His pupil was C. Aquilius Gallus, and through the

pupil of the latter, Ser. Sulpicius Rufus, the systematic development of the Law was greatly advanced, Cicero also contributing to it. Until then, legal knowledge had principally been propagated by oral tradition, and in some families (as e.g. the Aelii, Mucii, Porcii, Sulpicii, later on the Antistii) was quasi-hereditary, a circumstance which did much to create a special profession of jurists.

1. Sources: Pomponius de origine iuris, dig. 1, 2. Later on the Digests in general.—Corpus iuris anteiustinianei, Bonn 1835–41. GBruns, fontes iuris rom. antiqui, Freib. [5] 1886 (cur. THMommsen). EHuschke, Iurisprudentia anteiustiniana, Lps. [5] 1886. Collectio librorum iuris anteiustiniani, ed. PKrüger, ThMommsen, WStudemund, Berl. 1877 seq. III.

2. AFRudorff, röm. Rechtsgeschichte, Lpz. 1857. 59 II. OKarlowa, römische Rechtsgeschichte I, Lpz. 1885. RJhering, Geist des röm. Rechts auf den verschiedenen Stufen seiner Entwickelung, Lpz.[3] 1873–77 III. Mommsen, RG. 1[6], 430. 468. 2, 457. SWZimmern, Gesch. des röm. Privatrechts bis Justinian; especially I, i, Heidelb. 1826. WRein, das Criminalrecht der Röm. bis Justinian, Eisen 1844. HEDirksen, hinterlass. Schrr. z. Krit. u. Ausleg. d. Quellen d. röm. Rechtsgesch., Lpz. 1871 II. FDSanio, z. Gesch. d. röm. Rechtswissensch., Königsb. 1858 (see also § 166, 6d).

3. Among the Greeks legal training and knowledge were strangely neglected; Cic. de or. 1, 198. 253. At Rome the circumstances were more favourable; cf. Jhering, Geist des röm. Rechts 1, 300. Among the Romans legal knowledge penetrated even to the people; cf. the formulas of sponsio in cattle-bargains in Cato (RR. 144–150) and Varro (§ 133, 1). The more national a poet is, the more prominent the position the law holds in his writings. So especially in Plautus. But even Terence (Eun. prol. 10) thinks that a play of Luscius is condemned by proving a flagrant error in civil law in it. Cf. also the titles of togatae, Emancipatus, Iurisperita (perhaps also Ida=Icta) by Titinius and Afranius. It is a matter of course that business-men (e.g. M'. Curius, Cic. fam. 7, 29) possessed legal knowledge; later on we find the same related of several ladies, Iuv. 6, 244.

4. Cic. de or. 1, 212 *iuris consultus vere nominaretur . . . qui legum et consuetudinis eius qua privati in civitate uterentur et ad respondendum et ad cavendum peritus esset.* off. 2, 65 *in iure cavere, consilio iuvare atque hoc scientiae genere prodesse quam plurimis vehementer et ad opes augendas pertinet et ad gratiam. itaque cum multa praeclara maiorum tum quod optime constituti iuris civilis summo semper in honore fuit cognitio atque interpretatio.* Liv. 39, 40 *ad summos honores alios scientia iuris . . provexit.* Compared to oratory Cic. (Brut. 151; cf. or. 141. off. 2, 66) calls it the second art. On occasion he places it lower; cf. de or. 1, 236. Mur. 25. Connection with the pontificate (Cic. leg. 2, 47). Moreover there were many jurists distinguished for their social talent and wit (the Mucii, Aquilius Gallus, Cascellius, Trebatius) and for their character (Rutilius Rufus, the Mucii, Sulpicius Rufus, Cascellius, Antistius Labeo).

5. Clients (consultores) are said to *consulere*, and the consulti (*de iure*) *respondent* (Cic. Brut. 113), which they did either in their residence (Cic. de or. 2, 226. 3, 133) or while they *transverso foro ambulabant* (ib. 3, 133; cf. ib. 1, 246). Cic. Mur. 19 *Servius . . . urbanam militiam respondendi, scribendi, cavendi, plenam*

sollicitudinis ac stomachi, secutus est; . . . praesto multis fuit, multorum stultitiam perpessus est, adrogantiam pertulit, difficultatem exsorbuit By admitting younger men as listeners, pupils were trained, as was already the practice of Coruncanius. Cicero e.g. was the auditor of the augur Q. Scaevola. Many formulas had to be learnt by heart, Cic. de or. 1, 246.

6. Cicero writes to Trebatius (fam. 7. 19): *num ius civile vestrum ex libris cognosci potest? qui quamquam plurimi sunt, doctorem tamen usumque desiderant.* On the other hand de or. 1, 192 *neque ita multis litteris aut voluminibus magnis continentur. eadem enim sunt elata primum a pluribus, deinde paucis verbis commutatis etiam ab eisdem scriptoribus scripta sunt saepius.* Still more forcibly (but in joke) Mur. 28 *perpaucis et minime obscuris litteris continentur. itaque si mihi homini vehementer occupato stomachum moveritis, triduo me iuris consultum profitebor.*

7. The schematic arrangement of the Stoic philosophy necessarily influenced the jurists. The augur Q. Scaevola was in friendly intercourse with Panaitios (Cic. de or. 1, 45), and the pontifex Q. Scaevola shows the influence of the Stoics in his threefold division of the doctrine of the gods (August. civ. d. 4, 27) and in the title of a work, Ὅροι. Later on, the influence of Aristotle and the Stoics showed itself esp. in the view taken of the Law of Nature (as φύσει δίκαιον). MVoigt, das ius naturale I, Lpz. 1856. Hildenbrand, Rechts- und Staats-Philos. 1, 593. Laferrière, l'influence du stoïcisme sur la doctrine des Jurisconsultes rom., Mém. de l'acad. des sciences morales 10 (1860), 579. Cic. fam. 7, 12 considers jurisprudence irreconcilable with the Epicurean system.

49. As the main department of Roman jurisprudence, Civil law, was nearly independent of the constitution of the State, the change of this did not impede its development, but rather the monarchical concentration of legislation and judicature required technical advisers and interpreters all the more urgently. The age of Augustus possessed in C. Trebatius Testa and A. Cascellius, and in Q. Tubero and Alfenus Varus excellent jurists; under him the division of the jurisprudentes into Sabinians and Proculians commenced; at the head of the first was the yielding C. Ateius Capito, while the Proculians were headed by the republican M. Antistius Labeo. Augustus already gave to the responsa in part legal authority, but at the same time made the ius respondendi dependent on the Emperor. Under the following Emperors of the Julian dynasty flourished the jurists Masurius Sabinus, M. Cocceius Nerva, father and son, C. Cassius Longinus and Sempronius Proculus. Indispensable to the Emperors and undisturbed in their direction of the Civil law even in the worst periods, occupying, moreover, the highest places in the State, this profession was continually recruited by talented and high-principled men, by whose labours jurisprudence was developed to a minuteness unattainable to non-professionals, and who imparted to the law evenness and logical sequence. Though

even under the Flavian dynasty (Caelius Sabinus, Pegasus, Juventius Celsus the father), and under Nerva and Trajan (Celsus fil., Neratius Priscus, Priscus Javolenus, Titius Aristo) the number of eminent lawyers and professors of jurisprudence was very large, we find esp. after Hadrian, c. 130 until 230 A.D., a continuous series of the greatest jurists: Salvius Julianus, L. Volusius Maecianus, Sex. Pomponius, L. Ulpius Marcellus, Q. Cervidius Scaevola, and more especially the coryphees and classic authors of jurisprudence: Gaius, Aemilius Papinianus, Julius Paullus, Domitius Ulpianus, and Herennius Modestinus. Intellects of this excellence raised jurisprudence to a height compared with which all the labours of the Republican period appear but crude attempts; they imparted to their writings the distinctness, nay beauty of scientific works of art, and transformed the Roman Law, formerly the Law of a City, into a Law applicable to all humanity, almost without national peculiarities, and in which legal ideas have found their most distinct expression, a Law which has been the protection of the oppressed in virtue of the sentiments of humanity pervading it. Many traits, originally inequitable and harsh, they contrived to soften down or modify by explanation, though this also taught them to wrest the sense of the words.

About the middle of the 3rd century after Christ the productive power of jurisprudence ceased. No men of talent were then to be found, and after the Praetorian Edict had been condensed by Julianus (under Hadrian), ordinary ability sufficed for the administration of the law. In the 4th century only, literary activity recommenced, but it was confined to the collection of the sources of law, especially of the Imperial decrees, with which at the end of the 2nd century Papirius Justus had made a beginning. But now under Diocletian was formed the codex Gregorianus, followed, under Constantine, by the Fragmenta vaticana and the codex Hermogenianus. Under Theodosius II and Valentinian III the Roman Law of the Christian period began to be systematised, in the codex Theodosianus, which received legal authority a. 438 and was augmented between 448 and 468 by the Novellae of Theodosius and his successors. All these labours were concluded by the collection of legal documents commanded by Justinian and executed esp. by Tribonianus; first (529) the Codex Iustinianus, then (533) the Institutiones and Digest, a selection from the works of the principal jurists in 50 books, then (534) an enlarged edition of the Codex (repetitae praelectionis). The Novellae constitutiones Iustiniani are a private collection made after Justinian's death.

1. Popular notions of the jurist's task: *qui iuris nodos et legum aenigmata solvit*, Iuv. 8, 58. *Iurisconsulti, quorum summus circa verborum proprietatem labor est*, QUINT. 5, 14, 34. In reality the criminal law was far less developed than the civil law. Even in the Imperial period a certain knowledge of law was for some time general. See § 48, 3. APULEIUS met. 9, 27 makes a miller say: *non herciscundae familiae, sed communi dividundo formula dimicabo*, and he uses in the myth of Psyche (above § 47, 3) a good deal that is juridical both in matter and form (e.g. met. 6, 8. 22. 23) by way of parody. On the other hand we find the people scoffing at the exaggerated exactness (*nimia et misera diligentia*, dig. 2, 31, 88, 17) of the jurists, as e.g. in sepulchral inscriptions: *huic monumento dolus malus abesto et iurisconsultus* (or *ius civile*), ORELLI 4374. 4390 sq. 4821. Wilm. 277. Thus Or. 7236 Wilm. 2473 a *librarius* is praised *qui testamenta scripsit annos XVI sine iuris consulto*. A pantomimus of the time of Tiberius *qui primum invenit causidicos imitari* (Or. 6188 Wilm. 2627). The will of a pig (§ 28, 3) should also be mentioned here, though it may probably have originated in juridical circles, as did also the possibly contemporaneous lex convivalis addressed to Querolus (printed also in BÜCHELER'S Petr. p. [3]239); see BÜCHELER, Bonner ind. schol. 1877, 10 (below § 436, 9). Cf. also § 140, 1 on the lex Tappula.

2. The praefectus urbi was a jurist, and jurists composed the Imperial edicts (constitutiones). CAPITOL. Ant. Philos. 11, 10 *habuit secum praefectos, quorum et auctoritate et periculo semper iura dictavit. usus autem est Scaevola praecipue iuris perito.* LAMPRID. Alex. Sev. 16, 1 *neque ullam constitutionem sacravit sine XX iurisperitis et doctissimis ac sapientibus viris isdemque disertissimis non minus L.* But this number was not the usual one. The official position of the jurists obtained for them the reputation that they had principally an eye to the interests of the treasury (IUV. 4, 53 sqq.); but the most distinguished of them, Labeo, Cassius (TAC. A. 14, 43), Papinian (SPARTIAN. Carac. 8), were far from servile.

3. QUINTILIAN (12, 3) expressly defends the necessity of legal knowledge in orators and assures them (ib. 6 cf. 9) that the law is *non tam arduum quam procul intuentibus fortasse videatur*, but also speaks (ib. 11) against the jurists who despise eloquence and *se ad album ac rubricas transtulerunt et formularii vel . . leguleii esse maluerunt.* As a rule the orators understood nothing of the law, which was so difficult to handle in their phraseology (cf. § 45, 4); and in their arrogance they even thought that they could afford to make free with it (TAC. dial. 32. APOLL. SIDON. ep. 8, 16). The *causidici* and *iuridici* are contrasted in SENECA apocol. 12. But for all that, legal knowledge and eloquence were always thought of as in some way connected; LAMPRID. Alex. Sev. 16, 2 *si de iure aut de negotiis tractabat solos doctos et disertos adhibebat.*

4. The general ignorance in the Imperial period respecting the Republican time (cf. § 39, 1) extended also to the jurists; the iuris auctores of the Republic were soon denoted as veteres and forgotten. Celsus is the last who seems to have himself used the writings of the veteres anterior to Q. Mucius Scaevola. The writings of the veteres after Q. Scaevola were in all probability no longer used in the originals by Pomponius and his contemporaries, and hence Pomponius commits several errors in his survey of the old period.

5. POMPON. dig. 1, 2, 2, 47 *hi duo* (Labeo and Capito) *primum veluti diversas*

sectas fecerunt; nam Ateius Capito in his quae ei tradita fuerant perseverabat, Labeo ingenii qualitate et fiducia doctrinae, qui et ceteris operis sapientiae operam dederat, plurima innovare instituit. If, according to this, Labeo may be regarded as a Rationalist and Capito as a Positivist, RUDORFF (Röm. Rechtsgesch. 1, 182) also dwells on the fact that the Sabinians were inclined to the new system of government, while the Proculians adhered to the older foundations of law, and that this distinction lost its importance after Hadrian had caused the existing law to be codified by Julianus. Cf. BREMER, die Rechtslehrer (1868) 68. KUNTZE, Instit. und Gesch. des röm. Rechts 267. MVOIGT, das Aelius- und Sabinussystem und verwandte Rechtssysteme, Lpz. 1875 (Abh. d. sächs. Ges. d. Wiss. XVII).

6. In the juridical literature of the second and third centuries after Christ two principal varieties may be distinguished: text-books and opinions (responsa). The latter give exclusively the view of the adviser himself, while the text-books give not only the opinion held by their author, but also that of earlier authorities on law, as well as the Imperial decrees affecting the question, and aim in this at some degree of completeness. Externally they are founded chiefly on certain texts, either laws or earlier text-books. Hence the frequent occurrence of the titles *Ad edictum*, *Ad legem Iuliam*, as also *Ad Q. Mucium*, *Ad Vitellium*, *Ad Plautium* or the citation *Apud Labeonem;* e.g. *Cassius apud Urseium scribit* means: Cassius in his edition of the work of Urseius; *Marcellus apud Iulianum notat*= makes this comment on Julianus (dig.). Thus Paulus wrote *Notae ad Papinianum*, Ulpian *ad Marcellum*. *Ex Plautio*, *ex Cassio* denotes excerpts from these.

7. The place between text-books and opinions is filled by the Quaestiones originating from the legal questions which the listeners put to the teacher, concerning partly theoretical moot points, partly actual cases which were noticed by a student or by the teacher. This literature extended to the entire civil law. Labeo's Posteriora already belonged to it. MOMMSEN, Zeitschr. f. Rechtsgesch. 7, 83. 93.

8. Digesta is often used as a title for books, e.g. by Alfenus Varus, Juventius Celsus, Salvius Julianus, Ulpius Marcellus, Cervidius Scaevola. By it is meant the systematic grouping of the collective juridical writings of a lawyer (or school), whether proceeding from himself, or from some later writer. The original order is here abandoned in favour of the new systematic one. MOMMSEN, Z. f. Rechtsgesch. 7, 477. 480. 9, 82. On this cf. HPERNICE, Miscell. z. Rechtsgesch. u. Textkrit. 1 (Prag 1870), 1.—Scope of the juristic literature: the index auctorum for Justinian's Digesta includes 1539 books with three million lines (cf. constit. Δέδωκεν 1).

9. Instruction in law continued for some time longer to be unremunerated, or at least it had no legal claim to payment; see ULP. dig. 50, 13, 1, 5. The first teacher of law exclusively (*professor iuris civilis*) was Gaius. By him was founded a new branch of juridical literature, the Institutiones, an introduction to the study of law. After him Inst. were composed by Callistratus and Ulpianus; shorter ones by Paulus, and more complete by Florentinus and Marcianus. They came to a close with the Justinian. FPBREMER, die Rechtslehrer und Rechtsschulen im röm. Kaiserreich, Berl. 1868. HDERNBURG, d. Instit. des Gaius (1869) 3.—A certain M. Picarius Turranianus is mentioned as *magister iuris* in an African inscr. (eph. epigr. 5, p. 537). *Iuris studiosi* frequently in inscriptions CIL. 3, 2936. 10, 569. WILM. 2470. eph. epigr. 5, p. 411. Even a *studens* without further designation eph. epigr. 5, p. 527.

10. From the 4th cent. the science of law was applied practically only in the profession of advocate, and was merged in oratory. The astrologer and former

advocate Firmicus never mentions jurists among the other numerous professions which he names, but on the other hand e.g. 8, 27 in fin.: *advocati optimi et regum amici ac praecipui oratores.* According to him penmen, rather than lawyers, were employed in the Imperial council; see e.g. 8, 27 *regum interpretes vel magistros, scribas quoque et sacrarum* (Imperial) *litterarum officia tractantes.* 30 *litterarum officia tractantes, regibus notos et eorum scribas.* Cf. MAMERTIN. grat. act. 20, 1 *iuris civilis scientia, quae Manlios, Scaevolas, Servios in amplissimum gradum dignitatis evexerat, libertinorum artificium dicebatur* (by the aristocrats of the Byzantine Court). On the other hand of Julian *qui in oratoria facultate, qui in scientia iuris civilis excellit ultro ad familiaritatem vocatur* (ib. 25, 3). AMMIAN. 30, 4, 11 (a. 374) *secundum est genus eorum qui iuris professi scientiam, . . . ut altius videantur iura callere, Trebatium loquuntur et Cascellium* etc. ib. 16 (of the lawyers) *e quibus ita sunt rudes nonnulli ut numquam se codices habuisse meminerint. et si in circulo doctorum auctoris veteris inciderit nomen, piscis aut edulii peregrinum esse vocabulum arbitrantur.*

11. CFHOMMEL, Palingenesia librorum iuris veterum, sive Pandectarum loca integra . . . exposita et ab exemplari Taurellii Florentino accuratissime descripta, Lps. 1767 sq. III. HFITTING, d. Alter d. Schriften röm. Juristen von Hadr. bis Alex. Sev., Bas. 1860. Concerning the language of the jurists: HE DIRKSEN, manuale latinitatis fontt. iur. civ. rom., Berl. 1837 and his kl. Schrr. (§ 48, 2). WKALB, das Juristenlatein, Versuch einer Charakteristik auf Grund d. Digesten, Nürnb. 1886.

50. The Romans as a nation had not much talent for the study of Philosophy: abstract reflection seemed to their simple practical turn of mind little better than idling. All real philosophy they obtained from the Greeks, and this at a time when in Greece itself the great masters had been succeeded by Epigoni, who confined themselves to reproducing and spinning out in the traditional manner a limited stock of ideas. The first transplanter of Greek philosophical thought, Q. Ennius, took up (not to mention his Epicharmus) a production of the most shallow rationalism, the work of Euhemerus, and this note reverberates in Pacuvius and L. Accius. The disagreement of doctrines of this kind with the existing customs and religion caused a. 581/173 the expulsion of the Epicurean philosophers Alkaios and Philiskos, 593/161 the SC. de philosophis et rhetoribus (uti Romae ne essent), and 599/155 the hasty but still too long delayed departure of the Athenian ambassadors, the Academic Karneades, the Stoic Diogenes, and the Peripatetic Kritolaos, of whom the first especially made a deep impression on the younger generation by his eloquence and liberal sentiments. The far-seeing Stoic Panaitios was not long afterwards received by the younger Scipio, and through him and his disciple Poseidonios Stoicism gained admittance among the Romans. It was professed by the younger Laelius, Q. Aelius Tubero,

C. Fannius, Sp. Mummius, C. Blossius, P. Rutilius Rufus, Valerius Soranus, L. Aelius Stilo, by the jurisprudentes Q. Mucius Scaevola (the augur as well as the pontifex), L. Lucilius Balbus, Sex. Pompeius and Ser. Sulpicius Rufus, and finally the younger Cato; and in literature by Stertinius. Other Romans were won over to other systems by the Greeks into whose hands they chanced to fall; the (new) Academy especially found many adherents, on account of its plausible doctrines and its consequent utility for legal purposes, e.g. C. Aurelius Cotta (cos. 679/75), L. Lucullus, L. Tubero. M. Piso (cos. 693/61) and M. Licinius Crassus (cos. 684/70) inclined to the Peripatetic philosophy. The simplicity, moral laxity and self-sufficiency of the Epicurean philosophy recommended it especially to such natures as were glad to retire to leisure and quiet from the political agitations, e.g. in Cicero's time his friend Atticus, Papirius Paetus and M. Marius, and also Pansa. For this very reason this system was also the first to be represented in Latin literature, not only by Ennius and the communis historia of Lutatius in the time before Cicero, but also by Rabirius, Catius and Amafinius, and especially by Lucretius. Other adherents of the Epicurean philosophy were C. Velleius, L. Saufeius, L. Manlius Torquatus (praetor 706/48), Statilius, P. Volumnius, and to a certain extent also C. Cassius. A form of the Pythagorean philosophy corrupted with all sorts of superstitious elements found an apostle in Nigidius Figulus, and disciples (such as P. Vatinius). Much greater was the number of those who, following the example of the most distinguished Greek philosophers of this period, e.g. Antiochos of Askalon, combined several systems, as Varro the polyhistor sided with the Stoics in dialectics, theology and natural philosophy, with the Academy in ethics; and M. Brutus who, on the other hand, was a Stoic in ethics, and an Academic in all other respects. The eclectic tendency is especially exhibited in the numerous philosophical writings of Cicero.

1. A survey in Cic. Tusc. 4, 1–7; cf. de or. 2, 154 sq. Acad. pr. 2, 5. Quint. 10, 1, 123 sq.—Hepke, de philos. qui Romae docuerunt usque ad Antoninos, Berl. 1842. EZeller in his history of Greek philosophy and: Religion u. Philosophie b. d. Röm. in his Vorträge u. Abhh. 2 (Lpz. 1877), 93; esp. 106. Mommsen, RG. 2 6, 410. 3 6, 570. Also AStahr, Aristot. bei d. Röm., Lpz. 1834. Friedländer, Sittengesch. 3 5, 607.—CBuresch, consolationum a Graecis Romanisque scriptarum hist. crit., Lpz. Stud. 9, 1. On this see also AGercke in the Tirocin. philol. sodal. semin. Bonn. (Berl. 1883) 28.

2. The reflective bent of the Romans is shown by Appius Caecus' didactic

poem (§ 90, 5), by Cato's praecepta ad filium (§ 121, 2), and by the sententious character of the Mimi (§ 8, 6. 212, 4) etc. Their practical wisdom was apt to wear a fatalistic colouring: see L. Paullus in Liv. 45, 8 and Scipio Africanus in Cic. off. 1, 90. Ennius' saying is characteristic: *phílosophari est míhi necesse, at paúcis, nam omnino haúd placet* (Reliq. ed. Vahlen p. 145). The supposed compositions of Numa dug out in the year 573/181, containing *scripta philosophiae Pythagoricae*, were burnt, *quia philosophiae scripta essent*, Plin. NH. 13, 86. Cato the Elder was ὅλως φιλοσοφίᾳ προσκεκρουκώς (Plut. Cat. mai. 23). Cicero considers it his duty to justify his philosophical writings in almost every book of this kind, see especially off. 2, 2 sqq. Even Tacitus makes his Agricola (Agr. 4) say *se prima in iuventa studium philosophiae acrius, ultra quam concessum Romano ac senatori, hausisse*, and Gellius (5, 16, 5) considers that *degustandum ex philosophia, non in eam ingurgitandum.*

3. The Romans valued philosophy only as conducive to the formation of character, a source of instruction as to the moral duties of man, the things on the possession of which his happiness depends, and the means of obtaining them (Zeller, Vortrr. 2, 106). Thus Varro alleged as *causa philosophandi* that man thereby becomes *bonus et beatus*, and Cornelius Nepos (in Lactant. Inst. 3, 15, 10) adduces against the study of philosophy: *video magnam partem eorum qui in schola de pudore et continentia praecipiant argutissime, eosdem in omnium libidinum cupiditatibus vivere.* And Pacuvius already (in Gell. 13, 8, 4) has said: *ódi ego homines ígnava opera et phílosopha senténtia.* We must also keep in mind the general mediocrity of the Greeks to whom the Romans owed their philosophy. 'Thus it came to pass that the Romans became in philosophy merely worse pupils of bad masters' (Mommsen).

4. The various philosophical systems with regard to their fitness for oratorical purposes are discussed by Quintil. 12, 2, 24. The Stoic philosophy appeared to be the least applicable thereto; Cic. de. or. 3, 66. fin. 4, 78. parad. praef. 2. Brut. 114, 118. Quint. 10, 1, 84; cf. 12, 2, 25; Cic. parad. praef. 1: *animadverti saepe Catonem . . ., cum in senatu sententiam diceret, locos graves ex philosophia tractare abhorrentes ab hoc usu forensi et publico, sed dicendo consequi tamen ut illa etiam populo probabilia viderentur.* The new Academy on the contrary seemed to be most favourable to this object; see Cic. de or. 3, 80.

5. Cic. Vatin. 14 *tu qui te Pythagoreum soles dicere et hominis doctissimi nomen tuis immanibus et barbaris moribus praetendere.* But Vatinius can no more be numbered among the philosophers on account of this passage than Caerellia on account of Cic. Att. 13, 21, 5 *mirifice Caerellia, studio videlicet philosophiae flagrans, describit (libros meos) de tuis; istos ipsos de finibus habet;* cf. ib. 22, 3. Thus the lady in Hor. epod. 8, 15 has *libelli stoici inter sericos pulvillos.*

51. Augustus intentionally favoured the study of philosophy and even himself wrote Hortationes ad philosophiam. Besides him we know, however, only T. Livius, Crispinus, and Sextius the Elder as philosophical writers in his time. But philosophical training was possessed by, and manifested itself in, almost all the first writers of that period, e.g. Vergil, Horace and L. Varius. Many combined with it an interest in natural philosophy. The Epicurean philosophy was most in harmony with the tendency of the times, calling up, as it did, in the more serious minds a

feeling of sorrowful resignation. Even in the first century after Christ the Epicurean and Stoic philosophies remained the only systems represented at Rome, but then only a few (such as Aufidius Bassus) possessed that mental independence and self-reliance, which form the basis of the Epicurean philosophy; the majority turned to Stoic philosophy, some weakening it by dropping the harsher features of its system and its crotchety doctrines on cosmology, as Seneca does, others, e.g. Sextius the Younger, increasing its depth by adding to it theistic and Pythagorean ingredients. Men of the most decided characters, as Paetus Thrasea, Helvidius Priscus, and also the young Persius Flaccus, even augmented its ruggedness of doctrine and practice. Others at least observed the fashion of keeping a philosopher and having discussions with him. Rome in this way was flooded with philosophers, many of whom by their personal want of character brought philosophy itself into contempt. The number was small of men who, like the Cynic Demetrios, gave to others the example of an independent mind. Vespasian and Domitian banished the philosophers from Rome and Italy. In the second century also the Stoic system prevailed and was numerously represented in Rome, by Greeks as well as Romans, among the latter especially by Junius Rusticus; with M. Aurelius the Stoic philosophy appeared even on the throne. Others endeavoured to make philosophy popular, by extending their declamations to these subjects also, e.g. Apuleius. Many thought to increase their effect by a cloudy mysticism, arbitrarily styling itself Platonism, e.g. Taurus, Favorinus, and also Apuleius. The Neoplatonic philosophy of the 3rd century has no representative of note in Roman literature. The ascendancy of the Christian religion in the 4th century drove those who did not go over to it to the renewed study of the treasures of the old Greek philosophy, which were made more accessible by revision and translation, as e.g. by Augustine before he became a Christian, and especially by Boethius in the 6th century. By these labours they were transmitted to the nations of the West, whose mental food they formed during the Middle Ages.

1. *L. Varius* (or *Varus*) *Epicureus:* § 223, 3. Horace ridicules in his earlier poems the absurdities of the Stoic philosophy, and professes Epicurean doctrines; in the later ones he does justice to the seriousness and depth of Stoicism. Cf. § 235, 5. Liv. 43, 13, 1 *nihil deos portendere vulgo nunc credunt.* Under Caligula Πομ-

πήδιος, συγκλητικὸς μέν, τὰς ἀρχὰς δὲ διεληλυθὼς σχεδὸν πάσας, Ἐπικούρειος δὲ ἄλλως καὶ δι αὐτὸ ἀπράγμονος ἐπιτηδευτὴς βίου, IOSEPH. antiq. 19, 1, 5. In many epitaphs of the period this tendency manifests itself. The Sextii, father and son, wrote in Greek as well as Cornutus.

2. In the first century after Christ the majority studied philosophy *ut nomine magnifico segne otium velarent* (TAC. hist. 4, 5); even ladies dallied with philosophy: see L. FRIEDLÄNDER, Sittengesch. 1[5], 445. TAC. A. 14, 16 relates of Nero *etiam sapientiae doctoribus tempus impertiebat post epulas utque contraria adseverantium discordia frueretur. nec deerant qui ore voltuque tristi inter oblectamenta regia spectari cuperent.* This *tristitia* belonged to the philosopher's costume, as well as his long beard, his staff, and threadbare gown, which was adopted from the Cynics, cf. MARTIAL. 4, 53. IUV. 13, 121. Unfortunately the servile covetousness and moral despicability of very many individuals did not well agree with this spiritual appearance. QUINT. 1, prooem. 15 *voltum et tristitiam et dissentientem a ceteris habitum pessimis moribus* (see instances in Iuv. 2, 4. 65) *praetendebant.* On this arrogance cf. also 12, 3, 12. 5, 11, 39. But the common run of orators *sapientiae studium et praecepta prudentium penitus reformidant* (TAC. dial. 32). Cf. also QUINT. 11, 1, 35 *at vir civilis vereque sapiens, qui se non otiosis disputationibus, sed administrationibus reip. dediderit, a qua longissime isti qui philosophi vocantur recesserunt.* Similarly 12, 2, 6, cf. ib. 9 *hanc artem superbo nomine et vitiis quorundam bona eius corrumpentium invisam.* Popular quips: *facilius inter philosophos quam inter horologia conveniet* (SEN. apocol. 3, 3), and *numquam philosophum audivit* in PETRON. 71. Similar attacks against the Greek philosophers at Rome occur, however, as early as PLAUTUS, Curc. 2, 3, 9, and the same complaints recur in GELLIUS, e.g. 7 (6), 10, 5 *nunc videre est philosophos ultro currere ut doceant ad fores iuvenum divitum eosque ibi sedere atque opperiri prope ad meridiem, donec discipuli nocturnum omne vinum edormiant.* 13, 8, 5 *nihil fieri posse indignius neque intolerantius dicebat* (Macedo, familiaris meus) *quam quod homines ignavi ac desides, operti barba et pallio, mores et emolumenta philosophiae in linguae verborumque artes converterent et vitia facundissime accusarent intercutibus ipsi vitiis madentes.* In the same period APULEI. flor. 1, 7. CMARTHA, les moralistes sous l'empire romain . . . philosophes et poètes, Paris 1865. LFRIEDLÄNDER, Sittengesch. 3[5], 615. HSCHILLER, Nero 588.

3. ULPIAN. dig. 50, 13, 1, 4 *an et philosophi professorum numero sint* (who have a claim to payment for teaching)? *non putem, non quia non religiosa res est, sed quia hoc primum profiteri eos oportet, mercenariam operam spernere.*

4. CAPITOL. M. Antonin. philos. 2, 7. 3, 2 (see § 358, 2. 3). *L. Iunius Rusticus, philosophus stoicus*, ORELLI 1190. *C. Tutilius Hostilianus, philosophus stoicus, domo Cortona*, ib. 1191. *C. Matrinius Valentius, philosophus epicureus*, ib. 1192. *Gaius Stallius . . . ex epicureio gaudivigente choro* IRN. 3374 OR. 1193. *Iulius Iulianus . . . philosophus primus.* WILM. 2475. *Ti. Claudius Paulinus philosophus*, CIL. 3, 302. Cf. § 407, 6.

52. The Romans looked upon mathematics and astronomy as unprofitable studies. With the exception of a few amateurs, such as Sex. Pompeius and Sulpicius Gallus (cos. 518/166), they confined themselves to the lower kinds of computation and measuring. In the mathematical sciences the Romans were entirely dependent on the Greek masters, especially on Hero. The works of Varro are undoubtedly no exception. The only

partially preserved work on geometry by a Roman is that of Balbus written under Trajan. Sulpicius Gallus studied astronomy as an amateur, Varro as a polyhistor, and Nigidius Figulus from mystic tendencies. In the Imperial period astrology prevailed. Under Tiberius, Manilius made it the subject of a didactic poem. In the 3rd century of the Christian era Censorinus' treatise de die natali is of importance, in the 4th we have 8 books on astrology by Julius Firmicus Maternus, in the 6th Boethius' two books de institutione arithmetica (and de geometria).

1. The mathematical knowledge of the Romans corresponds in substance and form to the stand-point of Greek mathematics about the year 100 B.C. See MCantor, röm. Agrimens. (1875) 139. The idea of the Romans is shown by the meaning of mathematici=astrologi. The neglect of astronomy was punished in the Republican period by constant confusion in the calendar. Generalising Cic. Tusc. 1, 5 *nihil (apud Graecos) mathematicis illustrius ; at nos metiendi ratiocinandique utilitate huius artis terminavimus modum.* Arithmetic had also its place in the schools; see Hor. S. 1. 6, 72. E. 1, 1, 56. 2, 3, 325. Colum. 1, prooem. 5 *scholas geometrarum esse . . . ipse vidi.* Cf. in general MCantor, mathemat. Beiträge zum Kulturleben (1863), 168; Geschichte der Mathem. I, Lpz. 1881.

2. In Varro geometry was divided in theory into κανονική (*quae ad aures pertinet*, the basis of music), and ὀπτική (*quae ad oculos pertinet*, optics together with ἐπιπεδομετρία and στερεομετρία), in practice into gromatics and geography, see Ritschl, opusc. 3, 385.

3. A curious collection of problems geometrical (founded on Hero) and arithmetical, rather wanting in plan, and taken from sources already corrupt, bears the title: *Epaphroditi et Vitruvi Rufi architectonis;* first published by ASchott, Antw. 1616, subsequently esp. (from the cod. Arcerian. s. VI/VII, § 58, 3) by MCantor, Agrimens. (1875), 208 cf. 114. See also CBHase in Bredow's ep. Parisienses (Lpz. 1812), 201.

4. Firmic. Mat. math. 2, praef. (p. 15 ed. 1551): *Fronto noster* (perhaps the Stoic § 329, 3?), *Hipparchi secutus antiscia* (ἀντίσκια), *ita apotelesmatum sententias protulit tamquam cum perfectis iam et peritis loqueretur, nihil de institutione, nihil de magisterio praescribens. sed nec aliquis paene Latinorum de hac arte institutionis libros scripsit, nisi paucos versus Iulius Caesar* (=Germanicus see § 275, 7), *et ipsos tamen de alieno opere mutuatus. M. vero Tullius . . . etiam ipse de institutione pauca respondit. . . . Antiscia Hipparchi secutus est Fronto, quae nullam vim habent nullamque substantiam. et sunt quidem in Frontone praenuntiationis atque apotelesmatum verae sententiae, antisciorum vero inefficax studium . . . antiscia enim illa vera sunt, sicut et Navigius noster probat, . . . apotelesmata et Fronto verissime scripsit, quae Graecorum libris ac monumentis abundantissime continentur*, cf. 8, 5 *hi* (Aratus, Caesar, Tullius) *tantum nomina stellarum et ortus, non autem apotelesmatum auctoritatem ediderunt, ita ut mihi videantur non aliqua astrologiae scientia, sed poetica potius elati licentia docilis sermonis studia protulisse.* Thus Firmicus knows nothing of Manilius. He decides on undertaking the work *ne omni disciplinarum arte translata solum hoc opus extitisse videatur ad quod romanum non affectasset ingenium* (5, praef., p. 115).

5. Other writers on astrology in Ap. Sidon. c. 22 praef.: *Iulianum Vertacum, Fullonium Saturninum, in libris matheseos peritissimos conditores*; cf. ib. ep. 8, 11.

53. The Romans felt no pure interest in the objects of nature around them; neither would they spend their time in taking an unprejudiced view of them nor had they sufficient courage to do so. Hence they were always behindhand in natural philosophy and dependent upon the Greeks. Zoology and botany especially, which the latter had brought to such perfection, were but slightly cultivated, and chiefly in connection with agriculture. The writings of Nigidius Figulus remained without influence. In him, as in the other writers on the system of Augury and the Haruspicia (§ 42, 1), was to be found the strangest amalgamation of the observation of natural phenomena with superstition. In the Augustan period Pompeius Trogus edited the natural history of Aristotle, and probably also the botany of Theophrastus. Valgius Rufus and Aemilius Macer translated Alexandrine didactic poems on botanical and zoological subjects. In the encyclopaedias of Celsus and Pliny the Elder natural philosophy was also represented, and the Imperial time shows, at its commencement, a dilettante bent towards it, in its fondness for connecting moralising reflections with natural phenomena. This appears e.g. from Seneca's Quaestiones naturales. The following centuries were satisfied with mere translations of the Greek works on this subject.

1. Plin. NH. 25, 4 *minus hoc* (botany, pharmacology, toxicology etc.) *quam par erat nostri celebravere . . . primusque et diu solus idem ille M. Cato . . . paucis dumtaxat attigit . . . post eum unus illustrium tentavit C. Valgius . . . antea condiderat solus apud nos . . . Pompeius Lenaeus, Magni libertus . . . Pompeius . . . transferre ea* (Mithridates' prescriptions on poisons and antidotes) *sermone nostro libertum suum Lenaeum, grammaticae artis, iussit.* Pliny repeatedly (NH. 10, 5. 14, 11 cf. ind. auct. b. 8) quotes zoological and botanical notices from Cornelius Valerianus (see also 3, 108), which bear, however, the stamp of anecdotes. Similarly otherwise unknown are the writers whom the elder Pliny quotes among his authorities on botany, e.g. Domitius Calvinus (in the ind. auct. to b. 11. 18), Tergilla (ind. auct. to b. 14. 15, quoted 14, 147), Calpurnius Bassus (ind. auct. to b. 16–19. 21. 22), Dessius Mundus (ind. auct. to b. 17), Q. Birrius (ind. auct. to book 19), Vestinus (ind. auct. to b. 21. 22).

2. Pliny NH. 22, 15 *plerisque ultro etiam inrisui sumus ista* (botany, pharmacology) *commentantes atque frivoli operis arguimur* etc. The latter also especially from the point of view of a limited rhetoric, cf. praef. 13. On the later literature of pharmacy see below § 55 with n. 4 sq.

3. RAlbani, de hist. naturali ap. veteres, Dresden 1854. EHFMeyer, Gesch. d. Botanik (Königsb. 1854 sqq.) 1, 334. 2, 1.

54. Agriculture was a subject of great interest to the Romans, and besides their own experience they endeavoured also to utilise

that of foreign nations. Thus e.g. the work on agriculture by the Carthaginian Mago was, by order of the Senate, translated into Latin, and the only extant work of Cato the Elder is the de re rustica. In the 7th century U.C. we find other writers on agriculture, viz. Mamilius Sura, the two Sasernas (father and son), and Tremellius Scrofa, and by Varro the polyhistor we have also a work of this kind. Vergil's Georgics are a panegyric on this branch of human industry. At the same time Hyginus wrote on farming and bee-keeping, and Sabinus Tiro dedicated his work on horticulture to Maecenas. At the commencement of the Imperial period writing on agriculture occupied men of note such as Julius Graecinus, and with him Cornelius Celsus and Julius Atticus; the twelve books of Columella, written in the time of Seneca, have been preserved to us. The work of the brothers Quintilii, about the middle of the 2nd century A.D., was written in Greek. In the 3rd century Gargilius Martialis combined botany and pharmacology with agriculture, after the manner of Pliny and Celsus. The work of Palladius in 14 books, written in the 4th century, treats (towards the end) of forestry in elegiacs, just as Columella had given an epic form to his 10th book on horticulture. The cookery-book which bears the name of Apicius was compiled, about the middle of the 3rd century, from Greek sources.

1. Varro RR. 1, 1, 10 *hos (graecos scriptores de agricultura) nobilitate Mago Karthaginiensis praeteriit punica lingua, quod res dispersas comprehendit libris XXVIII, quos Cassius Dionysius Uticensis vertit libris XX ac graeca lingua Sextilio praetori misit . . . hosce ipsos utiliter ad VI libros redegit Diophanes* (cf. Gargil. Mart. in Mai's class. auct. 1, 406) *in Bithynia et misit Deiotaro regi.* See ib. 1, 17, 3. 1, 38, 1. 2, 1, 27. 3, 2, 13. Cic. de or. 1, 249. Plin. NH. 18, 22 *Poenus Mago, cui . . . tantum honorem senatus noster habuit Carthagine capta ut, cum regulis Africae bybliothecas donaret, unius eius XXVIII volumina censeret in latinam linguam transferenda, cum iam M. Cato praecepta condidisset, peritisque linguae punicae dandum negotium, in quo praecessit omnes vir clarissimae familiae D. Silanus.* Cf. ib. 17, 63. 80. 93. 128. 18, 35. 97. 21, 110.

2. Isid. orig. 17, 1, 1 *apud Romanos de agricultura primus Cato instituit* (the M'. Percennius Nolanus and the Manlii mentioned as authorities by Cato RR. 145. 151. 152 were probably practical farmers, not writers), *quam deinde M. Terentius* (Varro) *expolivit, mox Vergilius laude carminum extulit. nec minus studium habuerunt postmodum Cornelius Celsus et Iulius Atticus, Aemilianus* (Palladius) *sive Columella, insignis orator, qui totum corpus disciplinae eiusdem complexus est.* Cassiod. divin. lect. 28 *in agris colendis . . . inter ceteros Columella et Aemilianus auctores probabiles extiterunt* etc. More correctly Colum. 1, 1, 12–14 *ut agricolationem romana tandem civitate donemus . . . iam nunc M. Catonem Censorium illum memoremus, qui eam latine loqui primus instituit; post hunc duos Sasernas, patrem et filium, qui eam diligentius erudierunt; ac deinde Scrofam Tre-*

mellium, qui etiam eloquentem reddidit (to the Sasernae and Tremellius COLUM. 1, praef. 32 adds Stolo, see § 293, 4), *et M. Terentium, qui expolivit; mox Vergilium, qui carmine quoque potentem fecit. nec postremo quasi paedagogi eius meminisse dedignemur, Iulii Hygini, veruntamen ut Carthaginiensem Magonem rusticationis parentem maxime veneremur. nam huius XXVIII memorabilia illa volumina ex SCto in latinum sermonem conversa sunt. non minorem tamen laudem meruerunt nostrorum temporum viri, Cornelius Celsus et Iulius Atticus . . . cuius velut discipulus duo volumina . . . Iulius Graecinus . . . posteritati tradenda curavit.*—RREITZENSTEIN, de scriptorum RR. . . . inter Catonem et Columellam librr. deperditis, Berl. 1884.

3. COLUM. 12, 4, 2 *tum demum nostri generis postquam a bellis otium fuit quasi quoddam tributum victui humano conferre non dedignati sunt, ut M. Ambivius et Menas Licinius, tum etiam C. Matius, quibus studium fuit pistoris et coci nec minus cellarii diligentiam sui praeceptis instituere.* If the enumeration, as is possible, is chronological, Ambivius may be placed in the first half of the 7th cent. U.C. A certain Maenas is also mentioned in VARRO RR. 2, 3, 11. cf. 2, 1, 1. 2, 8, 1. On Matius, the contemporary of Cicero, see COLUM. 12, 44, 1 *quae C. Matius diligentissime persecutus est; . . . illi enim propositum fuit urbanas mensas et lauta convivia instruere. libros tres edidit, quos inscripsit nominibus Coci et Cellarii et Salgamarii.*

4. PLIN. NH. 19, 177 *Sabinus Tiro in libro Cepuricon* (Κηπουρικῶν) *quem Maecenati dicavit.* Cf. the ind. auct. to b. 18 (Sabino). Other authors of Κηπουρικά are, according to the ind. auct. to PLINY b. 19 Caesennius, Castricius, Firmus. Perhaps also Sergius Paulus (ib. b. 18)?

5. MACR. 3, 18, 7 *vir doctus Oppius, in libro quem fecit De silvestribus arboribus;* likewise ib. 3, 19, 4. He is probably the Oppius quoted by PLINY in the ind. auct. to b. 11 (zoological) and 11, 252. A grammarian (apparently) Oppius in FEST. 182[b], 133. Cf. § 41, 1 ad fin.

6. Curtius Justus is instanced by Gargilius Martialis in the Neapolitan fragment c. 2 and 4; Sextius Niger (§ 266, 7) in the St. Gallen fragment of Garg. Mart., ap. VROSE, Anecd. 2, 129; see his edition of Garg. (§ 411, 1) p. 139.

7. Collections of the Scriptores rei rusticae veteres latini by PVICTORIUS, Lugd. 1541 V, IMGESNER (adi. nott. varr. et lexicon rusticum), Lps.[2] (v. IAERNESTI) 1773. 74 II., especially by IGSCHNEIDER, Lps. 1794–97 IV.

55. Medical art was unknown at Rome during more than five centuries. The simple and invigorating way of living caused it to be but rarely wanted; in cases of need, there were domestic remedies and incantations good for man and beast. This was still the opinion of Cato the Elder, who inveighed against the Greek physicians, who resorted to Rome in constantly increasing numbers, and in whose hands the practice of scientific medicine remained almost exclusively, until the Arabs began to rival them. Only a small number of Latin works exist on medical subjects. Under Tiberius, Celsus wrote his encyclopaedia, and was thus obliged, although not a physician, to treat also of medicine. These books de medicina, which we still possess, are entirely dependent on Greek authors. Of a few Roman physicians who

wrote literary works we only know the names from Pliny. Pliny's own writings contain much concerning the history of medicine, and he devotes (beginning with book XX) to the healing efficacy of various objects in the natural kingdoms 12 books of his Natural History, which, in the 4th century A.D., were epitomised by an unknown author as the Medicina Plinii. The Empiricists Scribonius Largus (in the 1st century A.D.) and Serenus Sammonicus (at the beginning of the 3rd century) composed special works on pharmacology, the former treating, in a dry manner, of compound remedies, while the latter produced a popular compendium of domestic medicine in metrical form, like that of Vindicianus in the 4th century. In the 5th century the African Caelius Aurelianus translated the Methodician Soranus. The 4th and 5th centuries supply as well a number of stupid Empiricists, who propounded much superstition in unpolished language, e.g. Sex. Placitus, Marcellus (Empiricus), Theodorus Priscianus, the so-called Apuleius (Barbarus), and the supposititious Antonius Musa. In the 4th and 5th centuries we have also veterinary works by Pelagonius and P. Vegetius. From the 5th to the 8th centuries many medical works were translated into Latin for the use of the Germanic nations; one of the most remarkable of these works is that by Anthimus.

1. PLIN. NH. 29, 11 *milia gentium sine medicis degunt, nec tamen sine medicina, sicuti populus rom. ultra sexcentesimum annum, neque ipse in accipiendis artibus lentus, medicinae vero etiam avidus.* 12 *Cassius Hemina . . . auctor est primum e medicis venisse Romam Peloponneso Archagathum* (a. 535/219). 13 Cato's warning to beware of Greek physicians: *iurarunt inter se barbaros necare omnes medicina* (cf. PLUT. Cato mai. 23). 15 *profitetur* (Cato) *esse commentarium sibi quo medeatur filio, servis, familiaribus . . .* (17) *solam hanc artium graecarum nondum exercet romana gravitas in tanto fructu; paucissimi Quiritium attigere, et ipsi statim ad Graecos transfugae; immo vero auctoritas aliter quam graece eam tractantibus, etiam apud imperitos expertesque linguae, non est.* But the greater the number of quacks and cheats among the Greek physicians, the less respected was the whole profession; cf. *illa infelix monumentis inscriptio, turba se medicorum perisse* (PLIN. l. l. 11) and in VOPISC. Firm. 7, 4 the collocation: *sunt Aegyptii . . . mathematici, haruspices, medici.* On the other hand the Imperial court physicians knew how to make themselves respected.

2. The oculists also, whose names we learn from their seals, are, to conclude from their cognomina, most of them of Greek origin, and on account of the frequency of the names Julius and Claudius must belong to the 1st century and the first half of the 2nd century after Christ; CLGROTEFEND, die Stempel d. Augenärzte, Hannov. 1867; the new discoveries in JKLEIN, Jahrb. d. Altertumsfr. im Rheinl. 55, 93; further additions 57, 200 and elsewhere. AHÉRON DE VILLEFOSSE et HTHÉDENAT, cachets d'oculistes rom. I, Par. 1882. For elucidation see also WFRÖHNER, Phil. Suppl. 5, 87.

3. Among his Roman authorities on medicine PLINY NH. quotes in the ind. auct. to b. 28 *Granius medicus*, *Ofilius medicus* (both quoted 28, 42) and *Rabirius medicus* (28, 74), further in the ind. auct. to b. 29 *Caecilius medicus* (his *commentarii* 29, 85). MARCELLUS (EMPIR.) praef. enumerates among *veteres medicinae artis auctores latino sermone perscriptos: uterque Plinius* (Plin. the Elder and the so-called Plin. Valerianus) *et Apuleius Celsus et Apollinaris ac Designatianus, aliique nonnulli etiam proximo tempore illustres honoribus viri, cives ac maiores nostri, Siburius, Eutropius atque Ausonius.* CASSIOD. inst. div. litt. 31 *quodsi vobis non fuerit graecarum litterarum nota facundia, imprimis habetis Herbarium Dioscoridis, qui herbas agrorum mirabili proprietate disseruit atque depinxit. post haec legite Hippocratem atque Galenum latina lingua conversos, i.e. Therapeutica Galeni ad philosophum Glauconem destinata et Anonymum quendam qui ex diversis auctoribus probatur esse collectus. deinde Aureliani Caelii de medicina et Hippocratis de herbis et curis* (*cibis* VRose), *diversosque alios de medendi arte compositos quos vobis in bybliothecae nostrae sinibus reconditos . . . dereliqui.* MARCELL. EMPIR. p. 145. 216 mentions Nero's court physician, Marcellus, as a medical writer. Cf. GALEN 14, p. 459.—Dietetical works by Soranus (in the form of questions and answers), translated through Caelius Aur., by Theodorus Priscianus, Anthimus and others.—'*Dicta Marci medici ad * * virum clarissimum inter cetera sic:* etc.' from Bern. 109 s. X in HHAGEN, de cod. Bern. Tironianis, Bern 1880 p. 9.

4. The numerous writers on medicines (esp. on simple εὐπόριστα), fall into two divisions according as they classed their prescriptions by the natural kingdom from which they were taken, or by the suffering parts of the body which they were intended to affect. The first arrangement is adopted esp. by Sex. Placitus (animalia) and Ps.-Apuleius (herbae); but the majority, following the example of Pliny (NH. 25, 132), adopted the second system and began the enumeration with the head; thus Scribonius Largus, Serenus Sammonicus, Plinius Val., Marcellus Emp., Theodorus Priscianus.

5. Collections of the medici vett. lat. by Aldus (1547) and H. Stephanus (1567). Anonymus de re medica in Mai, class. auct. 7, 459 (fragment).—Collection of the writers on pharmacology by JCHGACKERMANN (Parabilium medicamentorum scriptt. ant., Nürnb. 1788).

6. KSPRENGEL, Gesch. d. Arzneikunde, b. 1[4] (by JRosenbaum) Lpz. 1846, 1, 199. JFCHECKER, Gesch. d. Heilkunde, vol. 2. HHÄSER, Gesch. d. Medizin 1[3] (Jena 1875), 254. RBRIAU, l'archiatrie rom. ou la médecine officielle dans l'empire rom., Par. 1877. HNANKE, lexicogr. Bemerkungen medizinisch-philologischen Inhalts, Phil. 32, 385. 577. On the medicina pliniana see § 411.

56. Military science and history were introduced into literature only in the Imperial period, and thus we have Sex. Julius Frontinus' Strategemata (under Domitian), Hyginus' work on encampments (cf. § 58), and (in the 4th century) Vegetius' work Epitoma rei militaris.

1. In the Republican time we may perhaps mention the defence of his strategical conduct in Spain and before Carthage addressed by Scipio Africanus the Elder in a Greek letter to King Philip: see POLYB. 10, 9, 3. Cf. § 46, 2.

2. VEGET. 1, 8 *compulit evolutis auctoribus ea me in hoc opusculo . . . dicere quae Cato Censorius de disciplina militari scripsit, quae Cornelius Celsus, quae Frontinus perstringenda duxerunt, quae Paternus diligentissimus iuris militaris adsertor in libros*

redegit, quae Augusti et Traiani Hadrianique constitutionibus cauta sunt. ib. 2, 3 *Cato ille maior . . . se reip. credidit profuturum si disciplinam militarem conferret in litteras . . . idem fecerunt alii complures, sed praecipue Frontinus, divo Traiano ab eius modi comprobatus industria.* Laur. Lyd. de magistr. 1, 47 μάρτυρες Κέλσος τε καὶ Πάτερνος καὶ Κατιλίνας (οὐχ ὁ συνωμότης, ἀλλ' ἕτερος), Κάτων πρὸ αὐτῶν ὁ πρῶτος, καὶ Φροντῖνος, μεθ' οὓς καὶ Ῥενάτος (Vegetius), Ῥωμαῖοι πάντες.

3. From Vegetius is copied the little book de vocabulis rei militaris ad Tacitum Aug. by the soi-disant Modestus (cf. n. 4) composed in the 15th century by Pomponius Laetus (or one of his pupils), together with whose work de magistratibus (and de legibus) it was originally brought out (anonymously). Peyron, notitia libr. bibl. Taurin. (1820) 85.

4. Vett. de re militari scriptores in unum redacti corpus, Wesel 1617. We find besides Frontinus and Modestus (n. 3.) printed in earlier editions of Vegetius, e.g. by Stewechius (Antv. 1585) and PScriverius (Antv. 1607).—MJähns, d. röm. Militärliteratur, Grenzboten 1878 Nr. 38.

57. In the department of Architecture, even in the Republican period, a literature was commenced by Fuficius, Varro and P. Septimius. Only the work of Vitruvius de architectura belonging to the Augustan period has been preserved.

1. Vitruv. 7, praef. 14 *animadverti in ea re ab Graecis volumina plura edita, ab nostris oppido quam pauca. Fuficius enim mirum de his rebus ni primus instituit edere volumen, item Terentius Varro de novem disciplinis* (see below § 166, 6, a) *unum de architectura, P. Septimius duo.* As architects of whom no written works are known to him, he mentions ib. 17 Cossutius and C. Mucius. Cf. CPromis, gli architetti e l'architettura presso i Romani (Mem. d. Turin. Akad. Ser. II, t. 27. 1873). AChoisy, rev. archéol. 28 (1874), 263.

2. Vitruv. 1, 1, 3 requires of the architect *ut litteratus sit, peritus graphidos, eruditus geometria, historias complures noverit, philosophos diligenter audierit, musicam scierit, medicinae non sit ignarus, responsa iurisconsultorum noverit, astrologiam caelique rationes cognitas habeat.*

3. Vitruv. 5, 1 *non de architectura sic scribitur ut historia aut poemata. . . . vocabula ex artis propria necessitate concepta inconsueto sermone obiciunt sensibus obscuritatem.*

58. The science of land-measurement, which at an early time became indispensable to the Romans for the purpose of encampments and for the distribution of land in lots, was, so far as we know, first treated independently by Varro. On account of the military colonies and the survey of the Empire under Augustus, the importance of the art of measuring the land was so increased that schools were instituted exclusively for this in the Imperial period, and a peculiar kind of literature, half mathematical and half juridical, was formed, extending from the first century after Christ to the sixth. The oldest of these literary land-measurers (gromatici, agrimensores) is Frontinus, whose

work was in the 5th century commented on by Aggenus Urbicus. Under Trajan, Balbus wrote his expositio; to the same reign belongs Hyginus, a little later is Siculus Flaccus. But M. Junius Nipsus, Innocentius, and others whose Latin is partly barbarous, belong perhaps to the 5th century. Many works of Boethius concerning these subjects are of doubtful authenticity. Other works again are anonymous.

1. Caesar summoned astronomers and geometers from Alexandria to Rome, and by them the works of Hero were introduced into Roman literature. With but unimportant exceptions all the formulas, calculations and arrangements for surveying land which are to be found in Roman authors can be traced back to passages in those works which have been handed down to us as written by Hero. MCantor, Agrimens. 86. Connection of the art of surveying with ecclesiastical affairs, see HNissen, Templum (Berl. 1869), 11; with jurisprudence, cf. Cic. Mur. 22. Cf. also Mart. 10, 17, 5 *mensorum longis . . . vacat ille libellis.*

2. Ps.-Boeth. Schrr. d. röm. Feldmesser 1, 403 *nomina agrimensorum: Igeni* (Hygini), *Iuli Frontini, Siculi Flacci, Ageni Urbici, Marci Iuni Nipsi, Balbi mensoris, Cassi Longini, Igini, Euclidis.* Extracts are also extant *ex libris Dolabellae, ex libris Latini* (also called *Latinus Togatus*), *ex libris Magonis et Vegoiae auctorum* (cf. p. 350 Lachm. *idem Vegoiae Arrunti Veltymno;* cf. § 77 and Müller's Etr. 2^2, 31. 312. 560. Nissen l.l. 10); also fragments of Faustus, Gaius, Innocentius (§ 447, 2), Mysrontius (? Dyspontius), Valerius, Vitalis.

3. The chief MS. is Arcerianus s. VI/VII in Wolfenbüttel.—Collections: by GGoesius (Rei agrariae auctores legesque, Amst. 1674), but especially: Die Schriften der röm. Feldmesser herausgg. u. erläutert von FBlume, KLachmann, ThMommsen u. ARudorff, Berl. 1848. 52 II.

4. Paul. Festi 96 *groma* (from *gnorma?* see FHultsch, JJ. 113, 767) *appellatur genus machinolae cuiusdam quo regiones agri cuiusque cognosci possunt, quod genus Graeci γνώμονα dicunt.* A gauging instrument therefore. Cf. in general Mommsen, Schr. d. röm. Feldm. 2, 174, WRein and EWölfflin, PRE. 1^2, 594, FHultsch in Ersch and Gruber's Enc. 1, 92, 97, MCantor, d. röm. Agrimensoren, Lpz. 1875, EStöber, d. röm. Grundsteuervermessungen nach d. lat. Text des gromat. Cod. insbes. des Hyg. Frontin. u. Nipsus, Münch. 1877, GRossi, groma e squadro ovvero storia dell' agrimensura italiana, Rome 1877. PdeTissot, les agrimensores dans l'anc. Rome, Par. 1879.

5. On the popular constituents in the language of the gromatici see AFPott, ZfAW. 1854, 219.

59. Weights and measures were first treated independently, sometimes in metrical form, in the Imperial period.

1. Metrologicorum scriptorum reliquiae; coll. rec. partim nunc primum ed. FHultsch. Vol. 2 (scriptores romani) Lps. 1866.

60. Geography was among the Romans first separately treated by Varro the polyhistor, next, probably, by Cornelius Nepos, but generally only as an addition or appendix to history,

the subject and its treatment remaining dependent on the Greeks except so far as individual knowledge added to their materials, as in Cato's Origines, in Caesar, and in Sallust. Some also described their travels and what they themselves had seen, e.g. Trebius Niger, Statius Sebosus, Turranius Gracilis. Under Augustus, Agrippa planned a large map of the world accompanied with explanations, and after his death this was actually executed and exhibited in a public hall in Rome. The careful, and in its way critical, labour of Pomponius Mela followed soon afterwards. Many continued to make separate contributions from their own observations, e.g. Seneca in his writings on (India and) Egypt, Corbulo and Mucianus on the East, Suetonius Paulinus for Africa, and on Germany (besides L. Vetus and Pliny) and Britain Tacitus' Germania and his Agricola. The geography of Pliny the Elder in books III to VI of his Natural History was more comprehensive. Seneca's Quaestiones naturales contain a kind of mathematical and physical geography, but no Roman after Pliny undertook any complete geographical work. Pliny's work was epitomised about Hadrian's time and enlarged with notices from other sources, and from this Solinus, in the 3rd century A.D., made his abridgment. Again in the 3rd century Iulius Titianus the Elder wrote his chorography. In the 4th century we have the geographical didactic poems of Avienus (orbis terrae and ora maritima) and Ausonius' Mosella. At the beginning of the 5th century Rutilius Namatianus wrote his Itinerarium (de reditu suo) in elegiac metre; about the same time (or at the end of the 4th century) Vibius Sequester wrote his schoolbook on the geographical names occurring in the standard poets. Of the same description is the compilation (in connection with a map) from the cosmography of the orator Julius Honorius. The cosmography current under the name of Aethicus Ister belongs to the middle of the 7th century; the work of the so-called Geographus of Ravenna to the end of the same century. Lists of the roads, stations and distances are found in the Itineraria, of which we have several in the 4th century, the It. Antonini, the It. Hierosolymitanum (from Burdigala to Jerusalem), and the It. Alexandri. The original of Peutinger's map may probably have belonged to the middle of the 3rd Christian century, and is indirectly founded on Agrippa's work. Frontinus' work de aquis urbis Romae (at the end of the 1st century) is limited to the narrow circle of the metropolis, as well as the Index of the regiones of Rome in the

4th century, which exists in two texts (Notitia regionum and Curiosum urbis).

1. Geographi lat. minores; coll. rec. proleg. instr. ARiese, Frankf. 1878. FUkert, Geographie der Griech. u. Röm. esp. 1, 1, Gotha 1816. EHBunbury, hist. of geography among the Greeks and Romans, Lond. 1879 II. HKiepert, Lehrb. d. alt. Geogr. (Berl. 1878), 7 sqq. HNissen, ital. Landeskunde 1, 17.

2. Maps, plans of towns, travelling maps, map of the island of Sardinia a. 580/174 dedicated in the temple of Mater Matuta: Liv. 41, 28. Varro RR. 1, 2, 1 *spectantes in pariete pictam Italiam.* Propert. 5, 3, 37. Agrippa's map of the World: § 220, 12. Auson. grat. act. 3, 9 p. 21 sch.: *ut qui terrarum orbem unius tabulae ambitu circumscribunt, aliquanto detrimento magnitudinis, nullo dispendio veritatis.* Eumen. pro restit. schol. 20 (see below § 220, 12). On the Peutingerian road and travelling map: § 412, 6.—Mommsen, Ber. d. sächs. Ges. d. Wiss. 3 (1851), 99.—The so-called Capitoline plan of the town in the beginning of the third century after Christ, engraved on marble, preserved in a fragmentary condition; best represented in HJordan's Forma Urbis Romae, Berl. 1874.

B. SPECIAL AND PERSONAL PART.

I.

THE EARLY HISTORY OF ROMAN LITERATURE.

To the Year u.c. 514. b.c. 240.

61. All written compositions in the oldest time exceeding the limits of mere registers had a certain rhythmical form, and were therefore carmina.

1. Carmen (old *casmen*, related to *Casmena* [*Cămena*], *Carmenta* and cognates) e.g. Liv. 1, 24. 26 (*lex horrendi carminis*). 32. 3, 64 (*rogationis carmen*). 10, 38 (an oath). 41. 39, 15 (*sollemne carmen precationis quod praefari magistratus solent*). Cic. Mur. 26 (*praetor ne . . . aliquid ipse sua sponte loqueretur ei quoque carmen compositum est*). leg. 2, 59 (XII tabb.). de or. 1, 245. Macrob. 3, 9, 6 sqq. (*carmen quo di evocantur*). Sen. cons. ad Marc. 13, 1 (*sollemnia pontificalis carminis verba*). Ritschl, opusc. 4, 298. HDüntzer, ZfGW. 11, 2. 12, 526 (cf. Phil. 28, 242). ORibbeck, JJ. 77, 201. HJordan, krit. Beitr. z. Gesch. d. lat. Spr. 167. EBährens, JJ. 135, 65.—Such a rhythmical system (in series, each containg four arses), often supported by alliteration, is shown e.g. in the very ancient farmer's prayer in Cato RR. 141 etc. RWestphal, Metr. d. Gr. 2^2, 36. JHuemer, älteste lat.-christl. Rhythmen 3. RPeter, de Rom. precationum carminibus in the Commentt. phil. in hon. Reifferscheidii, Bresl. 1884, 67. Cf. § 85.

2. WCorssen, origines poesis rom., Berl. 1846. RWestphal, d. älteste Form der röm. Poesie, Tüb. 1852. HNettleship, on the earliest Italian literature, in his lectures 45.—JWordsworth, Fragments and specimens of early Latin (down to Varro inclusively) with introductions and notes, Oxford 1874. FDAllen, Remnants of early Latin, Boston 1880.

62. The old Roman kind of rhythm is denoted by the name of saturnian, i.e. old Italian, verse. A division into two halves is its prominent feature. Further the accent (high-tone) seems to be of principal importance. Of the arses marked thereby there are three in each half of the verse, while the thesis may be suppressed and the avoidance of hiatus is not yet recognised. The thesis may be disyllabic. The loose structure of these lines is strengthened by alliteration. Another theory regards the verse as quantitative, determines its character from the point of view

of prosody in connection with the oldest scenic poets, and thus requires for the arses either one long or two short syllables, and assumes the following specimen of a saturnian:

˘ ´ ˘ – ˘ ´ ⏓ | ´ ˘ – ˘ ´ ⏓

Malum dabúnt Metélli Naévio poétae.

The saturnian verse was supplanted by the Greek metres of the scenic poets and Ennius, but survived for a long time in popular poetry; at Rome it seems to have gone out of use even sooner than elsewhere.

1. VARRO LL. 7, 36 *Fauni dei Latinorum . . .: hos versibus, quos vocant Saturnios, in silvestribus locis traditum est solitos fari futura* (cf. FEST. 225). MAR. VICT. GL. 6, 138 *versus cui prisca apud Latium aetas tamquam Italo et indigenae Saturnio sive Faunio nomen dedit.*

2. SERV. Verg. G. 2, 385 '*versibus incomptis ludunt*': *id est carminibus saturnio metro compositis; quod ad rhythmum solum vulgares componere consueverunt.* Cf. TEUFFEL, JJ. 77, 281. Opinion of NIEBUHR, KFHERMANN (Kulturgesch. 2, 57), RWESTPHAL (Griech. Metr. 2², 36; Gött. gel. Anz. 1884, 340); recently repeatedly combated: OKELLER, d. saturn. Vers als rhythmisch erwiesen, Prag 1883. 86 II. FRAMORINO, riv. fil. 1883, 425. RTHURNEYSEN, d. Saturnier u. s. Verh. zur spät. Volkspoesie, Halle 1885. HGLEDITSCH in IwMüller's Handb. 2, 577.—If so, the later popular songs would be a mere revival of the original prosody, long suppressed by art-poetry (see however WMEYER, rhythmische Dicht., Abhh. d. Münchn. Ak. 17, 269). Altogether the saturnian, when so viewed, forms a homogeneous link in the history of Indo-European popular poetry (see § 61, 1). Cf. WESTPHAL, l.l. 35. KBARTSCH, d. saturn. Vers u. d. altdeutsche Langzeile, Lpz. 1867. FALLEN, Zfvgl. Sprachf. 24, 572.

3. Quantitative theory. The later theories of metre seek to rank the saturnian verse entirely with the Greek metrical system. CAES. BASS. GL. 6, 265 *(saturnium) nostri existimaverunt proprium esse italicae regionis, sed falluntur. a Graecis enim varie et multis modis tractatus est . . . nostri autem antiqui, ut vere dicam quod apparet, usi sunt eo non observata lege nec uno genere custodito ut inter se consentiant versus, sed praeterquam quod durissimos fecerunt etiam alios breviores, alios longiores inseruerunt ut vix invenerim apud Naevium quos pro exemplo ponerem . . . optimus est quem Metelli proposuerunt de Naevio . . . 'Malum dabunt Metelli Naevio poetae'. hic enim saturnius constat ex hipponactei quadrati iambici posteriore commate et phallico metro.* CHARISIUS de versu saturnio: § 419, 4. The quantitative theory is represented by GHERMANN (Metrik § 525), KLACHMANN ('der Urheber der Bemerkungen in s. Bruders Abhh. de fontt. Liv. 1, 73. 2; de die Alliensi thes. 11, wie er mir selbst gesagt hat' MHERTZ), KOMÜLLER (ad Fest. p. 396), FRITSCHL (opusc. 4, 83 and elsewhere) and the scholars named further on in this note. Limitations and corrections of Ritschl's theory: FBÜCHELER JJ. 87, 330. ASPENGEL, Phil. 23, 81. THKORSCH, de versu Sat., Moscow 1868. The permanent benefit of Ritschl's researches has been to establish that the enquiry must start from the saturnians of the inscriptions (collected e.g. in BÜCHELER's anthol. epigr. lat. 3 [Bonn 1876], p. 3–11 and in HAVET l.l. The saturnians of Andronicus and Naevius are (notwithstanding LMüller's argument to the contrary) of secondary importance. But the single metrical form employed by a nation still without literary culture cannot have been tied down by a variety of

artificial and difficult rules, which could not be apprehended by the unaided ear. —LHavet, de saturnio Latinorum versu. inest reliquiarum quotquot supersunt sylloge, Par. 1880. LMüller, d. saturn. Vers u. s. Denkmäler, Lpz. 1885. E Bahrens, FPR. 6. 19. HUsener, altgriech. Versbau, Bonn 1887, 77.

4. Popular employment of this metre, detached examples in inscriptions etc. down to the middle of the 7th cent. u.c. Saturnians are frequently discernible in records preserved by the historians. Caes. Bass. GL. 6, 265 *in tabulis antiquis quas triumphaturi duces in Capitolio figebant.* Festus 162 s. v. navali corona. Caes. Bass. GL. 6, 265. Livius 40, 52 (a. 575/179). 41, 28 (a. 580/174). Schol. Bob. to Cic. Arch. p. 359 Or. (a. 620/134). Cf. § 83. 85. 90, 5. 115 and 163, 7. Saturnians are perhaps also to be found in Varro's Menippean satires, see LMüller, d. saturn. Vers 151.—Bücheler, JJ. 77, 61. Teuffel, ib. 281. WFröhner, Phil. 13, 208. EBährens, JJ. 129, 837. Among the Oscans and Paelignians the saturnian was also, according to the evidence of the inscriptions, the national metre. Cf. Bücheler, RhM. 30, 441. 33, 274. SBugge, altital. Studien (Christiania 1878) 83. This was likewise the case among the Umbrians, as appears from the assonances in the Igubine tables. See GFGrotefend, PRE. 4, 99. Westphal, älteste röm. Poesie 57; Metr. 2^2, 37. Concerning the alliteration in the saturnian see HJordan, krit. Beitr. z. Gesch. d. lat. Spr. 175. More on this subject § 93, 1.

63. As regards their subjects the monuments and compositions of the oldest time are chiefly practical; they partly relate to ritual, partly to political and historical matters, some being of a private, others of a public character. After the 4th century u.c. Law also gains some significance in literature.

From the year 390/364 there was a permanent stage in Rome; see § 6, 3. FDGerlach, griechischer Einfluss in Rom im 5. Jahrh. d. St., Bas. 1872.

a) Concerning Rites.

64. At the vernal festivals of the Salii in March these priests, during their processions, used to sing old ritual songs (axamenta) in honour of Mars and Quirinus, which had become unintelligible as early as the middle of the 7th century u.c. and were then accordingly annotated; the faithful preservation of these songs justifies the conclusion that they were committed to writing at an early time.

1. They are ascribed to Numa: Varro LL. 7, 3. Cic. de or. 3, 197. Hor. E. 2, 1, 86. Liv. 1, 20. Quint. 1, 10, 20. Ter. Scaur., GL. 7, 28. Diomed. GL. 1, 476. Both colleges of the Salii, the elder Palatini and the younger Collini (agonenses) had such songs. Serv. Verg. Aen. 8, 285 *duo sunt genera Saliorum, sicut in Saliaribus carminibus invenitur.* In gen. Marquardt, Staatsverw. 3^2, 427. Preller, röm. Mythol. 1^2, 355.

2. Quint. 1, 10, 20 *versus quoque Saliorum habent carmen.* Delivery of the songs *cum tripudiis sollemnique saltatu* Liv. 1, 20, 4; cf. Hor. C. 4, 1, 28.—Their obscurity, Hor. l.l. Quint. 1, 6, 40 *Saliorum carmina vix sacerdotibus suis satis intellecta: sed illa mutari vetat religio et consecratis utendum est.* Hence the commentary of L. Aelius Stilo (Varro LL. 7, 2. Fest. 141. 146. 210. 239), whereas that

of Sabidius (Schol. Veron. to Aen. 10, 241) rests only on Mai's arbitrary assumption. Preference of later antiquarians, Hor. l.l. Capitolin. M. Ant. 4. Symmach. ep. 3, 44.

3. Collection and explanation of the fragments, e.g. Bergk, opusc. 1, 477. Corssen, origg. poes. rom. 43. 55. Wordsw., EL. 564. FPR. 29. Cf. HJordan, krit. Beitr. z. Gesch. der lat. Spr. 211. LHavet, de versu Sat. 243; rev. d. phil. 4, 15.

4. In the time of the decay of the old religion even the praises of princes were inserted in the songs of the Salii, e.g. of Augustus (Dio 51, 20. Mon. Anc. 2, 21 ⟨*nomenque meum senatus consulto incl*⟩ *usum est in saliare carmen*=CIL. 3, p. 790. 791), Germanicus (Tac. A. 2, 83), Drusus (Tac. A. 4, 9), Verus (Iul. Cap. M. Ant. 21, 5) and Caracalla (Spartian. Carac. 11, 6).

65. The Arvalian brotherhood, who held their annual festival with solemn sacrifices, field-processions etc. in the second half of May, a short time before the harvest, had also their unvarying ancient songs, one of which, together with the minutes of a meeting of this order in A.D. 218, has been preserved. It was recited with lively dance-like movements (tripudium) and in alternate singing.

1. Very important fragments (14–241 A.D.) of the *acta collegii fratrum Arvalium* have been frequently found since 1570 in the grove of the dea Dia (who was worshipped by this brotherhood) near the 5th milestone of the via Campana (now the Vigna Ceccarelli), especially in 1777, and again in 1866 and following years. The principal of the early works is: G. Marini, gli atti e monumenti de' fratelli arvali, Rome 1795 II. Recent: Acta fratrum Arvalium quae supersunt, restituit et illustr. GHenzen. Acc. fragmenta fastorum in luco Arval. effossa, Berl. 1874 and CIL. 6, 2023 sqq. In addition to these other finds e.g. Ephem. epigr. 2, 211; bull. arch. 1882, 72. 201. 1883, 110; bull. di commiss. arch. di Roma 12, 4. 14, 361 Selection in Wilmanns 2870 sqq. Cf. in general Marquardt, röm. Staatsverw 3^2, 447. ThBirt in Roscher's Lex. d. Myth. 1, 970.

2. In the record of the year 218 (CIL. 6. 2104; cf. ib. 1, 28. Wilm. 2879. DIE. 392) we read: *Ibi sacerdotes clusi succincti libellis* (text-books) *acceptis carmen descindentes* (Weissbrodt, obss. in S. C. de Bacc. 31) *tripodaverunt in verba haec.* Here follows the text of the song. Facsimile of the same in Ritschl, PLM. Tf. 36 (also Jordan l.l. 192). Recent treatises concerning the chant: FBücheler, ind. schol., Bonn 1876, 3. LHavet, de versu Sat., Par. 1880, 218. HJordan, krit. Beitr. z. Gesch. d. lat. Spr. 189. MBréal, rev. crit. 1880, 123; mém. de la soc. de linguist. 4 (1881), 373. GÉdon, restit. et interpret. du chant des fr. Arv., Par. 1882; nouv. étude sur le chant Lémural (!), les fr. Arv. etc., Par. 1884. CPauli, altiatl. Studd 4 (1881), 1. LMüller, d. saturn. Vers 99.

66. 67. It may be safely assumed that other sacerdotal bodies also had their old hymns and litanies. There existed also ancient maxims and prophecies in saturnian metre, attributed by popular opinion to Faunus, Carmentis and others, many of which were collected at an early date, though far more were interpolated and forged.

1. ENNIUS ann. v. 222 V. *versibus quos olim Fauni vatesque canebant. vates* means a priestly singer (as opposed to *poeta*, the artistic poet): the origin of the word is obscure. MOMMSEN Herm. 16, 620, 4 even thinks it may be Gallic in its derivation. FEST. 325 *versus antiquissimi, quibus Faunus fata cecinisse hominibus videtur, Saturnii appellantur.* Similarly Carmentis gave ἐμμέτρους χρησμούς (PLUT. quaest. rom. 56), that is in the saturnius (VARR. LL. 7, 88). *Similiter Marcius et Publicius vates cecinisse dicuntur* (CIC. div. 1, 115). HOR. E. 2, 1, 26 *annosa volumina vatum*, and also PORPHYRIO: *veteres libros Marci vatis Sibyllaeque et similium.* Cf. FEST. 326 *ex libris sibyllinis et vaticinio Marci vatis.* CORSSEN, origg. 6. 162.

2. Marcius (CIC. l.l. LIV. 25, 12 and MHERTZ on that passage and JJ. 109, 268; MACR. sat. 1, 17. PLIN. NH. 7, 119. PORPHYR. l.l.; cf. FEST. 165: *in carmine Cn. Marcii*) lived some time (uncertain how long) before the second Punic war (*vates hic Marcius illustris fuerat* etc. LIV. l.l.). Several of this name are mentioned by CIC. div. 1, 89 (*Marcii fratres, nobili loco nati*). 2, 113 (*nec Publicio nescio cui, nec Marciis vatibus*). SERV. Aen. 6, 70. SYMMACH. ep. 4, 34 *Marciorum vatum divinatio caducis corticibus inculcata est.* Cf. § 84, 2. Reconstruction in saturnians of the specimens in LIVY l.l. by WESTPHAL, Form d. ält. röm. Poesie 58. But there are unmistakeable instances of the hexameter rhythm, and accordingly we must assume either a later recasting in hexameters (RIBBECK, JJ. 77, 204) or corruption (BÄHRENS FPR. 21). ISID. or. 6, 8, 12 (an improbable statement) *apud Latinos Marcius vates primus praecepta composuit, ex quibus est illud 'postremus dicas, primus taceas.'* Cf. WORDSW. EL. 288. FPR. 36. 294.

B) POLITICAL AND HISTORICAL DOCUMENTS.

68. The following treaties of alliance are mentioned in the Regal period: 1) the apocryphal treaty of Romulus with the Veientines of 100 years' duration; 2) Tullus Hostilius' treaty with the Sabines; 3) Servius Tullius' treaty with the Latins; 4) Tarquinius' (Superbus?) peace with Gabii.

1. DIONYS. antiq. 2, 55 στήλαις ἐνεχάραξε τὰς ὁμολογίας, according to Greek custom. — 2. DIONYS. 3. 33 στήλας ἀντιγράφους θέντες, cf. Hor. E. 2, 1, 24 sq.

3. DIONYS. 4. 26 στήλην κατασκευάσας χαλκῆν ἔγραψεν ἐν ταύτῃ etc., and it was γραμμάτων χαρακτῆρας ἑλληνικῶν, οἷς τὸ παλαιὸν ἡ Ἑλλὰς ἐχρᾶτο. Historical? cf. MOMMSEN, RG. 1[6], 216. IHNE RG. 1, 58. DETLEFSEN, Phil. 20, 448.—4. It was written on the hide of the ox then sacrificed, γράμμασιν ἀρχαϊκοῖς, and preserved in the temple of Sancus, DIONYS. 4, 58. Cf. PAUL. Festi 56. HOR. l.l. Mommsen is against connecting it with Tarquinius Superbus, RG. 1[6], 216. See also SCHWEGLER, RG. 1, 18. 21. 37. 43. 789.

69. In the oldest time of the Republic we find 1) the document comprising the maritime and commercial treaty with Carthage, supposed to date from a. U.C. 245/B.C. 509 the first year of the Republic; 2) the treaty with king Porsena; 3) the treaty of alliance with the Latins dating 261/493; 4) the Foedus Ardeatinum in the year 310/444. To these we may add 5) the

lex tribunicia prima of the year 261/493 and 6) the lex Icilia de Aventino publicando, of the year 298/456.

1. POLYB. 3. 22 *διαθῆκαι . . . ἃς καθ' ὅσον ἦν δυνατὸν ἀκριβέστατα διερμηνεύσαντες ἡμεῖς ὑπογεγράφαμεν. τηλικαύτη γὰρ ἡ διαφορὰ γέγονε τῆς διαλέκτου καὶ παρὰ Ῥωμαίοις τῆς νῦν πρὸς τὴν ἀρχαίαν ὥστε τοὺς συνετωτάτους ἔνια μόλις ἐξ ἐπιστάσεως διευκρινεῖν.* This frequently controverted statement of Polybios has been more and more confirmed by the inscriptions found in recent years, of which some date back to the 3rd cent. B.C. (§ 83).

2. PLIN. NH. 34, 139 *in foedere quod expulsis regibus populo rom. dedit Porsena nominatim comprehensum invenimus ne ferro nisi in agri cultu uteretur.*—3. CIC. Balb. 23, 53 *foedus . . . quod quidem nuper in columna ahenea meminimus post rostra incisum et perscriptum fuisse.* Cf. LIV. 2, 33. FEST. 166. DIONYS. 6, 95. MOMMSEN, Herm. 5, 231.—4. LIV. 4, 7. MOMMSEN, röm. Chronol.[2] 93.—5. FEST. 318, 30.—6. LIV. 3, 31. DIONYS. 10, 32. SCHWEGLER, RG. 2, 395.

70. The so-called leges regiae, supposed to be decrees and decisions of the Roman kings, and which partly affect an antique diction and are of a religious character, in reality represent traditional laws of a very high age, which were not, however, written down till a later time and were then arbitrarily assigned to single kings.

1. HEDIRKSEN, Versuche z. Krit. u. Ausleg. d. Quellen d. röm. Rechts (1823) 234. SCHWEGLER, RG. 1, 23. 572. 664. GBRUNS, fontes iur.[5] 1 sq. WORDSW., EL. 253. MOMMSEN, Staatsr. 2, 40. MVOIGT, d. leges regiae, Lpz. 1876. 77 II (Abh. d. sächs. Ges. d. Wiss. 7, 555. 643).

71. The collection of these supposed leges regiae was after its author called ius Papirianum. As the oldest ius civile coincides with the ius sacrum, the contents of that collection, with regard to some decrees in it, might to a certain degree be described as ius civile, but more strictly it consisted of sacerdotal rules. The collection seems never to have received an official sanction.

1. POMPON. dig. 1, 2, 2, § 2 *quae omnes (leges regiae) conscriptae exstant in libro Sextii Papirii, qui fuit illis temporibus quibus Superbus . . . is liber appellatur ius civile Papirianum . . . quod (Papirius) leges sine ordine latas in unum composuit.* ib. § 36 *fuit in primis peritus (iuris) P. Papirius, qui leges regias in unum contulit.* DIONYS. 3, 36 *αἱ περὶ τῶν ἱερῶν διαγραφαὶ (ἃς Πομπίλιος συνεστήσατο) μετὰ τὴν ἐκβολὴν τῶν βασιλέων εἰς ἀναγραφὴν δημοσίαν αὖθις ἤχθησαν ὑπ' ἀνδρὸς ἱεροφάντου Γαΐου Παπιρίου* etc. Cf. ib. 3, 70, 1. On the uncertainty respecting the personality and date of Pap. see SCHWEGLER, RG. 1, 24. Cf. OCLASON, JJ. 103, 719. Granius Flaccus' (§ 199, 7) *liber de iure Papiriano* is quoted by PAULUS dig. 50, 16, 144. Cf. WREIN, PRE. 4. 660. RSCHÖLL, XII tabb. 51. MVOIGT (see § 70, 1) p. 670.

72. The commentarii regum, though wrongly professing to be works of the kings themselves, seem to have contained de-

crees concerning the kingly privileges and functions, very ancient as to the facts themselves, and written down and collected in historical time.

1. Cic. p. Rab. p. r. 15 *ex annalium monumentis atque ex regum commentariis.* We find special mention of *commentarii Numae* (Liv. 1, 31) which Ancus Martius *in album elata proponere in publico iubet* (Liv. 1, 32, cf. Dionys. 3, 36). Ὑπομνήματα Νουμᾶ (Plut. Marcell. 8)=*libri Numae* (Piso ap. Plin. NH. 28, 14)=*leges Numae* (Serv. Aen. 6, 860)=*lex Pompilii regis in Pontificum libris* (Fest. p. 189). Cf. § 71, 1. So also *commentarii Servii Tullii* (Liv. 1, 60)=*discriptio classium* and *centuriarum* (Fest. 246. 249), and in its contents also=*censoriae tabulae* (Cic. orat. 156). Schwegler, RG. 1, 27; cf. 545. Mommsen, Staatsrecht 2, 10. MVoigt l. l. 647.

2. The books of Numa on religious and philosophical subjects, discovered a. 573/181, for which Piso and Hemina are the earliest authorities and which must be due to a forgery or mystification, are of a different character; this is the earliest example we have of such pretended 'finds' (ERohde gr. Roman 272, 2). Varro (de cultu deorum) ap. Augustin. civ. dei 7, 34. Liv. 40, 29. Plin. NH. 13, 84. EvLasaulx (on the books of king Numa) in his Studd. d. klass. Altert., Regensb. 1854, 92 and to the contrary Schwegler, RG. 1, 564

73. The priests made the most extensive use of writing; they framed rules for religious worship and ritual, made compilations of the rulings of the priestly colleges on cases, sacerdotal or administrative, which might serve as precedents for future occasions (libri and commentarii pontificum), and kept records of their meetings (acta, § 77).

1. Vague citations (*pontifices dicunt, docent, apud p. legimus* etc.) Varro LL. 5, 23. Colum. 2, 21, 5. Macr. sat. 3. 20, 2.—Val. Prob. GL. 4, 271 *in legibus publicis pontificumque monumentis.*

2. *Pontificum libri*, Cic. de or. 1, 193. Hor. E. 2, 1, 26. Fest. 189 *testimonio esse libros pontificum, in quibus sit* etc. Macr. sat. 1, 12, 21.—*pontificii libri*, Varr. LL. 5, 98. Cic. rep. 2, 54; cf. ND. 1, 84. Fest. 356.—*pontificales libri*, Sen. ep. 108, 31. Serv. Verg. Ecl. 5, 66. G. 1, 21. A. 12, 603; cf. Lyd. mens. 4, 20.—*libri sacri*, Serv. G. 1, 272. *libri sacrorum*, Fest. 141.—*commentarii sacrorum* (*pontificalium*), Fest. 165. 286. 360.—*commentarii pontificum*, Cic. Brut. 55. de dom. 136. Liv. 4, 3. 6, 1. Plin. NH. 18, 14. Quint. 8, 2, 12.—ἱεροφαντῶν γραφαί, Dionys. 8, 56. ἱεραὶ δέλτοι, ib. 1, 73. ἱεραὶ βίβλοι, ib. 10, 1.—The *indigitamenta* ('formulas used in invocation' see Corssen, de Volscorum ling., Naumb. 1858, 19), were in the keeping of the Pontifices, i.e. *pontificales libri*, Serv. G. 1. 21.—Were the *sacra Argeorum* mentioned by *Varro* LL. 5, 45 derived from the *libri pontificii?* See HJordan, röm. Topogr. 2, 237. 599.

3. Ambrosch, *de sacris Rom. libris*, Part I, Bresl. 1840 and d. Religionsbücher d. Röm., Bonn 1843 (Z. f. Kath. Theol.). Schwegler RG. 1, 31. ELübbert, quaest. pontificales, Berl. 1859, 79. EHübner, JJ. 79, 407. MVoigt (§ 70, 1) p. 648. AReifferscheid, JB. 1880 3, 274. PPreibisch, de libris pontificiis, Bresl. 1874; fragmenta libr. pontificiorum, Tilsit 1878.

74. The Pontifices, who possessed the art of keeping account of the time, arranged also the fasti, i.e. a list of the days for 'awards' or the administration of the law (dies agendi, dies fasti), this being part of the table of each month (Kalendarium), enumerating also the feasts, games, markets, sacrifices etc. falling on each day, to which were gradually joined first the anniversaries of disasters, and then other short notices of historical events, as well as observations on the rising of certain constellations. After these fasti had been made public (§ 88), private persons also undertook the compilation of fasti in the shape of tables or books, and they became the subjects of learned discussions. After the introduction of the Julian era (709/45) these publications became again official, and were made by the Emperor in his quality of pontifex maximus. We possess a number of fragments of calendars which were engraved or written (painted) at Rome and in neighbouring Italian towns, and which extend from the 8th century U.C. to the time of Claudius (from a. 723/31 B.C. to 804/51 A.D.). When the new chronology had become sufficiently familiar, the industry of private persons found there a new field. There are still two complete calendars in existence, an official one of the 4th century written by Furius Dionysius Philocalus A.D. 354, and a Christian revision of the official calendar, composed by Polemius Silvius (A.D. 448 sq.).

1. VARRO LL. 6, 29 *dies fasti per quos praetoribus omnia verba sine piaculo licet fari. . . contrarii horum vocantur dies nefasti, per quos dies nefas fari praetorem 'do dico addico,' itaque non potest agi.* Cf. ib. 6, 53. OVID. fast. 1, 48. LIV. 1, 19 *idem* (Numa) *nefastos dies fastosque fecit.* Cf. CIL. 1, p. 361.—SUET. Iul. 40 *fastos correxit, iam pridem vitio pontificum per intercalandi licentiam turbatos* = introduction of the Julian era; cf. Aug. 31. CAPIT. M. Antonin. 10 *fastis dies iudiciarios addidit.*—PETRON. 30 *altera tabula in poste triclinii praefixa habebat inscriptum lunae cursum stellarumque septem imagines pictas, et qui dies boni quique incommodi essent distinguente bulla notabantur.*—CIC. Phil. 2, 87 *adscribi iussit in fastis ad Lupercalia: C. Caesari . . . M. Antonium . . . regnum detulisse, Caesarem uti noluisse.* On Domitian's accession a committee of the senate was appointed *qui fastos adulatione temporum foedatos exonerarent,* TAC. H. 4, 40. Cf. CIL. 1, p. 377[b].

2. *Fulvius Nobilior* (§ 126, 1) *in fastis quos in aede Herculis Musarum* (a. 565/189) *posuit,* MACR. sat. 1, 12; cf. 13 extr. VARRO LL. 6, 33. CENSORIN. d. n. 20. 22. CHARIS. GL. 1, 138. Together with the announcements of the days and festivals they also gave explanations.

3. SUET. gramm. 17 *Verrius Flaccus statuam habet Praeneste, in inferiore (superiore) fori parte, circa hemicyclium in quo fastos a se ordinatos et marmoreo parieti incisos publicarat.* Remains of these fasti were found in 1771, not indeed in the forum of Praeneste, but more than 3 km. from the town, in the ruins of a Christian building belonging to a late period. HENZEN, bull. archeol. 1864, 70.—

Best edited in CIL. 1, p. 311. Cf. Bergk, JJ. 105, 37. Against the doubt of OHirschfeld (Herm. 9, 103) as to whether these fasti praenestini are an original work of Verrius, see Vahlen, ind. schol. Berol. 1877/78 p. 5.

4. Works entitled 'fasti' (Fest. 87, 19. Ovid. fast. 1, 657) were written by Junius Gracchanus, Cincius, Ovid (regarding calendars drawn from Ovid's fasti: § 249, 6), Nisus, Masurius Sabinus, Julius Modestus (de feriis), Cornelius Labeo etc. Festus 67. Macrob. sat. 1, 11, 50. Merkel's pref. to his edition of Ovid's Fasti p. liii. Mommsen, CIL. 1, p. 363.—Astronomical fasti of Clodius Tuscus § 263, 5.

5. The best collection of epigraphic fasti (hemerologia and menologia) is by Mommsen, CIL. 1, p. 293–360 (with archaeological commentarii, ib. p. 361–412). Additions: Ephem. epigr. e.g. 1, 33. 3, 5. 85. 4, 1.—The fasti of the city of Rome also CIL. 6, p. 625. Cf. Mommsen, Röm. Chronol. [2] 208. The Roman calendar of festivals is presented comprehensively, from inscriptional and literary sources, in JMarquardt's röm. Staatsverw. 3^2, 567.

6. Only the parts written in capitals in the calendars engraved on stone belong to the oldest Roman calendar, originally perhaps a part of the XII tables; all additions in small writing are later. Mommsen, RhM. 14, 82. 85; CIL. 1, p. 361 sq. The excerpts from the official calendar in those now extant are arbitrary and betray ignorance. Mommsen CIL. 1, p. 363^b.

7. On the Mons Albanus near Rome in the ruins of the temple of Juppiter Latiaris have been found remains of the annual tables of the Feriae Latinae (dating from 303/451 B.C. to 109 A.D.; now collected CIL. 6, p. 455. Cf. Mommsen, röm. Forsch. 2, 97. DeRossi, eph. epigr. 2, 93.—List of the festivals of the temple of Augustus at Cumae: CIL. 1, p. 310; Mommsen. Herm. 17, 631.

8. The official calendar in the middle of the 4th century of the Christian era was in the year 354 copied by the calligrapher Furius Dionysius Philocalus (§ 422, 2), who illustrated it with numerous pictures (published by Strzygowski, Jahrb. d. deutschen arch. Inst., Suppl. 1) and epigrams (see EBährens PLM. 1, 203). It was preserved in two copies, the one of which (Peirescianum, saec. VIII/IX) was again lost and now exists only in two copies of the 17th century (at Brussels and in the Vatican Library); of the 2nd (saec. IX), originally at Strasburg, now at Bern, only December is still extant, but at Vienna there is a complete copy of it made in 1480. The best edition is by Mommsen CIL. 1, p. 334 with his treatise on the chronicler of a. 354, in Abh. d. sächs. Ges. d. W. 1 (1850), 550, and the summary CIL. 1, p. 332.

9. The calendar of Polemius Silvius was written a. 448 sq. under Valentinian III and is addressed to the bishop Eucherius (§ 457, 6). In his Christian zeal the author has omitted all that seemed like pagan superstition, and added historical data (e.g. *nomina omnium provinciarum* of the year 385; see Seeck on the not. dign. p. 254. Riese geogr. 130) and grammatical and meteorological observations etc. of his own. It is preserved in a Brussels MS.; best edited, in correspondence with that of Philocalus, by Mommsen, CIL. 1, p. 335. See also his treatise on the Laterculus of Polemius Silvius, in the Abh. der sächs. Ges. d. W. 3 (1853), 231; on Cassiodorus, ibid. 8, 694, and the resumé CIL. 1, p. 333.

10. Besides these we have a rural calendar, containing the rustic business, festivals, the length of months and days etc. (menologium rusticum), in two versions, not differing materially: menol. rust. Colotianum and Vallense, edited CIL. 1, p. 358 and CIL. 6, 2305. 6.

75. From denoting lists of days and months, the name of fasti was also transferred to lists of years containing the names of the chief annual magistrates (fasti consulares), the triumphs held in each year (fasti triumphales), and the priests (fasti sacerdotales). Fragments of fasti in this sense of the word have likewise come down to us, and of these the fasti capitolini are by far the most important.

1. *Fasti* as lists esp. of magistrates, e.g. Liv. 9, 18: *in annalibus magistratuum fastisque.* Cic. Pis. 30 *hos consules fasti ulli ferre possunt?* ad Brut. 1, 15 *in fastis nomen adscribitur;* cf. Tac. A. 3, 17 *nomen fastis radere* (see Mommsen, Herm. 9, 273). Trebell. Gallien. 15 *Gallienum tyrannum in fastos publicos rettulerunt.*—Lists of consuls for convenient reference: Cic. Att. 4, 8[b], 2 *non minus longas iam in codicillorum fastis futurorum consulum paginulas habent quam factorum.*—KCichorius, de fastis consularibus antiquiss., Lpz. Stud. 9, 171.

2. The fasti capitolini (so called from the place in the Palace of the Conservatori on the Capitol which the fragments at present occupy) were a chronological list of the consuls, censors, dictators and magg. eqq. (fasti consulares in their principal contents); they were engraved about 720/34 on the outer wall of the Regia, the residence of the pontifex maximus, and separate additions were made to them, in the same place, up to about the year 766/13 A.D.: to these were added as an appendix (about the year 742/12), on neighbouring pillars, the list of triumphs, f. triumphales, more correctly acta triumphorum, then the register of ludi saeculares, terminating with those under Domitian (a. 841/88).

3. The fasti capitolini and the other fragments of consular and triumphal fasti preserved in inscriptions, belonging to the time of the Republic and of Augustus, best edited by WHenzen, CIL. 1, p. 415 (additions: Eph. epigr. 1, 42. 154. 2, 210. 3, 11. 4, 192. 253. On the Capitoline fasti cf. also OHirschfeld, Herm. 9, 93. 11, 154. Mommsen, röm. Forsch. 2, 58. BBorghesi, oeuvr. 9, 1.—Fasti of the fratres arvales from 752/2 to 790/37, containing the consuls and the praetor urb. and peregr. for each year, in the appendix to Henzen's Acta fr. Arval., Berl. 1874 and CIL. 6, 2295.—A comparative resumé of the statements of authors and the MS. and inscriptional lists of the consuls in the years 245/509 to 766/13 is given by Mommsen CIL. 1, p. 483. As a supplement to this JKlein, fasti consulares a Caesaris nece ad imp. Diocletianum, Lps. 1881.

4. The remains of the sacerdotal fasti (fasti augurum, saliorum Palatinorum, sodalium Augustalium Claudialium, sacerdotum Jovis propugnatoris etc.) of the city of Rome have been collected CIL. 6, 1976 sqq.

76. From the lists drawn up by priests and originally not intended for publication we should separate the annales pontificum, which were from the very beginning composed for publication, and also styled annales maximi, but not because they were kept by the pontifex maximus. He annually exhibited in public a white table, on which the memorable events of the year, with special mention of the prodigies (regularly mentioned from 505/249) were set down in the briefest possible manner. This was a very old custom and was observed until the 7th century U.C.

But when notes and publications of this sort by writers became more common, the official ones were discontinued. When they were collected and put into the shape of a volume, they formed a collection of 80 books. But as the place where they were kept, the official residence of the pontifex maximus (the Regia close to the temple of Vesta in the Forum), was repeatedly destroyed by fire, it follows that those parts of the collection which concerned the oldest time must have been restored from recollection and were less trustworthy, indeed the statements as to the very oldest times must have been mere fictions.

1. Paul. 126 *maximi annales appellabantur non* (?) ⟨*a*⟩ *magnitudine, sed quod eos pontifex maximus confecisset;* cf. Serv. Aen. 1, 377 (n. 2). Macr. sat. 3, 2, 17. Cic. Leg. 1, 6 *annales pontificum maximorum quibus nihil potest esse ieiunius*, and (after him) Quint. 10, 2, 7 *pontificum annales.* Cf. ὁ παρὰ τοῖς ἀρχιερεῦσι (thus Niebuhr for ἀγχιστεῦσι; deposited with the pont. max., therefore in the Regia; see § 75, 2) κείμενος πίναξ in Dionys. Hal. 1, 74. *Annales publici* in Cic. rep. 2, 28. Diomed. GL. 1, 484. The name maximi is no doubt of later origin, when there were also other annals by other authors and of less extent.

2. Serv. Aen. 1, 373 *ita annales conficiebantur: tabulam dealbatam quotannis pontifex maximus habuit, in qua praescriptis consulum nominibus et aliorum magistratuum digna memoratu notare consueverat, domi militiaeque, terra marique gesta, per singulos dies* (indicating the days [see n. 4] and in chronological order). *cuius diligentiae annuos commentarios in octoginta libros veteres rettulerunt eosque a pontificibus maximis, a quibus fiebant, annales maximos appellarunt.* Gell. 4, 5, 6 *in annalibus maximis, libro undecimo.* It is a question whether this publication in book form rendered the genuine substance of the official announcements. The few remaining fragments arouse suspicion: Bücheler, RhM. 41, 2.

3. Cic. de or. 2, 52 *ab initio rerum romanarum* (an exaggerated rhetorical phrase) *usque ad P. Mucium pontificem maximum* (c. a. 631/123 down to 640/114; see § 133, 4) *res omnes singulorum annorum mandabat litteris pontifex maximus referebatque in album et proponebat tabulam domi, potestas ut esset populo cognoscendi: ii qui etiamnunc annales maximi nominantur.* Their official character and the fact of their being designed for popular use produced intentional distortion as well as suppression of the historical truth; see HNissen, Krit. Unters. 97.

4. Cato ap. Gell. 2, 28, 6 *non lubet scribere quod in tabula apud pontificem maximum est, quotiens annona cara, quotiens lunae aut solis lumini caligo aut* ⟨*aliut*⟩ *quid obstiterit.* Cf. Cic. rep. 1, 25 *ex hoc die, quem apud Ennium et in maximis annalibus consignatum videmus, superiores solis defectiones reputatae sunt.* But the regular noting down of prodigies by the pontifices was introduced only after the year 505/249. JBernays, ges. Abh. 2, 307. OJahn's Obsequens p. XX.

5. Livy and, most likely, Dionysius do not seem to have made direct use of the ann. max.; see Schwegler RG. 1, 8, 11. Dionysius indeed says 4, 30 ἐν ταῖς ἐνιαυσίοις ἀναγραφαῖς κατὰ τὸν τεσσαρακοστὸν ἐνιαυτὸν τῆς Τυλλίου ἀρχῆς τὸν Ἀρροῦντα τετελευτηκότα παρειλήφαμεν: but these expressions may be meant to denote writers of annals; cf. 4, 7 (L. Piso Frugi ἐν ταῖς ἐνιαυσίοις πραγματείαις) and 15 (idem ἐν τῇ πρώτῃ τῶν ἐνιαυσίων ἀναγραφῶν).

6. JGHullemann, de annalibus maximis, Amsterd. 1855. EHübner, JJ. 79. 401. HPeter, hist. rom. rell. 1, viii.

77. Like the college of the pontifices, the augurs had likewise their books (libri or commentarii augurum). In the same manner there were libri Saliorum and commentarii XVvirorum. Besides this, the various colleges of priests kept their albums or fasti, being chronological lists of the priests as well as the minutes (acta) of their official transactions.

1. *Libri augurum*, e.g. Varro LL. 5, 21. 33. 58. 7, 51. Cic. rep. 1, 63. 2, 54. n. deor. 1, 72. 2, 11. de dom. 39. Gell. 13, 14, 1. Fest. 253. 322. Serv. A. 4, 45. 9, 20. *Commentarii augurum*, Cic. de div. 2, 42. Fest. 317. Serv. A. 1, 398. From these *libri augurales* the only connected piece preserved is a formula in Varro LL. 7, 8 (on this see HJordan, krit. Beitr. z. Gesch. d. lat. Sprache 89).—PRegell, de augurum publicorum libris, part. I, Bresl. 1878; fragmenta auguralia coll. PRegell, Hirschb. 1882; the same in Commentatt. in hon. A. Reifferscheidii, Bresl. 1884, 61. FABrause, libr. de discipl. augur. ante Aug. mortem rell. I, Lpz. 1875.

2. *Libri Saliorum*, Varro LL. 6, 14.

3. *Commentarii XVvirorum*, Censorin. 17, 9. 10. 11.

4. On the fasti sacerdotales see § 75, 4. On the acta fratrum arvalium see § 65, 1. Lex collegii Aesculapii et Hygiae of 153 A.D. in Or. 2417 Wilm. 320.

5. There existed Latin translations and editions of the books of ritual of the haruspices written in the Etruscan language (*Etruscae disciplinae libri*, *libri Tagetici*, after *Tages*, the promulgator of this doctrine, *Vegonici* after *Vegone*, *Begoe nympha*). Traces of a Latin version e.g. Serv. Aen. 1, 42, where the word *manubiae* is quoted from the libri Etruscorum, in the gromat. p. 348 Lachm. (a fragment of the †Vegone, see also § 58, 2), and even distinct traces of an hexameter version in Amm. Marc. 17, 10, 2 (OMüller's Etr. 2^2, 25. Bährens, FPR. 422).

78. The temporal magistrates also had their corresponding notes, partly such as were written by them (commentarii magistratuum), partly records of which they formed the subject (libri magistratuum). The first treated of the transactions of individual magistrates: commentarii consulum, quaestorum etc. The most important of this kind are the tabulae censoriae (sometimes inaccurately called libri censorii), registers of the status and property of the Roman citizens resulting from each census, as well as accounts of the state of the exchequer. The commentarii censorum, on the other hand, seem to have had a private character and purpose.

1. *Commentarii consulum*, Varro LL. 6, 88. To these belong also the saturnian line *Oriens consul magistrum povpuli dicat*, Vel. Long. GL. 7, 74; cf. Reifferscheid, RhM. 15, 627. *Commentarium vetus anquisitionis M. Sergii M'. f. quaestoris*, Varro LL. 6, 90. 91. 92.—On the general subject MVoigt (§ 70, 1) p. 653.

2. *Tabulae censoriae*, Varr. LL. 6, 86. Cic. orat. 156. de leg. agr. 1, 4. Plin. NH. 18, 11. Mommsen, Staatsr. 2, 380.—*Libri censorii*, Gell. 2, 10, 1; cf. τιμητικὰ γράμματα, Dionys. 4, 22.

3. *Commentarii εἰσαγωγικοὶ* (cf. Gell. 14, 7, 1) of former censors, which became hereditary in their families, as a kind of manual, Dionys. 1, 74; cf. § 2, 3. 80, 2.

4. Schwegler, RG. 1, 28. Mommsen, Staatsr. 1, 4. On the *commentarii aedilium* KWNitzsch, d. röm. Annalistik (1873) 210. 220.

79. Libri magistratuum was the name given to the lists of the magistrates of each year, and these may have been kept ever since the magistrates were changed annually. Part of them were written on linen and hence called libri lintei. These were kept on the Capitol in the temple of the Goddess of Memory and are repeatedly mentioned by Livy as one of the sources of his authorities.

1. Liv. 4, 7 *neque in annalibus priscis neque in libris magistratuum.* 39, 52 (*in mag. libris*); cf. 9, 18 (§ 75, 1).

2. Linen was one of the writing materials of the olden time, see e.g. Liv. 10, 38 *ex libro vetere linteo* of the Samnites. Plin. NH. 13, 69 *postea publica monumenta plumbeis voluminibus, mox et privata linteis confici coepta aut ceris.* Fronto ep. ad Caes. 4, 4 (p. 67 Nab.) *multi libri lintei, quod ad sacra attinet.* Symmach. ep. 4, 84. Cf. MVoigt l.l. 661.

3. *Magistratuum libri, quos linteos in aede repositos Monetae Macer Licinius citat*, Liv. 4, 20, 8; cf. ib. 7, 10. 13, 7. 23, 2. Documents written on this material must have been easily destroyed, and therefore those which Macer unsuspectingly made use of were probably later copies. HPeter, hist. rom. rell. 1, cccxlv.

c) Monumenta privata.

80. Private persons also at an early time put down notes for after-use, both in connection with their domestic accounts and independently of them, on events and incidents which appeared important for the clan, the family or the individual (especially in his official capacity.) While at first these notes were prompted solely by the desire of preserving the recollection of past events, they soon may have begun to have an admixture of individual predilection and a tendency to glorify special persons.

1. *Privata monumenta*, Liv. 6, 1.

2. Gell. 13, 20, 17 *quae ita esse . . . cognovimus cum et laudationes funebres et commentarium de familia Porcia legeremus.* Plin. NH. 35, 7 *tabulina codicibus implebantur et monimentis rerum in magistratu gestarum.* Fest. 356 *tablinum proxime atrium locus dicitur, quod antiqui magistratus in suo imperio tabulis ⟨eum implebant⟩.* Cf. also § 259, 10.

3. Niebuhr's view of the influence of family chronicles on our tradition requires at least strict limitation: there is no evidence for the existence of such family chronicles in the Republican period. Mommsen, RG. 1^6, 467. BNiese, Herm. 13, 411.—Schwegler, RG. 1, 12. E. Lübbert, de gentium rom. commentariis domesticis, Giessen 1873; de gentis Serviliae, Quinctiae, Furiae, Claudiae commentt. domest. Kiel 1875–78.—Cf. further § 78, 3.

81. To this kind belong the lists of ancestors and pedigrees (stemmata), the inscriptions (indices, elogia) under the ancestral busts, and the funeral laudations of departed members of the family (laudationes or orationes funebres), in all of which historical truth was often disregarded in favour of the purposes of a panegyric.

1. Families of secondary rank were eager to prove their relationship with noble families, and these themselves (e.g. the Antonii, Julii etc.) to carry their ancestral line back to the Trojans and to the gods. Festus 130. 166. Dionys. 4, 68. Plut. Fab. 1. Anton. 4. Num. 1. Plin. NH. 35, 8 *etiam mentiri clarorum imagines erat aliquis virtutum amor.* Cornel. Nep. Att. 18. Suet. Iul. 6. Vitell. 1 and elsewhere.

2. Suet. Galb. 3 *imagines et elogia generis.* Vitell. 1 *extatque elogi* (thus MHertz, de hist. 1871, 10: *que elogii* in the MSS., *Q. Eulogii* Casaubon) *ad Q. Vitellium . . . libellus* (§ 259, 10). Such inscriptions for a series of ancestral images (*elogia* i.e. ἐλεγεῖα) were in later times made from various sources, and from them probably were chiefly drawn the funeral orations so far as they related to ancestors. Augustus decorated the colonnades of the temple of Mars in his forum with the statues of heroes from Aeneas and Romulus downwards; the elogia on the pedestals of these (Hor. C. 4, 8, 13 already mentions them: *incisa notis marmora publicis, per quae spiritus et vita redit bonis post mortem ducibus*) are preserved partly in the original, partly in copies: CIL. 1, p. 277; eph. epigr. 3, 1. Wilm. 622 sqq. The historical material here employed is in part dubious, and evidently derived not only from original sources, but also from learned research (more or less honest). OHirschfeld, Phil. 34, 85. HHildesheimer, de libro de vir. illustr. U.R., Berl. 1880, 36. Inscriptions on statues or hermae in libraries, CIL. 1, p. 281. Literary elogia in metrical form by Varro, the elder Symmachus, and also AL. 831–855 PLM. 5, 396 (see § 357, 2). See further § 83. 90, 1. 115, 2.

3. GCurtius, d. Etymol. des Wortes elogium, kl. Schrr. (Lpz. 1886) 2, 230. AFleckeisen, JJ. 23, 3. Düntzer, ZfvglSprachf. 16, 275. HJordan, Herm. 15, 20; vindic. serm. lat. antiquiss., Kgsb. 1882, 19.

4. Liv. 8, 40 *vitiatam memoriam funebribus laudibus reor falsisque imaginum titulis, dum familia ad se quaeque famam rerum gestarum honorumque fallente mendacio trahunt;* cf. 4, 16 and Cic. Brut. 61 *nec vero habeo quemquam* (*Catone*) *antiquiorem, cuius quidem scripta proferenda putem, nisi quem Appi Caeci oratio haec ipsa de Pyrrho* (§ 90, 3) *et non nullorum mortuorum laudationes forte delectant. et hercules hae quidem extant. ipsae familiae sua quasi ornamenta ac monumenta servabant, et ad usum, si quis eiusdem generis occidisset, et ad memoriam laudum domesticarum et ad illustrandam nobilitatem suam. his laudationibus historia rerum nostrarum est facta mendosior. multa enim scripta sunt in eis quae facta non sunt* etc. The custom of such laudationes is ancient, Dionys. 5, 17. Plut. Poplic. 9; cf. Polyb. 6, 53 and Cic. de leg. 2, 62; cf. de or. 2, 44 sqq. Liv. 2, 47, 11 (a. 274/480). And see Quintil. 3, 7, 2. 11, 3, 153. Gell. NA. 13, 20, 17 (§ 80, 2). In the later time M. Aurelius and Verus *laudavere pro rostris patrem*, Capitol. Ant. phil. 7, 11.

5. At a comparatively early time such laudationes were published in book form. Such was that by Q. Caecilius Metellus (Plin. NH. 7, 139) on his father Lucius (a. 533/221), by Fabius Cunctator on his son (between 547/207 and 551/203, cf. Plut. Fab. 1), by M. Claudius Marcellus (Liv. 27, 27) on his father (546/208), Laelius on the younger Africanus etc. For a later period see § 195, 2. 210, 2 ad fin.; cf. § 220, 2. 275, 2.

6. The first non-official (cf. Liv. 5, 50, 7. Plut. Camill. 8) funeral oration on a woman (his mother) was pronounced by Lutatius Catulus (cos. 652/102), Cic. de or. 2, 44. After that time this became customary (Suet. Iul. 6), at least for women whose sons had risen to high positions (Plut. Caes. 5). Cf. § 267, 4. 356, 5.

7. Schwegler, RG. 1, 16. HGraff, de Rom. laudationibus, Dorpat 1862. EHübner, Herm. 1, 440. CMartha, l'oraison funèbre chez les Rom., in his études morales, Par. 1883.

82. There were also, in the very earliest times, songs in praise of the departed—some of them sung at the funeral procession to the accompaniment of a tibia (neniae), others at festival banquets by boys and later on by the guests in alternation, also to a tibia. Both these customs are of great antiquity, and the first, though in a degenerate form, existed also until later times; the second was dying out as early as several generations before the time of Cato the Elder.

1. Tac. A. 3, 5 *Veterum instituta, . . meditata ad memoriam virtutis carmina* etc.

2. Fest. 161. 163 *nenia est carmen quod in funere laudandi gratia canitur ad tibiam*; cf. Cic. leg. 2, 62 *nenia, quo vocabulo etiam apud Graecos cantus lugubres nominantur* (Poll. 4, 79 τὸ δὲ νηνίατον ἔστι μὲν Φρύγιον κτλ.). Quintil. 8, 2, 8. Originally they seem to have been sung at the funeral banquets and by the members of the family (cf. Suet. Aug. 100), later on, they were recited before the mourners' house, in the funeral procession, and at the place of burning by hired wailing-women, *praeficae* (so Naevius in Ribbeck Com.[2] 29 *haec . . . praeficast, quae sic mortuum collaudat;* Plaut. truc. 2, 6, 14 *praefica, quae alios collaudat* etc. Varro, LL. 7, 70 *mulier . . . quae ante domum mortui laudes eius caneret* and other passages), hence they became insipid and soon got into bad repute (*nenia, ineptum et inconditum carmen* etc. Non. 145, cf. Plaut. asin. 4, 1, 63. truc. 2, 1, 3. Petron. 47. 58. Capitol. Clod. Alb. 12 *neniis quibusdam anilibus occupatus*, and other passages in Teuffel, PRE. 5, 395). JWehr, de Rom. nenia (in the προπεμπτικὸν for ECurtius, Gött. 1868, p. 11).

3. Cic. Brut. 75 *utinam exstarent illa carmina quae multis saeclis ante suam aetatem in epulis esse cantitata* (*deinceps*, Tusc. 4, 3) *a singulis convivis* (a later custom adopted from the Greeks, Mommsen RG. 1[6], 222, 452) *de clarorum virorum laudibus in Originibus scriptum reliquit Cato!* Cf. Tusc. l.l. and 1, 3. Val. Max. 2, 1, 10. On the other hand, Varro says ap. Non. s. v. *assa voce: in conviviis pueri modesti ut cantarent carmina antiqua, in quibus laudes erant maiorum, et assa voce et cum tibicine.* Cf. also Hor. C. 4, 15, 25 *virtute functos more patrum duces . . . canemus*, and 1, 12. This is referred to Numa in Cic. de or. 3, 197. Quint. 1, 10, 20. Songs in praise of Romulus and Remus are mentioned by Dionys. 1, 79 (from Fabius Pictor: ὡς ἐν τοῖς πατρίοις ὕμνοις ὑπὸ Ῥωμαίων ἔτι καὶ νῦν ᾄδεται). Plut. Num. 5; of Coriolanus, by Dionys. 8, 62. Cf. CZell, Ferienschrr. 2, 170. 193.

4. Perizonius (Animadvv. histor. cap. 6) held these laudatory songs to have been one source of the Roman legendary history. Ribbeck, Gesch. d. röm. Dicht. 1, 8. Niebuhr was of opinion that these songs formed a continuous epic poem, and hence originated the theory that this epic poem was the source of our extant version of Roman history, which he thought would account for its poetical charac-

ter. On this view (which goes much too far and is now rightly discarded) see WCorssen, origg. 112. 162. Schwegler, RG. 1, 53. But on the other hand MAKrepelka Phil. 37, 450.

83. We have relics of a similar kind in the inscriptions on votive offerings, pillars, tombs and vessels, of which we possess a large number belonging to the first centuries of the Republic, partly through literary and partly through epigraphic records. Of the first kind are 1) the inscription on the linen coat-of-mail of Tolumnius dedicated by A. Cornelius Cossus a. 317/437 (326/428?) and seen even by Augustus; 2) the tabula triumphalis of the dictator T. Quinctius of the year 374/380; 3) the sepulchral inscription of A. Atilius Calatinus (cos. 496/258). Of the second class: 4) the dedication on a golden fibula, probably of the 3rd century u.c., found in a grave at Praeneste; 5) the inscription of Dvenos, of the 5th century u.c.; 6) the dedication of the Marsian Caso Cantovios, probably dating from the second Samnite war (428/326–450/304); 7) the three oldest of the epitaphs of the Scipios, the inscription in memory of L. Cornelius Cn. f. Scipio (cos. 456/298), his son L. Cornelius Cn. f. Scipio (cos. 495/259) and the elogium of the latter in saturnian lines; 8) the inscription on the columna rostrata erected to C. Duilius in honour of his naval victory over the Carthaginians a. 494/260; 9) the inscription on the oldest milestone preserved, about 500/254.—Of other inscriptions the epitaphs of the Furii at Tusculum, several Praenestine inscriptions on cists and mirrors, as well as dedications from the grove near Pisaurum etc., may belong to the 5th century u.c.

1. Liv. 4, 20.

2. Liv. 6, 29. Festus 363 (saturnian).

3. Cic. Cato 61 *carmen incisum in sepulcro;* cf. fin. 2, 116 (saturnian).

4. '*manios med fhefhaked numasioi*' (right to left) i.e. *Manius me fecit Numerio.* Discovered 1886; FDümmler, Röm. Mitteil. des deutsch. arch. Inst. 1887, 40. GLignana, ib. 139. Bücheler, RhM. 42, 317. EWölfflin, Arch. f. lat. Lexikogr. 4, 143.

5. On a small earthen vessel intended for funeral offerings on the Novendial, found in Rome (1880) near the Quirinal, is a curious ritualistic instruction written from right to left, with saturnian assonances; HDressel, ann. d. inst. arch. 52, 158. Bücheler, RhM. 36, 235. The text is given with critical notes in ESchneider's DIE. 1, 19. Other short dedications on very ancient vases from southern Etruria CIL. 1, 43 seqq. DIE. 1, 20 sqq.

6. On this alternate (*βουστροφηδὸν*) inscription (lines 1. 3. 4 from left to right, lines 2. 5 from right to left) on a bronze tablet, found in 1877 in the Fucine lake, cf. FBücheler, RhM. 33, 489. HJordan, Herm. 15, 5.

7. The epitaphs of the Scipios were discovered on the via Appia, a. 1614 and

1780, and have often been printed and explained. They are now found in Priscae Lat. Monum. t. 37–42. CIL. 1, 29–39 (also 6, 1284–1294). Wilm. 1, 537. DIE. 1, 88–93. Those belonging to the time anterior to 514/240 are in the CIL. 1 no. 29. 31. 32. On these epitaphs see Ritschl, opusc. 4, 213. Mommsen, RhM. 9, 462. RG. 1^6, 452. FBücheler, JJ. 87, 328; anthol. epigr. spec. 2, 6. LMüller, d. saturn. Vers 102 al. The Grecian tendencies of the Scipios show themselves also in the adoption of metrical epitaphs.

8. FRitschl, Inscriptio quae fertur columnae rostratae Duillianae, opusc. 4. 183. 204; PLMon. t. 95; also CIL. 1, 195. 6, 1300. Wordsw. EL. 170. DIE. 1, 391. The present text of the inscription cannot be the original, but dates from the time of the Empire; at the very best, it is the original text renewed and to a certain extent modernised (Ritschl, opusc. 4, 234), but the many forms of exaggerated archaism, standing side by side with later forms, as well as numerous material difficulties and its general prolixity, render Mommsen's view (CIL. 1, p. 40) more probable, viz. that the column originally had either no inscription at all, or only a very short and simple one, and that the extant inscription was made, when the monument itself was restored under Claudius, in accordance with accessible historical sources and with intentional imitation of the archaic style (esp. following the inscription of L. Aemilius Regillus relating to his naval victory at Myonnesos, Liv. 40, 52).

9. This milestone (milliarium) from the via Appia, now at Mesa, is published CIL. 10, p. 1019, no. 6838. DIE. 1, 283.

10. The tituli Furiorum CIL. 1, 65 DIE. 1, 60; the Praenestine CIL. 1, 54 DIE. 1, 41; those of Pisaurum CIL. 1, 167 DIE. 1, 68.—The inscriptions on coins, vessels, monuments etc. of this period, so far as preserved, have been collected in the CIL. vol. 1, where the pars prior (p. 1–40) contains the Inscriptiones vetustissimae, bello Hannibalico quae videntur anteriores. See also the selection: DIE. 1, 1–89. On the elogia § 81, 2.

84. The custom of a victorious army singing at their general's triumph ditties either praising or rallying him (carmina triumphalia), frequently in alternating form, is likewise very ancient.

1. Liv. 3, 29. 4, 20. 53. 5, 49. 7, 10. 17. 38. 10, 30. 39, 7. 45, 38. 43. Dionys. 2, 34. 7, 72. App. Pun. 66. Plut. Aemil. P. 34 (ὁ στρατὸς . . . ᾄδων τὰ μὲν ᾠδάς τινας πατρίους ἀναμεμιγμένας γέλωτι, τὰ δὲ παιᾶνας ἐπινικίους καὶ τῶν διαπεπραγμένων ἐπαίνους). Marcell. 8. Dio 43, 20. Vellei. 2, 67. Suet. Iul. 49. 51. Martial. 1, 4, 3 sq. Panegyr. incert. 9, 18 extr.—For the amoebaean form (*alternis versibus*) see Liv. 4, 53. Plin. NH. 19, 144. Cf. also § 3, 3. 11, 2 and 3.—The burden *io triumphe*, Varro LL. 6, 68. Tib. 2, 5, 118. Liv. 3, 29. Cf. Hor. C. 4, 2, 49 sq. Ov. trist. 4, 2, 51.

2. Cf. FPR. 330.—Zell, Ferienschr. 2, 148. GHBernstein, versus ludicri in Rom. Caesares priores compositi, Halle 1810. Guicherit, de carminibus Marciorum (§ 66, 2) et de carm. triumphal. milit. Rom., Leid. 1846.

85. The old weather-rules, incantations and magic lines and similar things bore likewise a popular character and were, as a rule, in saturnian rhythm.

1. Fest. 93 *in antiquo carmine: hiberno pulvere, verno luto grandia farra,*

camille, metes. Cf. MACR. sat. 5, 20, 18 *in libro vetustissimorum carminum . . . invenitur hoc rusticum vetus canticum: hiberno* etc. SERV. Georg. 1, 101. PLIN. NH. 17, 14 and 28, 29 *carmina quaedam exstant contra grandines contraque morborum genera* etc. Ib. 27, 131 (in free trochaic measure: *reseda, morbos reseda! scisne, scisne, quis hic pullus égerit radíces? néc caput nec pédes habeat*). CATO RR. 160. VARRO RR. 1, 2, 27 (charm against the gout) *terra pestem teneto, salus hic maneto* (saturnian). VERG. A. 4, 487. Buc. 8, 80. HOR. E. 2, 1, 138. TIB. 1, 2, 53. MOMMSEN RG. 1[6], 221. 459. Cf. § 11. Also BÜCHELER, RhM. 34, 343. BERGK, op. 1, 556.

D) LEGAL MONUMENTS AND LITERATURE.

86. The constantly increasing legal insecurity and inferiority in which the Plebeians found themselves, when compared with the Patricians, after the abolition of the royal power, led after many struggles at the beginning of the 4th century U.C. to the design and introduction of a common law of the country, by which the existing customs, most of them merely traditional and not fixed in writing, were at length systematised, and materially improved by the recently gained experience and the knowledge acquired of foreign states and laws; a process resulting in the legislation of the XII tables. Thus the civil law was regulated both theoretically and practically, laws of a religious and criminal character and some referring to the police being also included. These laws were at an early time commented upon, in order to keep them in harmony with practical law and the development of the language.

1. a. 300/454 lex Terentilia and the departure of three ambassadors for Greece. They returned a. 302/452, a legislative committee was then appointed (Xviri legibus scribundis), which commenced its functions in May 303; at first 10 tables were drawn up, and a. 304 two others were added. Hermodoros of Ephesus is said to have assisted them.

2. The legislation of Solon was fixed on as the model, CIC. leg. 2, 59. 64. Dig. 10, 1, 13. 47, 22, 4. PLUT. Sol. 21. 23. FHOFMANN Beitr. z. Gesch. d. griech. und röm. Rechts (Wien 1870), p. 1 sqq.

3. The XII tabulae were *fons omnis publici privatique iuris*, LIV. 3. 34. Cf. DIONYS. 10, 3. AUSON. op. 26, 61. TAC. A. 3, 27. The two last tables are frequently excluded from the usual praise, CIC. de rep. 2, 61. 63.

4. DIOD. 12, 26 βραχέως καὶ ἀπερίττως συγκειμένη. GELL. NA. 20, 1, 4 *eleganti atque absoluta brevitate verborum scriptae*, but also *quaedam obscurissima aut durissima* etc.

5. They were graven on bronze (LIV. 3, 57. DIONYS. 10, 57. DIOD. 12, 26). After the retreat of the Gauls (365/389) the consular tribunes ordered *foedera ac leges* (*erant autem eae XII tabulae . . .*) *conquiri quae comparerent* (LIV. 6, 1). Until the time of Cicero they were learnt by heart in the schools, CIC. leg. 2, 9. 59. In Diodoros' time (12, 26 διέμεινε θαυμαζομένη μέχρι τῶν καθ' ἡμᾶς καιρῶν) and

that of A. Gellius (20, 1) they were still in existence. As for the time of Cyprian, nothing certain appears from his rhetorical expression: ad Donat. 10 *incisae sint licet leges XII tabulis et publico aere praefixo iura praescripta sint,— inter leges ipsas delinquitur, inter iura peccatur*).

6. Commentators: Sex. Aelius Catus (Cic. leg. 2, 59. Top. 10. Pompon. dig. 1, 2, 2. § 38), L. Acilius (Cic. leg. l.l.), L. Aelius Stilo (§ 148, 1 sqq.), Ser. Sulpicius Rufus (dig. 50, 16, 237. Fest. 210, 322 cf. 174. 321. 376), Antistius Labeo (Gell. NA. 1, 12, 18. 7, 15, 1. 20, 1, 13), Valerius (Fest. 321. cf. 253. 355. RSchöll, XII tabb. p. 35), Gaius (of whose commentary 20 fragments have been preserved in the Digests).

7. Since Gothofredus (see Otto's Thesaur. iur. rom. 3, 1), the fragments of the XII tables have been collected and explained esp. by HEDirksen, Kritik u. Herstellung des Textes der Zwölftafelfragmente, Lpz. 1824. Legis XII tabb. reliquiae, ed. prolegomena add. RSchöll, Lps. 1866. MVoigt, d. XII Tafeln, Gesch. u. Syst. usw. nebst den Fragmenten, Lpz. 1884 II. Bruns, fontes [5] 14.—On the legislation of the XII tables see esp. Schwegler, RG. 3, 1.—OKarlowa, röm. Rechtsgesch. 1, 108.

87. The concession of the XII tables soon lost part of its value to the Plebeians by the cleverness with which the Patricians succeeded in obtaining the exclusive right of explaining and applying them. Especially their knowledge of the precise forms of legal proceedings (legis actiones), as well as of the days on which they were religiously admissible, was withheld from the Plebeians.

1. *Interpretatio legum, auctoritas prudentum, disputatio fori* (ius civile in a limited sense), Pompon, dig. 1, 2, 2. § 5. *Et interpretandi scientia et actiones apud collegium pontificum erant*, ib. § 6; cf. Val. Max. 2, 5, 2.

2. The legis actiones are partly older than the XII tables, esp. those *per sacramentum* and probably also the one *per iudicis* (*arbitrive*) *postulationem*; less probably those *per condictionem, per manus iniectionem, per pignoris capionem.* PRE. 4, 902. ASchmidt, de originibus legis actionum, Frieb. 1857. FLvKeller, röm. Civilproc., [6] v. AWach, Lpz. 1883 (and the literature there quoted).

3. Plin. NH. 33, 17 *diebus fastis, quos populus a paucis principum quotidie petebat*, cf. Cic. Mur. 25. Cf. § 74.

88. This state of things was improved by Cn. Flavius Anni f. as curule aedile a. 450/304 publishing, with the assistance of Ap. Claudius, a calendar of the religious festivals and the legis actiones: Fasti and ius Flavianum.

1. Liv. 9, 46 *Cn. Flavius . . . civile ius repositum in penetralibus pontificum evulgavit fastosque circa forum in albo proposuit ut quando lege agi posset sciretur.* Plin. NH. 33, 17 *Appii Caeci* (see § 90) *scriba, cuius hortatu exceperat eos dies consultando assidue sagaci ingenio.* Val. Max. 2, 5, 2.

2. *Legis actiones composuit*, Cic. Att. 6, 1, 8; cf. de or. 1, 186. Pompon. dig. 1, 2, 2. 7. *Hic liber, qui actiones continet, appellatur ius civile Flavianum*, Pompon. l.l.

Later on, it was supplemented and continued by Sex. Aelius, who *alias actiones composuit et librum populo dedit, qui appellatur ius Aelianum*; cf. § 125, 2. MVoigt (see § 49, 5) p. 328. Query whether there are extracts from the ius Flavianum in Probus de notis? Mommsen, Lpz. Ber. 1853, 133.

89. When the sources of the law had thus all become accessible, legal knowledge ceased to belong exclusively to the Patricians: among the earliest jurists we have, besides several Patricians, as the most eminent the Plebeians P. Sempronius Sophus and Tiberius Coruncanius, the first teacher of law.

1. Pompon. dig. 1, 2, 2. § 37 *fuit maximae scientiae Sempronius, quem populus rom. σοφὸν appellavit* (cos. 450/304, one of the first Plebeian pontifices 454/300, censor 455; PRE. 6, 974); *C. Scipio Nasica, qui Optimus a senatu appellatus est* (this must be an error, as the one who received, a. 550/204, the surname of Optimus, is in all other passages called Publ. and was consul 563/191; PRE. 2, 666), *cui etiam publice domus in sacra via data est, quo facilius consuli posset. deinde Q. Mucius* [? Bynkershoek conjectures *Maximus*] . . . § 38: *post hos fuit Ti. Coruncanius, qui, ut dixi* (§ 35), *primus profiteri coepit. cuius tamen scriptum nullum extat, sed responsa complura et memorabilia eius fuerunt* (*feruntur* Muretus). He was consul a. 474/280 and the first Plebeian pontifex maximus. PRE. 2, 722. ESchrader, Civilist. Magazin 5, 187.

2. It remains doubtful whether Sophus and Coruncanius owed their sacerdotal dignity to their legal knowledge or vice versâ; Mommsen, RG. 1[6], 469.

90. The most prominent figure of this period, in fact a man a century in advance of his own time, was Appius Claudius Caecus (censor 442/312, cos. 447/307 and 458/296), the great Patrician who abolished in the state the limitation of the full right of citizenship to landed proprietors, who broke through the old financial administration, from whom the Roman aqueducts and streets, the Roman jurisprudence, oratory and grammar date their beginning, and with whom begins also the first attempt at Latin prose-composition and at art-poetry.

1. His elogium: CIL. 1, p. 287 nr. 28 Or. 539 Wilm. 628. Plin. NH. 35, 12 *posuit in Bellonae templo* (founded by him a. 458/296) *maiores suos placuitque in excelso spectari et titulos honorum legi.* Frontin. aq. 1, 5 *Ap. Claudio Crasso censore cui postea Caeco fuit cognomen.* OHirschfeld, Herm. 8, 476.—Generally Mommsen, RG. 1[6], 454; Röm. Forsch. 1, 301.

2. Pompon. dig. 1, 2, 2, 36 *App. Claudius . . . maximam scientiam habuit. hic Centemmanus appellatus est. Appiam viam stravit et aquam Claudiam induxit, et de Pyrrho in urbem non recipiendo sententiam tulit* (the famous speech of a. 474/280, preserved long afterwards, see Cic. Brut. 55. 61. Cato m. 16. Sen. ep. 114, 13 Tac. dial. 18. 21. Quint. 2, 16, 7). *hunc etiam actiones scripsisse traditum est* (he rather suggested the legis actiones of Flavius; Mommsen considers *actiones* to be an interpolation), *primum de usurpationibus, qui liber non exstat. idem . . . R literam invenit* (i.e. distinguished the two sounds r and s in writing, cf. Mommsen, RG. 1[6], 470), *ut pro Valesiis Valerii essent et pro Fusiis Furii.* See, however, on this trans-

ition HJordan, krit. Beitr. z. Gesch. d. lat. Spr. (Berl. 1879) 104. The removal of z from the alphabet is also ascribed to him (Martian. Cap. 3, 261). HJordan l.l. 155. LHavet, rev. de philol. 2, 15. GMeyer, ZföG. 31, 122. Cf. § 93, 6.

3. *Sollers iuris atque eloquentiae consultus*, Liv. 10, 22; cf. 19. He was the first author who wrote down and published any prose work (see § 35, 1).

4. Cic. Tusc. 4, 4 *mihi Appii Caeci carmen, quod valde Panaetius laudat epistola quadam quae est ad Q. Tuberonem, Pythagoricum videtur.* Cf. Fest. 317 *in Appii sententiis.* Ps.-Sall. ad Caes. de rep. 1, 1, 2 *quod in carminibus Appius ait, fabrum esse suae quemque fortunae.* Thus perhaps *faber suae fortunae unusquisquest ipsus.* Priscian GL. 2, 384 *Appius Caecus: amicum cum vides, obl(iv)iscere miserias* etc. (a saturnian). FPR. 36.

II.

HISTORY OF ROMAN LITERATURE.

PART I.

THE TIME OF THE REPUBLIC AND OF AUGUSTUS.

First period: from Andronicus to the time of Sulla.

A. 514/240–670/84.

91. The centuries during which Rome possessed no literature are those of her real greatness. Her literature arose through the demands of school and stage, when the instruction gained by youths from accompanying their fathers to the market-place and into the Senate appeared no longer sufficient, and when the stage was expected to give continuous and more artistic exhibitions besides the customary uncouth farces and dances.

The Roman literature was from its very beginning under the influence of the Greek. The tentative beginnings of early Roman literary exertion could not develope and assert themselves, in contact with the externally isolated and internally perfect Greek literature which was penetrating into Rome. They were stunted and overpowered by the foreign influence even more than was the Roman faith under the pressure of the Greek. A Roman literature was first wakened into life by the Greek literature, and so developed itself at the expense of the genuine old Roman character.[1]) But what Roman authorship lost through this involuntary surrender, its foreign teacher amply repaid by severe training, by guarding it against countless errors, and by

---

[1]) Mommsen RG. 1⁶, 876.

directing it to the highest examples. The Romans however showed in literature their characteristic strength and genius for assimilation, and made the foreign forms entirely their own.

The acquaintance with the Greek language and customs is of high antiquity in Italy and Rome. The Latin alphabet is of Greek origin (see below), and likewise the Roman system of weights and measures. We find Greek influence powerful from the time of the Tarquins, and it is proved even by the constitution of Servius and the character of the ludi romani[2]); in religion it was fostered by the Sibylline books. Such names, too, as Cocles (Κύκλωψ), Catamitus (Ganymedes) indicate an early connection. At the beginning of the 4th century U.C. the Roman legislation was improved by using that of Solon, and in the course of that century a separate place for the Greeks (Graecostasis) was made in the Roman forum. After the conquest of Campania, at the beginning of the 5th century U.C., this influence increased considerably: such surnames as Philippus, Philo, Sophus, Agelastus, were no longer strange, the customs of reclining at dinner, of erecting monuments and epitaphs in memory of the departed, etc., were then adopted from the Greeks[3]); and when, at the close of that century, the contact with the Greek parts of the south of Italy became more frequent, the Roman nobles were already able to use the Greek language in their missions, the Roman sailors and traders having understood it even before. Through the numbers of Greek slaves and freedmen even the lower classes at Rome became acquainted with Greek.

Accordingly the effects were the more rapid and deep, when the first Punic war brought the manhood of Rome into close and lasting contact with Greek culture in Sicily. Thence a taste for refined enjoyments was imported, and it was probably no mere accident that, in the year after the close of the first Punic war (490/264–513/241), Andronicus was enabled to set up the drama at Rome, since which time performances were maintained continually. Even during the war with Hannibal (536/218–553/201) they went on uninterruptedly, inasmuch as most of Naevius' works and one half of Plautus' literary exertions (though perhaps the less fertile half) fall into the time of this war, in which the peculiar virtues of the Roman nation appeared once more in their most brilliant lustre. But when the fearful tension of all

---

[2]) MOMMSEN 1^6, 95. 228. [3]) MOMMSEN 1^6, 452. Cf. § 83, 7.

powers which was necessitated by it had relaxed, when the feeling of having escaped an immense danger and the exultation at a final victory increased the relish of all the enjoyments of life[4]), literature also struck deeper roots at Rome, especially as its respectability had been secured by the grant of corporate rights to the poetae as early as 548/206. It also chanced a. 550/204 that M. Cato brought Ennius to Rome: the future chief of the old Roman party brought him who was destined soon to be the champion of the partisans of Greek literature. Thenceforth Porcius Licinus' words (in Gellius 17, 21) were daily more fully realised:

Poenico bello secundo Musa pinnato gradu
Intulit se bellicosam in Romuli gentem feram.[5])

Patriotic men were grieved to witness the desertion of national customs and the increasing influence of the foreign element.[6])

The ambition of the aristocracy, increasing equally with their wealth, met the popular eagerness for sights half way; together with other popular amusements the dramatic performances were, therefore, eagerly attended; writing plays for them became a tolerably remunerative occupation, and thus besides and after Plautus we find Ennius, Pacuvius, Statius Caecilius, and Terence busily pursuing it. The wars with Philip III. of Macedonia (554/200–557/197) and still more the war with Antiochus (a. 563/191 sq.) contributed greatly to the downfall of the old Roman manners, though they also enlarged the intellectual horizon and put the conception of a universal Empire within nearer reach, increasing also the necessity of exchanging the original Roman character for Grecian civilisation and its cosmopolitan and refining tendencies. This, indeed, could not be done without mistakes. Unfortunately most Romans lacked the faculty of discriminating in the foreign element between the valuable or necessary and the inappropriate or harmful; without reserve or selection they threw themselves into the arms of Grecian civilisation, and were so dazzled by its brilliant lights that they overlooked its deep shadows. At first it was exclusively the

---

4) The Oscan Atellanae seem also to have come to Rome about this time; see § 9.

5) Cf. also Hor. E. 2, 1, 162.

6) Cato ap. Gell. 6, 2, 5 *si quis in poetica arte studebat . . . grassator vocabatur.* Cf. *otium graecum* Cic. or. 108.

nobles who adopted the new fashion; above all the circle of the Scipios esteemed and propagated Grecian culture, and also kept tolerably free from its exaggerations.[7] Africanus the Elder manifested his desertion of the old Roman mode of thought especially by his familiar saying: numquam se minus esse otiosum quam cum otiosus esset;[8] and the occupation of his leisure becomes manifest from the charge of his adversaries, esp. Q. Fabius, a. 550/204, that he spent his time over old books and in gymnastics.[9] Another very respectable advocate of the Grecian tendency was L. Aemilius Paulus (c. 527/227–594/160). They both wrote and spoke Greek fluently, as did also T. Quinctius Flamininus (cos. 556/198), Ti. Gracchus (cos. 577/177. 591/163), C. Sulpicius Gallus (cos. 588/166), Cn. Octavius and in general all the annalists of the war with Hannibal (Fabius Pictor, Cincius, Acilius). Q. Labeo (cos. 571/183) and M. Laenas (cos. 581/173) wrote verses.

Even Cato showed at least in Latin prose an eager literary activity, and he who had asserted that the Romans would forget how to act, under the influence of Greek literature,[10] was in his old age obliged to learn Greek himself. But already were the symptoms of the decay of the old Roman severity becoming more frequent,[11] so much so that a man of the old stamp, like T. Manlius Torquatus, felt strange and solitary in his native town.[12] With each generation, nay almost every year, these symptoms become more serious, in the breaking-up of family life, the contempt of law and order, and even of the national gods. The opposition of the adherents of the old system grew indeed in the same proportion; Cato the Elder especially waged fierce war against these tendencies in his censorship (a. 570/184).

But it was impossible to stop a process resulting from a

---

7) See Naevius ap. Gell. NA. 7 (6) 8, 5. Val. Max. 6, 7, 1.

8) Cic. off. 3, 1. Cf. ABaldi, die Freunde und Förderer der griech. Bildung in Rom, Würzb. 1875; d. Gegner der griech. Bildung in Rom, Burghausen 1876. ADupuy, de Graecis Romanorum amicis aut praeceptoribus, Brest 1879.

9) Liv. 29, 19 ad fin.

10) Cf. § 2, 1 and in Plin. NH. 29, 14 *quandoque ista gens suas literas dabit omnia corrumpet.*

11) Liv. 26, 2, 15 (a. 543/211) *eum* (Cn. Fulvius) *in ganea lustrisque, ubi iuventutem egerit, senectutem acturum.*

12) Liv. 26, 22, 9 (a. 543/211) *neque ego vestros mores consul ferre potero neque vos imperium meum.* Cf. the frequent complaints of Plautus about the growing *mores mali*, e.g. Trin. 30. 531. 1028.

thousand unavoidable circumstances, to oppose the great change then accomplishing itself with irresistible power, in the religion, life and customs, in the thoughts and actions of the nation. Though the new culture was made solely responsible for the evils of the time, yet this convenient reproach, which made it possible to shift the blame, was by no means proved. Besides, the means employed were often absurd and not to the purpose. Thus a. 581/173 the Epicurean philosophers Alkaios and Philiskos were banished from Rome, a. 593/161 the philosophers and rhetores latini were again expelled, a. 599/155 the Athenian ambassadors (whose chief was Karneades) were sent home as soon as possible. But then again a. 587/167 the Senate decoyed one thousand noble and highly educated Achaeans (Polybios among them) into Italy, and there detained them as hostages during 17 years. Altogether the policy of shameless selfishness, which was pursued by the Roman Senate during this period, and reached its climax in their abominable conduct towards the unhappy, prostrate city of Carthage [13])—the frivolous wars tending to nothing but aggrandisement and enrichment waged by Rome continuously after the second Punic war—destroyed the old Roman character far more effectually than Grecian art and philosophy could ever have done. Henceforth there was a fearful increase in internal corruption, immorality,[14]) bribery, an insatiable eagerness for riches, disregarding everything else and impudently setting aside laws, orders of the Senate and legal proceedings, making war unauthorised, celebrating triumphs without permission, plundering the provinces, robbing the allies. Ignominious treaties and conclusions of peace became more and more frequent. Instead of by character (virtus) as of old, Rome now extended its power by deceit, perfidiousness and diplomatic craft. A certain culture did indeed gradually spread itself even among the great multitude; a fact borne out by the mere occurrence [15]) of numerous foreign words in Plautus (and Ennius), and by the ludi scenici gaining the superiority over the circenses.[16]) But the plays of the palliata, which were the

---

[13]) On this Macchiavellian policy see CPeter, Studien zur röm. Gesch., Halle 1863, 115. Even such an ardent admirer of the Romans as Polybios is thereby repeatedly roused to outbursts of indignation; see 31, 18; cf. 31, 8. 12. 19 extr. 32, 2.

[14]) Cf. Polyb. 31, 24 and esp. 32, 11 (p. 1096 Bk.).

[15]) Mommsen RG. 1[6], 877.—FOWeise, d. griech. Wörter im Lat., Lpz. 1882: RhM. 38, 547. GASaalfeld, Tensaurus italo-graecus, Wien 1884 etc.

[16]) At the end of the Republic there were 66 days annually appropriated to festivals: of these 2 days were occupied with feasts (epulae), 16 days with ludi

principal food offered to the people in the dramatic exhibitions, could not do much towards preserving the old austerity of morals.[17])

92. The work nearly finished in the 6th century was completed in the 7th; the year 608/146 brought the destruction of Carthage and Corinth. With Carthage, the stimulus for continued valour and expertness in war disappeared for ever. The very man who was obliged to destroy Carthage, a man more far-seeing than the old zealot Cato, deplored its fall; the fall of Corinth and the abolition of Greek independence caused numbers of Greeks to emigrate to Rome, there to make up for the loss of their home. The peculiar Roman character had now come to an end, and for ever: Graecia capta ferum victorem cepit. From the 6th into the 7th century the noble figure of Africanus minor (569/185–625/129) attracts our attention, he who was the friend of Panaitios and Polybios; around him congregated all who tried to keep above water in this sea of egotism, greediness and immorality: among his contemporaries, besides Terence, his brother Q. Fabius Maximus (cos. 609/145), his brother-in-law Q. Aelius Tubero, M'. Manilius (cos. 605/149), the younger Laelius (cos. 614/140), D. Junius Brutus (cos. 616/138), L. Furius Philus (cos. 618/136), Sp. Mummius, Sex. Pompeius, P. Rupilius (cos. 622/132), C. Lucilius (born 574/180); among the younger men, the sons-in-law of Laelius, C. Fannius and Q. Mucius, as well as the younger Tubero, P. Rutilius, A. Verginius and others.[1]) But the stronger the opposition in which these circles found themselves in their thought and action to the dominant tendency, the more they fell into aristocratic seclusion and so much the less became their influence.

The rottenness of the nobility and the internal corruption of the upper classes became manifest in the Numantine war (611/143–621/133) and roused the Gracchi (621/133-631/123) to their efforts; they stand forth prominently in the war with Jugurtha (643/111–648/106) and enable the rude force of Marius,

---

circenses (and preparations), but 48 days with ludi scenici. In the calendar of a. 354 A.D. (§ 74, 8) there are marked 175 days for ludi, of these 10 gladiatorial, 64 circensian, but 101 scenic. MOMMSEN, CIL. 1, p. 378. FRIEDLÄNDER, SG. 2[5], 272.

[17]) Sometimes it becomes manifest that this culture was only a slight varnish, which gave way as soon as the rigour of discipline was relaxed. Cf. e.g. POLYB. 30, 13 (from ATHEN. 14, p. 615) in the year 587/167.

[1]) Cf. CIC. Lael. 101.

himself a man of insignificant intellect, to gain marvellous successes. His ignorance of Greek was exceptional in his time,[2]) especially among the ruling class;[3]) the performances of Greek plays at Rome in the original Greek attest the great extent of this knowledge. Many inscriptions of this period are written in the two languages, and the Romans, who formerly in their palliatae denoted themselves as barbari, now share the lead with the Greeks: they leading in politics, and the latter in culture. The Roman writers of the period acknowledge the superiority of the Greek literature, some by resigning all rivalry in formal polish, as Lucilius did, and others again by striving after correctness and elegance in a higher degree, as e.g. L. Accius; many were by blind imitation even led to shallow trifling, e.g. the erotic epigrammatists. The political situation led to increased extension and refinement of the popular amusements.[4]) The drama therefore still held the principal place in literary production. Tragedy was, in the 7th century, respectably represented by L. Accius; in the comedy palliata, togata, the artistic Atellana and Mimus succeeded each other rapidly, but in this succession attest a continuous descent, in accordance with the taste of the mob, to plebeian farces and to vulgar spectacular amusement. The epos was still kept up by the impulse it received in the middle of the 6th century (through Naevius and Ennius), without, however, deriving any further encouragement from contemporary history. In general, poetical production had nearly died out with the exception of the drama, and Lucilius and the erotic poets alluded to. The nation itself was destitute of poetical power and aspiration, nor did the internal disturbances admit of sufficient mental tranquillity. On the other hand, historical composition, oratory and jurisprudence were forced in the atmosphere of political strife and grew rapidly both in extent and depth. Among the historical writers the most remarkable in the 7th century U.C. are Piso Frugi, Antipater, Asellio, also the latest of the Annalists, Valerius Antias, Sisenna and Licinius Macer. The most brilliant orators, after C. Gracchus, are M. Antonius and L. Crassus. Jurisprudence is best represented

---

2) Sall. Iug. 85, 32.

3) P. Crassus, cos. 623/131, knew five Greek dialects: see § 133, 5 ad fin.

4) Cf. § 12, 2. The attempt at reform made by the censors of a. 639/115 was an exception and remained without further consequences; see § 9, 7.

by the two Q. Scaevolas, the augur and the pontifex. Learned investigation was carried on diligently in all branches after the middle of the 7th century, in prose as well as in verse, though, with the exception of L. Aelius Stilo, generally not by native Roman citizens.

93. As regards language and prosody these two centuries are a period of most active development, and include all the three grades through which Roman poetry passed, that of the saturnian, the dramatic and the dactylic poets. As early as the 6th century U.C. the Latin was in danger of falling into something like the Umbrian loss of endings, of weakening all its suffixes, losing its declensions, and thus passing even then into the condition of the Romance languages. Old Latin had a strong tendency to degrade the long vowels, especially when final. The high-tone, by giving importance to the accented syllable, often had the effect of weakening adjacent long syllables (whether long by nature or position) and reducing them to short ones. Especially in iambic words or combinations the long syllable was shortened by the accent falling on the short one. Final consonants were slurred in pronunciation and became less and less audible. The nasals blended readily with the following vowel and disappeared. Lastly, little words in common use were clipped by being mispronounced or only half sounded. The oldest poets, especially Plautus and the other dramatic writers, struggling with their foreign material and writing for the people, readily availed themselves of the licences, which the fluctuating pronunciation of everyday life afforded for their versification. In respect of metre they are equally negligent: they showed little sensitiveness regarding hiatus, in the theses (except the last) they put short or long syllables indifferently; indeed the saturnian verse allowed of the arses being quite suppressed: a liberty which the dramatic writers of course avoided under the guidance of their Greek models. They also delighted in alliteration, employing it for the sake of cohesion as well as for ornament.[1])

---

[1]) Even the later artistic poetry did not disdain alliteration, which always continued popular in prose phraseology. Recent writings: WEBRARD, d. Allitt. in d. lat. Spr., Bayr. 1882. CBOETTICHER, de allitt. ap. Rom. vi et usu, Berl. 1884. HJORDAN, Beitr. z. Gesch. d. lat. Spr. (Berl. 1879) 167. EWÖLFFLIN, d. allitter. Verbindd. d. lat. Spr., Münch. SBer. 188[illegible] 2, 1. GLANDGRAF, de figuris etym-

Ennius first strove for greater strictness in these points. S final was left disregarded even by him, and must have been almost inaudible before consonants in his time; only by the poets towards the close of the Republic was it recognised as a full sound. But in all other things Ennius has the merit of having resolutely put an end to this state of indecision and irregularity, by attributing a normal value to each sound in accordance with its accurate Roman pronunciation, and thus classifying every syllable according to its value as either long or short.[2]) In connection therewith a fixed rule was applied to thesis, and hiatus was systematically avoided. For his new prosody Ennius introduced also into Roman literature a new measure, the Greek dactylic hexameter. It is true, his influence extended only to the written language and the conversational language of the educated classes, which was formed on it; while the simple practice of everyday life for some time longer pursued its own peculiar development.[3]) Not only did the saturnian metre continue for some time even after the introduction of the hexameter, but there was even in the 7th century a kind of plebeian prosody, in which the hexameter was indeed employed, but with all the prosodiacal licences of the dramatic poets of the 6th century, adhering also to the practice of solving the arsis;

---

ologicis lat., Acta Erl. 2, 1. JBinz, Phil. 44, 262; see further under the several authors.

[2]) It must not be supposed that Ennius reformed the prosody on any rigid or arbitrary system. He rather rescued the language, in its transitional stage of development, from an early decline, which the older poets had prepared by admitting the licences of the popular speech.—The people apprehended the quantity of the syllables in virtue of their unerring linguistic instinct, not from any scholastic instruction. Cic. de orat. 3, 195 *omnes tacito quodam sensu sine ulla arte aut ratione quae sint in artibus ac rationibus recta ac prava diiudicant, idque . . . ostendunt magis in verborum numerorum vocumque iudicio, quod ea sunt in communibus infixa sensibus nec earum rerum quemquam funditus natura esse voluit expertem. itaque non solum verbis arte positis moventur omnes, verum etiam numeris ac vocibus. quotus enim quisque est qui teneat artem numerorum ac modorum? at in his si paullum modo offensum est ut aut contractione brevius fieret aut productione longius, theatra tota reclamant.* or. 173 *in versu theatra tota exclamant, si fuit una syllaba aut brevior aut longior. nec vero multitudo pedes novit nec ullos numeros tenet nec illud quod offendit aut cur aut in quo offendat intellegit: et tamen omnium longitudinum et brevitatum in sonis sicut acutarum graviumque vocum iudicium ipsa natura in auribus nostris collocavit.* parad. 3, 2.

[3]) The omission of final m and s occurs in inscriptions even in the first third of the 7th cent. u.c.—GÉdon, écriture et prononciation du Latin savant et du Latin populaire, Par. 1882. ESeelmann, d. Aussprache des Lat., Heilbr. 1885.

specimens of this we possess in the inscription of Mummius (§ 163, 8) and the so-called sortes Praenestinae.[4]) But to Ennius belongs the credit of having arrested the imminent breaking-up of the language, at least in literature, for several centuries.

The language itself was fixed about this time: so was its rendering in writing. The Latin alphabet[5]) is descended from the Greek alphabet used by the Chalkidian colonies in Campania (Kyme and Neapolis). This old Latin alphabet consisted of 21 letters, among which were C (in the 3rd place = gr. Γ), Z (in the 7th place), K, Q, X (this last at the end). K disappeared from use at a very early date, being represented by C instead. Later, when the need appeared for a distinction between the smooth (tenuis) and middle (media) gutturals, the freedman of Sp. Carvilius, cos. 520/234 and 526/228 (§ 128) invented the sign G by slightly altering the C, and put it in the place of the almost unnecessary and little used Z,[6]) which was only restored, (together with Y[7]) in the time of Cicero and was then placed at the end of the alphabet. Thus the alphabet of Carvilius likewise consisted of 21 letters. Other regulations of writing are connected with the names of poets, since in the fluctuating state of the Latin language and the scarcity of a fluent practice in writing, the poets had also to be grammarians, in order to express the spoken language accurately in writing.[8]) Thus Ennius is reported first to have employed the doubling

---

[4]) Ritschl, op. 4. 400. LMüller, d. saturn. Vers 80.

[5]) Cf. Mommsen, die unteritalischen Dialekte (Lpz. 1850), 3; RG. 1[6], 210; bull. 1882, 91. 101. Kirchhoff, Stud. z. Gesch. d. gr. Alphab.[4] 117. 127. 133. Ritschl, opusc. 4, 691. 765. WSchmitz, Beitr. z. lat. Sprach- u. Literaturkunde, Lpz. 1877. WDeecke in Baumeister's Denkm. d. kl. Altert. 1, 50.

[6]) Z was read by the ancients in the carmen Saliare (Vel. Long. GL. 7, 51, 6): we find it in the Dvenos inscription (§ 83, 5) and on coins of the end of the 5th cent. u.c. (DIE. 1, 9). After the loss of Z that sign was replaced till about the time of Cicero by S or SS. HJordan, Krit. Beitr. (Berl. 1879) 155 ascribes the removal of Z and the introduction of G to Appius Claudius (§ 90). The earliest extant inscriptions with G are not older than the time of Carvilius, so that no evidence can be deduced from them against the tradition. Cf. also LHavet, rev. d. philol. 2 (1878), 15.

[7]) The Chalkidian V (= υ) was employed in the old Latin alphabet to represent the Latin vowel u (and the Greek υ) as well as the labial spirant v. The digamma Ϝ, which was the equivalent of the latter sound in the Chalkidian alphabet, was utilised in the Latin for the labiodental spirant f. Y is not found in inscriptions before the end of the 7th cent. u.c.

[8]) Very much in the same way as the earliest compositors (esp. of Greek) were obliged to be scholars.

of consonants.[9]) L. Accius expressed the long quantity of the vowels AEU by doubling them,[10]) and Lucilius discriminated the two sounds I and EI—all with this result, that their example exercised a certain, though not always immediate or constant, influence on the orthography of the most important documents of their time.[11]) The vocalisation of Latin was systematised very gradually in these two centuries. In the older language the fluctuations are numerous and marked, especially between O and U, likewise between E and I (and also in respect of AI and AE, EI and I, OU and U). In the inscriptions O and E begin to give way about 520/234 in the case-endings and verb-endings where U and I were subsequently established. But it was only between 550/204 and 568/186 that U and I permanently prevailed over O and E,[12] though the sequences UV VU UU, and likewise the doubling of vowel I or the coupling of consonant and vowel I, were regularly avoided. The aspirates in Greek words were at first represented by the corresponding tenues; from 650/104 they began to be expressed by the signs CH TH PH.[13]) Here as well as in the adoption of Y and Z we notice the endeavour to assimilate Greek usage.

A. THE SIXTH CENTURY U.C.

I. Poets.

94. Andronicus (c. 470/284–550/204) came as a young man, most probably at the time of the capture of Tarentum (a. 482/272),

---

9) Fest. s.v. solitaurilia. The evidence of the inscriptions accords with this: though one example *Hinnad* CIL. 1, 530. 6, 1281 DIE. 1, 117 of a. 543/211 occurs before the time when Ennius wrote. But here the Greek name Ἔννα facilitated the doubling. Otherwise this is first found (and then along with the simple style) in the decree of L. Aemilius Paulus a. 565/189 (§ 123, 8) CIL. 2, 5041 DIE. 1, 96.—Ritschl. op. 4, 48. 231; pl. Excurse 1, 17. WWeissbrodt, specimen grammaticum (Cobl. 1869), 34; quaest. gramm. 2 (Braunsberg 1872), 10. EBährens, JJ. 127, 774.—The sicilicus (') is occasionally employed to indicate a doubled consonant (Mar. Vict. GL. 6, 8); see EHübner, Herm. 4, 413; exempla script. epigr. lxxvi.

10) This is supported by the inscriptions: the earliest example (*paastores*) a. 622/132 CIL. 1, 551. 10, 6950 DIE. 1, 275. Ritschl. op. 4, 142.

11) WWeissbrodt, specimen grammaticum, Cobl. 1869; quaest. gramm. 2, 3 (de simplic. et geminatis consonantibus latt.) by the same.

12) Ritschl, op. 4, 224. Mommsen, RhM. 9, 464.

13) These signs were also employed out of place and superfluously, and such mistakes were perpetuated in several instances throughout the Roman literature. E.g. the spelling *Bosphorus*. Cf. Catull. 84. Quintil. 1, 5, 20. AFleckeisen, JJ. 99, 656. 101, 458. On the representation of ϕ in Latin writing see Mommsen, Herm. 14, 65.

to Rome, and being a prisoner of war became the slave of a certain Livius, perhaps the same as the victor of Sena, M. Livius Salinator. He gained his living by private instruction in Latin and Greek, was manumitted and received the name of L. Livius Andronicus. For his pupils he translated the Odyssey into Latin saturnians, but awkwardly and not without flagrant mistakes. Being besides an actor, he wrote his own text-books; these he likewise translated from the Greek, esp. tragedies, in doing which he imitated the easier Greek measures and kept the popular alliteration. The first performance of a complete play of this kind took place a. 514/240, the year after the successful termination of the first Punic war. In the year 547/207 he was commissioned to prepare an intercessory hymn to the Aventine Juno; he composed, probably in the same year, a song of thanksgiving for victory, namely that of his patron at Sena. For his sake the poets received the grant of corporate rights, and a place was assigned them for their meetings and votive offerings in the temple of their tutelary goddess Minerva on the Aventine hill.

1. The praenomen L. (Gell. 6, 7, 11. 17, 21, 42. Fest. 297b, 7. Cassiod. see n. 2). The deviation of the praenomen from that of his former master is in accordance with the custom of this period; see EHübner in IwMüller's Handb. 1, 521. From a confusion with the name of the historian T. is several times erroneously given. (Non. 207, 23. 368, 25. Hieron. see n. 2.)

2. Cassiod. chron. ad a. 515/239: *his conss. ludis romanis* (at which the earliest stage-plays a. 390/364 appear to have previously taken place, § 6, 3) *primum tragoedia et comoedia a Lucio Livio ad scaenam data.* On the other hand a. 514/240 *Livius primus fabulam C. Claudio Caeci filio et M. Tuditano coss. docuit* ap. Cic. Brut. 72, who appeals to Atticus and to *antiqui commentarii* (§ 95, 4), and at the same time refutes the errors of Accius (§ 134, 7), who owing to a confusion of the second with the first capture of Tarentum stated that Andronicus had come a. 545/209 from Tarentum to Rome, and there first produced a piece a. 557/197 *C. Cornelio Q. Minucio coss. ludis Iuventatis quos Salinator Senensi proelio voverat.* For the date 514/240 cf. also Cic. Cato mai. 50 (with the following notice: *vidi* [the speaker being Cato b. 520/334] *Livium senem: qui . . . usque ad adulescentiam meam processit aetate*) and Gell. 17, 21, 42. An erroneous account is also given by Hieronym. chron. ad a. 1830 (Bongars. ad a. 1831) =567/187 (perhaps owing to a confusion of M. Livius Salinator, cos. 547/207, with C. Liv. Salin., cos. 566/188): *Titus Livius tragoediarum scriptor clarus habetur, qui ob ingenii meritum a Livio Salinatore, cuius liberos erudiebat, libertate donatus est.*

3. Sueton. gramm. 1 *antiquissimi doctorum, qui iidem et poetae et semigraeci erant,—Livium et Ennium dico, quos utraque lingua domi forisque docuisse adnotatum est—nihil amplius quam Graecos interpretabantur aut si quid ipsi latine composuissent praelegebant.*

4. Liv. 7, 2, 8 *Livius . ., qui ab saturis* (§ 6) *ausus est primus argumento fabulam serere, idem scilicet, id quod omnes tum erant, suorum carminum actor.* Cic. leg. 2, 39 *(theatra) quae solebant quondam conpleri severitate iucunda Livianis et Naevianis*

modis. From a good source the glossae Salomonis (§ 42, 9; see USENER, RhM. 28, 419): *Romae tragoedias comoediasque primus egit idemque etiam composuit Livius Andronicus, duplici toga* (laena=σύρμα, the train of Greek tragedy; see RhM. 23, 676) *involutus.*

5. The titles of the tragedies of Andr. are Achilles, Aegisthus, Aiax (mastigophorus), Andromeda, Danae, Equos Troianus (on this see RLALLIER, Mélanges Graux, Par. 1884, 103), Hermiona, Ino (for the choral hymn in this see § 13, 5), Tereus. The fragments collected in RIBBECK's trag.[2] 1–6. Comedies were Gladiolus, Ludius, Virgus (? RIBBECK proposes Verpus). Fragments in RIBBECK, Com.[2] p. 3 sq. Liv. Andron. et Naevi fabularum frag. emend. et adnot. LMÜLLER, Berl. 1885.

6. CIC. Brut. 71 *et Odyssia latina est sic tamquam opus aliquod Daedali e Livianae fabulae non satis dignae quae iterum legantur.* GELL. NA. 18, 9, 5 *offendi in bibliotheca Patrensi librum verae vetustatis Livi Andronici, qui inscriptus est* 'Οδύσσεια, *in quo erat versus primus* '*virum mihi, Camena, insece versutum.*' The Odyssia chiefly seems to be meant in the mention of the *carmina Livi* as a school-book used by Orbilius, HOR. E. 2, 1, 69. The Odyssey is quoted as one book (LIV. *in Odissia* and so forth; once only PRISC. GL. 2, 321 *in I Odissiae*). The fragments of the Od. e.g. in the collections of saturnians by HAVET and MÜLLER see § 62, 3. WORDSW. EL. 289. FPR. 37 and elsewhere.

7. LIV. 27, 37 (a. 547/207) *decrevere pontifices* (in expiation of a bad omen) *ut virgines ter novenae per urbem euntes carmen canerent, . . . conditum ab Livio poeta . . . carmen in Iunonem reginam* (of the Aventine) *canentes, illa tempestate forsitan laudabile rudibus ingeniis, nunc abhorrens et inconditum, si referatur . . .* — FEST. 333 *cum Livius Andronicus bello Punico secundo scripsisset carmen quod a virginibus est cantatum, quia prosperius resp.* (*res* MHERTZ) *populi rom. geri coepta est, publice adtributa est ei in Aventino aedis Minervae, in qua liceret scribis histrionibusque consistere* (MOMMSEN, Herm. 7, 309) *ac dona ponere, in honorem Livi, quia is et scribebat fabulas et agebat.* On this 'collegium poetarum' (§ 134, 2) see OJAHN, Lpz. Ber. 1856, 294. ARIESE, Heidelb. Philologenvers. (Lpz. 1866) 161. LMÜLLER, Q. Enn. 30. Hence the scribae histrionesque were ranked with the other collegia opificum and artificum. To this guild of poets the older and highly esteemed collegium tibicinum is very nearly related. MARQUARDT, röm. Staatsverw. 3[2], 138.

8. Livii Andr. fragm. coll. HDÜNTZER, Berl. 1835.—ALDÖLLEN, de vita Livii Andr., Dorp. 1838. TEUFFEL, PRE. 4, 1118. OGÜNTHER, ZfdGW. 14, 809. MOMMSEN, RG. 1[6], 881. RIBBECK, röm. Trag. 19; röm. Dicht. 1, 15.

9. Of the time of Livius, but not by him, is the *Nelei carmen* (GL. 1, 84, *ut in Odyssia vetere . . . et in Nelei carmine aeque prisco*), from which fragments in iambic metre are preserved through Festus and Charisius; (perhaps a tragedy). FPR. 53. RIBBECK's trag. [2] p. 233 seq. röm. Trag. 629.—A *carmen Priami* (in saturnians) VARRO LL. 7, 28. On this see HJORDAN, Beitr. z. Gesch. d. Lat. Spr. 133.

95. Cn. Naevius, a native of Campania, but of Latin extraction, was one of the actors in the first Punic war; he began to exhibit plays in the year 519/235, in general in the manner of Andronicus, but with more talent and originality, and with a preference for comedy. The inconsiderate candour with which

he assailed in them even leading statesmen (though he did this in a genuine Roman manner) caused him first to be thrown into prison and then to be exiled; he died in exile c. 555/199. In his later years he attempted a poetical treatment of the first Punic war, the events of which he had himself witnessed, and in this he used the saturnian measure. Through this national tendency of his, he also created a new kind of drama, the praetexta, and for centuries retained the kindly recollection of his nation. Even in the scanty fragments left to us we seem to feel the traces of a fresh, energetic, talented and self-possessed mind.

1. Gell. NA. 1, 24, 1 *trium poetarum illustrium epigrammata, Cn. Naevi, Plauti, M. Pacuvi, quae ipsi fecerunt* (but see § 115, 2) *et incidenda sepulcro suo reliquerunt . . . epigramma Naevi plenum superbiae campanae* (cf. Cic. leg. agr. 2, 91. Liv. 9, 6, 5) . . .: *Immortales mortales si foret fas flere, flerent divae Camenae Naevium poetam. itaque postquam est Orci traditus thesauro obliti sunt Romai loquier lingua latina.* Spurious portrait of Naevius: JJBernoulli, röm. Ikonogr. 1, 234.

2. Gell. 17, 21, 44 *anno post Romam conditam quingentesimo undevicesimo . . . Cn. Naevius poeta fabulas apud populum* (primum? but see Cic. Cato 50. Brut. 72, 73) *dedit, quem M. Varro in libris* (libro? cf. 1, 24, 3) *de poetis primo stipendia fecisse* (consequently N. was not himself an actor, see Mommsen, RG. 1^6, 899) *ait bello poenico primo, idque ipsum Naevium dicere in eo carmine quod de eodem bello scripsit.*

3. Gell. 3, 3, 15 *de Naevio accepimus fabulas eum in carcere duas scripsisse, Hariolum et Leontem, cum ob assiduam maledicentiam et probra in primores civitatis de graecorum poetarum more dicta, in vincula Romae a triumviris coniectus esset. unde post a tribunis plebis exemptus est, cum in his quas supra dixi fabulis delicta sua et petulantias dictorum, quibus multos ante laeserat, diluisset.* Ps. Ascon. on Cic. Verr. act. pr. 29 (p. 140 Or.) *dictum facete et contumeliose in Metellos antiquum Naevii est 'fato Metelli Romai fiunt consules,' cui tunc Metellus consul* (a. 548/206 see § 123, 2) *iratus versu responderat . . . 'dabunt malum Metelli Naevio poetae;'* see MWende, de Caeciliis Metellis 1 (Bonn 1875), 31. The imprisoned Naevius is mentioned with sympathy by Plaut. mil. 211: *ós columnatúm poetae esse indaudivi bárbaro, quoi bini custódes semper tótis horis óccubant* (cf. Paul. Festi 36, 2).

4. Hieron. chron. on a. 1816=553/201 *Naevius comicus Uticae moritur, pulsus Roma factione nobilium ac praecipue Metelli* (Metellorum?). Cic. Brut. 60 *his consulibus* (a. 550/204), *ut in veteribus commentariis* (in which? see § 94, 2) *scriptum est, Naevius est mortuus; quamquam Varro noster, diligentissimus investigator antiquitatis, putat in hoc erratum vitamque Naevi producit longius.* Varro was no doubt right; Naevius was born c. 485/269 or 490/264.

5. Tragedies: Andromacha, Danae, Equos troianus, Hector proficiscens, Hesiona (Aesiona), Iphigenia, Lycurgus. Fragments in Ribbeck, trag. ^{2} p. 6; in LMüller, see § 94, 5. Cf. Ribbeck, röm. Trag. 44.

6. Praetextae: Clastidium (on the victory won there by M. Marcellus a. 532/222; cf. § 14, 2) and Romulus. Ribbeck trag. ^{2} p. 277. MHaupt, op. 1, 189. Grauert, Phil. 2, 115. Röper, ib. 7, 591. LMüller, Q. Ennius 84.

7. Comedies: Acontizomenos, Agitatoria, Agrypnuntes, Appella, Ariolus, Astiologa, Carbonaria, Chlamydaria, Colax, Commotria, Corollaria, Dementes,

Demetrius, Dolus, Figulus, Glaucoma, Gymnasticus, Lampadio, Nagido, (Nautae?), Nervolaria, Paelax, Personata, Proiectus, Quadrigemini, Satura (? see n. 9), Stalagmus, Stigmatias, Tarentilla, Technicus, Testicularia, Tribacelus, Triphallus, Tunicularia. The fragments in Ribbeck, com.[2] p. 5, in LMüller see § 94, 5. Much is uncertain, esp. on account of the frequent confusion with Laevius, Livius and Novius. The plays with Latin titles may possibly be the later ones. But all belong to the palliata; Naevius, however, seems to have dealt more freely with the originals than even Plautus, and he already practised contamination (§ 16, 9. Ter. Andr. prol. 7).

8. Bellum punicum (poenicum). Cic. Cato 40 *si habet aliquod tamquam pabulum studii atque doctrinae, nihil est otiosa senectute iucundius . . . quam gaudebat bello suo punico Naevius!*—Suet. de gramm. 2 *C. Octavius Lampadio* (§ 138, 4) *Naevii Punicum bellum . . . uno volumine et continenti scriptura expositum divisit in septem libros.* Santra ap. Non. 170, 21 *quod volumen unum nos lectitavimus, id postea invenimus septemfariam divisum.* Also in the earlier quotations from Naevius' bell. pun. the work is quoted not according to books, but as a whole; see Bücheler, RhM. 40, 149. LMüller's edition of Ennius, p. xxii.—A certain Cornelius and Virgilius are mentioned as commentators by Varro LL. 7, 39.—Cic. Brut. 75 *Naevi . . . bellum punicum quasi Myronis opus delectat . . . et luculente quidem* (*Naevius rem scripsit*), *etiamsi minus quam tu* (Ennius) *polite.* The first two books contained the mythical history of Rome and Carthage (Anchises, Aeneas, Anna, Dido), and the third opened with the first Punic war. The subject was treated in a prosaic manner, much like the style of a mediaeval chronicle, but with rhyming a mythological framework after the Homeric manner (Juno as the enemy, Venus as the friend of the Trojans, Juppiter and Apollo take a personal part in the action). Horace's indignant question (E. 2, 1, 53): *Naevius in manibus non est et mentibus haeret paene recens?* may be supposed to relate to this heroic poem. The fragments ed. IVahlen, Lpz. 1854 and in LMüller's ed. of Ennius (cont. also quaestt. Naev. p. xx), see § 104, 6. FPR. 43. Wordsw. EL. 292.

9. Fest. 257[a], 29 *ut apud Naevium . . . in satyra*, etc. Perhaps a comedy (n. 7) as there were comedies similarly entitled by Atta and Pomponius? Others understand satires: fragments conjectured to belong thereto FPR. 51.—On the supposed preservation of Naevius down to the Middle Ages, see RFörster, RhM. 37, 485.—EKlussmann, Cn. Naevii vitam descripsit, reliq. coll., Jena 1843. PRE. 5, 396. Mommsen, RG. 1[6], 899. 892. 917. Ribbeck, röm. Trag. 44; röm. Dicht. 1 20. DdeMoor, Cn. Névius, Tournai 1877. JVillemain, l'instr. publ. 10 (1821), 142.

96. T. Maccius Plautus was born c. 500/254 in the Umbrian town of Sarsina (which, at that time, can hardly have been altogether Latinised), of free, but poor parents. Having at first worked for the stage at Rome, he lost his savings through speculation; he then for some time worked in a treadmill, and afterwards gained his subsistence by Latin versions of Greek comedies, until his death a. 570/184. Great uncertainty prevailed as to the number of his plays, especially when the public became accustomed to consider as Plautine any comedy of the palliata class, and of the time of Plautus (many of which probably existed only in stage copies). Varro divided them into three classes: 21 considered genuine by all, then those which were

probably genuine, and last of all spurious plays. Those of the first class (fabulae Varronianae) are no doubt those which we still possess.

1. Sarsina was the last town of Italy proper, which so late as 488/266 offered opposition to the Romans. The name T. Maccius (instead of M. Accius) was elicited from the Ambrosian MS. (at the end of Cas. Men. Epid.; Merc. 6) and GELL. 3, 3, 9 by RITSCHL, de nominibus Plauti, Parerga p. 3, and was defended by MHERTZ (T. Maccius Plautus or M. Accius Plautus? Berl. 1854: de Plauti nominibus epimetrum, Bresl. 1867), against GEPPERT, Jahn's Arch. 19, 262; cf. RITSCHL's ed. of Mercator p. XI. A recent defence of M. Accius by ECOCCHIA, riv. de filol. 13 (1884), 97; on the other side LMANTEGAZZA, Bergamo 1885, and especially CHRHÜLSEN, Berl. phil. Wochenschr. 1886, 420.—In Asin. prol. 11 (*Demóphilus scripsit, Máccus vortit bárbare*) the name *Maccius* is spelt either in the latter form, or in the forms *Maccis* or *Măcius*. BÜCHELER, RhM. 41, 12, pertinently conjectures that *maccus* here means 'buffoon' (§ 9, 3), and is a nickname given to Plautus as a writer of comedies, from which he on becoming a Roman citizen deduced for himself the family name of *Maccius* (CIL. 5, 2437. 6, 1056, 81. 10, 8148). *Plotus* (*Plautus*) meant in Umbrian a flat-footed man, FEST. 238; hence the only evidence for *Accius:* PAUL. Festi 239, 4 *poeta Accius, quia Umber Sarsinas* etc. (in FEST. 238ª, 34 only . . . *us poeta quia Umber* etc., is preserved).

2. CIC. Brut. 60 *Plautus P. Claudio L. Porcio coss.* (a. 570/184) *mortuus est, Catone censore.* In Cato 50 he mentions among the instances of the occupations of *senectus: quam gaudebat . . . Truculento Plautus, quam Pseudulo* (performed a. 563/191)! This agrees also with other data. Cf. RITSCHL, de aetate Plauti, Parerga p. 45. It must therefore be an error when HIERONYM. on Euseb. chron. 1817 (Bong. 1818) = 550/200 reports: *Plautus ex Umbria Sarsinas Romae moritur* (*moratur*, MHERTZ; others assume an error for *clarus habetur*).—GELL. 1, 24, 3, *epigramma Plauti, quod dubitassemus an Plauti foret* (§ 115, 2), *nisi a M. Varrone positum esset in libro de poetis primo: Postquam est mortem aptus Plautus, comoedia luget, scaena est deserta ac dein risus, ludus iocusque et numeri innumeri simul omnes conlacrimarunt.*

3. GELL. 3, 3, 14 *Saturionem et Addictum et tertiam quandam . . . in pistrino eum scripsisse Varro et plerique alii memoriae tradiderunt, cum pecunia omni quam in operis artificum scenicorum* (as a stage artificer) *pepererat in mercatibus perdita inops Romam rediisset et ob quaerendum victum ad circumagendas molas quae trusatiles appellantur operam pistori locasset.* HIERONYM. l.l. (see n. 2): *qui propter annonae difficultatem ad molas manuarias pistori se locaverat, ibi quotiens ab opere vacaret scribere fabulas solitus ac vendere.*

4. GELL. 3, 3, 11 *feruntur sub Plauti nomine comoediae circiter centum atque triginta.* SERV. praef. in Aen. p. 4, 15 Th.: *Plautum alii dicunt unam et viginti fabulas scripsisse, alii quadraginta, alii centum.* The last number is probably (as MHERTZ supposes) from a different source to the 130; RITSCHL, Parerga 126. 173 thinks otherwise. Gellius l.l. 12 *homo eruditissimus L. Aelius XXV eius* (*Plauti*) *esse solas existimavit.* Of Varro we are told ib. 3, 3, 1 sqq. that he distinguished his classes according to his personal feeling and judgment, as to whether a play was worthy of Plautus or not: (3) *nam praeter illas XXI quae Varronianae vocantur, quas idciro a ceteris segregavit, quoniam dubiosae non erant, sed consensu omnium Plauti esse censebantur, quasdam item alias probavit, adductus filo atque facetia sermonis Plauto congruentis, easque iam nominibus aliorum occupatas Plauto vindicavit.* RITSCHL conjectures that Varro put 19 plays in this second class (ἀντιλεγόμενα) and thus explains the number 40 in Servius, perhaps (p. 128): 22. Saturio; 23. Addictus; 24. Boeotia; 25. Nervolaria; 26. Fre-

tum; 27. Trigemini; 28. Astraba; 29. Parasitus piger; 30. Parasitus medicus; 31. Commorientes; 32. Condalium; 33. Gemini lenones; 34. Feneratrix; 35. Frivolaria; 36. Sitellitergus; 37. Fugitivi; 38. Cacistio (? Cocistrio GLöwe, prodrom. glossar. 291); 39. Hortulus; 40. Artemo. To the 3rd class (νόθα) may then belong (ib. p. 154): 1. Colax; 2. Carbonaria; 3. Acharistio; 4. Bis compressa; 5. Anus; 6. Agroecus; 7. Dyscolus; 8. Pago (? Phago JBPius, Paplago MHertz, rament. Gell. mant. Bresl. 1868, 20, Arpago, GLöwe, prodr. glossar. lat. 292); 9. Cornicula; 10. Calceolus; 11. Baccaria (on the name see Löwe l.l. 292); 12. Caecus aut Praedones. In Ritschl, opusc. 3. 177 is the commencement of a collection of fragments (Acharistio to Boeotia). Pl. fabb. deperditt. frgm. coll. FWinter, Bonn 1885. But that the 21 (only the last, Vidularia, is lost, see § 97, 21), which we still have are the Varronianae (of the first class, the ὁμολογούμενα) is of itself highly probable. Varro's authority brought it to pass that the plays acknowledged by him were treated with preference in copying and reading.

5. The origin of the critical difficulty appears from Gell. 3, 3, 13 *non dubium est quin istae* (all?) *quae scriptae a Plauto non videntur et nomini eius addicuntur veterum poetarum fuerint et ab eo retractatae atque expolitae sint ac propterea resipiant stilum plautinum.* This might apply only to plays of Andronicus and Naevius; see Ritschl, Parerga 96. In § 10 Gellius mentions also that in Varro's *liber de comoediis plautinis id quoque scriptum, Plautium fuisse quempiam poetam comoediarum*, whose plays had been mixed up with those of Plautus, on account of the similarity of the names (gen. *Plauti*), but this does not help us much: see Ritschl 95 sq. But MHertz (de Plautio poeta ac pictore, Bresl. 1867) has at least proved that such a Plautius did once exist. The principal cause of the confusion is (Ritschl 113) that the name 'Plautine' became a kind of collective appellation of the principal period of the palliata, the anonymous plays being put to the account of a famous name, or the managers also intentionally ascribing them to Plautus. Cf. Mommsen, RG. 1^6, 901.—On the whole question see Ritschl, the fabulae Varronianae of Plautus, Parerga 71.

97. The 20 extant plays are arranged in the MSS. in nearly alphabetical order, which has, however, been departed from in the case of the Bacchides in favour of chronological order. The following list contains their names according to the usual arrangement:—

For editions of the whole or parts see § 99, 11.

1) Amphitruo, the only Plautine play with a mythological (comic-marvellous) plot, treated with complete mastery over the language and with sparkling humour. Its original and the time of its composition are unknown.

1. There are confusions of persons as in the Menaechmi, but involving two pairs instead of one, and not as there owing to accidental resemblance, but in consequence of intentional imitation. On account of the mixture of divine and human characters the play is denoted as *tragicomoedia* in the prologus. The original belongs no doubt to the New Comedy, and was neither a play of Archippos (old Attic Comedy) nor of Rhinthon. See Vahlen, RhM. 16, 472. It was perhaps performed as late as the 4th and 5th century of the Christian era. See Arnob. adv. nat. 4, 35. 7, 33. Prudent. perist. 10, 226. Augustin. epist. 202. After act 4, 2 there is a

gap of several scenes, or 300 lines, caused by the loss of a quaternio; in the 15th century this was filled up by Hermolaus Barbarus in a manner very unsuccessful both as to form and contents.

2. Edited separately by FLindemann (Lps. 1834), FWHoltze (Lps. 1846). APalmer, Lond. 1890.—FOsann, der A. des Pl., RhM. 2 (1834), 305. Welcker, griech. Trag. 1478. Steinhoff, Proleg. zu Pl. A., Blankenb. 1872. 79 II. EHoffmann, de Pl. Amph. exemplari et fragm.; Bresl. 1848. JSchröder, de fragm. Amph. Plaut. I. Strassb. 1879. SBrandt, RhM. 34, 575. HKöstlin, Phil. 36, 358. ORibbeck, RhM. 38, 450. Mediaeval revision of the Amph. by Vitalis: § 436, 9.

2) Asinaria, with a farcical plot, but varied and lively characters and scenes of great comic power. It is taken from Demophilos' Ὀναγός, and was written c. 560/194.

1. On Prolog. v. 11. see § 96, 1. Ritschl, op. 2, 683, cf. JJ. 97, 212.—Ed. by EJRichter, Nürnb. 1833. Criticism: LHavet, rev. de phil. 6, 148. Ribbeck, RhM. 37, 54.

3) Aulularia, one of the best plays of Plautus, both in plot and in execution, containing the portrait of a miser. The conclusion is lost.

1. The original was no doubt a play of the New Comedy. On account of 3, 5 it must have been written after the abolition of the lex Oppia, i.e. after 559/195; Ladewig in ZfAW. 1841, 1085. GABWolff, proleg. ad Pl. A., Naumb. 1836. WWagner, de Pl. A., Bonn 1864. CMFrancken, het origineel v. Pl. Aul., Versl. en Mededeel. 2 (1882), 11.

2. Editions by Göller (Cologne, 1825), JHildyard (Lond. 1839), WWagner (Cambr. [2] 1876), EBenoist (Par. [5] 1878), CMFrancken (Groningen 1877).—OFLorenz, Collationen der codd. B. u. D. zur Aul. des Pl., Berl. 1872. HAKoch, JJ. 107, 839. GGötz, act. Lips. 6, 310. KDziatzko, RhM. 37, 261.—On the Querolus, an imitation of the Aulularia, see § 436, 9.

4. Captivi, a pathetic piece without female characters or love-intrigue, and without active interest (stataria), though well constructed and enlivened by the character of the parasite.

1. On the question, whether the parasite is a genuine addition of Plautus, see EHerzog, JJ. 113, 363. Separately edited by CEGeppert (Latin and German, Berl. 1859), JLUssing (Copenh. 1869), JBrix (Leipz. [4] 1884), with crit. app. and Bentley's emendatt. to the whole of Plautus (cf. § 99, 13) by ESonnenschein, Lond. (also Lpz.) 1880.

2. Lessing, Werke 3, 77. 127. Cf. WHertzberg, preface to his transl. p. xix. —JBrix, Emendatt. in Pl. Capt., Liegnitz 1862. BDombart, BlfdbayrGW. 5, 157. 197; JJ. 123, 185. ASpengel, Phil. 37, 415. FMartins, quaestt. Plaut. (cap. 2, 3), Halle 1879.

5) Curculio (guzzler), the comical name of the parasite in the play; the plot insignificant. Composed soon after 561/193.

1. Curc. 4, 2, 23 allusion to the lex Sempronia (Liv. 35, 7) of the year 561/193 Teuffel, Studien u. Char. (1871) 262. A kind of parabasis in 4, 1 is remarkable. On this HJordan, Herm. 15, 116.

2. Edition by CEGeppert (Lat. and Germ.), Berl. 1845.—LMercklin, Symb. exeget. ad Curc. Pl., Dorp. 1861. ASpengel, Phil. 26, 354. MVoigt, RhM. 27, 168. GGötz, RhM. 34, 603.. Fleckeisen, JJ. 121, 122. Ribbeck, Lpz. Ber. 1879, 80. Bücheler, RhM. 39, 285. WSoltau, Curc. act. III interpret., Zabern 1882.

6) Casĭna, adapted from the *Κληρούμενοι* of Diphilos, though with the addition of obscenities in coarse Roman taste, which may also have caused the loss of the concluding scenes. The extant play is no doubt an abridgment made for later performances, but the author of the prologue was evidently acquainted with the complete play.

1. Teuffel, Stud. u. Charakt. 257. Mommsen, RG. 1^6, 892 concludes from 5, 4, 11 that the play was written before the prohibition of the Bacchanalia (a. 568/186), against Ritschl, Parerga 191; cf. also R's Opusc. 2, 658.

2. The supposed theatre-ticket with the inscription *Casina Plauti* (Or. 2539) is spurious. Mommsen, Lpz. Ber. 1849, 286. FWieseler, Denkm. des Bühnenw. (Gött. 1850), 37 on t. 4, 13; de tesseris . . . theatralibus 1 (Gött. 1866), 3.

3. Edition (in us. lectt.) by Geppert, Berl. 1866.—ThLadewig, RhM. 3, 185. Mommsen, ib. 10, 122. Fleckeisen, krit. Miscellen (Dresd. 1864), 5. CFuhrmann, JJ. 99, 480. Geppert, on the Cas. in the cod. Ambr., ZfGW. 17, 625. Studemund, ib. 18, 526, and Emend. plaut. (1871) 3. 15. Fleckeisen and Ritschl, JJ. 103, 637. Bergk, kl. Schr. 1, 410. HAKoch, JJ. 105, 638. CMFrancken, Mnemos. NS. 7, 184.

7) Cistellaria, scarcely one half of which is preserved, perhaps also from a stage-edition. The plot is very much like that of the Epidicus.

1. In the prologue (1, 3, 54) a single mention of the still unfinished war with Hannibal.—Edition: LEBenoist, Lyon 1863.—ThLadewig, RhM. 3, 520. Teuffel, Stud. 260. Studemund, Emend. plaut. 1871, 7; Herm. 19, 456.

8) Epidicus, the plot varied, but somewhat complicated, and without much humour and vivacity. It must have been written after 559/195.

1. The complicated plot may perhaps be explained (according to Ladewig ZfAW. 1841, 1086, but against him RMüller l.l. 5 and LReinhardt in Studemund's Studien 1, 103, with JJ. 111, 194) by assuming contamination, and may itself account for the unfavourable reception of the play, whereas the poet (Bacch. 215) blames for this Pellio, the actor of the leading part (§ 16, 14).—2, 2, 40 presupposes the abolition of the lex Oppia sumptuaria (a. 559/195).

2. Editions by FJacob (Lüb. 1835) and CEGeppert, Berl. 1865.—RMüller, de Pl. Epidico, Berl. 1865. GLangrehr, de Pl. Epid. in the Miscellanea philol. (Gött. 1876) 9. GGötz, acta Lips. 6, 283. 322. CMFrancken, Mnemos. NS. 7, 184. ThHasper, ad Epid. coniectanea, Dresd. 1882. CSchredinger, obss. in Epid., Münnerst. 1884.—Translation by FJacob, Lüb. 1843.—On the plays nos. 1–8: GGötz, symb. crit. ad priores Pl. fabulas, Lps. 1877.

9) Bacchides, one of the best plays both in plan (esp. in the

masterly working-up of the intrigue) and as regards the characters. The first scenes were lost with the last part of the Aulularia between the 4th and 6th centuries A.D. The original was most likely Menander's *Δὶς ἐξαπατῶν.* It was performed a. 565/189.

1. On the contents and remains of the 2 or 3 scenes which are lost see RITSCHL, op. 2, 292. RIBBECK RhM. 42, 111. The bad supplements found in old editions are most probably by Antonio Beccadelli of Palermo (§ 99, 8).

2. Contamination is not probable; see TEUFFEL, stud. u. Charakt. 256. On supposed later revision see WBRACHMANN, Lpz. Stud. 3, 57 and EANSPACH, Bonn 1882, and against it PWEISE, Berl. 1883.—It must have been written before 568/186 on account of lines 53 and 1073 (allusion to the four triumphs of the year 565/189): see RITSCHL, Parerga 423. GGÖTZ, acta Lips. 6, 315.

3. The present placing of the play (after Epid.) dates only from the 5th century A.D., and is founded on line 214 R. RITSCHL, Parerga 391; cf. op. 2, 321. STUDEMUND, Festgruss z. Würzb. Philologenvers. (1868) 39.

4. Editions by FRITSCHL (Hal. 1835), GHERMANN (Lps. 1845).—Articles: RITSCHL, Parerga 391 and op. 2, 292. FVFRITZSCHE, Rostocker Sommerkatalog 1846. SCHNEIDEWIN, RhM. 2, 415. MHEMEIER, op. 2, 330. THLADEWIG, Phil. 17, 261. TEUFFEL, RhM. 30, 317; JJ. 113, 539.

10) Mostellaria (the haunted house), a play with a well-contrived plot and a variety of happily invented situations and well-drawn characters.

1. Probably adapted from Philemon's Φάσμα; cf. FEST. 162. 305 *Plautus in Phasmate.* RITSCHL, Parerga 159. 272. 431. Comic quotation of himself by Philemon, retained by Plautus v. 1149: *Si amicus Diphilo aut Philemoni es* etc. FLEO. Herm. 18, 560.

2. Editions by ALORENZ, Berl.[2] 1883. WRAMSAY, Lond. 1869. SBUGGE, Christiania 1873. EMORRIS, Bost. 1880. EASONNENSCHEIN, Cambr. 1884.—IASTAMKART, commentarius in Pl. Most., Amst. 1858.—Cf. LORENZ, Phil. 27, 543. ASPENGEL, ib. 28, 725. RELLIS, journ. of philol. 11, 161. FLEO, Herm. 18, 558.

11) Menaechmi, in all probability the most excellent of the Plautine comedies, describing the merry mistakes and complications arising from the very great resemblance of twin brothers. The original and time of this play are unknown.

1. *Argumentum sicelissat* (prol. 12) is said with reference to the birthplace of the twins only. It is very doubtful whether Poseidippos' Δίδυμοι (Ὅμοιοι) was the original (LADEWIG, Phil. 1, 275); see TEUFFEL, Stud. 263. RIBBECK, röm. Dicht. 1, 125. 2, 3, 60 bears out, in some degree, the supposition that it was composed before a. 539/215. In any case the Menaechmi is among the earliest of the plays of Plautus which have been preserved to us.

2. Editions by JHILDYARD (Cambr. 1840), CEGEPPERT (Lat. and Germ., Berl. 1845), JBRIX (Leipz.[3] 1880). WWAGNER (Cambridge 1878). JVAHLEN, Berl. 1882.—VAHLEN, RhM. 16, 631. 27, 173. Herm. 17, 599. 603. 610. TEUFFEL, Stud. u. Charakt.

263. LSchwabe, JJ. 105, 403. KDziatzko, ib. 107, 833. PLangen, de Men. prologo, Münster 1873; Phil. 33, 708. Ribbeck, RhM. 37, 531. JBrix, JJ. 131, 193. JHOnions, journ. of Philol. 1885, 53.

3. ALStiefel, d. Menächmenfabel, in the Symbolae philol. ad LSpengel., Münch. 1877; BlfdbayrGW. 15, 309. 340. ThZielinski, quaestt. com. 71.—PESonnenburg, de Men. Pl. retractatione, Bonn 1882. GGötz, RhM. 35, 481.

12) Miles gloriosus, the exaggerated portrait of a braggadocio, not without prolix passages, and rather careless as to the plot, but overflowing with most felicitous humour.

1. This is the traditional and correct title: see WHertzberg, transl. 356. ARiese, RhM. 22, 303.—Lessing, Works 7, 90 and Fleckeisen, RhM. 14, 628 preferred *Gloriosus*.—The original of the play, according to 2, 1, 8, is the Ἀλαζών of some Greek poet, and in the introductory scene also Menander's Κόλαξ (WABecker), or Diphilos' Αἱρησιτείχης (Ritschl). Cf. Teuffel, Stud. 273. Ribbeck, Alazon, Beitr. z. antiken Ethologie; together with the transl. of Pl. Mil. glor., Lpz. 1882.—The time is later than a. 550/204 (on account of v. 211 sq.) and earlier than 568/186 (on account of 1016). The play contains no lyrical portions; Ritschl, op. 3, 29.—For parallels to the story of the abduction: EZarncke, RhM. 39, 1.

2. Editions by ALorenz (Berl.[2] 1886), JBrix (Lpz.[2] 1882, together with JJ. 115, 337). ORibbeck, Lps. 1881. RYTyrrell, Lond.[2] 1885.

3. Ritschl, op. 2, 404 (de argumento acrosticho Mil. gl.). 3, 789. FVFritzsche, Rostocker Index Sommer 1850. MHaupt, op. 2, 135. 3, 399. Ribbeck, RhM. 12, 594. 29, 13. 36, 116. ASchöne, ib. 18, 157. HAKoch, JJ. 101, 61. Fleckeisen, ib. 101, 846. SBugge, Phil. 30, 636. ALorenz, ib. 30, 578. 32, 270. 406. FSchmidt, Unterss. üb. d. Mil. gl., JJ. Suppl. 9, 321. ThBirt, RhM. 40, 521.

13) Mercator, with a plot resembling the Casina, probably performed not before 558/196. Its original was Philemon's Ἔμπορος.

1. The time has been deduced from 3, 1, 28 by Ladewig, ZfAW. 1841, 1085; cf. Ritschl, Parerga 344. Critical contributions by Ritschl, op. 2, 395. JBrix, Phil. 12, 650. FBücheler, RhM. 15, 428. GGötz, ib. 31, 635. ORibbeck, emendatt. in Merc., Lps. 1883.—On the prologue see Dziatzko, RhM. 26, 421. 29, 63. LReinhardt, de retractatis fabb. Pl., Greifsw. 1872.=Studemund's Studien 1, 80.

14) Pseudŏlus, a mature production in its whole character and form, but rather loose in construction; performed a. 563/191.

1. On the form of the title Pseudŏlus (see the puns on *dolus* 1205. 1244) =Ψευδύλος OSeyffert, Phil. 25, 448. Fleckeisen, JJ. 93, 9. Cf. ib. 242. OLorenz, Phil. 35, 153. Against this and for Pseudulus Ritschl, op. 3. 7; cf. 3, 332.—Didascalia: *M. Junio M. fil. pr. urb.* (a. 563/191) *acta Megalesiis*. Accordingly the first performance took place on the consecration of the temple of the magna mater (cf. 2, 4, 19), on the 10th of April of that year (Ritschl, Parerga 286. 295). Cf. Cic. Cato 50 *quam (gaudebat in senectute) Truculento Plautus, quam Pseudulo!*—Bergk maintains that this comedy was an adaptation of a play of the Middle Comedy: RhM. 20, 290.

2. Editions by Romeijn (Daventr. 1836), ALorenz (Berl. 1876).—With Rud. and

Truc. denuo rec. et expl. FHBothe, Lps. 1840.— HUsener, Pseud. scaena secunda recogn., Greifsw. 1866. AKiessling, RhM. 23, 411. ALorenz, Phil. 35, 153. FSchmidt, in the Miscellanea philol. (Gött. 1876) 20. JBrix, JJ. 115, 327. JHilberg, ZföG. 28, 34.

15) Poenulus, not without blemishes in its plot and division, but famous for the Phoenician passage in it. It was performed 565/189. Its original was a play called **Καρχηδόνιος**, probably by Menander.

1. On the faults and chronology of this play see Teuffel, Stud. 274. Cf. LReinhardt in Studem. Stud. 1, 109. At a later performance the title was changed to *Patruus pultiphagonides* (prol. 54). The present fourth act (817 sqq.) should be placed before v. 439: GGötz, de compos. Poen., Jena 1883. The last scene exists in two texts, not agreeing with each other, but of about the same age; Ritschl, Parerga 601. ThHasper, de Poen. duplici exitu, Lps. 1868. Cf. GGötz, acta Lips. 6, 253. 326. CMFrancken, de Poen. compositione, Mnemos. 4 (1876), 146. GLangrehr, de Pl. Poen., Friedland 1883.

2. Edition by Geppert, Berl. 1864.— On the Punic (5, 1) recent notice by JGildemeister in Götz-Löwe's edition. GHennen, de Hannonis in Poen. precationis recensione punica, Marb. 1882.—Critical: Ritschl, op. 5, 552. HAKoch, JJ. 107, 241. GGötz, act. Lps. 6, 328. KSchueth, de Poen. quaestt. crit., Bonn 1883. On the prologue: OBenndorf, ZföG. 26, 83. JSommerbrodt, RhM. 31, 129.

16) Persa, a play describing the intrigues of slaves, with a simple plot, which is, however, in some respects carried out in a very lively manner.

1. ThLadewig, on the canon of Volc. Sed. 38 (composed a. 557/197). GGötz, die Aufführungszeit des Persa (a. 568/186), RhM. 30, 162.—Cf. the same writer acta Lips. 6, 297.—AvanJisendijk, de Plauti Persa, Utrecht 1884.

17) Rudens (the Cable), remarkable rather for the merry and witty execution of many scenes than the plot of the whole. The original by Diphilos. Time about 562/192.

1. Editions by FVReiz (Lps. 1789), CEChrSchneider (Bresl. 1824), FHBothe (see Pseud.), Geppert (Berl. 1846), LEBenoist (Par. 1864).

2. Teuffel, Stud. 276.—Kampmann, adnott., Oels 1830. CMFrancken, Mnemos. 3 (1875), 34. JBrix, JJ. 131, 200. On the prologue: KDziatzko, RhM. 24, 570. On the fishermen's chorus: see § 16, 3.

18) Stichus, performed 554/200 ludis plebeis, a bourgeois comedy without intrigue, second-rate.

1. The didascalia preserved in the cod. Ambros. calls the original Adelphoe Menandru. The play by Menander, reproduced in Terence's Adelphi, is out of the question on account of the difference of contents. Ritschl, Parerga 270 (who with KFHermann understands Menander's Φιλάδελφοι), Studemund l.l. and others consider the didascalia corrupt. It appears more probable that two different plays of Menander bore the name of Adelphi (cf. Schol. Plat. p. 276 καὶ Μένανδρος ἐν Ἀδελφοῖς β). See FSchöll, JJ, 119, 44.

2. Ritschl, Parerga 261. Bergk, op. 1, 36. Teuffel, Stud. 277. Dziatzko, RhM. 21, 82. ASpengel, Phil. 28, 728. WStudemund (de actae Stichi Plautinae tempore), comment. Mommsen. (Berl. 1877) 782. GGötz, acta Lips. 6, 302. HBuchholtz, Phil. 36, 720. FLeo, RhM. 39, 470.

19) Trinummus, a very pretty family piece, without female characters, of measured plan and tone (stataria). Exhibited not before 560/194. The original was Philemon's *Θησαυρός*.

1. Editions by GHermann (Lps. 1800 and 1853), Geppert (Latin and German, Berl. 1844. Lpz. 1854), JBrix (Lpz.[3] 1879), WWagner (Cambridge[2] 1875), ASpengel (Berl. 1875), CEFreeman and ASloman, Oxford 1883, ECocchia, Turin 1886.

2. Ritschl, de actae Trin. tempore, Parerga 339. De interpolatione Trin., ib. 511. MHEMeier, op. 2, 321. Bergk, kl. Schr. 1, 53. 615. FVFritzsche, Rostock Ind. 1849 sq. Studemund, der pl. Trin. im cod. Ambrosianus, RhM. 21, 574. Cf. Herm. 1, 304. 310. Contributions to the criticism of the text by ORibbeck, RhM. 27, 177. Teuffel, ib. 485. 28, 344. 31, 472. 632; JJ. 105, 831. Ritschl, op. 3, 146. FSchöll, acta Lips. 2, 457. GLöwe, JJ. 111, 533; coniect. Plaut., Lps. 1877, 61. HSchenkl, Wien. Stud. 2, 154.

3. Translated by FOsthelder (Speier 1852 sq.) and WWagner (Frankf. 1861).

20) Truculentus, performed about 565/189, defective in its present form as regards the characters, full of broad and unrestrained humour, somewhat prolix in parts. The principal character is a greedy meretrix.

1. Cic. Cato 50 (see § 96, 2). Teuffel, Stud. 279. LReinhardt in Studem. Stud. 1, 93 (de compositione Truc.). On the prologue see KDziatzko, RhM. 29, 51. Was the original the *Σικυώνιος* of Menander ?? FSchöll, l.l. 15, and in the praef. to his edition. Against this FSchmidt, GGA. l.l. Ribbeck, Alazon 79.

2. Editions by Göller (Cologne, 1824), FHBothe (see Pseud.), Geppert (Berl. 1863), ASpengel and WStudemund (Gött. 1868).

3. The MS. material is very corrupt. Criticism: CEChrSchneider, Vratisl. 1834. ASpengel, lectt. Plaut., Münch. 1866. JBrix, Epistula ad ASpengelium, Liegnitz, 1868. AKiessling, JJ. 97, 609. ThBergk, kl. Schr. 1, 680. Fleckeisen, JJ. 101, 616. 647. 709. 781. 848. 103, 460. 809. Cf. 105, 366. 569. 832. SBugge, ib. 107, 401; HAKoch, ib. 419. BDombart, Phil. 28, 731. JMähly, Blfdbayr. Gymn. 9, 113. FSchöll, acta Lips, 2, 458; divinationes in Truc., Lps. 1876. GGötz, acta Lips. 6, 288. GLöwe, coniectan. Plaut. 52. FSchmidt, Gött. gel. Anz. 1877, 951. Ribbeck, RhM. 37, 417. EBährens, JJ. 125, 473. KDziatzko, JJ. 127, 61. REllis, journ. of Phil. 12, 256.

4. GEGeppert, on the so-called Italian revision in the Truc., in his Plautine studies, 1 (1870), 87. EKellerhoff, complete text of the Truc. from the Paris MS. 7889 with the variants from F, and the collations by Geppert, Oldenb. 1886.

---

21) Vidularia, 'story of the travelling trunk,' perhaps after a *Σχεδία* (probably by Diphilos), very similar in its contents to the Rudens. Being the last play of the collection it was lost (only during the Middle Ages). Remains of it are extant in the Milan palimpsest. In addition there are quotations in some of

the grammarians. WSTUDEMUND, de Vidularia plautina, Greifsw. 1870; Verh. d. Karlsruher Philol.-Vers., Lpz. 1883, 33 (which contains also a complete collection of the fragments).

98. Plautus is wholly a comic and popular poet, with all the good and bad qualities of such. His position as a playwright, producing rapidly to make a living out of his employment, explains his frequently rough treatment of his Greek original, his dovetailing of two plays, and his carelessness as regards contradictions, improbabilities and the like. But Plautus is not merely a translator. His strength, like that of most comic poets and humorists, lies not in the plan of the whole but in the details. For the former he is entirely dependent on his models, to whom he is far from equal in constructive skill as regards the development of the story and in artistic insight generally. On the other hand, with these limitations, he shows masterly ability in recasting the old subject-matter in new language. In his hands the foreign material receives a Romano-Italic colouring, which spoils the delicate finish of the Attic delineation. His genius imprints on materials drawn from all manner of sources a distinct and uniform style, and a character of original power, robustness and freshness. The poet overflows with a profusion of wit and humour. Comic conceits crowd upon him, leading him away again and again from his models. His wit is often broad and strongly flavoured, but is rarely insipid. The poet is at his best in passages of repartee, which he successfully manages and modulates, according to the circumstances and characters, with variations of tone and tempo, either subdued or wrought to a pitch in neat and striking phraseology. Here Plautus is assisted by his perfect mastery of the language. In handling it he shows admirable ease and wealth of diction, though this indeed frequently degenerates into what, according to our taste, would appear gross redundancy. He employs, as the subject-matter of his plays itself necessitated, the transitional language of his time, which was exceedingly fluctuating in sound and form (§ 93). In prosody also he availed himself of the licences described above (p. 125 sq.), but his versification is thoroughly artistic, always easy, even in difficult metres (bacchii, cretics etc.), and often very harmonious. The large remains of Plautus which have fortunately been preserved to us are, therefore, irrespective of their literary importance, of extraordinary value for the history of the language.

1. On the characteristics of Plautus see e.g. LESSING, collected works, 3, 1,

Lachm., MOMMSEN, RG. 1[6], 901. 2, 432, RIBBECK, röm. Dicht. 1, 57. The plays are singly reviewed in RITSCHL's op. 2, 732 (by a lady).

2. Among the ancients CICERO is extravagant in his admiration (in ascribing to Plautus, off. 1, 104 the *iocandi genus elegans, urbanum, ingeniosum, facetum* in equal perfection with the Attic poets; APOLL. SIDON. 23, 148 even says: *Graios, Plaute, sales lepore transis*), while HORACE is too severe in his criticism (judging from artistic rules) E. 1, 1, 170 (here, e.g. *gestit enim* [Plautus] *nummum in loculos demittere, post hoc securus, cadat an recto stet fabula talo*). 1, 3, 270. See RITSCHL, neue plautin. Exkurse 1, 122; op. 3, 156. In the Augustan period the admirers of the archaic poets praised him for his vivacity and rapidity, for which they compared him to Epicharmos, thus at the same time palliating his frequent want of form; on the frequently misunderstood expression *properare ad exemplar Epicharmi* (HOR. E. 2, 1, 57) cf. ARISTOPH. Eccl. 583 ὡς τὸ ταχύνειν χαρίτων μετέχει πλεῖστον παρὰ τοῖσι θεαταῖς and THLADEWIG, on the canon of Volc. Sed. (1842) 19; Phil. 1. 276; and also LINGE, de Plauto properante ad ex. Ep., Ratibor 1827.

3. Chronology of the comedies. FWINDISCHMANN, RhM. 1 (1833), 110. FRITTER, Allg. Schulztg. 1830, 873. PETERSEN, ZfAW. 1836, 615. VISSERING, quaestt. Plautt. 1 (Amst. 1842), 94. RITSCHL, Parerga 177. 353 and elsewhere. Cf. supr. § 97.

4. His treatment of his Greek originals: in the action and general substance of the plays he adheres to them closely for the most part, insomuch that he often actually retains allusions in the original which the Roman public could not understand at all. The Greek colouring remains in the names, in the scene where the action takes place, in the customs which are carefully preserved; but the poet thinks nothing of suddenly dropping out of the Greek surroundings, though usually not beyond a few words and phrases. In formulas and idioms the originals are more freely dealt with. Allusions by Plautus himself to individual contemporaries (§ 95, 3) or actual events are rare. WABECKER, de com. rom. maxime Plaut. quaestt. (Lps. 1837), 82. RITSCHL, Parerga 271. FWFRITZSCHE, de graecis fontibus Plauti I, Rost. 1845. AKIESSLING, anall. Plaut. 1, 14. 2, 9. MSCHUSTER, quomodo Pl. attica exemplaria transtulerit, Greifsw. 1884. FOSTERMAYER, de historia fabulari in com. Pl., Greifsw. 1884.—AKESEBERG, quaestt. Pl. et Ter. ad religionem spectantes, Lps. 1884. THHUBRICH, de diis Plaut. et Ter., Königsb. 1883.

5. Allusions of a military and juridical nature are very frequent: KAMPMANN, res militares Pl., Bresl. 1839. ROMEIJN, loca nonnulla Pl. iure civili illustrata, Daventr. 1836. EIBEKKER, de emptione venditione quae Plauti fabulis fuisse probetur (Berl. 1853), and Loci Plautini de rebus creditis, Greifsw. 1861. GDEMELIUS, plautin. Studien, ZfRechtsgeschichte, 1 (1862), 351. 2, 177. Cf. § 48, 3. Lorenz on the Pseud. p. 28.—Pl. nowhere mentions Roman money: see WCHRIST, JJ. 97, 345. (On Men. 1161 *quinquagensiens*, see LSCHWABE, ib. 105, 418). On the nummi plumbei in Pl. OBENNDORF, ZföG. 26, 611. Cf. also GEPPERT, das plaut. Münzwesen, plaut. Studien 1, 41.

6. Actual discrepancies, inconsequences, improbabilities, negligences, are frequent in Pl.; they are only in a very slight degree to be explained or excused on the theory of later revision. See GEPPERT, plaut. Stud. 1, 61. PLANGEN, Berl. Stud. 5, 89.—Plautus, the quondam hodman and journeyman miller, succeeds best in the description of characters from the lower class, such as slaves, parasites and the like. His unfavourable view of the female sex partly reflects the vulgar opinion, but it is also partly imported from the originals, being a peculiarity of the New Attic comedy. LEBENOIST, de personis muliebribus apud Pl., Marseille 1862.—EBERTIN, de Plautinis et Terent. adolescentibus amatoribus, Paris 1879.

7. Plautine language, and early Latin in general (see also § 111, 6): lists of words, lexika, see § 99, 11. FWHoltze, syntaxis priscorum scriptorum ad Terentium, Lps. 1861. 62, II; suppl.: synt. scaenicorum qui post Ter. fuerunt, Lps. 1881. ELübbert, grammat. Studien, Bresl. 1867. 70, II. GSchmilinsky, de proprietate sermonis Pl. usu linguarum romanicarum illustrato, Halle, 1866. On the characteristics of the Plautine language e.g. Ribbeck, röm. Dicht. 1, 119.—Ritschl, plautin. Exkurse, op. 2, 436. 661; neue plautin. Exk. I (final d in early Latin), Lpz. 1869 (together with op. 3, 120. 155). ThBergk, Beitr. z. lat. Gramm. I (final d in early Latin), Halle, 1870. FUmpfenbach, meletem. Plautt. (de MED et TED accusativis; de iussivo temporis praeteriti), Giessen 1860. HPloen, de copiae verborum differentiis inter varia poesis rom. genera intercedentibus (Diss. Argent. 7, 233). EBallas, grammatica Pl., Berl. 1884 II. AGEngelbrecht, Wien. Stud. 6, 216.—HRassow, de Pl. substantivis, with an index of all the passages, JJ. Suppl. 15, 589. WFraesdorff, de comparativi gradus usu ap. Pl. Halle 1881.—ALuchs, Genetivbildung der latt. Pronom., in Studem. Stud. 1, part 2. SBrandt, de varia apud Rom. scaenic. genet. sing. pronominum forma ac mensura, Heidelb. 1877. FSchmidt, der Plur. des Pron. HIC bei Pl. u. Ter., Herm. 8, 478; de pronominum demonstrat. formis plaut., Berl. 1875 (cf. Studemund, JJ. 113, 57). Thurau, de pronominum demonstr. ap. Pl. usu, Rössel 1876. WNiemüller, de pronomm. IPSE et IDEM ap. Pl. et Ter., Halle 1886. AMahler, de pronominum personal. ap. Pl. collocatione, Griefsw. 1876. WKämpf, de pronomm. person. usu et colloc. ap. poett. scaen. Rom. (Berl. Stud. 3, 2). RKuklinski, critt. Plaut. (on TUTE, TETE, EPEDOL, ECASTOR etc.), Berl. 1884. MPennigsdorf, de QVISQVE et QVISQVIS pronominum ap. comicos usu, Halle 1878.—MPaul, quaestt, gramm. I: DE UNUS nom. num. ap. priscos scriptt. lat. usu, Jena 1884.—FSchultz, de obsoletis coniugationum Plaut. formis, Conitz 1864. RJonas, de verbis frequent. et intensivis apud comic. lat., Posen 1871. Meseritz 1872 II; zum Gebr. der vv. freq. u. intens. in d. ält. lat. Prosa (Cato, Varro, Sall.), Posen 1879 (see § 257, 15). CBesta, de verborum compositione Plaut., Bresl. 1876. FUlrich, de verbb. compositorum ap. Pl. usu, Halle 1880; die Composita bei Pl., Halle 1884. ENeumann, de compositorum a DIS- (DI-) incipientium ap. prisc. scriptt. vi et usu, Jena 1886. AGoerke, symb. ad vocab. Graeca in ling. Lat. recepta (in Plaut.), Königsb. 1868.—CFKampmann, de AB praepositionis usu Plaut., Bresl. 1842; de IN praep. usu Pl. 1845. FHarder, A und AB vor Konsonanten bei den Kom., JJ. 131, 882.—RObrikatis, de PER praepos. ante Cic. aetat. usu, Königsb. 1884.—HBocksch, de casuum attractione ap. Pl. et Ter., Bresl. 1865.—ASchaaf, de genetivi usu Pl., Halle 1881. ELoch, de genet. ap. prisc. scriptt. lat., Bartenst. 1880. HPeine, de dativi usu ap. prisc. scriptt. lat., Strassb. 1878. EBombe, de ablat. absol. ap. antiquiss. scriptores usu, Greifsw. 1877. WEbrard, de ablativi locativi instrumentalis ap. prisc. Lat. usu, JJ. Suppl. Bd. 10, 579. MRuge, de ablativi in vett. ling. ital. forma et usu locali, in GCurtius' Studd. 10, 586. WGoerbig, nominum quibus loca significantur usus Plaut. exponitur et cum Ter. comparatur, Halle 1883.—WOlsen, quaestt. Pl. de verbo substantivo, Greifsw. 1884. ThMeifart, de fut. exacti usu Pl., Jena 1885. FCramer, de perfecti coniunctivi usu potentiali ap. prisc. scr. lat., Marb. 1886. ABiese, de obiecto interno ap. Pl. et Ter. atque de transitu verbalium notionum, Kiel 1878. HHahn, de verborum cum praepositionibus compositorum ap. vett. Rom. poett. scaen. cum dativo structura, Halle 1878. ELoch, Gebr. des Imperat. bei Pl., Memel 1871. FLübker, de usu infinitivi Plaut., Schlesw. 1841 (=ZfAW. 1849, Nr. 14). WVotsch, de infin. usu Pl., Halle 1874. EWalder, der Infin. bei Pl., Berl. 1874. PBarth, de infinitivi ap. scaen. poett. lat. usu, Lpz. 1881. AFunck, d. Auslassung des Subj. Pron. im Acc. c. inf. bei d. latt. Kom., JJ. 121, 725; *animum inducere* im arch. Lat., JJ. 127, 487. JDem-

BITZER, de ratione quam Pl. potissimum et Ter. in reciproca actione exprimenda inierint, Krakau 1886. ASPENGEL, NONNE im Altlatein., Münch. 1867. HSCHUBERT, z. Gebr. d. Temporalkonjj. bei Pl., Lissa 1881. PSCHERER, de particula QUANDO ap. vetust. scriptt. lat., Strassb. 1883. OELSTE, de DUM particulae usu Pl., Halle 1882. GMRICHARDSON, de DUM part. ap. prisc. scriptt. lat. usu, Lpz. 1886. AKRAUSE, de QVOM coniunctionis usu et forma (esp. cap. 1), Berl. 1876. OKIENITZ, de QVIN particulae ap. prisc. Lat. usu, Karlsr. 1878; de QVI localis modalis ap. prisc. script. Lat. usu: JJ. Suppl. Bd. 10, 527. CSCHMIDT, de QUIN partic. usu Plaut., Marb. 1877. OWICHMANN, de QUI ablativo antiquo, Bresl. 1875. HSCHNOOR, quaestt. Pl. (parataxis, QUIN etc.), Kiel 1878; zum Gebr. von UT bei Pl., Neumünster 1885. THBRAUNE, obss. ad usum ITA SIC TAM (TAMEN) ADEO particularum Pl. et Ter., Berl. 1882. PRICHTER, de usu particularum exclamativarum ap. prisc. Lat., Strassb. 1874. CFUHRMANN, de particul. comparativarum usu Plaut. I, Greifsw. 1870; über d. Vergleichungssätze b. Pl., JJ. 97, 841. 101, 687; der Indik. in den indir. Fragesätzen, JJ. 105, 809. SSTEINITZ, de affirmandi particulis I: PROFECTO, Bresl. 1885. FSIGISMUND, de HAUD negationis ap. prisc. scriptt. usu, Commentatt. Ienens. 3, 215. EBECKER, de syntaxi obliquarum interrogationum ap. prisc. Lat. in Studem. Stud. 1, 113. JROTHHEIMER, de enuntiatis condicionalibus Pl., Gött. 1876. HBLASE, de modd. et tempp. in enunt. condicion. lat. permutatione, Diss. Argentor. 10, 57. OBRUGMANN, Gebr. d. condicionalen NI in d. alt. Lat., Lpz. 1887. JLANGE, de sententiarum temporalium ap. prisc. Lat. syntaxi I, Bresl. 1878. HKRIEGE, de enuntiatis concessivis ap. Pl., Halle 1884. CROTHE, quaestt. gramm. ad usum Pl. et Ter. spectantes (esp. on consecut. tempp. in final sentt. and indir. questions), Berl. 1876. 81 II. SCHMERL, der Prohibitiv bei Pl., Krotoschiner Jubel-Progr. 1887.—JBWEISSENBORN, parataxis Plautina, Burghaussen 1884.—EKELLERHOF, de collocatione verborum Pl., Strassb. 1881.—BGRAUPNER, de metaphoris Pl. et Ter., Bresl. 1874. AINOWRACLAWER, de metaphorae ap. Pl. usu, Rost. 1876. PLANGEN, d. Metapher im Lat. von Pl. bis Ter., JJ. 125, 673. 753; de execrandi formulis Pl., RhM. 12, 426; UTOR FRUOR FUNGOR POTIOR im ält. Lat., Arch. f. Lexikogr. 3, 329; plautin. Studien, Berl. 1887 (see § 99, 13). EFWORTMANN, de comparationibus Pl. et Ter. ad animalia spectantibus, Marb. 1883. FGOLDMANN, d. poetische Personifikation in d. Spr. d. alten Kom. I Plautus, Halle 1885.—EKÖNIG, de nominibus propriis ap. Pl. et Ter., Patschkau 1876 (cf. § 16, 1); quaestt. Pl. (names of places with prepp.), Patschkau 1883.—JSCHNEIDER, de proverbiis Pl. et Ter., Berl. 1878. FXPFLÜGL, d. Sprichw. b. Pl. u. Ter., Straubing 1880.

8. On the condition of the language as Plautus found it, and as it is reflected in his verses, see § 93. Even in the Ciceronian period Plautine prosody had ceased to be completely understood: CIC. or. 184 *comicorum senarii propter similitudinem sermonis sic saepe sunt abiecti ut non nunquam vix in eis numerus et versus intellegi posit* (cf. ib. 67). During a long period Plautus continued to be judged according to the standard of the language when fully developed and the laws of Greek prosody, and consequently was unfairly criticised. The historical examination of Latin, as it has been opened up, especially by Ritschl, first made possible the more correct estimate, which recognises in Plautus a master of the language as well as a highly skilled and versatile versifier. The more recent views of RITSCHL, op. 4, 400 (cf. 2, 444, 600) mark a decided improvement on the earlier system propounded in the proleg. to the Trin.[1] (Bonn 1848, reprinted op. 5, 285): see on this WCORSSEN, Ausspr. Vokal. u. Beton. d. lat. Spr. 2, 400. Other recent literature on the Plautine prosody and metre: JBRIX, Einleit. z. Trin. ([3]1879) p. 13. CFWMÜLLER, plautin. Prosodie, Berl. 1869; supplementary, Berl. 1871. HKOEHLER, de verborum accentus cum numerorum rationibus in trochaicis

septenariis Plautinis consociatione, Halle 1877. OBrugmann, quemadmodum in iamb. senar. Romani vet. verb. accent. cum num. consociarint, Bonn 1874. MW Humphreys, influence of accent in Latin iamb. trim., Americ. philol. associat. 1876, 1. CMFrancken, Woord- en Versaccent bij Pl., Versl. en Mededeel. 2, 4 (Amsterd. 1873). WMeyer, d. Beachtung des Wortaccents in d. altlat. Poesie, Abh. d. bayr. Akad. d. Wiss. 17, 1 (1884). ALuchs, commentatt. prosod. lat., Erl. 1883. 84 II. PSchrader, de particularum -ne, anne, nonne ap. Pl. prosodia, Diss. Argentor. 8, 225. EBelow, de hiatu Pl. I, Berl. 1885.

9. WStudemund, de canticis Pl., Halle 1863. FRitschl, op. 3, 1. 144; proleg. ad Trin.[1] and elsewhere. WChrist, metr. Bemerk. zu den cantica des Pl., SBer. d. bayr. Akad., phil. Kl. 1871, 41. JWinter, d. metr. Rekonstruktion d. pl. Cantica, Münch. 1880. ASpengel, de versuum cretic. usu pl., Berl. 1861; Reformvorschläge z. Metr. d. lyr. Versarten b. Pl. u. d. übr. Szenikern, Berl. 1882 (cf. § 99, 13). OSeyffert, de bacchiac. versuum usu pl., Berl. 1864. PESonnenburg, de verss. Pl. anapaest. in Exercitationis grammaticae spec. (Bonn 1881) 16. GVoss, de verss. anap. Pl., Strassb. 1882. PMohr, de iambico ap. Pl. septenario, Lps. 1873. ALuchs, quaestt. metr. plaut. in Studem. Stud. 1, 1.—RKlotz, zur Alliteration u. Symmetrie bei Pl., Zittau 1876. JBaske, de allitterationis usu Pl., Königsb. 1884. LBuchhold, de paromoeoseos (allitterationis) ap. vett. Rom. poett. usu, Lpz. 1883. ORäbel, de usu adnominationis ap. Rom. poett. com., Halle 1887. FLeo, RhM. 40, 2.

99. The Plautine plays maintained themselves on the stage for a long time after the poet's death, and most of the prologues were written for performances at the beginning of the 7th century U.C. His works became also at an early time the subject of learned labours, with regard both to the language and the explanation of the subject-matter, and here Varro's researches were prominent. The text of the plays is preserved in two versions, of which one is contained in the Ambrosian palimpsest (A), the other mainly in the so-called Palatine (Pfälzer) MSS. (BC).

1. The revivals of the Plautine plays doubtless occasioned considerable injury to the original text; too much blame, however, has been laid upon these recently (see the literature on the various plays, § 97), when the real or presumed shortcomings of the plays, both in composition and wording, have been attributed by a somewhat one-sided estimate to later versions (retractationes) produced for the purpose of revivals. PLangen, Berl. Stud. 5, 1.—On the continuance of the influence of Plautus in the later literature: CvReinhardstöttner, Plautus, spätere Bearbeitt. plautin. Lustspiele, Beitr. z. Vgl. Lit.-Gesch., Lpz. 1886 etc.

2. Prologues. Ritschl, Parerga 1, 180. Teuffel, Stud. u. Charakt. 256. 260. 273. ALRLiebig, de prol. Terent. et Plautinis, Görlitz 1859. CDziatzko, de prologis Pl. et Ter., Bonn 1864; die plaut. Prologe, Luzern 1867. ThLadewig, JJ. 99, 473. FMartins, quaestt. Pl. (cap. 1), Halle 1879.

3. We have two sorts of metrical summaries of contents (argumenta) to the Plautine plays: 1) acrostic (for all the plays except the Bacch.); they are the earliest, and on account of the close acquaintance with the Plautine method of

versification which they exhibit, may be considered to belong to the best period of Plautine studies in the 7th cent. U.C. (cf. § 159). 2) non-acrostic, which are later. These may perhaps (cf. § 109, 3) be by the grammarian C. Sulpicius Apollinaris (§ 357, 2) or more probably by some contemporary of his. Cf. RITSCHL, on the Trin.[1] p. CCCXVI.; op. 2, 404. FOSANN, ZfaW. 1849, 199. WSTUDEMUND, commentat. Mommsen. 803. CROPITZ, de argumentorum metric. lat. arte et orig., Lpz. Stud. 6, 204. 234. OSEYFFERT, JB. 1886, 2, 22.

4. Lists (indices) of the (genuine) plays of Plautus were, according to GELL. 3, 3, 1, made by L. Accius, Aelius (Stilo), Aurelius Opilius, Volcacius Sedigitus, Serv. Clodius, Manilius (§ 158, 1) and Varro; cf. the latter.—Sisenna and Terentius Scaurus were commentators of Pl. RITSCHL, Parerga 374; below § 156, 4. 352, 1.

5. Detailed points of the language of Plautus were commented on by the glossographers Aurelius Opilius, Ser. Clodius, Aelius Stilo, Flavius Caper, Arruntius Celsus. FRITSCHL, de veteribus Plauti interpretibus, in his Parerga 357. Remains of their works are to be found in the glossae Placidi and other collections of glosses. See RITSCHL, op. 3, 65. GLÖWE, prodromus corp. gloss. lat. 254; cf. § 42, 5. 6. On the commentaries on Plautus used in Nonius cf. ASCHOTTMÜLLER, symb. philol. Bonn. 823. Generally for the quotations from Plautus in Festus-Paulus see § 261, 8; for those in Nonius, § 390, 3.

6. An ancient Plautine glossary drawn up before the time of Priscian, see in RITSCHL, op. 2, 234; cf. ib. 228. 237. ASPENGEL, Plautus 50.

7. In the Middle Ages Plautus was hardly known. RPEIPER, Archiv f. Lit.-Gesch. 5, 495; RhM. 32, 516. Plautus is also unknown to Hrotswitha von Gandersheim, the imitator of Terence (about 960): see MHAUPT, op. 3, 587.—At the beginning of the 15th cent. the last 12 Plautine plays (Bacchides to Truculentus, see § 97) were lost. Only the first 8 (Amphitruo to Epidicus) were known; these were distributed in a great number of MSS., their order indeed being varied, but in the main alphabetical (RITSCHL, op. 2, 236). List of 43 extant MSS. of the first 8 plays (all s. XIV/XV) in GGÖTZ, symb. crit. 22. A manuscript of the last 12 was found in Germany about 1428 by Nicolaus of Trèves (concerning him see GVOIGT, Wiederbel. d. klass. Altert. 1², 259; in Italy it was first in the possession of Cardinal Orsini, now Vatic. 3870 s. XII, D in RITSCHL; see his op. 2, 19; facsimile in CHATELAIN, paléogr. d. classiq. lat. t. 4); this contains besides the 3 first plays (Amph. Asin. Aul.) and the first half of the fourth play (the Captivi). In the 16th cent. come into use the two MSS. of Camerarius, which at a later period were kept in the Heidelberg library (hence called Palatini), the vetus codex (B) s. X, which contains all the 20 plays (now in Rome, Vaticanus 1615; facsimile in CHATELAIN l.l. t. 2), and the decurtatus (C)—so called by Pareus—s. XI, now containing only the last 12 plays (since 1815 again kept in Heidelberg; facsimile in CHATELAIN t. 3. 4). D is from the same source as C. The most important version of the recension (n. 10), which is best preserved in BC, was the MS. used by ATurnebus, now unfortunately lost: its readings are collected in GÖTZ-LÖWE on the Poen. p. VII. For the first 8 plays we have also to take into account an Ambros. (E) s. XII/XIII (facs. in CHATELAIN l.l. t. 5) and a MS. in the British Museum (J) s. XI; see GGÖTZ, symbol. crit. ad priores Pl. fabulas, Lps. 1877; JJ. 113, 351; the same and GLÖWE, RhM. 34, 52. SONNENSCHEIN's (German) ed. of the Capt. p. 55. (English ed. p. 16 sqq. Excursus and Appendix.)

8. During the course of the 15th century was formed in Italy, probably at Naples at the instance of Alfonso I. (who reigned from 1435), an edition of the 20 plays in accordance with the requirements and taste of the period; this was done in a very arbitrary and ignorant manner, with numberless gratuitous alter-

ations, and it was circulated in numerous copies. The originator of this text was perhaps Antonio Beccadelli of Palermo: see on him GVoigt, Wiederbel. d. klass. Altert. 1^2, 480, and on his Plautine studies GScheps, BlfdbayrGW. 16, 97. To these interpolated MSS. belongs the Lipsiensis (F). Cf. Ritschl, op. 2, 23; and on the MSS. of Camerarius ib. 103. 125. 3, 80. 105. 5, 59. Ed. of the Trin. [2] p. viii.

9. Opposed to all these MSS., which are collectively based on the same original (and therefore show the same gaps and corruptions, e.g. Trin. 944–8), is the palimpsest (from Bobbio) of the Ambrosian library in Milan (cod. Ambros. G. 82 sup. s. IV/V), which however omits 7 of the plays entirely, while the others are in part very incomplete. Cf. AMai, M. Acci Plauti fragmenta inedita etc., Mediol. 1815 (also in Osann, Anal. crit. p. 205). Facsimile in Zangemeister-Wattenbach, Ex. codd. latt. t. 6 and in Chatelain l.l. t. 1.—FRitschl, op. 2, 167 and Proleg. z. Trin. [1] cap. i, vi, vii; Trin. [2] p. vii. Geppert, üb. d. cod. Ambros. u. s. Einfluss auf die plautinische Kritik, Lpz. 1847; Mitteilungen aus dem cod. Ambros. (Plautin. Stud. 2 Hft., Berl. 1871). WStudemund RhM. 21, 574 and Würzb. Festgruss (1868) 39; by whom the publication of the MS. has long been promised. New collation of A by GLöwe in the second edition of Plautus by Ritschl (n. 11): cf. also Löwe's coniectan. Plaut. ad cod. Ambros. maximam partem spectantia, Lps. 1877; cf. the same in Götz' edition of the Epid. p. v. See also HUsener JJ. 91, 263.

10. In comparison with the text given in the Ambros. that of the Palatini, often greatly varying from it, possesses a decidedly high independent value, though it has probably been overrated recently in depreciation of the Ambros., e.g. by Ritschl on the Trin. [2] p. xi.; op. 3, 791. Bergk, Beitr. z. lat. Gramm. 1, 129. AFleckeisen, JJ. 101, 709. BBaier, de Pl. fabb. recensionibus ambros. et palat., Bresl. 1884 (and OSeyffert, Berl.phWschr. 1886, 716). ELeidolph, commentatt. Ienens. 2, 208. In certain formulas the divergence between the two texts is almost uniform; Studemund, RhM. 21, 606. Cf. FSchöll, divin. in Truc., Lpz. 1876. MNiemeyer, de Pl. fabb. recensione duplici, Berl. 1877. On the antiquity, origin, and relative value of the two texts see conjectures in Leidolph l.l. 210.—Scanty traces of stichometric arrangement in the Trin. and Truc. Ritschl on the Trin. [2] p. lxv and KDziatzko, JJ. 127, 61.

11. Critical account of the editions and text of Plautus (down to Bothe) by Ritschl, op. 2, 1. The later Palatine MSS. were first employed by their owner Joach. Camerarius (chamberlain): separate editions by him from 1530; complete edition Bâle 1552; supplement to this 1553; see for Camerarius' editions of Plautus Ritschl, op. 3, 67 and GGötz, RhM. 41, 629. DLambinus' commentary (and text) was published in Paris 1576, FTaubmann's commentary Wittenb. 1605, subsequently (with more ample notices from the MSS. of Camerarius, since transferred to Heidelberg, and others) in 1612, and best (ex recogn. Iani Gruteri) in 1621.—Ed. JPhPareus, Francof. 1610; together with the (for the period) excellent collection of variants from the Palatine MSS. Neapoli Nemetum (Neustadt in the Palatinate) 1619 = Francof. 1623; and (without the collection of variants, but with a more complete enumeration of the fragments) Francof. 1641. By the same Pareus lexicon Plautinum, [2] Hanoviae 1634.—Ex rec. FGuieti ed. (unreliable) MdeMarolles, Par. 1658 (see EBenoist, le Plaute de FGuyet, Mél. Graux, Par. 1884, 461).—The vulgate (and verse-numeration) accepted down to Ritschl was founded on the edition of JFGronov (Leiden 1664. 1669. 1684; c. praef. Ernesti, Lps. 1760 II).—Ed. FHBothe, Berl. 1809–11 IV, and vols. 1 and 2 of the Poetae scen. lat. Halberst. 1821 = Stuttg. 1829 sq. IV.—Cum nott. varr. cur. JNaudet, Par. 1830 IV (vol. 4 index).—Rec. interpr. est CWWeise, Quedlinb.

1837. 1847 (with list of words, 2 ed. 1886) II, and Lpz. ap. Tauchnitz.—Epoch-making: ex rec. et cum apparatu critico FRitschelii, Tom. I (Prolegomena, Trin., Mil., Bacch.). II (Stich. Pseud. Men. Most.). III (Persa, Merc.), Bonn 1848–54. Simultaneously an edition of the text. (Cf. AFleckeisen, JJ. 60, 234. 61, 17. ThBergk, kl. Schr. 1, 1. 29. 106.) Second revision begun by Ritschl, continued by GLöwe, GGötz, FSchöll: I Trin. ([3]1884) Epid. Curc. Asin. Truc. 1871—1881. II Aul. Amph. Merc. Stich. Poen. 1882—1884. III 1 Bacch. 1886. 2 Capt. 1887. Rud. 1887.—Ex recogn. AFleckeiseni, Lps. 1859 II (10 plays). Rec. et enarr. JLUssing, Kopenh. 1875—1886 V (III, 1 Cas. Cist., has not yet appeared). Recogn. FLeo I (Amph. As. Aul. Bacch.), Berl. 1885.—Plaute. Morceaux choisis publ. par EBenoist, Paris [2] 1877.

12. Germ. transll.: Köpke, Berl. 1809. 1826 II. Rost (9 plays), Lpz. 1836; MRapp, Stuttg. 1838 sqq.; WHertzberg (Trin. Mil. Capt. Rud.), Stuttg. 1861; WBinder, Stuttg. 1862 sqq.; JJCDonner, Heidelb. 1864 sqq. III. Eng. Bonnell Thornton, Lond. 1769.

13. Textual criticism e.g.: PSchroeder, Bentley's Emendatt. z. Pl., Heilbr. 1880. EASonnenschein, Bentley's Plautine emendations (Anecd. Oxon. 1 [1883], 178); cf. above § 97, 4, 1. FRitschl, op. 2, 274. 3, 166 and elsewhere. AFleckeisen, exercit. Plaut., Gött. 1842; Phil. 2, 57; krit. Miscellen, Dresd. 1864; JJ. 95, 625; 107, 501 and elsewhere. JBrix, emendatt. Plaut., Brieg 1847. Hirschb. 1854; JJ. 101, 761. 131, 193 and elsewhere. ThBergk, op. 1, 1. 673 and elsewhere. ASpengel, T. Maccius Plautus; Kritik, Prosodie, Metrik, Gött. 1865 (see on this esp. Studemund, JJ. 93, 49). KHWeise, d. Komödien d. Pl., beleuchtet, Quedlinb. 1866. AKiessling, in d. Symb. phil. Bonn. 833; RhM. 24, 115; analecta pl., Greifsw. 1878. 81 II. SBugge, Tidskr. f. Philol. (Kopenh. 1867 sq.) 6, 1. 7, 1; Phil. 30, 636. 31, 247; opusc. philol. ad Madvig. (1876) 153. WStudemund, Festgruss zur Würzb. Philologenvers. (Würzb. 1868) 38; emendatt. Plaut., Greifsw. 1871 and elsewhere. OSeyffert, Phil. 25, 439. 27, 432. 29, 385; studia Pl. (Progr. d. Sophien-Gymn.), Berl. 1874. ALorenz, Phil. 27, 543. 28, 183. CEGeppert, plaut. Studien, Berl. 1870, 71 II. ALuchs, Herm. 6, 264. 8, 105. 13, 497. GGötz, acta Lips. 6, 235. GLöwe, coniectan. Pl., Lps. 1877. JLUssing, Nord. Tidskr. f. Fil. 5, 54. PLangen, Beitr. z. Krit. u. Erkl. d. Pl. Lpz. 1880; analecta Pl., Münst. 1882. 83 III; plautinische Studien, Berl. 1887. HSchenkl, Wien. SBer. 98, 609. AWeidner, adverss. Pl., Darmst. 1882. FLeo, RhM. 38, 1. 311; Herm. 18, 558. WAbraham, JJ. Suppl. 14, 179.

ALorenz, Berichte über die pl. Literatur seit 1873, JB. 1873, 341. 1874/75 1, 606. 1876 2, 1. 1878 2, 1. 1879 2, 1. 1880 2, 1. 1881 2, 1 and OSeyffert, ib. 1882 2, 33. 1886 2, 1.

100. Q. Ennius, born a. 515/239 at Rudiae in Calabria, served in the Roman army 550/204 in Sardinia, where M. Porcius Cato fell in with him and took him to Rome. Here he too gained his livelihood by teaching Greek, and translating Greek plays for the Roman stage, and won the favour of the elder Africanus. M. Fulvius Nobilior, cos. 565/189, took the poet with him into his province of Aetolia, as a witness and herald of his deeds. His son obtained for Ennius the Roman citizenship a. 570/184, by giving him a lot (at Potentia or Pisaurum) with the approval ot the people, as triumvir coloniae deducendae. Ennius died of gout a. 585/169.

1. The year of his birth is attested by Varro, Gell. NA. 17, 21, 43 (see § 101, 3); cf. Cic. Brut. 72. Tusc. 1, 3; see n. 2.—The poet himself mentions his birth-place ap. Cic. de or. 3, 168 *Nos sumu' Romani, qui fuimus ante Rudini:* cf. Cic. Arch. 22 *Ennium . . . Rudinum hominem.* Auson. grammaticom. 17. Hor. C. 4, 8, 20 *Calabrae Pierides.* Ov. AA. 3, 409 *Ennius . . . Calabris in montibus ortus.* Sil. It. 12, 393 *Ennius . . . antiqua Messapi ab origine regis . . . Miserunt Calabri: Rudiae genuere vetustae, Nunc Rudiae solo memorabile nomen alumno.* Serv. Aen. 7, 691 *ab hoc* (Messapo) *Ennius dicit se originem ducere.* Suid. v. Ἔννιος· ποιητὴς Μεσσάπιος. Therefore Rudiae (now Rugge) near Lupiae (the modern Lecce) in Calabria. Another Rudiae near Canusium in Apulia was by Strabo 6, p. 281 and Mela 2, 66 erroneously considered to be the birth-place of Ennius. Discussions on this question: ECocchia, riv. di filol. 13 (1884), 31. LMantegazza, Bergamo 1885. FTamborrino, Ostuni 1885.—Fest. 293 *quam consuetudinem* (*non geminandi litteras*, § 104, 5) *Ennius mutavisse fertur, utpote Graecus graeco more usus.* Suet. gramm. 1 *antiquissimi doctorum, qui iidem et poetae et semigraeci erant, Livium et Ennium dico* etc. Gell. 17, 17, 1 *Q. Ennius tria corda habere sese dicebat, quod loqui graece et osce et latine sciret.* He does not here specify the language of his native country, Messapian: the area of Oscan extended as far as Apulia and Lucania.

2. Corn. Nep. Cato 1, 4 *praetor provinciam obtinuit Sardiniam, ex qua quaestor superiore tempore ex Africa decedens Q. Ennium poetam deduxerat.* Cf. Hieron. ad Euseb. Chron. a. 1777=514/240 *Q. Ennius poeta Tarenti* (a mistake) *nascitur, qui a Catone quaestore Romam translatus habitavit in monte Aventino parco admodum sumptu contentus et unius* (? cf. Cic. de or. 2, 276) *ancillae ministerio* (cf. Varro LL. 5, 163 . . . *ligionem Porcius*—Licinus § 146, 4—*designat quom de Ennio scribens dicit eum coluisse Tutilinae loca*). FRitter, ZfAW. 1840, 370.

3. Cic. Arch. 22 *carus fuit Africano superiori noster Ennius; itaque etiam in sepulcro Scipionum putatur is esse constitutus ex marmore.* Liv. 38, 56 *Romae extra portam Capenam in Scipionum monumento tres statuae sunt, quarum duae P. et L. Scipionum dicuntur esse, tertia poetae Q. Ennii.* Cf. Welcker, Trag. 1360. Portrait of Ennius with the inscription Q. E.? Bernoulli, röm. Ikonogr. 1, 234.—Familiar relations with Scipio Nasica, Cic. de or. 2, 276.

4. Cic. Arch. 27 *ille qui cum Aetolis Ennio comite bellavit Fulvius.* Tusc. 1, 3 *oratio Catonis, in qua obiecit ut probrum M. Nobiliori quod is in provinciam poetas duxisset. duxerat autem consul ille in Aetoliam, ut scimus, Ennium.* Aur. Vict. illustr. 52, 3 *quam victoriam* (of Fulvius over the Aetolians) *per se magnificam, Q. Ennius, amicus eius, insigni laude celebravit.* Symmach. ep. 1, 21 *Q. Ennio ex aetolicis manubiis captiva chlamys tantum muneri data Fulvium decolorat* (cf. Bergk, Beitr. z. lat. Gramm. 1, 33, 1).

5. Cic. Arch. 22 *ergo illum . . . Rudinum hominem, maiores nostri in civitatem receperunt.* Brut. 79 *Q. Nobiliorem M. f.*, (§ 126, 2) . . ., *qui etiam Q. Ennium, qui cum patre eius in Aetolia militaverat* (inaccurate), *civitate donavit, cum triumvir coloniam deduxisset.* (570/184, see Liv. 39, 44). Cf. FRitter, l.l. 383. This explains Ennius' line: *nos sumu' Romani* etc. Cic. de or. 3, 168 (see n. 1).

6. Cic. Cato mai. 14 *annos septuaginta natus—tot enim vixit Ennius—ita ferebat duo quae maxima putantur onera, paupertatem et senectutem, ut eis paene delectari videretur.* Brut. 78 *hoc* (C. Sulpicius Gallus) *praetore ludos Apollini faciente, cum Thyesten fabulam docuisset, Q. Marcio Cn. Servilio coss.* (585/169) *mortem obiit Ennius.* Hieron. ad Euseb. Chr. ad a. 1849=586/168: *Ennius poeta septuagenario maior articulari morbo perit* (cf. Ennius ap. Priscian. GL. 2, 434 *numquam poetor nisi si*

podager; cf. also HOR. E. 1, 19, 7 *Ennius ipse pater numquam nisi potus ad arma prosiluit dicenda*; SEREN. SAMMON. 713 *Ennius ipse pater, dum pocula siccat iniqua, hoc vitio tales fertur meruisse dolores*), *sepultusque* (? cf. n. 3) *in Scipionis monumento, via Appia intra primum ab urbe miliarium. quidam ossa eius Rudiam ex Ianiculo translata adfirmant* (it may be, because a monument was there erected to him). His epitaph (see however § 115, 2) ap. CIC. Tusc. 1, 34 *aspicite, o cives, senis Enni imaginis formam. hic vestrum panxit maxima facta patrum* etc., cf. ib. 1, 117. Cato mai. 73.

101. His greatest renown Ennius gained as an epic poet, by his eighteen books of Annales, which related the traditional Roman history, from Aeneas' arrival in Italy down to the poet's own time, in chronological order, now recording the events in the dry tone of the chronicler, now depicting incidents such as were effective for poetry with forcible pathos and felicitous colouring. The work was meant to be a pendant to the Homeric poems, and was also considered as such by the Romans—though there can be no doubt that its artistic value was but very small. It was important on account of the introduction of the epic line of the Greeks into Roman literature, besides many other details in which the Homeric style was imitated. The poet appears to have composed this work in advanced age and published it gradually in separate parts.

1. VAHLEN, üb. d. Ann. d. Enn., Abh. d. Berl. Akad. 1886, and the literature quoted § 104, 6.

2. DIOMED. GL. 1, 484 *epos latinum primus digne scripsit Ennius, qui res Romanorum decem et octo complexus est libris, qui vel annales (in)scribuntur, quod singulorum fere annorum actus contineant, sicut publici annales quos pontifices scribaeque conficiunt, vel Romais* (according to REIFFERSCHEID JJ. 79, 157, a title invented in the Augustan time; MSS. *Romanis*), *quod Romanorum res gestas declarant.*

3. B. I–III: Introduction and Regal Period. IV–VI: foundation of the Republic, conquest of Italy, Pyrrhus. VII: the first Punic war, in a brief summary, as the subject had already been treated by Naevius, who was spoken of in the proem in a somewhat contemptuous manner; see CIC. Brut. 75. In book 7 a personal description, in which, in Stilo's opinion, Ennius portrayed himself. (GELL. 12, 4). VIII and IX: the war with Hannibal. X–XII: the Macedonian war and its results (to the year 558/196). With the twelfth book there was probably a winding-up of the previous contents; in the epilogue the poet spoke of himself: see GELL. 17, 21, 43 *consules Q. Valerius et C. Manilius, quibus natum esse Q. Ennium poetam M. Varro . . . scripsit eumque cum septimum et sexagesimum annum haberet* (therefore a. 582/172, three years before his death) *duodecimum annalem scripsisse, idque ipsum Ennium in eodem libro dicere* (see on this VAHLEN, die Ann. des Enn. 1886). Then a fresh continuation; XIII and XIV: the war with Antiochus (to the year 564/190). XV: Fulvius Nobilior in Aetolia (a. 565/189). Lastly a concluding group, opening also with a special proem, XVI–XVIII. PLIN. NH. 7, 101 (concerning *fortitudo* which had become a theme

for *poetica fabulositas*): *Q. Ennius T. Caecilium Teucrum fratremque eius praecipue miratus propter eos sextum decumum adiecit annalem.* Cf. Bergk, opusc. 1, 252. LHavet, l'histoire rom. dans le dernier tiers des Ann. d'Enn., Mél. de l'école des hautes études 1878, 21. Vahlen, d. Ann. d. Enn. 25. It cannot be ascertained from the fragments to what date the Annales were brought down. The latest event which they mention is the censorship of Fulvius and Lepidus 573/181 (Cic. de prov. cons. 20). The Annales were probably brought out gradually (in series of six consisting respectively of three books [?]).—Cf. on reminiscences of Ennius in Livy HHagen, JJ. 109, 271. WSieglin, Chronol. der Belager. v. Sagunt, Lpz. 1878. Bärwinkel, Ennius u. Livius, Sondershausen 1883.

4. Suet. gramm. 2 *Q. Vargunteius* (cf. § 41, 1) *annales Ennii, quos certis diebus in magna frequentia pronuntiabat.* Cf. ib. 8 *M. Pompilius Andronicus . . . adeo inops atque egens ut coactus sit praecipuum illud opusculum suum Annalium Ennii elenchorum XVI milibus nummum cuidam vendere.* For Gnipho's commentary on the Ann. see § 159, 5. Cic. opt. gen. or. 2 *licet dicere Ennium summum epicum poetam, si cui ita videtur.* Martial. 5, 10, 7 *Ennius est lectus salvo tibi, Roma, Marone et sua riserunt saecula Maeoniden.* In a Pompeian mural inscription is the beginning of a line from the Annales CIL. 4, 3135 (see Bücheler, RhM. 27, 474). Vitruv. 9, praef. 16 *qui litterarum iucunditatibus instinctas habent mentes non possunt non in suis pectoribus dedicatum habere sicut deorum sic Ennii poetae simulacrum.* Quint. 10, 1, 88 *Ennium sicut sacros vetustate lucos adoremus, in quibus grandia et antiqua robora iam non tantam habent speciem quantam religionem.* Cf. 2, 17, 24 *dicet notum illud* (words of Ennius): *Dum clavom rectum teneam;* cf. 9, 4, 115. Vulcac. Gall. Avid. Cass. 5, 7 *scis versum a bono poeta dictum et omnibus frequentatum: Moribus antiquis* etc. Gell. 18, 5, 2 (*Antonio*) *Iuliano nuntiatur anagnosten quendam, non indoctum hominem, voce admodum scita et canora Enni Annales legere ad populum in theatro* (at Puteoli). ib. 3 *Ennianistam . . . se ille appellari volebat.* 4 *quem cum iam inter ingentes clamores legentem invenissemus* etc. 7 *cumque aliquot eorum qui aderant 'quadrupes equus' apud suum quisque grammaticum legisse se dicerent,* etc. ib. 11 is mentioned a *liber summae atque reverendae vetustatis* (the Ann. of E.), *quem fere constabat Lampadionis* (§ 138, 4) *manu emendatum.* Spart. Hadr. 16, 6 *Ciceroni Catonem, Vergilio Ennium, Sallustio Coelium praetulit.* Macr. sat. 6, 9, 9 *quia saeculum nostrum ab Ennio et omni bibliotheca vetere descivit, multa ignoramus quae non laterent si veterum lectio nobis esset familiaris.*

102. Tragedies held the place of second importance amongst Ennius' productions. He seems to have translated Euripides in preference to other poets, perhaps attracted by his free thinking and his rhetorical and sententious manner. He also wrote praetextae and comedies, though he did not distinguish himself in this department.

1. We possess fragments of Achilles and (cf. Klussmann in Jahn's Archiv 11, 325. OJahn, Hermes 3, 191) Achilles Aristarchi, Aiax, Alcumeo, Alexander, Andromacha aechmalotis, Andromeda, Athamas (? FALange, quaest. metr. 16, 30; BSchmidt, RhM. 16, 599), Cresphontes, Erechtheus, Eumenides, Hectoris lutra (Bergk, op. 1, 295) Hecuba (FOsann, anal. crit. 126), Iphigenia, Medea exsul (cf. HPlanck, Ennii Medea illustr., Gött. 1807. FOsann, l.l. 79. JVahlen, Berl. ind. lect. 1877), Medea Atheniensis, Melanippa, Nemea Phoenix, Telamo, Telephus,

Thyestes. The fragments in RIBBECK, trag. lat.[2] p. 15. Cf. WELCKER, griech. Trag. 1373. RIBBECK, röm. Trag. 81, 212.

2. Glossae Salomonis (HUSENER, RhM. 28, 419. 22, 446): *tragoedias Ennius fere omnes ex graecis transtulit, plurimas ex Euripideis, nonnullus Aristarchiis.* Of the plays known to us Andromeda, Hecuba, Iphigenia, Medea exsul, Melanippa, Telephus, Alexander, Andromacha are certain to be translations from Euripides, and so are in all probability Erechtheus and Phoenix. The Eumenides (and Hectoris lutra?) was translated from Aischylos, Aiax probably from Sophokles, and one Achilles from Aristarchos. A comparison with the original plays shows that Ennius' were free translations, the plot being in the Iphigenia completed from Sophokles (contaminatio). See CIC. fin. 1, 4 *cum . . . fabellas latinas ad verbum e graecis expressas non inviti legant. quis enim tam inimicus paene nomini romano est qui Ennii Medeam aut Antiopam Pacuvii spernat aut reiciat, quod se isdem Euripidis fabulis delectari dicat?* de opt. gen. 18 *eidem . . . Andromacham aut Antiopam aut Epigonos latinas recipiunt; quod igitur est eorum in orationibus e graeco conversis fastidium, nullum cum sit in versibus?* GELL. 11, 4 *Euripidis versus sunt in Hecuba . . . hos versus Q. Ennius, cum eam tragoediam verteret, non sane incommode aemulatus est.* CIC. Brut. 78 proves that Ennius remained faithful to this occupation till his death.

3. The Sabinae (the rape of the Sabine women) was a praetexta by Ennius, as VAHLEN (RhM. 16, 580, cf. Enn. p. LXXXVIII) conjectures from JUL. VICTOR. p. 402, 30 Halm: *ut (in) Sabinis Ennius dixit;* against this BERGK, op. 1, 361. Cf. RIBBECK, röm. Trag. 205. The Ambracia also was probably a praetexta treating of the capture of that town by Ennius' patron, M. Fulvus Nobilior, a. 565/189. See RIBBECK, röm. Trag. 207; cf. VAHLEN, Enn. p. 153.

4. Ennius does not seem to have been very successful in the easy comic style. Of two comedies, Cupuncula (a tabernaria?) and Pancratiastes, we have slight traces; see RIBBECK com.[2] p. 4. VAHLEN, Enn. p. LXXXI and p. 153 sq. Volcatius Sedigitus (§ 147, 3) mentioned his name among the comic poets *antiquitatis causa.*

103. Ennius further published Saturae, i.e. a collection of miscellaneous poems in various metres. Parts of this work may be recognised in the Sota, Protrepticus, Heduphagetica, Epicharmus, Euhemerus and in the epigrams.

1. PORPH. Hor. S. 1, 10, 47 *Ennius quattuor libros saturarum reliquit.* Quotation from book 6 in DONAT. Ter. Phorm. 2, 2, 25 (?). The reference (OKELLER, Phil. 45, 389) to the σάτυροι of Timon of Phlius († 226 B.C.) as Ennius' model for names and subject-matter is of little service, as we know nothing of the character of those poems (cf. WACHSMUTH's sillogr. gr.[2] 25); moreover the poems of Ennius were called *saturae* not *saturoe* or *saturi*, and an amalgamation through Ennius of the ancient Italian with the Hellenistic conception (§ 6, 2. § 28) is improbable; lastly the Hellenistic contents of the satires (supposing the above-mentioned individual titles to have really formed part of the satires) do not prove the title to have been derived from Hellenistic sources. Metres: trochaic, iambic, sotadean, dactylic hexameters; it is neither probable nor attested that Ennius composed saturnians. The contents are didactic and include fables, e.g. that of the crested lark (Babr. 88) in trochaic tetrameters (§ 27, 1. RIBBECK, RhM. 10, 290; cf. the fable restored in the same metre by BÜCHELER, RhM, 41, 5 from Hygin. fab. 220).—APETERMANN, on Ennius' satires, Hirschb. 1851. 52. II.

2. GELL. 4, 7, 3 *Ennii versum* (trochaic) *ex libro qui Scipio inscribitur*, probably a constituent part of the saturae (Book 3?): certainly not a praetexta (as GRÖPER, de Ennii Scipione, Danzig 1868, supposed; cf. RHABAN. MAUR, above § 14, 2). The scanty fragments show chiefly carefully constructed trochaic septenarii (but also dactylic hexameters). Composed probably before the Annales, about 554/200 after Scipio's triumphant return from Africa (a. 553/201); there is no real ground for assigning to them a later date (VAHLEN, MÜLLER).

3. Sota (i.e. Σωτᾶς)=Sotades (Σωτάδης), from whom the sotadean metre has received its name. VARRO LL. 5, 62 *in Sota Ennii.* FEST. 356 *Ennius . . . in Sota* (the MS. has *nasota*). *Sota Ennianus* in FRONTO p. 61; *Ennius sotadico versu* PAUL. Festi 59.

4. Praecepta s. Protrepticus, a double title. Heduphagetica, on gastronomical matters, after the parody by Archestratos of Gela entitled ἡδυπάθεια. VAHLEN, RhM. 16, 581.

5. Epicharmus, a kind of didactic poem on subjects of natural philosophy, was probably so called after the Sicilian comic poet of that name, who was imagined as having delivered to Ennius, in the under-world, the Pythagorean philosophy propounded in the work. Was it only a version of a Greek book? It was in trochaic tetrameters.

6. Euhemerus, sive Sacra historia (cf. also HUSENER, RhM. 28, 408), a Latin version of the ἱερὰ ἀναγραφὴ of Εὐήμερος of Agrigentum (about 450/304), in which this fantastic system of explaning mythology was also applied to the gods of Italy. CIC. n. d. 1, 119 *Euhemerus, . . . quem noster et interpretatus et secutus est praeter ceteros Ennius.* AUGUSTIN. civ. d. 7, 26 (27) *totam de hoc Euhemerus pandit historiam quam Ennius in latinum vertit eloquium.* In the quotations of Lactantius (from a prose version) the original trochaic rhythm is often heard (?).—KRAHNER, Grundlinien zur Gesch. d. Verfalls etc. 37. MOMMSEN, RG. 1^6, 917. ERОHDE, gr. Rom. 220. B. TEN BRINK, Varronis locus de urbe Roma, accedunt Q. Ennii apologus Aesopicus (cf. n. 1) et reliquiae Euemeri versibus quadratis, Utr. 1855.

7. A few epigrams (in elegiacs), e.g. the supposed epitaph of Ennius (§ 115, 2), in VAHLEN Enn. p. 162; cf. p. xc.

104. Ennius possessed a decided impulse towards artistic perfection. His poems indeed frequently violate the laws of beauty and good taste; but in the new path chosen by him he had also very great difficulties to overcome, and by his hard position he was prevented from evenly developing his rich talents. This disproportion between his outer circumstances and inner capacities increased also his self-consciousness. In his own time he was a missionary of culture and free thought, and he turned the Roman language and poetry into the paths in which they continued for centuries afterwards. His poetic works show great versatility both in form and subject-matter, and we find him devoting himself besides to practical literary objects: thus he was occupied with fixing Latin orthography. Perhaps he was also the first to introduce short-hand writing (notae) in Latin.

1. The Augustan and Imperial poets ungratefully and unjustly dwell on Ennius' imperfect formal polish (AZINGERLE, Ovids Verhältn. 2, 1): HOR. E. 2, 1, 50. AP. 259. PROP. 5, 1, 61. OVID. Am. 1, 15, 19. VAL. MAX. 8, 14, 1. SEN. ep. 58, 5; cf. dial. 5, 37, 5. fragm. 110–114 H. MARTIAL. 11, 90. MACR. 1, 4, 17. A juster appreciation in OVID. trist. 2, 423 sq. *suo Martem cecinit gravis Ennius ore, Ennius ingenio maximus, arte rudis.* Cf. QUINT. 1, 8, 8. 10, 1, 40. Also SEN. fr. 114 H. *quidam sunt tam magni sensus Q. Ennii ut, licet scripti sint inter hircosos, possint tamen inter unguentatos placere.* MACR. 6, 3, 9 *nemo ex hoc viles putet veteres poetas quod versus eorum scabri nobis videntur. ille enim stilus Enniani saeculi auribus solus placebat* etc. QUINT. 10, 1, 88. FRONTO p. 114 *Ennius multiformis.* CICERO de or. 1, 198 and de prov. cons. 21 *summus poeta.* Tusc. 3, 45 *egregius poeta . . . praeclarum carmen.* But or. 36 *multa apud Ennium neglegentius.* Mur. 30 *ingeniosus poeta et auctor valde bonus.* Affected admiration also in VITRUVIUS; see above § 101, 4.—Cf. LUCR. 1, 118 sqq. MOMMSEN, RG. 1^6, 910. RIBBECK, röm. Trag. 77.

2. His self-consciousness: cf. his criticism on Naevius, CIC. Brut. 76. Ann. 3 sq. 15. Sat. 6 sq. But see also Ann. 551.

3. His rationalism (see § 103, 6) appears esp. from Trag. 353 *Égo deum genus ésse semper dixi et dicam caélitum, Séd eos non curáre opinor quíd agat humanúm genus*; *Nám si curent, béne bonis sit, mále malis, quod núnc abest* etc. . . .

4. Ennius gave commendable care to verse-construction, and is remarkably strict in regard to the slurring of vowels. LMÜLLER, Q. Ennius 228.—Conceits of versification and relatively faults of taste occur, e.g. exaggerated alliteration etc. Ann. 113 Vahl. 452. Trag. 337, 448. sat. 33 sq.; unsuccessful tmesis (586 *saxo cere- comminuit -brum;* cf. GL. 4, 565, 21), apocope (451 *replet te laetificum gau;* 561 *divum domus altisonum cael;* 563 *endo suam do.*—Acrostic: *Q. Ennius fecit.* CIC. de div. 2. 111.

5. Doubling of consonants: FESTUS 293 *nulla geminabatur littera in scribendo. quam consuetudinem Ennius mutavisse fertur, utpote Graecus graeco more usus, quod illi aeque scribentes ac legentes duplicabant mutas, semi⟨vocales et liquidas⟩*, cf. § 93, 9. See in general for Ennius' services to the language § 93. LMÜLLER, metr. 69.—Short-hand: SUET. p. 135 Rffsch. and from him ISID. orig. 1, 21 and a Cassel MS. of the notae Tironis et Senecae (§ 289, 8. WSCHMITZ, symb. phil. Bonn. 532): *vulgares notas Ennius primus mille et centum invenit. notarum usus erat ut quidquid pro contione aut in iudiciis diceretur librarii scriberent simul astantes, divisis inter se partibus quot quisque verba et quo ordine exciperet. Romae primus Tullius Tiro* etc. (see § 191, 4). Cf. WSCHMITZ, Beitr. 211; Verhandl. d. Trierer Philol.-Vers. (Lpz. 1880) 59. WDEECKE, RhM. 36, 577. It is curious that, at a period which witnessed the bare beginnings of regular rhetoric, the need for exact recording of speeches should have already made itself felt. These notae are therefore sometimes attributed to the later grammarian Ennius: similar doubts as to the authorship of *Ennii de litteris, syllabis, metris libri II* were entertained even in ancient times: see § 159, 13.

6. On Ennius in gen. RIBBECK, röm. Dicht. 1, 27. MOMMSEN, RG. 1^6, 918. LMÜLLER, Q. Ennius, eine Einleitung in das Stud. d. röm. Poesie, Petersb. 1884.—Ennianae poesis reliquiae, rec. JVAHLEN, Lps. 1854. Q. Enni carmm. reliquiae; acc. Cn. Naevi belli Poen. quae supersunt; emend. et adn. LMÜLLER, Petersb. 1885. FPR. 58.—On the supposed preservation of works of E. down to the Middle Ages see RFÖRSTER, RhM. 37, 485.—MHOCH, de Ennianorum Ann. fragm. a PMerula (in his ed. Leiden 1595) auctis, Bonn 1839. JLAWICKI, de fraude Pauli Merulae, Ennianorum annalium editoris, Bonn 1852. THBERGK, op. 1, 209–316. ORIBBECK,

RhM. 10, 265. VAHLEN, ib. 14, 552. 16, 571; Herm. 12, 253. 399. 15, 260; Berl. ind. lect. 1878. MOMMSEN, RhM. 16, 449. 17, 143. JMÄHLY, JJ. 75, 359. RUNGER, scheda Enniana, Halle 1875. LFRUTERIUS, RhM. 33, 244. LHAVET, rev. d. philol. 2, 93. 9, 112. 189 and elsewhere. LQUICHERAT, mélanges de philol. (Par. 1879), 244. EBÄHRENS, JJ. 129, 838. FRANCKEN, de zoneclips van Enn., Versl. en Mededeel. 1885 3, 1.—HJORDAN, quaestt. Enn., Königsb. 1885. EMAASS, Herm. 16, 380.

105. M. Pacuvius, the son of Ennius' sister, was born c. 534/220 at Brundisium, and under the guidance of his uncle, who brought him to Rome, he there carried on both the profession of a painter and the writing of serious dramas. After having exhibited plays there as late as 614/140, he returned to the South of Italy and died at Tarentum c. 622/132. Of his writings we know only the titles of 12 tragedies and one praetexta (Paulus). The fragments as compared with the tragedies of Ennius show on the whole more fluency and facility in language and verse, but sometimes likewise a tendency towards artificiality and eccentricity. The stage effect of his plays was great and lasting. The artistic judgment of Cicero's time still saw in Pacuvius Rome's greatest tragic poet.

1. CIC. Brut. 229 *Accius isdem aedilibus ait se et Pacuvium docuisse fabulam, cum ille octoginta, ipse triginta annos natus esset.* Accius was born 584/170. HIERON. ad Euseb. Chr. a. 1863 = 600/154 *Pacuvius Brundisinus tragoediarum scriptor clarus habetur, Ennii poetae ex filia* (erroneously instead of his sister, see Pliny l.l.) *nepos, vixitque Romae quoad picturam exercuit ac fabulas venditavit. deinde Tarentum transgressus prope nonagenarius diem obiit.* VARRO sat. menipp. 356 Büch.: *Pacvi* (*Pacvius, Paquius, Pacuius* bye-forms of the Oscan name *Pacuvius*: see LACHM. on Lucr. p. 306. MOMMSEN, unterital. Dial. 284) *discipulus dicor, porro is fuit Enni, Enniu' Musarum: Pompilius* (§ 146, 2) *clueor.* PLIN. NH. 35, 19 *celebrata est in foro boario, aede Herculis, Pacuvii poetae pictura. Ennii sorore genitus hic fuit, clarioremque eam artem Romae fecit gloria scenae.* GELL. 13, 2, 2 *cum Pacuvius grandi iam aetate et morbo corporis diutino adfectus Tarentum ex urbe Roma concessisset* etc. Epitaph of Pacuvius (certainly genuine, BÜCHELER, RhM. 37, 521) in GELL. 1, 24, 4 *Aduléscens tam etsi próperas te hoc saxúm rogat Ut sése aspicias, deinde quod scriptúm est legas. Hic súnt poetae Pácuvi Marcí sita Ossa. hóc volebam nescius ne esses. vale.* Cf. § 115, 2.

2. Tragedies: Antiopa (after Euripides), Armorum iudicium, Atalanta, Chryses, Dulorestes (OJAHN, Herm. 2, 229. CROBERT, Bild und Lied 185), Hermiona, Iliona, Medus, Niptra (after Sophokles), Pentheus, Periboea, Teucer (Protesilaus is extremely doubtful). The fragments are collected in RIBBECK, trag. 2 p. 75. Cf. WELCKER, Trag. 1380. TEUFFEL, Tüb. Progr. 1858, 7. RIBBECK, röm. Trag. 218.

3. The subject of the praetexta Paulus (RIBBECK trag.[2] p. 280) was no doubt L. Aemilius Paulus as conqueror at Pydna; OJAHN, Lpz. Ber. 1856, 301. RIBBECK, röm. Trag. 326.

4. GELL. 6 (7), 14, 6 *exempla in latina lingua M. Varro esse dicit ubertatis Pacuvium, gracilitatis Lucilium, mediocritatis Terentium.* FRONTO, however, p. 114 *mediocris*

Pacuvius. CORNIFICIUS ad Her. 4, 7 finds his forte in the messengers' recitals (*nuntii.*) CIC. de opt. gen. or. 1 *itaque licet dicere et Ennium summum epicum poetam et Pacuvium tragicum et Caecilium fortasse comicum.* Brut. 258 *illorum* (Laelius and Africanus minor) *aequales Caecilium et Pacuvium male locutos videmus*; cf. ad Att. 7, 3, 10. or. 155. LUCIL. ap. Non. 30 *tristis contorto aliquo ex Pacuviano exordio.* HOR. E. 2, 1, 55. QUINT. 10, 1, 97. PERS. 1, 77. MARTIAL 11, 91. TAC. dial. 20. A review of these judgments by TEUFFEL, Tüb. Progr. 1858, 11. Cf. OJAHN, Herm. 2, 234.

5. Pacuvius as a writer of satires: DIOMEDES GL. 1, 485 *satira . . . carmen quale scripserunt Pacuvius et Ennius.* Cf. PORPHYR. on Hor. sat. 1, 10, 46 *cum . . . Terentius Varro Narbonensis* (§ 212, 1) . . . *item Ennius . . . et Pacuvius huic generi versificationis non suffecissent.*—In general on Pacuvius MOMMSEN, RG. 2[6], 431. TEUFFEL, Caecil. Statius, Pacuvius etc. Tüb. Progr. 1858, 5. RIBBECK, röm. Trag. 334; röm. Dicht. 1, 166.

106. Statius Caecilius, a contemporary of Pacuvius of almost the same age, belonged by birth to the Celtic tribe of the Insubrians, and came to Rome probably as a prisoner of war between 554/200 and 560/194. After his manumission he associated himself especially with Ennius, whom he did not survive very long. Thus standing midway between Plautus and Terence, Caecilius seems in his comedies, which were adaptations from New Attic originals, to have at first adhered more to the manner of Plautus, and later on, in accordance with the Greek fashion of the period, to have conformed more to rules, though he always retained greater originality than Terence. His fragments show the usual manner of the palliatae, but not so many archaic forms as Pacuvius.

1. HIERON. ad Euseb. Chron a. Abr. 1838=575/179: *Statius Caecilius comoediarum scriptor clarus habetur, natione Insuber Gallus et Ennii primum contubernalis. quidam Mediolanensem ferunt. mortuus est anno post mortem Ennii III* (the number added by RITSCHL, op. 3, 233, in order to carry Caecilius' life down to the performance of Terence's Andria [§ 110, 1, 1]; *IIII* acc. to Dziatzko) *et iuxta eum in Ianiculo* (so RITSCHL l.l. instead of *iuxta Ianiculum*) *sepultus.* Cf. KFHERMANN, de script. ill. p. 3. GELL. 4, 20, 13 *Caecilius ille comoediarum poeta inclutus servus fuit et propterea nomen habuit Statius. sed postea versum est quasi in cognomentum appellatusque est Caecilius Statius.* Merely Caecilius he is called in CIC. de or. 2, 40. Brut. 258. de opt. gen. 2. ad Att. 7, 3, 10; Statius alone never, not even de or. 2, 257. —If Caecilius died a. 588/166 he may have been born c. 535/219, as he is nowhere numbered among the longaevi (RITSCHL, Parerga 183, note) and was therefore of a fit age for military service in 554/200 sqq.

2. At first he was not successful in his plays, see TER. Hec. prol. 2, 6 sqq. Later on, he was employed as an authority to pass judgment on plays offered for exhibition, SUET. vit. Ter. p. 28, 9. RITSCHL, Parerga 329.

3. Of the 40 titles of comedies known to us (RIBBECK's com.[2] p. 35) 16 agree with titles of Menander: Andria, Androgynos, Chalcia, Dardanus, Ephesio, Hymnis, Hypobolimaeus (Rastraria), Imbrii, Karine, Nauclerus, Plocium, Polu-

meni, Progamos, Synaristosae, Synephebi, Titthe. The titles themselves are divided into three classes; 1) merely Latin ones, in the manner of Plautus; 2) double titles, in Latin and in Greek; 3) merely in Greek, in the manner of Terence and Turpilius. The last by far preponderate in number. Hence it may be inferred that Caecilius at first treated his originals with great freedom, but afterwards adhered to them more and more closely.

4. Varro ap. Non. 374 *in argumentis Caecilius poscit palmam*; ap. Charis. GL. 1, 241 *πάθη Trabea, Atilius, Caecilius facile moverunt.* Cf. Hor. E. 2, 1, 59 and other notices in Teuffel, Tüb. Progr. 1858, 3. Being an Insubrian by birth and having come late to Rome, Caecilius could not be considered a competent authority for good Latin; Cic. ad Att. 7, 3, 10. Cf. Brut. 258 (§ 105, 4). Criticism: LFruterius, RhM. 33, 243.—In general see Mommsen, RG. 1[6], 902 and Teuffel, Caecilius Statius etc. Tüb. 1858, 1.

107. In the time of Caecilius, Trabea was another poet of palliatae, and perhaps also Atilius, who seems to have resembled him; so was the author of the Boeotia, Aquilius, and Licinius Imbrex. Luscius Lanuvinus was an older contemporary and rival of Terence.

1. Varro ap. Charis. GL. 1, 241 *πάθη Trabea, Atilius, Caecilius facile moverunt.* Cf. Ritschl, Parerga 194, who accordingly places the time of the two former before that of Caecilius, who came to Rome when a full-grown man. Trabea's nomen gentile is unknown, the praenomen Q. without any authority. Two fragments of lively tone and polished language are found in Ribbeck, com. [2] p. 31.

2. The scanty fragments of Atilius (p. 32 Ribb.[2]), as a poet of palliatae designated by the title of Misogynos, are more archaic. Cic. ad Att. 14, 20, 3 calls him *poeta durissimus* and so also Licinius (correctly *Licinus* § 146, 3; DDetlefsen, Phil. 42, 182 incorrectly writes *Lucilius*) ap. Cic. fin. 1, 5 calls Atilius who translated Sophokles' Elektra (cf. Suet. Iul. 84) '*Ferreum scriptorem: verum, opinor, scriptorem tamen Ut legendus sit*'. Thus the two may be presumed to be identical; see Ribbeck, röm. Trag. 608. It is less probable that he is identical with the actor L. Hatilius of Praeneste (§ 16, 14) who performed in the plays of Terence (at the beginning of the 7th century? Dziatzko, RhM. 21, 72).

3. The Boeotia (Boeotis? see Kock, com. gr. 2, 35), shown by its title to be a palliata, which was considered to be by a certain Aquilius even in (or before) Varro's time, was yet attributed by the latter to Plautus on account of its Plautine style (Gell. 3, 3, 3), though L. Accius had emphatically protested against this supposition (ib. 9). The historical allusions point to a. 580/174–600/154. Ritschl, Parerga 82. 123. 208. Ribbeck, com.[2] p. 33.

4. *Licinius Imbrex, vetus comoediarum scriptor, in fabula quae Neaera (in)scripta est*, Gell. 13, 23, 16. Cf. Paul. Festi 109. Non. 196, 24 *Licinius in Marte* (cf. Bergk, JJ. 101, 832)? Rather *Licinius Macer* (§ 156, 5). Volcac. Sedig. ap. Gell. 15, 24 *si erit quod quarto detur dabitur Licinio.* Perhaps identical with Licinius Tegula (§ 114, 3)?

5. Luscius Lanuvinus (Lavinius: see on this perhaps incorrect form Dziatzko on the Phorm., p. 100), the chief adversary of Terence (*malivolus vetus poeta*) who is bitterly attacked in all the Terentian prologues except the one to the Hecyra. He translated Menander's Φάσμα (Ter. Eun. prol. 9) and a Θησαυρός (ib. 10) by the same author (?) so faithfully as to preserve even details which were

sure to displease a Roman audience, and blamed Terence's deviations from his Greek originals and his additions from other Greek plays (§ 16, 9) as faults. TER. Eun. prol. 10. Cf. Andr. prol. 15. Heaut. 16. Phorm. prol. 1. Ad. 1. GRAUERT, Analekten 116. LADEWIG, Kanon des Volc. Sed. 12. RIBBECK, com.[2] 83.—On Plautius see § 96, 5.

108. P. Terentius Afer was a native of Carthage, but at an early age came to Rome, where he was the slave of a senator Terentius Lucanus, by whom he was educated like a free man, and soon manumitted. Perhaps on account of his African birth, he came into intimate relations with Africanus the Younger, a fact which gave rise to the rumour that the latter was the real author of his plays. After having exhibited six plays, Terence went to Greece (a. 594/160) in order to study there. He died there, while on his way home, a. 595/159, in the prime of life.

1. Our principal source is the extract from Suetonius' work de poetis (§ 347, 7) preserved by Donatus (§ 409, 3) in the introduction to his commentary on Terence, mostly a compilation of the frequently conflicting notices of the grammarians. See Ritschl's edition in Reifferscheid's Sueton. (Lpz. 1880), now also in his opusc. 3, 204. See also BERGK, Phil. 16, 627. HSAUPPE, Gött. Nachrichten 1870, 111. JVAHLEN, SBer. d. Berl. Ak. 1876, 789.

2. The notice in HIERON. ad Euseb. 1859=596/158 and the vitae (Norimbergensis, Ambrosiana) preserved in MS. are collectively derived from Sueton. (n. 1). RITSCHL, opusc. 3, 374. Only the very short addition to the vita of Suetonius by Donatus possesses an independent value (p. 35, 1 R.).

3. Terence came to Rome perhaps through a slave-dealer, who either bought or caught him in Africa. He cannot have been a prisoner of war, as he was born after the end of the second Punic war (553/201) and died before the commencement of the 3rd (605/149); see FENESTELLA in Suetonius l.l. BERGK, l.l. 628. AL. 734 PLM. 5, 385 *Romanis ducibus bellica praeda fui.*

4. The praenomen Publius he may have received either from his patron or from another protector, perhaps Africanus the Younger. Cf. CIC. fam. 13, 35, 1. Att. 4, 15, 1.

5. SUET. p. 27, 2 Reiff. *cum multis nobilibus familiariter vixit, sed maxime cum Scipione Africano et C. Laelio. quibus etiam corporis gratia conciliatus existimatur . . . non obscura fama est adiutum Terentium in scriptis a Laelio et Scipione, eamque ipse auxit numquam nisi leviter* (cf. prol. to Heaut. and Ad.) *refutare conatus.* The latter he may have done because the rumour was offensive to neither party. Comments on it in SUET. l.l. Cf. CIC. Att. 7, 3, 10 *Terentium, cuius fabellae propter elegantiam sermonis putabantur a C. Laelio scribi.* QUINT. 10, 1, 99 *licet Terentii scripta ad Scipionem Africanum referantur.* †VALLEGIUS in actione (§ 147, 3) ap. Donatus (SUET. p. 35, 5 R.). It is possible that, before publishing, Terence used to read his compositions in the circle of his friends and avail himself of their observations and suggestions. We may, at all events, consider this rumour as a sufficient warrant for the genuine Roman character of Terence's style and language. Cf. besides VAHLEN, MBer. d. Berl. Ak. 1876, 797.

6. SUET. p. 32, 4 *post editas comoedias nondum quintum atque vicesimum* (the

number *XXXV* is only in interpolated MSS., Ritschl, op. 3, 253) *egressus* (Ritschl, *ingressus*) *annum, causa vitandae opinionis qua videbatur aliena pro suis edere seu* (*studio* added by Ritschl) *percipiendi Graecorum instituta moresque, quos non perinde exprimeret in scriptis, egressus* (GBecker *in Graeciam profectus*) *est neque amplius rediit . . . Q. Cosconius redeuntem e Graecia perisse in mari* ⟨Fleckeisen, krit. Miszell. 59 here adds the words *sinu Leucadiae* and omits the words below⟩ *dicit cum C et VIII fabulis conversis a Menandro* (on this corrupt passage see Ritschl l.l. 257. EBährens and AFleckeisen, JJ. 113, 594. RPeiper, RhM. 32, 517. JHilberg, epistula ad Vahlen., Wien 1877, 17): *ceteri mortuum esse in Arcadia Stymphali* [*sinu Leucadiae*] *tradunt Cn. Cornelio Dolabella M. Fulvio Nobiliore coss.* (a. 595/159, following which Jerome writes ad a. 1859=596/158 *Terentius . . . moritur*), *morbo implicatum ex dolore ac taedio amissarum sarcinarum, quas nave praemiserat, ac simul fabularum quas novas fecerat.* Cf. Lucan. 5, 651 *oraeque malignos Ambraciae portus*, on which the Schol. observes: *malignos dixit, sive quia saxosi sunt sive quia Terentius illic dicitur periisse.* Auson. ep. 18, 16 *Arcadiae medio qui iacet in gremio.*

7. The date of his death was traditional (n. 6): but that Terence died in his 25th year and therefore was born about a. 570/184 has only been inferred by the Roman historians of literature, chiefly from the fact of his being a contemporary of Scipio (born a. 569/185) and of Laelius (§ 131, 1, 3): cf. Suet. p. 27, 6 *Nepos aequales omnes* (Ter. Scip. Lael.) *fuisse censet.* But the fact remains established even if Terence was several years older than these. Fenestella already asserted (Suet. l.l.) *utroque maiorem* (Terentium) *fuisse*, and Santra (Suet. l.l.) even calls Scipio and Laelius *adulescentuli* as compared with Terence. That he may have been born earlier there is evidence in the fact that the oldest of the plays (Andr.) was performed 588/166. That the elaborate purist Terence should have taken his place as a writer for the stage in his 18th year, is hardly credible, nor is it likely that his opponent, with whom he often quarrels in the prologues, would have omitted to reproach him with this precocity. KLRoth, RhM. 12, 183. HSauppe, Gött. Nachr. 1870, 114. CDziatzko, Ter. com. p. v.

8. Suet. p. 33, 4 *fuisse dicitur mediocri statura, gracili corpore, colore fusco* (Suet. l.l., cf. Verg. Moret. 32 *Afra genus, tota patriam testante figura, torta comam labroque tumens et fusca colore*). His portrait in vignette in the MSS. Vatic., Paris., Basilic., Ambr. (§ 109, 2) and also on a contorniate in Gotha, all unauthentic; equally unauthenticated is a bust with a mask (rather tragic than comic) on the right shoulder, which was found in 1826 in the neighbourhood of the site indicated by Suetonius, and which is now in the Capitoline Museum. Ann. d. Inst. archeol. 1840, p. 97 tav. GVisconti, iconogr. rom. 1, 317. JJBernoulli, röm. Ikonogr. 1, 68.—Suet. p. 33, 5 *reliquit filiam, quae post equiti rom. nupsit, item hortulos XX iugerum via Appia ad Martis* (cf. PRE. 1^2, 158; Wilmanns 320, 7).

109. All the six comedies written and exhibited at Rome by Terence are extant. The numerous MSS. are divided into two classes, the very ancient Bembine and those representing the text of Calliopius. His plays were also annotated; we possess only the commentaries of Donatus and Eugraphius. There are also important didascaliae to the plays (though in a very difficult text), and metrical arguments.

1. Suet. p. 28, 8 *scripsit comoedias sex, ex quibus primam Andriam* etc. Cf.

Auson. ep. 18, 15 on the number six: *protulit in scenam quot dramata fabellarum* etc.

2. Manuscripts: the best is Vatic. 3226 (A, s. IV/V, Bembinus; facsimile ap. Wattenb.-Zangem. t. 8 and 9; Chatelain t. 6): in competition with this are the other MSS. which are all derived from the text, sound in its basis but greatly damaged by arbitrary alterations, of the unknown grammarian Calliopius (of s. IV or III? CBraun, quaestt. Ter. 21. FLeo, RhM. 38, 321). The subscriptio (§ 41, 2 ad fin.) reads: *Calliopius recensui* and *feliciter Calliopio;* cf. OJahn, Lpz. Ber. 1851, 362. To these Calliopian MSS. belong among others Paris. 7899 (P), Vat. 3868 (C), Ambros. (F), Basilicanus (B), all s. X; further, as a separate group, important on account of their close connection with A: Victorianus (D, s. X in Florence) and Decurtatus (G, Vatic. 1640 s. XI/XII), Lps. s. X (OBrugmann, JJ. 113, 420. KDziatzko, RhM. 39, 340), Paris. 10304 s. XI (AFritsch Phil. 32, 446. Dziatzko l.l. 344). Facsimiles of MSS. BCDFGP are also to be found in Chatelain t. 7–11.—The MS. C is specially notable for its illustrations (to the Terentian comedies) which are based on old tradition (FLeo, RhM. 28, 335): partly reproduced in d'Agincourt, Hist. de l'art 5, pl. 35. 36. FWieseler, Denkm. d. Bühnenwesens, Gött. 1851, t. 10. Similar designs are to be found in F and P. Those in F ap. AMai, Plauti fragm. etc., Mail. 1815.—On the Terence MSS.: Ritschl, opusc. 3, 281. FUmpfenbach before his edition p. 1. CSydow, de fide librorum Ter. ex Calliopii recensione ductorum, Berl. 1878. FLeo, RhM. 38, 317. Dziatzko, RhM. 39, 339. WPrinzhorn, de libris Ter. qui ad recens. Calliopianam redeunt, Gött. 1885. WFörster, Lyoner fragm. zum Hautontim. s. VIII, ZföG. 26, 188.—EBartels, de Ter. ap. Nonium, Diss. Argentor. 9, 1 (see § 390, 3). On the quotations from Terence in Arusianus (they generally agree with D) HSchindler (n. 9) cap. 1.—ASteubing, anall. ad testimonia Terentiana, Marb. 1872.—Geppert, zur Gesch. der terentianischen Kritik, Jahn's Archiv 18, 28. JBrix, de Ter. libris mss. a Bentleio adhibitis, Brieg 1852. AWilms, de personarum notis in codd. Ter., Halle 1881 (§ 16, 8). FUmpfenbach, Phil. 32, 442.

3. For all the plays metrical tables of contents are preserved, consisting each of 12 senarii, which in the Bembine severally bear the superscription: *GSulpici Apollinaris periocha:* § 99, 3. 357, 2.—Commentators: Valerius Probus, Aemilius Asper, Helenius Acro, Aelius Donatus, Euanthius; doubtful are Arruntius Celsus and the writer, whose name is corrupt, mentioned ap. Donat. on Ter. Eun. 4, 4, 22: *Ego Adesionem sequor, qui recte intellexit* etc. Suringar, hist. crit. schol. lat. 1, 77. Ritschl, Parerga 361. The commentary of Donatus preserved to us (§ 409, 3) is also valuable for its comparative references to the Greek originals, but it is wanting for the Heauton timorumenos: to supply its place JCalphurnius wrote in the 15th cent. a commentary which has no value for us; FJLöffler, de Calphurnio (†1503) Ter. interprete, Diss. Argentor. 6, 261. The commentary of Eugraphius (§ 482, 2) is without independent value; HGerstenberg, de Eugraphio, Jena 1886. See the scholia of the cod. Bembinus ap. FUmpfenbach, Herm. 2, 337, and on them WStudemund, JJ. 97. 546. 125, 51. Cf. Umpfenbach's edition p. xxxvii.—*Differentiae* (synonyms) *Terentii* ap. HHagen, anecd. Helv. p. cxxxiii. A glossary to Ter. from Vat. 1471 s. IX was published by GGoetz, ind. schol. Ienens. 1885.

4. The didascaliae are preserved in a twofold text, viz. in that of the Bembine, and in the Calliopian (n. 2): with the latter are connected the praefationes of Donatus. The basis of both was a collection (originally more complete) of scenic notices, which had probably been compiled from official records (commentarii magistratuum, annales maximi) and literary research, most likely from Varro de actis scaenicis (§ 166, 5). Out of this the Bembine has preserved a selection, which,

though incomplete and confused, is not systematically or intentionally garbled; the Calliopian version on the other hand gives a deliberate and to some extent arbitrary selection, which is limited in each case to a single performance (the first). KDziatzko, RhM. 21, 87. Cf. generally Ritschl, Parerga 263. WWilmanns, de didascaliis Ter., Berl. 1864. Dziatzko, RhM. 20, 570. 21, 64. 39, 339. CSteffen, act. soc. Lips. 2, 152. FSchoell, RhM. 31, 469.—On the number of actors etc. in Ter. see § 16, 4. See also below n. 6.

5. The enumeration in § 110 follows the Bembine, which arranges the plays in the supposed order of their composition. This MS. alone marks this succession regularly with '*facta I*' (*prima* or *primo loco*) '*facta II*' etc. up to '*facta VI*,' whereas the other MSS. only three times give the number, but in so doing correspond with the Bemb. The illustrated MSS. CPF have the following succession: Andr. Eun. Heaut. Ad. Hec. Phorm., while DG have: Andr. Ad. Eun. Phorm. Heaut. Hec. Conjectures as to the cause of these differences of arrangement e.g. WWagner, JJ. 91, 291. FLeo, RhM. 38, 318. Cf. § 110, 6, n. 1. During the lifetime of Terence, according to the didascaliae, the following representations took place: a. 588/166 the Andria in April (lud. meg.). 589/165 Hecyra 1 (first time, lud. meg.). 591/163 Heauton timorumenos (lud. meg.). 593/161 Eunuchus (lud. meg.). Phormio (lud. rom. in September). 594/160 Hecyra 2 (second trial) and Adelphoe (at the funeral games for Aemilius Paulus). Hecyra 3 (complete performance; lud. rom.). Dziatzko, RhM. 21, 84. Cf. HPäckelmann, de ordine Ter fabularum, potissimum prologis adhibitis, Halle 1875.

6. ALRLiebig, de prologis Ter. et Plaut., Görlitz 1859. KDziatzko, de prologis Plaut. et Ter., Bonn 1863. GBoissier, les prologues de Ter., Mélanges Graux (Par. 1884) 79. ARoehricht, quaestt. scaen. ex. prologis Ter. petitae, Diss. Argentor. 9, 293.

7. Collective editions: Ed. princeps: Strassb. 1470. Edition s. l. et a. in Italy about 1470-75 (Jahn's Archiv 4, 325). Editions by Muretus (Venet. 1555), GFaernus (Florent. 1565), FLindenbrog (c. Donati et Eugraphii comm., Paris 1602; Francof. 1623), PhPareus, (Neust. 1619), JHBoecler (acc. comm. FGuieti, Strassb. 1657), in usum Delphini (with index of words, Par. 1675).—Ex rec. et c. not. RBentleji, Cantabr. 1726 (with vocabulary, reprint by EVollbehr, Kiel 1846; on Bentley's English MSS. of Ter. see FUmpfenbach, Phil. 32, 442. MWarren, Americ. journ. of philol. 3, 59). Comm. perp. illustr.; acced. Donat. Eugraphius etc., cur. AWesterhovius, Haag 1726 II (reprint by CStallbaum, Lps. 1830). Ed. FGBothe in Poet. scen. T. IV (Mannh. 1837). Illustr. NELemaire, Par. 1827 III. Cum schol. Donati et Eugraphii ed. RKlotz, Lps. 1838. 39. II.—Rec. AFleckeisen, Lps. 1857. With notes etc. by RStJParry, Lond. 1857; by WWagner, Lond. 1869. Ed. et apparatu crit. instruxit FUmpfenbach, Berl. 1870. Rec. KDziatzko, Lps. 1884.

8. Recent translations (German): by ThBenfey, Stuttg. 1837 sqq.; remodelled (Andr. Eun. and Ad.) Stuttg. 1854: by FJacob, Berl. 1845; JHerbst, Stuttg. 1854 sqq. JJCDonner, Lpz. u. Heidelb. 1864 II. In English verse, by GeoColman, Lond. 1802.

9. Criticism and explanation: GHermann, de Bentleio eiusque edit. Terent., in opusc. 2, 263. JKrauss, quaestt. Ter. crit., Bonn 1850. AKlette, exercitt. Ter., Bonn 1855. JBrix, de Ter. fabulis post Bentleium emendandis, Liegnitz 1857. ThLadewig, Beitr. z. Kritik des Ter., Neustrelitz 1858. EBrunér, quaestt. Ter., Helsingfors 1868; acta societ. scient. fennicae 9, 1 sqq. Madvig, advers. crit. 2, 12. FUmpfenbach, analecta Ter., Mainz 1874. HBosse, quaestt. Ter., Lps. 1875. WKocks, interpolationes Ter. in d. Festschr. des Friedr.-Wilh.-Gymn., Köln 1875,

27. MHoelzer, de interpolatt. Ter., Halle 1878. OSchubert, symb. ad. Ter. emendandum, Weim. 1878. HSchindler, obss. crit. et hist. in Ter., Halle 1881. ThBraune, JJ. 131, 65.—PBaret, de iure ap. Ter., Paris 1878.—Reviews of the literature on Ter. since 1873 by WWagner and ASpengel, JB. 1873, 445. 1874/75 1, 798. 1876 2, 356. 1877 2, 314. 1881 2, 177. 1884 2, 74. Cf. § 16, 2 sqq. 98., 7 sqq.

110. These six plays are as follows:

1) Andria, exhibited a. 588/166 at the Megalensian games, an adaptation of Menander's *Ἀνδρία* with additions from the same poet's *Περινθία*. The last scene exists in two texts.

1. In the Bemb. the didasc., together with the beginning of the play, is lost, but Donatus' titulus reports about the first and second performance (the latter between 611/143-620/134, by Q. Minucius and Valerius, Dziatzko, RhM. 21, 64). See Suet. vit. Ter. p. 28, 8 *primam Andriam cum aedilibus daret, iussus ante Caecilio recitare ad cenantem cum venisset, dicitur initium quidem fabulae, quod erat contemptiore vestitu, subsellio iuxta lectulum residens legisse, post paucos vero versus invitatus ut accumberet cenasse una, dein cetera percucurrisse non sine magna Caecilii admiratione.*

2. The prologue dates from the first performance, see Dziatzko, RhM. 20, 579. 21, 64: in his edition of the Phorm. p. 10. OBrugmann, JJ. 113, 417. WWagner, JB. 1874/75 1, 804. Cf. also HPäckelmann (see § 109, 5) 7.

3. On its relation to the original see Grauert, Analekten 173. KFHermann, Ter. Andr. quam fideliter ad Menandrum expressa sit, Marb. 1838. WIhne, quaestt. p. 5. ThBenfey's pref. to his translation. WTeuffel, Stud. u. Charakt. 280. KDziatzko, RhM. 31, 234. KBraun, quaestt. Ter., Jen. 1877. FKampe, § 111, 2.

4. Of the two texts of the conclusion the shorter is the genuine one; the more elaborate, which is missing from all the standard MSS., is certainly not Terentian. At the best it was composed for a later revival of the play. Ritschl, Parerga 583. ASpengel, Münchn. SBer. 1873, 620; ed. of the Andria, p. 148. KDziatzko, JJ. 113, 235. AGreifeld, de Andr. Ter. gemino exitu, Halle 1886.—On a third exitus in cod. Erlang. nr. 300 see FSchmidt, d. Zahl der Schauspieler bei Pl. u. Ter. 39. Cf. HKeil in Ritschl's opusc. 3, 280.

5. Editions: with copious notes by GPerlet, Ronneb. 1805; ex rec. FrRitteri, Berl. 1833; with critical and exegetical notes by RKlotz, Lpz. 1865; rec. et illustr. LQuicherat, Par. 1866. Annotated by ASpengel, Berl. 1875; CMeissner, Bernb. 1876. CEFreeman and ASloman, Oxf. 1886.

6. ASpengel, d. Composition der A. des T., Münchn. SBer. 1873, 599.—Vogel, Ter. Andr. in graecum conversa. P.I., Treptow 1864. Translated by F . . . x. (Felix Mendelssohn-Bartholdy), Berl. 1826.

2) Eunuchus, a clever contamination from Menander's *Εὐνοῦχος* and some parts of his *Κόλαξ*. The varied and lively plot obtained even in the poet's life-time a decided success for the play.

1. On its relation to the original see Grauert, Analekten 147. WIhne, quaestt. 15. WTeuffel, Stud. u. Char. 281. KBraun, quaestt. Ter., Jen. 1877. According

to PERS. sat. 5, 161 Thais was in the Εὐν. called Chrysis, Phaedria Chaerestratus, Parmeno Davus, and Gnatho in the Κόλ. was Struthias.

2. *Eunuchus bis die* (Ritschl: *deinceps*) *acta est meruitque pretium quantum nulla antea cuiusquam comoedia, i.e.* (see RITSCHL, op. 3, 240) *octo milia nummum*, SUET. vita Ter. p. 29 Rffsch.=RITSCHL, opusc. 3, 208. Cf. Auctar. Donat. ib. p. 35 (214), and DONATUS' praef. to the Eun. p. 10, 12 Rffsch. RITSCHL, Parerga 330. DZIATZKO, RhM. 21, 68.

3. The consuls of the year in which the play was first exhibited are not mentioned by Donatus; the Calliopian didascalia mentions M. Valerius (593/161), C. (?) Mummius (608/146); Fannius (593/161); the aed. cur. in Donatus and in the Calliopian rec. L. Postumius Albinus (cos. 600/154, consequently aedile c. 594/160), L. Cornelius Merula (probably the father of the consul of 667/87 who bears the same name) and the performance ludis megalensibus; but in the Bemb. M. Iunius (Brutus, the jurist, a praetorius? § 133, 2), and L. Iulius (Caesar, the father of the consul bearing the same name of 664/90?), ludis romanis. Hence we may draw conclusions as to two performances, a. 593/161 (coss. M. Valerius Messala, C. Fannius Strabo; aed. Albinus and Merula) and again 608/146 (coss. Cn. Cornelius Lentulus, L. Mummius Achaicus; aed. Iunius and Iulius). See DZIATZKO, RhM. 21, 66.—MHAUPT, opusc. 3, 457. 520. VAHLEN, Berl. ind. lect. 1883/84.—Transl. by GRAVENHORST, Hamb. 1852. Ed. (with Andr.) TLPAPILLON, Lond. 1870.

3) Heauton timorumenos, the self-tormentor, after Menander's play of the same title, without the use of another play; a comedy of intrigue, with a somewhat extravagant plot, little delineation of character and dry in tone.

1. *Ex integra graeca integra comoedia*, prol. 4; ib. 36 entitled *stataria*. Ἑαυτὸν τιμωρούμενος=*se crucians* (1, 1, 29), *se exercens* (1, 1, 94); *ipse se poeniens* (CIC. Tusc. 3, 65). In the titulus the MSS. give the more complete form *Heauton tim.*, and so do the grammarians in their quotations. This is therefore the proper title of the play, although in prol. 5 the shorter form *Hauton tim.* was used in speakin KDZIATZKO, RhM. 27, 159. Similar titles are Damoxenos' Ἑαυτὸν πενθῶν, Antiphanes' Ἑαυτοῦ ἐρῶν, Dexikrates' Ὑφ' ἑαυτῶν πλανώμενοι and the Ἐξ ἑαυτοῦ ἑστῶε translated by Caecilius.

2. The consuls of the year of performance in the Bemb.: Cn. Cornelius, Marcus (ought to be Manius) Iuvenius (i.e. Iuvencius, Iuventius); in the other MSS. M. Iunio, T. Sempronio, perhaps pointing to the year 591/163, in which Ti. Sempronius Gracchus II and M'. Iuventius Thalna were consuls, and to a revival under the consulship of some Cornelius (Cn. Cornelius Lentulus a. 608/146? P. Cornelius Scipio Nasica Serapio a. 616/138?). At the first performance (ludis megalensibus) perhaps aed. cur. L. Cornelius Lentulus (no doubt the ambassador of a. 592/162 in POLYB. 31, 23 and cos. 598/156) and L. Valerius Flaccus (cos. 602/152?) See DZIATZKO, RhM. 20, 574. 21, 68.

Annotated by WWAGNER, Berl. 1872; by ESSHUCKBURGH, Lond. 1878.—Criticism: CVENEDIGER, JJ. 109, 129. HBLÜMNER, JJ. 131, 805. LHAVET, rev. de phil. 10, 12.

4) Phormio, so called from the parasite in the play, the original by Apollodoros of Karystos being entitled Ἐπιδικαζόμενος.

The plot is interesting, the delineation of characters varied and detailed, the whole execution lively and merry.

1. On the title and original see prol. 25-28 together with Donatus, according to whom Apollodoros' play was rather entitled Ἐπιδικαζομένη. Cf. Meineke, hist. crit. com. gr. 464. Dziatzko, RhM. 31, 248.

2. The titulus in the Bemb. is: *acta ludis megalensibus Q. Caspione Gn. Servilio cos. Graeca Apollodoru Epidicazomenos. Facta est IIII.* In the cod. Vaticanus the coss. are G. Fannius, M. Valerius, and the same are given in Donat. praef. p. 14, 18 Rffsch. *M. Valerio et C. Fannio coss.*; the MSS. of the Calliopian class have also *ludis romanis.* The latter report the first exhibition a. 593/161, under the aediles Albinus and Merula; the Bemb. has a later revival, perhaps a. 613/141 (coss. Cn. Servilius Caepio and Q. Pompeius, this being more probable than a. 614/140, coss. C. Laelius and Q. Servilius Caepio). Dziatzko, RhM. 20, 575. 21, 70.

3. Ter. Phormio ed. CGElberling, Kopenh. 1861. Annotated by KDziatzko, Lpz.[2] 1885, by JBond and ASWalpole, Lond. 1879.—JWollenberg, Collation des Ph. aus e. Hs. des 13. saec. in Tours, ZfGW. 14, 888.

5) Hecyra, the mother-in-law, a play with a strange story, peculiar characters, and almost destitute of plot, and anything rather than a comedy; hence it was not to the taste of the Roman public and its performance was long attended with difficulties.

1. The plot turns only upon sentiment, and the final solution settles only sentimental difficulties. In his characters the Greek poet seems to have intended a deviation from the ordinary routine. The explanation of the plot is given through πρόσωπα προτατικά.

2. As the play is called Ἑκυρά and not *Socrus*, it is almost certain that it is (like the Adelphoe) an adaptation of a Greek play entitled Ἑκυρά. In agreement with this is Donatus' notice praef. p. 12 R.: *fabula Apollodori* (Carystii) *dicitur esse graeca*, esp. as he repeats it five times in his commentary, quoting the words of Apollodoros (cf. Meineke, fragm. com. gr. p. 1104, ed. min. Cobet, novae lect. 122.) The notice in the Bemb.: *graeca Menandru*, may perhaps have been caused by Apollin. Sidon. ep. 4 12, who mentions Menander's Ἐπιτρέποντες as a *fabula similis argumenti* (to the Hec.) At the very utmost, the πρόσωπα προτατικά might be assumed to have been taken from Menander's play. Teuffel in PRE. 6, 1700. Dziatzko, RhM. 21, 76, 80. Cf. FVFritzsche, lectt. Ter., Rost. 1860, p. 21. FHildebrandt, de Hec. Ter. origine, Halle 1884 (and on this FSchlee, WfklPh. 1885, 171).

3. The didasc. would agree with the facts, if it were *facta II* (it is, however, *V*). *acta ludis megalensibus Sex. Iulio Caesare* (cos. 597/157), *Cn. Cornelio Dolabella* (cos. 595/159 *aedilibus cur.*, *Cn. Octavio T. Manlio coss.* (a. 589/165). *primum acta sine prologo* (when the performance was interrupted by funambuli, prol. 1, 4). *relata est iterum L. Aemilio Paulo ludis funeralibus* (a. 594/160, with prol. 1); *non est placita* (cf. prol. 2, 33). *tertio relata est* (prol. 2) *Q. Fulvio* (cos. 601/153) *L. Marcio* (cos. 605/149) *aed. cur.* (at the ludi romani of a. 594/160). *placuit.* (This was followed by Terence's departure to the East.) See Dziatzko, RhM. 20, 576. 21, 72. Ritschl, op. 2, 237.

4. Two prologues, the first incomplete, written for the second performance, the second for the third. The latter was spoken by the manager Ambivius in his own

name (§ 16, 14) but was no doubt composed by Terence. HSCHINDLER (§ 109, 9) cap. 3. OAMDOHR, prologi Hec. Ter. . . . pertractantur, Frankfort on Oder 1873. WFIELITZ, RhM. 31, 304. FLECKEISEN, JJ. 113, 533.

6) Adelphoe, from Menander's Ἀδελφοί, with the addition of a scene from the beginning of Diphilos' Συναποθνήσκοντες. The simple and well-contrived plot, careful delineation of characters and prevailing cheerfulness, render this the most successful play of Terence. But the sceptical manner, in which at the close the new and old time are contrasted with each other, is not very pleasing.

1. *Acta ludis funeralibus Lucio Aemilio Paulo, quos fecere Q. Fabius Maxumus, P. Cornelius Africanus . . . facta sexta, M. Cornelio Cethego L.* (Anicio) *Gallo cos.* (a. 594/160). So according to the titulus. FOSANN, WWILMANNS, DZIATZKO (RhM. 20, 577. 21, 78), and SCHINDLER (§ 109, 9) cap. 2 in spite of *novam* v. 12, have tried to prove that this was not the first performance. For the other view see WWAGNER, JJ. 91, 289. The poet probably had his play in readiness at the time of the death of Paulus; its rehearsal would not be likely to require more time than all the other preparations for the funeral games. As to DONATUS' statement (praef. Ad. p. 7 Rffsch.): *hanc dicunt ex Terentianis secundo loco actam*, see § 109, 5. HBOSSE, quaestt. Ter. (Lps. 1874) cap. I: de tempore quo Ter. Ad. acta sit. HPÄCKELMANN, l.l. 27.

2. On its relation to the original see prol. 6 sqq. GRAUERT, Analekten 124. IHNE, quaest. 25. TEUFFEL, Stud. 284. WFIELITZ, JJ. 97, 675. See also above, § 97, 18, 1. On the conclusion see TEUFFEL, Stud. u. Charakt. 287. SPENGEL, in the preface to his ed. p. VIII. In gen. cf. KFHERMANN, de Ter. Adelphis, Marb. 1838= Jahn's Archiv 6, 65. KDZIATZKO, RhM. 31, 374.

3. Annotated by ASPENGEL, Berl. 1879. KDZIATZKO, Lpz. 1881. FPLESSIS, Par. 1884. ASLOMAN, Lond. 1886. EBENOIST et JPSICHARI, Par. [2] 1887.—AKLETTE, Symb. philolog. Bonn. 843. DGRÖHE, RhM. 22, 640.

111. Terence, the riper development of whose gifts was cut short by his early death, exhibits his character in his comedies as that of a rigid imitator, whereas Plautus notwithstanding his dependence on the Greeks is a creative poet. He faithfully adheres to his Greek originals, and avails himself of other Greek plays where he feels obliged to alter or curtail them and enliven the action. His plots are somewhat monotonous, nor is there much variety even in the names of his characters. He does not possess the liveliness, freshness and versatility of Plautus, but he is free from his extravagances. He succeeds best in quiet conversation, not so well in the language of passion, and he is sadly deficient in comic power. His plays are smooth in construction, the separate parts carefully adjusted and balanced, the style terse and refined, the characters carefully and consistently delineated. He

is a conscientious, sober artist, more to the taste of aristocratic connoisseurs than of the people. His language too shows everywhere smoothness and elegance, purposely rejecting antique forms and phrases. His verses are not so varied or lively as those of Plautus: Terence employs almost exclusively iambic and trochaic metres.

1. On Terence see in general MOMMSEN, RG. 2^6, 432. RIBBECK, röm. Dicht. 1, 131. Review of the plays (by a lady) in Ritschl's opusc. 2, 752.

2. His relation to his originals. *Duae (fabulae) ab Apollodoro* (of Karystos) *translatae esse dicuntur comico, Phormio et Hecyra: quattuor reliquae a Menandro.* So DONATUS' addition to Suet. vita p. 35, 10 R. So also the vita Ambros. (§ 108, 2). On his manner of using the Greek plays see MEINEKE ad Menand. p. 1. 19. 67. 98. 140. GRAUERT, Analekten 116. WIHNE, quaestt. Ter., Bonn 1843. THLADEWIG, üb. d. Kanon d. Volc. Sedig. (1842); Beitr. z. Kritik des Ter. (1858) p. 1–10. FKAMPE, d. Lustsp. d. Ter. (Andr. Eun. Heaut.) u. ihre gr. Originale, Halberst. 1884. GREGEL, Ter. im Verh. zu s. gr. Originalen, Wetzl. 1884. GVALLAT, quo modo Menandrum quoad praecipuarum personarum mores Ter. transtulerit, Par. 1887.—LHFISCHER, de Ter. priorum comicorum lat. imprimis Plauti sectatore, Halle 1875.

3. His want of originality manifests itself also in his frequent use of contamination, cleverly as he usually manages it. JKLASEN, quam rationem Ter. in contaminatis fabb. componendis secutus sit, I Adelphoe, Rheine 1886. Ter. generally altered the names of his originals, especially so as to denote by the name alone the character of the part ('typical names.') His lovers are called Phaedria, Charinus, Chaerea and Pamphilus; his girls Pamphila, Philumena, Bacchis; the slaves Geta, Syrus, Parmeno etc. This habit makes it difficult to retain a definite idea of individual characters and plays (EKÖNIG, above § 98, 7 ad fin.). Moreover, the love of a young man for a girl who finally turns out to be of free birth and is married by him, forms the plot of Andria, Eun., Heaut., Phormio; in the Hec. too there is a kind of ἀναγνωρισμός.—Terence changed the metres of his originals according to his pleasure or necessity.—The explanation of the plot was often facilitated by the introduction of πρόσωπα προτατικά, see § 16, 11.

4. QUINT. 10, 1, 99. *Terentii scripta . . . sunt in hoc genere elegantissima et plus adhuc habitura gratiae si intra versus trimetros stetissent* (because Ter. was destitute of spirit for a higher style). Poor puns: Andr. 218.—Eun. prol. 42. 45. Heaut. 218.—Heaut. 356. 379. 526. Hec. 543. Ad. 220. 427 etc. GELL. 6, 14, 6 *vera et propria . . . exempla in latina lingua M. Varro esse dicit . . . mediocritatis Terentium.*

5. AFRANIUS in Compitalibus 29 *Terenti numne similem dicent quempiam?* (RITSCHL, op. 3, 263), and perhaps also v. 30: *ut quidquid loquitur sal merumst!* CIC. ad Att. 7, 3, 10 *Terentium, cuius fabellae propter elegantiam sermonis* etc., and in Limone (ap. SUET. vita Ter. p. 34 Rffsch.): . . . *lecto sermone, Terenti, . . . Menandrum in medium nobis sedatis motibus affers* etc. Caesar (ib. see § 195, 3) . . . *puri sermonis amator. Lenibus atque utinam scriptis adiuncta foret vis, comica ut aequato virtus polleret honore cum Graecis neve hac despectus parte iaceres!* Caesar calls him, therefore, only *dimidiatus Menander.*

6. Linguistic. Cf. esp. above § 98, 7 (lit. on early Latin) EKÄRCHER, Prosodisches zu Plaut. und Terenz, Karlsr. 1846. ALIEBIG, de genitivi usu Ter.

Oels 1853; die hypothetischen Sätze bei Ter., Görlitz 1863. AHeinrichs, de ablativi apud Ter. usu et ratione, Elbing 1858. 60 II. CSchlüter de accus. et dativi usu Ter., Münster 1874. MSSlaughter, the substantives of Ter., Johns Hopkins Univ. Circ. 6 (1887), 77. PBarth, d. Eleganz des Ter. im Gebr. d. Adj., JJ. 129, 177. CRein, de pronominum ap. Ter. collocatione, Lps. 1879. PThomas, la syntaxe du futur passé dans T., Rev. de l'instruct. publ. Belge 19, 365. 20, 235. 325. 21, 2. EHauler, Terentiana; quaestt. cum specimine lexici, Wien 1862. AGEngelbrecht, Studia Ter., Wien 1883; Beobachtungen über. d. Sprachgebr. d. latt. Kom., Wiener Stud. 6, 216.—ChrGerdes, de translationibus Ter., Leer 1884. Cf. also n. 7.

7. Metrical (cf. also § 98, 9): The iambic and trochaic verses of Terence occur either in long regular series (stichic) or mixed in rapid and frequent alternation (lyrical). The lyric arrangement is found only at the beginning of scenes. Its laws have not yet been satisfactorily established in detail. But trochaic octonarii are invariably followed by other trochaic lines (Bentley's rule). Metres other than the iambic and trochaic occur only three times and each time in short passages: Andr. 481–485 (4 bacch. tetram. 1 iamb. dim.). 625–638 (1 dactyl. tetram. 9 cret. tetr. 2 iamb. dim. 2 bacch. tetram.). Ad. 610–616 (uncertain: choriambics preceded and followed by short iamb. and troch. series).—CConradt, de versuum Ter. structura, Berl. 1870; Herm. 10, 101; die metr. Kompos. der Komöd. des T., Berl. 1876) and on this KDziatzko, JenLZ. 1877, 59. ASpengel, JB. 1876 2, 372); JJ. 117, 401. BBorn, de diverbii ap. Ter. versibus, Magdeb. 1868. JDraheim, de iamb. et troch. Ter., Herm. 15, 238. OPodiaski, quo modo Ter. in tetr. iamb. et troch. verborum accentus cum numeris consociaverit, Berl. 1882. WMeyer, Wortaccent (see § 98, 8) 21. Über die Cäsuren des iamb. Trim. u. über dice face duce bei Ter. OSchubert, Weim. 1878 (§ 109, 9). FSchlee, de versuum in canticis Ter. consecutione, Berl. 1879. KMeissner, d. Cantica des Ter. u. ihre Eurhythmie, JJ. Suppl. 12, 465; d. stroph. Gliederung in d. stich. Partien bei Ter., JJ. 129, 289; de iamb. ap. Ter. septenario, Bernb. 1884.

8. Ethical: religious attitude etc. Treatises by Keseberg, Hubrich and others; see § 98, 4 ad fin.

112. The first writer of togatae of whom we know is Titinius, of a respectable plebeian family, a contemporary of Terence, whom he seems, however, to have survived. All his plays bear Latin titles and their plots prove them to have been tabernariae. The fragments show a broad and popular tone, a bold, lively and fresh manner reminding one of Plautus, while in consistent delineation of character Titinius was ranked with Terence, and applied his talent likewise, and especially, to the female rôles.

1. Varro ap. Charis. GL. 1, 241 ἤθη *nullis aliis servare convenit* (*contigit?*) *quam Titinio, Terentio, Attae.* Ritschl, Parerga 194 (cf. op. 3, 125) concludes from these words that Titinius was born before Terence; but as the latter commenced to write at an early age, and as the existence of togatae during Ter.'s literary career is improbable and cannot be proved, Tit. may have begun to write after the death of Ter.

2. Seren. Samm. med. 1037 sq.: *allia praecepit Titini sententia necti, qui veteri claras expressit more togatas.*

3. We know of 15 titles; the fragments in Ribbeck, com.² p. 133.—On Tit. see Neukirch, fab. tog. 97. Ritschl, Parerga 194. Mommsen, RG. 1⁶, 905.

113. Turpilius, also a contemporary of Terence, adhered to the palliata; he lived far into the 7th century U.C. He, like Terence, translated Greek plays of the New Comedy into Latin. The general tone in his fragments is more lively than in the lines of Caecilius and Terence; his diction abounds in popular elements, his metres are like those of Terence.

1. Hieron. ad Euseb. chr. a. 1914 (Amand. 1915)=651/103: *Turpilius comicus senex admodum Sinuessae moritur.*—The fragments in Ribbeck, com. ² 85.

2. Of the 13 titles known to us, all of which are in Greek, six agree with titles of Menander; the Demetrius was adapted from Alexis, Lemniae or Philopator perhaps from Antiphanes. It is probable that T. soon gave up writing for the stage, as the close of the 6th century U.C. coincides with the end of the palliata. Ritschl, Parerga 188.

114. Other poets of palliatae in this period were Juventius and Valerius and perhaps Vatronius, who was little esteemed; Licinius Tegula is mentioned as the author a. 554/200 of a sacred hymn, and we find the two consuls of the year 581/173, Q. Fabius Labeo and M. Popilius Laenas designated as poets.

1. *Iuventius comicus* in Varro LL. 7, 65, cf. 6, 50. *Iuventius in comoedia*, Gell. 18, 12, 2. *Iuventius in Anagnorizomene*, Fest. 298, rests on mere conjecture. Paul. (p. 299 M.) incorrectly substituted Terentius.—Ribbeck, com. ² p. 82 sq.

2. *Valerius in Phormione* ap. Priscian. GL. 2, 200, whom several authorities identify with Valerius Valentinus (§ 140, 1). Or perhaps identical with Val. Aedituus? The latter is called ap. Gell. 19, 9, 10 *vetus poeta*, and is mentioned before Licinius and Catulus. Cf. also § 86, 6 and 146, 2. Ribbeck, com.² p. 302 and LXXXVIII.—Concerning Vatronius (the name occurs repeatedly in inscriptions) Placidi gl. p. 13 Deuerl.: *Burrae Vatroniae, fatuae ac stupidae, a fabula quadam Vatroni auctoris quam Burra* (Πύρρα was the title of a play by Diphilos) *inscripsit vel a meretrice Burra.* FBücheler, RhM. 33, 309.—Unappropriated titles of palliatae: Adelphi, Hydria, Georgos; Ribbeck, com.² p. 112. Mention of an old (?) comedy in a letter from PCDecembrio to Niccolo Niccoli 1412–20 (printed in Mehus, epist. Travers. 35, 7 p. 1050) concerning the works which were possessed by the library of Giov. Corvini († 1438) in Milan: *ex antiquissimis libris vetustissimi, quos carie semesos ad legendum facesso: . . . comoedia antiqua, quae cuius sit nescio. in ea Lar familiaris* (as in Plaut. Aul. and especially in the Querolus § 436, 9) *multum loquax est: volt ne parasitus antelucanum cubet, ut plostrum vetus, pelves et rastros quatridentes ruri quam festinissime transferat; is ne volt parere quidem eo quod gallus nondum gallulat. meo denique iudicio vetustissima.* Cf. RSabbadini, della bibliot. di Giov. Corvini e d' una ignota commedia, Livorno 1886.

3. Livius 31, 12 in fin.: *decemviri . . . carmen ab ter novenis virginibus cani per urbem iusserunt* (in consequence of prodigies) *donumque Iunoni Reginae ferri. . . . carmen . . . tum condidit P. Licinius Tegula.* Cf. Ritschl, Parerga 197. 104. See also § 30, 1. 107, 4.—On Fabius and Popillius cf. § 125, 5.

115. Of the metrical inscriptions of the 6th century U.C. only a few of any length are preserved.

1. On the inscrr. in saturnians see § 62, 4. Among the epitaphs of the Scipios (cf. § 83, 7) nos. 30. 33 and 34 belong to this period (CIL. 1, p. 19 sq.).

2. The epitaphs of Naevius (in saturnians § 95, 1), preserved ap. Gell. 1, 24 and Cic. Tusc. 1, 34 (Enn.), of Plautus (in hexameters § 96, 2), Ennius (in elegiac metre § 100, 6 ad fin.) are not, as would appear, by the poets eulogised in them, but were composed at a later time by way of description of their literary characteristics. OJahn, Herm. 2, 242. Only the epitaph of Pacuvius (ap. Gell. l.l. in iambic senarii § 105, 1) is entirely in keeping (both in form and matter) with the actual contemporary epitaphs, and may very possibly have marked the poet's grave. Bücheler, RhM. 37, 521.

II. Prose-writers.

116. Of the earliest Roman historians, who wrote in Greek, (§ 2. 36) the oldest and most important is Q. Fabius Pictor, of the time of the second Punic war (born about 500/254). His *ἱστορία* extended from Aeneas down to his own time, treating of the latter at great length. Polybios and Dionysius frequently find fault with him; but the first uses him as his principal authority in the second Punic war, and Livy seems to follow him in more details than he confesses. Besides the Greek work, there was also a later version in Latin. Works on the ius pontificium are attributed to him with little or no authority.

1. Dionys. ant. 1, 6 *ὁμοίας δὲ τούτοις* (the Greek writers on Roman history) *καὶ οὐδὲν διαφόρους ἐξέδωκαν ἱστορίας καὶ Ῥωμαίων ὅσοι τὰ παλαιὰ ἔργα τῆς πόλεως ἑλληνικῇ διαλέκτῳ συνέγραψαν, ὧν εἰσι πρεσβύτατοι Κόϊντός τε Φάβιος καὶ Λεύκιος Κίγκιος, ἀμφότεροι κατὰ τοὺς φοινικικοὺς ἀκμάσαντες πολέμους. τούτων δὲ τῶν ἀνδρῶν ἑκάτερος οἷς μὲν αὐτὸς ἔργοις παρεγένετο διὰ τὴν ἐμπειρίαν ἀκριβῶς ἀνέγραψε, τὰ δὲ ἀρχαῖα τὰ μετὰ τὴν κτίσιν τῆς πόλεως γενόμενα κεφαλαιωδῶς ἐπέδραμεν.* Polyb. 3, 9 *κατὰ τοὺς καιροὺς* (of the second Punic war) *ὁ γράφων* (Fab. P.) *γέγονε καὶ τοῦ συνεδρίου μετεῖχε τῶν Ῥωμαίων.* Liv. 22, 7, 4 (at the battle of the Trasimene lake) *Fabium aequalem temporibus huiusce belli potissimum auctorem habui.* Cf. Eutrop. 3, 5 *L. Aemilio cos.* (529/225) *ingentes Gallorum copiae Alpes transierunt. sed pro Romanis tota Italia consensit traditumque est a Fabio historico, qui ei bello interfuit* etc. So also Oros. 4, 13. cf. Plin. NH. 10, 71. After the battle of Cannae (538/216) *Q. Fabius Pictor Delphos ad oraculum missus est* (Liv. 22, 57, 5, cf. 23, 11, 1 sqq.). Plut. Fab. Max. 18 *εἰς Δελφοὺς ἐπέμφθη θεοπρόπος Πίκτωρ συγγενὴς Φαβίου* (the Cunctator). App. Hann. 27 *ἡ βουλὴ Κόϊντον Φάβιον, τὸν συγγραφέα τῶνδε τῶν ἔργων, ἐς Δελφοὺς ἔπεμπε* etc. On his father and son see Haakh in PRE. 6, 2911, 31. 38. On the regard for his own family shown in his work, see Mommsen, röm. Forsch. 2, 278.

2. Liv. 1, 44, 2 *scriptorum antiquissimus Fabius Pictor*. 2, 40, 10 *Fabium, longe antiquissimum auctorem.* Dionys. 7, 71 *Κοΐντῳ Φαβίῳ βεβαιωτῇ χρώμενος καὶ οὐδεμιᾶς ἔτι δεόμενος πίστεως ἑτέρας. παλαιότατος γὰρ ἀνὴρ τῶν τὰ ῥωμαικὰ συνταξαμένων καὶ πίστιν οὐκ ἐξ ὧν ἤκουσε μόνον ἀλλὰ καὶ ἐξ ὧν αὐτὸς ἔγνω παρεχόμενος.* Dion. 1, 79 gives the legend of the foundation of Rome after Fabius. See Mommsen, röm. Forsch.

2, 9. On the other hand DIONYS. 4, 6 and 30 censures his *ῥᾳθυμία* in an insignificant detail. POLYB. 1, 14 says that he undertook the history of the Punic war *διὰ τὸ τοὺς ἐμπειρότατα δοκοῦντας γράφειν ὑπὲρ αὐτοῦ, Φιλῖνον καὶ Φάβιον, μὴ δεόντως ἡμῖν ἀπηγγελκέναι τὴν ἀλήθειαν. ἑκόντας μὲν οὖν ἐψεῦσθαι τοὺς ἄνδρας οὐχ ὑπολαμβάνω, στοχαζόμενος ἐκ τοῦ βίου καὶ τῆς αἱρέσεως αὐτῶν*, but Pictor (he says) was misled by his patriotic leaning to the Romans; cf. ib. 1, 58 and below. WÖLFFLIN, Antiochus 37. 39. 53 sq. POLYBIOS 3, 8 and 9 speaks of Pictor in his crotchety manner, influenced also perhaps by the rivalry between the Scipios and the Fabii. THLUCAS, Glogauer Progr. 1854, p. 10. HPETER, hist. rell. 1, LXXXIII. LIV. 1, 55, 8 *magis Fabio, praeterquam quod antiquior est, crediderim . . . quam Pisoni.* LIVY quotes him (besides this and the other passages already cited 1, 44, 2. 2, 40, 10. 22, 7, 4) at 8, 30, 9 and 10, 37, 14. It is uncertain whether Livy means especially Pictor when he mentions in a general manner *antiquissimos scriptores* or *priscos annales* or *vetustiores scriptores*; it is even doubtful whether, in large portions of his history, Livy made use of him directly as his chief authority (cf. E. HEYDENREICH, Fab. P. and Livius, Freib. 1878); likewise whether the portions of Diodorus which treat of Roman history are founded on Fabius Pictor (Diodorus mentions no other Roman historian, and mentions even him only once). This last question is answered in the affirmative by NIEBUHR, RG. 2, 192. 630, and MOMMSEN esp., röm. Forsch. 2, 273, has tried to prove it. For the other view see SCHWEGLER, RG. 2, 24. NITZSCH, Annalistik 226. BNIESE, Herm. 13, 412. CPETER zur Kritik d. Quellen d. ält. röm. Gesch. (Halle 1879) 118. EMEYER, RhM. 37, 610. LCOHN, Phil. 42, 1 etc. But Polybios. who frequently mentions Fabius (1, 14, 1 sqq. 1, 15, 12. 1, 58, 5. 3, 8. 3, 9), certainly made use of him. NIESE, Herm. 13, 410. GFUNGER, Herm. 14, 90; Phil. 39, 69. Especially too for the description of the Gallic invasions 2, 18 sqq. and in particular for the enumeration of the Italian forces 2, 24; see MOMMSEN, röm. Forschungen 2, 382. PLIN. NH. mentions Fabius in his ind. auct. to b. 10. 14. 15 and quotes him 10, 71. 14, 89.

3 The fragments of Pictor ap. HPETER, hist. rell. 1, 5. 109; hist. fragm. 6. 74. —WHARLESS, de Fabiis et Aufidiis rer. rom. scriptoribus, Bonn 1853; WNDURIEU, de gente Fabia (Leiden 1856) 165. HNISSEN, RhM. 22, 565. HPETER, hist. rell. 1, LXIX. THPLÜSS, JJ. 99, 239. KWNITZSCH, d. röm. Annalistik (1873) p. 267 and for the other view EHEYDENREICH l.l.

4. PLUT. Romul. 3 (cf. 8) *τὰ κυριώτατα* (of early Roman history) *πρῶτος εἰς τοὺς Ἕλληνας ἐξέδωκε Διοκλῆς ὁ Πεπαρήθιος, ᾧ καὶ Φάβιος Πίκτωρ ἐν τοῖς πλείστοις ἐπηκολούθησε.* The agreement in facts between Pictor and his contemporary Diokles may be more justly explained from their using the same sources (SCHWEGLER RG. 1, 412), or perhaps even by assuming that Diokles already made use of the Roman annalists. Cf. HPETER, hist. rell. 1, LXXX. MOMMSEN, röm. Forsch. 2, 279.

5. That Fabius Pictor did not commence his Greek work before the termination of the second Punic war is likely from the nature of the case, and also that he brought it down to the close of that war. The latter is rendered probable by APPIAN. Hann. 27 (see n. 1).

6. Latin passages are repeatedly quoted from Fabius Pictor as his authentic expressions, e.g. *spelunca Martis*, *lupus* as a feminine, *duovicesimo anno*, this last in a longer quotation ap. GELL. 5, 4, 3 (from a copy of the Annals of Fabius *bonae atque sincerae vetustatis*, of which the correctness was guaranteed by the vendor *in libraria apud Sigillaria*). Accordingly we are obliged to assume a Latin version. FRONTO, ep. p. 114 Nab. (§ 37, 5) can refer only to this Latin

version. This must, however, have been later than the original Greek, as it presupposes a higher development of Latin prose, the earliest work in which is Cato's Origines (hence perhaps in Cic. de or. 2, 51 *ut noster Cato, ut Pictor, ut Piso*, and ib. 53 *talis noster Cato et Pictor et Piso;* but de leg. 1, 6, where the historical fact is mentioned, in another order: *ad Fabium aut Catonem aut ad Pisonem*?). It may be doubted whether the Latin version was made by the author himself, or by another, perhaps also called Fabius. But the supposition that there were two famous annalists of the name of Fabius (Pictor) (HPeter, hist. rell. 1, LXXVI. CLXXVIII. Mommsen, röm. Forsch. 2, 378) is not supported thereby. Many scholars take this second to be the jurist Servius Fabius Pictor, others again Fabius Maximus Servilianus (cos. 612/142), of whom it is, at all events, certain that he wrote historical works. A Numerius Fabius Pictor, whose name was founded on the corrupt reading ap. Cic. de div. 1, 43 (*Aeneae somnium, quod in † numerum Fabi Pictoris graecis annalibus eiusmodi est*) disappears with the emendation by MHertz, philol.-klinischer Streifzug 32; RhM. 17, 579; JJ. 99, 768, *nostri*. But from Cicero's words we may also conclude that the Latin version of Fabius' annals did not contain the dream of Aeneas at all, or at least not at such length, that it was therefore a kind of abridgment. This was also divided (either by the author himself or somebody else) into books; the first book is quoted by Non. 518, 28; the fourth by Gell. 5, 4, 3.—LHolzapfel, röm. Chronol. 351. WSoltau, JJ. 133, 479.

7. The work of a certain Fabius Pictor de iure pontificio is more likely to belong to the jurist Serv. Fabius Pictor, than to the annalist Q. Fabius Pictor, notwithstanding Non. 518 *Fabius Pictor Rerum gestarum lib. I. . . . Idem iuris pontificii libro III.* Cf. § 133, 3.

117. Pictor's younger contemporary, L. Cincius Alimentus, praetor 544/210, wrote a similar work, also in Greek, and as it seems, not without critically availing himself of historical sources. This annalist has, however, become a somewhat uncertain figure by his being frequently confounded with a later writer of the same name.

1. Dionys. 1, 74 Λεύκιος Κίγκιος, ἀνὴρ ἐκ τοῦ βουλευτικοῦ συνεδρίου, (places the foundation of Rome) περὶ τὸ τέταρτον ἔτος τῆς δωδεκάτης ὀλυμπιάδος (Mommsen, röm. Chronol.[2] 315. Plüss p. 34 and JJ. 103, 385). Liv. 21, 38, 3 *L. Cincius Alimentus, qui captum se ab Hannibale* (at all events after his praetorship, prob. a. 546/208) *scribit.* 26, 23, 1 *praetorum inde comitia habita. P. Manlius Vulso . . . et L. Cincius Alimentus creati sunt.* 27, 7, 12 *legiones decretae: M. Valerio cum Cincio (his quoque est enim prorogatum in Sicilia imperium) Cannensis exercitus datus.* See also ib. 26, 28. 27, 5. 7. 8. 26. 28. 29. He was a plebeian: (his brother) M. Cincius Alimentus was tribune of the people a. 550/204. Liv. 29, 20.

2. Dionys. 1, 6 (see § 116, 1) and ib. 79 περὶ δὲ τῶν ἐκ τῆς Ἰλίας γενομένων Κόϊντος μὲν Φάβιος . . . ᾧ Λεύκιός τε Κίγκιος καὶ Κάτων Πόρκιος καὶ Πίσων Καλπούρνιος καὶ τῶν ἄλλων συγγραφέων οἱ πλείους ἠκολούθησαν. Liv. 7, 3, 7 *Volsiniis quoque clavos indices numeri annorum fixos in templo Nortiae etruscae deae comparere diligens talium monumentorum auctor Cincius adfirmat.* As Livy never elsewhere quotes any but historical works, this passage is probably, as MHertz and others think, to be taken as referring to the annalist Cinc. The arguments of Mercklin, Plüss (p. 17, 25) and HPeter (hist. rell. 1, xv) only show the possibility of an

allusion to Cincius the antiquarian (see n. 4). LIV. 21, 38, 3–5 *L. Cincius Alimentus . . . maxime auctor me moveret, nisi confunderet numerum Gallis Liguribusque additis . . . ex ipso autem audisse ⟨se⟩ Hannibale* etc. Cincius' statement is defended by FLACHMANN, de font. Liv. 2, 80; cf. PLÜSS. p. 5–8. HPETER, hist. rell. 1, CIX. The silence of other writers (e.g. Polybios) about him may be explained from the coincidence of his subject with the work of the more famous Fabius, and at all events does not prove these Greek annals by Cincius to have been a fabrication of the Augustan age (MOMMSEN, röm. Chronol. [2]315; RG. 1[6], 921).

3. The fragments of Cincius most recently ap. HPETER, hist. rell. 1, 40; frag. 32. MHERTZ, de Luciis Cinciis, Cinciorum fragm. ed., Berl. 1842. SCHWEGLER. RG. 1, 78. JTHPLÜSS, de Cinciis rerum rom. scriptoribus, Bonn 1865, cf. N. Schweiz, Mus. 6 (1866), 43. HPETER, hist. rell. 1, CI. CIX.

4. We find also attributed to Cincius (HERTZ l.l. 32. HUSCHKE, iurisprud. anteiust.[5] 84), a book de fastis (MACROB. 1, 12, 12, cf. Κίγκιος ἐν τῷ περὶ ἑορτῶν ap. LAUR. LYD. de mens. 4, 92 and ib. 4, 44 Κίγκιος ὁ Ῥωμαῖος σοφιστής), de comitiis (FEST. 241, 21), de consulum potestate (FEST. 241, 8), de officio iurisconsulti (from which FESTUS 173, 10. 321, 29, quotes a second book) mystagogica (a second book in FESTUS 363, 26), de re militari (the 3rd, 5th and 6th books are quoted by GELL. 16, 4), de verbis priscis (in FESTUS 214, 31. 277, 4. 330, 1). It seems, however, probable and has, moreover, been shown by MHERTZ l.l. 61, that all these political and antiquarian works are by a later learned jurist L. Cincius (FEST. 218, 18). HERTZ (with HPETER) places him in the time of Cicero (and Varro) and identifies him with the L. Cincius who occurs in the correspondence of Cicero; Plüss removes him into the Augustan period (§ 255, 6), a supposition supported by the enumeration in ARNOB. adv. nat. 3, 38 and CHARIS. GL. 1, 132 (*Varro et Tullius et Cincius*); cf. also GELL. 7, 15, 5 (*Aelii, Cincii, Santrae*) and FEST. 173 (*Cincius et Santra*). On the other hand see MACR. 1, 12, 12 sq. (*Cingius . . . Cingio etiam Varro consentit*) and FEST. 166. 174. 277 (*Cincius et Aelius*). 170 (*Santra, Aelius, Cincius*). He would, therefore, at least have been a younger contemporary of Cicero. Plüss also conjectures that this Cincius (c. 725/29) wrote annals, which were frequently (e.g. by Dionys. of Halic.) confounded with the works of the earlier annalist of the same name; this would be credible only if the younger Cincius also had written in Greek. Cf. HPETER, hist. rell. 1, CIV. CXIV.

118. The national tendencies in public life and in literature are in the 6th century U.C. most zealously represented by M. Porcius Cato, born at Tusculum a. 520/234, quaestor 550/204, aedilis 555/199, praetor 556/198, consul 559/195, censor 570/184, died 606/149. A firm and strong character, fully aware of his purposes and following them now with indomitable energy, now with cunning; eager for strife, and full of shrewd common sense, Cato is the archetype of an old Roman. But then he also betrays the influence of his time in the vanity with which he loved to show himself to the greatest advantage, and in his often glaring egotism. In politics he was without the farsightedness of his aristocratic adversaries, though no one surpassed him in well-meaning patriotism. In spite of the small esteem he professed for literary composition, he was a

prolific writer, and he is indeed the first real prose-writer of the Romans.

1. Cato's (=Sapiens) surnames: Censor, Censorius, Orator, later distinguished from the Uticensis by the addition of priscus or superior. For his manysidedness see Quint. 12, 11, 23 *M. Cato idem summus imperator, idem sapiens, idem orator, idem historiae conditor, idem iuris, idem rerum rusticarum peritissimus fuit.* Cf. Cic. de or. 3, 135. Brut. 294, and § 121, 2. Liv. 39, 40 gives an eloquent and admiring estimate of Cato, though he does not expressly mention his Origines. On his life and character see the biographies by Cornelius Nepos and Cicero's Cato, Plutarch's *βίος Κάτωνος*, Victor vir. ill. 47; of modern writers WDrumann, GR. 5, 97. PRE. 5, 1904. Mommsen, RG. 1[6], 812. ORibbeck, M. Porc. Cato Cens. als Schriftsteller, in the N. Schweiz. Mus. 1 (Bern 1861), 7. GVollertsen, quaestt. Caton. seu de vita Catonis eiusque fontt. atque de originibus, Kiel 1880. GCortese, de M. Porc. Cat. vita, operibus et lingua, Turin 1883 (in addition Grammatica Catoniana ib. 1883).—PWeise, quaestt. Catonian. capita V, Gött. 1887.

2. HJordan, M. Catonis praeter librum de re rustica quae extant, Lps. 1860. See also HJordan, Quaestt. Caton. capita II, Berl. 1856.

3. Cic. Brut. 69 of Cato: *cum ita sit ad nostrorum temporum rationem vetus ut nullius scriptum exstet dignum quidem lectione quod sit antiquius.* Cf. ib. 61 *nec vero habeo quemquam antiquiorem, cuius quidem scripta proferenda putem, nisi quem Appi Caeci oratio . . . et nonnullae mortuorum laudationes forte delectant.* But there is no doubt that Cato was the first who wrote and published a large number of works (some of them of great extent) in Latin prose.

4. Plut. Cato mai. 7 *εὔχαρις ἅμα καὶ δεινὸς ἦν, ἡδὺς καὶ καταπληκτικός, φιλοσκώμμων καὶ αὐστηρός, ἀποφθεγματικὸς καὶ ἀγωνιστικός.* With his red hair, his powerful voice, and the heavy blows which he dealt as an orator both in jest and earnest, Cato made a deep impression alike on friends and enemies.—On a statue with the inscription M · P · CATO · see Matz-Duhn, antike Bildwerke in Rom nr. 1289 and Bernoulli, röm. Ikonogr. 1, 289.

119. Cato, who until the end of his life took part in all public affairs in the most energetic manner, and opposed incessantly the predominant party and the Grecian tendencies of his age, had ample opportunity of exhibiting his native eloquence. He was also the first Roman who wrote down and published his speeches on a large scale. Cicero knew of more than 150 of them; we know of only 80, beginning in the year of Cato's consulship, either in fragments or from the events which caused them. These 80 are pretty equally divided between judicial and political speeches, delivered either before the senate or an assembly of the people. The fragments show spontaneous eloquence, and practice in all effective modulations, humour and earnestness, self-praise and cutting raillery.

1. Cornel. Nep. Cat. 3, 3 says inaccurately *ab adolescentia confecit* (rather *habuit*) *orationes.* More justly Cicero (Cat. mai. 38) makes him say: *causarum illustrium quascumque defendi nunc* (*in senectute*) *cum maxime conficio orationes.*

Among those known to us as published speeches we find some which we can prove never to have been actually delivered (in M'. Acilium of a. 565/189). Cf. § 44, 8.

2. Cic. Brut. 67 *refertae sunt orationes amplius centum quinquaginta, quas quidem adhuc invenerim et legerim, et verbis et rebus illustribus.* The titles and fragments preserved have been collected by HMeyer, orat. rom. fragm.[2] p. 11 (who increased the number to 93 speeches) and more lucidly by HJordan, Caton. q. exst. p. 33, cf. p. lxi (supplements ap. LMüller, RhM. 23, 541. 24, 331). Several of them dealt with cases of civil law. Speeches in self-defence: Liv. 39, 40 mentions among his *scripta omnis generis orationes pro se multae.* Of these we know only six (e.g. de innocentia sua, Gell. 20, 9), though we learn that Cato was 44 times accused by his adversaries without, however, sentence being once passed against him (Plin. NH. 7, 100. Victor vir. ill. 47, 7. Plut. Cat. 15 comp. 2. Val. Max. 3, 7, 7. Ampel. 19, 8). Speeches of this class were of course only improvised, nor did Cato like to hand down to posterity the charges raised against him. On his proems see § 44, 5.

3. Cato's speeches were long preserved by the rhetors and grammarians and the antiquarian fashion of the 2nd century (e.g. Hadrian *Ciceroni Catonem praetulit*, Spart. Hadr. 16, 6). In the 4th century of the Christian era they were known to Servius (ad Aen. 7, 259. 11, 301) and Marius Victorinus (Boeth. in Cic. Top. I p. 271 Or.).

4. The best characterisation of Cato's style is given by Gellius NA. 6, 3, 17 sqq. 52 sq., e.g. (53) *ea omnia distinctius numerosiusque fortassean dici potuerint, fortius atque vividius potuisse dici non videntur.* Cicero's descriptions (esp. Brut. 63, 293, and de or. 1, 171. orat. 152) are partly confused in their expressions, partly impaired by the endeavour to use Cato as shield and foil for himself. Quint. 2, 5, 21 expresses himself intelligently. ESchober, de Catone Cens. oratore, Neisse 1825. AWestermann, Gesch. d. röm. Bereds. 37.

120. Cato composed also the first Roman historical work in Latin prose, his seven books of Origines, commenced in the later years of his life and continued nearly until his death. The work comprised also the other tribes of Italy, including Upper Italy, at the same time dealing with ethnography and all sides of social life to an extent which remained without imitation. In all the rest, the work was in the manner of the Annalists, now brief, now extensive and even allowing space for the insertion of complete speeches by the author.

1. Cornel. Nep. Cat. 3. 3 *senex* (i.e. probably not before his sixtieth year, 580/174) *historias* (thus the Origines are called also by Serv. Aen. 6, 842. Plut. Cato 25) *scribere instituit. earum sunt libri VII. primus continet res gestas regum populi rom.; secundus et tertius unde quaeque civitas orta sit italica; ob quam rem omnes Origines videtur appellasse. in quarto autem bellum poenicum est primum* (perhaps with a summary account of the preceding years of the Republic), *in quinto secundum. atque haec omnia capitulatim sunt dicta* (according to the principal events, distinguishing memorable actions and sayings; cf. Mar. Vict. ad Cic. rhet. I p. 57 Or. *Sallustius . . . tribuit in libro I historiarum Catoni brevitatem: 'Romani generis disertissimus paucis absolvit,'* cf. Ampel. 19, 8). *reliqua quoque bella pari modo persecutus est, usque ad praeturam Ser. Galbae*

(rather until 605/149, see n. 2) *qui diripuit Lusitanos. atque horum bellorum duces non nominavit, sed sine nominibus res notavit. in eisdem exposuit quae in Italia Hispaniisque aut fierent aut viderentur admiranda* (i.e. memorable, θαυμάσια, παράδοξα). *in quibus* (probably the whole work) *multa industria et diligentia comparet, nulla doctrina* (no book-learning, see Jordan p. lx). On this suppression of the names of generals, which no doubt applies also to the Roman generals descended from the aristocratic families so little loved by the author, see besides Plin. NH. 8, 11 *Cato, cum imperatorum nomina annalibus detraxerit, eum elephantum qui fortissime proeliatus esset in punica acie Surum tradidit vocatum.*—Dionys. 1, 11 Πόρκιος Κάτων, ὁ τὰς γενεαλογίας τῶν ἐν Ἰταλίᾳ πόλεων ἐπιμελέστατα συναγαγών. Solin. 2, 2 *sed Italia tanta cura ab omnibus dicta, praecipue M. Catone* etc. Serv. Aen. 7, 678 *de Italicis urbibus Hyginus plenissime scripsit et Cato in originibus.* Fronto p. 203 Nab. *Cato . . . Italicarum originum pueritias illustravit.* Dionys. 1, 74 Κάτων Πόρκιος ἑλληνικὸν μὲν οὐχ ὁρίζει χρόνον (as the year of the foundation of Rome), ἐπιμελὴς δὲ γενόμενος εἴ καί τις ἄλλος περὶ τὴν συναγωγὴν τῆς ἀρχαιολογουμένης ἱστορίας ἔτεσιν ἀποφαίνει δυσὶ καὶ τριάκοντα καὶ τετρακοσίοις ὑστεροῦσαν τῶν Ἰλιακῶν. ὁ δὲ χρόνος οὗτος ἀναμετρηθεὶς ταῖς Ἐρατοσθένους (who placed the capture of Troy a. 1183) χρονογραφίαις κατὰ τὸ πρῶτον ἔτος πίπτει τῆς ἑβδόμης ὀλυμπιάδος (1183−432=751).

2. Festus 198 *Originum libros quod inscripsit Cato non satis plenum titulum propositi sui videtur amplexus, quando praegravant ea quae sunt rerum gestarum p. rom* Fronto p. 203 *Cato . . . qui . . . italicarum originum pueritias inlustravit.* The title of Origines (beginnings, original history) is most easily explained by assuming the first three books to have been at first published separately. Of the 7th book, at least, it is certain that it was composed and published after the others; see Cic. Brut. 89 *Lusitanis a Ser. Galba praetore* (a. 603/151) . . . *interfectis T. Libone tribuno pl.* (605/149) *populum incitante . . . M. Cato legem suadens in Galbam multa dixit; quam orationem in Origines suas rettulit, paucis antequam mortuus est diebus an mensibus.* See Cato ap. Cic. Cato mai. (the scene is laid a. 604/150) 38 *septimus mihi liber Originum est in manibus.* Gell. 13, 25 (14) 15 *Cato ex Originum septimo, in oratione quam contra Ser. Galbam dixit.* The publication of the first three books might have taken place c. 588/166, as the antiquity of Ameria was there fixed by reference to the war with Perseus (ended 586/168) (Plin. NH. 3, 114 *Ameriam . . . Cato ante Persei bellum conditam annis* dcccclxiii *prodit*). But Cato's speech pro Rhodiensibus (*quae et seorsim fertur et in quintae originis libro scripta est*, Gell. 6, 3, 7), contained in the 5th book, was also as early as a. 586/168. If therefore the original publication had been extended to 5 books, the title would have been chosen a parte potiori, as the introduction of the oldest history of the rest of Italy was after all peculiar to Cato, while in the early history of Rome he was preceded by Fabius Pictor, whom he sometimes merely copied (cf. Dionys. ant. 1, 79), and the history of the two Punic wars had also been related by that writer. Bergk, Progr., Halle 15th July 1865, p. 7 sq. holds that the publication of the Origg. was gradual.—He is classed with the Annalists ap. Cic. de or. 2, 51 (§ 116, 6), leg. 1, 6 *post annales pontificum maximorum . . . si aut ad Fabium aut ad . . . Catonem aut ad Pisonem aut ad Fannium aut ad Vennonium venias.* Plin. NH. 8, 11 (cf. n. 1) plainly calls the Origines annales. The insertion of speeches by the author was certainly a deviation from the manner of former annalists, Cato being altogether *haud sane detrectator laudum suarum* (Liv. 34, 15, 9). These speeches appear to have been expressly collected at a later time and thus (very much like those from Sallust's historiae) to have survived the work of which

they originally formed part (cf. JORDAN p. LVIII). The absence of names (n. 1) as well as the inequality of the treatment made it difficult for later writers to avail themselves of the work; hence they generally preferred to go back to Fabius Pictor.

3. Collection of the fragments of the Origines by HJORDAN p. 3 sqq. (cf. p. XIX). HPETER, hist. rell. 1, 51; fragm. 40.—VAHLEN, ZföG. 10, 480. WSOLTAU, WschrfklPh. 1886, 886. 916.—SCHWEGLER, RG. 1, 81. MOMMSEN, RG. 1^6, 922. HPETER, hist. rell. p. CXXVII.

121. Cato published his practical instructions on agriculture, sanitary rules, and oratory, perhaps also military art and law, as admonitions to his son. In the first three branches especially many practical sayings attest his quick observation. He also wrote for his son practical rules of life in verse and addressed letters to him. In the same way as he had published a collection of the witty sayings of others, his own were soon collected; in late Imperial times, moreover, collections of sentences were circulated under his name, as Cato was supposed to have embodied the old Roman philosophy (Catonis disticha).

1. OJAHN, on Roman Encyclopedias, Lpz. Ber. 1850, 263. 281. HJORDAN, Caton. q. exst. p. XCIX sqq.

1. In respect of the subject-matter, the most appropriate title for Cato's principal didactic work is praecepta ad filium (NON. 143, 7), We also find more general citations, e.g. ad filium, libri quos scripsit ad filium (SERV. Georg. 2, 95) or special designations either from the form (oratio, epistula) or the subject (de agricultura, de oratore). FSCHOELL, RhM. 33, 481 attempts to make the title Oraculum appear probable. The extent of the whole work is doubtful. Though Cato was *omnium bonarum artium magister* (PLIN. NH. 25, 4; cf. 14, 44 *insignis . . . claritate litterarum praeceptisque omnium rerum expetendarum datis generi romano*) and CIC. might justly say of him (de or. 3, 135): *nihil in hac civitate temporibus illis sciri discive potuit quod ille non cum investigarit et scierit tum etiam conscripserit*, it may still be questioned whether all this heap of information was contained in one and the same work. The libri ad filium must have contained precepts on agriculture; see JORDAN p. 78 sq. CI sq.; in the same way his warnings against Greek quacks (cf. § 55, 1) and several sanitary rules must have been addressed to his son (OJAHN p. 265. JORDAN p. 77 sq.); no less his rules for an orator (JORDAN p. 80), on account of which QUINT. 3, 1, 19 (see § 44, 3) declares him to be the first Roman who *condidit aliqua in hac materia.* It is quite probable that his instruction extended also to military art, and consequently the liber de re militari (JORDAN p. 80–82, cf. p. CII sq.) formed part of the praecepta ad filium (JAHN p. 270 sq.), though it is not borne out by the fragments, in which neither an address nor any attention to the capacity of a learner is to be found. See KÖCHLY and RÜSTOW, greich. Kriegsschriftsteller, 2 (1855), 61. This applies even more to Cato's juridical writings, which there is no doubt that he composed; (CIC. de or. 3, 135 *num quia ius civile didicerat causas non dicebat? aut quia poterat dicere iuris scientiam neglegebat? utroque in genere et elaboravit et praestitit.* POMPON. dig. 1, 2, 2, 38 *deinde*—after the Aelii—*M. Cato, princeps Porciae familiae, cuius et libri exstant, sed plurimi Marci* (see MOMMSEN ad loc.)

filii eius, ex quibus ceteri oriuntur (MOMMSEN *ordiuntur*). But as his son became more famous in that field, the citation in FESTUS 157 (*Cato in commentariis iuris civilis*) as well as CIC. de or. 2, 142 should be rather explained of him; see § 125, 6. The quotations undoubtedly belonging to the praecepta tend to show them as a kind of Vademecum for a young Roman, though with a peculiar colouring from the author's strong personality; they attest (as do the dicta) his wonderful talent for hitting the mark (e.g. *rem tene, verba sequentur; nihil agendo homines male agere discunt*) and are composed in a categorical style, almost like oracles. (PLIN. NH. 7, 171. COLUM. 11, 1, 26.)

3. Both the expressions *liber* and *carmen* render it improbable that the *liber Catonis qui inscriptus est carmen de moribus* (GELL. 11, 2, 2; cf. NON. 465) formed part of the praecepta. If it was in metre (see § 61, 1), it was far more probably in saturnian verses (RITSCHL, op. 4, 297. VAHLEN, ZföG. 10, 469. JORDAN l.l. p. CIII), against which however we have the fact that the scanty fragments are trochaic septenarii (EKÄRCHER, Phil. 8, 727; 9, 412. ABÖCKH, kl. Schrr. 6, 296), sotadeans (AFLECKEISEN, Catonianae poesis reliquiae, Lps. 1854) or even anapaests (BÄHRENS, FPR. 25, 57). LMÜLLER (d. saturn. Vers. 95) supposes Gellius to have made use of a late prose paraphrase (cf. § 103, 6).

4. Cato's letters to his son are mentioned by CIC. (off. 1, 10), and PLUTARCH (Cato mai. 20. Quaest. rom. 39), but the quotations do not show that they were part of the praecepta. It is uncertain whether Cato published letters addressed to others. JORDAN p. 83 sq. cf. p. CIV sq.

5. CIC. off. 1, 104 *multa multorum facete dicta, ut ea quae a sene Catone collecta sunt, quae vocant ἀποφθέγματα*. PLUT. Cato mai. 2 extr. μεθηρμηνευμένα (from the Greek) πολλὰ κατὰ λέξιν ἐν τοῖς ἀποφθέγμασι καὶ ταῖς γνωμολογίαις (witty sayings and maxims, perhaps two different varieties of the same class) τέτακται. See JORDAN p. CVI and 83, RhM. 14, 261 and JJ. 73, 384.

6. Cato's own dicta seem to have been collected soon after his death from personal recollection as well as from his writings (esp. speeches). Cicero and Cornelius Nepos must have known of such a collection; most have, however, been preserved by Plutarch; see the collection in JORDAN p. 97; cf. p. CVI sq. Thirteen sententiae Catonis from collections of apophthegms, see ap. WOLFFLIN, Senecae monita (§ 289, 10) p. 26.—At a much later time, nice discriminations of synonymous expressions were excerpted from his writings (esp. from the speeches) by grammarians, a proceeding which led to the mistake that he himself had written about Synonyms (differentiarum liber): JORDAN p. CVII sq. Cf. § 42, 4—On the disticha Catonis see § 398, 1.

122. Of all Cato's writings only his work de agri cultura has been preserved entire. The first systematic part is followed, in a somewhat discursive manner, by a large number of receipts, rules for housekeeping, formulas for sales and leases, for sacrifices and domestic medicine. A special charm lies in the homely severity and simplicity of this work, and in its honourable zeal for improvement, which always asserts itself in a tone of authority: short sentences thrown out like aphorisms, but of great precision, succeed one another. The text in question has lost almost all its archaic style, and shows many signs of confusion, but notwith-

standing it represents Cato's work as a whole, and not a later revision.

1. The text is found in the scriptores R.R.; see § 54, 7; and esp. Catonis de agri cultura liber, Varronis rerum rusticarum l. III. ex. rec. HKeilii I, Lps. 1884. The MS. text of Cato and Varro de R.R. preserved to us is founded on an old long lost MS. in the Library of S. Marco at Florence (Marcianus, § 380, 2), which APolitianus and PVictorius were able to use. Of this there is preserved Politianus' collation (now in Paris) and transcripts of the Marcianus, the earliest Paris. 6842 A s. xii/xiii, also Laur. 30, 10 s. xiv, Laur. 51, 4 s. xv, and others. Keil's praef. to his edition.—Translated by GGrosse (Halle 1787). Ganter (Donauesch. 1844).—That it was preserved in its original form (Klotz supposes it to have been formed gradually from notes made incidentally for private use) is maintained by Klotz (on Cato's work de r. r. in Jahn's Archiv 10, 5; cf. his history of Latin literature 1, 22), LDietze (n. 4) p. 4 sq., HJordan, DLit.-Z. 1882, 1529. 1885, 157, OSchöndörffer, de genuina Catonis de agri cultura forma I: de syntaxi Cat. Königsb. 1885; for the opposite view of a modernised revision HKeil, obss. in Catonis et Varronis de r. r. (Halle 1849), esp. p. 65. Textual criticism Keil l.l. and MBer. der Berl. Akad. 1852, 160 sq. HUsener, RhM. 19, 141.

2. Name of the work in the MS. text: de agri cultura. Thus also Varro RR. 1, 2, 28 *in magni illius Catonis libro qui de agri cultura est editus.* M. Aurel. to Fronto p. 69 *legi ex agri cultura Catonis.* On the other hand ap. Cic. Cato 54 *in eo libro quem de rebus rusticis scripsi.* Cf. Gell. 3, 14, 17 (*de agric.*), with 10, 26, 8 (*de re rust.*). KWNitzsch, ZfAW. 1845, 493 attempted to prove that the work was intended as a guide for the cultivation of one particular estate, that of C. Manlius near Casinum and Venafrum: but the few indications which favour this view are contradicted by the mass of evidence. See also RReitzenstein, de scriptt. R. R. p. 61. On the plants mentioned in the work see Meyer, Gesch. der Botanik 1, 341. On two magical formulas in it ThBergk, op. 1, 556.

3. Ch. 143 is eminently characteristic of the spirit and tone of the whole; it treats of the vilica, e.g. *ea te metuat facito. ne nimium luxuriosa siet. vicinas aliasque mulieres quam minimum utatur, neve domum neve ad sese recipiat. ad cenam ne quo eat neve ambulatrix siet. rem divinam ni faciat . . . scito dominum pro tota familia rem divinam facere. munda siet. villam conversam mundeque habeat* etc.

4. Language: Fronto p. 114 *verbis Cato multiiugis* (§ 37, 5), p. 155 *partim iligneis nucibus Catonis.* Quint. 2, 5, 21. Verrius Flaccus wrote de obscuris Catonis (Gell. 17, 6, 2 quotes b. 2). LDietze, de sermone Catoniano, Anklam 1871. GCortese: see § 118, 1. EHauler, Arch. f. Lexikogr. 1, 582. Schöndörffer: n. 1.

123. Of the contemporaries of Cato we know as orators Q. Fabius Maximus (Cunctator), Q. Caecilius Metellus, M. Cornelius Cethegus, P. Licinius Crassus (Dives), Africanus the Elder, the father of the two Gracchi, as well as L. Papirius and L. Paulus.

1. Q. Fabius Q. f. Q. n. Maximus Verrucosus, cos. 521/233, 526/228, 539/215, 540/214, 545/209; censor 524/230; dictator 537/217; PRE. 6, 2901. Cic. Cato m. 12 *multa in eo viro praeclara cognovi, sed nihil est admirabilius quam quo modo ille mortem filii tulit, clari viri et consularis. est in manibus laudatio; quam cum legimus, quem philosophum non contemnimus?* Plut. Fab. 1 διασώζεται αὐτοῦ λόγος ὃν εἶπεν ἐν τῷ δήμῳ τοῦ παιδὸς αὐτοῦ μεθ' ὑπατείαν ἀποθανόντος ἐγκώμιον. ib. 25: τὸ δ' ἐγκώμιον

. . . *αὐτὸς εἶπε καταστὰς ἐν ἀγορᾷ καὶ γράψας τὸν λόγον ἐξέδωκεν.* Whether the quotation '*Fabius Maximus: amitti quam apisci*' ap. PRISCIAN GL. 2, 380 belongs to it, is not certain: see HERTZ's note. His son (cos. 541/213) died probably not before a. 548/206; see PRE. 6, 2911, n. 32.

2. Q. Caecilius Metellus, cos. 548/206; PRE. 2, 23. PLIN. NH. 7, 139 *Q. Metellus in ea oratione quam habuit supremis laudibus patris sui L. Metelli*, cos. 503/251 and 507/247; dictator 530/224) . . . *scriptum reliquit* etc. Cf. CIC. Brut. 57. MWENDE, de Caeciliis Met. 1 (Bonn 1875), 18.

3. M. Cornelius Cethegus, cos. 550/204, † 558/196; PRE. 2, 686. As an orator he was praised by Q. Ennius, see CIC. Brut. 57–59. Cato 50. Enn. ed. VAHLEN p. 45. IV.

4. P. Licinius Crassus Dives, cos. 549/205, † 571/183; see TEUFFEL, PRE. 4, 1054. LIV. 30, 1, 5 *facundissimus habebatur seu causa oranda seu in senatu, ad populum suadendi aut dissuadendi locus esset; iuris pontificii peritissimus.* Cf. CIC. de or. 3, 134. Cato 50 *et pontificii et civilis iuris studium.*

5. Africanus the Elder, cos. 549/205 and 560/194, † 571/183 (see MOMMSEN, Herm. 1, 201); CIC. Brut. 77 *ipsum Scipionem accepimus non infantem fuisse.* LIV. 39, 52, 3 *tribunus pl. M. Naevius* (a. 567/187 or 569/185), *adversus quem oratio inscripta P. Africani est.* Cf. 38, 56. GELL. 4, 18, 6 *fertur etiam oratio quae videtur habita eo die a Scipione; et qui dicunt eam non veram* etc. Cicero did not accept it as genuine; see off. 3, 4 *nulla eius ingenii monumenta mandata litteris;* and no doubt it was of an apocryphal character, see HNISSEN, Krit. Unters. 51. MOMMSEN, Herm. 1, 163. 312. On his son see § 127, 3; on his son-in-law Nasica § 127, 4. Laelius, the friend of Africanus, is also praised as a political orator by SIL. IT. 15, 453.

6. Ti. Sempronius P. f. Ti. n. Gracchus, cos. 577/177 and 591/163, censor 585/169; PRE. 6, 978, 35. CIC. Brut. 79 *erat isdem temporibus Ti. Gracchus . . . cuius exstat oratio graeca apud Rhodios* (a. 589/165 or 593/161), *quem civem cum gravem tum etiam eloquentem constat fuisse.* Inscription attached to the forma Sardiniae insulae (§ 60, 2) dedicated by him after his triumph in Sardinia, ap. LIV. 41, 28. To him also was attributed (see n. 5) an apocryphal speech in defence of his father-in-law, Africanus the Elder; see LIV. 38, 56, 2 sqq. MOMMSEN, Herm. 1, 163. 212. In the MSS. of Cornelius Nepos (probably from the section de oratoribus romanis) two large fragments of a letter of his wife Cornelia to her son Gaius belonging to a. 630/124 are preserved, nor is there any doubt that there were letters by her current in antiquity (CIC. Brut. 211 *legimus epistulas Corneliae, matris Gracchorum: apparet filios non tam in gremio educatos quam in sermone matris.* Cf. QUINT. 1, 1, 6. PLUT. C. Gracch. 13 *ἐν τοῖς ἐπιστολίοις αὐτῆς*); but the genuineness of the fragments handed down to us has been doubted (AGLANGE, verm. Schr. 108. JSÖRGEL, Corneliæ . . . epistolarum fragmenta genuina esse non posse, BlfbayrGW. 3 (1866), 101. 144), though as it seems without sufficient reason. A rhetor would have made the mother of the Gracchi rather declaim for liberty and for revenge against the murderers of her son's brother (cf. § 45, 6); but he would never have succeeded in combining the manly energy of thought of an old Roman with a woman's tenderness and carelessness of style. See also LMERCKLIN, de Corneliae vita, moribus, epistolis, Dorp. 1845. CNIPPERDEY, op. 95. THBERGK, Phil. 16, 626. HJORDAN, Herm. 15, 530. The base of her statue in Octaviae operibus (PLIN. NH. 34, 31) was found in 1878; it bears the inscription CORNELIA | AFRICANI · F | GRACCHORUM (bull. arch. 1878, 209).

7. CIC. Brut. 170 *apud maiores nostros video disertissimum habitum ex Latio L. Papirium Fregellanum, Ti. Gracchi P. f. fere aetate; eius etiam oratio est pro Fregellanis coloniisque latinis habita in senatu.*

8. L. Aemilius L. f. M. n. Paulus, cos. 572/182 and 586/168, † 594/160; PRE. 1², 368. Cic. Brut. 80 *etiam L. Paulus, Africani pater, personam principis civis facile dicendo tuebatur.* Cf. Liv. 45, 8. Val. Max. 5, 10, 2 *quem casum* (the death of his sons) *quo robore animi sustinuerit oratione quam de rebus a se gestis apud populum habuit hanc adiciendo clausulam nulli ambiguum reliquit.* Cf. Liv. 45, 41. Plut. Aem. P. 36. A decree by him (*L. Aimilius L. f. inpeirator*) dated 19th Jan. 565/189 at the time when he held the supreme command in Spain, *utei quei Hastensium servei in Turri Lascutana habitarent leiberei essent*, on a bronze tablet found a. 1867 (now at Paris in the Louvre); see CIL. 2, 5041 and EHübner, Herm. 3, 243. Wordsw. EL. 171. DIE. 96.

124. Among Cato's younger contemporaries who were orators in the 6th century u.c. we must specially mention C. Sulpicius Gallus, on account of the extent and accuracy of his learning.

1. C. Sulpicius C. f. C. n. Gallus, cos. 588/166, † 604/150; see Cic. Brut. 90. PRE. 6, 1493. Cic. Brut. 78 *de minoribus C. Sulpicius Gallus maxime omnium nobilium graecis litteris studuit, isque et oratorum in numero est habitus et fuit reliquis rebus ornatus atque elegans.* Off. 1, 19 *videbamus in studio dimetiendi paene caeli atque terrae C. Gallum . . . quam delectabat eum defectiones solis et lunae multo ante nobis praedicere!* Pliny in the Ind. auct. of book 2 quotes him as a writer on astronomy, cf. NH. 2, 83 *in qua sententia* (that touching the mutual distances of the constellations) *et Gallus Sulpicius fuit noster.* Cf. ib. 2, 53 *ab imperatore productus ad praedicendam eclipsim* (in the night before the battle of Pydna 586/168), *mox et composito volumine.*

125. The most remarkable jurists of the 6th century u.c. are the two Aelii, Publius and especially his younger brother Sextus, the first writer of a juridical work. It was entitled Tripertita, and dealt with the XII tables, their explanation, and the formulae of law-suits. Besides these, we have Scipio Nasica, L. Acilius (or Atilius), Q. Fabius Labeo and Cato's son.

1. P. Aelius Q. f. P. n. Paetus, cos. 553/201, censor 555/199, † 580/174, PRE. 1², 332, 5. Pompon. dig. 1, 2, 2, 38 *deinde* (after Ti. Coruncanius) *Sex. Aelius et frater eius, P. Aelius, et P. Atilius maximam scientiam in profitendo habuerunt, ut duo Aelii etiam consules fuerint, Atilius autem primus a populo Sapiens appellatus est.*

2. Sex. Aelius Paetus Catus, cos. 556/198, censor 560/194. PRE. 1², 332, 6. Cic. de or. 1, 212 *eum* (*iuris consultum vere nominari*) *dicerem qui legum et consuetudinis eius qua privati in civitate uterentur et ad respondendum et ad agendum et ad cavendum peritus esset; et ex eo genere Sex. Aelium, M'. Manilium, P. Mucium nominarem.* Brut. 78 *Sex. Aelius, iuris quidem civilis omnium peritissimus, sed etiam ad dicendum paratus.* Cato 27 *nihil Sex. Aelius tale* (on old age), *nihil multis annis ante Ti. Coruncanius, nihil modo P. Crassus* (§ 123, 4), *a quibus iura civibus praescribebantur.* Pompon. l.l.: *Sex. Aelium etiam Ennius laudavit, et exstat illius liber qui inscribitur Tripertita* (fragments ap. Huschke, Iurispr. anteiust. ⁵ 1), *qui liber veluti cunabula iuris continet. Tripertita autem dicitur quoniam lege XII tabularum praeposita iungitur interpretatio* (cf. RSchöll, legis XII tabb. reliqq. p. 22), *deinde subtexitur legis actio. eiusdem esse tres alii libri referuntur, quos tamen quidam negant eiusdem esse, sed hos sectati ad aliquid Aeli Cati* (according to Huschke's emendation). Cf. ib.

7 *augescente civitate, quia deerant quaedam genera agendi, non post multum temporis spatium* (after Cn. Flavius) *Sex. Aelius alias actiones composuit et librum populo dedit, qui appellatur* (in later time) *ius Aelianum.* (§ 88, 2.) OKarlowa, röm. Rechtsgesch. 1,475. Attempt to determine the particular contents of the Tripertita by MVoigt, Abh. d. Sächs. G. d. Wiss. 7, 327, who also connects with this work the *Aeliana studia* ap. Cic. de or. 1, 193 (§ 148, 2).

3. Pompon. dig. 1, 2, 2, 37 *fuit maximae scientiae* (as a jurist) . . *Gaius* (?) *Scipio Nasica, qui Optimus a senatu appellatus est* (a. 550/204; cos. 563/191), *cui etiam publice domus in sacra via data est, quo facilius consuli posset.* Cf. § 89, 1.

4. L. Atilius is mentioned by Pomponius, see n. 1. But Cic. Lael. 6 (the authority followed by Pomp.) we read *scimus L. Acilium apud patres nostros appellatum esse Sapientem . . . quia prudens esse in iure civili putabatur.* Leg. 2, 59 *hoc* (*lessum* in the XII tables) *veteres interpretes Sex. Aelius, L. Acilius non satis se intellegere dixerunt.*

5. Q. Fabius Labeo, cos. 571/183. PRE. 6, 2912, 37. Cic. Brut. 81 *Ser. Fabius Pictor et iuris et litterarum et antiquitatis bene peritus; Quintusque Fabius Labeo fuit ornatus eisdem fere laudibus.* Suet. vita Terent. 4 (p. 31 sq. Rffsch.) *Santra Terentium putat . . . uti potuisse. . . Q. Fabio Labeone et M. Popillio, consulari utroque ac poeta.* Cf. 114, 3.

6. M. Porcius Cato (Licinianus), born c. 562/192, † 602/152; PRE. 5, 1910. Pomponius see § 121, 2. Gell. 13, 20 (19), 9 *ex maiore Catonis filio, qui praetor designatus patre vivo mortuus est et egregios de iuris disciplina libros reliquit.* Inst. 1, 11, 12 *apud Catonem bene scriptum refert antiquitas* etc. Ulp. dig. 21, 1, 10, 1 *Catonem scribere lego* etc. Paul. ib. 24, 3, 44 pr.: *Nerva et Cato responderunt, ut est relatum* etc. 45, 1, 4, 1 *Cato libro XV scribit* etc. He is principally known by the regula Catoniana, concerning legacies (dig. 34, 7).

126. One of the aristocratic adversaries of Cato, M. Fulvius Nobilior, composed and published fasti. His son Quintus, too, showed interest in literature.

1. The father was cos. 565/189 (in Aetolia), censor 575/179. Macr. 1, 12, 16 *Fulvius Nobilior in fastis quos in aede Herculis Musarum* (probably founded from the Aetolian booty, cf. Plin. NH. 35, 66. GBdeRossi, sul tempio d' Ercole e delle Muse nel portico di Filippo, bull. archeol. 1869 p. 3) *posuit Romulum dicit . . . Iunium mensem vocasse.* Cf. Macr. 1, 13, 12 *Fulvius id egisse M'. Acilium cos. dicit a. u. c. a. DLXII, inito mox bello aetolico.* Varro, LL. 6, 33 *ut Fulvius scribit et Junius* (on the name Aprilis). Censorin. d. n. 20, 2 *magis Iunio Gracchano et Fulvio et Varroni et Suetonio aliisque credendum.* ib. 4 *sive a Numa, ut ait Fulvius, sive, ut Iunius, a Tarquinio.* 22, 9 *Fulvius et Iunius auctores sunt* (on the Roman names of the months). Charis. GL. 1, 138 *Nobiliore. comparativa Plinius e putat ablativo finiri; antiquos tamen ait per i locutos, quippe fastos omnes et libros 'a Fulvio Nobiliori' scriptum* (?) *rettulisse.* See § 74, 2 and on his relations with Ennius n. 2 and § 100, 4, 5.

2. Cic. Brut. 79 *Q. Nobiliorem M. f. iam patrio instituto deditum studio litterarum, qui etiam Q. Ennium, qui cum patre eius in Aetolia militaverat* (see § 100, 4), *civitate donavit cum triumvir coloniam deduxisset* (a. 570/114), when *coloniae duae, Potentia in Picenum, Pisaurum in gallicum agrum deductae sunt*, Liv. 39, 44, 10; cf. § 100, 5. Liv. per. 49 *Q. Fulvius Nobilior ei* (i.e. Cato) *saepe ab eo in senatu laceratus respondit*

pro Galba (a. 605/149, at the same accusation of the Lusitanians). Quintus was consul a. 601/153, and censor probably 618/136.

127. A. Postumius Albinus, C. Acilius and the son of Africanus the Elder were historians in Cato's time, but all wrote in Greek. Albinus was a zealous advocate of the Hellenising movement, and even in his younger days dedicated his work to Ennius, the venerable apostle of that school. Africanus the Elder himself and Scipio Nasica furnished contributions to history.

1. A. Postumius A. f. Albinus, praet. 599/155, cos. 603/151; PRE. 5, 1941. POLYB. 39, 12, 1: Αὖλος Ποστούμιος . . . οἰκίας μὲν ἦν καὶ γένους πρώτου, κατὰ δὲ τὴν ἰδίαν φύσιν στωμύλος καὶ λάλος καὶ πέρπερος διαφερόντως. ἐπιθυμήσας δὲ εὐθέως ἐκ παίδων τῆς ἑλληνικῆς ἀγωγῆς καὶ διαλέκτου πολὺς μὲν ἦν ἐν τούτοις καὶ κατακορής, ὥστε δι' ἐκεῖνον καὶ τὴν αἵρεσιν τὴν ἑλληνικὴν προσκόψαι τοῖς πρεσβυτέροις καὶ τοῖς ἀξιολογωτάτοις τῶν Ῥωμαίων. τέλος δὲ καὶ ποίημα γράφειν καὶ πραγματικὴν ἱστορίαν ἐπεχείρησεν. Fragm. of an unknown historian (taken by GCORTESE from a MS. s. VI. published riv. di filol. 12 (1884), 396; and RhM. 39, 623): *cum eo tempore, ut narrat in historiae suae principio, duae quasi factiones Romae essent, quarum una graecas artes atque disciplinas adamabat, altera patriae caritatem praetexebat, acerrime ab illa stetit Albinus. hic Athenis studiosus audiendi versatus est adulescentulus, atque propterea graeca institutionem prae ceteris extollebat non sine quadam iactatione et petulantia. inde irae atque accusationes adversariorum, qui minus paterentur graecum sermonem in scriptionibus usurpari ad rem R. spectantibus. graece autem, ut scimus, historiam ille confecerat Q. Ennio poetae inscriptam* (therefore at latest in the year of Ennius' death 585/169). *ceterum satis in eo erat litterarum et philosophiae, cuius alumnam eloquentiam inculcandam aiebat* . . . (two illegible lines) *consulatu arrepto cum dilectu* (cf. LIV. per. 48). . . . Another quotation from the proem ap. GELL. 11, 8, 2 (apology for his Greek style; cf. POLYB. 39, 12, 4). This graecising Roman was naturally intolerable to the narrowly patriotic Cato. POLYB. 39, 12, 5. PLUT. Cato 12.—CIC. Acad. pr. 2, 137 *A. Albinum . . . doctum sane hominem, ut indicat ipsius historia scripta graece.* Brut. 81 *vivo Catone minores natu multi uno tempore oratores floruerunt. nam A. Albinus, is qui graece scripsit historiam, . . . et litteratus et disertus fuit.* From MACROB. 3, 20, 5 *Postumius Albinus annali primo de Bruto 'ea causa sese stultum brutumque faciebat'* etc., one feels tempted to assume the existence of a Latin version of the work; but the translation of those words may just as well belong to Macrobius' authority as the one in praef. 14 sqq. belongs to Cornelius Nepos (GELL. 11, 8, 5). At all events it seems that Albinus also in some way or other took in the earliest history.—SERV. Aen. 9, 710 *Postumius De adventu Aeneae et Lutatius* (§ 142, 4) *Communium historiarum Boiam . . . dicunt* appears to rest upon a misunderstanding. HPETER, hist. rell. 1, cxxv. 49. fragm. 37.

2. CIC. off. 3, 115 (*C.*) *Acilius qui graece scripsit historiam, plures ait fuisse qui in castra revertissent* (after the battle of Cannae). DIONYS. ant. 3, 67 (Γάιον Ἀκίλλιον ποιησάμενος. . . βεβαιωτήν). Isig. Nicae. (act. soc. phil. Lips. 1, 40) Ἀκύλιος ὁ Ῥωμαῖος ἱστορικός φησι κτλ. STRABO 5, p. 230 (if here for the MS. ὅγε Κύλιος we may read with SCHWEGLER, RG. 1, 80 ὅ γ' Ἀκύλιος; others suppose Coelius Antipater, see WSIEGLIN, Coel. Antip. 33; philol. Wochenschr. 1883, 1453). LIV. per. 53 *C. Acilius* (conjectural reading of MHERTZ, de Cinc. 12; RhM. 17, 579: the MSS. give *C. Iulius*) *senator graece res romanas scribit* (c. a. 612/142). He is certainly the C. Acilius senator who according to GELL. 6, 14, 9 (cf. PLUT. Cat. mai. 22) in the

year 599/155 served in the Senate as interpreter to the three Greek ambassadors and philosophers (§ 50 and p. 136). The work went back by way of introduction to the early history (Plut. Romul. 21 Γάιος Ἀκίλλιος ἱστορεῖ, πρὸ τῆς κτίσεως κτλ.) and was continued probably to the time of the author; the latest notice which we find in the few extant fragments relates to 570/184 (Dion. 3, 67).—Later on, the work was put into Latin by one Claudius: see Liv. 25, 39, 12 *Claudius, qui annales Acilianos ex graeco in latinum sermonem vertit.* Cf. 35, 14, 5 (a. 561/193) *Claudius secutus graecos Acilianos libros.* Presumably this translator (or borrower?) was no other than Claudius Quadrigarius (cf. § 155, 1). So Giesebrecht, Plüss, Mommsen, röm. Forsch. 2, 427, GFUnger, Philol. Suppl. vol. 3, 2, 4, GThouret, JJ. Suppl. 11, 156. HPeter, JJ. 125, 103.—Against this identification Sigonius, FLachmann, HNissen, HPeter (earlier hist. rell. 1, ccxcvii).—In general PRE. 1², 109. HNissen, krit. Unters. 39. HPeter, hist. rell. 1, cxix. 44; fragm. 34.

3. Cic. Brut. 77 *filius eius* (of Africanus the Elder), . . . *si corpore valuisset, in primis habitus esset disertus: indicant cum oratiunculae tum historia quaedam graeca, scripta dulcissime* (perhaps treating of his father's deeds? see Keller, der 2. pun. Krieg, Marb. 1875, 77. OGilbert, JJ. Suppl. 10, 393; or of the war with Antiochos 563/191? see Mommsen, röm. Forsch. 2, 513). Cato mai. 35 *ad paternam magnitudinem animi doctrina uberior accesserat.* Vellei. 1, 10, 3 *P. Scipioni, P. Africani filio, nihil ex paterna maiestate praeter speciem nominis vigoremque eloquentiae retinenti.* He became augur a. 574/180 (Liv. 40, 42, 13). His epitaph in saturnian metre CIL. 1, 33 calls him Flamen dialis (cf. Mommsen).

4. Plut. Aemil. Paul. 15 ὁ Νασικᾶς ἐπικαλούμενος Σκηπίων (cos. 592/162 and 599/155, censor 595/159; (PRE. 2, 667) . . γεγραφὼς περὶ τῶν πράξεων τούτων (in the war with Perseus) ἐπιστόλιον πρός τινα τῶν βασιλέων. Cf. ib. 16. Cic. Brut. 79 *P. etiam Scipionem Nasicam . . . habitum eloquentem aiunt.* Cf. Cato m. 50. On the similar work of Africanus the Elder see § 56, 1. Nissen, Unterss. üb. d. Quell. des Liv. 267.

128. The freedman Sp. Carvilius is a remarkable figure in the literary history of the 6th century u.c., one of the first who opened a public school at Rome and the arranger of the Roman alphabet of 21 letters.

1. Plut. quaest. rom. 59, p. 278 D πρῶτος ἀνέῳξε γραμματοδιδασκαλεῖον Σπόριος Καρβίλιος, ἀπελεύθερος Καρβιλίου τοῦ πρώτου γαμετὴν ἐκβαλόντος. The authorities fluctuate between 519/235 and 524/230 as the date of this first (arbitrary) divorce; see Ritschl, Parerga 68. On Carvilius' alphabet see above p. 127. Ritschl, op. 4, 226. HJordan, Beitr. z. Gesch. der lat. Spr. (Berl. 1879), 151. LHavet, rev. d. phil. 2 (1878), 17.

129. Among the prose Inscriptions of the 6th century the SC. de Bacchanalibus is the most prominent, both in language and in its subject-matter. It may, however, be stated that the number of these documents is but small, and that their significance belongs either to political history or to the history of the alphabet.

1. The SC. (more correctly epistula consulum ad Teuranos) de Bacchanalibus of the year 568/186 is copied and explained e.g. CIL. 1. 196. Prisc. Lat. Mon. pl.

18 (in facsimile). Bruns, fontes [5] 151. DIE. 97. WWeissbrodt, obss. in SC. de Bacc., Braunsb. 1879; miscell. epigr. numism. gramm., Braunsb. 1883, 10; Phil. 39, 558.—On the decree of L. Aemilius Paulus a. 565/189 see § 123, 8.—Among the epitaphs of the Scipios belong to this period CIL. 1, 35 on L. Cornelius Scipio, quaestor 587/167, † c. 593/161, and perhaps ib. n. 36 (c. 600/154 ?) on Scipio Asiagenus.

2. Decree of the praetor L. Cornelius Cn. f. (cos. 598/156 ?) to the Tiburtines (a. 595/159 ?), CIL. 1, 201. Bruns, font. [5] 157. DIE. 305. FBücheler, JJ. 105, 568. For the other inscriptions of the 6th century (from the beginning of the second Punic war) which it is possible to date, see the CIL. 1, 530–539. DIE. 1, 98 sqq. Two very ancient inscriptions from Luceria and Spoletium, threatening with punishment for the desecration of a sacred grove, are especially remarkable for the ancient linguistic forms. Ephem. epigr. 2, 205 and EBormann in the miscellanea Capitolina (Rome 1879), 5 (and bull. d. inst. arch. 1879, 67). DIE. 1, 94, 95. Bruns, fontes iur. rom. [5] 241. Bücheler, RhM. 35, 627. MBréal, mém. de la soc. de linguist. 4 (1881), 373. HJordan, quaestt. Umbr., Königsb. 1882; ann. dell' inst. 56, 5. A SC. of the year 584/170, relating to the affairs of the town of Thisbe in Boeotia, is preserved only in a Greek translation: Ephem. epigr. 1, 278. 2, 102. Bruns, fontes [5] 152.

B. THE SEVENTH CENTURY U.C.

(153–54 B.C.).

130. The first twenty years of the 7th century u.c. (601/153–620/134) are in the history of Rome taken up with wars, especially the Lusitanian (601/153–620/134, Viriathus) and the Numantine (611/143–621/133), in the shameful conduct of which the consequences of the year 606/146 (Carthage, Corinth) already appear. Literary studies were, therefore, very insignificant during this period.

131. These twenty years produced orators in Africanus the Younger, Laelius the Younger, Sulpicius Galba, L. Scribonius Libo, M. Lepidus, Furius Philus, Q. Metellus Macedonicus, and minor ones, e.g. the two Mummii.

1. P. Cornelius Scipio Aemilianus, Africanus (minor), born 569/185 (KFRoth, RhM. 12, 183), cos. 607/147 and 620/134, censor 612/142, † 625/129; PRE. 2, 662. Cic. Brut. 82 *C. Laelius et P. Africanus in primis eloquentes, quorum exstant orationes.* Lael. 96 *quanta illa (Scipionis) fuit gravitas, quanta in oratione maiestas! . . . sed . . . est in manibus oratio.* Cf. Mur. 58. de inv. 1, 5. de or. 1, 215. Brut. 258, off. 1, 116. *Scipionis oratiunculae* excerpted by M. Aurelius, according to Fronto 34 Nab. Among the fragments of his speeches (Meyer, or. fr. 1, 101) there are two somewhat more extensive, ap. Gell. 6, 11, 9. Macr. 3, 14, 7. Most of them very bitterly criticise the spreading corruption of morals. On his delivery see Cic. de or. 1, 255 *multi oratores fuerunt, ut illum Scipionem audimus et Laelium, qui omnia sermone* (conversational manner) *conficerent paullo intentiore.*—Aemilius Paulus' care for the Greek education of his children: Plut. Aem. Paul. 6; Plin. NH. 35, 135. Of the Macedonian spoils *μόνα τὰ βιβλία τοῦ βασιλέως* (Perseus) *φιλογραμματοῦσι τοῖς υἱέσιν ἐπέτρεψεν ἐξελέσθαι* (Plut. Aem. P. 28). Africanus possessed much general culture: Cic. Tusc. 1, 5 *Galbam, Africanum, Laelium doctos fuisse traditum est.* 2, 62 *semper*

Africanus Socraticum Xenophontem in manibus habebat: especially the Κύρου παιδεία, Cic. ad Q. fr. 1, 1, 23. C. Fannius in Annalibus ascribed to him (Socratic) irony; cf. § 137, 4. Cic. Acad. 2, 15. de or. 2, 270. Brut. 299. He was a friend of Polybios, Polyb. 32, 9 sq.; and Panaitios, Cic. Acad. 2, 5. p. Mur. 66. cf. de or. 2, 154. Vellei. 1, 13, 3. Plut. c. principibus esse philos. 1. 12 (4, 117 Wytt.); apophthegm. Scip. min. 13, 14 (1, 797 W.). Friendship with C. Laelius (e.g. Cic. de or. 2, 22. Hor. S. 2, 1, 71), Terence (§ 108, 5) and Lucilius (§ 143, 1 and 3). Mommsen, RG. 2^6 82. 429.

2. Q. Fabius Maximus Allobrogicus, nephew of the younger Scipio Africanus (cos. 633/121; PRE. 6, 2915, 46), recited the funeral speech on Africanus (his uncle), Cic. Mur. 75, which had been written by C. Laelius, who afterwards published it under his own name; see Schol. Bob. ad Cic. p. Mil. 16, p. 283 Or.: *super Africani laudibus exstat oratio C. Laeli Sapientis, qua usus videtur Q. Fabius Maximus in laudatione mortui Scipionis.* Cic. de or. 2, 341 (*Q. Tuberoni* [§ 139, 2] *Africanum avunculum laudanti scripsit C. Laelius*) appears to confuse two nephews of Afr.

3. C. Laelius (Sapiens), son of Laelius the elder § 123, 5, a few years older than Aemilianus (Cic. de rep. 1, 18 *Laelium quod aetate antecedebat observabat in parentis loco Scipio;* cf. Lael. 104); cos. 614/140. PRE. 4, 725.—Cic. Brut. 84 *ingeni, litterarum, eloquentiae, sapientiae denique, etsi utrique* (Africanus and Laelius) *primas, priores tamen lubenter deferunt Laelio.* Cf. ib. 82 (above n. 1) and de or. 1, 255. Brut. 83 *plurimum tribuitur ambobus, dicendi tamen laus est in Laelio illustrior, at oratio Laelii de collegiis non melior quam de multis quam voles Scipionis; . . . multo tamen vetustior et horridior ille quam Scipio.* de or. 1, 58 *Ser. Galbae et . . . C. Laelio, quos constat dicendi gloria praestitisse.* Brut. 94 *hanc ob causam* (because Laelius *limatius dicendi consectabatur genus*) *videtur Laeli mens spirare etiam in scriptis, Galbae autem vis occidisse.* 295 *de Laelio, cuius tu oratione negas fieri quidquam posse dulcius, addis etiam nescio quid augustius. nomine nos capis summi viri vitaeque elegantissimae verissimis laudibus.* Cf. de rep. 6, 2 *⟨oratio⟩ Laeli quam omnes habemus in manibus.* ND. 3, 43 *in illa aureola oratiuncula.* We do not know of any accusations by Laelius, but of political speeches, defences and panegyrics (see n. 2). Cf. HMeyer, orat. fr.[1] p. 96. Cic. Att. 7, 3, 10 *Terentii fabulae propter elegantiam sermonis putabantur a C. Laelio scribi;* cf. § 108, 5; fin. 2, 24 *Diogenem stoicum adulescens, post autem Panaetium audierat Laelius.* From his philosophical tendencies he was called σοφὸς (Lucil. ib.) or Sapiens (Brut. 213. off. 2, 40. 3, 16). Perhaps Coelius Antipater dedicated his history to him? See § 137, 5.

4. Ser. Sulpicius Galba, born c. 565/189 (*aetate paulum his*—Laelius and Africanus the Younger—*antecedens* he is styled by Cic. Brut. 82), censured on account of a disgraceful breach of faith committed by him in Lusitania (a. 604/150). In spite of this he was consul a. 610/144. PRE. 6, 1494. Cic. Brut. 82 states that he was the first Roman orator who employed artificial figures (*ut egrederetur a proposito ornandi causa, . . . ut communibus locis uteretur*), perhaps in order to hide his bad cause. He who was praised as *divinus homo in dicendo* was, on the other hand, *ignarus legum, haesitans in maiorum institutis, rudis in iure civili* (Cic. de or. 1, 40). His delivery was remarkable for great vivacity: *in agendo . . . vehemens atque incensus,* Brut. 88; *incitata et gravis et vehemens oratio,* ib. 93; *lateribus et clamore contendebat,* de or. 1, 255; *nihil leniter dixit,* or. 106; cf. Brut. 86 *atrocior acriorque Laelio;* 89 *elegantia in Laelio, vis in Galba;* de or. 3, 28 *gravitatem Africanus, lenitatem Laelius, asperitatem Galba, profluens quiddam habuit Carbo et canorum.* Therefore his speeches made less impression when read (Brut. 93 sq.). His style was also less polished (*exiliores orationes sunt et redolentes magis antiquitatem quam*

aut Laelii aut Scipionis aut etiam ipsius Catonis; itaque evanuerunt, vix iam ut appareant, Brut. 82; cf. ib. 295. Tac. dial. 18). Of the trib. pl. L. Scribonius Libo, who prosecuted Galba (605/145) for maladministration (see above), Cicero says (Brut. 90): *Libonem non infantem video fuisse, ut ex orationibus ejus intellegi potest.*

5. M. Aemilius Lepidus, qui est Porcina dictus (Cic. Brut. 95), cos. 617/137; PRE. 1², 357. Cic. l.l. *isdem temporibus fere quibus Galba, sed paulo minor natu, et summus orator est habitus et fuit, ut apparet ex orationibus, scriptor sane bonus.* Cf. ib. 295. 333. But he too shared Galba's ignorance of the law (de or. 1, 40). *Aemilius Porcina orator, in oratione uti lex Aemilia abrogetur*, Priscian. GL. 2, 474. Cornif. ad. Her. 4, 7 *allatis exemplis . . . a Laelio* (n. 3), *a Scipione* (n. 1), *Galba* (n. 4), *Porcina.* Quoted also GL. 5, 590, 3.

6. L. Furius Philus (cos. 618/136) *perbene latine loqui putabatur litteratiusque quam ceteri*, Cic. Brut. 108. He was a friend of Africanus the Younger, and familiar with learned Greeks (de or. 2, 154). He is quoted de leg. agr. 2, 64 along with Cato and Laelius among the men of wisdom (sapientes) inspired by the Stoa; cf. de or. 2, 154. p.Mur. 66. de rep. 3, 5. He was perhaps (MHertz, JJ. 88, 54) the author of a treatise founded on the sacred law, and is referred to Macrob. S. 3, 9, 6 sqq. *carmen (quo di evocantur) quod ille* (Sammonicus Serenus) *se in cujusdam Furii vetustissimo libro repperisse professus est.*

7. Q. Caecilius Metellus Macedonicus, cos. 611/143, censor 623/131, † 639/115; a political adversary of Africanus minor; PRE. 2, 23. MWende, de Caeciliis Met. (Bonn 1875) 36. Cic. Brut. 81 *Q. Metellus . . . in primis est habitus eloquens . . . cuius et aliae sunt orationes et contra Ti. Gracchum exposita est in C. Fanni annalibus.* Cf. § 141, 2.

8. Cic. Brut. 94 *fuerunt etiam in oratorum numero mediocrium L. et Sp. Mummii fratres, quorum exstant amborum orationes; simplex quidem Lucius et antiquus, Spurius autem nihilo ille quidem ornatior, sed tamen astrictior; fuit enim doctus ex disciplina Stoicorum.* Lucius was cos. 608/146 and destroyed Corinth; PRE. 5, 199; see § 163, 7. His younger brother Spurius accompanied him as legate to Achaia, and wrote *epistolas versiculis facetis ad familiares missas a Corintho* (Cic. Att. 13, 6, 4). Cf. § 25, 1.

9. Cic. Brut. 94 *multae sunt Sp. (Postumii) Albini* (cos. 606/148) *orationes.*—For others see § 132, 4. § 133, 4 and 5.

132. The historians of the first twenty years of the 7th century u.c. still clung to the manner of the older Annalists, but followed Cato's example in writing Latin. The earliest of them was L. Cassius Hemina, the most important L. Calpurnius Piso Frugi; both beginning with the foundation of Rome and concluding with their own time. Besides these, Fabius Maximus Servilianus belongs to this period. Trebius Niger wrote on subjects in natural history, as did the Spaniard Turranius Gracilis (date uncertain).

1. L. is called Hemina in Prisc. GL. 2, 482, 15. Schol. Veron. Aen. 2, 717. p. 91 K.—Censorin. d. n. 17, 11 (concerning the fourth secular games): *at Piso censorius et Cn. Gellius, sed et Cassius Hemina, qui illo tempore vivebat, post annum*

factos tertium adfirmant, viz. 608/146. Cass. is called *vetustissimus auctor annalium* in Pliny NH. 13, 84; cf. 29, 12 *Cassius Hemina ex antiquissimis auctor est primum e medicis venisse Romam* etc. The quotation *Cassius Hemina de censoribus libr. II.* (ap. Non. 346, 22) is not incredible. (MHertz. de hist. 1871, p. 2 sq.) Of his historical work, called both *Annales* and *Historiae*, four books are quoted. The oldest history was treated extensively in b. 1, comprising also other towns of Italy. The fourth book was entitled *bellum punicum posterior* (cf. *prior bellum* and *foedus prior* ap. Claud. Quadr. quoted by Prisc. GL. 2, 347, 7); the third book seems, therefore, to have treated of the first Punic war, while the second may have contained a short resumé of the Roman history down to the first Punic war (Vahlen, Enn. p. li n.). As Pliny in his list of authorities quotes him at book xii (arborum naturae), xiv (de peregrinis arboribus et unguentis), xxxii (on remedies), he seems also to have taken in various curiosities. Also sacerdotal and juridical works, and attempts at etymology. Fragments of his works, which it is sometimes difficult to keep apart from those of other Cassii, HPeter, hist. rell. 1, 95; fragm. 68. Concerning him Schwegler, RG. 1, 87. HPeter, hist. rell. 1, clxviii.

2. On the historian Libo see § 172, 6.

3. Q. Fabius Maximus Servilianus, cos. 612/142. Macr. 1, 16, 25 *Fabius Maximus Servilianus pontifex in libro XII negat oportere atro die parentare.* Possibly a confusion with Ser. Fabius Pictor (§ 133, 3). Schol. Veron. ad Georg. 3, 7 . . . *Servilianus historiarum scriptor.* Serv. Verg. Aen. 1, 3 *Fabius Maximus annalium primo.* Dionys. ant. 1, 7 ἃς οἱ πρὸς αὐτῶν ἐπαινούμενοι Ῥωμαίων συνέγραψαν, Πόρκιός τε Κάτων καὶ Φάβιος Μάξιμος καί Οὐαλέριος ὁ Ἀντιεὺς etc. As Polyb. 3, 8 seems to know no other historian of the gens Fabia besides Fabius Pictor, Servilianus appears to have begun to write only in his later years. WHarless, de Fabiis 37, cf. ib. p. 3. HPeter, hist. rell. 1, clxxxii and 114; fragm. 76.

4. L. Calpurnius Piso Frugi, trib. pl. 605/149, cos. 621/133, censor probably 634/120 (censorius, n. 1. Plin. NH. 13, 87; cf. Πίσων Λεύκιος ὁ τιμητικὸς in Dionys. 2, 38. 39. 12, 4). Perhaps the pupil of Panaitios? Philodem. syntax. philosoph. stoic. in the rivista di philol. 3, 544. ΕΙ . ΩΝ is probably to be completed Πείσων (MHertz). The adversary of the Gracchi. Piso's historical work began with Aeneas, if his name is rightly completed Schol. Veron. Aen. 2, 717 *additur etiam a L. Cassio et ⟨Pisone⟩ censorio* etc. It reached in the 7th book at least to a. 608/146 (Censorin. 17, 11). Annales is generally given as the title; Plin. only says l.l.: *L. Piso censorius primo commentariorum:* hence OJahn (Lpz. Ber. 1848, 429) and Plüss, de Cinc. 28 (in Dionysius also) distinguish two Pisos, while MHertz (philologisch-klinischer Streifzug, 1849, 15) distinguishes at least a second work of this Piso (of antiquarian contents); cf. for the other view HPeter, hist. rell. 1, cxciii. Piso certainly did not lack veracity (*gravis auctor* he is styled by Pliny NH. 2, 140) and the references to him, which are especially frequent in the first two books of Livy and Dionysius, do not always show good taste, but show on the whole simple and sober honesty, and also a tinge of rationalism antipathetic to Niebuhr's romantic mind. Cicero's judgment on Piso's style is unfavourable, but Gellius, a professed admirer of archaic style, pronounces the unmethodical sequence of his sentences to be charming. Brut. 106 *Piso et causas egit et multarum legum aut auctor aut dissuasor fuit, isque et orationes reliquit, quae iam evanuerunt, et annales sane exiliter scriptos.* Cf. de leg. 1, 6. de or. 2, 51 sqq. (above § 37, 5). On the other hand Gellius 7, 9, 1 *res perquam pure et venuste narrata a Pisone.* 11, 14, 1 *simplicissima suavitate et rei et orationis L. Piso Frugi usus est in primo annali.* His two instances show that Piso indulged in anecdotes; Pliny quotes him among his authorities at book 2 sq. (geography), 8 (animals), 12 to 18 (on

trees), 28 and 29 (medicine), 33 sq. (metals), 36 (stones). Cf. n. 1. Fragments in HPeter rell. 1, 118; fragm. 76. Liebaldt, de L. Calpurnio Pisone annalium scriptore, Naumb. 1836. Schwegler, RG. 1, 88. HPeter, hist. rell. 1, CLXXXVIII. CAldenhoven, Herm. 5, 151. LKeller, d. 2. pun. Krieg u. s. Quellen (Marb. 1875) 127, and for the opposite view OGilbert, Gött. GA. 1875, 343. HVirck, d. Quellen des Liv. und Dionys. Strassb. 1877, attempts to prove that Liv. 2, 1–21, 32–33 are derived from Piso. Klimke, Diod. u. d. röm. Annalistik, Königshütte O/S. 1881 maintains that Diodorus' Roman history is based on Piso. LCohn, Phil. 42, 1 shares this view.

5. Plin. NH. 9, 89 *L. Lucullo proconsule Baeticae* (a. 604/150) *comperta de polypis quae Trebius Niger e comitibus eius prodidit.* Cf. ib. 93 *ut ipsius Trebi verbis utar.* ib. 80 *Tr. N.* and 10, 40 *Trebius auctor est.* He is named as an authority for book 8, 9 (de aquatilium natura) and for book 32 (medicinae ex aquatilibus) and is quoted 32, 15.

6. Plin. NH. 3, 3 *a vico Mellaria Hispaniae ad promunturium Africae Album, auctore Turranio Gracile iuxta genito.* Hence he is placed first in the ind. auct. to b. 3, and also to b. 9 (cf. n. 5), and to book 18 (naturae frugum). Cf. 9, 11 *Turranius prodidit expulsam beluam in Gaditano litore.* 18, 75 *in Baetica et Africa* (hordei genus) *glabrum appellat Turranius.* The date of the Turranius here introduced is unknown. OHirschfeld, Phil. 29, 27, considers it not improbable that he may be identified with C. Turranius (praef. annonae under Tiberius and still under Claudius, † about 48 A.D. when almost a centenarian; PRE. 6, 2256, 6) and even with the dilettante writer of tragedies of the same name (§ 254, 3 ad fin.).

7. For Plin. books 31 and 32 a certain Sornatius (quoted 32, 68) is mentioned ind. auct. as well as Iacchus (§ 41, 1 ad fin.).

133. These twenty years possess great jurists in Manius Manilius, M. Junius Brutus, Ser. Fabius Pictor, and especially in P. Mucius Scaevola, cos. a. 621/133, an acute thinker, of an easy and studious disposition, rather than a man of action; it was he who finished the official Annales and perhaps published them in book form. They were eminent writers on their subjects, especially Manilius as the framer of deeds of purchase. Scaevola's brother also, P. Licinius Crassus Mucianus, cos. 633/131, was a legal authority, and so was C. Marcius Figulus.

1. M'. Manilius, cos. 605/149, one of the circle of Africanus minor.—Pompon. dig. 1, 2, 2, 39 *post hos* (Cato and his son) *fuerunt P. Mucius et Brutus et Manilius qui fundaverunt ius civile. ex his . . . libellos reliquit . . . Manilius tres* (see Zimmern, Gesch. d. röm. Priv.-R. 1, 276), *et exstant volumina scripta, Manilii monumenta.* Cic. de or. 1, 246 *Manilianas venalium vendendorum leges ediscere.* Varro RR. 2, 3, 5 *Manilius scriptum reliquit sic* (the formula of sponsio concerning the purchase of goats). ib. 2, 5, 11 *paulo verbosius haec* (formula of stipulation) *qui Manilii actiones sequuntur.* 2, 7, 6 *emtio equina similis fere ac boum, . . . ut in Manilii actionibus sunt perscripta.* LL. 7, 105 *nexum Manilius scribit omne quod per libram et aes geritur.* (In Varro RR. and LL. the best MSS. always give *Mamilius.*) Cic. fin. 1, 12 *disseretur inter principes civitatis, P. Scaevolam Maniumque Manilium, ab iisque M. Brutus dissentiet. . . . nosque ea scripta . . . legimus libenter.* Fam. 7, 22 *ut scires id . . . Sex. Aelium, M'. Manilium, M. Brutum sensisse.* Cf. ib. 7, 10, 2. p. Caecin. 69 *si ut*

Manilius statuebat, sic est iudicatum. GELL. 17, 7, 3 *Q. Scaevola patrem suum et Brutum et Manilium, viros adprime doctos, quaesisse ait* etc. Dig. 41, 2, 3, 3 *Brutus et Manilius putant* etc. As a jurist he is called *vir prudens* by CIC. rep. 1, 18, cf. Brut. 108 *nec multo minus* (than P. Scaevola) *prudenter* (*loqui putabatur*) *M'. Manilius.* de or. 3, 133 *M'. Manilium . . . vidimus transverso ambulantem foro, quod erat insigne eum qui id faceret facere civibus omnibus consilii sui copiam.* HUSCHKE, iurispr. anteiust. [5] 5.

2. M. Junius Brutus, *iuris peritissimus* (CIC. Brut. 130; cf. 175; *iuris civilis in primis peritus*, off. 2, 50). POMPON. l.l. 39 he is called praetorius and it is stated of him *septem libellos reliquit.* On the other hand CIC. de or. 2, 55, 223 *tres Bruti de iure civili libros tribus legendos dedit.* p. Cluent. 141 *tres excitavit recitatores cum singulis libris quos M. Brutus . . . de iure civili reliquit.* QUINT. 6, 3, 44 *tris excitavit lectores hisque* (*M. Bruti*) *dialogos dedit legendos.* The form of the dialogue appears from CIC. de or. 2, 224, where it is also said *ex libro tertio, in quo finem scribendi fecit* (M. Brutus); *tot enim, ut audivi Scaevolam dicere, sunt veri Bruti libri*, i.e. Scaevola was of opinion that the four other books were continuations of the original work by a jurist of the 7th century U.C. Cf. ZIMMERN, Gesch. d. röm. Priv.-R. 1, 276.—CIC. de or. 2, 142 *video in Catonis* (the younger) *et in Bruti libris nominatim fere referri quid alicui de iure viro aut mulieri responderint.* GELL. 6, 15, 1. 17, 7, 3. Dig. 49, 15, 4 (*inter Brutum et Scaevolam varie tractatum est*).

3. CIC. Brut. 81 *Ser. Fulvius* (cos. 619/135) *et una Ser. Fabius Pictor et iuris et litterarum et antiquitatis bene peritus.* GELL. 1, 12, 14 *in libro I Fabii Pictoris quae verba pontificem maximum dicere oporteat . . . scriptum est.* 10, 15, 1 *item castus multiplices* (*flaminis Dialis*), *quos in libris qui de sacerdotibus publicis compositi sunt, item in Fabii Pictoris primo scriptos legimus.* NON. 544 *Fab. Pict. libr. XVI* (the formula follows). 223 *Varro: commentario veteri Fabii Pictoris legi* (the rule follows). FEST. 250 *puilia saxa esse ad portum qui sit secundum Tiberim ait Fabius Pictor, quem locum putat Labeo* (the jurist Antistius Labeo) *dici* etc. MACR. 3, 2, 3 *Veranius* (§ 199, 6) *ex primo libro Pictoris* (cf. § 49, 6). NONIUS 518 *Idem* (preceded by a quotation from the annalist Q. Fabius Pictor) *iuris pontificii libro III*, confusing the two of the same name. See above § 116, 7. Gellius also seems from his way of quoting it to have ascribed the work de iure pontificio to the famous annalist Fabius Pictor. Cf. HPETER, hist. rell. 1, p. CLXXIX. 111. HUSCHKE, iurispr. anteiust. [5] 2. MHERTZ. JJ. 85, 47.

4. P. Mucius Scaevola, ὁ νομοδείκτης (PLUT. Gracch. 9), cos. 621/133; PRE. 5, 181. He and his brother Crassus (n. 5) sided with Ti. Gracchus (CIC. acad. pr. 2, 13).—POMPON. l.l. 39 (see n. 1). Supposing the order there (Mucius, Brutus, Manilius) to be not appreciative but chronological, Pomponius would appear to confound the father and the son; see PRE. l.l. 182. POMPON. l.l. relates moreover *ex his P. Mucius etiam decem libellos reliquit . . . illi duo* (Manilius and P. Mucius) *consulares fuerunt, P. autem Mucius etiam pontifex maximus.* The latter at least after 631/123; see CIC. de dom. 136. As such he seems to have done away with the writing of the official Annals by the pontifex maximus, which had become unnecessary on account of the private annalists; they extended at least only *usque ad P. Mucium pontificem maximum* (CIC. de or. 2, 52). At the same time he would seem to have superintended the collection and publication of the Annals as far as they existed; see § 76, 2 and 3. MOMMSEN, RG. 2^6, 453. The dignity of pontifex was connected with legal knowledge: CIC. de leg. 2, 47 (cf. 52): . . . *Scaevolae* (father and son, the latter cos. 659/95), *pontifices ambo et eidem iuris peritissimi* (cf. de leg. 2, 52). *saepe, inquit P. filius, ex patre audivi pontificem bonum neminem esse nisi qui ius civile cognosset.* de or. 1, 170 *P. Crassus, ille Dives . . . cum P. Scaevolae*

frater esset, solitus est ei persaepe dicere, neque illum in iure civili satis facere posse nisi dicendi copiam assumpsisset . . . neque se ante causas amicorum tractare atque agere coepisse quam ius civile didicisset. Brut. 108 *latine loqui putabatur . . . P. Scaevola valde prudentur et acute, paulo etiam copiosius.* de or. 1, 240 (of Crassus) *id quod ipse diceret et in P. Mucii, fratris sui, libris et in Sex. Aelii commentariis scriptum protulisse.* The existing instances of his decisions and sayings prove him to be as careful in defining (Cic. top. 24. 29. 37. 38) as powerful in casuistry (Cic. de leg. 2, 57. fin. 1, 12. Gell. 17, 7, 3. Dig. 24, 3, 66 pr. 49, 15, 4. 50, 7, 17; cf. 47, 4, 1, 15), especially also in pointing out how laws might be avoided in a legal manner (Cic. leg. 2, 53). But it was only by a party view that Nasica attributed to him the principle *fiat iustitia, pereat mundus* (Val. Max. 3, 2, 17 *tum Scipio Nasica: quoniam, inquit, consul, dum iuris ordinem sequitur, id agit ut cum omnibus legibus romanum imperium corruat* etc.). Rutilius Rufus (cos. 649/105) was trained by intercourse with him; see § 142, 2; his most brilliant pupil, however, was his son, cos. 659/95 (§ 154, 1).—Remains: Huschke, iurispr. [5] 6. ASchneider, die drei Scaevola Cic.'s, Münch. 1879.

5. P. Licinius Crassus Dives Mucianus, own brother of the preceding, but adopted by P. Crassus (cos. 549/205; see § 123, 4); cos. 623/131, † 624/130; PRE. 4, 1057.—Gell. 1, 13, 10 *is Crassus . . . traditur habuisse quinque rerum bonarum maxima et praecipua: quod esset ditissimus, quod nobilissimus, quod eloquentissimus, quod iurisconsultissimus, quod pontifex maximus.* Cic. de or. 1, 216 *P. Crassus idem fuit eloquens et iuris peritus* (likewise Brut. 127. Cato 50); ib. 240 *fuit Crassus in numero disertorum, sed par Galbae* (§ 131, 4) *nullo modo;* ib. 170 (see n. 4). Brut. 98 *P. Crassum valde probatum oratorem . . . accepimus, qui et ingenio valuit et studio et habuit quasdam etiam domesticas disciplinas. nam . . . cum esset P. Muci* (cos. 579/175) *filius fratremque haberet P. Scaevolam* (n. 4) *domi ius civile cognoverat. in eo industriam constat summam fuisse maximamque gratiam, cum et consuleretur plurimum et diceret.* He is mentioned among the jurists but with the praenomen L. (probably by confusion with the orator L. Crassus, § 152, 3) and wrongly placed (after Sex. Pompeius and others), Pompon. dig. 1, 2, 2, 40 *L. Crassus, frater P. Mucii* (who was cos. 621/133, see n. 4), *qui Mucianus dictus est.* In addition see Val. Max. 8, 7, 6 *P. Crassus, cum in Asiam ad Aristonicum regem debellandum consul venisset, tanta cura graecae linguae notitiam comprehendit ut eam in quinque divisam genera* (i.e. dialects) . . . *penitus cognosceret.* He of course understood Greek thoroughly previous to this.

6. Valer. Max. 9, 3, 2 *G. Figulum mansuetissimum, pacato iuris iudicio (studio?) celeberrimum,* son of the cos. 592/162 and 598/156, but who did not himself attain the consulship; hence his irritable question addressed to his consultores: *an vos consulere scitis, consulem facere nescitis?*

134. Among poets L. Accius (born a. 584/170 at Pisaurum, died at an advanced age) is especially famous as the author of numerous tragedies imitated from the Greek. The choice made by Accius manifests a just appreciation of the genuine tragic element, as well as a certain predilection for romantic incidents and the Trojan legends. These fragments are in a lively and impassioned tone, though frequently more cleverly turned than really pathetic. He dealt also with original Roman subjects in his praetextae Aeneadae s. Decius and Brutus. In prose he composed

nine books Didascalicon, Pragmaticon libri, Annales and Parerga. Resembling Ennius in versatility of forms and subject, liberal thought and consciousness of his own worth, Accius surpassed his predecessor in accuracy and polish.

1. Hieron. on Euseb. Chr. a. 1878=615/139 *L. Accius tragoediarum scriptor clarus habetur, natus Mancino et Serrano coss.* (584/170) *parentibus libertinis et seni iam Pacuvio Tarenti sua scripta recitavit. a quo et fundus Accianus iuxta Pisaurum dicitur, quia illuc inter colonos fuerat* (his father, as the deductio happened as early as 570/184) *ex urbe deductus.* Plin. NH. 7, 128 also mentions the poet as a Pisaurensis: *pretium hominis in servitio geniti maximum ad hanc diem fuit grammaticae artis Daphnin Attio* (thus Detlefsen, RhM. 18, 236: *daphni natio* the MSS.) *Pisaurense vendente et M. Scauro principe civitatis HS DCC licente.* The instruction of Accius imparted his great value to Daphnis (§ 41, 1. 142, 4). His father's patron was perhaps an ancestor of the knight T. Attius (Accius) of Pisaurum, the accuser of Cluentius (§ 179/15). Accii (and Attii) appear on inscriptions from Pisaurum, Olivieri marm. Pisaur. 1738. The forms *Accius* and *Attius* probably differ dialectically. In the MSS. that with cc greatly preponderates (see LMüller's Lucilius p. 320); on the other hand, in inscriptions the spelling of this name with tt is far the more frequent.—Portrait of Accius on a contorniate: Bernoulli, röm. Ikonogr. 1, 289 (cf. n. 2).

2. Cic. Brut. 229 *Accius isdem aedilibus* (c. 614/140) *ait se et Pacuvium docuisse fabulam, cum ille LXXX, ipse XXX annos natus esset.* pArch. 27 *D. Brutus, summus vir et imperator* (cos. 616/138), *Accii amicissimi sui carminibus templorum ac monumentorum aditus exornavit suorum,* on which the Schol. Bob. p. 359 observes *eius versus Saturnii a D. Bruto Gallaeco vestibulo templi Martis superscripti.*—Cornif. ad Her. 1, 24 *mimus quidam nominatim Accium poetam compellavit in scena. cum eo Accius iniuriarum egit. hic nihil aliud defendit nisi licere nominari eum cuius nomine scripta dentur agendo.* Cf. ib. 2, 19 *P. Mucius* (*iudex*) *eum qui L. Accium poetam nominaverat condemnavit.*—Plin. NH. 34, 19 *notatum ab auctoribus et L. Accium poetam in Camenarum aede maxima forma statuam sibi posuisse, cum brevis admodum fuisset.*—Cic. Brut. 107 *D. Brutus M. filius, ut ex familiari eius* (cf. leg. 2, 54) *L. Accio poeta sum audire solitus* etc. According to this passage Cicero knew Accius personally, and was in the habit of conversing with him on literary topics; this supposes Cicero to have been at least 20 years of age, so that Accius must have lived till about 668/86 and have attained an age of over 80 years. Cic. Phil. 1, 36 referring to the reproduction of Accius' Tereus (cf. ad Att. 16, 2, 3. 16, 5, 1) in the year 710/44: *nisi forte Accio tum plaudi et sexagesimo post anno palmam dari, non Bruto putatis.* Here Cicero is reckoning not from the death of Accius, but (roughly) from the first performance of the Tereus, which accordingly would fall about the year 650/104, about Accius' 66th year.—Val. Max. 3, 7, 11 *poeta Accius . . . Iulio Caesari, amplissimo ac florentissimo viro* (himself the author of tragedies, see § 153, 3) *in conlegium poetarum* (§ 94, 7) *venienti numquam adsurrexit, . . . quod in comparatione communium studiorum aliquanto se superiorem esse confideret.* Besides, Accius was about 40 years older than his fellow-poet.

3. Quint. 5, 13, 43 *aiunt Accium interrogatum, cur causas non ageret, cum apud eum in tragoediis tanta vis esset optime respondendi, hanc reddidisse rationem: quod illic ea diceret quae ipse vellet, in foro dicturi adversarii essent quae minime vellet.* In Cic. Planc. 59 he is called *gravis et ingeniosus poeta;* Sest. 120 *summus poeta.* The epithets *altus* (Hor. E. 2, 1, 56), *animosi oris* (Ovid. am. 1, 15, 19) etc. express his

tragic qualities in a general manner. Cf. GELL. 13, 2, 2 *cum Pacuvius . . . Tarentum concessisset, Accius, tunc haud parvo iunior, proficiscens in Asiam cum in oppidum venisset, devertit ad Pacuvium comiterque invitatus plusculisque ab eo diebus retentus tragoediam suam cui Atreus nomen est desideranti legit.* (3) *tum Pacuvium dixisse aiunt, sonora quidem esse quae scripsisset et grandia, sed videri tamen ea sibi duriora paulum et acerbiora.* (4) *ita est, inquit Accius, uti dicis; neque id me sane paenitet; meliora enim fore spero quae deinceps scribam.*

4. VELLEI. 1, 17, 1 *in Accio circaque eum romana tragoedia est.* Of the tragedies of A. about 45 titles are still known to us, the largest number we have of any Roman tragic writer, and probably nearly the whole number that he composed; in accordance with this the fragments of Accius are also the most numerous; the most celebrated plays were perhaps Atreus, Epigoni, Epinausimache, Philocteta.—The fragments in RIBBECK, trag.[2] p. 136. Enumeration of the titles and contents of the plays by TEUFFEL in the Tüb. Progr. 1858, 17. Cf. ORIBBECK, röm. Trag. 344. 599; röm. Dicht. 1, 177. FLEO on Sen. trag. 1, 158. KROBERT, Bild und Lied 133.

5. Of his praetextae (RIBBECK, trag. [2] p. 281; röm. Trag. 586) Decius (or Aeneadae) treated of the self-sacrifice of P. Decius Mus the Younger (a. 459/295), Brutus of the downfall of Tarq. Superbus and the creation of consuls.—VARRO LL. 6, 7 *ut in Bruto Cassii quod dicebat Lucretia 'nocte intempesta nostram devenit domum'*; cf. ib. 7, 72 *apud Cassium* (the same line follows here): therefore a praetexta of the same contents as the Brutus of Accius; hence, in spite of the name Cassius being twice transmitted to us, it is usually attributed to A.

6. The fragments of Accius other than dramatic (n. 7–10) see in LMÜLLER's Lucilius (1872) p. 303 (cf. p. 317). FPR. 266.

7. Didascalica (cf. e.g. Aristotle's διδασκαλίαι), a history of Greek and Roman poetry, with special attention to dramatic art and treating also of the poet's own times: very scanty fragments (down to b. 9). MADVIG, op. 1 (Copenh. 1834), 96. TEUFFEL, Tüb. Progr. v. 1858, 35. RIBBECK, röm. Dicht. 1, 267. The majority of the fragments preserved appear to be in sotadean metre (LACHMANN, kl. Schr. 2, 67. RITSCHL and others) and this is supported by GELL. 6. 9, 16 (cf. PRISC. GL. 2, 517, 5) *L. Accius in Sotadicorum l. I.* But the address to Baebius in CHARIS. GL. 1, 142, 1 is in prose (BÜCHELER, RhM. 35, 401): according to this b. 9 must have had a preface in prose (cf. the prose prologues in Mart. Auson. and others). But an unmistakable iambic senarius also occurs (PRISC. GL. 1, 253). BÜCHELER l.l. considers the main substance of the work to have been prose. GHERMANN, op. 8, 390 assumed trochaic tetrameters (cf. § 146, 3). On a bad mistake of Accius in connection with the history of literature, see § 94, 2.

8. Pragmaticon libri, in trochaic tetram. and on subjects connected with the history of literature and art.

9. PLIN. NH. ind. auct. to b. 18 (naturae frugum) *Attius qui Praxidicam* (so RIBBECK: *praxidica* the MSS.) *scripsit.* NH. 18, 200 *Accius in Praxidica* (so RIBBECK: *praxidico* the MSS.), *ut sereretur cum luna esset in ariete* etc.: therefore a work on agricultural subjects, and in agreement with this is the title: Praxidica=Persephone, invoked in the Orphic hymn 29, 5 as Πραξιδίκη . . . Δηοῦς θάλος ἁγνόν . . . ἱερὸν ἐκφαίνουσα δέμας βλαστοῖς χλοοκάρποις κτλ. ORIBBECK, RhM. 41, 631. A fragment in NON. 61, 19 from *parergorum lib. I* (two iambic senarii) treats of ploughing as does the fragment from the Praxidica of sowing, and is certainly also derived from the latter, which in Nonius is quoted not with the separate title but under the collective one (Parerga). But it is not very credible that these

parerga should have included all the works of Accius except the tragedies, and that we must thus explain the quotation *annali XXVII* (Fest. 146, 31; see n. 10); at the least it should have been worded *parergorum XXVII.*

10. Annales in the epic metre, from which mythological quotations (on Hermes and the Κρόνια) have been preserved. Bk. 1 and bk. 27 are quoted (the latter number probably too high and corrupt, see n. 9).

11. Evidence that he studied his language is to be found in many artificial words and usages in Accius' tragedies, especially his mode of employing alliteration (Teuffel, Progr. v. 1858, 32), and in the notice (Mar. Vict. GL. 6, 8) that he wrote *aggulus* (instead of *ang.*), did not use z and y, and denoted the long quantity of the vowels a, e and u by doubling them (§ 93, 10; perhaps this custom was adhered to by the elder Pliny, at least for the endings of the fourth declension? see DDetlefsen, symb. philol. Bonn. 712). Accius found the model for this duplication in other Italic dialects, e.g. the Oscan, Umbrian, Sabellian. Ritschl, op. 4, 142. 153. 361. 492. 687. Did Accius also set the example of replacing C by K before a and by Q before u? Cf. HJordan, krit. Beitr. z. Gesch. d. lat. Spr. (Berl. 1879), 125. Schady, de Mar. Vict. (1869) 13. M. Varro dedicated to him his work de antiquitate litterarum (§ 166, 6, e). Cf. Varro LL. 10, 70 *Accius haec in tragoediis largius a prisca consuetudine movere coepit et ad formas graecas verborum magis revocare, a quo Valerius* (see § 147, 1) *ait: Accius Hectŏrem nolet facere, Hectŏra malet;* and 5, 21 *apud Accium non terminus, sed termen.*

12. GBoissier, le poète Attius, Paris 1857. Teuffel, Caecilius Statius etc. Tüb. 1858, 14 and PRE. 1^2, 2008. Ribbeck, röm. Trag. 340. 602; röm. Dicht. 1, 177. Critical contributions by LFruterius, RhM. 33, 241.

135. The period of the Gracchi (a. 620/134–635/119) was a time of civil discord, which shook the state to its very foundations. In these excited times eloquence was a powerful weapon, though it availed nothing against brute force. Gracchus the Younger was in this period the most powerful master of language (a. 600/154–633/121). The kindling power of his speeches is plainly perceptible even in the few specimens now extant. Gaius' elder brother Tiberius (a. 591/163–621/133) was inferior to him in oratory as well as in other matters.

1. Ti. Sempronius Gracchus, born 591/163 or 592/162, popular tribune 621/133, during which office he was exasperated by the opposition raised against his well-intended reform-bills, soon deviated from legal methods, and was killed by the pontifex maximus P. Nasica (οὔπω τριάκοντα γεγονώς, Plut. G. Gracch. 1). Gaius was nine years his junior (Plut. Ti. Gr. 3. G. Gr. 1, consequently born 600/154 or 601/153), was triumvir agris dividundis 621/133 sqq., popular tribune 631/123–633/121: in the last year he succumbed to the cos. L. Opimius.

2. Common and characteristic features of both. Plut. Ti. Gr. 2 ἰδέᾳ προσώπου καὶ βλέμματι καὶ κινήματι πρᾷος καὶ καταστηματικὸς ἦν ὁ Τιβέριος, ἔντονος δὲ καὶ σφοδρὸς ὁ Γάϊος. . . . ὁ λόγος τοῦ μὲν Γαΐου φοβερὸς καὶ περιπαθὴς εἰς δείνωσιν, ἡδίων δ' ὁ τοῦ Τιβερίου καὶ μᾶλλον ἐπαγωγὸς οἴκτου. τῇ δὲ λέξει καθαρὸς καὶ διαπεπονημένος ἀκριβῶς ἐκεῖνος, ὁ δὲ Γαΐου πιθανὸς καὶ γεγανωμένος. τῷ δ' ἤθει . . . ὁ μὲν ἐπιεικὴς καὶ πρᾷος, ὁ δὲ τραχὺς καὶ θυμοειδής. Though the difference is perhaps drawn too sharply here,

there is no doubt that Gaius was more vehement, and he was embittered by his brother's fate. LIV. per. 60 *C. Gracchus . . . eloquentior quam frater.* DIO fr. 85 Bk. *ὁ Γράκχος τὴν μὲν γνώμην ὁμοίαν τῷ ἀδελφῷ εἶχεν . . . τῇ δὲ παρασκευῇ τῶν λόγων πολὺ αὐτοῦ προέφερεν.* VELLEI. 2, 6, 1 *ingenio eloquentiaque longe praestantior.* CIC. Brut. 333 *Gracchi in contionibus multo faciliore et liberiore genere dicendi (usi sunt quam superiores).* PLIN. NH. 13, 83 *ita sint longinqua monumenta Tiberii Gaique Gracchorum manus. apud Pomponium Secundum . . . vidi.*

3. Tiberius. CIC. Brut. 103 *fuit uterque* (Carbo and Tib.) *summus orator.* 104 *et Carbonis et Gracchi habemus orationes nondum satis splendidas verbis, sed acutas prudentiaeque plenissumas. fuit Gracchus . . . graecis litteris eruditus. nam semper habuit exquisitos e Graecia magistros, in eis iam adolescens Diophanen Mytilenaeum* (cf. PLUT. Ti. Gr. 8. 20), *Graeciae temporibus illis disertissimum.* de harusp. resp. 41 *Ti. Gracchus convellit statum civitatis: qua gravitate vir, qua eloquentia, qua dignitate!* APPIAN. b. c. 1, 9 *Τιβέριος Σεμπρώνιος Γράκχος, ἀνὴρ ἐπιφανὴς καὶ λαμπρὸς ἐς φιλοτιμίαν, εἰπεῖν τε δυνατώτατος.* That his participation in the Numantine stipulations was early turned to account in the schools of rhetoricians, appears from QUINT. 7, 4, 13 *interdum culpa in hominem relegatur: ut si Gracchus reus foederis numantini . . . missum se ab imperatore suo diceret.* MARTIAN. CAP. 5, 456 *remotio est cum obiectum crimen in alterum vel in aliud . . . removetur. in alium, ut Ti. Gracchus in Mancinum qui auctor faciendi foederis fuit.* It may, therefore, appear doubtful whether the arguments attributed to Tib. by Plut. (Ti. Gr. 9) as specimens of the *πιθανότης* and *πυκνότης τοῦ ἀνδρός* and Appian (b. c. 1, 9) are really drawn from his speeches or merely the exaggerations of rhetors and rhetorical historians (e.g. Fannius and Livy). Plutarch's source seems, however, actually to have contained specimens of the speeches of at least Gaius; cf. G. Gr. 4 extr.: *τοιαύτη μὲν ἡ πικρία τῶν λόγων ἦν αὐτοῦ, καὶ πολλὰ λαβεῖν ἐκ τῶν γεγραμμένων ἔστιν ὅμοια.* GCBIJVANCK, studia in Ti. Gr. hist., Leid. 1879. THGREVE, Krit. d. Quellen z. Leb. des Ti. Gr., Aachen 1883.

4. Gaius. General characteristics of his eloquence. PLUT. G. Gr. 1 *τὸν λόγον ὥσπερ ὠκύπτερα κατασκευαζόμενος ἐπὶ τὴν πολιτείαν . . . ἀπέδειξε τοὺς ἄλλους ῥήτορας παίδων* (infantium) *μηδὲν διαφέροντας.* 3 *ἰσχύων τῷ λέγειν ὡς ἄλλος οὐδείς.* 4 *ἦν δὲ καὶ μεγαλοφωνότατος καὶ ῥωμαλεώτατος ἐν τῷ λέγειν.* Cf. n. 2. CIC. de harusp. resp. 41 *C. Gracchus quo ingenio, qua eloquentia, quanta vi, quanta gravitate dicendi!* pro Font. 39 *exstat oratio hominis, ut opinio mea fert, nostrorum hominum longe ingeniosissimi atque eloquentissumi, C. Gracchi.* Brut. 125 *vir et praestantissumo ingenio et flagranti studio et doctus a puero, C. Gracchus. noli enim putare quemquam pleniorem aut uberiorem ad dicendum fuisse. . . . damnum illius immaturo interitu res romanae latinaeque litterae fecerunt.* 126 *eloquentia nescio an habuisset parem neminem. grandis est verbis, sapiens sententiis, genere toto gravis: manus extrema non accessit operibus eius; praeclare incohata multa, perfecta non plane.* TAC. dial. 18 *Catoni seni comparatus C. Gracchus plenior et uberior.* 26 *malim C. Gracchi impetum.* In Fronto's time the interest in Gracchus revived. FRONTO epist. p. 145 *tribunalia Catonis et Gracchi et Ciceronis orationibus celebrata.* p. 144 *contionatur Cato infeste, Gracchus turbulente, Tullius copiose. iam in iudiciis saevit idem Cato, triumphat Cicero, tumultuatur Gracchus, Calvus rixatur.* p. 54 *oratores veteres, quorum aut pauci aut praeter Catonem et Gracchum nemo tubam inflat.* His study of (C.) Gracchus' speeches appears also from p. 56. 61. 105. To this revived interest we owe the preservation of some valuable fragments of his oratory by GELLIUS, esp. NA. 10, 3, 3–5. 11, 10, 2–6. 11, 13, 3. 15, 12, 2–4. Dio again uses secondary sources, hostile to C. Gracchus, see fr. 85 Bk., where we also read: *πολλῇ μὲν πυκνότητι ἐνθυμημάτων, πολλῇ δὲ καὶ σφοδρότητι ὀνομάτων ἐπίπαν ἐδημηγόρει.*—MOMMSEN, RG. 2^6,

103. RSCHMIDT, Krit. der Quellen zur Gesch. der gracchischen Unruhen, Berl. 1864.

5. The manner of C. Gracchus' oratory: his delivery very lively (PLUT. G. Gr. 4; he advised modulation of the voice, CIC. de or. 3, 225. PLUT. G. Gr. 4 extr., de cohib. ira 6. cf. VAL. MAX. 8, 10, 1. QUINT. 1, 10, 27. GELL. 1, 11, 10 sqq. DIO fr. 85 Bk. AMMIAN 30, 4, 19); his gestures were excited, he would walk up and down and bare his arm, PLUT. Ti. Gr. 2. DIO l.l. CIC. de or. 3, 214 *quae sic ab illo esse acta constabit oculis, voce, gestu, inimici ut lacrimas tenere non possent.* His taunts aimed at the pride of the aristocrats and against individual opponents were sometimes very cutting. (SCHOL. VAT. in Cic. or. pFlacc. 16. p. 233 Or.; against Piso *C. Gracchi exstat oratio maledictorum magis plena quam criminum;* cf. CIC. pFont. 39). CIC. Tusc. 3, 48 *lege orationes Gracchi: patronum aerarii esse dices.* He chose the best expressions, CIC. de or. 1, 154.—GELL. 11, 13 2 *in eius orationis principio collocata verba sunt accuratius modulatiusque quam veterum oratorum consuetudo fert.* On his exordia see § 44, 5. CIC. Brut. 100 states that he employed the rhetor Menelaus from Marathus. Fragments of (17–19) speeches in MEYER, or. rom. fragm.[2] p. 227.

6. CIC. de div. 1, 36 *Ti. Gracchus P. f. . . . nonne, ut C. Gracchus, filius eius, scriptum reliquit, duobus anguibus domi comprehensis haruspices convocavit!* More accurately ib. 2, 62 *C. Gracchus ad M. Pomponium* (PRE. 5, 1876) *scripsit duobus anguibus domi conprehensis haruspices a patre convocatos.* Cf. PLUT. Ti. Gr. 1. From this it appears that the work in question had the form of a letter and was at all events no speech, but probably a political pamphlet. PLUT. Ti. Gr. 8 may perhaps refer to this: ὁ δ' ἀδελφὸς αὐτοῦ Γάϊος ἔν τινι βιβλίῳ γέγραφεν (the motive of Tiberius' leges agrariae). Cf. HPETER, hist. rell. 1, CLXXXV; fr. 117. BÖHME (n. 1) p. 4 sq.

136. Among the orators of this period were on the side of the Gracchi only the brothers Crassus (cos. 623/131) and Scaevola (cos. 621/133), Tiberius' father-in-law Appius Claudius (cos. 611/143) and M. Fulvius Flaccus (cos. 629/125), C. Papirius Carbo (cos. 634/120), and P. Decius (praetor 639/115), perhaps also C. Scribonius Curio (praetor 633/121); on the opposite side we find Ti. Annius Luscus (cos. 601/153), Q. Metellus (§ 131, 7), P. Nasica (cos. 616/138), L. Piso Frugi (§ 132, 4), P. Popilius (cos. 622/132), C. Fannius (cos. 632/122), Q. Aelius Tubero (§ 139, 2), the princeps senatus, M. Scaurus (cos. 639/115), M. Livius Drusus (cos. 642/112).

1. The two Mucii favoured Ti. Gracchus: § 133, 4.

2. *Appi Claudi volubilis, sed paulo fervidior erat oratio,* CIC. Brut. 108. *Ap. Claudius C. f. Polc(er)* on a terminus Gracchanus CIL. 1, 552, censor 618/136; PRE. 2, 410, 26.

3. CIC. Brut. 108 *in aliquo numero (erant) etiam M. Fulvius Flaccus et C. Cato . . ., mediocres oratores, etsi Flacci scripta sunt, sed ut studiosi litterarum* (literary dilettanti). PRE. 3, 532. 534.

4. C. Papirius C. f. Carbo, tr. pl. 623/131, praetor 629/125, cos. 634/120; PRE. 5, 1145. CIC. Brut. 104 *et Carbonis . . . habemus orationes* (§ 135, 3). 105

Carbo . . . est in multis iudiciis causisque cognitus. hunc . . . L. Gellius . . . canorum oratorem et volubilem (cf. de or. 3, 28) *et satis acrem atque eundem et vehementem et valde dulcem et perfacetum* (cf. Lael. 96) *fuisse dicebat; addebat industrium etiam et diligentem et in exercitationibus commentationibusque multum operae solitum esse ponere* (cf. Quint. 10, 7, 27 *C. Carbo etiam in tabernaculo solebat hac uti exercitatione dicendi*). 106 *hic optimus illis temporibus est patronus habitus.* Cf. 159 and 221 (*eloquentissumus homo*); 103 (*summus orator*). His culture seems, however, to have been exclusively rhetorical, as he, like Galba and Porcina (§ 131, 4 and 5) understood little of leges, instituta maiorum, and ius civile (Cic. de or. 1, 40). He was, moreover, unprincipled as well as talented; though a friend of C. Gracchus (Cic. Lael. 39. pMil. 8. Val. Max. 6, 2, 3) he as consul defended and praised his murderer L. Opimius (Cic. de or. 2, 106. 165. 169).

5. Cic. Brut. 108 *Flacci* (n. 3) *aemulus P. Decius fuit, non infans ille quidem, sed ut vita sic oratione etiam turbulentus* (he accused L. Opimius a. 634/120). PRE. 2, 879, 7.

6. Cic. Brut. 79 *et T. Annium Luscum, Q. Fulvi collegam* (in the consulship) *non indisertum dicunt fuisse.* Plut. Ti. Gr. 14 Τίτος Ἄννιος, οὐκ ἐπιεικὴς μὲν οὐδὲ σώφρων ἄνθρωπος, ἐν δὲ λόγῳ περὶ τὰς ἐρωτήσεις καὶ ἀποκρίσεις ἄμαχος εἶναι δοκῶν. Fest. 314 *T. Annius Luscus in ea . . . quam dixit adversus Ti. Gracchum.* He is perhaps the same Annius against whom Cato Major made a speech (Fest. 305). PRE. 1², 1022, 11.

7. P. Cornelius Scipio Nasica Serapio (cos. 616/138). Cic. Brut. 107 *Accius . . . illum . . . cum omnibus in rebus vehementem tum acrem aiebat in dicendo fuisse.* PRE. 2. 667, 13.

8. P. Popillius C. f. Laenas, cos. 622/132 (cf. CIL. 1, 550. PRE. 5, 1900, 10), *cum civis egregius* (in persecuting the adherents of T. Gracchus) *tum non indisertus fuit*, Cic. Brut. 95.

9. Cic. Brut. 99 *C. Fannius C. f., qui consul cum Domitio fuit* (a. 632/122; but cf. § 137, 4), *unam orationem de sociis et nomine latino contra C. Gracchum reliquit sane et bonam et nobilem.* Many indeed questioned whether Fannius was the author of this speech, and attributed it to C. Persius (*litteratus homo* Brut. l. l., *omnium fere nostrorum hominum doctissimus* de or. 2, 25. fin. 1, 7; as such he is mentioned in Lucilius 26, 2. 29, 99 M): others supposed that *multos nobiles quod quisque potuisset in illam orationem contulisse.* Both views are however opposed by Cic. Brut. l. l. Ib. 100 *cum Fannius numquam sit habitus elinguis. nam et causas defensitavit et tribunatus eius* (a. 612 or 613/142 sq.), *arbitrio et auctoritate P. Africani gestus, non obscurus fuit.* Passages from his speech against C. Gracchus ap. Cic. de or. 3, 183. Jul. Victor in Halm's Rhet. lat. min. 402. Charis. GL. 1, 143, 13. Moreover Cicero wrongly distinguishes between an orator C. Fannius C. f. and the C. Fannius M. f. mentioned below, § 137, 4; all the particulars (including Cic. de rep. 1, 18) are to be taken as referring to this Fannius M. f. Cf. ad Att. 16, 13, 2. Mommsen, CIL. 1, p. 158 and HPeter, hist. rell. 1, cciii.

10. M. Aemilius M. f. L. n. Scaurus, born a. 592/162 of a noble but poor family, by his energy, versatility and shrewdness gradually became the leader of the aristocratic party in the time after the Gracchi; cos. a. 639/115 and 647/107, censor 645/109, and from 640/114 princeps senatus, † c. 665/89. PRE. 1², 370. HPeter, hist. rell. 1, ccliii. As he was always careful of good appearances, he composed for this purpose an autobiography (*tres ad L. Fufidium libri scripti de vita ipsius.* Cic. Brut. 112, cf. 132, Plin. NH. 33, 21 and Val. Max. 4, 4, 11 according to Halm's emendation), though this was not much read, probably on account of its undisguised apologetic character (Cic. l. l.). It is possible that Cicero's recommendation

prolonged the existence of this work for a few centuries; curious expressions (such as *sagittis confictus, poteratur, possitur*) are quoted from Scaurus de vita sua down to the authority of Charisius (GL. 1, 146 *Scaurus libro III*) and Diomedes (see HPETER, hist. rell. 1, 185), and not only do we find notices taken from it in Val. Max. (4, 4, 11) and Frontinus (Strat. 4, 3, 13), but in so late a writer as Aurel. Victor the chapter on Scaurus (ill. 72) is indirectly derived from this source. Cicero knew also of speeches by him (Brut. 112 *huius et orationes sunt*), as it seems, both judicial and political. Brut. 111 *in Scauri oratione . . . gravitas summa et naturalis quaedam inerat auctoritas . . .* 112 *hoc dicendi genus ad patrocinia mediocriter aptum videbatur, ad senatoriam vero sententiam . . . vel maxime.* de or. 1, 214 *quamquam est in dicendo minime contemnendus, prudentia tamen rerum magnarum magis quam dicendi arte nititur* (in his public position).—From a speech against him (a. 663/9) by his bitter adversary Q. Servilius Caepio (§ 153, 8; PRE. 6, 117, 38) see quotations ap. DIOM. GL. 1, 103, 19. 196, 7. 224, 21.—Another of his opponents was C. Canius (*eq. R. nec infacetus et satis litteratus*, CIC. off. 3, 58), who defended Rutilius Rufus (§ 142, 1) when he was accused by Scaurus of having obtained office by fraudulent means. A witticism of Canius ap. CIC. de or. 2, 280. From him perhaps is the quotation ap. PAUL. Festi 369, 11 (*Gannius*)? Cf. § 19, 1.

11. M. Livius C. f. Drusus, trib. pl. a. 632/122, cos. 642/112; PRE. 4, 1108. *Vir et oratione gravis et auctoritate*, CIC. Brut. 109, cf. PLUT. G. Gr. 8 ἤθει καὶ λόγῳ καὶ πλούτῳ τοῖς μάλιστα τιμωμένοις . . . ἐνάμιλλος. Perhaps a writer on law. JJ. 85, 44; cf. HUSCHKE, iurispr. anteiust. [5] p. 95, 6.

12. C. Scribonius Curio, praetor 633/121, the first of three orators of the *familia Curionum, in qua tres continua serie oratores exstiterunt* (§ 153, 6. 209, 1. PLIN. NH. 7, 133; cf. also SCHOL. AMBR. in Cic. or. p. 330 Or.). Cic. de or. 2, 98 calls him *vel eloquentissimus temporibus illis.* More accurately Brut. 122 *fuit . . . sane illustris orator, cuius de ingenio ex orationibus eius existumari potest. sunt enim et aliae et pro Ser. Fulvio de incestu nobilis oratio. nobis quidem pueris haec omnium optuma putabatur.* Cf. ib. 124. A passage from it is quoted in CIC. de inv. 1, 80 = CORNIF. ad. Herenn. 2, 33. *Scripsit etiam alia nonnulla* (speeches) *et multa dixit et illustria, et in numero patronorum fuit*, Brut. 124. He was not made consul (CIC. Brut. 122); perhaps he had sided with the Gracchi.

137. Most of the **historians** of this period tried to rise above the style of the old annalists. Cn. Gellius and probably Tuditanus and Vennonius must be excepted, but the statement holds good all the more of C. Fannius (mentioned above as an orator), whose truthfulness is specially asserted by competent judges, and, in regard to style, of L. Coelius **Antipater**, whose history of the second Punic war was loaded with rhetorical ornament, but important in substance. To this period belongs also the conclusion of the official Annals and their publication in the shape of a book (§ 133, 4).

1. Γναῖος Γέλλιος (Gnaeus Gellius PLIN. ind. auct. b. 7) is quoted in the history of the Regal period by DIONYS. HAL. 2, 31. 76 cf. Γέλλιος 4, 6. 6, 11 (οἱ περὶ Γέλλιον). 7, 1. *Cn. Gellii annalem tertium* with a prayer of Hersilia in GELL. NA. 13, 23 (22), 13, cf. 18, 12, 6 *Cn. Gellius in annalibus.* ib. bk. 8, cap. 14 contained *verba quaedam ex Naevio poeta et Cn. Gellio non usitate collocata.* CENSORIN. d. n. 17, 11 *Piso censorius*

et Cn. Gellius. MACROB. 1, 16, 21 *Gellius annalium libro XV et Cassius Hemina.* CHARIS. GL. 1, 54 *Gellius in II . . . et in V . . . et in VII . . . idem Gellius XCVII* (? exc. Cauchii *XXVII*, cf. FMAIXNER, ZföG. 29, 332); ib. 55 (also 139): *Gellius libro XXIII* (? Cauch. *XXXVI*); in PRISC. GL. 2, 318 the same fragment from *Gellius libro XXX.* The work seems certainly to have been long and detailed: possibly this annalist is the same Cn. Gellius against whom Cato the Elder made a speech (GELL. NA. 14, 2, 21. 26), PRE. 3, 661. KNIPPERDEY, op. 399. OMELTZER, JJ. 105, 429. Mention is made of Gellius (Γέλλιοι and *Gellii*, see KNIPPERDEY l.l.) ap. DION. 1, 7. CIC. leg. 1, 6 (according to this he wrote *ad antiquorum languorem*): see § 37, 5 and HPETER, hist. rell. 1, CCXXXVIII. 165; fragm. 92.

2. The quotation *Sex. Gellius in origine gentis romanae* in the Origo g. rom. 16, 4 is spurious; cf. § 414, 5; the mention of *A. Gellius* (*agellius* in the MSS. *Asellio* OMELTZER) *historiarum lib. I* ap. NON. 194, 3 is also suspicious.

3. CIC. leg. 1, 6 *Fabium aut . . . Catonem aut Pisonem aut Fannium aut Vennonium.* Att. 12, 3, 1 *moleste fero Vennonii me historiam non habere.* DIONYS. HAL. 4, 15 ὡς Οὐεννώνιος ἱστόρηκεν.

4. CIC. Brut. 101 *alter* (see § 136, 9) *C. Fannius, M. f., C. Laeli gener* (but see CIC. Att. 12, 5, 3. HIRSCHFELD, l.l.) *et moribus et ipso genere dicendi durior. is Panaetium audiverat. eius omnis in dicendo facultas ex historia ipsius non ineleganter scripta perspici potest.* Cf. ib. 118 and above n. 3. He was the companion of Ti. Gracchus at the destruction of Carthage (PLUT. Ti. Gr. 4 τοῦ γε τείχους ἐπέβη . . . πρῶτος [Ti. Gracchus], ὥς φησι Φάννιος λέγων καὶ αὐτὸς τῷ Τιβερίῳ συνεπιβῆναι κτλ.) and (a. 612/142) in Spain (APPIAN. Hisp. 67). Trib. pleb. a. 613/141 (CIC. ad Att. 16, 13 C) ? cf. § 136, 9. About 625/129–629/125 praetor (Φάννιος Μάρκου υἱὸς στρατηγός, JOSEPH. ant. 13, 9, 2). This is certainly C. Fannius M. f. (CIL. 1, 560) Strabo, cos. 632/122, and therefore born about 580/174. VICTORIN. in Cic. rhet. 1, 28 p. 57 Or.=203, 27 Halm: *Sallustius . . . in libro I historiarum dat Catoni brevitatem . . . Fannio vero veritatem.* Highest number of books known: SCHOL. VER. ad Aen. 3, 707 *C. Fannius in VIII annali Drepanum modo, modo Drepana appellat.* The repeated mention of Drepana here evidenced points to the first Punic war (HIRSCHFELD l.l.). The other fragments refer to the period contemporary with the author (e.g. Cic. de or. 2, 270 *Fannius in annalibus suis Africanum Aemilianum . . . appellat* εἴρωνα=Brut. 299 *ut ait in historia sua C. Fannius.*) The work would appear to have been exhaustive, if the first Punic war was related only in bk. 8; see also CIC. Brut. 81 Metellus' speech *contra Ti. Gracchum exposita est in C. Fanni annalibus.* This is confirmed by the fact that M. Brutus (§ 210, 2) epitomised it: *epitome Bruti Fanniana an (?) Bruti epitoma Fanniorum*, CIC. Att. 12, 5, 3. HPETER, hist. rell. 1, 138; fragm. 87. PRE. 3, 421.—HPETER, hist rell. 1, CCII. OHIRSCHFELD, Wien. Stud. 6, 127.

5. CIC. leg. 1, 6 *Fannii aetate coniunctus Antipater paulo inflavit vehementius habuitque vires agrestis ille quidem atque horridas, sine nitore ac palaestra* etc. de or. 2, 54 *paululum se erexit et addidit historiae maiorem sonum vocis vir optimus, Crassi familiaris, Antipater: ceteri non exornatores rerum sed tantummodo narratores fuerunt . . . sed ipse Caelius neque distinxit historiam varietate colorum neque verborum collocatione et tractu orationis leni et aequabili perpolivit illud opus; sed ut homo neque doctus neque maxime aptus ad dicendum, sicut potuit, dolavit: vicit tamen superiores.* Brut. 102 *L. Caelius Antipater scriptor . . . fuit ut temporibus illis luculentus, iuris valde peritus, multorum etiam, ut L. Crassi* (born 614/140) *magister.* POMPON. Dig. 1, 2, 2, 40 *Caelius Antipater, qui historias conscripsit, sed plus eloquentiae quam scientiae iuris operam dedit.* His legal knowledge justifies the assumption of Roman nationality. At all events he was no freedman (see SUET. rhet. 3; above

§ 36, 3), but probably the son of one. (FLachmann, de font. Liv. 2, 19). That he belonged to the period of the Gracchi, appears from Cic. de div. 1, 56 *C. Gracchus multis dixit, ut scriptum apud eundem Caelium est, sibi in somnis . . . fratrem visum esse . . . hoc antequam tribunus pl. C. Gracchus factus est et se audisse scribit Caelius et illum dixisse multis.* Val. Max. 1, 7, 6 *Caelius etiam, certus romanae historiae auctor, sermonem de ea re ad suas aures illo adhuc vivo pervenisse scribit.* Vellei. 2, 9, 6 *vetustior Sisenna fuit Caelius.*—The date of his work is doubtful. In it, however, the death of C. Gracchus (a. 633/121) was mentioned (Cic. de div. 1, 56). Coel. Antip. ap. Plin. NH. 2, 169 says *vidisse se qui navigasset ex Hispania in Aethiopiam commercii gratia.* If this circumnavigator of Africa was Eudoxos of Cyzicus (Poseidonios ap. Strabo 2 p. 98 C. Mela 3, 90), which is uncertain notwithstanding the argument of KTNeumann, Phil. 45, 385, Coelius can hardly have composed his work earlier than about 644/110.

The work was dedicated to L. Aelius Stilo (§ 148): Cornif. ad Her. 4, 18 *quo in vitio* (in the verborum transiectio) *est Coelius* (the best MSS. vary between this spelling and Caelius) *assiduus, ut hoc est 'in priore libro has res ad te scriptas Luci misimus Aeli.'* FMarx, studd. Luciliana, Bonn 1882, 96. Cf. Cic. or. 230 *quod* (traicere verba) *se L. Coelius Antipater in prooemio belli punici nisi necessario facturum negat. . . . et hic quidem, qui hanc a L. Aelio* (so APopma: MSS. *a Lœlio;* but Laelius, who died soon after 629/125, can hardly have been alive when the history of Caelius appeared) *ad quem scripsit, . . . veniam petit, et utitur ea traiectione verborum et nihilo tamen aptius explet concluditque sententias.* Very likely a declaration to this effect was made at the beginning of the whole work, and not of some part of it, and probably it dealt with the second Punic war, to which most of the extant fragments (see n. 7) relate. Cf. Fronto p. 62 *rari veterum scriptorum in eum laborem . . . verba industriosius quaerendi se commisere . . . poetarum . . . maxime Ennius eumque studiose aemulatus L. Coelius.* Fronto p. 114 *historiam scripsere . . . verbis Cato multiiugis, Coelius singulis.* To this work perhaps belongs also p. 253 *necdum legi Coelianum excerptum nec legam (? reddam) priusquam ipse sensus venatus fuero.* Cic. de div. 1, 49 *hoc item in Sileni, quem Caelius sequitur, graeca historia est: is* (Silenus) *autem diligentissume res Hannibalis persecutus est.* This historical work of Coelius comprised 7 books. Book 1 described the years 536/218 sq., b. 2 538/216 sq., b. 3 began with 540/214 (see Gell. 10, 1, 3). In b. 6 was related Scipio's landing in Africa 550/204 (Non. 137). B. 7 contained the last three years 551/203–553/201. WSieglin l.l. 46. GFUnger, Phil. 40, 183.

6. Antipater was not deficient in critical faculty (Priscian. GL. 2, 383 *Coelius 'ex scriptis eorum qui veri arbitrantur' passive* ὑπολαμβάνονται) and love of truth (Liv. 21, 46, 10. 27, 27, 13): he availed himself of numerous native authorities, *e.g.* Fabius Pictor, Cato's Origines, Ennius (see n. 5), the laudatio of Marcellus (§ 81, 5); that he made use of the memoirs of the elder Scipio is conjectured by LKeller, d. 2. pun. Krieg u. s. Quellen, Marb. 1875; and Sieglin l.l. 54: but he had also recourse to opposition authorities, esp. to Silenus (n. 5; see HBujack, de Sileno scriptore Hannibalis, Königsb. 1859), which was a decided step in advance of the one-sided views which had thus far prevailed. Coelius gave special attention to the external form of his history, and no doubt the chief merit of his work consisted, in accordance with the intention of its author, in the lucid, skilfully chosen, ornate and copiously flowing diction. Thus the fragments indicate the interlarding of the work with speeches composed by himself (*e.g.* those of Carthaginians), and a propensity to amplification and to highly coloured descriptions (Liv. 29, 27, 13 sqq. Non. 137; frequent use of the praes. historicum), exaggerations, carelessness in regard to geography (Wölfflin l.l. 61)

and to numerical statements (Liv. 29, 25, 3 *Caelius ut abstinet numero ita ad immensum multitudinis speciem auget*), prominence given to the interpretation of dreams and portents (Wölfflin l.l. 75); he also showed enough partiality for the Romans; see Wölfflin l.l. 28. 38. 44. 78.—Livy in his third decade uses him far more often than he acknowledges; in opposition to JBSturm, quae ratio inter tertiam decadem Livii et Antipatri historias intercedat, Würzb. 1883, see LBauer, philol. Rundsch. 1884, 1578. He was also used by Plutarch (in the Fab. and Marcellus; see Soltau, de fontt. Plut. in sec. bello Punico enarrando, Bonn 1870. EWölfflin l.l. 28. 79) and especially by Cassius Dio (see M. Posner, quibus auctoribus in bello Hannibalico enarr. usus sit Cass. Dio, Bonn 1874). That Polybios made use of Coelius, who was his junior by a whole generation, as Sieglin (l.l. 69) holds, is not proved and is a priori improbable. On the other hand there appears evidence of his having been used in Valerius Maximus (HPeter, hist. rell. 1, ccxxiv. MKranz, Beitr. z. Quellenkrit. des Val. Max., Posen 1876, 24), in Frontinus and in the author of the short work de viris illustribus (§ 414, 4, Wölfflin l.l. 77, 80). In general cf. on the employment of Coelius' history, especially in Livy, KBöttcher, JJ. Suppl. Bd. 5, 351. HPeter, hist. rell. 1, ccxxv. ASchäfer, histor. Zeitschr. 23, 436. EWölfflin l.l. AvGutschmid, Lit. Centr. Bl. 1872, 1133. KWNitzsch, röm. Annalistik, Berl. 1873. OGilbert l.l. WSieglin l.l.—M. Brutus (cf. n. 4 ad fin.) had also epitomized this work (Cic. Att. 13, 8 *epitomen Bruti Caelianorum velim mihi mittas*, cf. Charis. GL. 1, 220 *Brutus et Coelius frequenter eo usi sunt*). Paulus (perhaps Julius Paulus in the time of Hadrian? see § 353, 4) elucidated Antipater (antiquated forms); cf. Charis. GL. 1, 143 *Paulus in Coelii hist*(*oriarum* or *-ae*) *libr. I*; cf. ib. 126. 217. 241.

7. Among the fragments of Coelius are many which relate to ethnology and geography, to legends and etymology. These can only be included in the history of the second Punic war, on the supposition that they formed part of digressions in that history: this is difficult on account of the comparatively large number of such notices. Hence first JMeursius, then ThPlüss (de Cinciis, Bonn 1865) and recently WSieglin l.l. have inferred that Coelius composed a second antiquarian work. On this theory Coelius' history would be earlier, while the antiquarian work, to which might be assigned the mention of C. Gracchus' death and the dedication to C. Laelius [see however n. 5], would be later. But no convincing evidence of two such works by Coelius can be produced; neither can this be proved from the *epitome Caelianorum* (see n. 6); it is likewise strange that the two works are not distinguished by special names (both would be quoted as historiae, the historical work being in addition called annales), and lastly that, for both, the number of books in the citations does not exceed VII. See, besides, for two works Sieglin l.l. and Phil.Wschr. 1883, 1451 EZarncke, WschrfklPh. 1886, 515; for the other view *e.g.* GFUnger, OGilbert, RPöhlmann, Phil. Anz. 10, 384 sqq. HPeter, JJ. 125, 97 and others.

8. Collection of the fragments of Antipater: HPeter, hist. rell. 1, 147; fragm. 98. OGilbert, die Fragm. des Coel. Antip., JJ. Suppl. Bd. 10, 365 and Sieglin, die Fragm. des Coel. Antip., ib. 11, 1.—Cf. in addition WGroen van Prinsterer (Leiden 1821) and BANauta (Leid. 1822); OMeltzer, de L. Coelio Antipatro, Lps. 1867. HPeter, hist. rell. 1, ccxiii. EWölfflin, Antiochus von Syrakus und Coelius Antipater (Winterthur 1872) 22; edition of Liv. XXI, p. viii. ThZielinski, d. letzten Jahre d. 2. pun. Kriegs, Lpz. 1880, 112.

9. Festus 158^b, 21 *cuius historiae auctor est Alfius libro I belli carthaginiensis.* HPeter, hist. rell. 1, ccxxxvi. ccclxvii.

138. In this period we have as antiquarians the annalist C. Sempronius Tuditanus (cos. 625/129) and M. Junius, a partisan of the Gracchi; the first was the author of an historical work and of libri magistratuum, the latter of a work de potestatibus. Another was Junius Congus. The poet L. Accius, who flourished about this time, was also a scholar (§ 134, 7. 8. 11). Others were especially busied in making the old literature accessible and intelligible, e.g. Lampadio and Vargunteius.

1. C. Sempronius C. f. C. n. Tuditanus, triumphed as consul Kal. Oct. 625/129 de Iapudibus (CIL. 1, p. 459, XXI). PRE. 6, 976. Cic. Brut. 95 *C. Tuditanus cum omni vita atque victu excultus atque expolitus tum eius elegans est habitum etiam orationis genus.* Dionys. 1, 11 οἱ λογιώτατοι τῶν ῥωμαϊκῶν συγγραφέων, ἐν οἷς ἐστι Πόρκιός τε Κάτων . . . καὶ Γάϊος Σεμπρώνιος καὶ ἄλλοι συχνοί. Cf. ib. 1, 13. The notice there given concerning the aborigines of Italy is probably taken from his history, as well as the one about Regulus in Gell. 7, 4, 1 and about the triumph of Flamininus (a. 560/194) in Plut. Flam. 14. Hence his work seems to have been after the manner of the Annalists in dealing both with archaic and contemporary history. Besides this, *Tuditanus libro III magistratuum* is quoted (Macrob. 1, 13, 21) on leap-years, and *in commentario XIII C. Tuditani* (Messala ap. Gell. 13, 15, 4) on the praetor, and to this work may also belong the notices concerning the nundinae (Macrob. 1, 16, 32) and the trib. pl. (Ascon. ad Cornel. p. 76 Or. 68 K-S.). In treating of leap-years, which were by many connected with Numa, the author may there also have referred to the supposed books of Numa found a. 573/181 (§ 72, 2), and we may therefore understand of the same work Plin. NH. 13, 87 *hoc idem tradit L. Piso censorius primo commentariorum . . . Tuditanus tertio decimo, Numae decretorum fuisse.* (HPeter, rell. 1, CCXI differs from this). Tuditanus is also mentioned Plin. NH. ind. auct. to bk. 12. The fragments ap. HPeter, hist. rell. 1, 142: fragm. 89.

2. Plin. NH. 33, 36 *idque duravit ultra C. Gracchum. Iunius certe, qui ab amicitia eius Gracchanus appellatus est, scriptum reliquit.* Censorin. d. n. 20, 2 *magis Iunio Gracchano et Fulvio et Varroni et Suetonio credendum;* cf. ib. 20, 4. 22, 9 (above § 126, 1). Varro LL. 6, 33 *ut Fulvius scribit et Iunius;* cf. ib. 5, 42. 48. 55. 6, 95 *in M. Iunii commentariis.* Ulp. dig. 1, 13, 1 pr.: *Gracchanus denique Iunius libro septimo de potestatibus,* from which Lyd. de magistr. 1, 24 Ἰούνιος Γρακχιανὸς ἐν τῷ περὶ ἐξουσιῶν. The work was addressed to his friend Pomponius, the father of Atticus (Cic. leg. 3, 49 *de potestatum iure . . . pluribus verbis scripsit ad patrem tuum M. Iunius sodalis, perite meo quidem iudicio et diligenter*). The scanty fragments show that Iunius endeavoured to combine the investigation of the subject-matter with definitions of terms; partiality to Gracchus is possible but cannot be traced in them. Nor can direct use of Gracchanus' work be proved after Varro. HEDirksen, Bruchstücke der röm. Juristen (Königsb. 1814) p. 56. LMercklin, de Iunio Gracchano, Dorp. 1840. 41 II. MHertz, de Cinciis (1842) 88. PRE. 4, 534. JBecker ZfAW. 1854, nr. 16. Huschke, iurispr. anteiust.[5] 8.

3. Lucil. ap. Plin. NH. praef. 7 *nec doctissimis. nam Gaium* (?) *Persium* (§ 136, 9) *haece legere nolo, Iunium Congum volo* i.e. (cf. § 143, 8) he objects to be read by learned scholars, but desires educated readers, and as such Junius Congus. Cic. de or. 1, 256 (the orator Antonius § 152, 1 says, a. 663/91) *historiam et prudentiam iuris publici et antiquitatis † iter et exemplorum copiam . . . a viro optimo et istis rebus instructissimo, familiari meo Congo* (*longo* in the MSS.) *mutuabor.* pPlanc. 58

(delivered a. 700/54) *neque fuit qui id* (some antiquarian matter) *nobis narraret, praesertim mortuo Congo* (*conco* in the MSS.). On this the Schol. Bob. 264 Or.: *ideo mentionem Congi videtur interposuisse, qui⟨a⟩ per illud tempus decesserat* (? this is only inferred from the *mortuo Congo;* Congus was probably older than Antonius, and must have been born about 600/154), *homo curiosus et diligens eruendae vetustatis. nam historicus ⟨non fuit⟩.* KLRoth, RhM. 8, 613. HPeter, hist. rell. 1, clxxiii. JBecker (see n. 2. ad fin.) connects him with Gracchanus; against this see CMFrancken, comm. crit. ad Lucil. 2 (1871), 86.

4. C. Octavius Lampadio was, according to Suet. gramm. 1 (see § 41, 1) the first who, at the suggestion of Krates of Pergamus (in Rome about 585/169), critically revised, lectured on and explained the works of the earliest Latin poets; he gave special attention to the poems of Naevius; he published afresh in 7 books Naevius' bellum punicum, which before was extant only in a single volume (Suet. gramm. 2, see § 95, 8). His editions were renowned and continued to be respected down to a late period (Fronto p. 20; see § 159, 10. Ennius' *annales Lampadionis manu emendati* ap. Gell. 18, 5, 11; see § 101, 4). Junior to Lampadio was Q. Vargunteius, who *certis diebus in magna frequentia pronuntiabat* Ennius (§ 101, 4) and who likewise handled the old poets technically as a grammarian (§ 41, 2, l. 12).

139. The Stoic philosophy was in the Gracchan period professed by C. Blossius of Cumae, the faithful friend of Ti. Gracchus, and by Q. Tubero (cos. 636/118), a man of high principles, though of one-sided mind, who was also a jurist. In the augur Q. Scaevola (cos. 637/117) legal knowledge preponderated over his Stoicism. Juridical works were in this period composed by C. Livius Drusus.

1. Plut. Ti. Gr. 8 *Διοφάνους τοῦ ῥήτορος καὶ Βλοσσίου τοῦ φιλοσόφου παρορμησάντων αὐτόν. ὧν. . . . ἦν . . . ὁ Βλ. αὐτόθεν ἐξ Ἰταλίας Κυμαῖος, Ἀντιπάτρου τοῦ Ταρσέως γεγονὼς ἐν ἄστει συνήθης καὶ τετιμημένος ὑπ' αὐτοῦ προσφωνήσεσι γραμμάτων φιλοσόφων.* Cf. ib. 20. Cic. Lael. 37. PRE. 1^2, 2399.

2. Q. Aelius Tubero, grandson of L. Aemilius Paulus and nephew of Africanus Minor, praetor probably 631/123, cos. suff. 636/118, a favourite pupil of Panaitios. His Stoicism, though not unfavourable to his juridical studies, was an impediment to his oratory, and as he carried it out most rigorously in practice, he appeared to his contemporaries as a crotchety personage; PRE. 1^2, 334. Cic. Lael. 37 *Ti. Gracchum remp. vexantem a Q. Tuberone . . . derelictum videbamus.* Brut. 117 *Q. Aelius Tubero fuit . . . nullo in oratorum numero, sed vita severus et congruens cum ea disciplina quam colebat, paulo etiam durior. . . ut vita sic oratione durus, incultus, horridus. . . . fuit autem constans civis et fortis et in primis C. Graccho molestus, quod indicat Gracchi in eum oratio. sunt etiam in Gracchum Tuberonis. is fuit mediocris in dicendo, doctissimus in disputando.* The belief that Laelius composed for him the funeral oration on his uncle Scipio Africanus (Cic. de or. 2, 341) is probably based on a confusion (§ 131, 2). Pompon. dig. 1, 2, 2, 40 *Q. Tubero, ille stoicus, Panaetii auditor, qui et ipse consul.* Cic. ap. Gell. 1, 22, 7 *nec vero scientia iuris maioribus suis Q. Aelius Tubero defuit, doctrina etiam superfuit,* explained by Gellius: *disciplinas enim Tubero stoicas et dialecticas percalluerat.* Panaitios himself, Hecaton and Poseidonios addressed philosophical writings to him. The juridical

writings of Q. Tubero in the Ciceronian period (see § 208, 1) are frequently based upon him.

3. Q. Mucius Q. f. Q. n. Scaevola, distinguished from his nephew of the same name (§ 154, 1) by the appellation of augur, born c. 595/159 (a. 625/129 he is *iam aetate quaestorius*, Cic. de rep. 18), cos. 637/117, died later than 666/88 (Val. Max. 3, 8, 5). PRE. 5, 183. He was no real orator (Cic. Brut. 102 *oratorum in numero non fuit;* cf. de or. 1, 39. 214. 234), much less a philosopher, though a friend of Panaitios (Cic. de or. 1, 45). His excellence lay in 'respondere de iure,' but he seems not to have written anything. Vellei. 2, 9, 2 *Q. Mucius iuris scientia quam proprie eloquentiae nomine celebrior fuit.* Cic. Brut. 102 *iuris civilis intellegentia atque omni prudentiae genere praestitit.* 212 *peritissimus iuris idemque percomis est habitus.* Atticus and Cicero as adulescentuli used to assist at his consultations (Cic. leg. 1, 13. Lael. 1. Brut. 306). With all his firmness of character he was at the same time an amiable person (*comiter, ut solebat*, Cic. de or. 1, 35 and 234 *eximia suavitate*), even a *ioculator* (ad Att. 4, 16, 3). But the Q. Scaevola, whom Pliny ep. 5, 3, 5 (§ 31, 1) mentions as the author of *lasciva carmina* (quoting from these de dub. nom. GL. 5, 575, 24 *Scaevola 'lassas clunes'*; cf. Charis. GL. 1, 101, 7), likewise the author of the epigram on Cicero's poem Marius (Q. Cic. ap. Cic. leg. 1, 2 *ut ait Scaevola de fratris mei Mario, 'canescet saeclis innumerabilibus'*), and lastly the Μούκιος Σκευόλας whose epigram on a bucolic subject is to be found Anth. Pal. 9, 217, is not he, but rather his son Q. Scaevola (trib. pl. 700/54; PRE. 5, 188), who a. 695/59 was among the cohors amicorum of the poetaster Q. Cicero. MHaupt, opusc. 1, 214.—ASchneider, die drei Scaevola Ciceros, Münch. 1879, 5.

4. C. Livius C. f. Drusus, the elder brother of the cons. of 642, 112 (§ 136, 11). Cic. Tusc. 5, 112 *C. Drusi domum compleri a consultoribus solitam accepimus; . . . caecum adhibebant ducem.* Val. Max. 8, 7, 4 *Livius Drusus, qui et aetatis viribus et acie oculorum defectus ius civile populo benignissime interpretatus est utilissimaque discere id cupientibus monumenta composuit.*

140. The bloody suppression of the Gracchic movement increased the haughtiness of the nobility to the highest degree and brought about the disgraceful acts of the war with Jugurtha (a. 643/111–648/106), but also called up an avenger in the person of C. Marius. In respect to literature, the years between 635/119 and 650/104 are the period in which C. Lucilius and L. Afranius flourished. To this period belong besides the tragic poet C. Titius, Atta the composer of togatae, the epigrammatists Pompilius, Valerius Aedituus and Catulus, the learned Q. Valerius Soranus, and Porcius Licinus.

1. The strange humourist Valerius Valentinus (from Vibo Valentia ?) seems also to belong to this period. Festus 363 *Tappulam legem* (§ 49, 1) *convivalem ficto nomine conscripsit iocoso carmine Valerius Valentinus, cuius meminit Lucilius hoc modo 'Tappulam rident legem concenae optimi.'* Val. Max. 8, 1, 8 *C. Cosconium Servilia lege reum* (c. 667/87) . . . *Valeri Valentini accusatoris eius recitatum in iudicio carmen, in quo puerum praetextatum et ingenuam virginem a se corruptam poetico ioco significaverat, erexit.* Cf. § 114, 2. F. Bücheler, Bonner Ind. lect. 1877, 5.—In the year 1882 was found in Vercelli a bronze fragment of a ⟨*lex*⟩ *Tappula*, a pot-house formulary drawn up quite in the legal style, but with comic nomenclature, etc.

(M. Multivorus, P. Properocius ⟨*L. Vinius Me*⟩ro; ⟨*pro trib*⟩u Satureia); it appears from the writing to belong to the Augustan time: probably a joke produced in some festive club in allusion to the lex Tappula, which had been famous from the time of Valerius. In l. 1 . . . *jus Tapponis f. Tappo.* The name Tappo seems to have had a scandalous significance (cf. CATULL. 104, 4). MOMMS., arch. Zeit. 40, 176; bull. arch. 1882, 186 (with facsimile). On the inscription AKIESSLING, conjectan. II, Greifsw. Vorl. Verz. 1884/85, IV. RIBBECK, röm. Dicht. 1, 232.

141. As orators of this period we have the grandson of the elder Cato, M. Cato (cos. 636/118), Q. Metellus (cos. 645/109), the Epicurean T. Albucius lashed by Lucilius, C. Galba, C. Fimbria (cos. 650/104), C. Titius, who has already been mentioned above as a tragic writer, and others.

1. GELL. 13, 20 (19), 10 *M. Cato M. f. M. n. is satis vehemens orator fuit multasque orationes ad exemplum avi scriptas reliquit et consul cum Q. Marcio Rege fuit* (a. 636/118) *inque eo consulatu in Africa . . . mortem obit.* Cicero in his Brutus does not mention him. Perhaps, however, his speeches may have been mixed up with those of his grandfather. See also FEST. 154, 25. PRISCIAN. GL. 1, 90 (*Cato nepos de actionibus ad populum ne lex sua abrogetur*).

2. Q. Caecilius Metellus Numidicus, cos. 645/109 (against Jugurtha), censor 652/102; PRE. 2, 30. VELLEI. 2, 9, 1 mentions him and Scaurus as second-rate orators of their time. Cf. CIC. Brut. 135. GELL. 1, 6, 1 *oratio Metelli Numidici* (rather *Macedonici*, see above § 131, 7; see MWENDE, de Caeciliis Met. 1875, 56) *gravis ac diserti viri, quam in censura dixit ad populum de ducendis uxoribus.* LIV. per. 59 *Q. Metellus censor censuit ut cogerentur omnes ducere uxores . . . extat oratio eius quam Augustus Caesar . . . in senatu recitavit.* Cf. SUET. Aug. 89 *recitavit . . . orationem Q. Metelli de prole augenda.* Cf. § 143, 4 in fin.

3. CIC. Brut. 131 *doctus etiam Graecis T. Albucius, vel potius paene Graecus . . . licet ex orationibus iudicare. fuit autem Athenis adolescens, perfectus Epicureus* (cf. nat. d. 1, 93) *evaserat.* There Q. Scaevola met him a. 633/121 and made fun of him, a scene described by Lucilius in his satires; see § 143, 4 in fin. CIC. fin. 1, 8. or. 149. VARRO Men. 127 Büch. *de Albuci subus Athenis* (Cf. Hor. E. 1, 4, 16). A. 651/103 he was accused and sentenced on account of extortions, whereupon he returned to Athens and lived there quietly as a philosopher (CIC. Tusc. 5, 108). Perhaps he then composed an Epicurean didactic poem, if he is the person to whom Fronto refers p. 113: *in poetis quis ignorat ut gracilis sit Lucilius, Albucius aridus, sublimis Lucretius?* MHERTZ JJ. 107, 338.

4. CIC. Brut. 127 *C. Galba* (quaestor 634/120) *Servi* (§ 131, 4) . . . *filius, P. Crassi* (133, 5) . . . *gener, . . . rogatione Mamilia, Iugurthinae coniurationis invidia, cum pro sese ipse dixisset, oppressus est* (a. 644/110). *extat eius peroratio, qui epilogus dicitur; qui tanto in honore pueris nobis erat ut eum etiam edisceremus.*

5. CIC. Brut. 129 *C.* (Flavius) *Fimbria . . . bonus auctor in senatu. idem tolerabilis patronus nec rudis in iure civili, et cum virtute tum etiam ipso orationis genere liber. cuius orationes pueri legebamus, quas iam reperire vix possumus.* Cf. de or. 2, 91.

6. As orators of the same period, though without detailed mention of published speeches, Cicero notices P. Scipio and L. Bestia (Brut. 128), C. Licinius Nerva (ib. 129), C. Sextius Calvinus, M. Brutus and L. Caesulenus (ib. 130), M. Silanus, M.

Aurelius Scaurus, A. Postumius Albinus, the flamen Albinus, Q. Caepio (ib. 135), C. and L. Memmii (cf. SALL. Iug. 30, 4), Sp. Thorius, M. Marcellus and his adopted son P. Lentulus (Brut. 136), L. Cotta (ib. 137); also L. Apuleius Saturninus (*seditiosorum omnium post Gracchos eloquentissimus*, ib. 224), C. Servilius Glaucia (ib.). Here belongs also C. Canius, see § 136, 10 ad fin.

7. MACROB. 3, 16, 14 *Gaius Titius, vir aetatis Lucilianae, in oratione qua legem Fanniam* (a. 593/161) *suasit*. CIC. Brut. 167 *eiusdem* (as M. Antonius and L. Crassus) *fere temporis fuit eques rom. C. Titius, qui meo iudicio eo pervenisse videtur quo potuit fere latinus orator sine graecis litteris et sine multo usu pervenire. huius orationes tantum argutiarum, tantum exemplorum, tantum urbanitatis habent ut paene attico stilo scriptae esse videantur. easdem argutias in tragoedias satis quidem ille acute, sed parum tragice transtulit*, see § 145, 1. These dates do not agree. If Titius flourished about a. 630/124, having been born about 600/154 (cf. FRONTO, ep. p. 20: *contigisse quid tale M. Porcio aut Q. Ennio aut C. Graccho aut Titio poetae?* and NOVIUS 68 Ribb. *in tragoedia Titi*), he might be described as a man *aetatis Lucilianae*, and at the same time *fere eiusdem temporis* as Antonius and Crassus, but that he should have spoken pro lege Fannia as early as 593/161 is hardly credible. Therefore either two persons called alike C. Titius are supposed (KW PIDERIT on Brut. p. 284) or the name in MACROB. is held to be corrupt (LMÜLLER, Q. Ennius 96). Perhaps, however, Macrobius only erred as to the name of the law; Titius spoke not for the Fannia but for one of the later leges sumptuariae, which completed the earlier law and increased its severity, perhaps the lex Aemilia sumptuaria 639/115 or the lex Licinia (cf. § 143, 1), which *in plerisque cum Fannia congruit* (MACROB. 3, 17, 8). The characterisation in Cicero (Brut. l.l.), especially with reference to the wealth of *argutiae* and *exempla* in the speeches of Titius, is well supported by the large fragment (in MACR. l.l.) of his speech for the sumptuary law (a description of the behaviour of the aristocratic youth of Rome): but this unrestrained vein of harsh satire and rude criticism hardly deserves praise as *urbanitas* and *stilus paene atticus*, nor on the other hand was it possible for Titius, who wrote tragedies, to have been *sine litteris graecis*; at most he might have been wanting in close acquaintance with Greek rhetoric. On the title of a tragedy (Protesilaus), of which the genuineness may be disputed, see RIBBECK, com. [2] 116.—HAYM, de C. Titio, Lauban 1832. MOMMSEN, RG. 2^6, 403. 454. BÜCHELER, Greifsw. Ind. lect. 1868/69 p. 4. RIBBECK, röm. Trag. 612; röm. Dicht. 1, 189.

142. A many-sided literary activity was in this period shown by the two optimates P. Rutilius Rufus (cos. 649/105) and Q. Lutatius Catulus (cos. 652/102): the noble Rufus was an adherent of the Stoic philosophy, an orator, an authority and a writer on questions of law, lastly the author of a history written in Greek, and of an autobiography. The somewhat desultory Catulus, in addition to his political and military labours, wrote an account of his life, and incidentally also playful epigrams. Other works attributed to him were probably written by his freedman Lutatius Daphnis. Sempronius Asellio likewise confined himself to the narration of events within his own experience, but endeavoured in intentional opposition to previous methods to introduce a more serious treatment of history. He undertook to treat at the same

time of the internal development of the state and aimed, evidently under the influence of Polybios, at presenting it in a pragmatic form.

1. P. Rutilius Rufus was born c. 596/158 (see Cic. Brut. 85 and Appian. Hisp. 88), and grew up in the circle of Africanus minor, under whom he (like Asellio and Lucilius) had served in the Numantine war (a. 620/134 sq.) as trib. mil. (App. Hist. 88, cf. Cic. de rep. 1, 17). As praetor (the year unknown) he was the author of the actio (Gai. inst. 4, 35) or constitutio (fragm. Vat. 1) Rutiliana, and the edictum on the rights of patrons (dig. 38, 2, 1, 1) and previously perhaps of the lex Rutilia on the rufuli (Fest. 261). Cos. 649/105, later (a. 662/92?) in return for his rigorous probity he was sentenced by the knights after a haughty Socrates-like defence, and went into exile to Mytilene and afterwards to Smyrna (Cic. pBalb. 28. Tac. A. 4, 43). Cicero saw him there a. 676/78 (Brut. 85, cf. de rep. 1, 13 and de d. nat. 3, 80), and there too he seems to have died (after 677/77); see AL'Oisel, vie de P. R. R., in Meermann's Thesaur. iur. 1, 359. Majansius, Comment. 2, 1. PRE. 6, 586. Löwe, P. Rutilii Rufi vita, Züllichau 1853. EHuschke, ZfCivilr. 14 (1856), 1. HPeter, hist. rell. 1, cclxi.

2. Vellei. 2, 13, 2 *P. Rutilium, virum non saeculi sui sed omnis aevi optimum.* Capitol. Gordian. 5, 5. Ammian. 30, 4, 6. Cic. Brut. 113 *Rutilius in quodam tristi et severo genere dicendi versatus est . . . multa opera multaque industria Rutilius fuit; quae erat propterea gratior quod idem magnum munus de iure respondendi sustinebat.* (114) *sunt eius orationes ieiunae, multa praeclara de iure; doctus vir et graecis litteris eruditus, Panaeti auditor, prope perfectus in stoicis.* Suet. Aug. 89 *libros totos . . . recitavit . . . ut orationem . . . Rutili de modo aedificiorum.* Diomed. GL. 1, 376 *P. Rutilius . . . pro L. Cesutio ad populum.* HMeyer, oratt.[2] 263. His legal knowledge he owed to P. Scaevola (§ 133, 4), see Cic. off. 2, 47; cf. Pompon. dig. 1, 2, 2, 40. From his juridical writings some fragments are quoted in the Digests (on the authority of Ulpian), but without further details; see dig. 7, 8, 10, 3. 33, 9, 3, 9 (cf. Gell. 4, 1, 22). 43, 27, 1, 2. SWZimmern, Gesch. d. röm. Privatrechts 1, 1, 280. Macrobius' notice 1, 16, 34 (*Rutilius scribit* etc.) about nundinae may be derived, through the medium of a work of Varro's, from a juridical work of Rutilius (hardly from his autobiography).

3. *P. Rutilius Rufus de vita sua* is quoted by Charisius (GL. 1, 120. 125. 130. 139. 146. 195) and Diomedes (GL. 1, 374. 376). The first repeats (120. 139) from his fifth book. Autobiographical relations are also indicated by App. Hisp. 88 Ῥουτίλιον Ῥοῦφον, συγγραφέα τῶνδε τῶν ἔργων (before Numantia), τότε χιλιαρχοῦντα, ἐκέλευσε etc. (hence Suidas v. Ῥουτίλιος), and Isidorus' notice (orig. 20, 11, 4) from Rutilius Rufus de vita sua agrees also with App. Hisp. 85. From the same work may be derived Plut. Mar. 28 ὡς δὲ Ῥουτίλιος ἱστορεῖ τὰ μὲν ἄλλα φιλαλήθης ἀνὴρ καὶ χρηστός, ἰδίᾳ δὲ τῷ Μαρίῳ προσκεκρουκώς, and Plut. Pompei. 37 ὁ Ῥουτίλιος ἐν ταῖς ἱστορίαις. But the embassy a. 599/155 (*aiunt Rutilius et Polybius*, Gell. 6, 14, 10) occurred in his earliest childhood, and the death of the elder Scipio (*Scipionem et Polybius et Rutilius hoc anno mortuum scribunt*, Liv. 39, 52, 1) was certainly before his birth, though it is not impossible that both these events were somewhere mentioned incidentally in his autobiography. At all events, side by side with the Latin version we must assume one in Greek, in which the personal standpoint was perhaps enlarged to an historical one. But it is more probable that the Greek version was an independent work. Cf. Athen. 4, p. 168 E (from Poseidonios' Apam.) Ῥουτιλίῳ τῷ τὴν ῥωμαϊκὴν ἱστορίαν ἐκδεδωκότι τῇ Ἑλλήνων φωνῇ. 6, p. 274 C Ῥουτίλιος Ῥοῦφος ὁ τὴν πάτριον ἱστορίαν γεγραφώς. 12, p. 543 B διαβόητος ἦν παρὰ Ῥωμαίοις καὶ

Σίττιος ἐπὶ τρυφῇ . . . ὥς φησι Ῥουτίλιος, an observation probably made on account of Rutilius' accuser Apicius (cf. ib. p. 168 E). Both works seem to have been composed at Smyrna; cf. Oros. 5, 17 extr. *Smyrnam commigrans litterarum studiis intentus consenuit.* In general see Suringar, de rom. autobiogr. 8. Nissen, krit. Untersuchungen (1863) 41. HPeter, hist. rell. 1, cclxv. 187; fragm. 120.

4. Q. Lutatius Catulus, born c. 602/152, cos. 652/102, who was with Marius victorious over the Cimbri at Vercellae, † 667/87. Cic. Brut. 132 *non antiquo illo more, sed hoc nostro . . . eruditus* (cf. de or. 2, 28). *multae litterae, summa non vitae solum atque naturae sed orationis etiam comitas, incorrupta quaedam latini sermonis integritas* (cf. 259. de or. 3, 29. off. 1, 113. Quint. 11, 3, 35). *quae perspici cum ex orationibus eius* (cf. § 81, 6) *potest tum facillume ex eo libro quem de consulatu et de rebus gestis suis conscriptum molli et xenophonteo genere sermonis misit ad A. Furium poetam* (§ 150, 1), *familiarem suum.* Plut. Mar. 25 ὅμοια δὲ καὶ τὸν Κάτλον αὐτὸν ἀπολογεῖσθαι . . . ἱστοροῦσι (Sulla?), cf. 26 ὡς τὸν Κάτλον αὐτὸν ἱστορεῖν λέγουσι, and 27 τὰ οὖν λάφυρα . . . ἀνενεχθῆναι λέγουσιν. HJordan (Herm. 6, 68) rightly connects this *liber* with the *latae Catuli litterae* in Fronto p. 126, as a political pamphlet in epistolary form. Perhaps he addressed this to the epic poet with the design of prompting his muse to eulogise his exploits; see HPeter, JJ. 115, 751. Two half-erotic epigrams of Q. Catulus ap. Gell. 19, 9, 14 and in Cic. nat. d. 1, 79. Hence included in the enumeration in Plin. ep. 5, 3, 5 (§ 31, 1).—In addition are generally attributed to Catulus Communes historiae (or Communis historia) in at least four books (Philarg. on Verg. G. 4, 564), whose author, in the three passages in which the work is mentioned or quoted, is called Lutatius. Without specification of the work Lutatius is also cited four times, the earliest mention being by Varro LL. 5, 150 and Verrius on the fasti Praenest. CIL. 1, p. 315. The quotations refer to etymology and antiquities, especially Italic. Probably it is incorrect to explain the title as equivalent to 'secular history' and to infer that the work was of a Euhemeristic tendency (see Serv. Aen. 10, 175, and ARiese, RhM. 18, 448); it was rather chosen in allusion to Timaios' κοιναὶ ἱστορίαι, and must be understood to denote a collection of Greek and Italic legends etc. (see Mommsen CIL. 1, 389). But the book is probably to be ascribed not to Catulus himself, but to his learned freedman (see § 41, 1. 134, 1. 150, 3) Lutatius Daphnis (see also OJahn, ad. Pers. p. 143).—In gen. PRE. 4, 1246. HOSimon, vita Lutatii Q. f. Catuli, Festschr. des Gymn. z. gr. Klost. (Berl. 1874) 81. HPeter, hist. rell. 1, cclxx. 191; fragm. 125 and JJ. 115, 751.—A Catulus is perhaps concealed in the commenta Bern. in Lucan. 1, 544 (p. 36 Usener) *sed hoc fabulosum esse inveni in libro Catulli qui* ⟨*in*⟩*scribitur permimo logiarum* (*perperomimologiarum* OCrusius, περὶ μιμολογιῶν LMüller, RhM. 24, 622) or in Serv. Verg. G. 2, 95 (*Catullus eam* [uvam Rhaeticam] *vituperat et dicit nulli rei esse aptam* etc.)

5. Sempronius Asellio. His praenomen is unknown; he cannot well be the L. Asellio who was praetor in Sicily a. 654/100. For the historian Asellio *sub P. Scipione Africano tribunus militum ad Numantiam* (620/134 sq.) *fuit* (like Rutilius Rufus and C. Lucilius) *resque eas quibus gerendis ipse interfuit conscripsit* (Gell. 2, 13, 3). Hence born at the latest 595/159. His work, written in his old age, came down at least to 663/91 (Gell. 13, 22, 8; death of M. Livius Drusus): it is uncertain whether Charis. GL. 1, 195 refers to 668/86 or 671/83.—Next to the very doubtful quotation *Asellio rerum romanarum XL* (XI? XX?) ap. Charis. GL. 1, 195 the highest number of books given is ib. 220 *Sempronius Asellio historiarum XIV*; the title is given more correctly ap. Gell. 13, 22 (21), 8 *Sempronius Asellio in libro rerum gestarum XIV.* The death of Ti. Gracchus (a. 621/133) was related in the 5th book (Gell. 2, 13, 2. 4), that of Livius Drusus (a. 663/91) in the 14th. Polemic

of Asellio against the customary treatment of history by the Annalists, and statement of his own principles ap. GELL. 5, 18, 8 (cf. § 37, 3) *nobis non modo satis esse video quod factum esset, id pronuntiare, sed etiam quo consilio quaque ratione gesta essent demonstrare . . . nam neque alacriores ad remp. defendundam neque segniores ad rem perperam faciundam annales libri commovere quiquam possunt. scribere autem bellum initum quo consule . . . sit* etc. . . . *non praedicare autem interea quid senatus decreverit aut quae lex rogatiove lata sit, . . . id fabulas pueris est narrare, non historias scribere.* That CIC. leg. 1, 6 places him together with Gellius and Clodius far below Antipater is due to the one-sided prominence which he gives to style, or to an insufficient acquaintance with Asellio's work. The fragments in HPETER rell. 1, 178; fragm. 108. Cf. KNIPPERDEY, op. 134. WSTELKENS, der röm. Geschichtschreiber S.A., Crefeld 1867. HPETER, hist. rell. 1, CCXLVIII. WEGGERT, S.A. quem locum quamque vim inter historicos rom. habuerit, Rost. 1869.

143. C. Lucilius, born probably 574/180 in the Latin town of Suessa Aurunca in Campania, of a well-to-do equestrian family, and belonged to the circle of Africanus the Younger. Holding himself aloof from political activity and in an independent position, Lucilius put down in his miscellaneous poems (Saturae) his reflections on what he saw or heard, and in them freely criticised the life of his contemporaries in its various sides—political, moral and literary—to a degree never attempted either by a comic poet before or a satirist afterwards. His fragments show a many-sided culture, acute thought, moral solidity, good humour and ready wit, but also indifference to style. Lucilius was a highly respectable and amiable representative of the new Roman character. He died in Naples 651/103.

1. HIERON. ad Euseb. Chr. a. Abr. 1870 (Freher. and Amand. 1869)=607/147 *Lucilius poeta nascitur.* Probably a confusion of A. Postumius Albinus and C. Calpurnius Piso (coss. 574/180) with Sp. Postumius Albinus and L. Calp. Piso (coss. 607/147.) So MHAUPT, see JJ. 107, 72. 365. VELLEI. 2, 9, 4 *celebre et Lucilii nomen fuit, qui sub P. Africano* (620/134 sq.) *Numantino bello eques militaverat.* Lucilius probably performed his first military service as one of the horsemen who were required to be furnished from Suessa (LIV. 29, 15, 5. MARX, stud. 92). HIERON. ad a. Abr. 1914 (Amand. 1915)=651/103 *Gaius Lucilius* (so cod. Middehill. s. VIII in SCHÖNE 1, p. 143: the other MSS. read *Lucius*) *satirarum scriptor Neapoli moritur ac publico funere effertur anno aetatis XLVI.* Against this statement as to his age see LMÜLLER, Lucil. p. 228; Leb. d. Luc. p. 3. There is no certain indication of any date later than 651/103, as nothing prevents our placing before 651/103 the lex Licinia sumptuaria mentioned by Lucilius (GELL. 2, 24, 10) and repealed already in 657/97 (see LLANGE, röm. Altert. 3, 70. 86). HORACE's (S. 2, 1, 34) mention of Lucil. as *senex* also shows that he lived to an advanced age. The dialogue in CIC. de orat. laid in the year 663/91 (see 1, 72. 2, 25) presupposes Lucilius to be dead.

2. IUV. 1, 20 *magnus Auruncae alumnus.* AUSON. ep. 15, 9 *rudes Camenas qui Suessae praevenis.*—HOR. S. 2, 1, 75 calls himself *infra Lucili censum*, on which PORPH.: *constat enim Lucilium avunculum maiorem Pompei fuisse.* VELLEI. 2, 29, 2 *fuit* [Cn. Pompeius] *genitus matre Lucilia, stirpis senatoriae*, this Lucilia was the

niece of the poet, and his brother, her father a Roman senator. MARX, stud. 92, 1. That Lucilius lived in easy circumstances is shown besides by ASCONIUS in Cic. Pis. p. 13 Or. 12 K-S.: *domus (Antiochi regis filio obsidi publice aedificata) postea dicitur Lucilii poetae fuisse;* see n. 1.

3. His relations with Africanus the Younger (569/185–625/129) and Laelius (cos. 614/140): HOR. S. 2, 1, 71–74; see the pretty anecdote in Acro ad loc. Other friends of his were (Postumius) Albinus, Granius (praeco). On the latter, a noted wit, see BÜCHELER RhM. 37, 521; see there too concerning an extant metrical epitaph, which possibly relates to this Granius. Enemies or at least such as were attacked by Lucilius: Mucius Scaevola, L. Cornelius Lentulus Lupus (cos. 598/156; see MARX, stud. 59), Caecilius Metellus (HOR. S. 2, 1, 67, that is, Q. Macedonicus § 131, 7) and his son C. Caprarius; see CIC. de or. 2, 267 (LMÜLLER ad Lucil. p. 297, MARX l.l. 89), T. Albucius (§ 141, 3), Hostilius Tubulus, Papirius Carbo, and others.—CIC. acad. 2, 102 *Clitomachus* (of Carthago, the Sceptic) *in eo libro quem ad C. Lucilium scripsit poetam.* CORNIF. ad Her. 2, 19 *C. Caelius iudex absolvit iniuriarum eum qui C. Lucilium poetam in scena nominatim laeserat.* Cf. OHIRSCHFELD, Herm. 8, 468.

4. In the quotations and elsewhere the poems are called *saturae:* the poet himself mentions them in one place as *ludus ac sermones* (fragm. 30, 56 M. 934 Lm.). There were 30 books. Only of books 21 and 24 are wanting fragments with the number of each book; of b. 25 only 2 words are preserved; of b. 23 only one hexameter. According to the remains books 1–20 were composed in hexameters; b. 22 in distichs; b. 26–27 in trochaic septenarii; b. 28–29 in troch. sept., iamb. senarii, dactyl. hexameters; b. 30 in hexameters. This voluminous work of a lifetime was published gradually, and the poet certainly (following the example of Ennius, Accius and others in the treatment of didactic subjects) began his satires in trochaic septenarii, next tried his skill in other metres, until he had proved the hexameter to be the most suitable, afterwards adhering entirely to it. Thus the last books are those which were first composed. In the earliest book (26) L. enlarged on his poetry in general, carried on (like Horace with Trebatius S. 2, 1) a dialogue with a friend concerning his readers, his inward impulse towards writing, his disinclination towards all other literary varieties but the satiric, etc.—Two chief groups may be distinguished among the books: b. 1–20, 21 (presumably) in hexameters and 26–30 in various metres. The collection in b. 1–21 is referred to by VARRO LL. 5, 17 *a qua bipartita divisione* (heaven and earth) *Lucilius* (so Scaliger: *Lucretius* Flor.) *suorum unius* (*unum* Flor. originating from the numeral I) *et viginti librorum initium fecit.* The passage which used formerly to be quoted in support of the bipartition of the Lucilian satirical work in CORNIF. ad. Her. 4, 18 *Lucilius* (*Coelius* in the MSS.) . . . *in priore libro* is rather applicable to Coelius Antipater: see § 137, 5; with the other application of the passage the dedication of part of the Lucilian satires to Aelius Stilo is also precluded.—Concerning the third group, book 22–25, all is uncertain owing to the scantiness of the remains. Perhaps, consisting of distichs, it was a supplement to b. 1–21, as was b. 30 (the earliest book in hexameters) to b. 26–29.—By whom and at what period the separate collections were united in a general one, whereby the earlier works were placed after those of the poet's riper years, is not ascertainable.—Date of composition of the satires: HOR. S. 2, 1, 63 proves that Scipio († 625/129) and Laelius († not long afterwards § 137, 5) were living when Lucilius wrote the satires in which he attacked Lupus and Metellus (Macedonicus, n. 3): this is confirmed by the remains of b. 26 sqq. in which the inveterate bachelor Lucilius inveighs against marriage, which during his censorship (623/131, § 131, 7) Metellus had strongly encouraged. According to

this b. 26–30 were composed about 623–625/131–129 (FMarx, stud. 91).—B. 1 after the death of Karneades († c. 626/128; see fr. 1, 12 M. 14 Lm.) and soon after the death of Lupus († c. 628/126), on which Lucilius supposes an assembly of the gods to sit in judgment.—After the publication of b. 1 Lucilius was subjected to the law of M. Junius Pennus tr. pl. 628/126, which banished the peregrini from Rome. After the repeal of this law by C. Gracchus 630/124 Lucilius probably returned to Rome (Marx, stud. 93).—The impeachment for extortion brought against Scaevola when augur (§ 139, 3) 634/120 by Albucius (§ 141, 3), was treated of by Lucilius chiefly in order to ridicule the over-refined oratory of the Graecising Albucius (perhaps in b. 2; see Marx, stud. 70).—B. 11 was composed after 644/110 (fr. 11, 19 M. 358 Lm. condemnation of L. Opimius). Lucilius was still writing after 647/107 (Cic. Brut. 160. 161. Marx, stud. 92).—vHeusde, Lucil. 251. CLachmann, kl. Schr. 2, 62. LMüller, Lucil. p. ix. FMarx, studia Lucil., Bonn 1882.

5. Lucilius' satires soon became the subject of learned annotations, e.g. by Laelius Archelaus and Vettius Philocomus (on this see § 148, 4). Suet. gramm. 14 *huius* (Curtius Nicia in the time of Cicero) *de Lucilio libros etiam Santra comprobat.* The eight ingenious lines by an unknown author before Hor. S. 1, 10 treat of critical efforts on the satires of Lucilius by a certain Cato, no doubt the Valerius Cato mentioned ap. Suet. gramm. 2 (§ 148, 4) and by a much decried *grammaticorum equitum doctissimus*; see the commentators on the passage. EBährens, commentar. Cat. 2, p. 9. FMarx, RhM. 41, 552. Critical editions of the Lucilian satires are vouched for by the anecd. Paris. de notis: see § 41, 2, l. 11. Gell. 2, 24, 5 *erraverunt quidam commentariorum in Lucilium scriptores.*

6. The satires of Lucilius were varied in substance as well as in form. They contained all kinds of humorous descriptions of the delights of the table and the wine-cup, love-stories (Porph. Hor. C. 1, 12, 10 *liber XVI Lucilii 'Collyra' inscribitur . . . de Collyra amica scriptus*), travelling adventures (iter Capuanum in b. 3, the model for the journey to Brundusium in Horace; on it see LVarges, Stettin 1836. OKeller, Phil. 45, 553), ridicule of all sorts combined with serious reflections; as an example of the latter see the fine interpretation of what is meant by *virtus* in Lactant. inst. 6, 5, 2 (fr. inc. 1 M. 1020ª Lm.), culminating in the words: (*virtus est*) *hos* (*homines moresque bonos*) *magni facere, his bene velle, his vivere amicum, commoda praeterea patriai prima putare, deinde parentum, tertia iam postremaque nostra.* Scipio was repeatedly eulogised by Lucilius: Hor. S. 2, 1, 16 (Trebatius to Horace) *iustum poteras* (*Caesarem*) *et scribere fortem, Scipiadam ut sapiens Lucilius.* This is especially confirmed by the fragments of b. 30 (5 sqq. M.) and of b. 14, in which the often mentioned mission of Scipio to the East (about 619/135) was related (Marx, stud. 81). The tendency towards ethical criticism, which made of L. the first satirist, generally predominated. Horace frequently compares himself with his great predecessor, whose high reputation was annoying to him. Sat. 1, 4. 1, 10. 2, 1 and elsewhere. Hor. S. 2, 1, 62 *est Lucilius ausus primus in hunc operis componere carmina morem;* 1, 10, 48 he calls him *inventor.* The words ib. 66 *rudis et Graecis intacti carminis auctor* must be taken to refer to Lucilius; cf. KFHermann, de satirae auctore ex sententia Horatii, Marb. 1841. Teuffel, RhM. 30, 623.—Hor. S. 1, 4, 6 *hinc* (on the old comedy) *omnis pendet Lucilius* is incorrect and unjust (cf. § 236, 4). Points of contact with the Greek comedy in L.: Marx, stud. 46. Archilochos is quoted 27, 50 M. 655 Lm. The assertion made by Lydus (magistr. 1, 41), that Lucilius attached himself to Rhinthon, evidently rests on some confusion.

7. The objects of Lucilius' criticism. That he *primores* (n. 3) *populi arripuit populumque tributim* (Hor. S. 2, 1, 69) is attested by the fragments, especially those of the earliest books (26 sqq.) Pers. 1, 114, *secuit Lucilius urbem te, Lupe, te Muci* (n. 3), *et genuinum fregit in illis.* Juv. 1, 165 *ense velut stricto quotiens Lucilius ardens infremuit, rubet auditor cui frigida mens est criminibus* etc. Schol. Persii 3, 1 *hanc satiram poeta ex Lucili libro IIII transtulit castigans luxuriam et vitia divitum.* Cf. Trebonius ap. Cic. fam. 12, 16 *qui magis hoc Lucilio licuerit adsumere libertatis quam nobis?* Apul. apol. 10 *C. Lucilium, quamquam sit iambicus, tamen improbarim quod Gentium et Macedonem pueros* (cf. Dziatzko, RhM. 33, 111) *directis nominibus carmine suo prostituerit.* ESzelinski, de nominibus personarum apud poetas sat. rom. (Königsb. 1862) p. 1. But also learned criticism and literary criticism in general: derision of the philosophers, e.g. the logical doctrines concerning the chief good (see the charming example inc. 69 M. 1060 Lm.), the flimsy rhetoric (n. 4 ad fin.).—Gell. 17, 21, 49 *Pacuvius . . . et Accius clariorque tunc in poematis eorum obtrectandis Lucilius fuit.* Hor. S. 1, 10, 53 *nil comis tragici mutat* (parodies) *Lucilius Acci? non ridet versus Enni gravitate minores?* on which Porph.: *facit autem Lucilius hoc cum alias tum vel maxime in tertio libro, meminit nono et decimo;* even the Greek poets (Euripides, Homer), are criticised by L., who also attacks the affected mannerism of several contemporaries in the use of Greek phraseology: fragm. 1, 43 M. 35ª Lm. *porro clinopodas lychnosque ut dicimus σεμνῶς ante pedes lecti atque lucernas.* He ridiculed especially the bombastic language of the tragedians and opposed Accius' innovations in language (*quare pro facie, pro statura, Accius status,* ap. Non. 226) and spelling, while he eliminated the duplication of a long vowel introduced by Accius (§ 134, 11), and retained ei for ē only in certain cases. Ritschl, op. 4, 153. LMüller ad Lucil. p. 211; Luc. Leb. u. W. 39. WCorssen, Phil. 18, 723. Marx, stud. 4.—Quint. 10, 1, 94 *eruditio in eo* (L.) *mira et libertas atque inde acerbitas et abundantia salis.* On the Greek words in Lucil. see Lachmann, kl. Schr. 2, 73 and RBouterwek, Phil. 32, 691.

8. His intermediate attitude and purpose of influencing a large circle. Cic. de or. 2, 25 *C. Lucilius, homo doctus et perurbanus, dicere solebat neque se ab indoctissimis neque a doctissimis legi velle; . . . de quo etiam scripsit: Persium* (§ 136, 9) *non curo legere, . . . Laelium Decumum volo.* fin. 1, 7 *nec vero, ut noster Lucilius, recusabo quominus omnes mea legant. utinam esset ille Persius! Scipio vero et Rutilius multo etiam magis. quorum ille iudicium reformidans Tarentinis ait se et Consentinis et Siculis scribere. facete is quidem, sicut alia; sed neque tam docti tum erant . . . et sunt illius scripta leviora, ut urbanitas summa appareat, doctrina mediocris.* Petron. 4 *schedium Lucilianae humilitatis.* Gell. 6, 14, 6 *vera et propria . . . exempla in latina lingua M. Varro esse dicit . . . . gracilitatis Lucilium.* Cf. Fronto p. 113 and 62.

9. Indifference as to form. Cf. Hor. S. 1, 4, 9 sqq. 1, 10, 1 sqq. 50 sqq. That which is here asserted (S. 1, 4, 9 sq,), *L. in hora saepe ducentos . . . versus dictabat stans pede in uno,* is confirmed by L. himself, e.g. fr. 11, 10 M. 342 Lm. *conicere in versus dictum praeconis volebam Grani* (n. 3). Especially in versification L. is free, yet without going beyond what is admissible; cf. LMüller, metr. lat. 71. RBouterwek, quaest. lucil.; comm. prosodiaca, metrica, critica, Elberf. 1867.

10. Full of self-importance Lucilius himself says (30, 4 M. 906 Lm.): *et sola ex multis nunc nostra poemata ferri;* contrary to the prevailing fashion of the Roman aristocracy he will remain just what he is: *publicanus vero et Asiae fiam scripturarius pro Lucilio, id ego nolo et uno hoc non muto omnia* (26, 16 M. 527 Lm.). The authority enjoyed by Lucilius even in the Augustan period (esp. among the national party) appears from the frequent and serious comparisons drawn by Horace

between L. and himself. Even at a still later time there were some who *Lucilium pro Horatio, Lucretium pro Vergilio legunt* (Tac. dial. 23); and those who esteemed poetical energy and originality above all were quite right in doing so.—Plin. NH. praef. 7 *Lucilius qui primus condidit stili nasum.* Quint. 10, 1, 93 *satira quidem tota nostra est, in qua primus insignem laudem adeptus Lucilius quosdam ita deditos sibi adhuc habet amatores ut eum non eiusdem modo operis auctoribus sed omnibus poetis praeferre non dubitent.*

11. Collection of fragments by FDousa, Leid. 1597 (frequently reprinted). EFCorpet, Par. 1845. FDGerlach, Zür. 1846. LMüller, Lps. 1872. CLachmann, Berl. 1876 (as a supplement to this FHarder's index Lucil., Berl. 1878; cf. also Lachmann, kl. Schr. 2, 62, 73). FPR. 139.—The glossaries (§ 42, 6) contain very valuable remains of Lucilian language: see concerning this esp. GLöwe, prodrom. gloss. lat. 293. Also GGötz, RhM. 40, 324. GGundermann, RhM. 41, 632. EBährens, JJ. 135, 483.

Criticism: LFruterius, RhM. 33, 246. EKlussmann, Phil. 16, 166. LMüller, metr. lat. passim (see p. 483); RhM. 17, 195. 26, 577; JJ. 97, 424. 438; Luciliana, Berl. 1884, and elsewhere; ORibbeck, RhM. 29, 118; Jen. LZ. 1877, 58. KDziatzko, RhM. 33, 94. RBouterwek, RhM. 21, 339 (see also n. 9). B. 9 by LFSchmidt, Berl. 1840. Bücheler, RhM. 39, 287. CMFrancken, coniectanea critica ad C. Lucilii librorum decadem I, Amsterd. 1869; ad dec. II et III, Amsterd. 1871; Mnemos. N. S. 1, 237. GLöwe in the commentatt. philol. (Lps. 1874) 239. MSchmidt, Miscellan. phil. (Jena 1876), 14. LQuicherat, rev. archéol. 32 (1876), 117. 358. 34 (1877), 1. HBuchholtz, RhM. 32, 114. HAJMunro, Journ. of Phil. 7, 293. FMarx in the exercitat. gramm. specim., Bonn 1881, 8; studia Lucil., Bonn 1882; RhM. 41, 549. JMStowasser, d. Hexam. des Lucil., Wien 1880; Wien. Studd. 3, 277. 5, 128. 252. 7, 36; Arch. f. lat. Lexikogr. 1, 117. 195.

12. On Lucilius: JACvHeusde, studia critica in C. Lucilium, Utr. 1842. Cf. KFHermann, Gött. GA. 1843, 361 (on which Heusde: Epistola ad C. F. H., de Lucilio, Utr. 1844). FDGerlach, historische Studien (Bas. 1847) p. 3. sqq. Teuffel, PRE. 4, 1181. Mommsen, RG. 2[6], 443. RBouterwek, de L. satirico, Merseb. 1871. LMüller, Leben u. Werke des L., eine Skizze, Lpz. 1876. Ribbeck, röm. Dicht. 1, 227.—CGiussani, quaestt. Lucil., Milan 1885.—Harder's Wortindex: see n. 11. MKleinschmidt, de Lucilii genere dicendi, Marb. 1883 (on which FMarx, Gött. GA. 1883, 1246). EFischer, de vocibus Lucil., Berl. 1881. HPetitjean, rôle de L. dans le progrès de la langue etc., Ann. de Caen 2, 4 (1886).

144. In the first half of the 7th century u.c. we find two writers of togatae, Atta and Afranius. We know eleven titles of plays, all Latin, by T. Quinctius Atta (died 677/77); the scanty fragments abound in archaisms and are lively and bold in style. Atta was praised for his consistent delineation of character. He appears to have also published a collection of epigrams in distichs.

1. Hieron. ad Euseb. Chr. a. Abr. 1940 (Freh. 1939)=677/77. *T. Quintius* (so cod. Middlehill. s. VIII. in Schöne 1, 144: *Quinticius*, the rest) *Atta scriptor togatarum Romae moritur sepultusque via Praenestina ad miliarium II.*—Diomed. GL. 1, 490, 8 *Atta togatarum scriptor;* ib. 490, 16 *togatas tabernarias in scenam dataverunt praecipue duo, L. Afranius et C. Quintius.*

2. Varro in Charis. GL. 1, 241 ἤθη *nullis aliis servare convenit quam Titinio,*

Terentio, Attae. FRONTO p. 62 *animadvertas particulatim elegantis Novium et Pomponium et id genus in verbis rusticanis et iocularibus ac ridiculariis, Attam in mulieribus.* In HOR. E. 2, 1, 79 Atta is an example of one of the antiqui whose influence survives in the present.

3. NON. (v. crines) 202 *Atta in epigrammatibus* (an hexameter follows); see MHAUPT, op. 3, 440. Cf. § 146.—ISIDOR. or. 6, 9 *Atta in Satura* (here follow iamb. senarii) is generally supposed to refer to a togata (cf. § 6, 2 ad fin.), BÄHRENS FPR. 274 to a satire.—In general concerning Atta NEUKIRCH, de tog. 153. PRE. 1², 2049. The fragments in RIBBECK ² 160.

145. L. Afranius was, both in fertility and artistic worth, the principal author of togatae; he was born about 600/154–610/144. Of his plays we know wellnigh all the titles, the Roman public having kept up their interest in them for a long time. He treated national subjects, but in Menander's spirit and partly in imitation of him. His plots belonged principally to the middle class and family life. In his style he knew, like Titinius, how to combine Plautus' popular manner with the correctness and elegance of Terence.

1. CIC. Brut. 167 *quem* (C. Titius, § 141, 7) *studebat imitari L. Afranius poeta, homo perargutus, in fabulis quidem etiam . . . disertus.* According to this Afranius was an orator at the same time that he devoted himself to writing togatae, as Titius combined oratory with the writing of tragedies. VELLEI. 2, 9, 3 *clara etiam per idem aevi spatium fuere ingenia, in togatis Afrani, in tragoediis Pacuvii atque Attii, usque in graecorum ingeniorum* (*tragicorum* OJAHN) *comparationem evecti.* Cf. 1, 17, 1. HOR. E. 2, 1, 57. QUINT. 10, 1, 100 *togatis excellit Afranius; utinam non inquinasset argumenta puerorum foedis amoribus, mores suos fassus.* In accordance with this AUSON. epigr. 67, 2 *repperit obscenas veneres vitiosa libido, . . . quam toga facundi scenis agitavit Afrani.* Plots of this sort, which were in the main excluded from the New Comedy, reflected the average morality of Rome in his day. MACROB. 6, 1, 4 *Afranius togatarum scriptor in ea togata quae Compitalia inscribitur non inverecunde respondens arguentibus quod plura sumpsisset a Menandro 'Fateor,' inquit 'sumpsi non ab illo modo, Sed ut quisque habuit conveniret quod mihi, Quod me non posse melius facere credidi, Etiam a Latino.'* CIC. fin. 1, 7 *locos quosdam, si videbitur, transferam. . . . cum inciderit ut id apte fieri posset, ut ab Homero Ennius, Afranius a Menandro solet.* SUET. v. Ter. p. 33, 8 *Terentium Afranius omnibus comicis praefert:* which agrees with his whole tendency, see § 17.

2. We know more than 40 titles; the most celebrated were Divortium, Emancipatus, Epistula, Fratriae, Privignus, Vopiscus. The fragments in RIBBECK, com.² 164.

3. Performance of his Simulans 697/57 (CIC. Sest. 118), of his Incendium under Nero (SUET. Ner. 11). In the Augustan period enthusiasts placed him on a level with Menander (HOR. E. 2, 1, 57); about the time of Hadrian (Julius?) Paulus devoted himself to his elucidation (CHARIS. GL. 1, 241. Cf. § 137, 6 in fin. 353, 4).—APULEI. also apol. 12 *pereleganter Afranius hoc scriptum reliquit.*

4. NEUKIRCH, fab. tog. 165. MOMMSEN, RG. 2⁶, 437. TEUFFEL, Caecilius Statius, etc. (Tüb. 1858) 37. RIBBECK, röm. Dicht. 1, 204.—Criticism: LFRUTERIUS, RhM. 33, 242. LQUICHERAT, mélanges en philol. (Par. 1879), 232.

146. The other varieties of poetry were little cultivated at this period, the epos perhaps only in the bellum Histricum of a certain Hostius. But epigram, being less troublesome, was practised in imitation of Greek (Alexandrine) models. Atta's collection of epigrams has already been mentioned above (§ 144, 3): others, chiefly of an erotic character, were composed by Pompilius, Valerius Aedituus, Porcius Licinus and Q. Lutatius Catulus (cos. 652/102); Licinus wrote besides a poem on a literary and historical subject in trochaic septenarii.

1. The few quotations from the bellum Histricum of Hostius only reach as far as b. 2. They indicate an imitation of Homer (Macr. 6, 3, 6) and a mythological clothing (Macr. 6, 5, 8). Cf. also Fest. 325, 5. 356, 21. Serv. Aen. 12, 121. Hostius is not likely to have treated of the Istrian war a. 576/178 sqq., which Ennius had already celebrated in his Annals (Bergk, kl. Schr. 1, 252. LMüller's Q. Ennius 179); he wrote rather concerning a later one, probably that of 629/125, in consequence of which Sempronius Tuditanus celebrated his triumph (§ 138, 1). See Bergk l.l. This poem, which never attained any special estimation, was composed in honour of the victor by Hostius, who was either under an obligation to him or desirous of obtaining his favour. To him probably refers Prop. 4, 20, 8 *splendidaque a docto fama refulget avo;* for the name of the Cynthia there addressed was in reality Hostia (§ 32, 3. 246, 1). Perhaps he is also alluded to by Priscian GL. 2, 270 *vetustissimi etiam 'hoc pecu' . . . dicebant. Hostilius in I annali* (an hexameter follows). Priscian's *vetustissimi* does not contradict this. AWeichert, poett. latt. rell. 3. Bergk, kl. Schr. 1, 252. LMüller, Q. Ennius 278.

2. The name of Pompilius is restored in Varro LL. 7, 28 *Pompili* (*Papini* Flor.) *ἐπιγραμμάτιον quod in adolescentem fecerat Cascam* (here follows an erotic jest in two distichs) and in Prisc. GL. 2, 90, where the same epigram is quoted from Varro: *Pompilius* (*pompnius*, *pomponius* in the MSS.) *in epigrammate.* From a book of epigrams may also very likely have been taken the senarius in Varro LL. 7, 93 *apud Pompilium* (on the strength of this tragedies are attributed to P., ARiese, Varr. sat. 183. Ribbeck's trag.[2] 227); cf. e.g. the iambics of Manilius § 158, 1. The epigram already quoted above § 105, 1, l. 6 sqq. was no doubt included in the same collection as a σφρηγὶς (in the sense of Theognis 19 sqq.). LHavet, rev. de phil. 7, 193.

3. Gell. NA. 19, 9, 10 *versus cecinit Valeri Aeditui, veteris poetae, item Porcii Licini et Q. Catuli, quibus mundius, venustius, limatius, tersius graecum latinumve nihil quidquam reperiri puto* (much exaggerated). In relation to the first epigram of Val. Aed. (ib. § 11) cf. HUsener, RhM. 19, 150. 20, 147. RPeiper, ib. 19, 311. FMaixner, ZföG. 34, 405. 36, 583. 38, 1.—On the epigram and other works of Q. Catulus, see § 142, 4.—To this period and to the same circle belongs an erotic epigram on a wall in Pompeii, published by Bücheler, RhM. 38, 474 *⟨Quid fi⟩t? vi me, oculi, posquam deduxstis in ignem*, etc. Cf. EBährens, JJ. 127, 798.

4. An epigram by Porcius Licinus in Gell. 19, 9, 13. Cf. 17, 21, 45 *Porcius Licinus serius poeticam Romae coepisse dicit in his versibus: Poénico bell6 secundo* etc. (above p. 120). Eleven trochaic senarii by him in Suetonius' vita Terentii, p. 27, 9 R. discuss in a bitter strain Terence's relations with Roman magnates, his servility and their want of consideration. Ritschl, Parerga 244. 622. 637; in

Reifferscheid's Suetonius 489=op. 3, 225.—Criticism: JVahlen, Berl. SBer. 1876, 789. Cf. also Charis. GL. 1, 129 '*fretus, huius fretus*' *Porcius Licinus* and Cic. fin. 1, 5 (§ 107, 2).

147. Q. Valerius from the Latin town of Sora was a many-sided and esteemed scholar (of the first half of the 7th century u.c.) in the department of linguistic and antiquarian research, and a precursor of Varro, who like him often employed the metrical form. Volcacius Sedigitus also was a didactic poet in the department of literary history.

1. Cic. de or. 3, 43 (the scene is laid in 663/91) L. Crassus says: *nostri* (the Romans themselves) *minus student litteris quam Latini.* Notwithstanding (he says) the most uneducated native Roman easily surpasses *litteratissimum togatorum omnium, Q. Valerium Soranum, lenitate vocis atque ipso oris pressu et sono.*—Varro (born 638/116) knew him personally and often refers to him as a weighty authority; cf. Gell. 2, 10, 3: Varro, questioned by Ser. Sulpicius (§ 174, 2) concerning the *favisae Capitolinae*, confesses that he knows nothing about the origin of the word, *sed Q. Valerium Soranum solitum dicere*, etc. Varro LL. 7, 31, *apud Valerium Soranum: vetus adagio est, o P. Scipio* († 625/129). From this he appears to have been a contemporary of L. Accius, and it becomes probable that he is the same Valerius whom Varro quotes LL. 10, 70 *Valerius ait: 'Accius* (§ 134, 11) *Hectōrem nollet facere, Hectŏra mallet,*' further 7, 65 *scrupipedas . . . dicit . . . Valerius a pede ac scrupea.* He must also be identical with the expositor of the XII tables (§ 86, 6) of the same name. Two hexameters (of Stoic character on Juppiter as the one and highest god) ap. Augustin. civ. d. 7, 9 in fin. (cf. Mythogr. Vat. 152 Bode): *in hanc sententiam etiam quosdam versus Valerii Sorani exponit idem Varro in eo libro quem seorsum ab istis de cultu deorum scripsit.* Plin. NH. praef. 33 *hoc ante me fecit* (viz. to add a table of contents to a book) *in litteris nostris Valerius Soranus, in libris quos ἐποπτίδων inscripsit.* He must have been born about 600/154. His two sons, Quintus and Decimus, are called by Cic. Brut. 169 *vicini et familiares mei, non tam in dicendo admirabiles quam docti et graecis litteris et latinis.* PRE. 6, 2342.—Distinct from the '*litteratissimus togatorum omnium*' is *tribunus plebei quidam Valerius Soranus*, who divulged the secret name of Rome and was punished with death by order of the Senate (Varro ap. Serv. Aen. 1, 277; cf. Plin. NH. 3, 65. Plut. qu. rom. 61, p. 278 F). EvLeutsch, Phil. 39, 90. 130.

2. Gell. 15, 24, 1 *Sedigitus* (in the ind. capp.: *Volcacius Sedigitus*), *in libro quem scripsit de poetis, quid de his sentiat qui comoedias fecerunt et quem ex omnibus praestare ceteris putet ac deinceps quo quemque in loco et honore ponat his versibus suis demonstrat.* Here follow 13 senarii, in which 10 poets of palliatae are enumerated in a very curious arrangement and with a dogmatic air (*contra si quis sentiat, nil sentiat*): ThLadewig (üb. d. Kanon des Volc. Sed., Neustrel. 1842) has endeavoured, but without success, to introduce some degree of rationality into this. HIber, de Volc. Sed. canone, Münst. 1865; see § 15, 4. If in Suet. vit. Terent. p. 33 R. the succession *Porcius* (Licinus), *Africanus, Volcacius, Cicero, Caesar* is chronological, as is probable, Volcacius may be assumed to have flourished after the middle of the 7th century u.c. Four senarii by Sed. on Terence in Suet. v. Ter. p. 29, 6 and 32, 10. The three senarii of a certain † *vallegius in actione* (concerning Scipio as the author of the Terentian comedies) which are quoted in Donatus' addition to Suet. v. Ter. p. 35, 5 R. belong also to Volcacius. Bücheler, RhM.

33, 492. F. Leo, ib. 38, 321. Cf. § 304, 3. According to this he appears to have summarily treated of the life and works of the poets in question, giving at the same time a kind of æsthetic criticism on them. He does not, however, appear to have gone beyond the time of the palliata, and merely for that reason it is unadvisable to place him so late as the time of Cicero. See further Ritschl, op. 3, 238.

3. Donatus' addition to Suetonius' Life of Terence p. 35 R.: *duos Terentios poetas fuisse scribit Maecius* (§ 193, 1), *quorum alter Fregellanus fuerit Terentius Libo*, and the other the comic poet.

148. But the most notable scholar and antiquarian of this period was the Roman knight L. Aelius Praeconius Stilo of Lanuvium. He adhered to Stoicism, and was the first to give solid instruction (to friends) in Latin literature and oratory, creating a scientific basis for the investigation of the Latin language and antiquities by going back to the oldest documents and commenting on them. The first Roman philologer, he bequeathed the purpose and results of his investigations to his pupil Varro. Simultaneously with Stilo, scholars of Greek origin pursued the same studies, e.g. Laelius Archelaus and Vettius Philocomus.

1. Suet. gr. 2 *instruxerunt auxeruntque ab omni parte grammaticam L. Aelius Lanuvinus generque Aelii Ser. Clodius* (§ 159, 9), *uterque eques rom. multique ac varii et in doctrina et in rep. usus.* (3) *Aelius cognomine duplici fuit; nam et Praeconinus, quod pater eius praeconium fecerat, vocabatur et Stilo, quod orationes nobilissimo cuique scribere solebat; tantus optimatium fautor ut Metellum Numidicum* (§ 141, 2) *in exilium comitatus sit* (a. 654/100). Cic. Brut. 205 *L. Aelius . . . fuit vir egregius et eques rom. cum primis honestus, idemque eruditissimus et graecis litteris et latinis antiquitatisque nostrae et in inventis rebus et in actis scriptorumque veterum litterate peritus. quam scientiam Varro noster acceptam ab illo auctamque per sese . . . pluribus et illustrioribus litteris explicavit.* (206) *sed idem Aelius stoicus esse voluit, orator autem nec studuit umquam nec fuit; scribebat tamen orationes quas alii dicerent, ut* (205 *Cottae pro se lege Varia*, a. 663/91) *Q. Metello *F., ut Q. Caepioni* (cf. ib. 169), *ut Q. Pompeio Rufo. . . .* (207) *his scriptis etiam ipse interfui, cum essem apud Aelium adulescens eumque audire perstudiose solerem.* Cornif. ad. Her. 4, 18 *Coelius* (§ 137, 5) *. . . In priore libro has res ad te scriptas, Luci, misimus, Aeli.* Varro in Gell. NA. 1, 18, 2 *L. Aelius noster, litteris ornatissimus memoria nostra*, and LL. 7, 2 *homo in primis in litteris latinis exercitatus.* Cf. also Gell. 10, 21, 2 *qui doctissimus eorum temporum fuerat, L. Aelius Stilo.* Plin. 33, 29. 37, 9. Verg. catal. 7, 3 *Valete . . . Et vos, Stiloque Tarquitique* (§ 158, 2) *Varroque, Scolasticorum natio madens pingui. Stiloque* was already conjectured by Heyne: the MSS. indicate *Selique*, but the Selii from Cic. acad. 2, 11 or fam. 7, 32, 2 cited by Ellis and Bücheler (RhM. 38, 514) are hardly in place here.—The MSS. frequently read Laelius instead of L. Aelius, e.g. Cic. fam. 9, 15, 2. acad. post. 1, 8. or. 230. de or. 1. 265? Plin. NH. 14, 93.—As according to the above L. Aelius was a friend of Coelius Antipater, and Cicero his pupil, he must have been born about 600/154 and seems to have reached an advanced age. Cf. Ritschl, Parerga 239.

2. His literary activity: *Aeliana studia* (*antiquitatis romanae*), Cic. de or. 1,

193? (MVoigt, Abh. d. sächs. Ges. d. Wiss. 7, 324, refers this to Sex. Aelius § 125, 2) cf. acad. post. 1, 8. Reference to (verbal) remarks of St. Varro RR. 3, 12, 6. LL. 5, 66. 101. 6, 7. Gell. NA. 12, 4, 5. His writings: *Aelii . . . interpretationem carminum Saliorum videbis et exiliter* (?) *expeditam et praeterita obscura multa*, Varro LL. 7, 2. Cf. Fest. 146 (v. manuos). 141 (v. molucrum). 210 (v. pescia). Corssen, orig. 48 and above § 64, 2.—His commentary on the XII tables: Cic. leg. 2, 52. Fest. 290 (v. sonticus morbus). RSchöll, leg. XII tabb. reliqq. 29 is of opinion that we should always understand Stilo where Aelius alone is quoted. Gell. NA. 16, 8, 2 *commentarium de proloquiis L. Aelii, docti hominis, qui magister Varronis fuit, . . . legimus. sed in eo nihil edocenter neque ad instituendum explanate scriptum est, fecisseque videtur eum librum Aelius sui magis admonendi quam aliorum docendi gratia.* His criticism and interpretation of the old Latin poets: he produced critical editions: see anecd. paris. de notis (above § 41, 2, l. 12) and Fronto p. 20 (below § 198, 3 in fin). An admirer of Plautus, Quint. 10, 1, 99. *Indices Aelii* (see n. below) *super his fabulis* (*Plauti*) *quae dicuntur ambiguae*, Gell. 3, 3, 1 and ib. 12 *homo eruditissimus L. Aelius XXV* (*comoedias*) *eius* (*Plauti*) *esse solas existimavit.* Cf. § 96, 4. 99, 4 and 5. Numerous etymological (*in quo . . . erravit aliquotiens*, Varro ap. Gell. 1, 18, 2) and grammatical observations of Stilo are collected in vHeusde 64.—JACvHeusde de L. Aelio Stilone; inserta sunt Stilonis et Servii Claudii fragm., Utr. 1839. Cf. Mommsen, RG. 2[6], 425. 456.

3. Suet. gramm. 2 (cf. § 41, 1) *ut Laelius Archelaus Vettiusque Philocomus* (*retractarunt ac legendo commentandoque etiam ceteris notas fecerunt*) *Lucili saturas familiaris sui* (so the MSS.: *familiaribus suis* Heusde), *quas legisse se apud Archelaum Pompeius Lenaeus* (§ 53, 1), *apud Philocomum Valerius Cato* (§ 200, 1) *praedicant.* As in the lives directly following, this humble degree of learned employment is contrasted with the higher, represented by Stilo (*instruxerunt*, etc., n. 1 above), and as, on the other hand, the pupils of these two (Lenaeus and Cato) belong to the time of Cicero, Archelaus and Philocomus may be considered to have flourished at about the same time as Stilo c. 630/124 sqq.—The same Archelaus is perhaps alluded to ap. Charis. GL. 1, 141, 33 *Q. Laelius ex principibus grammaticis librum suum ita inscripsit 'de vitiis virtutibusque poematorum.'*

149. The twenty years 650/104–670/84 again contain violent civil struggles, partly with the Allies, who in the Marsian war obtained for themselves complete equality with the Romans, partly between the revived popular party and the nobility, the latter fighting for their privileges and at length victorious through Sulla. The great activity stirred up by these struggles in the national domains of intellectual activity, in rhetoric and jurisprudence, produced splendid results. Oratory now became a matter of instruction and was also taught by natives. Historical writing was in the hands of the new Annalists, some showing themselves influenced by rhetoric, others swayed by party views.

1. Latini rhetores at Rome, see § 44, 9.—On the later Annalists see § 37.

150. In poetry also there was much activity; the Atellan farce was introduced into literature by Pomponius and Novius; Cn. Matius composed mimiambi and translated the Iliad; Laevius

(Melissus) began in jocular mythological erotic poems skilfully to imitate the various forms of Greek metres, even in their artificial refinements. This period possessed an epic poet in A. Furius of Antium, and a tragic poet in C. Julius Caesar Strabo. The idyllic poet Sueius also perhaps belongs to the same time. In this period (650/104–670/84) fell the youth of Cicero (b. 648/106) and Caesar (b. 654/100).

1. Q. Lutatius Catulus wrote *de consulatu et de rebus gestis suis* one book *ad A. Furium poetam, familiarem suum* (Cic. Brut. 132; see § 142, 4). Gell. NA. 18, 11 in the ind. cap. *ex carminibus Furi Antiatis;* ib. § 2: *Furium veterem poetam.* Gellius there quotes 6 hexameters from an epic and defends the poet against the reproach he had incurred for his clumsy formation of words. Cf. A. Weichert, poet. lat. rell. 348. JBecker, ZfAW. 1848, 597. KNipperdey, op. 499.—On other lines attributed to this Furius, see § 192, 9.

2. Varro LL. 7, 95 *apud Matium 'corpora Graiorum maerebat mandier igni'* (Hom. *A* 56). Cf. ib. 96 *ap. Matium 'obsceni interpres'* etc. (=*A* 62). Gellius, who hardly ever mentions Matius without complimenting him as a *doctus vir, homo impense doctus, vir eruditus* and so forth, quotes 7, 6, 5 *Cn. Matium . . . in II Iliadis;* 9, 14, 14 *Cn. Matius in Iliadis XXI* and ib. 15 *Matius in XXIII.* Cf. Charis. GL. 1, 117. 345. Diom. GL. 1, 345. Prisc. GL. 2, 334.—Terent. Maur. GL. 6, 397, 2416 *hoc* (in choliambics) *mimiambos Matius dedit metro; nam vatem eundem* (Hipponax) *est attico thymo tinctum pari lepore consecutus et metro.* This metre also appears in the scanty remains (e.g. 14 lines quoted in LMüller's Catullus [Lpz. 1870] 91), which point to cheerful descriptions of every-day life (in the form of dialogues), being probably analogous in subject-matter to many such (in Sophron.), in Lucilius and Varro (sat. Men.). The name (cf. μελίαμβοι, μυθίαμβοι) and subject are borrowed from the μιμίαμβοι, likewise in choliambics, of Herodas (see fragments in Bergk's poett. lyr. gr. 2^4, 508), who even at a later time, among the Romans, enjoyed a high reputation (Plin. ep. 4, 3, 4 concerning the Greek epigrams and iambics of one of his friends: *Callimachum me vel Heroden vel si quid his melius tenere credebam*). It must not be supposed that the μιμίαμβοι were of a purely dramatic character, nor that they were produced on the stage.—Wernsdorf, PLM. 4, 568. LCMAubert, de Matio mimiamb. auctore, Christiania 1844. Ribbeck, röm. Dicht. 1, 302. The fragments most recently FPR. 281.

3. Besides Matius, a certain Ninnius Crassus also translated the Iliad. Cf. Priscian. GL. 2, 478, 12 *Ninnius Crassus in XXIV Iliados,* and Non. 475, 14 *Crassus lib. XVI Iliados.* The same is alluded to by Prisc. GL. 2, 502, 24 † *nevius in Iliadis secundo* and Charis. GL. 1, 145, 21 † *neuius Cypriae Iliadis libro I.* According to the latter quotation he also translated τὰ Κύπρια ἔπη (in eleven books). The date of the poet is not known. FPR. 283.

4. Ausonius says in the epilogue to his cento nuptialis (p. 146, 11 Sch.) in justification of it: *quid antiquissimi poetae Laevii Erotopaegnion libros loquar?* Cf. Prisc. GL. 2, 281, 2 *idem vetustissimi . . . Laevius . . . Ennius.* Hence it is improbable that Laevius did not flourish till about 690/64, although the multiplicity of his metres would agree with this. The period above assigned to him is supported by the nature of Laevius' diction (cf. esp. Gellius 19, 7, 2), as well as by the order in which Gellius 19, 9, 7 places him among the Roman erotic writers: *Laevius . . . Hortensius . . . Cinna . . . Memmius* (cf. § 31, 1). And the

pleasantry on the lex Licinia sumptuaria (passed before 651/103, see LLange, röm. Altert. 2, 625. 3, 70; see § 143, 1) ap. Gell. 2, 24, 8 loses its point unless it is earlier than the repeal of this law, which took place before 657/97 (Lange l.l. 3, 86). Perhaps Prisc. GL. 1, 560 *Laevius erotopaegnion in IIII 'meminens Varro corde volutat'* alludes to the Polyhistor. With our date Bücheler agrees, JJ. 111, 306, as he places the mention of the phoenix (see below) by Laevius a few years later than the legendary account of this bird given by L. Manilius or Manlius (§ 158, 1), therefore about the year 660/94–665/89. Laevius is identified by Bücheler (RhM. 41, 11) with the individual who is mentioned in Suet. gramm. 3: *quem* (Lutatius Daphnis, § 142, 4 in fin.) *Laevius Melissus per cavillationem nominis* Πανὸς ἀγάπημα *dicit*, and we should prefer to ascribe to a Greek and a schoolmaster the attempt to adapt Latin for the first time to the artificialities of the later Greek prosody. By his contemporaries and immediate successors Laevius (as likewise Phaedrus at a later time) was intentionally neglected. He himself spoke of his critics as *vituperones subducti supercili carptores* (Gell. 19, 7, 16). Earliest mention in Fest. 206[b], 15.—His name was frequently confounded with Livius, Naevius, Laelius, Lepidus, Laevinus, even with Pacuvius. The name Laevius is very rare.—Porphyr. on Hor. C. 3, 1, 2 *Romanis utique non prius audita, quamvis Laevius lyrica ante Horatium scripserit; sed videntur illa non Graecorum ad lyricum characterem exacta.* Horace was silent concerning his long-forgotten predecessor, who had never attained any great consideration; he even passed over Catullus.—Gell. 19, 7, 2 *figuras habitusque verborum nove aut insigniter dictorum in Laeviano illo carmine.* L. especially delighted in bold and arbitrary coinages and combinations of words, after the manner of the earlier Roman poets, and the fragments generally show in their diction a foreign tendency. As regards the contents we find Greek legends playfully treated, and a variety of lyrical metres (iambic dimeters, trochaics, scazons, anapaests, dactylic tetrameters, phalaecian metre, ionics a maiore, a minore and others) freely dealt with and combined; lastly even the Alexandrine (cf. Simmias' πτέρυγες Ἔρωτος, Anth. Pal. 15, 24) trifle known as the pterygion phoenicis with increasing and diminishing lines, experiments with the number of the syllables, etc. See n. 5 and Bücheler, l.l.

5. Highest number of books: *Laevius* Ἐρωτοπαιγνίων *VI* ap. Charis. GL. 1, 204. Cf. ib. 288, 5, *in pterygio phoenicis Laevii novissimae odes Erotopaegnion.* Possibly we have subdivisions of this general title in the quotations *Laevius in Adone* (Priscian. GL. 2, 269, 6), *in Ione* (*Inone*, ib. 281, 3), *in Protesilaodamia* (Gell. 12, 10, 5. Non. 116. 209. Priscian. GL. 2, 242, 13; cf. *in Protesilao* ib. 484, 9; *in Laudamia* 496, 27), *in Sirenocirca* (302, 1, Non. 120), *in Centauris* (Fest. 206; Ribbeck, röm. Trag. 11), *Alcestis* (Gell. 19, 7, 2). *Laevius in polymetris* ap. Priscian. GL. 2, 258, 12.—AWeichert, de Laevio poeta, in d. poett. latt. 31. FWüllner, de Laevio, Münst. 1829; allg. Schulzeit. 1830 2, 1259. PRE. 4, 732. LMüller, de re metr. 75 and the fragments in his Catullus (Lps. 1870) p. 76, cf. p. xxxviii. FPR. 287. EBährens, Catullcommentar 6. Ribbeck, röm. Dicht. 1, 303. CHäberlin, Phil. 46, 87.

6. On Caesar Strabo see § 153, 3.—Sueius: the name is rare, cf. CIL. 1, 1183= 10, 5191. 7, 477? Only in Macr. do the MSS. give the poet his correct name, elsewhere it is corrupted into *suis, suemus, ueius* etc. Macrob. sat. 3, 18, 11 *huius rei idoneus adsertor est Sueius, vir longe doctissimus, in idyllio quod inscribitur Moretum. nam cum loquitur de hortulano faciente moretum*, etc., upon which he quotes from it 8 hexameters which in their hard, pedantic tone differ materially from the style of the (Vergilian) Moretum (cf. ib. 3, 19, 1 *Sueius poeta*). It is a question whether there is a connection between the moretum of S. and the μυττωτός (?) of

Parthenios of Nicaea (in Rome from about 681/73; see MEINEKE, anall. alex. 257 and below § 230, 3, 1)?—From Sueius' '*Pulli*,' relating to bird-breeding and the habits of birds, trochaic septenarii are quoted by Non. 139, 24. 513, 21. 72, 23. Perhaps the much mutilated fragments in VARRO LL. 7, 104 are from the same source.—MACROB. 6, 1, 37. 6, 5, 15 quotes two fragments (both times *Sueius in libro quinto*) perhaps from an epic poem. RIBBECK, röm. Dicht. 1, 306 would identify the poet with the knight M. Seius, aed. 680/74, a friend of Varro and Cicero, and the owner of a profitable bird-breeding establishment (PRE. 6, 921).—Fragments in MÜLLER's Lucilius p. 311. 322 (cf. p. xxx). FPR. 285. Cf. MHERTZ, Berl. Jahrbb. 1843, 232. LMÜLLER, RhM. 24, 553. ORIBBECK, ib. 27, 181; röm. Dicht. 1, 306. EBÄHRENS, miscell. crit. (Groning. 1879) 22.

151. The popular Atellane play became a branch of literary comedy, owing to Novius and L. Pomponius of Bononia, who introduced into the forms of the old popular play a similarity to the Palliata, while he preserved its popular comic character, which shrank from no coarseness (§ 9, 10). Of the two poets Pomponius appears to have been the more original and fertile.

1. MACROB. 1, 10, 3 *Novius, Atellanarum probatissimus scriptor*, and : *post Novium et Pomponium* (§ 10, 2). The same order is observed in Fronto (§ 144, 2); on the other hand VELLEIUS (see n. 4): *Pomp. . . . novitate inventi* etc. His praenomen is not known: frequent confusion with Naevius. *Novianae Atellaniolae* were excerpted by M. Aurelius according to FRONTO p. 34 Nab. Fragments (43 titles) in MUNK, fab. Atell. 165; cf. 117. RIBBECK, com.[2] 254.

2. Subjects of Novius: personae oscae (Duo Dossenni; Maccus copo, exul; Mania medica; Pappus praeteritus), classes and trades (Agricola, Bubulcus, Ficitor, Vindemiatores; Bubulcus cerdo, Fullones; Milites, Optio, Hetaera), country clowns (Milites Pometinenses), literary (v. 5. 26. 38. 67. 116, perhaps also a burlesque Phoenissae), mythological parodies (Hercules coactor). The titles Dotata (Dotalis?), Gallinaria, Lignaria, Tabellaria, Togularia, are apparently in the style of the old Palliata, while the Paedium is like the new Palliata. Besides this Exodium is also noteworthy (§ 6, 4); Mortis et vitae iudicium; Malivoli, Parcus, Surdus.

3. The farcical character and obscene jokes, frequent alliterations and popular forms and constructions, nay even the metres are common to Novius and Pomponius (n. 5). The comparative frequency of similes from child-life is peculiar to Novius (v. 41. 62. 65).

4. HIERON. ad Euseb. Chr. ad a. Abr. 1928=a. 665/89: *L. Pomponius Bononiensis, Atellanarum scriptor, clarus habetur.* VELLEI. 2, 9, 6 *sane non ignoremus eadem aetate* (as Valerius Antias and others) *fuisse Pomponium, sensibus celebrem, verbis rudem et novitate inventi a se operis commendabilem.* MACR. 6, 9, 4 *Pomponius, egregius Atellanarum poeta.* Cf. FRONTO, p. 62 (see § 144, 2). SEN. contr. 7, 3, 9 *auctorem huius vitii quod ex captione unius verbi plura significantis nascitur aiebat* (Cassius Severus) *Pomponium Atellanarum scriptorem fuisse.* EMUNK, de fab. Atell. (Lps. 1840) 93. PRE. 5, 1876. His fragments (70 titles) in MUNK, fab. At. 134. RIBBECK, com.[2] 225. Chronology: reckoning by victoriati; MOMMSEN, RG. 2^6, 439.

5. Subjects besides the Oscan figures (Bucco auctoratus, adoptatus; hirnea Pappi, Pappus agricola, praeteritus, sponsa Pappi; Maccus, Macci gemini, Maccus

miles, sequester, virgo) especially classes (Rustici, Fullones, Leno, Pictores, Piscatores, Pistor, Praeco, Medicus, and others), various tribes (Campani, Galli, Transalpini), satire political (Petitor, Pappus praeteritus, Praefectus morum) and sacerdotal (Aeditumus, Aruspex, Augur; Decuma fullonis); literary (Philosophia; cf. v. 83. 138. 181), also (perhaps as burlesques) mythological subjects (Agamemno suppositus, Marsya, and probably Atalanta, Sisyphos, Ariadne, VAHLEN, RhM. 16, 473, and perhaps Atreus). From animals are derived the titles Asina[ria], Capella, Vacca, Verres aegrotus (and salvos?), perhaps also Pecus rusticum (MHERTZ, JJ. 107, 339). Finally a play called Satura (§ 6, 2. 95, 9. 144, 3; this is also alluded to in NON. 112, 9 *Pomponius . . . saturarum*). Several titles are like those of palliatae (Adelphi, Synephebi, Syri, Dotata). Personal allusions v. 15. Intrigues of a very coarse description, e.g. girl's disguise, v. 57 sqq. 67 sq.; Maccus virgo; Nuptiae; Prostibulum. There are many obscene jokes and other immoral passages; puns and frequent alliteration; proverbs and other characteristics of a popular style. Metres: iambic senarii and septenarii, trochaic septenarii, and also (v. 164 sq.) cretics. Cf. on Novius and Pomponius RIBBECK, röm. Dicht. 1, 210.

6. Doubtless to an Atellana belonged the fragment ap. VARRO LL. 6, 68 *hos* (the rustici) *imitans Aprissius* (?) *ait 'io bucco, quis me iubilat? vicinus antiquus tuus.'*

152. The principal orators of this period are M. Antonius (a. 611/143–667/87), and L. Licinius Crassus (a. 614/140–663/91); the first was a self-taught man, who owed everything to his excellent memory, natural vivacity and quick imagination, and whose chief merit lay in his brilliant delivery. Crassus, a man of acute intellect, and juridical training, was for this very reason less taking as an orator than Antonius, though effective through his lucid exposition, and the charm of his genial wit and elegant language.

1. M. Antonius, M. f. M. n. (thus on a fragm. of the consular fasti, Ephem. epigr. 4, 253), born 611/143 (CIC. Brut. 161; cf. de or. 2, 364), praetor 651/103, consul 655/99, censor 657/97, killed by the partisans of Marius 667/87; see JASÖDERHOLM, de M. Antonio et L. Crasso oratoribus rom., Helsingf. 1853. PRE. 1^2, 1169. OENDERLEIN, de M. Antonio oratore, Lps. 1882. His style is described (besides de oratore, where he and Crassus are the two principal speakers) esp. CIC. Brut. 139–142 (cf. 207. 215. 301. 304), e.g.: *erat memoria summa, nulla meditationis suspicio . . . verba ipsa non illa quidem elegantissimo sermone . . . sed tamen in verbis et eligendis . . . et collocandis . . . nihil non ad rationem et tamquam ad artem dirigebat; verum multo magis hoc idem in sententiarum ornamentis et conformationibus. . . . actio singularis . . . gestus erat . . . cum sententiis congruens . . . vox permanens, verum subrauca natura. sed hoc vitium . . . in bonum convertebat. habebat enim flebile quiddam in questionibus aptumque cum ad fidem faciendam tum ad misericordiam commovendam.* As the general result CIC. Tusc. 5, 55 states: *omnium eloquentissimus quos ego viderim.* Cf. de or. 1, 172 *Antonii incredibilis quaedam . . . vis ingenii videtur, etiamsi scientia iuris nudata sit, posse se facile ceteris armis prudentiae tueri.*

2. M. Antonius purposely did not publish his speeches, of which that for

M'. Aquilius (a. 656/98) seems to have been the most famous, not merely (though he himself used to allege this as his reason) on account of lawyerlike shrewdness (§ 44, 4), but rather from the knowledge that they could not possibly produce the same effect when read as when heard. By mere chance, he published a small work de ratione dicendi of not much significance; see Cic. or. 18. Brut. 163. Quint. 3, 1, 19 (*hoc solum opus eius, atque id ipsum imperfectum, manet*). 3, 6, 45. A quotation from it is given by Cic. de or. 1, 94. orat. 18. Quint. 8. prooem. 13. 12, 1, 21. Plin. ep. 5, 20, 5. For notices on the speeches of Antonius see in HMeyer oratt. fragm.[2] 280.

3. L. Licinius L. f. C. n. (Ephem. epigr. 4, 253) Crassus, born (614/140, Cic. Brut. 161), made his début as orator a. 635 (*annos natus XXI*, Cic. de or. 3, 74; wrongly *XIX* in Tac. dial. 34; see KNipperdey, op. 323), a pupil of Caelius Antipater (§ 137, 5, l. 9); 636/118 leader of the colony to Narbo Martius, cos. 659/95, censor 662/92, in which office he took part in the expulsion of the rhetores latini (§ 44, 9), Cic. de or. 3, 93. Tac. dial. 35, † 663/91. PRE. 4, 1058, 18. Söderholm (n. 1). MÖtte, de L. Licinio Crasso, Lps. 1873.

4. The description given of Crassus by Cicero is less trustworthy, owing to Cicero's evident desire to identify himself with him, just as he also imitated him in the comedy of his Cilician triumph. This identification is pushed so far as to attribute to Crassus (2, 142, cf. 1, 190) even the intention of writing a work de iure civili in artem redigundo. In the same manner 1, 154 those exercises in style are attributed to him which Cicero himself went through in his youth (cf. Quint. 10, 5, 2). Especially the importance attached to the necessity of varied culture in an orator (e.g. 1, 156 sqq.) is due to this motive, as in reality we have no reason for assuming that Crassus in this respect differed materially from Antonius and other noblemen of his time. The description in Brut. 143–145. 148. 158–165 is much more probable; e.g. 143 *erat summa gravitas, erat cum gravitate iunctus facetiarum et urbanitatis . . . lepos; latine loquendi accurata et sine molestia diligens elegantia; in disserendo mira explicatio; cum de iure civili, cum de aequo et bono disputaretur, argumentorum et similitudinum copia.* 145 *ut eloquentium iurisperitissimus Crassus, iurisperitorum eloquentissimus Scaevola* (§ 154, 1) *putaretur.* 158 *vehemens et interdum irata et plena iusti doloris oratio . . . idem et perornatus et perbrevis.* 159 *iam in altercando invenit parem neminem. versatus est in omni fere genere causarum.* 162 *quin etiam comprehensio et ambitus ille verborum* (his sentences) *. . . erat apud illum contractus et brevis, et in membra quaedam, quae κῶλα Graeci vocant, dispertiebat orationem libentius* (cf. orat. 223). Tac. dial. 18 *Graccho politior et ornatior Crassus.* 26 *C. Gracchi impetum aut L. Crassi maturitatem.* Macrob. Sat. 5, 1, 16 *sunt stili duo; . . . unus est maturus et gravis, qualis Crasso adsignatur . . . alter huic contrarius, ardens et erectus et infensus, quali est usus Antonius.*

5. Published speeches of Crassus. Cic. or. 132 *Crassi perpauca sunt, nec ea iudiciorum.* Brut. 160 *orationis eius* (for the Vestal virgin Licinia, a. 641/113) *scriptas quasdam partes reliquit. . . . exstat in eam legem* (de colonia Narbonem deducenda) *. . . oratio.* 161 *haec Crassi* (pro lege Servilia) *cum edita oratio est* (a. 648/106), *. . . XXXIV tum habebat annos.* 162 *est etiam L. Crassi in consulatu* (a. 659/95) *pro Q. Caepione . . . non brevis ut laudatio, ut oratio autem brevis. postrema censoris oratio. in his omnibus inest quidam sine ullo fuco veritatis color.* 163 *vellem plura Crasso libuisset scribere.* 164 *multa in illa oratione* (pro lege Servilia) *. . . dicta sunt, plura etiam dicta quam scripta, quod ex quibusdam capitibus expositis nec explicatis intellegi potest. ipsa illa censoria contra Cn. Domitium collegam non est oratio, sed quasi capita rerum et orationis commentarium paulo

plenius. Cf. § 44, 7. MÖTTE l.l. 41. The simplicity of his style was not acceptable to later rhetoricians. Only through Cicero have a few passages from his speeches been preserved; see HMEYER, oratorum fragm.[2] p. 291. These specimens exhibit frequent use of anaphora and rhetorical questions and, as they are quoted on account of their vivacity, give an idea of Crassus' oratory from this side alone.

153. In addition to these two eminent orators this period possessed good speakers in the jurist Q. Scaevola (cos. 659/95) and L. Marcius Philippus (cos. 663/91); among the younger men the most eminent orators were L. Julius Caesar Strabo, who also wrote tragedies, C. Aurelius Cotta (cos. 679/75) and P. Sulpicius Rufus, besides whom we should also mention C. Scribonius Curio (cos. 678/76).

1. For Scaevola, see § 154, 1.

2. L. Marcius Philippus, born c. 610/144, cos. 663/91, censor 668/86, died after 677/77. PRE. 4, 1538. CIC. Brut. 173 *duobus summis, Crasso et Antonio, L. Philippus proxumus accedebat, sed longo intervallo tamen proxumus. . . . erat in Philippo . . . summa libertas in oratione, multae facetiae; . . . erat . . . graecis doctrinis institutus, in altercando cum aliquo aculeo et maledicto facetus* (cf. 166). As he used to improvise (CIC. de or. 2, 316) we know only a few dicta of his quoted from mere recollection, ap. CIC. off. 2, 73. de or. 3, 2. Sallust (hist. I) makes him deliver a speech against Lepidus (a. 676/78 sq.).

3. C. Iulius L. f. Caesar Strabo (CIL. 1, p. 278, IV, also Sesquiculus and Vopiscus, MAR. VICTOR. GL. 6, 8. VARRO RR. 1, 7, 10. CIC. Phil. 11, 11), aed. cur. (a. 664/90; CIC. Brut. 305. ASCON. p. 24 Or. [p. 22 K-S.], therefore born about 634/120); quaestor tr. mil. bis, Xvir agr. dand. adtr., iud., pontif. (according to the elogium CIL. l. l.), a. 667/87 killed by the partisans of Marius with his elder brother Lucius (cos. 664/90). CIC. Brut. 177 *festivitate et facetiis C. Iulius L. f. et superioribus et aequalibus suis omnibus praestitit, oratorque fuit minume ille quidem vehemens, sed nemo umquam urbanitate, nemo lepore, nemo suavitate conditior* (cf. de or. 2, 98. off. 1, 133. TUSC. 5, 55). *sunt eius aliquot orationes, ex quibus, sicut ex eiusdem tragoediis, lenitas eius sine nervis perspici potest.* de or. 3, 30 *novam quandam rationem attulit orationis. . . . res . . . tragicas paene comice, tristes remisse, severas hilare, forenses scenica prope venustate tractavit.* ASCON. l.l.: *idem inter primos temporis sui oratores et tragicus poeta bonus admodum habitus est. huius sunt enim tragoediae, quae inscribuntur Iuli.* Of the latter we know the titles Adrastus, Teuthras, Tecmessa; WELCKER, trag. 1398. RIBBECK trag.[2] 227: röm. Trag. 610. Cf. § 134, 3. The fragments of his speeches in MEYER[2] 330. PRE. 4, 426, 8.

4. C. Aurelius M. f. Cotta, born c. 630/124 (CIC. Brut. 301), 663/91–672/82 in exile, cos. 679/75, † 680/74 PRE. 1[2], 2164, 10. CIC. Brut. 182 *aetate inferiores paulo quam Iulius, sed aequales propemodum fuerunt C. Cotta, P. Sulpicius, Q. Varius, Cn. Pomponius* (cf. ib. 221. 308; on the other hand see de or. 3, 50), *C. Curio* (n. 6), *C. Carbo* (praetor 669/85, † 672/82; Brut. 221), *L. Fufius* (Brut. 222), *M. Drusus* (ib.), *P. Antistius* (ib. 226). . . . *ex his Cotta et Sulpicius cum meo iudicio tum omnium facile primas tulerunt.* See de or. 1, 30. or. 204. ASCON. p. 66 Or. (58 K–S.). CIC. Brut. 202 *inveniebat acute Cotta, dicebat pure ac solute. . . . nihil*

erat in eius oratione nisi sincerum, nihil nisi siccum atque sanum. (Cf. 317, or. 106. de or. 2, 98. 3, 31.) His interest in philosophy and adherence to the New Academy (and Antiochos) was in agreement with this methodical manner; see Cic. de deor. nat. 1, 16. 2, 1. de div. 1, 8. He did not publish any speeches (or. 132). *Cottae pro se lege Varia quae inscribitur, eam L. Aelius* (§ 148, 1) *scripsit Cottae rogatu*, Brut. 205; see 207 *Cottam miror, summum ipsum oratorem minumeque ineptum, Aelianas levis oratiunculas voluisse existumari suas.* Sallust (hist.) attributed to him an oratio ad populum rom. Meyer, oratt.[2] 339.

5. P. Sulpicius Rufus, a contemporary of the preceding, born c. 633/121, proscribed and killed by the party of Sulla as tr. pl. a. 666/88. PRE. 6, 1495, 35. Cic. Brut. 203 *fuit Sulpicius vel maxime omnium quos quidem ego audiverim grandis et, ut ita dicam, tragicus orator. vox cum magna tum suavis et splendida; gestus et motus corporis venustus; . . . incitata et volubilis, nec ea redundans tamen et circumfluens oratio. Crassum hic volebat imitari, Cotta malebat Antonium* (in accordance with Cicero's description of the rhetorical style of both one might feel tempted to reverse this); *sed ab hoc vis aberat Antoni, Crassi ab illo lepos.* Cf. de or. 1, 131. 2, 88. 96. 3, 31. de har. resp. 41. Brut. 205 (cf. or. 132) *Sulpici orationes quae feruntur, eas post mortem eius scripsisse P. Canutius putatur, aequalis meus, homo extra ordinem nostrum meo iudicio disertissimus. ipsius Sulpici nulla oratio est, saepeque ex eo audivi cum se scribere neque consuesse neque posse diceret.* On this Cannutius (the better spelling, Nipperdey, op. 307) Cic. Cluent 29. 50. 58. 73. 74; a fragment of the same ap. Prisc. GL. 2, 381, 12.

6. Cic. Brut. 207 *his duobus* (Cotta and Sulpicius) *eiusdem aetatis annumerabatur nemo tertius, sed mihi placebat* (Cn.) *Pomponius* (see n. 4) *maxume, vel dicam, minume displicebat.* 210 *erant tamen quibus videretur illius aetatis tertius Curio, quia splendidioribus fortasse verbis utebatur et quia latine non pessime loquebatur usu, credo, aliquo domestico. nam litterarum admodum nihil sciebat.* 213 sqq. See also there concerning his see-saw while speaking, which earned for him the nickname Burbuleius (Val. Max. 9, 14, 5. Plin. NH. 7, 55). Cf. § 136, 12. He is cited as *Curio pater* (cf. § 209, 1) ap. Prisc. GL. 2, 385, 11 and Plin. ind. auct. to b. 3 (geography). This C. Scribonius was tr. pl. 664/90, cos. 678/76, and died 701/53; PRE. 6, 879, 11. He was a bitter enemy of Caesar (Suet. Jul. 9. 49. 50. 52) and composed against him a political pamphlet in the form of a dialogue; see Cic. Brut. 218. He was also pontifex maximus; hence Varro's Logistoricus Curio de cultu deorum.

7. Cic. Brut. 174 *horum* (Antonius, Crassus, Philippus) *aetati prope coniunctus L. Gellius . . . nec erat indoctus . . . nec romanarum rerum immemor et verbis solutus satis. sed in magnos oratores inciderat eius aetas . . . ita diu vixit* (about a. 615/139–700/54) *ut multorum aetatum oratoribus implicaretur.* Cf. ib. 105 (*familiaris noster L. Gellius*). He was cos. 682/72, censor 684/70. PRE. 3, 662. LSchwabe, quaestt, catull. 112.

8. Besides those already named Cicero in his Brutus mentions a great number of those who were public speakers (*qui tantum in dicentium numero, non in oratorum, fuerunt*, 176) or only *clamatores* (182). He might have quoted nearly all those whose names appeared in the lists of magistracy, but he is somewhat careless as to chronological order, and only pours out his store of names, adding little to characterise them, e.g. 165 sq. 168 sq. 175 178–180. Those deserve most to be mentioned who in this period *apud socios et Latinos oratores habiti sunt* (169), viz. *Q. Vettius Vettianus e Marsis, Q. et D. Valerii Sorani* (see § 147, 1 in fin.), *C. Rusticelius Bononiensis*, and especially *omnium eloquentissimus extra hanc urbem T.*

Betutius Barrus Asculanus, cuius sunt aliquot orationes Asculi habitae et illa Romae contra Caepionem (§ 136, 10 in fin.) *nobilis sane, cui orationi Caepionis ore respondit Aelius* (§ 148, 1), Brut. 169. Ib. 304 are styled *oratores non illi quidem principes L. Memmius* (cf. ib. 136. 247) *et Q. Pompeius, sed oratores tamen.* The latter, *Q. Pompeius Rufus* (cos. 666/88) *etiam ipse scripsit eas* (*orationes*) *quibus pro se est usus, sed non sine Aelio* (ib. 206). Perhaps Prisc. GL. 2, 385, 10 may be a quotation from this.

154. Next to oratory, jurisprudence, a science in direct connection with it, showed most life in this time. It was brilliantly represented by the pontifex Q. Scaevola (cos. 659/95), one of the most pleasing Roman characters, accurate, varied and liberal, the ideal of a lawyer, to which vocation he devoted his life, as an advocate, adviser, teacher and writer; he was free from pedantry, eloquent, and of unyielding honour and unstained probity. He was the first to undertake a systematical treatise on jurisprudence, which was used and imitated by all subsequent writers. Independently of his writings, his memory was kept alive by his numerous pupils, among whom Lucilius Balbus and Aquilius Gallus were the most important. Side by side with him Sex. Pompeius, Aculeo, and Q. Cornelius Maximus were especially famous as jurists.

1. Q. Mucius P. f. (son of the one mentioned § 133, 4) P. n. Scaevola, friend of the orator L. Crassus (§ 152, 3) and his colleague in all his offices (e.g. in the consulship 659/95), excepting the censorship and the tribuneship; killed by the party of Marius a. 672/82; see SWZimmern, Privatrecht 1, 1, 284. PRE. 5, 184, 11. From his uncle of the same name (§139, 3) he was distinguished by the designation of pontifex maximus, e.g. Ascon. p. 67 Or. 59 K-S. *Q. Mucium Scaevolam pontificem max. eundemque et oratorem et iurisconsultum significat.* L. Crassus ap. Cic. de or. 1, 180 styles him *aequalis et ingenio prudentiaque acutissimus et oratione maxime limatus . . . atque, ut ego soleo dicere, iuris peritorum eloquentissimus, eloquentium iuris peritissimus.* His style was remarkable for perspicuity, elegance and conciseness; see Cic. de or. 1, 229. Brut. 145. 148. 163 (*Scaevolae dicendi elegantiam satis ex iis orationibus quas reliquit habemus cognitam*). Just as in the passages where Scaevola alone is mentioned and in a way almost proverbial (e.g. Hor. E. 2, 2, 89), we are justified in fixing on him especially as the most famous person of that name, he might also be that Scaevola whom Quint. 11, 2, 38 mentions on account of his strong memory. His anxiety for a systematic description of the ius civile, especially his work περὶ ὅρων (n. 2 in fin.), renders it probable that he adhered to the Stoa and that he was actually the *doctissimus pontifex* (maximus) *Scaevola* whose Stoic threefold division of the gods (poetical, philosophical and political gods) and other freethinking opinions on popular religion are quoted by Augustin. de civ. dei 4, 27 on Varro's authority; see EZeller, Vortr. u. Abhh. 2 (Lpz. 1877) 119: where, however, such opinions as these should not have been accounted for by the licence given for their publication, but rather as reflecting the constant candour and firm character of Scaevola.

2. Pompon. dig. 1, 2, 2, 41 *Q. Mucius, P. f. pontifex maximus, ius civile primus*

constituit, generatim in libros XVIII redigendo. See Gell. 6, 15, 2 *Q. Scaevola in librorum quos de iure civili composuit XVI°.* For the first time we meet here with a comprehensive, uniform and methodical system, in the place of the old interpretation of laws and casuistry, of legal opinions and precedents. See AFRudorff, röm. Rechtsgesch. 1, 161. OKarlowa, röm. RGesch. 1, 481. Cf. MVoigt, Abh. d. Sächs. Ges. d. W. 7, 337 (t. 1, attempted reproduction of the plan of the work). It was based on the purely Roman theory of the right of freely disposing of one's possessions, by a last will and among the survivors (*uti legassit super familia tutelave, ita ius esto*, dig. 50, 16, 120 comp. 122. Gell. 4. 1, 17. dig. 33, 9, 3 pr. 34, 2, 27 pr.), in succession to which the obligations arising from injuries and compacts were expounded (Gell. 6, 15, 2. dig. 17, 2, 30. 47, 2, 76, 1), and the system of legal prosecution (dig. 19, 5, 11); see Rudorff l.l. 161 sq. His work remained the basis of the legal works of the next period, which supplemented, developed and amended it. Cf. § 49, 6. Ser. Sulpicius e.g. wrote Notata Mucii (dig. 17, 2, 30 cf. Gell. 4, 1, 20 *in reprehensis Scaevolae capitibus.* Gai. Inst. 188. 3, 149), Laelius Felix Ad Q. Mucium (Gell. 15, 27, 1. 4), Gaius (1, 188) Ex Q. Mucio, and Sex. Pomponius (§ 350, 8) Ad Q. Mucium lectionum libri XXXIX; the latter work being frequently made use of in the pandects instead of Q. Mucius himself; it should no doubt also be understood dig. 41, 1, 53 sq. (Zimmern l.l. 287, n. 28). Besides this great work, Scaevola wrote also a Compendium, liber singularis Ὅρων (definitionum), probably a critical collation of regulae juris, four times quoted in the pandects (dig. 41, 1, 64. 43, 20, 8. 50, 16, 241. 50, 17, 73; cf. 35, 1, 7 pr. *Muciana cautio*), as the oldest work used there.—The fragments in EHuschke's iurispr.[5] 13.—ASchneider (§ 133, 4 ad fin.) 22.

3. Pompon. dig. 1, 2, 2. 42 *Mucii auditores fuerunt complures, sed praecipuae auctoritatis Aquilius Gallus, Balbus Lucilius, Sex. Papirius, G. Iuventius. . . . omnes tamen hi a Ser. Sulpicio nominantur, alioquin per se eorum scripta non talia exstant ut ea omnes appetant; denique nec versantur omnino scripta eorum inter manus hominum, sed Servius (eis) libros suos complevit.* Of these Gallus (§ 174, 1) certainly belongs to the Ciceronian period, Cicero himself having for some time attended the responsa of this (§ 139, 3) Q. Scaevola also (Lael. 1). Sex. Papirius and C. Iuventius are not known from other passages, though in Cic. Brut. 178 a certain T. Iuventius is noticed for his dry style of speaking; while at the same time is attributed to him *magna iuris civilis intelligentia.* L. Lucilius Balbus, *doctus et eruditus homo*, thoughtful, but slow (Cic. Brut. 154), was the former master of Ser. Sulpicius (§ 174, 2).

4. Other jurists besides Scaevola were Antipater (§ 137, 5), Q. Tubero (§ 139, 2) and Rutilius Rufus (142, 2), also Q. Lucretius Vispillo (*in privatis causis et acutus et iurisperitus*, Cic. Brut. 178) and Paulus (Pompon. l.l. 40: Cic. Lael. 101 more correctly has Aulus) Virginius, then Volcatius, the teacher of A. Cascellius (Plin. NH. 8, 144; cf. Mommsen on the dig. 1, 2, 2, 45), and probably also C. Sextius Calvinus (§ 141, 6), Pontidius (Cic. de or. 2, 275), and M. Buculeius (ib. 1, 179).

5. Sex. Pompeius, *Gnaei Pompei* (Magni) *patruus* (Pompon. dig. 1, 2, 2. 40); *praestantissimum ingenium contulerat ad summam iuris civilis et ad perfectam geometriae et rerum stoicarum scientiam* (Cic. Brut. 175 cf. de or. 1, 67. 3, 78. off. 1, 19).—Who is the Pompeius Sextus quoted (for old Lat. *numero = nimium*?) in Fest. 170[a], 25?

6. The Roman knight C. (Visellius) Aculeo (PRE. 6, 2679, 1 and 2), the friend of the orator L. Crassus (Cic. de or. 2, 2), according to Cic. de or. 1, 191, understood *ita ius civile ut ei* (except Q. Scaevola) *nemo de iis qui peritissimi sunt anteponatur*, and bequeathed his legal knowledge to his son C. Visellius Varro; Brut. 264. The

latter is here also praised as an orator; a fragment from one of his speeches ap. Prisc. GL. 2, 386, 7.

7. Q. Cornelius Maximus, known only as the teacher of Trebatius Testa (§ 207, 3), and from Cic. fam. 7, 17, 3 (*idem Q. Cornelio videbatur*, cf. ib. 7, 8, 2). See also Gai. Inst. 1, 136 (*Maximus*). dig. 33, 7, 16, 1 (*Cornelius*).

155. Among the Annalists of these ten years Q. Claudius Quadrigarius made a step in advance in that, passing over the early legendary tradition, he began his Roman history with the invasion of the Gauls. In other ways also he shows himself superior to Valerius Antias. The latter indeed in his very extensive work is the most important immediate predecessor of Livy, but with his wilful exaggeration both in descriptions and numerical statements, and his efforts to glorify his own family, he prominently represents the manner of the later Annalists. There is no trace of antiquarianism in his work. Cn. Aufidius again wrote his historical work in Greek.

1. Vellei. 2, 9, 6 *aequalis Sisennae Claudius Quadrigarius* (see n. 2). The person of Cl. is unknown. The name Quadrigarius, which cannot have been a proper Roman cognomen, does not occur in Livy but in Velleius, Seneca and later writers, and is probably a sort of literary nickname (conjectures as to its meaning ap. Unger l.l. 12; Mommsen, röm. Forsch. 2, 426). Gellius is the authority for Annales as the title of his chief work. As regards the number of books, the highest figure cited is *Q. Claudius in XXIII annali* ap. Gell. 10, 13, 4. The fragments of the first book prove that it treated of the conquest of Rome by the Gauls. This commencement of his work decidedly bears witness to the critical insight of the author, which is shown elsewhere, as well as to his attention to chronology and to internal affairs. In the description of battles (cf. n. 3) he does indeed quote in enormously high numbers the losses of the enemy (Liv. 33, 10, 9. 38, 23, 8. Oros. 5, 3, 2. 5, 20, 6), but this no doubt is not to be attributed merely to the historian, but chiefly to the exaggerated accounts of generals. (In contrast with the large numbers of the dead, observe the small numbers of prisoners—because this could be checked: Liv. 36, 19, 12. 36, 38, 8. 40, 28, 6. 40, 33, 6.) Cf. Unger l.l. 17. — In harmony with analogous work he seems to have carried his to his own period; book XIX treated of Sulla's war against Archelaos and Marius' seventh consulate (a. 667/87). The latest certain date is a. 672/82 ap. Oros. 5, 20 (*Claudius historicus*). The first book related the second war with the Samnites (at least down to a. 434/320), the third book gave the first, while books 5 and 6 gave the second Punic war. Hence the treatment of the subjects must have been very unequal: at first a mere summary of events, but gradually expanding as the writer approached his own time, embodying even speeches and, no doubt, entire letters (Gell. 1, 7, 9. 3, 8, 8). The narrative was lengthy even in details. The diction was archaic, the sentences full of bulky words, but short and close and crowded together without any adjustment, therefore very much to the taste of the time of Fronto; see Fronto ap. Gell. 13, 29, 2 *vir modesti atque puri ac prope cotidiani sermonis*, and ep. p. 114, 3 *historiam scripsere . . . Claudius lepide, Antias invenuste, Sisenna longinque.* Gell. 15, 1, 4 *Q. Claudi, optumi et sincerissimi scriptoris;* 9, 13, 4 *Q. Claudius . . . purissime atque inlustrissime simplicique et incompta orationis antiquae suavitate descripsit.*

Dionysius of Halicarnassus does not mention him; Livy quotes him ten times, sometimes differing from him. He seems to have made use of him, together with Val. Ant., esp. in the second half of the first decade, and in the fourth and fifth decades. See Unger l.l. We owe most of the fragments to Gellius; these are collected in HPeter, hist. rell. 1, 205; fragm. 136.—Quadrigarius is probably also the *Claudius qui Annales Acilianos ex graeco in latinum sermonem vertit* ap. Livy 25, 39, 12 (see § 127, 2). This translation and the Annales of Cl. must not be taken for one and the same work, as the Annales of Cl. begin with the incursion of the Gauls, while those of Acilius commenced with the foundation of Rome. At the most it may be doubted whether, on the ground of Liv. 25, 39, 12, we must suppose a 'translation' by Claudius of the work of Acilius, or whether we may not take this passage as well as Liv. 35, 14, 5 as referring to the employment of the Greek Annales of Acilius in the Latin Annales of Cl. Cf. HPeter, JJ. 125, 104. LCantarelli, riv. di fil. 12, 1.—Plutarch also Num. 1 Κλώδιός τις ἐν ἐλέγχῳ χρόνων —οὕτω γάρ πως ἐπιγέγραπται τὸ βιβλίον—κτλ, since he is referring to the loss of the older records ἐν τοῖς Κελτικοῖς πάθεσι τῆς πόλεως, probably means Cl. Quadr. (notwithstanding Appian. Gall. 1, p. 36 Bkk. ἐν χρονικαῖς συντάξεσι δοκεῖ Παύλῳ τῷ Κλαυδίῳ). Perhaps this treatise may have contained a chronological foundation and justification of the statements in the Annales? The Clodius mentioned in Cic. leg. 1, 6 (§ 37, 5) as a successor of Antipater is probably also to be identified with Cl. Quadr. See Unger l.l. 11.—On Claudius see Giesebrecht, über Q. Cl. Quadr., Prenzlau 1831. Nissen, krit. Unters. 39. HPeter, hist. rell. 1. ccxlv. cclxxxvii. ccxcviii. CFUnger, Phil. Suppl. 3, 2, 4 sqq.

2. Valerius Antias (probably descended from the L. Valerius Antias mentioned by Liv. 23, 34, 9), the author of a work called sometimes Annales, sometimes Historiae (or Historia) in at least 75 books (book 75 is quoted by Gell. 6, 9, 17; book 74 by Priscian, GL. 2, 489), beginning with the earliest history of Rome (Gell. 7, 7, 6; the second book treated of Numa, the 22nd of the sponsio of Ti. Gracchus, 618/136), reaching as far as the time of Sulla (for he mentioned the heirs of the orator M. Crassus, who died a. 663/91, Plin. NH. 34, 14). We have no exact information with regard to the date of Valerius. MVoigt, Abh. d. sächs. Ges. d. Wiss. 7, 776 maintains that Valerius did not compose his work until about 709/45, but this is contradicted by Vell. 2, 9, 6: *Vetustior Sisenna* (§ 156, 1) *fuit Caelius* (§ 137, 5), *aequalis Sisennae Rutilius* (§ 142, 3) *Claudiusque Quadrigarius* (above n. 1) *et Valerius Antias. Sane non ignoremus eadem aetate fuisse Pomponium* (§ 151, 4), etc.—Dionys. Hal. mentions him 2, 13 and 1, 7 (see § 37, 5) among the ἐπαινούμενοι of the Roman historians, and has taken much from him (e.g. what tends to the glorification of the Valerii); AKiessling, de Dionys. Hal. auct. 20. MVoigt l.l. 685. 777. Plutarch's Poplicola also seems to be drawn chiefly from him (HPeter, die Quellen Plut. 45 and hist. rell. 1, cccxviii), as also the elogium of M'. Valerius Maximus (OHirschfeld, Phil. 34, 87). Among Latin authors besides Liv. (see n. 3), Plin. NH. especially made use of him according to the ind. auct. in 9 books.—Fronto p. 114 *Historiam scripsere. . . . Antias invenuste* (§ 37, 5).

3. We known Val. Ant. however, chiefly through Livy, who mentions him more frequently (in 35 places in the existing books) and makes more use of him than of any of his predecessors, and even seems to have adopted from him the general plan of his work. In the first decades he follows him unhesitatingly and hence not only cites his exaggerated number of citizens (at the lustra), but is even confident as to 30,000 killed 7, 36, 13; 7, 37, 16 he speaks of *ad quadraginta milia*

scutorum; 9, 27, 14 *ad triginta milia caesa aut capta;* 9, 43, 17 *triginta milibus hostium caesis;* 9, 37, 11 even *caesa aut capta eo die hostium milia ad sexaginta* etc. Only 3, 5, 12 he has the modest observation: *difficile ad fidem est, in tam antiqua re, quot pugnaverint ceciderintve exacto adfirmare numero; audet tamen Antias Valerius concipere summas.* Cf. 3, 8, 10. But in the less obscure periods, where better sources were available (e.g. Polybios), Livy discovers the inaccuracy and bombast of his authority whom he has so far followed almost blindly, and now blames him with all the more bitterness of feeling, since the errors into which he had been led by Valerius could not be rectified, as he had already published the books in question (decades). In books 21–25 he never actually mentions his name (although he appears to have made use of him), but at 26, 49, 3 we read: *scorpiones maiores minoresque ad LX captos scripserim si auctorem graecum sequar Silenum, si Valerium Antiatem, maiorum scorpionum sex milia, minorum tredecim: adeo nullus mentiendi modus est.* 30, 19, 11 *Valerius Antias quinque milia hostium caesa ait. quae tanta res est ut aut impudenter ficta sit* (by Antias) *aut neglegenter* (by others) *praetermissa.* 36, 38, 6 *duodetriginta milia hostium caesa Antias Valerius scribit, capta tria milia et quadringentos, signa militaria CXXIV, equos MCCXXX . . . ubi ut in numero scriptori parum fidei sit, quia in augendo eo non alius intemperantior est, magnam victoriam fuisse adparet.* 33, 10, 8 *si Valerio quis credat, omnium rerum immodice numerum augenti, quadraginta milia hostium eo die sunt caesa, capta, ubi modestius mendacium est, quinque milia septingenti.* 38, 23, 8 *Valerius Antias, qui magis* (than Claudius) *immodicus in numero augendo esse solet.* See also 39, 43, 1 *Valerius Antias, ut qui nec Catonis orationem legisset et fabulae tantum sine auctore editae credidisset.* Whenever, therefore, Valerius is the only authority for a statement, Livy frequently adds *si Valerio credamus* (*credas*) (36, 19, 12. 39, 41, 6. 44, 13, 12) or merely names his authority (38, 50, 5. 39, 22, 9. 39, 56, 7), sometimes with an express reservation, e.g. 37, 48, 1 (*Valerius Antias auctor est rumorem celebrem Romae fuisse . . . rumoris huius quia neminem alium auctorem habeo, neque adfirmata res mea opinione sit nec pro vana praetermissa*) and 45, 43, 8 (*HS ducenties ex ea praeda redactum esse auctor est Antias . . . quod quia unde redigi potuerit non apparebat auctorem pro re posui*). It must be admitted that Valerius' lies in numerical statements are grossly absurd, it being quite usual with him to have 40,000 enemies and more killed in a battle (Liv. 33, 10, 8. 33, 36, 13. 34, 15, 9. 36, 19, 12. Oros. 4, 20). But at Tolosa he surpassed himself by giving as the number of the slain even *octoginta milia Romanorum sociorumque, . . quadraginta milia calonum atque lixarum* (Oros. 5, 16). That exaggerations of this kind were deliberate fictions, appears also from the fact that he very often stands absolutely alone in his statements; see Gell. 6, 19, 8 *Valerius Antias contra decretorum memoriam contraque auctoritates veterum annalium dixit.* Cf. ib. 6, 8, 6. Liv. 32, 6, 5 *Valerius Antias tradit . . . XII milia hostium eo proelio caesa . . . ceteri graeci latinique auctores . . . nihil memorabile actum . . . tradunt.* On his biassed version of the prosecutions of the Scipios, due to his veneration for the elder Africanus, see Mommsen, röm. Forsch. 2, 491.—The fragments in HPeter, hist. rell. 1, 237; fragm. 151.—HLiebaldt, de Valerio Antiate, Naumb. 1840. Schwegler, RG. 1, 90. Nissen, krit. Untersuch. 43. HPeter, hist. rell. 1, cccv. KWNitzsch, d. röm. Annalistik (1873) 346. MVoigt, Abh. d. sächs. Ges. d. Wiss. 7, 776.—ThFriedrich, Biogr. des Barkiden Mago, ein Beitr. z. Krit. d. Val. Ant., Wien 1880.

4. Cic. Tusc. 5, 112 *Cn. Aufidius praetorius* (his praetorship must fall about 650/104) *pueris nobis* (therefore perhaps 660/94) *et in senatu sententiam dicebat nec amicis deliberantibus deerat et graecam scribebat historiam et videbat* (*vivebat* Bentley)

in litteris. fin. 5, 54 *equidem e Cn. Aufidio praetorio, erudito homine oculis capto, saepe audiebam.* He attained a great age (Cic. de dom. 35). CIG. 2349 b (ὑπὸ Γναίου Αὐφιδίου Γναίου υἱοῦ τοῦ ἀντιστρατήγου) from Adramyttium probably refers to his son (PRE. 1², 2128, 5). No fragments of this graeca historia have been preserved; but it undoubtedly contained the history of Rome. WHarless, de Fabiis et Aufidiis rerum rom. scriptoribus (Bonn 1853) 46.

156. L. Cornelius Sisenna (635/119–687/67), wrote a history of the times nearest his own, mainly the period of Sulla, in a stiff archaic style. In addition he translated the narratives of Aristeides of Miletus. But Sisenna the commentator on Plautus is to be distinguished from the historian. The friend of the latter, C. Licinius Macer, went back in his Annales to the oldest time and rectified the accounts of it in various places by a diligent study of the sources, though he was too rhetorical and perhaps also too much influenced by a predilection for his own gens.

1. Sisenna must have been born about 635/119 (Roth, l.l. p. 4), was praetor 676/78 (SC. de Asclepiade, CIL. 1, p. 110, στρατηγοῦ κατὰ πόλιν καὶ ἐπὶ ξένων Λευκίου Κορνηλίου ⟨. . . υἱοῦ⟩ Σισέννα, cf. Cic. Cornel. 1, 18 with Ascon. p. 74 Or. 66 K-S.) and died 687/67 in Crete, where he was Pompey's legate in the war with the pirates (Dio 36, 1 Κορνήλιος Σισέννας, cf. Appian. Mithr. 95 Λούκιος Σισιννᾶς). CLRoth, L. Sisennae vita, Bas. 1834. HPeter, hist. rell. 1, cccxxiii.

2. Vellei. 2, 9, 5 *historiarum* (OJahn, *milesiarum* (see n. 3) *auctor iam tum* (about 646/108) *Sisenna erat iuvenis; sed opus belli civilis* (*=socialis?* ARiese l.l. 54) *Sullanique post aliquot annos ab eo seniore editum est* (therefore probably not before 680/74). Cic. Brut. 228 *inferioris aetatis* (than P. Antistius) *erat proximus L. Sisenna, doctus vir et studiis optumis deditus, bene latine loquens* (see however n. 3), *gnarus reip., non sine facetiis, sed neque laboris multi nec satis versatus in causis* (but he defended† Chirtilius [thus the name is given by the MSS.: variously edited C. Hirtilius, Hirtuleius, Rutilius] according to Brut. 260, and a. 684/70 he pleaded in behalf of Verres, see Cic. Verr. acc. 2, 110. 4, 43 cf. 4, 33 *L. Sisenna, vir primarius;* the latter he defended together with Hortensius, whose friend he was, Sen. controv. 1, pr. 19 and below § 157, 4); *interiectusque inter duas aetates Hortensi et Sulpici nec maiorem consequi poterat et minori necesse erat cedere. huius omnis facultas ex historia ipsius perspici potest; quae cum facile omnis vincat superiores* (?), *tum indicat tamen quantum absit a summo quamque genus hoc scriptionis nondum sit satis latinis litteris illustratum.* de leg. 1, 7 *Sisenna, eius* (Macer) *amicus, omnes adhuc nostros scriptores . . . facile superavit. is tamen neque orator . . . umquam est habitus et in historia puerile quiddam consectatur, ut unum Clitarchum neque praeterea quemquam de Graecis legisse videatur.* This comparison with one of the wildest historians of Alexander the Great is significant, though perhaps not quite just to Sisenna. Sallust, Iug. 95, 2 *L. Sisenna optume et diligentissime omnium qui eas* (Sullae) *res dixere persecutus parum mihi libero ore locutus videtur.* Varro named after him the Logistoricus *Sisenna de historia* (§ 166, 2).

3. We may form some estimate of the plan of the work from the statement (in Gell. 12, 15, 2): *nos una aestate in Asia et Graecia gesta litteris idcirco continentia mandavimus ne vellicatim aut saltuatim scribendo lectorum animos impediremus.* The title was Historiae, and the work embraced at least 12 books; beyond this number

we have only an isolated quotation in Non. 468, 10 *Sisenna hist. lib. XXIII* (of the year 672/82). This number can hardly be correct: in book 6 the narrative was already brought down to 666/88; so according to this Sisenna would have taken up 17 books with the remaining six years! Beyond the year 664/90 we are led by only a few fragments which treat of the oldest time (Aeneas etc.), Serv. Aen. 1, 108. 242. 11, 316, and which probably formed part of a prooemium (after the manner of Sallust). The fragments contain much detailed description, and traces of speeches (especially in book 4) and digressions (philosophical passages in the spirit of Epicurus): hence the treatment appears to have been lengthy (*longinque*, Fronto above § 155, 1, l. 30). Most of the fragments refer to the Marsian war (cf. Cic. de div. 1, 99) and are found in Nonius, whose quotations (chiefly from books 3 and 4) give us some idea of the crotchety archaisms of Sisenna; cf. Cic. Brut. 259 *Sisenna quasi emendator sermonis usitati cum esse vellet non . . . deterreri potuit quo minus inusitatis verbis uteretur . . . ille familiaris meus recte loqui putabat esse inusitate loqui*, and Varro ap. Gell. 2, 25, 9 *Sisenna unus 'adsentio'* (not *adsentior*) *in senatu dicebat;* cf. Quint. 1, 5, 13. Tac. dial. 23. Collection in HPeter, hist. rell. 1, 277; fragm. 175.—ARiese, d. Geschichtsw. d. Sis., in d. Festschr. z. 24. Philol.-Vers. (Lpz. 1865) 53. ASchneider, de Sis. hist. reliquiis, Jena 1882. Cf. OJahn, Herm. 2, 233.—Sisenna is characterised as a man of the world after the taste of Sulla, by his translation of Aristeides' coarse stories (Μιλησιακά, see OJahn, RhM. 9, 628); Ovid. trist. 2, 443 *vertit Aristiden Sisenna, nec obfuit illi historiae* (his story) *turpes inseruisse iocos.* Fronto ep. p. 62 *scriptorum animadvertas particulatim elegantis . . . Sisennam in lascivis.* Ten passages from book 13 of this work are to be found in Charisius (b. 2). Also in Peter's hist. rell. 297 and Bücheler's Petron.[3] 237.

As a commentator on Plautus a certain Sisenna is mentioned by Rufinus GL. 6, 560. 561 in his metrical notes: *Sisenna in commentario Poenuli Plautinae, Sisenna in Rudente, S. in Amphitryone, in Captivis, in Aulularia.* Quotations from Sisenna on the Amphitryo in Charisius GL. 1, 198, 26. 203, 27. 221, 6. 9. Cf. also ib. 107, 14. 120, 10. Peter, hist. rell. 297. This Sisenna is generally identified with the historian Sisenna, who would thus be the earliest commentator on Plautus. See Ritschl's Parerga 374. 376. 385. The preference of the historian (see above) for antiquated language might be considered to account for his occupying himself with Plautus; indeed it has been remarked (Ritschl l.l. 385) that, of the five fragments in Charisius, three treat of adverbs in -im, and that even in Sisenna's histories a preference is shown for such adverbia (Gell. 12, 15). But on the other hand it would be strange if such a person as the historian S. composed a series of commentaries on Plautus, especially as the extant specimens are very trivial. That in fact the Plautine S. is to be distinguished from the historian is shown by the fragment of the former in Charisius p. 221, 9 *Tractim Plautus in Amphitryone, ubi Sisenna 'pro lente' inquit 'non ut Maro georgicon IIII tractimque susurrant inquit,'* where, if we read it without prejudice, the quotation from Vergil evidently belongs to Sisenna. ThBergk, Phil. 29, 328 and FBücheler (lat. Deklin.[2], Bonn 1879, 123) distinguish between the two Sisennae; the latter, on account of the observation in Charis. p. 203, 27 (?), places the Plautine commentator in the period after Hadrian.—In general cf. concerning Sisenna Mommsen, RG. 3[6], 611. HPeter, hist. rell. 1, lii. cccxxviii.

4. C. Licinius L. f. Macer (on denarii of the time of Sulla, a. 670/84–673/81, see Mommsen, röm. Münzwesen 607; CIL. 1, p. 137. 434), the father of the orator and poet Calvus, who was born 672/82 (see § 213, 5), tr. pleb. 681/73, in which dignity Sallust (Hist.) attributed to him a speech ad populum; a. 688/66 he was charged with

extortions in his province, which he governed as propraetor, before the tribunal of Cicero who was then praetor, and being found guilty he committed suicide; PRE. 4, 1075, 1. Cic. Brut. 238 describes him as an orator in the following manner. *C. Macer auctoritate semper eguit, sed fuit patronus propemodum diligentissimus. huius si vita, si mores, si voltus denique non omnem commendationem ingeni everteret, maius nomen in patronis fuisset. non erat abundans, non inops tamen, non valde nitens, non plane horrida oratio; vox, gestus et omnis actio sine lepore; at in inveniendis componendisque rebus mira accuratio. . . . hic etsi etiam in publicis causis probabatur, tamen in privatis illustriorem obtinebat locum.*

5. In his judgment of Macer as a historian, Cicero's dislike of him appears even more strongly, de leg. 1, 7 *quid Macrum numerem? cuius loquacitas habet aliquid argutiarum, nec id tamen ex illa erudita Graecorum copia, sed ex librariolis latinis, in orationibus autem multa, sed inepta, elatio, summa impudentia.* This shows that Macer had embodied speeches (and perhaps letters, cf. Nonius 259 *Licinius Macer in epistola ad senatum,* unless this relates to Sallust's hist.) in his work, which seems to have been altogether diffuse. Livy's criticism 7, 9, 5 is of greater importance and credibility *quaesita ea propriae familiae laus leviorem auctorem Licinium facit. cum mentionem eius rei in vetustioribus annalibus nullam inveniam* etc., cf. also Dionys. 1, 7 (see § 37, 5). 6, 11 Λικίννιος καὶ οἱ περὶ Γέλλιον οὐδὲν ἐξητακότες οὔτε τῶν εἰκότων οὔτε τῶν δυνατῶν, and 7, 1 Λικίννιος καὶ Γέλλιος καὶ ἄλλοι συχνοὶ τῶν Ῥωμαίων συγγραφέων οὐδὲν ἐξητακότες τῶν περὶ τοὺς χρόνους ἀκριβῶς. His indifference to points of chronology would agree with the rhetorical character of the work. It is also very probable that the strong anti-aristocratic tendencies of the author manifested themselves in his work, though it does not seem to have treated of his own time. On the other hand, he drew directly from independent sources, unlike almost all his predecessors, though here he allowed himself to be misled by spurious documents. Cf. Liv. 4, 7, 12 *Licinius Macer auctor est et in foedere Ardeatino et in linteis libris* (see § 79, 3) *ad Monetae ea inventa.* 4, 20, 8 *quod tam veteres annales quodque magistratuum libros, quos linteos in aede repositos Monetae Macer Licinius citat identidem auctores.* 4, 23, 2 *in tam discrepante editione* (of the consuls) *et Tubero et Macer libros linteos auctores profitentur. neuter tribunos mil. eo anno fuisse traditum a scriptoribus antiquis dissimulat. Licinio libros haud dubie sequi linteos placet et Tubero incertus veri est.*

6. The title of Macer's work was no doubt Annales and, less accurately, Historiae. It certainly embraced the oldest time (Macrob. 1, 10, 17. Dionys. 2, 52; concerning the use made of Licinius by Dionys. Hal. see MVoigt, Abh. d. sächs. Ges. d. Wiss. 7, 756) and is mentioned by Livy (seven times) only in his first decade; the latest date, at which he mentions it, being a. 455/299. Even the number of the books is not known, reliable references being made only to books 1 and 2; then we have Priscian. GL. 2, 525, 3 *Aemilius Macer in XVI annalium: omnium* etc. (cf. Diomed. GL. 1, 369, 15 *Aemilius Macer: omnium* etc.), where it is just as probable that a confusion has taken place with Licinius Macer, as that the reverse has happened in Plin. NH. (see § 223, 7). Nonius 221, 11 *Licinius rerum romanarum lib. XXI* (neither the name nor the number can be relied upon) must be taken, as Hertz and others suppose, to refer to Clodius Licinius (§ 259, 6).—The fragments in HPeter, hist. rell. 1, 300; fragm. 190.—For one-sided praise of Macer see HLiebaldt, C. Licinius Macer, Naumb. 1848; for equally one-sided depreciation Mommsen, RG. 1^6, 434. 3^6, 613; cf. röm. Chronol.^{2} 88. 93 and röm. Forsch. 1, 315. Schwegler, RG. 1, 92 and HPeter, hist. rell. 1, cccxxxviii are more just. Cf. also KWNitzsch, röm. Annalistik 351.

157. Like Scaurus, Rutilius Rufus, and Catulus in the preceding epoch, the dictator L. Cornelius Sulla (a. 616/138–676/78) wrote an autobiography, commentarii rerum gestarum, in 22 books, which were after his death completed by his freedman Epicadus. Lucullus himself (a. 640/114–697/57), to whom these Memoirs were dedicated, wrote in his early years a history of the Marsian war, in Greek, and subsequently a certain C. Piso narrated the war between Sulla and Marius.

1. Sulla was cos. 666/88 and 674/80, dictator 672/82–675/79; † 676/78. PRE. 2, 669. ThLau, L. Cornelius Sulla, Hamb. 1855.

2. Plut. Lucull. 1 *Σύλλας τὰς αὑτοῦ πράξεις ἀναγράφων ἐκείνῳ* (Lucullus) *προσεφώνησεν*. Cf. ib. 4. Sull. 6. Sulla 37 *τὸ εἰκοστὸν καὶ δεύτερον τῶν ὑπομνημάτων πρὸ δυεῖν ἡμερῶν ἢ ἐτελεύτα γράφων ἐπαύσατο*. Suet. gramm. 12 *Cornelius Epicadus* (§ 159, 8) *L. Corneli Sullae dictatoris libertus calatorque in sacerdotio augurali, . . . librum quem Sulla novissimum de rebus suis imperfectum reliquerat* (therefore the others were completed) *ipse supplevit.* The title is given as *rerum gestarum* (Gellius) or *rerum suarum libri* (*de rebus suis*) or *commentarii* (*ὑπομνήματα*). *Sulla in XXI rerum suarum*, Priscian. GL. 2, 476. *In Sullae historia*, Cic. div. 1, 172. Sulla had taken pains in this work to exalt himself as a specially favoured protégé of the gods, and to disparage his opponents (esp. Marius). Plutarch has largely and incautiously availed himself of these Memoirs, esp. in his Lives of Sulla and Marius, and they have otherwise contributed to the detriment of historical truth; see HPeter, hist. rell. 1, cclxxvi. The fragments of the work ib. 1, 195; fragm. 127.

3. A Greek epigram by Sulla (on a statue of Aphrodite: two hexameters and a pentameter) ap. Appian. bell. civ. 1, 97.—Athen. 6, p. 261 C: *Νικόλαος* (Damasc.) *. . . Σύλλαν φησὶν . . . χαίρειν μίμοις καὶ γελωτοποιοῖς φιλογέλων γενόμενον . . . ἐμφανίζουσι δ' αὐτοῦ τὸ περὶ ταῦτα ἱλαρὸν αἱ ὑπ' αὐτοῦ γραφεῖσαι σατυρικαὶ κωμῳδίαι τῷ πατρίῳ φωνῇ* (cf. Plut. Sulla 2 and 36. Welcker, griech. Tragödien 1362). This statement arose perhaps from a mistaken representation of the fact, that under Sulla the Atellanae commenced to be written down; see § 10 and 151.

4. L. Licinius L. f. Lucullus (born c. 640/114, cos. 680/74, † 697/57; see his elogium in CIL. 1, p. 292. WDrumann, GR. 4, 120. PRE. 4, 1070): he possessed great mental culture. He was celebrated by *Cordubae nati poetae* (Cic. pArch. 26). Plut. Lucull. 1 *ὁ Λούκουλλος ἤσκητο καὶ λέγειν ἱκανῶς ἑκατέραν γλῶτταν, ὥστε καὶ Σύλλας* (see n. 2.) *. . . ἐκείνῳ προσεφώνησεν ὡς συνταξομένῳ καὶ διαθήσοντι τὴν ἱστορίαν ἄμεινον . . . λέγεται νέον ὄντα* (c. 666/88) *πρὸς Ὁρτήσιον τὸν δικολόγον καὶ Σισενναν τὸν ἱστορικὸν ἐκ παιδιᾶς τινος εἰς σπουδὴν προελθούσης ὁμολογῆσαι, προθεμένων ποίημα καὶ λόγον ἑλληνικόν τε καὶ ῥωμαϊκὸν, εἰς ὅ τι ἂν λάχῃ τούτων, τὸν Μαρσικὸν ἐκτελεῖν πόλεμον. καί πως ἔοικεν εἰς λόγον ἑλληνικὸν ὁ κλῆρος ἀφικέσθαι. διασώζεται γὰρ ἑλληνική τις ἱστορία τοῦ Μαρσικοῦ πολέμου.* Cf. Cic. Att. 1, 19, 10 *non dicam quod tibi ut opinor Panhormi Lucullus de suis historiis dixerat, se, quo facilius illas probaret romani hominis esse, idcirco barbara quaedam et σόλοικα dispersisse.* He never really employed his talents, nor did he ever attain to cultivated oratory, though Plut. Luc. 33 calls him *δεινὸς εἰπεῖν*. Cf. Cic. Brut. 222 (*oratorem acutum*) and Tac. dial. 37 (§ 171, 5).

5. He also took a certain interest in philosophy, cf. Plut. Luc. 1 *γενόμενος πρεσβύτερος ἤδη παντάπασιν . . . ἀφῆκε τὴν διάνοιαν ἐν φιλοσοφίᾳ σχολάζειν καὶ ἀναπαύεσθαι, τὸ θεωρητικὸν αὐτῆς ἐγείρας.* Cic. acad. pr. 2, 4 *maiore studio Lucullus cum omni litterarum generi tum philosophiae deditus fuit quamqui illum ignorabant*

arbitrabantur, nec vero ineunte aetate solum sed et pro quaestore aliquot annos et in ipso bello. . . . cum autem e philosophis . . . putaretur Antiochus, Philonis auditor, excellere, eum secum et quaestor habuit (a. 667/87 sq.) *et post aliquot annos imperator. . . . delectabatur autem mirifice lectione librorum de quibus audiebat.* Cf. de fin. 3, 7 sq.

6. PLUT. Mar. 45 Γάϊός τις Πείσων, ἀνὴρ ἱστορικός, whom he quotes as his authority for the death of Marius. As he is not mentioned again, we cannot decide which of the Calpurnii Pisones he was; at all events he is not the L. Piso mentioned § 132, 4; rather the cos. 687/67. HPETER, hist. rell. 1, CCCLXVIII. Cf. § 179, 13, 1.

158. To the epoch of Sulla belong also the Senator L. Manlius, who wrote a miraculous account of journeys in the manner of Euhemerus; likewise Tarquitius Priscus, who transplanted into Latin the Etruscan literature on divination. The freedman L. Voltacilius was the first man of servile birth who attempted historical writing at Rome. He was a partisan of the Pompeians and wrote political pamphlets for them. He also employed his sharp tongue in their interest.

1. DIONYS. ant. 1, 19 χρησμὸς ὅν φησι Λεύκιος Μάλλιος, ἀνὴρ οὐκ ἄσημος, αὐτὸς ἰδεῖν (at Dodona, here follow 4 Greek hex.). PLIN. NH. 10, 4 *primus atque diligentissime togatorum de eo* (the phoenix) *prodidit Manilius* (the MSS. here read *Mamilius*, but in the mention immediately following and in the ind. auct. to book X: *Manilius*) *senator ille maxumis nobilis doctrinis doctore nullo. . . . prodit idem Manilius . . . fuisse eius conversionis annum prodente se P. Licinio Cn. Cornelio cos.* (657/97) *CCXV.* Varro quotes this book; see LL. 5, 31 (*Mallius*); cf. ARNOB. adv. nat. 3, 38 (*Manilius*). MACROB. 1, 10, 4 (*Mallius*). ARN. l.l. mentions Manilius together with Granius, Aelius, Varro, Cornificius, and Cincius as writers on the novensiles. FEST. 334 *Sexagenarios ⟨de ponte olim deiciebant⟩ cuius causam Mani⟨lius hanc refert⟩.* Cf. also VARRO LL. 7, 16 (where see fragments of iambics on a mythological subject by a certain Manilius). 7, 28 (a facetious epigram of the same author in iambics; FPR. 283).—MOMMSEN, RhM. 16, 284 considers it possible that he may be the L. Manlius known from coins of Sulla as his proquaestor about 670/84 (MOMMSEN, röm. Münzwesen 595), and from various writers (LIV. per. 90. OROS. 5, 110. CAES. b. c. 3, 20. PLUT. Sertor. 12) as regent of Gallia Narbonensis about 677/77. It is also probable (RITSCHL, Parerga 242) that he is identical with the Manilius mentioned by Gellius (see § 99, 4) as the author of a catalogue of the genuine plays of Plautus.

2. MACROB. 3, 20, 3 *Tarquitius Priscus in ostentario arborario sic ait.* On the genuine Etruscan clan-name see WDEECKE on OMüller's Etr. 1^2, 470. On the cognomen see TAC. ann. 12, 59. 14, 46. Cf. MACR. 3, 7, 2 *est super hoc liber Tarquitii transscriptus ex ostentario tusco.* PLINY in the ind. auct. to b. 2: *ex . . . Caecina* (§ 199, 4) *qui de etrusca disciplina scripsit, Tarquitio qui item.* Cf. ib. 2, 199. Ind. auct. to b. 11. LYD. de ostent. 2 ⟨χρησόμεθα δὲ καὶ⟩ Ταρκύτῳ τῷ ⟨τελεστῇ⟩. AMMIAN. MARC. 25, 2, 7 (A.D. 363): *etrusci haruspices . . . ex Tarquitianis libris in titulo de rebus divinis id relatum esse monstrantes.* LACTANT. div. inst. 1, 10, 2 *hunc* (Aesculapium) *Tarquitius, de illustribus viris disserens, ait incertis parentibus natum* etc. An infusion of Euhemerism may be inferred. From his

work is probably also taken Serv. Verg. ecl. 4, 43 (=Macrob. 3, 7, 2). He is probably also referred to in Festus 274 v. *ratitum: Tarqui-* ⟨here is a lacuna⟩. In Verg. catal. 7, 3 he is mentioned with Stilo (? see § 148, 1 in fin.) and Varro as a representative of the *scholasticorum natio.* MHaupt, op. 2, 152. In a mutilated inscription (CIL. 11, 3370) T. appears to be mentioned with reference to his metrical Latin version of the Etruscan discipline (§ 75, 5; traces of metrical setting are to be found in the fragment in Macr. 3, 7). EBormann, in the archäol.-epigr. Mitteill. a. Östr. 1887 (who without sufficient grounds places the life-time of T. between 664/90–744/10). The praenomen M. (?) in the inscription is opposed to the otherwise obvious identification with C. Tarquitius P. f. Priscus (PRE. 6, 1614, 5. Mommsen, röm. Münzw. 600).—GSchmeisser, de etrusca disciplina (Bresl. 1872) p. 14; d. etr. Disziplin (§ 42, 1), Liegn. 1881, 5.

3. Suet. gramm. 27(=rhet. 3) *L. Voltacilius Pilutus servisse dicitur atque etiam ostiarius vetere more in catena fuisse, donec ob ingenium et studium litterarum manumissus accusanti patrono subscripsit. deinde rhetoricam professus Cn. Pompeium Magnum* (born 648/106) *docuit patrisque eius* (Cn. Pompeius Strabo, cos. 665/89 †667/87) *res gestas nec minus ipsius* (no doubt in his life-time) *compluribus libris exposuit, primus omnium libertinorum, ut Cornelius Nepos opinatur, scribere historiam orsus* (see § 36, 3). Hieron. ad Euseb. Chron. 1936=673/81: *Vultacilius Plotus latinus rhetor, Cn. Pompei libertus et doctor, scholam Romae aperuit.* His name shows that he rather was the freedman of a certain Voltacilius. This L. Voltacilius Pilutus or Plotus (born perhaps about 635/119) is probably in spite of the MS. variations in his praenomen and cognomen to be identified with M. Voltacilius (*uotacilius* in the MSS.) Pitholaus in Macr. 2, 2, 13, where a joke of his on the one-day consul (709/45) Caninius Rebilus is quoted (MHertz). Voltacilius as a partisan of Pompey ridiculed not only, as here, the followers of Caesar but even Caesar himself. Suet. Iul. 75 *Pitholai carminibus maledicentissimis laceratam existimationem suam civili animo tulit.* Bentley takes this Πειθόλαος also for the *Rhodius Pitholeon* (Πειθολέων; cf. Τιμόλαος and Τιμολέων, Ἀριστόλαος and Ἀριστολέων) ap. Hor. S. 1, 10, 22, of whom Porph. relates ad loc.: *huius modi* (i.e. in which were mixed *verba graeca orationi latinae*) *epigrammata effutivit magis quam scripsit . . . perquam ridicule graeca latinis admiscuit.*

4. On Trebius Niger and Turranius Gracilis see § 132, 5 and 6.

159. After the middle of the 7th century u.c., education and teaching seem to have gradually become more systematic, and we meet with an increased number of the names of those who in Rome as well as in the rest of Italy taught grammar and rhetoric, most of them indeed freedmen and of foreign birth. The majority were also writers on these subjects, and combined antiquarian and literary lore with their grammatical researches. A few gave a metrical form to their learned works; e.g. L. Accius, Porcius Licinus and Volcacius Sedigitus, also Valerius Soranus. In this period we may mention as the most eminent scholars L. Plotius Gallus, Sevius Nicanor, Aurelius Opilius, Antonius Gnipho and Pompilius Andronicus, Q. Cosconius, Ennius, Epicadus, Hypsicrates, Nicostratus, Servius Clodius and Staberius Eros.

1. Suet. gramm. 3 (§ 41, 1).

2. Suet. rhet. 2 (=gramm. 26) *L. Plotius Gallus primus Romae latinam rhetoricam docuit;* see § 44, 9. The date given by Suetonius (ap. Hieronym.), a. 666/88–677/77, is in agreement with Cicero's statement *pueris nobis* (ap. Suet. l.l. cf. Sen. controv. 2. pr. 5) or *extremis L. Crassi temporibus* (Quint. 2, 4, 42). Cf. M. Varro ap. Non. 79 *Automedo meus, quod apud Plotium rhetorem bubulcitarat, erili dolori non defuit.* According to Quint. 11, 1, 143, he had published a treatise de gestu. *Hunc eundem (nam diutissime vixit) M. Caelius . . . significat dictasse Atratino accusatori suo actionem* (Suet. rhet. 2).

3. Suet. gramm. 5 *Sevius* (see MHertz, JJ. 107, 340) *Nicanor primus ad famam dignationemque docendo pervenit fecitque praeter commentarios, quorum tamen pars maxima intercepta dicitur, saturam quoque, in qua libertinum se ac duplici cognomine esse* (see EHübner in IwMüller's Handb. 1, 521) . . . *indicat.* His satires appear therefore (like those of Lucilius and Horace) to have been portraitures of his own individuality. Suetonius quotes from them two hexameters, in which *s* final is disregarded metrically.

4. Suet. gramm. 6 *Aurelius Opilius* (Opillius), *Epicurei cuiusdam libertus, philosophiam primo, deinde rhetoricam, novissime grammaticam docuit. dimissa autem schola Rutilium Rufum* (§ 142, 1) *damnatum in Asiam secutus* (a. 662/92?) *ibidem Smyrnae simulque consenuit composuitque variae eruditionis aliquot volumina, ex quibus novem unius corporis . . . Musarum . . . inscripsisse se ait et numero divarum et appellatione* (cf. Gell. 1, 25, 17 *Aurelius Opilius in primo librorum quos Musarum inscripsit* like the rhetor Bion of Syracuse, see Diog. Laert. 4, 7, 58). To judge from the specimen given by Gellius, his Musae contained explanations of words, and to this work we should probably refer the numerous quotations in Varro LL. and esp. in Festus, where he is sometimes called Aurelius (Varro 7, 65. 70. 106. Fest. 68. 147 etc.), sometimes Opilius (Varro 7, 50. 67. 79. Fest. 85), sometimes also Aurelius Opilius (Fest. 141) and Opilius Aurelius (Fest. 163). See Egger, serm. lat. reliqq. p. 27 sqq. Usener, RhM. 23, 682. As an author of glosses he paid special attention to Plautus, though he cannot be considered a scholiast on that author. Gellius 3, 3, 1 also mentions him among the authors of indices to the Plautine plays, to which category his *libellus qui inscribitur Pinax* with the acrostich Opillius in the title (Suet. l.l.) would seem to belong. FOsann (l.l. p. 199) conjectured the acrostichs prefixed to the Plautine plays to have been derived from this source (cf. § 99, 3). Ritschl, Parerga 180. 239. 321. 364 xv. FOsann, Aurelius Opilius der Grammatiker, ZfAW. 1849, no. 25–28.

5. Suet. gramm. 7 *M. Antonius Gnipho, ingenuus in Gallia natus; sed expositus, a nutritore suo manumissus institutusque, Alexandriae quidem, ut aliqui tradunt, in contubernio Dionysi Scytobrachionis; quod equidem non temere crediderim, cum temporum ratio vix congruat* (this last statement is not proved: Dionysios of Mytilene ὁ σκυτοβραχίων wrote about 654/100. Gnipho may have been born about 640/114) *fuisse dicitur ingenii magni, . . . nec minus graece quam latine doctus. . . . docuit primum in D. Iulii* (born 654/100) *domo pueri adhuc, deinde in sua privata. docuit autem et rhetoricam, ita ut quotidie praecepta eloquentiae traderet, declamaret vero nonnisi nundinis. scholam eius claros quoque viros frequentasse aiunt, in his M. Ciceronem, etiam cum praetura fungeretur* (a. 688/66, cf. Macrob. 3, 12, 8) *scripsit multa, quamvis annum aetatis quinquagesimum non excesserit. etsi Ateius Philologus* (his pupil, Suet. gramm. 10, see § 211, 1) *duo tantum volumina de latino sermone* (cf. Quint. 1, 6, 23) *reliquisse eum tradit, nam cetera scripta discipulorum eius esse, non ipsius.* That Gnipho composed a commentary on Ennius' annals is

convincingly demonstrated by Bücheler, RhM. 36, 334 from the Schol. Bern. Verg. georg. 2, 119 '*acanthi*' *Gnifo commentatur annalium libro X* etc., cf. with Liv. 31, 45. Perhaps from the same work was derived the comment (now used in a wrong application) in Charisius GL. 1, 205, 1.—Cf. also Welcker, kl. Schr. 1, 436; cf. ep. Cycl.[1] 84. See also § 162, 5.

6. Suet. gramm. 8 *M. Pompilius Andronicus, natione Syrus, studio Epicureae sectae desidiosior in professione grammaticae habebatur. . . . itaque cum se in urbe non solum Antonio Gniphoni sed ceteris etiam deterioribus postponi videret Cumas transiit ibique in otio vixit et multa composuit.* He was driven by poverty to sell his chief work *annalium Ennii elenchi* (see § 101, 4), *quos libros Orbilius redemisse se dicit vulgandosque curasse nomine auctoris.*—Concerning his book-making a quite uncertain conjecture is advanced by ThGomperz, Wien. Stud. 2, 139.

7. Q. Cosconius, quoted as an authority in Suetonius' vita Terentii (p. 32, 13 Rffsch.); see § 108, 6. He is no doubt the same as the grammarian mentioned by Varro LL. 6, 36 and 89 (*Cosconius in actionibus*). Ritschl, op. 3, 256. Cf. MHertz, JJ. 85, 52.

8. Victorinus GL. 6, 209, 9 *Cornelius Epicadus* (cf. § 41, 4. 157, 2) *in eo libro quem de metris scripsit.* Charis. GL. 1, 110, 3 *Epicadus de cognominibus.* From an antiquarian work by him seems to be derived Macr. 1, 11, 47 (*de sigillaribus . . . Epicadus refert Herculem* etc.); cf. HPeter, hist. rell. 1, cclxxvii.

9. Ser. Clodius, eques rom. and son-in-law of L. Aelius; see § 148, 1. Plin. NH. 25, 24 *tradit M. Varro Ser. Clodium eq. rom.* etc. Suet. gramm. 3 *cum librum soceri nondum editum fraude intercepisset, ob hoc repudiatus secessit ab urbe.* After his death his half-brother Papirius Paetus presented Cicero with the papers and books left by him; see ad Att. 1, 20, 7 (*Ser. Claudius*) and 2, 1, 12 (both a. 694/60). Cf. ad fam. 9, 16, 4 (to Paetus) *Servius, frater tuus, quem litteratissimum fuisse iudico, facile diceret 'hic versus Plauti non est. hic est,' quod tritas aures haberet notandis generibus poetarum et consuetudine legendi.* Varro LL. 7, 106 (cf. 70 and 66) mentions him after Aurelius (above n. 4), whose whole direction he appears to have shared, being also a glossographer (Varro l.l. cf. Gell. 13, 23, 19 *in commentario Ser. Claudii.* Serv. Aen. 1, 52 and 2, 229 *Clodius commentariorum.* 1, 176 *Clodius scribit, commentariorum IV°*), as the author of a catalogue of the genuine plays of Plautus (Gell. 3, 3, 1). Cf. Ritschl, Parerga 242. 365.

10. *Staberius Eros . . . emptus de catasta* (cf. Plin. NH. 35, 199) *. . . temporibus Sullanis proscriptorum liberos . . . gratis in disciplinam recepit*, Suet. gramm. 13. Fronto p. 20 *quorum libri* (those of the old Roman authors) *pretiosiores habentur . . . si sunt a Lampadione* (§ 138, 4) *aut Staberio* (*scripti*). Priscian. GL. 2, 385 *Staberius de proportione.* He lived to be the master of Brutus and Cassius (Suet. l.l.). It was probably a mere fiction that Publilius, Manilius and he came to Italy *eadem nave* (Plin. l.l., who exaggerates in calling him *conditor grammaticae*, see § 212, 3).

11. Festus 347 v. senacula: *Nicostratus in libro qui inscribitur de senatu habendo.* Cf. LMercklin, Phil. 4, 428.—Macr. sat. 3, 12, 7 *est Octavii Hersenni* (mentioned between Varro and Antonius Gnipho) *liber qui inscribitur de sacris saliaribus Tiburtium, in quo . . . docet* etc.

12. Varro LL. 5, 88 *cohortem in villa Hypsicrates dicit esse graece χόρτον.* Cf. Paulus Festi 8 v. aurum, where erroneously *Hippocrates.* Gell. 16, 12, 6 *id dixisse ait* (*Cloatius Verus*) *Hypsicraten quempiam grammaticum, cuius libri sane nobiles sunt super his quae a Graecis accepta sunt.*

13. Suet. gramm. 1 *quod nonnulli tradunt duos libros de litteris syllabisque, item de metris ab eodem Ennio* (the poet, § 104, 5 ad fin.) *editos, iure arguit L. Cotta* (is he the same mentioned § 197, 9 ?) *non poetae, sed posterioris Enni esse, cuius etiam de augurandi disciplina volumina feruntur.* Did this grammarian Ennius also develope shorthand writing? see § 104, 5. Festus 352 v. topper; *Ennius vero sic: topper fortasse valet in Enni et Pacuvi scriptis.* Varro LL. 5, 86 (*foedus, quod fidus Ennius scribit dictum*) probably relates to him, and 5, 55 *nominatae, ut ait Ennius, Tatienses a Tatio.* See also § 41, 2, l. 12. Cf. besides Charis. GL. 1, 98 *erumnam Ennius* (*M. Ennius*? ARiese, JJ. 93, 465) *ait per e solum scribi posse.* MHertz, Sinnius Cap. 9; anal. ad carm. Hor. hist. 3, 9. Ribbeck, JJ. 75, 314.

14. Varro LL. 5, 55 *sed omnia haec vocabula* (*i.e. Titienses Ramnenses Luceres*) *Tusca, ut Volnius, qui tragoedias tuscas scripsit, dicebat.* Probably a grammarian, a native of Etruria, who, in order to demonstrate the literary capabilities of his decaying mother-tongue, composed tragedies in it. OMüller, Etr. 2^2, 293.—On Cincius see above § 117, 4.

160. About the middle of the 7th century the two Sasernae and, towards the end of the same century, Tremellius Scrofa, wrote on husbandry and domestic economy.

1. Saserna is a cognomen of the gens Hostilia (PRE. 3, 1530, 13). Colum. 1, 1, 12 (cf. § 54, 2) *post hunc* (Catonem) *duos Sasernas, patrem et filium, qui eam diligentius erudierunt.* Varro RR. 1, 2, 22 *sequar Sasernarum, patris et filii, libros. Sasernae* in the ind. auct. of Plin. NH. bk. 10 *Sasernae pater et filius*, ib. bk. 14. 15. 17. 18, cf. bk. 11 (*Saserna*) and 17, 199 *arbusti ratio mirum in modum damnata Sasernae patri filioque, celebrata Scrofae, vetustissimis post Catonem peritissimisque.* See Varro RR. 1, 16, 5 *Sasernae liber praecipit.* 1, 18, 2 *Saserna scribit.* 2, 9, 6 *quod in agri cultura* (this is the title of the work) *Saserna praecepit.* Columella 1, 1, 4 *id non spernendus auctor rei rusticae Saserna videtur adcredidisse. nam in eo libro quem de agricultura scriptum reliquit* etc. Perhaps the son may have completed and published the work left by his father in a fragmentary state. This treated (like Cato de r. r.) of various matters not directly connected with the theme but of importance to farmers, over which Varro frequently makes merry, e.g. RR, 1, 2, 22 sqq.

2. Varro R.R. 1, 2, 10 *collegam* (of Varro), *XXvir qui fuit ad agros dividundos Campanos* (a. 695/59) . . . *Cn. Tremellium Scrofam, virum omnibus virtutibus politum, qui de agri cultura Romanus peritissimus existimatur.* 2, 1, 11 *Scrofa noster, cui haec aetas defert rerum rusticarum omnium palmam.* He also wrote on this subject; see n. 1. Colum. 2, 1, 2 *Tremelli auctoritatem revereri, qui cum plurima rusticarum rerum praecepta simul eleganter et scite memoriae prodiderit* etc. Cf. ib. 1, 1, 12 *Scrofa Tremellius qui rusticationem eloquentem reddidit.* 2, 1, 4. Tremellius evidently attached much importance to elegant diction; hence the work of the practical Saserna was distasteful to him: Varro RR. 1, 2, 25 *Scrofa* (Sasernarum) *libros despiciebat.* In Varro RR. Scrofa, in bks. 1 and 2, takes the chief part in the dialogue. He is mentioned, always as Scrofa, by Pliny in the ind. auct. to the NH. bk. 11. 14. 15. 17. 18. PRE. 6, 2085, 5. He was also on terms of friendliness with Cicero and Atticus, who were nearly of the same age with himself. He attained the praetorship (Varro RR. 2, 4, 2) and was probably propraetor in Gallia Narbonensis (cf. Varro 1, 7, 8 and Mommsen in Reitzenstein l.l. 13).

3. It is quite uncertain whether the very experienced landowner C. Licinius

Stolo, who with Tremellius (n. 2) takes part in the discourse in VARRO RR. bk. 1 and who is mentioned with Cato, Saserna, Tremellius and Vergil by COLUMELLA 1, praef. 32 (see § 54, 2. 293, 4), wrote about husbandry. He was younger than Tremellius: VARRO RR. 1, 3 (Stolo to Tremellius) *tu et aetate et honore et scientia quod praestas, dicere debes.* RREITZENSTEIN, de scriptt. rei rust. inter Cat. et Colum., Berl. 1884, p. 8.

4. Otherwise unknown is Mamilius Sura, quoted by PLIN. NH. in the ind. auct. to bk. 8. 10. 11. 17–19, but in the text itself mentioned only at 18, 143 (*Cato . . . Sura Mamilius . . . Varro*). He is hardly to be connected with Aemilius Sura (see § 277, 5).—On M. Ambivius, Licinius Menas, and C. Matius see § 54, 3.

161. The whole period from 650/104 to 675/79 offered little leisure for philosophical studies; those, however, who pursued them, were as a matter of course Stoics, when jurists, and adherents of the New Academy, when orators, or perhaps also Peripatetics. The Epicurean system found adherents only among those who kept aloof from public life.

1. CIC. de or. 3, 78 *quid . . . C. Velleius afferre potest quam ob rem voluptas sit summum bonum quod ego non possim vel tutari . . . vel refellere . . . hac dicendi arte in qua Velleius est rudis? . . . quid est quod aut Sex. Pompeius* (§ 154, 5) *aut duo Balbi aut . . . qui cum Panaetio vixit M. Vigellius de virtute homines stoici possint dicere?* de nat. deor. 1, 15 *cum C. Velleio senatore, ad quem tum Epicurei primas ex nostris deferebant. . . . etiam Q. Lucilius Balbus, qui tantos progressus habebat in Stoicis ut cum excellentibus in eo genere Graecis compararetur.* In the same period we meet with Q. Catulus (§ 142, 4), C. Cotta (§ 153, 4) and L. Lucullus (§ 157, 4) adherents of Antiochos (Academy), somewhat later M. Piso (cos. 693/61), an older contemporary of Cicero (CIC. Brut. 230, cf. ASCON. in Pis. p. 15 Or. 14 K-S.) through the agency of the Peripatetic Staseas (CIC. de or. 1, 104) an adherent of this system (CIC. de n. deor. 1, 16. ad Att. 13, 19, 4); in a similar manner the triumvir M. Crassus was won over by Alexander Polyhistor (PLUT. Crass. 3). Besides those already mentioned, esp. Q. Scaevola (§ 154, 1), and of the earlier ones P. Rutilius Rufus (§ 142, 2) and L. Stilo (§ 148, 1), declared for the Stoa. Epicureans were, besides Velleius, T. Albucius (§ 141, 3) and Pompilius Andronicus (§ 159, 6). The author of the Rhetorica ad Herennium (§ 162, 2) also shows interest in philosophy.

2. The earliest Epicurean writers among the Romans, Amafinius, Rabirius, Catius, seem to belong to the time of Cicero, to judge from the manner in which they are spoken of by CIC. acad. post. 1, 2, 5. See below § 173.

162. An important literary production of Sulla's time survives in the four books of Rhetorica ad C. Herennium, a complete manual drawn from Greek sources; but the author looks at all things from the Roman point of view, omits all that the Roman regarded as unpractical refinement, and himself generally supplies the illustrations for the rhetorical figures. The mode of treating the subject-matter shows clear and independent thought as well as an original mind. The exposition is impeded by the

language. The author, an irreconcilable enemy of the nobility, would seem to have enjoyed an independent position in life. Tradition wrongly ascribes the work to Cicero. The name of the author was probably Cornificius.

1. For the characteristic features of the work see esp. 1, 1, *illa quae graeci scriptores inanis adrogantiae causa sibi adsumpserunt reliquimus; . . . nos ea quae videbantur ad rationem dicendi pertinere sumpsimus; non enim spe quaestus aut gloria commoti venimus ad scribendum, quemadmodum ceteri*, etc.; 4, 1 *quibus in rebus opus fuit exemplis uti nostris exemplis usi sumus et id fecimus praeter consuetudinem Graecorum qui de hac re scripserunt.* (Cf. in general the whole preface to bk. 4.) But the author has nevertheless made use of his recollections of speeches which he had read and heard for his illustrations. (See HJordan, Herm. 8, 75.) 4, 10 *nomina rerum graeca convortimus.* B. I. and II general observations and de inventione; bk. III de dispositione, pronuntatione, memoria; bk. IV. de elocutione (cf. 3, 1 *in quarto libro, quem, ut arbitror, tibi librum celeriter absolutum mittemus*). The author was an admirer of M. Antonius (see § 152, 1).

2. For the personal position of the author see 1, 1 *etsi negotiis familiaribus impediti vix satis otium studio suppeditare possumus, et id ipsum quod datur oti lubentius in philosophia consumere consuevimus, tamen tua nos, C. Herenni, voluntas commovit ut de ratione dicendi conscriberemus.* 4, 69 *simul lubenter exercemur* (Herennius and the author) *propter amicitiam, cuius initium cognatio fecit, cetera philosophiae ratio confirmavit.* 3, 3 *si quando de re militari aut de administratione reip. scribere velimus.* 4, 17 *haec qua ratione vitare possimus in arte grammatica . . . dicemus.* The author sides with the popular party. Cf. the catalogue of iniquities with which he upbraids the nobility in the last illustration of the adnominatio 4, 31, or the description of the murder of Ti. Gracchus 4, 68 as an example of the demonstratio. WWFowler, l.l. RvScala, JJ. 131, 221.—The second (very corrupt) example of brevitas (4, 68) is generally taken to refer to Sulla (see also Weidner on Cic. art. rhet. p. xvii.). According to this we should have to bring down the date of its composition, at least for the last book, to about 674/80, a supposition which involves us in great difficulties. These are removed if this exemplum (in accordance with the opinion of Jordan, Kröhnert, Bochmann l.l. WWFowler, Journ. of phil. 10, 197) is regarded as pointing to Marius. The deaths of Sulpicius 666/88 (see § 153, 5) and of Marius 668/86 are then the latest events mentioned in this Rhet. ad Her. We may perhaps conclude from 1, 20 that the work was written before 672/82. Cicero read it as early as 670/84 (see n. 3).

3. Numerous parts of the work are literally used by Cicero in his juvenile rhetorical treatise (de inventione); see § 182, 1, 3. The tripartite division of the insinuatio, e.g., described as new and original ad Her. 1, 16, is simply assumed by Cic. de inv. 1, 23. The very discrepancies found in many principal points (CLKayser, ed. p. ix. and Münchner Gel. Anz. 1852, 482), prove this agreement to have arisen from more than mere coincidence of the authorities used by both writers.

4. The form is clumsy, especially in the mode of connecting the sentences, in the use of particles, etc. The baldness of the style is shown chiefly in the frequent repetition of the same phrase. Cf. also EWölfflin, Phil. 34, 142. 144 and PhThielmann, de sermonis proprietatibus . . . apud Cornific. et in primi Cic. libris, Strassb. 1879; Herm. 14, 629.

5. In the MSS., including the earliest, the work is attributed to Cicero; the fact that Jerome, Fortunatianus, Priscian and others took the treatise for a production of Cicero (Kayser, ed. p. 12) only shows how uncritical they were. The assumption that Cornificius was the author, brought into vogue by CLKayser (Münchner Gel. Anz. 1852, 492 and in his edition), is supported by Quintilian. Cf. the latter 3, 1, 21 where, after mentioning Cicero, he says: *scripsit de eadem materia* (Rhetorica) *non pauca Cornificius, aliqua Stertinius*. He quotes various passages from Cornificius' work, esp. Latin renderings for Greek artistic terms (cf. n. 1), which are found in the Rhet. ad Her. in precisely the same manner. Thus Quint. 5, 10, 2 *ideo illud Cornificius contrarium appellat* = ad Her. 4, 25.—Quint. 9, 2, 27 *oratio libera, quam Cornificius licentiam vocat* = Her. 4, 48.—9, 3, 71 *Cornificius hanc traductionem vocat* = Her. 4, 20.—9, 3, 91 *et hoc Cornificius atque Rutilius σχῆμα λέξεως putant* = Her. 4, 35.—9, 3, 98 *adicit his . . . Cornificius interrogationem* etc. = Her. 4, 22–41. In other places Quintilian borrows illustrations from the same work without naming it, e.g. 9, 3, 31 (= Her. 4, 20). 56 (= Her. 4, 34). 70 (= Her. 4, 29). 72 (= Her. 4, 30). We know of several Cornificii in the time of Cicero, e.g. one who a. 680/74 was scriba to the praetor Verres (Verr. acc. 1, 150), a senator P. Cornificius (Ascon. in Mil. p. 37 Or. 32 K–S.) and Q. Cornificius, a. 685/69 tr. pleb. (Verr. act. prima 30 *Q. Manlium et Q. Cornificium, duos severissimos atque integerrimos iudices, quod tribuni pl. tum erunt, iudices non habebimus;* cf. Ascon. in tog. cand. p. 82 Or. 73 K–S. *vir sobrius ac sanctus*), 690/64 Cicero's competitor for the consulship (Cic. ad Att. 1, 1, 1) and mentioned as senator in Sall. Cat. 47, 4 and Cic. ad Att. 1, 13, 3. Kayser (ed. p. 6) declares in favour of the last-named as the author of this work.

6. The work was much used, copied and interpolated in the Middle Ages; for the MSS. containing it see Kayser's ed. p. xv. The lacunae in the earliest and best (Paris. 7714 s. IX, Wirceb. s. IX [–X], Bern. 433, Paris. 7231 s. X: facsimile of the Paris. 7714 and of the Bern. in Chatelain t. 16) are more or less supplied in the later MSS. (the best is Bamberg. 423, s. XII). On a (worthless) Durhamiensis s. XIII see FBJevons, Journ. of phil. 12, 209. Against CHalm, analecta Tull. I, Münch. 1852 and RhM. 15, 536, who looks upon the additions of the later MSS. as mere interpolations, cf. LSpengel, RhM. 16, 391; JSimon, die Hss. der Rhet. ad Her., Schweinf. 1863, 64 II; JvDestinon, de codd. Cornific. ratione, Kiel 1874.—ROstmann, de additamentis in Rhet. ad Her. antiquioribus, Bresl. 1876. KHoffmann, de verborum transpositionibus in Cornif. ad Her. libris, Münch. 1879.

7. Editions by PBurmann (with Cic. de inv.), Leid. 1761, and esp. Cornifici Rhetoricorum ad C. Herennium libri IV, rec. et interpretatus est CLKayser, Lps. 1854. Also in collective edd. of Cicero and in edd. of his writings on rhetoric. (§ 177, 5).—CHansel, JJ. 93, 851. OSievers, RhM. 28, 568. PLangen, Phil. 36, 445. 577. 37, 385. CGermann, emendd. Cornif., Darmst. 1880. CLKayser, Münchn. Gel. A. 1852, Nr. 59; Heidelb. JJ. 1854, 411; Phil. 12, 271. AKammrath, de rhett. ad Her. auctore, Holzminden 1858. Mommsen, RG. 2[6], 456. FBlass, d. griech. Bereds. von Alex. bis August (Berl. 1865), 121. RKrönhert, de rhet. ad Her., Königsb. 1873. HNetzker, Hermag. Cic. Cornificius quae docuerint de statibus, Kiel 1879; d. constitutio legitima des Cornif., JJ. 133, 411. FRoch, de Cornif. et Cic. artis Rhet. praeceptoribus, Bad. (Austria) 1884. HEBochmann, de Cornificii . . . rerum rom. scientia, Lpz. 1875.

163. Among the prose inscriptions of the years 600/145 to 670/84 we should especially mention the public documents, such as the tabula Bantina, lex repetundarum, lex agraria etc. The

inscriptions of this period in metrical form are partly still in the saturnian metre, partly in hexameters handled in a popular style, or in other Greek metres, especially the iambic senarius.

1. The tabula Bantina, a fragment of a bronze tablet in Naples, was found in 1790 at Bantia in Apulia, and on one side bears a Latin, on the reverse an Oscan text (not however agreeing with the Latin) of the years 621/133–636/118. The Latin text is the conclusion of a Roman (local) law. CIL. 1, 197. Bruns, font. iur. [5]51. DIE. 292.

2. Lex Acilia (formerly incorrectly Servilia) repetundarum of the year 631/123 or 632/122. CIL. 1, 198. Bruns, font. [5]53. DIE. 293.

3. To the period of the Gracchi probably belong also the fragments of a lex de quaestione perpetua. CIL. 1, 207. 208. Bruns, font. [5]116. DIE. 296, as well as the milestone of Popilius (cos. 622/132) CIL. 1, 551. 10, 6950. DIE. 275, and probably the inscription of L. Betilienus L. f. Vaarus of Aletrium, CIL. 1, 1166. DIE. 291.

4. The decision of the arbitrators Q. and M. Minucius in a dispute about boundaries between the Genuates and Viturii, of 637/117. CIL. 1, 199 and 5, 7749. Wilm. 872. Bruns. font. [5]325. DIE. 294.

5. Lex agraria of a. 643/111, formerly called lex Thoria (which was, however, about 635/119); preserved on the reverse of the lex repet. (above n. 2): CIL. 1, 200. Bruns, font. [5]72. DIE. 295.

6. Lex parieti faciendo of Puteoli, of a. 649/105, but cut as late as the Imperial period: CIL. 1, 577. 10, 1781. Bruns, font. [5]272. DIE. 306.

7. In saturnians: the titulus Mummianus (§ 131, 8) of the year 612/142 (CIL. 1, 541. 6, 331. Ritschl, op. 4, 82. DIE. 285, the inscription preserved is perhaps not the original, but a later and inexact repetition: see Bücheler, anthol. epigr. 3, p. 5); the epitaph of Maarcus Caicilius (CIL. 1, 1006. 6, 13696. Ritschl l.l. 735. Bücheler l.l. p. 9. DIE. 322); the inscription of Sora (CIL. 1, 1175. 10, 5708. Ritschl l.l. 130. Bücheler l.l. p. 5. DIE. 284); as also the epitaphs of the master baker M. Vergilius Eurysaces and his wife Atistia (CIL. 1, 1013 sqq. 6, 1958. Ritschl l.l. 749. Bücheler l.l. p. 10. DIE. 323) are probably intended to be in this metre, as well as perhaps CIL. 1, 1080 *amantissuma suis, fide maxsuma pia.* For other saturnian fragments in inscriptions see Bücheler l.l. p. 10.

8. In popular hexameters (above p. 126): the titulus Mummianus CIL. 1, 542. 9, 4672. DIE. 286, as well as the sortes falsely called Praenestinae (CIL. 1. 1438–1454. DIE. 370 sqq. Ritschl, op. 4, 395. Düntzer, Phil. 20, 368). In addition the epitaph of Cn. Taracius (CIL. 1, 1202. DIE. 334) and that of Protogenes (CIL. 1297. DIE. 333). A dactylic octometer CIL. 1480. No. 1038 also betrays dactylic metre. Nos. 1011 (DIE. 335) and 1220 (DIE. 336) are distichs, and so is no. 38 of the epitaphs of the Scipios (DIE. 93).

9. Among the inscriptiones lat. antiquissimae (CIL. vol. 1) the foll. are iambic: 1007 (in Bücheler, anthol. epigr. specim. 1 and 2—RhM. 27, 127—Nr. 20. DIE. 324). 1008 (Büch. 33. DIE. 327). 1009 (B. 22. DIE. 326). 1010 (81. DIE. 328). 1012 (34. DIE. 329). 1019 (45. DIE. 332). 1027 (Büch. in 27. DIE. 331). 1194 (23). 1267 (48. DIE. 330). 1273 (32). 1277 (80). 1306 (21. DIE. 325). 1422 (26). 1431 (84); probably trochaic CIL. 1459; LMüller, JJ. 97, 214.

PART II.

THE GOLDEN AGE OF ROMAN LITERATURE.

Ciceronian and Augustan Age, a. 671/83 b.c.–770/17 a.d.

A. Ciceronian age, a. 671/83–711/43.

163. The golden age of Roman literature is that period in which it reached its climax in the perfection of form, and for the most part also in the methodical treatment of the subject-matter. The period may be subdivided between two generations, in the first of which (the Ciceronian age) prose culminated, while poetry was principally developed in the second (the Augustan age).

In the beginning of the Ciceronian age, the overthrow of the popular party and the victory of the nobility were accomplished facts. But such a condition of affairs was both untenable and unjustifiable. Had the nobility been less degenerate and broken up by self-seeking, its domination might have been lasting; but the nation, in outward semblance risen to formidable power, owing to the extension of the Roman citizenship to all Italians, was in reality henceforth a blind tool in the hands of unscrupulous ambition. All was ripe for monarchy, though Sulla found it too troublesome to maintain his absolute power; even such an adventurer as Catiline dared to grasp at the prize, and had Cn. Pompey been possessed of greater firmness, he could scarcely have missed it; but the spoilt favourite of fortune was by his vanity and sensitiveness brought to a wavering and vacillating conduct, which ended in depriving him of the respect and confidence of both parties and served to smooth the way for Caesar, who was clear as to his purpose and the means of attaining it. The immediate result of this state of things was the first triumvirate (694/60); the sequel was the war between Pompey and Caesar, Pompey's death, Caesar's victory and monarchical sway. The insensate murder of Caesar led merely to a second death of the already defunct Republic, in a new civil war; the agony commenced again, and again a triumvirate was the next step to monarchy; the first triumvirs had exiled Cicero, the second killed him.

This period is not conspicuous for the same feverish excitement as the time of Sulla, the internal exhaustion of one of the contending parties, the nobility, being unequal to it; but there was no lack of stirring life. For a long time the contention of factions was continued with weapons drawn from the armoury of the mind, with speech and the pen, in the forum and in the Senate, even after brute force had gained the ascendancy and gladiators at first, and trained armies afterwards, were the real decisive agencies. Oratory and historical and political composition were, therefore, still predominant in this era. But the novel feature of it is that now one branch of literature after the other climbs to the height of art, as the prejudice which assumed that literary occupations were of no importance, and deeds alone worthy of attention, began to disappear. This fact attests the subjection of the Roman mind to the influence of the Greeks, which about this time became quite a settled fact and assumed larger proportions from year to year. It is true that there was no lack of men who stood true to their national colours: e.g. Varro; but they had less influence and formed only a small minority.

In the ruling circles the estrangement from the people and from the Roman modes of thinking was quite universal; the common aim of all being, as fast as possible, by any means whatever, whether robbery or venality, to get a chance of keeping pace with others in their senseless squandering. Appetites raised to an unnatural pitch were met by the over-refined culture of the Greeks, whose fashions at last became a positive necessity of life. Greeks were now in all houses, either as tutors, readers, or companions at home and on journeys; and frequently we find men of great mental culture and knowledge in the service of Roman magnates, from whom they knew how to obtain a large share of respect: Lucullus had Antiochos; M. Crassus, Alexander Polyhistor; L. Piso, Philodemos. Staseas, too, the companion of M. Piso, and Philagros, who lived with Metellus Nepos, seem to have been men above the ordinary run; Cicero had Diodotos, Lyson and Apollonios in his entourage; M. Brutus had Aristos, Strato, Posidonios and Empylos. The majority, of course, did not consider the relation a very serious one, on either side; the Greeks wanting to be rid of the trouble of providing for their maintenance, while the Romans merely wished to have philosophers, poets or men with ready pens among their courtiers.

But men of intellect, and those who had not merely inherited their riches and high station, perceived in Greek culture an excellent means of distinction, enabling them to surpass their predecessors, and exalt themselves, by superior achievements of their own. Even before this, exiles had chosen Greek towns by preference as their places of residence, e.g. Metellus and Rutilius Rufus; now it became the fashion for aspiring young Romans to make Eastern tours for the completion of their education, especially to the principal seats of philosophical and rhetorical schools, Athens, Rhodes and Mytilene; and at the close of the Ciceronian age it was even a necessary requirement of a superior education to visit a Greek University, as may be seen by the example of Cicero's son, Horace, L. Bibulus, Messala and others.

But besides the living Greeks of the period, Rome was also invaded by their ancestors in their immortal works; before this, Aemilius Paullus had after his victory over Perseus brought a Greek library to Rome; now, after the capture of Athens by Sulla, the library of Apellikon, and with it most of the writings of Aristotle and Theophrastos, arrived at Rome; Lucullus sent thither rich literary spoils from Pontus; henceforth there were real lovers and connoisseurs of books at Rome (e.g. Varro and Cicero), and gradually a book-trade was formed, Atticus for instance being a publisher and bookseller (§ 2, 2). Latin translations of Greek works increased. The higher classes did not, of course, require them, as they were quite conversant with Greek; but wider circles could be influenced only through the medium of translations. These were not now confined to dramatic literature; the aristocratic circles willingly left the people to their national amusements and delighted themselves with Greek performances. But the productions of Greek immorality and freethinking were now translated into Latin, e.g. the novels of Aristeides by Sisenna, and Epicurean works by Amafinius and others. At a later date, Cicero first and then Messala translated Greek works of a more serious character.

It was natural, and it was the fault of the Greek instructors themselves, that the genuine old Greek literature did not come into the hands of their Roman pupils, but only the lighter literature of the existing or of the previous generation. Hence the orators trained themselves not after the model of Demosthenes, but of the Greek rhetoricians of Asia Minor, where the Greek character was considerably alloyed with Orientalism; and when, at a subsequent time, the younger orators made Lysias their model, as though he represented the purest Attic type, they and their contemporaries added to the mistake by choosing the Alexandrines as their model in poetry. The Greek genius was, however, so marvellously rich and robust, that in spite of this it exercised an important influence, and did not make itself felt merely in the way of destruction; on the contrary, to its alliance with the Roman mind are due most literary productions of the period. The influence of the Greeks leaves clear traces in the variety and manysidedness, in the high estimation and popularity gained by literature, and especially in the great attention paid to form, an attention carried almost to an excessive worship of formal perfection at the close of the Ciceronian age.

The practical tendencies in literature and the influence of a time of great political excitement became conspicuous in the fields now especially selected for literary cultivation. Oratory above all now reached its climax. Even before, when Greek taste and art had influenced only individuals, the Romans might be said to have at least equalled the Greeks in the thorough treatment and powerful grasp of political and legal questions; and even at the beginning of this period Hortensius was a brilliant example of the high achievements attainable by Roman talent, though trained in a one-sided manner. By mere natural talent, it was scarcely possible to advance any further; but it was possible to progress in art and methodical training—an advance made by Cicero. Never tired of learning and ever working to cultivate his mind, he enlarged both the horizon and materials of oratory; he brought great accomplishments, a vivid knowledge of the rules of his art, and a refined perception of beauty and aptness in phraseology to bear upon a Latin style which, until then loose and straggling, he now endowed with order, method and variety. Such contemporaries as Caesar willingly acknowledged his superiority and classicality in this point. In the close of his life he had indeed to experience the charges of being antiquated, and too much in the Asiatic style, from a younger generation who claimed the name of Atticists exclusively for themselves, and in the period immediately following him Sallust and Asinius Pollio rebelled against his style. In the main points, however, he came out victorious, his phraseology, terms and constructions becoming the standard of classicality, and when Rome itself had long ceased to follow his example, it was honourably revived in later centuries.

In connection with the methodical development of oratory, its theoretical treatment, i.e. rhetoric, increased in importance. Here the Greeks were now the rulers, Hermagoras, Molon, Apollodoros and Theodoros; the manuals written by them were used for instruction either in the originals or in Latin translations, Valgius for example being the author of one of the latter. Cicero, who in his early years had followed the same track in his treatise de inventione, in his riper years pursued rather the plan of the rhetorica ad Herennium, leaving aside the technical disputes of the various schools, and enlarging the popular mode of dealing with his subject. This he did by replacing the sober, severe and methodical manner of his earlier work by interesting dialogues on the principal questions of rhetoric, made attractive and instructive by the rich stores of his knowledge and the variety and extent of his experience.

Political literature flourished in an almost equal degree. With the gradual increase of general education, the pen had become a power, and there were more than enough hands to wield it. All persons and events of importance during these years were, therefore, soon surrounded with a literature of pamphlets, memoirs, and biographies. We may also, perhaps, explain the great attention given to the religious ceremonies in treatises by A. Caecina, Appius Pulcher, Valerius Messala, Trebatius, from their importance in politics. A great deal of correspondence turned on politics, and historical composition was even more connected with this department, as may be seen from Caesar's example. Along with this political treatment of historical subjects, the old manner of the Annalists was still continued by a few, and particularly by Cornelius Nepos. Varro's historical works were large repositories of facts; M. Varro, Atticus and Cornelius Nepos wrote abridgments, all three furnishing also specimens of a comparative mode of historical composition, in which Greeks and Romans were compared with one another. The establishment of an official gazette (acta diurna) by Caesar (a. 695/59) and the invention of stenography (notae Tironianae) promoted the accumulation of materials for subsequent historians. In Sallust, this period possesses the representative of a new direction, in which a consciousness of the task of writing history as an art led to the imitation of Greek models in the description of facts and characters.

In proportion to the increase of general education scholarship and learning gained in importance. Varro especially, a man of honest national tendencies, collected in his long life astonishing stores of learning, and published them in his works in such abundance that subsequent centuries continued to draw upon them. After him, Valerius Cato, Nigidius Figulus and Santra enjoyed most authority, and even some aristocrats (e.g. Valerius Messala, cos. 701/53) contributed to the investigation of Roman antiquities. The teachers, as a class, derived as yet little personal advantage from the reviving zeal for education. Men of free birth rarely devoted themselves to that profession, e.g. Orbilius Pupillus, and he was never fond of it; the majority were freedmen of Greek descent, e.g. Curtius Nicias, Lenaeus, Ateius Praetextatus, Caecilius Epirota.

Besides these professors, Greece furnished Rome also with philosophers, who established there the practice of philosophical disputation and composition. In rare instances only were these occupations taken up with such zeal as in the case of Cato, who was a thorough Stoic, and Lucretius, who was a zealous Epicurean; the majority gathered from the various systems the fruits agreeable to their taste. Philosophical writers followed the example of the principal Greek philosophers of the time in adopting an eclecticism, the ingredients of which were mixed so as to suit individual inclination. M. Varro, for instance, adhered to the Academy in ethics, in all other departments to the Stoa; M. Brutus on the other hand was a Stoic in ethics, but in all things else an Academican, and Cicero delighted in setting one system against the other in philosophical disputation. Independently of the works of Lucretius, we possess in this period the philosophical writings of Cicero, which are principally remarkable for their form and the dexterity with which the Latin language is employed for the new subjects.

Poetry at first held a subordinate position in this age, and had nothing more to show than the incidental attempts of Varro, M. Cicero and Q. Cicero in this field. M. Varro, though thoroughly prosaic, was the most important of these writers, and on account of the great variety of metres used by him especially in his saturae Menippeae, and of the severe laws which he imposed upon himself, he may be accounted a precursor of the poets who imitated Alexandrine models. Poetry took a higher flight in the work to which Lucretius gave his life. His didactic poem, in spite of its thorough Roman austerity and archaic style, is pervaded by a spirit of freethinking and in its form keeps to the path pointed out by Ennius. The younger generation, though mainly following the Alexandrine poetry as their model, cultivated the various branches of poetry and attempted the most varied forms, which they thoroughly and perfectly mastered. At their head stands Catullus, the greatest lyric poet whom Rome had seen; along with him his friends Licinius Calvus and Helvius Cinna, and also Valerius Cato, Furius Bibaculus, Varro Atacinus and Cassius of Parma. The drama alone was not attempted by them; in their self-sufficient manner they turned away from the people and contented themselves with the appreciation of the school, their friends and connoisseurs. The stage was therefore limited to the old drama, and such excellent actors as the tragedian Aesopus and the comedian Roscius breathed new life into the plays of the tragic and comic poets of the 6th century U. C. Among the popular kinds, the Mimus became of importance in the course of the Ciceronian period as the most accurate representation of the licence of the capital. The Roman knight D. Laberius worked in this direction, and it was also made popular by the freedman and actor Publilius Syrus. Laberius gained for the Mimus a place in literature.

During this time the last remnant of national prosody disappeared. Final *s*, scarcely audible in actual pronunciation, and hence disregarded by Ennius before consonants (see p. 126), was by the poets of the Alexandrine school systematically and regularly treated as a full consonant, though even M. Varro and Lucretius had disregarded it in prosody, in a number of cases proportionally not very numerous. But the elision of final *m* before a following vowel was always retained.

The literary characters of the Ciceronian era differ very strongly according as they belong either to the first or second half of it, the older or younger generation. Those of the first half, whose youth fell during the terrible struggles between Marius and Sulla, preserved both in their life and literary productions a certain serious tone of mind. The close of the 7th century and the beginning of the eighth we know, from Cicero and Sallust, to have been a time of tempestuous excitement; it was the period of such persons as Clodius and Clodia, when dissoluteness was considered genius, and ancient Roman honesty had disappeared from life and literature.[1]) The younger generation, who grew up in this atmosphere and were speedily drawn into the whirlpool, were swallowed up by it, their strength was

---

[1]) Cic. pCael. 40 *haec genera virtutum non solum in moribus nostris, sed vix iam in libris reperiuntur.*

rapidly spent in sensual enjoyments, and they came to an early end. When contrasted with the old Roman writers, who preserved a patriarchal character even in the great age they attained, it seems strange that the authors of this epoch were so short-lived, e.g. Catullus, Calvus, Caelius Rufus, and likewise Lucretius and Sallust. In this respect as well as in their literary tendencies they were the precursors of such Augustan poets as Tibullus and Propertius, who however were depressed by the political conditions of their time. Those of them who arrived at a higher age did not reach their zenith until the time of Augustus, e.g. Trebatius, Asinius Pollio, Q. Tubero, C. Matius.

These two generations are also divided by their national and political tendencies. In the older generation there is a marked difference between the prose-styles of Varro and Cicero, the one representing antiquarian traditions, the other progress; in the younger generation Lucretius and Catullus show the same antithesis in poetry; the first national and bent upon his subject-matter, the other Hellenising and striving after perfection of form. As to principle, Cicero appears to be on the same ground with Catullus and his friends; but the same principle is there carried out with discretion, and here with one-sided exclusiveness, the fashionable poets slighting the antiquated Cicero, and he ridiculing the new poetasters, whose highest standard in eloquence was Lysias and in poetry Euphorion.[2]) In politics also the younger generation are divided, some being for the Republic—e.g. Catullus, Calvus, and the principal members of the conspiracy against Caesar, M. and D. Brutus, C. Cassius and Cassius of Parma—others belonging to Caesar's party, e.g. Sallust, C. Matius, Q. Tubero, M. Antony, Curio, Trebatius, Asinius Pollio etc.

It is, moreover, characteristic of this time that after the removal (in the Marsian war) of the last barriers between Rome and Italy, the Italian municipia showed an increasing interest in literature, which, from being merely Roman, gradually assumes the character of an Italian literature. When at length Gallia Cisalpina had been added to the rest and Italy had extended to its natural frontiers, talented men repaired thence to a larger arena. Catullus, Cornelius Nepos, Furius Bibaculus, Cassius (of Parma) and subsequently Aemilius Macer, Cornelius

---

[2]) Cic. orat. 161 (*poetae novi*). Att. 7, 2, 1 (*νεώτεροι* and *σπονδειάζοντες*, cf, § 213, 3. 214, 6. 230, 2, n. 2 ad fin.). Tusc. 3, 45 (*cantores Euphorionis*. Cf. also Quint. 12, 10, 12.

Gallus and T. Livius are natives of Upper Italy, Varro (Atacinus) and Pompeius Trogus even of Transalpine Gaul.[3]) Though nice ears pretended to perceive this or that peculiarity in these new Romans distinguishing them from real urbanitas,[4]) they certainly possessed greater vigour and earnestness. The proportionally slow development of the distant parts of Italy [5]) offered, moreover, the advantage of greater independence with regard to the ever-changing fashions of the metropolis, and this again led to a faithful adherence to really classic models,[6]) and from this source they often derived sufficient vitality to supply again the arteries of the metropolis when exhausted by its fitful restlessness.

Both the extent and the lasting influence of his literary activity secured to Cicero a central position in this period. Around him the older and part of the younger generation may be grouped. Among those somewhat older than himself we may mention Varro (born 638/116), Aquilius Gallus, the aristocrats M. Crassus (born anterior to 639/115), L. Lucullus (born c. 640/114), Hortensius (born 640/114), M. Piso (born c. 642/112), and Atticus (born 645/109), the translators of Epicurus (§ 173) and L. Albucius. Of the same age with Cicero are Cn. Pompey and D. Laberius (both born 648/106), Sulpicius Rufus, and of nearly the same age L. Lucceius, Q. Tubero, Q. Cicero (born 652/102), and Furius Bibaculus (born 651/103?). Besides these, Tiro, Trebatius Testa (born c. 665/89) and perhaps Nigidius Figulus (praetor 696/58) belong to the same school. Upon the younger men Caesar (born 654/100) exercises much power of attraction. Among these, nearer to Cicero in point of age are Lucretius (born 655/99), Cato Uticensis (born 659/95), C. Memmius (praetor 696/58), Cornelius Nepos (born c. 660/94), Valerius Cato (born c. 664/90), Hirtius, Oppius, Munatius Plancus, M. Calidius, C. Trebonius, Maecius Tarpa, C. Cassius, Valerius Messala. Orbilius Pupillus (though born as early as 640/114), only then began his career. Some even younger than these came into frequent contact with Cicero, in so far as they were adversaries of the monarchy just then rising; but they were sought by him

---

3) JJWLagus, studia latina provincialium, Helsingfors 1849. ABudinsky, d. Ausbreitung der lat. Spr., Berl. 1881. 4) Cic. Brut. 171.

5) Plin. ep. 1, 14, 4 *Brixia ex illa nostra Italia quae multum adhuc verecundiae, frugalitatis atque etiam rusticitatis antiquae retinet ac servat.*

6) Even Suet. gramm. 21 says: *in provincia . . . durante adhuc ibi antiquorum memoria, necdum omnino abolita sicut Romae.*

and did not court his favour. To these belong M. Brutus (born 669/85), D. Brutus (born later than 670/84), Calvus (born 672/82), and also Catullus (born 667/87). As concerns the party of Caesar, Cicero was in friendly intercourse with C. Matius (born c. 670/84), and Caelius Rufus (born c. 666/88); his relations with Asinius Pollio (born 670/84) are somewhat doubtful, but to Sallust (born 667/87) and M. Antony (born c. 671/83), he was decidedly hostile. The personal and political relations of Varro Atacinus (born c. 672/82) are not known.

The year 691/63, in which Cicero was consul, forms to a certain extent a turning-point in his life as well as in the relative position of the political parties. Hence we divide the whole period into two halves and assign to the first all those writers whose principal achievements (whether literary or personal) are anterior to that year, and to the second those who flourished after 691/63.

THE FIRST HALF OF THE CICERONIAN PERIOD. 671/83–691/63.

164. M. Terentius Varro, born a. 638/116 in the Sabine town of Reate, probably of a family of equestrian rank, from the very first devoted himself especially to the investigation of antiquarian lore and to literature, though he did not keep aloof from public life and was employed in public business (especially by Pompey) whenever a man of firm and trustworthy character was required. In the civil war also he fought in Spain on the side of the constitutional party against Caesar, who however after his victory designated him the librarian of the collection contemplated by him; M. Antony on the other hand (711/43) proscribed him. He escaped the danger and, laborious to his death, reached the age of almost 90 years. Varro was a writer of extensive learning, of marvellous fertility and versatile both in his subjects and form; we meet in him a peculiar mixture of the simple popular element and the most universal culture, of homely mirth and old-fashioned austerity. He was honourable in character, sober and upright, devoted to the good old time, keenly interested in all sides of the genuine old Roman life, but also accessible to Greek culture. His diction is vigorous and pithy, though stiff, often abrupt and disjointed, and regardless of symmetry and finish.

1. Varro wrote de sua vita libri III (cf. § 166, 3). Hieronym. in Euseb. chron.

ad a. Abr. 1901=638/116 *M. Terentius Varro filosofus et poeta nascitur.* The same ad 1990=727/27 *M. Terentius Varro filosofus prope nonagenarius moritur.* He is called *Reatinus* by Symmachus ep. 1, 2; cf. Varro RR. 2, praef. 6. 2, 8, 3. 5. 6. Incorrectly August. civ. d. 4, 1 *Romae natus et educatus.* His expressions in the Catus seem to apply to himself: *mihi puero modica una fuit tunica et toga, sine fasciis calciamenta, equus sine ephippio, balneum non cotidianum, alveus rarus.* He was a pupil of Stilo (§ 148, 1) and of Antiochos of Ascalon (Cic. acad. post. 1, 12), like Cicero. He was a friend of Cn. Pompey (Gell. 14, 7, 2 *Gn. Pompeius . . . M. Varronem, familiarem suum, rogavit* etc.) and Atticus (Cic. Att. 2, 25, 1. Varro RR. 2, 1, 25. 2, 2, 2), but never very intimate with Cicero, owing to their different characters (Roth l.l. 8). Letters to him by Cicero, fam. 9, 1–8. Triumvir (capitalis?), trib. pl. (Gell. 13, 12, 6); aedil. (Vitruv. 2, 8, 9; cf. Plin. NH. 35, 173). According to coins Pro Q(uaestore) of Pompey as proconsul, probably a. 678/76 in Spain against Sertorius (Roth l.l. 12), where he served at that time (Sall. hist. 2, fr. 42 *haec postquam Varro in maius more rumorum accepit*), certainly his lieutenant in the war against the pirates a. 687/67 (Varro RR. 2, praef. 7. Plin. NH. 3, 101. Flor. 1, 41, 10) and rewarded (Plin. NH. 7, 115. 16, 7) with a corona navalis (rostrata), probably (Roth l.l. 17) also in the war against Mithridates (a. 688/66). It seems that after this he became praetor (Themist. p. 453 Dind.: Βάρων τὴν ἑξαπέλεκυν ἦρχεν ἀρχήν, cf. Appian. b. c. 4, 47 ἐστρατηγηκώς), a. 695/59 he became a member of the commission of twenty charged with the execution of the lex Iulia agraria passed by the triumvirs (Varro RR. 1, 2, 10, cf. Plin. NH. 7, 176). a. 705/49 he was in company with Afranius and Petreius lieutenant to Pompey in Spain (Flor. 2, 13, 29) and, after the desertion of one of his legions, was obliged to surrender to Caesar (Caes. b. c. 1, 38. 2, 17–20) and seems to have had no further share in the rest of the war against him. In 707/47 Varro dedicated to him his Antiquitates rerum div. (Lactant. 1, 6, 7. Augustin. civ. d. 7, 35). He was designated librarian (Suet. Caes. 44; cf. Isid. orig. 6, 5, 1). M. Antony, who in 707/47 had been obliged by Caesar's order to render up an estate of Varro's which he had first seized (Cic. Phil. 2, 103) and again took possession of a. 710/44, proscribed him 711/43; but Fufius Calenus saved his life (App. b. c. 4, 47), though part of his library (Gell. 3, 10, 17) and his large estates were lost (at least it seems so, Roth l.l. 28 sq.). Val. Max. 8, 7, 3 *Terentius Varro . . . non annis, quibus saeculi tempus aequavit, quam stilo vivacior fuit. in eodem enim lectulo et spiritus eius et egregiorum operum cursus exstinctus est.* Plin. NH. 29, 65 *ni M. Varro LXXXIII vitae anno prodidisset* etc. ib. 7, 115 *Varronis* (in the public library of Asinius Pollio, § 219, 21, founded 716/38) *unius viventis posita est imago.* Cf. § 165, 1. JGSchneider, vita Varr., in his Scriptt. R. R. 1, 2, 217. PRE. 6, 1688. KLRoth, das Leben des Varro, Bas. 1857. GBoissier, la vie et les ouvrages de V., Par. 1861. ARiese, Phil. 27, 288.

2. General characterisation. Cic. Brut. 60 *diligentissimus investigator antiquitatis.* acad. post. 1, 9 *nos in nostra urbe peregrinantes . . . tui libri quasi domum reduxerunt. . . . tu aetatem patriae, tu discriptiones temporum, tu sacrorum iura, tu sacerdotum, tu domesticam, tu bellicam disciplinam, tu sedem regionum, locorum, tu omnium divinarum humanarumque rerum nomina, genera, officia, causas aperuisti plurimumque idem poetis nostris omninoque latinis et litteris luminis et verbis attulisti, atque ipse varium et elegans omni feri numero poema fecisti philosophiamque multis locis incohasti, ad impellendum satis, ad edocendum parum.* or. Phil. 2, 105. Ap. August. civ. dei 6, 2 *homo omnium facile acutissimus et sine ulla dubitatione doctissimus.* Irritably ad Att. 13, 18 (a. 709/45) *homo* πολυγραφώτατος *numquam me lacessivit* (challenged me by dedicating a work to me). Dionys. 2, 21 Τερέντιος Οὐάρρων . . .

ἀνὴρ τῶν κατὰ τὴν αὐτὴν ἡλικίαν ἀκμασάντων πολυπειρότατος. QUINT. 10, 1, 95 *Terentius Varro, vir Romanorum eruditissimus. plurimos hic libros et doctissimos composuit, peritissimus linguae latinae et omnis antiquitatis et rerum graecarum nostrarumque, plus tamen scientiae collaturus quam eloquentiae.* 12, 11, 24 *quam multa, paene omnia, tradidit Varro!* AUGUSTIN. civ. d. 6, 2 *M. Varro . . . tametsi minus est suavis eloquio, doctrina tamen atque sententiis ita refertus est ut in omni eruditione . . . studiosum rerum tantum iste doceat quantum studiosum verborum Cicero delectat.* Further: '*vir doctissimus undecumque Varro*' (TERENTIAN. MAUR. GL. 6, 409, 2846) *qui tam multa legit ut aliquid ei scribere vacasse miremur, tam multa scripsit quam multa vix quemquam legere potuisse credamus.* SEN. cons. ad Helv. 8, 1. APULEI. apol. 42 and others. PLUT. Romul. 12 *Οὐάρρωνα τὸν φιλόσοφον, ἄνδρα Ῥωμαίων ἐν ἱστορίᾳ βιβλιακώτατον.*

165. The total number of the works of Varro, according to a list ultimately to be traced to himself, amounted to about 620 books, belonging to 74 different works. Of the poetical works we can form an approximate idea as to which categories they belonged to only from the fragments of the saturae Menippeae (150 books), which fluctuate between the metrical and prose forms. Of the other poetical writings (saturae, pseudotragoediae and poemata) we know nothing but the names.

1. GELL. 3, 10, 17 *tum ibi addit (M. Varro in primo librorum qui inscribuntur Hebdomades), se quoque iam duodecimam annorum hebdomadam ingressum esse* (i.e. his age was more than 77 years) *et ad eum diem septuaginta hebdomadas librorum* (i.e. 490) *conscripsisse.* AUSON. profess. Burdig. 20, 1 *omnis doctrinae ratio . . . quantam condit sexcentis* (a round number) *Varro voluminibus.* A list of the works of Varro, which is wanting in arrangement both as to contents and chronology, but is derived from a good source, was given by Jerome in one of the (missing) letters ad Paulam (cf. HIERON. de vir. illustr. 54). Some quotations from it are contained in RUFIN. apol. 2, 20. But the original list was discovered in a MS. of the public library at Arras in the praefatio to Rufinus' translation of Origines' commentary on Genesis, and was first published and explained in the chief treatise on Varro's writings by RITSCHL, op. 3, 419. A facsimile of the MS. ib. 506. See also JBPITRA, spicil. Solesm. 3 (Par. 1855), 311 (cf. p. 1) and CHCHAPPUIS, Sentences de Varron et liste de ses ouvrages d'après différents manuscrits (Par. 1856) 117, where two Paris MSS. of the Homiliae in Genesim are used. Cf. RITSCHL, op. 3, 524. The list does not profess to be complete (*et alia plura, quae enumerare longum est. vix medium descripsi indicem, et legentibus fastidium est*), and contains 39, or (if we reckon singly the singulares libri X, the *μονόβιβλοι* which have been grouped together, and of which the contents cannot be determined) 48 numbers (with 490 single books), of which however 21 known to us from other sources are missing. The titles mentioned in this list will in the following list be marked thus *. Hence RITSCHL, op. 3, 485, fixes the whole number of Varro's works at 74, and calculates the number of books approximately at 620, whence we should have to assume the composition of 130 books during the last 11 or 12 years of Varro's life, which were, it is true, spent in perfect leisure. To the last part of his life belong by far the most important and extensive of his works, and to his earlier years we assign his poetical and rhetorical compositions, especially the saturae Menippeae and the logistorici. Remarkable are in Jerome's list the three *ἐπιτομαί* (which stand side

by side) of the Antiquitates (§ 166, 4 in fin.), the Imagines (p. 260, l. 18), the books de l.l. (§ 167, 2 ad fin.): did Varro arrange these himself? It is more probable that some later writer condensed the diffuse and inconvenient works for every-day use.

2. With regard to Varro's metrical compositions, we knew before the discovery of Jerome's list only epigrams on the Imagines and lines from the saturae Menippeae (see below). As in the Menippeae Varro founded himself on the Cynic Menippos, so he may in the *pseudotragoediarum libri VI, which were certainly not intended for the stage, have taken as his model the τραγῳδίαι of the Cynics Diogenes and Oinomaos or of the sillographer Timon. ERohde, gr. Rom. 249. OCrusius, lit. Centr.-Bl. 1887, 279. Ritschl, op. 3, 527. Riese, Varr. satt. 31.—Next *poematum libri X; cf. Diom. GL. 1, 400 *Varro in poetico libro.* Varro ap. Non. 428 *verba plura modice in quandam coniecta formam.*—*Satirarum libri IIII, perhaps in the manner of Lucilius and in contrast to the Menippean (n. 3) in verse throughout. Horace never mentions Varro as his predecessor in satire. Does he refer to him S. 1, 10, 47? Ritschl, op. 3, 431.—The existence of a didactic poem by Varro de rerum natura may be presumed from Quint. 1, 4, 4 (grammar cannot be *ignara philosophiae vel propter Empedoclem in Graecis, Varronem ac Lucretium in Latinis, qui praecepta sapientiae versibus tradiderunt*) and Lactant. div. inst. 2, 12, 4 (*Empedocles . . . de rerum natura versibus scripsit, ut apud Romanos Lucretius et Varro;* on Vellei. 2, 36, 2 *auctores carminum Varronem ac Lucretium*, see Riese, Varro p. 50), unless indeed Quintilian and Lactantius after him assumed the existence of a work of this kind from the words of Cicero (acad. post., see above p. 253, n. 2 l. 7). Cf. ARiese, Varr. satt. Men. 16. Reifferscheid's Suetonius 408.

3. *Satirarum Menippearum libros CL are mentioned by Hieronymus (n. 1) Quint. 10, 1, 95 *alterum illud etiam prius satirae genus, sed non sola carminum varietate mixtum condidit Terentius Varro* (cf. LMüller, RhM. 24, 140). Probus on Verg. Ecl. 6, 31, p. 14, 19 K.: *Varro . . . Menippeus* (Athen. 4, 160c Οὐάρρων ὁ Μενίππειος ἐπικαλούμενος), *non a magistro, cuius aetas longe praecesserat, nominatus, sed a societate ingenii, quod is quoque* (Menippus) *omnigeno carmine satiras suas expoliverat* (cf. ERohde, griech. Roman 249). Title of a satire by Varro Ταφὴ Μενίππου. Cic. acad. poster. 1, 8 (a. 709/45; Varro is the speaker): *in illis veteribus nostris quae Menippum imitati, non interpretati, quadam hilaritate conspersimus multa admixta ex intima philosophia, multa dicta dialectice.* ib. 1, 9 (Cicero addresses Varro, § 164, 2) *atque ipse varium et elegans omni fere numero poema fecisti*, a passage which probably refers to these Menippeae, although *poema* seems a curious title both as to the term and number by which to designate a work comprising 150 books and containing also prose. Gell. 2. 18, 7 *Menippus, cuius libros M. Varro in satiris aemulatus est, quas alii cynicas, ipse appellat Menippeas.* The Cynic Menippos of Gadara (about 250 b.c., concerning him CWachsmuth, sillogr. gr. [2] 78) had treated questions of social life and of philosophy σπουδογέλοιος in a jocular tone, and with frequent innuendos aimed at followers of other systems, in a prose work mixed with verse. His manner may still be recognised in his imitator Lucian. The mixture of prose and verse in Varro is seen from the fragments in addition to the passage in Probus (see also fragm. 58 B).—In the fragments of Varro's Menippeae there is especially frequent censure of the falling away of the present from the simplicity of early times. The form was motley (e.g. grotesque personifications of ideas); erudition and practical life, mythology and history, the past and the present supplied the subjects. Especially were to be found, as also in Menippos, ridicule of the philosophers (Armorum iudicium, λογομαχία, περὶ αἱρέσεων, ταφὴ Μενίππου, Periplu lib.

II περὶ φιλοσοφίας: this is the only one of the satires comprising several books) and many allusions to the Cynics (Cynicus, ἱπποκύων, κυνοδιδασκαλικά, κυνορήτωρ, ὑδροκύων; cf. GKnaack, Herm. 18, 148). The form frequently is a dialogue, and Varro seems to have sometimes introduced his own person (addresses *Varro, Marce* [562 B. 60. 175. 505]; cf. the titles Marcopolis, Marcipor and Bimarcus). As concerns the order of ideas, we should probably imagine it to a certain extent like Horace's Satires, loose and desultory. The whole was evidently one of the most characteristic productions of Roman literature, full of humour and spirit and in many points equal to the Lucilian satires; but the influence was not commensurate with the importance of the work, which was set aside as that of a whimsical person out of keeping with the times. Side by side with many peculiarities of popular composition (proverbs, puns, obscenities, alliteration, diminutives) we also meet with a liberal admixture of Greek, single words as well as whole lines. The metres used are of a varied character, and really *omni fere numero*, but treated with strict correctness. Iambic senarii prevail; besides these we have trochaics, halting iambics and trochaics, hexameters (and distichs), anapaests; but also sotadean lines (Lachmann's kl. Schr. 2, 48), galliambics, hendecasyllables, glyconeans, cretics, bacchiacs. Bücheler's Petronius (1882) p. 247. The greater number of fragments have been preserved by Nonius; those of the Eumenides are most numerous. Gellius is most useful in fixing the original contents and parts of the saturae Menippeae, hence the lists in Vahlen l.l. 203 and ARiese p. 38. As a rule, the titles are strange and arbitrary (e.g. Sesculixes, Papiapapae, Σκιαμαχία), sometimes Latin and sometimes Greek, not seldom taken from a proverb (*nescis quid vesper serus vehat; cras credo, hodie nihil; longe fugit qui suos fugit; mutuum muli scabunt;* ἄλλος οὗτος Ἡρακλῆς, δὶς παῖδες οἱ γέροντες and others), many are twofold, e.g. *Aborigines* περὶ ἀνθρώπων φύσεως; *Est modus matulae* περὶ μέθης; *Desultorius* περὶ τοῦ γράφειν etc. Such double titles e.g. also in the Cynic Oinomaos (n. 4. § 166, 2).—In 709/45 Cicero (acad. post. 1, 8) makes Varro call these satires *vetera sua*. But the publication of such a comprehensive work was naturally spread over a series of years: thus Varro wrote the Sexagessis only after his 60th year (see fragm. 485. 491. 493 sq. B.) and also the γεροντοδιδάσκαλος (181 sqq. B.) and the Tithonus περὶ γήρως (544 sqq. B.) evidently only as an old man. In the κοσμοτορύνη περὶ φθορᾶς κόσμου the battle of Thapsus (708/46) is probably mentioned. The Τρικάρανος (§ 166, 3), supposing it to belong here, was composed 694/60.—Otherwise unknown is Scantius in the fr. 142 B. *ut scribit S. 'horno per Dionysia'* (the name also Cic. Mil. 75. Plin. NH. 2, 240. Tac. ann. 4, 16. CIL. indd.).

4. Most recent collection of the remains of the satt. Men. by ARiese (Lpz. 1865) and FBücheler in the small ed. of Petronius ([3]Berl. 1882), p. 161. Criticism: JVahlen, in Varr. sat. Menipp. coniectanea, Lps. 1858; ORibbeck, RhM. 14, 102. FBücheler, RhM. 14, 419. 20, 401. LMüller, metr. poet. lat. and JJ. 95, 488. 507. JMähly, Varroniana (esp. for the Modius), Basel 1865. EBährens, RhM. 27. 490. LFriedländer in the Königsb. Ind. lect. 1873 sq. p. 3 sq. LHavet, rev. de phil. 6. 52. 7, 177. 193 and others.—LMercklin, die Doppeltitel der varron. Menippeae u. Logistorici, RhM. 12, 372; cf. Phil. 13, 713. ARiese, prolegg. to his ed.; in the symb. phil. Bonn. 479; RhM. 21, 109; Phil. 27, 316.—Mommsen, RG. 3[6], 603. Ribbeck, röm. Dicht. 1, 243.

166. Varro's prose-writings embraced almost all branches of knowledge and literature, oratory, history both general and literary, jurisprudence, grammar, philosophy, geography, husbandry etc. But in all this universal study, Varro always

kept his own country and its past steadily in view, and through that portion of his writings exercised an immense influence, both directly and indirectly. The Christian Fathers especially, and among them pre-eminently S. Augustine, studied and used him diligently. The most important prose works of Varro were his Antiquitates rerum humanarum et divinarum, which long survived in literature, the books de lingua latina, rerum rusticarum, the Encyclopaedia of the artes liberales (Disciplinarum libri) and his Imagines.

1. Speeches: *Orationum libri XXII, and *Suasionum libri III, the first probably exercises of the pen never delivered (some also pamphlets), possibly intended as laudationes (Varro's laudatio Porciae ap. Cic. Att. 13, 48, 2), the Suasiones perhaps of a political character. Each book seems to have contained only one speech. Ritschl, op. 3, 433. 492.

2. *Λογιστορικῶν libri LXXVI, discussions of philosophical (chiefly ethical) questions (λόγοι) with plentiful additions of historical instances (ἱστορίαι) derived from mythology and history, perhaps in the manner of Heraclides of Pontus, and like Cicero's Cato and Laelius serious and popular, in prose, some of them at least in the form of dialogues. Each piece bore a twofold title, the first part of which was the name of some person, either living or dead, who was connected with the subject-matter, and was perhaps the principal speaker, the second part indicating the contents in Latin; e.g. Catus de liberis educandis; Messala de valetudine; Curio de deorum cultu; Marius de fortuna; Orestes de insania; (Fundanius) Gallus de admirandis (cf. LHavet, rev. de phil. 7, 177); Sisenna de historia. They were probably written at an advanced age, at the end of the 7th and beginning of the 8th century u.c. So late a writer as Apoll. Sidon. ep. 8, 6 ad fin. says *Varronem logistoricum . . . misi.* Ritschl, op. 3, 403. 440. 482. 493. ARiese, Varr. sat. Menipp. 32. 53 and the fragments (those of the Catus very numerous) ib. 247. LKrahner, Varronis Curio de cultu deorum, Friedland 1851. LMercklin, Phil. 13, 728. ChChappuis, frag. des ouvrages de V. intitulés Logistorici, Hebdomades, . . . de forma philosophiae, Par. 1868.

3. Subjects of contemporary history: *Legationum libri III and *de Pompeio III, also *de sua vita libri III (Charis. GL. 1, 89, 28 *Varro de vita sua*); the first no doubt treated of Varro's own achievements as the legate of Pompey, in the war with the pirates, against Mithridates and in Spain; see § 164, 1. GOemichen, acta Lips. 3, 432; plinian. Studd. 27. RReitzenstein, Herm. 20, 517. The work on Pompey seems to have been in defence of him. Ritschl, op. 3, 436. Appian. b. c. 2, 9 (a. 694/60) *καί τις αὐτῶν* (of the triumvirs Pompeius, Caesar and Crassus) *τήνδε τὴν συμφροσύνην συγγραφεύς, Οὐάρρων ἐνὶ βιβλίῳ περιλαβὼν ἐπέγραψε* Τρικάρανον (cf. § 165, 3 ad fin.).

4. Works on Roman history. a) *Antiquitatum libri XLI (Jerome erroneously has XLV), a system of Roman antiquities, divided into two parts according to the subject-matter, rerum humanarum in 25 books (4 parts of 6 books each, with an introductory book); then (*quod prius exstiterint civitates, deinde ab eis res divinae institutae sint*, Augustin. civ. d. 6, 4), 16 rerum divinarum (5 parts of 3 books each, with one book to serve as introduction); see the account in Augustin. de civ. dei 6, 3; *XLI libros scripsit antiquitatum; hos in res humanas divinasque divisit, rebus humanis XXV, divinis XVI tribuit.* In the *res humanae* the author

took as the basis for his classification (cf. also VARRO ap. Non. 92, 11) the questions: *qui* (homines) *agant, ubi, quando, quid agant;* likewise in the *res divinae* the corresponding ones: *qui* (homines) *exhibeant, ubi, quando, quid exhibeant,* here is added the question: *quibus exhibeant* (sc. *deis*). From the summary of contents in AUGUSTIN. l.l. (especially accurate for the *res divinae*) results the following strictly systematised division of the whole work: I. RERUM HUMANARUM LIBRI XXV: book 1 general introduction (*librum unum singularem qui communiter prius de omnibus loqueretur in capite posuit*). Book 2–7 de hominibus. 8–13 de locis (geography of the Roman Empire, which was at a later time made use of by Verrius Flaccus, Pliny and others; RREITZENSTEIN Herm. 20, 516. 530). 14–19 de temporibus (see GELL. 3, 2, 1 *Varro in libro rer. human. quem de diebus scripsit.* SERV. Aen. 8, 526 *Varro de saeculis.* On this section HKETTNER, krit. Bemerk. zu Varro usw., Halle 1868, 14. OFGRUPPE, Herm. 10, 51). 20–25 de rebus (GELL. 1, 25, 1 *Varro in libro humanarum qui est de bello et pace*). II.—RERUM DIVINARUM LIBRI XVI: book 1 general introduction (*et istorum exordio unum singularem qui prius de omnibus loqueretur apposuit*). B. 2–4 de hominibus (2 de pontificibus. 3 de auguribus. 4 de xvviris sacrorum). 5–7 de locis (5 de sacellis. 6 de sacris aedibus. 7 de locis religiosis). 8–10 de temporibus (8 de feriis. 9 de ludis circensibus. 10 de ludis scenicis). 11–13 de sacris (11 de consecrationibus. 12 de sacris privatis. 13 de sacris publicis). 14–16 de deis (14 de deis certis. 15 de deis incertis. 16 de deis praecipuis atque selectis).—The rer. divin. libri were intended to counteract the decay of the religion of the State and were addressed ad Caesarem pontificem (AUGUSTIN. de civ. dei 7, 35. LACTANT. inst. 1, 6, 7) and seem, therefore, to have been published about the close of 707/47. Of the entire work there was also an abridgment: *ἐπιτομή antiquitatum, ex libris XLI [I] libri VIIII: see § 165, 1 in fin. Priscian seems to be the last who possessed the Antiqq. complete. RITSCHL, op. 3, 444. LHKRAHNER, de Varr. antiqq. . . . libris XLI, Halle 1834; ZfAW. 1852, 385. LMERCKLIN, Phil. 13, 731. The fragments are collected and explained by RMERKEL in his edition of Ovid's Fasti p. CVI. PMIRSCH, de Varr. antiqq. rer. humanarum libris (with a collection of fragments), Lpz. Studd. 5, 1 (compare OFGRUPPE, Phil. Wschr. 1883, 464). CHJFRANCKEN, fragmenta Varronis in libris Augustini de civ. dei, Leid. 1836. LÜTTGERT. Theologumena Varroniana a s. Augustino in iudicium vocata, Sorau 1858. 1859. LMERCKLIN, de Varrone coronarum Rom. militarium interprete praecipuo, Dorp. 1859. On the employment of the Antiq. rer. human. by later writers see OGRUPPE, commentat. Mommsen. 540.

b) *Annalium libri III, probably a chronological compendium like the annalis of Atticus and the chronica of Cornelius Nepos. RITSCHL, op. 3, 447. LURLICHS, Anfänge der griech. Künstlergesch. 35; die Quellenregister zu Plin. p. 17. That these annales (CHARIS. GL. 1, 105, 6. *Varro . . . in annali*) as well as the res urbanae (below, g) are a garbled selection from Antiquitates rerum humanarum is an untenable conjecture of OGRUPPE's, comment. Mommsen. 541. 550. 825.

c) *de vita populi romani (cf. Dikaiarchos' Βίος Ἑλλάδος; cf. VARRO RR. 1, 2, 16) libri IIII, dedicated to Atticus (CHARIS. GL. 1, 126), to judge from the fragments (collected by KETTNER p. 21) a kind of history of Roman civilisation. It was written perhaps about 711/43 (RITSCHL, op. 3, 450). BOISSIER l.l. 188. H KETTNER, Varronis de vita pop. rom. . . . quae exstant, Halle 1863.

d) de gente populi rom. 4 books; see ARNOB. adv. nat. 5, 8 *Varro . . . in librorum quattuor primo quos de gente conscriptos rom. pop. dereliquit, curiosis computationibus edocet ab diluvii tempore* (of Deucalion) *ad usque Hirti consulatum et Pansae* (a. 711/43) *annorum esse milia nondum duo.* They were therefore written a. 711/43 or shortly afterwards; an attempt to bring Roman chronology into accordance with that of other parts of history, and thus to fix the pedigree of the Roman nation (ROTH, Leben des Varro 27). This genealogy was, after a chronological introduction on the Sicyonian and Athenian dynasties (bk. 1 and 2), carried down to the Latin (bk. 3) and Roman (bk. 4) dynasties, great attention being paid to *quid Romani a quaque traxerint gente per imitationem.* (SERV. Aen. 7, 176; cf. RSCHÖLL, Herm. 11, 337.) This work was much used by S. AUGUSTINE in book 18 de civ. dei in the first half, see esp. c. 2. 13. FRANCKEN, fragm. Varr. 124. HKETTNER, varronische Studien (Halle 1865) 38; the fragments ib. 63 and in HPETER's hist. frag. 228.

e) de familiis troianis (families of patrician rank descended from Aeneas or his companions) in several books (SERV. Aen. 5, 704 *Varro in libris quos de familiis troianis scripsit.*) See RITSCHL, op. 3, 445. WHERTZBERG in the notes on his translation of the Aeneid 5, 116. p. 369.

f) Aetia (Αἴτια, after the example of Kallimachos), explanations (of the ratio, causa, the cur) of Roman customs and manners, especially those of private life, the principal source of Plutarch's Αἴτια ῥωμαϊκά; the only question is whether Plutarch made use of Varro himself, or only took Varronian materials at second hand. LMERCKLIN, Phil. 3, 267. 13, 710. GTHILO, de Varrone Plut. quaestt. rom. auctore praecipuo, Bonn 1853. JJWLAGUS, Plutarchus Varronis studiosus, Helsingf. 1847. RITSCHL, op. 3, 451. FLEO, de Plutarchi quaestionum roman. auctoribus, Halle 1864. PGLAESSER, de Varron. doctrinae ap. Plut. vestigiis, Lpz. Studd. 4. 157.

g) *rerum urbanarum libri III (cf. CHARIS. GL. 1, 133 *Varro de rebus urbanis III*), perhaps a history of the city of Rome, especially on questions of topography. RITSCHL l.l. 449. BOISSIER l.l. 169. OJAHN, Herm. 2, 235. HJORDAN, Topogr. d. Stadt Rom. 1, 1, 43.

h) tribuum liber (quoted by VARRO LL. 5, 56); used in the articles concerning the tribes in Festus? see LMERCKLIN, quaestt. Varr. (Dorpat 1852), 5.

All these works (b—h) form the completion and detailed explanation of the subject treated in the Antiqq. rerum humanarum, to which also belongs the Εἰσαγωγικὸς (cf. § 2, 3) ad Pompeium composed as early as 683/71 (*Pompeius cum initurus foret consulatum*, GELL.)—*ex quo disceret quid facere dicereque deberet cum senatum cousuleret* (GELL. 14, 7, 2). See § 166, 6, d. But the subject treated in the res divinae does not recur in any work of more special scope: the passage *Varro in augurum libris* (Macrob. sat. 1, 16, 19) is doubtful (perhaps we should read *libro* i.e. *antiquitatum*); see RITSCHL, op. 3, 480.

5. Works on literary history (cf. AKIESSLING, coniectan. III, Greifsw. 1886, III): *de bibliothecis III; *de proprietate scriptorum III (perhaps on questions of style, RITSCHL, op. 3, 463); de poetis (the Roman) in several books (GELL. 1, 24, 3 *epigramma Plauti . . . a M. Varrone positum in libro de poetis primo;* cf. 17, 21, 43. 45); *de poematis III (probably a treatise on poetic art); *de lectionibus III (seems to have dealt with recitation, RITSCHL l.l. 460); de compositione saturarum (NON. 67). Dramatic literature and Plautus were especially treated by Varro in a series of works (RITSCHL l.l. 455). Also *de originibus scenicis III; *de scenicis actionibus (exhibitions) III (acc. to JEROME; in CHARIS. GL. 1, 95 *Varro de actionibus scenicis V;* cf. de dub. nomin GL. 5, 590); *de actis scenicis III; (so in JEROME, i.e. concerning the dramatic records, the didascaliæ; this work was probably the source of the scenic notices which have been preserved; see § 109, 4 and FSCHOELL, RhM. 31, 471.—RITSCHL, op. 3, 457 wrote de actibus

scenicis=concerning the arrangement of the acts); *de personis (masks) III; *de descriptionibus (characters) III; *quaestionum Plautinarum V (possibly explanations of obscure expressions) and de comoediis Plautinis (perhaps on the genuine and spurious plays) several books (*M. Varro in libr. de comoediis Pl. primo*, Gell. 3, 3, 9). Servius Aen. 10, 894 (*ut etiam Varro in ludis theatralibus docet*) speaks rather of the book of the Antiqq. rer. div. treating de ludis scenicis (see above p. 258, l. 19) than of the treatise de scenicis actionibus.—Of special importance among the writings of Varro concerning literary history are

*Imaginum libri XV or Hebdomades, illustrated biographies, published about 715/39 (Gell. 3, 10, 17), containing, with the prose text, 700 portraits of Greek and Roman celebrities (kings and generals, statesmen, poets, prose-writers, professional men, artists, men famous in all branches of knowledge) with a (metrical) elogium on each. The first book seems to have formed the introduction with 14 types of the classes given in the succeeding books; the other 14 books (or 7 dyads, the even numbers for the aliens, especially the Greeks, the odd for the Romans) would seem to have contained 7 hebdomades or 49 imagines each ($14 \times 49 = 686 + 14 = 700$). There was also (most likely at a later date) a cheap (popular) edition, probably without portraits, *Ἐπιτομὴν ex Imaginum libris XV libros IIII. Cf. § 165, 1 in fin. Ritschl. op. 3, 554. Plin. NH. 35, 11 *imaginum amorem flagrasse quondam testes sunt Atticus ille Ciceronis* (see § 172, 2, d) *et M. Varro benignissimo invento, insertis voluminum suorum fecunditati septingentorum inlustrium aliquo modo imaginibus . . . inventor muneris etiam dis invidiosi, quando* (the celebrities as depicted) *in omnes terras misit ut praesentes esse ubique ceu di possent.* Gell. 3, 10, 1 *M. Varro in primo librorum qui inscribuntur hebdomades vel de imaginibus.* 3, 11, 7 *M. Varro in libro de imaginibus primo Homeri imagini epigramma hoc adposuit.* Symmach. epist. 1, 2 *scis Terentium . . . Reatinum . . . hebdomadum libros epigrammatum adiectione condiisse . . . in socerum . . . tibi delegamus epigrammata. nam et Varronis libri diversis notantur auctoribus.* Cf. ib. 1, 4. Auson. Mosell. 305 *forsan et insignes hominumque operumque labores* (of Greek architecture) *hic habuit decimo celebrata volumine Marci hebdomas.*—Perhaps the sketcher Iaia (Maia? Laia?) of Cyzicus supplied the illustrations? Cf. Plin. NH. 35, 147 and WFröhner, Phil. Suppl. 5, 18.—MHertz, Arch. Ztg. 8, 142. Ritschl, op. 3, 452. 508. 528. 544. 564. LMercklin in the Dorpater Ind. lect. 1857 (reprinted in Ritschl's op. 3, 530); RhM. 13, 460 and Phil. 13, 742. 15, 709. LUrlichs, RhM. 14, 607. JVahlen, JJ. 77, 737. MSchmidt, RhM. 20, 298.

Pliny derived from Varro many notices concerning the mechanical arts: but it is not demonstrable that Varro composed special treatises on the history of art. AFurtwängler, Plin. u. s. Quellen in der Kunstgesch. (Lpz. 1877), 56. ThSchreiber, de artificum aetatibus in Plin. NH., Lpz. 1872. GOehmichen, plinian. Studd. 106. 203.

6. Works on various departments of science (Ritschl l.l. 441).

a) *Disciplinarum libri IX, the first encyclopaedia in Roman literature on the artes liberales, as they had been developed by the Greeks, viz. 1 grammatica (Wilmanns, Varr. gramm. 98. 208), 2 dialectica, 3 rhetorica, 4 geometria, 5 arithmetica, 6 astrologia (OGruppe, Herm. 11, 237), 7? musica, 8 medicina, 9 architectura (cf. § 57, 1), out of which grew the seven artes liberales which are met with as early as S. Augustine and Martianus Capella. If we are justified in referring to bk. 8 the words of Pliny NH. 29, 65 (*cunctarer in proferendo ex his remedio ni M. Varro LXXXIII vitae anno prodidisset*), this work would seem to be one of Varro's latest compositions (Gruppe l.l. 239 argues otherwise). In general Ritschl, op. 3, 353. 441. 474. LMercklin, Phil. 13, 736.

b) The single departments comprised by Varro in his Discipl. libri were mostly again treated by him in special treatises, e.g. grammar (see below, e), philosophy, *de forma philosophiae libri III; perhaps also a single book de philosophia, see AUGUSTIN. civ. d. 19, 1; cf. RITSCHL, op. 3, 441. LKRAHNER, de Varrone ex Martiani satura supplendo, c. 1: de Varronis philosophia, Friedland 1846. These philosophical treatises were undoubtedly written after Cicero's Academica, i.e. after 709/45 (WILMANNS, Varr. gramm. libr. 9). There was also a special treatise on rhetoric (*Varro . . . in libro III Rhetoricorum*, PRISCIAN. GL. 2, 489), and also the *libri IX de principiis numerorum, which were no doubt in the Pythagorean spirit. On the geometria see § 52, 2. On gromatic (§ 58) the treatise de mensuris (PRISCIAN. GL. 2, 420. BOETHIUS de geometr. p. 1234): RITSCHL, op. 3, 475. 494.—*De valitudine tuenda liber I: was it an independent work or rather a logistoricus? (RITSCHL l.l. 440. 475).

c) Geographical. Besides the books 8–13 of the antiquitt. hum. (see above) the books de ora maritima (SERV. Aen. 1, 108. 112. 5, 19. 8, 710), which appear to have been directions for navigation (on coast-lines and coast-settlements, dangers and difficulties of navigation, wind and weather, ebb and flood tides etc.); called by VEGET. 5, 11 *libri navales*, by SOLIN. 11, 6 *opus quod de littoralibus est*. VARRO LL. 9, 26 probably himself refers to some part of the book *in libro quem feci de aestuariis* (i.e. on the subject of the ebb and flood tides). MOMMSEN on Solin. p. XIX.; Herm. 18, 161. DDETLEFSEN, commentt. Mommsen. 27. RREITZENSTEIN, Herm. 20, 523; 21, 240. OEHMICHEN, plinian. Studd. 47. ESCHWEDER, Phil. 46, 276.—Akin to this as regards its subject is the meteorological calendar for mariners *ephemeris navalis* (NON. 71, 19). Itiner. Alex. M. 6 *Varro Cn. Pompeio per Hispanias militaturo librum illum Ephemeridos sub nomine elaboravit* (therefore composed about 677/77). Besides this a second Ephemeris (agrestis or rustica?? RREITZENSTEIN, de scriptt. R. R., Berl. 1884, 44): PRISC. GL. 2, 256, 20 *Varro in ephemeride: postea honoris virtutum causa Iulii Caesaris . . . mensis Iulius est appellatus* (therefore written after 708/46). BERGK, RhM. 1, 367.

d) *de iure civili libri XV, probably denoting Roman private law; RITSCHL l.l. 444. This is supposed, without sufficient proof, to be a general introduction to Roman law and the principal source of Pomponius by FDSANIO, Varroniana in den Schriften der römischen Juristen, Lpz. 1867, 134, cf. ib. 211. The libri de gradibus (on the degrees of relationship), mentioned by SERV. Aen. 5, 410, seem to treat of a similar subject. Questions of antiquarian and political interest and also grammatical points were dealt with in the Epistolicae quaestiones, in at least 8 books (RITSCHL l.l. 477): in b. 4 of these epist. quaestt. was the epistula ad Oppianum, by which Varro replaced the commentarius εἰσαγωγικὸς (§ 166, 4 h) de officio senatus habendi, which he had formerly sent to Pompey, and which had been lost: GELL. 14, 7, 3. In addition (or contained in it?) letters ad (Iulium) Caesarem, ad Fabium, ad Fufium, ad Marullum, ad Neronem (all quoted in NON.), ad Serv. Sulpicium (GELL. 2, 10); lastly *ep. Latinae* (NON. 473, 20), *epistulis Latiniae* (NON. 419, 13, cf. *ep. latina* 121, 12, *ep. latina l. I.* 141, 14): addressed to Latins?? LHAVET, rev. de phil. 7, 176.—RITSCHL, op. 3, 476. 494.—Concerning the *rerum rusticarum libri III see § 168.

e) Besides the great work *de lingua latina libri XXV, see § 167, the following separate treatises dealt with grammar: de antiquitate litterarum (PRISCIAN. GL. 2, 8 *Varro in II de antiquitate litterarum*), addressed to the tragic poet L. Accius and therefore one of the earliest works of Varro (RITSCHL l.l. 469. 498. WILMANNS p. 117, 218); *de origine linguae latinae III (perhaps dedicated to Pompey; RITSCHL l.l. 470); περὶ χαρακτήρων (=τύπων, formation of words

HUsener, JJ. 95, 247), at least 3 books (Charis. GL. 1, 189 *Varro in III π. χ.*); *de similitudine verborum III (=de analogia, Ritschl l.l. 468); de utilitate sermonis (Charis. GL. 1, 123 *Varro de ut. s. IIII*), laying great weight on the principle of anomalia (Ritschl l.l. 469); lastly *de sermone latino V (Jerome; but Rufin. GL. 6, 555 *Varro de lingua latina ad Marcellum*, and ib. 556 twice *Varro in lib. VII de lingua latina ad Marcellum*, cf. Gell. 12, 6, 3. 12, 10, 4. 16, 12, 7. 18, 12, 8. Wilmanns, p. 47, 170), treating also of the metres (Ritschl l.l. 463, cf. Westphal, griech. Metrik 1[2], 116, 173) and the chief authority on orthography for the later grammarians. An epitome of the section on accents is contained in Sergius' explan. in Donat. GL. 4, 525; cf. Wilmanns 49, Lentz on Herodian 1, xxxi, FSchöll, act. Lips. 6, 5. Another in the Orthography of Terentius Scaurus GL. 7, 29; cf. HUsener, RhM. 24, 94. In general AWilmanns, de Varr. libris grammaticis scripsit relliquiasque subiecit, Berl. 1864.

167. Of all the works of Varro only two have come down to us, de lingua latina and rerum rusticarum libri III. But of the original 25 books de lingua latina only books V to X are in existence, and even those mutilated at the end of VIII and X, and at the beginning of VII and IX, not to speak of numerous interpolations and corruptions. The complete work dealt, in its first half, with the formation and inflexion of words, in its second with the syntax, and throughout the Alexandrine writers and Stoics were laid under large contributions. From the fifth book the work was dedicated to Cicero, whence it follows that it was written and published (at least in part) about 711/43, at the very latest. The subject-matter is often distorted by the arbitrary arrangement, the style is antiquated, jerky and uncouth, the numerous etymologies are no better than empirical word-play.

1. The strict and mechanical symmetry of the composition in the work de lingua latina (cf. § 116, 4 a) appears from the repeated reference to the scheme. 7, 110 *quoniam omnis operis de lingua latina tris feci parteis, primo quemadmodum vocabula imposita essent rebus* (etymology), *secundo quemadmodum ea in casus declinarentur* (declension and conjugation), *tertio quemadmodum coniungerentur* (syntax). Cf. 8, 1.—5, 1 *quemadmodum vocabula essent imposita rebus in lingua latina sex libris exponere institui. de his tris* (independently of the first book which contains the introduction, thus we get books 2–4) *ante hunc feci, quos Septumio* (*qui mihi fuit quaestor* is added by Varro 7, 109) *misi. in quibus est de disciplina quam vocant ἐτυμολογικήν. quae contra eam dicerentur, volumine primo* (b. 2); *quae pro ea, secundo* (b. 3); *quae de ea, tertio* (b. 4). *in his ad te* (Cicero) *scribam, a quibus rebus vocabula imposita sint in lingua latina, et ea quae sunt in consuetudine apud poetas.*—6, 97 *quoniam de hisce rebus tris libros ad te mittere institui, de oratione soluta duo, de poetica unum, et ex soluta ad te misi duo, priorem* (b. 5) *de locis et quae in locis sunt, hunc* (b. 6) *de temporibus et quae cum his sunt coniuncta: deinceps in proxumo* (b. 7) *de poeticis verborum originibus scribere incipiam.*—7, 5 *dicam in hoc libro de verbis quae a poetis sunt posita, primum de locis, dein de his quae in locis sunt, tertio de temporibus, tum quae cum temporibus sunt coniuncta.*—8, 24 *de quibus utriusque generis* (ἀναλογίας and ἀνωμαλίας) *declinationibus libros faciam bis ternos: prioris tris* (b. 8–10) *de earum declinationum disciplina, posterioris* (b. 11–13) *de eius disciplinae pro-*

paginibus. de prioribus primus (b. 8) *erit hic: quae contra similitudinem* (analogy) *declinationum dicantur, secundus* (b. 9), *quae contra dissimilitudinem* (anomaly), *tertius* (b. 10) *de similitudinum forma. de quibus quae expediero, singulis tribus; tum de alteris totidem scribere ac dividere incipiamus.* The books 14 to 25 treated of syntax (but see ARiese, Phil. 27, 296). Cf. Spengel pref. to his ed.[2] p. xxxiv. Wilmanns, de Varr. libris gramm. p. 22. ORibbeck (composition of b. 5–7), RhM. 41, 618. The fragments of the lost books are collected by Wilmanns, 141.

2. The dedication to Cicero covered books 5 to 25 (see however ARiese, Phil. 27, 297). Cf. Gell. 16, 8, 6 *M. Varro de lingua latina ad Ciceronem quarto vicesimo;* also Priscian. GL. 2, 540 *Varro in XXIIII ad Ciceronem.* The fact of the other books being already dedicated to Septumius (n. 1) would seem to prove that they were written before Varro decided to exchange with Cicero a series of dedications. As early as 707/47 he promised Cicero *magnam et gravem προσφώνησιν* (Cic. Att. 13, 12, 3), but did not get on as fast as Cicero desired, so that Cicero became impatient in 709/45 (*biennium praeteriit cum ille Καλλιππίδης assiduo cursu cubitum nullum processerit,* l.l.) and took Atticus' advice in starting himself by dedicating his Academica to Varro (Att. 13, 12, 3. 16, 1, 18). Varro's work was finished only after the publication of Cicero's Academica (a. 709/45), but no doubt a part was published before Cicero's death (close of 711/43). OMüller's supposition, that the work was perhaps published in an unfinished state after Varro's death, rests on insufficient evidence. See OMüller's praef. p. iii–xi and against his view LSpengel, Abhandl. der bayr. Akad. 7, 2, 443; Roth, Leben Varros 25 and Wilmanns, Varr. libr. gramm. 37. There was an epitome of this work: *ἐπιτομὴν de lingua latina ex libris X⟨X⟩V libri VIIII; see § 165, 1 ad fin.

3. Sole standard MS.: Laur. 51, 10 s. XI in Florence from Monte Cassino (Facsim. ap. Chatelain t. 12); from this, when it was still complete (Q.II=5, 118–6, 61 now missing), were copied the rest of the MSS. (all s. XV sq.). AGroth, de Varr. de LL. ll. cod. florentino (containing a complete collation), Diss. Argentor. 4 (1880), 81. The fragm. Casinense 361 s. XI to LL. 5, 41–57 also depends on the Laur.; HKeil, RhM. 6, 142. LSpengel, Abh. d. Münch. Akad. 7, 2, 475. GGötz, quaestt. Varron., Jena, 1886. Recent editions by LSpengel (Berl. 1826; [2]emend. app. crit. instr. praef. est LSpengel, ed. ASpengel, Berl. 1885) and OMüller (Lps. 1833; following the latter AEEgger, Par. 1837). Criticism (see Phil. 13, 684 and 27, 303) esp. by LSpengel, Abh. d. bayr. Ak. 7, 2, 429; de emendanda ratione librorum . . . de l.l., Münch. 1858; Phil. 17, 288. 32, 92. CLachmann, kl. Schr. 2, 163. Bergk, kl. Schr. 1, 571. WChrist, Phil. 16, 450. 17, 59. JNMadvig. advers. 2, 166. CFWMüller, ZfGW. 19, 421. 792. 867. HReiter, quaestt. Varron. gramm., Königsb. 1862; obss. crit. in Varr. de LL., Braunsb. 1884. ASpengel, Münch. SBer. 1885, 243. GGötz, Berl. PhWschr. 1886, 781.

168. Varro's three books rerum rusticarum, which we possess almost entire, are far more attractive to the reader. The first treats of agriculture, the second of cattle, the third of bird- and fish-breeding. Erudition and a long practical experience furnished the author (who was then 80 years old) with rich materials, and one feels how firmly and with what pleasure he handles these subjects with which he is thoroughly familiar. The whole is dressed up as a dialogue, in the manner of Cicero's philosophical writings, but far more graphic in scenery and

action; Varro largely availing himself of this opportunity to display his somewhat pedantic, but thoroughly kindly wit, especially in puns on the names of his characters.

1. R. R. 1, 1, 1 *annus octogesimus admonet me ut sarcinas colligam ante quam proficiscar e vita.* It was, therefore, written a. 717/37. The dialogue in b. 2 is supposed to take place in 687/67 (April 21st), in book 3 in 700/54; see 2, praef. 7. 3, 2, 3 (cf. Cic. Att. 4, 15, 5). Ib. 1, 1, 4 *scribam tibi* (his wife Fundania) *tres libros indices* (i.e. précis). This remained, though books 2 and 3 were dedicated to others, the latter to Q. Pinnius, the former to Turranius Niger, who perhaps also wrote on kindred subjects; see Diom. GL. 1, 368, 26 † *tyrannus* (*Turranius*, Keil) *de agri cultura primo.* 1, 1, 11 *quo brevius* (on account of the great number of predecessors) *de ea re conor tribus libris exponere, uno de agri cultura, altero de re pecuaria, tertio de villaticis pastionibus.* 1, 1, 12 (Varro's instruction proceeds) *ex radicibus trinis, et quae ipse in meis fundis colendo animadverti et quae legi et quae a peritis audii.* 2, praef. 6 *quoniam de agri cultura librum Fundaniae uxori propter eius fundum feci, tibi, Niger Turrani noster, qui vehementer delectaris pecore, . . . de re pecuaria breviter ac summatim percurram.* 3, 1, 9 *cum putarem esse rerum rusticarum . . . tria genera, unum de agri cultura, alterum de re pecuaria, tertium de villaticis, pastionibus, tres libros institui, e queis duo scripsi: primum ad Fundaniam uxorem de agri cultura, secundum de pecuaria ad Turranium Nigrum. qui reliquus est tertius, de villaticis fructibus, hunc ad te* (Q. Pinnius) *mitto, quod visus sum debere pro nostra vicinitate et amore scribere potissimum ad te.* Just as this continual insistence on the arrangement of the work is characteristic of Varro (cf. § 167, 1), so we have in this work also a frequent recurrence of his complaints about the loss of the ancient simplicity of manners. For the puns on proper names (Fundania, Fundilius, Agrasius, Agrius, Stolo, Scrofa, Vitulus, Vaccius, Merula, Passer, Pavo, Pica, Parra, Orata, Murena and others) see ASchleicher, meletem. Varron. 1 (Bonn 1846), 1–12.

2. On the MSS. cf. § 122, 1.—Critical ed. by HKeil; see § 122, 1. Other editions in the Scriptt. RR. (§ 54, 7) and in the opera Varronis (§ 169, 3).—Translation by GGrosse, Halle 1788.—HKeil, observatt. critt. in Catonis et Varronis de RR. libros, Halle 1849; obss. critt. in Varr. RR., Halle 1883; emendatt. Varr., Halle 1883. 84, II; de Petri de Crescentiis commodis ruralibus (on their worthlessness for the criticism of Varro), Halle 1885. HNettleship, Journ. of Phil. 7, 172. FZahlfeldt, quaestt. crit. in Varr. RR., Berl., 1881.

169. The other works of Varro do not seem to have been in existence beyond the 6th century of the Christian era. It is quite uncertain whether the so-called sententiae Varronis are really derived from Varro's writings.

1. On the relation of Martianus Capella to Varro see CBöttger, Jahn's Arch. 13, 590. LHKrahner, de Varrone ex Martiani satura supplendo, Friedland 1846. Isidorus does not derive the 36 passages in which he mentions Varro from Varro himself. HKettner, varronische Studien (Halle 1865) 2–37. From this circumstance we seem justified in drawing the conclusion that the age of Isidorus (§ 496) possessed no more of Varro than we have.

2. The Sententiae Varronis, about 160 (printed e.g. in ARiese, Varr. satt. 265), appear in the MSS. under various titles (Sententiae Varronis ad Papirianum Athenis audientem; Proverbia Varronis ad Paxianum: Sententiae Varronis ad Atheniensem auditorem morales atque notabiles; Varro ad Atheniensem audi-

torem; Liber Moralis quem Varro scripsit ad Ath. aud.; Varro in Moralibus or in libro Moralium). A good many among them may well be genuine sayings of Varro (see Riese l.l. p. x), but we have no trustworthy evidence by which to recognise and distinguish these. That the collection bears the name of Varro proves very little. As instances, e.g. 1 *di essemus ni moreremur.* 4 *cum natura litigat qui mori grave fert.* 10 *in multis contra omnes sapere desipere est.* 62 *eo tantum studia intermittantur ne omittantur.* 86 *sic multi libros degustant ut convivae delicias.* 151 *sic studendum ut propter id te putes natum;* it is true that all these sayings remind us even more of Seneca in style and spirit. Mercklin even conjectured that the Varro (p. 13, 24. 60, 22. 80, 11 Huemer) mentioned by the late grammarian Virgilius Maro (§ 452, 5) was the author. In the encyclopaedic works of the Middle Ages (e.g. Vicentii Bellovacensis Speculum historiale and doctrinale, Arnoldi de Hollandia Liber Vaticani) these sayings were much used. Literature: Sententias Varr. ed. et illustr. VDevit, Padua 1843. RKlotz, die Varro beigelegten Denksprüche, Jahn's Arch. 9, 582. HDüntzer, ib. 15, 193; cf. JJ. 54, 135. LMercklin, Phil. 2, 480. 13, 739. LQuicherat, pensées inédites de Varron, Bibl. de l'école des chartes 3, 1 (Par. 1849), 3. Sentences de Varr. et liste de ses ouvrages, d'après differ. mscrits, par ChChappuis, Par. 1856. Ritschl op. 3, 522.

3. A trustworthy collection and explanation of the whole of the remains of Varro's works is still wanting.—Early editions: Varronis opera cum notis JScaligeri, ATurnebi all., Par. 1569. 1585. Cum fragm. APopma, Leid. 1601; c. nott. varr., Dortr. 1619 (repeated ed. Bipontina 1788 II). Brunetti, frammenti minori di V., Venice 1874.—LMercklin and ARiese, die varronische Literatur vom J. 1826–1868, Phil. 13, 683. 27, 286.—On Varro's diction LStünkel, de Varr. verborum formatione, Strassb. 1876. AMüller, de priscis verborum formis Varr., Halle 1877. Compare the references § 98, 7.

170. Among the scholars of the period, the next place to Varro was held by P. Nigidius Figulus (praetor a. 696/58), whose extensive works dealt not only with grammar, but also with theology and various branches of natural science; yet, as his bent was mainly towards odd and occult subjects, he gained little influence, and was soon perfectly eclipsed by Varro.

1. P. Nigidius (Cic. p Sull. 42. Timae. 1. Plut. Cic. 20. an seni 27 and elsewhere) Figulus (see Schol. Lucan. 1, 639), praetor 696/58 (Cic. ad Qu. fr. 1, 2, 16), whence his birth-year cannot be fixed later than 656/98. Being a zealous partisan of Pompey, he was exiled by Caesar (Cic. fam. 4, 13 a. 708/46), Hieron. ad Euseb. Chron. a. Abr. 1972=709/45 *Nigidius Figulus Pythagoricus et magus in exilio moritur.* In conformity with his Pythagorean views he was conservative in his politics, and was useful to Cicero in his struggle with Catiline (p Sull. and Plut. l.l.). The Orphic mysticism and magic tendencies of the Pythagorean teaching of this period appear in Nigidius Figulus. Occult arts, recovering stolen objects (Apulei. mag. 42), and conjecturing at nativity (Suet. Aug. 94. Dio 45, 1) are mentioned of him. Conflicts with the police caused thereby may account for the sacrilegium Nigidianum in Ps. Cic. in Sall. resp. 5; see n. 3. Cf. Mommsen, RG. 3^6, 573.

2. MHertz, de P. Nigidii Fig. studiis atque operibus, Berl. 1845. Quaestt. Nigidianae by JKlein (de vita Nigidii, Bonn 1861) and JFrey (Rössel 1867). HRoehrig, de Nig. Fig. capp. II, Coburg 1887.—His fragments have been collected

by ARiccobonus (Bas. 1579), JRutgers (Var. lect., Leiden 1618, p. 246); those on astronomy by RMerkel, Ovid. Fast. p. lxxxvi sqq. ABreysig, de N. F. fragmentis apud schol. Germanici servatis, Berlin 1854.—FBücheler, RhM. 13, 177. CRobert, Eratosth. cataster. (Berl. 1878) 16.

3. Cic. Timae. 1 *fuit vir ille cum ceteris artibus, quae quidem dignae libero essent, ornatus omnibus, tum acer investigator et diligens earum rerum quae a natura involutae videntur. denique sic iudico, post illos nobiles Pythagoreos . . . hunc exstitisse qui illam (disciplinam) renovaret.* Gell. 4, 9, 1 *Nigidius Figulus, homo, ut ego arbitror, iuxta M. Varronem doctissimus.* Cf. ib. 4, 16, 1. 10, 11, 2 (*homo in omnium bonarum artium disciplinis egregius*). 11, 11, 1. 13, 26, 1. 5. 15, 3, 5. 17, 7, 4. Schol. Bob. Cic. Vatin. p. 317 Or. *fuit illis temporibus Nigidius quidam vir doctrina et eruditione studiorum praestantissimus ad quem plurimi conveniebant. haec ab obtrectatoribus veluti factio* (thus Bücheler, RhM. 34, 352: *actio* MS.) *minus probabilis iactitabatur, quamvis ipsi Pythagorae sectatores existimari vellent.* Serv. Aen. 10, 175 *Nigidius est solus post Varronem, licet Varro praecellat in theologia, hic in communibus* (cf. § 142, 4) *litteris. nam uterque utrumque scripsit.*

4. Commentarii grammatici probably in 30 books (Gell. 10, 5, 1 *P. Nigidius dicit in commentariorum undetricesimo*), often quoted ap. Gell. Non. and elsewhere, in which he treated of grammar in its widest sense, also of orthography, synonyms, etymology, with a tendency to investigate the causes of facts, frequently in imitation of Varro. In his etymologies he clung to the Latin, e.g. he derived *frater* from *fere alter.* Gell. 17, 7, 5 *anguste perquam et obscure disserit, ut signa rerum ponere videas ad subsidium magis memoriae suae quam ad legentium disciplinam.* 19, 14, 3 *Nigidianae commentationes non proinde* (like those of Varro) *in vulgus exeunt et obscuritas subtilitasque earum tamquam parum utilis derelicta est.*—He was perhaps the inventor of the method of indicating a long vowel by an apex, HUsener, RhM. 24, 107.—Quint. 11, 3, 143 *qui de gestu scripserunt circa tempora illa* (of the veteres), *Plotius Nigidiusque.*

5. Gell. 16, 6, 12 *P. Nigidius in libro quem de extis composuit.* 7, 6, 10 *Nigidius Figulus in libro I augurii privati.* Lyd. de ostent. 45 ὁ Νιγίδιος ἐν τῇ τῶν ὀνείρων ἐπισκέψει. Cf. ib. 27 (ἐφήμερος βροντοσκοπία . . . κατὰ τὸν Ῥωμαῖον Φίγουλον ἐκ τῶν Τάγητος), and on this CWachsmuth, praef. p. xxviii. Bergk, op. 1, 653. GSchmeisser, de etrusca discipl. (1872) 23.

6. Macrob. 3, 4, 6 *Nigidius de dis libro nono decimo* (hence at least 20 bb.). They embraced also questions of ritual, both Roman and foreign. The fragments are collected in Merkel's edition of the Fasti, p. clxxxv sqq.

7. His works on Natural Science. Cic. Timae. 1. (see n. 3). a) on Astronomy. Serv. Georg. 1, 43 *Nigidius in sphaera graecanica;* 218 *Nigidius commentario sphaerae graecanicae;* ib. 19 *Nigidius . . . sphaerae barbaricae.* On their relation see Bücheler, RhM. 13, 177.—b) *P. Nigidii in secundo librorum quos de vento composuit verba,* Gell. 2, 22, 31. *Nigidius de ventis IIII ait,* Schol. Bern. Georg. 1, 428. According to CWachsmuth (Lyd. de ost. p. xxiv), Lydus' observations on signs of the weather (ost. p. 19) are derived from this source.—c) On Zoology. Gell. 6, 9, 5 *P. Nigidius de animalibus libro II.* Macrob. 3, 16, 7 *Nigidius Figulus . . . in . . . libro de animalibus quarto.* Rutgers l.l. 270. Serv. Aen. 1, 178 *Nigidius de hominum naturalibus IIII* (on generation); in Plin. NH. he is mentioned as an authority for b. 6, 7–11 (zoology) and b. 16, and is quoted 15 times.—The existence of a treatise de terris is maintained by JKlein l.l. 25.

8. With Figulus there was formly identified, wrongly, an otherwise unknown author Βικέλλιος (Vicellius, cf. CIL. 8, 8974; or Vecellius? as the variant Βεκέλλιος

occurs twice; cf. the common name Vecilius, also Vecillius CIL. 9, 936. See also MOMMSEN, RhM. 18, 590). LAURENT. LYD. de ostent. 3 mentions him along with Figulus himself and other authors de etrusca disciplina, and ib. 54, where he gives in Greek from the Latin translation of Vicellius (Βικέλλιος ὁ Ῥωμαῖος) a fragment out of the Etruscan ritual hymns of the day. Cf. CWACHSMUTH Laur. Lyd. de ost. p. XXII.—A work on the Etruscan Discipline by a certain Fonteius, also otherwise entirely unknown, is mentioned in LYD. de ost. 3. A Βροντοσκοπία ἐκ τῶν Φοντηίου τοῦ Ῥωμαιου is reproduced ib. 39–41. LYD. de mens. 4, 2 mentions a treatise περὶ ἀγαλμάτων by the same author. He is again named elsewhere in LYD. de mens. 4, 53, de mag. in prooem., and at 2, 12. 3, 42. See JFSCHULTZE, quaestt. Lydian. 1, 38. WACHSMUTH l.l. p. XXI. LTRAUBE, var. libam. crit. (Münch. 1883) 37.

171. The most eminent orator of the aristocratic party was Q. Hortensius Hortalus (a. 640/114–704/50), as a man pliable and soft to effeminacy, as an orator long the most prominent on account of his choice and ornate style and elaborate elocution, until Cicero surpassed him. He also distinguished himself in literature, not only by publishing part of his speeches, but also by writing a treatise on general questions of oratory, and likewise Annales and erotic poems. Together with him, we may mention the following orators of the aristocratic party: the triumvir M. Licinius Crassus (a. 638/116–701/53), L. Licinius Lucullus (a. 640/114–697/57), M. Pupius Piso Calpurnianus (cos. 693/61), as well as Cn. Pompeius Magnus (a. 648/106–706/48), and a few others.

1. Hortensius was aedile 679/75, praetor 682/72, cos. 685/69; † 704/50, according to SEREN. SAMMON. 261 sqq. of an affection of the throat. CIC. Brut. 301 (*erat Hortensius*) *primum memoria tanta quantam in nullo cognovisse me arbitror* (see a specimen in SEN. controv. 1. praef. 19), *ut quae secum commentatus esset, ea sine scripto verbis eisdem redderet quibus cogitavisset.* . . . 302 *attuleratque minume volgare genus dicendi, duas quidem res quas nemo alius, partitiones, quibus de rebus dicturus esset, et collectiones eorum quae essent dicta contra quaeque ipse dixisset.* . . . 303 *vox canora et suavis, motus et gestus etiam plus artis habebat quam erat oratori satis.* 326 *Hortensius genere* (orationis asiatico) *florens clamores faciebat adolescens. habebat enim et Meneclinum illud studium crebrarum venustarumque sententiarum* . . . *et erat oratio cum incitata et vibrans tum etiam accurata et polita.* 327 *erat excellens iudicio volgi et facile primas tenebat adolescens.* . . . *sed cum iam honores et illa senior auctoritas gravius quiddam requireret, remanebat idem nec decebat idem; quodque exercitationem studiumque dimiserat, quod in eo fuerat acerrimum, concinnitas illa crebritasque sententiarum* . . . *vestitu illo orationis quo consueverat ornata non erat.* QUINT. 11, 3, 8 *diu princeps orator, aliquando aemulus Ciceronis existimatus est, novissime, quoad vixit, secundus.* To Cicero he always behaved with kindness and ungrudging recognition, though he was often misjudged by his sensitive rival.

2. Among the numerous speeches delivered by Hortensius in the course of 44 years (from 659/95), we know the subjects of 28; see LUZAC 119. MEYER, orat. rom.[2] 361. His speeches were published (e.g. pro Verre, QUINT. 10, 1, 23): CIC.

Brut. 324 (*dicendi genus quod fuerit in utroque orationes utriusque etiam posteris nostris indicabunt*). 328 *id declarat totidem quod dixit, ut aiunt, scripta verbis oratio.* or. 132 *dicebat melius quam scripsit.* Quint. 11, 3, 8 *actione valuisse plurimum . . . fides est quod eius scripta tantum intra famam sunt, . . . ut appareat placuisse aliquid eo dicente quod legentes non invenimus.*—Also Quint. 2, 1, 11 *communes loci . . . quibus quaestiones generaliter tractantur, quales sunt editi a Q. quoque Hortensio, ut Sitne parvis argumentis credendum?* cf. ib. 2, 4, 27. Priscian. GL. 2, 381, 10.

3. Vellei. 2, 16, 3 *maxime dilucide Q. Hortensius in Annalibus suis rettulit.* Cic. ad Att. 12, 5, 3 *de bono auctore Hortensio sic acceperam;* cf. 13, 32, 3 *ex Hortensio audieram;* by word of mouth? 13, 33, 3 *non temere dixit Hortensius.* For his erotic poems see Plin. ep. 5, 3, 5 (§ 31, 1). Ovid. trist. 2, 441 *nec minus Hortensi nec sunt minus improba Servi carmina.* Gell. 19, 9, 7 (§ 31, 1). Varr. LL. 8, 14 *Ortensius in poematis: cervix.* Cf. ib. 10, 78. Catull. 95, 3 and thereon LSchwabe, quaestt. Catull. 268.

4. LCLuzac, de Q. H. oratore, Leid. 1810. WDrumann, Gesch. Roms. 3, 81. PRE. 3, 1497.—Bust of Hortensius (Qvintvs Hortensivs) in the Villa Albani at Rome; engraved by JJBernoulli, röm. Ikonogr. 1, t. 4; also Ann. dell' inst. arch. 54, T. L.

5. Cic. Brut. 64, 230 *Hortensius . . . suos inter aequalis M. Pisonem* (n. 7), *M. Crassum, Cn. Lentulum* (cos. 682/72), *P. Lentulum Suram* (cos. 683/71) *longe praestitit.* Tac. dial. 37 *ex his* (i.e. *vetera quae et in antiquariorum bibliothecis adhuc manent et cum maxime a Muciano contrahuntur ac iam . . . edita sunt*) *intellegi potest Cn. Pompeium* (n. 8) *et M. Crassum non viribus modo et armis sed ingenio quoque et oratione valuisse, Lentulos* (n. 9) *et Metellos* (n. 10) *et Lucullos* (n. 6) *et Curiones* (§ 136, 12. 153, 6 and 209, 1) *et ceteram procerum manum multum in his studiis operae curaeque posuisse.* Of these, M. Licinius P. f. Crassus Dives was more than 60 years old in 699/55 (Plut. Crass. 17), praetor 682/72, cos. 684/70 and 699/55, censor 689/65, a member of the first triumvirate 694/60, † 701/58; see WDrumann, GR. 4, 71. PRE. 4, 1064. Cic. pMur. 48 *vir summa dignitate et diligentia et facultate dicendi.* Brut. 233 *mediocriter a doctrina instructus, angustius etiam a natura, labore et industria . . . in principibus patronis aliquot annos fuit.* This is exaggerated by Plut. Crass. 3.

6. For L. Lucullus see § 157, 4. His brother, M. Licinius Lucullus, after his adoption (by M. Terentius Varro) M. Terentius M. f. Licinianus Varro, cos. 681/73 (PRE. 4, 1074, 9), is mentioned by Cicero (Brut. 222) next to M. Octavius Cn. f. and Cn. Octavius M. f. (cos. 678/76) amongst political orators.

7. Cic. Brut. 236 *M. Piso* (cos. 693/61) *quidquid habuit habuit ex disciplina, maximeque ex omnibus qui ante fuerunt graecis doctrinis eruditus fuit. habuit a natura genus quoddam acuminis, quod etiam arte limaverat, quod erat in reprehendendis verbis versutum et sollers* (cf. ad Att. 1, 13, 2) . . . *is cum satis floruisset* (as an orator) *adolescens, minor haberi est coeptus postea; deinde ex virginum iudicio* (a. 681/73?) *magnam laudem est adeptus et ex eo tempore . . . tenuit locum tam diu quam ferre potuit laborem.* Ascon. on Cic. in Pis. p. 15 Or. 14 K.-S.: *Pupius Piso eisdem temporibus quibus Cicero, sed tanto aetate maior ut adolescentulum Ciceronum pater ad eum deduceret, quod in eo . . . multae inerant litterae. orator quoque melior quam frequentior habitus est.* Cic. fin. 5, 1 *cum audissem* (at Athens) *Antiochum, ut solebam, cum M. Pisone.* de nat. deor. 1, 16 *M. Piso si adesset,* the Peripatetic school also would be represented. ad Att. 13, 19, 4 (a. 709/45 when Piso was already dead): *confeci V libros περὶ τελῶν, ut . . . περιπατητικὰ M. Pisoni darem.* de or. 1, 204 *est apud M. Pisonem . . . Peripateticus Staseas.*

8. Cn. Pompeius Magnus, born 648/106, cos. 684/70, 699/55 and (sine collega) 702/52, triumvir 694/60, † 706/48. According to Tac. dial. 37 (see n. 5) there were written speeches by him in existence. Cic. Brut. 239 *maiorem dicendi gloriam habuisset nisi eum maioris gloriae cupiditas ad bellicas laudes abstraxisset. erat oratione satis amplus, rem prudenter videbat; actio vero eius habebat et in voce magnum splendorem et in motu summam dignitatem.* Vellei. 2, 29, 3 *sanctitate praecipuus, eloquentia medius.* Quint. 11, 1, 36 *Pompeius abunde disertus rerum suarum narrator.* Plut. Pompei. 1 πιθανότης λόγου. A letter by him from the beginning of the Civil war (a. 705/49) in Cic. ad Att. 8, 11 A. C. and 12 A–D.

9. The Lentuli mentioned by Tac. dial. 37 are no doubt the same as those spoken of by Cic. Brut. 230 (see n. 5), of whom Cn. Cornelius Lentulus Clodianus ib. 234 and the Catilinarian P. Cornelius Lentulus Sura ib. 235 are described as orators (cf. ib. 308 *Lentuli duo*). Also Cn. (Cornelius) Lentulus Marcellinus (cos. 698/56) ib. 247; P. Cornelius Lentulus Spinther (cos. 697/57) and L. Cornelius Lentulus Crus (cos. 705/49) ib. 268.

10. For the Metelli mentioned by Tac. dial. 37 (n. 5) cf. Cic. Brut. 247 *duo Metelli, Celer* (cos. 694/60; PRE. 2, 26, 15) *et Nepos* (cos. 697/57; PRE. 2, 27, 16), *non nihil in causis versati, nec sine ingenio nec indocti.* ad Att. 6, 3, 10 (a. 704/50) *orationem Q. Celeris mihi velim mittas contra M. Servilium.* Cf. ad. fam. 5, 4, 2.

11. For L. Lucceius see § 172, 5.

12. Other orators of this period, of whom it is not, however, related that their speeches were published, are mentioned by Cicero in his Brutus 237 (P. Murena, C. Censorinus, L. Turius). 239 (C. Piso, M'. Glabrio, L. Torquatus). 240 (D. Silanus, Q. Pompeius A. f. Bithynicus). 241 (P. Autronius, L. Octavius Reatinus, C. Staienus). 242 (C. and L. Caepasii, C. Cosconius Calidianus, Q. Arrius). 245 (T. Torquatus T. f. *doctus vir ex Rhodia disciplina Molonis*). 246 (M. Pontidius; M. Valerius Messala (Niger) cos. 693/61, see Mommsen, ephem. epigr. 3, 1). Erucius, the accuser of Sex Roscius (see § 179, 2), is called *Antoniaster* (i.e. a stupid imitator of the orator Antonius) by Cic. p. Varen. fr. 10, p. 232 Müll.=930 Or.

172. In the department of historical composition among the older contemporaries of Cicero his friend T. Pomponius Atticus (645/109–729/32) was especially distinguished, principally by his Annalis, a synchronistic Roman history in the somewhat meagre form of tables, probably with the addition of the contemporary history of foreign peoples, which had acquired importance in connection with that of Rome, and, as a supplement, the pedigrees of the chief Roman families. Besides him, Procilius, Hortensius, Lucceius, Sulpicius, L. Tubero, and others inferior to them composed historical works.

1. T. Pomponius Atticus, subsequently to his adoption by his uncle, Q. Caecilius Q. f. Pomponianus Atticus, a banker and publisher well known through Cicero's correspondence with him (§ 184, 2) and the panegyric biography by Nepos. It happens that Atticus is the earliest Roman bookseller of whom we know. By means of his slaves he carried on a wholesale business. Corn. Nep. Att. 13, 3 *namque erant in ea* (familia) *pueri litteratissimi, anagnostae optimi et plurimi librarii.* In his friendship with Cicero, Atticus was far from being merely the recipient.

Cicero had a great opinion of his judgment on questions of politics and of literature: ad Att. 1, 14, 3 *meis orationibus, quarum tu Aristarchus es.* 16, 11, 1 *nostrum opus tibi probari laetor; . . . cerulas enim tuas miniatulas illas extimescebam;* cf. 15, 14, 4.—JGHulleman, de Pomp. Att., Utr. 1838. GBoissier, Cicéron et ses amis, Par.[7] 1884. PRE. 1[2], 2094. EFialon, de T. Pomp. Att., Par. 1861.

2. Works of Atticus: a) Corn. Nep. Att. 18, 6 *unus liber graece confectus de consulatu Ciceronis;* cf. Cic. Att. 2, 1, 1 (a. 694/60) *tuus puer . . . mihi commentarium consulatus mei graece scriptum reddidit*).

b) Annalis. Cic. Brut. 13 *salutatio . . . illius libri quo me hic* (Atticus) *affatus . . . excitavit. . . . quo omnem rerum* (*nostrarum* is added by OJahn from 19; see, however, also or. 120) *memoriam breviter et . . . perdiligenter complexus est.* 15 . . . *ut explicatis ordinibus temporum uno in conspectu omnia viderem.* 19 *eis* (by Cicero's work de rep. of a. 700/54) . . . *ad veterum rerum nostrarum memoriam comprehendendam . . . incensi sumus* (Atticus). Cf. ib. 42. 44 (*te, quem rerum rom. auctorem laudare possum religiosissimum*). 74. orat. 120 *quem laborem* (to learn not only Roman history *sed etiam imperiosorum populorum et regum illustrium*) *nobis Attici nostri levavit labor, qui conservatis notatisque temporibus . . . annorum septingentorum memoriam uno libro colligavit.* ad Att. 12, 23, 2 *scriptum est in tuo annali.* Cf. Cornel. Nep. Hann. 13, 1 and Ascon. on Cic. in Pis. p. 13 Or. 12 K.-S. (*Atticus in Annali*). Schol. Veron. on Aen. 2, 717. Solin. Polyh. 1, 27. Cornel. Nep. Att. 18, 1 *summus . . . fuit . . . antiquitatis amator; quam adeo diligenter habuit cognitam ut eam totam in eo volumine exposuerit quo magistratus ordinavit. nulla enim lex neque pax neque bellum neque res illustris* (and literary, Cic. Brut. 72; see § 94, 2) *est populi rom. quae non in eo suo tempore sit notata, et . . . sic familiarum originem subtexuit ut ex eo clarorum virorum propagines possimus cognoscere.* FSchneider, de Attici annali ZfAW. 6 (1839), no. 5. The fragments in HPeter, hist. fragm. 214.

c) Corn. Nep. Att. 18, 3 *fecit hoc idem separatim in aliis libris, ut M. Bruti rogatu Iuniam familiam a stirpe ad hanc aetatem ordine enumeraverit* (though for this purpose it was necessary to invent much or to adopt many family fictions to the disadvantage of historical criticism; cf. § 80, 2. 81, 1, 4), *notans qui a quoque ortus quos honores quibusque temporibus cepisset. pari modo Marcelli Claudii de Marcellorum, Scipionis Cornelii et Fabii Maximi Fabiorum et Aemiliorum.* Cf. § 166, 4 e.

d) Imagines. Plin. NH. 35, 11 *imaginum amorem flagrasse quondam testes sunt Atticus ille Ciceronis edito de iis volumine et M. Varro* (also Plin. ind. auct. to b. 7. 33 Atticus is specified). Nep. Att. 18, 5 *attigit poeticen quoque . . . nam de viris qui honore rerumque gestarum amplitudine ceteros rom. populi praestiterunt exposuit ita ut sub singulorum imaginibus facta magistratusque eorum . . . quaternis quinisve versibus descripserit.*

3. Cic. ad Att. 2, 2, 2 (a. 694/60) *Dicaearchus . . . a quo multo plura didiceris quam de Procilio.* Varro LL. 5, 148 *a Procilio relatum.* 154 *ut Procilius aiebat.* Plin. NH. 8, 4 (notice of a. 673/81). Ind. auct. to b. 12, 13 (there Flavius Procilius according to HBrunn, de indic. plin., Bonn 1856, 21). Possibly the Procilius who was trib. pleb. 698/56. HPeter, hist. rell. cccLXII. 316 fr. 198.

4. For the annals of Q. Hortensius see § 171, 3. For Lucullus' history of the Marsian war see § 157, 4.

5. Cic. ad. fam. 5, 12, 1 (a. 698/56) to L. Lucceius Q. f.: *genus scriptorum tuorum, . . . vicit opinionem meam . . . ut cuperem quam celerrime res nostras monumentis commendari tuis.* (2) . . . *videbam italici belli et civilis historiam iam a te paene esse perfectam, dixeras autem mihi te reliquas res ordiri.* (3) . . . *gratiam*

illam de qua . . . in quodam prooemio scripsisti. (4) *si liberius* (frankly), *ut consuesti, agendum putabis* etc. Ascon. p. 92 Or. 81 K.-S.: *fecit Catilinam* (690/64) *reum inter sicarios L. Lucceius paratus* (ad dicendum) *eruditusque;* ib. 93 (82) *hoc Lucceius quoque Catilinae obicit in orationibus quas in eum scripsit.* These may be the 'scripta' which pleased Cicero and made him desirous to see his consulship treated by him, which Lucceius never carried out, though he had almost promised to do so (Cic. Att. 4, 6, 4). A letter by him to Cicero (a. 709/45) fam. 5, 14. PRE. 4, 1156. HPeter, hist. fr. 213.

6. Cic. Att. 13, 30, 3 (a. 709/45): *in Libonis annali quattuordecim annis post* (622/132) *praetor est factus Tuditanus quam consul Mummius.* 13, 32, 34 *eum* (Tuditanus) *video in Libonis praetorem.* 13, 44, 3 (a. 709/45) *Cottam* (§ 197, 9) *mi velim mittas. Libonem mecum habes.* This might be the same Libo to whom Varro dedicated a work in several books (*Varro ad Libonem primo,* Macrob. 3, 18, 13), viz. his own and Pompey's friend L. Scribonius Libo (PRE. 6, 881, 13). If so, Appian's words b. c. 3, 77 (ὧδε μέν τισι περὶ τοῦ Βάσσου δοκεῖ, Λίβωνι δ' ὅτι) would have to be understood of some one else or to be written Λιβίῳ as Perizonius has it; the events there related (belonging to the year 708/46) lead rather to the conclusion that the person in question was an adherent of Caesar. Cf. MHertz, Bresl. Ind. lect. 1864/65, p. 13. HPeter, hist. rell. cccLXIV. 318. fr. 198.

7. Cornel. Nep. Hann. 13, 1 *quibus consulibus interierit* (Hannibal) *non convenit. namque Atticus* (mentions a. 571/183) . . . *at Polybius* (a. 572) . . . *Sulpicius autem Blitho* (a. 573/181). Serv. Aen. 1, 6 *Saufeius Latium dictum ait quod ibi latuerant incolae* etc. Perhaps L. Saufeius the friend of Atticus (PRE. 6, 847): cf. e.g. Cic. Att. 14. 18, 4 (here a work of Saufeius appears to be mentioned), 15, 4, 3 (Saufeius as an Epicurean). Nep. Att. 12, 3 *L. Saufeii eq. R. aequalis sui, qui complures annos studio ductus philosophiae habitabat ⟨Athenis⟩.*

8. L. Aelius Tubero, the old friend and brother-in-law of M. Cicero, a. 693/61–696/58 lieutenant to Q. Cicero in Asia. PRE. 1², 335, 6. Cic. pLig. 104 *homo cum ingenio tum etiam doctrina excellens.* ad Q. fr. 1, 1, 10 (a. 694/60) *legatos habes . . de quibus honore et dignitate et aetate praestat Tubero, quem ego arbitror, praesertim cum scribat historiam, multos ex suis annalibus posse deligere quos velit et possit imitari.* It is doubtful whether this history was completed and published or descended to his son Q. Tubero (§ 208, 1) as a mere collection of materials. The first supposition is scarcely justified by the plural Αἴλιοι in Dionys. Hal. ant. 1, 7 (above § 37, 5). Varro named after him his logistoricus 'Tubero de origine humana.' Like Cicero, Tubero adhered especially to the (New) Academy, and the Sceptic Ainesidemos addressed to him his Πυρρώνειοι λόγοι (Phot. Bibl. 212, 1, p. 169 Bk.). HPeter, hist. rell. cccLVI. fragm. 199.

173. In the popular treatment of philosophical subjects in Latin, Cicero was preceded by Amafinius, Rabirius and T. Catius, but all three confined themselves to the Epicurean system, without any ornament of style, and faithfully copied from Greek sources. They had admirers and imitators.

1. Cicero's statements as to these predecessors of his exhibit little candour of judgment. Acad. post. 1, 5 *vides ipse . . . non posse nos Amafinii aut Rabirii similes esse, qui nulla arte adhibita de rebus ante oculos positis volgari sermone disputant . . . nullam denique artem esse nec dicendi nec disserendi putant.* (6) *iam vero physica, si Epicurum, i.e. si Democritum, probarem, possem scribere ita plane ut*

Amafinius. Tusc. 1, 6 *multi iam esse libri latini dicuntur scripti inconsiderate ab optimis illis quidem viris sed non satis eruditis. fieri autem potest ut recte quis sentiat et id quod sentit polite eloqui non possit* etc. 2, 7 *eorum qui se philosophos appellari volunt . . . dicuntur esse latini sane multi libri, quos non contemno equidem, quippe quos numquam legerim; sed . . . lectionem sine ulla delectatione neglego.* 4, 6 *C. Amafinius . . . cuius libris editis commota multitudo contulit se ad eam potissimum.* (7) *post Amafinium multi eiusdem aemuli rationis multa cum scripsissent Italiam totam occupaverunt . . . et facile ediscuntur et ab indoctis probantur.*

2. Rabirius is not mentioned except acad. 1, 5 (see n. 1), as he is probably not to be identified with the poet C. Rabirius (§ 252, 9).

3. Cic. fam. 15, 16, 1 (a. 709/45: *Catius Insuber* from Ticinum; cf. § 198, 1), *Epicureus, qui nuper est mortuus, quae ille Gargettius* (Epicurus) *et iam ante Democritus* εἴδωλα, *hic spectra nominat.* 15, 19, 2 *Epicurus, a quo omnes Catii et Amafinii, mali verborum interpretes, proficiscuntur.* Quint. 10, 1, 124 *in Epicureis levis quidem sed non iniucundus tamen auctor est Catius.* Plin. ep. 4, 28, 1 *imagines Corneli Nepotis et Titi Cati* (to be placed in a library, see § 198, 1). Porphyr. on Hor. sat. 2, 4 '*Unde et quo Catius?*' (in some of the headings of the satire the speaker is called M. Catius): *Catius Epicureus fuit qui scripsit quattuor libros de rerum natura et de summo bono.* ib. Acro on v. 48 (p. 287 H.): *irridet eum qui de opere pistorio in libro scripsit Catius Miltiades;* where Cruquius has: *irridet eum quod de op. pist. in suo libro scribit de se ipso: 'haec primus invenit et cognovit Catius Miltiades.*' Teuffel's Comm. on Hor. sat. 2, p. 114.

174. In point of solidity of character, the jurist C. Aquilius Gallus was a worthy pupil of the Pontifex Q. Scaevola, and his indifference to political life is characteristic both of the increasing aversion to that kind of life and the elevation of jurisprudence to an independent study then commencing. His pupil, Servius Sulpicius Rufus (649/105–711/43), far surpassed him in many-sided fertility; he was of a peaceful nature, averse to extremes, distinguished as an orator, respected as a scholar, nor was he a stranger to poetry, but his chief eminence consisted in his legal knowledge and in his numerous writings, by which he secured to himself a long-abiding influence on the development of jurisprudence. Jurists of the same period were P. Orbius and Precianus; C. Furius Camillus, too, was at least well versed in legal matters.

1. Plin. NH. 17, 2 *pulcherrima domus . . . C. Aquilii eq. R., clarioris illa etiam quam iuris civilis scientia.* Praetor 688/66 with Cicero, † before 710/44. PRE. 1^2, 1388. Cic. pCaec. 78 (a. 685/69): *iuris civilis rationem numquam ab aequitate seiunxit, . . . iustus . . . et bonus vir . . . ita peritus ac prudens ut ex iure civili non scientia solum quaedam verum etiam bonitas nata videatur.* Brut. 154. Pompon. dig. 1, 2, 2, 42 *ex quibus* (the auditores Mucii) *Gallum* (whom he previously calls *Aquilius Gallus*) *maximae auctoritatis apud populum fuisse Servius* (n. 2) *dicit.* Cf. § 154, 3. Ulpian also knew him only at second hand (dig. 19, 1, 17, 6 *Gallus Aquilius, cuius Mela refert opinionem, recte ait*), and in the Digest. where he is mentioned perhaps a dozen times, we never find a definite title quoted.

It is, therefore, possible that these quotations should be traced back to assertions made by his pupil Sulpicius Rufus as to oral responsa of Aquilius. Some legal forms are the only things which we know with certainty that Aquilius himself left in writing: e.g. especially the Aquiliana stipulatio et acceptilatio (inst. 3, 29, 2. dig. 46, 4, 18, 1), and formulae de dolo malo from the time of his praetorship (Cic. off. 3, 60. 61. nat. deor. 3, 74). SWZimmern, Gesch. d. röm. Privatrechts 1, 1, 287. Huschke, iurispr. anteiust.[5] 18.

2. Ser. Sulpicius Q. f. Rufus, of about the same age with Cicero (*aetates vestrae . . . nihil aut non fere multum differunt*, Cic. Brut. 150), praetor 689/65, consul (after he had been repulsed in 692/62) 703/51, appointed proconsul of Achaia 708/46 by Caesar, † 711/43 on a mission from Mutina. PRE. 6, 1497. Originally Rufus had studied rhetoric together with Cicero, and not until a. 677/77 had he despaired of rivalling him, upon which he turned his principal attention to jurisprudence, in which he brought about a considerable advance. Cic. Brut. 152 *existumo iuris civilis magnum usum . . . apud multos fuisse, artem* (method) *in hoc uno* (?). *quod numquam effecisset ipsius iuris scientia, nisi praeterea didicisset . . . dialecticam.* 153 *sed adiunxit etiam et litterarum scientiam et loquendi elegantiam, quae ex scriptis eius, quorum similia nulla* (*volumina multa* Koch, cf. Pompon, l.l.) *sunt, facillume perspici potest.* (154) *cumque discendi causa duobus peritissumis operam dedisset, L. Lucilio Balbo* (§ 154, 3) *et C. Aquilio Gallo, Galli . . . celeritatem subtilitate diligentiaque superavit, Balbi . . . tarditatem vicit expediendis conficiendisque rebus.* Pompon. dig. 1, 2, 2, 43 *institutus a Balbo Lucilio, instructus autem maxime a Gallo Aquilio, qui fuit Cercinae. itaque libri complures eius* (sc. Rufi) *exstant Cercinae confecti. . . . huius volumina complura exstant* (as late as the time of Pomponius). *reliquit autem prope CLXXX libros.* Brutus ap. Cic. Brut. 156 *audivi nuper* (a. 707/47) *eum* (Sulp. Rufus) *studiose et frequenter Sami, cum ex eo ius nostrum pontificium, qua ex parte cum iure civili coniunctum esset, vellem cognoscere.* For his learned correspondence with Varro: § 166, 6, d.

3. As a specimen of Rufus' rhetorical culture we may quote his letter of condolence to Cicero upon the death of Tullia (a. 709/45), fam. 4, 5; his account of the death of M. Marcellus ib. 4, 12 (a. 709/45) is a pattern of an historical relation. Quint. 10, 1, 116 *Ser. Sulpicius insignem non immerito famam tribus orationibus meruit.* 10, 7, 30 *feruntur aliorum quoque* (besides Cicero's sketches of orations) *et inventi forte, ut eos dicturus quisque composuerat, et in libros digesti, ut causarum quae sunt actae a Ser. Sulpicio, cuius tres orationes* (completed and published by himself) *exstant. sed hi de quibus loquor commentarii ita sunt exacti ut ab ipso* (Sulp.) *mihi in memoriam posteritatis videantur esse compositi* (different from Cicero's commentarii, which were edited by Tiro). Of these tres orationes Quintilian (4, 2, 106; cf. 10, 1, 22 and Festus 153) names one *pro Aufidia*, and another *contra Aufidiam* (6, 1, 20), if indeed the latter designation (instead of the former) be not due to a slip of the pen or an error of memory on Quintilian's part; see also FSchöll, RhM. 34, 86. In general see Meyer, or. rom.[2] 398; and above § 44, 12.—Quint. 10, 5, 4 *et illa ex latinis conversio multum et ipsa contulerit. ac de carminibus quidem* (turning Latin poems into prose) *neminem credo dubitare, quo solo genere exercitationis dicitur usus esse Sulpicius* (unless this be the orator mentioned § 153, 5). Pliny ep. 5, 3, 5 (see above § 31, 1) mentions also *Ser. Sulpicium* among the writers of erotic poems. See Ovid trist. 2, 441 (§ 171, 3).

4. Juridical writings of Sulpicius Rufus. (The fragments in Huschke, iurispr. anteiust.[5] 91). *Ser. Sulpicius iureconsultus, vir aetatis suae doctissimus, in libro de*

sacris detestandis secundo, Gell. 7, 12, 1. *Ser. Sulpicius in libro . . . de dotibus*, ib. 4, 3, 2. 4, 4, 1. Cf. dig. 12, 4, 8. 23, 3, 79, 1. Gell. 4, 1, 20 *Ser. Sulp. in reprehensis Scaevolae capitibus.* Commentary on the XII tables (§ 86, 6). Pompon. dig. 1, 2, 2, 44. *Servius duos libros ad Brutum perquam* (*Ad Brutum itemque?*) *brevissimos Ad edictum subscriptos reliquit.* Cf. Ulp. ib. 14, 3, 5, 1 *Servius libro primo Ad Brutum* (was it composed about 700/54? See MVoigt, Abh. d. sächs. Ges. d. Wiss. 7, 338). Perhaps also in Varro LL. 5, 40 *dividit in eo, Servius scribit Sulpicius* etc. A derivation of the word *religio* from *relinquere* is by Macrob. 3, 3, 8 ascribed to Ser. Sulpicius, by Gell. 4, 9, 8 to Masurius Sabinus (§ 281, 1). Plin. NH. 28, 26 *Servii Sulpicii . . . commentatio est, quamobrem mensa linquenda non sit.* It is several times quoted in the Digest, but direct extracts from his works do not occur. SWZimmern, Gesch. d. PRechts 1, 1, 290. RSchneider, de Ser. Sulp. Rufo, Lps. 1834 II. AFRudorff, RGesch. 1, 163. 235. OKarlowa, RG. 1, 483. On his Latinity JHSchmalz, ZfGW. 35, 90.

5. Pompon. dig. 1, 2, 2, 44 *ab hoc* (Sulp. Ruf.) *plurimi profecerunt, fere tamen hi libros conscripserunt: Alfenus Varus Gaius* (*Catus* according to Huschke's conjecture, see § 208, 3 ad fin.), *A. Ofilius, T. Caesius, Aufidius Tucca, Aufidius Namusa, Flavius Priscus, C. Ateius, Pacuvius Labeo* (§ 207, 6) *Labeonis Antistii pater, Cinna, Publicius Gellius* (?). *ex his decem libros octo conscripserunt, quorum omnes qui fuerunt libri digesti sunt ab Aufidio Namusa in CXXXX libros.* Among those here enumerated no writings are known of T. Caesius and Flavius Priscus. Cinna belongs to those of less note, mentioned as a writer on law dig. 23, 2, 6. 35, 1, 40, 1; so does Publicius, ib. 31, 50, 2. 35, 1, 51, 1. 38, 17, 2, 8 (*Africanus et Publicius*), though he probably is of later date, whence in Pompon. l.l. we should rather follow the editors in reading *Publius Gellius.* C. Ateius seems to be the same as the one of whom it is stated, dig. 23, 3, 79, 1: *Ateius scribit Servium respondisse*, and perhaps he may have been the father of the famous jurist C. Ateius Capito, who is called by Pompon. l.l. 47 a pupil of Ofilius. The father was trib. pl. 699/55 and praetor (perhaps 702/52); PRE. 1 [2], 1954, 2. *Servii auditores* (probably from the compilation of Aufidius Namusa) are quoted dig. 33, 4, 6, 1. 33, 7, 12 pr. 33, 7, 12, 6. 39, 3, 1, 6.

6. Cic. Brut. 179 *cuius* (i.e. T. Juventius, § 154, 3) *auditor P. Orbius, meus fere aequalis, . . . in iure civili non inferior quam magister fuit.* A. 691/63 he was praetor in Asia; cf. Cic. p. Flacc. 76. A certain Precianus iureconsultus, who was with Caesar in Gaul, Cic. fam. 7. 8, 2 (a 700/54). A certain Volcacius see § 154, 4. —C. Camillus, a clever jurist and business adviser of Cicero and his family; fam. 5, 20, 3 (a. 705/49), 14, 5, 2 (a. 704/50). 14, 14, 2 (a. 705/49) and elsewhere. He is probably identical with the Camillus who is jocularly styled a gourmet (fam. 9, 20, 2, a. 708/46) and newsmonger (Att. 13, 33, 4, cf. ib. 13, 6, 1, a. 709/45).

175. M. Tullius Cicero was born Jan. 3, 684/106 on his father's estate near Arpinum; he was the son of a Roman knight. He employed every means of studying rhetoric in all its branches, and pleaded his first cause under Sulla's dictatorship. To perfect himself still further, he spent two years (675/79–677/77) in Greece and Asia Minor, was then quaestor in Sicily 679/75, aed. cur. 685/69, praetor (urbanus) 688/66, and consul 691/63. The Catilinarian conspiracy, which broke out during Cicero's consulship and was suppressed by him, furnished

the triumvirs in 695/59 with a pretext for removing the obnoxious consular by means of his enemy P. Clodius. At the end of April 696/58 Cicero left Italy and lived in exile at Thessalonica and Dyrrhachium. On Aug. 4, 697/57 he was permitted to return, and arrived at Rome on Sept. 4. He was augur 701/53. From July 31, 703/51 until July 30, 704/50 he was entrusted with the administration of the province of Cilicia, as proconsul. On his return to Rome, the antagonism between Caesar and the Senate, with Pompey at its head, had already broken out; after long hesitation, he joined Pompey at Dyrrhachium (June 705/49), where he also stayed during the battle of Pharsalus (Aug. 9, 706/48). From the end of Sept. 706/48 until Sept. 707/47, Cicero lived at Brundisium, awaiting the victor's return and permission from him to go back to Rome. The years 708/46 and 709/45, which he was compelled to spend in political leisure, were all the more fertile in literary productions. The 15th March 710/44 recalled Cicero to political activity, but soon threw him into contention with M. Antony, which ended in his being proscribed by the second triumvirate, and killed Dec. 7, 711/43.

1. Biography of Cicero by Plutarch.—WHDSuringar, Cic. comm. rerum suarum s. de vita sua; acc. annales Ciceroniani, Leid. 1854. SMartini, Cic. autobiographia, Turin 1885.—Among modern works CMiddleton, life of Cicero, Lond. 1741 II. WDrumann, Gesch. Roms 5, 216–716. 6, 1–308. Teuffel, PRE. 6, 2182, and also (more complete and without references to authorities) in Studien u. Charakt. (1871) 289. CAFBrückner, Leben d. Cic. I: d. bürgerliche u. Privatleben, Gött. 1852. FDGerlach, Cicero, Bas. 1864 (against Mommsen, § 176, 2). WForsyth, life of Cic., Lond. 1864 II. ATrollope, life of Cic., Lond. 1880 II. GBoissier, Cicéron et ses amis, Par.[7] 1884.

2. AJäcklein, Cic.s Verbannung, Bamb. 1875. GRauschen, ephemerides Tull. ab exilio Cic. usque ad extremum annum 54, Bonn 1886. EOppenrieder, de Cic. proconsule Ciliciae, Augsb. 1853. Gd'Hugues, de Cic. in Cilicia proconsulatu, Strassb. 1859; sur le proconsulat de Cic., Paris 1876. FHoffman, Phil. 15, 662. CHartung, de proconsulatu Cic., Würzb. 1868. WSternkopf, de rebus a Cic. inde a tradita Cilicia usque ad relictam Italiam gestis etc., Marb. 1884. JZiehen, ephemerides Tull. a Mart. 49 a. Chr. usque ad Aug. 48 a. Chr., Budapest, 1887.

3. On the portraits of Cicero now extant, see JJBernoulli, röm. Ikonogr. 1, 132. Of the bust in Madrid with the inscription M · CICERO AN · LXIIII, which has lately become famous, the fragment with the inscription (CIL. 1, p. 281) is certainly genuine, but the head is modern. CAldenhoven, Arch. Ztg. 1885, 235. Bernoulli l.l. 2, vi. EHübner, Bildwerke in Madrid 115.

176. Cicero was endowed by nature with great talents, many-sided, and versatile; at the same time kind, generous and assi-

duously bent upon high aims; a thoroughly respectable character in a period pervaded by egotism. But he was formed of pliable stuff, accessible to all outward impressions without interior self-control to maintain his equanimity. His sensitiveness, his quick imagination and highly emotional temperament made him an amiable man and a great orator, in whom each string that was touched gave full and harmonious answer; his whole tone of mind qualified him especially to become the interpreter and transplanter of Hellenic elegance and formal refinement; but these same qualities made his character undecided, wavering between intense excitement and utter prostration, crotchety, moody, conceited, sensitive to sarcasm, afraid of danger and despairing in evil days. Others also might have their weak hours, but not many had them in such regular succession, and nobody else had the misfortune of bequeathing to posterity such authentic documents of the fluctuations of his mind. Cicero was always under the sway of the moment and therefore little qualified to be a statesman, yet he had not sufficient self-knowledge to see it or resignation to act accordingly. Hence the attempts he made to play a part in politics served only to lay bare his utter weakness. Here also he was full of good intentions, but he had neither the calm and acute judgment necessary to see the right path, nor the courage and perseverance required to follow it. Thus it happened that he was alternately used and then pushed aside, attracted and repelled, deceived by the weakness of his friends and the strength of his adversaries, and at last was threatened equally by both extreme factions between which he had tried to steer his way.

1. For the judgment of antiquity see especially Asinius Pollio in Sen. suas. 6, 24 *huius viri tot tantisque operibus mansuri in omne aevum praedicare de ingenio atque industria supervacuum est. . . . utinam moderatius secundas res et fortius adversas ferre potuisset! . . . sed quando mortalium nulli virtus perfecta contigit, qua maior pars vitae atque ingenii stetit, ea iudicandum de homine est.* Further the elogium of Velleius 2, 66 *Nihil tam indignum illo tempore fuit quam quod . . . Cicero proscriptus est abscisaque scelere Antoni vox publica est, cum eius salutem nemo defendisset qui per tot annos et publicam civitatis et privatam civium defenderat. Nihil tamen egisti, M. Antoni . . . rapuisti tum M. Ciceroni lucem sollicitam et aetatem senilem . . . , famam vero gloriamque factorum atque dictorum adeo non abstulisti ut auxeris. vivit vivetque per omnem saeculorum memoriam . . . citiusque e mundo genus hominum quam* ⟨*Ciceronis gloria ex hominum memoria umquam*⟩ *cedet.* Quint. 12, 1, 16. A writing of Asinius Gallus (§ 276, 3) against Cicero, and the reply by Claudius who was afterwards emperor (§ 286, 2), and the writing of Suetonius against Didymos (§ 347, 2).

2. In preceding centuries admiration for Cicero's style prevented an unpre-

judiced criticism of his character and political career. See, on the other hand, FGaliani, correspondance inédite (Par. 1818), 1, 295 (cf. Ritschl, op. 3, 701). This was, however, more than sufficiently made up for by WDrumann, GR. 6, 411, who criticised Cicero's character on all its sides, accurately, it is true, but in a carping spirit and suppressing all extenuating circumstances. ThMommsen, RG. 3^6, 619 tried, if possible, to surpass Drumann in exaggerated diction and unhistoric bitterness.

177. Cicero possessed, to a wonderful extent, the power of appropriating and assimilating to his own individuality foreign ideas and dressing them up anew in an easy and pleasant style. Owing to this gift, he amplified Roman literature by introducing into it several new departments which had previously not been attempted; he became the creator of a standard prose, which was so rich and refined and so eminently suited to the genius of the Latin language that it was impossible to surpass it in subsequent centuries. But the ease with which he threw off his productions tempted him to write fast and too much, and to cover with a facile style the want of serious studies and real learning. Cicero succumbed to this temptation at least during his leisure-time in 709/45 and 710/44. The real business of his life Cicero exhibits in his speeches, where indeed his talent shows to the greatest advantage. His speeches were carefully prepared beforehand and generally edited subsequent to their delivery. The knowledge and experience gained in this career were utilised by him in his rhetorical treatises. His theoretic compositions he also extended to other fields, first to political science, then to ethics, and the philosophy of religion, and he even attempted the simpler parts of theoretic philosophy. Besides all this, his extensive personal connections and the habit of thinking pen in hand led to a very voluminous correspondence.

1. Chronological arrangement of Cicero's principal writings: a. 673/81 pro Quinctio.—674/80 pro Roscio Amerino.—684/70 Verrinae.—685/69 pro Caecina.—688/66 de imperio Cn. Pompei.—691/63 consular speeches: de lege agraria, pro Rabirio, in Catilinam, pro Murena.—692/62 pro Sulla, p. Archia.—695/59 pro Flacco.—697/57 sq. orations post reditum.—698/56 pro Sestio, in Vatinium, pro Caelio, de provinciis cons., pro Balbo.—699/55 in Pisonem, de oratore.—700/54 de republica, pro Plancio, p. Rabirio Postumo.—702/52 pro Milone, de legibus.—708/46 Brutus, Paradoxa, Orator, pro Marcello, p. Ligario, partitiones oratoriae.—709/45 pro Deiotaro, de finibus, Academica, Tusculanae.—710/44 de natura deorum, Cato maior, de divinatione, de fato, topica, de optimo genere oratorum, Laelius, de officiis, Philippicae I–IV.—711/43 Philippicae V–XIV.

2. ELange, quid de ingenio, litteris, poetis Graec. Cic. senserit, Halle 1880. EScholimeyer, quid Cic. de poetis Rom. iudicaverit, Halle 1884. RWurzer, de Cic. tragoediae rom. iudice, Czernowitz 1885. IKubik, de Cic. poetarum lat. studiis,

Diss. Vindob. 1, 237. AKiessling, coniectan. III, iv. JSchäfler, BlfbayrGW. 20, 285. ChCauseret: § 181, 2.

3. General writings on Cicero's diction (for the more special see under different departments and works). Dictionaries: MNizolii thesaurus Cic. (Brix. 1535), Bas. 1559; Venet. 1570 and elsewhere, e.g. Patav. 1734 (cur. JFacciolati); Lond. 1820 III. Clavis Cic., ed. IAErnesti (in his edition and separately, last ed. by AHRein, Halle 1831). Lex. Cic. by ChrGSchütz, Lps. 1817 (vol. 18. 19. of his ed.).—RStürenburg, Materialien zu einem lex. Cic., Hildburgh. 1854. FHeerdegen, de fide Tulliana (i.e. on the word fides in Cic.), Erl. 1876.—EFrohwein, d. Perfectbildd. auf vi bei Cicero, Gera 1874. OSchüssler, de praepp. ab ad ex ap. Cic. usu, Hannov. 1880; z. Lehre v. den Präpp. bei Cic. (in with Acc.), Hann. 1881. ChrJänicke, d. Verbind. der Substantive durch Präpp. b. Cic., Vienna 1866. Grossmann, de particula quidem (esp. in Cic.), Königsb. 1880; de particulis ne—quidem, Allenst. 1884. Stamm, d. Partikelverb. et quidem bei Cic.. Rössel 1885. AKlein, de adiectivi assimulati ap. Cic. usu, Bresl. 1879. HAnz, Ciceros Sprachgebr. in der Bez. des gemeins. Prädikats bei mehreren Subjekten, Quedlinb. 1884. FNieländer, d. factitive Dat. bei Cic., Krotoschin 1878. HLieven, die consecutio temporum d. Cic., Riga 1872. AMotschmann, doctrinam de tempp. consec. quam exposuit HLieven exemplis Cic. oratt. veram esse, Jena 1875. MWetzel, de consec. tempp. Cic., Gött. 1877. FHoppe, d. Conjunctiv der conjug. periphr. act. usw. bei Cic., Gumbinnen 1879 (cf. § 189, 5). WOGutsche, de interrogationibus obliquis ap. Cic., Halle 1885. JPriem, d. irrealen Bedingungssätze bei Cic. u. Cäs., Phil. Suppl. 5, 261. WKriebel, der Periodenbau bei Cic. u. Liv., Prenzl. 1873. EJWSchuppe, de anacoluthis Cic., Berl. 1860. KAhlén, de subiectis rei ap. Cic. cum verbis quae actionem significant coniunctis, Upsala 1879. JTheobald, de annominationis et alliterationis ap. Cic. usu, Bonn 1853.—HGenthe, de proverbiis a Cic. adhibitis, commentatt. Mommsen. 268.

4. The apparatus criticus for Cicero (in ms.) by GGarantoni in Ravenna: CHalm, Münch. GA. 26 (1848), 285; by HLagomarsini (more than 80 vols., see WvHumboldt's works 5, 253. 264); qu.: where now preserved?—CHalm, zur Hss.-Kunde der cic. Schrr., Münch. 1850; RhM. 9, 321; Jahn's Arch. 15, 165 and elsewhere.—JGBaiter, Phil. 20, 335. 507. CMFrancken, ad Cic. palimpsestos, Mnemos. 11, 374. 12, 57. 283. 393. 13, 43. 288. HDeiter, de Cic. cod. Leid. 118, Emden 1882; de Cic. codd. Vossianis 84 et 86, Aurich 1885 etc.—On the knowledge and study of Cicero's works in the early Middle Ages see PSchwenke, Phil. Suppl. 3, 402.—For details see under the separate works.

5. Complete editions of all the works: Venet. Junt. 1534–37 IV by PVictorius. Venet. Ald., by PManutius 1540–46 IX. A DLambino emend. et aucta, Paris 1566 IV and subsequently. Cum notis varr. cura JGGraevii, Amst. 1684 sqq. XI; not finished. Cum clavi Cic. ed. JAErnesti, Lps. 1737 sqq. VI; last edition 1820 sqq. V. Cum delect. comm. (stud. JOliveti), Par. 1749 IX; Genev. 1743 sqq.—E rec. Graevii (cura GGaratonii), Neap. 1777 sqq. (unfinished). Recogn. ChrGSchütz, Lps. 1814 sqq. XX.—Rec. JCOrelli, Zürich 1826–30 IV; editio altera emendatior, cur. JCOrelli, JGBaiter, CHalm, Zürich 1845–62 IV; with the ed. I (and II) as vol. 5: Cic. scholiastae, C. Marius Victorinus, Rufinus, C. Julius Victor, Boethius, Favonius Eulogius, Asconius Pedianus, scholia Bobiensia, scholiasta Gronovianus, edd. JCOrelli and JGBaiter 1833, and as vol. 6–8 Onomast. Tullianum, 1836–38 III.—Cic. opera omnia uno volumine ed. CFANobbe, Lpz.[2] 1850.—Recogn. RKlotz, Lpz.[2] 1863–71 XI vols. in V partes (vol. 11: index nominum); recently revised by CFWMüller, Lps. 1878 sqq., up to the present date there have appeared P. I Vol. I scripta rhett. (rec. WFriedrich), P. II Vol. I–III oratt., P. IV Vol. I–III philos.—Edd. JGBaiter et CLKayser (Lps. 1861–69 XI, in b. 11 ind. nom.).

177[a]. Even in his early youth Cicero made attempts in various departments of literature. He composed, among other poems, one in trochaic tetrameters entitled Pontios Glaukos, he translated in the metre of the original Aratos' *Φαινόμενα*, the *Οἰκονομικός* of Xenophon, and other works. He even attempted theoretical writing, and about the year 670/84 he put together an immature work on rhetoric, as it seems, after Hermagoras and Cornificius (§ 162). The only two books which he completed treat of the materials of oratory, de inventione, and hence are generally so entitled.

1. PLUT. Cic. 2 *ἐρρύη πως προθυμότερον ἐπὶ ποιητικήν, καί τι ποιημάτιον ἔτι παιδὸς αὐτοῦ διασώζεται Πόντιος Γλαῦκος ἐν τετραμέτρῳ πεποιημένον. Admodum adolescentulus* (nat. d. 2, 204) Cic. translated the Φαινόμενα of Aratos; after which, perhaps not before 694/60 (HJORDAN, krit. Beitr. z. Gesch. d. lat. Spr. 299) he translated the Προγνωστικά of the same poet. In addition to detached fragments of both, which are nearly all to be found as quotations in Cicero himself, a large fragment of the Phainomena (of 480 vv.) has been independently preserved (esp. Harl. 647 s. IX. Dresd. 183 s. X). The whole printed, e.g. BAITER-KAYSER 11, 96. CFWMÜLLER 4, 3, 360. PLM. 1, 3. The scholia on Cic. Arat. preserved in the above-mentioned Harl. were published by JVOGELS, Crefeld 1884. 87 II. Cf. AREIFFERSCHEID ann. d. inst. archeol. 1862, 108; Bresl. ind. schol. 1885/86, 11.—Whether the other poems of Cicero belong to his youth cannot be determined.—GSCHÜTZ, quaestt. crit. ad Cic. Arat., Neuruppin 1868.

2. CIC. off. 2, 87 *Xenophon in eo libro qui Oeconomicus inscribitur quem nos, ista fere aetate cum essemus qua es tu nunc* (in his twenty-first year) *e graeco in latinum convertimus.* The translation was in three books. SERV. Georg. 1, 43. MACR. 3, 20, 5. Cf. CIC. de sen. 59. PLIN. NH. 18, 224. COLUM. 12, praef. 7 and 1, 6. GELL. 15, 5, 8. HIERON. apol. adv. Ruf. 2, p. 227 Bas. and elsewhere (LÜBECK, Hieron. quos noverit scriptt. 26). The remains: BAITER-KAYSER 11, 50. CFW MÜLLER 4, 3, 307. QUINT. 10, 5, 2 *vertere graeca in latinum . . . id Cicero ipse frequentissime praecipit, quin etiam libros Platonis atque Xenophontis edidit hoc genere translatos* (cf. HIERON. ad Eus. chron. praef. p. 1, 5 Sch.). On the translations of Plato's Timaeus und Protagoras see § 186, 9 and 9[a].

3. De inventione: CIC. de or. 1, 5 *quae pueris aut adolescentulis nobis ex commentariolis nostris incohata* (he left them unfinished) *ac rudia exciderunt vix hac aetate digna et hoc usu, quem ex causis . . . tot tantisque consecuti sumus.* Cf. 1, 23. QUINT. 3, 6, 60 *Cicero his pulcherrimos illos de oratore libros substituit.* The MSS. (in the best of them the title is wanting, the Würzburg MS. has the subscription *explicit liber rhetoricae*) call the work Rhetorica, so does PRISCIAN GL. 2, 81. 469. 489. 545 (*Cicero in I rhetoricon* and similar instances). In Quintilian also this title may be discerned, or rather the title Rhetorici which was probably current as well (sc. libri; cf. Pliny's *studiosi III*, see § 312, 2): 2, 15, 6 *in rhetoricis, quos sine dubio ipse non probat.* 3, 1, 20 *rhetoricos suos.* 3, 5, 14 *ex Cic. rhetorico I . . . ipse hos libros improbat.* 3, 6, 50 (*Cicero in libris rhetoricis*=de inv. 1, 10) and 58 (*in primo Ciceronis rhetorico*). HIERONYM. adv. Rufin. 1, p. 137 *lege ad Herennium Tullii libros, lege Rhetoricos eius aut . . . revolve tria volumina de oratore.* QUINT. 2, 14, 4 *cum M. Tullius etiam in ipsis librorum quos hac de re* (on rhetoric) *primum scripserat titulis graeco nomine utatur.* The appellation 'Ars

rhetorica' which, in accordance with a few passages in it and with Quint. 3, 6, 64 (cf. besides Jul. Vict. 429, 12 H) AWeidner has given to the work (in his ed. p. VI) is incorrect; and the title 'rhetorice' (supported by AEussner, BlfbayrGW. 16, 1) is not satisfactorily proved.

4. Cic. de inv. 2, 4 *quod quoniam nobis voluntatis accidit ut artem dicendi perscriberemus, non unum aliquod proposuimus exemplum, cuius omnes partes . . . exprimendae nobis necessario viderentur, sed omnibus unum in locum coactis scriptoribus quod quisque commodissime praecipere videbatur excerpsimus* etc. Hermagoras is mentioned 1, 8. 12. 16. 97. Quint. 3, 6, 59 *sunt velut regestae in hos commentarios quos adolescens deduxerat scholae, et si qua est in his culpa, tradentis est.* ib. 3, 11, 10. 18 (*in Rhetoricis Hermagoram est secutus*). FBader p. 18–24.

5. By the fact that Cornificius ad Herennium (§ 162) was made use of, and by the passage in Cicero's de or. 1, 5 (see n. 1) the date of composition is pretty well fixed. RPhilippson, JJ. 133, 421. It is certain that Cicero himself published the work (AEussner, BlfBayrGW. 16, 2). On the employment of Cornificius cf. LSpengel, RhM. 18, 495. CLKayser, Münch. GA. 1852 no. 59 sqq. and Bader l.l. 6. KHoffmann (§ 162, 6). FRoch (§ 162, 7). ARömer, JJ. 119, 831. Weidner (pref. to his ed. p. viii) wrongly denies Cicero's dependence on the Rhet. ad Her., which he takes to be later than Cicero's work.—PhThielmann, de sermonis proprietatibus . . . ap. Cornificium et in primis Cic. libris (de inv. pQuinct. pSRosc.), Strassb. 1879.

6. Commentary of Marius Victorinus (§ 408, 6) on the work. Excepta ex Grillii commento (§ 445, 7) in Halm, Rhet. lat. min. p. 596.—On a (worthless) mediaeval commentary by a certain Theodoricus *Brito, homo barbaricae nationis* on Cic. de inv. see PThomas, Mél. Graux 41. Cf. Suringar, hist. schol. lat. 1, 212. REllis, Journ. of phil. 9, 61. 13, 86. ERohde, JJ. 123, 426. Bücheler, RhM. 38, 637. 39, 168.

7. The best MSS. are those of Paris (7774 A), Würzburg and St. Gallen (facsim. Chatelain t. 18), all s. IX: on them see EStröbel, Phil. 45, 469. To these must be added the numerous quotations in the later rhetoricians.—ALinsmayer, varias lectt. ad Cic. libr. I de inventione congessit, Munich. 1853. On a Würzburg fragm. (2, 90–95) GScheps, BlfbayrGW. 23, 432.—Separate editions: cum not. varior. by PBurmann, Leid. 1761 (reprinted by FLindemann, Lpz. 1828). Cic. artis rhetoricae libri II rec. AWeidner, Berl. 1878.—FBader, de Cic. rhett. libris, Greifsw. 1869. AKnackstedt, de Cic. rhetoricorum libris ex rhetoribus lat. emendandis I, Gött. 1873; II Helmstedt 1874. Weidner introd. to his ed. p. xxii.

178. As a speaker, Cicero had extraordinary natural aptitudes; the extreme versatility of his mind, his lively imagination, his quick sensibility, his uncommon formal talent, his inexhaustible richness of expression, a felicitous memory, the gift of incisive and amusing wit, a splendid voice and impressive figure, all contributed to render Cicero an excellent orator. But he himself did everything to attain the very highest perfection: it was only after long and laborious preparation, theoretical and practical, that he made his début as an orator, nor did he ever rest and think himself perfect, but was always working on, and never pleaded a cause without careful preparation; each success was to

him only a step to another still higher achievement, and by continual meditation and study he kept himself fully prepared for his task and the means of accomplishing it. Hence he succeeded, as is now universally admitted, in gaining a place beside Demosthenes, or at all events immediately after him, though he does not come up to the moral earnestness and consequent impressiveness of the Attic orator. But Cicero surpasses him in variety and splendour, where he is more akin to the Asiatic School than to the Attic. He commands such abundance of words as sometimes to become diffuse, though often, where he is verbose, it is to cover the weakness of his arguments. His great strength lies in his style; it is clear, refined, concise and apt, perspicuous, elegant and brilliant. He commands all moods, from playful jest to tragic pathos, but is most successful in the imitation of conviction and feeling, to which he gave increased efficacy by his fiery delivery; hence he pleaded especially in criminal causes. Sometimes, of course, his rhetoric degenerates to a mere study of effect, and the grandeur of his words serves only to hide the poverty of thought and the badness of the cause. It is true, he was not over-scrupulous as to the causes he pleaded, but this feature he shares with the advocates and lawyers of all times. In their general effect, we are often dissatisfied with his speeches, since they are frequently deficient in acuteness and distinctness; but we must allow him to be highly impressive in details.

1. Cicero's description of himself Brut. 321 *cum propter adsiduitatem in caussis et industriam tum propter exquisitius et minime vulgare orationis genus animos hominum ad me dicendi novitate converteram. nihil de me dicam, dicam de ceteris, quorum nemo erat qui* (like myself) *videretur exquisitius quam vulgus hominum studuisse litteris quibus fons perfectae eloquentiae continetur; nemo qui philosophiam . . . ius civile . . . memoriam rerum Romanarum teneret, . . . nemo qui breviter arguteque incluso adversario laxaret iudicum animos atque a severitate paulisper ad hilaritatem risumque traduceret, nemo qui dilatare posset atque a propria ac definita disputatione hominis ac temporis ad communem quaestionem universi generis orationem traducere, nemo qui delectandi gratia digredi parumper a caussa, nemo qui ad iracundiam magno opere iudicem, nemo qui ad fletum posset adducere, nemo qui animum eius . . . quocumque res postularet impellere;* Cic. orat. 108 *nemo orator tam multa ne in graeco quidem otio scripsit quam multa sunt nostra, eaque hanc ipsam habent quam probo varietatem;* cf. Quint. 10, 1, 105–112. 12, 1, 19–21. 12, 10, 12–15.—Quint. 6, 3, 3 *non solum extra iudicia sed in ipsis etiam orationibus habitus est* (*Cic.*) *nimius risus affectator.* Cf. Macrob. 2, 1, 13. Drumann, GR. 6, 599. AHaacke, de Cic. in orationibus facetiis, Burg 1886.

2. FHand in Ersch and Gruber's Encycl. 1, 17, 213. Drumann, GR. 6, 588. FBlass, die griech. Beredsamkeit (1865) 125. AHaacke, de dispositione orationum Cic., Burg 1873.

3. A collection of Cicero's orations in which each speech formed a book by itself seems indicated by such citations as Charis. GL. 1, 368, 28 *Cicero causarum decimo tertio;* Quint. 5, 10, 98 *Cicero pro Caecina . . . et alia in eodem libro plurima.*—On the MSS. of the orations see the references under each. Collective MSS. containing more than one oration are e.g. the following: Vatic.-Basilic. S. Petri H 25 s. VIII/IX (facsim. in Chatelain t. 26) contains Pis., Font., Flacc., Philipp.; Paris. 7794 s. IX (Chat. t. 23) contains pridie quam iret in exilium (§ 180, 6), post red. in sen., post red. ad Quir., de domo, Sest., Vatin., de prov. cons., de har. resp., Balb., Cael.; the same 10 orations together with the Caesarianae (§ 179, 41, 1) are to be found in the Brussels MS. 5345 s. XII; in the Monac. 18787 s. X (Chatelain t. 27) Philipp., pro imp. Pomp., Mil., Sull., Planc., Caec., Marc.—More comprehensive collections especially in the later MSS. e.g. Wolfenbüttel. 205 s. XV (containing 38 speeches; Wrampelmeyer, cod. W. collatus, Hannover and Clausthal 1872–81 VI); Laur. 48, 25 s. XV (Chatelain t. 24) gives 41 speeches; Vatic.-Palat. 1525 s. XV (Chatelain t. 25) contains most of the speeches, etc.—The speeches, or separate groups of them, were often arranged alphabetically in the earlier MSS. (cf. Niebuhr on Cic. pFont., Rome 1820, 67; see § 179, 3, 2), often chronologically (so e.g. in the above-mentioned Paris 7794 and Bruss. 5345; HJordan, quaestt. crit., Königsb. 1886, 3; cf. § 295, 2. 374, 5). Groups of speeches on similar subjects (Verrinae, Catilinariae, Caesarianae, Philippicae) had a tendency to separate from the rest.

4. On the commentary of Asconius see § 295, 2; the scholia Bobiensia § 295, 4. The so-called scholiasta Gronovianus (see also § 177, 5 l. 10) extant only in the Leid. Voss. Q. 138 s. X, an amalgamation of heterogeneous commentaries, gives elucidations on Verr. 2, 1, 1–62 (this is the earliest portion, about s. V, like the Bobbio-scholia, § 295, 4); on div. in Caec.; Verr. 1, 16–20; Verr. 1, 1–45; Catil. II–IV; Lig.; Marc.; Deiot.; Rosc. Am.; de imp. Pomp.; Mil. ThStangl, der sog. Gronovscholiast, Prague 1884. GLandgraf on Cic. Rosc. p. 3 (§ 179, 2. 2). Mommsen, RhM. 16, 140.—Other early editors and commentators of Cic. are Fronto, Flavius Caper, Volcacius, Statilius Maximus. Also Sacer: see § 179, 19, 1. Cf. Prisc. GL. 3, 316, 2 *commentatores probatissimi* (of the orations).—ThStangl, zur Textkritik der Scholiasten cic. Reden, RhM. 39, 231. 428. 566.

5. Complete editions of the speeches by PManutius (Ven. 1546 III), DLambinus (Ven. 1570 III), IGGraevius (cum nott. varr., Amsterd. 1695–99 III), RKlotz (Lps. 1835–39 III), GLong, with notes, Lond. 1855–62 IV.

6. Selected speeches for the use of schools e.g. by JNMadvig (12 Speeches Copenh.[4] 1858). CHalm (and GLaubmann) (18 Reden erklärt, Berl.[4–12] 1882–86 VII) and others.—Recent editions of orationes selectae: that of the Halle Waisenhaus ([21] 1883 cur. OHeine); CHalm (18 speeches Berl. [2] 1887), AEberhard and W Hirschfelder (19 speeches Lpz.[2] 1879, see also AEberhard, lection. Tull. I, Lps. 1872). HNohl., Lpz. 1884 sqq. III.—Criticism on the speeches: Madvig, advers. 2, 194. 3, 111. CALehmann, Herm. 14, 212. 451. 621. 15, 348. 567. WG Pluygers, Mnemos. NS. 8, 345. HKarsten, spicil. crit. (Leid. 1881) 3. AWeidner, advv. Tull., Dortm. 1885.

7. Linguistic works on the speeches: HMerguet, Lexikon zu den Reden d. Cic., Jena 1873–84 IV.—DRohde (§ 195, 10). GHatz, Beitr. z. lat. Stil. (d. Hendiadys in Cic.s Reden), Schweinfurt 1886. JStraub, de tropis et figuris in oratt. Demosth. et Cic., Aschaffenb. 1883. ARoschatt, d. Gebr. der Parenthesen in Cic's Reden u. rhett. Schrr., Acta semin. Erl. 3, 189. Cf. § 179, 1, 1.

8. Cicero's speeches (all), translated by CNOsiander, Stuttg. (Metzler). Selected

speeches translated by GWendt, Stuttg. (Metzler, Klass. d. Alt.) 1858; EJenicke, Lpz. (Engelmann) 1858 sqq.; JSiebelis, Stuttg. (Hoffmann) 1861 sqq.

179. The extant speeches of Cicero are in chronological order, as follows:

1) pro Quinctio, delivered a. 673/81, an action in iudicio, in which Cicero's client was driven to the necessity of being the accuser, and demanded the decision in his favour of a previously formed sponsio praeiudicialis. The action was only an incident in the main suit, concerning an accusation of debt against Quintius, founded on an agreement for partnership. Cicero does not appear to have won his cause.

1. In the earlier speeches Cicero clings somewhat narrowly and rigidly to the scholastic rules, especially to the rhetoric of Cornificius (§ 162), while the phraseology appears in certain respects commonplace as well as archaic in comparison with Cicero's later and thoroughly formed style. In these speeches also he is often very diffuse, for his forte never lay in terseness.—EWölfflin, Phil. 34, 142. GLandgraf, de Cic. elocutione in oratt. pQu. et pRosc. Am., Würzb. 1878. H Hellmuth, de sermonis proprietatibus in Cic. prioribus (from 673/81–685/69) oratt., Acta semin. Erl. 1, 101. PhThielmann, see § 162, 4; by the same writer stilist. Bemerk. zu den Jugendwerken Cic.'s, BlfbayrGW. 16, 202. 352. Ernst, de genere dicendi et composs. rhetorica in prioribus Cic. oratt., Neuruppin 1885. Cf. inf. No. 26, 1, l. 6.

2. In publication, Cicero himself seems to have omitted the third part of the speech pQuinctio, which dealt with a point of inferior importance; cf. § 44, 7.—Drumann, GR. 3, 82. 5, 232. FLKeller, Semestria ad M. Tull. Cic. 1, 1 (Zür. 1842); also Bachofen, in Richter's Jahrb. 1842, 961, and Mommsen, ZfAW. 1845, 1086. SJERau, disput. juridica ad Cic. pQu., Leid. 1825. JFrei, der Rechtsstreit des P. Quinctius, Zür. 1852. SBenfey, zur jurist. Erkl. d. Rede pro Q., Phil. 10, 126. WOetling, Cic.'s Quinctiana, z. Verständnis u. zur rhetor. Würdigung, Oldenb. 1882. RKlotz, adnotatt. ad Cic. or. Quinct., Lps. 1862.

3. With the exception of inconsiderable fragments in the Turin Palimpsest, s. IV/V (see APeyron, Cic. oratt. p. Scauro etc. p. 214, cf. § 180, 2) this speech is only preserved in later MSS. s. XV., e.g. in the Bern. 214, Genev. 101 and in the Paris MSS. collated in Keller (n. 2).

2) pro Sex. Roscio Amerino, a. 674/80, a successful defence against a charge of parricide. The cause was a difficult one inasmuch as the real adversary was a favourite of the dictator Sulla, and the mere fact that Cicero notwithstanding took up the defence, as well as his boldness toward Sulla, combined with tact, in conducting the case, told in his favour. This speech also is constructed in strict accordance with scholastic rules, diffuse in style and rhetorically embellished.

1. Cic. Brut. 312. 316. Orat. 107. Quint. 12, 6, 4. Drumann, GR. 5, 234.

ANIKL, abundantiam iuvenilem in or. pR. A. apparentem notavit, Kempten 1836. EWÖLFFLIN, Phil. 34, 142. GLANDGRAF, see § 179, 1, 1.

2. The oration was known already to Petrarch. AHORTIS, Cic. nelle opere de Petr., Trieste 1878. Subsequently it was discovered by Poggio (about 1415) in Gallis together with the pro Murena (likewise the speeches pCaec., de leg. agr., in Pis., pRab. Post., pRab. perduellionis reo, pRosc. com.): accordingly there are only late copies e.g. Wolfenbüttel. 205, Monac. 15734, Lag. 26, Laur. 48, 25 (=Lag. 25; CHATELAIN t. 24).—Separate editions by EOSENBRÜGGEN (with introd. and commentary, Brunswick 1844), GWGOSSRAU (Quedlinb. 1853), CHALM (Ausgew. Reden I, Berl.[10] 1886), SKARSTEN (Utr. 1861), FRICHTER (Lpz.[2] 1877 by AFLECKEISEN, cf. the same JJ. 93, 548). Published and explained, together with the schol. Gronov., by GLANDGRAF, Erl. 1884. A school edition by the same writer, Gotha 1882. EHDONKIN (after Halm), Lond.[2] 1882.—Criticism: AEBERHARD, lect. tull. 1 (1872), 5. HWRAMPELMEYER, cod. Wolfenb. 2, XXII.

3) pro Q. Roscio Comoedo, according to the ordinary assumption delivered a. 678/76. The speech turns upon a slave (Panurgus), whom the prosecutor, C. Fannius Chaerea, had sent to Roscius for the purpose of histrionic study, the agreement being that the profit anticipated from the art of the slave should be divided between the master and teacher. But a certain Flavius, having killed Panurgus, had paid damages first to Roscius and then to Fannius, which are now to be divided between the two.

1. UNTERHOLZNER, d. Rede f. d. Schausp. R., in Savigny's Zeitschr. 1, 248. GFPUCHTA, civilistische Schriften (1851) 272. GEHEIMBACH, observatt. iur. rom. (Lps. 1834) 18. EHUSCHKE in Richter's krit. Jahrb. 1840, 481. MAvBETHMANN-HOLLWEG, röm. Civilproz. 2 (Bonn 1865), 804. JBARON, Zeitschr. d. Savigny-Stift. 1, 116. ERUHSTRAT, ib. 3, 34. DRUMANN, GR. 5, 346, who gives the date as not earlier than 686/68. See for a different calculation LANDGRAF (§ 179, 1, 1), app. 1.

2. The beginning of the speech, together with the close of that pro C. Rabirio perduellionis reo (no. 19), which in the MS. found by Poggio (see above no. 2, 2) immediately preceded it, has been lost in consequence of a few leaves having fallen out. See BAITER-HALM Cic. 2, III.—MSS. Laur. 48, 25. Monac. (bibl. Electoral. 68) and others.—Or. pR. C. ed., adnott. illustr. CASCHMIDT, Lps. 1839.—Translated by EOSENBRÜGGEN, in Jahn's Archiv. 11, 554.

4) pro M. Tullio, delivered before reciperatores a. 682/72 or 683/71, a suit in Tullius' name against a neighbour of his, a veteran soldier of Sulla's, P. Fabius, who had destroyed Tullius' country house in the territory of Thurii.

1. TAC. dial. 20 *quis* (nunc) *de exceptione et formula perpetietur illa immensa volumina quae pro M. Tullio aut A. Caecina legimus?* Cf. JUL. VICTOR p. 240 Or.= 419 Halm. SCHOL. BOB. pMil. p. 278 Or.—DRUMANN GR. 5, 258 assigns the speech to a. 682.

2. Preserved only in a very incomplete form in two palimpsests s. IV/V at

Turin and Milan: first edited by APeyron and AMai, see § 180, 2. See the same section for CBeier's edition.—PhEHuschke's text and commentary in JGHuschke's anal. lit. (Lps. 1826) 77. Keller, semestr. 1, 3, 653 (with a new collation of the palimpsests). PKrüger, Herm. 5, 146.—CBeier, iurispr. in Cic. p. T., Jahn's Jahrb. 1 (1826), 214. FKvSavigny, verm. Schrift. 3, 228.

5) Divinatio (in Caecilium), by which Cicero (a. 684/70) secured to himself the right of appearing as accuser of Verres (opposing Hortensius), in the place of the harmless Q. Caecilius Niger who had been put forward by Verres; and

6–11) in Verrem, on account of his exactions in his praetorian province of Sicily, 6 speeches in two actiones. In the first actio on the 5th August 684/70 Cicero delivered the first oration as an introduction to the prosecution proper. After this during the nine days which the case occupied he brought in the counts of the accusation one by one, giving merely the heads, and letting the witnesses and documents plead for themselves. Then, when the defendant, foreseeing the adverse verdict, had voluntarily gone into exile, Cicero elaborated his rich materials in the five books of the actio secunda: de praetura urbana, de iurisdictione Siciliensi, de frumento, de signis, de suppliciis. In these orations, which were never actually delivered, Cicero speaks as if Verres had put in an appearance at the second hearing (accusatio), and as if these speeches might still influence the final decision. They rank among the finest of Cicero's orations on account of the richness of the subject-matter, and the liveliness and lucidity of the exposition.

1. Caecilius (of Sicily) was ἀπελευθερικὸς ἄνθρωπος, ἔνοχος τῷ ἰουδαΐζειν (Plut. Cic. 7). LFriedländer, Sittengesch.[5] 3, 578. Hence Cicero's witticism: *quid Iudaeo cum verre?* (Plut. l.l.).—JWSluiter, de Cic. div. in Caec., Leid. 1832.

2. Drumann, GR. 5, 263. 327. Ps.-Ascon. p. 97–213 Or. Schol. Gron. p. 382–495 Or. König, de Cic. in Verr. artis operum aestimatore, Jever 1863. WGöhling, de Cic. artis aestimatore, Halle 1877. HDegenkolb, die lex Hieronica . . ., Beitr. z. Erkl. d. Verrinen, Berl. 1861. WGPluygers, emendatt. in Cic. Verr. act. II. l. 2 et 3 (Leid. 1855) and lectt. Tull. (ib. 1856) p. 3–43. LSchwabe (on Verr. IV), Phil. 30, 311. KLehrs, wissensch. Mon.-Bl. 1878, 45. CJacoby, Phil. 41, 178.

3. The most important MSS. of the Verrinae are the Paris 7774 A s. IX (now only for b. 4 and 5: but at one time it contained all the Verrinae: EThomas, rev. de phil. 9, 167. Facsim. Chatelain t. 31, 1), the Vatican palimpsest (Regin. 2077 s. IV? facsim. Zangem. and Wattenb. pl. 4. Chatelain t. 32), Paris 7776 s. XI (Chatelain t. 31, 2), Lagom. 29 and 42, two Wolfenbüttel MSS. (dependent on the Paris 7774 A; on this cf. HNohl, Herm. 20, 56) and others. A leaf of a palimpsest (s. III?) for Verr. 2, 1, 44–45 in Turin (Chatelain t. 30). Cf. NMadvig, op. ac. 1, 323. CHalm, Münch. Gel. Anz. 1853, no. 29–33. Notwithstanding its age the Vatican palimpsest must be used with caution. HMeusel, utri Verrinarum codici

maior fides habenda sit, Palimps. Vat. an Regio Paris., Berl. 1876. CFWMüller's Cic. 2, 1, xl.—HKarbaum, de auctor. et fide grammaticorum lat. in constit. lect. in Verr., Diss. Hal. 6, 71.—Editions of the Verr. by CGZumpt (Berl. 1831: the text by itself, ib. 1830), GLong (with a commentary, Lond.[2] 1862). Separate editions of b. II by Creuzer and Moser, Gött. 1847.—Speech against Caecil. and against Verr. IV and V, explained by CHalm (ausgew. Reden II, Berl.[8] 1882). The same speeches singly by FRichter and AEberhard (Div. in Caecil. Lpz.[2] 1879). Div. and in Verr. act I by WEHeitland and HCowie, Camb. 1877, the same by JRKing, Lond. 1887.—B. IV and V by EThomas, Par. 1886. 85. B. IV translated from the text of KLehrs by OPfundtner, Königsb. 1879.

12) pro M. Fonteio, a. 685/69, an actio repetundarum, not completely preserved.

1. We owe the greater part of what is preserved to the Vatic.-Basilic. (see § 178, 3). Niebuhr (§ 180, 2) added from the palimps. Palatino-Vaticanus 24 s. V (Chatelain t. 32) new fragments of the first part (see these also in AMai's class. auct. 2, 363); others from a MS. s. XII in Cues near Trêves have been added by JKlein (cf. § 180, 2) p. 57.—On the substance of the speech see Drumann, GR. 5, 329. ARSchneider, quaestt. in Cic. p. Font., Lps. 1876.

13) pro Caecina, a. 685/69, delivered before reciperatores, on a suit concerning an inheritance, at least the letter of the law being on Cicero's side.

1. Cic. orat. 102. Cf. Tac. dial. 20 (above p. 284, l. 4 from the end). Quint. 5, 10, 98. The advocate of the defendant (L. Aebutius) was C. Piso.

2. The best MSS.: Monac. 18787 (Tegernseensis) s. XI, Berolinensis (Erfurtensis) s. XII (cf. EWunder, variae lectt. librorum aliquot Cic. ex cod. Erfurt., Lps. 1827 p. 87), fragments in the Turin palimps., see above no. 4, 2.—Separate editions by CAJordan (Lps. 1847, supplement to this de cod. Tegernseensi, Lps. 1848).—PhEHuschke in JGHuschke's analect. lit. 164. Drumann, GR. 5, 335. FLKeller, semestr. lib. II (Zür. 1843) and also Mommsen, ZfAW. 1845. no. 136. CAJordan in his prolegg., and for the contrary view OZeyss, ZfAW. 1848, 865. AHGZimmermann, de A. Caecina (1852), p. 6. RKlotz, adnott. ad Cic. Caecin., Lps. 1866. 67 II. JNMadvig, udsigt of phil.-hist. samf. virksomh. 1878/80, 11. CMFrancken, Mnemos. 9, 245.

14) de imperio Cn. Pompei, delivered a. 688/66 when Cicero was praetor, in support of the lex Manilia. The praise of Pompey is somewhat exaggerated, the arrangement is scholastically strict, but the style is masterly.

1. Cic. de or. 102. Fronto p. 221. Cf. Schol. Gronov. p. 437–442 Or.—MSS. are the Erfurtensis (see above no. 13, 2), then the Tegerns. which is here incomplete (above no. 13, 2) and to supplement it the Hildeshemensis s. XIII (HNohl, Herm. 21, 193) and others. Drumann, GR. 5, 356. ANikl, levitatem et fallaciam argumentationis in Cic. or. etc. ostend., Kempten 1842. Bauermeister, Cic. Rede de imp. P. nach ihrem rhet. Werte, Luckau 1861. Editions by CBenecke (Lps. 1834), CHalm (Lps. 1849 and ausgew Rdn. I, Berl.[10] 1866), GWGossrau (Quedlinb. 1854), FRichter (Lpz.[3] 1883 by AEberhard). ADeuerling, Gotha 1884. ASWilkins (after Halm), Lond.[2] 1885.

15) pro A. Cluentio Habito, defence against a charge of poisoning. a. 688/66.

1. QUINT. 2, 17, 21 *Cicero se tenebras offudisse iudicibus in causa Cluentii gloriatus est.* Cf. ib. 4, 5, 11. 6, 5, 9. 11, 1, 61–63. 74. APOLL. SID. ep. 8, 10 *M. Tullius . . . pro Cluentio ipse se vicit.*—MSS.: Monac. 15734, Laur. 48, 12 and 51. 10; Wolfenbutt. 205. Fragments in the Turin palimpsest.—Editions by JCLASSEN, Bonn 1831, WRAMSAY, Oxf.[3] 1883. WYFAUSSET, Lond.[2] 1888.—Discussions of the legal points DRUMANN, GR. 5, 360. CNIEMEYER, der Prozess gegen Cl., Kiel 1871. CBARDT, zu Cic.s Cluentiana. Neuwied 1878. HNETTLESHIP, Lectures and Essays (Lond. 1885) 67.

16–18) The three speeches de lege agraria contra P. Servilium Rullum, the earliest of Cicero's consular speeches (a. 691/63), combating the immoderate proposals of the popular tribune Servilius to appoint a (democratic) committee of ten with the most extensive powers concerning the purchase and distribution of land in Italy. His proposal (which was also directed against Pompey) is impugned by Cicero apparently on a democratic basis. The first speech was delivered in the Senate on Jan. 1, only the conclusion being extant, the second and third (short) are addressed to the people, while a fourth speech (likewise short) has not come down to us.

1. A summary of his consular speeches is given by CICERO himself Att. 2, 1, 3. QUINT. 2, 16, 7.

2. Best MSS.: Pithoeanus, Erfurtensis (see above no. 13, 2), Erlangens. 38. HEBELING, codicis Lagom. 9 auctoritas in oratt. de lege agr., cum mantissa de cod. Paris. 7774, Brunswick 1863.—Rec. et expl. AWZUMPT, Berl. 1861 (cf. FRICHTER, JJ. 87, 251).—DRUMANN, GR. 3, 152. LLANGE, röm. Altert. 3, 231. MOMMSEN, RG. 3[6], 182.—HCGEBHART, obss. in Cic. de l. agr., Hof 1851. HSCHWARZ, miscellanea philol. (Lps. 1878), 3–24; coniectan. critt. in Cic. oratt. (Hirschb. 1883). HTKARSTEN, Mnemos. NS. 6, 283. 432. HAENICKE, on Cic.'s speeches de lege agr., Stettin 1883.

19) pro C. Rabirio perduellionis reo, a. 691/63.

1. Incompletely preserved (the conclusion is missing, see above no. 3, 2) in late MSS. which rest upon Poggio's discoveries see above no. 2, 2; in addition Niebuhr in 1820 published a few fragments from a palimps. Palatino-Vaticanus (§180, 2).—An early commentator ap. CHARIS. GL. 1, 211, 20 *quod iudicii genus* (Rabirius perduell. reus is previously mentioned) *Sacer in eandem orationem M. Tullii ab Horatio sumptum ait* etc.—On this subject cf. MOMMSEN, RG. 3[6], 169. RLALLIER, rev. hist. 12 (1880), 257. HWIRZ, JJ. 119, 177. HPUTSCHE, d. genus iudicii der Rede Cic. pRab., Jena 1881.—Separate ed. by WEHEITLAND, Cambr. 1882.

20–23) The four speeches in L. Catilinam, treating of the Catilinarian conspiracy, the first delivered in the Senate on Nov. 8. 691/63 and charging Catiline with his latest steps; the second, of Nov. 9, informing the people of the events in the Senate and of Catiline's departure from Rome; the third, of the evening of Dec. 3, acquainting the people with the imprisonment of the Catilinarians left at Rome and the evidence of the letters seized on the Allobroges; the fourth pronounced in the Senate on Dec. 5, and recommending the immediate execution of the prisoners.

1. On the events themselves see esp. DRUMANN GR. 5, 377. EHAGEN, Catilina, Königsb. 1854. MOMMSEN, RG. 3[6], 175; Herm. 1, 434. FBAUR in the Progr. v. Buchsweiler 1875; Württ. Korresp.-Bl. 1870, 24. 193. 252. LLANGE, röm. Altertümer 3 (1871), 216. CHACHTMANN, die chronol. Bestimmung von Cic. in Cat. I u. II, Seehausen 1877. AWEIDNER, Phil. Anz. 8. 410. AWZUMPT, JJ. Suppl. vol. 7, 577 and esp. CJOHN, die Entstehungsgesch. der Catilinar. Verschwörung, ibid. 8, 703. 782; JJ. 131, 841. JOGOREK, wann hat Cic. in Cat. I u. II gehalten? Rudolfswert 1878. 79 II. AKÜHN, quo die Cic. or. in Cat. I habuerit, Bresl. 1885.—EvSTERN, Catil. u. d. Parteikämpfe in Rom der Jahre 66–63, Dorp. 1883.

2. FAWOLF was probably joking when he disputed the genuineness of one of these speeches, though even later on he upheld this view, always ambiguously, of altera ex mediis duabus. Acting on this hint, ingenious writers insisted on 'demonstrating' the spuriousness first of or. 2 or 3, then of 4, and lastly even of 1! This dust-cloud of criticism has long since been laid. On this question see the appropriate observations of DRUMANN, GR. 5, 470. Also MADVIG, Op. acad. 2, 338. WBÄUMLEIN, ZfAW. 1838, 66. EHAGEN, de Cic. Catilinariis ad . . . Gottholdium, Königsb. 1851. Moderate criticism, which does not presume spuriousness on the ground of any seeming or even actual defect, will be obliged to leave these speeches to Cicero.

3. These orations are preserved in very numerous MSS., some exceedingly corrupt; among the best are e.g. Laur. 45, 2 s. XIV=Lagom. 62 (CALEHMANN, Herm. 14, 625. CFWMÜLLERS Cic. 2, 2, LXIV), Ambros. C. 29 inf. s. X (BAITER, Phil. 20, 335. Facsim. CHATELAIN t. 28, 3), the Monacenses 15964 s. XI (CHATELAIN t. 27, 3), 4611 s. XII, 7809 s. XIII.—Editions by CBENECKE (Lpz. 1828), CHALM (Ausgew, Rdn. III, Berl.[12] 1886), FRICHTER (Lpz.[4] 1882 by AEBERHARD). KHACHTMANN, Gotha [2] 1886. APASDERA, Turin 1885. ASWILKINS (after Halm with many additions), Lond.[2] 1879.

24) pro L. Murena, a successful defence of the consul elect L. Licinius Murena, who was prosecuted under the lex Tullia de ambitu (Nov. 591/63). It is not very convincing, but ingenious and lively, with all sorts of witticisms on jurisprudence and Stoicism, representatives of which were then Cicero's opponents, Ser. Sulpicius Rufus and M. Cato; the speaker likewise cleverly plays upon the jurors' dread of Catiline gaining the consulship. The speech does not, however, appear to have been delivered in quite the same form in which it was published.

1. In 57 only the headings of the sections *de Postumii criminibus*, *de Servii*

adolescentis are given; see § 44, 7. There are also a few accidental gaps in our text towards the end, e.g. 73. 80. 85.

2. QUINT. 11, 1, 69 sq. PLUT. Cic. 35. DRUMANN, GR. 4, 187. 5, 477. NIEBUHR, kl. Schr. 2, 213. BOOT, de emendanda et explicanda Cic. or. pMur., Mnemosyne 5, 347. GSOROF, de Cic. pM. or. comment. critica. I, Potsd. 1861. Other critical contributions by JFCCAMPE (JJ. 93, 179) and TEUFFEL (ibid. 99, 856. 101, 821. 103, 264. 504. 723. 105, 668). LURLICHS, RhM. 33, 153. CMFRANCKEN, Mnemos. NS. 5, 295. JVÖLKEL, JJ. 113, 506. WHROSCHER, JJ. 131, 377. AGRUMME, Cic. or. pMur. dispositio, Gera 1887.

3. The MSS., which are of late date throughout, are all derived from the one brought to Italy by Poggio (see above no. 2, 2). CHALM, die Hss. zu Cic. pMur. Münch. SBer. 1861, 1, 437. On the Wolfenbüttel. 205 see WRAMPELMEYER (§ 178, 3) P. II–IV, Hannov. 1874–78.—Editions: Rec. et explicavit AWZUMPT, Berl. 1859 (discussions concerning it between CHALM and AWZUMPT in the ZfGW. 14, 881. 15, 337. 16, 337. 833). Explained by GTISCHER (Berl. 1861), CHALM (Ausgew. Rdn. VII, Berl.[4] 1883), HAKOCH (and GLANDGRAF, Lpz.[2] 1885), WEHEITLAND, Camb.[2] 1877.—Translated by GWENDT, Stuttg. 1869.

25) pro P. (Cornelio) Sulla, of the year 692/62, a successful defence against a charge of participation in the Catilinarian conspiracy.

1. SCHOL. BOB. p. 359–369 Or. GELL. 12, 12, 2.—Best MSS.: Monac. 18787 (Tegernseensis) and Palatino-Vaticanus 1525.—GEJEVERTS, de Cic. or. p. Sylla, Nymwegen 1835. MSEYFFERT, ep. crit. ad C. Halmium de Cic. p. Sulla et Sest. orr., Berl. 1848, together with HALM, JJ. 55, 30. CCAMPE, Beitr. zur Kritik des Cic. 1 (Greiffenberg 1860), 21.—Editions by KHFROTSCHER (Lps. 1831; commentary 1832), CHALM (Lps. 1845 and Ausgew. Rdn. VII, Berl.[4] 1883), FRICHTER (and GLANDGRAF, Lpz.[2] 1885), JSREID (Cambr. 1882).

26) pro Archia, delivered a. 692/62 in defence of the contested citizenship of Archias.

1. The speech abounds in declamation and its genuineness was questioned on that ground by CWSCHRÖDER (Lpz. 1818), who was opposed by FPLATZ (Seebode's krit. Arch. 1820–22); but JCWBÜCHNER (Schwerin 1839. 1841) raised new doubts, which were answered by JLATTMANN (Gött. 1847); yet why should not Cicero have indulged in declamation? Cf. IHSCHNEITHER, Mnemosyne 5, 115; also TAC. dial. 37 *nec Ciceronem magnum oratorem P. Quintius defensus aut Licinius Archias faciunt: Catilina et Milo et Verres et Antonius hanc illi famam circumdederunt.*

2. Best MSS.: Bruxellensis (Gemblacensis) 5352 s. XI/XII (Facsim. CHATELAIN t. 33), Erfurtensis s. XII (see above no. 13, 2).—Editions by RSTÜRENBURG (Lps. 1832. Lpz. 1839), CHALM (Ausgew. Rdn. III, Berl.[12] 1886), FRICHTER (Lpz.[3] 1884 by AEBERHARD), ÉTHOMAS (avec une nouvelle collation de Gemblac. etc.), Paris 1883. PTHOMAS, Mons 1882. JSREID, Cambr.[2] 1884.

3. For explanations see SCHOL. BOB. p. 353–359 Or. FJACOBS in Ersch and Gruber's Allg. Enc. I, 5, 137. DRUMANN, GR. 4, 199. SCHNEITHER, Mnemos. 5, 113. CAUTENRIETH, Blfbayr GW. 3, 322.

27) pro L. (Valerio) Flacco, of a. 695/59, a successful defence against an actio repetundarum raised by D. Laelius.

1. MACROB. 2, 1, 13 *pro L. Flacco, quem repetundarum reum ioci opportunitate*

de manifestissumis criminibus exemit. is iocus in oratione non exstat: mihi ex libro Furii Bibaculi notus est.—There is at the beginning of the speech a lacuna which AMai has partially filled in by the aid of the scholiasta Bobiensis (§ 295, 4) and from a cod. Ambros. (§ 180, 2). The chief MS. is the Vatic. Basilic. s. VIII/IX (§ 178, 3), which however contains only § 39-54 (new collation ap. AReifferscheid, Bresl. ind. schol. 1885/86). Also Mon. 15734, Bern. 354. There is no extant MS. evidence for § 75-83: according to the account of KPeutinger they were first printed, from a MS. which is now lost, in the edition of ACratander, Basel 1528. Cf. Mommsen, Herm. 18, 160.—WOetling, librorum mss. Cic. pFlacco condicio, Hameln 1872.—Drumann, GR. 5, 619.—WGPluygers, lect. tull. (Leid. 1856), 44. CAJordan, annotatt. critt., Soest 1868. JFCCampe, zu Cic. p. Fl., Progr. v. Greiffenberg 1879. HTKarsten, Mnemos. NS. 7, 300. RDareste, Mél. Graux (Par. 1884) 7.—An annotated edition by AduMesnil, Lpz. 1883.

28-31) Four speeches post reditum, viz. (28) oratio cum senatui gratias egit; (29) cum populo gratias egit; (30) de domo sua ad pontifices, to prove the invalidity of the consecration of the site of his house by Clodius and his legal claim to its restitution, all three of September 697/57; (31) de haruspicum responsis, of a. 698/56 and caused by the declaration of the haruspices, that sacred institutions were being violated, a declaration explained by Clodius of Cicero's house (as a consecrated site), but which Cicero applies to Clodius himself.

1. The first speech is an expression of thanks for the efforts of the Senate in favour of Cicero's return (ad Att. 4, 1, 5). For the third speech cf. ad Att. 4, 2, 2. Quint. 10, 1, 23; for the fourth Ascon. p. 69 Or. 62, K.-S. (de arusp. responso) and Quint. 5, 11, 42.

2. The second speech, ad Quirites, cannot be proved genuine by external arguments, and there are various reasons to suspect it on internal grounds. MLange, de Cic. altera post reditum oratione, Lpz. 1875; IwMüller, JB. 1874/75, 1, 689.—The other three are undoubtedly genuine, though they have been frequently impugned. JMarkland (Remarks on the epistles of Cic. to Brutus etc. with a dissertation upon four orations ascribed to Cic., Lond. 1745, cf. Wolf's edition p. xlvii) was strongly supported in his doubts by FAWolf (Cic. quae vulgo feruntur oratt. IV etc., Berl. 1801), whose views were adopted by Schütz, Orelli, CLKayser (in the edition by him and Baiter 4, IX) and others. Various discussions thereon. More recent literature: Drumann, GR. 2, 300. 311. GLahmeyer, orat. de harusp. resp. habitae originem Tullianam etc., Gött. 1849; WHoffmann, de fide et auctor. orat. Cic. de har. resp., Burg 1878 (in answer to the arguments for spuriousness advanced by SPPompe van Meerdervoort, ad or. q. Cic. fertur de har. resp., Leid. 1850). ADietzsch, über die Halmsche Ausgabe der Reden Ciceros in ihrer Bedeutung für die Untersuchung der angefochtenen Reden, RhM. 12, 529. CHOGrotenfeldt, de or. Cic. de domo inventione et dispositione, Helsingf. 1879. CRück, de Cic. or. de domo, Munich. 1881.—LLange, spicil. in Cic. de domo, Lps. 1880. HJordan, quaestt. crit., Königsb. 1886.

3. The best MS. is the Parisinus 7794 s. IX (see concerning it CHalm, RhM. 9, 321), also Erlang. 38 Bruxell. 5345 s. XII.—HWagner, Cic. or. post red. in

senatu rec., scripturae var. adiecit, prolegomenis instruxit, annotationibus . . . explanavit, defendit, Lps. s. a. (1858).—Criticism: HTKarsten, Mnemos. NS. 7, 399.

32) pro P. Sestio, of March 698/56, a successful defence against a suit de vi, in which Cicero avails himself of all the resources of oratory. The orator speaks, however, at greater length of himself and the aristocratic party than of the accusation and the accused.

1. ad Q. fr. 2, 4, 1 *Sestius noster absolutus est a. d. V. Id. Mart., et . . . omnibus sententiis absolutus est. . . . scito nos in eo iudicio consecutos esse ut omnium gratissimi videremur. nam defendendo et moroso homini cumulatissime satis fecimus et . . . Vatinium . . . concidimus.*—Schol. Bob. p. 291-313 Or. JNMadvig, op. ac. 1, 411. 524. Drumann, GR. 5, 664. ASWesenberg, obss. in or. S., Viborg 1837. CFHermann, vindiciae lect. Bern. in Cic. Sest., Gött. 1852. WPaul, ZfGW. 28, 305. HProbst, JJ. 97, 351. HWrampelmeyer, librorum mss. qui Cic. orr. p. Sest. et pro Cael. continent ratio, Gött. 1868; Cod. Wolfenb. 2 (1874), p. xxix. LUrlichs, RhM. 33, 150. EOppenrieder, zu Cic. pSest., Augsb. 1877. EOrtmann, ZfGW. 33, 417. MHertz, z. Krit. v. Cic. pSest., JJ. Suppl. 13, 33. OKimmig, de Sestianae interpolatt., Heidelb. 1882. LRoersch, rev. de l'instr. publ. Belge 1883, 285.

2. Chief MS.: the Paris. 7794 s. IX, also Bruxell. 5345 s. XII. Monac. 15734 and others. Editions by OMMüller (Köslin [2] 1831), JCWLotzbeck (Baireuth 1829, with p. leg. Man.), Orelli (with p. Cael., Zür. 1832, also prefixed to the Zürich Lectionskatal. 1834 and Heidelb. 1835), CHalm (Lps. 1845, also Ausgew. Rdn. IV, Berl. [6] 1886), HAKoch (Lpz. [2] 1877 by AEberhard). RBouterwek, Gotha 1883. HAHolden, Lond. 1883.

33) (Interrogatio) in P. Vatinium testem, connected with the suit against Sestius, in which Vatinius had been a witness for the prosecution. This speech was also successful.

1. Cic. ad Qu. fr. 2, 4, 1 (see no. 32, 1). Schol. Bob. p. 315-324 Or. Drumann GR. 5, 682.—The MSS. correspond to those for the pro Sestio.—Edition by CHalm, Lps. 1846. Cf. JNMadvig, op. acad. 1, 508.

34) pro M. Caelio (§ 209, 5), of a. 698/56, full of *esprit* and cutting witticisms, especially against the real prosecutrix, the ill-famed Clodia; a speech of much importance for our knowledge of Roman morals.

1. MSS.: Paris. 7794 s. IX (Facsim. Chatelain t. 23), Erfurt., Bruxell. 5345, Harleian. 4927 (collated by EBährens, rev. de phil. 8, 33), all s. XII: for certain passages cf. besides the Milan and Turin palimpsests, see § 180, 2.—LSchwabe, quaestt. Catull. 63. 66. JNMadvig, op. acad. 1, 375. ASWesenberg, krit. Bemaerk. til Cic.s Cael., Viborg 1836. HWrampelmeyer (see no. 32, 1 and § 178, 3). WOetling, librorum mss. Cic. or p. C. . . condicio . . eiusdem Caelianae virtutes et vitia, Gött. 1868. CBarwes, quaest. tull. spec. I ad Cael. or. spectans, Gött. 1868. CMFrancken, Mnemos. 8, 201. FSchöll, RhM. 35, 542. Bährens l.l.

35) De provinciis consularibus, delivered about the end of May 698/56, in order to obtain the prolongation of the governorship of Gaul for Caesar.

1. MSS. as for no. 34.—Drumann, GR. 5, 706. Mommsen, RG. 3[6], 323. Madvig, op. 2, 1. EMüller, Einleit. zu Cic. de pr. cons., Kattowitz 1886.—Explained by GTischer, Berl. 1861.

36) pro L. (Cornelio) Balbo, of a. 698/56, the defence of an intimate friend of Caesar (and Pompey) against the charge of arrogation of the rights of citizenship.

1. MSS. as for no. 34.—Madvig, op. 2, 13. WPaul, stud. Ciceroniana, Berl. 1875, EJullien, étude sur Cic. pBalbo, Lyon 1881; de L. Corn. Balbo, Paris 1886. JHoche, de L. Cornelio Balbo p. I, Rossleben 1882. AGasquy, de Cic. pBalbo oratione sive de civitatis jure ex Cic. libris, Paris 1886.—Edition by JSReid, Cambr. 1879.

37) In L. (Calpurnium) Pisonem, of a. 699/55, delivered in the Senate, a speech of monstrous vehemence.

1. Ascon. p. 1–17 Or. 1–15 K.-S. The commencement has been lost. Eleven fragments of it were published for the first time from the MS. at Cues (see above no. 12, 1), by JKlein, d. Hs. des Nic. C. (Berlin 1866) 49. Only incomplete versions of the correct text of the speech have been preserved in the Turin palimpsest and the cod. Vatic. Basilican. (§ 178, 3) s. VIII; the latter however only contains § 32–74 together with a few old scholia (published by AReifferscheid, Bresl. ind. schol. 1885/86, 10); the more complete MSS. e.g. Monac. 15734, the Erfurtensis etc., show a great deterioration, embodying numerous glosses.

2. Drumann, GR. 6, 4. CMFrancken Mnemos. 12, 61. JBake, schol. hypomn. 4, 298.

38) pro Cn. Plancio, of a. 700/54, against a charge of bribery.

1. Schol. Bob. p. 253–273 Or.—Manuscripts: Monac. 17787 (Tegernseensis), Erfurtensis.—Drumann, GR. 6, 45.—HKeil, obss. in Planc., Erl. 1864. CCampe, JJ. 95, 265.—Editions by GGaratoni, Bologna 1815, EWunder, Lps. 1830, EKöpke, Lpz.[3] 1887 (by GLandgraf), HAHolden, Lond. 1881, GBBonino, Turin 1887.

39) pro C. Rabirio Postumo, the defence (probably unsuccessful) of a partisan of Caesar against a well founded charge of extortions, a. 700/54.

1. Quint. 3, 6, 11. 4, 2, 10. Cf. Suet. Claud. 16.—All the MSS. (e.g. Monac. 15734, Ambros. C 121 inf.) are derived from that brought from Italy by Poggio, and are therefore late and untrustworthy.—Drumann, GR. 6, 71. CHalm, über Ciceros Rede pro R.P., Abh. d. Münch. Ak. 7, 3, 621. BtenBrink, Phil. 11, 92; Mnemos. NS. 2, 80.

40) pro T. Milone on the murder of Clodius, which is represented as an act of self-defence on the part of Milo, a. 702/52. It

is not, however, the speech actually delivered (which was not successful), but a subsequent revision of it, a real masterpiece of oratorical art.

1. Ascon. p. 31–55 Or. 26–49 C.-S. (ed. ill. Frotscher, Freiberg 1845). Quint. 6, 5, 10. 10, 5, 20. Schol. Bob. p. 275–290. Schol. Gron. p. 443 sq. Cf. below § 210, 2 ad fin. and § 268, 6.—Chief MSS.: Monac. 18787 (Tegernseensis, Facsim. Chatelain t. 27), Erfurtensis (from this WFreund, Bresl. 1838 published the speech pMil. in a lithographic facsimile); also for some passages the Turin palimpsest is important. Editions by EOsenbrüggen ([2]Hamb. 1872 by HWirz), CHalm (Ausgew. Red. V, Berl.[9] 1885), J. and AWagener (Mons [2] 1876), FRichter (Lpz. [3] 1881 by AEberhard). RBouterwek, Gotha 1887. JSPurton, Camb. 1877.—Translated into Greek by WBirkler, Stuttgart 1860.

2. AFGCurth, de artificiosa forma or. p. M., Berl. 1833. LSpengel, ZfAW. 1843, 432. HMeusburger, qua tenus Cic. in or. pMil. observaverit praecepta rhetorica, Ried 1882.—CWex, zu Cic. p. M., JJ. 83, 207. LLange, obss. ad Cic. or. Mil., Giessen 1864. 65 II.

3. The speech as actually delivered had also been preserved. Ascon. 36, 24 Or. 42, 21 K.-S. *manet illa quoque excepta* (by short-hand writers) *eius oratio*. Quint. 4, 3, 17. Schol. Bob. 276, 10 *et extat alius* (Ciceronis) *praeterea liber actorum pro Milone*. A fragment of this first speech occurs ap. Quint. 9, 2, 54 and Schol. Bob. 346, 13. HGaumitz, zu den Bobienser Cic.-Scholien, Dresd. 1884, 1.

41) pro M. Marcello, a. 708/46, addressed to Caesar in the Senate for the purpose of obtaining the recall of an old adversary of his (§ 202, 5).

1. The three speeches pMarc. Lig. Deiot. were even in ancient times coupled together as "Caesarianae"; see Non. 437, 9 *M. Tullius in Caesarianis* (=pMarc. 2). Serv. Aen. 11, 438 *Cicero in Caesarianis* (= pDeiot. 12). Prob. GL. 4, 27, 18 *Cicero . . . in Caesarianis* (= pDeiot. 41) and elsewhere.

2. The speech pMarc. also, in spite of quotations and other evidence, has not escaped the attacks of scepticism. FAWolf in particular has expended all his ingenuity in the attempt to prove that the speech is bad (which must be granted) and therefore not Ciceronian; see the pref. to his edition (Berl. 1802). CLKayser (in his and Baiter's edition of Cicero 5, viii) concurred with Wolf. Recent answers to Wolf FHahne, orat. pMarc. defendit, Jena 1876 (also IwMüller, JB. 1877, 2, 248) and HSchwanke, de Cic. quae fertur or. pMarc., Erl. 1886.

3. Schol. Ambr. p. 347 sq. Schol. Gronov. p. 418 sqq. Or. Drumann, GR. 6, 262.—Manuscripts: Bruxellensis 5345 (Gemblacensis), Erfurtensis, Ambros. C 29 inf. s. X. Admont. 383 s. XII (collation by MPetschenig, ZföG. 34, 1).—Explained (together with Ligar. and Deiot.) by FRichter (Lpz. [3] 1886 by AEberhard).

42) pro Q. Ligario, a public intercession with Caesar in favour of this exiled partisan of Pompey, a. 708/46.

1. CGuttmann, de earum quae vocantur Caesarianae orationum Tullian. genere dicendi, Greifsw. 1883, attempts (following UvWilamowitz, Herm. 12, 332) to show that Cicero in the speech pro Marcello before Caesar poses as an Asiatic, but in the speeches pLig. and pDeiot. as an Atticist (pr. 67 supr), out of consideration for Caesar!

2. Schol. Ambros. p. 371 sq. Schol. Gron. p. 414 sqq. Or.—The MSS. as for no. 41, 3.—Editions by AFSoldan (Hanau 1839), CHalm (Ausgew. Rdn. V, Berl. [9] 1885), FRichter (see no. 41, 3).—Translation with notes by HKratz, Stuttg. 1869. Criticism: HJordan, quaestt. crit., Königsb. 1886, 3.

43) pro rege Deiotaro, in defence of the king of Galatia of that name against the charge of attempting to murder Caesar, delivered at Caesar's residence, October 709/45.

1. Schol. Ambr. p. 372. Schol. Gron. p. 421 sqq. Or.—MSS. as for no. 41, 3, and in addition the Gudian. 335 s. X in Wolfenbüttel.—Editions by KHFrotscher (Lps. 1835), AFSoldan (Hanau 1836), CHalm (Ausgew. Rdn. V, Berl. [9] 1885), FRichter (see no. 41, 2).

44–57) In M. Antonium orationum Philippicarum, libri XIV, of the years 710/44 and 711/43. In the first (2 Sept. 710/44) the speaker endeavours to justify his long absence from the stage of political life and complains of a recent attack on the part of his 'friend' M. Antony. When Antony had been roused by this, on 19 Sept., to make a speech in the Senate in which he attacked the whole political career of Cicero (who was, however, absent), the orator wrote a reply in the form of an answer returned on the spot, but which was not published until after Antony's departure from Rome—the second Philippica. In the third (Dec. 20), he recommends that the Senate should award special praise to D. Brutus and Octavianus for resisting the consul, M. Antony, and this having been obtained, Cicero the same evening announced the resolution to the people, in the fourth speech. The fifth speech (1 Jan. 711/43) has for its purpose to recommend the award of special honours to those adversaries of M. Antony and to declare him an enemy of the state. The first half of this prosposal having been passed on 4 Jan., but an attempt at mediation being contemplated in the place of the second half, Cicero announced this to the people on the same day, in the sixth speech. The seventh (end of Jan.) is intended again to urge the immediate declaration of war against M. Antony, and in the eighth (beginning of February) he blames the adoption of an unsatisfactory compromise after that attempt had failed, and puts forth positive proposals of his own. In the ninth he again attacks M. Antony and advocates special distinctions and honours to be awarded to Ser. Sulpicius. In the tenth speech (end of Feb. at latest) the subsequent confirmation of the measures taken by M. Brutus in Macedonia and Greece is recommended. The eleventh (middle of March 711/43) is an unsuccessful argument in favour of committing the punishment of Dolabella (who had executed C. Trebonius, one of the assassins of Caesar) to C. Cassius, himself one of the assassins. In the twelfth, which almost immediately followed the preceding, Cicero attempts to prevent the second embassy to M. Antony (which had been decided on) and to free himself from all share in it. In the thirteenth (20 March 711/43) he defends his warlike policy against the peaceful counsels of M. Lepidus and Munatius Plancus. In the fourteenth and last (22 April 711/43) he recommends the celebration of a great thanksgiving on account of the victory gained over M. Antony near Forum Gallorum, and honours to the victorious generals. The tone of these Philippics is angry, and the lively, impassioned language does not eschew strong and coarse expressions.

1. The chief MS. is the Vatic.-Basilican. H 25 s. IX (§ 178, 3) (FDeycks, de Cic. Philippic. oratt. cod. Vatic., Münster 1844), next Monac. 8787 (Tegernseensis) s. XI and others. On a Phil. MS. in Cheltenham GNutt, Academy no. 679, 332.—Editions of the Phil.: by GGWernsdorf (Lps 1821 sq. II; verb. Text ib. 1825), by JRKing, [2]Oxf. 1877; the second (which is especially famous, Iuv. 10, 125) published separately by Wernsdorf (with a translation, Lpz. 1815), JGantrelle Par. [2] 1882, GLanson, Par. 1881, AEPeskett, Cambr. 1887. The first and second explained by CHalm (Ausgew. Rdn. VI, Berl. [6] 1881) and HAKoch (Lpz. [2] 1879 by AEberhard). The second, edited after Halm, with corrections and additions, by JEBMayor, Lond. [6] 1878.

2. JMittermayr, Beitr. zur Erkl. der ersten phil. R. (Aschaffenb. 1841); to the second (ib. 1843. 45). CCampe, Phil. 10, 627; JJ. 91, 163. Against AKrause's doubts concerning the genuineness of the fourth speech (Cic. Phil. IV expl. et Ciceroni derogavit, Berl. 1839, and Jahn's Archiv 13, 297) see CAJordan, ZfAW. 1840, 611. Schuster, vindiciae Cic. or. Phil. quartae, Lüneb. 1851 sq. SChrSchirlitz, Cic. Phil. nona, Wetzlar 1844. On the chronology OESchmidt, de epist. Cassian. 25. 27. 34. Criticism: CGCobet, Mnemos. NS. 7, 113. ThGomperz, Wien. Studd. 2, 143.—OHauschild, de sermonis proprietatt. in Cic. oratt. Phil., Diss. Halens. 6, 223.

180. Besides these 57 speeches we possess fragments of about 20 more, and we know the titles of 30 others delivered by Cicero. In addition to these there are a number of laudations which were published, but never pronounced, viz. of Caesar (a. 698/56), Cato the Younger (a. 708/46) and his sister Porcia (a. 703/51).

1. Important fragments have been preserved: a) of the two Cornelianae (pro C. Cornelio de maiestate, a. 689/65, see Ascon. p. 56–81 Or. 50–72 K.-S. and Quint. 8, 3, 3; cf. 6, 5, 10. 10, 5, 13. RGBeck, quaestt. in Cic. p. C. Cornelio orationes, Lps. 1877); b) of the oratio in toga candida, a. 690/64 delivered in the Senate, cf. Bücheler, Q. Cic. p. 9. PKötschau, de Cic. or. in toga candida, Lps. 1881; in the time of Asconius (p. 84 K.-S.) there were in circulation answers to this speech of Cicero, which had been forged by his enemies in the name of Catiline and An-

tony; c) of the speech pro Aemilio Scauro, a. 700/54, see DRUMANN, GR. 6, 36. ASCON. p. 18–30 Or. 16–25 K.-S. SCHOL. BOB. p. 373–376 Or. HGAUMITZ, de Scauri caussa repetundarum et de Cic. pScauro, Lpz. Stud. 2, 249. Criticism: CMFRANCKEN, Mnemos. NS. 11, 375; d) in Clodium et Curionem; RGBECK, Einl. u. Dispos. zu Cic. in Clod. et Cur., Zwickau 1886.

2. The principal MSS. of the fragments of orations are: Ambros. R 57 sup. s. V. palimps. (facsim. CHATELAIN t. 29, 1), Taurinensis A II 2 (CHATELAIN t. 29, 2), Vatic.-Palat. 24 s. V (CHATEL. t. 32, 2).—Collective editions of the fragments of some of the speeches: Sex orationum partes ineditae, ed. AMAI, Milan² 1817; Auctor. class. 2, 277. Oratt. p. Fonteio et C. Rabir. fragmenta ed. BGNIEBUHR, Rome 1820. Oratt. p. Scaur., Tull. et in Clod. fragmenta inedita ed. APEYRON, Stuttg. 1824 (with commentatio de biblioth. Bobiensi by APEYRON, p. III; inventarium librorum monasterii S. Columbani de Bobio, p. 1, and annotationes on it, p. 70). Oratt. p. Tull., in Clod., p. Scauro, p. Flacco fragmenta ined. coll. CBEIER, Lps. 1825, with Indd. (edited by GHERTEL), Lpz. 1831. JKLEIN, üb. eine Handschr. des Nik. v. Cues nebst ungedruckten Fragm. Cic. Reden, Berl. 1866.—The fragments of the speeches in the complete editions e.g. in BAITER-KAYSER 11, 1 and in CFW MÜLLER 4, 3, 231. CHALM, Beitr. z. Berichtig. u. Ergänzung der cic. Fragmente, Münch. SBer. 1862 2, 1. FBELIN, de Cic. Orationum deperditarum fragmentis, Par. 1875.—List of the speeches of which there are no fragments extant e.g. in CFWMÜLLER 4, 3, 289.

3. Sketches and schemes of speeches by Cicero were published from his papers by his freedman Tiro. QUINT. 10, 7, 30 *quod fecisse M. Tullium commentariis ipsius apparet.* ib. 31 *Ciceronis ad praesens modo tempus aptatos* (*commentarios*) *libertus Tiro contraxit.* Cf. ib. 4, 1, 69 *Cicero pro Scauro ambitus reo, quae causa est in commentariis* (*nam bis eundem defendit*), *prosopopoeia . . utitur.* HIERONYM. apol. ad Rufin. 2, 469 Vall. (*in commentariis causarum, pro Gabinio*). CFWMÜLLER's Cic. 4, 3, 291.

4. For Cicero's laudatio Caesaris see ad Att. 4, 5; for his laudatio Porciae ib. 13, 37, 3. 13, 48, 2.—ad Q. fr. 3, 8, 5 *Serrani Domestici filii funus perluctuosum fuit a. d. VIII Kal. Dec.* (J. 700/54), *laudavit pater scripto meo.*

5. PLUT. Caes. 54 ἔγραψε Κικέρων ἐγκώμιον Κάτωνος, ὄνομα τῷ λόγῳ θέμενος Κάτωνα. FSCHNEIDER, de Ciceronis Catone minore, ZfAW. 1837, Nr. 140. CGÖTTLING, de Cic. laudatione Catonis et de Caesaris Anticatonibus, op. 153. BAITER-KAYSER 11, 67. CFWMÜLLER 4, 3, 327. The contents of this laudation of Cato gave some offence to Caesar (ad Att. 12, 40, 1. 13, 27, 1), though he fully admitted its excellence in point of form (ib. 13, 46, 2); he therefore caused Hirtius to write a reply and even wrote an Anticato himself (see § 195, 7). M. Brutus, on the other hand, thought Cicero's treatise somewhat cold and narrow in spirit, Cicero (from prudential motives) having confined himself to Cato's private character; hence he too (beg. of 709/45) wrote a Cato (§ 210, 2. ad fin.).

6. The spurious speech pridie quam in exilium iret (extant in very good MSS. e.g. the Paris, 7794, Brux. 5345, Erfurt.) see e.g. in BAITER-KAYSER 11, 156, and in CFW MÜLLER 4, 3, 425. On the supposititious speeches of Sallust and Cicero against each other, see below § 205, 6. The speech which CASSIUS DIO 44, 23–33 attributes to Cic. was (to judge from its contents) written by the historian himself; FSTRAUMER, de Cic. q. f. or. ap. Cass. Dion., Chemnitz 1872.

181. In the theory of rhetoric, Cicero was a disciple of the Greeks. After an unsuccessful attempt in his youth, in his

mature age he wrote original works on rhetoric, not in order to develope the theory of it, but to show his own position in the history of Roman oratory and defend his style against his adversaries. Here he succeeded in setting forth the principal doctrines in popular form. In his opposition to the barren schematism of scholastic rhetoric, Cicero even drifted into the extreme of mere empiricism and frequently missed distinctness of definition.

1. On Cicero's position in relation to Asiatic and Attic oratory see p. 67. OHarnecker, JJ. 125, 601. 129, 42.—CWPiderit, Kunstwert der rhetorischen Schriften Cic.s JJ. 82, 503. LSpengel, RhM. 18, 495. HJentsch, Aristotelis ex arte rhetorica quid habeat Cicero, Berl. 1866; de Aristotele Cic. in rhetorica auctore, Guben 1874. 75 II. ChCauseret, sur la langue de la rhétorique et de la critique littéraire en Cic., Par. 1887.—Über die Benutzung der ciceron. Rhetorica bei den späteren Rhetoren ThStangl, BlfbayrGW. 19, 184. 277. 334. GWüst, de clausula rhetorica quae praecepit Cic. qua tenus in oratt. secutus sit, Diss. Argentor. 5, 227. EMüller, de numero Ciceroniano, Kiel 1886.—DWollner, d. aus der Krieger- u. Fechter-Sprache entlehnten Wendd. in den rhetor. Schrr. d. Cic. Quint. Tac., Landau 1886.—Criticism: ThStangl, BlfbayrGW. 18, 245. WGPluygers, see § 178, 6.

182. The extant rhetorical works of Cicero in chronological order are as follows:

1) Rhetorica, (Rhetorici, de inventione): see § 177[a], 3.

2) De oratore libri tres, written a 699/55, in the form of a dialogue between the two greatest orators of the preceding period, L. Crassus and M. Antonius, and several others, supposed to take place a. 663/91. By this form the treatment has gained in facility, comprehensiveness and vivacity, and Cicero avoids dry systematic explanation and the necessity of himself deciding in favour of one style, though it is evident that his characters pronounce only his own views. The work is far from attaining the dramatic art of a Platonic dialogue, nevertheless it ranks with the most finished productions of Cicero on account of its varied contents and its excellent style. The first book treats of the studies necessary to an orator, the second of the treatment of the subject-matter, and the third of the form and delivery of a speech.

1. Cic. ad Att. 13, 19, 4. fam. 1, 9, 23 cf. 7, 32, 2. Above § 152, 4.—FEllendt introd. to his edition 2, vii. CAFBrückner, quid Cic. in libris de or. ex Isocrate et Aristotele mutuatus sit, Schweidnitz 1849. CWPiderit, zur Krit. u. Exegese v. Cic. de or., Hanau 1857—58 II. JBake, Mnemos. 7, 97. GSorof, Phil. 21, 654; Vindic. Tull., Berl. 1866. FThAdler, locos quosdam libr. I et II emend., illustr., Halle 1869. Ritschl, op. 3, 814. HRubner, krit. Beitr. zu Cic. de orat., Hof 1874. WFriedrich, JJ. 111, 859; quaestt. in Cic. de or., Mühlhausen 1885; JJ. 135, 73. PLangen, de locis nonnull. in Cic. de orat. l. I, Münst. 1876 II. HMuther, JJ. 129, 593; Beitr. z. Emend. von. Cic. de or., Coburg 1885. Madvig., adv. crit. 3, 85. JRoby, Journ. of phil. No. 29, 57.

2. The treatises de oratore, Brutus and orator (cf. below no. 3, 2. no. 4, 2) have been transmitted to us in a twofold version, which rests on the one hand on the old codex Laudensis, found at Lodi in 1422, which after being transcribed was again lost. Direct copies from the Laud. are, for the three works, Vatican.-Ottobon. 2057 (written in Nov. 1422); for Brut. and Or. Florent. Magliabecch. I, 1, 14 (written 1423); for de orat. and Or. Vatic.-Palat. 1469. Discussions on the Laudensis and the copies from it: DDetlefsen, Kieler Phil.-Vers. 1869, 94. FHeerdegen, RhM. 38, 120; JJ. 131, 105. 245; BlfbayrGW. 22, 98. Also in the introd. to his edition of the Or. ThStangl WschrfklPh. 1884, 1209; BlfbayrGW. 21, 24. 118. RSabbadini, Guarino Veronese e le opere rhetoriche di Cic. (WschrfklPh. 1886, 749); Mus. di antichità class. 2 (1887), 22. The copies of the Laud. alone give the work de oratore entire (integri): that treatise and the orator are also preserved in a mutilated state in MSS. which are good in other respects (codices mutili), e.g. in the most important of this class, the Abrincensis s. IX (see FWSchneidewin, Phil. 10, 758, Heerdegen, proleg. z. Orator, facsim. Chatelain t. 19), in the Harleian. 2736 s. IX/X and others. EStröbel, Cic. de orat. codd. mutilos examinavit, Acta semin., Erlang. 3, 1.—Concerning Lagom. 32 on de or. I SpVassis, Athens 1884.—Editions e.g. by RJFHenrichsen (Copenh. 1830) and esp. by FEllendt (Königsb. 1840 II). Also rec. IBake, Amsterd. 1863. Annotated by CWPiderit, Lpz.[6] 1886 (with contributions by GHarnecker); by GSorof, Berl.[2] 1882. B. I. II. by ASWilkins, Lond. 1879. 81.—Translated by Dilthey and FBaur, Stuttg. 1859; RKühner, Stuttg. 1858.

3) Brutus de claris oratoribus, written in the beginning of 708/46, a pragmatic history of Roman oratory, highly valuable on account of the abundance of the historical materials contained in it, as well as many pertinent and vivid sketches of character, and information in regard to Cicero's studies. The form of a dialogue is handled with greater ability than in the philosophical works; though there are imperfections of style, great and small, here and there.

1. At the commencement (26 sqq.) is the summary of the history of oratory among the Greeks. The number of Latin orators discussed amounts to nearly 200, and, on principle, only those who are deceased are treated of (231). Of living orators only Caesar, Sulpicius Rufus, M. Marcellus (§ 202, 5) and Cicero himself are discussed. Cf. Brut. 319. or. 23. Quint. 10, 1, 38. Tac. dial. 30. Above § 153, 8. 171, 12.

2. The extant manuscripts (all s. XV) are derived from the lost Laudensis (§ 182, 2, 2).—Editions by HMeyer and GBernhardy (Halle 1838), CPeter (Lpz. 1839), EEllendt (Konigsb. 1825 and especially 1844), OJahn (Berl.[4] 1877 by AEberhard), CBeck (Cambridge in Massachusetts[3] 1853), CWPiderit (annot. Lpz.[2] 1875), rec. ThStangl, Prague 1886. MKellog, Boston and Lond. 1889.

3. JBake, schol. hypomn. 3, 311; Mnemos. 6. 421. CWPiderit, zur Krit. u. Exegese v. Cic. Brut., Hanau 1860. 1862 II. (JCFCampe), Beitr. z. Krit d. Cic. 1 (Greiffenberg 1860), 1-21. JMähly. RhM. 20, 637. HJordan, die Einleitung des cic. Brut., Herm. 6, 196. WFriedrich, JJ. 107, 845. 121, 137. AWeidner, Phil. 38, 63. Madvig, adv. crit. 3, 100. FNesemann, z. Textkrit. des Brut. u. Or., Lissa 1882. Fleckeisen, JJ. 127, 208. EBährens, rev. de phil. 10, 70. JSimon, krit.

Bemerkk. zu Cic. Brut., Kaiserslautern 1887. JStangl, WschrfklPh. 1888, 559. 595. —MNaumann, de fontt. et fide Bruti Cic., Halle 1883.—Translated by WTeuffel, Stuttg. 1850.

4) Orator ad M. Brutum, Cicero's 'last word' on rhetoric, giving his ideal of an orator, though of greater value for various details and isolated remarks than for completeness and systematic arrangement; it was also written a. 708/46.

1. Cic. ad fam. 6, 18, 4. 15, 20, 1. div. 2, 4.—Ad Att. 14, 20, 3 and fam. 12, 17, 2 called *de optimo genere dicendi* from its contents.

2. The MSS., like those for the books de oratore, fall into two classes, one of which consists of the copies from the cod. Laudensis, while the others are codices mutili. Cf. § 182, 2, 2 and the literature there quoted; also § 182, 3, 2. CStegmann, de oratoris Tull. mutilis ll., Jena 1875. Oratoris Tull. codicem Erlang. (303, olim 39) contulit ChrHörner, Zweibr. 1878. HRubner, de oratoris Tull. cod. Laurentiano (50, 1 s. XV), Speier 1882.—Editions by HMeyer, Lps. 1827, FGöller, Lps. 1838, CPeter and GWeller, Lpz. 1838, OJahn, Berl.[3] 1869, KWPiderit, Lpz.[2] 1876. Rec. FHeerdegen, Lpz. 1884. By JESandys, Lond. 1885.

3. IBake, de emendando Cic. or., Leiden 1856. KWPiderit, Eos 1, 401. 2, 168; JJ. 91, 372. 765. HSauppe, quaestt. tull., Gött. 1857. HEckstein, observatt. gramm. ad Cic. orat. c. 45–48, Lps. 1874. WFriedrich, JJ. 121, 142. 123, 177; Phil. 44, 666. FNesemann (see above 3, 3) JCHBoot, Versl. d. Akad. v. Amsterd. 1882 2, 11. EBährens, rev. de phil. 10, 70. LHavet, ibid. 10, 155. Madvig, adv. 3, 95.—Translated by Teuffel (Stuttg. 1861), JSommerbrodt (Stuttg. 1870).

5) Partitiones oratoriae (or de partitione oratoria), written a. 708/46, or 709/45, a survey of the whole department of rhetoric in the form of questions (put by the author's son) and answers; a rather dry catechism.

1. Quint. 3, 3, 7. Drumann, GR. 6, 293. Best MS. Paris. 7231 s. XI (facsim. in Chatelain t. 22); then Paris. 7696 s. XII. Erlang. 848 s. XV. Rhediger. s. XV and others. EStröbel, z. Hss.-Kunde u. Krit. von Cic. Partitt. oratt., Zweibr. 1887. Edition by KWPiderit (with notes, Lpz. 1867).—KWPiderit, zur Kritik von Cic. p. or., Hanau 1866; JJ. 95, 275. HSauppe, Gött. GA. 1867, p. 1863. WFriedrich, Phil. 47, pt. 2.

6) Topica ad C. Trebatium, an explanation of Aristotle's Topics, at least according to the author, for the use of forensic orators, written down from memory a. 710/44 during a voyage from Velia to Regium.

1. Cic. top. 5 *ut veni Veliam . . . haec, cum mecum libros non haberem, memoria repetita in ipsa navigatione conscripsi tibique ex itinere misi.* Cf. ad fam. 7, 19. Quint. 3, 11, 18. 5, 10, 64 (*scribens ad Trebatium ex iure ducere exempla maluit*). —Manuscripts: Leid. 84 and 86 (§ 184, 2, 3), Einsidl. 324 s.X (Chatelain t. 21), two SGall. s. X 830 (facsim. Chatelain t. 21). 854. FBücheler, Phil. 21, 123. Regarding Boethius' commentary on this work: see § 478, 5.—ChABrandis, RhM. 3 (1829), 547. JJKlein, de fontibus topp. Cic., Bonn 1844. HJentsch, Aristotelis ex arte

rhet. quid habeat Cicero 2, 25. MWALLIES, de fontt. top. Cic., Halle 1878. CHAMMER, de Cic. topicis, Landau 1879. IwMÜLLER, JB. 1880 2, 218.

7) De optimo genere oratorum, forming the introduction to a translation of Demosthenes' and Aeschines' speeches for and against Ctesiphon, perhaps of the same date (710/44).

1. This translation was intended to prove to the Romans that the greatest Attic orators employed a kind of eloquence differing entirely from that of the insipid Lysias, who was at this period specially recommended for imitation as the purest Attic model (see p. 67. 245. 250). Cicero at § 10 mentions his speech pro Milone; cf. ASCON. p. 31 Or. 26, 6 K.-S.—Chief MS. SGall. 818 s. XI (CHATELAIN t. 20).—Ed. cum comment. ASTATII, Löwen 1552; (together with topp. and partitt.) by GHSAALFRANK, Regenst. 1823; OJAHN in his Orator.

183. Cicero studied philosophy originally only as a means of assisting his rhetorical training, and it was not until his last years, when he saw himself stopped in his political and rhetorical career, that he wrote a number of philosophical works within a short time, partly for the sake of occupation and to divert his mind from the existing state of things. In these, he rendered his Greek originals in a loose and unmethodical manner, even committing numerous mistakes, e. g. frequently confounding the Academic and Peripatetic philosophers. His study of the original authorities was mainly confined to late Greek philosophers, while he had only an imperfect acquaintance with Plato and Aristotle. The most difficult problems he left aside, and he carefully avoided strict definitions. He was eclectic as to the different systems. He preferred, however, the plausible doctrines of the New Academy on account of their practical utility to a lawyer, as this school renounced positive definitions and was content with the statement of pros and cons and the investigation of probabilities; in ethics he inclined to the idealism of the Stoics, though softening down their asperities; he was repelled by the moral laxity of the Epicureans. The material value of these works is far surpassed by the merit of their form, for Cicero was the first Roman writer who treated philosophical subjects in Latin in an easy and elegant manner and thereby became the creator of a Latin philosophical style. His philosophical writings are, as a rule, conceived as dialogues, though these are somewhat monotonous, as the form is not seriously sustained; they are wanting in dramatic skill and subtlety, and are mere abstracts of the originals worked into their present dialectic frame.

1. Tusc. 2, 9 *itaque mihi semper Peripateticorum Academiaeque consuetudo de omnibus rebus in contrarias partes disserendi non ob eam caussam solum placuit quod aliter non posset quid in quaque re veri simile esset inveniri, sed etiam quod esset ea maxima dicendi exercitatio.* paradox. prooem. 2 *nos ea philosophia plus utimur quae peperit dicendi copiam et in qua dicuntur ea quae non multum discrepent ab opinione populari.* Cf. Brut. 161. 315. 322. Tusc. 4, 7. 5, 82. nat. deor. 1, 6–15.

2. ad Att. 12, 52, 3 *dices, qui talia conscribis?* Ἀπόγραφα *sunt, minore labore fiunt; verba tantum affero, quibus abundo;* cf. fam. 13, 63, 1. He expressly declares that he used his own discretion and taste, de fin. 1, 6. 7. off. 1, 6. But there is not the same degree of dependence in all his works; it is greatest in the departments of natural philosophy and dialectics, and least in questions of practical morals and experience. RHirzel, l.l. 1, 1.

3. He quite misunderstands the Platonic Ideas in the Orat. 7–40. With regard to Aristotle's Nicomachean Ethics he says de fin. 5, 127 *quare teneamus Aristotelem et eius filium Nicomachum, cuius accurate scripti de moribus libri dicuntur illi quidem esse Aristotelis, sed non video cur non potuerit patris similis esse filius*, words which may well make us doubt whether Cicero had ever seen the work in question, see Madvig ad loc. For other particulars see Brut. 120. 149. fin. 5, 7 sq. 14, 21 (*antiquis, quos eosdem Academicos et Peripateticos nominamus*), 23 extr. et passim.

4. Ciceronis hist. philosophiae antiquae etc., collegit, FGedike, Berl.³ 1815. HRitter and LPreller, hist. philosophiae graecae et romanae (ed. FSchultess, Gotha⁶ 1887) 427. JFHerbart, die Philosophie des Cic., kl. Schrr. (Lpz. 1842) 1, 11. RKühner, Cic. in philosophiam merita, Hamb. 1825. ABKrische, Forschungen, vol. 1, Gött. 1840. HRitter, Gesch. der Philos. 4, 103. Drumann, GR. 6, 650. EZeller, Philos. d. Griechen 3, 1³, 648. ChABrandis, Gesch. d. gr. röm. Philos. 3, 2, 248. FÜberweg, Grundriss 1⁵, 257. RHirzel, Unterss. zu Cic. philos. Schriften, Lpz. 1877–1883 III. CThiaucourt, essai sur les traités philosophiques de Cic. et leurs sources grecques, Par. 1885. JACvHeusde, Cic. φιλοπλάτων, Utr. 1836. FGloël, üb. Cic.s Studium des Platon, Magdeb. 1876. FSaltzmann, Cic.s Kenntnis der platon. Schrr., Cleves 1885, 86 II. Ritter üb. Cic.s Bekanntschaft mit aristotel. Philosophie, Zerbst 1846. MMvBaumhauer, de Aristotelis vi in Cic. scriptis, Utr. 1841. WThomas, de Aristotelis ἐξωτερικοῖς λόγοις deque Ciceronis Aristotelio more, Gött. 1860. Burmeister, Cic. als Neuakademiker, Oldenb. 1860. EHavet, pourquoi Cic. a professé la philos. académique, Séanc. et trav. de l'acad. d. sc. mor. et polit. 1884, 660. CHartfelder, de Cic. epicureae doctrinae interprete, Karlsr. 1875. GBehncke, de Cic. Epicureorum philosophiae existimatore et iudice, Berl. 1879. CMBernhardt, de Cic. graecae philosophiae interprete, Berl. 1865. VClavel, de Cic. Graecorum interprete; acc. Ciceronianum lexicon Graeco-Latinum, Par. 1869. FVLevius, six lectures introductory to the philosophical writings of Cic., Lond. 1871. JWalter, Ciceronis philosophia moralis, Prague and elsewhere, 1878–1883 II.

5. There is no manuscript containing all Cicero's philosophical works; but a more comprehensive collection can be shown to have existed, which included de nat. deor., de div., Tim., de fato, top., parad., Lucullus, de leg. From it are derived the MSS which are now most important: two Leidenses (Vossiani 84 s. X and 86 s. XI; cf. § 177, 4), the Laurentianus S. Marci 257 s. X. (HEbeling, Phil. 43, 705) and the Vindob. 189 s. X. Cf. in regard to these CFWMüller, JJ. 89, 127. 261. 605. AReifferscheid, RhM. 17, 295.—More than 600 excerpts from Cicero's philosophical works, compiled by a certain Presbyter Hadoardus, in the Vatic.-Regin.

1762 s. IX: they contain only materials already familiar. See on this ENARDUCCI, bull. delle scienze matem. 15 (1882), 512; rendiconto dell' Acad. dei Lincei 1885, 152. WHDSURINGAR, de onlangs gevonden fragm. v. Cic., Leid. 1883 and esp. PSCHWENKE, Phil. Suppl. 5, 399 (containing a reprint of the collection). On Cratanders (§ 187, 5) MSS. for Cic.'s philosoph. writings KLEHMANN, WschrfklPh. 1888, 472.—Collective ed. of Cicero's philosophical writings cum scholiis et coniectt. PMANUTII, Ven. 1546 II. The editions by JDAVIS (Cambridge 1736 sqq. VI; ed. RGRATH, Halle 1804–20 VI) and JAGÖRENZ (Lpz. 1809–13 III) were never completed. The most recent critical revision is by THSCHICHE, Prague 1884 sqq.

6. KVAUCHER, in Cic. libros philosophicos, Lausanne 1864. 65 II. MHAUPT, op. 2, 358. JJEEP, de locis nonnullis philosoph. Cic., Wolfenb. 1868. JVAHLEN, ZföG. 24, 241. ABRIEGER, Beitr. z. Krit. einiger philos. Schriften (esp. Cato, Lael., de nat. deor.) des Cic., Posen 1874. WFRIEDRICH, JJ. 127, 421.—HMERGUET, Lexikon zu den philosoph. Schr. Cic.s, Jena 1887 sqq. Literary reviews of Cicero's philosophical works by THSCHICHE in ZfGW. 1880. 1882. PSCHWENKE, JB. 1883 2, 74. 1886 2, 267.

184. Cicero himself enumerates his philosophical works de divin. 2, 1–3. The following is a chronological list of those extant:

1) De republica, forming so to say the transition from Cicero's practical life to philosophical writing, written a. 700/54 sqq., and published before his departure for Cilicia (703/51), in six books, of which, however, scarcely the third part has come down to us.

1. CIC. de div. 2, 3 *his libris adnumerandi sunt sex de rep., quos tum scripsimus cum gubernacula reip. tenebamus.* Cf. fam. 8, 1, 4. Att. 5, 12, 2. 6, 1, 8. leg. 3, 4. Tusc. 4, 1.

2. The composition of the work may be traced in Cicero's letters. His original plan was to introduce only defunct persons as interlocutors, but this was changed upon the advice of Cn. Sallustius (§ 192, 1), he himself and his brother becoming the speakers; subsequently, however, he reverted to his first idea, laid the scene a. 625, 129 and made Africanus minor, Laelius, and others the principal speakers. See ad Qu. fr. 3, 5 and 6, 1 sq. JPRICHARZ, de politicorum Cic. librr. tempore natali, Würzb. 1829. The form of the whole is an attempt to imitate the Platonic dialogues. See DRUMANN GR. 6, 83.

3. In this work Cicero resorted to Plato and Dikaiarchos (Aristotle), Polybios, Theophrastos and others, embodying in it also his personal political experience. Suetonius defended this book against the attacks of Didymos, see SUID. v. Τράγκυλλος (§ 347, 2). MSGRATAMA, de Cic. de rep. et de legg. libris, Grön. 1827. JvPERSIJN, de politica Cic. doctrina in libris de rep., Amst. 1827. KSZACHARIÄ, über Cic.s Bücher vom Staat, Heidelb. 1823. RISCHUBERT, quos Cic. de rep. I et II auctores secutus sit, Würzb. 1883.

4. Part of the sixth book, the dream of Scipio, was at an early period separately circulated and annotated, the latter especially by Macrobius (see § 444, 4), also by Favonius Eulogius (cf. § 443, 4). Hence the Somn. Scip. is also reprinted in the editions of Macrobius. Chief MSS. of the text (and of Macrobius' commentary): Paris. 6371 s. XI, Bamb. s. XI, Monac. 6362 s. XI, 14436 s. XI and others. AGGERN-

HARD, de Cic. somn. Scip., opusc. latt. p. 373. On Cicero's authorities see PCORSSEN (below no. 8, 2). A Greek translation by Maximus Planudes (about 1330), see in PHCHESS, Cic. Cato etc. ex gr. interpr., Halle 1832 p. 70, sqq., published also by FBRÜGGEMANN, Conitz 1840 and in MOSER's ed. p. 547, lastly (beginning with 1, 16) in MATTHAEI, brev. hist. animal., Mosc. 1811, 91. Separate ed. by CMEISSNER, Lpz.[3] 1886.

5. Except from single fragments the work was not otherwise known until AMAI discovered in a Vatican palimpsest (Vatic. 5757 s. IV? Facsimile in ZANGEMEISTER and WATTENBACH, pl. 17, CHATELAIN t. 39, 2, also in PFAFF l.l.) very considerable portions which he published, Rome 1822 (and Stuttg. 1822), also in Class. auct. Rome 1828, 1, 1–386 and again in Rome in 1846. After him CGSCHÜTZ (Lpz. 1823), CFHEINRICH (Bonn 1823; ed. maior, cum comm. crit. in libr. I, Bonn 1828), GHMOSER (Frankf. 1826), FOSANN (Gött. 1847). GNDURIEU, schedae Vaticanae, in quibus retractatur palimpsestus Tullianus de rep. (Leid. 1860) p. 1–126. On the great value of the second writer of the palimpsest, see ASTRELITZ, de antiquo Cic. de rep. librorum emendatore, Gnesen (Breslau) 1874. RBELTZ, d. hs. Überlieferung von Cic. de rep., Jena 1880. KPFAFF, de diversis manibus quibus Cic. de rep. libri in cod. Vat. correcti sunt (after a fresh collation by AMAU), Heidelb. 1883. CMFRANCKEN (§ 177, 4).—Translated by GHMOSER (in Metzler's collection of Roman prose writers 22 sq.).

2) De legibus, probably commenced a. 702/52 sq., immediately after the completion of the preceding work, with the purpose of adding *νόμοι* to his *πολιτεία*; resumed 708/46, but never completed or edited by the author; he never mentions it in his letters, or elsewhere. Originally it may have consisted of six books, of which, however, we possess only three, with a few fragments of the others. Even the extant part has several lacunae, and if Cicero himself had published the work, he would no doubt have added one of the prefaces of which he always had a stock on hand; as it is, the work opens abruptly in the form of a dialogue. The first book, which contains a kind of system of natural law, is carefully elaborated, but the ideas are somewhat superficial and confused: in the following parts much is only sketched. In addition to Plato, some of the Stoics especially served him as authorities; in the form of the dialogue he repeated the attempt to imitate Plato; yet throughout the work much attention is paid to the state of law at Rome. The second book treats of the drawing up of laws and the ius sacrum, in which the style of the old laws is successfully imitated; the third is de magistratibus; the fourth was to be de iudiciis. Concerning the contents of the rest we can only make uncertain conjectures.

1. The year 702/52 is also indicated as the time when Cicero began the work by the allusions to historical events (e.g. Cicero's augurship, see 2, 32; the death of Clodius, ib. 42), though there is no absolute certainty on this point, as these allusions

may belong to the character of the situation. The work, however, was not then completed (the interruption being caused by the administration of Cilicia and the Civil Wars); cf. Brut. 19 *ut illos de rep. libros edidisti nihil a te sane accepimus*, and Tusc. 4, 1 de rep. is mentioned, but not de legibus. It was resumed 708/46, see fam. 9, 2, 5 *modo nobis stet. . . et scribere et legere πολιτείας et, si minus in curia atque in foro, at in litteris et libris. . . navare remp. et de moribus ac legibus quaerere.* But even then the work was again abandoned, perhaps in consequence of Cicero's increasing interest in systematic philosophy or merely owing to other literary engagements. The preface is wanting, contrary to Cic.'s general theory *in singulis libris utor prooemiis*, Att. 4, 6, 2; cf. 16, 6, 4. Vahlen on the other hand attributes the serious corruptions of the text to the character of the archetype from which all the MSS. are derived. The original extension to 6 books is partly attested by the analogy of the work de rep., partly by the citation in Macrob. sat. 6. 4, 8 *Cicero in quinto de legibus.* DuMesnil, page 6. 10 of his edition argues unconvincingly for 8 books.

2. On the date of composition see (besides the editions) CPeter in his ed. of the Brutus (1839) p. 264. EHorrmann, de tempore quo Cic. libros de legg. scrips., Detmold 1845. OHarnecker, JJ. 125, 601. In general CFFeldhügel, über C. de legg., Zeitz 1841. Drumann, GR. 6, 104. Critical: CHalm, JJ. 79, 759, JVahlen, ZföG. 11, 1. 12, 19, AReifferscheid, RhM. 17, 269, ABaumstark, Phil. 19, 633, EHuschke, Zeitschr. f. Rechtsgesch. 11, 107, LUrlichs, RhM. 33, 154. EHoffmann, JJ. 117, 709. AEussner, JJ. 115, 620.

3. Chief MSS.: Vossiani 84 s. X and 86 s. XI, Heinsianus 118 s. XI, all in Leiden: concerning them HDeiter, see § 177, 4 l. 6. See besides HJordan, Beitr. 225; quaestt. Tull., Königsb. 1884. WFriedrich, Phil. Anz. 15, 515. PSchwenke, JB. 1886 2, 313.—Editions by JDavis (Cambr. 1727. 1745, published again by RGRath, Halle 1818. vol. 5), JAGörenz (Lpz. 1803), GHMoser and FCreuzer (Frankf. 1824), JBake (Leid. 1842), CFFeldhügel (Zeitz 1852 sq. II). Ex recognitione IVahlen, Berl.[2] 1883. In Huschke's iurisprud. anteiust.[5] (1886) 19. Explained by AduMesnil, Lpz. 1879. Col commento di GSichirollo, Pad. 1885. The specimens of ancient laws inserted by Cicero, together with linguistic elucidations of the archaisms contained in them, are reprinted in HJordan, krit. Beitr. z. Gesch. d. lat. Spr. 230.—Translated by CAFSeeger (Metzler's collection) and AWZumpt (Klotz' translation of the philosophical works, t. 2).

3) Paradoxa, written in April 708/46, immediately after the Brutus, before the arrival at Rome of the news of the death of M. Cato, and previously to the Orator. On account of its smallness the little treatise is not specially mentioned de div. 2, 1–4. It contains an exposition, rather rhetorical than philosophical, of six striking theorems of the Stoic system.

1. From the above dates will be understood the rectifications of Parad. 2 implied in fin. 4, 52, and of Parad. 5 in fin. 3, 33 sq. CMorgenstern, prolegg. in Cic. P. in Seebode's Misc. critt. 1, 1, 386. Drumann, GR. 6, 288. OHeine, zu Cic. Parad., Phil. 10, 116.

2. Manuscripts: Voss. 84 and 86. Vindob. 189 see § 183, 5. Cf. DDetlefsen, Wiener SBer. 21, 110. JHuemer, ZföG. 36, 589.—Editions by AGGernhard (with the Cato, Lpz. 1819). JBorgers (Leid. 1823). JCOrelli (with the Tusc., Zür.

1829), GHMoser (Gött. 1846).—Translated by FBaur (Stuttg. 1854), RKühner (Stuttg. 1864). Greek translation by DPetavius (Par. 1653 and in PhCHess, Cic. Cato etc. see above no. 1, 4) and by JMorisoto (ed. WFWensch, Halle 1841).

4) While in his Paradoxa Cicero as yet occupies the position of a rhetor, the Consolation, his next philosophical work, was due to a personal motive and domestic calamity, his daughter's death. It was composed a. 709/45, with the assistance of Crantor's treatise *περὶ πένθους*.

1. See ad Att. 12, 14, 3. 12, 20, 2. Tusc. 1, 65. 3, 76. 4, 63. divin. 2, 3, 22. Plin. NH. praef. 22 etc.—The fragments in Baiter-Kayser 11, 71 and CFW Müller 4, 3, 332. Cf. CHalm, Beitr. zu den cic. Fragm. p. 32. FSchneider, de consolatione Cic., Bresl. 1835. Drumann, GR. 6, 319. BASchulz, de Cic. consolatione, Greifsw. 1860. Did Cicero himself transcribe this consolatio in the Tuscul. I and III? See CBuresch, Lpz. Stud. 9, 94; cf. the same writer as regards its employment by Jerome in ep. 60 ad Heliodorum concerning the death of Nepotianus.

2. M. Tullii Cic. Consolatio, liber nunc primum repertus et in lucem editus, Colon. 1583 was a forgery. (It is also printed e.g. in Klotz' ed. of Cic. 4, 3 372.) Cf. Schulz l.l. 58.

5) In his Hortensius Cicero furnished a kind of preface to the series of philosophical writings projected by him, in order to justify this occupation in his own eyes and those of others and, if possible, to win successors. The Hortensius is also lost with the exception of a number of fragments.

1. Cic. de div. 2, 1 *cohortati sumus ut maxime potuimus ad philosophiae studium eo libro qui est inscriptus Hortensius.* Cf. Augustin. conf. 3, 4, 7 sq. 8, 7, 17 *lecto Ciceronis Hortensio excitatus eram studio sapientiae* etc. Trebell. Salon. Gallien. 2 *M. Tullius in Hortensio quem ad exemplum protreptici scripsit.* On the relation of the H. to the Aristotelian *προτρεπτικός* cf. JBernays, d. Dialoge des Aristoteles (Berl. 1863) 116. JBywater, Journ. of philol. 2 (1869), 55, 7 (1877), 64. HUsener, RhM. 28, 395. RHirzel, Herm. 10, 80.—The fragments in Baiter-Kayser 11, 55 and CFWMüller 4, 3, 312. Cf. WCrecelius, JJ. 75, 79. CHalm, Beiträge etc. p. 35. FSchneider, Jahn's Arch. 11, 536. Drumann, GR. 6, 322.

2. The Hortensius was still nominally extant in the 11th and 12th centuries in the island of Reichenau, and in the monastery of Bec in France. As, however, during the Middle Ages Cicero's Lucullus (cf. p. 307) went by the name of *liber ad Hortensium* or *ad Hort. dialogus*, the above statement is more probably to be taken in connection with it. KSchenkl, Phil. 31, 563. AHortis, Cicerone nelle opere del Petrarca 51–53. PThomas, rev. de philol. 3 (1879), 152; Athenaeum belge 2 (1879), 155. GVoigt, Wiederbeleb. d. class. Altert. 1^2, 39.

6) De finibus bonorum et malorum, in 5 books, written in the first part of 709/45, immediately before the Academica, and dedicated to Brutus, a compilation on the doctrines of the Greek sects concerning the supreme good and evil, one of the

main questions of practical philosophy, just as the Academica treat of the chief subject of theoretical philosophy, viz. the theory of knowledge. Cicero's authorities for this work are later representatives of the respective schools. His judgment is not guided by fixed principles; but in point of careful elaboration this work deserves, perhaps, the first place among the philosophical writings of Cicero.

1. Cic. de div. 2, 2 *cum fundamentum esset philosophiae in finibus bonorum et malorum, perpurgatus est is locus a nobis quinque libris, ut quid a quoque et quid contra quemque philosophum diceretur intellegi posset.* ad Att. 13, 12, 3 *περὶ τελῶν σύνταξις*. Cf. ib. 13, 19, 3. 13, 21, 4. 12, 6, 2. de leg. 1, 52. Drumann, GR. 6, 323.

2. The work is arranged in three conversations, in which Cicero himself is the central figure, according to the example of Aristotle, all the other speakers being deceased at the time: in the first conversation (books I and II), supposed to take place in 704/50, they are L. Manlius Torquatus and C. Valerius Triarius, the first of whom explains the Epicurean doctrine (b. I) which Cicero (b. II) attempts to refute. In the second conversation (books III and IV), assigned to 702/52, the younger Cato states the doctrine of the Stoics (b. III), which Cicero (b. IV) shows to agree in all essential points with that of Antiochos of Ascalon; in the third conversation (b. V), laid in 675/79, appear M. Pupius Piso, who sets forth the system of the Academics and Peripatetics, L. Tullius Cicero and others.

3. In general cf. the prolegomena by Madvig, Görenz and others. RHirzel (§ 183, 4) 2, 567 (and PSchwenke, phil. Rundsch. 1883, 43). HNFowler, Panaetii et Hecat. fragm. (Bonn 1885) 13. CHartfelder (see § 183, 4), p. 8. 21.

4. Manuscripts: Palatino-Vaticanus 1513 s. XI (Facsim. Chatelain t. 43, 1), then Palat. 1525 s. XV, Erlangensis, Paris. 6331 s. XII (Facsim. Chatelain t. 43, 2; new collation by CThurot, rev. crit. 1870 1, 17 and ONigoles, rev. de philol. 4, 35) and others. See on these Madvig's Proleg. On the value of the so-called deteriores ThSchiche, Jahresber. zu ZfGW. 33, 187, ONigoles l.l., FGustafsson, Herm. 15, 465. JMaschka, un. cod. (Malfatti s. XIII) del Cic. de fin., Rovereto 1882.—Editions by JDavis (Cambridge 1728. 1741. Oxf. 1809, in Rath's ed. vol. 1), JAGörenz (Lpz. 1813), Orelli (with Acad., Zür. 1827), FWOtto (Lpz. 1831) and especially JNMadvig (Copenh. 1839. [3]1876). Also HAlanus (Dublin 1856). Explained by DBöckel (Vol. 1, Berl. 1872), HHolstein (Lpz. 1873). Revised and explained by JSReid, III (Vols. I, II preparing)—GFSchömann, op. 3, 390. GFUnger, Phil. 20, 372. 21, 481. LVaucher (see § 183, 6). DBöckel, Frauenfeld 1863. OHeine, JJ. 93, 245. IwMüller, Erl. 1869. 70 II. CGCobet, Mnemos. NS. 3, 92. FVGustafsson, de Cic. de fin. l. I, Helsingf. 1878. AduMesnil, JJ. 115, 753. PLangen, ad non nullos locos Cic. de fin. adnott., Münst. 1888.

5. Translated by JGDroysen, Lpz. 1841. FBaur (Stuttg. 1854, Class. d. Alt. 1854). JHvKirchmann, Berl. 1875. JSReid (vol. 3 of his edition, Lond. 1883).

7) Academica, written a. 709/45, originally in two books, named after (Q. Lutatius) Catulus and (L. Licinius) Lucullus, subsequently in four books. Of the first edition the second book (Lucullus) has been preserved, of the second (Academica posteriora) the first part of the first book and various fragments. The Lucullus contains the doctrines of Antiochos and Philo

concerning knowledge, the Catulus seems to have embraced those of Karneades and a general exposition of the Old and New Academy. The beginning of the second edition contains general observations and a survey of the history of philosophy from Socrates to Arkesilas, the predecessor of Karneades and Philo. Cicero devoted a special exposition to the doctrines of the Academy, because he was specially attracted by its system (§ 183), and in the absence of other works, his treatise is one of our principal sources for it.

1. Together with Catulus and Lucullus, Hortensius and Cicero were introduced as speakers in the first edition; subsequently however Cicero substituted Cato and M. Brutus; and when Atticus wrote informing him that Varro was offended because Cicero had never yet dedicated anything to him, the whole work was once more completely re-written, divided into four books and dedicated to Varro. In this second edition Cicero made Varro the exponent of the views of Antiochos, and reserved to himself those of Philo. Atticus had already had the first edition copied, when Cicero resolved to re-write it. On the relations of the two editions to each other see especially ad Att. 13, 13, 1 *ex duobus libris contuli in quattuor. grandiores sunt omnino quam erant illi, sed tamen multa detracta. . . . multo haec erunt splendidiora, breviora, meliora.* 13, 16, 1 *illam ἀκαδημαϊκὴν σύνταξιν totam ad Varronem traduximus. primo fuit Catuli, Luculli, Hortensii. deinde . . . eosdem illos sermones ad Catonem Brutumque transtuli. ecce tuae litterae de Varrone, nemini visa est aptior* 'Αντιοχεία *ratio.* Cf. ib. 13, 12, 3. 13, 18. 13, 19, 3. 5. 13, 21, 4. 13, 32, 3. fam. 9, 8. off. 2, 8. QUINT. 3, 6, 64. PLIN. NH. 31, 6. Above § 167, 2. Cf. p. 305, no. 5, 2. Various conjectures on this subject in THBIRT, antikes Buchwesen 354.

2. ACRANITZ, de libr. Acad., Lps. 1809 and in Acta soc. Lips. 2 (1812), 165. CHRABRANDIS, RhM. 3 (1829), 543. DRUMANN, GR. 6, 327. ABKRISCHE, üb. Ciceros Akademika, Gött. 1845. HDIELS, doxogr. gr. (Berl. 1879) 119. KFHERMANN, Phil. 7, 466. CJHENGSTRAND, de libris Cic. academicis, Ups. 1860. RHIRZEL (§ 183, 4) 3, 251.

3. Manuscripts for the Lucullus Flor. Marc. 257 s. X. Voss. 84 and 86 and the Vindob. 189 see § 183, 5; for the Acad. posteriora the earliest MS. is Paris. 6331 s. XII (§ 184, 6, 4), the others are late, of s. XV, e.g. an interpolated Gedanensis.—Editions by JDAVIS (Cambridge 1725. 1736; in RATH Vol. 3), GÖRENZ (t. II, 1810), ORELLI (with de fin., Zür. 1827); Text revised and explained by JSREID, Lond.[2] 1885.—Translated by GHMOSER (Stuttg. Metzler), by JSREID, Lond. 1880.

8) Tusculanae disputationes, so called after Cicero's estate at Tusculum, where the conversations are supposed to have taken place. They were begun in 709/45 and finished and edited 710/44, subsequent to de finibus and anterior to de divinatione and de fato. The work is in five books and dedicated to M. Brutus; it treats of the troubles which beset human happiness, and how to surmount them. As to the authorities made use of by Cicero we have so far no certain knowledge.

1. Cic. ad Att. 13, 32, 2 *Dicaearchi περὶ ψυχῆς utrosque velim mittas et καταβάσεως. Τριπολιτικὸν non invenio et epistulam eius quam ad Aristoxenum misit. tres eos libros maxime nunc vellem; apti essent ad id quod cogito* (cf. Tusc. 1, 24). 15, 2, 4 *quod prima disputatio Tusculana te confirmat sane gaudeo.* 15, 4, 3. Contents: Cic. div. 2, 2 *libri Tusculanarum disputationum res ad beate vivendum maxime necessarias aperuerunt. I enim est de contemnenda morte, II de tolerando dolore, III de aegritudine lenienda, IV de reliquis animi perturbationibus, V . . . docet ad beate vivendum virtutem se ipsa esse contentam.*

2. RKühner's Prolegg. and Cic. in phil. mer. 111. Drumann, GR. 6, 347. Emendations by ASWesenberg (Viborg 1830. 1841. 1843 sq.), JBake (schol. hypomn. vol. 4). OHeine, de Cic. Tusc. disp., Halle 1854; de fontibus Tusc. disp., Weim. 1863. JSchlenger, Phil. 12, 280. JJeep, de locis quibusdam Tusc. disp., Wolfenb. 1865. FGustafsson, Herm. 17, 169. HMuther, JJ. 85, 491; über die (rhetorische) Composition des 1. und 5. Buchs v. Cic. Tusc., Coburg 1862. GZietzschmann, de Tusc. disp. fontibus, Halle 1868. CHartfelder (see § 183, 4) p. 18. 43. PCorssen, de Posidonio Rhodio Ciceronis in l. I Tusc. et in somnio Scipionis auctore, Bonn 1879; RhM. 36, 506. RHirzel (§ 183, 4) 3, 342. PHPoppelreuter, quae ratio intercedat inter Posidonii περὶ παθῶν πραγματείας et Tusc. disputt. Cic., Bonn 1883. RHoyer, de Antonio Ascalonita, Bonn 1883. XKreuttner, Andronici περὶ παθῶν I, Heidelb. 1884. HNFowler, Panaetii et Hecat. fragm. (Bonn 1885) 8. HDiels, RhM. 34, 487. FSaltzmann (§ 183, 4), II, appendix.

3. Manuscripts: Gudian. 294 s. IX–X, Paris. 6332 s. X (Facsim. Chatelain t. 44, 1), Bruxell. 5351 s. XII. On the (worthless) Leid. Lips. 30 s. XII HDeiter Phil. 42, 171.—Editions: JDavis (Cambr. 1709. 1723, and later, in Rath vol. II), FAWolf (Lpz. 1792. 1807. 1825), RKühner (Jena[5] 1874), Orelli (with the Paradoxa, Zür. 1829), RKlotz (Lpz. 1835. Addenda and Corrigenda, Lpz. 1843). GHMoser (Hanover 1836 III), CFSüpfle (Mannh. 1845), GTischer ([8] 1884. 87 II, by GSorof), MSeyffert (emend., comment. criticos adi., Lps. 1864), OHeine (explained, Lpz.[3] 1881), CMeissner (explained, Lpz. 1873), LWHasper, Gotha 1883.—Translated by FBaur, Stuttg. 1854. RKühner, Stuttg. 1855.

9) Timaeus, a free reproduction of Plato's dialogue, the outward dress being changed; written after the Academica, a. 709/45 or 710/44, and extant only in an incomplete form.

1. Priscian. GL. 2, 463, 19 *Cicero in Timaeo.* The title *De universo* is unauthenticated. Probably this translation was intended to form part of a large work on natural philosophy, in which Nigidius Figulus was to represent the Pythagorean doctrine (Hermann p. 8. 13 sq.). For the considerable fragment extant see Baiter-Kayser 8, 131. CFWMüller 4, 3, 214.

2. The fragment was included in the collection of philosophical writings mentioned above (§ 183, 5), hence it was preserved in the two Vossiani and the Vindobon., and in the Monac. 528 s. XI., besides other MSS.—In general cf. Drumann GR. 6, 353. KFHermann, de interpretatione Timaei Plat. dial. a. Cic. relicta, Gött. 1842. Hochdanz, quaestt. crit. in Tim. Cic., Nordhausen 1880.

9a) About the same period Cicero appears to have made a close translation of the Platonic Protagoras.

1. Cic. fin. 1, 7 expressly says in reference to translating Plato literally:

id (ad civium meorum cognitionem Platonem aut Aristotelem transferre) neque feci adhuc (until a. 709/45) *nec mihi tamen ne faciam interdictum puto.* These last words appear to point to plans, one of which Cicero carried out in the Protagoras: the express statement above quoted can only be evaded by the very far-fetched supposition that he has here left unmentioned the translation of Protagoras which he made in his youth, because it was written by Cicero merely as an exercise, and not brought out by the author himself, but published only after his death. RPhilippson, JJ. 133, 423. vHeusde, Cic. φιλοπλάτων 92. 274. Drumann, GR. 6, 354. PSchwenke, JB. 1886 2, 314. KFHermann, de Tim. Cic., Gött. 1842, 3.—*Cicero in Protagora*, Prisc. GL. 2, 182. 247. 402. Donat. Ter. Phorm. 4, 3, 6.—Hieron. ad Pammach. 1, 308 Vall. and ad Sunn. et Fret. 1, 643. The fragments: Baiter-Kayser 11, 54. CFWMüller 4, 3, 310.

10) De natura deorum, in 3 books, written in 710/44, after the Tusculanae, though already commenced in 709/45. This work is also dedicated to M. Brutus. The conversation is supposed to have taken place in the feriae Latinae of a. 677/77, C. Velleius representing the Epicureans, Q. Lucilius Balbus the Stoics, and C. Aurelius Cotta the Academics. If Cicero wrote this work with the practical aim (perhaps in conscious opposition to the free-thinking of Lucretius) of showing the value of a reasonable religion, he certainly failed in that object with the Roman public. For here also Cicero was content to translate and superficially adapt late Greek authorities, and took no pains to digest them seriously. Hence there is no lack of contradictions, inequalities, confusion and desultoriness, which mark the work as one of the least satisfactory of Cicero's writings.

1. Cic. div. 2, 3 *quibus* (Tusc.) *editis tres libri perfecti sunt de natura deorum.* HDiels, doxogr. gr. p. 121 is for the title *de deorum natura* in accordance with the citations in the grammarians. Cf. ib. 7. Att. 13, 39, 2 *libros mihi . . . mittas, et maxime Φαίδρου περὶ θεῶν* et Παλλάδος. Drumann, GR. 6, 349. JVahlen, ZföG. 24, 241. On Philodemos as an authority for book I LSpengel, Abh. d. Münchner Akad. 10, 1. 1863, HSauppe, de Philod. de pietate, Gött. 1864. The section Cic. de n. d. 1, 25–41 with a collation of the corresponding passages from Philodemos in HDiels' doxographi graeci (Berl. 1879), 529. Cf. ib. 121.

2. ABKrische, Forschungen 1, 34. RHirzel, Unterss. (§ 183, 4) I De nat. deor., Lpz. 1877. PSchwenke, Quellen v. Cic. d. n. d., JJ. 119, 49. 129. BLengnick, ad emendandos Cic. de n. d. quid ex Philodemo περὶ εὐσεβείας redundet, Halle 1872. HNFowler, Panaetii et Hecat. fragm., Bonn 1885, 10. PWendland, Arch. f. Gesch. d. Phil. 1, 206.

3. Manuscripts: Leid. Voss. 84 and 86 (Chatelain t. 39, 1; cf. HDeiter, RhM. 37, 314; also PSchwenke, JB. 1883 2, 94; see besides § 177, 4). Vindob. 189 (Chatel. t. 38, 1; see § 183, 5). Flor. Marc. 257 (Chatel. t. 37), all s. X (-XI), also Leid. Heins. 118 s. XI (Chatel. t. 38, 2; cf. § 177, 4). On the Vatic. Pal. 1519 s. X HEbeling, Phil. 43, 702.—Editions by JDavis (Cambr. 1718. 1723 and subsequently; in Rath vol. VI), LFHeindorf (Lps. 1815), GHMoser and FCreuzer (Lps. 1818), CGSchütz (Halle 1820), FAst (Munich 1829), GFSchömann (Berl.[4] 1876), with introduction, appar. crit. and commentary by JBMayor, and a new collation of

several of the English MSS. by JHSwainson, Cambr. 1880–85 III. (These MSS. are of little value.) Explained by AGoethe, Lpz. 1887. By AStickney (after Schömann), Boston, 1889.—Book 2 by MCThiaucourt and by FPicavet, both Par. 1886.

4. Criticism: Schömann (op. 3, 274. 280. JJ. 111, 685), Heidtmann (ep. crit. ad Schömannum, Stettin 1856: Zur Krit. u. Interpret. v. Cic. n. d., Neustettin 1858), RKlotz (adn. critt., Lips. 1867. 68 III). PStamm, de Cic. de n. d. interpolatt., Bresl. 1873. JForchhammer, Nord. Tidskr. f. filol. 5, 23. JDegenhart, Bemerkk. zu Cic. de n. d., Aschaffenb. 1881. PSchwenke, JJ. 125, 613. AGoethe, JJ. 129, 30. JBMayor, Journ. of philol. 12, 1. 248. KJNeumann, RhM. 36, 155.—Translated by GHMoser (Metzler's collections), RKühner (Stuttg., Hoffmann).

5. Only a joke was intended in the pamphlet entitled Cic. de n. d. liber quartus ex pervetusto cod. . . . ed. PSeraphinus (i.e. HHCludius in Hildesheim, gest. 1835), Bonon. (Berl.) 1811.

11) Cato maior or de senectute, dedicated to Atticus and hastily thrown off at the end of the year 709/45 or the beginning of 710/44. The dialogue is supposed to have taken place a. 604/150. The form is, however, unimportant; the work may rather be styled a continuous lecture in praise of old age, on the basis of materials compiled from Greek authors. Cicero manifests his sympathy in his careful delineation of Cato's character.

1. Cic. div. 2, 3 *interiectus est etiam nuper liber is quem ad nostrum Atticum de senectute misimus.* Att. 14, 21, 3 *legendus mihi saepius est Cato maior ad te missus. amariorem enim me senectus facit.*—On the date of composition ThMaurer, JJ. 129, 386.

2. PJvanderTon, C. m. explicatur et e graecis potiss. fontibus illustr., Löwen 1821; comm. ad quaest. de Cic. Cat., Löwen 1822. HJNassau, adnotatt. in libr. Cic. de sen., Gröningen 1829. Drumann, GR. 6, 350. GSchneider, ZfGW. 33, 689.

3. Manuscripts: Leid. Voss. F. 12 s. X (Mommsen, Berl. SBer. 1863, 10), Paris. 6332 s. X (above no. 8, 3), Laur. 50, 45 s. X, Monac. 15964 s. XI, Rhenaug. 126 s. XII (JGBaiter, Phil. 21, 535. 675; cf. GLahmeyer, Phil. 23, 473; cf. 21, 284. Facsim. Chatelain t. 40, 2). On Leid. Voss. O. 79 s. IX/X (Chatel. t. 41, 1) and Voss. F. 104 s. XIV see WGemoll, Herm. 20, 331; on Italian (unimportant) MSS. of the Cato (and Laelius) see FRamorino, riv. di filol. 15, 247. BDahl, z. Hss.-Kunde u. Kritik des cic. Cato I: codd. Leid.; II: codd. Parisini, Christiania 1885. 86. KTomanetz, Wert u. Verh. der Hss. v. Cic. Cato, Hernals 1883. 86 II.

4. Editions: AGGernhard (with Parad., Lps. 1819), FWOtto (Lps. 1830), RKlotz (Lpz. 1831). JNMadvig (Copenh. 1835), GTischer (Halle 1847), JSommerbrodt (Berl.[10] 1885), CNauck (Berl. 1855), GLahmeyer (Lpz.[4] 1877), CMeissner (Lpz.[2] 1885), JLey (Halle 1883), ThSchiche (with Lael., Prague[2] 1887), TKArnold (after Sommerbrodt), Lond. 1853, GLong (Lond. 1880), JSReid (Cambr.[2] 1883), WHeslop (with Lael.), Oxf. 1884, ESShuckburgh (Lond. 1886), EWHowson (Lond. 1887), LHuxley (Oxf. 1890), AStickney (with Lael., New York 1887).—Criticism: JMähly, N. schweiz. Mus. 6, 243, CMeissner, JJ. 103, 57. 131, 209, AOtto (on interpolation) in d. phil. Abhh. f. MHertz, Berl. 1888, 94. ChrLütjohann, RhM. 37, 496.

5. Greek translation by ThGaza in Hess (above no. 1, 4) p. 3 sqq.; German translations e.g. by KGBauer, Lpz. 1841, FJacobs (in Klotz' translation of Cic.'s. philos. works, part 2) and others.

12) De divinatione, in two books, a supplement of the work

on the nature of the gods, in which the subject of divine revelation and its perception by mankind is treated of; published a. 710/44, after the Cato maior and subsequent to Caesar's death, and represented as a conversation at the villa at Tusculum between Cicero and his brother. The first book contains the doctrine of the Stoics (compiled from Poseidonios περὶ μαντικῆς), the second the tenets of the Academics (probably chiefly following Kleitomachos). The popular notions and the political corporations connected with them are leniently dealt with, but, even in his quality of Augur, Cicero furnishes much valuable material, though his personal scepticism is often sufficiently evident in his humorous mode of treating the subject.

1. Definition of divinatio 1, 9 *earum rerum quae fortuitae putantur praedictio atque praesensio;* see Gell. 4, 11, 1. Tennemann, Gesch. d. Philos. 5, 121. Drumann, GR. 6, 352. Höfig, Cic.s Ansichten von der Staatsreligion, Krotoschin 1865. ThSchiche, de fontibus libr. Cic. de div., Jena 1875. KHartfelder, d. Quellen v. Cic. de div., Freiburg i. Br. 1878; RhM. 36, 227. PCorssen (above no. 8, 2) p. 13. HDiels, doxogr. 224.—On the question whether Cic. made use of Coelius Antipater see OMeltzer, JJ. 105, 430 f.

2. Manuscripts: corresponding to those for de nat. deor., see above no. 10, 3, also Vatic. Palat. 1519 s. X (Chatelain t. 40, 1; cf. HEbeling, Phil. 43, 702).—Editions by JDavis (Cantabr. 1721 and later; ed. Rath, Halle 1807), GHMoser (Frankf. 1828), LGiese (Lps. 1829).—APolster, quaestt. critt. in Cic. de div., Kattowitz 1874. FZöchbauer, zu Cic. de Div. (b. 2), Hernals 1878. PStamm, adnott. ad Cic. de div., Rössel 1881. FDrechsler, ZföG. 37, 101.—Translated by GHMoser (Stutt. Metzler), RKühner (Stuttg. Hoffmann).

13) De fato, the last of Cicero's treatises on the philosophy of religion, and likewise written a. 710/44. The author impugns the views of the Stoics on the εἱμαρμένη, taking himself the side of the Academics. This treatise has come down to us in a mutilated form. As his authorities Cicero mentions specially Chrysippos, also Poseidonios, Kleanthes, Diodoros, Karneades and others. The de fato is valuable as a collection of materials, but the style betrays hurry and the writer does not arrive at any settled results.

1. Cic. de div. 2, 3 *quibus* (de n. d. and de divin.), *ut est in animo, de fato si adiunxerimus, erit abunde satisfactum toti huic quaestioni.* de fat. 2 *Hirtius noster, cos. designatus . . post interitum Caesaris.* Gell. 7, 2, 15. Macrob. sat. 3, 16, 4. Drumann GR. 6, 353. MMeinecke, de fontt. . . Cic. de fato, Marienwerder 1887. AGercke, Chrysippea, JJ. Suppl. 14, 689.

2. Manuscripts as those for the Lucullus, above no. 7, 3. The cod. Turonensis (ChThurot, bibl. de l'école des hautes études, fasc. 17) perhaps a transcript from the Vindob. (IBruns).—Editions (with de divin.) by Davis, Moser; in particular by JHBremi (Lps. 1795).—Translation by Moser (in de divin.).

3. Nuovi frammenti del Cicerone de fato di recente scoperti in palimpsesti dal LCFerrucci, Modena 1853, repeated in his Fabularum libri tres, Forocornelii 1867. His pretended discovery is printed and deservedly exposed by Ritschl, op. 3, 674. Cf. also FWSchneidewin, Gött. gel. Anz. 1853, 1917. GLinker, ZföG. 5, 81. 423.

14) Laelius or de amicitia, inscribed to Atticus, written after the Cato maior and previously to the work on duties, like them in the year 710/44. The conversation is conducted by Laelius the Younger and his sons-in-law, C. Fannius and Q. Mucius Scaevola, the subject being treated in connection with the recent death (625/129) of Africanus minor, the intimate friend of Laelius. Cicero has largely availed himself of Theophrastos' work on the same subject, also of Chrysippos and (indirectly?) the Ethics of Aristotle. Some fault may be found with the logical arrangement of the treatise, but on the whole it is interesting and practical.

1. Cic. off. 2, 31 *de amicitia alio libro dictum est.* Gell. 17, 5, 1 *Cicero in dialogo cui titulus est Laelius vel de amicitia.* ib. 1, 3, 10 *eum librum* (Theophrastos' περὶ φιλίας) *M. Cicero videtur legisse cum ipse quoque librum de amicitia componeret.* RFBraxator, quid in conscribendo Cic. Lael. valuerint Arist. Eth. Nic. de amicitia libri, Halle 1871.

2. The best MS. is a codex s. IX/X formerly in the possession of FDidot in Paris (on it see Mommsen, RhM. 18, 594), qu. where is it now?; also Monac. 15514 s. X, Gudian. 335 s. X, Laur. 50, 45 s. X (Chatel. t. 42) and others. EVogel, collatio trium codd. Cic. de am. Monacensium, Zweibr. 1839.—More recent critical and explanatory editions e.g. by AGGernhard (Lps. 1825), CBeier (Lps. 1828), RKlotz (Lpz. 1833), MSeyffert (Lpz.[2] 1876 by CFWMüller, cf. the same ZfGW. 33, 14), CWNauck (Berl.[9] 1884), GLahmeyer (Lpz.[4] 1881). ThSchiche (see no. 11, 4). AStrelitz, Gotha 1884. GLong (Lond. 1880), JSReid (Cambr.[2] 1883), ASidgwick (Lond.[2] 1883), ESShuckburgh, Lond. 1885. CMeissner, Lpz. 1887 (and in JJ. 135, 545). AStickney (above no. 11, 4).—AGGernhard, op. 323. OFKleine, adnott. in Cic. Cat. mai. et Laelium, Wetzlar 1855. CEPutsche, Phil. 12, 293. EWeissenborn, Gedankengang v. Cic. Lael., Mühlh. in Thür. 1882.—Translated e.g. by AASchreiber and GFWGrosse (Halle 1827), FKvStrombeck (Brunswick 1827, with the rest of the so-called minor works), in Greek by DPetavius in Hess (above no. 1, 4) 99.

15) De gloria in two books, finished at the close of July 710/44; it is not extant.

1. Cic. off. 2, 31 *nunc dicamus de gloria, quamquam ea quoque de re duo sunt nostri libri.* Cf. Att. 15, 27, 2. 16, 2, 6. 16, 3, 1 (cf. PSchwenke, JB. 1886 2, 298). 16, 6, 4. Gell. 15, 6, 1. Drumann, GR. 6, 355. FSchneider, melet. in Cic. de gl., ZfAW. 1839, no. 28.—Petrarch asserted that he possessed the work (ep. senil. 15, 1, p. 1049 Basil. *libros Cic. de gloria ab hoc habui. . . . singulares libri II de gl. quibus visis me ditissimum existimavi. . . . novi nihil praeter illos de gl. libros II et aliquot orationes aut epistolas*); but see GVoigt, Wiederbel. des class. Altertums 1^2, 41. Cf. also FHand, Ersch and Gruber's allg. Encykl. 1, 17, 238. AHortis, Cic. nelle opere del Petrarca (Trieste 1878) 53. The fragments in Baiter-Kayser 11, 69 and CFWMüller 4, 3, 330.

16) De officiis, in three books, addressed by Cicero to his son Marcus. This work also is due to the leisure forced upon Cicero by Mark Antony subsequent to Caesar's death, a. 710/44, and like its fellows was written off rather rapidly. Cicero's principal authorities were the Stoics, especially Panaitios in the first two books, and probably Poseidonios in the third. The whole is seasoned and enlivened with numerous illustrations from Roman history, a feature which occasions some unevenness of treatment. The moral views are those of a practical politician, and for this very reason not much higher than the conventional Roman standard.

1. Off. 1, 6 *sequimur . . potissimum Stoicos, non ut interpretes, sed, ut solemus, e fontibus eorum iudicio arbitrioque nostro quantum quoque modo videbitur hauriemus.* Cf. 2, 86. 3, 7. 51. 63. 89. 91. Att. 15, 13, 6 *nos his φιλοσοφοῦμεν (quid enim aliud?) et τὰ περὶ τοῦ καθήκοντος magnifice explicamus προσφωνοῦμεν que Ciceroni.* 16, 11, 4 *τὰ περὶ τοῦ καθήκοντος, quatenus Panaetius, absolvi duobus. illius tres sunt. . . . eum locum Posidonius persecutus est. ego autem et eius librum arcessivi et ad Athenodorum Calvum scripsi ut ad me τὰ κεφάλαια mitteret.* GELL. 13, 28, 1.

2. ChGARVE, philosophische Anm. und Abhandl. (Bresl.[6] 1819). RKÜHNER, Cic. mer. p. 108. DRUMANN, GR. 6, 357. CJGRYSAR, prolegg. ad Cic. libr. de off., Cologne 1844. CJDAHLBÄCK, de off. Cic. comm., Upsala 1860. ADESJARDINS, les devoirs de Cicéron, Par. 1865. FCADET, examen du traité des devoirs de Cicero, Par. 1865. RHIRZEL (§ 183, 4) 2, 721.

3. Criticism: JHELLER, Phil. 12, 302, HSAUPPE, coniect. Tull., Gött. 1857, GFUNGER, Phil. Suppl. 3, 1, 13, CTHUROT, rev. d. phil. 1, 86, JFORCHHAMMER, Tidskr. f. filol. 4 (1880), 200, CBELDAME, rev. de phil. 5, 85, REINHARDT, interpolatt. in Cic. off. I, Oels 1885.

4. Manuscripts: Bern. 391 s. X (CHATELAIN t. 45, 1), Paris. 6601 s. X (CHATEL. t. 45, 2), Ambros. C. 29 inf. s. X (see JJ. 111, 221), Bamb. s. X. Wirceb. s. X, Leid. Voss. Q. 71 s. X (CHATEL. t. 45, 4), then Harlei. 2716 s. IX (very incomplete), Bern. 104 s. XIII (EPOPP, acta sem. phil. Erl. 3, 245), Palat. 1531 s. XII (EPOPP, de Cic. de off. cod. palat. 1531, Erl. 1886); cf. GFUNGER, Phil. Suppl.-Bd. 3, 1, 3. On Paris. 6347 s. IX/X a fragment (2, 72–3, 11; facsim. CHATEL. t. 44, 2) ECHATELAIN, rev. de phil. 5, 135. On Ambr. F. 42 s. XII see RSABBADINI, la critica del testo del de off. Cic., Catania 1888.—Editions by JGGRAEVIUS (cum nott. varr. Amsterd. 1688. 1710. Naples 1771), JFHEUSINGER (Brunswick 1783; repet. suisq. animadverss. auxit CThZUMPT, Brunswick 1838), JFDEGEN (Berl.[4] 1848, ed. by EBONNELL), AGGERNHARD (Lps. 1811), CBEIER (Lps. 1820 sq. II, together with Indd., Lps. 1831), GOLSHAUSEN (Schlesw. 1823), RSTÜRENBURG (Lps. 1834. 1843), CGZUMPT (small ed. Brunswick[2] 1849). GFWLUND (Copenh. 1849), GFUNGER (Lpz. 1852), JvGRUBER (Lpz.[3] 1874), OHEINE (Berl.[6] 1885), CFWMÜLLER (Lpz. 1882), TATHACHER, New York, 1857. HAHOLDEN (Cambr.[5] 1884), ThSCHICHE (Prague 1885).—Translations e.g. by JJHOTTINGER, Zür. 1820. AWZUMPT, Lpz. 1841, GGÜBELEN and FBAUR, Stuttg. 1856, RKÜHNER, Stuttg. 1859.

17) De virtutibus, most probably (on account of its similar contents) written not much before or after the work on duties, i.e. in the year 710/44.

1. HIERON. in Zach. 1, 2 (6, 792 Vallars.) *quattuor virtutes, . . ., de quibus plenissime in officiorum libris Tullius disputat scribens proprium quoque de quattuor virtutibus librum.* CHARIS. GL. 1, 208, 15 *Cic. in commentario de virtutibus.* AUGUSTIN. de trin. 14, 11.—BAITER-KAISER 11, 76; CFWMÜLLER 4, 3, 340.—DRUMANN, GR. 6, 359.

18) De auguriis, of unknown date, though at all events later than 703/51, when Cicero became an augur.

1. According to DRUMANN, GR. 6, 352 it was composed a. 710/44 after the treatise de divin. The fragments BAITER-KAYSER 11, 55, CFWMÜLLER 4, 3, 312.—CHARIS. GL. 1, 105. 122. 139 *Cicero de auguriis.* SERV. Aen. 5, 738 *Cicero in auguralibus* (libris).—On Cicero's translation of Xenophon's οἰκονομικός see § 177a, 2; of Plato's Protagoras see § 184, 9a.

185. In the department of jurisprudence, just as in philosophy, Cicero was a mere amateur, though well-informed. He was too much of an orator and too little accustomed to strict definitions to find in it a welcome field for the display of his powers. Notwithstanding, he composed a treatise de iure civili in artem redigendo, which perhaps he originally intended to form a part of the de legibus, and treated by itself on failing to complete that work.

1. Ad fam. 7, 30, 2, in defining proprius, Cicero mixes up the notions of possession and property. On Cicero's knowledge of jurisprudence see besides a variety of earlier treatises: WSZIMMERN, Gesch. d. Privatr. 1, 1, 288 and others. DRUMANN, GR. 6, 644. PLATNER, de partt. Cic. rhett. quae ad ius spectant, Marb. 1829. GDE CAQUERAY, les passages de droit privé dans . . . Cicéron, Rennes 1857. ADESJARDINS, de scientia civili apud Cic., Beauvais 1858. AGASQUY, Cic. iurisconsulte, Paris 1886. Cf. § 48, 4 and 6.

2. QUINT. 12, 3, 10 *componere aliqua de iure coeperat.* GELL. 1, 22, 7 *M. Cicero in libro qui inscriptus est de iure civili in artem redigendo.* Cf. also Cicero's judgment of himself, de or. 2, 142 sqq., where he disguises himself under the mask of Crassus (§ 152, 4): *est nobis pollicitus ius civile, quod nunc diffusum et dissipatum esset, in certa genera coacturum et ad artem facilem redacturum.* CHARIS. GL. 1, 138 *Cicero de iure civili.* On the treatise cf. HEDIRKSEN hinterlass. Schrift. 1, 1. DRUMANN, GR. 6, 107.—BAITER-KAYSER 11, 55. CFWMÜLLER 4, 3, 311.

186. Cicero attempted even historical composition, and de leg. 1, 5 sq. (cf. de or. 2, 51–63) he sharply criticises the style of the historians of the time, hinting that he himself was qualified to introduce a great change in this department. It is true that Cicero possessed an unusual fund of historical knowledge, and this is fully displayed in his orations as well as in his philosophical and rhetorical writings, particularly in his Brutus: but here also his rhetorical bent and the difficulty he experienced in losing sight of his own self were much against him, and many

casual expressions prove his lax opinions as to the real task of the historian. It appears credible that, had he lived longer, he might have turned to this branch of literature; as it is, he wrote only memoirs on his consulship, a Secret History (which was, perhaps, never finished), and Admiranda—all which writings have been lost.

1. PLUT. Cic. 41 διανοούμενος, ὡς λέγεται, τὴν πάτριον ἱστορίαν γραφῇ περιλαβεῖν καὶ πολλὰ συμμῖξαι τῶν ἑλληνικῶν καὶ ὅλως τοὺς συνηγμένους λόγους αὐτῷ καὶ μύθους ἐνταῦθα τρέψαι etc. CORN. NEP. fragm. Guelf. (cod. Gud. 278, p. 99, 29 NIPP.): *ille* (Cic.) *fuit unus qui potuerit et etiam debuerit historiam digna voce pronuntiare, quippe qui oratoriam eloquentiam rudem a maioribus acceptam perpoliverit, philosophiam ante eum incomptam latinam sua conformarit oratione. ex quo dubito, interitu eius utrum res publica an historia magis doleat.*—Though Cicero is fully aware *primam esse historiae legem ne quid falsi dicere audeat* (de or. 2, 62; cf. ib. 62–64. leg. 1, 5), he often acts differently. Thus of Lucceius he expects (fam. 12, 3): *amori nostro plusculum etiam quam concedit veritas largiare;* and orat. 37. 66 (cf. ib. 125) he places historiae in the γένος ἐπιδεικτικόν of eloquence, nor would he seem to know any other kind of historical composition than that of the school of Isokrates. Accordingly he asserts (Brut. 66) that Philistos and Thukydides (!) were eclipsed by—Theopompos! See on this subject § 36, 7.—DRUMANN, GR. 6, 677. SCHWEGLER, RG. 1, 93. FDGERLACH, d. röm. Geschichtschr. 96. KBERNS, Cic.s Ansicht v. d. Gesch., Attendorn 1880.

2. Commentarius consulatus sui graece compositus (ὑπόμνημα τῆς ὑπατείας), Att. 1, 19, 10. 1, 20, 6. 2, 1, 1. 2; written a. 694/60, at which period Cicero was also busy with a Latin treatise on the same subject (ad Att. l.l.). Cf. PLUT. Caes. 8. Crass. 13. DIO 46, 21. CFWMÜLLER's Cic. 4, 3, 398. HPETER, hist. fragm. 209. This ὑπόμνημα is one of the chief authorities for Plutarch's Cicero. AHLHEEREN, histor. Schrr. 3, 23. 417. PWEIZSÄCKER, JJ. 111, 417. GTHOURET, Leipz. Stud. 1 306. ESCHMIDT, de Cic. comm. de consulatu graece scripto a Plut. expresso, Jena 1885. Cf. § 189, 3. The same subject-matter was also treated of in an *epistula non mediocris ad instar voluminis scripta quam Pompeio in Asiam de rebus suis in consulatu gestis miserat Cicero* (SCHOL. BOB. p. 270 Or.). pSulla 67 *epistulam meam quam ad Pompeium de meis rebus gestis et de summa re publica misi.*

3. Ἀνέκδοτα, commenced as early as 695/59 (Att. 2, 6, 2), resumed after the death of Caesar on Atticus' advice (Att. 14, 14, 5. 14, 17, 6. 15, 2, 2. 15, 4, 3. 15, 13, 3. 15, 27, 2. 16, 2, 6) and edited after the author's death. This work is that referred to by DIO 39, 10 (cf. 46, 8): βιβλίον τι ἀπόρρητον συνέθηκε καὶ ἐπέγραψεν αὐτῷ ὡς καὶ περὶ τῶν ἑαυτοῦ βουλευμάτων ἀπολογισμόν τινα ἔχοντι. ASCON. p. 83 Or. 74 K.-S. *Cic. in expositione consiliorum suorum* (cf. AUGUSTIN. c. Iulian. 5, 5). CHARIS. GL. 1, 146 *Cic. in ratione consiliorum suorum.* BOETH. de inst. mus. 1, 1 *Tullius in libro quem de consiliis suis composuit.* CFWMÜLLER's Cic. 4, 3, 338. PETER l.l. 209. Cf. DRUMANN, GR. 6, 360. OHARNECKER, JJ 123, 184.

4. Admiranda (PLIN. NH. 31, 12. 51; cf. 7, 18. 85. 29, 60. COLUM. 3, 8, 2), of unknown date. The fragments BAITER-KAYSER 11, 76. CFWMÜLLER 4, 3, 340. Cf. the Greek θαυμάσια and παράδοξα.

5. PRISCIAN. GL. 2, 267, 5 *Cicero in Chorographia* (with the variants (*h*)*ortogr.*, *cosmogr.*, *chronogr.*). Acting upon Atticus' advice, Cicero had actually studied geography a. 695/59; see Att. 2, 4. 6. 7. 9. 12. 14. 22.

6. Cicero's witticisms (cf. § 178, 1 in fin.) were eagerly collected by others; he

himself observed complacently that his merry conceits found admittance even in Caesar's collection of ἀποφθέγματα (§ 195, 5). C. Trebonius published a separate collection of Cicero's *facete dicta* (§ 210, 9). On a similar but more comprehensive collection by Tiro, see § 191, 2. QUINT. 8, 6, 73 *Ciceronis est in quodam ioculari libello* (an epigram follows). Collection of matter contingent to this subject in CFW MÜLLER 4, 3, 341.

7. A satirical pamphlet of Cicero's, aimed under a false name at his mortal enemy, is mentioned in SCHOL. BOB. p. 268 *exstat libellus Ciceronis qui ita inscribitur 'Edictum L. Racili tr. pl.', quod sub nomine ipsius Cicero scripsit in invectionem P. Clodi.*—The admonitory epistle *Orpheus ad M. filium Athenas* (or *de adolescente studioso*) is a forgery; see AWEICHERT, de L. Vario etc. 297.—There are also apocryphal writings: 'Synonyma,' the composition of an anonymous early grammarian, of some interest for Cicero's style and phraseology (cf. EBÄHRENS ap. JWBECK, de different. scriptt. lat. 18), already quoted in ISIDOR. 6, 473 Arev. and extant in old MSS. (e.g. Leid. Voss. F. 24 s. IX, Bern. 178 s. IX): see HAGEN l.l. CXVII. CXX. Printed in Orelli [2] 4, 1063. WLMAHNE, Cic. . . . Synonyma ad L. Veturium sec. editt. Romanas denuo excudi curavit, Leid. 1850 and: sec. edit. Parisinam denuo exc. cur., ibid. 1851. Specimens of these Synonyma are given from a separate MS. by LBACHMANN, zur Hss.-Kunde, Rost. 1854, 17. A similar work is the Differentiae sermonum Ciceronis, from Berne MSS. s. IX u. X published by HHAGEN, anecd. Helvet. (Lps. 1870) 275; cf. ibid. CXVII. Cf. also § 42, 4. Also de notis (ORELLI [2] 4, 939), etc.

187. The four collections of the correspondence of Cicero which have come down to us, counting in 90 letters addressed to Cicero, contain altogether 864 pieces, and are, both in personal and political contents, an inexhaustible treasury of contemporaneous history, though partly such that their publication was not favourable to Cicero. In the case of a man accustomed to think as rapidly and feel as vividly as did Cicero, and who was strongly impelled to give vent to his thoughts and feelings either orally or in letters to a familiar friend such as Atticus, a correspondence of this kind affords a very deep but sometimes erroneous insight into his heart. Hence his accusers derive the greater part of their materials from these letters.

1. The earliest letter dates from 686/68, the latest July 28th, 711/43, not a single one from the time of Cicero's consulship being preserved. FRONTO ad M. Antonin. p. 107 *omnes Ciceronis epistulas legendas censeo, mea sententia vel magis quam omnes eius orationes. epistulis Ciceronis nihil est perfectius.* Cf. also above § 46, 1.

2. In the letters to Atticus and other familiar acquaintances Cicero writes very freely, those addressed to more distant acquaintances are generally cautious and careful in style. BRABEKEN, Cic. in s. Briefen usw., Hanover 1835. ad fam. 9, 21, 1 *quid tibi ego videor in epistulis? nonne plebeio sermone agere tecum? . . . epistulas vero cotidianis verbis texere solemus.* ASTINNER, de eo quo Cic. in epistolis usus est sermone, Oppeln 1879 III. KRAUSE, stilist. Bemerkk. aus Cic.s Briefen, Hohenst. 1869. GLANDGRAF, BlfbayrGW. 16, 274. 317. RYTYRRELL, introd. to his ed. of the epistles 1, LXXVII. EZIMMERMANN, de epistulari temporum usu Cic., Rastenb.

1886. 87 II. PMeyer, de Cic. ad Att. sermone, Bayreuth 1887.—RBoltzenthal, de graeci sermonis proprietatibus in Cic. epistt., Cüstrin 1884.—EOpitz, quo sermone ei qui ad Cic. litteras dederunt usi sint, Naumb. 1879. JHSchmalz, ZfGW. 35, 87; die Latinität des Vatinius, Mannh. 1881.—Chronology: JvGruber, de temporibus atque serie epistolarum Cic., Strals. 1836. GRauschen, ephemerides Tullianae rerum inde ab exilio Cic. (Mart. 696/58) usque ad extremum annum 700/54 gestarum, Bonn 1886. AEKörner, de epistulis a Cic. post reditum (a. 697/57) ad finem a. 700/54 datis, Lps. 1886. LMoll, de tempp. epistt. Tull. quaestt. (a. 703/51–704/50), Berl. 1883. WSternkopff, quaestt. chronol. de rebus a Cic. inde a tradita Cilicia provincia usque ad relictam Italiam gestis deque epistulis intra illud tempus (a. 704/50 et 705/49) datis acceptisve, Marb. 1884. ERuete, d. Correspondenz Cic.s in den JJ. 710/44 u. 711/43, Marb. 1883. See further under the separate collections.

3. Cicero himself never collected his letters, much less did he edit them, but even in his life-time friends of his had formed some such design. Cf. ad Att. 16, 5, 5 (a. 710/44) *mearum epistularum nulla est συναγωγή. sed habet Tiro instar LXX, et quidem sunt a te quaedam sumendae. eas ego oportet perspiciam, corrigam; tum denique edentur;* and to Tiro he writes (fam. 16, 17, 1 a. 708/46) *tuas quoque epistolas vis referri in volumina.* After Cicero's death, his correspondence was very zealously collected and edited, first of all no doubt by Tiro, who even during Cicero's life-time had planned the collection of his letters. Cornelius Nepos, in a part of his life of Atticus written before 720/34 (Att. 16, 3), knows from private communication (for he himself says that they were not yet published) the letters to Atticus (see § 188, 2, 2); they had, it would seem, already been compiled for publication. The earliest mention which we have of a published letter from the Ciceronian correspondence is found in Sen. suas. 1, 5=fam. 15, 19.

4. Atticus brought about the publication of the Ciceronian letters addressed to him (§ 188, 2); Tiro appears to have published the rest gradually (above n. 3). The two chief collections, those of Atticus and of Tiro, each excluded the contents of the other (the two exceptions fam. 8, 16=Att. 10, 9 A; fam. 9, 14=Att. 14, 17 A only prove the rule) and both editors suppressed their own letters to Cicero.—Tiro arranged the correspondence according to the persons addressed, and published the correspondences thus collected in one or more books according to the amount of the materials; matter insufficient to form a volume by itself and detached letters were disposed of in collective volumes (letters to two or more correspondents); earlier collections, which had been published previously, were supplemented with letters which had either been written or become accessible at a subsequent time. To this Tironian collection belong the extant collections *ad Q. fratrem* (§ 188, 3), and *ad Brutum* (§ 188, 4) of which last only a small portion is preserved; and in particular the so-called collection *ad familiares* (§ 188, 1) has been formed from portions of the Tironian collective edition. Thus we account for such quotations as Gell. 1, 22, 19 *in libro epistularum M. Ciceronis ad L. Plancum* (i.e. the person addressed at the beginning of book 10 and prominent throughout) *et* (and in particular) *in epistula Asini Pollionis ad Cic.* etc. (=fam. 10, 33, 5); cf. 12, 13, 21 *in libro M. Tullii epistularum ad Ser. Sulpicium* (=fam. 4, 4, 4). Non. 83, 30 *Cicero ad Varronem* (i.e. the person addressed at the beginning of the book) *epistula Paeti* (rather *ad Paetum*=fam. 9, 20, 3).—Also the collections which are known to us only by quotations belonged to this Tironian edition: Nonius cites p. 450 b. 9 (437 b. 7; 37 b. 5) *ad Hirtium;* 293 b. 4 *ad Pompeium* (the two quotations=Cic. ad Att. 8, 11 D, 2, 3; but the quotation in Nonius is probably founded on a mistake. LGurlitt, Berl. ph. Wschr. 1887, 891. Cf. besides § 186, 2), 286 and 436 b. 3 *ad Caesarem*, 329 and 426 b. 3 *ad Caesarem iuniorem*, 92 b. 3 *ad Pansam*,

509 b. 2 *ad Axium* (cf. FRONTO p. 107. PRE. 1², 2202, 2; mentioned also in the SC. de Oropiis, Herm. 20, 270), 275 b. 2 *ad filium;* again MACROB. 2, 1, 14 quotes b. 2 *ad Cornelium Nepotem;* likewise PRISCIAN. GL. 2, 490 b. 1 *ad Calvum* (OHARNECKER, JJ. 125, 604). There are also quoted (without the number of the book being specified) Ciceronian letters *ad Catonem* (NON. 264 [=ad fam. 15, 4, 2]. 273 [ib. 15, 3, 2]. 438), *ad M. Titinium* (SUET. rhet. 2), *ad Hostilium* (CHARISIUS GL. 1, 110), *ad Caerelliam* (QUINT. 6, 3, 112; cf. AUSON. p. 146 Sch.)—There are also mentioned ἑλληνικαὶ (πρὸς Ἡρώδην, πρὸς Γοργίαν, πρὸς Πέλοπα τὸν Βυζάντιον etc.) in PLUT. Cic. 24 (NAKE p. 10). On Cicero's correspondence with the young Octavian see LGURLITT, Berl. phil. Wschr. 1887, 1616. The scanty remains of these collections have recently been collected in BAITER-KAYSER 11, 38 and CFWMÜLLER 4, 3, 292.—BNAKE, hist. crit. Ciceronis epistularum, Bonn 1861. RFLEIGHTON, hist. crit. Cic. epp. ad fam., Lps. 1877; and esp. LGURLITT, de Cic. epistulis earumque pristina collectione, Gött. 1879; JJ. 121, 609.

5. Cicero's letters were diligently read during several centuries (see the list of citations in NAKE, hist. crit. 38), and abridgments of them were also made: FRONTO ad Antonin. p. 107, 7 *memini me excerpsisse ex Ciceronis epistulis ea dumtaxat quibus inesset aliqua de eloquentia vel philosophia vel de rep. disputatio; praeterea si quid elegantius aut verbo notabili dictum videretur;* cf. ib. 107, 2. Perhaps we may possess the remains of an abridgment of the letters ad fam. in the text of the leaf of the Turin palimpsest containing ad fam. 6, 9, 1–2. 6, 10, 1–6 (new collation by PKRÜGER, Herm. 5, 146). But the letters were much less widely read and for a much shorter period than most of the other writings of Cicero. We find only isolated traces of MSS. of them existing or utilised during the Middle Ages (ORELLI in the introd. to his ed. p. VI; also MHAUPT, op. 3, 588. GVOIGT, RhM. 36, 474). They came again into circulation when Petrarch in 1345 rediscovered in Verona the letters to Brutus (b. 1; cf. § 188, 4, 1), Q. Cicero, the letter to Octavian (§ 185, 5) and the letters to Atticus (PETRARCAE epp. de reb. fam. 24, 3). The MS. in which Petrarch found these letters (in the above order) has again been lost, only a copy taken directly from it being extant (now cod. Medic. 49, 18 s. XIV, facsimile in CHATELAIN t. 34, 2). This however is not the copy, which, as we know, Petrarch made for himself (see GVOIGT and AVIERTEL l.l.): the one still extant, which was made by several copyists (FRÜHL, RhM. 36, 21. LMENDELSSOHN, JJ. 121, 863), belonged to a younger contemporary of Petrarch, the Florentine chancellor of state Coluccio Salutato. Pasquino de Capellis his colleague in Milan had procured it for him there. In that city, at the time in question, there were in the possession of Galeazzo Visconti, Duke of Milan, both the cod. Veronensis of the letters ad Att. etc. and the Vercellensis (see n. 6) of those ad fam.—Valuable also is the cod. Tornaesianus (z), (now lost), from which Lambinus gives us the most trustworthy information; it is no more derived from the cod. Medic. 49, 18 (M), (FHOFMANN 26. FSCHMIDT in the Festgruss für HHeerwagen, Erl. 1882, 18), than is a certain cod. Escurial. s. XIV/XV; and similarly the specially important marginal notes in Cratander's edition (c), Basel 1528, are derived from some MS. which is older than the Med. (FHOFMANN 26. 30), viz. probably from the Würzburg MS. s. XI, which is lost all but a few leaves (cf. LSPENGEL, Münchn. Gel. Anz. 1846, 917. 926. KHALM, RhM. 18, 460. GSCHEPSS, BlfbayrGW. 20, 7. 111) or from one very much like it. Cf. also KLEHMANN, WschrfklPh. 1888, 470. On the other hand the variants of the 'decurtatus' and 'Crusellinus' which were formerly highly valued and which SBOSIUS gives, are founded on forgeries by Bosius: see MHAUPT, op. 2, 83. D DETLEFSEN, JJ. suppl. vol. 3, 111). On the MSS. of the 15th cent. and the edd. principes of a. 1470 (the Romana and the Jensoniana=R and I) see HOFMANN 48.

OESCHMIDT, die hs. Überlieferung der Briefe ad Att. Q. Cic. Brut. in Italien, Abh. d. sächs. Ges. d. Wiss. 10, 271; WschrfklPh. 1187, 1014 (against KLEHMANN, ib. 1887, 506. 1403, who imagines that he has discovered MSS. of the epp. ad Att. independent of the Med.); RhM. 40, 611; JJ. 137, 179. HEBELING, Phil. 42, 403. 45, 369.

6. The letters ad familiares were not also discovered by Petrarch, as was formerly supposed in accordance with a misleading statement of Flavius Blondus (Italia illustrata p. 346 ed. Bas.: *Petrarcha epistolas Ciceronis Lentulo inscriptas*—the collection ad fam. is thus entitled from its first letter—*Vercellis reperisse gloriatus est;* AVIERTEL, RhM. 36, 150). Petrarch in fact knew only the one collection of letters discovered by him in Verona (see above n. 5). A MS. of the collection ad familiares was discovered at Vercelli and was already known about 1390. Coluccio Salutato procured through Pasquino (n. 5) a copy of this MS. also; now codex Med. 49, 7 (CHATELAIN t. 36). Its original, formerly the Vercellensis, is likewise preserved as the cod. Med. 49, 9 s. IX/X (CHATELAIN t. 34, 1; on its age see FRÜHL, RhM. 36, 25. LMENDELSSOHN, JJ. 121, 864. 129, 845). Since Orelli this Mediceus was regarded as the authority for all existing MSS. of the letters ad familiares (with the exception of the Turin fragment above n. 5, l. 7). This view has been discredited, since the discovery of MSS. which furnish a tradition independent of the Med.: Harleiani 2682 s. XI and 2773 s. XII (cf. THOEHLER in BAITER-KAYSER's Cicero 9, p. v. FRÜHL, RhM. 30, 26; Wissensch. Monatsbl. 1878, 25), Erfordiensis (now in Berlin fol. 252 s. XII, cf. § 179, 13, 2, which already EWunder regarded as independent of the Med.), Paris. 17812 s. XII (CHATELAIN t. 35) and Turon. 688 s. XII/XIII, probably derived from it (ChTHUROT, Cic. ad fam. notice sur un inscr., Par. 1874. LMENDELSSOHN, Mélanges Graux 169). On fragments of a MS. s. XII (?) see AGOLISCH, Phil. 26, 701. GVITELLI, framm. di un cod. epp. ad fam., Mus. ital. 1, 156.—On the diplomatic history of the letters see ORELLI's hist. crit. epist. Cic. introd. to his ed.[2] p. v. CECSCHNEIDER, de cod. Med. epp. Cic. ad fam. auctoritate, Bresl. 1832. FHOFMANN, d. krit. Apparat von Cic.s Briefen an Att., Berl. 1863. DDETLEFSEN, JJ. 87. 551. MHAUPT, op. 2, 83. 112. AVIERTEL, die Wiederauffindung von Cic.s Briefen durch Petrarca, Königsb. 1879; JJ. 121, 231. GVOIGT, Leipz. SBer. 1879, 41; Lit. Centr. Bl. 1879, 1425.—OSTREICHER, de Cic. epp. ad fam. emendandis. in the commentatt. phil. Ienens. 3 (1884), 97. LMENDELSSOHN, JJ. 121, 864. 129. 108. 845; Phil. 45, 152.

7. Emendationes Cic. epistolarum by ASWESENBERG (Copenh. 1840; emend. alterae, Lps. 1873) and HAKOCH (Putbus 1855; RhM. 12, 268). FBÜCHELER, RhM. 11, 509. JKRAUSS, Cologne 1866. Lps. 1869 II. JFREY, Rössel 1873. 75 II. OHIRSCHFELD, Herm. 5, 296. JCGBOOT, obss. crit. ad Cic. epp. (acad. reg. Nederl.), Amsterd. 1880. GGPLUYGERS, Mnemos. 9, 113. PSTARKER, symb. critt. ad Cic. epp., Bresl. 1882. CALEHMANN, quaestt. Tull. I: de Cic. epistulis, Prague 1886. MADVIG, adv. critt. 3, 133. ChNISARD, notes (esp. historical) sur les lettres de Cic., Par. 1882. —Review of the literature on Cicero's letters: KSCHIRMER, Phil. 45, 133.

8. Collective editions of the letters: rec. ASWESENBERG (Lps. 1872. 73 II). The correspondence of Cicero (chronologically arranged, with commentary, etc.); by RYTYRRELL, I Lond.[2] 1885. II 1886.

9. Translations by CMWIELAND (and FDGRÄTER), Zür. 1808–21 VII; by GHMOSER and others (in the Metzler collection, small vols. 51–76), CLFMEZGER (Stuttg. Hoffmann 1859 sqq.). By WMELMOTH and WHEBERDEN, Lond. 1854. G. EJEANS, Lond.[2] 1887.

10. Selections with annotations by FHOFMANN and GANDRESEN, Berl.[5] 1884,

[2]85 II, KFSüpfle (Karlsruhe[8] 1880 by EBoeckel), AWatson, Oxf.[2] 1874, JFrey, Lpz.[3] 1881. EStJParry, Lond. 1867. JEYonge, Pt. I. Lond. 1870. CEPritchard and ERBernard, Lond. 1872. GEJeans, Lond. 1882. JHMuirhead, Lond. 1885.—Translated in the Metzler Klass. d. Alt., Stuttg. 1854.

188. The collections extant are as follows:

1) Epistulae (ad familiares), 16 books of the years 692/62–711/43, arranged according to the persons to whom they are addressed (with the exception of book XIII), but without consistent attention to chronology.

1. The traditional title of this collection is (according to the subscriptiones in the Med.) simply *M. Tulli Ciceronis epistularum ad P. Lentulum* (=b. 1), ad *C. Curionem* (b. 2), *ad App. Claudium* (b. 3), *ad Ser. Sulpicium* (b. 4) etc. after the chief, or at least the first person addressed in the respective books. Cf. n. 2 and § 187, 4. The usual designation *ad familiares* is not attested by any MS. (cf. on this Suet. Iul. 56 [§ 195, 8]); late MSS. and old editions give the title *epistolae familiares* (cf. Quint. 1, 1, 29. Gennad. v. ill. 63). The name *ad diversos* which was formerly widely accepted is also unauthenticated (cf. Hieron. v. ill. 69. 99. 135 [§ 434. 2]. Gennad. v. ill. 92).

2. The third book contains only letters to Appius Claudius Pulcher, b. 8 only letters from M. Caelius (§ 209, 6) to Cicero, b. 14 only letters from Cicero to Terentia and the other members of his family, b. 16 exclusively letters to Tiro (the editor): here too are quite unimportant ones addressed to the latter, some which merely relate to Tiro but are not addressed to him (16, 16); b. 13 contains mere letters of recommendation.—The collection consists of portions of the Tironian collective edition of the letters (§ 187, 4): how just these portions came to be combined into a larger group, when and by whom this was done, has not been explained.

3. On the MSS. see § 187, 6. Editions e.g. by PManutius (Ald. 1575 and other edd., his commentary specially edited by GCRichter, Lpz. 1779, 80 II), JGGraevius (cum notis variorum, Amsterd. 1677. 1693 II and other edd.), ChCellarius and GCorte (Lpz.[3] 1771), JAMartyni-Laguna (vol. I Lps. 1804; beginning of the commentary in Jahn's Archiv. 2 [1833], 249, 365 and with PVictorii curae tertiae in epp. ad fam. II. by JCOrelli, Zür. 1840). Cf. § 187, 8.

4. The letters not by Cicero (Clarorum virorum epist. etc.) with notes by BWeiske (Lpz. 1792). Ep. ad. L. Lucceium (5, 12) ed. ill. CHFrotscher, Annaberg 1838 (on this see also CECSchneider, Bresl. 1837. Willmann, Halberst. 1883). M. Caelii Rufi et M. Tullii Ciceronis epp. mutuae ed. WHDSuringar, Leid. 1845. —HAKleijn, obss. in Cic. ad fam., Leid. 1860. RJacobs, ad Cic. ad fam. l. XIII, JJ. 85, 732, JMüller, z. Krit. u. Erkl. der Br. Cic. an P. Lentulus, Innsbr. 1862. FOudendorpii scholia in selectas epp. ad fam. ed. JALiebmann (Lps. 1839). BNake, der Briefwechsel zw. Cic. u. Caelius, JJ. 89, 60; zw. Cic. u. D. Brutus, JJ. suppl. vol. 8, 647; de M. Caeli Rufi epist. libro, in der Symb. philol. Bonn. 373; de Planci et Cic. epistulis, Berl. 1866. LGurlitt, d. Briefwechsel zw. Cic. u. D. Brut., JJ. 121, 609. OESchmidt, de epistulis et a Cassio et ad Cassium datis quaestt. chronologicae, Lps. 1877. LMendelssohn, JJ. 133, 64. CGCobet (fam. and Att.), Mnemos. 8, 182. LPurser, Hermath. 11, 277. Proposed emendations to b. 10 by MGitlbauer, Wiener Stud. 1, 75; to b. 8 Teuffel, RhM. 29, 364.

2) Ad Atticum, likewise in 16 books, commencing with a.

686/68 and terminating a few months before Cicero's death. These are confidential letters, in which the writer expresses himself with entire freedom, and frequently in language intelligible only to his correspondent. They read partly as monologues. These letters (without the answers of Atticus) were doubtless not published until after Atticus' death, though prepared by him for publication.

1. Cic. ad Att. 8, 14, 2 *ego tecum tamquam mecum loquor.*

2. The commencement is inaccurately determined by Corn. Nepos Att. 16, 3: XVI (the MSS. XI) *volumina epistularum ab consulatu eius* (Cicero) *usque ad extremum tempus ad Atticum missarum. quae qui legat non multum desideret historiam contextam eorum temporum . . . omnia de studiis principum, vitiis ducum, mutationibus rei publicae perscripta sunt. non enim Cicero ea solum quae vivo se acciderunt futura praedixit, sed etiam quae nunc usu veniunt, cecinit ut vates.* The correspondence during the last months of Cicero's life was perhaps suppressed out of regard for Octavianus (see BNake, hist. crit. p. 17, n. 30). Owing to a similar precaution and perhaps out of modesty (§ 187, 4 l. 5) Atticus' replies were left out, though they are often indispensable to a full understanding of Cicero's letters, and had been carefully preserved by Cicero (Att. 9, 10, 4). Atticus was actuated by the same motive in keeping back the publication until after his own death (a. 722/32), as appears from Corn. Nep. l.l. From the circumstance that on the one hand Asconius in his commentary on Cicero (§ 295, 2, composed about 808/55) does not mention the letters ad Att. 2 while on the other hand Seneca ad Lucil. 97, 118 (§ 289, 5) already quotes from them, FBücheler, RhM. 34, 352, conjectures that the correspondence with Atticus was not published until about A.D. 60. In that case the epp. ad Att. would have been made public only a whole century after Cicero's death, which is against all historical probability. Cf. also the quotation in Seneca de brevit. vitae 5 (written before a. 49) *quam flebiles* (Cicero) *voces exprimit in quadam ad Atticum epistula . . . 'quid agam hic quaeris? moror in Tusculano meo semiliber.' alia deinceps adicit quibus et priorem aetatem complorat et de praesenti queritur et de futura desperat*, where however Lipsius (the quotation not being found in our collection) plausibly conjectures *ad Axium* (§ 187, 4). At all events the wording of the passage in Seneca would go to prove that Seneca had read the letter itself, and would contradict Bücheler's assumption that the quotation refers to Cic. ad Att. 13, 31, 3 *semiliberi saltem simus*, and that the incorrect quotation was communicated to Seneca from the collection ad Atticum prior to its publication.

3. On the MSS. see § 187, 5.—On a transposed leaf at the end of b. 4 see Mommsen, ZfAW. 1845, 779.—Editions by PManutius (Venice 1547 and subsequently), PVictorius (Florence 1571), JGGraevius (Amsterd. 1684. 1693. 1727 II), JCGBoot (rec. et adn. ill., Amsterd. [2]1886). Cf. § 187, 8.—ThSchiche, z. Chronol. v. B. 15 ad Att. in d. Festschr. d. Friedr.-Werderschen Gymn., Berlin 1881, 225; zu Cic. ad Att. 2. Teil, Berl. 1883. OESchmidt, JJ. 129, 331.—RMücke, de locis aliquot graecis in Cic. epp. ad Att., Ilfeld 1878. Critical contributions by FSchmidt, BlfbayrGW. 12, 235; zur Kritik u. Erkl. d. Briefe Cic. ad Att., Nürnb. 1879. CGCobet (§ 188, 1, 4). AOtto, RhM. 41, 364.

3) Ad Quintum fratrem, three books dating from 694/60–

700/54. Here there is no doubt that we possess all that was ever published.

1. On the MSS. see § 187, 5.—The confusion in book 2, which arose from a transposition of every two double leaves of the original MS., was set right by MOMMSEN, ZfAW. 1844, 591.—Editions by JHOFFA (Heidelb. 1843); also with the letters ad Brut. by PMANUTIUS (Frankf. 1580 and subsequently) and cum notis variorum; acc. Q. Cic. de petit. cons. c. comm. Valerii Palermi, Hagae Com. 1725.

2. Ep. 1, 1 of a. 694/60, which amounts to a long and elaborate essay (on provincial administration), a sort of complimentary return for his brother's epistle de petitione (§ 190, 4).

4) Correspondence between M. Brutus and Cicero, very incompletely preserved.

1. This correspondence at one time comprised 9 books, and the one now extant as b. 1 was originally the ninth and last. NON. 421, 31 *Cic. . . . ad Brutum lib. VIIII. 'L. Clodius, tr. pl. des.* etc.'=our CIC. ad Brut. 1, 1, 1. For book 1 (properly 9) the principal MSS. are the Medic. 49, 18 (in this the subscriptio reads: *Ad Brutum epistolarum liber primus explicit. incipit ad Q. epistolarum primus*) and the MS. which Cratander used; see § 187, 5.—To this first book (18 letters) Cratander in 1528 added seven letters *quod a Ciceroniana dictione abhorrere non videbantur et in vetusto codice primum locum obtinerent*, which since Schütz have been denoted as the second book. No MS. of them is known to exist. AVSTRENG, de Cic. ad Brut. epistt. libro II, Helsingfors 1885. Cratander's words show that in the cod. vetustus the 7 new letters preceded the so-called b. 1, hence it is probable that originally they also belonged to b. 9 (or b. 8). In agreement with this is the fact that the letters of the so-called second book relate to the time before the battle of Mutina, those of the first to the time succeeding it. Another fragment from b. 8 in NON. 527, 25, who 296, 8 also quotes book 7. See a quotation from b. 1 ap. SERV. Aen. 8, 395. LGURLITT, JJ. 131, 561. KWERMUTH, quaestt. de Cic. epp. ad Brut. l. IX, Basel 1887 (together with LGURLITT, Berl. philol. Wochenschr. 1887, 1086).—For editions see above no. 3, 1.

2. AMM. MARC. 29, 5, 24 quotes ad Brut. 1, 2, 5 as Ciceronian (*Tullianum illud*). PLUT. Brut. 53 τὸ ἐπιστόλιον (Βρούτου), εἴπερ ἄρα τῶν γνησίων ἐστί: but on the genuineness of this (non-extant) letter in particular and of the Ciceronian epistle ad Brut. 1, 9 see MOMMSEN, Herm. 15, 102. The spuriousness of both books was first maintained by JTUNSTALL (epistola ad C. Middleton, Cambr. 1741, and Observations etc., Lond. 1745), and esp. by TMARKLAND (Remarks etc. Lond. 1745), while their authenticity was successfully defended by CMIDDLETON (the epp. of Cic. and Brut. with a dissertation, Lond. 1743) and recently by KFHERMANN; cf. his vindiciae latinitatis epp. Cic. ad Br., Gött. 1844; Gött. gel. Anz. 1844, 1934. 1845, 961. 1310; defence of the authenticity of the letters etc., Abh. der Gött. Ges. d. Wiss. 2, 189. 3, 143; Vindiciarum Brutinarum epimetrum, Gött. 1845. Against Hermann AWZUMPT, de Cic. et Bruti mutuis epp. quae vulgo feruntur, Berl. 1845; Berl. Jahrb. 1845. 2, no. 91 sqq. and recently FBECHER, de Cic. quae feruntur ad Brut. epistulis, Jena 1876; RhM. 37, 576; Phil. Suppl. 4, 502; Phil. 44, 471. PMEYER, üb. d. Frage der Echtheit des Briefwechsels Cic. ad Brut., Zürich 1881; Phil. Wochenschr. 1883, 1313; WschrfklPh. 1884, 423. However, these attempts to disprove the Ciceronian origin of these letters have been confuted on all points, and their authenticity is more firmly established than ever. The objections

raised against this collection are of small consequence, chiefly contradictions between Cicero's confidential judgments on certain persons and the assertions made by him in public or at other times. The simple style of the Brutus letters, which are quite free from turgid rhetoric, does not favour the assumption of forgery and quite agrees with Brutus' Attic tendency. Cf. § 210, 1 sqq. Cf. e.g. MADVIG, adv. 3, 197. CGCOBET, Mnemos. N. S. 7, 262. OESCHMIDT, JJ. 127, 559. 129, 617; WschrfklPh. 1884, 261. ERUETE (§ 187, 2 ad fin.); Phil. Rundsch. 1884, 593. LGURLITT, Phil. Anz. 1883, 720; Phil. Suppl. 4, 551; JJ. 121, 610. 129, 855. KSCHIRMER, Phil. Anz. 13, 765; die Sprache des Brutus in den bei Cic. überlieferten Briefen, Metz 1884.

3. Only the two letters 1, 16 and 17 are very suspicious and are probably a production of the rhetorical school. KNIPPERDEY, Abh. d. sächs. Ges. d. Wiss. 5, 71. RHEINE, de Cic. et Bruti epistulis mutuis, Lps. 1875. OESCHMIDT, de epist. Cass. (§ 188, 1, 4) 57 and esp. LGURLITT, Phil. Suppl. 5, 591 (who however should not have impugned 1, 15, 3–11).

5) There is no doubt as to the spuriousness of the letter ad Octavianum.

1. The letter is found e.g. in the Med. 49, 18 (§ 187, 5), in Berol. 252 (Erford.) s. XII (§ 179, 13, 2), it was to be found in Cratander's MS. (above no. 4, 1) and is printed in the editions of Cicero; e.g. in BAITER-KAYSER 10, 465. CBERNS in the commentatt. phil. semin. Lips. (Lps. 1874) 177.

189. Cicero practised poetry incidentally from his early years, chiefly with a view to forming his style. His talent for literary form made metrical composition very easy to him. At a riper age he composed an epic on Marius, but he was strangely blinded by his burning desire for fame, which induced him to make himself and his life the subject of epics, greatly to the disadvantage of his reputation.

1. On Cicero as a poet cf. SEN. exc. controv. 3 praef. 8 *Ciceronem eloquentia sua in carminibus destituit.* SEN. de ira 3, 37, 5. TAC. dial. 21. JUV. 10, 124 '*o fortunatam natam me consule Romam!' Antoni gladios potuit contemnere, si sic omnia dixisset.* MART. 2, 89, 3 *Carmina quod scribis Musis et Apolline nullo Laudari debes: hoc Ciceronis habes.* PLUT. Cic. 40 (on improvising). SCHOL. BOB. 305 Or. DRUMANN, GR. 6, 681. FMFRANTZEN, de Cic. poeta, Abo 1800. vHEUSDE, Cic. φιλοπλάτων (Utr. 1836) 25. 34. RIBBECK, röm. Dicht. 1, 296. HSCHENKL, de Cic. poeta, in the Jahresber. des Vereins 'Mittelschule,' Vienna 1886. MGROLLMUS, de Cic. poeta I: de inscriptt., argumentis, tempp. singulorum carmm., Königsb. 1887. JKUBIK (§ 177, 2) 241. The fragments e.g. in BAITER-KAYSER 11, 89. CFWMÜLLER 4, 3, 350. FPR. 298.

2. On his youthful attempts, the Pontios Glaukos and his translation of Aratos, see § 177a, 1. The date of some of his other works is uncertain. IUL. CAPITOL. Gordian. 3, 2 *adulescens cum esset Gordianus . . . poemata scripsit . . . et quidem cuncta illa quae Cicero edidit Marium* (n. 3) *et Aratum et Halcyonas* (cf. NON. 65 *Cicero † alcyon*, 2 hex. follow) *et Uxorium* (carpet-knight?) *et Nilum* (Casaubon: *Limona* see below). *quae quidem ad hoc scripsit ut Ciceronis poemata nimis antiqua viderentur.*—SERV. buc. 1, 57 *Cicero in elegia quae † talia masta inscribitur* (an hexameter follows; *Thalia maesta* HEINSIUS, Θαυμαστά MHERTZ, *Italia maesta* LURLICHS, Eos 1, 151).—Cicero also made metrical translations of portions

of Homer (de div. 2, 63. de fin. 5, 49), Aischylos (Tusc. 2, 23), Sophokles (ib. 2, 20) and others.—Suet. vita Ter. p. 34, 2 R. *Cicero in Limone* (Λειμών=*Pratum*; Plin. NH. praef. 24. Gell. NA. praef. 6. Suid. s. v. Πάμφιλος· . . . ἔγραψε λειμῶνα· ἔστι δὲ ποικίλων περιοχή): here follow four hexameters on Terence as a felicitous adapter of Menander; accordingly their contents must have been literary criticism, cf. Ritschl. op. 3, 263.—Epigrams: Plin. ep. 7, 4, 3 (*epigramma* [*lascivum lusum*; cf. *Auson.* op. 28, 4, 9 p. 146 Sch.] *Ciceronis in Tironem suum*; cf. Grollmus l.l. 49). Quint. 8, 6, 73.

3. Quint. 11, 1, 24 *in carminibus utinam pepercisset* (had indulged less in self-laudation), *quae non desierunt carpere maligni.* Here should be mentioned his three books *de suo consulatu* in epic metre. Schol. Bob. 267, 19 Or. Att. 2, 3, 3; cf. 1, 19, 10 (*poema expectato ne quod genus a me ipso laudis meae praetermittatur*). de div. 1, 17–22: here is a considerable fragment, a speech of Urania, which shows how the contemporary subject-matter was tastelessly decked out with tawdry mythology. From this work or the following are derived the two famous lines (n. 1): *O fortunatam natam me consule Romam* (Quint. 9, 4, 41 and elsewhere) and *Cedant arma togae, concedat laurea laudi* (off. 1, 77 and elsewhere) Drumann, GR. 5, 601. JMähly, Phil. 25, 544. Ribbeck, röm. Dicht. 1, 296.—Also the epic de temporibus meis, likewise in three books (composed about 699/55). Cf. fam. 1, 9, 23 (still unpublished a. 700/54). ad Q. fr. 3, 1, 24. 2, 13, 2. 2, 15, 5. Att. 4, 8b. 3. Drumann, GR. 6, 20. —Cicero wrote besides, a. 700/54, an eulogistic poem on Caesar as the conqueror of Britain; ad Q. fr. 3, 1, 11 (poema ad Caesarem). Cf. 2, 13, 2. 3, 4, 4. 3, 8, 3. 3, 9, 6 (*quod me hortaris ut absolvam, habeo absolutum suave, mihi quidem uti videtur, ἔπος ad Caesarem*). Cf. Drumann GR. 3, 322. Lastly, the epic poem Marius, Att. 12, 49, 1. leg. 1, 1 is probably of the same period. The latter passage shows clearly that the date of its composition (702/52) was not long after that of the Marius. MHaupt, op. 1, 211. Grollmus l.l. 22 holds a different opinion. At all events the subject, the glorification of the popular leader, does not oblige us to suppose an earlier date for the poem (so Ribbeck l.l.). It was just in 700/54 sqq. that Cicero was courting Caesar's favour, often in an undignified fashion. It is quite probable that at that time a panegyric on Marius, his countryman, his relative, Caesar's predecessor in the leadership of the popular party and who was also closely connected with Caesar by marriage, would appear expedient to Cicero, who always loads Marius with praise; and he was an expert writer, who could easily surmount the difficulties of the task. The passage in a letter (Att. 2, 15, 3 a. 695/59) is no evidence for an earlier date.

4. Most recent collections of the Ciceronian fragments in Baiter-Kayser vol. 11 (1868) and CFWMüller 4, 3 (1879), 231. CHalm, Beitr. z. Berichtig. u. Ergänzung der ciceron. Fragm., Lpz. 1862 (=Münch. SBer. 1862 2, 1). JMähly, ZföG. 21, 821. FHoppe, zu den Fragmenten u. der Sprache Cic.s, Gumbinnen 1875.

190. Cicero's younger brother, Quintus (a. 652/102–711/43), took much interest in literature, especially in poetry, and seems to have resembled his brother in facility of composition, but he never attained any distinction. He undertook an annalistic work, and translated tragedies of Sophokles and the like. We possess by him the commentariolum petitionis, a missive addressed to his brother Marcus, composed early in 690/64, and a few letters.

1. The official career of Q. Cicero seems to justify the assumption of 652/102 as the year in which he was born. He was aedile 689/65, praetor 692/62, governed Asia from 693/61 to 696/58, was Pompey's legate in Sardinia 698/56, Caesar's in Gaul and Britain 700/54–702/52, his brother's in Cilicia 703/51; he was with the latter proscribed, and killed together with his son 711/43; see Drumann, GR. 6, 719. WPütz, de Q. Cic. vita et scriptis, Düren 1833. CHBlase, de Q. Cic. vita, Bedburg 1847. PRE. 6, 2234. FBücheler, Q. Cic. reliqq. p. 1–24.

2. Schol. Bob. on Cic. pArch. p. 354 Or.: *fuit enim Q. Tullius non solum epici verum etiam tragici carminis scriptor.* Cic. Att. 2, 16, 4 (a. 695/59): *Q. frater . . . me rogat ut annales suos* (hardly in a metrical form) *emendem et edam.* ad Q. fr. 2, 11, 4 (a. 700/54) *Callisthenem et Philistum . . . in quibus te video volutatum . . . sed quod adscribis: aggrederisne ad historiam? me auctore potes.* 2, 15, 4 (a. 700/54) *o iucundas mihi tuas e Britannia litteras! te vero ὑπόθεσιν scribendi egregiam habere video. quos tu situs, quas naturas rerum et locorum, quos mores, quas gentes, quas pugnas, quem vero ipsum imperatorem habes!* (Hence we may conclude that it was intended to become an epic poem.) *ego te libenter . . . adiuvabo et tibi versus quos rogas . . . mittam.* 3, 4, 4 (a. 700/54) *sine ulla mehercule ironia loquor, tibi istius generis in scribendo priores partes tribuo quam mihi.* Cf. 3, 5 and 6, 7 (a. 700/54) *quattuor tragoedias XVI diebus absolvisse cum scribas tu quidquam ab alio mutuaris? et πάθος* (see Usener, RhM. 22, 459) *quaeris cum Electram et † trodam* (*Troadas* Schütz. *Troilum? Aëropam* Bücheler) *scripseris? . . . sed et istas et Erigonam mihi velim mittas.* ib. 3, 1, 13 *in ea* (epistula) *nihil erat novi praeter Erigonam, quam si . . . accepero scribam ad te quid sentiam; nec dubito quin mihi placitura sit.* 3, 9, 6 *ne accidat quod Erigonae tuae, cui soli Caesare imperatore iter ex Gallia tutum non fuit.* There was an Ἠριγόνη by Sophokles. Cic. de fin. 5, 3 *tum Quintus: . . . Sophocles . . ., quem scis quam admirer quamque eo delecter.* ad Q. fr. 2, 15, 3 (a. 700/54) Συνδείπνους Σοφοκλέους, *quamquam a te factam fabellam* (a satyric drama? see Ribbeck, röm. Trag. 620) *video esse festive, nullo modo probavi.* fam. 16, 8, 2 *ego* (Q.) *certe singulos eius* (Euripides) *versus singula testimonia puto.* Ribbeck, röm. Dicht. 1, 190.

3. Three letters of Q. Cicero to Tiro, fam. 16, 8 (a. 705/49). 26. 27 (a. 710/44) and one (ib. 16, 16) to his brother Marcus (694/60?). Together in Bucheler (n. 4) p. 64. Cf. also Cic. ad Q. fr. 2, 14, 2 *in brevi epistula πραγματικῶς valde scripsisti.* 3, 1, 19 *epistulam tuam aristophaneo modo valde et suavem et gravem.*

4. The missive to his brother Marcus, when he was a candidate for the consulate a. 690/64, throws light on the place-hunting, which was then carried on very vigorously; the writer perhaps making use of Theophrastos περὶ φιλοτιμίας (Cic. ad Att. 2, 3, 3). Its plan is correct but pedantic, the diction is dry and insipid (Bücheler, p. 3, 7 sq.). The similarity to the speech in toga candida, to the one for Murena, and to the first letter from M. to his brother Quintus (1, 1) is remarkable. For these and other arguments against the authorship of Q. (and for the letter having been written by a rhetorician of the first century after Christ) see AEussner, commentariolum petitionis examinatum atque emendatum, Würzb. 1872. See however against this view HWirz, philol. Anz. 5 (1873), 499 and RYTyrrell, the letters of Q. Cic., Hermathena 5 (1877), 40; and his edition of the Ciceronian letters (§ 187, 8) 1, p. lxv. The best MSS. are Harleian. 2682 s. XI (see EBährens, misc. crit. 23) and Berol. 252 s. XII (see Bücheler p. 11). Printed as an appendix to the letters ad Q. fratr. Separate editions by Valerius Palermus (§ 188, 3, 1), CGSchwarz (cum animadv., Altorf 1719), JHoffa (perpet. adnot. illustr., Lps. 1837). JWTijdemann, in Q. Cic. de pet. cons. adnotatt., Leid. 1838 sq. Q.

Cic. rell. recogn. FBücheler, Lps. 1869. The text in Eussner l.l. p. 24; scholia critica ib. p. 36.

5. Ausonius ecl. 17 p. 16 Sch. gives after one of his own poems for the sake of comparison 16 (20) hexameters by Q. Cicero on the twelve signs of the Zodiac; the same in Bücheler l.l. 68. AL. 642. FPR. 315. Baiter-Kayser's Cic. 11, 138. CFWMüller 4, 3, 405.—The epigram on women, which late MSS. (AL. 268. PLM. 4, 359) attribute to a certain Cicero, properly belongs to Pentadius (§ 398, 5).

191. Cicero's freedman and friend, M. Tullius Tiro, long survived his patron and carefully cultivated his memory. He wrote his biography, published his orations and letters, and perhaps also collected his witticisms. He wrote comprehensive works himself of a grammatical character, and seems to have also dabbled in poetry. His name has become well known through the notae Tironianae.

1. Cic. fam. 16, 4, 3 *innumerabilia tua sunt in me officia: domestica, forensia; urbana, provincialia; in re privata, in publica; in studiis, in litteris nostris.* 16, 17, 1 *κανὼν esse meorum scriptorum soles.* Cf. Att. 7, 5, 2. Gell. 6, 3, 8 *Tiro Tullius, M. Ciceronis libertus, sane quidem fuit ingenio homo eleganti et haudquaquam rerum litterarumque veterum indoctus, eoque ab ineunte aetate liberaliter instituto adminiculatore et quasi administro in studiis litterarum Cicero usus est.* ib. 13, 9, 1. 15, 16, 2. He was manumitted a. 700/54 (Cic. fam. 16, 16). A. 704/50 he was *adulescens* (ad Att. 6. 7, 2). Hieronym. on Euseb. Chron. ad a. Abr. 2013 (Freher. 2012) = 750/4 *M. Tullius Tiro, Ciceronis libertus, qui primus notas commentus est, in Puteolano praedio* (cf. Cic. fam. 16, 21, 7) *usque ad centesimum annum consenescit.* JCd'Engelbronner, de Tirone, Amst. 1804. ALion, Tironiana, in Seebode's Arch. 1824, 246 and (cf. § 220, 9) Gött. 1846. Drumann, GR. 6, 405. PRE. 6, 2207. PMitzschke, M. Tull. Tiro, Berl. 1875.

2. Ascon. p. 49 Or. 43 K.-S. *ut legimus apud Tironem libertum Ciceronis in libro IIII de vita eius.* His work bore the character of an apology for Cicero, and sought to clear his memory from detraction. Plutarch, who cites it (Cic. 41. 49), has no doubt availed himself of it in part of his Βίος Κικέρωνος: see HPeter, Quellen Plutarchs 129. Tac. dial. 17. Gell. 4, 10, 6.—ib. 15, 16, 2 *a Tirone . . . librorum patroni sui studiosissimo.* HPeter, hist. fragm. 212. A MS. of Cic.'s orations revised by him is mentioned Gell. 1, 7, 1 (*in oratione Cic. V in Verr., libro spectatae fidei, Tironiana cura atque disciplina facto*) and 13, 21, 16 (*in uno atque in altero antiquissimae fidei libro Tironiano*). A memento of this activity is preserved in the subscriptio of Statilius Maximus (§ 374, 5). Quint. 10, 7, 31 (§ 180, 3). On his activity as the editor of collections of Cicero's correspondence see § 187, 3 and 4. He was also the reputed author of a collection of *ioci Ciceronis.* Quint, 6, 3, 5 *utinam libertus eius Tiro aut alius quisquis fuit, qui tris hac de re libros edidit, parcius dictorum numero indulsissent* etc. Macrob. S. 2, 1, 12 *liberti eius libros quos is de iocis patroni composuit.* Schol. Bob. in Sest. p. 309 Or. *hoc etiam dictum . . . Tullius Tiro . . . inter iocos Ciceronis adnumerat.* Cf. § 186, 6.

3. Gell. 6, 3, 10 (*Tiro*) *epistulam conscripsit ad Q. Axium, familiarem patroni sui, confidenter nimis et calide, in qua sibimet visus est orationem* (of Cato the Elder) *pro Rhodiensibus acri subtilique iudicio percensuisse* (no doubt in maiorem gloriam patroni). 10, 1, 7 *quod . . . Tiro Tullius . . . in epistula quadam enarratius scripsit ad hunc fere modum.* 13, 9, 2 (*Tullius Tiro*) *libros complures de usu atque*

ratione linguae latinae, item de variis atque promiscuis quaestionibus composuit. in his esse praecipue videntur quos graeco titulo Πανδέκτας *inscripsit. ibi de his stellis . . . hoc scriptum est* (here follows a quotation of some length). This work was probably also used by PLIN. NH., who in the ind. auct. for b. 2 (universe, constellations etc.) quotes *Tullius Tiro.* CHARIS. GL. 1, 297 '*novissime*' *Tiro in pandecte non recte ait dici* etc. CIC. fam. 16, 18, 3 (a. 709/45): *tu* (Tiro) *nullosne tecum libellos? an pangis aliquid Sophocleum? fac opus appareat.*

4. SUETONIUS (ed. Rffsch. p. 135) and from him ISIDORUS orig. 1, 21 and a Cassel MS. of the Notae Tironis et Senecae (§ 289, 8. WSCHMITZ, symb. philol. Bonn 532): *vulgares notas Ennius primus mille et centum invenit . . .* (see § 104, 5). *Romae primus Tullius Tiro, Ciceronis libertus, commentatus* (perhaps *commentus*, see above note 1) *est notas, sed tantum praepositionum. post eum Vipsanius, Philargyrus* (the freedman of Agrippa—§ 220, 10—? see OLEHMANN l.l. 12) *et Aquila, libertus Maecenatis* (also in DIO 55, 7; see § 220, 8) *alius alias addiderunt. denique Seneca contracto omnium digestoque et aucto numero opus effecit in quinque milia.*

5. Under the title of *Notae Tironis* (*Tyronis*) *et Senecae* (n. 4) we possess an extensive collection of abbreviations for shorthand, of various dates and divided into six commentarii, first published by GRUTER in his Thesaurus inscriptionum, Heidelb. 1603. Manuscripts: cod. Cassellanus (from Fulda) s. VIII, Paris. 190 s. IX and others (see below). Cf. UFKOPP, palaeograph. crit. (Mannh. 1817) § 331 and ZEIBIG l.l. 37; see also THSICKEL, Urk. d. Karolinger 1, 326; the Göttweih. lexic. Tironianum, Wiener SBer. 38 (1861), 3. On the Tiron. Notae see especially the researches of WSCHMITZ, collected in his Beiträge zur lat. Sprach- und Lit.-Kunde (Lpz. 1877) 179–306; also by the same author: RhM. 33, 321; de Romanorum tachygraphia and on the notae Matritenses in the Panstenographikon 1 (1869), 3. 91; the notae Bernenses in 75 fol. plates with prolegg. and index ib. 1 (1874), 193. 337; on Lat. tachygraphy, Verh. d. Phil.-Vers. at Trêves 1879, 59; in the Festschrift Rhein. Schulmänner z. Begrüss. d. Trierer Phil.-Vers. 1879, 53; Studd. z. lat. Tachygr., Cologne 1880; monumenta tachygr. cod. Par. 2718, Hanover 1882. 83 II; by the same and GLOEWE, Ausg. der Notae Escorialenses in Lit.-Bl. des sächs. stenograph. Instit. no. 5 (1879). JWZEIBIG, Gesch. und Lit. der Geschwindschreibkunst, Dresd.[2] 1874. OLEHMANN, de notis Tir. et Senecae, Lps. 1869. P MITZSCHKE, quaestt. Tiron., Rostock 1875. FRUESS, d. Tachygraphie d. Römer, Munich 1879; L und die Durchschneidung in den Tiron. Noten, Neuburg a/D. 1883. HHAGEN, de cod. Bern. (109) notis Tironianis, Bern. 1880.—A description of the old stenography (of Tullius) s. XII (by John of Tilbury) in VROSE, Herm. 8, 303.

6. An epigram by another freedman of Cicero, Tullius Laurea, in honour of his former master, ap. PLIN. NH. 31, 7. Three Greek epigrams by the same AP. 7, 17. 7, 294. 12, 24.

192. Besides Varro, Hortensius, the two brothers Cicero, and some others, the satirist L. Abuccius and the didactic writer Egnatius (de rerum natura) wrote in metre, as also, perhaps, Volumnius and Ninnius Crassus. Quintipor Clodius seems to have been a late imitator of the Graeco-Roman comedies. Of greater importance was the Roman knight D. Laberius (a. 649/105–711/43), who attempted, with signal success, to give a literary importance to the popular farce, the mimus (§ 8). According to tradition M. Furius Bibaculus of Cremona was of about the

same age as Laberius; in reality he was probably younger and belongs to the following generation § 204 sqq. He was the author of comic and satirical poems in the manner of Catullus, and of an epic poem on Caesar's Gallic war (perhaps of an Aethiopis); lastly of a prose work (Lucubrationes, containing anecdotes, etc.

1. Varro RR. 3, 2, 17 *L. Abuccius* (the best reading in both passages, see Keil ad loc.; cf. MHertz, JJ. 107, 338), *homo, ut scitis, adprime doctus, cuius Luciliano charactere sunt libelli, dicebat* etc. Cf. ib. 3, 6, 6 *Hortensius, . . quem secuti multi, ut quidem Abuccius aiebat.* According to Varro's language, Abuccius was already dead in 700/54 (see § 168, 1, l. 3). Macrob. sat. 6, 5, 2 *Egnatius de rerum natura libro primo* (after *Accius in Philoctete* and before *Lucretius in secundo*); also ib. 12 (after Livius, Ennius, Accius, before Cornificius). One of the hexameters quoted there is remarkable for the fact of final *s* being discarded. Bergk, op. 1, 430.—EBährens, anal. Catull. 45; comment. Catull. 219 and others identify this E. without sufficient evidence with the one mentioned in Catull. 38, 19. 39, 1. —Cic. ad Q. fr. 2, 9, 3 (a. 700/54) *sed cum veneris, virum te putabo* (cf. § 203, 2) *si Sallustii Empedoclea legeris, hominem non putabo* (Vahlen, Berl. ind. lect. 1881/82, 3). ASchöne, JJ. 93, 751 takes this to relate to Sallust the historian; Teuffel, PRE. 6, 703, 3 holds that it relates to Cn. Sallustius (in Cicero's letters, cf. § 184, 1, 2).—GL. 5. 574 *cyma: alii cymam, ut Volumnius 'stridentis dabitur patella cymae'.* This hendecasyllabic line is attributed by EBücheler, JJ. 111, 126 to P. Volumnius Eutrapelus (PRE. 6, 2743) mentioned by Cicero.—Ninnius Crassus: § 150, 3.

2. Non. 448 *Varro in Bimarco: cum Quintipor Clodius tot comoedias sine ulla fecerit Musa, ego unum libellum non edolem?* The expression *comoediae* renders it probable that they were palliatae. Cf. § 15, 1. The same is also mentioned ap. Non. 117 *Varro epistula ad Fufium* (§ 166, 6 d, l. 12) '*Quintiporis Clodi † ant foriae* (*Antipho eris* Bücheler and LMüller) *ac poemata eius gargaridians dices: "O Fortuna, o Fors Fortuna"*' (= Ter. Phorm. 841, where the line is given to Geta, a slave of Antipho).

3. The 44 titles of his plays which we know and the fragments prove the complete absorption of all the other kinds of comedy in the mimus. Besides the titles resembling palliatae (see § 8, 4) we meet also many derived from qualities and professions, e.g. Augur, Catularius, Centonarius, Colorator, Fullo, Piscator, Restio, Salinator, Staminariae (? Wölfflin, RhM. 43, 308); intrigues and character plays such as Aries, Cancer, Carcer, Imago, Nuptiae, Paupertas, Taurus; Aulularia, Caeculi, Galli, Gemelli, Late loquentes, Sorores, Stricturae, Virgo; Cretensis, Tusca; Anna Perenna, Lacus Avernus, Compitalia, Natal, Parilia, Saturnalia. The allusions to *Pythagorea dogma, Cynica haeresis, Democritus, Necyomantia* (710/44; cf. in fr. 63 the witticism on Caesar's schemes and regulations) plainly indicate the high culture of the writers of mimi; but there is also much evidence to show the connection of the mimus with the prevailing immorality of the time. Laberius was very bold in forming new words, see e.g. Gell. 16, 7. Tert. de pall. 1. Some peculiarities were plebeian (Gell. 19, 13, 3). Laberius v. 55 gives the explanation: *versorum, non numerum* (*numerorum* Bücheler, *numorum* Dziatzko) *numero studuimus.* The prosody of his senarii is the same as that of the poetae scenici and, as a rule, they are fluent; he has also trochees, and in some isolated places bacchiacs. The fragments: in Ribbeck's com.[2] 279.

Towards the close of Laberius' life, Caesar severely humiliated him, evidently as a penalty for his Republican candour (cf. e.g. MACROB. 2, 7, 4. 5), and generally on account of his sharp tongue, SEN. contr. 7, 3, 9. MACR. 2, 3, 10. 2, 6, 6. Caesar, acting in this matter as a thoroughly malignant tyrant, obliged the poet, who until then had indeed written mimes for the ludi given by the magistrates (cf. MACR. 2, 6, 6), but was precluded by his position as an eq. Rom. from taking part in them himself, to go on the stage and that as a competitor in the mimic impromptu-play to which Publilius Syrus had challenged his rivals (§ 212, 3). SUETON. Iul. 39 *ludis* (a. 709/45) *D. Laberius eques rom. mimum suum egit.* Cf. the chief passage on Laberius in MACROB. sat. 2, 7: there § 2 *Laberium, asperae libertatis equitem rom., Caesar . . . invitavit ut prodiret in scenam et ipse ageret mimos, quos scriptitabat.* The impressive prologue to this compulsory performance (a. 709/45) has been preserved in MACROB. 2, 7, 3 (from GELL. 8, 15). Laberius was defeated and would have sustained a defeat even had he won the prize; *statimque* (Caesar) *Publilio palmam et Laberio anulum aureum* (so as to restore to him outwardly his knighthood, which had become void by his performing) *cum quingentis sestertiis dedit* (the honour to the Greek freedman, the money to a Roman knight!). Cf. GELL. 17, 14, 2 *C. Caesarem ita Laberii maledicentia et adrogantia* (according to Caesar) *offendebat ut acceptiores sibi esse Publilii quam Laberii mimos praedicaret.* Laberius himself recognised that his time was over: *non possunt primi esse omnes omni in tempore: summum ad gradum cum claritatis veneris, consistes aegre . . .: cecidi ego, cadet qui sequitur* (MACR. 2, 7, 9). In the prologue, a. 709/45, Laberius says he is 60 years old (*ego bis tricenis annis actis sine nota Eques Romanus e Lare egressus meo Domum revertar mimus*), hence he was born about 649/105. HIERON. on Eus. Chron. ad a. Abr. 1974 = 711/43 *Laberius mimorum scriptor decimo mense post C. Caesaris interitum Puteolis moritur* (therefore Jan. 711/43). On Lab. CJGRYSAR, der röm. Mimus (1854) 290. MOMMSEN, RG. 3^6, 590. RIBBECK, röm. Dicht. 1, 218.

4. HIERON. on Euseb. Chron. ad a. Abr. 1914 = 651/103 (in the cod. Amand. and Freher. a. 1915 = 652/102). *M. Furius poeta cognomento Bibaculus* ('Bibber'; earlier Furii with this cognomen in LIV. 22, 49, 16. VAL. MAX. 1, 1, 9) *Cremonae nascitur.* On the perverted orthography (intended to save the poet's honour) *Vivaculus* in PLINY NH. praef. 24 (see below) cf. TEUFFEL on Hor. sat. 2, 5, 40 p. 135. QUINT. 10, 1, 96; *iambus . . . cuius acerbitas in Catullo, Bibaculo, Horatio . . . reperietur.* DIOMED. GL. 1, 485 (see § 33, 1). TAC. A. 4, 34 *carmina Bibaculi et Catulli referta contumeliis Caesarum leguntur: sed ipse divus Iulius, ipse divus Augustus* (therefore Bibaculus wrote against him) *et tulere ista et reliquere.* The fragments of Bib. (hendecasyllabics, iambics, hexameters) in LMÜLLER's Catullus (1870) p. 89. FPR. 317. The hexameter in SCHOL. JUV. 8, 16 (*Bibaculus: Osce senex Catinaeque puer, Cumana meretrix*) may have belonged to an epigram. Mention of Valerius Cato (§ 200, 1) and Orbilius (below n. 5 and 6; § 200, 3). RIBBECK, append. Verg. p. 7 takes him to be the author of Verg. catal. 5.—PLIN. NH. praef. 24 speaking of the choice of titles of books says: *nostri . . . facetissimi lucubrationum* (*inscripserunt*), *puto quia Bibaculus erat et vocabatur:* according to this the title was facetiously chosen. Hence in all probability MACROB. sat. 2, 1, 13, *is iocus* (of Cicero a. 695/59) . . . *mihi ex libro Furii Bibaculi notus est* (§ 179, 27, 1). To this work should be referred the notice *Messala Corvinus in quadam epistola . . . non esse sibi dicit rem cum Furio Bibaculo, ne cum Ticida quidem aut litteratore Catone* (SUET. gramm. 4). BÄHRENS, commentar. Cat. p. 13.

5. On HOR. s. 2, 5, 40 (a. 724/30) *seu pingui tentus omaso* (cf. Gl. Philox. *omasum . . . τῇ τῶν Γάλλων γλώττῃ*) *Furius hibernas cana nive conspuet Alpes* PORPH. remarks: *hic versus Furi Bibaculi est. ille enim, cum vellet Alpes nivibus plenas describere, ait*

'*Juppiter hibernas cana nive conspuit Alpes*' (this line is quoted by Quint. 8, 6, 17 as an instance of a *dura translatio*). Acro ad loc. more circumstantially: *Furius Bibaculus in pragmatia belli gallici* '*Juppiter* etc.' From this epos are probably derived the hexameters (11) quoted in Macrob. 6, 1, 31–34. 44. 6, 3, 5. 6, 4, 10 (FPR. 318) as Vergil's models: among which are 6 on martial subjects. Macrobius quotes them from *Furius in I* (and *IV*) *annali;* and *Furius in sexto, decimo, undecimo.* Further Schol. Vers. Aen. 9, 379 ⟨a lacuna⟩ *in annalibus belli gallici* (an hexameter follows). It is improbable that these clever verses should have been written by the antiquated Furius of Antium (§ 150, 1). E. Bährens, comment. Catull. 21.—To Furius Bibaculus has also been referred with some probability Hor. s. 1, 10, 36 *turgidus Alpinus ingulat dum Memnona, dumque diffingit Rheni luteum caput;* on which Acro: *Bibaculum quendam poetam Gallum tangit*, who, according to this, besides the bellum gallicum denoted by *Rheni luteum caput* must also have composed an Aethiopis, or must at least have inserted in the bell. gall. a pompous comparison relating to the death of Memnon; Porphyrio ad loc. used to read as follows: [*Cornelius Alpinus Memnona*] *hexametris versibus nimirum describit:* but the words in brackets are not found in the best copies.—As regards the attribution of the bellum gallicum to Bibaculus, there is an obstacle in the fact that in his iambics he attacked Caesar (n. 4: or perhaps Bibaculus attacked Augustus only, and not Caesar), while in the epos he is supposed to have eulogised him; in the iambics he is terse and caustic, while in the epos he appears turgid and insipid: but this obstacle will not appear insuperable to anyone who reflects on the frequent alternations of political sympathy and antipathy in stirring times, and does not forget the exigencies of the different styles (*e.g.* terseness for epigrams, exuberance and elevation of style for epic poetry).

6. Bibaculus lived at least until 730/24, for he alludes to Orbilius' (born 640/114, § 200/3) senile weakness of memory (*vixit prope ad centesimum aetatis annum amissa iam pridem memoria, ut versus Bibaculi docet: 'Orbilius ubinam est, litterarum oblivio?'* Suet. gr. 9. He also outlived Valerius Cato's (§ 200, 3) *summa senectus* (Suet. l.l.). According to Hieronymus (n. 4) Bibaculus was born 651/103, he would therefore himself have been an octogenarian, when he thus expressed himself concerning the infirmity of the old Orbilius: this is hardly credible. Moreover the lines on Cato (§ 200, 1) prove that the writer is a considerably younger man. Besides, his epigrams are in tone, versification, and Republican attitude near akin to those of Catullus, Calvus and their associates, and his references to Cato (*mei . . . Catonis*, Suet. l.l.) indicate that he belonged to that circle. Hence Nipperdey's conjecture (op. 500) is plausible, that the date assigned for his birth by Hieronymus is wrong, and that Bibaculus was about 20 years younger.—AWeichert, de M. Furio Bibaculo, in his rell. poett. Rom. 331. Nipperdey, op. 498. Ribbeck, röm. Dicht. 1, 343. AWissowa, die der Dichter Furius betr. Stelle in Hor. s. 2, 5, Bresl. 1867. GCamozzi, riv. di filol. 16, 161.

THE SECOND HALF OF THE CICERONIAN PERIOD,

COMPRISING THE YEARS 691/63–711/43.

193. In the course of these years, during which the political storm spent itself in the Civil war, Caesar became very prominent. But within this period we may again notice two distinct generations. The elder generation produced the historians Caesar, Cornelius Nepos, Caesar's continuator Hirtius, and Oppius; the scholars and professors Valerius Cato and Orbilius; the Stoic Cato; the orators Calidius and Memmius; lastly the poet Lucretius.

194. C. Julius C. f. C. n. Caesar was born on July 13, 654/100. As he was related to Marius, his life was in danger when Sulla was victorious; a. 674/80 sqq. he served in Asia, and commenced his oratorical and political career with charges of extortions against members of the nobility; he then continued his studies at Rhodes a. 679/75, became quaestor (687/67) in Hispania ulterior, aedile 689/65, pontifex maximus 691/63, was praetor 692/62, propraetor in Hispania ulterior 693/61 sq., consul 695/59, having previously concluded a. 694/60 the first triumvirate with Pompey and Crassus, and having throughout followed the plan of presenting himself as the man of the people. In the years 696/58–704/50 Caesar was proconsul in Gaul, which country he subjugated and re-organised, while at the same time he greatly increased his own resources and formed an army, highly trained and faithful to himself. By means of this army he gained absolute power in the years 705/49–708/46 (cos. II 706/48, III 708/46), a fact openly acknowledged by his being consul sine collega (IV 709/45, V 710/44) and dictator reip. constituendae. In 710/44, March 15, he succumbed to the blows of his murderers.

1. Sources for the life of Caesar are: his commentarii, SUETONIUS' divus Iulius, PLUTARCH's βίος Καίσαρος, APPIAN's Ἐμφύλια. On the sources of the two last see HPETER, Quellen Plutarchs (1865) 119. GTHOURET, Leipz. Stud. 1, 324.—DRUMANN, GR. 3, 129. PVLIMBURG-BROUWER, Caesar en zijne tijdgenooten, Gröningen 1844–46 III. MOMMSEN, RG. vol. 3. KÖCHLY and RÜSTOW, Einl. zu Caes. üb. d. gall. Krieg (1857) p. 9 (until a. 703/51). (NAPOLÉON III), histoire de Jules César, Paris 1865. 66 (with an atlas) II (continued by STOFFEL, see § 196, 10). JAFROUDE, Caesar, a sketch, Lond.[2] 1886. ATROLLOPE, Introd. to the Commentaries of Caesar, Lond. 1870.—On the portraits of Caesar JJBERNOULLI, röm. Ikonogr. 1, 145 (who likewise 2, VI pronounces the expressive basalt bust in Berlin to be undoubtedly modern).

195. Caesar possessed the most varied talents: a great politician and a great general, his clear mind and the iron energy of his will qualified him to be the ruler of an age not able to rule itself. This task he conceived at an early time and pursued it with the whole power of his intellect, with cunning and boldness, with quiet perseverance and farsighted calculation. But the very qualities which made him the ruler of Rome were not likely to make him a brilliant writer. Handling his language, as he did, with complete mastery both in speaking and writing, he still used it only as a means of attaining definite political aims, and both his subjects and his style were controlled by those aims and by the unimaginative cast of his mind. For this reason, he himself thought little of his own oratory, though in his time he was surpassed only by Cicero, being distinguished for precision, good taste and vivacity of style and delivery; if possible, he thought even less of his verses, though his metrical compositions were not confined to his youth. His precise thinking is attested by his treatises on grammatical correctness, while his jovial disposition appears from his collection of witticisms; political ends were served by the pamphlets against Cato, who had been set up as the martyr of the Republic, as well as by Caesar's most important literary achievement, the commentarii. His astronomical work (de astris) probably arose from his rectification of the calendar.

1. On Caesar as an orator see Cic. Brut. 252 *de Caesare . . . ita iudico, . . . illum omnium fere oratorum latine loqui elegantissime* (see below n. 4), *nec id solum domestica consuetudine . . . sed . . . multis litteris, et eis quidem reconditis et exquisitis, summoque studio et diligentia est consecutus.* 261 *splendidam quandam minumeque veteratoriam rationem dicendi tenet, voce, motu, forma etiam magnifica et generosa quodammodo.* Fronto ep. p. 123 *Caesari facultatem dicendi video imperatoriam fuisse.* Quint. 10, 1, 114 *C. Caesar si foro tantum vacasset, non alius ex nostris contra Ciceronem nominaretur. tanta in eo vis est, id acumen, ea concitatio ut illum eodem animo dixisse quo bellavit appareat; exornat tamen haec omnia mira sermonis, cuius proprie studiosus fuit, elegantia.* Tac. A. 13, 3 *dictator Caesar summis oratoribus aemulus.* Suet. Iul. 55 *post accusationem Dolabellae* (a. 677/77; there is an error in the MSS. of Tac. dial. 34) *haud dubie principibus patronis annumeratus est.* See also Quint. 12, 10, 11 (§ 44, 12). Vellei. 2, 36. Tac. dial. 21 (n. 2). Apulei. apol. 95. Plut. Caes. 3. On Caesar's style Hirtius, b. g. 8, praef. 7, says: *erat in Caesare facultas atque elegantia summa scribendi.*

2. Caesar's speeches. Cic. Brut. 262 *orationes eius mihi vehementer probantur, compluris autem legi.* Tac. dial. 21 makes his eulogist of the new (Imperial) oratory say: *concedamus C. Caesari ut propter magnitudinem cogitationum et occupationes rerum minus in eloquentia effecerit quam divinum eius ingenium postulabat, . . . nisi forte quisquam Caesaris pro Decio Samnite . . . ceterosque eiusdem lentitudinis*

ac teporis libros legit. Gell. 4, 16, 8 *C. Caesar, gravis auctor linguae latinae, . . . in Dolabellam actionis I lib. I* (the MSS. are here corrupt). 5, 13, 6 *in oratione quam pro Bithynis* (CNipperdey, op. 327. 449) *dixit hoc principio usus est* (cf. Iul. Rufin. 8, p. 40, 24 Halm). 13, 3, 5 *repperi in oratione C. Caesaris qua Plautiam rogationem suasit* (a. 684/70?). Cf. Non. 354. Schol. Bob. 297 *Caesaris orationes contra hos* (Memmius and Domitius, a. 696/58) *extant, quibus et sua acta defendit et illos insectatur.* ib. 317 *ibi* (in the Senate) *habitae sunt tres illae orationes contra Domitium et Memmium.* Suet. Iul. 64 *in amitae laudatione* (a. 686/68) . . . *sic refert.* 55 *orationes aliquas reliquit, inter quas temere quaedam feruntur*, e.g. that *pro Metello* (§ 44, 8) and *apud milites in Hispania.* The fragments of C.'s speeches and the authorities concerning them are collected in Meyer's oratt. rom.² p. 408, in Nipperdey's Caes. (of 1847) 749 and in Dinter's ed. 3, 118.

3. Caesar's poems. Tac. dial. 21 *nisi qui et carmina eorundem* (of Caesar and M. Brutus) *miratur. fecerunt enim et carmina et in bibliothecas rettulerunt, non melius quam Cicero, sed felicius, quia istos fecisse pauciores sciunt.* Suet. Iul. 56 *feruntur et a puero et ab adulescentulo quaedam scripta, ut 'Laudes Herculis,' tragoedia Oedipus, item 'Dicta collectanea.' quos omnes libellos vetuit Augustus publicari.* ib. *reliquit et . . . poema quod inscribitur 'Iter,' (quod fecit) . . . dum ab urbe in Hispaniam ulteriorem quarto et vicensimo die pervenit* (a. 708/46). Of his poetical works there are extant only six hexameters, from a literary criticism on Latin comedy, where he treats pertinently of Terence (Suet. v. Ter. p. 34, 7 Rff.). Plin. ep. 5, 3, 5 (§ 31, 1) justifies the inference that Caesar also wrote erotic poems (epigrams?). Cf. besides Plut. Caes. 2 ποιήματα γράφων.—The poem on a vegetable (!) formerly attributed to Caesar on the strength of Plin. NH. 19, 144 is disposed of by the correct reading of the passage: *olus quoque silvestre triumpho divi Iuli carminibus praecipue iocisque militaribus celebratum, alternis quippe versibus exprobravere lapsana* (λαψάνῃ) *se vixisse apud Durrachium, praemiorum parsimoniam cavillantes. est autem id cyma silvestris.*

4. Sueton. Iul. 56 *reliquit et de analogia duos libros, . . . (quos) in transitu Alpium, cum ex citeriore Gallia conventibus peractis ad exercitum rediret, . . . fecit* (in the winter of 701/53 sq.?). Fronto p. 221 . . . *C. Caesarem . . . duos de analogia libros scrupulosissimos scripsisse, . . . de nominibus declinandis, de verborum aspirationibus et rationibus.* Cic. Brut. 253 *qui etiam in maxumis occupationibus ad te* (Cic.) . . . *de ratione latine loquendi accuratissime scripserit.* Gell. 19, 8, 3 *C. Caesar, . . . vir ingenii praecellentis, sermonis praeter alios suae aetatis castissimi, in libris quos ad M. Ciceronem de analogia conscripsit.* Suid. s. v. Γάιος Ιούλ. Καίσ. refers to the work as τέχνη γραμματική. We have evidence how here too Caesar showed himself to be practical and undisturbed by scholastic pedantry in the rule which Gell. 1, 10, 4 quotes from the first book *habe semper in memoria et in pectore ut tamquam scopulum sic fugias inauditum atque insolens verbum.* The fragments in Nipperdey's Caes. (1847) p. 753, in Dinter's ed. 3, 125. FSchlitte, de C. Iulio Caesare grammatico, Halle 1865 (the fragments p. 13). ChrHauser, Caes. bell. gall. et bell. civ. cum praeceptis grammaticis ab eodem scriptore in libris de anal. traditis comparatio, Villach 1883. Cf. Köchly(-Rüstow), Einl. zu Caes. b. g. p. 90.

5. Cic. fam. 9, 16, 4 (a. 708/46) *audio Caesarem, cum volumina iam confecerit ἀποφθεγμάτων, si quod afferatur ad eum pro meo quod meum non sit reicere solere.* Suet. Iul. 56 (above n. 3) mentions *dicta collectanea.*

6. Astronomy. Macr. 1, 16, 39 *Iulius Caesar siderum motus, de quibus non indoctos libros reliquit, ab aegyptiis disciplinis hausit.* Plin. NH. in the ind auct. to b. 18 among the Latin authors: *ex . . . L. Tarutio, qui graece de astris scripsit,*

Caesare dictatore, qui item. He actually mentions him repeatedly in b. 18, and he is also referred to by Ptolemy and Lydus. To the same work (or to a portion of it?) refer Schol. Lucan. Phars. 10, 185 *quia suus* (Caesaris) *liber quem composuit de computatione non inferior libro Eudoxi sit;* cf. ib. 187 *est autem liber fastorum divi Iulii Caesaris qui ordinationem continet secundum auctoritatem Chaldaeorum, quem in senatu recitavit.* Nipperdey's ed. 757. Dinter 3, 130. Pliny's words leave it doubtful whether the work was in Greek or Latin, and Suetonius' silence on this work would also seem to lead to the conclusion that it was not really written by Caesar himself, but merely compiled at his order and from his suggestions, and published (under his name?) by some one else, perhaps a Greek. Cf. Mommsen, röm. Chron.[2] 78. 66. 295. EHuschke, röm. Jahr 116.

7. Suet. Iul. 56 *reliquit et de analogia duos libros et Anticatones totidem . . . (quos) sub tempus Mundensis proelii* (17 March 709/45) *fecit.* Juv. 6, 338 *duo Caesaris Anticatones.* This treatise was an answer to Cicero's panegyric on Cato (§ 180, 5), combined with much flattery of Cicero (Plut. Caes, 3. Cic. 39. Plin. NH. 7, 117), and bitter animosity against Cato, who, in order to deprive the Republican party of their hero, was ridiculed and maligned (Plut. Caes. 54. Cato min. 36. 52. 54. Plin. ep. 3, 12). Cicero expressed himself to Caesar on this work very favourably (Att. 13, 50, 1. 13, 51, 1), though he changed after Caesar's death (top. 94). WSieglin, phil. Wschr. 1883, 1455. Cf. HWartmann, Leben des Cato (1858) 161. Roulez, rev. de l'instr. publ. en Belge 19, 2 (on a MS. of the Anticatones said to have been extant in Liège in the 16th cent.).

8. Caesar's correspondence was of course very extensive, and there were indeed several collections of his letters made and published after his death, many of them in cypher (the key is given by Sueton. Iul. 56; cf. Gell. 17, 9, 3). Suet. l.l. *epistulae quoque eius ad senatum exstant. . . . exstant et ad Ciceronem, item ad familiares domesticis de rebus* etc. Gell. 17, 9, 1 *libri sunt epistularum C. Caesaris ad C. Oppium et Balbum Cornelium, qui rebus eius absentis curabant.* The various references to Caesar's correspondence with these and others in Nipperdey's Caes. (1847), 766, in Dinter 3, 137. Letters of Caesar to Cicero and others in Cic. Att. 9, 6 A. 7 C. 13 A. 16. 10, 8 B.

9. Linguistic: Caesarlexika by HMeusel, Berl. 1884 sqq. (the best); RMenge and SPreuss, Lpz. 1885 sqq. only for the genuine works; also SPreuss, vollst. Lexikon zu d. pseudo-caesar. Schr. [b. g. 8, b. alex.; b. afr. u. hisp.], Eisenach 1884); HMerguet, Jena 1886.—OEichert, Wörterbuch zu Caes., Hann.[9] 1887.—ChrHauser: § 195, 4 ad fin. WDittenberger, Herm. 3, 375 (esse with partic. fut. act.). FHThFischer, die Rectionslehre bei C., Halle 1853. 54. ALehmann, de verborum compositt. ap. Caes. Sall. Tac. cum dativo structura, Breslau 1863. A Bergaigne, la place de l'adjectif épithète dans etc., Mél. Graux 536. DRohde, adiectivum quo ordine ap. Caes. et in Cic. oratt. coniunctum sit cum substantivo, Hamb. 1884. CKossak, de ablat. abs. usu ap. Caes., Gumbinnen 1858. Reinhardt, d. tempp. u. modi bei Caes., Heilbr. 1859. AHug, d. consec. tempp. des praes. hist. zunächst bei Caes., JJ. 81, 877. 125, 281; RhM. 40, 397. FWania, d. praes. hist. in Caes. b. g., Vienna 1885. GIhm: § 333, 16. PUhdolph, d. Tempp. in konjunktiv. Nebensätzen der or. obl. b. Caes., Leobschütz 1885. JPriem: § 177, 3 l. 19. R Schwenke, Gerundium und Gerundivum b. Caes. u. Nep., Frankenb. i/Schl. 1882. CGörlitz, Gerund. u. Supin. bei Caes., Rogasen 1887. AProcksch, Gebr. d. Nebensätze bei C. I, Bautzen 1870; d. consec. tempp. b. C., Eisenb. 1874. AThOséen, de voce quod ap. Caes. I, Lund 1878. DRinge, z. Sprachgebr. des Caes. (et que atque ac), Gött. 1880. Ilg on antequam und priusquam in Caes., Württ. Korr.-Bl. 33, 460. FKnoke, hic and nunc in the or. obl. (in Caes.), Bernb. 1881. RMenge,

JJ. 137, 67. KLorenz, Anaphora u. Chiasmus in Caes. b. g., Creuzb. 1876. Kitt, obss. gramm. in Caes., Braunsb. 1875. HHartz, Beitr. z. Sprachgebr. d. Caes., Frankf. a. O. 1875. FFröhlich, Realistisches u. Sprachliches zu Caes., in the Festschr. z. Zürich. Phil.-Vers. 1887. (Alleged) differences of languages between b. g. VII and b. g. I–VI: GIhm, Berl. ph. Wschr. 1886, 1010. Cf. § 196, 11 ad fin.

196. Of Caesar's literary works only his Memoirs (commentarii) are preserved. These contain the history of the first seven years of the Gallic war in seven books, and the history of the Civil war down to the Alexandrine war in three books, and lie midway between a mere collection of materials, or the rapid and sketchy remarks of a diary, and a carefully elaborated historical work. But artless and unpretentious as the form is, it is equally attractive in its brevity, perspicuity and definiteness; while the substance, which is manifestly the direct product of the events, is most carefully weighed and meditated. Without any flagrant violation of truth, the author knows thoroughly how to interpret the facts in his favour or, if more convenient, to pass them over in silence; without ever boasting or sacrificing the semblance of an objective 'historia,' he perfectly succeeds in displaying his personal merits to the greatest possible advantage, in justifying his actions and clearing his motives. The books on the Gallic war were published on its termination, a. 703/51; those on the Civil war do not seem to have been finished.

1. Suet. Iul. 56 *reliquit et rerum suarum commentarios gallici civilisque belli pompeiani.* Cic. Brut. 262 *etiam commentarios quosdam scripsit rerum suarum valde quidem probandos, nudi enim sunt, recti et venusti, omni ornatu orationis tamquam veste detracta: sed dum voluit alios habere parata unde sumerent qui vellent scribere historiam, ineptis gratum fortasse fecit qui volent illa calamistris inurere: sanos quidem homines a scribendo deterruit: nihil enim est in historia pura et illustri brevitate dulcius.* Hirtius b. g. 8, praef. *Caesaris nostri commentarios rerum gestarum Galliae . . . contexui* etc. *constat inter omnes nihil tam operose ab aliis esse perfectum quod non horum elegantia commentariorum superetur. qui sunt editi ne scientia tantarum rerum scriptoribus desit adeoque probantur omnium iudicio ut praerepta, non praebita facultas scriptoribus videatur. . . . ceteri quam bene atque emendate, nos etiam quam facile atque celeriter eos perfecerit scimus.* Sueton. Iul. 56 *Pollio Asinius parum diligenter parumque integra veritate compositos putat, cum Caesar pleraque et quae per alios erant gesta temere crediderit et quae per se vel consulto vel etiam memoria lapsus perperam ediderit, existimatque rescripturum et correcturum fuisse* (§ 221, 6). The latter can only apply to the bell. civ.; see Köchly-Rüstow, Einl. z. gall. Krieg 93. Various misrepresentations of facts are pointed out e.g. by Drumann, GR. 3, 756. Cassius Dio is entirely at one with Caesar in his account of the conquest of Gaul; HHaupt, Phil. 41, 152. DGJelgersma, de fide et auctorit. Cassii Dionis, Leid. 1879. Strabo 4, p. 177 calls the work ὑπομνήματα, Plut. Caes. 22 (and Symmach. ep. 4, 18 and Arator ep. ad Parthen. 39) ἐφημερίδες (cf. Appian. Celt. 18 ἐν ταῖς ἰδίαις—for which Wölflinn, phil. Anz. 5, 181, reads ἐφημέριος—

ἀναγραφαῖς τῶν ἰδίων ἔργων), Suid. (s.v. *Γάιος Ἰούλιος Καῖσαρ*) *περὶ τοῦ ἰδίου βίου*.—By a strange mistake the commentarii were already at an early period attributed to Suetonius; e.g. by Orosius 6, 7 *hanc historiam Suetonius Tranquillus plenissime explicuit, cuius nos competentes portiunculas decerpsimus* (here follows an extract from Caesar), and Apoll. Sid. ep. 9, 14 (§ 349, 1) certainly includes the commentarii under the *opera Suetonii:* at the same place on account of the preface being addressed to Balbus by Hirtius, Ap. Sid. designates bell. gall. b. 8 as *Balbi ephemeris!* In several early MSS. of the commentarii they appear under the name of Suetonius. Cf. Roth's Suet. p. ci. The error probably arose from the title being taken to refer not to the wars described by Caesar, but to those conducted by him, so that Suetonius, as Caesar's biographer, was supposed to be the chronicler of his deeds.

2. The manuscripts of the commentarii are divided into two classes, the one (α), which is on the whole preferable, contains only the eight books de bello gallico, the other (β), which likewise possesses a high independent value, gives all the books with the continuations. To the first (the 'integri' or 'lacunosi') belong esp. Paris. 5763 (Floriacensis) s. IX/X (Chatelain t. 46; from this MS. are copied the Leid. Voss. Q. 53 s. XI, Chatel. t. 50, 1) and its duplicate Vatic. 3864 s. XI, Bongars. I in Amsterdam s. IX/X, Paris. 5056 (Moysiacensis) s. XI (Chatel. t. 47) and others; to the second (the so-called 'interpolati') belong the Paris. 5764 (Thuaneus) s. XI/XII (Chatel. t. 48; MGitlbauer, phil. Streifzüge, Freib. 1886, 460), Vatic. 3324 (Ursinianus) s. XII, Vindob. 95 s. XIII (Chatel. t. 50, 2) and others. The division into two classes was made at an early time: Orosius made use of MSS. of the second class for his abstract of the b. g. (n. 1). RSchneider, ZfGW. 39, Jahresber. 154. The worthless scholia in Caes. et Sall. (ed. EHedicke, Quedlinb. 1879) from a cod. Paris. s. IX usually follow class β. On the cod. Ashburnham. (now in Florence) s. X (it belongs to the first class, but is complete, and it counts the bella from b. 1–13, giving to the b. c. only 2 instead of 3 books), see ThStangl, Phil. 45, 213. The close of bell. gall. VIII and of b. hispan. is not extant in any MS.; bell. civ. has many lacunae. On the MSS. of both classes see Nipperdey's ed. 1847, p. 37. HJHeller, Phil. 17, 492. 19, 466. 31, 316; Phil. Suppl. 5, 388. AFrigell and AHolder introd. to their edd. DDetlefsen, Phil. 17, 649. WDittenberger, Gött. gel. Anz. 1870, 14. BDinter, quaestt. Caesar., Grimma 1876 (cap. I de codd. Caes.). HWalther, de Caess. codd. interpolatis, Grünb. 1885. RSchneider and HMeusel, ZfGW. 39, Jahresber. 151. 173. ibid. 40, Jahresber. 262.—In MS. subscriptiones (e.g. in the Floriac., Ashburnham. and many others are minutes concerning the production of critical editions of the bell. gall. (cf. p. 59, l. 5 from the end): *Iulius Celsus Constantinus v. c. legi* and *Flavius Licerius Lupicinus legi* (Sirmond, notae ad Ennod. p. 78, rightly takes the latter to be the son of Euprepia, the sister of Ennodius (§ 479); cf. Ennod. ep. 2, 15. 23. 3, 28. 6, 26. dict. 8 p. 488).

3. Editions of the commentarii with the continuations by ILipsius, Antv. 1585, IIScaliger, Leid. 1606. GJungermann, c. nott. varr., Frankf. 1604. JGoduinus, Par. 1678 (with ind. verbb.). Ex rec. IDavisii, Cantabr. 1706. 1727. C. nott. var. ed. IGGraevius, Leid. 1713 II. Likewise cura FOudendorpii, Leid. 1737 (and Stuttg. 1822 II).—Rec., optt. codd. auct. ann., quaestt. criticas praemisit CNipperdey, Lps. 1847. Annot. crit. instruxit FDübner, Par. 1867 II.—Texts by C Nipperdey (Lps.[4] 1881), EHoffmann (Vienna [2] 1888), FKraner (Lps. 1861), FDübner (Par. 1866), JKWhitte, Copenh.[3] 1877. BDinter (Lps. 1864–76 III [I [2] 1884] with the fragments) and others.

4. German translations e.g. by ABaumstark (Stuttg.. Metzler), and (the Gall. war) by HKöchly and WRüstow (Berl.[6] 1886).—On a Greek translation (published by GJungermann, Frankf. 1606, by ABaumstark, Freib. i. B. 1834), which was

formerly considered to be of critical value, but which was only made from R STEPHANUS' ed. Par. 1544, see HJHELLER, Phil. 12, 107.

5. NAPOLÉON (I), précis des guerres de César, Par. 1835. WRÜSTOW, Heerwesen u. Kriegführung Caesars, Gotha 1855; Nordhausen 1862. MJÄHNS, Caes. Commentarien in ihrer lit. und kriegswissenschaftlichen Folgewirkung, Militär-Wochenbl. 1883, Beiheft 7, 343 sqq.—On the credibility of Caesar's Comm. BRESEMER (Berl. 1835), FWINKELMANN (Jahn's Archiv 2, 533), FEYSSENHARDT (JJ. 85, 755), FSECK (de . . . fide, Essen 1860. 64 II). HRAUCHENSTEIN (n. 9), PETSCH, d. hist. Glaubwürdigk. v. Caesars b. gall., Glückst. 1885. 86 II and others. Cf. n. 8. —Criticism: BDINTER, Phil. 34, 710; quaestt. Caes., Grimma 1876. OSCHAMBACH, Mühlhaus. 1877. MADVIG, advers. 2, 246. FHARTZ, coniectan. Caes., Altona 1886 and many others. Cf. n. 11.

6. On the date of publication of the books of the Gallic war see CESCHNEIDER in Wachler's Philomathie 1, 184 (they were composed in the winter of 702/52 sq. and published probably in the spring of 703). Cf. GMEZGER, üb. d. Abfassungszeit v. Caes. bell. gall., Landau 1875. FKEBEC, quo tempore scripserit Caes. librr. de b. gall., Odessa 1881. This vindication was intended to calm imminent tempests and impress the popular mind with an idea of Caesar's fitness for great emergencies. As Caesar had carried on his expeditions without special command of the Senate, he constantly endeavours to represent them as necessary measures of defence. His memoirs embrace only the events of war, which he relates as a Roman would do to Romans, without sentimentality and without disguising the cruelty and perfidiousness employed against tribes defending their rights and independence. We perceive a certain pride on the part of the writer in describing the exploits of his faithful partisans. He carefully abstains from injuring the popular tendency of his work by going too much into military details. A critical epitome of the contents in KÖCHLY and RÜSTOW, Einl. z. gall. Krieg 51. PETERSDORFF, Caesar num in bello gallico enarrando non nulla e fontibus transscripserit, Belgard 1879. Cf. KVENEDIGER, JJ. 119. 786, also HSCHILLER, BlfbayrGW. 16, 389.

7. Editions of the bellum gallicum: CECSCHNEIDER (rec. et ill., Halle 1840–55 II; only b. I–VII), AFRIGELL (rec., codd. contulit, comm. instr., Upsala 1861 III), recens. AHOLDER (with an ind. verb. to b. I–VII), Freib. i. B. 1882.—MSEYFFERT, Halle[3] 1879. FKRANER and WDITTENBERGER, Berl.[14] 1886. HRHEINHARD, Stuttg.[5] 1886. ADOBERENZ and BDINTER, Lpz.[8] 1886. JKWHITTE, Havniae[4] 1886. MGITLBAUER, Freib. 1884. RMENGE, Gotha 1883 (in addition quaestt. Caes., Eisenach 1883). JPRAMMER, Prague[2] 1888. HWALTHER, Paderb.[2] 1887. GLONG, Lond.[2] 1868. CE MOBERLEY, Oxf. 1871. AKISBISTER, Lond. 1866. AGPESKETT, Camb. 1878. Bks. 1–3 JHMERRYWEATHER and CCTANCOCK, Lond. 1879. LSCHMITZ, Lond. 1878. Bk. 7 (illustrated) WCOCKWORTHYCOMPTON, Lond. 1889. ALLEN and JUDSON, Boston, 1889 (illustrated).

8. Explanatory works. APLATEN, de fide et auctoritate Caes. b. gall., Leignitz 1854. HKÖCHLY and WRÜSTOW, Einl. z. Caes. gall. Krieg, Gotha 1857. BMÜLLER, zu Caes. b. g., Kaiserslaut. 1877. WPAUL, ZfGW. 32, 161. 35, 275; Berl. phil. Wschr. 4, 1209. 1241. 1273. JCLAURER, Schwabach 1883–86 III; BlfbayrGW. 21, 19. 508. HBAUMANN, Vienna 1885. BHORNER, Wiener-Neustadt 1878. 1879 II.—CWGLÜCK, die keltischen Namen bei Caes., Munich 1857. HJHELLER, de nominibus celticis in Caes., Phil. 17, 270.—Geographie des transalpinischen Gallien von IvHEFNER (Munich 1836). AvGÖLER, Caesars gall. Krieg u. Teile s. Bürgerkriegs, Freib.[2] 1880 II. AvCOHAUSEN, Caes. gg. d. Germanen am Rhein, Jahrbb. der rheinl. Altert. Fr. 43, 1. WRÜSTOW, Atlas zu Caes. gall. Kr. Stuttg. 1868.

CFMeyer and AKoch, Atl. zu Caes. b. g., Essen 1879. AvKampen, descriptiones nobiliss. ap. class. locorum ser. I: xv ad Caes. b. g. tabb., Gotha 1883. FTVine, Caesar in Kent, Lond. 1886. HPJudson, Caesar's army (illustrated), Boston, 1888.

9. Since Napoleon III (§ 194, 1) devoted his studies to this subject, France has made innumerable geographical and military contributions to it. Enumeration and criticism of the works in question by HJHeller, Phil. 19, 465. 22, 99. 285. 26, 652. 31, 314. 511. KThomann, der Französ. Atlas zu Caes. b. g. (see § 194, 1, l. 7), Zür. 1868-74 III.—EDesjardins, géogr. de la Gaule Romaine, Par. 1876–78 II. JMaissiat, Cés. en Gaule, Par. 1865–81 III. JSchlumberger, Caesar u. Ariovist, Colmar 1877. CvKampen, die Helvetierschlacht bei Bibracte, Gotha 1878. H Rauchenstein, d. Feldz. Caes.s gg. die Helvetier m. Abh. üb. d. Glaubwürdigk. v. Caes. b. gall., Jena 1882. KvVeith in d. Mon. Schr. f. d. Gesch. West-Deutschl. vol. 4. 5. 6 and others. ThBergk, z. Gesch. u. Topogr. d. Rheinlande, Lpz. 1882, 1. 25.

10. The three books of the bellum civile are unmistakably weaker, they are less carefully elaborated and contain many undoubted traces of negligence and inaccuracy. Moreover the text, for which one class of MSS. (§ 196, 2) is wanting, is in a most deplorable condition. On this subject see FHofmann, de origine b. c. Caesariani, Berl. 1857, and ThMommsen, die Rechtsfrage zw. Caes. u. dem Senat, Abh. d. Bresl. hist.-philol. Ges. 1 (1857), 1. AvGöler, see n. 8. RSchneider, Ilerda, Berl. 1886.

Stoffel, hist. de Jul. César, Guerre civile; continuation of the work of Napoleon III (§ 194, 1) (with Atl.), Par. 1888 II. JvHefner, Geographie zu Caesars b. c., Munich 1836. LHeuzey, opérations militaires de Cés. étudiées sur le terrain par la mission de Macédoine, Par. 1886.—HGlöde, die Glaubwürdigk. C.s im b. c., Kiel 1871. Cf. n. 8. Strenge, d. tendenziöse Charakter v. Caes. b. c., Lüneb. 1873. 75 II. OBasiner, de b. c. Caes., Dorp. 1883.

11. Editions of the b. c., with notes etc. by JCHeld (Sulzbach[4] 1857), ADoberenz and BDinter, Lpz.[5] 1884. FKraner and FHofmann, Berl.[9] 1885. CEMoberley, Oxf. 1873.—Criticism: JNGForchhammer, de vera . . . emendandi ratione (Havn. 1852), HHartz (Züllichau 1864), LVielhaber (Vienna 1864), WH Roscher, JJ. 115, 559, KSchnelle, ib. 562, EHerzog, JJ. 117, 621 and others.

Recent controversy as to Caesar's authorship: (HMosner) num Caesar b. c. scripserit, Culmbach (1865). Heidtmann, Essen 1867. RWutke, quaest. Caesarianae, Neisse[2] 1885. RMenge, de auctoribus comm. de b. c. (2, 1–16) qui Caesaris nomine feruntur, Weim. 1873 (2, 1–4. 8–16 are said to be by Trebonius, see § 210, 9). Cf. HHartz, phil. Anz. 6, 202; AEussner, Blfbayr GW. 10, 205; JB. 1881 2, 230. AHug, JB. 1873, 1169. BDinter, quaestt. Caesar, Grimma 1876, 32 attempts to prove Hirtius to be the author of 3, 108–112.—The attempts of Menge (see above), Petersdorff, Venediger (n. 6 ad fin.) and others to prove from variations of idiom, style etc. in the commentarii, that Caesar literally embodied the reports sent to him by the legates, have been unsuccessful. Caesar, when composing this work, of course availed himself, when necessary, of the materials which were to be found in his military bureau, including the despatches of his officers and the reports which he himself had made to the Senate (cf. b. g. 2, 35. 4, 38. 7, 90. Suet. Iul. 56), but in the description of the services of the legates and of their reports the same spirit, language, and style prevail as in the rest of the work.

197. After Caesar's death his nearest friends thought it incumbent upon them to describe also those expeditions which he had not narrated himself, being his last year in Gaul, and the

Alexandrine, African and Spanish wars. It is evident that they are by different writers. The history of the Spanish war betrays an utter want of style, that of the African war being superior to it in that respect; but while the first is awkward and uncouth, the second is written in a distorted and inflated style. The account of the eighth year of the war in Gaul is by A. Hirtius. The narrative of the Alexandrine war also shows an educated writer who endeavours to imitate Caesar's style, but it is doubtful whether Hirtius or perhaps C. Oppius was its author. The bellum Africum and Hispaniense must be by persons who had taken part in the war, though perhaps only in an inferior position, and whom Caesar's friends had asked to write down their reminiscences of it, perhaps that they might some day be used as the basis for a more artistic narrative.

1. SUET. Iul. 56: *Alexandrini Africique et Hispaniensis (belli) incertus auctor est. alii Oppium putant, alii Hirtium, qui etiam Gallici belli novissimum imperfectumque librum suppleverit.* See the praefatio to b. g. VIII expressly ascribed by SUET. l.l. to Hirtius: *coactus adsiduis tuis vocibus, Balbe, . . . rem difficillimam suscepi. Caesaris nostri commentarios rerum gestarum Galliae non cohaerentibus superioribus atque insequentibus eius scriptis contexui* (i.e. 'I have re-established the context by filling up with b. g. VIII the wide gap between b. g. VII and b. c. I'), *novissimumque imperfectum ab rebus gestis Alexandriae confeci usque ad exitum non quidem civilis dissensionis, cuius finem nullum videmus, sed vitae Caesaris . . . mihi ne illud quidem accidit ut Alexandrino atque Africano bello interessem. quae bella . . . ex parte nobis Caesaris sermone sunt nota.* Hence it appears that this continuation was written after Caesar's death, at a time when a war with M. Antony had become probable and it was indeed impossible to foresee any end of the Civil war; it is also clear that it was written by an intimate friend of Caesar, but not by Cornelius Balbus, whence we are left to choose between C. Oppius and A. Hirtius. The latter is mentioned (see above) unequivocally as the author of b. g. VIII by Suetonius, so also the MSS. (*Hirtii incipit liber VIII* and so forth). In the pref. to b.g. VIII Hirtius announces his intention (which is here supposed to have been already carried out) of describing all the wars down to Caesar's death. But as Hirtius was killed on the 27th April 711/43, he was unable to bring his scheme to completion. He only got as far as the close of b. g. VIII (and perhaps of b. alex., cf. however n. 6). After his death Caesar's intimate friends took care that the rest of the wars of Caesar should not remain unchronicled, and in order to make the series outwardly complete they added the bell. (alex.) afr. and b. hisp., which were written at their behest by persons who had taken part in those wars. DRUMANN, GR. 3, 76. CNIPPERDEY, de supplementis commentariorum Caesaris, Berl. 1846 = ed. Caes. 1847, p. 8. KÖCHLY-RÜSTOW, Einl. z. gall. Krieg 105. Cf. PETERSDORFF, ZfGW. 34, 215. HSCHILLER, BlfbayrGW. 16, 246, AEUSSNER, JB. 1883 2, 136.

2. Both Hirtius and Oppius possessed the education necessary for attempting historical composition, but both were too accomplished writers to be the authors of the bell. hisp. and afr. Hirtius was caused by Caesar, a. 709/45, while in Spain, to write an answer to Cicero's panegyric on Cato, in the form of an epistle to Cicero, full of flattery of the latter (CIC. Att. 12, 40, 1. 41, 4. 44, 1. 45, 3. 47, 3). A

short letter from Hirtius to Cicero is found in Cic. Att. 15, 6. The fragments of Hirtius e. g. in Dinter's ed. of Caesar 3, 159.

3. Oppius was also a writer. In particular, he wrote a life of Caesar, quoted by Plut. Pompei. 10 (Ὀππίῳ μὲν, ὅταν περὶ Καίσαρος πολεμίων ἢ φίλων διαλέγηται, σφόδρα δεῖ πιστεύειν μετ' εὐλαβείας) and 17 (on Caesar's personal courage), as well as by Suet. Iul. 53 (*circa victum C. Oppius adeo indifferentem docet ut* etc.). Hence may be derived the quotation in Plin. NH. 11, 104 (*C. Marium . . . Oppius auctor est*) concerning Marius' severity to himself. Cf. Suet. Iul. 53. *C. Oppius . . . librum edidit, non esse Caesaris filium quem Cleopatra dicat.* Oppius appears to have been made use of in the first part of Plutarch's biography of Caesar. GThouret, Leipz. Studien 1, 346. Also Charis. GL. 1, 147, 3 *Oppius de vita Cassii* (*Caesaris* HPeter), *idem de vita prioris Africani* (Gell. 6, 1, 2). It may be supposed that the work named in the first place was directed against the assassin of Caesar, C. Cassius, while the latter contained a comparison between Caesar and Africanus the Elder, which would most likely be in Caesar's favour (Mommsen, röm. Forsch. 2, 502). This Oppius (not the legate mentioned b. afr. 68, 4) was believed by many to have been concerned in the continuation of the Caesarian commentarii; see Suet. Iul. 56 (above n. 1); this could be possible only as regards the bell. alex. (cf. however n. 6); bell. afr. and hisp. show so low a degree of culture that they cannot well be attributed to Oppius (n. 7, 8); and for both works such authorship is precluded by the fact that the writers took part in the wars, whereas Oppius was at that time in Rome (as was the elder Balbus, n. 4).—FRCKrebs, lectt. Diodor., Hadamar 1832 p. 35.

4. L. Cornelius Balbus of Gades (§ 179, 36), to whom Hirtius' letter before b. g. VIII is addressed, seems to have written on Caesar; see Suet. Iul. 81 *cuius rei* (omens of Caesar's death) . . . *auctor est Cornelius Balbus, familiarissimus Caesaris*, an expression which scarcely allows us to think of Balbus minor (§ 209, 4); (HPeter, hist. fragm. p. xxi takes a different view). On Sid. Apoll. 9, 14 (*quis . . . Balbi ephemeridem* [on Caesar] *adaequaverit*) cf. § 196, 1 in fin. Letters from Balbus maior to Cicero of 705/49 ap. Cic. ad Att. 8, 15 A. 9, 7 B. 9, 13 A; one written conjointly with Oppius ib. 9, 7 A. Cf. FFröhlich, n. 7 below, and EWölfflin, phil. Anz. 5 (1873), 180. EJullien, de L. Corn. Balbo maiore, Par. 1886. JHoche, de L. Corn. Balbo p. I., Rossleben 1882.

5. The arrangement of bell. gall. VIII is good, the language of the best period, though the style lacks Caesar's vigour and is rather languid, lifeless and monotonous (Nipperdey 1847, p. 13). This appears especially in the periods (preference for *cum*, connection through the relative etc.) and in the construction. EFischer, B. 8 des b. g. u. das b. alex., Passau 1880 (also HSchiller, phil. Anz. 11, 89).

6. The bellum alexandrinum (incorrectly so called after c. 1–33) shows, when compared with b. VIII de b. g., greater command of style and, perhaps owing to the increased interest of the subject, a more lively colouring, but its peculiarities of diction bear a striking resemblance to b. g. VIII (e.g. the absence of *licet, quamvis, antequam*); but it also shows a distinct difference on many points, so that it is hazardous to attribute it also to Hirtius, as Nipperdey does. The authorship of Hirtius (and of Oppius, who next to him would have the strongest claim, n. 3 ad fin.) is negatived, though not absolutely, by two passages (3, 1, 19, 6) which seem to attest the participation of the author in the Alex. war, whereas Hirtius (and Oppius) did not take part in it (b. g. 8, praef. 8).

7. In the bell. africanum on the other hand, the narrative is more circumstantial and chronological on the surface; the author, politically irresponsible,

manifests clumsily his reverence for Caesar, and parades his hatred of the Pompeians; the diction is careless and sometimes vulgar (e.g. the incorrect use of the plupf.); the writer attempts to be grandiloquent without success, his command of words is limited (e.g. *interim* occurs 68 times), and he employs expressions and constructions (e.g. frequently the *hist. inf.*) foreign to Hirtius (NIPPERDEY p. 15). Cf. n. 2. It is probably the work of some subaltern who took part in the war. FFRÖHLICH, das b. afr. sprachl. u. hist. behandelt, Brugg 1872. AKÖHLER, see n. 8.—ChTISSOT, la campagne de César en Afrique, Mém. de l'acad. des inscr. 31 (1884), 2.

8. The bell. hispaniense also is minute, betraying indeed incapacity to distinguish between essential and useless details; the superficial parts of the narrative are amplified to an intolerable extent; idioms belonging to the popular language are here more numerous, including a false use of the plupf. and of the conjunctive in relation to the indicative, several peculiar usages (*quod* instead of the accus. c. inf., *bene multi* and so forth); even gross blunders are common. There is hardly a trace of period and style. The author's want of education is brought into strong relief by the numerous citations (e.g. from Ennius) which he introduces (NIPPERDEY, p. 24), and by his grandiloquent orations and descriptions of battles. JDEGENHART, de b. Hisp. elocutione et fide, Würzb. 1877. AKÖHLER, de b. afr. et hisp. latinitate, Acta semin. phil. Erl. 1. 367. The corruptions of the text may perhaps be partially due to the hasty composition of the work. NIPPERDEY p. 33.—CECSCHNEIDER, nova bell. hisp. recensio, and de indagando belli hisp. scriptore, Bresl. 1837.—CFLEISCHER, obss. critt. de b. hisp., Meissen 1876. 85 II; JJ. 117, 273. 119, 849 and in the Meissener Festprogr. 1879.

9. L. Aurunculeius Cotta, Caesar's legate in Gaul († 700/54 or 701/53; PRE. 1^2, 2183) wrote according to ATHEN. 6, p. 273 περὶ τῆς Ῥωμαίων πολιτείας σύγγραμμα, ὃ τῇ πατρίῳ ἡμῶν (a Roman is speaking) γέγραπται φωνῇ, which is quoted l.l. in reference to the expedition to Britain (699/55). BÜCHELER, JJ. 111, 136. CIC. Att. 13, 44, 3 (a. 709/45) *scire omnia non acerbum est, vel de Cotta . . . Cottam velim mihi mittas* (to the Tusculanum). *Libonem* (§ 172, 6) *mecum habeo et habueram ante Cascam:* the latter words seem to relate to an otherwise unknown historical work by a certain Casca (perhaps one of the two brothers P. and C. Servilius Casca, PRE. 6, 1120, 46. 47). Cf. § 159, 13.

198. Cornelius Nepos was born in Upper Italy, and was a friend of both Cicero and Atticus and also of his younger countryman Catullus. His life may be said to fall between 655/99 and 730/24. Besides erotic poems, three books of Chronica were his earliest work, but he seems also to have written a geographical treatise. His other writings show that he was influenced by Varro, for they were directed to the history of manners and customs and had a biographical and moral tendency. In this way he wrote five books of Exempla, and the elaborate biographies of Cato the Elder and Cicero, and especially his last and most comprehensive work de viris illustribus, in at least sixteen books, in which the lives of Romans and foreigners were placed in parallel juxtaposition. The parts of it which we possess, the work de excellentibus ducibus exterarum gentium and the biographies

of Cato and of Atticus (being an extract from his work de historicis latinis), are often valuable for their lucidity of arrangement, unpretentious tone, and fair and sympathetic judgments; but they hardly attain even a moderate level of accuracy and trustworthiness as historical essays, and are equally inferior in style, owing to the frequency of popular and colloquial idioms.

1. His praenomen is unknown. According to Auson. op. 23, 9 he was a native of Gaul. Plin. NH. 3, 127: *Nepos, Padi accola.* Plin. ep. 4, 28, 1 to Vibius Severus: *Herennius Severus . . . magni aestimat in bibliotheca sua ponere imagines municipum tuorum, Cornelii Nepotis et T. Catii* (the Insubrian, § 173, 3). As of the four Insubrian towns (Ptol. 3, 1, 33) only one, Ticinum, is on the Po, it is possible that this should be considered to be the birthplace of C. N. (Mommsen, Herm. 3, 62). GFUnger, Abh. d. Münch. Akad. 16, 1, 135 takes a different view.

2. For chronological data Hieronym. ad Pammach. 12 (2, 419 Vall.): *refert . . . Cornelius Nepos se praesente . . . eam pro Cornelio . . . defensionem peroratam* (a. 689/65, see § 180, 1[a]). Plin. NH. 9, 137 *Nepos Cornelius, qui divi Augusti principatu obiit* (cf. 10, 60), *me, inquit, iuvene violacea purpura vigebat . . . nec multo post rubra Tarentina. huic successit dibapha Tyria. . . . hac P. Lentulus Spinther aedilis curulis* (a. 691/63) *primus in praetexta usus improbabatur.* Cf. ib. 36, 59. 2, 169 *Nepos Cornelius auctor est Eudoxum quendam sua aetate, cum Lathyrum regem* (Ptolomaeus VIII Lathyros 637/117–674/80) *fugeret* etc. A. 710/44 he lost a son, who was then *puer* (Cic. Att. 16, 14, 4). From the passages quoted, as well as from the admiration with which he looks up to Atticus (b. 645/109), we may conclude that Nepos was born about 655/99. Corn. Nepos 25, 19, 1 (*quoniam fortuna nos superstites ei esse voluit*) does not (as Unger l.l. 136 supposes) prove him to have been of the same age as Atticus. For some unknown reason Hieron. on Eus. Chron. does not mention him until a. Abr. 1977=714/40: *Cornelius Nepos scriptor historicus clarus habetur.* He survived Catullus (Att. 12, 4) and Atticus († 722/32; Att. 19, 1), but we do not know how long he lived after the publication of his supplement to the life of Atticus (see p. 344, l. 18).—It is a question whether Nepos is mentioned with Atticus (§ 172, 1) as a bookseller in Fronto. See p. 20 Nab. *quorum* (of authors) *libri pretiosiores habentur et summam gloriam retinent, si sunt a Lampadione* (§ 138, 4) *aut Staberio* (§ 159, 10) *aut . . . aut . . . aut Aelio* (§ 148, 2) . . . *aut Attico aut Nepote.*

3. For his relations to Atticus, Cicero and Catullus see Att. 13, 7 *saepe propter familiaritatem domesticis rebus interfuimus.* Atticus living 658/86–689/65 in Athens, their *familiaritas* cannot have commenced before 690/64.—Gell. 15, 28, 1 exaggerates: *Cornelius Nepos . . . M. Ciceronis ut qui maxime amicus familiaris fuit.* For Cicero's correspondence with Nepos see p. 318 l. 3. A fragment in Suet. Iul. 55; from a letter of Nepos to Cic. in Lactant. inst. 3, 15, 10 (see § 50, 3). See also Cic. ad Att. 16, 5, 5. 16, 14, 4. Catullus was perhaps recommended to his compatriot on coming to Rome and was patronised, and even mentioned by him (n. 4) in his Chronica; see Catull. 1, 3.

4. Lost writings, 1) Erotic poems. Plin. ep. 5, 3, 6 *a bonis inter quos vel praecipue numerandus est P. Vergilius, Cornelius Nepos . . . non quidem hi senatores, sed sanctitas morum non distat ordinibus.*—2) Chronica. Catull. 1, 5 *iam tum cum ausus es unus Italorum Omne aevum tribus explicare chartis, Doctis, Iuppiter, et laboriosis.* Gell. 17, 21, 3 *Cornelius Nepos in primo chronico* (cf. 17, 21, 1 *ex libris qui chronici appellantur*). Auson. ep. 16 *apologos Titiani et Nepotis*

chronica, quasi alios apologos (nam et ipsa instar sunt fabularum) . . . misi. That Saturn should have been treated as a human being (MIN. FEL. Oct. 21, 4) points to Euhemerism. The whole work was probably a chronological abridgment such as Atticus and Varro composed, only perhaps giving a fairer proportion of space to non-Roman subjects (e.g. the lives of Greek heroes, such as Alexander the Great, and poets such as Homer and Archilochos). A few fragments from it in CHALM's edition (1871) 119. HPETERS hist. rom. fragm. 218.—According to Catull. l.l. these Chronica do not appear to have been published later than 691/63 (cf. SCHWABE, quaestt. Catull. 296): the words as there given *unus Italorum* suggest that Nepos wrote his abridgment earlier than did Varro and Atticus their similar works, which is certain as far as Atticus is concerned (§ 172, 2, b).—3) Exempla. CHARIS. GL. 1, 146 *Nepos exemplorum II.* GELL. 6, 18, 11 *Cornelius Nepos in libro exemplorum quinto . . . litteris mandavit.* The quotations from it (in HALM l.l. 120. PETER fragm. 224) seem to prove that the author had, in the spirit of Varro, contrasted old Rome with the city in his own time. Mamurra († 709/45?) was mentioned, and perhaps from it was also taken SUET. Aug. 77 *non amplius ter bibere eum solitum super cenam in castris apud Mutinam Cornelius Nepos tradit.* Pliny may have used it; see LURLICHS, die Quellenregister d. letzten Bücher des Plin. (Wurzb. 1878) 6.—4) Biography of Cato. CORN. NEP. Cat. 3, 5 *huius de vita et moribus plura in eo libro persecuti sumus quem separatim de eo fecimus rogatu T. Pomponii Attici, quare studiosos Catonis ad illud volumen delegamus.*—5) Life of Cicero, a panegyric, probably composed after his death. GELL. 15, 28, 2 *Cornelius Nepos . . . M. Ciceronis ut qui maxime amicus familiaris fuit . . . in librorum primo quos de vita illius composuit errasse videtur.*—6) A work on geography, as it would seem, in the manner of the Paradoxographi (cf. Cicero's Admiranda, above § 186, 4), without critical sifting of the reports but giving the distances. PLIN. NH. 5, 4 *minus profecto mirentur portentosa Graeciae mendacia de his . . . prodita qui cogitent nostros nuperque paulo minus monstrifica quaedam . . . tradidisse, . . . quaeque alia Cornelius Nepos avidissime credidit.* Further notices of the work in HALM l.l. 126. FCIPOLLA, Nepote e le scienze naturali, Riv. di fil. 11, 372.—7) SUET. gramm. 4 *Cornelius Nepos libello quo distinguit litteratum* (the learned grammarian) *ab erudito* (the scholar): was it a separate treatise or perhaps the preface to the grammatici illustres (p. 343, l. 21 from the end)?

5. SUETON. ap. Hieron. 2, 821 Vall.: (*de viris illustribus scripserunt*) *apud Latinos . . . Varro* (in his Imagines), *Santra, Nepos, Hyginus et . . . Tranquillus.* GELL. 11, 8, 5 *in libro Corneli Nepotis de inlustribus viris XIII* (on Cato; GCORTESE has attempted, but not convincingly, to connect with this the fragment quoted above § 127, 1 l. 8 sqq.; see BÜCHELER, RhM. 39, 623). CHARIS. GL. 1, 141 *Cornelius Nepos inlustrium XV* and: *Cornelius Nepos inlustrium virorum libro XVI;* cf. ib. 220, *Nepos de inlustribus viris II.* References to this are found in CORN. NEPOS himself: Dion 3, 2 *sed de hoc in eo libro plura sunt exposita qui de historicis graecis conscriptus est.* Besides this, a book on the Roman historians: of this there are extant the vitae of Atticus and of Cato (Censorius) with the heading *ex libro Cornelii Nepotis de latinis historicis* and under the same heading fragments of the letters of Cornelia, the mother of the Gracchi (§ 123, 6 l. 9): in this latter instance the specification of the book is certainly erroneous; Nepos could treat of the Gracchi only in a book *de latinis oratoribus.* NIPPERDEY, op. 99. Lastly on Cicero as an historian (§ 186, 1 l. 3) a notice in the cod. Guelferb. Gud. 278 s. XIII *Cornelius Nepos in libro de historicis latinis.* Cf. also SUET. rhet. 3 (§ 158, 3 l. 6). The book de lat. hist. was published during the life-time of Atticus (between

719/35 and 721/33); Nepos added the conclusion when a new edition was brought out after his death (722/32): Att. 1, 19 sqq. *hactenus Attico vivo edita a nobis sunt. nunc . . . reliqua persequemur;* perhaps after the battle of Actium (a. 723/31), in consequence of which Octavian received the title of imperator; see 19, 2 *in affinitatem pervenit Imperatoris, Divi filii.* Mommsen, mon. Ancyr. p. 53.

Praef. 8 *in hoc exponemus libro de vita excellentium imperatorum.* 15, 4, 6 *uno hoc volumine vitam excellentium virorum complurium concludere constituimus quorum separatim multis milibus versuum complures scriptores ante nos explicarunt.* 23, 13, 4 *tempus est huius libri facere finem et Romanorum explicare imperatores, quo facilius collatis factis qui viri praeferendi sint possit iudicari.* Among the foreign *imperatores* the Greek (20) are those first treated of, then comes a supplement: then after a short survey of the Greek kings who were also *imperatores,* Hamilcar and Hannibal. Cf. 21, 1, 1 *hi fere fuerunt graecae gentis duces* (among their number the Carian Datames) *qui memoria digni videantur, praeter reges; namque eos attingere noluimus quod omnium res gestae separatim sunt relatae* (in the *book de regibus*). This work on Greek heroes (vitae 1–20) is dedicated to Atticus (praef. 1, 1): the supplement was added (perhaps in a new edition) at a later time, after the death of Atticus (722/32; Hann. 13, 1 *Atticus—scriptum reliquit*).—A book *de poëtis latinis* is indicated by quotations in Sueton. vita Terent. p. 27, 6. 31, 2 R., one *de grammaticis* perhaps in Suet. gramm. 4 (see n. 4 fin.).—According to this the viri illustres were classed according to the departments in which they distinguished themselves, and under these departments foreigners (the title of the book now extant is *de excellentibus ducibus exterarum gentium*) and Romans were treated of together, just as in Varro's Imagines (above p. 260 l. 15). The quotations from non-extant books in Halm l.l. 121. Peter, hist. fragm. 219. It is improbable that artists (painters etc.) were also treated of in this work, and that, as Brunn and Furtwängler (see § 313, 3) recently maintained, Pliny availed himself of them in his NH. LUrlichs, d. Quellenregister zu Plin. letzten Büchern (Würzb. 1878). For a characteristic description of the whole work cf. also 16, 1, 1 *vereor . . . ne non vitam eius enarrare, sed historiam videar scribere.* 15, 1, 3 *cum exprimere imaginem consuetudinis atque vitae velimus.* 25, 19, 1 *rerum exemplis lectores docebimus . . . suos cuique mores plerumque conciliare fortunam.* Moral reflections 8, 2, 3. 8, 3, 2. The work frequently used by Plutarch: Marcell. 30. Pelop. et Marcell. comp. 1. Lucull. 43.

6. Gell. 15, 28, 1 expresses himself coolly *Cornelius Nepos rerum memoriae non indiligens.* Quintilian does not mention him in his list of the Roman historians, and Pliny (n. 4, fin.) charges him with credulity. The work which we possess entirely bears out this estimate of his literary position. It is difficult to find out his reason for selecting this or that general among the duces or imperatores and omitting such men as Brasidas, Aratos, Philopoimen, Kleomenes III and others; nor is his lengthy treatment in harmony with the importance of the events; he neglects important authorities, e.g. Herodotos. The authorities whom he mentions (e.g. Deinon, Polybios, Seilenos, Theopompos, Thukydides, Timaios, Xenophon) are not always those of whom he has chiefly made use. Ephoros e.g. is not named, but is much used (in the Lys. Themist. Paus. Alc.; perhaps Valerius Antias was also employed; see HHaupt. de auct. de vir. ill. libro 40; § 414, 4). He employs his authorities negligently and sometimes mistakes their meaning. The order of the duces and the arrangement of events in the biographies are void of plan, without just discrimination of important and unimportant facts; serious historical and geographical errors and confusions are frequent; chronology is often neglected and undue attention devoted to curious anecdotes. See on this

Nipperdey's larger edition, and GFUnger l.l. 146. The tenor of the whole is rhetorical, and he characterises his generals in a onesided manner, generally dwelling on their good sides; in most cases the person in question is described as the greatest in his way. His style belongs to the genus tenue and is to a certain extent graceful so long as it keeps within short periods; but whenever the author attempts long periods, he signally fails. His command of phrases and words is not very great. Some expressions deviate from the classical usage, though they do not justify any attempt to assign the work to a later date. A period in which side by side with Cicero and Caesar Varro and even the authors of the bell. afric. and hispaniense ranked as literati, and which before long produced Vitruvius, could well have a writer like Cornelius Nepos. All leads to the conclusion that he was a kind-hearted, honest man and author, though of moderate abilities. Cf. Nipperdey's Introd. (1849) xxi. xxviii.

7. The above account assumes the book on the generals to be a work of Cornelius Nepos: the MSS. however entitle it *Liber Aemilii Probi de excellentibus ducibus exterarum gentium* and name Cornelius Nepos only as the author of the Atticus and Cato (p. 343, l. 7 from the end). OGifanius (in his edition of Lucretius, Antw. 1566, p. 394[a]) recognised that the duces should also be attributed to Cornelius. The occasion for this false appellation was given by a commonplace epigram, printed also e.g. AL. 783. PLM. 5, 83, which, for some unknown reason, is given in the MSS. after the Hannibal. This however does not apply to the book on the generals, but is a dedicatory poem for a collection of poetry (8 *carmina*) which a certain Probus (10) sends to the Emperor Theodosius (I or II? v. 2. 3. 8. 12): Probus himself, his father and grandfather (11)—probably three copyists and calligraphers—compiled the *corpus* (11). This epigram then gave rise to the erroneous subscription which follows it in the MSS. *Aemilii Probi de exc. duc. ext. gent. liber explicit*, and this again occasioned the incorrect heading mentioned above. Bergk, Phil. 12, 580, has attempted to explain part of the name to be due to a misapprehension of EM (endavi) PROBVS. WFRinck and others have laboured hard to prove that this (Aemilius) Probus under Theodosius was the author of the doubtful vitae. But such attribution is precluded on historical grounds and by the evidence of style: among other reasons because Ampelius (§ 359, 1) cap. 14. 15. 33 notoriously availed himself of the book of heroes (abstracts from this book are likewise found in the Schol. Bob. p. 311. 312 Or., where also the work itself is mentioned by name as 'de viris illustribus' p. 311, 10. 312, 18). The vitae of Cato and of Atticus, which are uncontestably by Cornelius Nepos and are contained side by side with the book on the generals in all the good MSS., show the same characteristics in substance and diction, and the same kind of generalisation and the same tendency to exculpate and exalt the heroes described, which are found in the duces. The author's survey of the political circumstances of his time is perfectly applicable to the close of the Republic. (Eum. 8, 2. Ages. 4, 2. Cato 2, 2 and elsewhere. GGemss, ZfGW. 37, Jahresber. 390.) The view advanced by GFUnger, der sogen. Cornelius Nepos, Abhandl. d. Münch. Akad. 16, 1 (1881), attributing the book on the generals to Hyginus (§ 262) is untenable; see against this BLupus, JJ. 125, 379. HRosenhauer, phil. Anz. 13, 733. CWagener, phil. Rundsch. 1882, 907. AMayr, stimmt der Cato u. Att. des Nep. in Spr. u. Stil mit den vitae ducum überein?, Cilli 1883. There is also no sufficient reason for assuming the present work to be a late abstract from the original of Cornelius Nepos. Madvig, op. 2, 123. Lachmann, kl. Schr. 2, 188. Fleckeisen, Phil. 4, 345. KNipperdey (1849) p. xxxvi. Thyen, de auctore vitarum C. N. quae feruntur, Osnabr. 1874 holds this view. Cf. also HHaupt, de auctoris de viris illustribus (below § 414, 4) libro (Würzb. 1876) 39.

8. The MSS. are very defective. Of MSS. of the best class only one has been preserved, the cod. Parcensis in Löwen s. XV (CLRoth, RhM. 8, 626; cf. Phil. 26, 706), and even from this the vita Attici and the fragments of Cornelia's letters (p. 343, in fin.) are missing; other representatives of the same class were the cod. Danielis or Gifanii, the best of all; also the Leidensis Boecleri (see n. 9), the Batavicus from which (probably by ICaucus) the Utrecht ed. of 1542 was compiled: all these MSS. have now disappeared and are known to us only in a few not very exact collations. Of the second considerably inferior class of MSS. the best is the Gudianus 166 s. XII/XIII in Wolfenbüttel: the numerous other MSS., generally very corrupt, are of s. XV. Cf. de librorum numero et auctoritate in CLRoth's ed. (1841) p. 207. 251. Nipperdey's ed. of the text p. 3. The Excerpta Patavina, reprinted in Roth l.l. 190, should be noticed, see JFreudenberg, JJ. 111, 495.

9. Principal editions by DLambinus (Par. 1569), ASchott (cum notis varr., Frankf. 1608), Böcler (Strassb. 1640. 1656), AvStaveren (Leid. 1734. 1773. Stuttg. 1820 II, cur. WHBardili). JHBremi (with notes, Zür.[4] 1827).—First critical edition by CLRoth, Aemilius Probus etc.; praemissa sunt Rinckii prolegomena, Bas. 1841. Explained by CNipperdey (larger ed.), Lpz. 1849 (2nd edition by BLupus, Berl. 1879). Revision by CNipperdey, Berl. 1867 (the text with a short critical apparatus). Apparatu critico adiecto ed. CHalm, Lps. 1871.—Textum constit. CGCobet, Leid. 1881 (and the same writer Mnemos. 9, 303. 360). Rec. et verbb. ind. add. MGitlbauer, Freib. i. B. 1883. Rec. et emend. AWeidner, Prague[2] 1888.

School editions (with German notes and [or] lexicon e.g. by JSiebelis und MJancovius, Lpz.[11] 1885, CNipperdey (small ed. Berl.[9] 1885 by BLupus). FWHinzpeter (Bielef.[7] 1886). AMonginot, Par.[3] 1886. LEnglmann Munich. 1881. GGemss, Paderb. 1884. WMartens, Gotha 1886. KErbe, Stuttg. 1886. With English notes: OBrowning, Oxf. 1868. JFMacmichael, Lond. 1873. JTWhite, Lond. 1867. TBLindsay, New York, 1889.

Editions of the text e.g. by CHalm and AFleckeisen (Lps.[2] 1884, with a lexicon by HHaacke.[9] 1887). GAndresen, Prague 1884 (with a lexicon by KJahr). Lexicons by GAKoch and KEGeorges, Hanover[5] 1885. OEichert, Bresl.[10] 1879.—Completed (i.e. with corrections of the mistakes in diction and substance) by KVölker and WCrecelius, Lps.[3] 1886. EOrtmann (Lpz.[4] 1886). FVogel (Berl.[3] 1885 by KJahr). JLattmann (Gött.[5] 1876).

10. Criticism: AFleckeisen (Phil. 4, 308). HWHeerwagen (collect., Baireuth 1849), especially CNipperdey, spicilegia crit in C. N., in his op. Berl. 1877, 1-196.—JArnoldt, JJ. 105, 561. 109, 277. JFreudenberg, JJ. 111, 495. GOsthelder, Beitr. z. Nep., Kaiserslaut. 1879. GGPluygers, Mnemos. 8, 345. CGCobet, ib. 9, 47. 303. 360. JJCornelissen, ib. 11, 232.

11. WFRinck, saggio di un esame critico etc., Venice 1818; re-written in CLRoth's edition. CFRanke, comm. de C. N. vita et scriptis, Quedlinb. 1827. GEFLieberkühn, de auctore vitt. quae sub nomine C. N. feruntur, Lps. 1837; vindiciae librorum iniuria suspectorum, Lps. 1844 (defensio C. N. contra Aem. Pr. librarium). RHanow, de Corn. Nep., Züllichau 1850. HWHeerwagen, Münch. Gel. Anz. 1846, no. 28. ALinsmayer, de vit. exc. duc., Munich 1859. LGrasberger, zur Würdigung des C. N., Eos 1, 225. AEussner, BlfbayrG. 7, 335. De fontibus et auctorit. C. N. v. JPHisely (Delft 1827), RHEWichers (Gröningen 1828), AEkker (acta soc. Rheno-Traiect. 3, 1828, 193). JFreudenberg, quaestt. hist. in C. N., Cöln 1839; Bonn 1842. Cf. WFricke, d. Quellen Plut.s im Alkib., Lpz. 1869. PNatorp, quos auctores in ultimis belli peloponn. annis describendis secuti sint . . . Cornelius Iustinus, Strassb. 1876; ZföG. 27, 561. WKlotz, die Quellen z.

Phokion im . . . Nepos, Lpz. 1877. GFRICKE, de fontt. Plut. et Nep. in v. Phocionis, Berl. 1883. MMOHR, d. Quellen d. Plut. u. Nepotischen Themist. usw., Berl. 1879. RSCHUBERT, die Quellen Plutarchs, JJ. Suppl. 9, 647. GOETHE, die Quellen des Nep. zur griech. Gesch., Gr.-Glogau 1878. LHOLZAPFEL, Unterss. üb. d. griech. Gesch. von 489–413 (Lpz. 1879), 52. 80.—Zur vita Alcibiadis JWIGGERS (Lps. 1833), Catonis AFRSvHEEMFRA (Leid. 1825), Attici JHELD (Prolegomena, Bresl. 1826), Hannibalis JASBACH, anall. hist. et epigr. lat. (Bonn 1878) 34.

12. Lexicons, indices see above n. 9. ADORNHEIM, Beitr. z. Latinität d. N., Detmold 1861. BLUPUS, der Sprachgebrauch des N., Berl. 1876. WIGNATIUS, de verborum cum praeposs. compositorum ap. N., Liv., Curt. cum dat. structura, Berl. 1877. JEIDENSCHINK, der Infinitiv bei N., Passau 1877.

199. During this period a number of persons in high position made augury the subject of literary works, probably from political motives. Such was Appius Claudius (cos. 700/54), who busied himself with necromancy, second-sight and occult matters, as also did C. Marcellus, M. Messala (cos. 701/53) and L. Caesar, and also Veranius. Learned men such as Granius Flaccus and Aufustius wrote on kindred subjects, L. Caecina especially, and others, on the Etruscan system of divination. L. Tarutius devoted himself to astrology.

1. Appius Claudius Ap. f. Pulcher, augur from 695/59, cos. 700/54, censor 704/50, † 706/48. PRE. 2, 412, 41 and Bull. dell' inst. arch. 1860, 225. 1861, 63. CIL. 1, 619. CIC. Brut. 267 *Appius Claudius, collega et familiaris meus, . . et satis studiosus et valde cum doctus tum etiam exercitatus orator et cum auguralis tum omnis publici iuris antiquitatisque nostrae bene peritus fuit.* Tusc. 1, 37 *ea quae meus amicus* (temporarily) *Appius νεκυομαντεῖα faciebat.* div. 1, 132 *psychomantia, quibus Appius . . . uti solebat.* fam. 3, 4, 1 (a. 703/51) to him: *illo libro augurali quem ad me amantissime scriptum suavissimum misisti.* leg. 2, 32 *est . . . inter Marcellum* (C. Claudius Marcellus, cos. 704/50 or the cos. of 705/49) *et Appium, optimos augures, magna dissensio* (*nam eorum ego in libros incidi*), *cum alteri placeat auspicia ad utilitatem esse reip. composita, alteri disciplina vestra* (*augurum*) *quasi divinare videatur posse.* That the latter was the opinion held by Appius appears clearly from div. 2, 75. FEST. 298 (v. *sollistimum*) *Ap. Pulcher in auguralis disciplinae libro I ait.* Cf. besides CIC. fam. 3, 9, 3. 3, 11, 4.

2. M. Valerius Messala (Rufus, see below), cos. 701/53; PRE. 6, 2347. MACR. 1, 9, 14 *M. Messala, Cn. Domitii in consulatu collega idemque per annos LV augur, de Iano ita incipit* (cf. LYD. mens. 4, 1). GELL. 13, 14, 5 sq. (on the pomerium). 13, 15, 3 *liber M. Messalae auguris de auspiciis primus* (a considerable fragment follows). 13, 16, 1 *Messala in eodem libro de minoribus magistratibus.* FEST. 161 *Messala augur in explanatione auguriorum.* 253 . . . *ssala in expla.* 351 *Messala augur ait* (cf. 379, 18).—Ib. 321 (a passage in the XII Tables is being explained) *ne Valerius* ⟨*quidem Messala*⟩ *in XII explanati*⟨*one rem expedivit. hic ta*⟩*men in eo libro qu*⟨*em de dictis in*⟩*volute inscribit*, etc. 355 . . . *tione XII ait.* It is doubtful whether this Valerius, whose cognomen Messala rests only on an emendation, is to be identified with the writer on augury. Huschke conjectures Valerius Soranus (§ 147, 1). Cf. § 86, 6. Below § 222, 3 ad fin. Cf. RSCHÖLL, XII tabb. p. 37. HUSCHKE, iurispr. anteiust.[5] 103. This Messala, who was augur for fifty-five years, and therefore

must have reached a very advanced age, is no doubt the same who is repeatedly mentioned by Pliny as *Messala senex* (cf. ind. auct. b. 35 *ex . . . Messala oratore* [222], *Messala sene.* 34, 37. 35, 8, here too together with Messala orator), who in other passages of Pliny is called Messala Rufus (ind. auct. b. 7, 34; quoted 7, 173). PLIN. NH. 35, 8 *similis causa Messalae seni expressit volumina illa quae de familiis condidit* etc. A fragment of it ib. 34, 137. HPETER JJ. 127, 107; hist. fr. 265.

3. PRISCIAN. GL. 2, 380, 3 *Lucius Caesar: 'certaeque res augurantur.'* FEST. 161 *maiorem consulem L. Caesar putat dici eum qui* etc. This determines more precisely the quotations in PRISCIAN. GL. 2, 270 (*Caesar in auguralibus*) and MACR. 1, 16, 29 (*Iulius Caesar XVI° auspiciorum libro negat nundinis contionem advocari posse*). Perhaps the consul of a. 690/64 (PRE. 4, 425, 7, the elder brother of the one named above § 153, 3) † 667/87. HUSCHKE, iurispr. anteiust.[5] 102.

4. FEST. 289 *Veranius in eo qui est auspiciorum de comitiis.* As according to this Veranius had already been made use of by Verrius Flaccus, it would seem that he belongs to the Republican period; at all events he is not later than Augustus. EHÜBNER, ephem. epigr. 2, 73, conjectures that he is the legate of Germanicus, Q. Veranius mentioned in TAC. ann. 2, 56 and elsewhere. FESTUS 158 *Veranius in libro⟨quem inscripsit priscarum vo⟩cum*, according to Ursinus' emendation. Cf. ib. 203. 205. 250. 253. 348. MACR. 3, 6, 14 *Veranius pontificalium eo libro quem fecit de supplicationibus;* cf. ib. 3, 5, 6 *in pontificalibus quaestionibus.* 3, 2, 3 *Veranius ex primo libro Pictoris* (cf. § 116, 7) on *porricere.* 3, 20, 2 *Veranius de verbis pontificalibus.* Veranius Flaccus appears quite isolated in SUET. Aug. 86 (§ 209, 12), hence it has been proposed to read Verrius Flaccus or Granius Flaccus: but better support may be found for Veranius along with Flaccus as cognomen in MACR. 1, 15, 21 (*Verrium Flaccum, iuris pontificii peritissimum, dicere solitum refert Varro*), where for chronological reasons it cannot be Verrius who is referred to. OHIRSCHFELD, Wien. Stud. 3, 110. Cf. also § 222, 3 in fin.

5. Pliny ind. auct. to b. 2: *Caecina, qui de etrusca disciplina* (*scripsit*, esp. on divination from lightning). Remains of this work in SEN. nat. qu. 2, 31–49. PLIN. NH. 2, 137–138, in FEST. SERV. and others. The same writer is also probably the authority for PLIN. NH. 11, 197 *Caecinae Volaterrano dracones emicuisse de extis laeto prodigio traditur;* cf. 10, 71. CIC. fam. 6, 6, 3 (a. 708/46 or 709/45 addressing Caecina) *si te ratio quaedam etruscae disciplinae, quam a patre . . . acceperas, non fefellit.* The family (*Ceicna* in Etr.) came from Volaterrae in Etruria (see above), where it was among the most powerful; OMÜLLER, Etr. 1[2], 486. SEN. nat. quaest. 2, 56, 1 *haec* (on fulguratio) *apud Caecinam invenio, facundum virum et qui habuisset aliquando in eloquentia nomen, nisi illum Ciceronis umbra pressisset.* Cf. SCHOL. VERON. on Aen. 10, 198 (p. 103 Keil). CIC. fam. 6, 9 (a. 708/46) *et patre eius . . . plurimum usi sumus et hunc a puero, quod et spem magnam mihi afferebat summae . . . eloquentiae et vivebat mecum coniunctissime . . . etiam studiis communibus, semper dilexi.* He appears not to have composed this work till a later time. It is somewhat difficult to discriminate father and son in the various passages. The father appears to be that Caecina (§ 179, 13) whom Cicero defended a. 685/69 (when he was about 40 years old). SUET. Iul. 75 *Auli Caecinae criminosissimo libro . . . laceratam existimationem suam civili animo tulit.* Yet Caesar had banished him from Italy on that account, notwithstanding that the attack belonged to the time of open war: *armatus adversario male dixi*, says Caecina himself in the lively letter (a. 708/46) in CIC. fam. 6, 7 with which he accompanies a work (written in Sicily), intended to effect his recall from banishment (it was in prose, possibly in the form of a letter to Caesar). It was entitled 'Querelae'; see ib. 6, 6, 8 (*Caesar*) *mitis clemensque natura, qualis exprimitur praeclaro illo libro querelarum tuarum.* Caesar appears to

have pardoned him after the African war (b. afr. 89). He is recommended in a letter a. 708/46 Cic. fam. 6, 9. 13, 66 *hominibus omnibus mecum studiis officiisque coniunctissimi;* the recipient is to assist him *in reliquiis veteris negotiationis* (in Asia, cf. fam. 6, 6, 2. 6, 8, 2) *colligendis.* Drumann, GR. 6, 279. AHGZimmermann, de A. Caecina scriptore, Berl. 1852. GSchmeisser, de etrusca discipl. (Bresl. 1872), 23; die etr. Disziplin, Liegn. 1881, 13.

6. Pliny NH. in the ind. auct. to b. 11 (insectorum genera): *ex auctoribus . . . Iulio Aquila, qui de etrusca disciplina scripsit* (perhaps Maecenas' freedman in Dio 55, 7, 6? see OMüller, Etr. 2[2], 34), *Tarquitio* (see § 158, 2), *qui item, Umbricio Meliore* (of Etruria, the court haruspex of the emperor Galba), *qui item.* The latter is also mentioned as an authority for b. 10 (volucrum naturae). Cf. NH. 10, 19 (*Umbricius haruspicum in nostro aevo peritissimus*). Tac. hist. 1, 27. OMüller l.l. 2[2], 13. 34. GSchmeisser, etr. Diszipl. 25. 27.—Arnob. 3, 40 *Caesius et ipse* (like Nigidius, already mentioned § 170) *disciplinas etruscas sequens Fortunam arbitratur et Cererem Genium Iovialem ac Palem* (*esse penates*) etc. Otherwise unknown (unless he may be identified with the jurist mentioned § 174, 5 l. 3; this view is now accepted by MHertz, Berl. phil. Wschr. 1888, 302): the name points to Etruria. GSchmeisser, etr. Disziplin 31. GWissowa, Herm. 22, 53.

7. Censorin. d. n. 3, 2 *Granius Flaccus in libro quem ad Caesarem de indigitamentis scriptum reliquit.* Paul. dig. 50, 16, 144 *G. Fl. in libro de iure papiriano* (§ 71, 1) *scribit.* Cf. Macr. 1, 18, 4 (*Varro et Gr. Fl.*). Fest. 277 (*Gran.*). Solin. 2, 40 (*Granius tradit*). Arnob. 3, 31. 38. 6, 7 (unless Granius Licianus, § 359, 4 is meant in Sol. and Arn.). The *Graccus* quoted in Festus 214[b], 23 for a term used in the science of lightning is probably a mis-spelling for *Granius.* GSchmeisser, quaestt. de etr. disc., Berl. 1872, 26.

8. Paul. Festi (therefore Verrius Flaccus) 94 *Aufustius genius, inquit, est deorum filius* etc. Prisc. GL. 2, 383 *Aufustius: omnia argumentata nomina* etc. Hence the extract (from Varro) GL. 7, 35 *abnesti fusti grammatici liber ad Asinium Pollionem* should also be written: *Aufusti gramm.*; HUsener, RhM. 24, 101. 104. 111.

9. Cic. div. 2, 98 *L. Tarutius Firmanus, familiaris noster, in primis Chaldaeicis rationibus eruditus, urbis nostrae natalem diem repetebat* etc. Cf. Plut. Romul. 12. Lyd. mens. 1, 14 (Ταρρούτιος ὁ μαθηματικός). Plin. ind auct. to b. 18 *ex L. Tarutio qui graece de astris scripsit* (§ 195, 6). Mommsen, Chronol.[2] 145.

10. On Cornelius Balbus see § 209, 4.—Otherwise unknown is a certain Titius, who is twice mentioned as an authority on sacerdotal dress by Festus 205, 2 *offendices ait esse Titius nodos quibus apex retineatur et remittatur. At Veranius* (above n. 4) . . . 289, 22 *Titi⟨us autem ait quod ex lana fiat⟩ sucida alba vesti⟨mentum dici ricam idque esse⟩ triplex* etc. If he were identical with the one named in Macr. 3, 11, 5 (*Tertius cum de ritu sacrorum multa dissereret,* cf. MHertz, de Cinciis 39) we should have to assign him a date later than Vergil.

200. Other scholars were also teachers: such was the influential critic P. Valerius Cato, who founded a school and who, in addition to grammatical works, wrote poems on mythological subjects. He lived in poor circumstances. The bucolic-erotic poems Dirae and Lydia, which have come down to us in the alleged Vergilian remains, have been without sufficient reason attributed to Cato. In a similar position was the sour

but markedly original L. Orbilius Pupillus of Beneventum (a. 640/114–c. 737/17), and freedmen such as Curtius Nicias.

1. SUET. gr. 11 *P.* (the praenomen in the ind. gramm. p. 98, 9 R.) *Valerius Cato, ut nonnulli tradiderunt, Burseni cuiusdam libertus ex Gallia* (cisalpina?): *ipse libello cui est titulus 'indignatio'* (perhaps in verse?) *ingenuum se natum ait et pupillum relictum eoque facilius licentia Sullani temporis* (672/82–674/80) *exutum patrimonio.* According to this, as the Roman only attained his majority in his 25th year, we should fix the date of Cato's birth about 654/100: it must not be brought down too late, as C. was among Philocomus' students (§ 148, 3) and as a teacher of the 'new school' of poets, he must have been considerably senior to them. Cf. also § 192, 6. SUET. l.l. (Cato) *docuit multos et nobiles visusque est peridoneus praeceptor, maxime ad poeticam tendentibus, ut quidem apparere vel his versiculis potest 'Cato grammaticus, Latina Siren, qui solus legit ac facit poetas'* (i.e. he reads them aloud, cf. § 41, 1 l. 12, and thereby establishes their reputation), *is scripsit praeter grammaticos libellos etiam poemata, ex quibus praecipue probantur Lydia et Diana. Lydiae Ticida* (§ 213, 1) *meminit* (hence Suetonius was not himself acquainted with them) '*Lydia doctorum maxima cura liber*' (accordingly a work of Alexandrine erudition like Cinna's Smyrna § 213, 3), *Dianae Cinna 'Saecula permaneat nostri Dictynna Catonis'* (cf. LSCHWABE, obss. in Cirin, Dorp. 1871, 4): his pupils and friends criticised him with rather too much partiality (see Bibaculus immediately below). SUET. l.l. proceeds: *vixit ad extremam senectam, sed in summa pauperie et paene inopio, . . . postquam Tusculana villa creditoribus cesserat.* Here follow two epigrams of Bibaculus (§ 192, 4) on the contrast between Cato's needy outward circumstances (*mei . . . Catonis*) and his intellectual worth: he attributes to him *tantam sapientiam* and calls him *unicum magistrum, summum grammaticum, optimum poetam* ending with: *En cor Zenodoti, en iecur Cratetis!* Concerning Cato's critical labours on Lucilius see § 143, 5: Cato had been initiated in his Lucilian studies by Vettius Philocomus, see § 148, 3. Cf. also SUET. gramm. 4 *Valerium Catonem, poetam simul grammaticumque notissimum.* OVID trist. 2, 426 seems to allude to the erotic subjects of his poems: *et leve Cornifici parque Catonis opus.* Cf. LSCHWABE, quaestt. Catull. 305. NIPPERDEY, op. 491. BERGK, Beitr. z. lat. Gramm. 1, 126, 2.

2. The collection of the so-called Vergilian carmina minora (§ 229, 1) contains, besides other matters, the Dirae (183 hex.), an imprecation occasioned by the loss of an estate during the civil wars. As the second part (v. 104–183) takes the form of a lament for his beloved Lydia, JScaliger, Näke and others have conjectured Valerius Cato to be the author. But neither Cato's minority nor the Sullan period (n. 1) tally with this poem, which rather alludes to the agrarian distributions of a. 713/41. Cf. KFHERMANN, ges. Abh. 114. RMERKEL, on the Ibis p. 364. It was attributed to Vergil because he also had lost his estate 713/41; but there is no further agreement between this poem and Vergil either in mode of thought, poetic peculiarities or other circumstances.—RIBBECK (röm. Dicht. 1, 311) indeed takes Valerius Cato for the author of both poems, but believes him to have composed them only when the agrarian distribution of 713/41 again brought to his mind the injury which he had suffered during the Sullan proscription of 673/81. After forty years! But all the characteristic features of the poem go to prove that it was the reverse of such a reminiscence. Moreover the immoderation of youth or of undisciplined grief betrays itself throughout the poem, which is monotonous and unpleasing on account of the piling of one imprecation on another. How different would be the language of a sexagenarian, in whose memory the recollection of a long-past sorrow was reawakened! As the events of the year 713/41 are in themselves a sufficient explanation of the poem, the name of Lydia

is the thin thread on which Scaliger's theory hangs. And here we are warned to be circumspect by the title of the Indignatio, which would at once be coupled with the Dirae, but that this is precluded by the definite list of contents given by SUET. l.l. FJACOBS, verm. Schrr. 5, 639, saw that the poem must be divided into two parts, 'Dirae' and 'Lydia'; its strophic arrangement marked by refrains, and in the Bembine MS. by rubricated initials, was discovered by KFHERMANN l.l. 118; cf. HKEIL, Haller ALZ. 1849, no. 61. FCGÖBBEL, de ephymn. (Gött. 1858) 48; die stroph. Compos. d. Dirae, Warendorf 1861; Valeri Catonis carmina, rec. notisque instruxit . . . praemissus est lib. de Dir. compos. stroph. emendatus, Warendorf 1865. There is no certain trace of a second speaker and alternating singing; the Battarus of the Dirae is only the person addressed, and has no further individuality; the occasion and author are evidently the same in both poems (cf. also Dir. 20 with Lyd. 13); in the Dirae, it is stated that the separation from Lydia who remains on the estate (Dir. 41. 89. 95) renders its loss doubly painful, but the connection between Lydia and the estate is not explained. In the 'Lydia' the estate is envied the possession of the beloved girl, whose unmerited loss is bewailed, with much display of mythological learning, and in the sentimental, effeminate tone of some of the elegiac poets of the Augustan age, to the beginning of which both these poems clearly belong.—Editions: cf. § 229, 5 in BURMANN's Anth. lat. 2, p. 649 and WERNSDORF's PLM. 3, 1. Rec. et ill. CPUTSCHE, Jena 1828. Val. Catonis carmina cum animadvv. AFNAEKII; acc. . . . de V. C. eiusque vita ac poesi . . . diss., Bonn 1847. Further in ORIBBECK's App. Vergil. (Lpz. 1868) p. 165 (cf. p. 22. 50). MHAUPT's ed. of Vergil., Lpz.² 1873, p. 576. BÄHRENS PLM. 2, 73.—Cf. ORIBBECK, röm. Dicht. 1, 309. Criticism: MSCHMIDT, Phil. 8, 190; FCGÖBBEL, ZfGW. 20, 584. 22, 750; HAUPT, op. 3, 613; RELLIS, Journ. of philol. 8, 72; Americ. journ. of phil. 1887 (on Vatic. 3269 s. XV).

3. SUET. gr. 9 *L.* (the praenomen in the ind. gramm. p. 98, 7 R.) *Orbilius Pupillus Beneventanus . . . primo apparituram magistratibus fecit, deinde in Macedonia corniculo, mox equo meruit, functusque militia studia repetiit . . .; ac professus diu in patria quinquagesimo demum anno Romam consule Cicerone* (a. 691/63) *transiit, docuitque maiore fama quam emolumento. namque iam persenex pauperem se . . . quodam scripto fatetur* (see however SUET. gr. 8). *librum etiam cui est titulus † perialogos* (*peri alogon* Beroaldus, περιαλγής Toup) *edidit continentem querelas de iniuriis quas professores neglegentia aut ambitione parentum acciperent* (from this is probably taken PRISC. GL. 2, 381, 1 *Orbilius 'quae vix ab hominibus consequi possunt'*). *fuit autem naturae acerbae . . . etiam in discipulos*, for which he cites Horace (ep. 2. 1, 71) and Domitius Marsus (§ 243, 1). *ac ne principum quidem virorum insectatione abstinuit. . . . vixit prope ad centesimum aetatis annum* (§ 192, 6) *. . . statua eius Beneventi ostenditur in Capitolio . . . marmorea habitu sedentis ac palliati appositis duobus scriniis. reliquit filium Orbilium et ipsum grammaticum professorem.* Mention of passages in his works ib. 4 and 8. Cf. § 159, 6. Many writers (REISIG, NIPPERDEY, THSCHMID, Phil. 11, 54 and others) consider him to be the *grammaticorum equitum doctissimus*, whose acerbity is by Horace sat. 1, 10, 4 contrasted with the refinement and mild judgment of Valerius Cato (§ 143, 5).—AGLANGE, verm. Schrr. 182.

4. SUET. gramm. 14 *Curtius Nicia adhaesit Cn. Pompeio et C. Memmio; sed cum codicillos Memmi et Pompei uxorem de stupro pertulisset proditus ab ea Pompeium offendit domoque ei interdictum est. fuit et Ciceronis familiaris* (in support of which he quotes his epp. ad Dolabellam [=fam. 9, 10, 1 where he says *Niciam nostrum*] and ad Att. 12, 26, 2 of a. 709/45 *nosti Niciae nostri imbecillitatem, mollitiam, consuetudinem victus*). *huius de Lucilio libros* (cf. § 143, 5) *etiam Santra comprobat.*

201. The Stoic system was ennobled by Cato the Younger (a. 659/95–708/46) who openly professed it and realised its principles in his words, life, and death. The rigidity of the Stoic philosophy was in perfect agreement with the unyielding obstinacy of Cato's character, which was inseparable from a certain onesidedness and narrowness of mind.

1. M. Porcius Cato, the great-grandson of Censorius, was born 659/95, trib. pleb. 692/62, praetor 700/54, and died by his own hand at Utica after the battle of Thapsus, in April 708/46. Though wanting in political acumen and mental energy, he deserves great respect for his faithfulness, firmness and unselfishness in serving the cause of the Republic. Cf. PLUTARCH's Cato minor, which is probably derived from Paetus Thrasea (§ 299, 7). His character is delineated in SALL. Catil. 74. VELLEI. 2, 35, 2 is exaggerated; cf. DRUMANN, GR. 5, 153. PRE. 5, 1911, 20. HKÖCHLY, ak. Vorträge 1, 53. HWARTMANN, Leben d. Cato v. Utica, Zür. 1858. MOMMSEN, RG. 3[6], 459. FDGERLACH, Cato der jüngere, Bas. 1866.

2. Erroneously HIERON. Eus. Chron. on a. Abr. 1948 (Amand. 1949)=685/69. *M. Porcius Cato stoicus philosophus agnoscitur.* CIC. Brut. 118 *stoici . . . traducti a disputando ad dicendum inopes reperiuntur. unum excipio Catonem, in quo perfectissimo stoico summam eloquentiam non desiderem.* 119 *habet a stoicis id quod ab illis petendum fuit, sed dicere didicit a dicendi magistris eorumque more se exercuit.* leg. 3, 40 *nec est umquam longa oratione utendum, nisi aut peccante senatu . . . tolli diem utile est aut cum tanta causa est ut opus sit oratoris copia ; . . . quorum generum in utroque magnus noster Cato est.* For the use which he made of philosophy see § 50, 4. QUINT. 11, 1, 36 *Cato eloquens senator fuit.* PLUT. Cato min. 5 ὁ λόγος νεαρὸν μὲν οὐδὲν οὐδὲ κομψὸν εἶχεν ἀλλ' ἦν ὄρθιος καὶ περιπαθὴς καὶ τραχύς. ib. 23 τοῦτον μόνον ὧν Κάτων εἶπε διασώζεσθαί φασι τὸν λόγον (the speech against the Catilinarians), as he says that the cos. Cicero caused it to be taken down in writing, if indeed this be not a confusion with the speech attributed to him by Sallust (Catil. 52); cf. VELLEI. 2, 35, 3. FSCHNEIDER, de Catone Uticensi oratore, ZfAW. 1843, 112. Cato wrote iambics (τῷ πικρῷ προσχρησάμενος τοῦ 'Αρχιλόχου) against Metellus Scipio, who had deprived him of his bride, see PLUT. Cat. min. 7. The only composition by him which we possess is his letter to Cicero a. 704/50, fam. 15, 5.

3. PLIN. NH. 7, 113. *Uticensis Cato unum ex tribunatu militum* (a. 687/67) *philosophum, alterum ex Cypria legatione* (a. 696/58) *deportavit* (to Rome). He was very intimate with the Stoic philosophers Antipatros of Tyre (PLUT. 4), Athenodoros (ib. 10 and 16), Apollonides (ib. 65 sq.), but also with the Peripatetic Demetrios (ib.) and with Philostratos (ib. 57).

4. Immediately on his death Cato's character became a subject of political controversy; see § 180, 5. 195, 7. 215, 2. 220, 3. But even under the Julian dynasty the opposition delighted in glorifying Cato and his death both in verse and in prose; see AL. 397 sqq. PLM. 4, 58.

202. The most distinguished orators of this period were especially M. Calidius, one of the pioneers and chief representatives of the new Attic school, and the talented but profligate C. Memmius, who also attempted metrical composition and is known through his connection with Lucretius and Catullus. As

speakers may be mentioned C. Manilius and P. Sestius, M. Claudius Marcellus, M. Favonius and the well-known enemy of Cicero, P. Clodius.

1. Hieron. Eus. Chron. ad a. Abr. 1953=690/64 *Apollodorus Pergamenus* (cf. § 44, 10) . . . *praeceptor Calidii et Augusti;* ib. 1960=697/57 *M. Calidius orator clarus habetur* (he was at that time praetor, Cic. p. red. in sen. 22. Cass. Dio 39, 11) *qui bello postea civili* (a. 707/47) *Caesarianas partes secutus* (cf. Caes. b. c. 1, 2), *cum togatam Galliam regeret, Placentiae obiit.* Unsuccessful candidature for the consulship a. 704/50 (LMoll, de tempp. epp. Cic., Berl. 1883 p. 1). A minute description of his characteristics as an orator in Cic. Brut. 274–278, in which one feels that Cicero is stating his case against an important representative of the rival school (see p. 67. 246). Here we read e.g.: *non fuit orator unus e multis, potius inter multos prope singularis fuit, ita reconditas exquisitasque sententias mollis et pellucens vestiebat oratio . . . accedebat ordo rerum plenus artis, actio liberalis, totumque dicendi placidum et sanum genus. . . . aberat . . . illa laus qua permoveret atque incitaret animos, quam plurimum pollere diximus. nec erat ulla vis atque contentio.* Here too Cicero ridicules the negligent, weak and listless tone (*tam solute, tam leniter, tam oscitanter*) of the accusations of Calidius (cf. Cael. ap. Cic. fam. 8, 9, 5 *Calidius in accusatione satis frigidus*). Cf. Vellei. 2, 36, 2. Quint. 12, 10, 11 (*subtilitas*). 39. Speeches by him: in Q. Gallium ambitus reum (690/64; cf. AEussner, comment. petit. 1872, 21; two fragments from this Fest. 309, 31. Non. 208, 27; Cicero defended the accused, Brut. 277. Ascon. p. 78, 29 K.-S.); de domo Ciceronis (697/57; § 179, 30. Quint. 10, 1, 23); pro M. Aemilio Scauro (700/54, he was for the defence, with five others, amongst whom was Cicero, see § 180, 1, c; Ascon. p. 18, 10); pro libertate Tenediorum (700/54 with Cicero, Bibulus, Favonius, Cic. ad Q. fr. 2, 9, 2); pro se ambitus reo against two Gallii, who took their revenge for a former prosecution (703/51, Cael. ap. Cic. fam. 8, 4, 1. 8, 9, 5 *Calidius in defensione sua disertissimus*). Cf. PRE. 2, 74. 3, 644. HMeyer, oratt. fr.[2] 436. UvWilamowitz, Herm. 12, 333. 367. ERohde, RhM. 41, 176. OHarnecker, JJ. 125, 607.

2. Cic. Brut. 247 *C. Memmius L. f.* (the surname *Gemellus* is incorrect, see BBorghesi, oeuvr. 1, 152. Mommsen, röm. Münzw. 597) *perfectus litteris, sed graecis, fastidiosus sane latinarum; argutus orator verbisque dulcis, sed fugiens non modo dicendi verum etiam cogitandi laborem.* Yet his erotic poems (§ 31, 1; cf. Ovid. trist. 2, 433 *Memmi carmen*) do not seem to have been in Greek. He was a trib. pl. 688/66. As praetor (696/58) he opposed Caesar, but was subsequently gained over by him (Suet. Iul. 73 *Gai Memmi, cuius asperrimis orationibus non minore acerbitate rescripserat, etiam suffragator mox in petitione consulatus fuit*). He was propraetor in Bithynia a. 697/57 sq., when Helvius Cinna and Catullus were in his cohors (§ 213, 2. 214, 4), a. 701/53 he was accused of ambitus when a candidate for the consulship; he then went to Greece into exile and there died about 705/49. PRE. 4, 1755, 8. Mommsen, Münzw. 597. Cf. below p. 355 l. 4 from the end. FB(ockemüller), Grenzboten 1869 2, 129.

3. C. Manilius, as trib. pl. 688/66 the author of the lex Manilia, for which Livy made him deliver a *contio bona* (Liv. ep. 100.) PRE. 4, 1482, 6.

4. P. Sestius, quaestor 691/63, tr. pl. 697/57, propraetor in Cilicia a. 704/50 (Plut. Brut. 4), afterwards on Caesar's side. On the tediousness of his speech against Antius in a causa civilis see Catullus 44, 10. Cicero, who defended him a. 698/56 (see § 179, 32), thought little of his talents (*ἰδιώτης* Plut. Cic. 26; *nihil umquam legi scriptum σηστιωδέστερον*, Att. 7, 17, 2). PRE. 6, 1128, 6.

5. M. Claudius **Marcellus**, cos. 703/51 (Cass. Dio 40, 58 ἀλλ' ὅ τε Μάρκελλος ὁ Μάρκος καὶ ὁ Ῥοῦφος ὁ Σουλπίκιος [§ 174, 2], ὁ μὲν διὰ τὴν τῶν νόμων ἐμπειρίαν, ὁ δὲ διὰ τὴν τῶν λόγων δύναμιν ᾑρέθησαν), † 709/45; also praised as an orator Brut. 248, special prominence being given to the fact that he took Cicero as his model. He is accordingly included in the small number of living orators who are there mentioned (see § 182, 3, 1). Cf. besides § 179, 41. PRE. 4, 1520, 12.—L.Herennius Balbus, a joint prosecutor of M. Caelius (698/56. Cic. pCael. 25) and one of the prosecutors of Milo (702/52. Ascon. p. 35 Or. 30 K.-S.).

6. P. **Clodius** Pulcher, quaestor a. 693/61, tr. pl. 696/58, † 702/52; see Drumann, GR. 2, 199. CWElberling, de P. Cl. P., Copenh. 1839. IGentile, Clodio e Cicerone, Milan 1876. Cic. pCael. 27 *P. Clodius . . . cum inflammatus ageret . . . voce maxima, tametsi probabam eius eloquentiam, tamen non pertimescebam; aliquot enim in causis eum videram frustra litigantem.* A. 700/54 he appeared as the prosecutor of Procilius and the defender of M. Scaurus.

7. M. **Favonius** (Drumann, GR. 3, 32. PRE. 3, 437), aedile 701/53, praetor 705/49, † 712/42, the servile imitator of the younger Cato (§ 201), a man who was offensive alike to friend and foe, is frequently mentioned as an orator. Cic. Att. 2, 1, 9 *accusavit Nasicam* (694/60) *honeste* (SHRinkes reads thus: the MSS. have *inhoneste*) *ac moleste* (Malaspina thus: the MSS. *modeste*) *tamen dixit ita ut Rhodi videretur molis potius quam Moloni operam dedisse*, ad Q. fr. 2, 9, 2 (*pro Tenediorum libertate* 700/54; see § 202, 1). Probably it is he who is also referred to in Gell. 15, 8, where a passage against luxury is given *ex oratione Favorini, veteris oratoris, non indiserti viri*, delivered by him *cum legem Liciniam de sumptu minuendo suasit:* this then would not be the lex Licinia sumptuaria mentioned above § 141, 7 l. 18. 143, 1 l. 13, but rather the lex Licinia Pompeia, which was brought forward 699/55 but subsequently withdrawn by its proposers (Cass. Dio. 39, 37).

203. T. **Lucretius** Carus (probably born 658/96, died 15 Oct. 699/55), in his didactic poem de rerum natura in six books treated of physics, psychology and (though briefly) of Epicurean Ethics. Though it must be conceded that it was no happy idea to embody in poetry such a dry and mechanical doctrine, yet his devoted attachment to his lord and master Epicurus, the noble apostolic inspiration with which he preaches the Epicurean creed as the means of salvation from the darkness of superstition, the honest zeal with which he impugns false idols, the fervent tone of deep conviction in which he promises to set men free from the fear of the gods, of their own passions and of death, and to bestow on them truth and inward peace, all this is elevating to witness. The mental power and perseverance evinced in his struggle with his hard subject-matter deserve indeed the greatest admiration. In many passages the poet's high genius breaks through all the fetters of his original design. As if for relief from his severe abstract reasoning, he often pauses to introduce, with happy effect, picturesque illustrations from nature and human life. Still the tone pervading the

whole work is sad and mournful and in many passages even bitter. The poet makes us feel the disappointed hopes and the painful intellectual struggles, which he has gone through. The style is unequal: often heavy, cramped and stiff, but as often vivid, striking and trenchant, sometimes of glowing vehemence, sometimes of a ruggedness which possesses a peculiar attraction; in spite of all defects, the performance of a master of language. His mode of thought and writing was averse to his own time and directed to a better past; hence he received little attention in his own age; and though later writers were greatly influenced by him, antiquity was never able to realise the grandeur and sublimity of this figure among the poets. Many peculiarities of the work should be explained from the fact that it was not completed and edited by the author himself.

1. Hieronym. Euseb. Chr. ad a. Abr. 1922 (thus Amand. and Freh.: ad a. 1923 Bern.) = 659/95 *T. Lucretius poeta nascitur, qui postea amatorio poculo in furorem versus, cum aliquot libros per intervalla insaniae conscripsisset, quos postea Cicero emendavit, propria se manu interfecit anno aetatis XLIIII* (therefore 703/51). Jerome has probably in this case, as he frequently does, fixed the date of birth too late by a year, see Marx l.l. 139. Donat. vita Vergil. 2 implies a different date for his death: *usque ad virilem togam quam XVII* (correctly *XV*) *anno natali suo* (15 Oct.) *accepit isdem illis consulibus iterum duobus quibus erat natus* (that is to say 699/55, Cn. Pompeio II. and M. Licinio Crasso II), *evenitque ut eo ipso die Lucretius poeta decederet*, and this explicit statement going back to Suetonius certainly may be accepted with confidence. In favour of this date may be alleged that Cicero's words on Lucretius in a. 709/54 (vid. n. 2), relative to his edition of the poem, presuppose the poet's death. Therefore *anno aetatis XLIIII* must be wrong: L. must have died in his 42nd year. In the Munich MS. 14429 s. X we find the notice: *Titus Lucretius poeta nascitur sub consulibus. anñ* XX U. *II añ Virgilium.* Attempts at elucidation by HUsener, RhM. 22, 444; 23, 678; further arguments concerning the date of his birth and death FPolle, Phil. 25, 499. 26, 560. HSauppe, quaestt. Lucret. Gött. 1880, 3. JWoltjer, JJ. 129, 134 and esp. FMarx, RhM. 43, 136.

That Lucretius lost his reason and committed suicide in that state, is quite credible, considering the frame of mind which appears in the poem. There is nothing to justify the assumption (of Teuffel among others) that this terrible end was merely invented for the atheist by believers. One involuntarily compares the similar fate of Tasso, Hölderlin, Lenau, FRaimund, FHebbel, ALindner and others. The cause assigned for his malady, the love-philtre, is about as preposterous as similar empirical opinions to account for diseases at the present day. On the other hand, there is probably a germ of truth in the statement that Lucretius wrote *aliquot libros per intervalla insaniae.*—Of the rest of the poet's life we know nothing, as Lucretius is quite silent concerning himself. Of his contemporaries he only mentions Memmius, to whom he dedicates his work: 1, 26 *te sociam* (Venus, whom the atheist inconsistently invokes) *studeo scribendis versibus esse, quos ego de rerum natura pangere conor Memmiadae nostro, quem tu, dea, tempore in omni omnibus ornatum voluisti excellere rebus* (Venus crowned by

Cupido is found on coins of the Memmii, HSauppe, Phil. 22, 182). Memmius is usually identified with the one mentioned above § 202, 2. From his mode of mentioning Memmius, and from the cognomen Carus which is otherwise unknown in the gens Lucretia (it is altogether doubtful CIL., 9, 1867), it is a probable inference that Lucretius was not of good birth, but perhaps the son of a freedman, or an emancipated slave. FMarx in the exercitat. gramm. spec., Bonn 1881, p. 8.—AKannengiesser, JJ. 131, 59. SBrandt, JJ. 131, 601. He had nothing to do with the new school of Roman poets (Cato, Catullus etc.), as is sufficiently evident from his peculiarities of style and metre (n. 5).—His portrait on a gem (impronte gemm. del Instit. 2, 78; bull. 1831, 112)? engraved as frontispiece in Munro's edition: Bernouilli, röm. Ikonogr. 1, 235.

2. By *Cicero* Jerome (see n. 1 l. 4) no doubt meant the famous orator and not his brother Quintus, nor is there any other argument in favour of the latter. At most doubts might be raised against the credibility of the whole story (see KGneisse, de vv. in Lucr. repetitis 46) on account of Cicero's absolute silence, seeing that it is by no means a failing of his to be silent on his own performances; he never quotes Lucretius. Cicero's opinion on Lucretius: ad Q. fr. 2, 9, 3 (a. 700/54) *Lucreti poemata* (cf. Gell. 1, 21, 5 *in carminibus Lucreti* and Vellei. 2, 36, 2) *ut scribis ita sunt: multis luminibus ingenii, multae tamen artis*, i.e. 'I agree with your view that ⟨even though the work as a whole leaves much to be desired⟩ yet there are many instances of genius in it, and the art displayed throughout is very considerable.' The passage has been needlessly cumbered with emendations. The words immediately following in Cicero, which according to the MSS. refer to Sallust's Empedoclea (192, 1), are made by many writers, by alterations in the text, to apply to Lucretius: *sed cum* ⟨Bergk adds *ad umbilicum*⟩ *veneris* (*finieris* MHertz), *virum te putabo; si Sallustii Empedoclea legeris, hominem non putabo.* On the whole of this passage see FPolle, Phil. 25, 501. Bergk, op. 1, 425. Vahlen, ind. lect. 1881/82, 3. HNettleship, Journ. of phil. 13, 85. IKubik, diss. Vindobon. 1, 341. At all events, Cicero's part was not very important, and it might almost seem that he was half ashamed of being sponsor to such a dangerous work. His action does not go very far to confirm the otherwise dubious assertion (ap. Plin. ep. 3, 15, 1) *M. Tullium mira benignitate poetarum ingenia fovisse.* It would be more just from Lucretius imitations of Cicero's Aratea (see Munro on Lucr. 5, 619) to infer the existence of a certain connection between the two. See also Nep. Att. 12, 4 *quem post Lucretii Catullique mortem multo elegantissimum poetam nostram tulisse aetatem* etc. Ovid. am. 1, 15, 23. trist. 2, 425. Vitruv. 9, 3. Vellei. 2, 36, 2 *auctores carminum Varronem ac Lucretium.* Quint. 10, 1, 87. *Macer et Lucretius legendi quidem, sed non ut phrasin, i.e. corpus eloquentiae, faciant. elegantes in sua quisque materia, sed alter humilis, alter* (Lucr.) *difficilis.* Stat. silv. 2, 7, 76, *docti furor arduus Lucreti.* Horace shows his acquaintance with Lucretius in several passages in his Satires, e.g. 1, 1, 13 (Lucr. 2, 104. 5, 164). 118 (Lucr. 3, 938). 1, 3, 38 (Lucr. 4, 1153). 1, 5, 101 (Lucr. 5, 82). 1, 6, 4 (Lucr. 3, 1028). 18 (Lucr. 3, 69). ep. 1, 16, 38 (Lucr. 2, 1005). c. 1, 26, 6 (Lucr. 4, 2). Even c. 4, 7, 15 the *bonus Ancus* (Lucr. 3, 1025) is again found. E. Göbel, ZföG. 8, 421. JAReisacker, Hor. u. sein Verh. zu Lucr., Bresl. 1873. AWeingärtner, de Horatio Lucretii imitatore, Halle 1874. Gell. 1, 21, 7 *non verba sola, sed versus prope totos et locos quoque Lucreti plurimos sectatum esse Vergilium videmus.* Cf. § 228, 6 in fin. So too Vergil G. 2, 490 sqq. may be supposed to think especially of Lucretius. RWöhler, d. Einfluss d. Lucr. auf die Dichter d. august. Zeit. I (Vergil), Greifsw. 1876. Influence on Ovid, see AZingerle, Ovids Verhältn. 2, 12; more considerable on Manilius (§ 253, 5 ad fin.). The archaists of the 1st century of the Christian era preferred Lucretius to

Vergil (Tac. dial. 23). JJessen, über Lucr. und sein Verhältnis zu Catull (c. 64) und Späteren (esp. Arnobius), Kiel 1872. Cf. § 214, 6. On the use made of Lucretius by the Panegyrists see SBrandt, RhM. 38, 606.—On the chronology of the work: book 4 must have been written after 685/69: for in 4, 73 sqq. is mentioned the covering over of the theatre with vela, which first occurred in that year; b. 6 after 695/59: for 6, 109 are mentioned the *carbasina vela* covering the theatre, which were only introduced at that time (Plin. NH. 19, 23). Cf. FMarx in the exercitat. gramm. spec. 13. SBrandt, JJ. 131, 601.

3. Characteristics of the work. The deepest veneration for Epicurus: 3, 3 *te sequor, o Graiae gentis decus . . .* (9) *tu pater, es rerum inventor . . . tuisque ex, inclute, chartis, floriferis ut apes in saltibus omnia libant, omnia nos itidem depascimur aurea dicta, aurea perpetua semper dignissima vita.* Sympathy with Empedokles: 1, 729 *nil tamen hoc* (Emp.) *habuisse* (Siciliam) *viro praeclarius in se . . ut vix humana videatur stirpe creatus.* Allusion to Ennius: 1, 117. Lucretius is so firmly convinced of the truth of his doctrine that he looks upon the errors of others with compassion and self-congratulation (2, 7–13), and he is so certain of the merit of his enterprise that he is engaged on it night and day (1, 143. 4, 966 sq.) and forgets all the difficulties of his subject (1, 413 sqq. 921) and the treatment of it in Latin (*propter egestatem patrii sermonis* 1, 140. 832. 3, 261), in the hope of renown (1, 922), which he claims with charming naïveté *primum quod magnis doceo de rebus et artis relligionum* (cf. 63 sqq. 84 sqq. 2, 44, where *mortis timores* are mentioned) *animos nodis exsolvere pergo; deinde quod obscura de re tam lucida pango carmina, musaeo contingens cuncta lepore* (1, 930–933); and also on account of the novelty of his attempt (1, 926 *avia Pieridum peragro loca nullius ante trita solo iuvatque novos decerpere flores*, cf. 2, 1023 sqq.), which should be understood only in reference to Roman literature. A certain melancholy pervades his whole system, see e.g. 3, 870–977 and other passages. JReisacker, der Todesgedanke . . bes. bei Epikur und Lucretius, Trêves 1862. His instincts are attested by many touching descriptions of scenes of human life (1, 938 sqq. 2, 1163 sqq. 3, 907 sqq. 5, 223 sqq.) and of nature (2, 29 sqq. 144 sqq. 352 sqq.).

4. Authorities and system. Chief fund of information on the Epicurean philosophy: Epicurea ed. HUsener, Lps. 1887. FALange, Gesch. des Materialismus[2] 1, 99. 139. JBRoyer, les arguments du matérialisme dans L., Par. 1883. IBruns, Lucrez-Studien, Freib. 1884. FSiemering, quaestt. Lucrett., Königsb. 1867 II. JWoltjer, Lucr. philosophia cum fontibus comparata, Groningen 1877. FBockemüller, Studd. zu Lucr. u. Epik., Stade 1877. GLohmann, quaestt. Lucr. (cap. II de ratione inter Lucr. et Epic.), Brunswick 1882. PRusch, de Posidonio Lucretii auctore (in b. 6), Greifsw. 1882; Lucr. u. die Isonomie, JJ. 133, 777. EHallier, Lucr. carm. e fragmentis Empedoclis adumbratum, Jena 1857. ABästlein, quid L. debuerit Empedocli, Schleusingen 1875. JMasson, the atomic theory of L., Lond. 1884. WHMallock, introd. to Lucr., Lond. 1876. JVeitch, Lucr. and the Atomic theory, Glasg. 1875. ABrieger, de atomorum Epicurearum motu principali, in the phil. Abhh. f. MHertz, Berl. 1888, 215. ThBindseil, quaestt. Lucr., Anclam 1867; de omnis infinitate ap. Lucr., Eschwege 1870. WHörschelmann, observatt. Lucr. alterae, Lips. 1877 (on the inane in Lucr.; also GTeichmüller, RhM. 33, 310). CGneisse, das omne bei L., JJ. 121, 837. FHöfer, zur Lehre von der Sinneswahrnehmung in Lucr. IV, Stendal 1872. AJReisacker, quaestiones Lucr., Bonn 1847; Epicuri de animorum natura doctrina a Lucretio tractata, Cologne 1855. MEichner, adnott. ad Lucr. . . . de animae natura doctrinam, Berl. 1884. HHempel, die Ethik des L., Salzwedel 1872. Diebitsch, d. Sittenlehre des L., Ostrowo 1886.

5. Diction and metre. FWAltenburg, de usu antiquae locutionis in Lucr., Gotha 1857. CWFProll, de formis antiquis Lucr., Bresl. 1859. RSchubert, de Lucr. verborum formatione, Halle 1865. RBouterwek, Lucr. quaestiones gramm. et crit., Halle 1861. FWHoltze, syntaxis Lucr. lineamenta, Lps. 1868. HKeller, de verbb. c. praeposs. compositis ap. L., Halle 1880. EReichenhart, d. subordinierenden caus. Conjj. bei L. I, Frankenthal 1881; II BlfbayrGW. 18, 98; der Inf. bei L., Act. Erlang. 4, 457. KGneisse (on porro), JJ. 123, 489. FPolle, de artis vocabulis (philosophical technical terms) quibusdam Lucr., Dresd. 1866. CGLStädler, de sermone Lucr., Jena 1869. EKraetsch, de abundanti dicendi genere Lucr., Berl. 1881. JVahlen, obss. quaed. sermonis Lucr., Berl. Vorl.-Verz. 1881 f. CWolff, de Lucr. vocabulis singularibus, Halle 1878. FSchroeter, die Conditionalsätze des L., Jena 1874. GKühn, quaestt. Lucr. gramm. et metr., Bresl. 1869. EBüchel, de re metrica Lucr., Höxter 1874. ThBirt, hist. hexametri lat., Bonn 1876, 20.

6. Incompleteness (gaps, repetitions, ambiguous constructions), etc. As to the extent of this and the care of the editor, opinions differ (see HPurmann, JJ. 67, 658. FPolle, Phil. 25, 503), but there is no doubt as to the fact itself or the greater polish of the early books (2–3) when compared with the others. FBockemüller, Stud. zu Lucr. u. Epikur (Stade 1877) 1, 17. HStürenburg, de Lucr. libro primo, acta Lips. 2, 367. FNeumann, de interpolationibus Lucr., Halle 1875. AForbiger, de L. carmine a scriptore serioris aetatis pertractato, Lps. 1824. AKannengiesser, de L. versibus transponendis, Gött. 1878. KGneisse, de versibus in Lucr. carmine repetitis, Strassb. 1878. GLohmann (n. 4) p. 3 de repetitionibus. ThTohte, JJ. 119, 541.—On the Proemium (of b. 1) see JVahlen, Berl. SBer. 1878, 479. HSauppe, quaestt. Lucr. 1880, 11. FSusemihl, Greifsw. 1884; Phil. 44, 745.

7. On Lucretius and his work see e.g. LGrasberger, de Lucr. carmine, Munich 1856 (de L. philosophia 5–21; de arte L. 21–41), and especially CMartha, le poème de Lucr.; morale, religion, science, Par.[4] 1885.—Mommsen, RG. 3[6], 594. ABrieger, in the Gegenwart 8 (1875), 169. Ribbeck, röm. Dicht. 1, 273.

8. Ancient commentators: Valerius Probus (§ 300, 4). Hieronym. in Ruf. (2, 472 Vall.), see § 41, 4. Cf. JSteup, de Probis 81.—In the Middle ages Lucretius appears to have been completely forgotten; JJessen, Phil. 30, 236. Cf. MHaupt, op. 3, 641.

9. All the MSS. of Lucretius may be traced back to the long lost archetype (about s. IV–V, without separate division of words), of which in the 9th cent. there were still three copies extant. Of these we still possess one, the Vossianus F. 30 s. IX in Leyden ('oblongus'; facsimile in Chatelain t. 56. 57), see EGöbel, RhM. 15, 401. From the second copy, very similar to the oblongus, which Poggio brought from Germany to Italy, are descended the numerous Italian MSS., which are for the most part greatly interpolated; lastly, from the third are derived the Vossianus Q. 94 s. X ('quadratus') in Leyden (Chatelain t. 58) and the fragments at Copenhagen and Vienna (eight schedae Havnienses and ten Vindobonenses. Chatelain t. 59. 60), see RJFHenrichsen, de fragm. Gottorpiensi Lucr., Eutin 1846. EGöbel, RhM. 12, 449. See esp. Lachmann's commentary p. 3. Also FPolle, Phil. 25, 528. 517.—JWoltjer (new examination of the Leidenses), JJ. 119, 769. He makes an unsuccessful attempt to trace back to a still earlier archetype than that of Lachmann: against this see ABrieger, JJ. 127, 553.—One of the interpolated Italian MSS. is the Monac. 816[a] s. XV, once in the possession of PVictorius (cod. Victorianus): the corrections in this are probably due to IPontanus' pupil, MMarullus († 1500); see LSpengel, Münchn. Gel. Anz. 33 (1851), 771.

WChrist, quaest. Lucr., Munich 1855. EGöbel, quaest. Lucr. crit., Salzb. 1857; RhM. 12, 453. De cod. Victor. by HSauppe (Gött. 1864) and RBouterwek (Halle 1865). Munro's ed. p. 7. 27. FPolle, Phil. 25, 518.

10. On the basis of these MSS. the text of Lucretius was first restored by Lachmann in his epoch-making revision, which however presumed too much on corruption in the text and accordingly went much too far in the way of emendation: Lucretii de rerum natura libri sex. CLachmannus recensuit et emendavit, Berol. 1850 ([4] 1871): also CLachmanni in L. libros commentarius, Berol. 1850 ([4] 1882; index copiosus to the commentary by FHarder, Berl. 1882).—Numerous critical contributions: JMarkland, Hermath. 7, 153. HPurmann (Bresl. 1846. Naumb. 1849. Lauban 1858, 1860. Cottbus 1867. Phil. 3, 66. 7, 733. JJ. 115, 273), JSiebelis (Lps. 1844), HLotze (Phil. 7, 696), WChrist (Munich 1855), JJessen (Gött. 1868, p. 10–40), EGöbel (Bonn 1854), JNMadvig (op. 1, 305. adv. crit. 2, 22), JBernays (RhM. 5, 533; 8, 159), ThBergk, op. 1, 423 sqq., FSusemihl and ABrieger (Phil. 14, 550. 23, 455. 623. 24, 422. 25, 67. 27, 28. 29, 417. 32, 478. 33, 431. 44, 61), LMüller (ib. 15, 157), ThBindseil (de L. libr. I et II qui sunt de atomis; Halle 1865, on 1, 951–1113, Berl. 1870), FPolle (Phil. 25, 269), FBockemüller (Lucretiana, Stade 1868), JLUssing, Tidskrift f. Filol. b. 7 (Copenh. 1868), PLangen (Phil. 34, 28), WHörschelmann (obss. critt. in Lucr. libr. II, act. Lps. 5, 1, see above n. 4; cf. ABrieger, JJ. 111, 609), ThTohte, JJ. 117, 123, JWoltjer, JJ. 119, 769 (also ABrieger, JJ. 127, 553). 125, 471. CMFrancken, JJ. 121, 765. SBrandt, ib. 771. AKannengiesser, JJ. 125, 833; Phil. 43, 536. JPPostgate, Journ. of philol. 16, 124.—Cf. the notices by FPolle, Phil. 25, 484. 26, 290. 524. ABrieger, JB. 1873, 1097. 1876 2, 159. 1877 2, 62. 1879 2, 186. 1881 2, 148. 1884 2, 171.

11. Editions (cf. Munro 1, p. 3–23). Aldina I (1500) cura HAvancii; cum comm. IBPii, Bonon. 1511. Iuntina (cura PCandidi), Flor. 1512. Cum comm. DLambini, Par. 1564. 1570. Francof. 1583 and later. Cum collectan. OGifanii, Antv. 1566 and later. Cum notis ThCreech, Oxon. 1695 and later. Cum notis varr. ed. SHavercamp, Leid. 1725 II. Ed. CWakefield, Lond. 1796 III, Glasg. 1813 IV (cf. Madvig, op. 1, 306). Ed. HCAEichstaedt, Vol. I (Prolegg., Text, Index) Lps. 1801. Ed. AForbiger, Lps. 1828. Principal edition: Rec. et emend. CLachmann, cum commentario, Berl. 1850. II (see n. 10). Ed. JBernays, Lps. 1852. With notes and a translation by HAJMunro, Cambr.[4] 1886 III (together with an ed. of the text). Edited and explained by FBockemüller, Stade 1873. 74 II (and Studien zu L. und Epikur, Stade 1877 and other works). Commentary on b. 1 by JBernays in collected treatises (Berl. 1855) 2, 1.—With introd. and notes to l. I. III. V by FKelsey, Boston 1884. B. 5 av. comment. crit. et explic. par EBenoist et Lantoine, Par. 1884. Bks 1–3, WLee, Lond. 1884.

12. Translations (German) by CLvKnebel (Lpz. 1821 and 1831), WBinder (Stuttgart 1868 sq.), MSeydel (Munich 1881).

204. The younger generation, whose prime falls into the stormy time of the Civil War between Pompey and Caesar, and who were obliged to share these broils, derived therefrom a passionate and excited character in life as well as in literature. Imbued with the results of the earlier mental culture and with Greek refinement, conscious moreover of their own power, these men courageously tried new paths and even endeavoured to equal the Greeks themselves in literature. Sallust in history, and

Catullus in poetry, show how successful these attempts were, both being men of much the same age and only the most prominent of a considerable number: in poetry, Varro Atacinus, and Licinius Calvus, the latter nearly equalling Catullus; in another branch we should mention the Syrian Publilius; in prose, M. and D. Brutus, Caelius Rufus, Cornificius, Curio, Furnius, and many others. Even a lady, Hortensia, appears among the orators, and other ladies, like Catullus' Lesbia, wrote poems. All these writers and orators tend towards a common standard, which was the chief literary characteristic of their generation, viz. naturalness, simplicity and plainness, though sometimes they pursued it so intentionally as to become artificial by the excess of it. In poetry, they imitated the Alexandrine poets, sometimes even in the subject-matter. Epic poems on mythological subjects were written by Valerius Cato (Diana), Catullus (Epithalamium Pelei), Calvus (Io), Cinna (Zmyrna), Cornificius (Glaucus), Caecilius (Cybele); epithalamia and hymenaeal poems by Catullus, Calvus and Ticidas. It was in equal harmony with Alexandrine poetry and with the loose manners of the time and these circles, that almost every one of these poets should write erotic poetry. In politics, however, they were divided, and political motives were strong everywhere. As this stirring time produced an entire literature of its own, so poetry followed the men and the movements of the day with its productions; historical composition betrayed the influence of politics from beginning to end, and oratory even then began to suffer in consequence by being stinted in its range of subjects.

1. Epigrams on contemporaneous events see § 31, 2. Iambics § 33, 2. Trochaics e.g. on the death of Crassus: § 11, 2 ad fin. Cic. ad Q. fr. 2, 3, 2 (a. 698/56) *cum omnia maledicta, versus denique obscenissimi in Clodium et Clodiam dicerentur.* Anonymous epigrams in praise of Caesar and esp. his expedition to Britain from the cod. Voss. 86 AL. 419–426. PLM. 4, 59–71.

2. To this generation belongs (in addition to Bibaculus § 192, 4) Maecius. Pompey intrusted to him, a. 699/55, the selection of the plays to be performed at the dedication of his theatre. Cic. fam. 7, 1, 1 *nobis erant ea perpetienda quae Sp. Maecius probavisset* (here the Med. reads: *quae s. p.* [so according to Baiter, but *sp.* according to Mommsen, Herm. 15, 114] *maecius* i.e. *Sp. Maecius*, as in the Schol. Cruq. p. 735b we read *Spurius Metius Tarpa;* the reading *quae scilicet P. Maecius* in PVictorius, and HJordan, Herm. 8, 89 is wrong). Hor. sat. 1, 10, 38 mentions Tarpa as holding an official appointment (perhaps that of magister collegii) at public readings of the poets in the collegium poetarium (§ 94, 7. 134, 2). On this cf. Porph. *nam hi fere qui scenae scribebant ad Tarpam* (previously referred to as *Maecius Tarpa*) *velut emendatorem ea adferebant.* Cf. Verhandl. d. Heidelb. Philol.-

Vers. 163. Nipperdey, op. 503. We must not assign an earlier date to Maecius, since he is mentioned in Hor. AP. 287 as still living, and the young Piso (§ 239, 7) is for his future poems referred to the judgment of Maecius (*Maeci iudicis*). He may have been born about 665/89–670/84. In Donatus' appendix to Suetonius' vita Ter. p. 25 R. *duos Terentios poetas fuisse scribit Maecius*, the same Tarpa is probably intended.

205. C. Sallustius Crispus of Amiternum (a. 668/86–720/34) devoted the last years of his eventful life after Caesar's death to historical composition. At first he wrote a monograph on the conspiracy of Catiline (bellum Catilinae), more from literary sources than the original documents, but with a manifest attempt at impartiality. His treatment of the subject is not sufficiently accurate in respect of the facts and the chronological order of the events, aiming chiefly at exploring their inner sequence, the tone of the age and the motives of the leading men, which are neatly and epigrammatically presented in high-strained, peculiar and sometimes conceited phraseology. His Jugurtha exhibits the same general merits and defects, but is more evenly planned, more polished in style and founded on more careful research. It contains an objective description of the Roman oligarchy in its deepest degeneracy. The story is graphically developed and makes a stronger impression on the reader's mind because of the calmer and cooler spirit which the historian here assumes. His last work, and the largest and most mature, consisted of five books of Historiae, commencing with the year of Sulla's death (676) and carried down to 687, though they were perhaps never completed. This work was planned in the same way as the two smaller treatises, but the only remains of it are four speeches, two letters and fragments (considerably increased of late). Two letters ad Caesarem senem de republica and the invectiva Sallusti in Ciceronem (to which there is also Ciceronis in Sallustium responsio) are wrongly ascribed to Sallust.

1. The spelling *Sallustius* has the best authorities in its favour and is in accordance with etymology.—Hieronym. on Euseb. chr. ad a. Abr. 1930=667/87 (in cod. Freher. ad 1931=768/86) *Sallustius Crispus scriptor historicus in Sabinis Amiterni nascitur;* and ad 1981=718/36, *Sallustius diem obiit quadriennio ante actiacum bellum.* Chron. pasch. 1 p. 347 Dind. (perhaps after Phlegon's Ὀλυμπιονῖκαι, Reifferscheid Suet. 381): . . . ὑπάτων Μαρίου τὸ ζ' καὶ Κίννα τὸ β' (668/86) Σαλούστιος ἐγεννήθη καλάνδαις ὀκτωβρίαις, and p. 359, ὑπ. Κενσωρίνου καὶ Σαβίνου (a. 715/39) Σαλούστιος ἀπέθανε πρὸ τριῶν ἰδῶν μαΐων (13 May). Gell. 17, 18 *M. Varro . . . in libro quem scripsit 'Pius aut de pace' C. Sallustium scriptorem seriae illius et severae orationis, in cuius historia notiones censorias fieri atque exerceri videmus, in adulterio deprehensum ab Annio Milone loris bene caesum dicit* (after Sallust's death, Varro † 727/27) *et cum dedisset pecuniam dimissum.* Cf. Porph. Hor. sat. 1, 2, 41. Serv. Aen. 6, 612.

Cic. in Sall. invectiv. 14.—Trib. pl. 702/52. Was he leg. pro quaest. in Syria 704/50? Mommsen, Herm. 1, 171. He was expelled from the Senate by the censors 704/50 (Cic. in Sall. invectiv. 16. Dio 40, 63); reinstated 705/49 by Caesar, through his reappointment to the quaestura (Cic. in Sall. 17; cf. 21). 706/48 he commanded a legion in Illyria (Oros. 6, 15, 8). 707/47 negotiator on behalf of Caesar with the insurgent legions in Campania (App. b. c. 2, 92. Dio 42, 52, 1). 708/46 praetor (b. afr. 8. 34) and proconsul in Africa; bell. afr. 97. In this position he enriched himself by exactions; see Cic. in Sall. 19. Dio 43, 9. He was the possessor of the horti Sallustiani. Tac. ann. 3, 30 *Crispum equestri ortum loco C. Sallustius, rerum Rom. florentissmus auctor, sororis nepotem in nomen adscivit* etc. (cf. Hor. carm. 2, 2. sat. 1, 2, 48)—Portraits? Bernoulli, röm. Ikonogr. 1, 200.

2. Sall. Cat. 4 *ubi animus ex multis miseriis atque periculis requievit et mihi reliquam aetatem a re publica procul habendam decrevi . . . statui res gestas populi R. carptim ut quaeque memoria digna videbantur perscribere . . . igitur de Catilinae coniuratione quam verissume potero paucis absolvam.* The work is called *bellum Catilinae* in Quint. 3, 8, 9 and in the subscription of the Paris. Sorb. 500 (see n. 8), cf. also the passage in Suidas n. 7; it is called *b. Catilinarium* or rather *b. Catulinarium* (on this see EWölfflin, Arch. f. lat. Lexicogr. 1, 277) in the superscription of the Paris. Sorb.; composed after Caesar's death (53. 54), published about 712/42. Many historical and chronological inaccuracies in it have been pointed out. Cicero is treated with much tact, in that he is neither overpraised nor blamed; but the writer's personal partiality for Caesar appears in some places. General introductions, digressions and speeches; following the example of Greek writers (*C. Sallustius in bello iugurthino et Catilinae nihil ad historiam pertinentibus principiis orsus est* Quint. 3, 8, 9). RDietsch, quo tempore quoque consilio Sallustius Catilinam scripserit, Grimma 1856. WIhne, Würzb. Philol.-Vers. (Lpz. 1869) 105. HDübi, de Cat. Sall. fontt. ac fide, Berne 1872; JJ. 113, 851. CJohn, Entstehungsgesch. der Catil. Verschw., JJ. Suppl. B. 8, 701; RhM. 31, 401. CBuresch in the comm. Ribbeckianae 219. JBesser, de Catil. coniur., Lps. 1881. ELang, d. Strafverfahren gegen d. Catilinarier und Caesars und Catos darauf bezügliche Reden bei Sall., Schönthal 1884. See also § 179, 20, 1.

Editions by FKritz, ed. illustr., Lps. 1828. RDietsch, Lpz. 1864. JHSchmalz, Gotha [2] 1886. PThomas, Brussels 1884. AMCook, Lond. 1884. BDTurner, Lond. 1887.—AEussner, Lpz. 1887.—Translated by CHolzer, Stuttgart 1868. Criticism and explanation: CWNauck (the preface), Königsb. i/d. NM. 1850. JKvičala, ZföG. 14, 579. AEussner, RhM. 27, 493. Ritschl, op. 3, 818. Nipperdey, op. 452 and others.

3. Iug. 5 *bellum scripturus sum quod P. R. cum Iugurtha gessit, primum quia magnum et atrox variaque victoria fuit, dehinc quia tunc primum superbiae nobilitatis obviam itum est. Bellum iugurthinum* (thus in the superscription of the Paris. Sorb., ap. Quint. 3, 8, 9), probably chiefly following the memoirs of Sulla, Scaurus and Rutilius, making use of Sisenna (Iug. 95, 2) and of other authorities (ib. 17, 7 *ex libris Punicis qui regis Hiempsalis dicebantur nobis interpretatum est*), but the work is not very reliable in its geography and ethnography. The political point of view (ib. 5, 1) predominates, but does not lead the writer into partiality. The speeches of Memmius (c. 81) and Marius (c. 85) are excellent portraitures of political situations. The work concludes with a significant glance at Marius. The plan (introduction, digressions and speeches) is on the whole the same as in the Catiline; phrases are frequently repeated from the Catiline and from the Jugurtha itself; but the single parts are in better proportion to each other. WIhne, ZfGW. 34, 47. HWirz, d. stoffl. und zeitl. Gliederung des Iug., in d. Festschr. d. Zür.

Kantonsschule z. Philol.-Vers. in Zürich 1887, 1.—Editions by ChGHerzog, Lpz. 1840. OEichert, Bresl. 1867. PThomas, Brussels 1877. JHSchmalz, Gotha [2] 1886. WPBrooke, Lond. 1885.—RDietsch, obss. criticae in Iug. partem extremam, Grimma 1845. Widmann, de Memmii oratione, Blaubeuren 1857. Mommsen, Herm. 1, 427; on the chronology of the war see the same author, RG. 2^6, 146. 155. On the other side HFPelham, Journ. of philol. 7 (1877), 91.—Translated (in German) by CHolzer, Stuttg. 1868. Editions of the Catiline and Jugurtha by GLong (with the chief fragments of the Histories, by JGFrazer) Lond.[2] 1890. CMerivale, Lond.[2] 1858. WWCapes, Oxf. 1884. Translation, with notes, by AWPollard, Lond. 1882.

4. The Historiae were, as far as the subject is concerned, a continuation of Sisenna's work. The history of Sulla was purposely omitted (Iug. 95, 2). It extended *bis senos per annos* (Auson. op. 13, 2, 61). That it opened with a. 676/78 is quite certain (the first words were *Res populi rom. M. Lepido Q. Catulo coss. ac deinde militiae et domi gestas composui;* cf. also Auson. l.l.), nor does anything in the fragments lead us beyond a. 687/67. Here too the author aimed at historical impartiality; see § 206, 2. For rhetorical purposes, perhaps in the 2nd century after Chr., a collection was prepared of all the Sallustian speeches (15) and letters (6) arranged according to their order of succession in the Bella and Historiae (HJordan, Herm. 6, 74): in this are preserved 4 speeches (Lepidi, Philippi, Cottae, Macri) and 2 letters (Cn. Pompei, Mithridatis) from the Historiae. This collection is extant in a complete form in Vatican. 3864 s. X. (facsim. in Chatelain t. 54, 2), where is the observation: *C. Crispi Sallusti orationes excerptae de bellis explicit feliciter. C. Crispi Sallusti orationes excerptae de historiis incipit feliciter.* JCOrelli, hist. crit. eclogarum ex Sall. hist., Zür. 1833. EWölfflin, Phil. 17, 154 and esp. HJordan, RhM. 18, 584. There are also extant considerable fragments of b. 2 and 3, preserved by means of portions of a MS. of s. IV/V, which are to be found at Berlin, Rome and especially at Orleans, and are proved to belong to the hist. by the fact that the commencement of the speech of Cotta and the close of Pompey's letter (see above l. 11) recur in them; the fragmentum Berolinense (found at Toledo, first published by GHPertz, Abh. d. Berl. Akad. 1847, Berl. 1848, first recognised as a fragment of Sallust by KLRoth, RhM. 8, 433); the fragmenta Vaticana Reg. 1283 (facsimile in Zangem.-Wattenbach's Exempla t. 7 and in Chatelain t. 51; cf. HJordan, de vaticanis Sall. hist. l. III reliquiis, Herm. 5, 396. 14, 634. EHauler, Wien. Stud. 10, 136); the fragmenta Aurelianensia (cod. 196 M) discovered and deciphered by EHauler 1886; cf. the same author Wien. Stud. 8, 315; Rev. de philol. 40, 113; Wiener SBer. 1886, 615 and his edition of all the Orléans fragments in the Wien. Stud. 9, 25: the whole is also found in Jordan's ed.[3] 1887 p. 127. These fragments refer to the years 679/75–681/73.—The Historiae were made use of by Livy and others, by Plutarch and Cassius Dio, and especially by Julius Exuperantius (§ 445, 3). More recent collections of the fragments of the Hist. by FKritz (disposita suisque comm. illustrata, Lps. 1853; and newly arranged and explained, Erfurt 1856), again in Dietsch's ed. v. 1859 Vol. 2 (n. 9; additions in the RhM. 18, 478. 19, 147). For the speeches, letters and fragments independently preserved (vid. supr.) see especially HJordan's Sallust.[3] 1887, 111. Cf. HJordan, de Sall. hist. libri II reliquiis, Königsb. 1887.—Sall. oratt. et epistt. ex hist. ed. JCOrelli, Zür. 1831 (and frequently). GLinker, Sall. hist. prooemium . . . restituere tentavit, Marb. 1850. JCSchlimmer, hist. rerum. gest. in hist. Sall. libris, Utr. 1860. Cf. RKlotz in Jahn's Arch. 15, 362.—Criticism: Madvig, adv. 2, 293. LLange, de Philippi orationis ap. Sall. loco, Lps. 1879. On an hitherto unknown old copy of the oratt. and epistt. see LLange, Leipz. Stud. 2, 290.

5. The same Vaticanus 3864 (n. 4 l. 12) has preserved an oration and an epistle ad Caesarem senem de re publica, both no doubt of the Imperial period and the productions of rhetorical schools, both unreal and obviously written in imitation of Sallust's diction, with exaggerated archaic spelling. The epistle is very prolix and partly contains the same propositions as the oration, but has no further connection with it. They seem to be treatises on the same theme, from different points of view, but (to judge from the similarity of their arrangement, spirit, language and many phrases) certainly of the same age, if not by the same author, which is the opinion of Orelli and Jordan; the latter places him in the time between the Flavii and Antonini, while Orelli fixes on the age of Fronto and supposes Fronto to be the author of the collection of the orations and letters of Sallust. Cf. Teuffel, Tübinger Doctorenverzeichn. v. 1868, p. 13. HJordan, de suasoriis ad Caes. senem de rep. inscriptis, Berl. 1868. OHartung, de Sall. epistolis ad Caes. senem, Halle 1874. CSpandau, eine Salluststudie, Baireuth 1869 asserts the Sallustian origin of both works; that of the epistle is affirmed equally unconvincingly by LHellwig, de genuina Sall. ad Caes. epistula cum incerti alicuius suasoria iuncta, Lps. 1873. See against this FVogel, act. semin. Erlang. 1, 341. KSchenkl, ZföG. 22, 668. The best text in Jordan's Sallust [3] 1887, 141.

6. The reciprocal invectivae (this title and that of controversiae are traditional; suasoriae would be more correct. LGurlitt, Phil. Suppl. 5, 597) of Sallust and of Cicero were composed for each other, and are the work of one and the same rhetorician, who for the adornment of these wordy orations borrowed many details from the political ribaldry of the period immediately following Cicero's and Sallust's death. The analogies between the invect. in Tull. and Dio 46, 1 sqq. and the invect. in Tull. 5 with epist. ad Caesar. senem de rep. 9, 2 are probably due to the employment of the same authorities. The invectiva in Tullium is unsuspectingly quoted as Sallustian by Quintilian (4, 1, 68; 9, 3, 89; and 11, 1, 24). Subsequently also by Donatus and Servius (see the latter on Aen. 6, 623). The invectiva in Sallustium (20) by Diomed. GL. 1, 387 *de perfecto* (cf. *comedor*) *ambigitur apud veteres, comestus an comesus et comesurus. sed* † *Didius* (so the MSS.: *Tullius* Jordan, *Epidius* GLinker; see § 211, 4) *ait de Sallustio 'comesto patrimonio.'* Cf. Corradi, quaestura 85, ChGHerzog (Programme v. Gera 1834 sqq.), Teuffel l.l. (1868) 14, HJordan, Herm. 11, 305, FVogel, act. semin. Erlang. 1, 325. Extant in early MSS. in Wolfenbüttel (Gud. 335 s. X), London (Harl. 2716 s. IX/X; 2682 s. XI; 3859 s. XII) and Munich (19472 s. XI, 4611 s. XII). On an Admont. MS. s. XII MPetschenig, ZföG. 34, 1. Revisions of the text by GBaiter in Orelli's Cic. 2^2, 1421; Baiter-Kayser's Cic. 11, 147 (in CFWMüller's Cic. 4, 3, 315) and esp. in HJordan's Sallust ([3]1887) 155.

7. Old commentators. Aemilius Asper (Lyd. de magistr. 3, 8 *Αἰμίλιος ἐν τῳ ὑπομνήματι τῶν Σαλλουστίου ἱστοριῶν.* Charis. GL. 1, 216, 28 *Asper commentario Sallustii Historiarum I*). Suidas v. Ζηνόβιος : Ζηνόβιος σοφιστὴς παιδεύσας ἐπὶ Ἀδριανοῦ Καίσαρος ἔγραψε . . . μετάφρασιν ἑλληνικῶς τῶν Ἱστοριῶν Σαλουστίου τοῦ ῥωμαϊκοῦ ἱστορικοῦ τῶν καλουμένων αὐτοῦ Βελῶν (Bella). An anonymous commentator on the Catiline is mentioned by Suringar, hist. schol. 1, 254. Besides a collection of the speeches (see n. 4) there was perhaps (AvGutschmid) a collection of the geographical sections of Sallust. Cf. KMüllenhoff, Deutsche Altertumskunde 1, 75. —Praise of the Sallustian topographical descriptions in Licinianus below § 206, 4 ad fin. and Avien. ora marit. 36 *inclitam descriptionem qua locorum formulam imaginemque . . . paene in obtutus dedit lepore linguae.*

8. Manuscripts. On the transmission of the speeches and letters contained

in the Historiae see n. 4.—The MSS. of the Bella are divided into two classes. The older gives a better text, but has a gap in Iug. 103, 2 to 112, 3. Its best representatives are first Paris. 16024 (Sorb. 500) s. X (Chatelain t. 52, 2), next Paris. 16025 (Sorb. 1576) s. X (Chatelain t. 52, 2); to this class belong e.g. Gruter's lost Nazarianus, and the Leid. Voss. 73 s. XI, which, though decidedly corresponding with the first class, yet contains the missing chapters, at first hand, in the right place. The later class of MSS. (which have been greatly interpolated) fill up the large gap in the Iug. and contain besides much genuine matter (Cat. 6, 2. Iug. 21, 4. 44, 5) which is omitted from the first class: the best representative of this class is Monac. 14477 s. XI. The text of the speeches and letters in Vatic. 3864 (see n. 4) is often arbitrarily altered. For the differing theories as to the relation of these two classes to each other, see KLRoth (RhM. 9, 129, 630), RDietsch in his ed. of 1859, and EWölfflin (Phil. 17, 519, and against him EBrentano, de C. Sallustii Crispi codd. recensendis, Frankf. 1864 p. 2 sqq.), H. Jordan (on Vat. 3864, in the Herm. 1, 231; on the cod. Nazarianus, ib. p. 240; cf. 3, 460. 11, 330), HWirz, de fide et auctorit. cod. Sall. Paris. 1576, Aarau 1867; Phil. Anz. 7, 151; ZfGW. 31, 272. KNipperdey, op. 540. MHertz, JJ. 95, 318. AWeinhold, quaestt. Sall. maxime ad libr. Vat. 3864 spectantes, in the Acta Lips. 1, 183. FChThDieck, de ratione quae inter Sall. cod. Vat. 3864 et Paris. 500 intercedat, Halle 1872. GBöse, de fide et auctoritate cod. Sall. Vat. 3864, Gött. 1874. OAnhalt, quae ratio in libris recensendis Sall. recte adhibeatur, Jen. 1876. AEussner, Phil. 25, 343 and in Würzb. Festgruss (1868) 158. 184; JB. 1877 2, 156. LKuhlmann, de Sall. cod. Par. 500, Oldenb. 1881; quaestt. Sall. crit., Oldenb. 1887. ANitschner, de locis Sall. qui ap. scriptt. et grammaticos vett. leguntur, Gött. 1884. On a worthless Rostock MS. OClason, JJ. Suppl. 7, 243 (previously collated in Classical journ. 19 [1791], 144); on a worthless Rostock fragment of the Iug. Phil. 39, 363; on other fragments at Montpellier and Paris. 10195 s. XI (Chatel. t. 53) MBonnet, Herm. 14, 157.

9. Editions e.g. Bâle 1538 (by Glareanus). Ed. LCarrio, Antv. 1573, 1580. JGruter, Frankf. 1607. JWasse, Cantabr. 1710. E rec. et c. notis GCortii, Lps. 1724 (a reprint Lps. 1825 sqq.). Rec. et cum notis varr. ed. SHavercamp, the Hague 1742 II (a reprint by CHFrotscher, Lps. 1828 III). FDGerlach (recogn., varr. lectt., commentarios et indd. adiecit, Bas. 1823—41 III; denuo rec. atque ed., Bas. 1832; rec., adnot. crit., indicibus hist. et gramm. instruxit; acc. historicorum vett. roman. fragm. a CLRoth collecta, Bas. 1852 II; the revised text, introductory treatise, and selected readings, Stuttg. 1870), FKritz (ad fid. codd. rec. c. comm., Lps. 1828. 1834 f. II with an ind., and the fragmenta 1853; recogn. et succincta annot. illustr., Lps. 1856), EWFabri (with notes, Nürnb.[2] 1845), JCOrelli (Zür. 1840 and 1853), RDietsch (Lps. 1843–1846; large critical edition, Lps. 1859 II; with German notes, I. Lpz. 1864) RJacobs (Berl.[9] 1886 by HWirz).

Texts by GLinker (Vienna 1855), AEussner (Biblioth. Teub., 1887). AScheindler, Prague 1883, IPrammer, Vienna 1886 (likewise sallust. Miszellen, Vienna 1887) and especially HJordan (with a trustworthy critical apparatus, Berl.[3] 1887).

10. Critical and explanatory works: GLinker, Emendationen zu Sall., Wiener SBer. 13 (1854), 261. HJordan, Herm. 1, 229. AEussner in the Würzb. Festgruss (1868) 158, and exercitt. Sallust., Würzb. 1868. KNipperdey, op. 542. GUngermann, Bemerkk. zu Sall., Rheinbach 1878; JJ. 119, 554. PhKlimscha, ZföG. 29, 166: sallust. Miszellen, Kremsier 1883. CMeiser, BlfbayrGW. 19, 451. 20, 485. ThOpitz, JJ. 131, 267. AWeidner, advers. Sall., Dortm. 1886. FUber (§ 206, 9). Mollweide, glossae Sall., Strassb. 1887.

11. Translations e.g. by LNeuffer (Lpz. 1819), CCless (Stuttg. 1855 and 1865 II), RDietsch (Stuttg. 1858).

206. Sallust was the first Roman historian who wrote in obedience to fixed rules. Leaving the tracks of his Roman predecessors, he found his models among the Greeks, where he was especially interested and influenced by Thukydides. He followed the Greek historian in selecting subjects taken from the history of his own time. Though he did not succeed in reaching the elevated stand-point, the penetrating criticism and objective tone of his model, he may be allowed to rival Thukydides in truthfulness and impartiality. Even in the outward arrangement of his work he reminds the reader of Thukydides, especially in his introductory remarks and the speeches which he intersperses, and which serve to characterise the whole position of affairs and the principal actors. There is, however, in the Roman historian, a predominance of the rhetorical element which frequently interferes with the historical style, and the narrative is overloaded with general reflections. Sallust excels in delineations of character and the representation of the motives of the age; a constant increase of literary power in this respect is manifest from the Catiline to the Histories. Herein, as well as in the great care bestowed upon formal polish, he had no predecessor among his countrymen, while among his successors only Tacitus is to be compared to him. Like Thukydides, though perhaps not to the same extent, Sallust was no fast writer and took great pains with his works. Like his great model, he endeavours to be brief, sententious and concise, to such a degree as to become obscure and involved; in many details of his diction he purposely deviated from the usage of his time, and moulded his style in imitation of Greek analogies and of archaic writers, especially Cato the Elder. His archaic diction and rhetorical colouring gained Sallust great authority in the time of Fronto, and again at the close of the 4th and in the 5th century of the Christian era.

1. MART. 14, 191 *primus romana Crispus in historia.* QUINT. 2, 5, 19 *Livium a pueris magis (legi velim) quam Sallustium, etsi hic historiae maior est auctor, ad quem tamen intellegendum iam profectu opus sit.*—VELLEI. 2, 36, 2 *aemulum Thucydidis Sallustium.* QUINT. 10, 1, 101 *nec opponere Thucydidi Sallustium verear.* SEN. suas. 6, 21 *hoc* (a summary of character in relating the death of an eminent person) *semel aut iterum a Thucydide factum, item in paucissimis personis usurpatum a Sallustio.* It is significant that Sallust chose Thukydides for his pattern among the Greek historians, but that very fact explains why his imitation could not be successful in the most important points. Sallust held opposite political views and was as decided an adherent of the Democratic party as Thukydides was of the Aristocracy; gravity and dignity are, moreover, natural to Thukydides, and artificially acquired by

Sallust. It has often been remarked that Sallust's tone is at variance with the facts of his life. This was in ancient times asserted with great vehemence by Lenaeus (§ 211, 3), who *tanto amore erga patroni* (Cn. Pompey's) *memoriam exstitit ut Sallustium historicum, quod eum oris probi, animo inverecundo* (i.e. as a hypocrite) *scripsisset, acerbissima satura laceraverit, lastaurum et lurconem et nebulonem popinonemque appellans* (perhaps a hexameter '*lastaurus lurco nebulo ⟨turpis⟩ que popino*'? and from a Menippean satire? Bücheler, Petr. ed. min. [3] p. 243) *et vita scriptisque monstrosum, praeterea priscorum Catonis verborum ineruditissimum furem* (Sueton. gramm. 15 cf. below n. 8, l. 10). But even such an honest man as Gellius (see § 205, 1 l. 11) remarks that actions like those in Milo's house can scarcely be thought possible from the austere tone of Sallust's works; hence Macrobius (sat. 3, 13, 9) calls Sallust *gravissimus alienae luxuriae obiurgator et censor.* Symmachus also (ep. 5, 68) calls him *scriptor stilo tantum probandus; nam morum eius damna non sinunt ut ab illo agendae vitae petatur auctoritas.* Lactantius (inst. d. 2, 12 *quod quidem non fugit hominem nequam Sallustium, qui ait* '*nostra omnis vis* etc.' [Cat. 1, 2], *recte, si ita vixisset ut locutus est. servivit enim foedissimis voluptatibus suamque ipse sententiam vitae pravitate dissolvit*) judges unjustly, as Sallust's moral sayings were posterior to his immoral life, and instead of being refuted thereby, might rather be considered as the result of better experience and subsequent repentance. There is no reason to doubt the sincerity of this change of mind, though it was somewhat late, when Sallust had already secured the fruits of his past life, and could look forward to nothing else but literary renown. But his past life may have left to him a certain pessimism betrayed by the historian, a disposition to trace the acts of others to bad motives, a kind of dissatisfied misanthropy. See also JWLöbell, zur Beurteilung des Sall., Breslau 1818.—For assistance in his historical work Sallust caused the scholar Ateius (§ 211, 1) to prepare for him a *breviarium rerum omnium romanarum* (cf. HJordan, krit. Beitr. z. Gesch. d. lat. Spr. 352).

2. His veracity. Catil. 4, 2 *statui res gestas populi rom. . . . perscribere, eo magis quod mihi a spe, metu, partibus reip. animus liber erat.* 4, 3 and 18, 1 *quam verissume potero.* Hist. 1, 6 *neque me divorsa pars in civilibus armis movit a vero.* Hence Augustin. civ. dei 1, 5 *Sallustius, nobilitate veritatis historicus.* Isidor. orig. 13, 21, 10 *Sallustius, auctor certissimus.* But Sallust did not aspire to completeness and accuracy in details (Oros. 7, 10, 4. Vopisc. Firm. 6, 3); the dates he gives are often indefinite (*interea, isdem temporibus, dum haec aguntur*): he conceals the chronological frame-work of his narrative rather than gives prominence to it. The connecting middle terms in relation to facts are often omitted. Sallust's sober and free thought made him silent on the subject of the miracles and wonders mentioned by Livy.

3. On his prooemia see § 205, 2 l. 13. WMPahl, de prooemiis Sall., Tüb. 1859, RKuhn, die Einl. zu Sall. Cat. u. Jug., Tauberbischofsheim 1868. HJordan, krit. Beiträge 353. Sallust indulges much in neatly formulated commonplaces. Fronto p. 48 Nab. *gnomas egregie convertisti, hanc quidem quam hodie accepi prope perfecte, ut poni in libro Sallustii possit.* Among the letters occurring in Sallust that of Lentulus to Catiline (Cat. 44) is historical (cf. Cic. in Cat. 3, 12), and the same may be presumed of those of Catiline (c. 35) and of Pompey to the senate.

4. All the speeches in Sallust are impressive and powerful and far more adapted to the peculiar character of the speaker than those in Livy. Yet they are not authentic. Catiline's address to his companions may be shown from Cic. pMur. 25 and Plut. Cic. 14 to have been different; nor does anything of what Cic. Att. 12, 21 (cf. pSest. 61. Vellei. 2, 35, 3. Plut. Cato min. 23) alleges from Cato's speech in the Senate occur in the one attributed to Cato by Sallust. Hence it appears that

the other speeches also should be looked upon as such compositions as Thukydides 1, 22 declares his own to be. Those of Sallust, however, produce a greater rhetorical effect (cf. § 44, 6 in fin.) and display more art than those of the early Attic historian. When, therefore, the rhetor Seneca controv. 3, praef. 8 says: *orationes Sallustii in honorem historiarum leguntur*, this is the one-sided judgment of a scholastic rhetor who could discover too little of his unreal figures in the energetic speeches of our historian. On the other hand, LICINIANUS' judgment is perverse at least as far as the reason goes which he adduces for it (p. 42 sq. ed. Bonnensium): *Sallustium non ut historicum puto sed oratorem legendum. nam et tempora reprehendit sua et delicta carpit et contiones inserit et dat in censum* (*et dat praecepta et* NMADVIG) *loca, montes, flumina et hoc genus amoena et culta et comparat* (*et culte comparat* HJORDAN) *disserendo. . . .* See also above § 36, 5 Trogus' opinion concerning the Sallustian speeches. HSNORR v. CAROLSFELD, d. Reden u. Briefe bei Sall., Lpz. 1888.

5. Opinions concerning Sallust's diction. Ateius exhorted Asinius Pollio (*ut*) *vitet maxime obscuritatem Sallustii et audaciam in translationibus* (SUET. gr. 10). On the latter quality see QUINT. 9, 3, 12. SEN. contr. 9, 1, 13 (see n. 6). GELL. 10, 26.—GELL. NA. 4, 15, 1 *elegantia orationis Sallustii verborumque fingendi et novandi studium* (cf. 1, 15, 18 *novatori verborum Sallustio;* ib. 6, 17, 8. 10, 21, 2) *cum multa prorsus invidia fuit, multique non mediocri ingenio viri conati sunt reprehendere pleraque et obtrectare. in quibus plura inscite aut maligne vellicant.* Cf. 10, 26. QUINT. 10, 3, 8 *sic* (slowly) *scripsisse Sallustium accepimus, et sane manifestus est etiam ex opere ipso labor.*

6. His brevity. SEN. contr. 9, 1, 13 *cum sit praecipua in Thucydide virtus brevitas, hac eum Sallustius vicit et in suis illum castris cecidit. . . . ex Sallusti sententia nihil demi sine detrimento sensus potest.* L. SEN. ep. 19, 5 (=114), 17 *Sallustio vigente amputatae sententiae et verba ante exspectatum cadentia et obscura brevitas fuere pro cultu.* QUINT. 4, 2, 45 *vitanda est etiam illa Sallustiana, quamquam in ipso virtutis locum obtinet, brevitas et abruptum sermonis genus.* 10, 1, 32 *illa Sallustiana brevitas, qua nihil apud aures vacuas atque eruditas potest esse perfectius.* 102 *immortalem illam Sallustii velocitatem.* GELL. 3, 1, 6 *Sallustium, vel subtilissimum brevitatis artificem.* MACROB. sat. 5, 1, 7 *breve* (*dicendi genus*), *in quo Sallustius regnat.* STAT. silv. 4, 7, 55 *Sallusti brevis.* APOLL. SIDON. carm. 2, 190. 23, 151. APULEI. apol. 95 (*parsimonia*).

7. His Graecisms. QUINT. 9, 3, 17 *ex graeco translata vel Sallustii plurima.* We find echoes especially of Thukydides' orations, and some orations of Demosthenes, Xenophon's Cyropaedia and Memorabilia, the Menexenos and the 7th epistle of Plato. GERLACH's ed. 3, 331. POPPO's Thukyd. 6. 372. SDOLEGA, de Sall. imitatore Thucyd., Demosth. aliorumque scriptorum graec., Bresl. 1871. EMOLLMANN, quatenus Sall. e scriptorum graec. exemplo pendeat, Königsb. 1878. FROBOLSKI, Sall. in conformanda oratione quo iure Thucydidis exemplum secutus esse videatur, Halle 1881.

8. The archaisms consist chiefly in phrases such as *multi mortales, prosapia* and others. Cf. Lenaeus p. 415 l. 14. Augustus in SUET. Aug. 86 *verbis quae C. Sallustius excerpsit ex originibus Catonis.* SUET. gramm. 10 (cf. § 211, 1) *Asinius Pollio in libro quo Sallustii scripta reprehendit ut nimia priscorum verborum affectatione oblita.* Cf. GELL. 10, 26, 1 *Asinio Pollioni in quadam epistula quam ad Plancum scripsit et quibusdam aliis C. Sallustii iniquis.* Asinius also asserted that Aleius collected *antiqua verba et figuras* for the use of Sallust (see also above n. 1 ad fin.): see § 211, 1 l. 12 from the end. An epigram in QUINT. 8, 3, 29 *et verba antiqui multum furate Catonis, Crispe, iugurthinae conditor historiae.* FRONTO epist. p. 62

M. Porcius eiusque frequens sectator C. Sallustius. Cf. ib. p. 36. SERV. Aen. 1, 6 *Cato in originibus hoc dicit, cuius auctoritatem Sallustius sequitur* (Catil. 6). Thus Iug. 31, 1=Caton. reliq. p. 27, 1 JORD. 85, 8=p. 50 J. FDELTOUR, de Sallustio Catonis imitatore, Par. 1859. GBRÜNNERT, de Sall. imitatore Catonis, Sisennae aliorumque vett. historicorum rom., Jena 1873. But these archaisms are not genuinely pre-Catonian; they are intended to give stateliness and pathos to the narrative. PSCHULTZE, de archaismis Sall., Halle 1871. The antiquarian colouring is also stronger in the later works (esp. Hist.) than in the earlier ones; see EWÖLFFLIN, Phil. 34, 146; also HJORDAN, krit. Beitr. 350.

9. The formation and connection of Sallust's sentences is very simple and commonplace, sometimes even monotonous, esp. the frequent recurrence of *igitur* at the beginning of a sentence. Sallust repeats certain favourite expressions continually. Some are no doubt affectations, e.g. *paucis tempestatibus* (Iug. 96, 1) instead of *brevi tempore*. The impression of simplicity is chiefly caused by the frequent use of the historic infinitive. In his sentences Sallust is fond of rapid changes of construction, of subject and expression. Ind. verb. in DIETSCH's ed. 1859. OEICHERT, Wörterb. zu Sall., Hanover [3] 1885. References in GERLACH 3, 307. LCONSTANS, de sermone Sall., Par. 1880. NOSTLING, de elocutione Sall., Upsala 1862. BADSTÜBNER, de Sall. dicendi genere, Berl. 1863. ALAWS, de dicendi genere Sall., Rössel 1864. KKRAUT, d. vulgäre Element in d. Spr. des Sall., Blaubeuren 1881. IURI, quatenus ap. Sall. sermonis lat. plebeii aut cotidiani vestigia appareant, Par. 1885. FZEITFUCHS, de orthographia Sall., Sondersh. 1841. AANSCHÜTZ, selecta capita de syntaxi Sall., Halle 1873. LHELLWIG, zur Synt. des S. I, Ratzeb. 1877. FGROSSMANN, d. Gebr. der Kasus b. Sall., Berl. 1886. GÖRLITZ, de genetivi usu Sall., Schrimm 1878. A HERCHER, d. Gebr. d. Accus. b. S., Gera 1878. OCHRIST, de abl. Sall., Jena 1883. ALEHMANN, de verborum compositorum structura, Bresl. 1863. Leobschütz 1884. FBUSSMANN, de temporum et modorum ap. S. usu, Greifsw. 1862; obss. Sall., Hamm 1871. CHÜBENTHAL, de usu infinit. hist. ap. Sall. et Tac., Halle 1881. On the use of the particles in Sall. see FHELM, cf. § 333, 16. FBALÁZS, de disponendis enuntiatorum et periodorum partibus ap. S., Hermannst. 1873. KMEYER, d. Wort- u. Satzstellung b. Sall., Magdeb. 1880. DROHDE, adiectivum quo ord. ap. Sall. coniunctum sit cum substant., Hamb. 1887. WLILIE, obss. gramm. in Sall., Jauer 1870. FUBER, quaestt. Sall. gramm. et crit., Berl. 1882. KBRAUN, Beitr. z. Statistik des Sprachgebr. Sall.s im Cat. u. Iug., Düsseld. 1885.

10. The distinct peculiarities of Sallust provoked opposition, while they could not fail to attract a period fond of admiring and courting abstruseness. The reaction was manifested not only by Lenaeus and Asinius Pollio (n. 1 and 5) but by Livy, who was at the opposite pole to Sallust as a historical writer. SEN. contr. 9, 1, 14 (p. 399 and 449 K.) *T. Livius tam iniquus Sallustio fuit ut hanc ipsam sententiam, et tamquam translatam et tamquam corruptam dum transfertur, obiceret Sallustio.* But Tacitus felt himself akin to Sallust, whom he calls (ann. 3, 30) *rerum romanarum florentissimus auctor*, and it is easy to perceive to what extent he is influenced by Sallust. In the time of Augustus, Sallust was imitated by Arruntius, without taste and with exaggeration (§ 259, 7). See JSELLGE (§ 258, 11) on Trogus and Justinus' imitation of S. The age of Fronto was greatly attracted by a writer so piquant and so highly flavoured with archaisms. We find him frequently mentioned in the correspondence of Fronto and M. Aurelius. We meet repeatedly with the combination of Cato, Sallust and Cicero (p. 93. 105. 149), the rhetorical character of Sallust being mentioned with special emphasis. His antitheses (p. 107. cf. 108 sqq. 162) and his apophthegms (p. 48) are quoted admiringly. Under the influence of the taste of his time and owing to his natural good temper, Gellius

repeatedly (3, 1. 4, 15. 10, 26) takes Sallust's part against his adversaries. In the 4th and 5th centuries Sallust again found many imitators, such as L. Septimius (Dictys § 423, 4), Aurelius Victor (§ 414, 2), Hegesippus (§ 433, 5), Augustinus (EWölfflin, Phil. Anz. 11, 35); Sulpicius Severus too (§ 441, 2) is fond of Sallustian turns of expression, and Exuperantius (§ 445, 3) may almost be styled a Sallustian Cento. In Atil. Fort. GL. 6, 275, 15 we read *ille*=Sallust. On these imitators see FVogel, ὁμοιότητες Sallustianae, in acta sem. phil. Erlang. 1, 313; and quaestt. Sall. II, ib. 2, 405. Cf. besides EWölfflin, Herm. 9, 254. In the Middle Ages Sallust was highly popular and esteemed (Wölfflin, phil. Anz. 11, 35).

11. General literature on Sallust. JWLöbell, zur Beurteilung des Sall., Bresl. 1818. FDGerlach, hist. Studien (Hamb. 1841) 286; Geschichtschreiber d. Röm. (Stuttg. 1855), 103; de Sall. vita et scriptis, introd. to his ed. 1852, p. xiii. HUlrici, Charakteristik der antiken Historiographie 125. DeGerlache, études sur Salluste, Brussels[2] 1859. Teuffel, Tübinger Doctorenverz. v. 1868 p. 1–21. RDietsch, Stuttg. Philologen-Versamml. (Stuttg. 1857) 27. ThVogel, de Sall. vita, moribus ac scriptis, Mayence 1857. MJaeger, de vita Sall., Salzb. 1879; de Sall. moribus et scriptis, Salzb. 1884. ThRambeau, Charakt. der hist. Darstell. des Sall. I, Burg 1879.

207. In the field of jurisprudence, Caesar designed to collect the whole existing ius civile in a Corpus, in which task he was assisted by the learned lawyer A. Ofilius, whose literary exertions extended over the entire domain of law. After him, the most eminent jurist of this age was Cicero's young friend, C. Trebatius Testa, whose life extends into the Augustan age and who was the teacher of Antistius Labeo. Of about the same age as Cicero was the jurist A. Cascellius, a man of republican character, distinguished by his originality and wit.

1. Suet. Iul. 44 (*destinabat*) *ius civile ad certum modum redigere atque ex immensa diffusaque legum copia optima quaeque et necessaria in paucissimos conferre libros.* Isid. orig. 5, 1, 5 *leges redigere in libros primus cos. Pompeius instituere voluit, sed non perseveravit, obtrectatorum metu* (probably of the Jurists). *deinde Caesar coepit id facere, sed ante interfectus est.*

2. A. Ofilius, a pupil of Ser. Sulpicius, see § 174, 5. Pompon. dig. 1, 2, 2, 44 *ex his auditoribus plurimum auctoritatis habuit Alfenus Varus et A. Ofilius, ex quibus . . . Ofilius in equestri ordine perseveravit. is fuit Caesari familiarissimus et libros de iure civili plurimos et qui omnem partem operis fundarent reliquit. nam de legibus vicensimae primus* (FDSanio, rechtshist. Abh. 1845, 78: *de legibus XX libros*) *conscripsit: de iurisdictione idem edictum praetoris* (cf. dig. 2, 7, 1, 2. 43, 20, 1, 17. 43, 21, 3, 10) *primus diligenter composuit.* (45) . . . *ex his Trebatius peritior Cascellio, Cascellius Trebatio eloquentior fuisse dicitur, Ofilius utroque doctior.* Among his pupils were Tubero (ib. 46) and Ateius Capito (47). In the Digests is cited *Ofilius libr. V iuris partiti* (32, 55, 1. 4. 7), *Of. libr. XVI actionum* (33, 9, 3, 5. 8), *Of. ad Atticum* (50, 16, 234, 2). He is mentioned as a jurist by Cic. fam. 7, 21 (a. 710/44) and perhaps Att. 13, 37, 4 (a. 709/45); cf. fam. 16, 24, 1 (a. 710/44). AFRudorff, röm. Rechtsgesch. 1, 164. EHuschke, Z. f. gesch. Rechtswiss. 15, 186.

3. Pompon. dig. 1, 2, 2, 45 *fuit eodem tempore* (with Ofilius) *et Trebatius, qui idem* (*item* or *quidem*? or *Trebatius, Quinti C. M. auditor. fuit ex* etc.) *Corneli Maximi* (§ 154, 7) *auditor fuit. ex his Trebatius peritior* etc. (see n. 2) . . . *Trebatii complures* (*libri exstant*), *sed minus frequentantur.* 47 *Antistius Labeo . . . institutus est a Trebatio.* C. Trebatius Testa was born about 665 at Velia in Lucania, came to Rome as an adolescens and there became acquainted with Cicero, who recommended him to Caesar in Gaul a. 700/54 (fam. 7, 5), to improve his fortune. In Gaul he remained for at least one year. Of this period we have Cicero's letters to him, fam. 7, 6–18; also of a. 710/44 ib. 21. 20. 19 and of uncertain date ib. 22. Hence he remained on Caesar's side, as a moderate and conciliatory ally, and he played the same part under Augustus; see Hor. sat. 2, 1. Justinian inst. 2, 25 pr. *dicitur Augustus convocasse prudentes, inter quos Trebatium quoque, cuius tunc auctoritas maxima erat.* He seems to have been still living about a. 740/14. Porphyrio on Hor. l.l. *ad Trebatium scribit equitem romanum* (this he may have become through Octavianus; Teuffel on Hor. sat. 2, 1, 29). *hic est Trebatius iuris peritus, qui locum obtinuit* ⟨*inter poetas*, a trait quite in harmony with the character of an easy bon-vivant, but which is missing in the authoritative Monac.⟩ *et aliquot libros de civili iure composuit et de religionibus novem* (or rather *XI?*). The latter in Gell. 7, 12, 4 *C. Trebatius . . . in libro de religionibus secundo;* Macr. 3. 7, 8 (*Trebatius religionum libro nono*) and 3, 3, 5 (*Trebatius libro decimo religionum*); cf. ib. 1, 16 28. 3, 3, 2. 4. 3, 5, 1. Serv. Aen. 11, 316 (*Trebatius de religionibus libro VII*). Traces of his legal writings, especially of his commentary on the Edictum aedilium curulium occur in the Digests (4, 3, 18, 3. 21, 1, 6, 1. 21, 1, 12, 4. 21, 1, 14, 3; cf. Gell. 4, 2, 9). Cf. besides dig. 11, 7, 14, 11. 32, 100, 1, 4. 41, 2, 3, 5. 43, 24, 22, 3. SWZimmern, Gesch. des PRechts 1, 1, 297. OStange, de C. Tr. T. et eius loco inter aequales, Berl. 1849. PRE. 6, 2078. Teuffel's commentary on Hor. sat. II (Lpz. 1857), p. 10. The fragments in Huschke, iurisprud. anteiust.[5] 100.

4. Pompon. l.l. 45 *A. Cascellius* (perhaps the son of the person of that name mentioned in Cic. pBalbo 45, Val. Max. 8, 2, 1? see Mommsen l.l.), *Quintus Mucius Volosii auditor, denique in illius honorem testamento Publium Mucium nepotem eius reliquit heredem.* The corrupt words are probably (cf. Mommsen ad loc., Herm. 15, 114) to be read as follows: *A. Cascellius, Volcacii* (cf. Plin. HN. 8, 144 *Volcacium nobilem qui Cascellium ius docuit*), *Q. Muci* (§ 154, 1) *auditoris, auditor.* See also PRE. 5, 188. Further notice of Cascellius in Pompon. l.l. *fuit autem quaestorius, nec ultra proficere voluit, cum illi etiam Augustus consulatum offerret, ex his* etc. (note 2). *Cascellii scripta non exstant nisi unus liber bene dictorum* (perhaps a collection of his witticisms by some one else; cf. § 121, 6. 191, 2. 195, 5). As he appears (Αὖλος Κασκέλιος Αὔλου υἱὸς Ῥωμιλία) in the SC de Oropiis a. 681/73 (§ 218, 3) among those who had a seat in the Senate, he must have held the quaestura before that year: therefore he was born 650/104 at latest. Mommsen, Herm. 20, 282. Val. Max. 6, 2, 12 *Cascellius, vir iuris civilis scientia clarus, quam periculose contumax! nullius enim aut gratia aut auctoritate compelli potuit ut de aliqua earum rerum quas triumviri dederant formulam componeret, hoc animi iudicio universa eorum beneficia extra omnem ordinem legum ponens. idem cum multa de temporibus liberius loqueretur* (under Augustus) . . . *duas res . . . magnam sibi licentiam praebere respondit, senectutem et orbitatem.* See also Hor. AP. 371: is he mentioned there as still living? see Mommsen, Herm. 15, 114. 20, 282. Quint. 6, 3, 87. Macr. 2, 6, 1 (*Cascellius iuris consultus urbanitatis mirae libertatisque habebatur*, where a joke of his of the year 698/56 is quoted). He is probably the author of the *iudicium Cascellianum sive secutorium* in Gai. inst. 4, 166. 169. He is quoted 13 times in the dig.; see OLenel, palingenes. iur. civ. 107.

EGLagemans, de A. Cascellio, Leid. 1823. SWZimmern, Gesch. d. PRechts 1, 1. 299. HEDirksen, hinterlass. Schrr. 2, 435.

5. *L. Valerius iureconsultus, ex domesticis atque intimis familiaribus* of Cicero (fam. 3, 1, 3 of a. 702/52), witty like his contemporary and colleague Trebatius (ib. 1, 10), and as it seems a native of Apulia (*Apuliam tuam*, ib. of a. 700/54). Not improbably he is meant ib. 7, 11, 2 (a. 701/53, in a letter to Trebatius): *si diutius frustra afueris, non modo Laberium sed etiam sodalem nostrum Valerium pertimesco. mira enim persona induci potest Britannici iureconsulti;* whence we cannot conclude with certainty that he actually wrote mimi (§ 8, l. 3). It may be that he is the Valerius (cf. § 147, 1) who is mentioned as a commentator on the twelve Tables (§ 86, 6). Cf. § 199, 2.

6. Pompon. dig. 1, 2, 2, 44 (cf. § 174, 5) *ab hoc* (Ser. Sulpicio, § 174, 2) *plurimi profecerunt, fere tamen hi libros conscripserunt . . . Pacuvius Labeo Antistius* (Mommsen omits *Ant.*) *Labeonis Antistii* (§ 265, 1) *pater.* On the praenomen of his father (Pacuvius) see MHertz on Priscian. GL. 2, 384 and JJ. 91, 215. The same is intended in Gell. 5, 21, 10 *prima epistula* (of Sinnius Capito) *scripta est ad Pacuvium Labeonem.* He was one of the plotters of Caesar's murder, † 712/42. Cf. Appian. b. c. 4, 135 (ἐπὶ σοφίᾳ γνώριμος). PRE. 1^2, 1163, 21.

208. Q. Aelius Tubero wrote a historical work extending to his own time; he was also an orator, but especially esteemed as a writer on Jurisprudence. In point of formal perfection, he was in the last mentioned branch surpassed by P. Alfenus Varus of Cremona (cos. 715/39). The jurist C. Aelius Gallus touched upon the department of the grammarians in drawing up a list of legal terms with explanations. C. Matius, a knight and intimate friend of Caesar and Augustus, took interest in literature and himself wrote—though only on gastronomy.

1. Pompon. dig. 1, 2, 2, 46 *post hos* (Ofilius, Trebatius) *quoque* (*Q.* acc. to Mommsen) *Tubero fuit, qui Ofilio operam dedit; fuit autem patricius* (*prius patronus?* the Aelii were Plebeians) *et transiit a causis agendis ad ius civile, maxime postquam* (end of 708/46) *Q. Ligarium accusavit nec obtinuit apud C. Caesarem. . . . Tubero doctissimus quidem habitus est iuris publici et privati et complures utriusque operis libros reliquit; sermone tamen antiquo usus affectavit scribere et ideo parum libri eius grati habentur.* The other works of T. were also in archaic style. Quintilian had read his accusation of Ligarius (10, 1, 23. 11, 1, 80 cf. 78. 5, 13, 20. 31). Gell. 14, 2, 20 mentions among his juridical writings (*praecepta Aelii Tuberonis*) *super officio iudicis*, whence probably ib. 14, 7, 13 *in libro IX Tuberonem dicere ait* (cf. ib. 14, 8, 2). Tubero's views are quoted dig. 32, 29, 4. 33, 6, 7 pr. (Ofilius, Cascellius, Tubero). 33, 10, 7, 1. 2. PHSaaymans Vader, de Q. Aelio Tub. eiusque in pandectis fragmentis, Leid. 1824. He is mentioned as a historian (Τουβέρων Αἴλιος, which should not be understood of his father, see § 172, 8) by Dionys. 1, 80 who calls him δεινὸς ἀνὴρ καὶ περὶ τὴν συναγωγὴν τῆς ἱστορίας ἐπιμελής; cf. ib. 1, 7 and Liv. 4, 23, 1 (*Val. Antias et Q. Tubero*). *Tubero lib. XIV historiarum* quoted by Nonius 481. His work extended from the oldest time down to at least the beginning of the war between Pompey and Caesar. For the citations from it see HPeter's hist. rell. 1, 311; fragm. 199. He seems to be the Q. Tubero quoted by Pliny as an authority for b. 2, 18 (cf. ib. 18, 235 and Schol. German. p. 132 Br.) and 36. Gell. 6, 9, 11 *Aelium*

quoque Tuberonem libro ad C. Oppium scripto. 'occecurrit' dixisse Probus adnotavit. PRE. 1², 336, 7. HPeter, hist. rell. 1, ccclv.

2. Sueton. Galb. 3 *avus* (of the Emperor Galba, who was born Dec. 24, 751/3) *clarior studiis quam dignitate* (*non enim egressus praeturae gradum*) *multiplicem nec incuriosam historiam edidit.* Plut. Romul. 17 ὡς Ἰόβας φησὶ Γάλβαν Σουλπίκιον ἱστορεῖν. Oros. 5, 23 *fuisse tunc* (a. 678/76) *Pompeio XXX milia peditum . . . Galba scribit, Sertorium autem LX m. ped. . . . habuisse commemorat.* He is probably also referred to by Plin. NH. ind. auct. to b. 36 *C. Galba.* The opinion advanced by GIVossius de hist. lat. 1, 18 (also maintained by GFUnger, Abh. d. bayr. Ak. 16, 1, 154), that this Sulpicius Galba should be identified with Sulpicius Blitho (§ 172, 7), is improbable. HPeter, hist. rell. cclxvii. fragm. 237.

3. P. Alfenus Varus; on the praenomen P. see Henzen, CIL. 1, 467. Pompon. dig. 1, 2, 2, 44 *ex his auditoribus* (of Ser. Sulpicius, § 174, 2) *plurimum auctoritatis habuit Alfenus Varus . . . ex quibus Varus et consul fuit* (suff. a. 715/39). He is probably identical with the Alfenus mentioned in Catullus (30); perhaps also the Varus of the same author (10, 22); see MHaupt. op. 1, 97. AKiessling, commentt. Mommsen. 354; cf. however § 213, 4. Again, he is probably the same Varus who attended Siron's philosophical lectures together with Vergil (§ 224, 3. Schol. Veron. on Verg. ecl. 7, 9. Serv. on ecl. 6, 13. Aen. 6, 264), and the Alfenus Varus who was Octavianus' legate a. 714/40, and promised (ecl. 6) to protect Vergil's estate near Mantua (cf. ecl. 9, 27), and identical with the *Alfenus vafer* in Hor. sat. 1, 3, 130, who *omni abiecto instrumento artis clausaque taberna* yet (potentialiter) *sutor erat*, on which Porphyrio: *urbane Alfenum Varum Cremonensem deridet, qui abiecta sutrina quam in municipio suo exercuerat Romam petiit magistroque usus Sulpicio icto ad tantum dignitatis pervenit ut et consulatum gereret et publico funere efferretur.* Gellius 7, 5, 1 *Alfenus ictus, Ser. Sulpicii discipulus rerumque antiquarum non incuriosus, in libro digestorum XXXIV°, coniectaneorum autem II°* (on these two titles see LMercklin, Phil. 19, 653). Dig. 3, 5, 20 pr. *apud Alfenum libro XXXVIII° digestorum.* According to the Florent. Index, there were altogether 40 books of his Digesta, a collection of responsa (of Serv. Sulpicius, Heimbach, Z. f. RGesch. 2, 340. Mommsen on dig. 19, 2, 27) transferred by Aufidius Namusa to his collection (§ 174, 5). The editors of the Digesta of Justinian only knew and made use of the work of Alfenus in two epitomes, the one by Paulus (§ 377, 4: *Alfeni digesta a Paulo epitomata, Pauli epitomae Alfeni digestorum*) following the original arrangement of the work, the other by an anonymous writer, who adhered to the arrangement of the edictum perpetuum (*Alfeni digesta*). Cf. OLenel, palingenesia iur. civ. 37. Of some importance is the lengthy extract dig. 5, 1, 76, as it attests the writer's philosophical training (*quod, ut philosophi dicerent, ex particulis minimis consisteremus*); other fragments show an acquaintance with Greek, and nearly all are in a simple and easy style. EOtto, P. Alfenus Varus in Thesaur. iur. rom. 5, 1631. SWZimmern, Gesch. d. PRechts 1, 1, 295. EHuschke, Z. f. gesch. Rechtsw. 15, 187 (who, in the corrupt reading *Alfenus Varus Gaius* in Pomponius l.l., is inclined to change the last word into *Catus*). PRE. 1², 768, 3.

4. Gell. 16, 5, 3 *C. Aelius Gallus in libro de significatione verborum quae ad ius civile pertinent secundo* (a definition of *vestibulum*)=Macr. 6, 8, 16, who merely adds *vir doctissimus.* Dig. 50, 16, 157 *C. Aelius Gallus libro I de verborum quae ad ius civile pertinent significatione* (a definition of *paries* and *via*). An abbreviated title ap. Serv. georg. 1, 264 *Aelius Gallus de verbis ad ius civile pertinentibus vallos . . appellat*; and Festus 218ᵇ *postliminium receptum Gallus Aelius in libro primo signifi-*

cationum quae ad ius pertinent ait esse eum qui etc.: 273[a] *reus nunc dicitur qui causam dicit . . . at Gallus Aelius libro II significationum verborum quae ad ius pertinent ait: reus est qui* etc. 302[b] *saltum Gallus Aelius l. II significationum quae ad ius pertinent ita definit;* 352[b] *flumen recte dici ait Aelius Gallus libro II quae ad ius pertinent.* The quotations never exceed the second book, and FESTUS 352, 5 ⟨*nota*⟩*vit Aelius in XII* ⟨*tabulis*⟩ *signi*⟨*ficare*⟩ relates to Aelius Stilo (§ 148, 2); see RSCHÖLL, de legis XII tabb. reliqq. 29. Perhaps the arrangement was alphabetical. "Aelius Gallus" or "Gallus Aelius" is quoted by Festus 19 times besides the quotations already given. This extensive use as well as the combination of *nunc* and *at Gallus Aelius* p. 273[a] show that Gallus' work was employed by Verrius Flaccus. *Gallus Aelius* in GAIUS dig. 22, 1, 19 pr.; *C. Aelius* in PRISCIAN. GL. 2, 382, 1 (see LACHMANN, kl. Schr. 2, 248). CWEHEIMBACH, C. Aelii Galli Icti fragmenta rec. et illustr., Lps. 1823. EHUSCHKE, iurisprud. anteiust.[5] 94. PRE. 1^2, 337.

5. C. Matius, born c. 670/84, the faithful friend of Caesar, especially adapted by his mild and sober manner to his mediating position, though he did not enter into political factions or public business. He transferred his love for Caesar to Octavianus, and seems to have died as late as a. 750/4; see PLIN. NH. 12, 13 *primus C. Matius ex equestri ordine, divi Augusti amicus, invenit nemora tonsilia intra hos LXXX annos.* EVLEUTSCH, ZfAW. 1834, 164. PRE. 4, 1643. CIC. fam. 7, 15, 2 (a. 701/53) *C. Matii, suavissimi doctissimique hominis.* 11, 27, 5 (a. 710/44) *ut haec φιλοσοφούμενα scriberem tu me impulisti . . . omnia me tua delectant. sed maxime maxima cum fides in amicitia . . . tum lepos, humanitas, litterae.* Apollodoros of Pergamon dedicated his Ars (manual of Rhetoric) to him; QUINT. 3, 1, 18. A letter to Cicero (fam. 11, 28, of a. 710/44) is a faithful reflection of his noble disposition and fine culture. A letter addressed to Cicero by Matius aud Trebatius together (a. 704/49) is found ad Att. 9, 15 A. His work on gastronomy was probably written under Augustus (cf. § 54, 3), and his interest in such subjects is significant of his inoffensive character and love of refined enjoyment. *Minutal Matianum* (hachis à la Matius) was named after him, APIC. 4, 174, also the *mala Matiana.* COLUM. 5, 10, 19. 12, 45, 5. PLIN. NH. 15, 49 and elsewhere.

209. Among the other adherents of Caesar several may be mentioned either as orators or writers of letters still extant: e.g. the talented, but dissipated C. Scribonius Curio (trib. pleb. 704/50), Q. Cornificius, the triumvir M. Antony (671/83–724/30) and L. Balbus. Men of wavering political opinions were the clever M. Caelius Rufus and the unprincipled L. Munatius Plancus (cos. 711/42); C. Furnius, who was legate to the latter for a long time, was also an orator, and likewise the young L. Sempronius Atratinus (cos. 720/34), Q. Volusius, Annius Cimber, and also by Hortensia there was in the 1st century of the Christian era a published speech extant.

1. VELLEI. 2, 48, 3 *C. Curio trib. pl.* (704/50; son of the Curio mentioned § 153, 6; † 705/49) . . . *eloquens, audax, suae alienaeque et fortunae et pudicitiae prodigus, homo ingeniosissime nequam et facundus malo publico.* PRE. 6. 880, 11. For the date of his birth see a conjecture below, n. 5. His character as an orator is given by CIC. Brut. 230 *ita facile soluteque verbis volvebat satis interdum acutas, crebras quidem certe sententias ut nihil posset ornatius esse, nihil expeditius. atque hic*

parum a magistris institutus naturam habuit admirabilem ad dicendum; industriam non sum expertus; studium certe fuit. There were speeches by him in existence in the time of Tacitus: see dial. 37 (§ 171, 5). MEYER, orat. rom.² p. 481. Letters from CIC. to him fam. 2, 1–7 (of a. 701/53 and 703/51).

2. HIERON. ad. Eus. Chron. a. Abr. 1976=713/41 *Cornificius poeta a militibus desertus interiit . . . huius soror Cornificia, cuius insignia exstant epigrammata.* Chronological reasons oblige us to identify him with Q. Cornificius, the quaestor of Caesar (propraetor 706/48), who fell in Africa fighting against T. Sextius; he was also on friendly terms with Cicero, who addressed to him fam. 12, 17–30 in 709/45–711/43; see DRUMANN, GR. 2, 617. PRE. 2, 710, 3. Cicero somewhat pointedly (fam. 12, 18, 1) places him among the *magni oratores* and (ib. 12, 17, 2) recommends his Orator to his kind reception: *in quo saepe suspicatus sum te ab iudicio nostro, sic scilicet ut doctum hominem ab non indocto, paullulum dissidere.* ib. 12, 20 *me amabis et scripto aliquo lacesses.* He is no doubt identical with the poetical friend of Catullus (c. 38), who wrote erotic poems (*leve Cornifici . . . opus*, OVID. trist. 2, 436), whence a hendecasyllabic line in MACR. 6, 4, 12 and a fragment of dactylic metre (perhaps from an epic) ib. 6, 5, 13 (*Cornificius in Glauco*). Cf. § 233, 3 ad fin. LSCHWABE, quaest. Catull. 298. It is doubtful whether *Cornificius in primo de etymis deorum* (PRISC. GL. 2, 257, 6) should be understood of him: from this MACR. 1, 9, 11 (*Cornificius Etymorum libro III*) quotes curious derivations of the names of gods and a citation of CIC. de nat. deor. 1, 17, 9. 33. 62. 1, 23, 2. Other quotations in FEST. 123. 166. 170. 194. 282 and in other places in SERVIUS, LACTANTIUS etc. It is incomprehensible how Cornificius could find time or thought for these works in Syria and Africa, during the years 709/45 and 713/41. These writings should rather be attributed to a grammarian of the same name in the Augustan period, perhaps to that Cornificius Gallus whose somewhat pedantic epigram on Vergil is quoted by CLEDONIUS, GL. 5, 43, 2: *ordea qui dixit* (ge. 1, 210) *superest ut tritica dicat.* THBERGK, op. 1, 545. JBECKER, ZfAW. 1847, 1060.

3. The triumvir M. Antony, see DRUMANN, GR. 1, 64. PRE. 1², 1174. Possessing a defective education, he often fell in his speeches into a false kind of pathos and became turgid, obscure and faulty (SUET. Aug. 86 *M. Antonium . . . ea scribentem quae mirentur potius homines quam intellegant;* cf. CIC. Phil. 2, 101. 3, 21 sq. Att. 10, 8 sq. 11, 3 sq.). It would perhaps be too much to call him on that account an adherent of the Asiatic school (PLUT. Ant. 2. 43 cf. SUET. l.l.). His letters to Cicero of a. 705/49 (Att. 10, 8 A. 10, 10, 2) and 710/44 (14, 13 A.; cf. also CIC. or. Phil. 8, 25 sqq. 13, 22 sqq.) are in a natural style. PLIN. NH. 14, 148 *M. Antonio. is enim . . . avidissime adprehenderat hanc palmam* (capacity for drinking), *edito etiam volumine de sua ebrietate . . . exiguo tempore ante proelium actiacum id volumen evomuit* (cf. DRUMANN, GR. 1, 516. SCHELLE l.l. 2). To this, as well as to his correspondence with Octavian (specimens of which are given by SUETONIUS, e.g. Aug. 69), relates OVID ex Pont. 1, 1, 23 *Antoni scripta leguntur.* ESCHELLE, de M. Antoni triumviri quae supersunt epp. I, Frankenb. i. S. 1883.

4. ASINIUS POLLIO writes to Cicero (fam. 10, 32, 3 a. 711/43) *Balbus quaestor . . . ludis* (which he caused to be given at Gades) *praetextam de suo itinere ad L. Lentulum procos. sollicitandum* (705/49 to get him to leave Pompey and return to Rome, Att. 8, 9, 4. 8, 11, 5. 8, 15 A, 2. 9, 6, 1. VELLEI. 2, 51, 3) *posuit. et quidem cum ageretur flevit, memoria rerum gestarum commotus.* ib. 5 *praetextam* (of B.) *si voles legere, Gallum Cornelium* (§ 232), *familiarem meum, poscito.* See WELCKER, gr. Trag. 1402. RIBBECK, röm. Trag. 625; röm. Dicht. 1, 194. This Balbus is the one called Balbus minor to distinguish him from his uncle (§ 197, 4) L. Cornelius P. f.

Balbus, whose life extended far into the Augustan period (he certainly was living 741/13), who was cos. suff. 722/32 and who triumphed a. 735/19 as proconsul ex Africa; DRUMANN, GR. 2, 608. PRE. 2, 694. According to VELLEI. l.l. he likewise *ad pontificatum adsurrexit* and had a literary turn, whence it is not impossible that he is the Cornelius Balbus quoted by SERV. Aen. 4, 127 on hymenaeus and to whom relates MACR. 3, 6, 26 *Cornelius Balbus* ἐξηγητικῶν libro XVIII° (cf. HPETER, hist. fragm. p. XXI).

5. M. Caelius M. f. Rufus. PLIN. NH. 7, 165 *C. Mario Cn. Carbone III cos.* (a. 672/82) *a. d. V Kal. Iunias M. Caelius Rufus et C. Licinius Calvus eadem die geniti sunt, oratores quidem ambo, sed tam dispari eventu.* But to judge from the manner in which Cicero speaks of them (Brut. 273. 279) they cannot have been quite of the same age; more probably Caelius was the elder, as according to CIC. pCael. 18 he already in 695/59 *per aetatem magistratus petere potuit,* and his official career agrees with this (698/56 already a member of the council of his native town CIC. Cael. 5; quaest. between 698/56–700/54, tr. pl. 702/52, aed. cur. 704/50, praet. 706/48). Hence Caelius must have been born c. 666/88. Instead of Caelius Pliny should perhaps have mentioned Curio (n. 1). His native place was a municipium of which the name is most likely concealed by some corruption of the MS. in CIC. pCael. 5. Cf. NIPPERDEY, op. 299. KWEGEHAUPT, Cael. Ruf. 4.

6. Caelius was, as a young man, introduced by his father to Cicero and Crassus (pCael. 9. 39. 72), with whom he thus found himself in close connection. This circumstance made Cicero lenient towards Caelius' loose morals and luxurious life; he even defended him a. 698/56 (see § 179, 34) against some charges brought by Clodia (§ 214, 3), whose dissolute circle he had frequented for some time before breaking with her. During Cicero's absence in Cilicia (703/51) Caelius was his appointed correspondent at Rome: the letters (17 in number; letter 16 in duplicate; cf. Att. 10, 9 A.) are collected in the eighth book of Cic. epp. fam. Caelius exhibits in them a dashing and acute, though somewhat malicious judgment of persons and facts, though he is never quite clear in his own position; the style is lively, humorous, and original, condescending to the use of popular expressions, and not aiming at polish and elegance. Cf. § 188, 1, n. 2 and 4. On the outbreak of the Civil War, Caelius was obliged by his debts to join the camp of Caesar, who appointed him praetor in 706/48. As such he intended to introduce tabulae novae, but was deposed and soon afterwards killed. He is probably identical with the Rufus in Catullus; see LSCHWABE, quaest. Catull. 64. 85. 133 and the commentators on CAT. 69. 77. Cf. DRUMANN, GR. 2, 411. WWEGEHAUPT, das Leben d. M. Cael. Ruf., Bresl. 1878. HWIESCHHÖLTER, de M. Caelio Rufo oratore, Lpz. 1886.—FBECHER, d. Sprachgebr. d. Caelius, Ilfeld 1888. FBURG, de M. Cael. Rufi genere dicendi, Freibg. i/B. 1888.

7. On his oratorical power CIC. Brut. 273 *splendida et grandis et eadem inprimis faceta et perurbana . . . oratio. graves eius contiones aliquot fuerunt* (also 704/50 as aedile *de aquis,* FRONTIN. aq. 76; from this a fragm. GL. 5, 590, 21), *acres accusationes tres* (directed against C. Antonius 695/59, L. Sempronius Atratinus the father, iterum, 698/56; a. 703/51 against Q. Pompeius Rufus, and also in his character of patronus of the peregrinus Pausanias, plaintiff in a case of extortion), *defensiones* (esp. 698/56 *pro se* against Atratinus, also *pro Saufeio* 702/52) *. . . sane tolerabiles.* Hence QUINT. 6, 3, 69. 10, 1, 115; *asperitas Caelii* ib. 10, 2, 25; cf. TAC. dial. 18. 21 (*sordes verborum, hians compositio, inconditi sensus*). 25 (*amarior*). He seems to have followed the Atticists in preference to Cicero's style, though Cicero had taught him the principles of rhetoric in his youth (n. 6). VELLEI. 2, 68, 1 *M. Caelius, vir eloquio animoque Curioni* (n. 1) *simillimus, sed in utroque perfectior, nec minus*

ingeniose nequam. Sen. de ira 3, 8, 6 *Caelium oratorem fuisse iracundissimum constat.* Quintilian, Pliny (ep. 1, 20, 4), and Tacitus (dial. 21. 25) were acquainted with his speeches. The fragments see in Meyer, orat. rom.[2] 460. A very lively description from one of his speeches is given by Quint. 4, 2, 123. Witticisms on Clodia ib. 8, 6, 53. OHarnecker, Berl. ph. Wschr. 1884, 225 (where however Cic. Brut. 273 ad fin. is erroneously held to be the authority for Caelius' desertion to the side of the Atticists); WschrfklPhil. 1886, 1098.

8. L. Munatius Plancus, Caesar's legate and appointed by him consul in 712/42; after Caesar's death he went over to the side of the Senate, after a little hesitation, then joined Antony and when his star began to set, Octavian, with whom he could afford to remain, owing to his steady good fortune. He was censor 732/22, but generally despised. PRE. 5, 204, 9. CLRoth, über M. Pl., Erklärung der Inschrift auf dem Mausoleum in Gaeta (CIL. 10, 6087), in the Mittheilungen of the Basle Altert.-Ges. 4 (Bas. 1852). AWdeKlerck, disq. de etc. Utr. 1855. HAKleijn, de L. et T. Munatiis Plancis, Leid. 1857. Suet. rhet. 6 and Plin. NH. 7, 55 call him *orator; orator insignis habetur* in Hieronymus ad a. Abr. 1992=729/25; *summa eloquentia* Cic. fam. 10, 3, 3 cf. 13, 29, 1. Ascon. 33 Or. 28 K.-S. Non. 221. His rhetorical training, but also his vanity, appear from his letters to Cicero (fam. 10, 4. 7–9. 11. 15. 17 sq. 21. 23 sq.) of a. 710/44 and 711/43, which are exceedingly well written and abound in cadences, antitheses etc. (*verborum et sententiarum gravitas*, ib. 10, 12, 1. 16, 1. 19, 1), but often cloak a very ambiguous spirit under fair phrases.

9. Hieron. ad Euseb. Chron. a. Abr. 1980=717/37 *Furnii pater et filius clari oratores habentur, quorum filius consularis ante patrem moritur.* Cf. Tac. dial. 21 (a corrupt passage) *nec unum* (of the antiquarians) *de populi ganuti* (=*Canuti?* § 153, 5 ad fin.) *aut Atti, de Furnio et Toranio* (*Coranio*, otherwise unknown) *quique alii in eodem valetudinario haec ossa et hanc maciem produnt.* The father (C. Furnius) was a friend of Cicero; tr. pleb. 704/50; legatus to L. Plancus (n. 8) a. 710/44 sq. with whom he joined Antony, to whom he adhered until the battle of Actium. He was pardoned by Octavian and a. 725/29 *adlectus inter consulares* (Dio 52, 42). Cic. fam. 10, 26, 2 (*qui alienas causas tam facile discas*) attests that he was an orator, and Plut. Anton. 58 even calls him δεινότατος εἰπεῖν Ῥωμαίων. Hor. sat. 1, 10, 86 *te, candide Furni*, seems to relate to him, on which Acro *hic historiarum elegantia claruit* (subsequently). A trait of egregious flattery towards Octavianus by his son (cos. 737/17) is related by Sen. de benef. 2, 25, 1.

10. L. Sempronius L. f. Atratinus (cos. 720/34, triumphed 12. Oct. 733/21 as procos. ex Africa (CIL. 1, p. 461). Hieronym. on Eus. chron. ad a. Abr. 1996=733/21 *Atratinus, qui XVII natus annos Caelium* (n. 7) *accusaverat* (a. 698/56; he was therefore born 681/73), *clarus inter oratores habetur. ad extremum morborum taedio in balneo voluntate exanimatus heredem reliquit Augustum.* Cicero (pCael. 2) calls him his *necessarius*, and says of him (ib. 8) *ornate docteque dixisti;* ib. 15 he styles him *disertus adolescens.* As a speaker in the Senate he is mentioned side by side with Messala in Joseph. b. iud. 1, 14, 4. PRE. 6, 973, 8.

11. Vatinius to Cicero, fam. 5, 10 a, 2 (a. 709/45): *defenditur* (*Catilius*) *a Q. Valusio, tuo discipulo.* PRE. 6, 2745, 5.

12. Cic. Phil. 11, 14 *T. Annius Cimber Lysidici filius* (therefore son of a slave or freedman), a follower of M. Antony, through whose assistance he became praetor (ib. 13, 26). Concerning his literary tendency see the epigram on him Verg. catal. 2 (and Quint. 8, 3, 23), which already to Ausonius (op. 27, 13, 5) had lost its meaning: *Corinthiorum* (i.e. with the hall-mark of antiquity) *amator iste verborum,*

Iste iste rhetor, *iamque*, *quatenus totus Thucydides*, *tyrannus Atticae febris* (the exacting instructor in distempered Attic), *Tau* (?) *gallicum* (perhaps on account of the Gallic extraction of Annius Cimber), *min* (μὶν) *et sphin* (σφὶν) *et—male illi sit* (an execration on dealers in grammatical curiosities): *ita omnia ista verba miscuit fratri* (as a draught which was fatal to him: Annius Cimber was accused of fratricide: Quint. l.l. Cic. Phil. 11, 14. 13, 26). According to this he seems to have carried on the profession of a teacher before beginning his political career. He is also mentioned as an antiquarian by Octavianus in Suet. Aug. 86 to M. Antony: *tu dubitas Cimberne Annius an Veranius Flaccus imitandi sint tibi?* i.e. probably: you only waver between A. C. and Ver.'s pontificalia verba (§ 199, 4) and hence you write—in the language of Cato. JGHuschke, de Annio Cimbro, Rost. 1824 and esp. Bücheler, RhM. 38, 507. Cf. also § 19, 1 ad fin.

13. Caesar's favourite, the knight Mamurra of Formiae, † 709/45 (Cic. Att. 13, 52, 1; cf. also OHirschfeld, Herm. 5, 299), was active in literature, and seems to have been a poet; see Catullus 57, 7 and 105. Cf. § 214, 5. LSchwabe, quaest. Catull. 187. 226.

14. Val. Max. 8, 3, 3 *Hortensia, Q. Hortensi* (§ 171, 1) *filia, cum ordo matronarum gravi tributo a triumviris* (a. 711/43) *esset oneratus nec quisquam virorum patrocinium eis accommodare auderet, causam feminarum apud triumviros et constanter et feliciter egit; repraesentata enim patris facundia impetravit ut* etc. Cf. Appian. b. c. 4, 32. Quint. 1, 1, 6 *Hortensiae Q. filiae oratio apud triumviros habita legitur non tantum in sexus honorem.*

210. Among the members of the conspiracy against Caesar M. Iunius Brutus, an honest man, but without intellectual distinction, was the most active in literature, especially in philosophy and oratory; the style of D. Brutus and that of C. Cassius are known to us from their letters to Cicero. The same correspondence introduces us to Cassius of Parma and C. Trebonius, who were also writers of poetry. Ampius Balbus, Actorius Naso, and Tanusius Geminus wrote historical works hostile to Caesar.

1. M. Iunius Brutus. Plutarch's Brutus. Drumann, GR. 4, 18. PRE. 4, 518. 532. JSlevogt, de M. Bruti vita et scriptis, Petersb. 1870. Cic. Brut. 324 of Hortensius: *annis ante decem causas agere coepit* (i.e. a. 659/95, see Brut. 229 *L. Crasso Q. Scaevola coss. primum in foro dixit*) *quam tu* (Brutus) *es natus.* The birth-year which would be inferred from this (669/85) is at variance with Vellei. 2, 72, 1 *hunc exitum M. Bruti XXXVIIum annum agentis* (a. 712/42) *fortuna esse voluit* (cf. Liv. per. 124 *annorum erat circiter XL*). This would lead us to infer 675/79 or 676/78 as the year in which Brutus was born, and this assumption is presupposed by the story that Caesar (born 654/100) was himself the father of Brutus. Hence KNipperdey's conj. (op. 301), *ante sedecim* in Cicero l.l. has much probability. Cf. Nep. Att. 8, 1 *occiso Caesare . . . sic M. Bruto usus est ut nullo ille adolescens aequali familiarius quam hoc sene* (Atticus born 645/109). As early as 703/51 Brutus was a son-in-law (Cic. fam. 3, 4, 2) to App. Claudius (§ 199, 1). Aur. Victor ill. 82 *Athenis philosophiam, Rhodi* (not attested by any other writer) *eloquentiam didicit* (Pammenes, and Aristos, the brother of Antiochos, instructed him at Athens, Cic. Brut. 332. Orat. 105. Acad. post. 1, 12. Plut. Brut. 2), *Cytheridem mimam cum Antonio et Gallo poeta amavit* (cf. § 232, 1 and HFlach

JJ. 119, 793). . . . *civili bello* . . . *Pompeium secutus est, quo victo veniam a Caesare accepit et procos.* (?) *Galliam* (cisalp.) *rexit* (a. 708/46); a. 710/44, he became praetor (urb.) through Caesar; † after the battle of Philippi, a. 712/42.—Portraits: Bernoulli, röm. Ikonogr. 1. 187.

2. Cicero is accustomed to exaggerate his praises of M. Brutus (e.g. Brut. 22) both as Caesar's favourite and afterwards as his murderer; he dedicated to him de finibus, Paradoxa, de nat. deor., Tusc., Orator and Brutus. They differed as to their theory of style; cf. Cic. Att. 15, 1 b, 2 *ego secutus* (Med.: *solus*) *aliud* (iudicium de optimo genere dicendi) *sum*, and Tac. dial. 18 *ex Calvi* (§ 213, 6 ad fin.) *et Bruti ad Ciceronem missis epistulis* (§ 46, 5. OHarnecker JJ. 125, 604) *facile est deprehendere Calvum quidem Ciceroni visum exsanguem et aridum, Brutum autem otiosum atque diiunctum* (*discinctum*), *rursusque Ciceronem a Calvo quidem male audisse tamquam solutum et enervem, a Bruto autem,* . . . *tamquam fractum atque elumbem.* His diction is described by *gravitas* (Quint. 12, 10, 10. Tac. dial. 25). He endeavoured to attain to a rhythmical flow of prose (Quint. 9, 4, 76); hence Cicero's criticism in his Orator. Both Quint. 10, 1, 123, who says that in his philosophical writings *multo quam in orationibus praestantior suffecit ponderi rerum*, and Tac. dial. 21 agree, the latter saying; *Brutum philosophiae suae relinquamus. nam in orationibus minorem esse fama sua etiam admiratores eius fatentur. nisi forte quisquam* . . . *Bruti pro Deiotaro rege* (cf. Cic. Brut. 21. ad Att. 14, 1, 2) *ceterosque eiusdem lentitudinis ac teporis libros legit, nisi qui et carmina eorundem miratur; fecerunt enim et carmina* (see § 195, 3). Cf. Stat. silv. 4, 9, 20 *Bruti senis oscitationes* (tedious speeches). Other published speeches of Brutus: *de dictatura Pompei* (Quint. 9, 3, 95) of a. 703/51; his speech delivered on 17 March 710/44 on the Capitol (Cic. Att. 15, 1 b, 2), and other *contiones Bruti* (*falsa quidem in Augustum probra, sed multa cum acerbitate habent*, Tac. A. 4, 34); his declamation pro Milone (*orationem Brutus exercitationis gratia scripsit*, Quint. 10, 1, 23 cf. 10, 5, 20. 3, 6, 93. Ascon. p. 42 Or. 36 K.-S. Schol. Bob. p. 276); laudatio of his father-in-law App. Claudius (Diomed. GL. 1, 367) and of his uncle M. Cato (Cic. Att. 13, 46, 2. cf. 12, 21, 1). Schol. Lucani 2, 234 ed. Usener and § 220, 3. Meyer, orat. rom.[2] 446.

3. On his philosophical works see Cic. acad. post. 1, 12. He had an inclination to the Old Academy, Cic. Brut. 120. 149. We find notices of a treatise de virtute (dedicated to Cicero, see fin. 1, 8. Tusc. 5, 1. Sen. consol. ad Helv. 9, 4 sqq. cf. 8, 1), περὶ καθήκοντος (Sen. Ep. 95, 45; cf. *M. Brutus de officiis* ap. Priscian. GL. 2, 199), de patientia (Diomed. GL. 1, 383).—His abridgment of the Annals of Fannius and Antipater (see § 137, 4 and 6 in fin.) was probably an early work, as was also his abridgment of Polybios (Plut. Brut. 4. Suid. s. v. Βροῦτος. ἔγραψεν . . . Πολυβίου τοῦ ἱστορικοῦ βίβλων ἐπιτομήν; see § 257, 8).

4. Letters. (*M.*) *Brutus in epistulis* (Quint. 9, 4, 75. Diomed. GL. 1, 388. Priscian. ib. 2, 474; cf. Plin. NH. 33, 39: *M. Bruti in Philippicis campis epistolae reperiuntur, frementes fibulas tribunicias ex auro geri*), *ad Caesarem* (Charis. GL. 1, 130), *ad Ciceronem* (Tac. dial. 18). On the correspondence of Brutus and Cicero § 188, 4.—The letters of Brutus in Greek are the production of a rhetorician (e.g. in RHercher's epistolographi Graeci, Par. 1873, p. 177), of which Plutarch availed himself as though genuine in his Brutus 2. Cf. Suidas s. v. Βροῦτος. RHercher, Phil. 8, 187. 9, 592. IFMarcks, symb. ad epistologr. gr. (Bonn 1883) 23.—Brutus' verses (see Tac. dial. 21, above n. 2) seem to have been erotic according to the enumeration in Plin. ep. 5, 3, 5 (above § 31, 1).—Had the rhetorician Empylos, the familiar friend of Brutus (probably identical with his namesake from Rhodes, see Cic. ap. Quint. 10, 6, 4), composed in Latin that μικρὸν μέν, οὐ φαῦλον δὲ σύγγραμμα περὶ τῆς Καίσαρος ἀναιρέσεως ὃ Βροῦτος ἐπιγέγραπται (evidently a defence of the deed)?

5. D. Iunius Brutus, executed by M. Antony in the summer of a. 711/43. His letters to Cicero in 710/44 and 711/43 (ad fam. 11, 1. 4. 5–11. 13a. 19. 20. 23. 26) are sad specimens of the want of thought and courage continually exhibited by him after the assassination of Caesar. DRUMANN, GR. 4, 9. PRE. 4, 513, 19. BNAKE, d. Briefwechsel zw. Cic. und D. Brut., JJ. Suppl. 3, 647.

6. C. Cassius Longinus, somewhat older than M. Brutus (PLUT. Brut. 29. 40), a. 701/53 sqq. quaestor in Parthia, 705/49 tr. pleb.; appointed in 710/44 praetor together with M. Brutus; †after the battle of Philippi (712/42). He was of a hard, trenchant character, but egotistical and without higher aims (cf. PLUT. Brut. 29. comp. cum Dione 1. Brut. 37 *Κάσσιος τοῖς Ἐπικούρου λόγοις χρώμενος καὶ περὶ τούτων ἔθος ἔχων*). Among his letters to Cicero, fam. 15, 19 (a. 709/45) is a good-humoured echo of Cicero's previous letter; 12, 11–12 (a. 711/43) are official reports, partly calculated to flatter Cicero. A quotation from *C. Cassii epistula . . . ad Dolabellam* in CHARIS. GL. 1, 123, 13. Cf. DRUMANN, GR. 2, 117. PRE. 2, 194, 11. OESCHMIDT, de epp. et a Cassio et ad Cassium datis, Lps. 1877.

7. Cassius Parmensis, after being one of the assassins of Caesar, held a command in Asia (a. 711/43). He gives an account of his doings in a letter full of flattery, in which he also imitates Cicero's style, fam. 12, 13. He was executed after the battle of Actium, 723/31. DRUMANN, GR. 2, 161. PRE. 2, 200, 20. PORPHYRIO on Hor. ep. 1, 4, 3 [*scribere quod Cassi Parmensis opuscula vincat*] *hic est Cassius qui in partibus Cassii et Bruti cum Horatio tribunus militum militavit. quibus victis Athenas se contulit* (first 723/31). *Q. Varius ab Augusto missus ut eum interficeret, studentem repperit et perempto eo scrinium cum libris tulit. unde multi crediderunt Thyestem Cassii Parmensis fuisse* (the latter statements are due to a confusion between the officer Q. Attius Varus, cf. b. g. 8, 28, 2. b. c. 3, 37, 6, and the tragic writer L. Varius, § 223, 2: see also PORPH. Hor. sat. 1, 10, 62). *scripserat enim multas alias tragoedias* (? cf. *opuscula* in Horace) *Cassius.* ACRO (p. 390 H.) *Epicureus fuit et poeta . . . satiras scripsit. . . . aliquot generibus stilum exercuit. inter quae opera elegia et epigrammata eius laudantur.* A passage in SUET. Aug. 4 from an abusive letter of Cass. Parm. to Octavian. From an *epistula Cassi Parmensis ad M. Antonium* ap. PLIN. NH. 31, 11. An iambic verse by a certain Cassius ap. QUINT. 5, 11, 24. Praetexta Brutus by a Cassius: see § 134, 5 ad fin. A WEICHERT, de L. Varii et Cassii Parmensis vita et carminibus, Grimma 1836. WELCKER, d. gr. Tragödien 1403. (The hexameters entitled *Cassii Orpheus* in FEA's Horace 2, p. 216, WERNSDORF's PLM. 2, 310 are the work of the Italian Antonius Thylesius saec. XVII, see WEICHERT l.l. 198.)

8. To about the same time as Cassius Parmensis belongs the improviser Cassius Etruscus mentioned by HOR. sat. 1, 10, 69; see KIRCHNER ad loc.

9. C. Trebonius, quaestor 694/60, trib. pl. 699/55, Caesar's legate in Gaul a. 700/54 sqq. and on his side in the Civil War; praet. urb. 706/48; cos 709/45; killed by Dolabella in Febr. 711/43. PRE. 6, 2083, 9. A. 707/47 he appears to have made a collection of Cicero's puns and witty sayings; cf. fam. 15, 21, 1–3, e.g. *liber iste quem mihi misisti quantam habet declarationem amoris tui! primum quod tibi facetum videtur quidquid ego dixi, . . . deinde quod illa . . . fiunt narrante te venustissima. quin etiam ante quam ad me veniatur risus omnis paene consumitur.* In his letter to Cicero (fam. 12, 16, a. 710/44) he speaks of the elder and younger Cicero with great attachment and forwards to them *versiculi* (perhaps iambics against M. Antony), on the free tone of which he observes: *turpitudo personae eius in quam liberius invehimur nos vindicabit* (3). His request is (4): *tu, sicut mihi pollicitus es, adiunges me quam primum ad tuos sermones.* Cf. also § 196, 11.

10. T. Ampius Balbus, trib. pl. 691/63, praetor 696/58, a friend of Cicero (see the speech pro T. Ampio, QUINT. 3, 8, 50), and a zealous partisan of Pompey; PRE. 1^2, 920, 2. Some criticism on Caesar from the historical work of Ampius in SUET. Iul. 77; cf. CIC. fam. 6, 12, 5 (a. 708/46) *cum studium tuum consumas in virorum fortium factis memoriae prodendis.*—M. Actorius Naso was, according to SUETON. Iul. 9 (cf. 52 *Naso*), the author of a work on Caesar or the time of the Civil War. SUETON. in his d. Iul. quotes only contemporaries of Caesar as his authorities; MHAUPT, op. 1, 72.—On Tanusius § 212, 7.

211. The scholars and teachers had as such only a small share in the political struggles. The most important of them was the Greek L. Ateius Praetextatus, a manysided and prolific writer, who styled himself 'Philologus'; besides him may be mentioned Santra, who wrote on the history of literature; also Cn. Pompeius' freedman Lenaeus, Epidius, Sextus Clodius and Gavius Bassus. Statius Sebosus, who wrote an account of his travels, perhaps belongs to the same period.

1. SUETON. gramm. 10 *L.* (the praenomen in the ind. p. 98 R; cf. 1. 2 from the end) *Ateius Philologus libertinus Athenis est natus.* At the capture of Athens 668/86 he was probably allotted to the centurion M. Ateius (PLUT. Sulla 14) and was by him subsequently manumitted. Born about 655/99 (GRAFF l.l. 396): as he was of assistance to Asinius Pollio when writing his history (see below and § 221, 3), he must have lived at least until 725/29. SUET. l.l.: *hunc Capito Ateius* (§ 265, 3 the grandson of his emancipator), *notus iuris consultus, inter grammaticos rhetorem, inter rhetores grammaticum fuisse ait. de eodem Asinius Pollio, in libro quo Sallustii scripta reprehendit ut nimia priscorum verborum affectatione oblita, ita tradit: 'in eam rem adiutorium ei fecit maxime quidem Ateius Praetextatus, nobilis grammaticus latinus, declamantium deinde auditor atque praeceptor, ad summam Philologus ab semet nominatus'. ipse ad Laelium Hermam* (perhaps the same who is mentioned § 148, 3 ad fin. Concerning auct. ad Her. 1, 18 cf. CLKAYSER, Phil. 12, 273) *scripsit se in graecis litteris magnum processum habere, in latinis non nullum, . . . audisse Antonium Gniphonem* (§ 159, 5) *. . . praecepisse autem multis et claris iuvenibus, in quis Appio quoque et Pulchro Claudiis fratribus* (cf. § 199, 1), *quorum etiam comes in provincia* (in Cilicia and the prov. of Asia) *fuerit. Philologi appellationem assumpsisse videtur quia . . . multiplici variaque doctrina censebatur. quod sane ex commentariis eius apparet, quamquam paucissimi exstent. de quorum tamen copia sic altera ad eundem Hermam epistola significat: 'Hylen nostram, quam omnis generis coegimus, uti scis, octingentos in libros'. coluit postea familiarissime C. Sallustium et eo defuncto Asinium Pollionem, quos historiam componere aggressos alterum* (Sallust) *breviario rerum omnium romanarum, ex quibus quas vellet eligeret, instruxit, alterum* (Asinius) *praeceptis de ratione scribendi. quo magis miror Asinium credidisse antiqua eum verba et figuras solitum esse colligere Sallustio, cum sibi sciat nil aliud suadere quam ut noto civilique et proprio sermone utatur vitetque maxime obscuritatem Sallustii et audaciam in translationibus* (=μεταφοραῖς). His personal conviction as to the best style need not however have hindered Ateius from drawing up, at Sallust's express order, both this breviarium and also a collection of archaic phrases. FEST. 181 *Ateius Philologus in libro glossematorum*, and he quotes, without mentioning from what work, ib. 166. 173. 181. 313. 352. 375. CHARIS. GL. 1, 134, 4 *Ateius Philologus* πινάκων *III.* CHARIS. GL. 1, 127, 17 *Ateius Philologus librum suum sic edidit*

inscriptum 'an amaverit Didun Aeneas' (GRAFF l.l. 308). Ateius is also cited PLIN. HN. ind. auct. to b. 4 and as L. Ateius ib. to b. 3, further PRISC. GL. 2, 383. 8. SERV. Aen. 1, 601. HGRAFF, mélanges gréco-rom. de l'acad. de St. Pétersb. 2, 274.

2. SUET. gramm. 14 *huius* (of Curtius Nicias, § 200, 4) *de Lucilio libros etiam Santra comprobat.* Cf. MARTIAL. 11, 2, 7 *salebrosum Santram.* HIERONYM. de vir. illustr. (2, 821 Vall.) praef.: *fecerunt hoc idem* (i.e. they wrote *de viris illustribus*) . . . *apud Latinos Varro* (born 638/116), *Santra, Nepos* (born c. 655/99), *Hyginus* (born c. 690/64). GELL. 7, 15, 5 *ne si Aelii quidem, Cincii et Santrae dicendum ita censuissent.* VERRIUS FLACCUS (ap. FESTUS 277) and QUINT. 12, 10, 16 mention Santra in reference to questions of literary history. SUETON. vit. Terent. (p. 31, 10 R; *Santra Terentium existimat* etc. FESTUS 277 *quam rem* (on reciniati mimi planipedes) *diligenter exsequitur Santra libro II de antiquitate verborum.* SCHOL. VERON. Aen. 5, 95 (p. 95 K.) *Santra de antiquitate verborum libro III ait* etc. ad Aen. 2, 171 (p. 86) *ut Santra antiquitatium libris.* NON. 170, 21 *Santra de verborum antiquitate III* (or *l. II*)*: quod* (Naevius' b. punicum, see § 95, 8) *volumen unum nos lectitavimus et postea* (in other MSS.) *invenimus septemfariam divisum.* From *Santra nuntiis* (*nuptiis* RIBBECK) *Bacchiis* Nonius (see RIBB. trag.[2] p. 228, röm. Trag. 616) quotes four (incomplete) senarii, at least three of which are constructed after a strict Hellenic model. To judge by his name Santra was not of Italic birth (LMERCKLIN, Phil. 3, 344, takes him to have been an African, on account of MART. 6, 39; but see ib. 7, 20, 1).—LLERSCH, ZfAW. 1839, Nr. 13 sq. 43; Sprachphilosophie 3, 165. AE EGGER, lat. serm. vet. reliqq. 18. LPRELLER, ausgew. Aufsätze 377. BÜCHELER, RhM. 40, 148.

3. SUET. gramm. 15 *Lenaeus, Magni Pompei libertus et paene omnium expeditionum comes, defuncto eo filiisque eius* (Sextus died last, a. 719/35) *schola se sustentavit* . . . *ac tanto amore erga patroni memoriam exstitit ut Sallustium historicum* . . . *acerbissima satura laceraverit* (see § 206, 1). *traditur autem puer adhuc Athenis subreptus refugisse in patriam,* . . . *verum* . . . *gratis manumissus.* He also wrote on pharmacology (*Pompeius Lenaeus Magni libertus* PLIN, NH. 25, 5); see § 53, 1.

4. SUET. gramm. 28 *M.* (so in the Ind. gramm. p. 99 R., but see below) *Epidius calumnia notatus ludum dicendi aperuit docuitque inter ceteros M. Antonium et Augustum* (also Vergil, see § 224, 3). *quibus quondam C. Cannutius* . . . *malle* [*se*] *respondit Isaurici esse discipulum quam Epidii calumniatoris. hic Epidius ortum se a C. Epidio Nucerino praedicabat.* PLIN. NH. in the ind. auct. to b. 17 *C. Epidio* and 17, 243 *qualibus ostentis Aristandri apud Graecos volumen scatet,* . . . *apud nos vero C. Epidi commentarii, in quibus arbores locutae quoque reperiuntur.* HPETER, RhM. 22, 153. Was GL. 6, 79, 18 (*quid ais, Epidia?* etc.) perhaps also referred to?? EBÄHRENS, PLM. 327. Cf. also § 205, 6.

5. SUET. gramm. 29 = rhet. 5 *Sex Clodius e Sicilia, latinae simul graecaeque eloquentiae professor* (cf. *Sabinum* [*Sextum*?] *Clodium uno die et graece et latine declamantem* in SEN. controv. 9, 3, 13), *male oculatus et dicax par oculorum in amicitia M. Antonii triumviri extrisse* (?) *se aiebat.* . . . *a quo* (*M. Antonio*) *mox consule* (a. 710/44) *ingens etiam congiarium accepit.* Cf. CIC. Phil. 2, 43 (*rhetorem* . . . *salsum hominem*). 3, 22. ad Att. 4, 15, 2 (a. 700/54) *vereor ne lepore te suo detineat diutius rhetor Clodius.* LACTANT. inst. 1, 22, 11 *Sex. Clodius in eo libro quem graece scripsit.* ARNOB. adv. gent. 5, 18 *Sex. Clodius sexto de diis graeco.* On the other hand the Clodius cited in SERVIUS on Aen. 1, 176 *Clodius commentariorum quarto,* cf. ib. 52. 2, 229) is probably Clodius Tuscus (§ 263, 5). JBERNAYS, Theophrastos' work on piety p. 10.

6. A grammarian Gavius Bassus is also quoted as the author of works *de origine verborum et vocabulorum* (Gellius 2, 4, 3. 3, 19, 1. 5, 7) in at least 7 books (ib. 11, 17, 4) *de verborum significatione* (Macr. 3, 18, 2), *commentaria* (Gell. 3, 9. 18, 3), *de diis* (Macr. 1, 9, 13 cf. 3, 6, 17. Lyd. de mens. 4, 2; cf. Quint. 1, 6, 36. Lactant. inst. 1, 22, 9). As according to Gell. 3, 9, 8 he still saw at Argos the equus Seianus, the last proprietor of which, C. Cassius, died 718/36, he seems to belong to this period (at the very latest to the Augustan time.) JKretzschmer, de font. Gell. p. 99 sq.—In Fest. 166ᵇ, 3. 170ᵇ, 27. 355ᵃ, 7 a certain Curiatius as an explainer of words. Cf. LMercklin, de Varr. tralaticio scrib. genere, Dorp. 1858, 8.

7. Statius Sebosus is mentioned by Pliny in the ind. auct. for b. 2 and 9 and simply called Sebosus in b. 3. 5–7. 12. 13. Notices are given on his authority ib. 6, 201 (the time of a voyage to the insulae Hesperidum) and 9, 46 (the wonders of the river Ganges). EEHudeman, ZfAW. 1852, no. 3. A certain Sebosus is mentioned by Cicero, Att. 2, 14, 2. 2, 15, 3 (a. 695/59), as a friend of Lutatius Catulus and a troublesome neighbour.

212. Poets of this time who, as far as we know, kept aloof from political contention were P. Terentius Varro of Atax (a. 672/82–717/37) and Publilius Syrus; Varro first narrated in an epic poem Caesar's war in the country of the Sequani (bellum Sequanicum) and composed saturae: he subsequently became more famous as a tasteful and dexterous adapter of Alexandrine epic and didactic poems (Argonautae, Chorographia, and others); he was also an elegiac poet. Publilius Syrus (perhaps a native of Antioch) wrote for the stage, with much success, mimi which were still performed under Nero, a rich mine of proverbial philosophy, from which maxims were extracted in the 1st Christian century; this collection was enlarged from other sources in the beginning of the Middle Ages. A contemporary of these two poets was the wide-ranging epic poet (Annales) Tanusius Geminus, from Upper Italy, who was brought by Catullus into bad repute; he subsequently turned his attention to history, and after Caesar's death he treated in an Historia of the most recent events in Rome.

1. Hieronym. on Euseb. Chron. ad a. Abr. 1935=672/82 *P. Terentius Varro vico Atace* (Porphyrio on Hor. l.l. explains more correctly *ab Atace fluvio dictus*, now Aude) *in provincia Narbonensi nascitur. qui postea XXXV*[um] *annum agens graecas litteras cum summo studio didicit.* Hor. sat. 1, 10, 46 *hoc* (Satire) *erat experto frustra Varrone Atacino . . . melius quod scribere possem.* From this it appears that Varro was no longer living when this satire was written (a. 718/36, see Teuffel, RhM. 4, 111). Varro probably wrote satires in the earlier and patriotic period of his life, to which also his bellum Sequanicum seems to belong (Prisc. GL. 2, 497 *P. Varro belli Sequanici libro II*, followed by an hexameter). The subject was especially familiar to Varro both as regards period and locality;

it probably treated of Caesar's war against Ariovistus (696/58), who had established himself in the territory of the Sequani, Caes. b. g. 1, 30–54.

2. Quint. 10, 1, 87 *Atacinus Varro in iis per quae nomen est assecutus interpres operis alieni, non spernendus quidem, verum ad augendam facultatem dicendi parum locuples.* Vell. 2, 37, 3 *auctoresque carminum Varronem ac Lucretium*, unless it is M. Varro who is there alluded to, see § 165, 2 in fin. Quintilian refers to Varro's Argonautae, a free version of the Ἀργοναυτικά of Apollonios of Rhodes. Prob. Verg. G. 2, 126 *Varro qui quattuor libros de Argonautis edidit;* Schol. Veron. ad Verg. Aen. 2, 82 p. 84 K. *Varro Argonautarum primo;* Prob. Verg. G. 1, 14 *traditur . . . in corpore Argonautarum a Varrone Atacino;* Audax GL. 7, 332, 7 *Varro . . . in Argonautis*, also mentioned approvingly by Ovid am. 1, 15, 21. AA. 3, 335. trist. 2, 439. ex Pont. 4, 16, 21 (? cf. § 252, 1). Prop. 3, 34, 85. Stat. silv. 2, 7, 77. Sen. controv. 7, 2, 28 *illos optimos versus Varonis*=Apoll. Rh. 3, 748 sq. Literal borrowing from Ennius: Serv. Verg. Aen. 10, 396. RUnger, epist. de Varr. Atac., Friedl. 1861.—He wrote also a geographical work, in hexameters, of which the name is concealed ap. Prisc. GL. 2, 100, 15 in the corruption *(h)ort(h)ographia*: this has long since been rightly corrected to *chorographia* (others read *cosmographia*). After a general introduction (e.g. on the motions of the heavenly bodies, constellations and zones) Europe (Fest. 381, 4 *Varro in Europa?*), Asia and Africa were treated of successively, the work of Alexander of Ephesus (surnamed ὁ Λύχνος) being probably the original: cf. GRöper, Phil. 18, 433. Meineke, anal. Alex. 374; used by Plin. NH. b. 3–6 (geography, *ex . . . Varrone Atacino*). Ritschl, op. 3, 432. HFlach, Hesych. Mil. onomatol. p. 37 is wrong.—Also an Ephemeris: Schol. Leid. ad Verg. G. 1, 397 p. 222 Serv. Lion. *Varro in ephemeride* (so in Bergk: vulg. *epimenide.* Perhaps there is in the title a confusion with the Ephemerides of the Reatine author; cf. § 166, 6, c ad fin.) '*nubes * vellera lanae stabunt*' *sic et Aratus* (viz. 938): to the same version by Aratus belong the seven well constructed hexameters in Serv. Verg. G. 1, 375 (=Arat. 942. 954 sqq.). Bergk, RhM. 1, 372.—In his elegiac writings Varro shared the erotic tendency of the Alexandrine poets. Prop. 3, 34, 85 *haec quoque perfecto ludebat Iasone Varro, Varro Leucadiae maxima flamma suae, haec quoque lascivi cantarunt scripta Catulli* etc. Ovid trist. 2, 439 *is quoque phasiacas Argo qui duxit in undas non potuit Veneris furta tacere suae.* These are, however, the only traces of his elegies, as his successors obscured him; it is hardly probable that his un-Roman origin deprived him of influence.—An epigram (AL. 414. PLM. 4, 64) on the tomb of the rich Gaul Licinus (who died as late as Tiberius; Schol. Iuv. 1, 109. PRE. 4, 1081) may have been attributed to Varro on account of their being compatriots (it was entitled: *Terentii Varronis Atacini;* cf. Schol. Pers. 2, 36 *non invenustum Varronis epigramma*). Horace l.l. is our sole witness as to Varro's satires. FWüllner, de P. Terentii Varronis Atacini vita et scriptis, Münster 1829. Here are also collected the scanty fragments, and in Riese, Varr. Menipp. 261. FPR. 332. Cf. Ribbeck, röm. Dicht. 1, 345.

3. Hieron. ad. Euseb. Chron. 1974=711/43 (the year in which Laberius died, see § 192, 3): *Publilius* (so the cod. Amand.: *Publius* in the others) *mimographus natione Syrus Romae scaenan tenent.* On the correct name *Publilius* (instead of *Publius*) see Sillig on Plin. l.l. EWölfflin, Phil. 22, 439. Plin. NH. 35, 199 *talem (pedibus cretatis) Publilium † lochium* (*Antiochium* OJahn, Phil. 26, 11), *mimicae scaenae conditorem, et astrologiae consobrinum eius Manilium Antiochum* (cf. § 253, 2 ad fin.), *item grammaticae Staberium Erotem eadem nave advectos videre proavi* (cf. ib. 8, 209). Macr. 2, 7, 6 *Publilius, natione Syrus, cum puer ad patronum domini esset adductus, promeruit eum non minus salibus et ingenio quam forma.* (7)

ob haec et alia manumissus et maiore cura eruditus, cum mimos componeret ingentique adsensu in Italiae oppidis agere coepisset, productus Romae per Caesaris ludos (a. 709/45) *omnes qui tunc scripta et operas suas in scenam locaverant provocavit ut singuli secum posita invicem materia pro tempore contenderent. nec ullo recusante superavit omnes, in quis et Laberium.* (8) *unde Caesar adridens hoc modo pronuntiavit 'favente tibi me victus es, Laberi, a Syro' Publilio palmam . . . dedit. tunc Publilius ad Laberium recedentem ait 'quicum contendisti scriptor hunc spectator subleva'* (in Publilius' further contest with other competitors). Publilius must therefore have challenged his fellow actors to a mimic improvisation. EHOFFMANN, RhM. 39, 471. Syria excelled in the art of improvisation, see WÖLFFLIN l.l. 443. GELL. 17, 14, 1 *Publilius mimos scriptitavit. dignus habitus est qui subpar Laberio iudicaretur.* (3) *huius Publilii sententiae feruntur pleraeque* (om. MACR. 2, 7 10) *lepidae et ad communem sermonum* (om. MACR.) *usum commendatissimae* (MACR.: *adcommodatissimae*), *ex quibus sunt istae singulis versibus circumscriptae* etc. SEN. controv. 7, 2, 14. 7, 3, 8 (*quae apud eum melius essent dicta quam apud quemquam comicum tragicumque aut Romanum aut Graecum*). SEN. de tranq. an. 11, 8 *Publilius, tragicis comicisque vehementior ingeniis, quotiens mimicas ineptias et verba ad summam caveam spectantia* (addressed to the gallery) *reliquit, inter multa alia cothurno, non tantum sipario, fortiora et hoc ait.* epist. 8, 8 *quantum disertissimorum versuum inter mimos iacet! quam multa Publilii non excalceatis, sed cothurnatis dicenda sunt!* Cf. § 8, 6. Publilius seems also to have added allusions to his time. See CIC. Att. 14, 2, 1. Cf. besides CIC. fam. 12, 18, 2 and the other authorities on Publilius in WMEYER's ed. p. 1.

4. The fact that only two titles of plays by Publilius are known (NON. 133, 7 *Publili putatoribus* [the pruners] and PRISC. GL. 2, 532, 25 *Publius in † murmunthone*) is accounted for by the fact that he was chiefly an actor and improvisatore, and therefore only stage-copies of his plays were in circulation. The numerous pithy sayings contained in them were collected and published in the 1st century of the Christian era (GELLIUS 17, 14 already knows of such a collection). Of the 14 one-line apophthegms from Publilius given by GELLIUS l.l., all (except one) recur in collections still extant, and here we also find the 5 sayings attributed to Publilius by the two Senecas. Accordingly the contents of these collections are rightly traced to Publilius, as regards their fundamental substance, although no MS. mentions him as their author, and this is confirmed by the collection of excerpts in cod. Veron. 168 s. XIV (*Flores moralium autoritatum*), which gives 60 lines with the following references to their origin: *Publius, ex sententiis Publii, Publius Syrus, Publius mimus.* Hence the original title may have been: *Publilii Syri mimi sententiae.* Of these 60 lines 16 are not known from other sources. WMEYER, die Samml. d. Spruchverse (1877) 47. 61; however SMAFFEI, de' teatri antichi e moderni (Verona 1753) 118, had already published from the same MS. 12 out of those 16 lines (see GLOEWE, RhM. 34, 624).—The extant collections contain about 700 sayings (single lines, mostly iambic senarii, but also some trochaic septenarii) and they consist of heterogeneous abstracts from an original collection, which was alphabetically arranged and contained perhaps 1000 lines, from which (directly or indirectly) the writer of the cod. Veron. drew his materials.

5. The first revision (in WMEYER Σ) e.g. in the Parisini 2676 s. X–XI and 7641 s. X, Turic. (=Rheinaug. 95) s. X, gives 265 apophthegms from A–N. To replace the second half, which had been lost at an early date (it contained the sayings from O–V), 149 apophthegms in prose, taken chiefly from Seneca de moribus (§ 289, 10), were added. This entire collection was entitled after its better known

author *Sententiae* (or Proverbia) Senecae. The second revision (II) contained more than 450 lines; the Vaticano-Palatinus 239 s. X–XI includes the letters A–I. The remainder is to be found in the Frisingensis (see below). The third (Z), which has been much remodelled, exists in a Turic. C 78 s. X from C–V: the beginning of it (A–D) is given in Monac. 6369 s. XI: altogether 137 sayings, amongst them 50 which are not to be found in the other collections. Edited in a complete form by WMeyer, SBer. d. Münch. Ak. 1872 2, 538. On the Vatic. Reg. 1762 s. IX, which resembles the Monac., see WMeyer, Abh. d. Münch. Ak. 17, 1, 22.—The most complete Corpus (Ψ) is that which has resulted from combining the first and second revision, the cod. Frisingensis (now Monac. 6292) s. XI, altogether 649 lines. The Frisingensis was already made use of (by JGretser) in the Ingoldstadt ed. of 1600.—As nearly all the sayings are rules of common prudence and every-day experience, and as Seneca (ep. 33, 7) writes: *pueris sententias ediscendas damus*, it appears credible that this collection was used in the schools. Thus Hieronymus epist. ad Laetam 107 (1, 679 Vall.) quotes the line *Aegre reprehendas quod sinas consuescere* (now proved by the cod. Veron. to be by Publilius) and he adds: *legi quondam in scholis puer.*—The earlier editions (see Wölfflin, Phil. 22. 454. WMeyer's ed. p. 14) are now useless on account of their confusion of the various parts, and of many interpolations. First documentary edition: Publilii Syri sententiae ad fid. codd. optt. nunc primum rec. EWölfflin, Lps. 1869. Revisions by ORibbeck in the Com. lat.² p. 309 (together with p. lxxxix. cxxxiii; Jen. LZ. 1874, 446; LCentr.-Bl. 1880, 1044 and against this rightly WMeyer, Beobacht. des Versaccents, Abh. d. Münch. Akad. 17, 1, 21) and ASpengel (recensuit, Berl. 1874). New revision by WMeyer, Lpz. 1880 (with complete critical apparatus and ind. verborum).—Publ. Syr. sententiae, dig. rec. ill. OFriedrich; acc. Caecilii Balbi, Pseudosenecae, proverbiorum falso inter Publilianas receptae sententiae et recognitae et versibus adstrictae, Berl. 1880. Cf. also especially WMeyer, die Sammlungen der Spruchverse des Publilius, Lpz. 1877; likewise Wölfflin, Phil. 11, 191. 16, 618. 22, 437; phil. Anz. 9, 51. ANauck, Mélanges gréco-rom. (Petersb. 1872) 3, 2. CHartung, Phil. 37, 569. A few observations on the MS. copies, EBährens, miscell. crit. (Groningen 1879) 18.

6. From the original collection (n. 4 ad fin.) a series of Publilius-sayings was transmuted into a collection of apophthegms, which we now possess in MS. in a duplicate (longer and shorter) form (e.g. in the Frisingensis, now Monac. 6292 s. XI; Paris. 2772 s. X). Printed as Caecilii Balbi de nugis philosophorum quae supersunt nunc prim. ed. Wölfflin, Bas. 1855. The name of this author and this title, which Wölfflin following ChPetersen, Verh. d. Kasseler Phil.-Vers. 1844, 109, gave to the collection from Joannes Saresber. (Policrat. 3, 14), which had been handed down without a name, are founded on an error: see AReifferscheid, RhM. 16, 12 and Wölfflin himself ib. 615 and PRE. 1², 244. The so-called Caecilius Balbus is mainly an ancient Latin translation of a Greek collection of maxims: see WMeyer, die Samml. d. Spruchv. d. Publ. Syr. 45, JScheibmaier, de sententiis quas dicunt Caecilii Balbi, Munich 1879. On the lines from Publilius interpolated in this collection at a later time see Meyer l.l. 44. Scheibmaier l.l. 27. Also OFriedrich (n. 5) 10. 81.

7. Sen. ep. 93, 9 *paucorum versuum liber est* (the short life of Metronax), *et quidem laudandus atque utilis. annales Tanusii scis quam ponderosi sint et quid vocentur. hoc est vita quorundam longa et quod Tanusii sequitur annales.* This *quid vocentur* is an allusion to Catull. 36, 1 *annales Volusi, cacata charta* (cf. ib. 6 *electissima pessimi poetae scripta;* 19 *plena ruris et inficetiarum*, and 95, 7 *Volusi annales Paduam morientur ad ipsam*, i.e. in the author's native place) and Volusius

is a disguise of the real name of Tanusius; MHaupt, op. 1, 71. LSchwabe, quaestt. Cat. 278. Against PESonnenburg, who in the histor. researches for ASchäfer, Bonn 1882, 158, disputes the identification of Volusius=Tanusius see LSchwabe, JJ. 129, 380.—After Caesar's death this Tanusius wrote an historia (§ 210), mentioned by Suet. Iul. 9 (*Tanusius Geminus in historia*), Strabo 17, 829 (where instead of Γαβίνιος ὁ τῶν Ῥωμαίων συγγραφεύς we should according to the best MS. read Τανύσιος, cf. BNiese, RhM. 38, 601) and Plut. Caes. 22. This historia treated of the most recent events, and was not favourable to Caesar. Perhaps the Geminus mentioned in Macr. sat. 1, 16, 33 is likewise this same Tanusius, see Schwabe, JJ. l.l. 385.—HPeter, hist. rom. fr. 239. RUnger, de Tanusio Gemino annalium scriptore, Friedland 1855.

8. Catullus (14, 18. 19. 22, 1) mentions likewise other (inferior) poets of his time, such as Aquinus (cf. Cic. Tusc. 5, 63), Caesius, Suffenus. LSchwabe, quaestt. Cat. 257 and the interpreters ad ll.

9. Nep. Att. 12, 4 *L. Julium Calidum, quem post Lucretii Catullique mortem multo elegantissimum poetam nostram tulisse aetatem vere videor posse contendere, neque minus virum bonum optimisque artibus eruditum post proscriptionem equitum* (after the list of the proscribed belonging to the equestrian order had been already closed) *propter magnas eius Africanas possessiones in proscriptorum numerum a P. Volumnio praefecto fabrum Antonii absentem relatum expedivit* (Atticus). Nepos amicably overrates this poet, who is mentioned nowhere else. He is possibly to be identified with the L. Julius from Africa, whom Cicero (fam. 13, 6, 3 a. 698/56) recommends to Valerius Orca procons. Afr.

213. Ticidas, the author of erotic poems (on Perilla), appears to belong to the same circle, as well as C. Helvius Cinna, who in his mythological epic poem of Zmyrna laboriously plodded along in the track of the erudite Alexandrine poets, and also another friend of Catullus, the talented, original, and incisive writer C. Licinius Calvus (a. 672/82–707/47), a man equally eminent as juridical pleader and poet, and who in both departments purposely bridled his abundant vivacity by rigorous attention to form. In oratory he followed the New Attic school, and in poetry he succeeded in combining the correctness of the Alexandrine school with an impassioned treatment of his subject, both in love and hatred, in the manner of Catullus and closely approaching him.

1. Ovid trist. 2, 433 (after Catullus and Calvus, before Cinna) *quid referam Ticidae, quid Memmi carmen, apud quos rebus abest nomen nominibusque pudor?* Apul. apol. 10 *accusent . . . Ticidam similiter, quod quae Metella erat Perillam scripserit.* A pentameter by Ticidas in praise of Valerius Cato's Lydia is quoted by Suet. gr. 11, and Ticidas is mentioned ib. 4 together with Furius Bibaculus and (Valerius) Cato. Prisc. GL. 2, 189, 2 '*sole*' (as vocative) *quoque antiqui. Ticidas* (so in the MSS., in Suet. gr. 11 we have the nominative *Ticida*) *in hymenaeo: felix lectule talibus sole amoribus.*

2. C. (Catullus 10, 30) Helvius (Gell. 19, 13, 5) Cinna was the companion of Catullus in the suite of the praetor Memmius (§ 202, 2) in Bithynia (Catull.

10, 29, Cinnae fr. 3 Müll.). Very little besides this is known of his life. Perhaps he was a fellow-countryman of Catullus. Cf. Cinna ap. Gell. 19, 13, 5 *at nunc me Genumana* (the Cenomani lived near Verona and Brixia) *per salicta bigis raeda rapit citata nanis.* Kiessling l.l. 353 conjectures Brixia to have been his birthplace: here the gens Helvia was numerously established according to the inscriptions. Plut. Brut. 20 calls Cinna, the Caesarian tribune of the people, who, being mistaken for L. Cornelius Cinna (PRE. 2, 691, 2) was killed in consequence at Caesar's funeral (710/44), a ποιητικὸς ἀνήρ to distinguish him from that Cornelius Cinna (he is called *C. Helvius Cinna* by Val. Max. 9, 9, 1, *Helvius Cinna* by Suet. Iul. 85, cf. 52. Cassius Dio 44, 50). Accordingly it is very probable a priori that our poet and his namesake and contemporary, the tribune of the people, are identical. A difficulty indeed arises from the fact that the tribune of the people was a partisan of Caesar, inasmuch as we should rather have expected a hostile attitude towards Caesar in the friend of Catullus, which is confirmed by the circumstance that Catullus' poem 113, an attack on Caesar, is addressed to Cinna: but perhaps Cinna like Catullus (§ 214, 5) and Calvus (§ 213, 7) had subsequently been reconciled with Caesar. He must certainly have become one of his most zealous partisans: cf. besides § 192, 5. Verg. ecl. 9, 35 is not necessarily opposed to the statement of Plutarch, since that passage need not imply that Cinna was still living at the date of the composition of the poem (714/40). Kiessling l.l. 353. On Cinna's reputation as a poet cf. also Valgius in schol. Veron. Verg. ecl. 7, 22 (§ 233, 1). Ribbeck's theory (röm. Dicht. 1, 343), that Cornelius Cinna, and not Helvius Cinna, was killed at Caesar's funeral is incompatible with the authorities on the subject; see LSchwabe, Phil. 47, 169.

3. His principal work was his Smyrna (Zmyrna), in which he treated of the unnatural love of Smyrna (Myrrha) for her father Kinyras, the subject being in the manner of the Alexandrine poets. Cinna devoted nine years to this poem (Catull. 95. Quint. 10, 4, 4. Philargyr. on Verg. ecl. l.l. Porphyr. Hor. AP. 388) in spite of its inconsiderable length (Catull. 95, 9. Serv. Verg. ecl. 9, 35 *Smyrnam, quem libellum decem annis elimavit*), a fact equally characteristic of his lack of real poetical talent and his industry in formal polish. Philargyr. l.l. (in Lion's Servius 2, p. 327) states the result of all this: *fuit autem liber obscurus adeo ut et nonnulli eius aetatis grammatici* (L. Crassicius § 263, 2 is here referred to) *in eum scripserint magnamque ex eius enarratione sint gloriam consecuti. quod obscurus fuerit etiam Martialis ostendit in illo versu* (10, 21, 4) '*non lectore tuis opus est, sed Apolline libris: iudice te melior Cinna Marone fuit.*' Ovid trist. 2, 435 places him among the erotic poets *Cinna quoque his comes est* (cf. n. 1); we are justified in refusing credit to Gellius (see § 31, 1) both in his statement that these poems were *illepida* and that C. was *non ignobilis neque indoctus poeta* (Gell. 19, 13, 5). Lyrical poems by him in Gell. 9, 12, 12 *Cinna in poematis* (choliambic); also 19, 13, 5 (hendecasyllabics). Non. 87, 27 *Cinna in epigrammatis*; in Isidor. orig. 6, 12, 2 we have an epigram by Cinna, written to accompany a present, a copy of Aratus' Φαινόμενα which he had brought with him from Bithynia (n. 2). In Charis. GL. 1, 124 four hexameters from Cinna's Propempticon Pollionis (for the young Asinius Pollio § 221, on the occasion of his journey to Greece, see Kiessling l.l. 352). A commentary on or introduction to this poem by Hyginus (Charis. GL. 1, 134, 12 *Iulius Hyginus in Cinnae propemptico*). Parthenios, who was at that time living in Rome and had great influence on the Roman poets (§ 150, 6. 230, 2, 3. 230, 3, 1), also wrote a προπεμπτικόν (Steph. Byz. s. v. Κώρυκος. πόλις Κιλικίας. Παρθένιος προπεμπτικῷ.) Was Cinna in close connection with him? Parthenios ἐλήφθη ὑπὸ Κίννα (perhaps the father of the poet? see Kiessling l.l. 352) λάφυρον, ὅτε Μιθριδάτην Ῥωμαῖοι

κατεπολέμησαν (SUID. s. v.).—In general AWEICHERT, poett. latt. vitae etc. (Lps. 1830) 147; the remains of Cinna's poems ib. 187, in LMÜLLER's Catullus 87. FPR. 323.—AKIESSLING, de C. Helvio Cinna poeta in the commentt. Mommsen. 351. RIBBECK, röm. Dicht. 1, 341.

4. Another friend of Catullus, Caecilius in Novum Comum, was—according to CATULLUS 35, 13—likewise engaged on a poem (an epic, or perhaps galliambic? § 214, 6 l. 15) of a mythological character on Kybele, but we do not know if it was ever finished and published.—To this group also belongs Varus, Catullus' literary friend (22; cf. 10), who is generally identified with Alfenus Varus (§ 208, 3): it is quite as probable that he is the friend mentioned by HIERONYMUS a. 1994 (Freherian. a. 1993)=731/23: *Quintilius Cremonensis Vergili et Horati familiaris moritur*, whose death is referred to by HORACE c. 1, 24 (*ad Vergilium*), who has also AP. 438 raised a monument to him as a skilful art-critic; PORPHYR. ad loc.: *hic erat Quintilius Varus Cremonensis* (*poeta Cremonensis* Acro and comment. Cruquii) *amicus Vergilii, eques Romanus.* LSCHWABE, quaestt. Catull. 289.—From the Cretica of an unknown author (*de qua in creticis † versibus*) see four hexameters ap. HYGIN. fab. 177? cf. the editors ad loc. BÄHRENS misc. crit. 19. FPR. 327.

5. C. Licinius Macer (CIC. ad Q. fr. 2, 4, 1) Calvus (with two surnames: see DRUMANN's GR. 4, 195), the son of the annalist Licinius Macer (§ 156, 4), VAL. MAX. 9, 12, 7. He was born May 28, 672/82: see § 209, 5. Cicero's letter to Trebonius, fam. 15, 21, 4 (a. 707/47) presupposes the recent death of Calvus, cf. below the passage from CIC. Brut. (composed 708/46). SENECA contr. 7, 4, 7 *erat* (*Calvus*) *parvolus statura, propter quod etiam Catullus in hendecasyllabis* (53, 5) *vocat illum 'salaputtium disertum'* (cf. for this word *C. Iulius P. f. Salaputis* CIL. 8, 10570). Hence OVID trist. 2, 431 *exigui Calvi.* General characterisation of Calvus CIC. Brut. 279 *facienda mentio est . . . duorum adolescentium qui, si diutius vixissent, magnam essent eloquentiae laudem consecuti*, namely C. Curio (§ 209, 1) and C. Licinius Calvus. 283 *Calvus . . . orator fuit cum litteris eruditior quam Curio tum etiam accuratius quoddam dicendi et exquisitius afferebat genus. quod quamquam scienter eleganterque tractabat, nimium tamen inquirens in se atque ipse sese observans metuensque ne vitiosum colligeret etiam verum sanguinem deperdebat. itaque eius oratio nimia religione attenuata doctis et attente audientibus erat illustris, a multitudine autem et a foro . . . devorabatur.* (284) *Tum Brutus, atticum se, inquit, Calvus noster dici oratorem volebat; inde erat ista exilitas, quam ille de industria consequebatur.* ad. fam. 15, 21, 4 *genus quoddam sequebatur in quo, iudicio lapsus quo valebat, tamen assequebatur quod probarat. multae erant et reconditae litterae, vis non erat. . . . de ingenio eius valde existimavi bene.* Cf. TAC. dial. 18 (see § 210, 2). QUINT. 10, 1, 115 *inveni qui Calvum praeferrent omnibus . . . est* (*Calvi*) *et sancta* (cf. 12, 10, 11) *et gravis oratio et frequenter vehemens quoque. imitator autem est Atticorum fecitque illi properata mors iniuriam.* SEN. contr. 7, 4, 6 *Calvus, qui diu cum Cicerone iniquissimam litem de principatu eloquentiae habuit, usque eo violentus actor et concitatus fuit ut in media eius actione surgeret Vatinius reus et exclamaret 'rogo vos, iudices, num si iste disertus est ideo me damnari oportet?' . . . solebat praeterea excedere subsellia sua et impetu latus usque in adversariorum partem transcurrere. . . . compositio quoque eius in actionibus ad exemplum Demosthenis riget: nihil in illa placidum, nihil lene est, omnia excitata et fluctuantia.* Another feature, his precise phraseology, is mentioned by TAC. dial. 25 (*adstrictior*), APUL. apol. 95 (*argutiae*); but FRONTO p. 114 Nab. says: *in iudiciis . . . Calvus rixatur.*—SUET. Aug. 72 *habitavit primo in domo quae Calvi oratoris fuerat.*

6. TAC. dial. 21 *ipse mihi* (as a champion of the modern oratory) *Calvus, cum unum et viginti, ut puto, libros* (i.e. speeches) *reliquerit, vix in una et altera oratiuncula*

satisfacit. nec dissentire ceteros ab hoc meo iudicio video: quotus enim quisque Calvi in Asitium aut in Drusum legit? at hercle in omnium studiosorum manibus versantur accusationes quae in Vatinium inscribuntur ac praecipue secunda (which shows that there were at least three) *ex his oratio: est enim verbis ornata et sententiis, auribus iudicum accommodata.* ib. 34 *uno et vicesimo* (*aetatis anno*) *Caesar Dolabellam, altero et vicesimo Asinius Pollio C. Catonem, non multum aetate antecedens Calvus Vatinium iis orationibus insecuti sunt quas hodie quoque cum admiratione legimus.* Cf. Quint. 12, 6, 1 *cum . . . Calvus, Caesar, Pollio multum ante quaestoriam omnes aetatem* (which was then the thirtieth year) *gravissima iudicia susceperint.* Calvus acted several times as the accuser of P. Vatinius, the first time a. 696/58 (ex lege Licinia Iunia ?), then de ambitu e lege Tullia (a. 698/56 ?), and again lege Licinia de sodaliciis in July 700/54, when Cicero defended the accused; lastly, perhaps a fourth time (de vi ?) also a. 700/54, when Cicero was one of the witnesses in favour of Vatinius (ad. fam. 1, 9, 4. 19); see KNipperdey, op. 330. GMatthies, de Calvi in Vatin. accusationibus, in the commentt. philol. (Lps. 1874) 99. Bährens, commentar. Cat. p. 264. BSchmidt, Catull. p. lv. In the same way Calvus defended P. Sestius a. 698/56 (Schol. Bob. p. 292), and at another time Messius, and according to Sen. l.l. the epilogue to this speech was *non tantum emollitae compositionis sed infractae.* Tac. dial. 23 *isti* (antiquarians) *qui rhetorum nostrorum commentarios fastidiunt, oderunt, Calvi mirantur:* we hear, except this, nothing of works on rhetoric by Calvus: perhaps this may be an allusion to the learned correspondence on questions of oratory which Calvus carried on with Cicero; cf. Tac. dial. 18 (see § 210, 2). For the name cf. the commentariolum petitionis of Q. Cicero (§ 190, 4). Nipperdey l.l. 313 reads *L. Aeli* (§ 148) instead of *Calvi.* OHarnecker, JJ. 125, 604.

7. Seneca contr. 7, 4, 7 *carmina quoque eius* (of Calvus), *quamvis iocosa sint, plena sunt ingentis animi*, as a specimen of which he quotes a cutting saying against Pompey; cf. Schol. Lucan. 7, 726. Suet. Iul. 73 *Gaio Calvo post famosa epigrammata* (cf. ib. c. 49) *de reconciliatione per amicos* (Catullus ? cf. § 214, 5) *agenti ultro ac prior scripsit.* We know of hendecasyllabics *in poematis*, e.g. against Q. Curius PRE. 2. 787, 8), and choliambics (against Tigellius). There were also erotic poems; see § 31, 1. Ovid trist. 2, 431 *par* (like Catullus' poems on Lesbia) *fuit exigui similisque licentia Calvi, detexit variis qui sua furta modis.* Cf. Prop. 3, 25, 4. 3, 34, 89 *haec etiam docti* (hence probably in the manner of the Alexandrine poets) *confessa est pagina Calvi, cum caneret miserae funera Quintiliae* (Catull. 96, 6), who probably was his wife. Cf. Diomed. GL. 1, 376, 1 *Calvus alibi* (*lib. I* ARiese, JJ. 105, 755) *ad uxorem* (see however HKeil ad loc.). These lamentations on the death of his wife (elegies) seem indicated by such fragments as Charis. GL. 1, 101 (*Calvus in carminibus*). Prisc. GL. 2, 170 *Calvus in epithalamio* (dactylic lines), Charis. GL. 1, 147 *Licinius Calvus in poemate* (glyconic). Part of his poems were devoted to his friends; cf. Charis. GL. 1, 77, 3 *Calvus ad amicos* (does this mean a poetical epistle ?): *ne triclinarius.* Also an epic poem Io, Serv. Verg. ecl. 6, 47. 8, 4 *Calvus in Io*, (Probus) GL. 4, 226, 8. 234, 32, perhaps founded on Kallimachos' Ἰοῦς ἄφιξις? Schneider's Callim. 2, 33.—Martial. 14, 196 *Calvi de aquae frigidae usu* probably, to judge from the context, refers to a (didactic) poem (MHertz). Cf. Friedländer, Mart. 2, p. 300.—The remains of his poems are given in Lachmann's (p. 85) and LMüller's (p. 13) Catullus, in Weichert l.l. 131. FPR. 320.—He agrees with Catullus in many points, and is therefore frequently mentioned with him e.g. Hor. sat. 1, 10, 19. Prop. 3, 25, 4. 3, 34, 87. Ovid am. 3, 9, 62 (*cum Calvo, docte Catulle, tuo*). trist. 2, 431. Plin. ep. 1, 16, 5. 4, 27, 4. Gell. 19, 9, 7. Poems by Catullus addressed to him: 14. 50. 96. Cf. LSchwabe, quaestt. Catull.

255. In general see AWeichert, poetar. latt. vitae etc. 89. RUnger, Valg. Ruf. (1848) 47. FPlessis, essai sur Calvus, Caen 1885. ORibbeck, Gesch. d. röm. Dicht. 1, 313.

214. C. Valerius Catullus of Verona (a. 667/87–c. 700/54) is the greatest lyric poet of Roman literature. Though he followed at first the track of the Alexandrine poets, he subsequently developed in the most varied forms a rich lyric talent, which was ripened by his bitter experience of life and his love for Lesbia. He is one of the few Romans to whom poetry was a necessity of their being; he was and could be nothing but a poet. His early death prevented him from attaining to consummate excellence, maturity, and unblemished beauty; he remained a youth, passionate both in love and hatred, hot-blooded and reckless, unreserved in his attachments and intensely sensitive, ideal and yet coarse, tender and yet venomous, boldly spurning the bars of manners and modesty, a loyal loveable child of nature. But the directness with which the poet reveals his whole richly gifted temperament delights and fascinates his reader. The larger Catullus' poems are (with the exception of c. 61), the less they are successful, and the poet does not handle dactylic metres quite easily: on the other hand he is masterly in the lighter lyrical forms. The harmony of substance and form, the refinement and transparent clearness of the thoughts are incomparable, as are the grace, strength and warmth of feeling in the shorter pieces, especially his hendecasyllabics and iambics, which springing from the mood of the moment evidence the true nobility of a born poet.

1. The good MSS. only give his cognomen and birth-place (*Catulli Veronensis liber*). His praenomen rests on the authority of Apul. apol. 10 (*accusent C. Catullum quod Lesbiam pro Clodia nominarit*) and Hieron. chron. a. Abr. 1930=667/87 *Gaius Valerius Catullus scriptor lyricus Veronae nascitur*. The gentile name also is given ap. Suet. Iul. 73. Porphyr. on Hor. sat. 1, 10, 19. Charis. GL. 1, 97 (cf. MHaupt, op. 2, 68). Varro LL. 7, 50 (cf. LSchwabe, JJ. 101, 350). The praenomen Q. in some of the MSS. (it has long been set aside in Plin. NH. 37, 81) has no warrant. Scaliger's conjecture in the poem 67, 12 (*Quinte*) is tempting, but not therefore right. See LSchwabe, quaestt. Catull. 6, 11. Munro, criticisms of Cat. 68. KPSchulze, ZfGW. 34, 360. Birth-place Verona, see also Ovid am. 3, 15, 7. Plin. NH. 36, 48. Mart. 1, 61, 1. 10, 103, 5. 14, 195 and elsewhere. Cf. Cat. 39, 13. Of a respected and wealthy family: relations between Catullus' father and Caesar, Suet. Iul. 73 (below n. 5). Valerii are very numerous in upper Italy, and especially in Verona: Valerii Catulli are rare; *M. Annius Valerius Catullus* CIL. 5, 4484 (Brixia). *L. Vallerius Catullus M⟨essalinus⟩* ib. 5, 7239 (Susa), according to Borghesi, op. 5, 528, a descendant of the poet's brother; cf. *L. Valerius Catullus* Cohen, méd. impér.[2] 1, 142 no. 536. *Valerius Catullus* Suet. Calig. 36. CIL. 14, 2095.—He had an estate at Sirmio, c. 31 and at Tibur, c. 44.

2. For the year of his death see Hieron. l.l. a. Abr. 1959 = 696/58 but in the codd. A(mand.) P(etav.) F(reher.) not until 1960 = 697/57: *Catullus XXX aetatis anno Romae moritur.* Hieronymus (or rather Suetonius) is therefore consistent (see n. 1) in the year of his birth and death: yet it appears from Catull. 113, 2 that the latter is erroneously placed (696/58 or) 697/57 *consule Pompeio . . . nunc iterum* (a. 699/55); cf. 55, 6. 11, 12 and 29, 20 (after the autumn of 699/55); whether 53, 2 applies only to the second half of 700/54 remains doubtful, as Calvus had once before prosecuted Vatinius, see above § 213, 6. A date beyond 699/55–700/54 is indicated only by c. 52 *sella in curuli Struma Nonius sedet, per consulatum peierat Vatinius,* as Vatinius was not consul until the close of a. 707/47. But he calculated on being consul long before (and even used to swear 'ita consul fiam, ut haec vera sunt'), see Cic. in Vat. 6. 11; cf. Schol. Bob. p. 315 Or.; and these vain hopes of Vatinius were further strengthened by the agreement of the triumvirs at Luca (a. 698/56, cf. Cic. Att. 4, 8b, 2). Cf also Ellis, commentary on Cat. p. 142. It should also be observed that the years 700/54–707/47, especially 702/52 and 705/49, would furnish Catullus with abundant matter for cutting epigrams; but as there is no trace at all of them in his poems (cf. on the collection of them n. 7), it appears that he did not live until 702/52 sqq. On the other hand it is certain that Catullus died very young (Ovid Am. 3, 9, 61 *iuvenalia cinctus tempora . . . docte Catulle,* in Elysium). If we place his death a. 700/54 or 701/53, he actually died young, as the doubts against the year 667/87 as that of his birth cannot be substantiated. The erroneous computation of the year of his death by Hieronymus probably arose from an inexact or garbled statement in Suetonius as regards the number of years of Catullus' life. The conjecture in BSchmidt, Cat. p. lxii that Catullus lived between 672/82–702/52, is arbitrary. Cf. in general Schwabe, quaestt. Cat. 33.

3. His liaison with Lesbia. Prop. 3, 34, 87 *haec quoque lascivi cantarunt scripta Catulli, Lesbia quis ipsa notior est Helena.* Ovid trist. 2, 427 *sic sua lascivo cantata est saepe Catullo femina, cui falsum Lesbia nomen erat. nec contentus ea multos volgavit amores in quibus ipse suum fassus adulteriumst* (his infidelity, ARiese, JJ. 105, 753). Martial. 8, 73, 8 *Lesbia dictavit, docte Catulle, tibi* and others. Apuleius (see n. 1) attests that her real name was Clodia. An early and very probable conjecture identifies her with the notorious Clodia (born c. 660/94), elder sister of P. Clodius (born c. 661/93). This woman, who was conspicuous for her beauty and wit, was unhappily married to her cousin, Q. Caecilius Metellus Celer, cos. 694/60, who died (perhaps through his wife) 695/59, a man known to us also by his touchy and arrogant letter to Cicero (fam. 5, 1, a. 692/62); cf. also Cic. Att. 1, 18, 1 *Metellus non homo, sed litus atque aer et solitudo mera;* see PRE. 2, 26, 15. 420, 45. A strong argument for identifying Lesbia with this Clodia occurs in c. 79, where beside *Lesbia* (= Clodia) a certain *Lesbius* (therefore = Clodius) *pulcher* is mentioned, with special allusion to the cognomen of P. Clodius Pulcher. Against the previous doubts of ARiese (JJ. 105, 747, who however now hardly maintains his views, see his ed. p. xiii) and others as to the identity of the two, see KPSchulze, ZfGW. 28, 699. EBährens, analecta Catull. (Jena 1874) 3; comm. in Catull. p. 31. CMFrancken, Lesbia-Clodia, Verslag. en Mededeel. d. Amsterd. Akad. 2, 11 (1879). FSchöll, JJ. 121, 481. BSchmidt, Catull. p. vii. Clodia, well versed in all the arts of love, knew how to lure the passionate and brilliant young provincial into her net, where she held him fast for several years (perhaps from 693/61-696/58, Schwabe, quaestt. Catull.), so that he addressed his most fiery songs to her; nay after breaking with her returned to her again and again, until his eyes were opened. Several attempts have been made to trace the history of this connection with the help of Catullus' poetry; see the commentators and WThJungclaussen, on the chronology etc.

(Itzehoe 1857) 8. SCHWABE, quaestt. Catull. 71. 358. RIBBECK, Catullus (1863) 29. 56. WVORLÄNDER, de Catulli ad Lesbiam carminibus, Bonn 1864. TTKROON, quaestt. Cat., Leid. 1864. RWESTPHAL, Catullus' poems (Breslau 1867) 33. 100. Westphal's fancy as to erotic relations between Clodia (Lesbia) and Cicero (!) has been impugned by GFRETTIG, Catulliana 1 (Bern. 1868), 3. HHHESKAMP, de C. vita et ordine quo carmina amatoria sunt scripta, Münster 1869.

4. Catullus stayed in Bithynia in the train of the propraetor Memmius (§ 200, 2) together with Helvius Cinna and others, from spring 697/57 till 698/56, but without the desired profits: see c. 10, 6. 28, 7. 31, 5. 46, 1. SCHWABE, quaestt. Catull. 153. PWEHRMANN, fasti praet. 62. 64. On his journey back he visited the tomb of his brother, who had previously died in Troas: c. 101. (cf. 65, 1. 68a, 19. 68b, 91) SCHWABE, l.l. 176.

5. As a friend and an enemy: Catullus was in especially close relations with Calvus (§ 213, 5): 14, 1 *Ni te plus oculis meis amarem, iucundissime Calve.* 50. 53. 96. Accordingly later writers frequently mention C. and Calvus together as compeers both in poetry and in friendship; see the numerous passages specified above § 213, 7 in fin. p. 390 l. 2 from the end. He was also a friend of Cinna (§ 213, 2): 10, 30. 95. 113. An ironical thanksgiving to the patronus omnium Cicero 49 (perhaps this was an allusion to his defence of Vatinius, see § 213, 6); cf. BSCHMIDT, Cat. p. XL.—Attacks on Caesar and his adherents. SUET. Iul. 73 *Valerium Catullum, a quo sibi versiculis de Mamurra* (§ 209, 13. CAT. 29 end of 699/55, and especially c. 57; see also OJAHN, Herm. 2, 240) *perpetua stigmata imposita non dissimulaverat, satis facientem eadem die adhibuit cenae hospitioque patris eius sicut consueverat uti perseveravit.* See TAC. ann. 4, 34 (above § 192, 4). Besides this, c. 94. 105. 114. 115 (cf. 29, 13) are specially directed against Mamurra, whom the poet after his reconciliation with Caesar calls Mentula. Catullus is not a politician, he is altogether wanting in appreciation of public affairs: but like his companions among the literary neo-Roman youth he was a raisonneur, an oppositionist, who formed his opinions not on real but on personal grounds. See on the whole question SCHWABE, quaestt. Catull. 182, and CPLEITNER, Catulls Gedichte an und über Caesar und Mamurra kritisch behandelt, Speier 1849. RvBRAITENBERG, Cat.'s Verhältnis zu s. Zeit, Prague 1882.

6. The learned poems of Catullus are chiefly imitations of Alexandrine poems or in Alexandrine style: to them he owes the surname of *doctus* LYGD. (Tib.) 3, 6, 41. MART. 1, 61, 1. 7, 99, 7. 8, 73, 11. 14, 152. To the same class belongs the short and laboriously constructed epic on the nuptials of Peleus and Thetis (c. 64); in its plan and versification, its method of psychological delineation, by which the narrative is thrown into the shade (cf. also 63. 68), and in a host of separate details it imitates the Alexandrine manner, but it must not be looked upon as a mere translation (so RMERKEL ad Ov. Ib. p. 360; ARIESE, RhM. 21, 498; more correctly in his edition p. 154). It contains an imitation of Euphorion (§ 32, 1. p. 250, 2)? 64, 30 *Oceanusque, mari totum qui amplectitur orbem* = EUPHOR. fr. 158 Mein. Ὠκεανός, τῷ πᾶσα περίρρυτος ἐνδέδεται χθών. Cf. also OSCHNEIDER, Callim. 2, 791. KPSCHULZE, JJ. 125, 208. In this poem spondaic endings (n. 9) and alliteration are especially frequent. There is again the translation of a Sapphic epithalamium (c. 62), and the translation of Kallimachos' elegy on the hair of Queen Berenike (c. 66) with a dedication to Hortensius (c. 65; cf. 116, 2), and above all, the poem on Attis (c. 63) in galliambic metre, a masterpiece in spirit and form, which is likewise dependent on Alexandrine models (on Kallimachos according to UvWILAMOWITZ, Herm. 14, 194). Cf. MHAUPT, op. 2, 75. KPSCHULZE, de Catullo Graecorum imitatore, Jena 1871.

PWeidenbach, de Catullo Callimachi imitatore, Lps. 1873. WHenkel, de Catullo Alexandrinorum imitatore, Jena 1883. The poem on Allius is also Alexandrine (c. 68[b]) especially in its design. C. 61 is also translated from Sappho, but is altered to suit the personal motive and is made to refer to Lesbia.—A second class of poems treats of personal concerns, and on these the poet's fame has chiefly been founded and now justly rests. To this belong the epistle to Manlius (c. 68[a]), and the dialogue with a door (c. 67), an extract from the chronique scandaleuse of Verona, both in elegiac metre, and especially the lyrical poems (proper) and the iambic poems. With true tact these refrain from learned allusions, they attract the reader by unpretending simplicity, and are the spontaneous effusions of love or hatred (85 *odi et amo*), friendship or enmity, showing now genial warmth, now caustic bitterness (Quint. 10, 1, 96 *iambi acerbitas in Catullo.* Cat. 36, 5 *truces iambi*). Like everything else in Catullus, so even the sensuality and rudeness of the lawless, unseasoned youth are wholesome (*lascivus Catullus*, Prop. 3, 34, 87. Ov. trist. 2, 427; cf. Mart. 1, praef.): they eschew mere lewdness, but the 'naughty darling of the Graces' not infrequently condescends to unpleasant ribaldry and repulsive coarseness.—To his most successful creations belongs the magnificent hymn on the marriage of Manlius Torquatus (c. 61), which exhibits the Roman spirit and Roman usage in the most graceful Grecian garb. Remains of nuptial songs in the same (glyconic) metre among the fragments of his fellow-scholars Calvus and Ticidas. The hymn on Diana (c. 34) may have been composed for some religious ceremony.—Imitation of Lucretius in Catullus? Munro on Lucr. 3, 57; critic. of Cat. 72. JJessen, über Lucr. u. s. Verh. zu Catull, Kiel 1872. ABrieger, JB. 1873, 1098.

7. As the nature of the subject-matter proves, Catullus' poems were first published separately—a fact evidenced by the reference to c. 5 and 7 in c. 16, 12; cf. 54, 6 *irascere iterum meis iambis.* The *liber Catulli* (so in the MSS.; cf. n. 1; also Terent. Maur. 2899) counts 2286 lines, therein considerably exceeding the average compass of poetical 'books': the most voluminous books after these are those of Lucretius, now comprising on an average 1235 lines (the highest number 1457 in b. 5). From this and from the unmistakeable tripartite division of the present book (n. 8), we should incline to the belief that the book as we have it is the result of the subsequent amalgamation of three separate books; the dedicatory poem to Cornelius Nepos, accompanying a *libellus*, would be perfectly suitable as the preface to a single book; but neither separate books nor a plurality of books are ever cited, and the quotation is only in a few instances further defined as regards metre and subject; Sen. contr. 7, 4, 7. Charis. GL. 1, 97, 13 *Cat. in hendecasyllabis* (=c. 42, 5. 53, 5). Non. 134, 21 *Cat. priapeo* (?=fragm. 2). Caes. Bass. GL. 6, 262, 19 *Cat. in anacreonto.* Quint. 9, 3, 16 *C. in epithalamio* (=c. 62, 45). All this does not oblige us to assume that there were formerly several books, nor does this follow from the fact that Mart. 11, 6, 16 (cf. 4, 14, 13) designates Catullus' work with the name of 'passer' in reference to the first specially famous poems. EBrunér l.l. (see n. 13) p. 603. Ellis. comm. p. 1. JSüss, act. sem. Enlang. 1, 21. ThBirt, antikes Buchwesen 401 and the writers cited in n. 8. At most we might conclude from the nature of the book with its various fragmentary, disconnected and confused contents, that the edition prepared by the poet was after his death enlarged, by some friend, into a general edition, his literary remains being used for the purpose. The extant collection certainly contains almost everything appertaining to Catullus which was known in ancient times. Most of the so-called Catulline 'fragments' are founded on errors. Schwabe's Catullus 1866 p. 169. 1886 p. 102. JSüss in the acta semin. phil. Erlang. 1, 15. Against Bähren's

assumption of a prose work by Catullus (from Serv. Verg. ge. 2, 95 and Varro LL. 6, 6) see HPeter, JJ. 115, 749.—The book must, according to the indications as to the date contained in the collection (see n. 2), have been published c. 700/54. Possibly this took place in the first quarter of the year, if Cicero ad Q. fr. 2, 13, 4 (in June 700/54) refers to Cat. 25, 2 (see CBarth. adv. 38, 7 p. 1730. FBücheler, Greifsw. ind. schol. 1868/69 p. 16). Cf. also HAJMunro, criticisms of Cat. p. 71. Cic. Att. 13, 25, 3 (709/45) is perhaps an allusion to Cat. 3, 9 and 15, 1, 1 (710/44) to Cat. 3, 16. Earliest quotation from Catullus (62, 1 *vesper adest*) in Varro LL. 7, 50 (*dicit Valerius*, according to LSchwabe, JJ. 101, 350). Catullus at once attained a high reputation; cf. Nep. Att. 12, 4; the parody on Cat. 4 in Verg. catal. 8; Hor. sat. 1, 10, 19; Prop. 3, 25, 4; Vell. 2, 36, 2 *neque ullo in suscepti operis sui carmine minorem Catullum* and the other Testimonia in Schwabe's Catullus 1886 p. vii sq. Catullus blamed by Asinius Pollio: § 221, 6. On the imitation of Catullus in later writers (especially in the Priapea, in Ovid, in Ausonius, and most of all in the Ciris and in Martial: ADanysz, de scriptorum rom. studiis catull., Bresl. 1876; cf. JSüss, acta sem. Erl. 1, 6. Pauckstadt (§ 322, 7) and the summary in Schwabe's Catullus (1886) p. vii sqq.

8. According to the traditional arrangement of the poems, which in its origin is no doubt due to Catullus himself, the long poems occupy the middle of the collection (c. 61–68) and are surrounded by shorter ones, the iambic and melic poems (hendecasyllabics, choliambics, sapphic strophes etc.) preceding; they are followed by the elegiacs (epigrams), to which c. 65–68 form the transition, just as c. 61 leads from the first to the second part. In several instances the arrangement of the poems is determined by the attempt at diversity, and kindred subjects are separated by extraneous matter. For further details JvGFröhlich, Abh. der Münch. Akad. 3, 3, 691. RWestphal, Catulls Ged., Bresl. 1867, p. 1. JSüss, act. sem. Erlang. 1, 23. 28. KPSchulze, Catullforschungen in the Festschr. d. Friedr.-Werderschen Gymn., Berl. 1885, 195. Bährens, commentar. p. 57. BSchmidt, Cat. p. lxxxix. ASeitz, de Cat. carmm. in tres partes distribuendis, Rastatt 1887.

9. The diction of Catullus is distinguished for its extraordinary clearness, simplicity and elegance: in the learned and graecising works indeed we meet with much that is stiff and artificial (e.g. 64, 18 *nutricum tenus*, cf. τίτθη and τιτθός; 64, 8 *diva . . . retinens in summis urbibus arces;* cf. πολιοῦχος Ἀθάνα and other instances), also much antiquarian lore, turned to especially good account in the Attis: but in his best examples, the short occasional poems, C. lays aside all this, and to them apply Macaulay's words (Life 1, 468): "no Latin writer is so Greek." In them the free and easy sermo urbanus (e.g. frequent deminutiva) is developed with charming naturalness. Indices verborum to Sillig's, Döring's (1834), Ellis' (1878) and Schwabe's (1886) edd. FHeussner, obss. gramm. in C. librum, Marb. 1869 KHupe, de genere dicendi C., P. I, Münst. 1871. GOverholthaus, syntaxis Catull. capp. II, Gött. 1875. BZiegler, de C. sermone quaestt., Freib. i. B. 1879. ELehmann, de adjectivis compositis ap. Cat. Tib. Prop. Verg. Ovid. Hor., Königsb. 1867. FSeitz, de adiectivis poetarum latt. (beginning with Catullus) compositis, Bonn 1878. EDuderstadt, de particularum (=Praeposs.) usu ap. Cat., Halle 1881. FDressler, de troporum ap. Cat. usu, Vienna 1882. RFisch, de Cat. in vocabulis collocandis arte, Berl. 1875. EClemens, de Cat. periodis, Gött. 1886. Cf besides the works cited § 32, 4, 5.—Metrical system: Catullus handles the most varied metres (esp. *versus minuti*; cf. Ser. Augur, in Plin. ep. 4, 27, 4) with the sure touch of a master (*elegantissimus poetarum* Gell. 6, 20, 6), who never indulges too freely in the occasional licence permitted him, nor fears to avail himself of it (cf. Plin. NH. praef. 1; Plin. ep. 1, 16, 5), avoiding artificiality and paltriness. He is least

successful with hexameters, and the distichon especially is not yet polished to Ovid's degree of euphony. In his hexameters so-called spondiaci frequently occur in imitation of the Alexandrine model, sometimes even three in succession 64, 78–80; cf. Cic. Att. 7, 2, 1 *hunc σπονδειαζοντα si cui voles τῶν νεωτέρων* (see p. 250, 2) *pro tuo vendita*, cf. § 230, 2, 2). Of the lyric metres (iamb. trim., tetram., choliamb.; phalaeceus; glycon. asclep. mai.; str. sapph.; galliambi), the Phalaeceum hendecasyllabum, Catullus' favourite metre, is by far the most frequent and the most happily used: there is even one instance of its being used in strophes and with a spondee instead of a dactyl (55), which is without precedent elsewhere. The galliambi are especially effective (c. 63; cf. n. 6, such occur already in Varro § 165, 3; see also § 213, 4 l. 1), and so are the swift and trenchant pure iambics (c. 4. 29). AReeck, de C. carminum re grammatica et metrica, Bresl. 1872. CFANobbe, de metr. Cat., Lps. 1820–21 II. JBaumann, de arte metr. Cat., Landsb. a/W. 1881; and on this LMüller's ed. p. lix, see also ThBirt, hist. hex. lat. (1876) 23. OFranke, de artificiosa carm. Cat. compositione (acc. HUseneri epimetrum de c. lxviii), Greifsw. and Berl. 1866 (cf. also REllis in his ed.[2] p. 223 de aequabili partitione carminum Catulli, and ORibbeck, NSchweiz. Mus. 1, 213). CZiwsa, die eurhythmische Technik des Cat., (Hernals) Vienna 1879. 1883 II; der Intercalar bei Cat., Wien. Stud. 2, 298. 4, 271.

10. Manuscripts. Gellius 6, 20, 6 complains of *libri* (of Catullus) *de corruptis exemplaribus facti*. In the glossaries (§ 42, 5) Catullus is but very little used; see on this LSchwabe, JJ. 131, 803. During the Middle Ages he was almost forgotten. The statement of GVoigt (Wiederbeleb. d. klass. Altert. 2[2], 335) that Servatus Lupus, abbot of Ferrières († c. 862), had read Catullus, is founded on a misconception: see LSchwabe, Herm. 20, 495.—All the collective MSS. extant of the liber Catulli are late—only c. 62 occurs in the anthology of the cod. Par. 8071 (Thuaneus) s. IX–X (see the facsimile in Chatelain t. 14)—and all are derived from a certain cod. Veronensis, of which Rather, bishop of Verona, a. 965, availed himself; this was not heard of for a long time afterwards, until about the beginning of the 14th century it was again discovered in Verona and made use of by certain writers; it was also copied at a considerably later time, and was then again lost. The earliest and best MS. that can be proved to be a direct copy of the V(eronensis) is the Paris. 14137 (Germanensis) of a. 1375 (facsim. in Chatel. t. 15); most nearly related to this G(ermanensis) is the O(xoniensis), probably copied direct from the V about a. 1400, in the Bodleiana (Canonicianus 30, facsim. in Ellis' ed.[2] p. 146); this is specially important, because in it the original writing has not undergone numerous alterations, as is the case in the G, owing to erasures and emendations. As regards the other MSS. (about 70), concerning which see Ellis' prolegg. and Schwabe's ed. 1886 p. v sqq., it has not been demonstrated by how many and what links they are connected with the cod. Veron. Bähren's view (see analecta catull. 31 and the prolegg. in his ed. p. xvi) that all the MSS. (except O) are derived directly or indirectly from G, is untenable: see LSchwabe, Jen. Lit.-Zeit. 1875, 513 and BSchmidt, ib. 1878, 207; Cat. p. ciii. RSydow, de recensendis Cat. carmm., Berl. 1881. Attempts to investigate the earliest condition of the original manuscript (e.g. as regards the number of lines, the corruptions, lacunae, and transpositions) in Lachmann's ed. Haupt's op. 1, 35. Heyse, Übers. 279. Bergk, RhM. 15, 507. FBöhme, qu. cat. 2. Westphal l.l. 12, 23. Ellis' ed.[2] 135. RFisch, Wschrfkl Phil. 1884, 152. 180. On the critical history of the Catulline poems see MHaupt, op. 1, 2, 276. ThHeyse, Catull. übers. (1855) 279. LSchwabe, in the transactions of the Meissen Philologenvers. (Lpz. 1864) 111; in the Dorpat Ind. lect. 1865; introd. to his ed. (1866) p. i and Phil. 24, 351. REllis and EBährens intr. to their editions,

the latter also in his analecta catull. (Jena 1874) 22. EAbel, die Catullrecension des Guarinus, ZföG. 34, 161; Viertelj.-Schr. f. d. Kult. d. Renaiss. 1, 521 and also RSabbadini, riv. di filol. 13, 266; codd. latini posseduti da Guarino Veronese p. 10.—AGehrmann, de rat. crit. inde a Lachmanno in emend. Cat. adhibita, Braunsb. 1879.

11. Editions: on the oldest see Ellis, introd. to his ed.[2] p. lix. Ed. Ald. (by HAvancius) Ven. 1502. 1515. Cum comm. AMureti, Ven. 1554. Achillis Statii, Ven. 1566. Cum castigationibus IIScaligeri, Par. 1577 and subsequently. (The cod. Cuiacianus of a. 1467, which was used by Scaliger and has been greatly over-estimated, has recently reappeared in England: REllis, Hermathena 3, 124 and in his ed. of Catullus[2] p. liv). Cum comm. IsVossii, Lond. 1684, JAVulpii (Patav. 1710. 1737), FWDöring, Lps. 1788–1792 II, smaller edition, Altona 1834. Recogn. ISillig, Gott. 1823. Epoch-making: Ex rec. CLachmanni, Berol. 1829. [3]1874. Recogn. LSchwabe, Gissae 1866; ad optimos codd. denuo collatos recogn. LSchwabe, Berl. 1886. Recogn., app. criticum, prolegomena, appendices addidit REllis, Oxon.[2] 1878. Also REllis, a commentary on Cat., Oxf. 1876 (LSchwabe, JJ. 117, 257, gives addenda). Recens. et interpretatus est EBährens, Lps. 1876–85 II (Revision of the Bährens collation of the MSS; of the G by MBonnet, rev. critique 1877, 57, of the O by KPSchulze, Herm. 13, 50). Traduit en vers par E Rostand, texte revu av. un commentaire (only down to poem 63) par EBenoist, Par. 1880–82. Edited and explained by ARiese, Lpz. 1884.—The text by MHaupt (Cat. Tib. Prop., Lps.[5] 1885. JVahlen cur.), REllis (Lond. 1866), LMüller (Cat. Tib. Prop., Lps. 1870). BSchmidt, Lpz. 1887 (besides this an ed. maior with prolegg.).— Select poems, with introductions etc. by JPSimpson, Lond.[2] 1886. AHWratislaw and FNSutton (with Tib. and Prop.), Lond. 1869.

12. Translated e.g. by ThHeyse (with Lat. text, Berl. 1855), WHertzberg and WTeuffel (a selection in the Class. d. Alt., Stuttg. 1855; in a more complete form in the röm. Dichter, ib. 1862, with introd. and notes), RWestphal (C.'s Gedichte in ihrem geschichtlichen Zusammenhange übersetzt und erläutert, Bresl. 1867; Catulls Buch der Lieder, Bresl. 1884. FPressel, Berl.[2] 1884. Cranstoun (with notes), Lond. 1867. REllis, Lond. 1871. ThMartin (with notes), Lond.[2] 1875.

13. Essays on Cat. in general and concerning the subject-matter. CGHelbig, deutsche Jahrbb. 1842, 1213 (zur Charakteristik des C.). WThJungclaussen, zur Chronologie der Gedichte des C., Itzehoe 1857. LSchwabe, quaestt. Catullianarum liber I, Gissae 1862 (Vol. 1, 1 of his first ed.). EBrunér, de ordine et temporibus carminum C., Acta soc. sc. Fennicae 7 (Helsingf. 1863), 599. ORibbeck, C. Val. Cat., eine literarhistorische Skizze, Kiel 1863; Gesch. d. röm. Dicht. 1, 312. BRichter, de Catulli vita et carminibus P. I, Freiberg 1865. Mommsen RG. 3[6], 332. 600. MHaupt, in his Biogr. v. Belger, Berl. 1879, 238. Teuffel, preface to the translation (1862) p. 6. ACouat, étude sur Catulle, Par. 1875. HNettleship, characteristics of Cat., in his lectures and essays, Lond. 1885 p. 84. JDavies, Catull. Tib. and Prop., Lond. 1870. VVaccaro, Cat. e la poesia, Palermo 1885. HHHeskamp (n. 3).

14. Contributions to criticism and elucidation: J. Markland's unedited conjectures, Hermath. 7, 153. MHaupt, op. 1, 1. 73. 2, 67. 121. JvGFröhlich, Abh. d. Münch. Ak. 3, 3, 691. 5, 3, 235. 6, 2, 259. Ritschl, op. 3, 593. RKlotz, emendd. C., Lps. 1859; de Cat. c. iv, Lps. 1868. Zehme, de Cat. c. lxiii, Lauban 1859. JPohl, lectt. Cat. I Münster 1860, II Sigmaringen 1866. PBoehme, quaestt. C., Bonn 1862. EFritze, c. lxiv rec. et ill., Halberst. 1863. AWeise, zur Kritik

von C. c. 68. 65. 101, Naumb. 1863; krit. u. erkl. Bemerk. zu c. 68, Zeitz 1869. ThBergk in Rossbach's ed., Leipz.[2] 1860; RhM. 15, 507; emendatt. C., Halle 1864. LSchwabe, coniecturae C., Dorpat 1864. HAKoch, in the symb. philol. Bonn 315. GFRettig, Catulliana, 1868–71 III. JMähly, JJ. 103, 341. JAndre, de C. c. lxiv, Rostock (Gotha 1873). RPeiper, Catullus, Beitr. zur Kritik, Bresl. 1875. K Pleitner, des C. Hochzeitsgesänge krit. behandelt, Dillingen 1858; Studien zu C., Dillingen 1876 (cf. also n. 5 ad fin.). HAJMunro, criticisms and elucidations of Catullus, Cambridge 1878; journ. of philol. 8, 333. 9, 185. 11, 124. 141. AKiessling, analecta Cat., Greifsw. 1877. EBährens, JJ. 115, 409 and analecta Cat., Jen. 1874. EEichler, quo iure Cat. c. 68 in duo carmina dirimatur, Oberhollabrunn 1872. HMagnus, JJ. 111, 849 (the unity of c. 68). 113, 402. 115, 415; JB. 1887 2, 145 sqq. KRossberg, JJ. 115, 127. 841. OHarnecker, ZfGW. 33, 72; Beitr. z. Erkl. des Cat., Friedeberg Nm. 1879; Cat.s 68stes Ged., ib. 1881; qua necessitudine coniunctus fuerit cum Cic. Catullus, ib. 1882; Phil. 41, 465; JJ. 133, 273; BlfbayrGW. 21, 556. KPSchulze, ZfGW. 34, 369; researches on Catullus in the Festschr. of the Friedr.-Werder Gymn., Berl. 1881, 195; JJ. 125, 205. APalmer, Hermath. 3 (1878), no. 6. 7, 134. RRichter, Catulliana, Lpz. 1881. FSchöll, JJ. 121, 471. MSchmidt, JJ. 121, 777. JVahlen, ind. lect. Berol. 1882. ATartara, animadvv. in Cat. et Liv., Rome 1881. AArlt, Cat. Ged. 36, Wohlau 1883. HMonse, zu Cat., Waldenb. i. Schl. 1884. CJacoby, Phil. 44, 178 (c. 49). ABonin, d. 62ste Ged. des Cat., Bromb. 1884. HBlümner (c. 30), JJ. 131, 879. JPPostgate, Mnemos. 14, 433. FHermes, Frankf. a/O. 1888. ABDrachmann (c. 67), WschrfklPh. 1888, 538.

215. This turbulent and factious age employed the power of the pen and valued its influence. Not only were the political speeches more and more frequently published, in order to reach a wider circle of hearers, but the hostile factions attacked each other also in separate pamphlets. M. Varro, C. Scribonius Curio, and A. Caecina wrote such pamphlets against Caesar. Others again used the events of the day for ventilating their party views. Funeral speeches especially (laudationes) were used for these purposes. Cato's death at Utica gave rise to quite a literature of its own: Cicero, M. Brutus, M. Fadius Gallus, and Munatius wrote in praise of him, and against him were A. Hirtius, Caesar himself, Metellus Scipio, and at a later time Augustus. In the same way Cato's daughter, Porcia, became on the occasion of her death the subject of laudations by M. Varro, Lollius, and Cicero. Some employed a metrical form (epigrams and lampoons).

1. On Varro's Τρικάρανος in 694/60 see § 166, 3 ad fin. On Curio's pamphlet in a. 695/59 see § 153, 6. A. Caecina see § 199, 5. On the poetical attacks against Caesar see § 158, 3 l. 6 from the end. 192, 4. 213, 7. 214, 5.

2. On the pamphlets called forth by the death of Cato (a. 708/46) see Wartmann, Leben des Cato von Utica (Zür. 1858) 145. On Cicero's Cato see § 180, 5. As a supplement M. Brutus wrote his pamphlet, see § 210, 2. For Hirtius' Anticato see § 197, 2; on Caesar's Anticatones § 195, 7. The panegyric of M. Fadius Gallus was probably published in July or August 709/45; see Cic. fam. 7,

24, 2; cf. 25, 1. Cato's friend Munatius Rufus σύγγραμμα περὶ Κάτωνος ἐξέδωκε, ᾧ μάλιστα Θρασέας (§ 299, 7) ἐπηκολούθησεν. PLUT. Cat. min. 37 cf. 25. VALER. MAX. 4, 3, 2 *id Munatius Rufus, Cypriacae expeditionis* (Cato's 696/58) *fidus comes, scriptis suis significat.* On the other hand Metellus Scipio had in Cato's lifetime published βιβλίον βλασφημίας κατέχον τοῦ Κάτωνος, ib. 57. On Augustus' work see SUETONIUS Aug. 85 *multa varii generis prosa oratione composuit, ex quibus nonnulla in coetu familiarium velut in auditorio recitavit, sicut rescripta Bruto de Catone, quae volumina cum iam senior ex magna parte legisset, fatigatus Tiberio tradidit perlegenda.*

3. Porcia, the daughter (not the sister, as MOMMSEN, Herm. 15, 99 argued; see FRÜHL, JJ. 121, 147) of Cato Uticensis and wife first of M. Bibulus (see § 255, 2), and then of M. Brutus. Her illness is mentioned by BRUTUS ep. ad Cic. 1, 17, 7; and when she had resolved in her husband's absence διὰ νόσον καταλιπεῖν τὸν βίον (PLUT. Brut. 53), Brutus quarrelled with his friends at Rome for not having prevented her (ὡς ἀμεληθείσης ὑπ' αὐτῶν, PLUT. l.l.). A letter of condolence of Cicero to Brutus, ep. ad Brut. 1, 9. The story that after the death of her husband she swallowed burning coals is an invention of later rhetoricians. CIC. Att. 13, 48, 2 (a. 709/45) *laudationem Porciae tibi misi correctam. . . . et velim M. Varronis et Lollii mittas laudationem. Lollii utique; nam illam legi; volo tamen regustare.*

216. The daily news was after a. 695/59 regularly published in the acta, the minutes of the Senate in the acta senatus, and the public and private events in the acta populi or acta diurna. The latter were a kind of official journal, with a specially appointed editor; they were daily exhibited in public, copied by entrepreneurs and sold by them. We do not possess any genuine fragments of the latter kind of acta.

1. SUETON. Iul. 20 *inito honore* (of the consulship, a. 695/59) *primus omnium instituit ut tam senatus quam populi diurna acta confierent et publicarentur.* Acta of itself denotes the transactions themselves, especially those of magistrates, and as an abbreviation (instead of *commentarii actorum*) it means a written account of them. Before Caesar, only the decrees of the Senate used to be written down and, in special cases, published; but Caesar published also the transactions of the Senate. To take minutes of them was the constant practice of the whole Imperial period (even A.D. 438 we hear of *gesta in senatu urbis Romae de recipiendo codice Theodosiano*), but the publication was prohibited by Augustus (SUET. Aug. 36 *auctor et aliarum rerum fuit, in quis, ne acta senatus publicarentur*). These minutes contained also the motions made in the Senate, the reports and despatches as they arrived, in the Imperial period also the speeches of the Emperors read by the quaestor, and the acclamations of the senators. The minutes were written down at first by senators specially commissioned by the consul and subsequently the Emperor, afterwards by the curator actorum senatus, after Hadrian by the official ab actis senatus. These acta senatus were kept in the Imperial archives (tabularium), where they seem to have been accessible only to senators (and for definite purposes), or in separate parts of the public libraries, which were accessible only by special permission of the praefectus urbi. Some transactions of the Senate were admitted into the acta populi and thereby became generally accessible. EHÜBNER, JJ. Suppl. Bd. 3, 564, and a brief account in WREIN, PRE. 1^2, 132. 147. Also e.g. VLECLERC, des journaux chez les Romains, Par. 1838. WA SCHMIDT, in his Zeitschr. für Geschichtswiss. 1 (1844), 303. GEFLIEBERKÜHN, de

diurnis Rom. actis (Weim. 1840) and epist. crit. ad LeClercium (Lps. 1844). JWA Renssen, de diurnis aliisque Rom. actis, Gröningen 1857. CZell, Ferienschriften N. F. 1 (Heidelb. 1857), 1. Mommsen, röm. Staatsrecht 3, 1017.

2. The Roman public advertiser, the acta diurna populi, is also called acta diurna or acta populi rom. or acta populi or acta publica, acta urbana, rerum urbanarum acta, acta urbis, diurna populi rom., or diurna (e.g. Iuv. 6. 483) or acta (e. g. Iuv. 2, 136) briefly; the Greek writers merely call them τὰ κοινὰ ὑπομνήματα or simply ὑπομνήματα. The communication of the news of the day to those who were absent had been a private affair before Caesar, and even afterwards this was carried on privately: but Caesar made it regular and official. This was so much suited to the requirements of travellers and such as lived abroad, nay even of the very inhabitants of the huge capital, that the publication was continued uninterruptedly and did not cease until the seat of the Empire was transferred to Constantinople. The contents of these acta were partly official (such as events concerning the reigning family, decrees of the Emperors and of the magistrates, decrees or discussions of the Senate, and other facts interesting to the general public, e. g. perhaps news as to the winners in the chariot contests? Friedländer, SG. 1[5], 290), partly private, containing family news of all kinds, advertisements of births, marriages, divorces, deaths etc. communicated to the editor, frequently in a very subjective tone (e.g. of a widower *saucius pectus* Quint. 9, 3, 17). The official compilation was published in albo, and just as people used to copy the annals (above § 76), these acta were multiplied by scribes and communicated to their subscribers. After some time had elapsed, the original was transferred to the archives, where it could be used for literary purposes. The acta Muciani (§ 314, 1) and Acholii (§ 387, 1), were extracts from the originals. On account of their voluminous extent, the acta can scarcely have existed in a complete form in private libraries, and even at the very first they may have been read only in extracts. See EHübner l.l. 594, and in Rein l.l. 134.

3. The eleven fragments of acta populi first published by Pighius (1615) in his Annales 2, 378 and commonly called fragmenta Dodwelliana from their principal defender, Dodwell (praelect. Camden., Oxon. 1692, p. 665), are a forgery of the 15th century. Against their genuineness see especially PWesseling, Probabilia (Franeker 1731) p. 354 and JAErnesti, in his edition of Suetonius (Lps. 1748). HHeinze, de spuriis actorum diurnorum fragmentis I, Greifsw. 1860. Cf. CZell, Ferienschrr. NF. 1, 109. But Lieberkühn (especially in his Vindiciae librorum iniuria suspectorum, Lps. 1844, p. 1=Epistola . . . ad Le-Clercium) attempted to defend their genuineness; see n. 1 ad fin.

217. A peculiar position midway between critical and merely narrative daily literature is held by letters, of which we possess a considerable number in this period in the collections forming part of Cicero's works, most of them by Cicero himself, but many also by other contemporaries.

1. On the letters see § 46; on those of Caesar see § 195, 8; on those of M. Brutus see § 210, 4.

2. On the Ciceronian collections see § 187 and 188. Besides Cicero's own letters they contain letters by his brother Quintus (§ 190, 3), by his son (fam. 16, 21. 25), M. Brutus (§ 188, 4. cf. § 210, 4), Ser. Sulpicius (§ 174, 2; JHSchmalz, ZfGW. 35, 90), M. Marcellus (fam. 4, 11; Schmalz l.l. 128), Q. Metellus Celer (§

214, 3), Q. Metellus Nepos (fam. 5, 3), Vatinius (ib. 5, 9. 10; JHSchmalz, d. Latinität des Vatinius, Mannheim 1880), L. Lucceius (§ 172, 5), A. Caecina (§ 199, 5), Pompeius Bithynicus (fam. 6, 16), M'. Curius (fam. 7, 29; JHSchmalz, ZfGW. 35, 137), M. Caelius Rufus (§ 209, 6), Dolabella (fam. 9, 9; Schmalz ZfGW. 35, 131), Munatius Plancus (§ 209, 8), Ser. Sulpicius Galba (fam. 10, 30), C. Asinius Pollio (§ 221, 5), Lepidus (fam. 10, 34. 35), D. Brutus (§ 210, 5), C. Matius (§ 208, 5), C. Cassius (§ 210, 6), Cassius Parmensis (§ 210, 7), P. Lentulus (fam. 12, 14. 15), C. Trebonius (§ 210, 9), M. Cato (§ 210, 2). HHellmuth, die Sprache der Epistolographen Ser. Sulp. Galba u. L. Corn. Balbus, Würzb. 1888. Also enclosed in letters to Atticus, we have letters of Cn. Pompeius (§ 171, 8), Caesar (§ 195, 8), Balbus (§ 197, 4), M. Antonius (§ 209, 3).

218. Not one of the Latin inscriptions of a. 670/84–710/44 is in saturnian metre. Among the prose-inscriptions the most important are the lex Cornelia de XX quaestoribus of a. 673/81, the Senatus-consultum de Asclepiade, Polystrato, Menisco in amicorum formulam referendis of a. 676/78, the lex Antonia de Termessibus of a. 683/71, the lex Rubria de civitate Galliae cisalpinae c. 705/49, and the lex Iulia municipalis of a. 709/45, besides the inscription of a. 710/44 relating to the colony of Urso (Osuna).

1. For the undated metrical inscriptions of the 7th century u.c. see § 163, 7–9.

2. The lex Cornelia of Sulla the dictator (CIL. 1, 202. PM. 29. Bruns font.[5] 88. DIE. 307), of about a. 673/81 (cf. Tac. ann. 11, 22), is partly preserved on a brass tablet, which was dug up under the ruins of the temple of Saturn at Rome.

3. The SC. by which Asclepiades and his associates are declared *viri boni et amici* is written in Latin (very incompletely preserved) and Greek: CIL. 1, 203. PM. 30. Bruns font.[5] 158. DIE. 308. The SS CC de Oropiis of a. 681/73 (Mommsen, Herm. 20, 268. Bruns[5] 162) and de Aphrodisiensibus a. 712/42 are extant in Greek only. CIG. 2, 2737. Bruns[5] 167.

4. The lex Antonia confirms the independence of the town of Termessus maior in Pisidia: CIL. 1, 204. PM. 31. Bruns[5] 91. DIE. 309.

5. The lex Rubria: CIL. 1, 205. PM. 32. Ritschl, op. 4, 34. Bruns[5] 95. DIE. 311.—A new fragment, perhaps of this same law, has been found at Ateste: Mommsen, Herm. 16, 24. Bruns[5] 100.

6. The lex Iulia municipalis of Caesar intended to regulate the legal state of municipal towns: CIL. 1, 206. PM. 33, 34. Bruns[5] 101. DIE. 312. HNissen, RhM. 45, 100. The most important treatise on it is by Savigny, verm. Schrr. 3, 279.—A lex municipalis is also contained in the lamina Tudertina, which belongs to the Augustan period, and the lamina Florentina; see CIL. 1, p. 263. Bruns[5] 148. 149.

7. Lex coloniae Genetivae Iuliae s. Ursonensis of a. 710/44, but in its actual form dating probably only from the end of the first Christian century; it was discovered a. 1871 sqq. in very considerable fragments at Osuna. HNissen, l.l.

MRdeBerlanga, Malaga 1873. 76. EHübner and Mommsen, ephem. epigr. 2, 105. 221. 3, 89. Bruns [5] 119 and ZfRechtsgesch. 12, 82. 13, 383. CRe, Rome 1874. ChGiraud, Par. 1875. FBücheler, Jen. LZ. 1877, 137. CMFrancken, Versl. en Mededeel. d. Akad. Amsterd. 2, 10 (1880).

8. The rogatio Hirtia (of a. 708/46?) is mentioned in the brass tablet CIL. 1, 627 sq. p. 184.

9. Among the dated inscriptions of a. 670/84–710/44 (CIL. 1, 573–626) we should especially mention those of the time of Sulla (nos. 584–586 and 587–589, of the populus Laodicensis af Lyco, populus Ephesius and Λυκίων τὸ κοινόν), such as the boundary-stone of M. Terentius Varro Lucullus (PRE. 4, 1074, 9) no. 583 DIE. 270; the Campanian votive tablet (no. 573 DIE. 310) in which *in servom Iunonis Gaurae contulerunt* (a. 683/71), and the inscription of Furfo (no. 603, Bruns [5] 241. Wilm. 105. DIE. 304 [b] a. 696/58), the latter remarkable for its boorish Latin; HJordan, Herm. 7, 201; Beitr. z. Gesch. d. lat. Spr. 250.

10. Leaden projectiles for slings (glandes) with inscriptions relating, amongst other subjects, to the siege of Henna (621/133), Asculum (a. 664/90 sq.), Perusia (a. 713/41 sq.), the latter containing some coarse jokes of the soldiers, e.g. *peto Octaviani culum; L. Antoni calve, Fulvia, culum pandite; L. Antoni calve, peristi C. Caesarus victoria; esureis et me celas.* CIL. 1, 644 sqq. ThBergk, Inschriften röm. Schleudergeschosse, Lpz. 1876. EDesjardins, les balles de fronde de la république, Par. 1874–75. Latest complete critical edition: KZangemeister, glandes plumbeae latine inscriptae, ephem. epigraph. vol. 6 (1885).

11. So-called tesserae gladiatoriae, up to the present about one hundred, of the years 658/96 b.c. down to 827/74 a.d.; also a few earlier ones reaching back to about 640/114. Their coming into vogue is probably connected with the official recognition of the gladiatorial games in the consulate of P. Rutilius 649/105 (Bücheler, RhM. 38, 476. Mommsen, Herm. 21, 273). The remarkable inscription on them (now certain) spectavit has not yet been explained. Lists: CIL. 1, 717–774. 776[b]; in Ritschl's treatise on the subject op. 4, 572. Addenda: eph. epigr. 3, 161. 203; bull. arch. 1879, 252. 1880, 141. 1882, 8. 1884, 11. cf. also Friedländer, SGesch. 2^5, 477 and esp. Mommsen, Herm. 21, 266, AElter, RhM. 41, 517; Berl. Wschr. 1888, 1004, PFMeier, RhM. 42, 122, FHaug, Berl. Wschr. 1888, 763.

12. Bricks with dates from municipal towns (Veleia) of the years 678/76–743/11 in the CIL. 1, p. 202.

13. Imprecations (devotiones) of the Republican period in the CIL. 1, 818–820. DIE. 386 sqq.; cf. CWachsmuth, RhM. 18, 560. WHenzen, bull. arch. 1866, 252. Mommsen, Herm. 4, 281. GBdeRossi, bull. arch. 1880, 6. CStornaiuolo, bull. 1880, 188.

14. Sepulchral inscription on L. Manneius Q. (libertus) medicus, φυσικὸς οἰνοδότης according to the method of Asklepiades of Prusa (PRE. 1^2, 1845), therefore probably in the time of Pompey, CIL. 1, 1256. 10, 338.

15. A jocular mural inscription at Pompeii: *Urnannia (?) pereit de taberna. sei quis eam rettulerit dabuntur* etc. in the CIL. 1, 1254. 4, 64. Another found in the same town and bearing an exact date: *C. Pumidius Dipilus heic fuit a. d. V. nonas octobreis M. Lepid. Q. Catul. cos.* (a. 676/78), ib. 1, 590. 4, 1842.

B. THE AUGUSTAN AGE
(711/43 B.C.–767/14 A.D.).

219. The battle of Actium and the death of M. Antonius terminated the century of the Civil Wars; Octavianus was now the monarch acknowledged by all. But he was prudent enough to avoid the rocks on which his great predecessor had been wrecked, and did not openly discard the traditions of the Republic; its exterior forms were retained, but gradually changed so as to become the vehicles of Imperial power. Thus the Augustan period presents a twofold aspect, in that it contains the decay of the old and the formation of the new institutions, the death of the Republic and the development of the Monarchy. This ambiguous character is plainly perceptible in the foremost men of the time: Asinius Pollio, Messalla and Horace fought and played a part in the time of the Republic, and Vergil had in his early years written poetry in the manner of Catullus. But, on the whole, Octavianus' task was greatly facilitated by fortune. Most of the enemies of the Monarchy had been carried off by death, and those who survived had no vigour or spirit, nor were they backed by the people, who were tired of the long struggles. Cleopatra's disgraceful sway over M. Antonius led many into the camp of Octavianus, e.g. M. Messalla, Cn. Domitius Ahenobarbus (cos. 722/32), L. Sempronius Atratinus (cos. 720/34).[1]) One after the other made his peace with the new state of things[2]). The jurists Cascellius and Labeo were the most refractory, but as they were comparatively harmless, they were allowed to do as they pleased, though the more pliable Ateius Capito was favoured in preference to them. Asinius Pollio never perhaps ceased to resent the comparative insignificance to which the Monarchy had condemned him, but his courage evaporated in mere taunts. Horace also long kept aloof from the Monarchy, but he gradually

---

[1]) Horace also made this serve to justify his political conversion, which was really necessitated by his connection with Maecenas; cf. epod. 9. carm. 1, 37. Vergil (Aen. 8, 688) and the other Augustan poets likewise prefer to give prominence to this national point of view; cf. OVID. met. 15, 826. PROP. 4, 11, 29. 41. MANIL. astr. 1, 914.

[2]) SEN. de clem. 1, 10, 1 of Augustus: *Sallustium et Cocceios et Deillios et totam cohortem primae admissionis ex adversariorum castris conscripsit. iam Domitios, Messalas, Asinios, Cicerones, et quidquid floris in civitate erat, clementiae suae debebat.*

became sincerely reconciled to it. Matius, Trebatius Testa, L. Varius and also Vitruvius were favourable to Caesar's heir from the very beginning; Publilius Syrus, Ticidas, and Vergil were politically inoffensive. Munatius Plancus worshipped success. The longer the Monarchy existed, the more freely it disposed of rewards and punishments, the more it attracted, and at last there was quite a rivalry in toadying.[3]) Such characters as Labeo and Labienus were soon considered crotchety; they were either misunderstood or laughed at. The official hypocrisy, which continued the old forms and names in spite of the complete change of their meaning, diffused a spirit of untruth through the upper classes and through the literature of the time; this was further increased by the empty declamation, which began to take the place of oratory. Another result of the hypocritical character of the government appears in the increased sensitiveness of the ruler himself as to unwelcome revelations, and in the exertions made by him to bury the past in oblivion and consolidate the new institutions. Owing to these tendencies, literature was partly circumscribed, partly degraded to a servile 'instrumentum regni.'

Oratory suffered most under these conditions. The restrictions, which weighed upon it even under Caesar, became permanent and continually heavier. Public life was extinguished, all political business passed into the hands of the monarch, the meetings of the people became rarer and less important, the courts more and more subservient and mechanical. Only the transactions of the Senate and the civil lawsuits before the Court of the Centumviri offered a field to the exertions of orators; but the Senate was cramped by the presence of the Emperor and the servility of the great majority of its members, and very frequently all discussion was cut short by decisions and orders from the prince: even the authority of the Centumviri in its narrow sphere was gradually encroached upon by the growing power of the praefectus urbi. The two orators who survived the Republic, Asinius Pollio and M. Messalla, lost their ground completely; those who did not prefer silence were obliged to submit

---

[3]) Tac. ann. 1, 2 of Augustus: *ubi militem donis, populum annona, cunctos dulcedine otii pellexit, insurgere paulatim, munia senatus, magistratuum, legum in se trahere, nullo adversante, cum ferocissimi per acies aut proscriptione cecidissent, ceteri nobilium, quanto quis servitio promptior, opibus et honoribus extollerentur ac novis ex rebus aucti tuta et praesentia quam vetera et periculosa mallent.*

to the new mode, and to become elegant speakers without real aims or subjects, in a word, mere declaimers. [4])

The other branch of literature which had attained a high perfection under the Republic, namely historical composition, likewise suffered seriously. [5]) At first M. Brutus was freely defended in memoirs written by his friends, Messalla and Volumnius, but after the battle of Actium Asinius Pollio soon perceived that it was advisable to close his work on the Civil Wars with the battle of Philippi. Contemporary history was impeded by the cessation of publicity and the sequestration of public documents. [6]) To a still greater extent the possibility of pronouncing unbiassed judgments on historical characters was reduced. Hence writers selected subjects removed by time or locality, as did Pompeius Trogus [7]), Fenestella and L. Arrun-

---

[4]) Cf. § 45 with note 1.

[5]) Cf. § 39, 1. SEN. vol. 3, p. 437 Hse. *ab initio bellorum civilium, unde primum veritas retro abiit.* SUET. Claud. 41, *historiam in adulescentia, hortante T. Livio, . . . scribere adgressus est . . . coepitque a pace civili, cum sentiret neque libere neque vere sibi de superioribus tradendi potestatem relictam, correptus saepe et a matre* (Antonia) *et ab avia* (Livia). SEN. contr. 2, 4, 13 should therefore be taken with great restrictions: *tanta sub divo Augusto libertas fuit ut praepotenti tunc M. Agrippae non defuerint qui ignobilitatem exprobrarent.*

[6]) Cf. § 216, 1 l. 10. 18.

[7]) With the historical works of the Imperial period in Greek and Latin, we have the Latin inscriptions (see § 40); preserved in countless numbers, and daily augmented by fresh discoveries, they present for our investigation of all public and private affairs under the Empire a source of instruction especially direct, many-sided and valuable. In what follows only isolated inscriptions, which are also remarkable as bearing on literary history, can be mentioned in their proper place. On their different varieties and classes see the summaries in the collections of ORELLI and WILMANNS (§ 40, 2). Here may be mentioned, more on account of their external form than for the importance of their contents, the Privilegia militum veteranorumque de civitate et conubio, of which up to the present time over 60 have been found, reaching from the time of Claudius to that of Diocletian; they are best edited CIL. 3, p. 843. Specimens e.g. in WILMANNS 2862 sqq. BRUNS, font.[5] 231. We have besides the wax tablets found in 1875 in Pompeii containing receipts for sums of money paid out by the auctioneer and farmer L. Caecilius Iucundus, dating from the years 15. 27 and 53–62 A.D., published by GDEPETRA, atti dei Lincei 2, 3, Rome 1876. MOMMSEN, Herm. 12, 88; giorn. d. scavi di Pompei 1879, 70. HERMANN, z. Gesch, d. rom. Quittungen, Berl. 1883. Specimens in BRUNS font.[5] 275. They exhibit many points of resemblance to the wax tablets of Siebenburg, which have long been well known (best edited CIL. 3, p. 921). A few similar business documents from Pompeii (a. 61 A.D. concerning the property of a certain Dicidia Margaris) were found in 1887. MOMMSEN, Herm. 23, 157. VSCIALOJA e ALIBRANDI, nuove tavolette cerate pompejane, Bull. dell' istit. di diritto rom. 1. (1888) 5. EECK, neue pompej. Geschäftsurkunden, ZfRb. 22, 60. 151.

tius; Livy also, specially qualified in his capacity as a friend of Augustus and, generally, as a moderate critic and felicitous narrator, to pick his way per ignes suppositos cineri doloso, though he brought Roman history down to his own time, yet felt a repulsion from the present and an attraction towards the heroic times and great characters of the past. The Greeks had greater inducements to historical labours. Their nationality kept them from political broils, their language precluded them from gaining direct influence upon the nation at large, they easily adapted themselves to the existing state of things and turned it to their own account: hence they found at Rome a fertile field of literary activity. Besides Timagenes of Alexandria and Nikolaos of Damascus there wrote under Augustus and partly at Rome Diodoros of Sicily, Dionysios of Halicarnassus, Juba king of Mauretania and Strabo the geographer, and besides the historians other learned Greeks: the rhetoricians Caecilius of Cale Acte, Hermagoras, Apollodoros of Pergamon, the philosophers Areios of Alexandria and Athenodoros of Tarsus, the grammarians Didymos Chalkenteros, Tryphon, Philoxenos, the poets Parthenios of Nicaea, Krinagoras of Mitylene and many others.

As concerns Jurisprudence, Augustus succeeded in gaining it for the Monarchy by rendering the right of giving juridical consultations (until then merely left to the confidence of the public) dependent on the consent of the prince,[8]) and also granting to these responsa the same importance which was formerly attached to the edict of the praetor [9]). In the possession of these privileges, the jurists devoted themselves to the cultivation of their science, and even then the personal enmity of Labeo and Capito laid the foundation of the two schools of the Sabinians, the adherents of Capito, and the Proculians who followed Antistius Labeo.

The extinction of public political life was still more favourable to the development of art-poetry and erudition.

---

[8]) Pompon. dig. 1, 2, 2, 47 (49) *ante tempora Augusti publice respondendi ius non a principibus dabatur, sed qui fiduciam studiorum suorum habebant consulentibus respondebant. . . primus divus Augustus, ut maior iuris auctoritas haberetur, constituit ut ex auctoritate eius responderent.*

[9]) Gaius inst. 1, 7 *responsa prudentium sunt sententiae et opiniones eorum quibus permissum est iura condere. quorum omnium si in unum sententiae concurrant, id quod ita sentiunt legis vicem optinet.* Sen. ep. 94, 27 *iurisconsultorum valent responsa, etiam si ratio non redditur.*

Whereas formerly the Romans had admitted literary activity only in the second rank to fill up their otium, now that the negotia of the Republican time had been so greatly reduced, it became with many a serious life-task. Poetry especially was now zealously studied as an art [10]), and Hellenic finish was a regular requirement. The form of the poems became of greater importance, as the range of subjects was narrowed deliberately or under compulsion and subjected to various limitations. Prosody and metre were still treated with the rigour introduced by the new school of the Ciceronian period, and the reasonable severity of the Greek models was often surpassed by a pedagogic correctness which regulated everything by line and rule. Elision was treated in a more and more careful and laboured manner. [11]) But the gain in art was a loss in popularity: poetry was written for a select circle of friends and connoisseurs and for posterity; and sneers at the people plainly show that there was no sympathy between the writers and their nation. [12]) But the greater the estrangement between the poets and the nation, the more were they driven to the upper classes; these art-poets became court-poets, and this caused a further increase of the disfavour in which they were held. Hence the Augustan poets, especially Horace, are continually striving against a hostile current in favour of the old national poets, a tendency naturally connected with the general dissatisfaction at the political aspect of the time. Not until the older generation had died off, could the new school gain firm ground. [13])

Independently of this general assistance derived from the existing political situation, the representatives of the new school of poetry were also assisted by the rulers themselves, partly from dilettantism, partly from political calculation. Augustus did not forget to encourage the poets [14]), and his favour-

---

[10]) The making of verses was actually studied; see § 200, 1. Mart. 4, 61, 3, *in schola poetarum dum fabulamur.*

[11]) LMüller, de re metr. p. 74 and 281. WCorssen, Vocalismus 2, 199. Ovid, the author of the Culex, Grattius and Manilius are especially strict in this respect. Cf. also MHaupt, op. 1, 88. 359.

[12]) *malignum spernere volgus*, Hor. c. 2, 16, 39. Cf. 3, 1, 1 *odi profanum volgus et arceo.* ep. 1, 19, 37 *non ego ventosae plebis suffragia venor;* cf. sat. 1, 4, 72. 1, 6, 15. 1, 10, 73. ep. 2, 1, 18. Ps.-Vergil. catal. 11, 64 *pingui nil mihi cum populo.* Ps.-Tibull. 3, 3, 20 *falso plurima volgus amat.*

[13]) Hor. c. 4, 3, 14 *et iam dente minus mordeor invido.*

[14]) Suet. Aug. 89 *ingenia saeculi sui omnibus modis fovit.*

ites became the centres of literary circles which, though not without rivalry and quarrels [15]), were held together and influenced by their common relations to Augustus. First of these should be mentioned the circle of Maecenas, in which Horace was not the oldest, but the most distinguished member on account of his independent character, acute mind and poetical talent. Other members of the same circle were Vergil and L. Varius, Plotius Tucca, Quintilius Varus, Aristius Fuscus, Valgius Rufus, Domitius Marsus, Melissus, and others [16]), and at a later time, when Horace had almost entirely withdrawn from Rome, Propertius [17]), who is never mentioned by Horace, joined it. This whole circle was decidedly in favour of the existing government, and all its members were gradually imbued with these views. The circle of Messalla was less forward in politics, and in the writings of the principal member of it, Tibullus, the name of Augustus does not occur a single time. Other members of it were Messalla's brother (Horat. sat. 1, 10, 85), Aemilius Macer, Lygdamus, Sulpicia, the author of Ciris and of the elegy on Messalla, [18]) Lynceus (§ 244, 3), and in part also Ovid. [19]) Asinius Pollio was chiefly conspicuous as a critic, and on account of his repeated opposition to the government only the most independent members of other circles, e.g. Horace, ventured to join him. When Augustus was left alone and was no longer under the necessity of putting restraint

---

15) Cf. Sen. controv. 2, 4, 12. Something like this is reflected in Agrippa's judgment on Vergil's poetical manner. Donatus' vita Verg. 44 (62) *M. Vipsanius a Maecenate eum suppositum appellabat novae cacozeliae repertore* (Var. *repertorem*), *non tumidae nec exilis, sed ex communibus verbis atque ideo latentis.* On the other hand see the favourable opinions on Vergil by Maecenas in Sen. suas. 1, 12. 2, 20.

16) Cf. Hor. sat. 1, 10, 81, ep. 1, 3. See also Ovid. trist. 4, 10, 41. Mart. 8, 56.

17) On the other hand Propertius himself never mentions Horace, though he alludes to him in several passages (see § 246, 2). Ovid also, who likewise frequently shows points of similarity with Horace (§ 247, 7), passes him over in his enumeration A A. 3, 333, and not until his death does he allow him the somewhat scanty praise: *tenuit nostras numerosus Horatius auris* (trist. 4, 10, 49.) Verrius Flaccus also, and at a later time Velleius Paterculus never mention Horace. It may be that Horace occasionally showed his mental and social superiority in a way offensive to younger men. It is noteworthy that in the Pompeian mural inscriptions there occur passages from Vergil, Ovid, Propertius, the Priapeia, Tibullus, and even from Lucretius and Ennius (see § 101, 4; cf. CIL. 4, p. 259), but none from Horace. On the scanty reminiscences of Horace among the inscriptions see MHertz, anal. ad carm. Hor. hist. 3, 18. Cf. § 240, 1.

18) Vergil. catal. 11.

19) Cf. ex Pont. 1, 7, 28 to Messalinus: *nec tuus est genitor nos infitiatus amicos, hortator studii causaque faxque mei.* trist. 4, 4, 27.

upon himself, having already gained a firm footing, when all his friends and advisers had preceded him in death, when he had lost those to whom he had been attached within his private family circle and only those whom he disliked were left, and he had become sensitive and intolerant in his old age, then and only then some acts occurred that remind us of the Octavianus of the proscriptions, who preferred to rid himself once and for all of what gave him trouble, and then he dealt summarily with obnoxious men such as Labienus, Cassius Severus, and Ovid. In his earlier years men of talent had rather to be on their guard against allowing his kindness to turn them from their own paths.[20]) His care for scholars was shown by the forming of public libraries, the first of which, in atrio Libertatis, was founded by Asinius Pollio after his Dalmatian triumph (a. 715/39); Octavian followed this up with the library in porticu Octaviae, and a second one near the temple of the Palatine Apollo (a. 726/28)[21]).

As a result of this favour designedly shown to literary activity we meet in the Augustan period with an immense number of real and would-be poets [22]) at Rome, even among the female sex (e.g. Sulpicia, Cynthia and Perilla), while recitations of literary productions before a select audience (though not long afterwards

[20]) Friedländer, SGesch. 3^5, 386.

[21]) During the period following, the founding of new libraries in Rome was a common occurrence. In the notit. reg. Urbis (§ 412, 7) the number of public libraries is given collectively as 28: only six are known to us by name: besides the three already named in the text (mentioned together by Ovid, trist. 3, 1, 60. 69, 72) there is also the bibliotheca domus Tiberianae, the bibl. Pacis founded by Vespasian, and the bibl. Ulpia of Trajan: Marquardt, röm. Privataltert. 1, 116. OHirschfeld, Verwalt. 1, 187. Nor were such libraries wanting in the small towns. Pliny presented a library to Comum his native town (ep. 1, 8, 2). Tibur possessed in Herculis templo a *bibliotheca satis commode libris instructa* (Gell. 19, 5, 4: cf. 9, 4, 13). In addition there were in rich houses and villas a multitude of private libraries, often of very considerable extent. Sen. dial. 9, 9, 4 *quo innumerabiles libros et bibliothecas, quarum dominus vix tota vita indices perlegit?* The collection of Serenus Sammonicus numbered 62,000 volumes.—It is remarkable how little prominence is given to booksellers under the Empire. Only very few isolated notices about them are to be found. The Sosii fratres are mentioned by Horace ep. 1, 20, 2. AP. 345; Sen. de benef. 7, 6, 1 mentions Dorus librarius as a dealer in MSS. of Cicero and Livy. Tryphon is under Domitian the publisher of Quintilian (§ 325, 6) and of Martial (4, 72, 2. 13, 3, 4). In Martial are mentioned in addition Atrectus (1, 117, 13), Secundus libertus Lucensis (1, 2, 7) and Q. Polius Valerianus (1, 113, 6). *M. Ulpius Aug. lib. Dionysius bybliopola* Orelli 4154. *Sex. Peducaeus Dionysius bybliopola* CIL. 6, 9218.

[22]) Hor. ep. 2, 1, 108.

anybody who chose to come was welcome[23]), and declamations, gradually became substitutes displacing the old meetings of the people. These recitationes may indeed have had some relation to the old collegium poetarum[24]) : but Asinius Pollio was the first who used them to make up for the loss of his public sphere[25]), and indeed they agreed so well with the spirit of the time, that they never afterwards went out of use and soon became the decisive test of the success of writers, though venal applause also served to deceive many inferior talents as to their value.

Among the various branches of poetry, epic poetry was especially cultivated and perfected by Vergil, together with the kindred branches of didactic poetry and idylls. In reference to contemporary events, epic poetry naturally assumed a panegyric character. Satire was regenerated by Horace, but, constrained by circumstances to eschew political hostilities, it was soon limited to personal, literary and social subjects and soon afterwards disappeared from the arena altogether, though the poetical epistles of a later period were merely an innocent reproduction of it: in the former product of his earlier, and in the latter product of his riper years, Horace produced by far his best work. He himself indeed set a higher value on his lyrical (melic) poetry. But however much we may recognise in this masterly method and fine artistic perception, extensive culture, mature judgment, etc., yet all this skill could not compensate for the want of lyrical feeling and creative power.—Elegy was developed with much success; here the Romans were at least the equals of their Greek models. Cornelius Gallus was the first to cultivate erotic elegy, and Tibullus subsequently imparted to his poems the lucidity and loveliness of the productions of the Greek mind. Propertius enriched this department by his vigour and versatility in the poetry of passion, and in Ovid we meet with a graceful ease and perfection of form which seem to vie with the naughtiness

---

23) SEN. controv. 10, praef. 4, *T. Labienus . . . declamavit non quidem populo sed egregie. non admittebat populum, et quia nondum haec consuetudo erat inducta et quia putabat turpe ac frivolae iactationis.*

24) Cf. § 94, 7. 134. 2.

25) SEN. controv. 4, praef. 2. *Pollio Asinius nunquam admissa multitudine declamavit* (cf. n. 23), *nec illi ambitio in studiis defuit: primus enim omnium Romanorum advocatis hominibus scripta sua recitavit.* SUET. Aug. 89 *recitantes et benigne et patienter audiit, nec tantum carmina et historias sed et orationes* (e.g. SEN. controv. 2, 4, 12) *et dialogos.* On the arrangement of these recitationes cf. SEN. epp. 95. TAC. dial. 9. PLIN. ep. 8, 12. IUV. 7, 10. SUET. Claud. 41. KLEHRS, populäre

of the contents. The drama, however, no longer prospered.[26]) Tragedy in the hands of contemporary poets became erudite, was seldom admitted to the stage and took refuge in the study; genuine comedy could not thrive. The trabeata of Melissus remained isolated. When the stage required artistic comedy or tragedy, recourse was had to revivals of the plays of early masters. The effete multitude, however, preferred coarse farces (Atellanae, mimi) and especially the ballet (pantomimes, § 8, 13), which was patronised everywhere, even by Maecenas.

Even prose lost ground in this period. Livy, indeed, was a writer of the first rank, as far as style is concerned; but even in him, a certain poetical colouring of his style showed a marked deviation from the Ciceronian standard, which indicated the approach of the silver age. The other prose-writers are mostly specialists and rather intent upon their subjects than their style: for example Iulius Hyginus, Verrius Flaccus, Sinnius Capito, Vitruvius Pollio, and the jurists Antistius Labeo, Ateius Capito, and others. Philosophy lacked neither motive nor interest. Augustus himself wrote Hortationes ad philosophiam, and Livy composed philosophical treatises. Vergil intended to give himself up to philosophy, and Horace actually did so; the author of Ciris and Lynceus and also Iccius were enthusiasts for it. But only Sextius was what may be called a technical writer on philosophy, and he wrote in Greek. The others merely valued philosophy for practical guidance, and most of them started with the conviction of the emptiness of all human splendour and wisdom. From this they drew, according to their disposition and humour, either serious or loose conclusions, but always arrived at the result that it would be vain and foolish to struggle against the existing constitution and against the religion of the time. What was in reality the effect of outward necessity, i.e. entire abstinence from public activity, was now adopted by the majority as their free choice, and the principle of egotism was developed to a system of subjectivism and a kind of practical philosophy which finds its most eloquent and straightforward representative in Horace. By this voluntary recognition of the actual barriers the literature of this time assumed the character of obsequious submission and resignation.

Aufsätze (1856) 175. ThHerwig, de recitatione poetarum ap. Rom., Marb. 1864. Friedländer, SGesch. 3^5, 372. ERohde, griech. Roman 306. LValmaggi, riv. di filol. 16, 65. See also § 324, 1.

26) Cf. above p. 249.

Altogether the equality of the influencing circumstances causes a certain uniformity among the writers of the Augustan period. In its beginning there was indeed a difference between the older generation, whose youth had passed under the Republic and during the Civil Wars, and the younger generation that had entirely grown up under the Monarchy; but very soon peace and a mild despotism extended their relaxing influence over all alike, and both young and old vie in lauding the happiness of an iners vita, the slumber by the side of the murmuring brook 27); they wasted time and art in amorous dallying with members of the demi-monde; in moments of surfeit they longed for the healthy simplicity of nature, and endeavoured to stifle the sense of their lost liberty and self-respect by pompously proclaiming their immortality. But the clear intellect of Horace, penetrating with quiet insight the hollowness and hypocrisy of the whole period, derived therefrom a tone which shows itself sometimes as mild irony, sometimes as sadness, and sometimes too as deep-seated disgust.

This difference of the two generations was most pronounced in the field of public speaking, where the few orators who survived the downfall of the Republic were succeeded in the younger generation only by rhetoricians: in these the memory of the olden time was at first still alive, for example, in Cassius Severus and partly in the elder Seneca; but the other coryphees of declamation and rhetoric in the Augustan period, such men as Porcius Latro, Albucius Silus, Iunius Gallio, Cestius Pius, Rutilius Lupus and others, can scarcely be distinguished in their manner from those of the succeeding century. 28)

I. The Leading Men.

220. All the leading men of this time took an active share in literature. Augustus (691/63 B.C.–767/14 A.D.) wrote several

27) Teuffel on Horace sat. 2, 6, 61. p. 164.

28) AWSchmidt, Gesch. der Denk- und Glaubensfreiheit im ersten Jahrh. der Kaiserherrschaft (Berl. 1847), p. 35. 260 sqq. 290 sqq. (a caricature). GBernhardy, röm. Lit. (Brunswick 1872) 5 254. JFCCampe, literar. Tendenzen u. Zustände zu Rom zur Zeit des Horaz, JJ. 103, 463. 537. ThPlüss, politische u. sittl. Ideale im Reiche d. Aug., ibid. 109, 67. LFriedländer, SGesch. 3⁵, 329. HBlaze de Bury, les femmes et la société au temps d'Auguste, Paris 2 1876. GBoissier, l'opposition sous les Césars, Par. 2 1885; la religion rom. d'Auguste aux Antonins, Par. 1884 II.

OHaube, de carmm. epicis saec. Augusti, Bresl. 1870; cf. § 19, 3 with supple-

works in metrical form, even more in prose, especially in the shape of Memoirs, and a survey of his own reign, most of which we possess in the incomparable monumentum Ancyranum, which (in its contents, scope and composition) is just as unique as the man, whose honours in and services to the state during a reign of 57 years it records with justifiable pride. For a long time afterwards letters by him were in circulation. Maecenas (circ. 685/69–746/8) was notorious as a prose-writer for his artificial style and also wrote trifles in various metres. Agrippa (691/63–742/12) wrote Memoirs; he caused a map to be made of the whole Empire, and wrote commentarii to explain it.

1. C. Octavius C. f., born 691/63, adopted by Caesar in his last will and hence called Caesar Octavianus. The battle of Actium was 723/31. The title of Augustus he bore from the beginning of 727/27, †767/14. AWeichert, de imp. Caesaris Augusti scriptis, Grimma 1835 sq. II; Imp. Caes. Aug. operum rell. I., Grimma 1846.

2. Suet. Aug. 84 *eloquentiam studiaque liberalia ab aetate prima et cupide et laboriosissime exercuit. . . . neque in senatu neque apud populum neque apud milites locutus est umquam nisi meditata et composita oratione. . . . pronuntiabat dulci et proprio quodam oris sono.* 86 *genus eloquendi secutus est elegans et temperatum, vitatis sententiarum ineptiis atque concinnitate, . . . praecipuamque curam duxit sensum animi quam apertissime exprimere.* Tac. ann. 13, 3 *Augusto prompta ac profluens quaeque deceret principem eloquentia fuit.* Fronto ep. p. 123 *Augustum . . . eleganter et latine, linguae etiamtum integro lepore potius quam dicendi ubertate praeditum puto.* He pronounced a parentation on his avia Julia in his twelfth year (Suet. 8. Quint. 12, 6, 1. Nikol. Dam. Aug. 3), on M. Marcellus a. 731/23 (Dio 53, 30. Serv. Aen. 1, 712), on Agrippa a. 742/12 (Dio 54, 28), on his sister Octavia a. 743/11 (Dio 54, 35. Suet. 61), Drusus a. 745/9 (Suet. Claud. 1. Liv. per. 140. Dio 55, 2).

3. Suet. Aug. 85 *multa varii generis prosa oratione composuit, ex quibus nonnulla in coetu familiarium velut in auditorio recitavit, sicut rescripta Bruto de Catone* (cf. § 215, 2), . . . *item hortationes ad philosophiam* (conjectures on this in HDiels, doxog. gr. 83), *et aliqua de vita sua, quam tredecim libris, Cantabrico tenus bello* (727/27–730/24) *nec ultra exposuit.* Suid. v. Αὔγουστος Καῖσαρ· ἔγραψε περὶ τοῦ ἰδίου βίου καὶ τῶν πράξεων βιβλία ιγʹ. Plut. compar. Demosth. c. Cic. 3 ὁ Καῖσαρ ἐν τοῖς πρὸς Ἀγρίππαν καὶ Μαικήναν ὑπομνήμασιν; cf. Brut. 27. 41 (ἐν τοῖς ὑπομνήμασιν). Serv. Verg. buc. 9, 46 *Augustus in lib. II de memoria vitae suae;* Aen. 8, 696 *Aug. in commemorationae vitae suae.* dig. 48, 24, 1 *Aug. lib. X de vita sua.* Ps.-Plin. de medic. 1, 18 *ex commentariis Caes. Augusti.* Tertull. de an. 46 *in vitae illius* (so

---

ment. APick, de adiectivo praedicativo ap. Aug. poetas latt., Halle 1879. PRichter, de usu particularum exclamativarum ap. poetas Aug. aequales, Hagenau 1878 (cf. p. 144 l. 12). OErdmann, die lat. Adjective mit dem Gen. bei den Schriftst. des 1. Jahrh. n. Chr., Stendal 1879. ASommer, de usu participii fut. act. ap. aevi Augustei poett., Halle 1881. JSchäfler, die syntaktischen Gräcismen bei den august. Dichtern, Munich 1883. FSeitz, de fixis poett. Lat. epithetis, Elberf. 1890.

GVossius: the MSS. read *in vitelliis*) *commentariis* (of Augustus) *conditum est.* The fragments of this work in HPeter's hist. fr. 252. Suet. Claud. 1 *nec contentus elogium tumulo eius* (of Drusus) *versibus a se compositis insculpsisse, etiam vitae memoriam prosa oratione composuit* (Augustus). Quotations from his letters in Suet. Iul. 56 (*brevem admodum ac simplicem*). Aug. 69. 71. 76. 86. Claud. 4. gramm. 16. Tac. dial. 13 (to Vergil, cf. § 228, 1 l. 23). Letters to Horace are mentioned in Suetonius' life of the poet. A letter to Maecenas in Macr. 2, 4, 12 (cf. OJahn, Herm. 2, 247) and in Sueton.'s vita Horatii. *Augustus in epistulis ad C. Caesarem*, Quint. 1, 6, 19, cf. ib. 1, 7, 22.

4. Suet. Aug. 101 *tribus voluminibus, uno mandata de funere suo complexus est, altero indicem rerum a se gestarum, quem vellet incidi in aeneis tabulis quae ante Mausoleum* (the tomb erected by Augustus for the Imperial family a. 726/28, in the Campus Martius close to the Tiber; cf. Dio 56, 33) *statuerentur, tertio breviarium totius imperii, quantum militum sub signis ubique esset, quantum pecuniae in aerario et fiscis et vectigaliorum residuis.* Tac. ann. 1, 11 *proferri libellum recitarique iussit* (*Tiberius*). *opes publicae continebantur, quantum civium sociorumque in armis, quot classes, regna, provinciae, tributa aut vectigalia et necessitates ac largitiones. quae cuncta sua manu perscripserat Augustus addideratque consilium coercendi intra terminos imperii.* The breviarium is to be connected with the libellus mentioned by Tac. l.l. and it contained matters essential to the statistics of the Imperial administration. Perhaps the *discriptio Italiae totius in regiones XI* which was used by Pliny b. 3 and 4 (ind. auct.: *ex divo Augusto*) and which Plin. NH. 3, 46 attributes to Augustus, was a portion of or a supplement to the above-named work. DDetlefsen, comment. Mommsen. 33. GOemichen, plin. Stud. 48. Bormann l.l. 33. CJullian, le breviarium de l'emper. Aug., Mél. d'archéol. et de l'hist. de l'école franç. de Rome 3 (1882), 149. Cf. Riese, geogr. lat. p. x and see below n. 13. OCuntz, de Augusto Plinii geographicorum auctore, Bonn 1888. —Augustus' sepulchral inscription, in Suet. l.l. *index rerum a se gestarum*, has been preserved to us by a copy of it having been engraved (to right and left of the door) on the marble wall of the vestibule of the temple of Augustus and Roma at Ancyra in Galatia; a Greek translation adorned the outer wall of the temple cella at the same place. A second copy of this translation existed at Apollonia in Pisidia, in a temple dedicated to the Julian Imperial family, CIG. 3971. Waddington on LeBas, voyage, inscr. 3, 1194. Mommsen in the CIL. and the various editions. Of this very scanty remains are extant, whereas of the inscriptions at Ancyra (Monumentum Ancyranum), both the translation and the original, there are such considerable fragments, that the substance of the whole, except for a few unimportant gaps, is clearly established. The title of the Mon. Anc. (not the original one) reads in the Latin rendering: *Rerum gestarum divi Augusti quibus orbem terrarum imperio populi Romani subiecit et inpensarum quas in rem publicam populumque Rom. fecit, incisarum in duabus aheneis pilis quae sunt Romae positae* (see Suet. l.l.), *exemplar subiectum.* The inscription was completed a few months before the death of Augustus 767/14.—The best edition according to the most recent impression of the fragments (cast in plaster by KHumann 1882, now in the Berlin Museum) is by ThMommsen, res gestae divi Augusti ex monum. Ancyr. et Apollon. iterum edidit, Berl. 1883 ([1]1865). See also CIL. 3, 769 sqq. The remains of the mon. Anc. in GPerrot and EGuillaume, exploration archéol. de la Galatie et de la Bithynie, Paris 1862. Res gestae divi Augusti, ed. ThBergk, Gött. 1873. Handy editions: by ThMommsen, Berl. 1883. RCagnat et CPeltier, Par. 1885. On the importance of the mon. Anc., and on critical and linguistic points see: EBormann, Bemm. z. schriftl. Nachlass des K. Aug., Marb. 1884. JSchmidt,

Phil. 44, 442. 45, 393. 46, 70. HNissen, RhM. 41, 481. UvWilamowitz, Herm. 21, 623. OHirschfeld, Wien. Stud. 7, 170. Mommsen, in v. Sybel's hist. Zeitschrift NF. 21 (1887), 385. EWölfflin, Münch. SBer. 1886 2, 53. PGeppert, on the monum. Ancyr., Berl. 1887. LCantarelli, bull. arch. commun. di Roma 17, 3, 57. JPlew, Quellenunterss. z. Gesch. d. K. Hadr., with app. on the Mon. Anc., Strassb. 1889. A decree of Augustus de aquaeductu Venafrano, extant in an inscription at Venafrum. CIL. 10, 4842. Bruns font.[5] 222.

5. Suet. Aug. 85 *poetica summatim attigit. unus liber exstat, scriptus ab eo hexametris versibus, cuius et argumentum et titulus est Sicilia; exstat alter aeque modicus epigrammatum, quae fere tempore balinei meditabatur.* From this a very spicy epigram in Mart. 11, 20. A feeble epigram (an invitation to enjoy life, also in PLM. 4, 122) entitled *Octã. aug̃.* published by HHagen, RhM. 35, 569 from Bern. 109 s. X, is probably mediaeval. *tragoediam magno impetu exorsus, non succedenti stilo, abolevit, quaerentibusque amicis* (Macr. 2, 4, 2 mentions L. Varius), *quidnam Aiax ageret, respondit Aiacem suum in spongiam incubuisse.* Suidas v. Αὔγουστος Καῖσαρ (1, 851 B.): ἔγραψε καὶ τραγῳδίαν Αἴαντός τε καὶ Ἀχιλλέως. The latter work, if indeed it is to be distinguished from the former, no doubt shared the fate of his Ajax. Cf. Sophocles ed. Dindorf (Oxon. 1860) 8. p. 208. He composed fescenninae against a certain Pollio (Asinius Pollio § 221, 1 or the glutton Vedius Pollio, PRE. 6, 2419? HPeter, JJ. 119, 422; cf. § 5, 4). A school essay on the theme: 'Reflections of Augustus on Vergil's will' AL. 672, PLM. 4, 179, (cf. above § 45, 9). EBährens, anall. Cat. 66. EChatelain, rev. de philol. 4, 79 on Paris. 1623 b. s. X.

6. C. (cf. Vell. 2, 88, 2. Tac. ann. 14, 53. Dio 49, 16) Maecenas L. f. Pom(ptina): this full name in Gruter inscr. p. 945, 10. Maecenas is the name of the gens (*mehnate* Etr. occurs in Perusia). He appears to have been related on the female side to the aristocratic race of the Cilnii (of Arretium). EBormann, ind. lect. Marb. 1883 p. iii. Tac. ann. 6, 11 *Cilnium Maecenatem, equestris ordinis;* in Macr. 2, 4, 12 Augustus jocularly calls Maecenas among other things *ebur ex Etruria, lasar Arretinum. . . . Cilniorum smaragde;* otherwise we have up to the present time no evidence for Cilnii at Arezzo, Müller-Deecke, Etrusk. 1, 484. Maecenas was born id. April (Hor. c. 4, 11, 14–20) probably between 680/74 and 690/64. Augustus liked to employ him on diplomatic missions when there was need of mediation and reconciliation, for which Maecenas' easy pacific temperament was peculiarly adapted. His lack of real ambition (in spite of great though harmless vanity) fitted him for positions of trust, such as he occupied in Rome after the battle of Actium, while in war he never played an important part. He died a. 746/8. (Dio 55, 7.)

7. The best description of his character is given by Vell. 2, 88, 2: *C. Maecenas, equestri sed splendido genere natus, vir ubi res vigiliam exigeret sane exsomnis, providens atque agendi sciens, simul vero aliquid ex negotio remitti posset, otio ac mollitiis paene ultra feminam fluens.* He receives a one-sided treatment from Seneca, who parades against him his (theoretical) Stoic philosophy. Especially epist. 114, 4 *quomodo Maecenas vixerit notius est quam ut narrari nunc debeat, quomodo ambulaverit, quam delicatus fuerit, quam cupierit videri, quam vitia sua latere voluerit. quid ergo? non oratio eius aeque soluta est quam ipse discinctus? non tam insignita illius verba sunt quam cultus, quam comitatus, quam domus, quam uxor* (Terentia from a. 731/23. Teuffel, ZFAW. 1845, 608)? *magni vir ingenii fuerat* (ep. 92, 35 he even says: *habuit ingenium et grande et virile*, and 19, 9 *ingeniosus vir*) *si . . . non etiam in oratione difflueret. videbis itaque eloquentiam ebrii hominis, involutam et*

errantem et licentiae plenam. He subjoins (5) a specimen of *Maecenas de cultu suo*, and adds (6): *non statim cum haec legeris hoc tibi occurret hunc esse qui solutis tunicis in urbe semper incesserit? . . . hunc esse qui . . . in omni publico coetu sic adparuerit ut pallio velaretur caput exclusis utrimque auribus . . . ? hunc esse cui . . . comitatus hic fuerit in publico, spadones duo . . . ? hunc esse qui uxorem miliens duxit, cum unam habuerit?* etc. Cf. ep. 19, 9. 92, 35. 101, 10. 120, 19. dial. 1 (de provid.), 3, 10. Iuv. 1, 67.

8. Prose works: *Maecenas de cultu suo* see n. 7. Sen. ep. 19, 9 *Maecenas in eo libro qui Prometheus inscribitur.* Charis. GL. 1, 146 *Maecenas in dialogo II.* Prisc. GL. 2, 536 *Maecenas in Octaviam.* Serv. Aen. 8, 310 *Maecenas in Symposio, ubi (cui) Vergilius et Horatius interfuerunt, cum ex persona Messalae de vino loquere-tur ait.* Aelian. fragm. 108 p. 239 Herch. ἐν τῷ συνδείπνῳ τῷ τοῦ Μαικήνα (cf. RHirzel, RhM. 43, 316). Sen. benef. 4, 36, 2. Did Maecenas also write historical works? His intention is indicated by Hor. c. 2, 12, 9 *tuque pedestribus dices historiis proelia Caesaris, Maecenas.* From this Serv. georg. 2, 41 jumps to the conclusion that the intention was carried out. But Plin. NH. 7, 147 quotes Maecenas together with Agrippa as authorities for an occurrence in the life of Augustus (§ 220, 14). Moreover Plin. NH. 9, 25 *pigeret referre ni res* (of the tame dolphin at Puteoli) *Maecenatis et Fabiani* (§ 266, 10) *et Flavi Alfii* (§ 268, 9) *multorumque esset litteris mandata.* Plin. ind. auct. b. 9, 32. 37 *ex . . . Maecenate.* —Poetical works: Serv. georg. 2, 42 *constat Maecenatem . . . plura composuisse carmina.* An hexameter in Sen. ep. 92, 35. Charis. GL. 1, 79 *Maecenas in X* (cf. GL. 5, 575, 1), probably also GL. 5, 591, iamb. trim. in Caes. Bass. GL. 6, 263, 1. In Sen. ep. 101, 11 are quoted glyconeans of Maecenas. Hendecasyllabics addressed to Horace in Sueton. vita Hor. and in Isidor. orig. 19, 32, 6. Galli-ambics in Diomed. GL. 1, 514 and Caes. Bass. GL. 6, 262. The poetical fragments: FPR. 338. FHarder, d. Fragmente des Mäcenas, Berl. 1889.—Witticisms of Augustus on Maecenas' style (*calamistri*, Tac. dial. 26) in Sueton. Aug. 86 and Macr. 2, 4, 12. Strangely Dio 55, 7 πρῶτος σημεῖά τινα γραμμάτων πρὸς τάχος ἐξεῦρε καὶ αὐτὰ δι' Ἀκύλου ἀπελευθέρου συχνοὺς ἐξεδίδαξεν. See however above (§ 191, 4).

9. JHMeibom, Maecenas, sive de C. Cilnii Maecenatis vita etc., Leid. 1653. ALion, Tironiana et Maecenatiana, sive Tironis (§ 191, 1) et Maecenatis frag-menta ac de vita et moribus utriusque, Gött.[2] 1846. PSFrandsen, C. Cilnius Maecenas, eine histor. Untersuch., Altona 1843. WEWeber, Q. Horatius Flaccus (Jena 1844) p. 143. HJMatthes in his symbolae literariae 5, 1. Friedländer, SGesch. 3[5], 389. Cf. also § 229, 3. There are no authentic portraits of Maec. extant: Bernoulli, röm. Ikonogr. 1, 237.

10. M. Vipsanius Agrippa, born 691/63, hence of the same age as Octavianus, whose friend he was from boyhood, cos. 717/37, censor and cos. II a. 726/28, cos. III a. 727/27. He was Octavianus' best general and admiral, and also successful as a diplomatist, especially in the East; he was faithful and trustworthy, but knew his importance well enough and would not bear anybody above himself except Caesar's heir; in a. 733/21 he became Augustus' son-in-law: † 742/12.

11. He possessed rhetorical training, and a. 711/43 prosecuted C. Cassius as one of the assassins of Caesar (Plut. Brut. 27 cf. Vell. 2, 69, 5) and even later appeared as a defender (Sen. contr. 2, 4, 12 p. 201 K.); see also Plin. NH. 35, 26 *exstat eius oratio magnifica et maximo civium digna de tabulis omnibus signisque publicandis.* In literature he had a somewhat coarse (Plin. l.l.: *M. Agrippa, vir rusticitati propior quam deliciis*), but healthy taste (cf. above § 219, 15), and in his subjects showed a practical tendency. Frontin. aquaed. 98 *M. Agrippa . .*

descripsit quid aquarum publicis operibus, quid lacibus, quid privatis daretur. ib. 99 *qui ex commentariis Agrippae aquas haberent.*

12. Map of the World: PLIN. NH. 3, 17 . . . *Agrippam quidem in tanta viri diligentia praeterque in hoc opere cura, cum orbem terrarum urbi spectandum propositurus esset* (also from the patriotic point of view, in illustration of the greatness of the Empire and of the services of those who had extended it), *errasse quis credat et cum eo* (the publisher with the author) *divum Augustum? is namque complexam eum porticum ex destinatione et commentariis M. Agrippae a sorore eius incohatam peregit.* From this it would appear that Agrippa left only the sketch of a chart and chorographic commentarii, but in his will enjoined his sister (Paula) to have his great map made for a public porticus (the Vipsania, cf. PLIN. NH. 6, 139. TAC. hist. 1, 31), an injunction subsequently carried out by Augustus himself. The commentarii, which are specially based on road surveys and books of travel, have been much used by PLIN. NH. (ind. auct. to b. 3–6 *ex . . . M. Agrippa*, he is there quoted over thirty times), MELA and others, also by STRABO (see PARTSCH l.l. 42): a collection of passages relating thereto in PHILIPPI, de tabula Peutinger., Bonn 1876 p. 30 and in RIESE'S Geographi lat. p. 1–8. From these works of Agrippa are derived (though not immediately, AVGUTSCHMID, Lit. Centr.-Bl. 1877, 860) two geographical lists of names (compiled as an elucidation to school maps, at latest about a. 400) with scanty notices concerning boundaries and the size of the various countries, the Dimensuratio provinciarum (published by ESCHELSTRATE, antiq. eccl. 2, 525, AMAI, class. auct. 3, 410, ESCHWEDER, Beiträge zur Chorogr. des Aug. 1, 6 and RIESE, geogr. lat. 9) and the so-called Divisio orbis (published by SCHWEDER l.l. and Riese l.l. 15), which again has been largely used by Dicuil (§ 453, 5). Cf. also n. 13.—Agrippa's map was no doubt reproduced in various parts of the Empire: it is probably of such a copy, intended for Augustodunum (Autun), that we read in EUMENIUS pro instaur. schol. 20 a. 296: *videat in illis porticibus iuventus et quotidie spectet omnes terras et cuncta maria . . . si quidem . . . illic instruendae pueritiae causa . . . omnium cum nominibus suis locorum situs spatia intervalla descripta sunt* etc. ib. 21 *nunc demum iuvat orbem spectare depictum.* The tabula Peutingeriana also is indirectly derived from Agrippa's model (§ 412, 6). Cf. HBAZIN, rev. d'archéol. 1887 2, 325 on an inscr. taken from a geographical monument: *audi, viator; si libet, intus veni; tabula est aena quae te cuncta perdocet.*

13. That Agrippa was commissioned by Augustus to undertake a geographical survey of the whole Empire, and as a result of this produced the map and commentarii, is unlikely and cannot be proved. The statements in the so-called Divisio p. 14 R.: *orbem divus Augustus primus per chorographiam ostendit* and ISIDORUS 5, 36, 4 *Augustus Romanum orbem descripsit* assume too much. Augustus' breviarium totius imperii and discriptio regionum Italiae (§ 220, 4; see also below § 344, 4 the passage from the liber col. p. 239) rather served administrative and financial purposes; see also DETLEFSEN, comment. Mommsen. 33. So did the survey of the Empire ordered by Augustus and carried on during some 20 years by four Greeks; our only evidence for this is Julius Honorius and the pretended Aethicus in RIESE, geogr. lat. p. 21 and 72. Meanwhile Agrippa naturally had the geographical materials, which these undertakings brought to light, at his command for those works which were founded principally on the measured distances on the roads. FRITSCHL, op. 3, 743. CHPETERSEN, RhM. 8, 161. 377. 9, 85. 422. KMÜLLENHOFF, d. Weltkarte u. Chorographie des August, Kiel 1856 (and AVGUTSCHMID, RhM. 12, 619); Herm. 9, 182. JPARTSCH, d. Darst. Europas in dem geogr. Werke des Agr., Bresl. 1875. ESCHWEDER, Beitr. z. Kritik

d. Chorogr. des Aug., Kiel 1876. 78. 83 III; die Concordanz der Chorographien des Pompon. Mela und des Plin., Kiel 1879. Riese's proleg. to the geogr. Lat. p. vii. DDetlefsen, Unterss. z. d. geogr. Büchern d. Plin. 1: d. Weltkarte des M. Agrippa, Glückst. 1884. FPhilippi, z. Reconstruct. der Weltk. d. Agr., Marb. 1880; in the hist. researches for ASchäfer 239.

14. Agrippa wrote an autobiography. Philargyr. on Verg. georg. 2, 162 *Agrippa in secundo vitae suae dicit excogitasse se ut ex Lucrino lacu portum faceret.* Cf. Plin. NH. 7, 148 (*Augusti*) *Philippensi proelio morbidi fuga et triduo in palude aegroti et, ut fatentur Agrippa et Maecenas* (n. 8) *aqua subter cutem fusa turgidi latebra.* 36, 121 *adicit ipse* (Agrippa) *aedilitatis suae* (721/33) *commemoratione* etc. —PSFrandsen, M. Vipsanius Agrippa, eine hist. Unters., Altona 1836. DvLakeren-Matthes, de Agr. meritis, Amsterd. 1840. JHvEck, quaestt. hist. de A., Leiden 1842. APreuner, PRE. 1^2, 599. AFMotte, sur M. Agrippa, Ghent 1872.

221. Next to these leading men, Asinius Pollio and Valerius Messalla were in the Augustan period the most prominent on account of their past career and position among their contemporaries. C. Asinius Pollio (a. 678/76–758/5 A.D.), who in the Civil Wars exerted himself for Caesar and Antony, fell out with the latter without going over to Octavianus, then retreated from political life, supported science and art with great magnificence and devoted himself to literature. At first he wrote tragedies, then a history of the Civil Wars after the first triumvirate. But he was principally an orator: both in this capacity and as a writer he affected antique severity, and when his sphere as an orator was restricted, he found a substitute in the public recitations. By keeping aloof from politics this hard, strong-willed man contrived to maintain his peculiar position as well as a nominal independence, while within the domain of literature he was a very severe critic, by way of compensation for his lack of political influence.

1. C. Asinius Cn. f. Pollio (on the mode of spelling Pollio or Polio see e.g. Lachmann on Lucr. 1, 313; Ritschl, PM. p. 81; op. 3, 249. 5, 771), born 678/76, prosecuted C. Cato (in his 22nd year, Tac. dial. 34) a. 700/54, praetor 709/45, cos. 714/40. As consul he fought against the Parthines and Dalmatians; capture of Salonae (Spalato) and his triumph ex Parthineis a. d. VIII Kal. Nov. 715/39 (act. tr., CIL. 1, p. 461. 478. Hor. c. 2, 1, 16). Having subsequently fallen out with Antony (Charis. GL. 1, 80 *Asinius contra maledicta Antonii*), Asinius thought too well of himself to join Octavianus (who was much junior to him) or to submit to him (Vell. 2, 86, 3), and until his death he held aloof from him without open opposition or real submission. Hieron. ad Euseb. chron., a. Abr. 2020 = 758/5 A.D. *Asinius Pollio orator et consularis, qui de Dalmatis triumphaverat, LXXX aetatis suae anno in villa Tusculana moritur.* This is confirmed by Sen. contr. 4, praef. 5, according to which passage Pollio was alive A.D. 4, and Tac. dial. 17 *Asinius paene ad extremum* (*Augusti principatum*) *duravit.* KNipperdey, op. 288. On the first public library, which he founded and decorated with the portraits of celebrated authors (Plin. NH. 35, 10): § 219, 21. He also admitted

the public to his art-collections (PLIN. NH. 36, 33). On the recitations introduced by him see § 219, 25.

2. The poems of Pollio. His relations with Catullus (CAT. 12) and Cinna (§ 213, 3 l. 20); with Horace (n. 3). *Carmina Sophocleo digna cothurno*, i.e. tragedies, either written or about to be written at the time of Vergil's ecl. 8, 10 (a. 715/39), cf. ib. 3, 86 (*Pollio et ipse facit nova carmina*). HOR. sat. 1, 10, 42 sq. (c. a. 718/36) *Pollio regum facta canit pede ter percusso* (in iambic trimeters). c. 2, 1, 9 (a. 724/30 or 725/29, *paulum severae Musa tragoediae desit theatris*, while Asinius was writing his history of the Civil Wars. That Asinius actually published tragedies appears from TAC. dial. 21 *Asinius . . . videtur mihi inter Menenios et Appios studuisse; Pacuvium certe et Accium non solum tragoediis sed etiam orationibus suis expressit: adeo durus et siccus est.* That they were acted is indicated by the expression *theatris* used by HOR. l.l., but we are without further information concerning them. There seems to be an error in SERV. Verg. ecl. 8, 10 *alii ideo hoc de Pollione dictum volunt quod et ipse utriusque linguae tragoediarum scriptor fuit.* Asinius wrote also erotic poetry, according to PLIN. ep. 5, 3, 5 (above § 31, 1), cf. 7, 4, 4. Out of all these poems there has only been preserved the fragment in CHARIS. GL. 1, 100, 24 *Polio* '*Veneris antistita Cuprus.*' Cf. FHARDER, JJ. 137, 368.

3. History of the Civil Wars from the first triumvirate (a. 694/60, *Metello consule*, HOR. c. 2, 1, 1) and as it seems simply called historiae (SEN. suas. 6, 15 *Pollio in historiis suis;* ib. 6, 25 *in historiis eius* and *ne historias eius legere concupiscatis;* cf. VAL. MAX. 8, 13 ext. 4). It treated of the battle of Pharsalus (SUET. Iul. 30 and elsewhere), of that of Thapsus, of Cato's death (HOR. c. 2, 1, 24 sqq.), of the war in Spain (SUET. Iul. 55), Cicero's death (SEN. suas. 6, 24) and perhaps also (vid. inf.) of the battle of Philippi (cf. TAC. ann. 4, 34 *Asinii Pollionis scripta egregiam eorundem*—Cassius and Brutus—*memoriam tradunt*). There are no quotations relating to the broils between Octavianus and M. Antony; this may indeed be due to mere chance, but it is also possible that Asinius looked upon the history of that period as *periculosae plenum opus aleae* (HOR. c. 2, 1, 6) and therefore decided not to include it, and finished with a. 712/42 or a still earlier date: this is confirmed by the work being designated in Suidas (see below) as a narrative of the Civil War between Caesar and Pompey. The statement of Suidas (see below), that the work comprised 17 books, might well be explained by the supposition that the volumes and years coincided with each other, the narrative reaching from the middle of 694/60–710/44, that is, to the death of Caesar. As b. 1 contained the introduction and the second half of a. 694/60, so b. 17 would contain the beginning of a. 710/44, and would close with a passing survey (in which would be the eulogy of Cicero, Brutus and Cassius, see above) of the most recent times. According to HOR. c. 2, 1–8. 17 Asinius was at work on his historiae about the year 724/30 or 725/29. The passage in PRISC. GL. 2, 386, 9 *Asinius* '*cuius experta virtus bello Germaniae traducta ad custodiam Illyrici est*' cannot, if the name *Asinius* is correct, refer to Tiberius, as is generally supposed, as he was not sent to Illyria until 760/7, after the death of Asinius (PRE. 6, 1934). The third book is quoted by VAL. MAX. 8, 13 ext. 4 *Asinius Pollio, non minima pars romani stili, in tertio historiarum libro.* The wording of the work was not rhetorical (see SEN. suas. 6, 25 *adfirmare vobis possum nihil esse in Asinii historiis eius hoc quem rettuli loco*—concerning Cicero, see above—*disertius*): Ateius (§ 211, 1) in the *praecepta de ratione scribendi*, which he gave *Asinio historiam componere aggresso*, had advised him successfully *ut noto civilique et proprio sermone*

utatur (see also n. 4). The fragments in HPETER, hist. fr. 262 (the only considerable fragment is the judgment on Cicero, § 176, 1). PLIN. NH. ind. auct. b. 7 *ex . . Asinio Pollione.* These historiae of As. were used by Plutarch in his Life of Caesar and by Appian de bell. civ., see JAWIJNNE, de fide et auctor. Appiani in bell. civ., Gron. 1855. FEYSSENHARDT, JJ. 85, 757. HPETER, die Quellen Plutarchs, Halle 1865, 124; JJ. 119, 420. PBAILLEU, quomodo App. in b. c. l. II–V usus sit Asinii historiis, Gött. 1874. GTHOURET, Leipz. Studien 1, 324. Cf. also CWICHMANN, de Plut. Antonii et Bruti fontibus, Bonn 1874. SUIDAS' two articles on Ἀσίνιος Πωλίων Ῥωμαῖος (1, 786 ed. Bernh.) and on Πωλίων, ὁ Ἀσίνιος χρηματίσας, Τραλλιανός (2, 2, 387) are full of errors (concerning which see various criticisms in TEUFFEL, PRE. 1², 1868, 25. HPETER, JJ. 119, 422. THOURET l.l. HFLACH, RhM. 36, 316). According to these the consul Asinius Pollio would have written the first history of Greece in Latin (πρῶτος Ἑλληνικὴν ἱστορίαν Ῥωμαϊκῶς συνεγράψατο), which is manifestly an error and must rest on a confusion (AvGUTSCHMID, RhM. 36, 316 supposes a confusion with Pompeius Trogus); again we read of the same A. P.: ἱστορίας Ῥωμαϊκὰς συνέταξεν ἐν βιβλίοις ιζ', on the other hand of Pollio of Tralles that he composed a work περὶ τοῦ ἐμφυλίου τῆς Ῥώμης πολέμου ὃν ἐπολέμησαν Καῖσάρ τε καὶ Πομπήιος. Here it is evident that the history of the Civil War between Caesar and Pompey belongs rather to the consul, and that it is this work which is alluded to as the 17 books ἱστορίαι Ῥωμαϊκαί. GLANDGRAF, Unterss. zu Caes. u. s. Fortsetzern, Erl. 1888, has made the 'important discovery' that Asinius Pollio is the author of the bell. afr. (§ 197, 7) and the reviser and publisher of the Caesar-Hirtius remains (bell. gall. VIII, bell. civ., bell. alex.): will this theory really obtain any adherents?

4. On Pollio as an orator, both judicial and political (Hor. c. 2, 1, 13), subsequently as a declaimer, see the passages in HMEYER, orat. rom.² p. 487–491 and FBLASS, die griech. Bereds. von Alex. 141. SEN. epist. 100, 7 *compositio Pollionis Asinii salebrosa et exsiliens et ubi minime exspectes relictura. denique omnia apud Ciceronem desinunt, apud Pollionem cadunt, exceptis paucissimis quae ad certum modum et ad unum exemplar adstricta sunt.* QUINT. 10, 1, 113 *multa in Asinio Pollione inventio, summa diligentia, adeo ut quibusdam etiam nimia videatur, et consilii et animi satis; a nitore et iucunditate Ciceronis ita longe abest ut videri possit saeculo prior.* See the account (exaggerated from the point of view of the speaker) in TAC. dial. 21 (above n. 2), cf. 25 (*numerosior Asinius*). But in his rhetorical displays he was *floridior aliquanto* (SEN. contr. 4, praef. 3) than in his judicial speeches. Specimens of them are given by the elder Seneca; a collection of the fragments of the judicial speeches in MEYER l.l. 491. Among the latter the later ones are all defensive speeches. PIN. NH. praef. 31 *cum diceretur Asinius Pollio orationes in eum* (Plancum, § 209, 8) *parare quae ab ipso aut liberis post mortem Planci ederentur* etc. The accounts of his style and his opposition to Cicero (QUINT. 12, 1, 2) would characterise A. P. as an adherent of the Atticists (p. 245), from whom he is, however, distinguished by QUINT. 10, 2, 7.

5. Other prose-works by Pollio. As a philosophical writer (or penman?) Pollio is mentioned by SEN. ep. 100, 9. *Asinius Pollio ad Caesarem I* ap. CHARIS. GL. 1, 131, 3. Cf. n. 6. There are only three letters extant of a. 711/43, from A. P. to Cicero, CIC. fam. 10, 31–33. JHSCHMALZ, d. Sprachgebr. des A. P., in the Festschr. z. Karlsruher Philol.-Vers. 1882, 76. From CHARIS. GL. 1, 84, 5, PRISC. GL. 2, 513, 7 and others, MHAUPT, op. 2, 67, infers the existence of grammatical works by A. P. to which he assigns his literary and aesthetic opinions (see below n. 6), also CHARIS. GL. 1, 97, 11 *Asinius in Valerium* (i.e. Catullus, cf. § 214, 7 ad fin.). Against this see BERGK, op. 2, 751. JSTEUP, de Prob. 71.

6. Pollio as a critic. SEN. contr. 4, praef. 3 *illud strictum eius* (of A. P.) *et asperum et nimis iratum in censendo* (so OJAHN: *incendio suo* in the MSS., *ingenio suo* KIESSLING) *iudicium adeo cessabat* (in the declamations of A. P.) *ut in multis illi venia opus esset quae ab ipso vix impetrabatur* (cf. PLIN. NH. 36, 33 *Asinius Pollio fuit acris vehementiae*). Some sharp criticisms on rhetoricians by As. in SEN. rhet. see ed. KIESSL. p. 532[b]. As his judgment on Cicero (§ 176, 1) was no doubt derived from the historiae, so the one on Caesar's commentaries (SUET. Iul. 56; see § 196, 1) appears to be derived from the same source; the censure of Cicero (SEN. suas. 6, 15) is from a speech (SEN. l.l.) and perhaps also the one on an expression of Labienus (QUINT. 9, 3, 13, cf. ib. 4, 1, 11). Besides this, see SUET. gramm. 10 *Asinius Pollio in libro quo Sallustii scripta reprehendit* (cf. § 206, 5). This 'liber' was possibly in the form of letters, cf. GELL. 10, 26, 1 *Asinio Pollioni in quadam epistola quam ad Plancum* (n. 4) *scripsit . . . dignum nota visum est quod* (*Sallustius*) *in primo historiarum* etc. Cf. n. 5. This 'liber' may have contained also his criticism on Cicero's style (QUINT. 12, 1, 22) and his censure of the Paduan smack of Livy's diction (QUINT. 1, 5, 56. 8, 1, 3), perhaps the rejoinder to a remark of Livy *de oratoribus qui verba antiqua et sordida consectantur et orationis obscuritatem severitatem putant* (SEN. contr. 9, 25, 26).—In general see JRTHORBECKE, de C. A. P., Leid. 1820. DRUMANN, GR. 2, 2. FJACOB, A. P., Lüb. 1852. OHENDECOURT, de vita, gestis et scriptis A. P., Löwen 1858. TEUFFEL, PRE. 1^2, 1859. BLUZZATO, ricerche storiche su C. Asin. Poll., Padua 1867. FAAULARD, de Asin. Poll. vita et scriptis, Par. 1877. HPETER, JJ. 119, 420. JHSCHMALZ, Sprachgebr. des Asin. Poll. Munich[2] 1890. See addenda to § 197, 7.

222. M. Valerius Messalla (a. 690/64 B.C.–761/8 A.D.) served Octavianus with fidelity and sincerity, but without debasing himself. As an orator he was on a level with Pollio, but there was somewhat of hauteur and affectation about him, and he showed the jealous pride of a member of the old nobility. He subsequently busied himself with antiquarian and grammatical investigations e.g. concerning phonetics, and here he condescended to minute philological details. In his younger days he strongly felt the tendency of his time in admiring Greek literature; he translated Greek, and himself wrote in Greek both in verse and prose (memoirs).

1. M. Valerius M. f. (of the consul 693/61; see § 171, 12. BBORGHESI, op. 1, 407, MOMMSEN, ephem. epigr. 3, 4) Messalla Corvinus. HIERONYM. ad a. Abr. 1958=695/59 *Messala Corvinus orator nascitur et T. Livius Patavinus scriptor historicus;* and ad a. Abr. 2027=764/11 A.D. *Messala Corvinus ante biennium quam moreretur ita memoriam* (cf. PLIN. NH. 7, 90) *ac sensum amisit ut vix pauca verba coniungeret, et ad extremum . . . inedia se confecit, anno aetatis LXXII* (Frerianus *LXXVII*). The date of his death (A.D. 11) is certainly wrong, as Ovid, who was exiled in Dec. 761/8 A.D., was still at Rome when Messalla died (OVID. Pont. 1, 7, 27–30): whence it is evident that Messalla must have died not later than 761/8. Supposing him to have been 72 years old, he must have been born a. 689/65 or 690/64, and must have been of the same age as Cicero's son (CIC. Att. 1, 2, 1), together with whom (and Horace, born end of 689/65) Messalla studied at Athens (a. 709/45 sq.). Messalla was appointed consul 1 Jan. 723/31, Cicero on the ides of September 724/30). KNIPPERDEY, op. 289. BBORGHESI, op. 1, 408. HSCHULZ, de

Val. Mess. aetate, Stettin 1886, is of opinion that in giving the date of Messalla's birth (cf. § 143, 1) Hieronymus erred owing to a confusion of two pairs of consuls, viz. *Caesare et Figulo* (coss. 690/64) and *Caesare et Bibulo* (coss. 695/59). The statement in Tac. dial. 17 *Corvinus in medium usque Augusti principatum . . . duravit*, is no doubt erroneous: see Nipperdey l.l. 297. After the defeat at Philippi (a. 712/42) he went over to Antony, but was soon disgusted with his revels (Plin. NH. 33, 50. Charis. GL. 1, 129, 7 *Messala contra Antonii litteras*; ib. 104, 18 *M. Messala de Antonii statuis*) and made his peace with Octavianus (App. b. c. 4, 38), who received him with open arms and (a. 718/36 sqq.) employed him in several affairs; a. 723/31 he was even appointed consul in the place of Antony. Messalla henceforth remained faithful to Octavianus, without, however, betraying his former friends and principles (cf. Plut. Brut. 53). Περὶ Ἄκτιον ναυαρχήσας (App. b. c. 4, 38). His victory on the Atax (§ 212, 1) over the Aquitanians on his birthday (Tib. 1, 7) and his triumph (ex Gallia, a. d. VII Kal. Oct.) 727/27. Hieron. chron. ad a. Abr. 1991=728/26: *Messala Corvinus primus praefectus urbis factus sexto die magistratu se abdicavit, incivilem potestatem esse contestans;* cf. Tac. ann. 6, 11. Nipperdey op. 283. Curator aquarum a. 743/11, Front. aq. 99 cf. 102. A. 752/2 he moved that Augustus should receive the title of pater patriae (Suet. Aug. 58).

2. As early as 711/43 Cicero ad Brut. 1, 15, 1 writes of Messalla: *cave putes probitate, constantia, cura, studio reip. quidquam illi esse simile; ut eloquentia, qua mirabiliter excellit, vix in eo locum ad laudandum habere videatur. quamquam in hac ipsa sapientia plus apparet: ita gravi iudicio multaque arte se exercuit in verissimo genere dicendi. tanta autem industria est tantumque evigilat in studio ut non maxima ingenio . . . gratia habenda videatur.* The expression *verissimum genus dicendi* shows that Messalla had not joined the New Attic School, but followed the manner of Cicero. Cf. Tac. dial. 18 *Cicerone mitior Corvinus et dulcior et in verbis magis elaboratus.* Quint. 10, 1, 113 *Messala nitidus* (cf. 1, 7, 35) *et candidus et quodammodo praeferens in dicendo nobilitatem suam, viribus minor.* Sen. controv. 2, 12, 8 *fuit Messala exactissimi ingenii quidem in omni studiorum parte, latini utique sermonis observator diligentissimus.* In Sen. apocoloc. 10, 2 he is called *disertissimus vir.* Suet. Tib. 70 *in oratione latina secutus est Corvinum Messalam, quem senem adolescens observarat. Messala orator* is frequently mentioned in Plin. NH.: 7, 90. 10, 52 and elsewhere. On Messala's introductions see Quint. 4, 1, 8 and Tac. dial. 20 ad init. His speech against Aufidia (defended by Ser. Sulpicius, † 711, see § 174, 3) was known to Quintilian (10, 1, 22). See further Meyer, orator. fragm. [2]510. OGruppe, quaest. Ann. (1873) 35.

3. Quint. 10, 5, 2 *vertere graeca in latinum veteres nostri oratores optimum iudicabant . . . id Messalae placuit, multaeque sunt ab eo scriptae ad hunc modum orationes, adeo ut etiam cum illa Hyperidis pro Phryne difficillima Romanis subtilitate contenderet.* Hor. c. 3, 21, 9 *socraticis madet sermonibus.* He wrote bucolic poems in Greek and, as it seems, in the allegorical manner of Vergil's Bucolics: the author of catal. Verg. 9, (11; cf. § 230, 5 n. 1) lauds them to the skies. On account of these or of other poems Pliny ep. 5, 3, 5 (above § 31, 1) places him among the erotic poets. The existence of Memoirs by Messalla (perhaps in Greek) concerning the battle of Philippi etc. may be inferred from Plut. Brut. 40. 42. 45, and Appian also seems to have used them (cf. e. g. b. c. 4, 38. 121). Suet. Aug. 74 *Valerius Messala tradit* etc. Plin. NH. 33, 50 *Messala orator prodidit* etc. Tac. ann. 4, 34. Pliny NH. in the ind. auct. of b. 9 (*ex . . . Messala Corvino*). 33 (*ex Corvino*). 35 (*ex Messala oratore*).—Plin. NH. 35, 8 *extat Messalae oratoris indignatio, quae prohibuit inseri genti suae Laevinorum alienam imaginem.*—Disquisitions in

epistolary form: SUET. gramm. 4 *eosdem litteratores vocitatos Messala Corvinus in quadam epistula ostendit.* QUINT. 1, 7, 35 *ideo minus Messala nitidus quia quosdam totos libellos non verbis modo singulis sed etiam litteris dedit?* cf. ib. 23 *Messala in libro de S littera.* 9, 4, 38 *quae fuit causa et Servio . . . subtrahendae S litterae* (at the end of a word, when the next word began with a consonant), *quod reprehendit Luranius* (*Veranius* BERGK, cf. § 199, 4), *Messala defendit.* Cf. ib. 1, 5, 15. RSCHÖLL (leg. XII tab. p. 36) supposes this treatise rather to refer to Messala the augur (§ 199, 2).

4. Poems in honour of Messalla: TIB. 1, 7 and others; a panegyric in TIB. 4, 1 (see § 245, 3). Elegia ad Messalam § 230, 5, n. 1.—In general see the treatises by CvHALL, Amsterd. 1820 II. LWIESE, Berl. 1829. JMJVALETON, Gröningen 1874. LFONTAINE, Versailles 1878. Cf. also EBÄHRENS, tibull. Blätter (Jena 1876) 49.—The treatise de progenie Augusti Caesaris, which bears the name of Messalla, is a production of the 15th cent., last edited by CHTZSCHUCKE, Lps. 1793, and RMECENATE, Rome 1820. Cf. HJORDAN, Herm. 3, 426 and esp. CFWEBER (and JCAESAR) de Mess. libello de pr. A., Marb. 1873. 74 II.

II. POETS.

223. The earliest of the poets of the Augustan period is L. Varius Rufus (c. 680/74–740/14), an admirer of Caesar, then of Octavianus, on both of whom he composed epic poems: but his celebrity was chiefly obtained by his tragedy of Thyestes (a. 725/29), and by his friendship with Vergil and Horace, especially by editing the former's Aeneid. Of about the same age with him, and also a friend of Vergil, was Aemilius Macer of Verona († 738/16), the author of didactic poems in the manner of Nicander, Ornithogonia, Theriaca and probably also on a botanical subject (de herbis).

1. That Varius was nearly of the same age with Helvius Cinna (§ 213, 2) and certainly older than Vergil, appears from VERG. ecl. 9, 35 *neque adhuc Vario videor nec dicere Cinna digna.* An epic poem on Caesar, de morte, specimens of which (12 hexameters) are given by MACR. 6, 1, 39. 6, 2, 19. FPR. 337. Hence HOR. sat. 1, 10, 51 *forte epos acer ut nemo Varius ducit.* An epic poem by Varius in praise of the deeds of Agrippa (and Octavianus) is meant by HOR. c. 1, 6, 1–4, and this hope was fulfilled according to PORPHYRIO on Hor. ep. 1, 16, 25 *versus 'Tene magis* etc.' . . . *sunt notissimo ex panegyrico Augusti;* ACRON ib.: *haec enim Varius de Augusto scripserat.* As an epic poet he is mentioned together with Vergil by HOR. ep. 2, 3, 55. Perhaps he also wrote elegies; PORPH. on Hor. c. 1, 6, 1 *fuit L. Varius et ipse carminis et tragoediarum* (but only his Thyestes is known) *et elegorum* (or *elegiarum*) *auctor, Vergilii contubernalis.* As a tragic poet he is mentioned by MART. 8, 18, 7. When Horace wrote ep. 2, 1, 247 (c. a. 742/12) Varius was dead.

2. A scholion in the Paris. 7530 s. VIII states (after the heading *Incipit Thuestes Varii*) *Lucius Varius cognomento Rufus Thyesten tragoediam magna cura absolutam post actiacam victoriam Augusti ludis eius* (a. 725/29 cf. DIO 51, 19. 21) *in scaena edidit. pro qua fabula sestertium deciens* (as a donation from the Emperor) *accepit.* FWSCHNEIDEWIN, RhM. 1, 106. 2, 638. A quotation from it in QUINT. 3, 8, 45. Two anapaestic fragments without mention of the play in RIBBECK, trag.[2]

229. QUINT. 10, 1, 98 *Varii Thyestes cuilibet graecarum comparari potest.* TAC. dial. 12 *nec ullus Asinii aut Messalae liber tam illustris est quam Medea Ovidii aut Varii Thyestes.* PHILARGYR. on Verg. ecl. 8, 10 *Varium, cuius exstat Thyestes tragoedia, omnibus tragicis praeferenda.* WELCKER, Trag. 3 (1841), 1426.

3. His relations to Augustus (HOR. ep, 2, 1, 245; he is probably also meant by QUINT. 6, 3, 78 *L. Vareus* [so in the MSS.] *Epicurius, Caesaris.* i.e. of Augustus—*amicus*, § 51, 1), Maecenas (paneg. in Pis. 238 *Maecenas tragico quatientem pulpita gestu evexit Varium;* cf. MART. 8, 56, 21. 12, 4, 1), Horace (whom Varius introduced to Maecenas, HOR. sat. 1, 6, 55; cf. 1, 5, 40. 93. 1, 9, 23. 1, 10, 81. 2, 8, 21. 63) and Vergil. A follower of the Epicurean Philodemos: AKÖRTE, RhM. 45, 172. For his edition of the Aeneid see § 228, 2. A work on Vergil, QUINT. 10, 3, 8 *Vergilium paucissimos die composuisse versus auctor est Varius.* Cf. GELL. 17, 10, 2 *amici familiaresque P. Vergilii in iis quae de ingenio moribusque eius memoriae tradiderunt.*—On the tragedy of Tereus (the Progne of GREG. CORRARIUS, Ven. 1558), falsely ascribed to Varius, see WEICHERT, de L. Vario 118.—AWEICHERT, de L. Varii et Cassi Parmensis vita et carminibus, Grimma 1836. RUNGER, de Valgii Rufi poematis (Hal. 1848) p. 296; L. Varii de morte eclogae reliquiae, Halle 1870. 78 II.

4. HIERONYM. on Eus. Chron. a. Abr. 2001 (in the cod. Bern. 2002)=738/16 *Aemilius Macer Veronensis poeta in Asia moritur.* SERV. Verg. ecl. 5, 1 *Mopsus (intellegitur) Aemilius Macer Veronensis poeta, amicus Vergilii.* OVID. trist. 4, 10, 43 *saepe suas volucres legit mihi grandior aevo quaeque necet serpens, quae iuvet herba Macer.* CATON. dist. 2, praef.: *quodsi mage nosse laboras herbarum vires, Macer haec tibi carmina dicit.* QUINT. 10, 1, 87 *Macer et Lucretius legendi quidem, sed non ut phrasin . . . faciant; elegantes in sua quisque materia, sed alter* (Macer) *humilis, alter difficilis.* ib. 56 *Nicandrum frustra secuti Macer atque Vergilius* (cf. § 241, 1 ad fin.) ? 12, 11, 27 *neque post Lucretium ac Macrum Vergilius.* 6, 3, 96 *Ovidius ex tetrastichon Macri carmine librum in malos poetas composuit* (but cf. § 252, 3). TIB. 2, 6, 1. MANIL. astr. 2, 43.

5. A hexameter from *Macer Aemilius ornithogonias secundo* quoted in DIOMED. GL. 1, 374, 21; cf. NON. 220, 18 *Licinius Macer in ornithogonia.* 518, 25 *Aemilius Macer in ornithogoniae libro I.* ISIDOR. orig. 12, 7, 19. SCHOL. BERN. Lucan. 9, 701 *serpentum nomina aut a Macro sumpsit de libris theriacon (nam duos edidit) aut* etc. CHARIS. GL. 1, 81, 18 *Macer theriacon;* cf. ISIDOR. orig. 12, 4, 24. RUNGER, Phil. 47, 555. Other quotations of a more vague character ap. SERV. Aen. 1, 435. SCHOL. BERN. georg. 2, 160. CHARIS. GL. 1, 65, 7. 107, 4. 113, 11. 14, also 72, 17. 100, 33; the two passages last cited and de dub. nom. GL. 5, 576, 5 ?) seem to be from his work on botany (UNGER p. 11). The fragments in FPR. 345. *Macer de herbis* was perhaps still known early in the Middle Ages: BÄHRENS, PLM. 3, 104. The work set down by BECKER, catal. bibl. antiq. 74, no. 82 as *Nucer de herbis* in the catalogue of the convent library at Blaubeuren s. XI/XII must be the so-called Macer Floridus *de viribus herbarum* (see below); cf. also BECKER l.l. 117, 481 *liber Macri de virtutibus herbarum.* PLINY NH. mentions Macer as one of his authorities on b. 9. 10. 11. 17, and it is therefore probable (UNGER p. 16) that also in b. 19. 21. 22. 28. 29. 32, where the list of authorities mentions Licinius Macer in reference to a similar subject, we have the same confusion of names as in NON. 220, 18 and DIOMED. GL. 1, 369, 15 (above § 156, 6).—For Macer in general see BROUKHUSIUS on Tib. 2, 6. p. 274. MAFFEI, Verona illustr. 3, 2, 41. RUNGER, de Macro Nicandri imitatore, Friedl. 1845.—The name of Macer Floridus or (Aemilius) Macer is erroneously given to the composition (in hexameters) of a certain French physician Odo Magdunensis (of Meun-sur-Loire) de viribus herbarum. X; see AEBERT, Lit. d. MA. 3, 351. VROSE, Hermes 8, 63.

224. P. Vergilius Maro was born at Andes near Mantua on Oct. 15, 684/70, in modest circumstances, but received a careful education. When, a. 713/41 and 714/40, his paternal estate had repeatedly been granted to veteran soldiers of Octavianus, the intercession of influential friends effected either restitution or indemnification. After that time, Vergil lived partly at Rome, partly in Campania (at Naples), in many ways impeded by his weak health, but gradually becoming possessed of comfortable means. After the completion and publication of his Bucolica (713/41–715/39) and Georgica (717/37–724/30), and when the Aeneid was already far advanced (he began it 725/29), Vergil wished to go to Athens and Asia for the further elaboration of his work, but at Athens he was persuaded by Augustus to return, and soon afterwards fell ill and died at Brundisium, Sept. 21, 735/19, shortly before the close of his fifty-first year.

1. Sources. a) Vita Vergilii de commentario Valeri Probi sublata, in HKeil, M. Valerii Probi comm. (Halle 1848) p. 1 and in Reifferscheid's Suetonius p. 42 cf. p. 398. OJahn's Persius p. cxli. This is a carelessly made abstract, but keeps free from fabulous fictions; ARiese, de commentario Vergil. Probi p. 24. Ribbeck, JJ. 87, 351.—b) Donatus' vita Vergilii ap. Reifferscheid l.l. p. 54 and HHagen suppl. vol. 4, 734; various readings from a Paris MS. in EWölfflin, Phil. 24, 153. It is prefixed to Aelius Donatus' commentary on Vergil (§ 409, 4), and is mostly derived, as is shown by diction and style, from Suetonius de viris illustribus, who himself owed most to the conscientious Asconius (§ 295, 2), who was in his turn indebted to the works of L. Varius (§ 223, 3) and C. Melissus (n. 4); it contains much valuable information, but is interpolated with additions from the commentary of Servius, especially several nonsensical fictions of the Middle Ages, which in the later MSS. are added to the original text. Cf. Reifferscheid l.l. 399. Hagen l.l. 676. JWBeck, JJ. 133, 502. The metrical work of Phocas is entirely dependent on Donatus' vita: see § 472, 4.—c) Hieronymus on Euseb. Chron. ad a. Abr. 1948. 1959. 1964. 1999 (or to the years immediately following). Also from Suetonius.—d) The vita bearing the name of Servius (prefixed to his commentary on the Aeneid), but which is not the genuine life mentioned by Servius in his introduction to the Bucolics p. 3, 25. 29 Thilo; see Reifferscheid l.l. 399. ORibbeck in his edition of the text of Vergil p. vii.—Finally we possess a vita of slight value in some MSS. of Vergil, e.g. two Bernese, a Monacencis and a Reginensis; see Reifferscheid l.l. 52. Hagen l.l. 745. A vita (without value) from a MS. at St. Paul in Carinthia s. VIII MPetschenig, Wien. Stud. 4, 168.—HNettleship, ancient lives of Vergil: with an essay on the poems of V., Lond. 1879.

2. Name. The inscriptions of the Republic and the first centuries of the Christian era are in favour of *Vergilius* (not *Virgilius*), so also the older MSS., e.g. the Medicean, and the Greeks also write almost invariably Βεργίλιος or Οὐεργίλιος. The earliest dated instance of the spelling *Virgilius* is saec. V a.d. (see § 439, 1). In the Middle Ages, from about saec. IX, the spelling *Virg.* began to be favoured, chiefly because of fictitious derivations of the name (from *virgo* or *virga*), and in the 14th and 15th centuries this became quite victorious. But even then Angelus

Politianus proved it to be an error. It has been defended by FSCHULTZ, orthogr. quaestt. (Paderb. 1855) p. 42. JOBERDICK, Studd. z. lat. Orthogr., Münst. 1879, 13; WschrfKlPh. 1889, 348. On the other side see EHÜBNER, JJ. 77, 360. HHAGEN, ib. 95, 608. THCREIZENACH, ib. 97, p. 294. FRITSCHL, op. 2, 779. Cf. THBERGK, Phil. 28, 441. JPOHL, in the Progr. of Linz am Rhein 1871, 14. But in German (and correspondingly in Eng. Fr. Ital. etc.) the poet is called 'Virgil.'

3. For the data as to the life of Vergil see esp. RIBBECK in his edition of the text (Bibl. Teubn. Lps. 1867) p. VIII, cf. also GTHILO introd. to his ed. Vergil's mother was called Magia Polla. His father was mercennarius or figulus and by his exertions gradually made a small fortune. The poet received his instruction at Cremona, after 696/58. After the assumption of the toga virilis (15 Oct. 699/55, § 203, 1) he went to Milan, and in 701/53 to Rome, where he *studuit apud Epidium oratorem* (§ 211, 4) *cum Caesare Augusto* (vita Bern.), though he pleaded only once. He engaged all the more zealously in the study of philosophy, in which he and (Alfenus) Varus (§ 208, 3) attended the Epicurean Siro (Σείρων, MHAUPT, op. 3, 334 and MADVIG on Cic. fin.[2] p. 336); he likewise studied mathematics and natural philosophy, also medicine. May he have lived in the neighbourhood of Tarentum?? PROP. 3, 34, 67. EHEYDENREICH in the commentatt. philol. semin. Lips. (1874), 20. It is not known when he returned to his native place. A. 713/41 the allotments of agri were extended from Cremona to the neighbouring territory of Mantua by the limitator Octavius Musa, and Vergil's paternal estate was assigned to a centurio called Arrius. Asinius Pollio and Cornelius Gallus interceded with Octavianus. At the end of the Perusine war, Octavianus replaced Pollio in Gallia transpadana by Alfenus Varus, a man devoted to him, who indeed promised to protect Vergil, but did not prevent the primipilaris Milienus Toro from possessing himself of his paternal estate, on which occasion Vergil was nearly killed by a certain Clodius. Vergil and his father then fled to an estate formerly belonging to Siro (Catal. 10). Cornelius (Gallus) and (Aemilius?) Macer advised him to go to Rome, where the poet, who had meanwhile become known through his Bucolics, was indemnified through Maecenas' intercession, perhaps in Campania (estate near Nola, GELL. 6, 20, 1). At the end of 715/39 Vergil was already so familiar with Maecenas that he could introduce Horace into his circle. A. 717/37 both met on the Iter Brundisinum, HOR. sat. 1, 5, 40. Horace addressed to Vergil c. 1, 3 (a προπεμπτικὸν for an Athenian journey of Vergil's, not for the last), 1, 24. 4, 12? Cf. BÜCHELER, coniectanea, Bonn 1878, 14. EWÖLFFLIN, Phil. 39, 367. —The rest of Vergil's life is not remarkable for any events of public interest. DONAT. vita 35 (51) *dum Megara . . . ferventissimo sole cognoscit languorem nactus est eumque non intermissa navigatione* (from Greece to Italy) *auxit ita ut aegrior aliquanto Brundisium appelleret, ubi diebus paucis obiit, XI Kal. Oct. C. Sentio Q. Lucretio coss.* Cf. HIERON. ad a. 2000. *Ossa eius Neapolim translata sunt.* A life of 52 years is assigned to him by Donatus and the vita in HHAGEN, JJ. Suppl. 4, 745; also AL. 560. 566. (PLM. 4, 129. 130).—The plot of land on which Vergil's grave was situated became subsequently the property of Silius Italicus (§ 231, 12 l. 9. 320, 1; cf. MART. 11, 48. 49). ECOCCHIA, la tomba di Virg., Turin 1888.

4. Personal appearance. DONATUS' vita 8 (19) *corpore et statura fuit grandi, aquilo colore, facie rusticana, varia valetudine. nam plerumque a stomacho* (HOR. sat. 1, 5, 49) *et a faucibus ac dolore capitis laborabat, sanguinem etiam saepe reiecit.* His portrait as a frontispiece to his works: MART. 14, 186 *Ipsius et vultus prima tabella gerit.* We do not possess any trustworthy portraits of the poet. Cf. BERNOULLI, röm. Ikonogr. 1, 246. DCOMPARETTI, Virgilio 1, 184. Portrait on the mosaic at Trèves, representing the Muses (Arch. Ges. Berlin, Sitz. 9. Dec. 1888).

DONATUS' vita 16 (27) *in sermone tardissimum ac paene indocto similem eum fuisse Melissus tradidit.* ib. 28 (43) *pronuntiabat autem* (his compositions) *cum suavitate tum lenociniis miris.*

5. Personal circumstances. DONATUS' vita 13 (24) *possedit prope centiens sestertium ex liberalitatibus amicorum* (HOR. ep. 2, 1, 246 with SCHOL. MART. 8, 56, 5. SERV. Aen. 6, 862) *habuitque domum Romae Esquiliis iuxta hortos Maecenatianos, quamquam secessu* (TAC. dial. 13) *Campaniae Siciliaeque plurimum uteretur.* As Vergil lived very moderately, he might easily leave a considerable fortune. DONATUS 37 (56) *heredes fecit ex dimidia parte Valerium Proculum fratrem alio patre, ex quarta Augustum, ex duodecima Maecenatem, ex reliqua* (each $^1/_{12}$) *L. Varium et Plotium Tuccam.* Vergil had never been married.

225. Vergil was a childlike, innocent and amiable character, tender, sincere, and peaceful, a good son and faithful friend, honourable and high-minded, full of devotion both to persons and ideal interests, but not competent to grapple with the tasks and difficulties of practical life. If he had enemies notwithstanding, they were not personal adversaries, but opponents in regard to his political and literary position. Something similar to his personal character may be traced in his works. He is most successful in such subjects as call for or admit of a genial treatment, for instance, inanimate nature, his native country, family-ties, or love. But, weak and pliable as he was, and groping for his themes without the sure instinct of genius, he allowed himself to be led on to subjects for which his talent was imperfectly adapted. He collected his materials for these, and studied the Greek authors with the pertinacity of a scholar; he worked up his design and polished his diction deliberately and exactingly with the industry of a miniature-painter, and he did actually obtain—in the opinion of his contemporaries and of the following centuries—the highest honours both for epic and didactic poetry, and his manner and style became for a long period the models for Roman poets.

1. See for the details of the above characterisation TEUFFEL, PRE. 6, 2648.

2. His character as a man. Horace (sat. 1, 5, 54) calls Vergil *optimus* and (ib. 1, 5, 40) *anima candida.* See DONATUS' vita, e.g. 11 (22): *et ore et animo tam probum constat ut Neapoli Παρθενίας vulgo appellatus sit ac si quando Romae, quo rarissime commeabat, viseretur in publico sectantes demonstrantesque se subterfugeret in proximum tectum.* There is nothing in the scandal recorded by DONATUS 9 (20) on his love-affair with his favourite slave Alexander (=Alexis in ecl. 2. MART. 5, 16, 2, on which see Friedländer) and with Kebes, as well as with Plotia Hieria, an amica of L. Varius (HHAGEN in RIBBECK's prolegg. p. VI, who might also have quoted the Greek name as evidence; see also EWÖLFFLIN, Phil. 24, 154). Ib. 12 (23) *bona cuiusdam exulantis offerente Augusto non sustinuit accipere.*

3. Donat. 43 (61) *obtrectatores Vergilio numquam defuerunt.* As such he mentions Numitorius with his Antibucolica (§ 226, n. 1), the Aeneidomastix of Carvilius Pictor (Serv. ecl. 2, 23 *hunc versum male distinguens Vergiliomastix vituperat*), Herennius, who *tantum vitia eius*, Perellius Faustus, who *furta (eius) contraxit. sunt et Q. Octavi Aviti* ὁμοιοτήτων (*homoeotheleuton* in the MSS.) *octo volumina, quae quos et unde versus transtulerit continent*, ib. 43–45 (61–63). To these we should add Bavius and Mevius (§ 233, 2), Anser a partisan of Antony (very doubtful, see below § 233, 3), Cornificius (§ 209, 2 ad fin.), subsequently Caligula (Suet. Cal. 34) and others. Echoes of these hostile criticisms in Macr. sat. 1, 24, 6. 3, 10–12 and especially 5, 3–16 on supposed furta by Vergil. On the other hand, Asconius Pedianus wrote a liber contra obtrectatores Vergilii, Donatus 46 (64). Cf. Ribbeck's prolegomena 96 and below § 295, 2.

4. Hor. sat. 1, 10, 45 *molle atque facetum Vergilio annuerunt . . . Camenae.* Descriptions of inanimate nature occur in the ecl. and georg., also Aen. 5, 213. 9, 435. 11, 68; of a semi-idyllic character are also Aen. 4, 803 sqq. 11, 456; cf. 12, 473. He describes some plants in a strikingly picturesque manner, EMeyer, Gesch. d. Botanik 1, 374. His patriotic warmth ge. 2, 136. Aen. 6, 809. 842. He sympathises with family happiness and the grief of a mother ge. 2, 523. Aen. 6, 680. 8, 408. 9, 283. 475; cf. also the pathetic passage on Marcellus at the end of Aen. 6 (860). The whole fourth book of the Aeneid attests Vergil's sense of love, and this may be pronounced the most successful part of the whole. There is hardly a trace of sarcasm in Vergil, see WHertzberg on Aen. 12, 321. But cf. also p. 445, l. 27. All his characters bear the stamp of mild humanity, free from harshness and ruggedness, but also devoid of energy. ECollilieux, la couleur locale dans l'Énéide, Par. 1881, has counted in Vergil 20 expressions for joy and happiness occurring in 314 passages, against 58 which express pain and sorrow, in 1071 passages!

5. Quint. 10, 3, 8 *Vergilium paucissimos die composuisse versus auctor est Varius* (§ 223, 3); cf. ib. 10, 1, 86 *curae et diligentiae vel ideo in Vergilio plus* (than in Homer) *est quod ei fuit magis laborandum et quantum eminentibus vincimur fortasse aequalitate pensamus* (but this very *aequalitas*, if there is nothing to interrupt it, ends by becoming monotonous). Gell. 17, 10, 2. Donat. vita 22 (33) cf. 34 (49). To the Georgics Vergil devoted at least 7 years, and on the Aeneid he had already bestowed at least 10 and thought of devoting to it another *triennium continuum* (Donatus 35 = 51), after which time he wished to leave off writing and to devote himself to a contemplative life (*ut reliqua vita tantum philosophiae vacaret*, Donat. l.l.). Writing poetry was to him a labour, the end of which he longed to see. The unpractical scholar often betrays himself in Vergil's poems, e.g. ge. 1, 281. 3, 26. 4, 408. PhWagner in Heyne's ed. 4 p. 590. WHertzberg on Aen. 8, 660. 708. 726. As to his want of originality, see our observations on each of his poems and the collections by FUrsinus, Virgilius collatione graecorum scriptorum illustratus, Antv. 1568, Leov. 1747. FGEichhoff, études grecques sur Virgile, Paris 1825 III. Also WRibbeck in his brother's edition. RWöhler, Einfl. des Lucrez. auf die Dichter der august. Zeit I (Virgil), Greifsw. 1876.

6. In his political views, Vergil was a thorough Augustan. It is true, he fondly glances back at Rome's great past (*Vergilius, amantissimus vetustatis*, Quint. 1, 7, 18), but in his own time he rejoices above all at the restoration of peace and takes every opportunity of praising the author of the new order. Yet he has been spared the charge of servility which has been brought against Horace with so much noise, perhaps because he was looked upon as less politically accountable. Compared

with Antony, the cause of Octavianus appears also to Vergil (see above p. 403, n. 1) to be the national cause, Aen. 8, 685 sqq. A philosophical theory of life is nowhere prominent; here also all is resolved into tender-heartedness. See however ALDENHOVEN, über den virgilischen Fatalismus, Ratezeb. 1850. RDIETSCH, theologumenon Vergilianorum particula, Grimma 1853. GBOISSIER, la religion romaine 1 (Par. 1874), 250. 178.

7. Language, metre etc. (see also below under the separate works): Indices verborum by NERYTHRAEUS, CRUAEUS and others see § 231, 10. GAKOCH (and KEGEORGES), Wörterb. zu Verg., Hanov. [6] 1885. JBGREENOUGH, a special vocabulary to Virg., Lond. 1883. PHWAGNER, quaestt. Verg. in Heyne's ed. 4, p. 383.—RWOTKE, alte Formen bei V., Wien. Stud. 8, 131. EVFEISTMANTEL, die Deklin. der griech. Eigennamen bei Verg., Baden 1867. ESIEGEL, die nom. propria (Greek forms) in der Aen., Budweis 1887. PETERSSON and UDDGREN, de syntaxi Verg. quaestt., Upsala 1853. PHSPITTA, quaestt. Verg. (on the use of the plural to designate a single object or conception), Gött. 1867. FSASS, de numero plurali (in Verg.), Kiel 1873. ESEYSS, d. Plur. der substant. Abstr. in V.s Aen., Iglau 1882. FANTOINE, de casuum syntaxi vergil., Par. 1883. CRANTZ, der Accus. bei V., Düren 1871. HDITTEL, der Dativ bei V., Innsbruck 1873. HKERN, z. Gebr. d. Abl. b. V., Schweinfurt 1881. CSCHÜLER, quaestt. Verg. (c. 2: de abl. usu V.), Greifsw. 1883. WVSTELTZER, d. Gebr. des Inf. bei Verg., Nordhausen 1875. CHJÄNICKE, die sog. Gräcismen im Gebr. des Inf. bei Verg., Oberhollabrunn 1874. FMAIXNER, de infinitivi usu Verg., Leipz. (Agram) 1877. HKRAUSE, de Verg. usurpatione infinitivi, Halle 1878. EWEISSENBORN, d. Satz u. Periodenbau in V.s Aen., Mühlhausen i/Th. 1879. JLEY, Verg. quaestt. spec. I: de temporum usu (that is on the peculiar use of the praes. hist. and perf.), Saarbrücken 1877; ZfGW. 36, 111. PLACEK, de RE in compositis in Verg. Aen., Budweis 1882. MKRAFFT, z. Wortstellung V.s, Goslar 1887. PVBOLTENSTERN, d. Wortstellung, bes. die Stell. d. Präpp. in V.s Aen., Dramb. 1880. Über die Wortsymmetrie i. d. Aen. JKVIČALA, neue Beitr. z. Erkl. d. Aen. (1881) 274; üb. d. Alliteration in d. Aen. (with great exaggerations), ib. 293.—STSOBIESKI, Vergil u. Ovid nach ihren Gleichnissen, Lemberg 1861. THEPPELIN, die Vergleichungen V.s, Lahr 1862. WHORNBOSTEL, die Gleichnisse bei V., Ratzeb. 1870. HOUBEN, de comparationibus Verg., Düsseld. 1876. AKRONDL, quae potiss. V. similitudinibus illustraverit, Prerau 1878. GKOPETSCH, de comparatt. Verg., Lyck 1879. CASPERS, de comparatt. Verg., Hagenau 1883. ZIMMERMANN, BlfdbayrGW. 1870, 221. CGJACOB, de epithetorum nonnullorum ap. Verg. vi et natura, Cologne 1829; quaestt. epicae, Quedlinb. 1839. LCHOLEVIUS, epitheta ornantia ap. Verg. et posteriores I, Königsb. 1865. LÜNZNER, üb. Personificationen in V.s Ged., Gütersloh 1876. WHERTZBERG's Aeneis (Stuttg. 1859) p. XIV (on V.'s employment of hypallage, metonymy and hendiadys). RBRAUMÜLLER, üb. Tropen u. Figuren in V.s Aen., Berl. 1877. 82 II. THLADEWIG, de V. verborum novatore I, Neustrelitz 1869. HLÖWE, de elocutione Verg., Grimma 1873. Cf. also § 282, 6.—On Vergil's great care in polishing his lines, see LMÜLLER; de re metr. 140. 183. 190. Also WGOSSRAU, de hexam. Verg. in his ed. MWDROBISCH, Lpz. SBer. 1866, 75. 1868, 18. 138. 1871, 1. 1872, 1. 1873, 7. CSCHAPER, de georg. a Verg. emend. 39. THBIRT, hist. hex. lat. 39. JWCLOUGH, the hexameter of V., Boston 1880. PKLEINECKE, de penthem. et hephthemimere caesuris a Verg. (esp. in ecl. et georg.) usurpatis, Halle 1882. JWALSER, ZföG. 33, 1 (caes. κ. τρίτ. τροχ.). IDRAHEIM, de Verg. arte rhythmica, JJ. 129, 70. THFRANZEN, d. Untersch. des Hex. b. V., u. Hor., Crefeld 1881. EALBRECHT, wiederholte Verse u. Versteile b. V., Herm. 16, 393 (with addenda, ZfGW. 36, Jahresber. 243).

226. The extant poems of Vergil are in the following list arranged according to the date of their composition.

The number of lines in the whole of the Vergilian poems is given in an epigram (AL. 717 PLM. 4, 178) as 12,847. Our Vergil MSS. give 12,912 lines. On the variation see ThBirt, Buchwesen, 174.

1) Bucolica, ten poems. written 713/41–715/39, imitations, partly almost translations, of Theokritos, but with an artificial admixture of persons and events of contemporaneous history. The symmetrical composition of these poems cannot be doubted, but neither can a uniform strophic arrangement be demonstrated.

1. Donatus' vita 19 (30) *cum res romanas incohasset offensus materia* (cf. Serv. ecl. 6, 3 *Aeneidem aut gesta regum Albanorum, quae coepta omisit nominum asperitate deterritus*) *ad bucolica transiit, maxime ut Asinium Pollionem Alfenumque Varum et Cornelium Gallum celebraret, quia in distributione agrorum . . . indemnem se praestitissent.* 25 (40) *bucolica triennio . . . perfecit.* Cf. Prob. p. 7, 7 K. *cum certum sit eum, ut Asconius Pedianus dicit, XXVIII annos natum*,—i.e. end of 712/42—*bucolica edidisse;* cf. Serv. ecl. p. 3, 26 Th. Servius' vita Verg. p. 2, 8 Th. *tunc ei proposuit Pollio ut carmen bucolicum scriberet, quod eum constat triennio scripsisse et emendasse.* Don. 26 (41) *bucolica eo successu edidit ut in scena quoque per cantores crebro pronuntiarentur* (cf. Tac. dial. 13. Serv. ecl. 6, 11). 43 (61) *prolatis bucolicis Numitorius quidam rescripsit antibucolica, duas modo eclogas, sed insulsissime,* παρῳδήσας, *quarum prioris initium est 'Tityre, si toga calda tibi, quo tegmine fagi?', sequentis 'Dic mihi, Damoeta, cuium pecus? anne latinum? non, verum Aegonis nostri sic rure locuntur.'* The individual poems are called in the MSS. *eclogae* (eglogae): cf. § 29, 1. 273, 1. Amongst them, ecl. 10 is confessedly the last composed; ecl. 1 and 9, 4 and 8, and 6 contain hints for fixing their date of composition; of 5 it may at least be stated that it was written after 2 and 3, in both of which, and in ecl. 7, which is similar, the bucolic subject-matter is least alloyed with historical allusions, for which reason they are perhaps the earliest pieces of the whole collection. See Ribbeck, prolegg. p. 1. CSchaper (JJ. 89, 633. 769; de ecl. Verg. interpr. et emend., Posen 1872; de georg. a Verg. emendatis, Berl. 1873; in his introd. to Ladewig's ed.; symb. Ioachim. [Berl. 1880] 1, 3; JB. 1882 2, 133) has advanced the erroneous opinion that ecl. 4. 6. 10 are considerably later than the others which were composed between 712/42–716/38, and that they were not written until between 727/27–729/25. Against this see Ribbeck l.l. p. 13. RBitschofsky, quibus temporibus quoque ordine Verg. eclogas composuerit, Stokerau 1876. EKrause, quib. tempp. quoque ordine V. ecl. scripserit, Berl. 1884. APrzygode, de ecl. V. tempp., Berl. 1885. AFeilchenfeld, de V. buc. tempp., Lpz. 1886. The Bucolica appear to have been published separately at first and they had separate headings (ecl. 6, 12). From georg. 4, 566 it is evident that in publishing the whole collection Vergil himself assigned the first place to ecl. 1, and thus perhaps the whole arrangement may be due to him; cf. Ov. am. 1, 15, 25.

2. With regard to Theokritos the eclogues show a procedure very much like the contamination in the poets of palliatae (§ 16, 9): e.g. ecl. 3 is constructed after Theokritos id. 4 and 5; ecl. 8 after Theokr. id. 1 and 2. A comparison with the Greek poet is rarely in favour of the Roman imitator, and in many places it is very evident how Theokritos is spoilt, cf. e.g. 8, 43 by the side of Theokr. 3, 18.

Altogether these rustic poems are the least successful works of the poet; they are devoid of all rustic freshness, the heavy air of the study is rather suggested in the affected formality of the style, the superficiality of the characterisation, the want of dramatic life, the confusion between the ostensible and the deeper meaning, and the constant admixture of things unsuited to the Graeco-Sicilian form which the poet has adopted. Tityrus (ecl. 1) and Menalcas (ecl. 5. 9) properly denote Vergil himself, Daphnis (ecl. 5) is Caesar; in ecl. 3, 84 there is a sudden transition from bucolic surroundings to Pollio and Bavius and Mevius (§ 225, 3) etc. Ecl. 4, the bombastic and exaggerated prophecy of a new golden age, is entirely foreign to the bucolic style. Cf. CPeter, Gesch. Roms 3, 105.—Gell. 9, 9, 4 sqq. GAGebauer, de poett. graec. bucol., imprimis Theocriti, carmm. in eclogis a V. expressis, vol. I. Lps. 1861; quatenus V. in epithetis imitatus sit Theocritum, Zwickau 1863. EBüttner, d. Verh. v. V.s ecl. zu Theokr., Insterb. 1873.

3. The fashionable theory of strophic composition was applied to the eclogues by ORibbeck, JJ. 75, 65, and subsequently in his editions; likewise WHKolster, V.s Eklogen in ihrer stroph. Gliederung nachgewiesen mit Commentar, Lpz. 1882. RMaxa, ad stroph. Verg. compositionem (zu ecl. 10), Trebitsch 1878; d. stroph. Glieder. in V.s ecl. 2 u. 10 nachgewiesen, Treb. 1882. Cf. RPeiper, JJ. 91, 344. 95, 456. 97, 167. Westphal, griech. Metrik 2 (1868), xviii and the sober opinion of PhWagner, Phil. Suppl. 1, 396. This hypothesis cannot hold its ground against an unprejudiced examination of the eclogues themselves. That which is a matter of course in the amoebaean songs (e.g. 3, 60. 7, 21) should not be extended to the poems as a whole. See also Madvig, adv. 2, 29. 110. Haag, de ratione strophica carm. buc. Verg., Berl. 1875.

4. Vergil's rustic poems (text, transl. and explanation) by JHVoss (I and II Buc., III and IV Georg.) Altona 1789–97 (²1800–30) IV. Ecl. and georg. by ChAnthon, Lond.² 1882. By ASidgwick, Cambr. 1887. Virg. Buc. erkl. v. EGlaser, Halle 1876. Kolster's commentary on the buc. see n. 3.—A translation by CNOsiander, Stuttg. 1834 and 1853. FWGenthe, V.s Ekl. metr. übers. m. Einl. üb. V.s Leben u. Fortleben als Dichter u. Zauberer etc., Lpz.² 1855. A translation (with georg. and youthful poems) by WBinder, Stuttg. 1856 and HDütschke (ecl. and georg.), Stuttg. 1884. In English verse by CSCalverley, Camb. 1866. SPalmer, Lond. 1883.

5. PHofmann-Peerlkamp, ad Virgilium (ecl. and georg.), Mnemos. 10, 1. 113. 229. 367. ThLadewig, Beurteilung der Peerlkampschen Bem. z. d. ländl. Gedd. V.s, Neustrelitz 1864.

6. CSchaper, de eclogis Verg. interpretandis et emendandis, Posen 1872. EGlaser, V. als Naturdichter u. Theist; Einl. zu Buk. u. Georg., Gütersloh 1880. —GBippart, Beitr. z. Erkl. u. Krit. d. V. (ecl. 1 und 2), Prague 1869 (=Abh. d. k. böhm. Ges. d. Wiss. 6, 2). FDChanguion, Virgil and Pollio, an essay on V.s ecl. 2–5, Basle 1876. PWFreymüller, die messianische (! see however § 231, 4) Weissagung in V.s ecl. 4, Metten 1852. GFSchömann, op. 1, 50. LGiesebrecht, Damaris 2 (1861), 197. WGebhardt, ZfGW. 28, 561. RHoffmann, de V. ecl. IV. interpretanda, Rossleben 1877. ThPlüss, JJ. 101, 146. 115, 69. PAHWimmers, de Verg. ecl. quarta, Münst. 1874. OHellinghaus, de V. ecl. IV, Münst. 1875. OGruppe, Culte und Mythen 1, 687. MSonntag, z. Erkl. virg. Ekl. (4 and 10), Frankf. a/O. 1886. RMaxa, ZföG. 34, 249. On ecl. 6 GKettner, ZfGW. 32, 385. HFlach, JJ. 117, 633. CSchaper, ib. 859. On ecl. 8 FCGöbbel, de V. ecl. VIII, de Theocr. id. I et II etc., Warendorf 1862. JVahlen, Berl. ind. lect. 1888. EvLeutsch, Phil. 22, 214. RPeiper, JJ. 89, 456. JHuemer, ZföG. 28, 421. On ecl. 2. 4. 10 EGlaser,

Verh. der Geraer Phil.-Vers. (Lpz. 1879) 55; phil. Anz. 9, 646; JJ. 121, 247. GGevers, die 10 Ecl. des V. eine Parodie, Verden 1864 (also PhWagner, JJ. 91, 773). HFlach, JJ. 119, 791.—StSteffani, Archaismen u. Vulgarismen in V.s ecl., Mitterb. 1884. KBrandt, de re metr. in ecl. V., in the Festschr., Salzwedel 1882. —Literary reviews (on the Ecl. und Georg.) by H and ThFritzsche, JB. 1873, 308. 1874/75 1, 254. 1876 2, 128. 1877 2, 76. CSchaper ib. 1882 2, 112. See also § 228, 9 ad fin. Edition by FHermes, Dessau 1890. Ecl. 4: CPascal, Turin 1888. Ecl. 8: M. Sonntag, WschrfKlPh. 1888, 1413.

227. 2) Georgica, four books, written 717/37–724/30. The first book treats of agriculture, the second of the cultivation of trees, the third of domestic animals, and the fourth of bees. It is a didactic poem, written at the behest of and dedicated to Maecenas, but on a subject so well suited to the personal inclinations and gifts of the poet, that in it the pre-eminent qualities of the Vergilian muse were able to develop themselves most freely and luxuriantly. The subject is treated with evident love and the enthusiasm which belongs to thorough knowledge, and glorified and idealised as much as its character permitted, so that even the didactic parts are not essentially different in tone from those which are purely poetical. The poem has thus been rendered the most perfect of the larger productions of Roman art-poetry.

1. Donatus' vita 20 (31) *deinde* (after his Buc.) *edidit georgica in honorem Maecenatis.* 25 (40) *georgica septem . . . perfecit annis.* (cf. Serv. vita Verg. p. 2, 9 Th. *item proposuit Maecenas georgica, quae scripsit emendavitque septem annis.*) 27 (42) *georgica reverso post actiacam victoriam Augusto atque Atellae reficiendarum faucium causa commoranti per continuum quadriduum legit, suscipiente Maecenate legendi vicem quotiens interpellaretur ipse vocis offensione.* We see that the work was quite ready (about the middle of a. 725/29); it was fit for publication and may have been so for several months already. That the publication was then not delayed much longer, appears probable on account of the beginning of the elaboration of the Aeneid. A second edition by Vergil himself may be inferred from Serv. ecl. 10. 1 *fuit autem* (Cornelius Gallus, see § 232) *amicus Vergilii, adeo ut quartus georgicorum* (*liber*) *a medio* (l. 315 sqq.) *usque ad finem eius laudes teneret, quas postea* (after Gallus' disgrace and death, a. 727/27) *iubente Augusto in Aristaei fabulam commutavit.* See on georg. 4, 14 *sciendum . . . ultimam partem huius libri esse mutatam. nam laudes Galli habuit locus ille qui nunc Aristaei et Orphei continet fabulam, quae inserta est postquam irato Augusto Gallus occisus est* (the statements are impugned by EKlebs, de scriptoribus aet. Sullanae, Berl. 1876, p. 66. JWang, de Serv. ad V. ecl. 10, 1 et georg. 4, 1 annotatis, Klagenfurt 1883). A proposal of this kind would never have been made to Horace, much less would he have acted on it. But Vergil yielded to it, and a second edition was accordingly published about 729/25, this re-issue being of course intended for publicity. But it is in itself probable that the poet introduced other changes also, and some traces seem to point to this quite positively (Ribbeck, prolegg. 23. 24. 30); but they cannot have been very thorough, as even in the present shape of the work no allusion carries us earlier than 717/37 or later than 724/30 or 725/29

(ib. p. 14). A third edition may be inferred from DONATUS' vita 40 (53) *Vario ac simul Tuccae scripta sua sub ea condictione legavit ne quid ederent quod non a se editum esset*, as this implies authority to republish the Bucolics and Georgics. It may be granted that in a third edition by another hand and after two different earlier editions some errors might arise; but it is preposterous to speak of the unfinished state of the Georgics, as both beginning and end show that the poet, for his part, completed the work. The criticism in RIBBECK's Prolegg. p. 31–48 touches only insignificant details, or proves, if anything, that the poem might perhaps have been made more perfect than it actually is. ATITTLER, die Zeit der Veröffentlichung der Georg., Brieg 1857. CSCHAPER, de georgicis a Vergilio emendatis, Berl. 1873 (date of composition 723/31–725/29, when it was published, new ed. 729/25; against this ORIBBECK. Jen. LZ. 1874, 315. EGLASER, JJ. 109, 570). FBORGIUS, de tempp. quibus Verg. georg. scripta et perfecta sint, Halle 1875. CONINGTON, journ. of phil. 1, 54. 124.

2. For the subject-matter Vergil availed himself of his personal observation and experience in his youth. But his whole bent of mind would also induce him to consult other works, especially as both Greek and Roman literature abounded in works on agriculture (see § 54). SERV. georg. 1, 43 *sane sciendum Xenophontem scripsisse unum librum oeconomicum, cuius pars ultima agriculturam continet. de qua parte multa ad hoc opus Vergilius transtulit* (? see MORSCH l.l. 84) *sicut etiam de georgicis Magonis Afri* (§ 54, 1), *Catonis* (§ 122), *Varronis* (§ 168), *Ciceronis quoque libro tertio oeconomicorum* (§ 177ª, 2), *qui agriculturam continet.* On Hyginus see § 262, 3. QUINT. 10, 1, 56 *quid? . . . Nicandrum* (for the fragments of his γεωργικά see OSCHNEIDER, Nicandrea, p. 79) *frustra secuti sunt Macer atque Vergilius?* and MACR. 5, 22, 9 *Nicander huius est auctor historiae* (in georg. 3, 391); cf. SERV. georg. 2, 215. In the passage from Quintilian quoted above, it is not allowable to write (with RUNGER) *Macer atque Valgius* (§ 241, 1); this is shown by the words in QUINTILIAN immediately following: *quid? Euphorionem transibimus? quem nisi probasset Vergilius idem, numquam* etc. Cf. HMORSCH l.l. 52. OSCHNEIDER l.l. p. 74. MACR. 5, 2, 4 *vulgo nota sunt quod* (*Vergilius*) *Theocritum sibi fecerit pastoralis operis auctorem, ruralis Hesiodum et quod in ipsis georgicis tempestatis serenitatisque signa de Arati phaenomenis traxerit.* GELL. 9, 9, 3 *scite et considerate Vergilius, cum aut Homeri aut Hesiodi aut Apollonii aut Parthenii* (cf. ib. 13, 27, 1) *aut Callimachi aut Theocriti aut quorundam aliorum locos effingeret, partem reliquit, alia expressit.* PROB. in georg. p. 42, 13 K. *hanc universam disputationem* (georg. 1, 233) *certum est Vergilium transtulisse ab Eratosthene, cuius liber est hexametris versibus scriptus, qui Hermes inscribitur.* PLIN. NH. 18, 321 *Vergilius etiam in numeros lunae digerenda quaedam putavit, Democriti secutus ostentationem.* But the constant use of one principal author cannot be proved.—AKNOCHE, Verg. graeca exempla in georg., Lips. 1877. HMORSCH, de graec. auctoribus in georg. a Verg. expressis, Halle 1878. KBRANDT, de auctoribus quos in componendis georg. libr. adumbraverit Verg., Salzwedel 1884.—According to SUIDAS v. Ἀρριανός a certain Arrianos composed μετάφρασιν τῶν γεωργικῶν τοῦ Βεργιλλίου ἐπικῶς. Cf. MEINEKE, anal. alex. 370. COLUMELLA is an ardent admirer of the Georg. (3, 1, 1. 7, 1, 3. 10, praef. 3 and v. 433 sqq.).

3. Editions by GWAKEFIELD, Cantabrig. 1788, JHVOSS (see § 226, 4), EGLASER, Halle 1872, JMARTYN, transl. and notes, Lond. 1811, TKEIGHTLEY (with Bucol.), Lond. 1848, CSJERRAM (forthcoming).—Translations by FWGENTHE (Quedlinb. 1829). CNOSIANDER (Stuttg. 1835 and 1853). FOvNORDENFLYCHT (Bks. 1–3, Bresl. 1876). RDBLACKMORE, Lond. 1871 (verse). JWMACKAIL, Lond. 1889 (with Ecl., prose). On the Georgica see in HEYNE-WAGNER's ed. 1, 265 and others. OHANOW, schedae

crit. ad V. georg., Lissa 1863; ZfGW. 17, 78. FBockemüller, V. G. nach Plan u. Motiven erklärt, Stade 1873. KBossler, z. Erkl. v. V. Georg., Darmst. 1872. Mommsen, zu den Scholien der Georg., RhM. 16, 422; cf. 17, 143. HSeemann, annotatt. in ge. 4, 1-314, Neisse 1870. WHKolster, JJ. 125, 693. 133, 349. IvanWageninen, de Verg. georg., Utr. 1888. HRostagno, Verg. quae rom. exempla secutus sit in georg., Flor. 1888.—On the metre of the Georg. cf. Schaper (n. 4 in fin.) p. 40 together with ORibbeck, Jenaer LZ. 1874, 316.

228. 3) Aeneis, twelve books, commenced c. 725/29 but not completed when the poet died (a. 735/19) and published by L.Varius and Tucca contrary to his express desire. The Aeneid turns on the fortunes of Aeneas, the founder of a second Ilium and indirectly of Rome, and the ancestor of the Julian family. The great difficulties, which are inseparable from the literary epic, were in the case of Vergil heightened by the subject he had chosen. Naevius and Ennius in their heroic poems narrated to the Romans the great deeds of their forefathers and thus could count upon the sympathy of their readers: Vergil undertook to interest them in a hero who was neither a Roman nor an Italian, whose connection with Rome was based on a literary legend, or even on an imposition, a hero whose personality, whose deeds had no hold on the people, and on whose behalf Vergil had to awaken an interest in his readers by inventing for him artificial links and connections both with the past and the present. He could not, as did the Greeks, draw materials ready to his hand from the living spring of legend or from history, but was obliged to amass them laboriously for himself, and to cast them in a poetic mould, struggling as best he could with the barren and intractable Italian tradition. For this purpose the poet partly availed himself of the Greek epic writers, and partly relied on his extensive studies of native legends, customs, traditions and localities; he blended Greek and Italian characteristics, and thus formed for his narrative a background which, though consistent, was artificial and far removed from the Homeric truth to nature. On the whole, whoever compares Vergil with his unapproached and unapproachable model, Homer, will find him sadly wanting in the creative and inventive faculty, fresh resource, simplicity and vivacity. The events are but superficially explained, for the action, except in the second and fourth book, is halting, the personages are not sharply defined and characterised and distinct from one another, and the hero himself is weak and leaves us indifferent. Yet in spite of all this Vergil succeeded in creating for his country a national and patriotic although somewhat courtly epic, which did

ample justice to the times in which he lived, and for which his contemporaries and posterity rewarded the poet with extravagant admiration. And indeed, unreserved praise is due to the solemn, dignified, and truly Roman tone and colouring of the whole, to the splendour of the descriptions, to the psychological analysis, where the rhetorical and lyrical bent of the poet manifests itself in peculiar delicacy and deep insight, and lastly to the gorgeous richness and masterly handling in diction and versification. Roman and Romance ears have always been charmed with this aristocratic elegance, and we feel at least the music of his sonorous and beautiful lines.

1. From the promise georg. 3, 46 (*mox tamen ardentis accingar dicere pugnas Caesaris*, etc.) we should rather infer an epic poem in honour of Octavianus, but with the Emperor's approbation (or according to Servius at his desire) the subject was extended. About 728/26 Propertius was already acquainted with this extension of the design: see Prop. 3, 34, 61. Cf. Donat. 30 (45), ib. 25 (40) *Aeneida XI perfecit* (relatively speaking) *annis*. 23 (34) *Aeneida prosa prius oratione firmatam digestamque in XII libros particulatim componere instituit, prout liberet quidque, et nihil in ordinem accipiens.* (23=35) *ac ne quid impetum moraretur quaedam imperfecta transmisit, alia levissimis verbis veluti fulsit, quos per iocum pro tibicinibus interponi aiebat ad sustinendum opus, donec solidae columbae advenirent.* Hence we learn that Vergil attacked the poetical elaboration of his prose-sketch in various places, just as his inclination prompted him, not keeping to the order of his design. By this method of work a quantity of rather incongruous matter must have been produced, and also, in the course of time, poetic motives may have become transformed and new ones introduced: it was intended that these irregularities should be removed and smoothed down (§ 225, 5) in the three years' revision which Vergil contemplated. CHäberlin, Phil. 47. 310. Conjectures as to the earlier or later elaboration of the separate books in FConrads' work (n. 4). HGeorgii, on b. 3 of the Aeneid (Festschr. der Gymn. Württemb., Stuttg. 1877, 63), RSabbadini, riv. di fil. 15, 1. Donat. 30 (45) *Aeneidos vixdum coeptae tanta exstitit fama ut Sex. Propertius non dubitaverit sic praedicare* (see above), (31=46) *Augustus vero—nam forte expeditione Cantabrica* (a. 729/25) *aberat—supplicibus atque etiam minacibus per iocum litteris efflagitaret ut 'sibi de Aeneide prima carminis ὑπογραφὴ vel quodlibet κῶλον mitteretur.' cui tamen multo post perfectaque demum materia* (which does not include diction and style of the whole) *tres omnino libros recitavit, secundum, quartum et sextum.* GBoissier, rev. de phil. 8, 1 conjectures not without probability that the Aeneid was published a. 737/17 (cf. n. 2 l. 8), as Horace first mentions the legend of Aeneas in the carm. saec. (cf. Kiessling on Hor. c. saec. 49) and afterwards with increasing frequency. Cf. § 234, 6 ad fin.

2. Donatus' vita 39 (62) *egerat* (*Vergilius*) *cum Vario, prius quam Italia decederet, ut si quid ipsi accidisset Aeneida combureret; at is ita facturum se pernegarat; igitur in extrema valitudine assidue scrinia desideravit crematurus ipse; verum nemine offerente nihil quidem nominatim de ea cavit.* (40=53) *ceterum eidem Vario ac simul Tuccae* (*Plotius Tucca* Donat. 37=56) *scripta sua sub ea condicione legavit ne quid ederent quod non a se editum esset.* (41=59) *edidit autem auctore Augusto Varius, sed summatim emendata, ut qui versus etiam imperfectos sicut*

erant reliquerit. Hieronym. on Euseb. chron. a. Abr. 2000=737/17 *Varius et Tucca, Vergili et Horati contubernales, poetae habentur inlustres* (we do not know from other sources that Tucca was himself a poet), *qui Aeneidum postea libros emendarunt sub lege ea ut nihil adderent.* Serv. prooem. to Aen. p. 2, 10 Th. *postea ab Augusto Aeneidem propositam scripsit annis XI; sed nec emendavit nec edidit, unde eam moriens praecepit incendi. Augustus vero, ne tantum opus periret, Tuccam et Varium hac lege iussit emendare* (cf. Donat. vita V. 37=56) *ut superflua demerent, nihil adderent tamen.* Doubtful instances of their editoral labour are quoted by Serv. Aen. 2, 567. 588 (cf. Serv. prooem. Aen. p. 2, § 22 Th.). 4, 436. 5, 871. 7, 464. Nisus in Don. v. Verg. 42 (60). Ribbeck, prolegg. 90. *Superflua demere* can only be understood of various readings etc., but cannot be traced now with anything like certainty. But see also Gell. 17, 10, 6 *quae procrastinata sunt ab eo, ut post recenserentur, et absolvi quoniam mors praeverterat nequiverunt, nequaquam poetarum elegantissimi nomine atque iudicio digna sunt. itaque cum morbo oppressus adventare mortem videret petivit oravitque a suis amicissimis impense ut Aeneida, quam nondum satis elimavisset, adolerent.*

3. The conjecture of LLersch (Süddeutsche Schulzeit. 4, 2, 88 and Mus. d. rhein-westphäl. Schulm. 3. 1845) that the Aeneid was originally calculated to fill 24 books, each of the size of a book of the Georgics, and that the present division was not by Vergil himself, is only supported by the analogy of the Homeric poems (though this may also have prevented a modest poet like Vergil from fixing on the number 24), but is contradicted by the express testimony of Donatus (or rather Suetonius), vita 23 (34). See also ThBirt, antik. Buchwesen 295. The opinion that Vergil intended to pursue his subject beyond the death of Turnus, to the final settlement of Aeneas in Latium, is at variance with all the information we possess, which implies only a qualitative incompleteness, and with distinct hints in the poem itself: see 12, 803. 819. 833. See WHertzberg's Aeneid p. iv.

4. In a work confessedly unfinished and destined by its author to destruction it is a mere matter of course that—besides the great artistic blemishes (see n. 5)—there should be blemishes in detail, incongruities, gaps, contradictions, errors of memory and calculation. JMarkland already (praef. to Stat. Silv. ad fin.) observes that in the Aeneid *nonnulla sunt contradictoria, multa languida, exilia, nugatoria, spiritu et maiestate carminis heroici defecta*, and Peerlkamp (in his ed. of the Aen., Leid. 1843) explained these defects in his peculiar manner, by inferring the existence of interpolations in the passages at fault. Incongruities in the first six books are pointed out by FConrads, quaestt. Virg., Trèves 1863; cf. CSchüler, quaestt. Verg., Greifsw. 1883, 1. Throughout the whole poem ORibbeck, prolegg. p. 59, follows the example of Peerlkamp, and even attempts the hopeless task of discriminating what blemishes may be due to the imperfect state of the poem, and which to interpolation. Cf. also ThLadewig, einige Stellen des V., Neustrelitz 1853. ThBergk, griech. Lit.-Gesch. 1, 539. That all the books (though to a different extent) are in an unfinished state is proved by the imperfect lines (about 60). which occur in all. Cf. on this HWendland, ZfGW. 29, 385. WGebhardi, JJ. 119, 566. On an early completion (before Seneca) of such a half line see Bücheler, RhM. 34, 623. The attempts to explain the incomplete lines as the result of artistic intention and a metrical innovation of the poet have been unsuccessful. So Serv. Aen. 4, 361 *et oratorie ibi finivit ubi vis argumenti substitit* (cf. Sen. suas, 2, 20. AEussner, Phil. 43, 466); also MZille, die unvollendeten Verse der Aen., Lpz, 1865, reprinted in his transl. of the Aen., Lpz. 1868, 361. AWeidner's Comment. on Aen. I and II p. 27. FWMünscher, die unvollst. Verse in V.s Aen., Jauer 1879.

5. The belief that the Romans were descended from a Trojan colony, led by Aeneas into Latium, in the Sibylline books called Aeneadae, may perhaps originally have been caused by the Greek worship of Aphrodite on the coasts of Italy, and subsequently formulated and fostered in the vain nobles by flattering Greeks, but it was officially utilised at Rome as early as the first Punic war: see JUSTIN. 28, 1, 5. SUET. Claud. 25. This connection with the Trojans subsequently became one of the standing beliefs with Roman historians and poets. ASCHEBEN, de poetis Aeneae fugam atque fata ante Virgilium describentibus, Münstereifel 1828. JAHILD, la légende d'Enée avant Virgile, Par. 1883. FCAUER, d. röm. Aeneassage von Naev. bis Virg., JJ. Suppl. 15, 95; de fabb. graecis ad Romam conditam spect., Berl. 1884. EWÖRNER, d. Wanderungen des Aen., bei Dion. Hal. u. Virg., Lpz. 1882. HNETTLESHIP, journ. of phil. 9, 29, and in general SCHWEGLER, RG. 1, 279, esp. 307. PRELLER-JORDAN, röm. Myth. 2, 310. MZOELLER, Latium u. Rom. (Lpz. 1878) 70. But this legend had not received special treatment before Vergil. In the time of Augustus, the national motive was still further increased by the interest of the reigning dynasty, whose legendary tradition was that Aeneas through his son Iulus=Ascanius was the ancestor of the gens Iulia. Vergil chiefly dwells on this providential mission of his hero, and forgets to represent him acting. Throughout, Vergil formed his hero much in imitation of himself: soft-hearted, given to tears (cf. § 225, 4 ad fin.), full of piety, accessible to the noblest feelings, but without personal energy, always led and pushed on by the gods or by others. As the frail progenitor of a princely race he is anxiously watched by the gods and, conscious of his great task, he shuns dangerous adventures as much as possible. This is indeed a critical position for the hero of an epic poem, and it is this radical defect which renders a great part of the Aeneid flat and lifeless, not to say oppressively dull. Besides this, the whole legend of Aeneas, in its relation to Rome, was an artificial production, which had no roots in national tradition, no ramification with public life, and Vergil had first to gain such connection for it. He endeavours to keep down all doubts by consistently and intentionally identifying Trojan and Hellenic traits with those of Italy, and by blending legend and history; but through this something untrue, contradictory and characterless has invaded his narrative, an uncertainty in the whole foundation and atmosphere not to be repaired by any local colouring, which Vergil certainly endeavoured to realise and frequently did realise (see below). The language and tone of the Aeneid in contrast with the simplicity of Homer appear constantly stilted, the average style of the poem is so artificially elevated as to leave no room for a successful gradation to a climax in really pathetic passages, and in spite of a multitude of brilliant points, one misses a just distribution of light and shade through the whole. WHERTZBERG, pref. to his review of the Aen. p. IX. This want could not be overcome by the faithful scholarly industry which Vergil devoted to his work: we must acknowledge it in spite of all the sympathy with which Vergil's personality and his performance inspire us, and we must not subscribe to that adoring admiration of hidden beauties in which a hysterical aestheticism has recently indulged. Cf. Vergil's own confession in his letter to Augustus in MACR. 1, 24, 11 *paene vitio mentis tantum opus ingressus mihi videor, cum praesertim . . . alia quoque studia ad id opus multoque potiora impertiar.*—Vergil honestly strove by immersing himself in the past, and by the study of the works of Cato, Varro and others to give to his work a local Italian tone. In MACR. 1, 24, 16 the poet's knowledge of *ius pontificium* and *ius augurale* conspicuous in the Aeneid is praised; 3, 1, 6 sqq. the same praise is given in reference to *inferorum deorum cultus*; 3, 2, 7 to his *profunda scientia*, as seen in his *verborum proprietas* in descriptions of sacrifices, etc. 1, 24, 18 it is stated that he

astrologiam totamque philosophiam . . . operi suo . . . adspersit. So also Serv. Aen. 6, 1 *totus quidem Vergilius scientia plenus est* etc.; on 2, 57 *saepe dictum est Vergilium inventa occasione mentionem iuris pontificii facere in quacunque persona.* See also Niebuhr, röm. Gesch. 1³, 112. 217.—General praise of the Aeneid, and of Vergil, in Ovid. am. 1, 15, 25. AA. 3, 337. rem. am. 396. trist. 2, 533. Prop. 3, 34, 65 (see on this EHeydenreich, de Propertio Vergilii praecone in d. commentatt. philol. semin. [Lips. 1874] 1). Quint. 10, 1, 56. 86. Stat. Theb. 12, 816 and others.—ChVdeBonstetten, voyage sur la scène des dix derniers livres de l'Énéide, Geneva 1804—13 II. HTöpfer, Virg. geographia in Aen., Arnstadt 1828—34 IV. LLersch, de morum in V. Aen. habitu, Bonn 1836; die Idee u. antiquar. Bed. d. Aen., Mus. d. rhein-westph. Schulm. 2, 1. 18; antiquitt. Verg. ad vitam populi rom. descriptae, Bonn 1843. ECollilieux, la couleur locale dans l'Énéide, Par. 1881. AGöbel, JJ. 89, 658. ChMuff, antiquitt. rom. in Aen., Halle 1864. ANoël, Virgile et Italie, Par. 1865. ABougot, de morum indole in V. Aen., Par. 1876.

6. Macr. 1, 24, 18 *praedicarim quanta de Graecis cautus et tamquam aliud agens modo artifici dissimulatione modo professa imitatione transtulerit.* But Asconius defended Vergil against charges *circa historiam fere et quod pleraque ab Homero sumpsisset* (vita 46=64). From the Homeric poems Vergil derived his whole epic economy and method as well as numerous details (forging of weapons, description of the shield etc.), and especially the device of commencing with the latter part of the wanderings of Aeneas and making him describe his preceding adventures by way of episode; in the same way, b. 6 is entirely in the style of the Odyss. b. 11 and the first half of the Aeneid (the wanderings) may be said to be in imitation of the Odyssey, while the second half (the battles) imitates the Iliad. Its whole tone and spirit are, of course, diametrically opposed to that of Homer. Recent literature besides the works quoted § 225, 5: LMüller, de re metr. 219. 223. 307. 322. PRichter, de Verg. imitatore poett. Graec., Rost. 1870. MWilms, qua ratione Verg. in Aen. aut locuturum aliquem aut locutum esse indicaverit, Duisb. 1865. EEichler, d. Unterwelt V.s. ZföG. 30, 600. 721. DRiccoboni, quib. in rebus V. Hom. aliosque imitatus singulare ingenium prodat, Ven. 1879. 80 II. FHermann, V.s Aen. verglichen m. Hom., Dresden 1879–81 III. HBouvier, vgl. Erkl. der Schildepisoden in Hom. Il. u. V. Aen., Oberhollabrun 1881. JLuniak, de homericis similitudinibus ap. V., Journ. d. russ. Min. d. Volksaufkl. 1881. KNeermann, ungeschickte Verwendung hom. Motive in d. Aen., Ploen 1882. PCauer, z. Verständnis der nachahmenden Kunst des V., Kiel 1885. The substance of the second book is taken from the Cyclic poets (Pisander? Macr. 5, 2, 4,) and b. 4 is imitated from the fourth book (Jason and Medea) of Apollonios Rhodios. Among the Roman poets, Vergil has especially availed himself of Ennius (e.g. 6, 846), as has been shown by Servius in many passages of his commentary, and by Macr. 6, 1 (see CABentfeld, d. Einfluss des Enn. auf V., Salzb. 1875); likewise *non verba sola sed versus prope totos et locos quoque Lucreti plurimos sectatum esse Vergilium videmus* (Gell. 1, 21, 7 cf. Macr. l.l.). On the other hand the coincidences of expression with Naevius, Furius (§ 192, 5) and other Roman epic poets are probably accidental.

7. CGHeyne, de carmine epico Virg., in his ed. 2, 1; de rerum in Aen. tractatarum inventione, ib. 37; censura eorum quae in Aen. oeconomia reprehendi possunt, ib. 3, 854. PFTissot, études zur Virg., comparé avec tous les poètes épiq et dramat. des anc. et des modernes, Par. 1826 IV. WYSellar, the Roman poets of the Augustan age: Virgil, Oxf. ² 1883. DComparetti (§ 231, 12 in fin.). HNettleship, lectures and essays 97; cf. also § 224, 1 ad fin. Segrais, l'Én. par rapport à l'art de la guerre (Mém. de l'acad. des inscr. Vol. 24, Napoleon I also,

guerres de César 209 has accused Vergil of great ignorance). RWiechmann, de Aen. libri II compositione, Potsd. 1876. HGeorgii, on b. 3 of the Aen., in the Festschr. der württemb. Gymnasien (Stuttg. 1877) 63; die politische Tendenz der Aen., Stuttg. 1880. ThPlüss, d. Reiz erzählender Dicht. und die Aen., Basle 1882; V. und die epische Kunst, Lpz. 1884. Cf. also n. 1.

8. Recent separate editions of the Aen. by CThiel (with elucidations, Berl. 1834. 1838 II), PHofman-Peerlkamp (ed. et adnot., Leid. 1843 II), GWGossrau (illustr., Quedlinb.[2] 1876), WGebhardi and PMahn (for students, Paderb. 1880 sqq.), OBrosin (Gotha 1883), RSabbadini (Turin 1885).—On b. I. and II. a commentary by AWeidner, Lpz. 1869. L. I–VI by LSchmitz, Lond. 1879. TLPapillon and AEHaigh, Oxford, 1890.

9. FConrads, quaestt. Verg., Trèves 1863; ventorum ap. Verg. turbae, Essen 1872. Madvig, adv. crit. 2, 29. HNettleship, suggestions introductory to the Aen., in his lect. and essays 97. WKloučeк (see § 231, 11). ThPlüss, JJ. 103, 396. 111, 635. 115, 69. 121, 545. 125, 46. 403. 849. CWNauck, notes on V. Aen. 1, 1–405, Königsb. NM. 1862; Aen. 1, 406–760, ib. 1869; Aen. 2, 1–400, ib. 1874; ZfGW. 28, 709. 29, 75. HBrandt, zur Krit. u. Exegese v. V. Aen. I–III, Bernb. 1876; ZfGW. 28, 82. KKappes, notes on V. Aen. (B. I–IV) I Freib. i. Br. 1859. II Const. 1863. III Donauesch. 1870. IV ib. 1871. JKvičala, Vergilstudien (esp. on Aen. I–VI), Prague 1871; neue Beitr. z. Erkl. d. Aen., Prague 1881. JHenry, a voyage of discovery in the Aen. I–VI, Dresd. 1853; in German in his Adv. Virgiliana, Phil. 11, 480. 597. 12, 248. 13, 629. 17, 627; Aeneidea, or critical and other remarks on the Aen., I Lond. 1873; II Dublin 1879. WGebhardi, zum 2. Teil der Aen., Meseritz 1879; ZfGW. 32, 200; JJ. 119, 561. KPöhlig, Beitr. z. Krit. u. Erkl. zur Aen. B. I u. II, Seehausen 1871. 80 II. FWMünscher, Phil. 39, 173. HFlach, zur Chronologie von Aen. B. III, JJ. 107, 853. JStanko, de Victorii commentariis ineditis in Aen. l. IV, Munich 1851. GKettner, B. 5 der Aen., ZfGW. 33, 641. KZacher (on Aen. 1, 406), JJ. 121. 577. FSchöll, RhM. 41, 18. PCorssen, RhM. 41, 242. GHeidtmann (l. II), in the Festschr. v. Wesel 1883; Beitr. zur Emend. der Aen. (1, 695 sqq.), Wesel 1884; Emendationen (!!) zur Aen. I u. IV, Coblenz 1885. EGross Krit. u. Exeg. z. Aen., Nürnb. 1883. GSchroeter, z. Krit. u. Erkl. d. Aen., Glogau 1885 II. EBährens, JJ. 129, 391. 131, 385. 135, 259. 807. ThOesterlen (see § 240, 9).—Literary reviews by EBährens, JB. 1873, 211. 1874/75 1, 216. 1876 2, 149. 1877 2, 50. 1878 2, 113. 1879 2, 140. HGenthe, ib. 1880 2, 144. 1883 2, 185. PDeuticke (also on Buc. and Georg.), ZfGW. 36, Jahresbericht 100; 39, Jahresber. 233. CSchroeter, Beiträge z. Krit. u. Erkl. der Aen. III, Neisse 1888. LHavet, Aen. 6, 618 sqq. rev. de phil. 12, 145. RSabbadini, studi critici sulla Eneide, Lonigo 1889. EBrandes (B. 6 and 8), JJ. 141, 59. 141.

10. Translations by CLNeuffer (Frankf. 1816, Stuttg. 1830 sqq.), WBinder (Stuttg. 1857), and esp. by WABHertzberg (see also his introd. and notes), Stuttg. 1859. In English (prose), by JWMackail, Lond. 1885, (verse) by JConington, Lond.[6] 1881, WMorris, Lond. 1876, WJThornhill, Dublin 1886.

229. Besides these great and undoubtedly genuine works of Vergil we possess also a number of smaller poems, which bear his name with less justice.

1. Donatus' vita 17 (28) *poeticam puer adhuc auspicatus in Balistam ludi magistrum ob infamiam latrociniorum coopertum lapidibus distichon fecit: 'monte sub hoc etc.' deinde catalecton et priapeia* (§ 230, 5, 2) *et epigrammata et diras, item cirim*

(*et cupam* adds Bährens) *et culicem cum esset annorum XVI.* (Here follows an analysis of the latter). 19 (30) *scripsit etiam de qua ambigitur Aetnam* (see § 307). *mox cum res romanas incohasset . . . ad bucolica transiit.* Donatus (i.e. Suetonius) would therefore seem to consider all these poems as works of Vergil's youth. The so-called Servius (introd. to the Aen. p. 1, 8 Th.) *primum a Vergilio hoc distichon factum est in Balistam latronem: 'monte* etc.' *scripsit etiam septem sive octo libros hos: cirin, Aetnam, culicem, priapeia, catalepton* (so cod. Paris, *catelepton* V. Burmanni: *catalecton* the rest of the MSS., see § 230, 5, 1), *epigrammata, copam, diras* (§ 200, 2). According to this the poems had probably been formed even before Suetonius into a collection, which bore the name of Vergil. In our MSS. it is entitled *Virgilii iuvenalis ludi libellus* or *septem ioca iuvenalia Virgilii.* These poems have come down to us with a strong admixture of foreign matter. The extant MSS. go back to an original collection, which consisted of the works named by Servius and Donatus, arranged in the following order: culex, dirae, copa, Aetna, ciris, priapea (83–85), catelapta. To these were then added est et non, de viro bono, de rosis nascentibus, moretum (see n. 2 sqq.) and others. Epigrammata (specially mentioned by Servius and Donatus) is only a secondary title for catalepta (thus catal. 4, 9 is quoted by Mar. Victorin. GL. 6, 137 as *Vergilius iambico epigrammate*). More or less complete or valuable manuscripts of this collection, especially: Rhedig. s. XV. Vatic. 3252 s. IX, Paris. 7927 s. X, 8069 s. X, 8093 s. XI; Trevirensis (or Augustanus) 998 s. XI; Cantabrig. s. X/XI, Paris. 17177 (fragm. Stabulense s. XI); Bruxellensis 10675 s. XII; Leid. Voss. O. 81, Monac. 18895, Guelferb. Helmst. 332; the latter s. XV. On these see Näke, Ribbeck, Bährens, l.l. c.c.—On Ambr. D. 267 inf. s. XV see RSabbadini, la critica . . . delle poesie ps.-vergiliane, Catania 1888, 39.—ANäke, de Vergilii libello iuvenalis ludi app. to his Valer. Cato p. 221. ORibbeck, appendix Vergil. proleg., LMüller, praef. Cat. p. xli. EBährens, JJ. 111, 137; Tibull. Blätter 49; PLM. 2, 38 (who conjectures this collection to be the dilettante production of a small society of poets who met in Messalla's house, and supposes it to have been published perhaps under the Emperor Claudius). RPeiper, Catullus (Breslau 1875) 63. See also Bährens, JJ. 117, 120. MSonntag, die append. Verg., Frankf. a/O. 1887.

2. Of the three poems *De viro bono, Est et non, De rosis nascentibus* (printed e.g. in Ribbeck's append. Verg. p. 181. AL. 644–646), which were not included (see n. 1) in the original collection of the so-called youthful poems of Vergil, the first and second belong to Ausonius (cf. on their transmission CSchenkl in his ed. p. 149. 150), and *De rosis* also was attributed by HAleander in the Paris ed. of 1511 ex fide vetusti codicis to Ausonius. From its language and style it cannot have been composed before the 4th cent. Cf. RPeiper, JJ. Suppl. 11, 210. 305. Schenkl's Ausonius p. xxxvi. 243.—On equally slight grounds other works are in various MSS. attributed to Vergil: AL. 781 PLM. 4, 160 *ad puerum* (a prayer to be heard), epigrams AL. 256–63 PLM. 4, 156. AL. 782 PLM. 4, 160. AL. 663 PLM. 4, 161. Aldhelmus de metr. p. 232 (cf. p. 284) *Virgilius libro quem paedagogum praetitulavit, cuius principium est 'Carmina si fuerint* etc.' cf. AL. 675 PLM. 4, 161.

3. Two elegies on the death of Maecenas (Ribbeck, app. Verg. 193 AL. 779 PLM. 1, 125), transmitted to us as one and the same, but the work of two authors (EWagner, de Martiale poett. August. imitatore, Königsb. 1880, 42), also bear in MSS. the name of Vergil: their careful construction combined with poverty of substance makes it probable that they belong to the 1st century of our era; cf. § 251, 5. The extant MSS. go back as far as the 10th cent. In late MSS. (Leid. Voss. O 96 and Vatic. 3269 s. XV) we have the subscription: *finit elegia inventa*

(c. a. 1455) *ab enoch* (Enoche da Ascoli, see GVoigt, Wiederbel. d. class. Altert. 1, 258. 2, 201) *in Dacia* (=Denmark). Bährens l.l. EChatelain, rev. de phil. 4, 80. KSchenkl, Wiener Stud. 1, 65. 2, 69. LMüller, de re metr. 52; RhM. 23, 657. Ribbeck's app. V. 61. EHübner, Herm. 13, 239. ThBirt, hist. hex. (Bonn 1876) 66; RhM. 32, 397; de halieut. Ovid. 8. MHertz, anal. ad Hor. carm. hist. 3, 10. FBücheler, coniectanea (Bonn 1878) 13. Textual criticism: Mähly (§ 251, 5) p. 13–18. REllis (gives the readings of the Vatic. 3269), Amer. journ. of phil. 9, 265. ACima, Riv. di fil. 17, 383.

4. Under the head of works in prose by Vergil, only his correspondence with Augustus is known to us; it was probably published at the instance of Augustus. Specimens from it in Donatus' vita Verg. 31 (46) and in Macr. 1, 24, 11 (above p. 437 l. 24). Tac. dial. 13 (*testes Augusti epistulae*), Claudian. carm. min. 2 (41), 23 *dignatus tenui Caesar scripsisse Maroni*), and the opinion of the elder Seneca, contr. 3, praef. 8 *Vergilium illa felicitas ingenii in oratione soluta reliquit.*

5. Editions of the carmina minora e.g. by JJScaliger (Virgilii appendix, Lyons 1573 and frequently), JSillig (in b. 4 of the Heyne-Wagner ed.), ORibbeck (vol. 4 of his Verg. = Appendix Vergiliana, Lps. 1868), in MHaupt's V.-ed. Lpz.[2] 1873 and in Bährens' PLM. 2, Lpz. 1880.—Cf. JMähly, Heidelb. Jahrbb. 1870, 769. 801. Bücheler, RhM. 45, 321.—Transl. and explained by WABHertzberg, Stuttg. 1856.

230. Among these lesser poems is

1) Culex, which is so far attested that it is certain that Vergil in his youth wrote a small epic poem of this name, and on very much the same subject as the poem now extant; but the character of the latter renders it most probable that we have here an imitation—written a few decades after Vergil's death—which has taken the place of the original poem, which Vergil himself destroyed.

1. Besides Donatus (see § 229, 1) we may quote the following testimonies in favour of the composition of a Culex by Vergil: Sueton. vita Lucani (p. 50 Rffsch.) *ut praefatione quadam aetatem et initia sua cum Vergilio comparans ausus sit dicere: 'et quantum mihi restat ad culicem!'* Cf. Stat. Silv. 2, 7, 73 *haec primo iuvenis canes sub aevo, ante annos culicis maroniani.* Statius seems to have been of opinion that Vergil wrote his Culex at the age of XXVI (not XVI) years. Stat. Silv. 1 praef. *et culicem legimus et batrachomyomachiam etiam agnoscimus; nec quisquam est illustrium poetarum qui non aliquid operibus suis stilo remissiore praeluserit.* It appears that his impression was that he still possessed Vergil's Culex, though he did not think much of its poetical value. Mart. 14, 185 (after two epigrams on the Batrachomyomachia): *accipe facundi culicem, studiose, Maronis, ne nucibus positis Arma virumque legas.* Therefore there must have been a separate edition of the Culex, of which Martial did not question the Vergilian origin; see also 8, 56, 19 *protinus Italiam concepit et Arma virumque qui modo vix culicem fleverat ore rudi.* Nor did Nonius 211 *labrusca, genere feminino, Verg. in bucolicis* (5, 7); *neutro Vergilius in culice* (v. 53).

2. On account of the MS. authority and because of these early and positive testimonies, we might easily conclude the Culex now extant to be the work of the youthful Vergil, and amongst others who held this view were Näke (on Val. Cat.

Dir. 1, p. 227), Teuffel (PRE. 6, 2657), Ribbeck (RhM. 18, 100; app. Verg. p. 20). But to this opinion, though in itself very plausible, may be opposed the most cogent reasons. First and foremost we are struck by frequent imitations of Vergil's genuine poems (see FBaur l.l. 571), though these are not so undisguised as in the Ciris. Again, the poem is just as crude in regard to composition and execution as it is masterly in its careful and elegant metrical treatment. On this see WHertzberg p. 51, on the strictness of elision, which is not in keeping with Vergil's later manner, FBaur l.l. 368. ThBirt, de halieut. Ovid. 49. It is not possible to attribute these peculiarities to Vergil's youthfulness; this would also have betrayed itself in the metre. We should rather interpret this technical elaboration side by side with clumsiness in all other respects as a proof that the poem is by some other author. Lastly, the original motive of the poem can only have been the idea that the gnat could not rest in Hades and therefore asked the shepherd (whose life it had saved) for a decent burial. But this very motive, without which the poem loses its consistency, is wanting in the extant Culex, being suppressed in the effort to give the fullest possible description of Hades. So nothing is left us but to assume that Lucan, Martial, and Statius were mistaken in identifying the extant Culex with the one written by Vergil, even if the origin of the former could be traced back to the Augustan period (so LMüller, metr. 42. 217. 317; RhM. 23, 658. FBaur l.l. Bährens PLM. 2, 28). WHertzberg places it in the first half of the 1st century of our era, between Ovid and Persius. Heyne attempted to reconcile the various views by supposing the Vergilian Culex to have been preserved, but disfigured by strong interpolations: this untenable opinion has been pushed to extreme lengths by RHildebrandt (Studd. auf d. Geb. d. röm. Poesie u. Metr. I: V.s Culex, Lpz. 1887). Cf. in general WHertzberg, introd. to his transl. p. 5. FBaur, JJ. 93, 357. RHildebrandt l.l. Also ThBirt, ad hist. hex. (Bonn 1876) 41; de halieut. Ov. 47.

3. On the MSS. of the Culex see § 229, 1; cf. also REllis, journ. of phil. 16, 153.—Criticism: MHaupt, op. 1, 38. 55. 3, 63. 258. Ribbeck, RhM. 18, 100. REllis, Americ. journ. of phil. 3, 271. RUnger, journ. of phil. 16, 310.

2) Ciris, the account of the treacherous conduct of the Megarian princess Scylla toward her father Nisus, and her transformation into the bird Ciris. This small epic poem seems to have arisen in the circle of Messalla, and is dedicated to his son (cos. 751/3). The author draws largely upon Vergil's poetry, but still more shows himself to be the pupil and imitator of Catullus, and repeatedly reminds us of passages in Lucretius and others. In its refined descriptions of psychic conditions the poem recalls Vergil's manner. The metrical treatment is less careful, but the style more lively.

1. Nothing can be adduced in favour of the Vergilian origin of the composition, but everything is against it, nor does the author himself attempt to foist it upon Vergil, but in the opening lines of the poem gives an extensive statement as to his personal circumstances. He represents himself as a man of advanced age, who after an eventful (political) life would fain retire from public life and write a didactic poem on Epicurean philosophy. His name is unknown. Cornelius Gallus, whom JHVoss hit upon (so as to make Vergil guilty of theft from the

Ciris!), cannot have written it: (see WHERTZBERG l.l. p. 53); it might rather be the Lynceus of Propertius (§ 244, 3). The conjecture (by TEUFFEL, PRE. 6, 2657) that Messalla (v. 54) who is v. 36 addressed as *iuvenum doctissime* is the eldest son of the orator Messalla, Messalinus (§ 267, 6), cos. 751/3, has been accepted by WHERTZBERG l.l. p. 55, RIBBECK, app. p. 16 and LSCHWABE, observatt. in Cir. (Dorp. 1871) p. 3. The poem then would seem to have been written somewhere near 735/19–740/14, in about the 50th year of the author. On the possibility of its having been written in the Augustan age, see also LMÜLLER, de re metr. p. 42.

2. The poem is an elaboration of the theme expounded in Vergil's lines ge. 1, 406–409, which for this reason form the close (see SCHWABE 1871 p. 2). In its general character, however, it approaches nearer to the manner of Catullus (in his poem 64), than to that of Vergil; the setting is as it were borrowed from Catullus, the suggestion from Vergil, so that it has almost the appearance of a cento compiled from both writers. The purloining from all the works of Vergil (from whom are taken 11 lines in their entirety and 8 with only the change of one word) and from Catullus (esp. de nupt. Pel. et Thet. and the longer elegies) is traced by JSCHRADER, emendationes (Leovard. 1776) 33. 63. SILLIG, in Heyne-Wagner's Verg. 4 p. 155. LSCHWABE, l.l. EBÄHRENS, JJ. 105, 833; PLM. 2, 186. JSÜSS, acta semin. Erlang. 1, 8. There also occur detached phrases from other poems of the circle of Catullus (§ 213); the predilection for spondaic lines (see SCHWABE, l.l. 9) is also in keeping with the usage of that circle. Deviations from Vergil's usage, especially in the use of the particles, FJACOB on Prop. p. 165 and in SILLIG, l.l. p. 143. HAUPT, op. 1, 121. Deviations from his metrical system, WHERTZBERG l.l. p. 51 n. (see his whole introduction). Cf. also RIBBECK, app. Verg. 16.

3. The poem, as far as its subject-matter is concerned, probably imitates Greek (Alexandrine) originals: we have evidence for this in the Greek character of the mythology and style (ESIECKE, de Niso et Scylla in aves mutatis, Berl. 1884), the fact of its concluding with a transformation, the etymologieal derivation of the name ciris (from κείρειν, v. 488) and much besides. But it cannot be a translation: this supposition is precluded both by the proem (1–100) and the imitations of Catullus and Vergil. Perhaps it was modelled on Parthenios. See SCHOL. and EUSTATH. on Dionys. Perieg. 420. AMEINEKE, anal. alex. 270. EROHDE, gr. Rom. 93. See also WHELBIG, arch. Z. 24, 196.—EHOFFMANN (RhM. 40, 150) wrongly supposes Ov. Ib. 447 *quibus exiguo est volucris devota libello* etc. to refer to the ps.-Vergil. Ciris.

4. On the MSS. see § 229, 1.—Criticism and explanation: MHAUPT, op. 1, 55. 3, 75. 261, RIBBECK, RhM. 18, 112, LSCHWABE, in Cirin observatt., Dorpat 1871; JJ. 107, 617, MHERTZ, JJ. 103, 860, EBÄHRENS, ib. 105, 833. 107, 773. AWALTZ, de carmine Ciris, Paris 1881. RUNGER, d. Prooem. d. Cir., Halle 1881; electa e Ciris commentariis, Halle 1885; journ. of phil. 16, 310. MKREUNEN, prolegg. in Cirin, Utr. 1882. AZINGERLE, kl. phil. Abh. 3 (Innsbr. 1881), 23 (Ovid and the Ciris). RELLIS, Americ. journ. of phil. 8, 1. 399.

3) Moretum (the rural breakfast), a pleasant idyll of the time of Vergil and perhaps translated by him from a Greek poem of Parthenios, full of vivid and detailed description and amiable humour, the form being masterly.

1. The Moretum is missing in Donatus' and Servius' enumeration of the lesser Vergiliana. On the other hand it is found in MS. collections of these (see § 229, 1 and below n. 2). JGVOSSIUS, de poet. gr. 9, states that in a cod. Ambr. this poem

bore the heading: *Parthenius moretum scripsit in Graeco, quem Virgilius imitatus est.* This may perhaps account for the fact that the fresh and lively style and vivid description (Teuffel, PRE. 6, 2658. Hertzberg, transl. p. 95) and the candid undisguised appellation of things observed in this poem do not agree with Vergil's general manner. Hertzberg (l.l. p. 95. 100. 101) has justly concluded from the name of Simylus, the metre of v. 18 and from v. 116, that the Greek original was pretty faithfully translated. The 124 hexameters of this poem describe how the peasant Simylus rises at dawn, bakes his bread, prepares his mess of herbs in the mortar and then sets to work. Sueius also had written a Moretum (§ 150, 6), and it is not altogether improbable that the desire to surpass Sueius influenced Vergil in attempting the same task again. At all events the poem belongs to the best time of Roman literature, as appears e.g. from the estimation in which the lactuca is held v. 76 as compared with the time of Martial (Mart. 13, 14, 1): see Stauder, ZfAW. 1853, 290. Cf. Lachmann on Lucr. p. 326. MHaupt, op. 1, 39. Hertzberg's Introduction 93. Ribbeck app. p. 14.

2. On the MSS. see § 229, 1; also Vindob. 134 s. XI, Monac. 21562 s. XI/XII, 305 s. XI/XII.—FWSchneidewin in Jahn's Arch. 2, 426. ChrJahn ib. 4, 627. MHaupt, op. 1, 36. Stauder, ZfAW. 1853, 289. OSieroka, JJ. 109, 395. EBarth, Sprache und Versbau des Mor., Horn 1879. KvReichenbach, d. Echtheit d. M., Znaim 1883. REllis (Heinsius' codex Moreti), journ. of phil. 18, 273.

4) Copa ("mine hostess"), a short elegy of the best time, in style and diction quite according with Vergil's manner, but much less resembling him in its sprightly contents and tone; many passages of it remind the reader of Vergilian expressions.

1. The poem (19 distichs) has been transmitted to us among the lesser Vergiliana; Charisius also considered it to be by Vergil; see GL. 1, 63, 11 *quamvis Vergilius librum suum Cupam inscripserit.* Cf. Lachmann on Lucr. p. 164. On the points of difference in diction and tone between the Copa and the Vergilian poems see Hertzberg, transl. p. 103. The small compass of the Copa precludes us from drawing any conclusion from the construction of the metre: this yields no decisive evidence either for or against Vergil, but we notice a certain agreement with Propertius. Hertzberg l.l. 104. ThBirt, hist. hexam. lat. (Bonn 1876) 51. There is certainly no reason for removing the poem beyond the Augustan period. V. 27 *cantu rumpunt arbusta cicadae*=georg. 3, 328; v. 35 *cineri ingrato*=Aen. 6, 213; cf. *umbrosis harundinibus* (v. 8) with Aen. 8, 34 *umbrosa harundo.* V. 31= Calpurn. ecl. 11, 46. Ribbeck, app. p. 14.

2. The MSS. correspond to those of the Moretum, see § 229, 1 and above 3, 2.—CDIlgen, animadvv. in Virg. Copam, Halle 1820. MHaupt, op, 1, 143. KZell, Ferienschrr. 1, 5. WMüller, Rom und die Römerinnen 2, 171.

5) Catalepton (κατὰ λεπτόν), a collection of fourteen poems in elegiac and iambic metre and on various subjects. Only a few of them are attested as coming from the poet himself, but only very few can be positively proved to be not by him. This much may be stated, that all belong to the period of Vergil.

1. This collection is in the MSS. entitled *Ve(i)rgilii catalepton* (see n. 2). In the so-called Servian vita it is, according to the best tradition, called *cata(cate)-lepton*, sometimes *catalecton*: so also in Donatus' vita: see § 229, 1; cf. 301, 4.

AUSONIUS, grammaticomast. (op. 27, 13, 5 see § 209, 12) *Dic quid significent catalepta* (so the best MSS., see SCHENKL ad loc.: the rest give *catalecta*) *Maronis? in his* (2, 3) *al Celtarum posuit, sequitur non lucidius tau.* The original title was κατὰ λεπτόν, after the precedent of Aratos, who had called a collection of 'trifles' by this name (see vita Arati p. 55, 84 Westerm. ἔγραψε δὲ καὶ ἄλλα ποιήματα . . . καὶ εἰς Μύριν τὸν ἀδελφὸν ἐπικήδειον καὶ διοσημεῖα καὶ Σκυθικὸν [?] καὶ κατὰ λεπτὸν ἄλλα and STRABO 10, 486 Ἄρατος ἐν τοῖς κατὰ λεπτόν. From this *cata lepton* was derived by an abuse *catalepta* and finally *catalecta* (κατάλεκτα= 'collected poems' does not occur elsewhere). THBERGK, op. 2, 745. RUNGER, JJ. 113, 429. The explanations of the name as catalepta=κατάλειπτα 'poems left behind' (by EBÄHRENS JJ. 111, 142. 150; Tibull. Bl. 53; cf. PLM. 2, 36) or=καταληπτά (by RPEIPER, Catullus, Bresl. 1875, 65) are untenable.—In the collection no. 1. 3 (in praise of Alexander the Great; BÜCHELER l.l.) 4. 7. 8. 9. 11. 14 are in elegiacs, 6. 10. 12 and 13 are in iambics, 2 and 5 in choliambics. Immediately after the collection there follows in the MSS. an epigram by the compiler (AL. 777 PLM. 2, 177), which ends thus: *Illius* (of Vergil) *haec quoque sunt divini elementa poetae Et rudis in vario carmine Calliope.* This then agrees with the heading in the MSS. (see above). No. 2 (on Annius Cimber see § 209, 12) is attested authentic by QUINT. 8, 3, 28 and Ausonius (see above). A definite proof against Vergil's authorship is furnished only by no. 13, the first lines of which contain allusions to personal circumstances of the author which are at variance with those of Vergil. The servile elegy to Messalla (§ 222) no. 9 of a. 727/27 cannot be by Vergil (on account of v. 17), but should be assigned to a tiro displaying his mythological learning and imitating rather Ovid's than Vergil's manner. RIBBECK (app. p. 12) ascribes it to Lygdamus (§ 245, 4), a conjecture at least more credible than RUNGER's plea for Valgius (de Valg. Ruf. 304). Ed. et comm. instr. PHWAGNER, Lps. 1816. Poem no. 14, although it relates to the Aeneid and speaks in the name of Vergil, is hardly by him; BÜCHELER, RhM. 38, 523. The acerbity of the iambic poems (especially no. 6, 12 and 10) is not much in harmony with Vergil's later soft character, but may be sufficiently explained by the fire of youth, the general excitement of the period, and the example of Catullus. These poems, the quotation from Catullus in 6, 6, further no. 10, the parody of Catullus' poem 4 in derision of P. Ventidius (pr. 710/44, cos. 711/43. BÜCHELER, RhM. 38, 518. RKLOTZ, de Cat. c. IV eiusque parodia Verg., Lps. 1868), and the choliambics no. 5, also a reminiscence of Catullus in no. 4, lead to the assumption of a period in Vergil's poetical development in which he was under the influence of Catullus' manner and style. Nos. 5 and 8 are in perfect agreement with Vergil's personal circumstances; nos. 1. 4. 7. 11 are addressed to men of his acquaintance. On the whole question see FNÄKE, Valer. Cato p. 221. WHERTZBERG's introd. to his translation of the Catal. p. 108, RIBBECK app. p. 6. MHAUPT, op. 2, 147 and esp. BÜCHELER, RhM. 38, 507.

2. At the beginning of this collection of 14 poems, and included under the same title as belonging to it (see n. 1), we find in all the MSS.—and accordingly also in RIBBECK's append. p. 147. PLM. 2, 158—three poems, '*Vere rosa*' consisting of two distichs (cf. MART. 8, 40), '*Ego haec*' in iamb. senarii, '*Hunc ego*' in the priapic metre, all priapea as regards their contents and supposed to be spoken by Priapus. These are the priapea mentioned by Donatus and Servius (see § 229, 1) among the Vergiliana. Cf. also DIOMED. GL. 1, 512 *Priapeum* (sc. metrum) *quo Vergilius in prolusionibus suis usus fuit.* The two last (which might really have been youthful attempts of Vergil) used formerly (from Victorius and Muretus down to Döring and Sillig) to be enumerated among the Catulline works as poems 20 and 19, and besides this all three used to be placed at the end of the collection

of priapea (§ 254, 5), e.g. in LMüller's ed. as nos. 83, 84, 85; Bücheler's Petron. [3]1882, 157. Cf. WHertzberg's transl. p. 110, JEWernicke, Priapeia (Thorn 1853) p. 9. 108, FBücheler, RhM. 18, 415, Ribbeck, app. Verg. p. 4,—The fact that Plin. ep. 5, 3, 6 mentions P. Vergilius (§ 31, 1) among the *boni* who wrote erotic *lusus* is counterbalanced by the silence of Ovid, who trist. 2, 535 mentions only Aen. IV and the Bucolics in this department.

231. Vergil obtained from the first the highest reputation: his poems were at an early time admitted into schools, imitated, translated, and commented on: one of the earliest and most important commentators was M. Valerius Probus, a later one Servius. We still possess the commentary of the latter, and fragments of other works in the various collections of scholia. But Vergil's poems were also used for centos, and superstition employed them for the purpose of consulting them as an oracle. They were, moreover, industriously multiplied. Vergil himself was in popular belief gradully turned into a magician, upon whose name all nations of the West accumulated their fantastical fictions and legends for a long time in the Middle Ages.

1. Suet. gramm. 16 *Q. Caecilius Epirota* (§ 263, 1) . . . *primus dicitur* . . . *Vergilium et alios poetas novos praelegere coepisse.* Quint. 1, 8, 5 *optime institutum est ut ab Homero atque Vergilio lectio inciperet.* Oros. 1, 18 *Aeneae* . . . *adventus in Italiam quae arma commoverit* . . . *ludi litterarii disciplina nostrae quoque memoriae inustum est.* Augustin. civ. dei 1, 3 *apud Vergilium, quem propterea parvuli legunt ut videlicet poeta magnus omniumque praeclarissimus atque optimus teneris ebibitus animis non facile oblivione possit aboleri.* Iul. Capitol. Clod. Albin. 5, 2 *fertur in scholis saepissime cantasse inter puerulos* '*Arma amens*,' etc. (Aen. 2, 314). Macr. sat. 1, 24, 5 *Vergilianos versus, qualiter eos pueri magistris praelegentibus canebamus.* (Auson.) epigr. 137, 1 *Arma virumque docens atque Arma virumque peritus.* Augustin. confess. 1, 17, 27 cf. 1, 13, 20 shows that it was school-practice to turn passages from Vergil into prose.—On the other hand, themata Vergiliana were set as metrical exercises; cf. n. 2 and § 230, 2, 2. 427, 1.

2. Ovid often alludes to Vergil (see AZingerle, Ovids Verhältn. 2, 48). The Aeneid (2, 77) is also quoted by Phaedrus, fab. 3, praef. 27; by Juvenal 2, 99. 3, 197. 9, 102. See Wehle, obss. in Petr. 44. Ribbeck prolegg. 200. Livy derives much of his diction from Vergil, Tacitus even more; see EWölfflin, Phil. 26, 130. Verses on Vergil AL. 507–518 PLM. 4, 120. AL. 555–566 PLM. 4, 128. For the use made of Vergil in the schools of the rhetoricians see Sen. suas. 3, 5 (*solebat Fuscus ex Vergilio multa trahere*). Serv. Aen. 10, 18 *et Titianus et Calvus* (*Catulinus* Floriac.) *qui themata omnia de Vergilio elicuerunt et deformaverunt ad dicendi usum* (§ 364, 4). Cf. n. 1 and Ribbeck prolegg. p. 188. Passages from Vergil were found scribbled on the walls at Pompeii: see CIL. 4, p. 259. Addenda: ephem. epigr. 1, 53. giorn. d. scavi 1, 281. 2, 35. On a spoon (arch. Ztg. 1848, 110*) was found engraved ecl. 2, 17; on a relief at the Villa Albani Aen. 1, 607 above the head of a seller of game, OJahn, Lpz. SBer. 1861, 365. On a brick from Italica near Seville is inscribed Aen. 1, 1–2 CIL. 2, 4967, 31. For the use of Vergilian passages on tombstones see Marini fratr. Arv. p. 826; papiri dipl. p. 332. Quotaticns incidental to everyday life, Suet. Dom. 9. Dio 75, 10. Lamprid. Diadum.

8, 7. VOPISC. Tac. 5, 1. Car. 13, 3. APUL. apol. 56 and many other instances. LFRIEDLÄNDER, SGesch. 3[5], 334.—Ancient illustrations to Vergil or in imitation of him: on the MS. illustrations see n. 9. On wall-paintings in Campania: Aeneas and Dido (Aen. 1, 715; cf. MACR. 5, 17, 5): WHELBIG, Wandgem. Campaniens no. 1381; cf. bull. arch. 1881, 29 and the mosaic from Halicarnassus (Aeneas and Dido in the chase=Aen. 4, 151) bull. 1860, 105. Laocoon (Aen. 2, 200): ann. dell' inst. arch. 47, tav. O. Aeneas and Polyphemus (Aen. 3, 655): giorn. degli scavi 3 (1877) tav. 6. Aeneas admiring the weapons brought to him by Venus (Aen. 8, 608): HELBIG no. 1382. Aeneas wounded and cured by Venus (Aen. 12, 398): HELBIG no. 1383. Cf. HELBIG, Unterss. üb. d. Wandmalerei 4. HHEYDEMANN, Arch. Z. 29. 122.

3. An inscr. from Rome in ORELLI 1179 WILM. 2481 *Q. Glitius Felix, Vergilianus poeta*, cf. § 251, 1 (also WILM. 2488 *medicus asclepiadius*). But all the Roman epic and didactic poets are more or less imitators of Vergil. The beginning of a cento-like employment of Vergil's poems may be traced as early as in the Ciris; see § 230, 2, 2. For later examples see § 26, 2.

4. Vergil's poems were consulted as oracles, and resorted to for advice in difficult positions of life, and sortes Vergilianae were even publicly kept in the temples, see IUL. CAPITOL. Clod. Albin. 5, 4: *in templo Apollinis Cumani . . . cum sortem de fato suo tolleret, his versibus ei dicitur esse responsum* (Aen. 6, 857). LAMPRID. Alex. Sev. 4, 6 *huic sors in templo Praenestinae talis exstitit* (Aen. 6, 882). 14, 5 *ipse . . . Vergilii sortibus huiusmodi illustratus est* (Aen. 6, 848). SPARTIAN. HADR. 2, 8 *cum sollicitus . . . Vergilianas sortes consuleret 'Quis procul* etc.' (Aen. 6, 808) *sors excidit*. TREBELL. POLL. Claud. 10, 4 *cum in Apennino de se consuleret responsum huiusmodi accepit* (Aen. 1. 265); *item cum de posteris suis* (Aen. 1, 278); *item cum de fratre* (Aen. 6, 669), In the Middle Ages (at the close of which Vergil found an ardent admirer in Dante, cf. COMPARETTI, Virg. nel med. evo 1, 256 and below n. 12) the fourth eclogue was on account of its prophetic tone interpreted of the Messiah; THCREIZENACH, die Aen., die 4 Ekl. u. d. Pharsalia im MAlter, Frankf. a. M. 1864. FPIPER, Virgilius als Theolog und Prophet des Heidentums in der Kirche, Berl, 1862 (evangel. Kalender for 1862, 17). Vergil was even said to have had a hand in the conversion of the Emperor Constantine; cf. ROSSIGNOL, Virgile et Constantin le grand, Paris 1845. DCOMPARETTI (see n. 12) vol. 1.

5. Arrianos (see § 227, 2, in fin.) translated Vergil. SEN. consol. ad. Polyb. 8, 2 *Homerus et Vergilius, tam bene de humano genere meriti quam tu et de omnibus et de illis meruisti, quos pluribus notos esse voluisti quam scripserant*. On Avienus see § 420, 6; on Titianus and Calvus § 364, 4.

6. On the commentators of Vergil see RIBBECK prolegomena critica cap. 9, p. 114, where we find discussions on Q. Caecilius Epirota, Pollio, C. Iulius Hyginus, (Iulius or Aufidius, see § 282, 1) Modestus, L. Annaeus Cornutus, Aemilius Asper, M. Valerius Probus, Flavius Caper, Urbanus, Velius Longus, Q. Terentius Scaurus, Caesellius Vindex and Sulpicius Apollinaris, Helenius Acro, Haterianus, Aelius Donatus, Carminius, Avienus, Servius, the so-called commentarii of Probus, Iunius Philargyrius, the scholia Bernensia and scholia Veronensia. To this may be added HHAGEN's introd. to his edition of the scholia Bernensia JJ. suppl. vol. 4, 696. JKIRCHNER, JJ. suppl. 8, 471. On each of these grammarians see below, in the period to which they belong. In a MS. s. XIV at Padua 'Fulgentius super Bucol. et Georg. Virgilii,' certainly not by the mythologist Fulgentius (§ 480), see EJUNG-

MANN, quaest. Fulg. 61. JMDozio, Cynthii Cenetensis (of the 15th cent.) in Vergil. Aen. commentar. (Aen. I, II, III first edited by AMai, auct. class. 7, 323) e cod. Ambros., Milan 1845.

7. For the scholia Bernensia (on Buc. and Georg.) see § 472, 9: there too concerning both are the explanationes bucolicorum of Junius Philargyrius (Filargirius) and the georgicorum expositiones handed down in the Laur. 45, 14. Paris. 7960 and Leid. 135 (G in Burmann-Lion). The (fragmentary) scholia Veronensia on the Aeneid were first published by AMai (Virgilii intpp. vett., Milan 1818), then in Lion's Servius 2, 305; best ed. by HKeil, M. Valerii Probi in Virg. buc. et georg. commentarius (p. 1–68); acc. scholiorum Veronensium (p. 71–108) et Aspri quaestionum Vergil. (p. 111–115) fragm., Halle 1848. In addition HKeil, RhM. 6, 369 and FBücheler (and AHerrmann), JJ. 93, 65. AHerrmann, d. Veroneser Vergilscholien, Donauesch. 1869. 1871 II. Cf. also GThilo, RhM. 14, 535. 15, 119. ThMommsen. RhM. 16, 137.—Glossary on Vergil, see GLöwe, prodrom. gloss. 164. ABoucherie, fragm. d'un commentaire (very late, and in barbarous Latin) sur Virg. (ecl. and ge. 1, 1–222), Montpellier 1875.

8. Various metrical arguments, chiefly of s. IV/V, for Vergil's works have been preserved: decasticha on the books of the Aen. under the name of Ovid: AL. 1 PLM. 4, 161. Hexasticha on the Aen. by Sulpicius Apollinaris: § 357, 2. Pentasticha on the Aen. AL. 591 sqq. PLM. 4, 136. Tetrasticha on all the works: AL. 2 (cf. 654) PLM. 4, 173 (cf. 444, frequently attributed to Ovid). Monosticha on the Aen. AL. 1 PLM. 4, 176 and AL. 634 PLM. 4, 151; similar ones for all the works AL. 874 PLM. 4, 177. Hemistichia on the Aen. PLM. 4, 178.—Arguments by a certain Modestinus *in antiquissimo Vergilii codice?* Burmann, z. Anth. lat. 2, 188 p. 372.—Cf. LMüller, RhM. 19, 114. 23, 654. Ribbeck, prolegg. Verg. 369. JMähly, ZföG. 22, 331. ROpitz, Lpz. Stud. 6, 282. 298.—Fragments of a mediaeval argument of the Aeneid in distichs from a Bern. s. XII/XIII in HHagen, JJ. 111, 696.

9. Manuscripts of Vergil: Gell. 9, 14, 7 tells us of persons who had inspected *idiographum librum Vergilii* (on ge. 1, 208). Hyginus in Gell. 1, 21, 2 himself collated on ge. 2, 247 a *liber qui fuerit ex domo atque familia Vergili.* We possess (in a more or less complete state) seven very ancient MSS. of Vergil in capital writing (the exact date is rather uncertain, as is the case with all manuscripts in capitals). 1. The 'Mediceus' 39, 1 (M in Ribbeck) s. V at Florence, with the celebrated Subscriptio (cf. § 473, 6): *Turcius Rufius Apronianus Asterius v. c. et inl. ex comite domest. protect. ex com. priv. largit. ex praef. urbi patricius et consul ordin.* (a. 494) *legi et distincxi codicem fratris Macharii v. c. . . . . XI. kal. Mai Romae* (here follow 8 distichs, AL. 3 PLM. 5, 110, facsimile in Ribbeck's Vergil. 4, p. 206). A copy of this MS. by PFFoggini, Flor. 1741. Facsimile in Zangemeister-Wattenbach's exempl. codd. lat. pl. 10, Palaeograph. society pl. 86, Chatelain t. 66, 1.—2. The 'Palatinus' (P) Vaticanus 1631, s. IV-V ?, facsimile in Zangem.-Wattenb. pl. 12. Palaeogr. soc. pl. 115. Chatelain pl. 64.—3. The 'Romanus' (R), Vatican. 3867, s. IV-V ?, in it 16 illustrations to Vergil, published by Bottari (see on no. 4) p. 5. 29. 41. 43 and by Agincourt, hist. de l'art 5, pl. 63–65; PDe Nolhac, les peintures des MSS. de Virg., in the Mél. de l'école franç. de Rome 1884, pl. 11. 12; cf. EPlatner in the description of Rome 2, 2, 347. Text-facsimile in Zangem.-Wattenb. l.l. pl. 11. Pal. soc. pl. 113. 114. Chatelain pl. 65.—4. The 'schedae Vaticanae' (F), Vatic. 3225, put back without cogent reasons into the second century of our era, a copy of this MS. by GGBottari. Rome 1741, in which are (after drawings by PGBartoli, which are now in Windsor, see AMichaelis, arch. Zeit. 32, 67) the illustrations of the MS. (originally 50), mostly

belonging to the Aeneid; there are better specimens in AGINCOURT, hist. de l'art 5, pl. 20–25. PDENOLHAC l.l. p. 5–10. Cf. EPLATNER l.l. 345. Text-facsimile in ZANGEM.-WATTENB. l.l. pl. 13. Palaeogr. soc. pl. 116. 117. CHATEL. pl. 63. —The following MS. fragments are of insignificant extent: 5. Schedae Berolinenses (A), s. IV?, three leaves; to the same MS. (at one time in St. Denis) there originally belonged four leaves, now Vatic. 3256. Published by GHPERTZ, Abh. der Berl. Akad. 1863, 97. Nachtrag, Berl. SBer. 1864, 278, cf. JHENRY, JJ. 95, 419. Facsimile in ZANGEM.-WATTENB. pl. 14. CHATEL. pl. 61.—6. schedae Sangallenses 1394 (G), Facsim. ZANGEM.-W. pl. 14a. CHATEL. pl. 62.—7. schedae rescriptae Veronenses 40 (V). Facsim.: CHATEL. pl. 75, 1.—Together with these earliest MSS. we have the later ones: the cod. Gudianus (γ) s. IX three Berne MSS. (a, b—facs. CHATEL. pl. 67—c) of s. IX and X, besides (of s. X–XII) the codex Minoraugiensis (m). On these MSS., their connection, derivation from the same original etc. see RIBBECK, prolegomena ad Verg. (1866) 218 sqq. Other recent literature on the Vergil MSS.: JHENRY, Aeneidea 1, Lond. 1873, p. XI–LX. On a Prague MS. of s. IX, see JKVIČALA, Vergilstudien, Prague 1878 (with a complete collation). On a Vatic. s. X init. written by Rahingus, a monk of Flavigny in Burgundy, see LDELISLE, Mél. d'archéol. et d'hist. 6 (1886), 239. AJVITRINGA, de cod. Aen. Daventriensi (s. XV, valueless), Daventer 1881. MHECHFELLNER, eine Innsbrucker Virgil-Hs. (valueless), Innsbr. 1880. ECHATELAIN, un important fragm. de Virg. (Paris. 7906) in d. Mél. Renier, Art. 5.

10. Complete editions of Vergil's poems. Cf. the Notitia literaria in HEYNE-WAGNER 4, 635, SCHWEIGER, class. Bibliogr. 2, 2, 1145, ENGELMANN-PREUSS, bibl. class. 2, 693. On the earliest see also JHENRY, Aeneidea 1, LXI–LXXXV. Ed. princ. Rome about 1469. Ven. ap. Ald. 1501 and frequently. Cum comment. Donati, Servii etc. per GFABRICIUM, Bas. 1551 and frequently. Argumentis, explicc. et notis illustr. a JLDE LA CERDA, Madrit. 1608–17 III. E rec. DHEINSII, Leid. 1636. Rec. NHEINSIUS, Amst. 1664. 1676. Interpretat. et notis illustr. CRUAEUS, in us. Delph., Par. 1675 etc. (with an ind. verbb.). Cum Serv., Philarg. etc. et nott. varr. ed. PBURMANN, Amsterd. 1746 IV (in vol. 4 is the ind. verbb. by NERYTHRAEUS, first published at Ven. 1537). Variet. lect. et perpet. adnot. illustr. a CGHEYNE, Lps. 1767–75 IV; ³Lps. 1798–1800 VI (with a good glossary by AWSCHLEGEL); ⁴Lpz. 1830–41 V (cur. PHWAGNER, vol. 4: Carmina minora [Copa, Ciris, Culex, Moretum, rec. JSILLIG], Wagneri quaestt. Vergil., notitia literaria. Bd. 5: V. carmina ad pristinam orthographiam revocata, acc. Wagneri orthogr. Vergiliana etc.). Rec. et illustr. AFORBIGER, Lps. ⁴ 1872–75. Perpetuo comm. ad modum JBond explicuit FDÜBNER, Paris (Didot) 1858. Recensuit ORIBBECK, Lps. 1859–68 V (Prolegomena critica 1866, I Buc. et Georg. 1859, II. III Aen. 1860. 62; IV Appendix Vergiliana 1868). Vergile, texte latin . . . avec un commentaire crit. et explicatif etc., par EBENOIST, Par.² 1876 III. With a commentary by JCONINGTON, revised by HNETTLESHIP, Lond.⁴ 1881–83 III. Explanatory school editions by PHWAGNER (breviter enarravit, Lps.³ 1861), THLADEWIG (Berl. ⁷⁻¹⁰ 1882–86 III by CSCHAPER, cf. the same writer ZfGW. 31, 65). EBENOIST, Par.⁴ 1880, BHKENNEDY, Lond.² 1879, KKAPPES (Lpz.⁴ 1887). With introd. and notes by TLPAPILLON, Lond. 1882 II. ASIDGWICK, Camb. 1890. Translations (prose) by JCONINGTON (Lond.³ 1882), by JGLONSDALE and JLEE (Lond.¹² 1890).

Editions of the text by HPALDAMUS (Lpz. 1854, with introd.), MHAUPT (Lps.² 1873), THLADEWIG (cura PDEUTICKE Berl. ² 1889), ORIBBECK (with introd., Lps. 1867). GTHILO (with introd. and short apparatus, Lpz. 1886). WKLOUČEK, Prague 1886. 87.

11. PHWAGNER, quaestt. Verg. (in Heyne's ed. 4, 383) and lectt. Verg., Phil.

Suppl. 1, 307; together with Phil. 15, 351. 16, 537. 17, 170. WKloůček, Miszellen zu V., Leitmeritz 1870–73 II; critical and exegetical notes on V. (esp. Aen.), Prague 1879; ZföG. 35, 588; Vergiliana, Smichow 1882. 83. JKvíčala (n. 9 in fin.). RBentley's observations on V., communicated by EHedicke, Varia, Progr., Quedlinb. 1879 and AStachelscheid, RhM. 35, 312; ZföG. 35, 588. OGüthling, curaeVerg.; add. GLinkeri emendatt. Verg., Liegnitz 1886. AKirsch, quaestt. Verg. crit., Münst. 1886.

12. Vergil continued to be kept in remembrance by the literature of the whole of the Middle Ages. French, and following them, German elaborations of the subject-matter of the Aeneid occur after the 12th cent. (le Roman d'Eneas by Benoît de Saint-More; Eneit by Heinrich von Veldeke). Towards the close of the Middle Ages, Dante's († 1321) divina commedia transfigured and glorified the poet so that he ceased to belong to the earth. But he also plays a great part in the speech of the people, in popular books and so forth. The great respect in which Vergil, in his quality as a poet, was held by posterity and which manifested itself also in the reverence paid to his burial-place (§ 224, 3 ad fin. Plin. ep. 3, 7, 8; cf. Mart. 11, 48 sq. Stat. silv. 4, 4, 51), the superstitious use made of his poems (above n. 4), and the interpretation of his name (from *virga*, a magic wand) and that of his mother (*Magia*, § 224, 3), caused the gradual evaporation of Vergil's real character into that of a mythical being. In Donatus' vita we meet with indications of this, § 3–5, and in the later additions 8–18, 69 sq. and 78; the more we descend into the Middle Ages (esp. after saec. XII), the stranger the exaggerations, the greater the resemblance of Vergil to such figures as Faustus or Theophrastus Paracelsus. But Vergil always appears as a benevolent genius fond of assisting poor humanity. Only a Roman lady, who had wickedly cheated his love, must feel his revenge. Conformably to the romantic confusion of all names and times, Vergil was now placed under the fabulous Emperor Octavianus, now under King Servius (in the Seven Wise Men), now under Titus (Gest. Rom. c. 57), now under Darius at Rome (ib. c. 120), even in Brittany under King Arthur, or he is represented as the son of a knight of 'Campania in the Ardennes' and of a daughter of a Roman Senator under the Emperor Remus, who killed his uncle Romulus and was succeeded by his son Perseus, in whose reign Vergil studied at the University of Toledo (German popular chapbooks p. 3–7). The scene of his exploits is at Rome and especially Naples, whence the Vergil legend originated. At Rome he performs miracles chiefly at the request of the Emperor, who, after a vain struggle, appoints him his chief Senator, and the aim of his deeds is to insure the safety of the State (Salvatio Romae) and internal order. But at his beloved Naples, which he founded and placed on eggs at the bottom of the sea, he voluntarily provides for the welfare of the town (even driving away snakes and flies, providing good meat, etc.). In the 15th cent. these inventions are brought to a close in the chronicle (ly myreur des histors) of Jean d'Outremeuse and in the Faits merveilleux de Virgile (last printed in Geneva 1867). Principal work: DComparetti, Virgilio nel medio evo, Livorno 1872 II (in German by HDütschke, Lpz. 1875); it contains reprints of the most important documents 2, 169. GZappert, Virgil in Mittelalter, Vienna 1851 (Denkschriften der Wiener Akad. II). KLRoth, der Zauberer Virgilius in FPfeiffer's Germania 4 (1859), 257; cf. KBartsch, ib. 237 and FLiebrecht, ib. 10, 406. CGMilberg, Memorabilia Verg. (Meissen 1857), and Mirabilia Verg. (Meissen 1867). STunison, Virgil in the Middle Age, Cincinnati, 1889. Lastly the treatises by Genthe already quoted (§ 226, 1, 4), Piper and Creizenach (above n. 4).

232. Cornelius Gallus of Forum Julii (684/70–727/27), the

friend of Vergil's youth, was the first Roman poet who (apart from learned translations) devoted himself exclusively to the erotic elegy of the Alexandrines. Through the favour of Octavianus he was raised to high military and political positions, became too ambitious, and finished his life in a tragic manner at an early age.

1. Praenomen: C. and Cn. in the MSS. ap. EUTROP. 7, 7; C. in HIERON. chron. a. 1985 (from Eutrop.).—ASINIUS POLLIO ap. Cic. ad fam. 10, 32 extr. (a. 711/43) *Gallum Cornelium, familiarem meum.* PROBUS on Verg. buc. p. 6, 1 K. *insinuatus Augusto per Cornelium Gallum, condiscipulum suum, promeruit (Vergilius) ut* etc. VERG. ecl. 10 (a. 715/39) is addressed to him, and from this it appears that even then he had written poetry and experienced the faithlessness of his mistress Lycoris (see § 210, 1 in fin.) cf. v. 2–6. 10. 22. 42. 72. Thereon SERVIUS observes: *Gallus ante omnes primus Aegypti praefectus fuit, poeta eximius. nam et Euphorionem . . . transtulit in latinum sermonem* (cf. also on buc. 6, 72) *et amorum suorum de Cytheride scripsit libros quattuor . . . fuit autem amicus Vergilii, adeo ut quartus Georgicorum a medio usque ad finem eius laudes teneret* (see on this § 227, 1) . . . *hic Gallus amavit Cytheridem meretricem, libertam Volumnii, quae eo spreto Antonium euntem ad Gallias est secuta* (cf. the scholion in the cod. Medic. of Vergil [§ 321, 9, 1] on ecl. 10, 2 in ZANGEMEISTER-WATTENBACH's exempla codd. lat. pl. 10); AUR. VICT. ill. 82 (§ 210, 1). On the personality of Lycoris see HFLACH, JJ. 119, 793. WKOLSTER, JJ. 121, 626. Cf. also § 227, 1 and § 224, 3. PROB. on ecl. 10, 50 *Euphorion, . . . cuius in scribendo secutus colorem videtur Cornelius Gallus.* Cf. AMEINEKE, anall. Alex. 24. 78 and above p. 250, 2. OVID. trist. 2, 445 *nec fuit opprobrio celebrasse Lycorida Gallo.* Cf. rem. am. 765. MART. 8, 73, 6. QUINT. 10, 1, 93 calls him *durior* as an elegiac poet. Only a single pentameter of Gallus is extant in VIB. SEQ. p. 5, 21 Burs. Cf. also § 209, 4. 230, 2, 1.—We possess also by Parthenios of Nicaea (printed e.g. in HERCHER's Erotici gr., Lps. 1858, 1, 3) a little book περὶ ἐρωτικῶν παθημάτων, in which erotic legends from Greek sources have been collected for the use of Cornelius Gallus (αὐτῷ σοὶ παρέσται εἰς ἔπη καὶ ἐλεγείας ἀνάγειν τὰ μάλιστα ἐξ αὐτῶν ἁρμόδια), to whom the work is dedicated by the author. ERОHDE, gr. Roman 113.

2. Gallus took part in the war against Antony, DIO. 51, 9. SUET. Aug. 66 *Cornelium Gallum, quem ad praefecturam Aegypti* (a. 724/30) *ex infima fortuna provexerat* (cf. DIO. 51, 17. STRAB. 17 p. 819. EUTROP. 7, 7) . . . *ob ingratum et malevolum animum domo et provinciis suis interdixit. Gallo et accusatorum* (§ 252, 8) *denuntiationibus et senatus consultis ad necem compulso* etc. HIERON. chron. a. Abr. 1990=727/27 *Cornelius Gallus Foroiuliensis* (probably from Forum Julii in Gallia Narbonensis, now Fréjus) *poeta, a quo primum Aegyptum rectam supra diximus, XLIII aetatis suae anno propria se manu interfecit.* Cf. Ov. trist. 2, 446. am. 3, 9, 63. PROPERT. 3, 34, 91. DIO 53, 23. AMM. MARC. 17, 4, 5.—SUET. gr. 16 *Q. Caecilius Epirota . . . ad Cornelium Gallum se contulit vixitque una familiarissime . . . post deinde damnationem mortemque Galli*, etc. Cf. § 263, 1.—WABECKER, Gallus 1³, 16. CCHCVÖLKER, de C. G. vita et scriptis, I Bonn 1840; II Elberf. 1844. ANICOLAS, de la vie et des ouvrages de C. G., Par. 1851. CPASCAL riv. di filol. 16, 399.

3. The 4 poems (fragments), first published by AMANUTIUS 1590, of Gallus (reprinted in WERNSDORF, PLM. 3, 183 and in RIESE's AL. 914–917) have long been recognised as a forgery. An unknown writer (probably himself the forger) in the

year 1587 sent from Thessalonica to AStatius in Rome: 1) *Galli poetae clariss. elegia in antiquo Ovidii codice reperta, sed multis in locis a tineis corrupta* (=914 R.). 2) *versus quattuor sine authore et titulo* (=915). 3) *carmen imperfectum, sed valde elegans ut facile ab eadem officina profectum videretur cum hoc titulo 'de duabus sororibus ex Illyrio'* (=916). Statius having cautiously reserved his opinion, the forger appears to have brought a second thoroughly digested specimen under the notice of other writers with more success. Cf. EChatelain, rev. de philol. 4, 69; also Riese on the AL. 2, xxxiii. xl, not. 28.—An epigram (AL. 242 PLM. 4, 183: a petition to Augustus not to allow the Aeneid to be destroyed in spite of Vergil's will) is also attributed to Gallus in the Vatic. 1575, s. XI and in late MSS., incorrectly, as is shown by its contents; FJacobs (anth. gr. vol. 13, p. 897) likewise incorrectly assigned to Cornelius two epigrams from the Greek anthology 5, 49. 16, 89 bearing the superscription Γάλλου (perhaps more correctly Αἰλίου Γάλλου?).

233. Another friend of Vergil and, as it seems, a writer of elegies was Codrus (perhaps a pseudonym). The poets Bavius and Mevius were enemies of the poet. But as regards Anser, such hostility is not proved; he was an adherent of M. Antony and wrote erotic poetry.

1. Verg. ecl. 7, 21 *nymphae . . . Libethrides, . . . mihi carmen quale meo Codro concedite: proxima Phoebi versibus ille facit.* Cf. ib. 25. 5, 11. Similarly Valgius says of him (Schol. Veron. Verg. ecl. 7, 22; cf. JJ. 93, 66) *Codrusque ille canit quali tu voce canebas atque solet numeros dicere, Cinna, tuos; dulcior ut nunquam Pylio profluxerit ore Nestoris aut docto pectore Demodoci.* See Unger, Valg. p. xi. Idle guesses at his real name (Cornificius or Cinna or even Vergil) are given by the old commentators on the passage. The most likely suggestion would be the Roman name of Cordus. See RUnger, Valg. 405.

2. Hieronym. in Eus. chron. ad a. Abr. 1982=719/35 *M. Bavius* (the MSS. here, as frequently elsewhere, read *Vavius*) *poeta, quem Vergilius in bucolicis notat, in Cappadocia moritur.* Porphyrio on Hor. epod. 10, 1 *hic est Mevius importunissimus poeta, quem et Vergilius cum simili contumelia nominat;* and on sat. 2, 3, 239 *de hoc* (the son of Aesopus the actor, § 13, 4) *Mevius poeta scribit.* Verg. ecl. 3, 90 *qui Bavium non odit, amet tua carmina, Mevi;* on which Servius observes: *pro poena ei contingat ut diligat Meviüm peiorem poetam. nam Mevius et Bavius pessimi fuerunt poetae, inimici tam Horatio quam Vergilio. unde Horatius* (epod. 10, 1). Similarly Philargyrius, probably from Suetonius: *duos sui temporis poetas dicit pessimos, quorum carmina ob humilitatem abiecta sunt . . . ex quibus Bavius curator fuit, de quo Domitius in Cicuta* (§ 243, 2) *refert* (that he lived with his brother in peace and community of goods, until the latter extended also to his wife). Serv. on ecl. 7, 21 *ut sit . . . Thyrsis . . . Virgilii obtrectator, scilicet aut Bavius aut Anser* (n. 3) *aut Mevius pessimi poetae.* On georg. 1, 210 *reprehensus Vergilius dicitur a Bavio et Mevio hoc versu 'hordea qui dixit superest ut tritica dicat'* (cf. ecl. 5, 36): this satirical line is attributed by Cledonius GL. 5, 43, 2 to a certain Cornificius Gallus: cf. § 209, 2 ad fin. and below n. 3 in fin. Cf. generally § 225, 3. Weichert, poetar. lat. vitae etc. 308. The more correct spelling is *Mevius*, not *Maevius:* cf. Mommsen, arch. Ztg. 27, 123; and the Indices to the CIL. vol. 1. 2. 3. 5. 8. 10. 12 and 14 s.v. *Mevius*, further ib. 6, 44. 21814 sqq. and elsewhere.

3. Ov. trist. 2, 435 *Cinna* (§ 213, 2) *his* (erotic writers such as Ticidas and Memmius) *comes est Cinnaque procacior Anser.* He is called *poeta* in Serv on

Verg. ecl. 7, 21 (see n. 2). He is doubtless the same concerning whom CICERO (Phil. 13, 11) jokes: *ii qui nunc Mutinam oppugnant, D. Brutum obsident, de Falerno Anseres depellantur.* According to this he was a zealous partisan of M. Antony. SERVIUS on Verg. ecl. 9, 36 *alludit ad Anserem quendam Antonii poetam, qui eius laudes scribebat* (cf. GL. 7, 543, 21) . . . *de hoc etiam Cicero* (l.l.) . . . *ipsum enim agrum* (*Falernum*) *ei donarat Antonius.* From this passage of Servius is derived the notice published in the glossarium edited by CBARTH, advers. 37, 5 p. 1681 (and following this in LION'S Servius 2 p. 373) and by MOMMSEN, Herm. 8, 67 (from a Vatic. s. XV): *Anser quidam Antonii poeta fuit, qui eius laudes scriberet, de quo Ci. in Philippicis dixit 'ex agro Falerno anseres depellantur,' quem scilicet agrum donarat Antonius.* It is merely owing to some error or corruption that BARTH here reads: *de quo Mel in Philippica Ciceronis dixit*, which is completed Melissus and has been taken to refer to Aelius Melissus (§ 352, 4). MOMMSEN l.l. 74. Perhaps these statements of Servius are founded merely on inference, but it must certainly be due to a misconstruction that SERVIUS l.l. states: *quem ob hoc* (as a partisan of Antony) *per transitum carpsit* (*Vergilius*). For the words (ecl. 9, 35) *neque adhuc Vario videor nec dicere Cinna digna, sed argutos inter strepere anser olores* no more refer to the poet Anser than do the words of PROPERTIUS 3, 34, 84 *anseris indocto carmine cessit olor.* The same misconstruction may easily have led to the statement of SERVIUS on ecl. 7, 21 (see n. 1) that Anser belonged to the obtrectatores Vergilii. The same sort of mistake occurs also in the appendix to DONATUS' vita Verg. 67 (in REIFFERSCHEID'S Sueton. p. 66): *coaevos omnes poetas ita adiunctos habuit ut, cum inter se plurimum invidia arderent, illum una omnes colerent, Varius, Tucca, Horatius, Gallus, Propertius. Anser vero, quoniam Antonii partes secutus est, illum non observasse dicitur. Cornificius* (n. 2, in fin. and § 209, 2 ad fin.) *ob perversam naturam illum non tulit.* Against WEICHERT, poett. latt. vitae etc. p. 159 see RUNGER, de Ansere poeta, Neubrandenb. 1858. EHEYDENREICH in the Commentatt. phil. semin. phil., Lps. 1874, 14.

234. Q. Horatius Flaccus, born 8 December 689/65 at Venusia, was the son of a freedman; he received his instruction at Rome and subsequently (perhaps a. 709/45) at Athens. When M. Brutus came there in August 710/44, he also won the young Horace over to his cause. Horace received from him an appointment as tribunus militum and accompanied him in Macedonia and Asia, until the battle of Philippi (autumn 712/42) precipitately ended his military career. He availed himself of the amnesty to return to Rome, and having lost his paternal estate by the distribution of the land among the veterans, he purchased the position of a quaestorian scribe. He now began to publish his Satires and Epodes, through which he became known in literary circles. In the spring of 716/38 he was introduced by Vergil and L. Varius to Maecenas, and he was admitted to his circle in the winter of 716/717=38/37 B.C. Thus it came to pass that he accompanied Maecenas on his journey to Brundisium, a. 717/37. From Maecenas he received, c. 721/32, an estate in

the Sabine country, and probably through him he was also introduced to Octavianus, who by his liberality set the poet free from all cares concerning his livelihood, and would gladly have attached him to his service and society. In his middle age Horace also composed lyrical poems, in his later years epistles. He died within a short time after Maecenas, on 27 November 746/8, and was buried near him.

1. The poems of Horace contain abundant information on his life. We derive also a number of important facts from the biography of the poet by Suetonius preserved in MSS of Horace (§ 347, 7). It was at an early time prefixed to copies of his poems, especially such as contained scholia. From the latter interpolations were soon added to the vita, e.g. on the *speculatum cubiculum* (from Schol. ep. 1, 19, 1; see KFRoth, RhM. 13, 531. AReifferscheid, Sueton. p. 389). On the other hand, this use of Suetonius' work entailed its being abbreviated, e.g. in the enumeration of the poems of Horace (OJahn ap. Reifferscheid p. 390). The text of the vita e.g. in KLRoth's ed. of Suetonius p. 297; cf. p. lxxx, and the same writer in RhM. 13, 517. FRitter introd. to his ed. of Horace p. v. AReifferscheid, Suetoni rell. (Lps. 1860) p. 44, cf. p. 387. Cf. Acro on c. 4, 1, 1 (*ut refert Suetonius in vita Horatii*) and Porph. on ep. 2, 1, 1 (*cuius rei etiam Suetonius auctor est*). Porphyrio on sat. 1, 6, 41 mentions a biography of Horace by himself *patre libertino natum esse Horatium et in narratione quam de vita illius habui ostendi.*—The other MS. vitae are worthless, Reifferscheid l.l. 387. An enumeration and criticism of these in CKirchner, novae quaestt. hor., Naumb. 1847, 42.

2. Among modern biographies of Horace we mention especially JMasson, vita Horatii, Leid. 1708. ChMitscherlich's introduction to his ed. of the Odes p. cxliv, CPassow, on the life and period of Horace, before his ed. of the Epistles. CFranke, fasti hor. p. 5. deWalckenaer, hist. de la vie et des poésies d'H., Par. 1840. 1858 II. WTeuffel, Horaz (Tüb. 1843) p. 1–13; PRE. 3, 1465. ANöel des Vergers, vie d'Horace, Par. 1855 (also in the introd. to Didot's Horace ed. 1855). LMüller, Hor., e. literarhistorische Biographie, Lpz. 1880.—JMay, d. Entwicklungsgang d. Hor. von 41–33 v. Chr., Constance 1871; von 35–30 v. Chr., Offenburg 1883–87 II. Oertner, H.s Bemerkk. über sich selbst in d. Satt., Gross-Strelitz 1883. FOnesotto, Orazio come uomo, Padua 1888. ACima, Orazio e Mecenate, in Saggj di studj lat., Florence 1889, 1. ALasson, de iudiciis Hor. de suae et prioris aetatis poetis, Stryj 1888. EVoss, d. Natur in d. Dichtung des Hor., Münstereifel 1889. Cf. § 235, 1.

3. His praenomen Quintus is mentioned by Horace sat. 2, 6, 37; his nomen carm. 4, 6, 44. ep. 1. 14, 5; his cognomen Flaccus epod. 15, 12. s. 2, 1, 18; Martial mentions the poet only under his cognomen (1, 107, 4. 8, 18, 5. 12, 4, 1). The day on which Horace was born (*sexto idus decembris*) is given by Suetonius, the month we know from ep. 1, 20, 27; the year from epod. 13, 6. c. 3, 21, 1. ep. 1, 20, 27; the birth-place from s. 2, 1, 34. Venusia was in Apulia on the frontier of Lucania: s. 2, 1, 34 *Lucanus an Apulus anceps.* Martial is wrong in repeatedly (5, 30, 2. 8, 18, 5. 12, 94, 5) mentioning Horace as having been been in Calabria. The rank of his father: *libertinus et* (*auctionum*) *coactor* s. 1, 6, 6. 45. 86. ep. 1. 20, 20. The statement that his father was a salsamentarius (in Suet. vita Hor.) may possibly rest on some slander circulated by the maligners of the poet; AKiessling, coniectan. I. (Greifsw. 1883), 7. On his bringing up s. 1, 6, 72. 1, 4, 105. Instruction, ep. 2, 1, 69. 2, 2, 41. Tribunus militum, s. 1, 6, 48. On his campaigns with Brutus and

his flight at Philippi, see c. 2, 17, where v. 10 (*relicta non bene parmula*) does not exclude the possibility of a previous valiant defence (cf. ep. 1, 20, 23) and only describes the necessary consequence of all defeats (cf. e.g. Liv. 39, 20 *quattuor milia militum amissa . . . et arma multa, quae quia impedimento fugientibus per silvestres semitas erant passim iactabantur*). Horace could not prevent the general flight, nor was he so intimately connected with the cause of Brutus that his honour should have obliged him to court death. Sueton.: *victis partibus venia impetrata scriptum quaestorium comparavit.* Cf. sat. 2, 6, 36 (and ep. 1, 14, 17). The loss of his paternal estate is mentioned ep. 2, 2, 50: then *paupertas impulit audax ut versus facerem*, i.e. (with jocular mockery of his own poetic turn) 'poverty made me fearless, so I attempted to write verse in order that I might become known and get into a better position.' Cf. Fritzsche, Hor. serm. 1, p. 3, 2.

4. The commencement of his acquaintance with Maecenas s. 1, 6, 41–61; cf. 2, 6, 40. He got the Sabine estate a. 721/33; see Teuffel's commentary on sat. II p. 63. cf. ib. p. 158. GFGrotefend, RhM. 3, 471. Suet. v. Hor.: *vixit plurimum in secessu ruris sui Sabini aut Tiburtini: domusque eius ostenditur circa Tiburni luculum* (cf. c. 1, 7, 13). The Sabine estate is mentioned esp. epod. 1, 25. s. 2, 3, 5. 308. 2, 6, 1. 16. 60. c. 1, 17. ep. 1, 16, 1–14. There is voluminous early literature concerning the situation of this estate; among more recent works ANoël des Vergers (see n. 2) in Didot's Horace p. xxiii. PRosa, bull. dell' inst. arch. 1857, p. 105: cf. ib. p. 30. 151. See archäol. Ztg. 16, 155*: JJ. 77, 479. WPfitzner, Parchim 1864. CJullian, la villa d'Hor., Mél. de l'école franç. de Rome 3 (1883), 82. GBoissier, nouv. promenades archéol.: Horace et Virgile, Par. 1886, p. 1. HStich, BlfbayrGW. 20, 416.—A spring on his estate (s. 2, 6, 2. ep. 1, 16, 12) was called by Horace fons Bandusiae (Πανδοσία?) after one near Venusia associated with youthful recollections, c. 3, 13. Cf. Strodtmann, pref. to his translation of the lyrical poems 59.

5. According to his own statements Horace was in person the very reverse of Vergil (§ 224, 4), short (s. 2, 3, 309. ep. 1, 20, 24) and fat (ep. 1, 4, 15; cf. Aug. ep. in Suet.). In his youth he had dark hair (ep. 1, 7, 26, cf. c. 2, 11, 15. 3, 14, 25). Was he delicate? Aug. to Hor. in Suet.: *Si per valetudinem tuam fieri possit* (or did Horace merely make this a pretext in order to remain free?). He was afterwards troubled with hypochondriacal fits (ep. 1, 8). A certain well-to-doness seems to be indicated by some expressions, e.g. on his library (s. 1, 6, 122. 2, 3, 11. 2, 6, 61. ep. 1, 7, 12. 1, 18, 108), his journeys (ep. 1, 15, 1; cf. 1, 7, 11), his slaves (s. 1, 6, 116. 2, 7, 118) and his parasites (see 2, 7, 36). Suet. vita Hor.: (*Augustus Horatium*) *una et altera liberalitate locupletavit.* On the (very dubious) portraits of Horace see Visconti, iconographie rom. 1, 389 (pl. 13) and JBernoulli, röm. Ikonogr. 1, 250.

6. The earliest poems of Horace (from about his 25th to 35th year) are the epodes and the satires. Of the latter, so far as we can now ascertain, b. 1 was finished a. 719/35, book 2 a. 724/30, while the epodes were concluded in the same year. Next follow, among the works of his riper years, first the first three books of the odes, published 731/23; then book 1 of the epistles a. 734/20; after this the carmen saeculare for the secular festival of a. 737/17, which also in the MSS. stood alone (after the epodes); lastly book 4 of the odes, concluded 741/13: Horace only resumed lyrical poetry in response to high influences. Suet. vita Hor.: *Horatium* (*Augustus*) *coegit propter hoc* (that is *propter Vindelicam victoriam Tiberii Drusique privignorum suorum* a. 739/15; cf. c. 4, 4. 14) *tribus carminum libris ex longo intervallo quartum addere* (c. 4, 1, 6 the poet calls himself a man of fifty). Perhaps at the same time as b. 4 of the odes Horace wrote b. 2 of the epistles (consisting of

letters 1 and 2). The liber de arte poetica, if we assume Porphyrio's statement concerning the personality of the Pisones to be correct, must be placed in the latter years of Horace (cf. § 239, 7).—Literature concerning the chronology of the poems of Horace: JMasson, vita Horatii (1708); hist. crit. de la république des lettres (Amst. 1714) 5, 148. Bentley in the preface to his ed. p. xxv has dealt with it summarily but pertinently. CKirchner, quaestt. Hor. (Naumb. 1834) p. 1–41. GFGrotefend, in Ersch and Gruber, Allg. Encykl. 2, 10 (1883), 457; die schrifstellerische Laufbahn des H., Han. 1849. A new investigation by CFranke, fasti horatiani, Berl. 1839; with an epistola Lachmanni, p. 235 (also in his kl. Schrr. 2, 77). The whole question reviewed by Teuffel, Prolegomena zur horaz. Chronologie, ZfAW. 1842, 1103; die Abfassungszeit der Epoden, ib. 1844, 508. 1845, 596; der Satiren, RhM. 4, 93. 208. WChrist, fastorum Horat. epicrisis, Munich 1877. WThStreuber, Chronologie der horaz. Dichtungen, Bas. 1843. CGZumpt, introd. to Wüstemann's ed. of the sat. p. 20 (cf. RhM. 4, 224). ORibbeck, Episteln p. 83. JVahlen, über die Zeit u. Abfolge der Literaturbriefe der Hor., MBer. d. Berl. Ak. 1878, 588 (together with ThMommsen, Herm. 15, 103). HNettleship, transact. of Oxf. philol. soc. 1882/83, 21. CBrandes, de editione satt. Hor., Halle 1885. OTüselmann, quaestt. chronol. Hor., Ilfeld 1885. GGaebel, de H. epp. l. I tempp., Stettin 1888. AKrawutschke, tempp. Hor. carmm. ll. I–III, Troppau 1889.—On the (real and supposed) connections between the poems of Horace and those of Vergil see HDüntzer, JJ. 99, 313. MHertz, anal. ad carmm. Hor. hist. 1, 12. AKiessling in his and Wilamowitz' philol. Unterss. 2, 113. ERosenberg, ZfGW. 36, 675.

7. The order of the poems of Horace is in the MSS. (usually) the following: carminum libri I–IIII, de arte poetica liber, epodon liber, carmen saeculare, epistularum libri I–II, sermonum libri I–II. The order to which we are now accustomed (carmm. [+carm. saec.], epodi, satt., epp., a. p.) was meanwhile not unknown to antiquity, cf. Diom. GL. 1, 528, 34 and § 352, 1. In each book we notice a certain endeavour to give due prominence in the arrangement to the poems addressed to the poet's most valued friends (see below); as for the rest, in the epodes the poems in the same metre are placed together, while in the odes they are separated; at least two sapphic odes (25 in 103) are never found placed immediately together; only alcaic odes, which are more numerous (37 in 103), are frequently found in company (1, 16. 17. 26. 27. 34. 35. 2, 13–15. 19. 20. 3, 1–6. 4, 14. 15). With this exception there is in the odes only a single instance (3, 24. 25) of two poems of the same metre occurring together. In b. 1 the same metre does not recur until c. 10, and book 1, c. 1–11 parades, so to speak, before the reader all the metres employed by Horace in the odes, with the exception of three, each of which only occurs once (2, 18. 3, 12. 4, 7). Horace addresses his very first odes to his aristocratic and distinguished friends (1, 1 to Maecenas, 2 to Augustus, 3 to Vergil, 4 to Sestius, who was consul in the year when this was published 731/23, 6 to Agrippa, 7 to Plancus). In b. 2 c. 1–10 alcaic and sapphic poems succeed each other in regular interchange. This arrangement was all the more practical as the poems were originally separated from each other only by the difference of metre, not by headings (cf. § 240, 3). On this striving for alternation, and the other motives for the arrangement of the poems see Bücheler, coniectanea, Bonn 1878, 15. AKiessling, philol. Unterss. 2, 48. PKSchulze, JJ. 131, 865. ERosenberg, BlfbayrGW. 18, 335. AElter, Wiener Studd. 10, 158.—HStephanus, diatribe de titulis et ordine librorum Horatii, in his ed. of Horace. SCahn, trias quaestionum hor. (Bonn 1838) p. 1–17. Teuffel, ZfAW. 1842, 1108. AHerrmann, curae hor., Celle 1861. ARiese, JJ. 93, 474. Ribbeck, Episteln p. 82.

235. Horace is a highly sensitive nature, in which intellect predominates. It would be idle to expect in him great flights of imagination, idealism of thought and feeling, inspiration, or even anything inspiring. We find in him rare lucidity, calmness and sagacity of mind, a searching knowledge of his own self and of other persons and situations. Trustworthy and faithful towards friends, he is bitter towards his enemies. His sense of independence disgusted him with the capital and endeared to him the quiet of country life. His political opinions and his conduct towards Augustus are a continual compromise between this feeling of independence and his perception of what was possible and what necessary under the circumstances. Here also he hit upon the difficult via media, neither degrading himself nor offending others. He was not a member of the Opposition, but he observed political decency. His views were those of a mature mind, which had got over the passions of youth and could face death intrepidly. Hence his tone changes from joyous love of the pleasures of human life to calm resignation of the enjoyments refused to us: he seldom cares to rise above neutral moods and subdued tones. The aim constantly pursued by Horace is quiet equability, undisturbed by the storms of passion, by external occurrences or by the demands of other men. His intellect sharpened his taste and imparted to his style its peculiar lucidity, which we miss only in those parts where he cannot render his own impressions. Nothing is more foreign to him than exaggeration and bombast. His knowledge of the limitation of human existence makes him talk humorously of himself, and ironically of all who deem themselves great; and it is seen to best advantage in his vein of good-natured raillery.

1. WTeuffel, Charakteristik des Horaz (Lpz. 1842), esp. p. 35; on Hor. (Tüb. 1868) p. 34. WEWeber, Q. Hor. Fl. als Mensch u. Dichter, Jena 1844. SKarsten, Q. Hor. Fl., transl. from the Dutch (Utr. 1861) by MSchwach Lpz. 1863. FDGerlach, Leben u. Dichtung des Horaz, Bas. 1867. OWeissenfels, Horaz, s. Bedeutung usw., Berl. 1885; cf. § 234, 2.

2. His relations with his friends. In the most important passage (sat. 1, 10, 81) Horace mentions as his friends in learned and aristocratic Rome the following: Plotius § 228, 2, Varius § 223, 1, Maecenas, Vergilius, Valgius § 241, Octavius § 255, 5, Fuscus § 242, 1, Viscorum uterque § 242, 1, Pollio § 221, Messala § 222 'cum fratre' § 267, 1, Bibulus § 255, 2, Servius § 242, 3, Furnius § 209, 9. At the same place (sat. 1, 10, 78) Horace also mentions some of his literary adversaries, who were however entirely obscure writers, and who seem to have made even less impression on the public than did the assailants of Vergil (§ 225, 3): Pantilius, Demetrius, who played off the early writers—Catullus and Calvus—against Horace

(cf. s. 1, 10, 18), Fannius (the poetaster; cf. s. 1, 4, 21) and Tigellius Hermogenes (cf. s. 1, 10, 18). FJacobs, verm. Schr. 5, 3. Frandsen, Maecenas (1843) p. 193. GFGrotefend, des Horaz Freunde u. Bekannte, Phil. 2, 280. HPaldamus, Horaz u. Maecenas, ZfAW. 1848, Nr. 113. FJacob, Horaz u. s. Freunde, Berl. 1852 II. JGFEstré, Horatiana prosopographia, Amsterd. 1846. FHanna, zur Prosopogr. Hor., Krems 1885. 86 II. SJaffe, de personis horat., Halle 1885.

3. Concerning Horace's relations with Augustus, Suetonius relates some interesting particulars, which show how greatly Augustus endeavoured to gain the poet in his favour, and how slow the latter was to conform to his wishes. The same appears from the fact that the poems were kept back so very long in spite of the numerous personal relations implied by Horace's intimate intercourse with Maecenas, it appears again when he broke his silence, since his communications merely contain facts, and steer clear of the writer's personal convictions. In those cases in which Horace could not possibly avoid urgent demands, external compulsion is easily felt in the tone of the poems in question. It is not to be denied that he at last did homage to success. But he did not yield to these demands until the monarchy was firmly established, when it would have been scarcely wise to keep aloof much longer, and even then he acted with dignity, not disowning old friends, nor stooping to denounce those who were differently minded from himself. It has been maintained entirely without grounds (CPeter, Gesch. Roms 3, 110) that Horace recommended temperance and unambitious enjoyment of life especially to those men whose high descent, riches or pride might inspire Augustus with distrust. Literature: Wieland's introd. to ep. 2, 1. FJacobs, verm. Schrr. 5, 318. Giesebrecht, quid de Horatio senserit Augustus, Prenzlau 1829. Feldbausch, de Horatio non adulatore, Heidelb. 1839 (cf. Teuffel, JJ. 28, 327). WEWeber, Horaz als Mensch (1844) p. 168. OJahn, aus der Alt.-Wiss. (Bonn 1868) p. 300 and others.

4 With regard to the morality of Horace, it may be granted that only in his later and more mature poems his views as to sexual relations rise above those of his period. But not all passages in the odes touching this point should be understood literally (cf. c. 1, 6, 19 *cantamus vacui sive quid urimur*); on the contrary most of his 'mistresses' owe their existence only to the poet's fancy and to his literary studies. He was preserved from seriously giving himself up to women by his cool, sagacious temperament, so that he should rather be called a depiser of women than one of their votaries. Literature: Lessing, Rettungen des Horaz (Werke 4, 215; ed. of 1857 8, 1). Teuffel, de Horatii amoribus, Jahn's Archiv 6, 325. 7, 648; Charakteristik des Horaz 85. HDüntzer, Krit. u. Erklär. d. Hor. 3, 35. WEWeber in Jahn's Archiv 9, 248.

5. We may speak of the philosophy of Horace in so far as we mean his general views of the world, and so far as Horace assumed a certain position towards the two principal systems then current at Rome, the Epicurean and Stoic philosophy. At first a decided follower of Epicurus (study of Epicurus and Lucretius: AKiessling, coniectanea 3 (Greifsw. 1886), vii. s. 1, 6, 101=Lucr. 5, 83. Cf. besides ep. 1, 4, 16) and adversary of Stoicism, Horace betrayed even then (s. 1, 3. 2, 3. 7) a certain interest in the latter system by his repeated recurrence to it (cf. Teuffel on sat. 2, 7. p. 175). In spite of his hedonistic views of life Horace had a philosophical bent and gradually came to esteem the moral earnestness of the Stoic system independently of its strange excrescences; he gradually ceases to combat it and assimilates more and more of it (cf. ep. 1, 1, 17), though he never really became a convert, but rather maintained towards the various systems a critical attitude or

the eclectic position of a dilettante (ep. 1, 1, 14). c. 1, 34 is rather the expression of a transient mood than the result of a thorough change of mind. The conversion supposed to have taken place then does not prevent the poet calling himself *Epicuri de grege porcum* (ep. 1, 4, 16) even later. But c. 2, 2, 19 proves that when he was turned forty (c. a. 730/24) he began to render more justice to the Stoic system. Recent literature: JHBFortlage, de praeceptis Hor. ad artem beate vivendi spectantibus, Osnabrück 1835. AArnold, das Leben des Hor. und sein philosoph., sittl. u. dichterischer Charakter, Halle 1860. ThVogel, die Lebensweisheit des Hor., Meissen 1868. AJReisacker, Hor. in s. Verhältn. zu Lucrez u. in s. kulturgeschichtl. Bedeutung, Bresl. 1873, see also Weingärtner § 240, 10. RChrRiedl, Hor. Welt- und Lebensanschauung, Trieste 1873. AKirchhoff, d. Stellung des Hor. zur Philos., Hildesh. 1873. FABeck, Hor. als Kunstrichter u. Philosoph, Mayence 1875. HWeise, de Hor. philosopho, Colberg 1881. KMaier, d. philosoph. Standpunkt des Hor., Kremsier 1888.

6. Horace has been reproached with a certain degree of inaccuracy in matters of history, especially Roman; but what is adduced in proof of this is not very sound (cf. also e.g. OKeller, Epileg. zu Hor. 326). The worst passage is c. 4, 8, 17, where the *incendia Carthaginis* are attributed to Scipio Africanus the Elder, which is as bad a confusion as if 'a Prussian poet had attributed the capture of Paris to Frederick the Great' (Haupt, op. 3, 49); but that line is altogether to be suspected as a late interpolation. It is not correct to assume the same confusion s. 2, 1, 71 (cf. Cic. de or. 2, 22), while it is simply preposterous to suppose that Hor. s. 1, 6, 21 is an allusion in bad taste to the old Appius Caecus (§ 90): Horace is here evidently alluding to the severe (cf. also p. 362, l. 3) censorship (Dio 40, 63) of App. Claudius Pulcher 704/50 (§ 199, 1), who proceeded rigorously in the Senate against the sons of freedmen; those proceedings Horace had witnessed at the age of fifteen and, himself the son of a freedman, had retained them in his memory. The rest of the supposed blunders (c. 1, 12, 37. s. 1, 6, 12. ep. 1, 6, 40. AP. 276) are no more satisfactorily proved.

236. The branch of poetry first cultivated by Horace was satire (sermones). Following in the wake of Lucilius, Horace employed satire to display his own individuality and his personal views on various subjects. But after the horrible events of the preceding years, it was not possible to touch upon political topics without tearing open scarcely healed wounds, and a writer who had been a partisan of the conquered side could only keep silence on politics to avoid damaging his character. Hence the subjects of Horace and the aims of his criticisms are exclusively social and literary. The satirist rests his satire on a serious basis, and endeavours to gain proselytes for his ethic ideal by assailing those who disfigure it; but this he does with the weapons of jest, treating what is perverse and objectionable as merely ridiculous. The method of discussion is disguised by an appearance of laxity, though it is anything but planless. The poet with good reason avoids direct exposition. Most of the satires of the second book are dressed up as dialogues or in a dramatic

form, and show a more mature artistic faculty than those of the first. As regards his form, Horace voluntarily confined himself to epic metre, this being indeed most in harmony with the general didactic character of his satires, and also recommended by the example of Lucilius. In his verse Horace succeeded in attaining the lightness and unconstraint proper to satirical poetry. The satires are (together with the epistles, which see) the masterpiece of the poet: in them we see in their fullest and finest development his gift for description, his lively and striking diction and characterisation, his cultivation as a man of the world, and lastly his fine free humour, thoroughly at home with men and the human heart, which with happy ease and without blustering or scolding holds up the mirror to all the follies of his time.

1. On the position of the satires in the MSS. see § 234, 7. These are both in the headings and subscriptions of the MSS. entitled without exception *sermones* (see also § 239, 1). But Horace includes under this name (=tittle-tattle) both his satires (see 1, 4, 42. ep. 1, 4, 1) and his epistles (ep. 2, 1, 4. 250), because both approach the manner of the sermo, the every-day language of cultivated people (sat. 1, 4, 56; cf. *Musa pedestris*, sat. 2, 6, 17. ep. 2, 3, 95). But as the epistles are also *sermones*, it becomes more advisable to designate the satires as *satirae*, especially as s. 2, 1, 1. 2, 6, 17 show that this appellation is in conformity with the poet's intention while it characterises better the position which these poems occupy in literature and their relation to the predecessors and successors of Horace in this department of poetry.

2. Editions of all the Satires (independently of the complete editions of the works § 240, 8). Translated, with notes and introductions by CMWieland, Lpz. 1786. II. [4]1819; the translation also at Bresl. 1881. Explained by LFHeindorf, Bresl. 1815 (EFWüstemann, Lpz. [2]1843; Döderlein [3]1859). Critically revised, translated, and explained by CKirchner, I. Strals. 1829. Translated and explained by WEWeber, edited by WTeuffel, Stuttg. 1852. Critically revised, and translated with explanatory commentary by CKirchner. Lpz. 1854–57 II (the commentary on b. 2 by WTeuffel). Latin text and German translation by LDöderlein, Lpz. 1860. Recensuit PHofmann-Peerlkamp, Amsterd. 1863. Explained by HFritzsche, Lpz. 1875. 76, II; by APalmer, Lond. 1883; by KOBreithaupt, Gotha 1888.—Poetic sermones, Lat. and German with notes by JSStrodtmann, Lpz. 1855. Satires and epistles, in German with notes and introductions by EMunk, Berl. 1867. Sermones aliquot a MHertzio germanice redditi, Bresl. 1875.

3. Recent editions and discussions of individual satires (cf. Teuffel, on Horace 1868, 11) e.g.: 1, 1 (by FAWolf), Berl. 1813 (= kl. Schrr. 2, 992); KReisig's Vorless. üb. Sat. 1, 1, edited by EFEberhard, Cob. 1840; FGumpert, Buxtehude 1888; FAEckstein, familiaris interpretatio, Lps. 1865; on allusions to Vergil's georgica in 1, 1 see MHertz, anal. hor. 1, 12. 1, 3 MSchmidt, JJ. 121, 249. 1, 4 ChCron, epist. ad EOppenrieder, Augsb. 1880. 1, 5 EDesjardins, rev. d. philol. 2, 144. ABischoff, Landau 1880. AWaltz, ann. de Bordeaux 2, 2, 256. 1, 6 PWillems, notes de crit. et d'exégèse, Brussels 1873. 1, 9 FGumpert, Buxtehude

1881. HRoby, journ. of philol. 13, 233. 2, 1 AArlt, Wohlau 1883. 2, 3 FTeichmüller, Versuch einer Sichtung von Hor. Sat. 2, 3, Berl. 1872. EKammer, JJ. 111, 61. 2, 5 HBlümner, RhM. 34, 166.—JApitz, coniectan. in Hor. satt., Berl. 1856. CNipperdey (de locis quibusd. Hor. ex libro I satt.), op. 469. TMommsen, Bemerkungen zu Hor. Sat. I, Frankf. 1871. ALowinski, zur Krit. der hor. Satt., Deutsch-Krone 1889. Sat. 1, 9: JBMispoulet, rev. de philol. 12, 1. 2, 8: JHembold, Mühlhausen i/Els. 1888.

4. DHeinsius, de sat. Hor. liber, in his ed. of Hor., Leid. 1612 and elsewhere. Manso in the supplements to Sulzer 4, 446. BGNiebuhr, Brief an einen Philologen, published by Jacob p. 135. Teuffel, Charakteristik des H. (1842) p. 47. FABeck, das Wesen der horaz. Satire, Giessen 1859. ESzelinski, de nominibus personarum . . . apud poetas satiricos rom. (Königsberg 1862) p. 10–42. ThFritzsche, Menipp und Horaz, Güstrow 1871; Phil. 32, 744. HFritzsche, ed. of Hor. sat. 1, p. 28. 2, p. 90. Arndt, Hor. sitne imitatus Menippum, Harburg 1884. AHeinrich, Lukian u. Hor., Graz 1885. MAHerwig, Hor. quatenus recte de Lucilio iudicaverit, Halle 1873. JJIltgen, de Hor. Lucilii aemulo, Montabaur 1872. LTriemel, üb. Lucil. u. s. Verh. zu Hor., Kreuzn. 1877. RYTyrrell, Hor. and Lucil., Hermath. 4, 355. VZawadzki, qua tenus in satt. Hor. videatur imitatus esse Lucilium, Erl. 1881. FHanna, der apolog. Charakter der hor. Satt., Nikolsb. 1878. 79 II; cf. § 235, 2. ERowe, quo iure Hor. in satt. Menippum imitatus esse dicatur, Halle 1888. RHeinze, de Horatio Bionis imitatore, Bonn 1889. HSchröder, Beziehungen auf Tagesereignisse u. Polemisches in Hor. Satt., in d. Festschr. d. Strassb. protest. Gymn. 1888. AEHousman, journ. of phil. 18, 1 (Satt. and Ep.)—Metrical and linguistic works on the satires: see e.g. AKiessling introd. to his ed. 2, xiv. On the construction of the Horatian hexam. see e.g. FCHultgren, JJ. 107, 150. Vogel, d. Struktur des hor. Hex., Düren 1887. ThFranzen, d. Unterschied d. Hex. bei Virg. u. Hor., Cref. 1881.—FBarta, sprachl. Studd. z. d. Satt. d. Hor., Linz 1879. 81 II. Bäker, d. Metaphern i. d. Satt. d. H., Strals. 1883.

237. The epodes, which were written about the same time as the satires are, like these, of an aggressive character; they are, however, directed against individuals, while the satires contain criticisms of general application. Horace appears here as an ardent and skilful imitator of Archilochos and his versification. Besides the acerbity and animosity which form a characteristic feature of this kind of poetry, Horace imitated also its peculiar *αἰσχρολογία*. The whole collection forms a book of studies, the satirical element of which Horace developed in the sermones, the formal (melic) element in the odes, in both cases with greater success. The later pieces of this collection are more quiet and mature and approach the style of the carmina, just as many of the latter might well be ranged among the epodes in regard to form and contents.

1. *Iambi* is the name which Horace himself gives to the collection dedicated to Maecenas 14, 7 (*deus nam me vetat inceptos olim, promissum carmen, iambos ad umbilicum adducere*): cf. c. 1, 16, 3. 24. ep. 1, 19, 23. 2, 2, 59. Therefore the last epode 17 (in iambic trimeters) is entitled to form part of this collection. The name of

ἐπῳδοί and τὰ ἐπῳδά, *epodon liber*, is an addition of the grammarians, taken from the metrical character of most of the pieces. The name of epode subsequently became usual for all those kinds of metre in which a long and short line (the latter called ὁ ἐπῳδός sc. στίχος) are combined, especially an iambic trimeter and dimeter, e.g. epod. 1–10. Thus e.g. SCHOL. HERMOG. in Walz's Rhetores gr. 7, 820 ἐστὶ δὲ ἀεὶ τὸ ἐπῳδὸν βραχύτερον τοῦ πρὸ αὐτοῦ στίχου συλλαβὰς τέτταρας. The single poems are called by PORPHYRIO *eglogae* (see § 226, 1 l. 14). For the relation of these poems to Archilochos see ep. 1, 19, 23–25. The treatment of the trimeter in Horace exactly agrees with the manner of Archilochos. But epod. 16, the earliest of all the lyrical poems (a. 714/40), shows exclusively pure iambics (and no elision in the hexameter) after the manner of Catullus (4, 29). As regards the intimate connection of the latest epodes with the earliest odes cf. epod. 9 with c. 1, 37. A spirit similar to that of most of the epodes appears also in c. 3, 15; and c. 1, 4. 7. 28. 2, 18. 4, 7 might as well form part of the epodes, as far as their metrical form goes—but that collection was already completed when the odes were composed. The four-line strophe (§ 238, 4) is not employed in the epodes, neither is it possible to trace in them any antistrophic arrangement.

2. PHBUTTMANN, Mythologus 1, 318. VANDERBOURG's ed. 2, 2, 549. CFRANKE, fasti hor. 43. WFÜRSTENAU, de carm. hor. chronologia 11. TEUFFEL, ZfAW. 1884 sq. (see § 234, 6). MAXT, zur Erkl. u. Krit. der hor. Epoden, Creuzn. 1846. LEIDLOFF, de epodon Hor. aetate, Holzminden 1856. FMARTIN, de Hor. epodorum ratione antistrophica et interpolationibus, Posen 1860. Cf. against this ABUTTMANN, ZfGW. 16, 673. 753. CBECK, de vera epodon horat. indole, Troppau 1873. On epod. 2 see AMMANN, Bruchsal 1888; epod. 9 GFALTIN, JJ. 131, 617; epod. 14 JCPOHL, ZfGW. 33, 575. OHARNECKER, ib. 36, 428.

238. When Horace was already midway between thirty and forty, he resolved to use the technical skill and mastery of style, which he had acquired in composing his epodes, for the purpose of transplanting Alkaios and Sappho into Roman soil. He was thus employed for at least eight years, and the result is the first three books of the carmina, to which he subsequently added a fourth, under external pressure, after a long interval. Being the production of the ripest years of Horace, and of refined artistic consciousness, the lyrical poems are in point of form the most perfect of his creations, remarkable for the thoughtful lucidity of their design, the care and finish of the work, the evenness of the execution (showing preference for a tripartite arrangement), the severe regularity, beauty and harmony of the verses and the delicate linguistic perception. But they are not the immediate expression of inner experience which the poet puts forth to relieve and unburden himself of it, nor are they the outpouring of inspiration and overflowing imagination; they chiefly manifest a clear, calm and mature mind and careful reflection on the questions of life. There are not, however, wanting indications of tameness and frigidity; some turns and

expressions are rather prosaic and affected, and art is too often distorted into artificiality; we meet with exaggerations quite at variance with the poet's general good taste, and repetitions occur in the whole collection, but with especial frequency in the additional fourth book. These faults appear most of all in those poems which are either mere abstract compositions or even written to order; but when Horace's heart was interested, he often rose to real beauty. He began his lyric poetry with imitations of Greek works, gradually attempted independent composition in their spirit, and last of all treated original subjects, chosen from contemporary history, or manifestations of his own mind, in the Greek moulds.

1. Self-criticism of Horace: *operosa parvus carmina fingo*, c. 4, 2, 31. In epod. 11 and 14 he confesses that love prevented him from working (writing), and c. 1, 1, 19. 29 harmless enjoyment of life is contrasted with poetical studies. Again s. 1, 4, 39 Horace excepts himself from the number of real poets, though in other places he speaks complacently of his lyrical performances (especially in the last poems of books 2 and 3 of the odes): but the great care and industry bestowed upon his compositions, and the renown he gained by them, gave him a right to do so. Characterisation of Horace as a lyric poet in MHaupt's op. 3, 52.

2. The lyrical poems of Hor. are entitled *carmina* in the MS. headings and subscriptions, and likewise in the later grammarians, in whom however the name *odae* also occurs. Horace never employs the word *ode*. He repeatedly calls his poems *aeolium* or *lesbium carmen*, e.g. c. 3, 30, 13. 4, 3, 12. 1, 26, 11. 1, 32, 4; cf. 4, 6, 35. Their connection with Aeolic melic poetry (in which Catullus preceded him) is indeed their chief characteristic, and it is a special merit of Horace that he fell back upon the genuine classical melic poets of the Greeks, such as Alkaios, Sappho, and Anakreon—an immense gain in naturalness. Yet he did not do so throughout and consistently, but in place of nature he often started with artificial and rhetorical, or even academic motives. Cf. also AKiessling, on the reception of the Odes of Horace in the first century, in the Verhandl. d. Kieler Philologenvers. (Lpz. 1870) p. 28. As translations (metrical imitations) we may safely consider 1, 9 and 18, as well as the beginning of 1, 37. In all these instances we see how far Horace was from the fresh native energy of his originals, but also how clearly—showing himself in this rather a scholar than a poet—he knew what he had to omit or change and what to adopt, what minute attention he gave to his transitions and connections, and to the working out of details, and how he brings his poem within the immediate scope of his reader by adding traits of contemporary history. But independently of the intentional imitations we meet also with frequent reminiscences of Greek poets, which however we must not suppose to have been deliberately collected with bee-like industry.—On Horace's relation to the Greeks see GFGrotefend, die Originalität des Horaz in s. Oden, ZfAW. 1844, no. 19. ThArnold, de Horatio Graecorum imitatore, Halle 1845; die griech. Studien. d. H., Halle 1855. 1856. Göbel, Hor. u. Euripides, ZfGW. 1, 298. HHGarcke, Hor. carm. libri I collatis scriptoribus graecis illustrati specimen, Halle 1853. 1860; quaestionum de graecismo Hor. pars prior, Halle 1860. EThallwitz, de Hor. Graecorum imit. I, Lps. 1874. JFCCampe, Hor. u. Anakreon, Phil. 31, 667. (An attempt at a Greek translation of the odes of Horace by BArnold, Munich 1858.) See further § 240, 10.

3. In his treatment of the metres which he imitates we find various divergences in Horace as compared with his Greek models: here Horace has not been (as used to be supposed) exclusively influenced by the peculiarities of the Latin tongue (e.g. its wealth of spondees); he has been guided likewise by the rules of metre at that time prevailing and circulated in various text-books: the poet's practice accords noticeably with these theories in several points, e.g. in his preference for the long syllable in many instances and in his treatment of the caesura. WChrist, d. Verskunst des Hor. im Lichte der alten Überlieferung, Münch. Sitzungsberichte 1868, 1 sqq. AKiessling, introd. to his edition of Horace 1, vii. GSchultz, Herm. 22, 270. But adherence to theory will not in itself account for the gradually increasing strictness in the radical use of the spondee. C. 1, 15 (ascl.) is shown to be one of the very earliest attempts by the fact that at v. 36 Horace still employs the trochaic basis instead of the spondaic. In the same way in the anacrusis of the alcaic line Horace has admitted a short syllable five times in the first book, three times in the second, twice in the third, while he avoids it in the fourth. With regard to the caesura we find in Horace strict regularity: e.g. in the alcaic and sapphic line of eleven syllables he places the caesura each time after the fifth syllable, because according to the theory which he follows the joining between the two parts of the line occurs at this place. A careful study of Horace's treatment will also show that he steadily laboured at the perfection of the outward form of his poetry. In his alcaic strophes Horace gives to the third line of nine syllables in the odes of the first two books, as he does to the first two lines of the strophe, the caesura πενθημιμερής (i.e. division of 5+4). But subsequently he came to the conclusion that this rendered the line monotonous (the general defect of the Horatian metres), hence in the third and fourth books he carefully avoided this caesura of the third line and replaced it by others (especially the division of 6+3, sometimes also 7+2, with separate division of the first part). Cf. CLachmann's note on Franke's fasti hor. 238. The πενθημιμερής in the sapphic strophe which is used in b. 1–3 almost exclusively (see above) has, in the fourth book and the carm. saec., to share with the caesura κατὰ τρίτον τροχαῖον. Division of the word at the end of the third line in the same strophe does not occur in the fourth book or in the carm. saec. Horace is here more strict than in b. 1–3 with regard to elision (Lachmann on Lucr. p. 219). Cf. AWaltz (§ 240, 10). OTüselmann (§ 234, 6 in fin.) 17.—On the metres of the Horatian odes in general see summaries before the editions and Teuffel introd. to GLudwig's new translation of the odes (Stuttg. 1860), 24. A comparison of the Hor. metres with the Greek originals in CBock, de metr. Hor. lyricis, Kiel 1880. See in addition EUrban, Vorbemerkk. z. e. Hor.-Metrik, Insterb. 1885. HSchiller (for the use of schools, Lpz.[2] 1875). RKöpke, Berl.[3] 1886. On the elisions (synaloephae) see KLehrs, Horatius (1869) p. i–xxii and JSchultz, die prosodia satiricc. Rom., Königsb. 1864. FLindemann, de hiatu in versibus Hor. lyricis, Zittau 1825. Cadenbach, de alliterationis apud H. usu, Essen 1838. On the metre of c. 1, 10 ThKock, RhM. 41, 315. ThReichardt, de metrorum lyric. Hor. artificiosa elocutione, Marb. 1889.

4. Strophic arrangement is peculiar to the idea of an ancient μέλος. Hence we meet with it in the odes of Horace. Yet not only in Pindar, but also in Alkaios and Sappho we often see sense and grammatical construction carried beyond the limits of the strophes (Westphal, gr. Metrik 2^2, p. 295), so that there is nothing strange in Horace taking the same liberty; and even e.g. in the fourth book (which is otherwise more strict in its construction, see n. 3), in his favourite metre, the alcaic, he allows the close of the strophe to coincide with that of the sense more rarely than in b. 1–3 (Kiessling in the philol. Unterss. 2, 82; intr.

to his ed. 1, xv). The smallest compass of a strophe embraces two lines, like the elegiac distich, and the epodes of Archilochos and Horace keep within this. But the sapphic and alcaic strophes consist of four lines each, likewise those forms of the asclepiadean metre in which three asclepiadean lines are joined to a glyconean, or two asclepiadean lines and one glyconean are joined to a pherecratean. If an asclepiadean is joined to a glyconean line, the result is a strophe of two lines; cf. however c. 3, 9 the dialogue with speech and rejoinder each of 4 lines in 3 groups; if the asclepiadeus minor or maior is simply repeated through the whole poem, we have an apparently monostichic composition. But after the suggestion of Wetzel, CLachmann (kl. Schrr. 2, 84) and AMeineke (pref. of his edition) have made the observation that not only with the latter metres, but also in the carmina which resemble epodes, in fact in all the poems of the four books (except the very corrupt c. 4, 8, see also § 235, 6), the number of the lines is divisible by four, from which they drew the probable though not absolutely certain conclusion that Horace himself always designed his poems in strophes of four lines each. On the influence of this discovery on the criticism of Horace see LDöderlein, Reden (1860) p. 388. 403. Cf. also WFörster, quaestt. hor. 2 (Brünn 1870), 3. CBock, de Hor. metr. lyricis, Kiel 1880, 55.

5. Ovid. trist. 4, 10, 49 *tenuit nostras numerosus Horatius aures, dum ferit ausonia carmina culta lyra.* Petron. 118 *Horatii curiosa felicitas.* Quint. 10, 1, 96 *lyricorum* (rom.) *Horatius fere solus legi dignus. nam et insurgit aliquando et plenus est iucunditatis et gratiae et variis figuris et verbis felicissime audax.* Paneg. in Pis. 229. Fronto p. 23 Nab. (*memorabilis poeta*). Apoll. Sidon. ep. 8, 11. carm. 9, 218–222. Jani pref. to his edition 1, civ. Manso in his additions to Sulzer 5, 301. RHanow, ist H. ein kleiner Dichter? Halle 1838. AStahr, in the Hall. Jahrb. 1840, 1652. Teuffel, ib. 1841, no. 106–112, and Charakter. d. H. (Lpz. 1842), 13. 73. AGGernhard, de compositione carminum Hor., Weim. 1841–1842 II. ELTrompheller, Beiträge z. Würdigung d. horaz. Dichtweise, Coburg 1855–74 V. CPrien, d. symmetrische Bau der Oden d. Hor., RhM. 13, 321. FMartin, de aliquot Hor. carminum ratione antistrophica et interpolationibus, Posen 1865. Here, as well as in the epodes, Martin simply proceeds upon the plan of eliminating as spurious all passages which are at variance with his assumed laws of symmetry; so also CPrien, FJSchwerdt, and others. Such mechanical views of the general poetical method of Horace have been wrongly deduced from the strictly systematic arrangement of several of his lyric poems.—FPeters, z. Wortstellung in den Oden d. H., Münster 1870.

6. Horace's predilection for the same number (three) in his illustrations is very conspicuous, just as he also frequently repeats himself; Teuffel, on Horace (1868) 18. Prosaic illustrations and turns occur e.g. 3, 1, 25. 34 sqq. 3, 4, 69 sq. 3, 5, 12. 3, 11, 18 sq. 4, 4, 37 sq. Prosaic particles like *ergo* (epod. 2, 9), *quodsi* (1, 1, 35. 3, 1, 41. epod. 2, 39. 10, 21. 11, 15. 14, 13), *atqui* (1, 23, 9. 3, 5, 49. 3, 7, 9), *quatenus* (3, 24, 30), *eius atque* (3, 11, 18 cf. 4, 8, 18), also probably *namque* (1, 22, 9. 1, 34, 5. 4, 1, 13). An elevated tone does not suit Horace, and whenever he strikes upon it, he soon drops it again; sometimes indeed one may doubt whether this is not done with intentional humour, e.g. when he says of Venus 4, 1, 21 sq.: *naribus duces tura*, or ib. 4, 7, 5 sq. 2, 20, 9 sqq. It sounds like parody to read in a sapphic ode of *teretes surae* (2, 4, 21) or in an alcaic ode of *olentis uxores mariti* (1, 17, 7). Bad taste of this kind appears in *auritae quercus* (1, 12, 11 sq.), the *libido quae solet matres furiare equorum* (1, 25, 13 sq.), *clavi trabales* etc. (1, 35, 18 sqq.), *hydrops* and *aquosus languor* (2, 2, 13 sqq.) and in the rude expressions 2, 5, 2 sqq. 2, 11, 21. 3, 11, 19. 4, 13. epod. 9, 35. In the same way *vitrea Circe* (1, 17, 20) and *purpurei olores* (4,

1, 10) are not exactly elegant epithets. See OKELLER, RhM. 19, 211.—It also happens frequently that Horace overdoes his illustrations, heaping one upon another with the immoderation of a rhetorician: cf. 1, 1. 3, 1, 9 sqq. 41 sqq. 3, 27, 1–16. epod. 2. Neither 2, 20 nor 3, 30 can be called moderate. Learning is put in quite out of its proper place 2, 17, 13–20. 2, 18, 35 sqq. Exception may be most frequently taken to the long odes, where Horace's inadequate talent for lyric poetry becomes most conspicuous. TEUFFEL, die horazische Lyrik und deren Kritik, Tüb. 1876, 18 makes an attempt to arrange the odes and epodes in order of merit: he distinguishes four degrees: 1. imperfect poems, in which the deficiencies preponderate, the majority being youthfully immature, unmeasured or forced (14 poems). 2. Medium work not without defects (considerable either in number or character), in which however good work preponderates (80). 3. Good examples, without important defects (24). 4. Excellent work, with decided preeminence both in substance and form and (almost) without any real defects (3 poems, viz. c. 3, 7. 9. 29). Goethe's language (RIEMER's Mitteil. 2, 643) is equally exaggerated and incorrect, where he says that he recognises Horace's poetical talent only in regard to technical and linguistic perfection, i.e. successful imitation of the Greek metres and poetical diction, and this combined with a fearful realism, devoid of any real poetry, especially in the odes; and so are GRUPPE's dictum (Minos 412) 'Horace is himself only in his odes' and KLEHRS' paradoxical opinion (N. Schweiz. Mus. 1861, 64) 'The real Horace is never found in his odes.' On the contrary, the same individuality which is seen in the satires and epistles appears to all intents and purposes in the odes; whence we should also explain the good and bad qualities of the latter. An impartial criticism on Horace's lyrics by GBERNHARDY, Berl. Jahrbb. 1835, 750. LEHRS, Horatius p. LXXV, justly says, 'we should learn not to exaggerate the poetical character of Horace and even be prepared to meet with great defects.' But he does not act up to this maxim; see n. 7. Cf. also the remarks in MHAUPT's op. 3, 52.

7. An opinion which still widely obtains starts with the assumption that Horace is a faultless lyrical poet. An attempt is made to support this by arbitrary construction (recently either a vapid mystic-melancholy interpretation has been adopted which readily discovers deep sentiment, or else a humoristic one, which, when at fault, detects charming sallies and conceits): while others assert that the Horatian poems have been very largely interpolated. It is of course open to each writer and to every age to praise or to blame the poet according to their own standard, but it is absurd to pretend to judge solely by the criterion of modern aestheticism, what is and what is not the work of the poet. The strong rhetorical alloy in the odes is often displeasing to us, while it delighted the Romans. The absence of a dominant motive and of warm feeling, which seems to us a defect, was to the Romans amply compensated by the musical and artistic quality of the language in its metrical mould. Again, it has been forgotten that Horace produced his odes by slow, deliberate polishing, remodelling and gradual elaboration (§ 238, 1, 2. KIESSLING l.l.), and likewise that the poet reckoned upon careful readers, capable of following up concealed allusions. It became usual to declare spurious everything which contradicted the unfounded assumption of the perfection of the odes. But it must be confessed that, even after the most extensive omissions, much remains which might justify renewed objections, and consequently new omissions, so that we should never have done with them. This method of holding interpolators responsible for everything which did not exactly suit the casual reader (no trouble being taken to prove the possibility of such interpolation) caused the poems to be unjustly criticised; passages which deserved no blame at all were treated superciliously and immoderately censured. The first writer who, following certain

predecessors such as DLAMBINUS, TFABER and especially FGUYET (see his objections enumerated in the Phil. 35, 479), applied this fixed idea of the absolute perfection of Horace's lyrical poems in a one-sided way, even making it the test of the genuine or spurious origin of the whole or part of the odes, was the Dutch scholar PHOFMAN-PEERLKAMP (ed. of the odes of 1834). Cf. GBERNHARDY, Berl. Jahrbb. 1835, 737. TEUFFEL, Peerlkamp und seine Bestreiter, JJ. 41, 438; Jahrbb. der Gegenwart 1843, no. 50 sqq. = Correspondenzblatt f. d. württemb. Gelehrtenschulen 1859, 196; über Horatius (Tüb. 1868), 20; die horaz. Lyrik u. deren Kritik, at the Tübingen Philol.-Versammlung, Tüb. 1876, p. 1. MADVIG, adv. crit. 1, 93. LMÜLLER, JJ. 87, 171. 176; Gesch. d. class. Philol. in den Niederl., Lpz. 1869, 13. Among those who followed in the wake of Peerlkamp must be mentioned FMARTIN (in the Posen Programme of 1844. 1858. 1860. 1865; cf. n. 5 and 9 and § 237, 2), AMEINEKE (in his ed.), CPRIEN, GLINKER (ed. of 1856 and in the transactions of the Breslau, Frankfort, Meissen, Halle, Innsbruck, Wiesbaden and Gera Philologenversammlung; quaestt. Hor., Festschr. z. Tübinger Jubiläum, Prague 1877 etc.), OFGRUPPE (Minos; on the interpolations etc., Lpz. 1839; Aeacus, Berl. 1872; cf. TEUFFEL, RhM. 28, 634 and on Gruppe's self-contradictions MHERTZ, JJ. 93, 577), KLEHRS (Horatius, Lpz. 1869) and others. Cf. besides KGESELL, de interpolatt. mythol. ap. Hor., Bonn 1865. On the other side ABISCHOFF, hor. Lyr. I. Schaffh. 1872, 81. NMADVIG, adv. crit. 2, 50; SCHEELE, Horatiana, Merseb. 1874. IOLSSON, Lund 1882. 1885 and others.—More circumspect investigators have long since recognised that only a few passages necessitate the assumption of interpolations: PHBUTTMANN, Mythologus, 2, 364, MHAUPT, op. 3, 42 (cf. CHRBELGER, MHaupt als akad. Lehrer [Berl. 1879], 137), also LMÜLLER in his editions, AKIESSLING, zur Interpol. u. Interpretation der Oden, in his and Wilamowitz' phil. Unterss. 2, 75; cf. also SHEYNEMANN, de interpolationibus in carm. Hor. certa ratione diiudicandis, Bonn 1871 (against this FAHOFFMANN, vindic. Venusinae, Neisse 1873). A review of the atheteses of Peerlkamp and his followers in the odes in THFRITZSCHE, de interpol. hor. 1, Güstrow 1873; a supplement on FGUYET, Phil. 35, 477.

8. Recent separate editions of the odes (and epodes) (cf. the general editions § 240, 8) by CHDJANI (Lps.[2] 1809 II), CHWMITSCHERLICH (Lips. 1800 II), CFPREISS (Lpz. 1805–1807 IV), CHVANDERBOURG (ad fidem XVIII MSS. Paris. rec. etc. Par. 1812 II), PHOFMAN-PEERLKAMP (Harlem 1834; [2]Amsterd. 1862. Cf. above n. 7), FLÜBKER (commentary on b. I–III, Schlesw. 1841), THOBBARIUS (Jena 1848), CIGRYSAR (Vienna 1853), LMÜLLER (with notes, Giessen 1882), JMMARSHALL, Lond. 1874, TEPAGE, Lond.[4] 1890, ECWICKHAM, Lond.[2] 1887, AFRIGELL ([2]Upsala 1888; also adnott. ad H. carmm., Ups. 1888), EROSENBERG, Gotha 1883.

9. Reviews of and discussions on single odes, esp. recent ones: 1, 1–4 EANSPACH. Cleves 1888. 1, 1 by GHERMANN, op. 8, 395; CHRJAHN, Lpz. 1845; cf. JJ. 43, 462; HSCHWALBE, Eisleben 1865; ALOWINSKI, Deutsch-Krone 1878; Miscellen, Deutsch-Krone 1886; JCHFCAMPE, JJ. 101, 125; ADÖRING, Phil. 33, 713; HSTÖPLER, Darmst. 1881; LREINHARDT, JJ. 129, 429. THPLÜSS, JJ. 133, 115. 1, 2 (and 2, 13 sq.) by HRUNGE, Osnabr. 1871; EBENOIST, rev. de phil. 2, 62. 1, 1. 3. 12. 20 GBOISSIER, rev. de phil. 2, 204. 1, 3 JBARTSCH, JJ. 109, 275; EROSENBERG, ZfGW. 35, 396. 1, 3. 4, 12 EWÖLFFLIN, Phil. 39, 367. 1, 4 THPLÜSS, JJ. 133, 785. 1, 6 THPLÜSS, JJ. 129, 139; MGITLBAUER, philol. Streifz. 1, 125. 1, 4 and 12 AREIFFERSCHEID, anall. hor., Bresl. 1870. 1, 7 JBARTSCH, JJ. 111, 701; KSCHENKL, ZföG. 29, 1; AREIFFERSCHEID, Bresl. ind. schol. 1879/80, 1; 1884/5, 11. 1, 12 JBERNAYS, op. 2, 300; MHAUPT, op. 3, 55; THPLÜSS, JJ. 107, 111; WHERBST, JJ. 111, 119; JSTRENGE, Friedl. i. M. 1882; THKOCK, Herm. 17, 497. 1, 5–12 EANSPACH, Cleves, 1889. 1, 14 RUNGER, JJ. 115, 763; THPLÜSS, JJ. 129, 853. 1, 16 KNIEMEYER,

JJ. 133, 129. 1, 20 AKiessling, Wiesbad. Philol.-Vers. 142; cf. Phil. Anz. 8, 447. 1, 20. 30. 2, 11. 4, 3 FAEckstein, scholae Horat., Lpz. 1869. 1, 22 KSteffen, Lpz. 1882. 1, 22 and 3, 8 ARuhe, Münst. 1873. 1, 25 ThPlüss, JJ. 127, 493. 1, 28 BGWeiske, JJ. 12, 349; CPrantl, Munich 1842; AMeineke, Phil. 5, 171; LDöderlein, Erlang. Philol.-Vers. 51; cf. 59; CGöttling, ges. Abhh. 2, 214; JMähly, RhM. 10, 127; FMartin, Posen 1858; HJHeller, Phil. 16, 731; AMeyer, Festschr. v. Parchim 1877, p. 45; FAdam, Patschkau 1881; LCantarelli, riv. di filol. 11, 86; AReifferscheid, Bresl. ind. schol. 1884/85, 12; ThPlüss, JJ. 133, 123. 1, 32 EBrocks, Schwetz 1881. 1, 34 GLinker, Wiesbad. Philol.-Vers. 167. 1, 34. 3, 1 Kern, Ulm 1878. 1, 37 HProbst, Essen 1871. 2, 1 FRitschl, op. 3, 602; FMartin, Posen 1858; ThPlüss, JJ. 117, 641; GBoissier, ann. de la fac. de Bordeaux, 1, 80. 2, 2 KFisch, Frauenfeld 1883. 2, 5 ThPlüss, JJ. 131, 272. 2, 6 JCFCampe, JJ. 115, 136; ThPlüss, JJ. 117, 137; JBartsch, ib. 111, 703; ALuchs, Erl. 1888. 2, 7 VValentin, Frankf. 1887. 2, 11 ThPlüss, JJ. 119, 209. 2, 12 JProschberger, BlfbayrGW. 23, 201. 2, 13 WHRoscher, JJ. 135, 676. 2, 19 ThPlüss, ZfGW. 35, 720. 2, 20 ThPlüss, JJ. 123, 189. 3, 1–6 HWarschauer, de Hor. l. III, 1–6 carmm. p. I (esp. on 3, 3), Bresl. 1877. In addition ThPlüss, ZfGW. 33, 707; ERosenberg, ZfGW. 34, 309; ThMommsen, preuss. Akad. 24 Jan. 1889. 3, 3 CLStruve, op. 2, 339; CKiesel, Düsseld. 1845; FBamberger, op. 200; RRauchenstein, N. schweiz. Mus. 1, 129; HSchwalbe, Eisl. 1863; ERosenberg, JJ. 133, 344. 3, 4 GSchepss, BlfbayrG. 24, 185; ATeuber, JJ. 139, 147. 3, 5 sq. 16 sq. Scheele, Merseb. 1874. 3, 8 ARuhe, Münst. 1873; FHarder. JJ. 129, 412. 3, 11 FNäke, op. 1, 73. 3, 12 KLachmann, kl. Schr. 2, 84; PKnapp, JJ. 115, 326; LQuicherat, mélanges (Par. 1879) 59. 3, 25 Th Plüss, Pforta 1879. 3, 27 ThSchäfer, Lpz. 1868; ThPlüss, ZfGW. 32, 649; LBolle, JJ. 134, 578; RBlack, Class. review, 3, 3 p. 107. 3, 30 ESchulze, JJ. 135, 621; EAnspach, JJ. 137, 383. 4, 2 and 8 FSüss, St. Pölten 1883. 4, 2 KZiwsa, ZföG. 31, 246; Bücheler, RhM. 44, 317. 4, 6 FBücheler, RhM. 14, 158. 4, 7 FMartin, Berl. 1837; HProbst, JJ. 131, 140. 4, 8 KLachmann, kl. Schr. 2, 95; GHermann, op. 8, 401; AKiessling, Greifsw. 1874; JHäussner, Freib. i. Br. 1876; HJordan, Herm. 14. 270.; AWVerrall, journ. of phil. 17, 145. 4, 11 MGitlbauer, philol. Streifz. 1, 130. Carm. saecul.: JWSteiner, Kreuzn. 1841; CFHermann, de loco Apollinis in c. s., Gött. 1843; AKühn, Bresl. 1877; HBesser, JJ. 133, 692. MMessina Faulesi, il carm. sec. de Or., Catania 1889.—Critical, linguistic and other writings on Horace's odes, e.g. in Lachmann's kl. Schr. 2, 81, Madvig's adv. 2, 50, Bücheler's coniectanea (Bonn 1878) 10; RhM. 37, 226. ThFritzsche, Beitr. z. Krit. des Hor., Güstrow 1877. RUnger, analecta Hor., Halle 1877. HThPlüss Horaz-studien . . . über horaz. Lyrik, Lpz. 1882. ERosenberg, d. Lyrik des H., Gotha 1883. WGebhardi, ästhet. Commentar z. d. lyr. Dichtt. d. Hor., Paderborn 1885. FBobrik, Horaz. Entdeckungen (!!) u. Forschungen I, Lpz. 1885 (compare FCurschmann, Darmst. 1885). AWVerrall, Studies . . . in the odes of H., Lond. 1885. JJCornelissen, Mnemos. 16, 293. LBolle, d. Realien in den Oden d. H., Wismar 1882, and others.

10. Translations of the odes especially by KWRamler (Berl.[2] 1818 II), WBinder (Stuttg.[4] 1855), v.d.Decken (Brunswick 1838 II), JSStrodtmann (with Lat. text and notes, Lpz. 1852), GLudwig (Stuttg. 1853. 1860), ABacmeister (Stuttg. [1871]), ThKayser (Od. and Epod., text and transl. with notes, Tüb. 1877), CBruch, Minden 1855.—50 odes translated in EGeibel's class. Liederbuch, Berl.[4] 1882. 12 odes and epodes transl. by LMüller, Petersb. 1882. English verse: JConington, Lond.[10] 1888. By various translators: ed. CWFCooper, Lond. 1880. SdeVere, Lond.[3] 1888.

11. The musical settings of some of the odes are extant, proving that Horace

was occasionally sung in convents: see ORELLI-BAITER's ed. 2, p. 915. KIRCHNER, novae quaest. Hor. 37.—RVLILIENCRON, d. horaz. Metren in deutschen Compositt. des 16. Jahrn., Lpz. 1888.

239. The epistles are written in the same metre as the satires; they share with the latter the general character of sermones and together with them constitute the most remarkable production of the muse of Horace. In freshness and liveliness they are indeed inferior to the satires, and in not a few passages they are mere prose done into verse as regards their structure, but they atone for these defects by a more mature tone and form, refinement, and moderation of view, and conscious power. Now portraying the character of the author, now absorbed in the immediate purpose of a letter, now dealing with a given subject in quite a didactic style, they are distinguished sometimes by the nice tact with which difficult questions touching personal or social relations are treated, sometimes by their abundance of sound, suggestive matter. The latter especially applies to the letters (in b. 2 and in the epistle de arte poetica extant in a separate form) in which Horace's literary views are defended with much warmth and in some passages with partiality, his contention being that the Romans ought to fall back upon the genuine Greek models and endeavour after their formal polish rather than imitate the negligence and disregard of form peculiar to the old Roman poets. The most famous of these epistles is the one addressed to the brothers Piso, in which a number of aesthetic questions are dealt with in a very sensible manner, somewhat on Greek lines, but with considerable originality.

1. The epistles speak of themselves (ep. 2, 1, 250) as *sermones* (i.e. in antithesis to compositions in an elevated style), though this is not meant to stand for their title, which is constantly given as *epistulae* by the grammarians and MSS. Cf. PORPHYR. on ep. 1, 1, 1 *Flacci epistularum libri titulo tantum dissimiles a sermonum sunt. nam et metrum et materia verborum et communis adsumptio eadem est;* the same writer sat. 1, 1, 1 *quamvis saturam esse hoc opus suum Horatius ipse confiteatur* (sat. 2, 1, 1), *tamen proprios titulos voluit ei adcommodare. nam hos priores libros duos sermonum, posteriores epistularum inscripsit. in sermonum autem vult intellegi quasi apud praesentem se loqui, epistulas vero quasi ad absentes missas.*

2. Regarded as the expression of the poet's moods, the letters present great variety; cf. ep. 1, 8 with 7 and 10; 1, 15 with 14. On the whole they show a more highly matured art, and this even in details; for instance, elisions in the epistles are comparatively far less numerous (by about $\frac{2}{5}$) than in the satires. JJEEP, de elisionibus Horat., Wolfenbüttel 1844. Long vowels are very rarely elided before short (i.e. invariably short, which AMICHAELIS, comment. Mommsen. 428 disregards) in the epistles (and never in the AP.). MHAUPT, op. 1, 91; cf. 121. LACHMANN on Lucr. p. 77. Cf. also THBIRT, hist. hex. lat. Bonn 1876, 38.

3. Separate editions of the epistles (cf. the collective editions § 240, 8). Explained by FEThSchmid, Halberst. 1828. 30 II (without Ars poet.). Commentariis uberrimis instructas ed. SObbarius, Lps. 1837–47 II (without book II). With an introduction etc., by ORibbeck, Berl. 1869 (against this e.g. OLemcke, Jena 1874). By ASWilkins, Lond.[3] 1889. B. 1 by ESShuckburgh, Cambr. 1888. With Satt. and AP., by ECWickham (forthcoming).

4. Latin and German by JSStrodtmann (Lpz. 1854), LDöderlein (Lpz. 1856. 58 II). Other translations: by CMWieland (Dessau 1782. Lpz. 1837 II. Bresl. 1883), CPassow (Lpz. 1833; without AP.), JMerkel (Aschaffenb. 1841), WEWeber and WTeuffel (Stuttg. 1853. 1859), FList, Erl. 1883. CBardt, Bielef. 1887. JConington (Lond.[7] 1888, with Satt., in verse).

5. CMorgenstern, de sat. et epist. hor. discrimine, Lpz. 1801. CPassow (see n. 4) cxxxix n. 178. 180. 282. Teuffel, Charakteristik des Hor. (1842) 61. Düntzer, Kritik u. Erkl. 3, 73. WEWeber, Horatius (1844) 281. Schierenberg, die Personen der Briefe d. Hor., Detmold 1846. Manso, Hor.'s. Beurtheil. d. älteren röm. Dichter, in his Miscellaneous Essays and Treatises (Bresl. 1821) 87. KReichel, Hor. u. die ältere röm. Poesie, Pressb. 1852. ABarkholt, Horatii de vett. Rom. poetis sententiae, Warburg 1876. EMeissner, d. Kampf d. H. für eine bessere Geschmacksrichtung in der Poesie, Dresd. 1867. Berning, d. Geist der horaz. Briefe, Recklingsh. 1856. LDöderlein, translation p. 78. KLehrs, Horatius (1869) p. clvii. WHKolster, die Episteln des H. welche ersichtlich Antwortschreiben sind, Meldorf 1867.

6. Hofman-Peerlkamp, adnott. ineditae ad Hor. epp., Mnemos. 14, 305. HKeck, de Hor. epist. libro I critica ad L. Doederleinum epistola, Kiel 1857. HMuther, Beitr. z. Erkl. u. z. Emendation der horaz. Epp., Cob. 1864. FPahle, zur Erkl. von Epp. I, JJ. 97, 185. 269. LCMAubert, adnott. in I H. epp. libr., Tidskr. f. fil. 9, 170. MBedjanić, de H. epp. l. I, pars I, Serajewo 1883. FCBirch, Tidskr. f-filol. 8, 161. 9, 186.—Revisions of and discussions on particular epistles: 1, 1 APlanck, Corr.-Bl. f. d. württemb. Gel.-Sch. 31, 521. 1, 1 and 7 LDrewes, JJ. 113, 705. 1, 2 the same writer in JJ. 111, 705. 1, 5 ThFritzsche, Phil. 42, 769. 1, 6 APlanck, württ. Corr.-Bl. 32, 542. 1, 6 and 10 OLemcke, Jena 1874. 1, 6. 10. 16 GBippart, Prague 1887. 1, 7 by RHasper, Naumb. 1874; ThÖsterlen, württ. Corr.-Bl. 29, 283. 1, 11 and 14 JChFCampe, Phil. 29, 448. 1, 11 Teuffel, RhM. 27, 347; AKnütgen, Oppeln 1882; AReifferscheid, Bresl. ind. schol. 1884/85, 15; GFaltin, JJ. 137, 567. 1, 12 JArnoldt, JJ. 101, 619; JChFCampe, JJ. 115, 129; ASchubert, Anklam 1879. 1, 14 WGillischewski, Lauban 1885. 1, 15 MSchanz, Verhandl. d. Würzb. Philol.-Vers. (Lpz. 1869) 115; Courtoy, rev. de l'instr. publ. en Belg. 11, 4; RDuncker, JJ. 129, 57. 1, 16–18 PGeyer, de Hor. ep. 1, 16–18, Jena 1872. 1, 18 JBaron, Iambor 1881. 1, 19 FClausen, Jena 1868. 1, 20 OMüller, ein Begleitschreiben des H. zu s. Sermonen, Berl. 1876. 2, 1. 2 and AP. JVahlen, die Zeit u. Abfolge der Literaturbriefe des H., SBer. d. Berl. Akad. 1878, 688, compare ThMommsen, Herm. 15, 103; AKeissling, Griefsw. ind. lect. 1887/88. 2, 1 by KZell, Heidelb. 1819; HRiedel, Groning. 1831; JVahlen, ZföG. 22, 1. 254 (against Ribbeck, ib. 241). 24, 18; JNFischer, ZföG. 35, 481. KMacke, JJ. 137, 697. 2, 2 ALowinski, scholae crit. in H. ep. 2, 2, DKrone 1875; JVahlen, ZföG. 25, 12; AOPrickard, transact. of Oxf. philol. soc. 1886/87, 9.

7. In the MSS. the liber de arte poetica follows immediately after the odes (§ 234, 7). This work is already quoted by Quintilian (8, 3, 60 *Horatius in prima parte libri de arte poetica*); cf. Symmach. ep. 1, 4. Apoll. Sid. carm. 22 (*lyricus Flaccus in artis poeticae volumine*), and 9, 220. Prisc. GL. 3, 254, 16 (*Horatius de*

arte poetica). Charis. GL. 1, 202, 26. 204, 5 includes the Ars poet. among the epistles, and since HStephanus and Cruquius it has been accounted the third epistle of b. 2. This epistle is usually considered to be among the latest works of Horace, or is even taken to be the very last (cf. Teuffel's transl., Stuttg. 1859, 304 together with ARiese, JJ. 93, 476; see also above n. 2 ad fin.). See however AMichaelis, commentat. Mommsen. 420, who for reasons not quite conclusive holds (with Reenen) that the Horatian Pisones are Cn. Calpurnius Piso (cos. 731/23) and his sons (coss. 747/7 and 753/1) and believes the Ars poetica to have been composed simultaneously with the first book of the epistles, about 734/20. Cf. also Mommsen, Herm. 15, 114. 20, 282. HNettleship, journ. of phil. 12, 43.—Porphyrio at the commencement (p. 344 Meyer): *hunc librum, qui inscribitur de arte poetica, ad L. Pisonem qui postea urbis custos fuit* (=cos. 739/15) . . . *eiusque liberos misit* . . . *in quem librum congessit praecepta Neoptolemi* τοῦ Παριανοῦ *de arte poetica, non quidem omnia, sed eminentissima.* This distinct statement of Porphyrio precludes the conjecture of Meineke, who suggests the work of that Alexandrian writer περὶ ἀστεϊσμῶν, though again it does not oblige us to believe that Horace availed himself of such an inferior authority on a subject of which he was complete master. But Aristotle's treatise on poetry could neither be ignored nor overlooked by Horace; a parallelism between Aristotle's poetica and this epistle, though partly exaggerated, is given by Streubner, l.l. 72.

8. Editions of the Ars poetica e.g. by FvPHocheder (Passau 1824), PHofman-Peerlkamp (Leid. 1845). MAlbert (Par. 1886). Various experiments in criticism by Peerlkamp, JGOttema (Löwen 1846), Gruppe, Ribbeck (against him Reger, die AP. des Hor., Passau 1873), Lehrs, MSchmidt and others (see n. 9). See also Teuffel, RhM. 28, 493; LSpengel, Phil. 33, 574. Translations (cf. n. 4 and 9) by AArnold (Berl. 1836) and another AArnold (in rhyme, Erfurt 1853. Halle 1860), JMähly (Jahn's Archiv 19, 436: röm. Lyr. [1880] 60), ThKayser, Stuttg. 1888 and others.

9. Explanatory treatises on the Ars poetica. VanReenen, dissertat. philol. crit. etc., Amst. 1806. Eichstädt, quo tempore et ad quos scripta sit, Jenae 1811. Bosch, curae secundae in Hor. epist. ad Pis. Jenae, 1812; cf. Ernesti Parerga p. li. EMüller, Gesch. der Theorie der Kunst bei den Alten 2 p. 269–284. WTh Streuber, Basl. 1839. Lindemann, Zittau 1841 II. FJacob, on the relation of the Epistles of Horace to his Satires (Lüb. 1841), 7. Teuffel, on the character of Horace (1842) 64. GBernhardy, prooemium de Hor. ep. ad Pis., Halle 1847. AMichaelis, de auctoribus quos Hor. in arte poetica secutus esse videatur, Kiel 1857; die horaz. Pisonen, commentatt. Mommsen. 420. BBüchsenschütz, Phil. 12, 150. LSpengel, ib. 18, 94. AKiene, Composition der etc., Stade 1861, likewise VValentin, Frankf. 1876. FABeck, Beitr. zur Würdigung der AP., Giessen 1863. FBeck, die Ep. an d. P. nach ihrem Zusammenhang etc., Eos 1, 196. JVahlen, ZföG. 18, 1. MSchmidt, horazische Blätter, Jen. 1874 p. 1–57. EBährens, miscell. critt. (Grön. 1878) 35. VZambra, l'epistola ai Pisoni, Trent 1875–79 IV. OWeissenfels, ästhet.-krit. Analyse der AP., Görlitz 1880. Adam, Cic.'s Orat. u. Hor. AP., Urach 1882. GFaltin, Berl. phil. Wschr. 1884, 1223; Horazstudien I: d. Zusammenh. d. ep. ad Pis., Neuruppin 1886. GAntonibon, studj sull' A.P. di Oraz., Bassano 1888. l' A.P. commentata da GBBonino, Turin 1888.

240. The poems of Horace obtained immediate recognition, and maintained their position throughout antiquity. Their use as a text-book for schools contributed to this in a great degree.

The necessity of having numerous copies of them rendered interpolation extremely difficult, and any attempts of this kind were soon rejected and remained without influence upon the text. These poems were also commented on at a very early time by Julius Modestus, Valerius Probus, Q. Terentius Scaurus, Helenius Acro, Pomponius Porphyrio, perhaps also Claranus. Scholia by Porphyrio are extant. Those which bear the name of Acro are of a later period. The number of MSS. of the works of Horace is very considerable, but none of them goes beyond the ninth century.

1. Horace himself (ep. 1, 20, 17) prophesied that he would become a school-author, and as early as in the time of Juvenal (7, 226) he had regularly taken that position. On the reception and spread of H.'s works in the 1st cent. see JHLMeierotto, de rebus ad auctores quosdam class. pertinentibus dubia, Berl. 1785. SHeynemann, de interpolatt. in carm. Hor., Bonn 1871. AKiessling, Verh. der Kieler Philol.-Vers. 1869, 28. Cf. § 219, 17. § 332, 4. Hor. is often cited by Quintilian who, as well as other authors, quotes passages (e.g. c. 1, 12, 40 in Quint. 9, 3, 18; c. 2, 17, 17 in Persius 5, 45) which have been doubted by the hypercritical wisdom of modern times; Caesius Bassus and Martial also quote him. List of the quotations from Horace in the editions of Ritter and Keller-Holder, WDillenburger, testimonia zu Horaz, ZfGW. 22, 322. Cf. Haupt, op. 3, 47. Besides Persius (see § 302, 4) Horace had for his imitators esp. Seneca (tragedies), Statius, Ausonius, and Martial, Claudian, Prudentius etc. HPaldamus, de imitatione Horatii (Greifsw. 1851). AZingerle, zu spät. lat. Dichtern 1 (Innsbr. 1873), xii and 1; Ovids Verhältn. zu s. Vorgäng. 3 (Innsbr. 1871), 9 and esp. MHertz, analecta ad carminum Hor. historiam, Bresl. 1876–82 V.

2. Suetonius (Reiffersch. p. 47) *venerunt in manus meas et elegi sub titulo eius et epistola prosa oratione quasi commendantis se Maecenati. sed utraque falsa puto* (see § 46, 7). *nam elegi vulgares, epistola etiam obscura, quo vitio minime tenebatur.* These attempted deceptions were so strongly rejected by general tradition, that they do not even survive in a single MS., nor do we perceive any fluctuation as concerns the extent of the existing works. No doubt Horace himself suppressed his youthful Greek poems (see 1, 10, 31). The two new odes asserted by Pallavicini to have been discovered by him in the Vatican library (printed 1788 in Villoison animadv. ad Long. p. 310, and in the Gentleman's magazine, also in Jani's edition 1 p. cvi; Preiss 1, 110, Peerlkamp p. xxviii and elsewhere) are the production of a very late time; cf. Vanderbourg 1, 356. Ballenstedt, Hanover 1788. A dissertation concerning two odes of Hor., London 1789. Richter, vita Horatii p. 127.

3. Commentaries: Hieronym. apol. c. Rufin. 1, 16 (cf. § 41, 4) *puto quod puer legeris . . . commentarios . . . et aliorum in alios, Plautum videlicet, Lucretium, Flaccum* etc. The vita in the Bern. 363 (B) and Paris. 7975 (γ), with which Pseudo-Acro introduces his expositions, says: *commentati in illum sunt Porphyrion* (§ 374, 3), *Modestus* (§ 231, 6. 282, 1) *et Helenius Acron* (§ 374, 1) *omnibus melius.* On Valerius Probus § 300. On the supposed commentator of Horace, C. Aemilius, see FHauthal, RhM. 5, 516.—The Scaurus quoted by Porphyrio on sat. 2, 5, 92 is no doubt Q. Terentius Scaurus § 352, 1. On the supposed Chalcidius § 407, 5.

The headings of the poems in the MSS. sometimes only name the recipient (*ad Maecenatem, ad d. Augustum* etc.) sometimes they add in Greek technical terms a designation of the metre (*monocolos, dicolos, tetracolos* etc.) and of the contents (*encomiastice, erotice, hymnus, paraenetice, pragmatice, proseuctice, prosphonetice* and so forth). Not one of these notices is by the poet himself: but in several of the designations of recipients we can discern the traces of an expert scholar of a good period; cf. esp. the heading to c. 1, 4 *ad Sestium Quirinum*, owing to which it has been feasible to fix this name (that of the consul of a. 731/23) in a fragment of the fasti Capit. (CIL. 1, p. 441). AKiessling, de horatian. carmm. inscriptionibus, Greifsw. 1876. WHenzen, ephem. epigr. 3, 15. Those data concerning contents and metre, which are entirely external in their character, are derived from the schools, in which Horace was treated of and commented upon according to the canons of rhetoric. EZarncke, de vocab. graecanicis in inscriptt. carmm. Horat., Strassb. 1880; JJ. 123, 785.—There were writers *qui de personis horatianis scripserunt* (Porph. on sat. 1, 3, 21. 91), who have been made use of in Porphyrio's commentary: the notices from this have been collected by AKiessling, de personis horat., Greifsw. 1880.

The so-called Commentator Cruquianus is a collection of glosses from among his MSS., especially the Blandinii (n. 5) and other authorities (amongst them more recent ones, e.g. the Basle editions of 1527 and 1555) carelessly compiled by JCruquius; cf. Cruquius on ep. 1, 18, 15 (p. 581 a): *Blandin. antiquissimus, ex quo comment. descripsimus.* A number of scholia formerly only known from the comm. Cruq. are to be found in the Paris. 7975 s. XI (n. 6): cf. HJordan l.l. 3 and AKurschat, unedierte Horaz-Scholien d. Par. 7975 (γ) zu c. l. IV, epod., carm. saec., sat. l. I, Tilsit 1884. The comm. Cruq. contains many excellent notices not to be found elsewhere. KZangemeister, RhM. 19, 333. WHirschfelder, quaestt. hor. spec., Berl. 1862; ZfGW. 18, 568. FMatthias, quaestt. Blandinianae, Halle 1882, 29. HJordan, de commentatore Hor. Cruquiano, Königsb. 1883.—In the Vindob. 213 s. X–XI are preserved scholia on the Ars poetica by Alcuin (or belonging to his school), founded on the so-called Acron (see § 374, 2), cf. Schol. Vindob. ad Hor. a. p. ed. JZechmeister, Vienna 1877; cf. OKeller, ZföG. 28, 516. See for similar scholia on the AP. and other epistles in the Monac. 14693 s. XI, JHuemer, Wien. SBer. 96, 506.

4. Editions of the scholia by GFabricius (Basle 1555), by FPauly (Prague 1858 sq. II, see on these JMützell, ZfGW. 9, 850; cf. FPauly, Beitr. zu Porph., Prague 1876; new additions Prague 1877) and by FHauthal, Berl. 1864. 1866 II (cf. OKeller, JJ. 91, 175. Hauthal, ZfGW. 20, 398). Porphyrionis commentarii in Horatium, rec. WMeyer, Lps. 1874 (see the same author in Beitr. z. Krit. des Porph., Munich 1870). Concerning the scholia see WHDSuringar, hist. crit. scholiastarum latt. Vol. III, Leid. 1835. WDillenburger, Horatiana, Aachen 1841. WTeuffel, RhM. 3, 473. CKirchner, novae quaestt. hor. 1847, 59. CLRoth, RhM. 13, 517. GLinker, ZföG. 9, 813. HUsener, de scholiis horat., Berne 1863. OKeller, RhM. 19, 154; symbola philolog. Bonnens. (Lps. 1867) 491. ESchweikert, de Porphyrionis et Acronis scholiis horat., Münst. 1865; de Acrone qui fertur Hor. scholiasta, Cobl. 1871. MGitlbauer, Porphyrion's text of Horace in his phil. Streifzügen 120.—Textual criticism MPetschenig, ZföG. 22, 649. 27, 721. 30, 801; Progr. of Klagenfurt 1872; of Graz 1873. Critical estimate of the Schol. of HRUnger, JJ. 115, 490. WAHoffmans, in schol. hor. quaestt. Münst. 1874.

5. The number of the MSS. of Horace amounts to about 250, most of which come from France. In Italy the MSS. of Horace are much more scarce, and almost

all of late date. Horace was not really acclimatised in Germany until the middle of the 10th century; previous to this period the odes especially were known only to the most learned scholars in the convents (see EVoigt l.l. 27). Of the 1175 hexameters of the ecbasis captivi (a beast-epic of s. X edited by EVoigt, Strassb. 1875. Cf. AEbert, Lit. d. MAlt. 3, 276. CBursian, Gesch. d. class. Phil. in Deutschl. 49; Münch. SBer. 1873, 457) 250 are derived from Horace (esp. from the satt. and epp.).—Enumerations of the MSS. e.g. in Keller-Holder, praef. to vol. I and II.—The codices Blandinii, which were in the Abbaye de St. Pierre au mont Blandin (at Ghent) and perished when it was destroyed a. 1566, we know (apart from insignificant notices in the miscell. of PNannius?) only through the information supplied by JCruquius in his separate and collective editions (see n. 8) of Horace: see on this KZangemeister, RhM. 19, 321 and ESchweikert, Cruquiana, MGladbach 1879. Cf. also JMützell, ZfGW. 9, 850. KHalm, ib. 946. FRitter, ib. 11, 359 and against him HDüntzer, ib. 11, 927. 18, 876. Among these codd. Blandinii the antiquissimus is by RBentley, KLachmann (ad Lucret. p. 37), MHaupt (see e.g. op. 3, 45), KZangemeister (RhM. 19, 321) and others rightly considered to be the principal basis for the formation of the text, while ThBergk (op. 1, 737. JJ. 83, 861) maintained that the statements of Cruquius on his MSS. of Horace were partly falsifications. The latter opinion has been adopted by OKeller (RhM. 18, 281. 19, 634; Epilegomena zu Hor. 292. 800). See the palaeographic juggling in AHolder, Herm. 12, 501 in order to get rid of the awkward reading in the Bland. antiquiss. (s. 1, 6, 126), which in itself shows the superiority of this MS. over the others; another 'methodical' essay with the same intention in OKeller, Epileg. 483. Unfortunately the text of the Blandine MSS. of Cruquius has been transmitted incompletely, superficially and with numerous errors and confusions; but there is neither evidence nor likelihood of his having falsified it. The still extant cod. Divaei, now Leid. 127 A s. XII, has likewise been used by Cruquius, also with great carelessness, but without falsification: JHäussner, phil. Rundschau 1883, 233. FMatthias, quaestt. Bland. 52. Recent treatises: WDittenberger, ZfGW. 35, 321. WMewes, de codicis Hor. Blandin. vetustiss. natura et indole, Festschr. d. Friedr.-Werderschen Gymn., Berl. 1881, 51 (compare RKukula, phil. Rundsch. 1882, 1001); der Wert des cod. Bland. Vetust., Berl. 1882. FMatthias, quaestt. Blandiniarum capp. III, Halle 1882. PHöhn, d. cod. Blandin. antiquiss., Jena 1883. JHäussner, Cruquius u. die Horazkritik, Bruchsal 1884; phil. Rundsch. 1884, 430. RCKukula, de Cruquii codice vetustissimo, Vienna 1885.

6. Among the MSS. of Horace preserved to us (of which not one was written in uncial letters, the Blandin. antiquiss. had *barbarissimos characteres*, see Cruq. on sat. 2, 7, 64, therefore was likewise not in uncials) the following are notable for their antiquity and excellence: Bernensis 363 [Bongarsianus] s. VIII–IX (B in Keller-Holder; on critical marks in this MS. see HHagen, Züricher Philol.-Vers. 1887), Sueco-Vaticanus 1703 [from Weissenburg in Alsace] s. IX–X (R), Harleian. 2725 [Graevianus] s. IX–X (δ). Harleian. 2688 s. IX–X (d), Paris. 7972 [Mentelianus] s. IX–X (λ), Paris. 10310 [Augustodunensis, Autissiodorensis] s. IX–X (π) (Chatelain, rev. de phil. 12, 13; MHertz, anall. ad hist. Hor. 5, 24); Argentoratensis s. (IX–) X, burnt a. 1870 (D), Einsidlensis 361 s. X ineuntis (ε), Paris. 7973 s. X in. (u), Ambrosian. O 136 [from Avignon] s. X in. (a), Dessaviensis s. X in. (ν), Leid. 28 [from Beauvais] s. X in. (l), Paris. 7900ᵃ [Puteaneus] s. X, a few leaves of this are in the town library at Hamburg, see AKiessling, Jen. LZ. 1875, 158 (A), Turicensis s. X (τ), Paris. 7974 s. X (φ), Paris. 7971 s. X. (ψ), Lips. s. X (L), Paris. 7975 s. XI (γ), Mellicensis s. XI (M) and others. Photographic facsimiles of most of these MSS. (and of a few others) in Chatelain, paléogr. des class. lat. pl. 76–90.

—In 8 MSS. (e.g. in A, λ, l, and also in the Gothanus s. XV, in which alone of all the MSS. sat. 1, 6, 126 agrees with the Bland. vetustiss.) we find after the epodes the following subscriptio: *Vettius Agorius Basilius Mavortius v. c. et inl. excom. dom. excons. ord. legi et ut potui emendavi conferente mihi magistro Felice* (§ 452, 6) *oratore urbis Romae* (OKELLER, Epilegom. 415. 785). Cf. below § 477, 3.—Hitherto it has not been feasible to establish an authentic pedigree for the MSS. Certain more or less closely related groups may indeed be distinguished among the mass, but the differences between these groups are so slightly marked, their readings are so mixed and interchanged, that the decision between the various readings of the earliest MSS.—for these, of the MSS. named above, especially B and R, must naturally first be consulted—rests less upon the fact of their belonging to this or that group than upon other grounds, such as the poet's language elsewhere, and the logic and cohesion of the passage. The text has been transmitted, on the whole, with very remarkable uniformity, and the very numerous quotations from Horace (see n. 1) in later authors show no important divergence from our MSS. There is not much scope for conjectural criticism in the Horatian text.—MHAUPT, op. 3, 45 'the MSS. of Horace are the better the nearer they approach to the earliest of the lost Blandines . . . It is one of the laws of Horatian criticisms that there be no unnecessary departure from this Blandine MS., even where it is unsupported.' AKIESSLING, de horat. carm. inscript. (Greifsw. 1876) p. 8. LMÜLLER, pref. to his ed. of Hor. (Lpz.[2] 1879) p. VII. OKELLER, RhM. 19, 225. 33, 122; Epileg. p. VII. 790 and in the prefaces of the ed. mai. (cf. besides JJ. 133, 509) distinguishes 3 classes of MSS. (he reckons e.g. in I: MRγDτ; in II: AB, the revision by Mavortius; in III: φψδ). TEUFFEL, z. Beurtheil. der Hss. des H. in the Begrüss.-Schrift f.d. Tübinger Philol.-Vers. (Tüb. 1876) p. 19 unites in one Keller's classes I and II, see on this KELLER, RhM. 33, 127.

7. Horace's influence on German literature: see TEUFFEL, Charakt. d. H. (1842) 50. HFRITZSCHE, JJ. 88, 163. CLCHOLEVIUS, Gesch. d. deutsch. Poesie nach ihren antiken Elementen 1 (Lpz. 1854), 335. 469. 488. 2 (1856), 75. 435. ALEHNERT, d. deutsche Dichtung d. 17. u. 18. Jahrh. in ihrer Bez. z. Hor., Königsb. 1882.

8. Complete editions. The ed. princ. (fol.) s. l. et a., (though printed in Italy about 1470–73). Further may be mentioned: with the commentary of CHR LANDINUS, Flor. 1482. GFABRICIUS, Bas. 1555. With MURETUS' Comm., Ven. 1555. DLAMBIN's ed., Lugd. 1561 II. Par. 1567. 1579. 1587 II and frequently; reprinted Coblenz 1829 II. Ed. HSTEPHANUS 1577 and subsequently. JCRUQUIUS (Cruucke), first separately Od. b. IV, Brügge 1565; epod. and carm. saec. 1567; satt. 1572, then complete Antverp. 1578 (see n. 5); (subsequently with JDOUSA's commentary) 1597 and 1611. Ed. LTORRENTIUS, Antv. 1608. DHEINSIUS, Leid. 1612 and frequently. Ed. MDEMAROLLES, Par.[2] 1660 (in this are FGUYET's atheteses, reprinted Phil. 35, 478; otherwise Marolles is entirely untrustworthy; JURI, un cercle savant au XVII siècle: FGuyet, Par. 1886). (WHERTZ, de Hor. exemplari olim Guyetiano I. Bresl. 1889.) A translation into French, with crit. and histor. notes by DACIER, Par. 1681 X; Amstel.[4] 1727.—Leading epoch-making work: ed. RBENTLEY, Cantabrig. 1711 (republished Amsterd. 1713. 1728. Lps. 1764. 1826. Berl. 1869 II). Ed. ACUNINGHAM, Hag. Com. 1721. Chronol. arrangement, French translation and notes by NCSANADON, Par.[2] 1756 VIII. JMGESNER (after WBAXTER, Lond.[2] 1725), Lps.[2] 1772. GWAKEFIELD, Lond. 1794 II. JFHABERFELDT, Vorless. üb. die class. Dichter der Römer, Lpz. 1800 IV. CFEA, Rome 1811 II; denuo rec. FHBOTHE, Heidelb. 1821. 1827. FWDÖRING, Lps. 1803 (Vol. I, cur. REGEL [5] 1839; Vol. II., [3]1836); ed. minor, Lps. 1830. JCORELLI, Berl.[4] 1885 sqq. (by WHIRSCHFELDER). At the same time an editio minor ([6] 1881–84 by WHIRSCHFELDER). HDÜNTZER,

Kritik. u. Erklär. der horaz. Gedichte (without Text), Brunsw. 1840-45 V; with the text, Brunsw. 1849. Explanatory school edition Paderb. 1868 sq. WDILLENBURGER, Bonn[7] 1881. Explained by CWNAUCK, and GTAKRÜGER (and GKRÜGER), Lpz.[12-11] 1885 II. Cum novo comm. ad modum JBONDII (with illustrations) Par. (Didot) 1855. Ad codices saec. IX et X exact. comm. critico et exeget. illustr. ed. FRITTER, Lps. 1856 sq. II. In us. scholarum brevi annot. instr. FRITTER, Lps. 1857. Ed. with notes, by AJMACLEANE (Lond. 1869), by JEYONGE (Lond. 1867). Cura WHMILMAN, Lond. 1868.—Recensuerunt OKELLER (cf. RhM. 18, 271. 19, 211) et AHOLDER, Lps. 1864-70 II; ed. minor, Lps. 1878. In addition, OKELLER, Epilegomena zu Hor., Lpz. 1879-80.—With a commentary by ECWICKHAM, Vol. I[2], Oxf. 1878. Edited with special regard to the spurious passages and poems by KLEHRS, Lpz. 1869; a supplement to this, Lpz. 1871. Explained by HSCHÜTZ, Berl.[2] 1880-83 III. Expl. by AKIESSLING, Berl. 1884-88 III. By AWALTZ, Par. 1887.

Editions of the text e.g. by AMEINEKE, Berl.[2] 1854. MHAUPT (and JVAHLEN), Lps.[4] 1881 (compare HAUPT, op. 3, 42 and JVAHLEN, Berl. ind. lect. 1886). GLINKER, Vienna 1856. Recogn. et praefatus est LMÜLLER, Lps.[2] 1879 (cf. RhM. 25, 561), ed. min. ib. 1885 and (ed. nitida) ib. 1874 (cf. LMÜLLER, lectiones Hor. in the Petersb. Mél. Gréco-rom. 3, 688) and Chicago 1882. Ed. FAECKSTEIN, Bielef. 1876 (editio bibliophilorum). Ed. MPETSCHENIG, Prague 1883, edd. OKELLER et JHÄUSSNER, Prague 1885.—Illustrated edition by MILMAN, Lond. 1850. Hor. opera illustrated from antique gems by CWKING, the text revised with an introduction by HAJMUNRO, Lond. 1869. See also above the Paris ed. of 1855.

9. Recent general explanatory works on the poems of Horace e.g. JHORKEL, analecta Horat., Berl. 1852. ELTROMPHELLER, Beiträge (§ 238, 5). GBIPPART, Beitr. z. Krit. u. Erkl. d. H., Prague 1864. AKIESSLING, Hor. Kleinigkeiten, Bas. 1867. RUNGER, emendatt. Hor., Halle 1872; analecta H., Halle 1877. MADVIG, advers. 2, 51. THFRITZSCHE, Beitr. z. Krit. des Hor., Güstrow 1877. GSÄNGER, Verbesserungen z. Texte d. H., Kiew 1878-81 III. EBÄHRENS, lectt. Hor., Grön. 1880. GSTIER, Horatiana, Zerbst 1884. HNETTLESHIP, lectures and essays 143. THÖSTERLEN, Studd. z. Verg. u. Hor., Tüb. 1885; Komik u. Humor bei H., Stuttg. 1885-87 III. OJÄGER, Nachlese zu H., Cologne 1887 etc.– FSFELDBAUSCH, zur Erkl. d. H.; Einleitt. in die einzelnen Gedichte, Heidelb. 1851-1853 III.

10. Language etc.: indices by THTRETER, Antw. 1576; DAVEMAN, Brunswick 1667. The latter, augmented by JVERBURG, is repeated in the ed. of Bentley's Horace of a. 1713 and others (e.g. also in the ed. published at Lpz. 1826); again (augmented) in FRITTER's edition; new indices (by WREGEL) in Döring's ed. of 1836 and especially (by KZANGEMEISTER) in the Berlin ed. of Bentley's Horace of a. 1869. Separate indices for the lyrical poems and for the satires and epistles in KELLER-HOLDER's ed. maior.—JHMERNESTI, clavis horatiana, Lps.[2] 1823 III. GAKOCH, Wörterb. zu Hor., Hanov.[2] 1879.—GEBELING, de casuum usu Horatiano, Wernigerode 1866; de imperativi usu Hor., ib. 1870. HDITTEL, de dativi ap. Hor. usu, Landskron 1878. EOTT, d. Congruenz des Präd. m. mehreren Subjecten im Numerus bei H., Böhm. Leipa 1887. Abt. 2, 1888. FTEETZ, de verbb. compositorum ap. H. structura, Halle 1885. JAVOIGT, d. Gebrauch des Adjectivs bei H., Halle 1844. OLAUTENSACH, analecta hor. grammatica (on the connection between the noun and its attribute), Greifsw. 1878. FWDAHLEKE, de usu infinitivi hor. I, Bresl. 1854. FJHESTER, de infinitivi . . . ap. Hor. usu, Münst. 1858. HOINDEBETOU, de usu infinitivi Hor., Upsala 1875. AGRABENSTEIN, de interrogationum enuntiativarum usu Hor., Halle 1883. LUNTERBERGER, die syntaktischen Gräcismen bei H., Brixen 1877. ARUHE, de ornamentis elocutionis quibus

in componendis carmm. Hor. usus est, Coesfeld 1879. OCerny, das epitheton ornans in den hor. Oden, Brünn 1878. HEggers, de ordine et figuris verborum in H. carmm., Löwen 1877. GBeste, de generis dicendi inter H. carmina sermonesque discrimine, Münst. 1876. FBarta, sprachl. Stud. zu d. Satt., Linz 1879.—HHabenicht, d. Allitteration b. H., Eger 1885. AWeinhold, quaestt. Hor., Grimma, 1882.—JNeuss, quaestt. hor. gramm., Münst. 1870. ARothmaler, de Hor. verborum inventore, Berl. 1862. CZangemeister, de Hor. verbis singularibus, Berlin 1862. AWeingärtner, de Hor. Lucretii imitatore, Halle 1874. AWaltz, des variations de la langue et de la métrique d'H. dans ses différents ouvrages, Par. 1881. On the metre: see the summary before the various editions and e.g. the writings cited § 238, 3. 239, 2.

11. Translations of the whole of the poems into German by JHVoss (Heidelb. [2] 1820 II), KGNeumann (Trèves [2] 1868), JSStrodtmann (Lpz. [2] 1860), WBinder (Stuttg. 1855), FOvNordenflycht (Berl. 1861. Bresl. 1874. 1881) and others.—Hor. in neuen metrischen Übersetzungen, ausgewählt von ThObbarius, Paderb. [3] 1872. English (verse), by ThMartin, II. Lond. 1881: (prose), by JGLonsdale and JLee, Lond.[3] 1890.

241. On friendly terms with Horace was C. Valgius Rufus, cos. 742/12, the author of elegies and epigrams, a work on herbs, a Latin version of the rhetoric of Apollodoros of Pergamon his master, and of grammatical disquisitions in epistolary form.

1. C. Valgius C. f. Rufus was in the year 742/12 cos. (suff.) with P. Sulpicius Quirinus; see JKlein's fasti cons. for that year. Porphyrio on Hor. c. 2, 9 *Valgium consularem, amicum suum* (cf. v. 5), *consolatur morte delicati pueri graviter adfectum.* To judge from the tone of this poem, he was probably younger than Horace. He belonged to the circle of Maecenas; Hor. s. 1, 10, 82. Perhaps he is meant by the Pyrrhus (πυρρὸς = rufus) of Hor. c. 3, 20 (Bamberger). paneg. ad Messal. (Tib. 4, 1) 179 *est tibi qui possit magnis se accingere rebus Valgius, aeterno propior non alter Homero*, words at least expressive of the expectations cherished of his talent for epic poetry in these circles; cf. Hor. c. 2, 9, 18 (probably of a. 727/27). Schol. Veron. on Verg. buc. 7, 22 (p. 74, 10 Keil) *similiter hunc Codrum in elegiis Valgius honorifice appellat et quadam in ecloga de eo ait* etc. (see § 233, 1). Servius ib.: *Codrus poeta eiusdem temporis fuit, ut Valgius in elegiis suis refert*; ad Aen. 11, 457 *Valgius in elegis.* Isidor. orig. 19, 4, 8 (*Valgius:* a distich). Unger, Valg. l.l. 233. In these poems Valgius had probably also sung of and bewailed his favourite slave Mystes (Hor. c. 2, 9, 9). Charis. GL. 1, 108, 7 *Valgius in epigrammatis* (a phalaecean verse follows). Unger considers Valgius to be also the author of the elegy on Messalla, see § 230, 5, n. 1 l. 24. Philargyr. on georg. 3, 177 (*ut Valgius ait*) quotes two hexameters, which Unger l.l. 265 assigns to alleged Bucolica by Valgius.

2. A book on herbs: Plin. NH. 25, 4 *post eum* (see § 53, 1) *unus illustrium temptavit C. Valgius eruditione spectatus, imperfecto volumine ad divum Augustum, incohata etiam praefatione religiosa, ut omnibus malis humanis illius potissimum principis semper mederetur maiestas.* According to this the work must nevertheless have been published (which e.g. HMorsch, de Verg. ge. 52 erroneously denies). C. Valgius is also quoted by Pliny among his authorities for b. 20–27 (medicinal botany). For RUnger's conjecture on Quint. 10, 1, 56 *Macer atque Valgius* (instead of *Vergilius*) see § 227, 2.

3. Gell. 12, 3, 1 *Valgius Rufus, in secundo librorum quos inscripsit de rebus per*

epistulam quaesitis, lictorem dicit a ligando appellatum esse. CHARIS. GL. 1, 108, 28 (*Valgius de rebus per epistulam quaesitis solitaurilia dicta ait esse* etc.); ib. 135, 23 (*Valgius de rebus per epist. quaes.* in support of *lacer*). Hence also ib. 102, 10 (*et Valgius et Verrius et Trogus de animalibus lacte dicunt*) and 143, 24 (*secunda ratio, qua Plinius ait Valgium niti*). UNGER l.l. 163. DIOM. GL. 1, 387, 6 *Valgius de translatione (ait): comesa* (not *comesta*) *patina.* It is not likely that this formed part of his version of the τέχνη of Apollodoros of Pergamon (§ 44, 10. 202, 1. 208, 5. 243, 3. 268, 3. 276, 6; also SEN. contr. 2, 5, 11 *Attico Vipsanio, Apollodori discipulo*). QUINT. 3, 1, 18 (see § 44, 10). 3, 5, 17 (*causam finit Apollodorus, ut interpretatione Valgii, discipuli eius, utar, ita*). 5, 10, 4 (*epichirema Valgius aggressionem vocat*). RITSCHL, op. 3, 269 calls attention to the iambic rhythm of the quotations from Valgius' Ars in QUINT. 3, 5, 17 (cf. § 243, 3). See also UNGER l.l. 145. Vague quotations in SEN. ep. 51, 1 (*Aetnam quare dixerit Messala unicum, sive Valgius, apud utrumque enim legi*). In the little book de dubiis nominibus GL. 5, 586 we read: *Vallius 'perfusam pelvem,'* where HAUPT conjectures Valgius.—WEICHERT, poetar. lat. vitae etc. 209. RUNGER, de C. Valgii Rufi poematis, Halle 1848 (510 with XVIII pp.!). The scanty fragments also in FPR. 342.

242. Other friends of Horace, who themselves wrote in metre, were Aristius Fuscus, the two Visci, Fundanius, Servius Sulpicius and Florus, and Titius and Iullus Antonius.

1. Heading of HOR. c. 1, 22 *ad M. Aristium Fuscum.* In the same way HOR. ep. 1, 10 is addressed to him (heading: *ad Fuscum Aristium grammaticum*, cf. PORPHYR. on sat. 1, 9, 60 *Arist. Fuscus praestantissimus grammaticus illo tempore et amicus Horatii fuit*); cf. sat. 1, 9, 61. 1, 10, 83. PORPH. on ep. 1, 10 *ad Aristium Fuscum scriptorem comoediarum;* but in part of the MSS. of ACRO on ep. 1, 10, 1 (p. 422 H.): *alloquitur Aristium scriptorem tragoediarum*, which renders the whole notice dubious. The Varronian excerpt GL. 7, 35 relates to Aufustius; see § 199, 8.—Together with him HOR. s. 1, 10, 83 mentions among his learned friends *Viscorum uterque:* on this the comment. Cruq. (=Porphyrio; see AKIESSLING ad loc.): *Visci duo fratres fuerunt optimi poetae et iudices critici, quorum pater Vibius Viscus* etc.

2. HOR. s. 1, 10, 40 *arguta meretrice potes Davoque Chremeta eludente senem* (hence palliatae) *comis garrire* (at recitationes) *libellos unus vivorum, Fundani.* Cf. PORPH. ad loc.: *solum illis temporibus Gaium Fundanium dicit comoediam bene scribere.* Cf. also HOR. s. 2, 8, 19.

3. HOR. s. 1, 10, 86 *te dicere possum* (among the *docti et amici*) . . . *Servi.* Perhaps he is identical with the Ser. Sulpicius whom PLINY (ep. 5, 3, 5; see § 31, 1) enumerates among the writers of erotic poetry; cf. OVID. trist. 2, 441 *nec sunt minus improba Servi carmina.* As far as the time is concerned, he might be the son of the jurist Serv. Sulpicius Rufus (§ 174, 2), the husband of *Valeria Messalarum* (that is of Corvinus § 222 and of Potitus cos. 722/32) *soror* (HIERON. adv. Iovin. 1, 46 Vall.) and the father of Tibullus' Sulpicia (§ 245, 3). Cf. MHAUPT, op. 3, 502.

4. HOR. ep. 1, 3 and 2, 2 are addressed to Julius Florus, who was according to PORPH. on ep. 1, 3, 1 a *saturarum scriptor, cuius sunt electae ex Ennio, Lucilio, Varrone saturae.*—HOR. ep. 1, 3, 9 *quid Titius, romana brevi venturus in ora? Pindarici fontis qui non expalluit haustus, fastidire lacus et rivos ausus apertos? . . . fidibusne latinis Thebanos aptare modos studet auspice Musa an tragica desaevit et ampullatur in arte?* We do not know whether anything of the kind was ever finished. He is probably also referred to by TIB. 1, 4, 73. 74 (see

EHübner, Herm. 14, 309). He is perhaps the son of M. Titius, cos. suff. 723/31 (PRE. 6, 201). See also § 254, 3. At all events he belongs to Horace's junior friends. See FJacobs, verm. schrr. 5, 344. Teuffel, translation of the epistles of Horace (Stuttg. 1859) 208.

5. Of Albinovanus Celsus also (schol. Hor. ep. 1, 8), the *comes* and *scriba* of (Tiberius) Nero (ib. 2) about a. 734/20, who is warned (ib. 1, 3, 15) to beware of plagiarism, it is unknown whether he ever published his poems. He may be the Celsus whose death is mourned by Ovid Pont. 1, 9. Cf. ib. 37–40 to Fabius Maximus: *multos habeas cum dignus amicos, non fuit e multis quolibet ille minor; si modo nec census nec clarum nomen avorum, sed probitas magnos ingeniumque facit.* He was probably a relation of Albinovanus Pedo § 252, 6; see EHübner, ephem. epigr. 2, 33.

6. Iullus Antonius (on the praenomen *Iullus*, which is now established by inscriptions, and is also found in Hor. c. 4, 2, 2 and must be read there, see Chr Hülsen, Berl. phil. Wschr. 1888, 667. Cf. Mommsen, röm. Forsch. 1, 35. Herm. 24, 155. FBücheler, RhM. 44, 317. Borghesi, op. 1, 468), *triumviri* (M. Antonius) *filius* (Suet. gr. 18, cf. § 263, 2), born c. 710/44; praet. 741/13; cos. 744/10; † 752/2. PRE. 1^2, 1181, c. According to Acro on Hor. c. 4, 2, 33 *heroico metro* Διομηδείας *XII libros scripsit egregios, praeterea et prosa aliqua*, cf. comm. Cruq. ad loc.—Cf. AKiessling, de horat. carmm. inscriptt. p. 6.

243. Domitius Marsus, (700/54–750/4?) a younger contemporary of Horace, is never mentioned by the latter; he made himself known by a collection of pointed epigrams (Cicuta) and comic narratives and wrote a treatise on the application of wit in oratory (de urbanitate). He also wrote an epic (Amazonis) and perhaps erotic elegies (on Melaenis).

1. Marsus possibly enjoyed like Horace the instruction of Orbilius (§ 200, 3), though scarcely at the same time with Horace. He was still living after 735/19 (in which year Vergil and Tibullus died), but had long been deceased at the time of Ovid's exile, (a. 761/8 a.d.); see Ovid. Pont. 4, 16, 3 *famaque post cineres maior venit; et mihi nomen tunc quoque cum vivis adnumerarer* (before my exile) *erat; cum foret et Marsus magnique Rabirius oris* etc. For his relations to Augustus or his intimate friends, especially Maecenas, see Mart. 8, 56, 21 (cf. § 223, 3): *quid Varios Marsosque loquar ditataque vatum nomina?* ib. 7, 99, 7 (n. 2). Horace's silence concerning him (cf. § 219, 17) may possibly have originated in the offence taken by the self-conscious and sensitive satirist at the acerbity of the epigrammatist. (Perhaps Hor. c. 4, 4, 20 is in ridicule of the Amazonis of Marsus; see MHaupt, op. 3, 332). It was easier to get on with such sterling men as Vergil and Tibullus; Marsus' epigram on the death of Tibullus; see § 245, 1.

2. He is often mentioned by Martial as his predecessor, e.g. in the preface to 1 concerning the *lasciva verborum veritas: sic scribit Catullus, sic Marsus, sic Pedo, sic Gaetulicus* etc. 5, 5, 5 *sit locus et nostris aliqua tibi parte libellis, qua Pedo, qua Marsus, quaque Catullus erit.* 7, 99, 7 *nec Marso nimium minor est doctoque Catullo.* 8, 56, 24 *Vergilius non ero, Marsus ero.* 2, 71, 3. 2, 77, 5 (*Marsi doctique Pedonis saepe duplex unum pagina tractat opus*). The collection of his Epigrams was entitled Cicuta (Bergk: Scutica). Philarg. on Verg. buc. 3, 90 *Domitius in Cicuta:* here follows an epigram on Bavius (§ 233, 2) and his brother, recently supplemented from a Paris MS.: see HSauppe, Lpz. SBer. 1852, 135, and the dis-

cussions on it, Phil. 13, 222. 14, 217. 19, 150; RhM. 15, 132. 152. 18, 476. 633. JJ. 99, 268. From the same are probably derived the hexameters on Orbilius (Suet. gr. 9) and Caecilius Epirota (ib. 16), the incomplete line ap. Prisc. GL. 2, 168, 16, as well as the hemistich ap. Diom. GL. 1, 319, 13. RUnger, epistola de Marsi Cicuta, Friedl. 1861.

3. Charis. GL. 1, 72, 4 *Marsus fabellarum VIIII* (hexameter): perhaps anecdotes, miscellaneous trifles in verse, like much in Lucilius and Horace?—Quint. 6, 3, 102 *Domitius Marsus, qui de urbanitate diligentissime scripsit.* From this are derived the definitions of *urbanitas* and the *urbanus* ib. 104 sq. Cf. ib. 108 (*Marsi, hominis eruditissimi*) and 111 (*dictum Pompeii, quod refert Marsus, in Ciceronem*). This work has perhaps been made use of by Macr. sat. b. 2, see GWissowa, Herm. 16, 499.—Mart. 7, 29, 7 *et Maecenatis Maro cum cantaret Alexin, nota tamen Marsi fusca Melaenis erat:* accordingly the composition of erotic elegies is usually attributed to Marsus: epigrams might also be alluded to (n. 2).—Mart. 4, 29, 7 *saepius in libro numeratur Persius uno quam levis* (perhaps on account of his erotica) *in tota Marsus Amazonide* (Welcker, ep. Cykl. 1, 319); see n. 1 in fin.—Marsus is probably also indicated by Quint. 3, 1, 18 *ceteras missa ad Domitium epistola non agnoscit* (Apollodoros of Pergamon). Cf. § 241, 3. *Marsus poeta* is mentioned by Plin. NH. as an authority for b. 34 (*aeris metalla*): conjectures concerning this in Urlichs, d. Quellenregister zu Plin. (Würzb. 1878), 11.—Weichert, poett. latt. vitae etc. p. 241. The fragments also FPR. 346.

244. Among the poets of this period we should also mention Pupius, the author of lacrimose tragedies, and Maecenas' freedman C. Melissus, the inventor of a new learned variety of the national Roman comedy (the trabeata) and the editor of a voluminous collection of anecdotes. Propertius' Lynceus seems also to have published poems.

1. Hor. ep. 1, 1, 67 *ut propius spectes lacrimosa poemata Pupi.* On this Acro (p. 364 H.) *tragoedi vel tragoediographi. Pupius tragoediographus ita adfectus spectantium movit ut eos flere compelleret, unde distichon fecit: 'Flebunt amici et bene noti mortem meam; nam populus in me vivo lacrimavit satis.* It seems more probable that these senarii contain a joke made on him by others and placed to his account.

2. Suet. gramm. 21 *C.* (*Cn.* in Acro, see § 254, 3) *Melissus Spoleti natus ingenuus, sed ob discordiam parentum expositus, cura et industria educatoris sui altiora studia percepit ac Maecenati pro grammatico munere datus est. cui cum se gratum et acceptum in modum amici videret, quamquam asserente matre, permansit tamen in statu servitutis, . . . quare cito manumissus et Augusto insinuatus est, quo delegante curam ordinandarum bybliothecarum in Octaviae porticu suscepit. atque, ut ipse tradit, sexagesimum aetatis annum agens libellos Ineptiarum, qui nunc Iocorum inscribuntur, componere instituit, absolvitque CL, quibus et alios diversi operis postea addidit. fecit et novum genus togatarum inscripsitque trabeatas* (above § 17, 1). Ovid. Pont. 4, 16, 39 *tua cum socco Musa, Melisse, levis.* Lachmann proposed to take paneg. in Pis. 237 *Maecenas alta tonantis* (*apta togatis* Lachm.) *eruit et populis ostendit nomina Grais* (*acumina Gai* Lachm.) in reference to the trabeata of Melissus, see Haupt, op. 1, 406, and against him Bücheler, RhM. 36, 336 and below § 246, 4. These *ineptiae* or *ioci* were a collection of witty sayings, in which earlier ones (e.g. those of Cato § 121, 6, of Tiro § 191, 2, of Caesar § 195, 5, of Furius Bibaculus § 192, 4; cf. besides § 207, 4. 243, 3) were included, sifted and added to. His

literary activity must belong to the later Augustan period. HIERON. chron. ad a. Abr. 2013=750/4 B.C. *Melissus Spoletinus grammaticus agnoscitur.* PLIN. NH. 28, 62, *triennio Maecenatem Melissum accepimus silentium sibi imperavisse.* He is probably the same Melissus who is named as his authority by PLINY in b. 7 (man), 9 (aquatic animals), 10 (birds), 11 (insects), 35 (painting), and also the *Melissus, qui de apibus scripsit* (see FGLÖCKNER, RhM. 33, 159), mentioned by SERV. Aen. 7, 66. By the same author may also be the notice on Vergil in DONATUS' vita (see § 224, 4). But the references in SERV. Aen. 4, 146 (*hos Melissus ab Homero Achabas appellari ait*), POMP. GL. 5, 287 (on pronunciation) and gramm. de dub. nom. GL, 5, 575 (*clibanus generis masculini, ut Melissus docet*), should rather be traced back to the grammarian Aelius Melissus (§ 352, 4) in the time of Gellius.

3. To Lynceus (with a fictitious name), an older friend, who had formerly been attracted to philosophy and tragic poetry, PROPERTIUS 3, 34 gives the advice that he should devote himself to the Alexandrine erotic elegy. Cf. THBIRT, RhM. 32, 409. OHAUBE, de carm. ep. 29. See also § 230, 2, 1.

245. Among the elegiac poets of the Augustan age, Albius Tibullus (c. 700/54–735/19) followed indeed the Alexandrine poets in his almost exclusive choice of erotic subjects, but he discarded their inevitable aroma of learning and based his poems on warm and real feeling. Being less remarkable for power and talent than for depth and sentiment, he generally prefers a medium key. But though he is perfectly natural and his diction exceedingly simple, Tibullus succeeds in imaging each successive mood in lively hues, and expresses the fluctuations of feeling with consummate art. His genial and gentle spirit is agreeably impressed on his poetry, his passion for the peaceful calm of rural life, his yearning after true love impart to his elegies a strain of tender melancholy. His most perfect poems are those to Delia. In others it is discernible that the poet was surprised by an early death before he had finally polished them. The first editor added to this collection, consisting of two books, a third, which comprised besides Tibulline poems elegiac poems by other members of the circle of Messalla, among which we should mention the song in praise of Messalla, the elegies of a certain Lygdamus and those of Sulpicia.

1. We have in our best MSS. of Tibullus (n. 7) and at one time it was also to be found in the original (perhaps it might be traced back to Sueton. de poetis; cf. EBÄHRENS, tib. Blätter [Jena 1876] 3. AREIFFERSCHEID, JB. 1880 3, 284. EHILLER, Herm. 18, 351): *Domitii Marsi* (§ 243, 1; this heading is found only in the best MS. F, see n. 7): '*Te quoque Vergilio comitem non aequa, Tibulle, Mors iuvenem campos misit ad Elysios, Ne foret aut elegis molles qui fleret amores Aut caneret forti regia bella pede.*' *Albius Tibullus eques R.* (*eques regalis* in the MSS.) *insignis forma* (HOR. ep. 1, 4, 6) *cultuque corporis observabilis, ante alios Corvinum Messalam* (§ 222, 1) *oratorem* (*originem* in the MSS.) *dilexit, cuius et contubernalis aquitanico*

bello (a. 726/28 sq.) *militaribus donis donatus est. hic multorum iudicio principem inter elegiographos obtinet locum* (cf. QUINT. above § 32, 1). *epistolae quoque eius amatoriae quamquam breves* (those of b. IV ?) *omnino utiles* (*subtiles* BÄHRENS) *sunt. obiit adulescens, ut indicat epigramma supra scriptum.* Thus according to Domitius Marsus T. died 735/19 at the latest, being still *iuvenis.* OVID. trist. 4, 10, 51 *Vergilium vidi tantum nec amara Tibullo tempus amicitiae fata dedere meae. successor fuit hic tibi, Galle* etc. (above § 32, 1), ib. 2, 463 *legiturque Tibullus et placet et iam te* (Augustus) *principe notus erat.*—The praenomen of the poet is unknown; it was perhaps A.—He seems to have been well off originally (el. 1, 1, 41; cf. 4, 1, 183?), but to have suffered afterwards through the agrarian distributions of a. 713/41; he got, however, into comfortable circumstances, perhaps through the recommendation of Messalla (HOR. ep. 1, 4, 7. 11. cf. TIB. 1, 1, 49 sqq. 77 sq.). When Messalla was going to Asia, Tibullus at first refused to join him (el. 1, 1), but subsequently travelled after him (1, 3, 9), and remained ill at Corcyra (1, 3, 3). HORACE addressed to Tibullus c. 1, 33 and ep. 1, 4 (against this BÄHRENS, tib. Bl. 7; see however KPSCHULZE, ZfGW. 31, 658. LGRASBERGER l.l. WMEWES, ZfGW. Jahresber. 5, 85); OVID. am. 3, 9 is a poem on his death. Relations between Tibullus and Propertius: ZINGERLE, kl. philol. Abhh. 2, 84. WOLSEN in the commentatt. sodal. philol. Gryphiswald. 27. FWIDDER, de Tib. codd. 35; see § 246, 2 ad fin.—HAWSPOHN, de Tib. vita et carmm. I, Lpz. 1819. NOESTLING, de Tib. vita et carmm., Upsala 1860. LGRASBERGER, JJ. 125, 838.

2. Tibullus himself mentions as his mistresses Delia (and Marathus, b. 1) and Nemesis (b. 2); OVID. am. 3, 9, 31 *sic Nemesis longum, sic Delia nomen habebunt, altera* (Nemesis, see v. 57 *me*—Nemesis is the speaker—*tenuit moriens deficiente manu*) *cura recens, altera primus amor.* MART. 8, 73, 7 *fama est arguti Nemesis formosa Tibulli.* 14, 193, 1. APUL. apol. 10 *accusent . . . Tibullum quod ei sit Plania in animo, Delia in versu* (cf. *planus*=δῆλος; a gens Plania is not otherwise known). In HOR. c. 1, 33, 2 Glycera is named as a mistress of Tibullus. Fragments of the *miserabiles elegi* he wrote on her are perhaps to be found in TIB. 4, 13 sq. (if indeed Glycera is not rather one and the same with Nemesis, see AKIESSLING on Hor. l.l.). Cf. TEUFFEL, Stud. (1871) 347. SPOHN l.l. 32. HA DIETERICH, de Tibulli amoribus, Marb. 1844. ORICHTER, RhM. 25, 518. GDONCIEUX, de Tib. amoribus, Par. 1887. ESCHEIDEMANTEL, commentatt. Ribbeck. 373 (Marathus odes). See also n. 3.—Epigrams on this (?) Delia are to be found AL. 451 sq. PLM. 4, 80. 81.

3. In the MSS. the Tibulline collection is divided into three books: most editions reckon four, by a subdivision of the third (we here quote in accordance with this, the usual method). B. 1 (10 elegies, principal subject: Delia [and Marathus]) was published by the poet himself. B. 2 (6 elegies, chief subject: Nemesis) probably published soon after the poet's death. B. 3 adds to these earlier collections of the Tibulline poems in two books a supplement, which belonged to the family of Messalla, containing works both by Tibullus and by other authors, first 6 elegies (=3, 1–6 Lygdamus and Neaera, see n. 4), then (here begins b. 4) panegyricus Messallae (=4, 1), then 5 short familiar elegies of Tibullus (=4, 2–6) relating the love between Sulpicia (Messalla's niece, cf. § 242, 3) and Cerinthus (=Cornutus 2, 2. 2, 3), variations on the theme already announced in the 6 charming poetical letters by Sulpicia herself which follow (=4, 7–12; TEUFFEL, Stud. 365; on the supposed heading *Sulpicia* before 4, 8 see EHILLER, RhM. 29, 106). A short elegy and an epigram (=4, 13. 14) form the close.—Among these poems the earliest is the Panegyricus Messallae (4, 1) of a. 723/31. If this ode were really by Tibullus (whose authorship is not expressly certified in the MSS.),

it would represent to us the poet's period of Alexandrine transition. It is built after the method of Greek hymns (OCrusius, WschrfklPhil. 2, 1299; Zürich Phil.-Vers. 265), it attests a certain talent, but still more evidently unripe taste and low views, and betrays the exaggeration and want of tact peculiar to a youth just come from the schools of the rhetoricians, features by which some scholars have with good reason been led to deny Tibullus' authorship of it; see Lachmann, kl. Schr. 2, 149. EBährens, tib. Blätter 41. ThBirt, hist. hex. lat. 49. HHartung, de paneg. ad Mess. pseudo-tibulliano, Halle 1880. Cf. in favour of the Tibulline authorship Teuffel, Stud. 352. FTeufel, de Catulli etc. vocibus sing. (1872) 43 and FHankel, act. societ. phil. Lips. 5, 45. VVaccaro, de αὐθεντίᾳ Tib. in Mess. paneg., Palermo 1887. Of pretty much the same kind, though somewhat superior (OCrusius l.l.), is the poem on the triumph of Messalla (a. 727/27) 1, 7. Similarly the elegies on Marathus (1, 4. 9. 8) and 1, 10 show mistakes and faults (especially 1, 4 the same far-fetched mythological allusions and the same rhetorical manner as 1, 7), though they also exhibit a decided progress in the artistic grouping of the subject-matter (Teuffel, Stud. 355). But the highest stage of the poetical development of Tibullus, his literary prime, was attained in his elegies on Delia (1, 1. 3. 5. 2. 6) perhaps a. 730/24 sqq. They form a cycle containing a piece of genuine biography, a complete romance. Cf. ORichter, RhM. 25, 518. Bährens, tib. Bl. 16. ORibbeck, RhM. 32, 445. GGötz ib. 33, 145. FLeo l.l. 10. On the same eminence we may place the elegies treating of the love of Sulpicia (4. 2–6). On the other hand, those elegies of the second book lack final polish, which treat of Tibullus' liaison with Nemesis (Teuffel l.l. 370). In general see KLachmann, kl. Schr. 2, 149. OFGruppe, röm. Elegie, Lpz. 1838, and WHertzberg, Hall. Jahrbb. 1839 1, 1009. Passow, de ordine temporum quo libri I elegias scripsit Tib., in his op. (Lps. 1835) p. 280. RSchultz, quaestt. in Tib. l. I. chronologicae, Lps. 1887. FKindscher, Chronol. d. Gedd. T.s, ZfGW. 13, 289. APetersen, de libri IV Tib. elegiis earumque auctore, Glückst. 1849. AZingerle, on the Sulpicia elegies, in his kl. philol. Abh. 1, 22. 2, 45. Also WWölfflin, act. semin. Erl. 1, 100. JNMosl, Sulpiciae el. V, in the symb. phil. ad LSpengel, Munich 1877, 17. More on the subject n. 9. On the arrangement of the poems (variatio etc.) KPSchulze, JJ. 131, 860. GDoncieux, corrections a Sulpicia, rev. de phil. 12, 26.—RUllrich, studia Tibull. de libri II editione, Berl. 1889; JJ. Suppl. 17, 385.—SEhrengruber, de paneg. Mess. pseudo-tibull., Kremsmünster 1889.

4. Of the six elegies collected in the so-called third book, five treat of the love between Lygdamus and Neaera, the sixth (3, 5) is an epistle to friends. The author (born 711/43; see 3, 5, 17) is a younger contemporary and imitator of Tibullus in particular (see Liese l.l. 8; Kleeman l.l. 55), who however lacks his spirit and is altogether only moderately gifted, in every respect different from Tibullus (Teuffel, Stud. 372). Ovid cannot be the author of these poems (ib. 378; there is an attempt to prove that 3, 5 at least is the work of Ovid in the Phil. Anz. 10, 184). A still unsolved problem is the imitation which occurs 3, 5, 15-20 of three passages in Ovid (am. 2, 14, 23. 24. a. a. 2, 670. trist. 4, 10, 6—the latter only concluded 765/12!) together with the inferences to be drawn from it. Lygdamus is probably an assumed name; perhaps the author desired to characterise himself by this name (cf. *Albius* and λύγδος, λύγδινος, *lygdos*, *lygdinus*) as a follower of Tibullus. But our author certainly belonged to the circle of Messalla, hence also his elegies were added to those of Tibullus, in consequence of which his personality remained entirely obscure (Teuffel, Stud. p. 381). Conjectures concerning this literary circle of Messalla and the formation of the corpus Tibullianum in its midst in Lachmann, kl. Schr. 2, 150. FHaase, Berl. Jahrbb.

für wissensch. Krit. 1837. 40. Bährens, tib. Bl. 47; JJ. 111, 137. ThBirt, antikes Buchw. 426. EHiller, RhM. 18, 343. In general cf. AEichstädt, de Lygdami carmm., Jena 1819. 1823 sq. 1835. RTörnebladh, de elegiis Lygdami, Calma 1861. CStumpe, de Lygd. elegiis, Halle 1867. LBolle, de Lygd. carmm., Gött. 1873. Lierse, die Unechtheit v. Tib. B. 3, nebst Untersuch. üb. d. Conjunctt. d. Tib. u. Lygd., Bromb. 1875. SKleemann, de libri III carmm. quae T. nomine circumferuntur, Strassb. 1876. CBöhlau, de Lygd. carmm., Neustettin 1877. CBiuso, la questione del terzo libro di Tib., Rieti 1883. Cf. also § 230, 5, n. 1, l. 28. GDoncieux, rev. de philol. 12, 129.

5. On the two Priapea attributed to Tibullus see § 254, 5.

6. The opinions of Ovid amor. 1, 15, 27 *donec erunt ignes arcusque Cupidinis arma discentur numeri, culte Tibulle, tui*, Vell. 2, 36, 3 . . . *Tibullusque et Naso, perfectissimi in forma operis sui* and Quintilian (10, 1, 93; see § 32, 1). Like Horace, Tibullus also is fond of tripartite arrangement: see FRitschl, op. 3, 633. Bubendey, qu. Tib. 9. It is not however advisable to exaggerate a native feeling for symmetry into mechanical calculation, as HBubendey, quaestt. Tib., Bonn 1864; die Symmetrie der röm. Elegie, Hamb. 1876, and CPrien, JJ. 83, 149, and: Symmetrie u. Responsion d. röm. Elegie, Lüb. 1867, 3–36. Cf. JRiemann, de compos. stroph. Tib., Cob. 1878. HGroth, quaestt. Tib., Halle 1872. HFritzsche, quaestt. Tib., Halle 1875. HTKarsten, de T. elegiarum structura, Mnemos. 15, 211. 305. 16, 39. In connection with this exaggerated idea of symmetry, or from magnifying the difficulties of explanation and so forth, the empirical method of resorting to transposition remained for some time in favour: it has now gradually fallen into deserved discredit.—Tibullus deals very gracefully with his pentameters, in which he always contrives a pleasing parallelism with the preceding hexameter, while at the same time he succeeds in being novel and attractive. Tibullus furnishes the first example, on a large scale, of the limitation of elisions, even such as are not at all objectionable: this was attempted by Horace, see § 237, 1; he was followed by Ovid, the author of the Culex, Grattius, Manilius, and later poets. For other details concerning Tibullus' poetical individuality see LDissen's prolegg. p. xxxvii, in Gruppe l.l. p. 3 and in Teuffel's studies 384. MKrafft, de artibus Tib. et Lygd. in versibus concinnandis, Halle 1874. On the metre see LMüller's ed. p. xxvii. RBoltzenthal, de re metr. et de genere dicendi Tib., Cüstrin 1874. SKleemann (cap. iv and v, see n. 4). BLinke, Tib. quantum in poesi eleg. profecerit comparato Catullo, Luckau 1877. BEhrlich, de Tib. elocutione, Halle 1880. JStreifinger, de syntaxi Tib., Würzb. 1882. HIber, de dativi usu Tib., Marb. 1888. MHansen, de tropis et figuris ap. T., Kiel 1881. RStehle, de Tib. puri sermonis poetici cultore, Strassb. 1886. Cf. also § 32, 4 and 5.

7. Manuscripts: Tibullus had disappeared early in the Middle Ages, cf. REhwald, Phil. 46, 639. The earliest trace of a MS. of Tibullus is contained in a library catalogue of the 9th cent. (see Haupt, op. 3, 426. GBecker, catalogi biblioth. 42) *Albi Tibulli lib. II.* (cf. n. 3), later on we find traces of a (Veronese) MS. of Tibullus in William of Pastrengo (1290–1365) and in the flores moral. autor. of a. 1329 (§ 212, 4). MHaupt, op. 1, 276. WMeyer, Spruchverse des Publ., Lpz. 1877, 61. All the MSS. still extant are, like those of Catullus and Propertius, of a late date, the majority of them being interpolated especially by the Italians of the 15th cent. (e.g. JAurispa † 1459, JPontanus † 1503 and ThSeneca in Ancona about 1420, see a letter by the latter in Bährens' ed. p. viii). The best MSS. extant are a certain A(mbrosianus) R 26 sup. s. XIV (once in the possession of Coluccio Salutato, § 187, 5. 246, 5) and V(aticanus) 3270 s. XIV/XV. On the estimation of these and other MSS. (in particular the G(uelferbytanus) s

XV, whose value has been exaggerated by Bährens) see Bährens pref. to his ed. p. vii; JJ. 119, 473. KRossberg, JJ. 119, 74. GGötz, RhM. 36, 141. EHiller pref. to his ed. p. v; RhM. 37, 567; Phil. Anz. 14, 24. MRothstein, de Tib. codd., Berlin 1880. RLeonhard, de codd. Tib., Munich 1882. FWidder, de Tib. codd., Lahr 1824. PhIllmann, de Tib. cod. Ambrosiano, Halle 1886.—More correct and of much greater antiquity was the *fragmentum peroptimum Cuiacii* (F) made use of by Scaliger, but which commenced only with 3, 4, 65 (or a few verses earlier): Scaliger's collation of this is in Leiden, see CMFrancken, verslagen en meded. Amsterd. 10, 33; EHiller, RhM. 29, 97; JJ. 127, 273. On the second, quite late Cuiacianus of Scaliger, which contained Cat. Tib. Prop. see § 214, 11 l. 4.—Besides the complete MSS. there are extant two varieties of excerpts, which are of importance, even though the verses quoted have often been arbitrarily altered for the purposes of selection. The most valuable are the excerpta Frisingensia (Monac. 6292) s. XI. printed in LMüller's ed. of Tib. p. viii; JJ. 99, 63; cf. Protzen l.l. 3. A second collection of excerpts (perhaps of s. IX/X) has been preserved in various copies, the earliest and fullest is Paris. 7647 (Thuaneus) s. XII/XIII in Meyncke l.l. 381, and again Paris. 17903 (Nostradam. 188) s. XIII ib. and in Wölfflin l.l. 155 and in Prozen l.l. 22. From this second collection are also derived the excerpts used by Scaliger (who probably made use of the Thuaneus itself) and that of Vincentius of Beauvais († about 1264) in his speculum doctrinale b. 5–7 (cf. ORichter, de Vincentii Bellovacensis excerptis Tib., Bonn 1865 and Meyncke l.l. 370. 372. 452. On other excerpts from the same source see LMüller's ed. p. vii, Bährens ed. p. xiii, cf. besides GLöwe, RhM. 37, 145. Cf. Lachmann, kl. Schr. 2, 146. CMFrancken, in den verslagen en meded. Amsterd. 10 (1866), 30; JJ. 99, 207. EWölfflin. Phil. 27, 152. LMüller, JJ. 99, 63 and in his ed. EProtzen, de excerptis Tib., Greifsw. 1869. GMeyncke, d. Pariser Tibullexcerpte, RhM. 25, 369.

8. Editions: e.g. JJScaliger (with Cat. and Prop.), Par. 1577 and elsewhere. (JBroukhusius), Amsterd. 1708 (with ind. verbb.). JAVulpius, Padua 1749. CGHeyne, Lps.[4] 1817 (ed. EFCWunderlich; supplem. by LDissen 1819). JHVoss (corrected from MSS., Heidelb. 1811), JGHuschke (Lps. 1819 II). First critical edition: ex rec. CLachmanni, Berl. 1829. Explicuit LDissen, Gött. 1835 II (cf. on it CLachmann, kl. Schr. 2, 145). Tib. eleg. libri II; acc. Pseudotibulliana, recens. Aem. Bährens, Lpz. 1878. Tib. elegiae cum carmm. pseudotibull. ed. EHiller, acc. index verborum, Lps. 1885.—Texts by MHaupt (§ 214, 11), ARossbach, Lps. 1855, and LMüller, Lps. 1870.

9. Recent contributions in criticism and explanation (see also n. 3): CLachmann, kl. Schr. 2, 42. 102. FARigler (annott. ad. T., Potsdam 1839–44 III), FHaase (de tribus Tib. locis transpositione emendandis, Breslau 1855 and against this MHaupt, op. 3, 36), ODrenckhahn (criticism on T., Putbus 1862), FRitschl (on Tibullus 1, 4. op. 3, 616. Also GBubendey, Hamb. 1876 [see n. 6], EHübner, Herm. 14, 307, Westphal, Cöslin 1880), ORibbeck (de Tib. 1, 1 et Prop. 3, 34, Kiel 1867), Kindscher (on 1, 10; RhM. 17, 148), OKorn (on 1, 6 and 2, 5, ib. 19, 497; cf. WWagner, ib. 20, 314; Korn, ib. 471: de codice archetypo carm. Tib., ib. 20, 167), WWisser (quaest. Tib. Lps. 1869; on 2, 5, Eutin 1874), CPrien (JJ. 101, 689), RRichter (de Tib. tribus primus carm., Zwickau 1873; de quarti lib. Tib. elegiis, imprim. de quinta, Dresd. 1875), HGroth, (quaestt. Tib., Halle 1872, esp. on 4, 2 sqq. and 1, 4), ESeiler (Halle 1872, on 1, 2), EDietrich, quaestt. Tib. (on the transpositions in 1, 1) et Prop., Marb. 1873, CMFrancken, Mnemos. NS. 6, 174, Bährens, tib. Blätt. (Jena 1876) 64. JVahlen (on 2, 5. 1, 4. 1, 1), Berl. SBer. 1878, 343. FLeo, in Kiessl.-Wilamow. phil. Unterss. 2, 1. EMaass (2, 5. 2, 2), Herm. 18, 321.

480. ChKnappe, de Tib. 4, 2–4, 12, Gött. 1880. GLarroumet de IV Tib. libro, Par. 1882. CMFrancken, Mnemos. 13, 176.—HMagnus, JB. 1887 2, 301. GBelling (Tib. 2, 4) Phil. 47, 378. RBaumgartner, Wien. Studd. 11, 323.

10. Metrical translations by Count Reinhardt (Zür. 1783), FKvStrombeck (Gött.[2] 1825), JHVoss (Tüb. 1810), WTeuffel (Stuttg. 1853; repeated in part in the röm. Elegiker, ib. 1855, Class. d. Alt., p. 73). WBinder (Stuttg. 1862), AEberz (Frankf. 1865). GFischer (in modern metre), Ulm 1882. English (verse) by JCranstoun (with notes and life of the poet), Lond. 1872.

246. Sextus Propertius (c. 705/49–739/15) was a native of Umbria, but educated at Rome and admitted to the circles of Maecenas, after he had made himself known by his book on Cynthia. Besides this book, which was the first to be published, three (or four) others (although much damaged and curtailed) are still extant. Like Tibullus, Propertius is almost exclusively an elegiac and erotic poet, but far more than Tibullus he is a disciple of the Alexandrine school, brimful of mythological learning and frequently obscure; but he greatly surpasses his models in vivacity and originality as well as in glowing fervour. However strong his feelings, he has a still stronger reserve of thought to keep them in their place, and of art wherewith to embody them in his poems. His diction and metre are likewise nervous, but the sequence of his ideas is often desultory. The contents of the last book are in remarkable contrast with those of the others; especially in its more descriptive, semi-didactic poems on Roman (Italian) subjects somewhat in the manner of Ovid's Fasti. These (together with a few which are rather political) show us the poet in a new aspect as a Roman who looks with pride upon his country's past and present, eulogising it with patriotic ardour.

1. The poet calls himself (eight times) simply Propertius, and the other authors allude to him similarly: only Donat. vita Verg. 45 calls him Sex. Propertius; cf. besides AL. 264 PLM. 4, 158. The Neapolitanus (n. 5) has the heading *Incipit Propertius*; other MSS. before b. 1 *Incipit monobiblos Propertii Aurelii Nautae ad Tullum*, which cannot be credited: *monobiblos* is taken from Mart. 14, 189 (see n. 1 ad fin.), *Nautae* from the erroneous reading in Prop. 3, 24, 38 *Properti . . . navita* (for *haud ita*) *dives eras*, lastly *Aurelius* probably arose from a confusion with Prudentius (§ 436, see the same mistake GL. 5, 576, 22) and was copied from the MSS. into spurious inscriptions (from Ameria: *L. Aurelio Propertio L. f.*, and from Hispellum: *Sext. Aurel. Propert. Sex. f. Lom.*). MHaupt, op. 1, 280, cf. ThMommsen, Lpz. SBer. 1849, 261. 266. His home was Umbria (see 1, 22, 9. 5, 1, 64. 121), and probably the town of Asisium (5, 1, 125 *scandentisque asis*, which Lachmann rightly corrects *Asisi*, kl. Schr. 2, 248; cf. below § 332, 4), where Propertii have been discovered in inscriptions (MHaupt l.l. 282). EMattoli, la patria di Prop. ed il Torti rivendicato, Città di Castello 1886. GUrbini, la

patria di Prop., Torino 1889 (for Spello). WYSellar, Class. review, Nov. 1890 (for Assisi). The year in which he was born is not known and can only be approximately guessed at by various combinations. Propertius is certainly younger than Tibullus and older than Ovid; see trist. 4, 10, 53 sq. (above § 32, 1) and 2, 465 *invenies eadem* (as in Tibullus) *blandi praecepta Properti . . . his ego successi.* Hence it appears that he was born between 700/54 and 710/44. On the other hand, no allusion leads us beyond the year 739/15 (5, 6 to the quinquennales 738/16 and 5, 11, 65 to P. Cornelius Scipio, cos. a. 738/16). There are, however, not many of these allusions. The designation of Octavianus as Augustus shows that the poems in question were written later than January 727/27, *modo Gallus mortuus* (3, 34, 91) after a. 727/27 (cf. § 232/2). The early loss of his father and injury to his property by the agrarian distribution of 713/41; 5, 1, 127, cf. 3, 34, 55. Delicate health (and early decease) are indicated by frequent dwelling on death (e.g. 2, 1, 71. 2, 8, 17. 3, 13, 17. 3, 15, 54. 3, 24, 35. 4, 16, 21. 4, 21, 33). We perhaps possess a portrait of Propertius in a double Hermes (in the Villa Albani and the Vatican, see Visconti, iconogr. rom. pl. 14, 3. 4) which unites the head of a youthful, beardless, nervous, and delicate-looking Roman with that of a Greek poet (Kallimachos? Philetas?), see EBrizio, ann. dell' inst. arch. 1873, 105; CRobert, arch. Zeit. 38, 35. This same Roman head is also perhaps still extant in Madrid. Friedrichs-Wolters, Berliner Gipsabgüsse no. 1637.—The conclusions to be drawn from the poet's statements about his amores are very uncertain. His first love after the assumption of the toga virilis (at the age of 15 or 16) was Lycinna; 4, 15, 6. This was succeeded by his love for Cynthia (about 725/29 sqq.); this had already lasted two or three years when 4, 15 was written; see ib. v. 7; five years to the time of the (perhaps final) rupture in 4, 25, 3 (cf. *multos annos* 2, 8, 13), in which we may include the period of estrangement mentioned 4, 16, 9 (cf. 1, 1, 6). Cynthia was older than Propertius (3, 18, 19; cf. § 214, 3) and died before him (5, 7, 3). Apul. apol. 10 *accusent . . . Propertium, qui Cynthiam dicat, Hostiam dissimulet.* Cf. § 146, 1 in fin. In general Martial. 8, 73, 5 *Cynthia te vatem fecit, lascive Properti.* 14, 189 (with the heading *Monobiblos Properti*) *Cynthia facundi carmen iuvenale Properti, accepit famam nec minus ipsa dedit.* Iuv. 6, 7. Cf. Prop. 3, 25, 3. 3, 34, 93. AMarx, de Prop. vita et librorum ordine temporibusque, Lps. 1884. GUrbini, vita, tempi, elegie di Prop. I, Foligno 1884.

2. On his relation to Ovid, who repeatedly mentions Prop. with hearty appreciation, see trist. 4, 10, 45 *sape suos solitus recitare Propertius ignes, iure sodalicio qui mihi notus erat.* On the numerous points of resemblance to Propertius in Ovid see AZingerle, Ovid u. s. Vorgänger 1 (Innsbr. 1869), 109. JAWashietl, similitud. Ovid., Vienna 1883, 160. It is even possible that Ovid may have been prompted to write his Heroides by Prop. 5, 3 (cf. § 248, 3) and his Fasti by 5, 2. 4. 9. 10 (see n. 4); cf. § 249, 6 ad fin. He was on friendly terms e.g. with the younger (Volcacius) Tullus, the nephew of the cos. 721/33; see 1, 1, 9. 1, 6, 2. 1, 14, 20. 1, 22, 1. 4, 22, 2. Not until after the publication of the first book does he seem to have been introduced to Maecenas; in it we find no allusion to relations between the poet and the leading men and circles. Addressed to Maecenas are 2, 1 (v. 17) and 4, 9; in the latter elegy he refuses a request to write on greater subjects, but at the end (if indeed this part belongs to the poem; see Heimreich l.l. 23) he promises poems on national subjects (probably like the greater number in book 5). Propertius, like Vergil (§ 224, 5), lived on the Esquiline (4, 23, 24), perhaps with Maecenas; but such familiarity as existed between Maecenas and Horace was rendered impossible by the difference of age. We find phrases in praise of Augustus such as *arma deus Caesar dites meditatur ad Indos* (4, 3, 1); *Caesar dum canitur, quaeso,*

Iuppiter ipse vaces (5, 6, 14); *vix timeat salvo Caesare Roma Iovem* (4, 11, 66); *lacrimas vidimus ire deo* (5, 11, 60. To understand this cf. 3, 15, 40 *nocte una quivis vel deus esse potest*. 4, 9, 45 *haec urant scripta puellas meque deum clament et mihi sacra ferant;* also 3, 34, 18. 46). Warm praise of Vergil and of the as yet unpublished Aeneid: 3, 34, 61. Reminiscences of Verg. Georgica e.g. Prop. 4, 13, 41 =Verg. georg. 1, 21. Prop. 4. 24, 15=georg. 1, 303. Cf. EReusch l.l. 121. 140. MRothstein, Herm. 24, 1. Horace is never mentioned by him, nor is Tibullus; but we often meet in Propertius with reminiscences of Horace, e.g. 3, 24, 17 *hoc erat in primis*=Hor. s. 2, 6, 1; Prop. 4, 2, 17 *pyramidum sumptus ad sidera ducti* cf. Hor. c. 3, 30, 2; 4, 9, 17 *est quibus eleae concurrit palma quadrigae* cf. Hor. c. 1, 1, 3; 4, 23, 23 *i puer et citus haec*=Hor. s. 1, 10, 100; with 5, 6, 65 cf. Hor. epod. 9, 23; with ib. 79 (*sero confessum foedere Parthum*) Hor. c. 3, 8, 22; with 1, 6, 11 (*horam possum durare*) Hor. ep. 1, 1, 82; with 4, 13, 60 (*frangitur ipsa suis Roma superba bonis*) Hor. epod. 16, 2 etc. Cf. Meierotto, de rebus ad auctores quosd. class. pertinent. dubia (Berl. 1785), 143. EReisch, Wien. Stud. 9, 120. We might rather be justified in concluding from Horace's silence as to Propertius that the calm mind of Horace was not much attracted by the passionate manner of the young elegiac poet. Cf. § 219, 17. 243, 1. Possibly Hor. ep. 2, 2, 90 sqq. is intended to satirise Propertius (JPPostgate, Sel. eleg. of Prop. p. xxxii).—Imitations of Tibullus: AZingerle, Ovid u. s. Vorgänger 1, 55. 98. 101. 103. 132 and elsewhere. BKuttner (see n. 4 ad fin.) 72. AMarx l.l. 41 and above § 245, 1. Reminiscences of Catullus: HMagnus, JJ. 115, 418. Quintilian's opinion of Prop.: § 32, 1. Ov. a. a. 3, 333 *teneri . . . Properti*. tr. 5, 1, 17 *blandique Propertius oris* (cf. 2, 465). Mart. 8, 73, 1 *lascive Properti*. 14, 189 *facundi . . . Properti*.

3. It was divided into books, the first of which was published separately by the author himself (hence, at the close of b. 1 c. 22, the poet introduces himself to the reader): 2, 3. 4 *turpis de te iam liber alter erit*; 3, 24, 1 *cum sis iam noto fabula libro et tua sit toto Cynthia lecta foro*. The title *Propertii Cynthia*, *monobiblos* in the MSS. is therefore just, as far as the matter itself is concerned, see n. 1 l. 4. The first book shows remarkable indifference with respect to the concluding pentameters in three or more syllables, and in the books following these occur more and more rarely; Propertius here has regard to the more skilful (Ovidian) metrical construction. The second book contains much that is fragmentary.—Lachmann (ed. of 1816 p. xxi and in the ed. of 1829) has divided the second book into two. According to this arrangement b. 1 of the manuscripts = b. 1 in Lachmann; b. 2, 1–9 MS. = b. 2 Lachm.; b. 2, 10–34 MS. = b. 3 Lachm.; b. 3 MS. = b. 4 Lachm.; b. 4 MS. = b. 5 Lachm. In Lachmann's ed. of 1829—from which we quote—and likewise in Haupt's editions, only the numbers of the books are set down according to Lachmann's arrangement, but the counting of the poems and of the lines has been retained from the vulgate. In favour of the division of b. 2 Lachmann advances especially 3, 13, 25, where Propertius says in picturing to himself his funeral: *sat mea sit magna, si tres sint pompa libelli, quos ego Persephonae maxima dona feram;* a passage which must, therefore, belong to the third book although in the MSS. it is in b. 2; see however e.g. EReisch, Wien. Stud. 9, 94. Lachmann begins a new book with 2 (3 Lachm.), 10: this poem is evidently intended to form the dedication of a book to Augustus (corresponding with 2, 1 to Maecenas): b. 2 in Lachmann is indeed comparatively rather short (it may have been incompletely preserved, see also ThBirt, RhM. 32, 393, AOtto, JJ. 131, 411), but b. 2 of the MSS. is on the other hand disproportionately long. It is more important that the only quotation from Propertius with a reference to the number of the book (in Nonius 169, 32 *Propertius elegiarum libro III 'iam liquidum nautis aura secundat*

iter'=3 [4 Lm.], 21, 14) tells against Lachmann and for the enumeration of the MSS., although it is very easy to write *IIII* instead of *III*. ThBirt, antikes Buchw. 413; RhM. 38, 199 a remodelling of Lachmann's theory: first collection Cynthia, monobiblos, published and consisting independently; a second later collection of 4 books: b. 1 (=MS. b. 2, 1–9 incomplete; see above), b. 2 (=MS. 2, 10–34), b. 3 and 4 as transmitted in the MSS. Cf. also Hertzberg in his ed. 1, p. 213. ChrHeimreich, quaestt. Prop. 22 (and compare Heydenreich, quaestt. Prop. 22). Lütjohann, qu. Prop. 77. CBrandt (n. 7) cap. 3. Bährens pref. to his ed. p. xl. FPlessis, études 97. JPruszinsky, de Prop. carmm. in libros distribuendis, Pesth 1886. EReisch, Wien. St. 9, 95.—The date of composition of the several poems cannot usually be exactly determined, and the date of publication of the books is also uncertain: b. 1 perhaps in the middle of 726/28; b. 2+3 (in this 3, 31 was written immediately after the dedication of the temple to Apollo on the Palatine 9th Oct. 726/28, and in the closing poem 3, 34 Cornelius Gallus (§ 232, 1) † 727/27 is mentioned as *modo mortuus*) about 728/26–729/25; b. 4 (in this 4, 18 on the death of Marcellus (n. 4), † 731/23) about 732/22–733/21; b. 5 (in this 5, 11 on Cornelia, † 738/16) about 738/16–739/15. See besides BEschenburg in the liber misc. soc. Bonn. (1864) 83. Bährens l.l. xlv, and the treatises by AMarx (n. 1. ad fin.), RScharf (n. 7), KKirchner (n. 4), FPlessis, étud. 195, EReisch, Wien. Stud. 9, 106 and many others.

4. Among the Alexandrine poets Propertius mentions as his models especially Kallimachos and Philetas (4, 1, 1. 4, 3, 52. 5, 1, 64. 5, 6, 3). He rendered them admiring homage and imitated them zealously, both as regards the legendary materials they employed and individual poetical images and phrases, although it is very difficult to give proof of this owing to the fragmentary condition of the Alexandrine literature, and e.g. many of the reminiscences of Kallimachos are only to be recognised from the reflection of them in Paulus Silentiarus (AReifferscheid, JB. 1880 3, 271). Cf. in general Hertzberg 1, p. 186. AOtto, de fabulis Prop. I, Bresl. 1880, II, Gross-Glogau 1886. FMallet, quaestt. Prop., Gött. 1882. In point of natural character, these scholar-poets were really the antipodes of Propertius with his rich imagination. and indeed the flames of his passion often rise above his mythological manner: but that which after all attracted him towards them was their mastery over form, and this very adherence is proof sufficient that in spite of his sensuous fervour Propertius maintained his intellectual self-command. He was almost too apt a pupil of his models; when he has moved, elevated and carried away his readers, it suddenly occurs to him to return to the Alexandrine manner: mythological names, stories and allusions are rattled off in strange medley, and the reader's interest cools. Propertius' poetical gifts less than any had need of external props; but his impetuous nature imposed on itself this scholastic ballast, so as not to be driven without goal or helm on the sea of passion. It was Propertius who inspired the Roman elegies of Goethe, who says later on in Riemer, Mittheil. 2, 646 'Propertius' elegies . . . the greater part of which I have reread, have strongly stirred my nature, as works of this kind usually do, and given me a desire to produce something of the same kind, etc.' His books, the inexhaustible life of the huge metropolis, and his own exuberant fancy supplied our poet, however monotonous a life he might chance to lead, with the abundance of ideas which distinguishes him from Tibullus, but they also destroyed the even balance of his powers, the harmony of his colouring, and the clear steadiness of his thoughts.

The poems on Italian or Roman subjects are to be found in the last book: Propertius' intention is to celebrate Rome in a work to which 5, 1 forms the introduction: we there find v. 67 *Roma, fave, tibi surgit opus: date candida, cives, omina et inceptis dextera cantet avis: sacra diesque canam et cognomina prisca locorum: has meus ad metas sudet oportet equus.* Cf. besides 4, 3, 3 sqq. 4, 9, 49 sqq. Hence these must have been αἴτια in imitation of Kallimachos adapted to Italy. Propertius probably undertook the work at the solicitation of Maecenas: 4, 9, 49 and paneg. in Pisonem 237 *Maecenas alta Tonantis eruit et populis ostendit nomina Grais, carmina Romanis etiam resonantia chordis*, on which see Bücheler, RhM. 36, 336 and EReisch l.l. 136 (cf. § 244, 2). Propertius, however, did not complete the work. We have fragments of it in 5, 2 (Vertumnus). 4 (Tarpeia). 9 (Hercules and Cacus). 10 (Iuppiter Feretrius). Varro, no doubt, principally supplied the subject-matter for these poems. MTürk, de Prop. carminum quae pertinent ad antiquitatem Rom. auctoribus, Halle 1885.—With these poems are connected to some extent those on the most recent and contemporary events: 5, 6 (on the battle of Actium). 11 (on the death of Cornelia, † 738/16): the last-named poem, 'the queen of elegies,' as it has been called, of most touching and thrilling beauty, was perhaps designed to ornament the grave of the deceased (cf. v. 36 *in lapide hoc uni nupta fuisse legar*. Cf. EHübner, commentatt. Mommsen., Berl. 1877, 98; Herm. 13, 423. Separate editions by Hofman-Peerlkamp, Amsterd. 1865 (cf. LMüller, JJ. 91, 777). Further 4, 4 (on Augustus' armaments against the Parthians 732/22?). 4, 18 (on the death of the young Marcellus, † Sept. 731/23; Bücheler, RhM. 39, 621, cf. Verg. A. 6, 865 sqq.). The last book is proved by its increased severity of metrical treatment to be the latest composition of the writer (KKirchner l.l. cap. 4), but it was probably not published by the poet himself. Cf. RMerkel on Ovid's Fasti p. ccxlviii. LMüller ed. p. xiii. xlvii. See also § 332, 4. The Propertian origin of b. 5 is contested with insufficient reason by DCarutti (Prop. Cynthia, cum libro IV qui Propertii nomine fertur, Hagae Com. 1869, p. xxxiv). Cf. the same writer, Mem. dell. Acad. di Torino 2, 26 (1868), 23. A vindication of the tradition by RVoigt, de quarto (V) Prop. libro, Helsingf. 1872 and KKirchner, de Prop. l. V, Rost. 1882; Festgabe f. WCrecelius, Elberf. 1881, 62. RScharf (n. 7) 62. Cf. also Reisch l.l. 123.—On the rhetorical element in P.'s method see the references in Hertzberg's prolegg. p. 105. On the refined construction of his elegies Hertzberg ib. p. 80–103; and, with much exaggeration, KMüllenhoff (allg. Monatsschrift 1854, 186; see now the same author Herm. 13, 423) and CPrien (Symmetrie u. Responsion d. röm. Elegie, Lüb. 1867, 36). ODrenckhahn, stroph. Composition in b. 3 d. Prop., ZfGW. 22, 177. 257; in b. 4, Stendal 1868.—On the succession and arrangement of the poems (variatio, etc.) cf. KPSchulze, JJ. 131, 867. AOtto, Herm. 20, 552. On the metre of Prop. cf. Eschenburg, observ. p. 1, ChrLütjohann, comm. propert. 96, ThBirt, hist. hexam. lat. (1876) 26 and LMüller's ed. p. xlvii, Postgate (n. 6) p. cxxvi. Cf. also § 32 4 and 5.—On the diction cf. besides Hertzberg, Postgate (n. 6) p. lxxxix and others, BKuttner, de Prop. elocutione quaestt., Halle 1878. PHeymann, in Prop. quaestt. gramm. et orthogr., Halle 1883. Frahnert, zum Sprachgebr. des P. (on Supina, Gerundia, Participia), Halle 1874. AHörle de casuum usu Prop., Halle 1887. NMButler, the postpositive et in Prop., Americ. journ. of philol. 12, 349. AWagner, de syntaxi Propertiana, Passau 1888. WAEdwards, d. syntakt. Gräcismen bei Pr., Geneva 1889. WSchneider, de Prop. sermonis novatore et amplificatore, Strassb. 1888. ASpandau, de serm. Prop. I, Lps. 1888. HSpindler, syntaxeos Prop. capp. II (de verbi tempp. et modis), Marb. 1888.

5. Propertius' works are very rarely cited by later authors and were unknown during the Middle Ages, hence we do not find him quoted in anthologies etc. (see Bährens' ed. p. 197). There are extant at the present time only late and

for the most part very corrupt MSS., derived from one and the same original, which has disappeared. A MS. of Propertius belonging to Petrarch is the first mentioned. It is about this MS. or a transcription of it that Coluccio Salutato is concerned (§ 187, 5) in a letter of a. 1374 (see MHAUPT's op. 1, 277). Comparatively the most correct version is the cod. Neapolitanus, now in Wolfenbüttel Gud. 224, s. XII/XIII?; facsimile of 6 pages of the Neapol. in FPlessis, études sur Prop., Par. 1884. On the history of the Neapolitanus see PDENOLHAC, bibl. de FOrsini, Par. 1887, 233. The MSS. (Laur. 36, 49 s. XV, Leidensis Voss. 38 s. XIV, Ottoboniano-Vaticanus 1514 s. XV, Daventriensis 1792 s. XV) preferred by BÄHRENS (in his ed.) do not merit this preference above the Neapol., and only the two latter should be ranked with but after it. FLEO, RhM. 35, 441. AKIESSLING, DLZ. 1880, 231. APALMER, Hermath. 7 (1881), 40. KROSSBERG. JJ. 127, 65. RSOLBISKY, de codd. Prop., Jena 1882 (=diss. Ienens. 2, 139). CWEBER, de auctoritate codd. Prop., Hagen 1887. The Groninganus s. XV, which was formerly much valued, also abounds in interpolations; see HKIEL, obss. 11. MHAUPT, op. 2, 53. CHRHEIMREICH, quaestt. Prop. (Bonn. 1863) p. 2. WGRUMME, de codd. Prop. Groning. et Neapol., Aurich 1869. CHR LÜTJOHANN, comment. propert. p. 3. EHEYDENREICH, quaest. Prop. 37. On the Propertian MSS. generally see HERTZBERG's ed. 1, p. 231, LMÜLLER's ed. p. IV together with RhM. 27, 162. EBÄHRENS' ed. p. IV. FPLESSIS, étud. s. Prop. p. 1. On the re-discovered Cuiacianus of Scaliger: § 214, 11 (collated with Propertius in PALMER's ed. [n. 6] p. 139).—On a cod. Corsin. s. XV see HSCHENKL, Wien. Stud. 3, 160.

6. Editions (see HERTZBERG 1, p. 248, PLESSIS l.l. p. 47) e.g. JSCALIGER, Par. 1577 (and elsewhere). JPASSERATIUS, Par. 1608 (with a full ind. verb. and a commentary). JBROUKHUSIUS, Amsterd. 1727. JAVULPI, Padua 1755 II. PBURMANNUS (and LVSANTEN), Utr. 1870.—CLACHMANN, Lps. 1816 with a commentary; ed. of the text Berl. 1829. FJACOB, Lps. 1827. WAHERTZBERG, Halle 1843–45 III (cf. HKEIL, ZfAW. 1845, 519). Recens. EBÄHRENS, Lps. 1880, rec. APALMER, Lond. 1881. FAPALEY, Lond.[2] 1872 (also b. 5 with verse transl., Lond. 1866.) JPPOSTGATE, Select elegies, ed. with introd., notes etc., Lond. 1881.—Texts by HKEIL, Lps. 1850. MHAUPT (§ 214, 11). LMÜLLER (§ 214, 11).

7. The obstacles which the poet offers to rapid comprehension, the uneven method of his composition, which develops the ideas now by anticipation, now by retrospect, here passing over the connecting details, there throwing them in as afterthoughts—all this has caused Propertius to be loaded with useless conjectures, and it has been attempted to mend the text by numerous arbitrary transpositions. Recent contributions to criticism and explanation: HKEIL, observatt. crit. in Prop., Bonn 1843. FJACOB, Phil. 2, 446. 3, 552. RUNGER, anall. Philetaea et Propertiana, Neubrandenb. 1850; anall. Propert. etc., Halle 1851; Phil. 19, 319; emendd. Prop., Friedland 1868. MHAUPT, op. 2, 52. 101. 3, 205. 513: in Belger's Biogr. of Haupt (Berl. 1879) 249 and elsewhere. WFISCHER, de locis quibusd. Prop., Bonn 1863. CHRHEIMREICH, quaestt. Prop., Bonn 1863; novae quaestt. Prop. in the symb. philol. Bonn. 669. HAKOCH, symb. phil. Bonn. 321. BESCHENBURG in the liber miscellaneus (Bonn 1864), 83; obss. crit. in Prop., Bonn 1865. CHRLÜTJOHANN, commentatt. Prop., Kiel 1869 (esp. on b. 5). RELLIS in the professorial dissertations of University College, London 1871–72. 1872–73; journ. of phil. 15, 12. AKIESSLING, coniectan. Prop., Greifsw. 1875. EHEYDENREICH in commentatt. phil. sem. Lips. (1874) p. 3 on 3, 34 (see TEUFFEL, Jen. LZ. 1875, 453); quaestt. Prop., Lps. 1875; Übersichten über die neuere Prop.-Lit., JB. 1886 2, 139. 1887 2, 83. KWEBER, quaestt. Prop. (on interpolation), Halle 1876. EBÄHRENS, misc. crit. (Groning. 1879) 70. CROSSBERG, lucubratt. Prop., Stade 1877; JJ. 127,

64. CESandström, emendatt. in Prop., Lucan., Valer. Fl., Ups. 1878. HKnauth, quaestt. Prop., Halle 1878. CPeiper, quaestt. Prop., Creuzburg 1879. HAJMunro, journ. of phil. 6, 28. JPPostgate, ibid. 9, 62. JJCornelissen, Mnemos. NS. 7, 98. INMadvig, adv. crit. 2, 62. APalmer in Hermathena b. 1 sq., Dublin 1873 sq. 11, 318. EDietrich, quaestt. Tib. et Prop. (transpositions in 2, 6. 2, 8. 2, 11). Marb. 1873. LKrahner, Phil. 27, 58 (on 5, 1). FLeo, RhM. 35, 431. CBrandt, quaestt. Prop., Berl. 1880. LPolster, qu. P., Ostrowo 1881. RScharf, qu. P., Gött. 1881. JWeidgen, qu. P., Cobl. 1881–82 II. JVahlen, Beitrr. z. Berichtigg. des P., Berl. SBer. 1881, 335. 1882, 263, (on 1, 8. 2, 1); die Pätus-Elegie d. P. (4. 7), ib. 1883, 69; Berl. ind. schol. 1886/87. AOtto, die Versumstellungen bei Prop. I, Glogau 1884; die Versumstellungen b. Prop. 4, 1–4, in the commentatt. in hon. Reifferscheidii, Bresl. 1884, 11; BerlphWschr. 5, 481; d. Reihenfolge d. Gedd. d. Prop., Herm. 20, 552; neue Beitr. z. Erkl. d. Prop., Herm. 23. 21. ThKorsch, de interpolatt. Prop., Nord. Tidskr. f. fil. 5, 257. FAPaley, journ. of phil. 16, 183. WEHousmann, ibid. 16, 1. Ribbeck, RhM. 10, 481. OTappe, anall. ad Prop. l. I, in the Festschr. d. Königst. Realsch., Berl. 1882, 75. GKühlewein, in the Festpr. an HHeerwagen, Erl. 1882, p. 1. ThBirt (b. I), RhM. 38, 196. FPlessis, études critiques sur Prop. et ses élégies, Par. 1886; Propertiana. extr. du bull. de la fac. de Poitiers, Par. 1886. HFleischmann, Wien. St. 10, 150. AKiessling, commentariolum Propert. (on 5, 11), Greifsw. 1889.

8. On Propertius see e.g. Gruppe, röm. Eleg. 1, 274. FJacob, Properz, Lüb. 1847. WTeuffel, PRE. 6, 99. MHaupt, op. 3, 205. ThFKylander, Prop., en lit.-historisk Studie I, Upsala 1877. Postgate (n. 6) in his introduction. Plessis, étud. 281. Bücheler, Properz, in the deutsche Revue 8 (1883), 187.

9. Translations by CLvKnebel (Lpz. 1798; new ed. Lpz. 1882 Reclam), FCvStrombeck (Brunswick 1822), JHVoss (Brunswick 1830), WHertzberg (Stuttg. 1838; ausgewählte Elegien, Class. d. Alt. 1855, p. 137), FJacob (Stuttg.[2] 1868). In English (verse) 6, JCranstoun, Lond. 1875.

247. P. Ovidius Naso, of an equestrian family at Sulmo (a. 711/43 B.C.—770/17 or 771/18 A.D.), received an extensive rhetorical training, but at an early age devoted himself exclusively to poetry, for which he possessed an uncommon formal talent. Yet he remained rhetorical even in poetry, dallying with thought and subject-matter, rejoicing in brilliant figures and witty turns, without any seriousness, higher aims or firmness, indifferent to the claims and problems of life, but ingenious, piquant and original, showing unsurpassed mastery in all points of form, and inimitable lightness, adroitness and grace. In his first period he treated almost exclusively of sensual love, in the manner of the Alexandrine elegiac poets, though he always imparted to mythology, elegy and didactic poems a dash of irony by his frivolous selection of subjects. In his second period he wrote on subjects of Greek mythology and Italian legends, in nearly the same manner, but with greater care and earnestness. The works of his third period were composed at Tomi, and contain endless

complaints about his exile alternating with humble prayers for pardon.

1. Ovid's description of himself: tr. 4, 13. His name rests on the authority of the MSS.; he often calls himself Naso, e.g. am. 1, 11, 27. 2, 1, 2. He was born 20 March (trist. 4, 10, 13. cf. fast. 3, 813) 711/43 (trist. 4, 10, 6 cf. Hieron. on Eus. chron. a. Abr. 1975) at Sulmo (am. 3, 15, 11. Pont. 4, 14, 49 and elsewhere) in Paelignis (am. 2, 1, 1. 2, 16. 37. 3, 15, 3. 8 and elsewhere), being the second son of a well-to-do (trist. 2, 113) father. His brother died as early as 730/24 at the age of 20 (ib. 4, 10, 31). He studied rhetoric: see Sen. controv. 2, 10, 8 *hanc controversiam memini ab Ovidio Nasone declamari apud rhetorem Arellium Fuscum, cuius auditor fuit; nam Latronis admirator erat, cum diversum sequeretur dicendi genus. habebat ille comptum et decens et amabile ingenium. oratio eius iam tum nihil aliud poterat videri quam solutum carmen. adeo autem studiose Latronem audiit ut multas illius sententias in versus suos transtulerit . . .* (9) *tunc autem cum studeret habebatur bonus declamator. . . .* (12) *declamabat autem Naso raro controversias, et non nisi ethicas; libentius dicebat suasorias. molesta illi erat omnis argumentatio. verbis minime licenter usus est, nisi in carminibus, in quibus non ignoravit vitia sua, sed amavit. . . . adparet summi ingenii viro non iudicium defuisse ad compescendam licentiam carminum suorum, sed animum. aiebat interim decentiorem faciem esse in qua aliquis naevos fuisset.*—Ov. tr. 1, 7, 1. 8 mentions portraits of himself (busts and gems).

2. The official career of Ovid: (twice) XXvir, i.e. triumvir capitalis (trist. 4, 10, 33) and decemvir (stlitibus iudic., fast. 4, 383), a member of the court of the centumvirs (trist. 2, 93. Pont. 3, 5, 23); judge (trist. 2, 95). There are, however, but very slight traces in his writings of special knowledge of the ius civile. A further continuation of this career was prevented by Ovid's laziness and preference for poetry (trist. 4, 10, 35). He undertook a journey to Athens, Asia, and Sicily (trist. 1, 2, 77. Pont. 2. 10, 21). He was twice married at an early age and soon divorced (trist. 4, 10, 69); his third wife, Fabia (cf. HPeter on Ov. fast. 6, 802), remained faithful to him in exile. Ovid had a legitimate daughter who was twice married, trist. 4, 10, 75; cf. 1, 3, 19. Sen. dial. 2, 17 *Fidum Cornelium, Nasonis Ovidi generum.* This daughter cannot be the Perilla alluded to in trist. 3, 7, whose poetical taste was encouraged by Ovid. VLoers, de Ovidii filia, RhM. 1 (1833), 125. ΣΚΣακελλαρόπουλος, ἡ θυγάτηρ τοῦ Ὀβιδίου in the Ἀττικὸν ἡμερολόγιον 1879, 14. SGOwen on trist. p. xvii, xxix. Friends and intimates: Propertius (trist. 4, 10, 45), Gallio (Pont. 41, 1. Sen. suas. 3, 7. p. 27 K.), Hyginus (Suet. gr. 20), the poets Ponticus, Bassus, Macer, Sabinus, Tuticanus (see § 252, 1 sqq.), Cotta (§ 267, 6), Graecinus (am. 2, 10. Pont. 1, 6), Atticus (am. 1, 9, 2. Pont. 2, 4) and others; MKoch, prosographiae Ovidianae elementa, Bresl. 1865. OHennig, de Ovidii sodalibus (=the contemporary poets mentioned in Ovid), Berl. 1883 and further references § 250, 1.

3. His exile. *Decem lustris peractis* (trist. 4, 8, 33 cf. 4, 10, 95. Ibis 1) *Tomitas quaerere me laesi principis ira iubet* (tr. 4, 10, 97). In Elba he received the first news of his prosecution (Pont. 2, 3, 83). He was *relegatus, non exsul* (tr. 2, 137), and hence retained his fortune (Ibis 24). The description of his departure from Rome tr. 1, 3. It took place towards the end of 761/8 A.D. In December Ovid was on the Adriatic (trist. 1, 11, 3) and it was probably only in the spring of 762/9 that, after a long and tedious voyage (tr. 1, 10), he arrived at Tomi: he passed there as *sexta bruma* the winter of 767/14 (Pont. 4, 13, 40). HBrandes, JJ. 115, 353, CSchrader, ib. 846, EMeyer, ZfGW. 32, 451. GGräber, quaestt. Ovid. 1, Elberf.

1881, III. ThMatthias, JJ. 129, 201. GNick, Phil. Anz. 12, 194 and other references § 250, 1. The cause consisted in *duo crimina, carmen et error* (tr. 2, 207). The first of these, his immoral and dangerous ars amandi, is often mentioned by Ovid, who attempts to justify himself (esp. in b. 2 of the tristia, specially addressed to Augustus, ib. 3, 1, 7. Pont. 2, 9, 69. 2, 10, 15. 3, 3, 69. 4, 13, 41. Ibis 6 and elsewhere), and hence Apoll. Sidon. c. 23, 157, Vict. epit. 1, 27 mention his *tres libellos amatoriae artis* as the sole cause of his exile (Ovid. Pont. 4, 13, 42 says *prima causa*). It is indeed quite credible that Augustus should have been highly displeased with a work so greatly opposed to his attempts to promote marriage and a moral life (tr. 2, 7 *carmina fecerunt ut me moresque notaret iam demum visa Caesar ab arte meos*. 2, 212 *arguor obsceni doctor adulterii*). But ten years had passed since the first appearance of it, and the immediate cause must have consisted in quite a different error. Concerning this (his *error*, not *scelus* tr. 1, 3, 37. 3, 1, 52. 4, 10, 90. Pont. 3, 3, 75; cf. 1, 6, 25. 2, 9, 75) Ovid always speaks in mysterious expressions. Even the reason given for his silence, his unwillingness to renew Augustus' pain (trist. 2, 209 cf. 3, 6, 27), shows that the latter must have felt offended in his personal interests (cf. tr. 2, 133 *tristibus invectus verbis . . . ultus es offensas . . . ipse tuas*). And as Ovid blames his eyes as the guilty part (tr. 2, 103 *cur aliquid vidi, cur noxia lumina feci! cur imprudenti cognita culpa mihi est!* cf. 3, 5, 49 *inscia quod crimen viderunt lumina plector, peccatumque oculos est habuisse meum;* ib. 3, 6, 27. Pont. 3, 3, 74), it is highly probable that he witnessed without preventing the guilty act of some member of the Imperial family, perhaps under the erroneous impression (*partem nostri criminis error habet*, tr. 3, 5, 52) that Augustus himself knew of it and connived at it. This was probably the younger Julia's (Augustus' grand-daughter) adulterous connection with D. Silanus (Tac. ann. 3, 24). Julia was banished in the same year as Ovid (Tac. ann. 4, 71): Silanus was disgraced and went into voluntary exile (Tac. ann. 3, 24): the principal blame was perhaps laid upon Ovid, against whom Augustus may have been still predisposed on account of his ars amandi. The whole of Ovid's works (not only the ars, cf. v. 65) were removed from the three public libraries (§ 219, 21), see trist. 3, 1, 60 sqq.—ThDyer, in the Classical Mus. 1847, p. 229. GBoissier, rev. des deux mondes 69 (1867) p. 580. CLRoth, württ. Corresp.-Bl. 1854, 185. ADeville, sur l'exil d'Ovide, Par. 1859. EAppel, quibus de causis Ovid relegatus sit, Lps. 1872. Minich, atti dell' inst. Veneto di scienze 6, 5, 10 (1881). GSchömann, Phil. 41, 171. EKörber, de Ov. relegationis causis, Petersb. 1883. JHuber, d. Ursachen d. Verbannung Ov.'s, Regensb. 1888. EThomas, rev. de phil. 13, 47.

4. The manner in which Ovid bore his exile can only be compared with the meekness of Schubart when broken down by a lengthy imprisonment; his complaints resemble those of Cicero in his exile; his crouching to Augustus is carried to a délire d'adulation (Boissier). In losing Rome, he had lost himself. He now confines himself to the request that at least some other place of exile may be assigned to him (e.g. trist. 2, 577. Ibis 18), or again he cries to be pardoned and recalled. Augustus was already softened or tired out by the continual prayers of Ovid, but he died (Pont. 4, 6, 25 sq.), and his successor's cold heart was inaccessible to sighs and flatteries (Pont. l.l. 17). So it came that Ovid died at Tomi (on the Black Sea, in Moesia, the modern Kustindje): Hieron. on Eus. chron. a. Abr. 2033=770/17 A.D. (in the Amand. as early as a. 2032, in the Bongars. not until a. 2034) *Ovidius poeta in exilio diem obiit et iuxta oppidum Tomos sepelitur*. ThMatthias, JJ. 129, 214 conjectures from fast. 1, 223 that Ovid must have died during the first four months of 771/18; cf. Merkel on Ov. fast. p. CCLXVII.

5. The MS. vitae Ovidii (esp. Vindob., Vat. and Farnes.) are of no value, but Ovid's own poems are excellent sources for his life, especially trist. 4, 10. Among modern biographies the best is JMasson, Ovidii vita ordine chronologico sic delineata ut poetae fata et opera veris assignentur annis etc., Amstelod. 1708. A detailed and elaborate account is given by EvLeutsch, in Ersch and Gruber's Allg. Enc. 3, 8 (1836), 39.—ENageotte, Ovide, Dijon 1872.—No authentic portraits of Ovid (cf. n. 1 ad fin.) are extant: JJBernoulli, röm. Ikonogr. 1, 287.

6. On the character of Ovid: Sen. controv. 2, 10 (above note 1) and 9, 28, 17 *Ovidius nescit quod bene cessit relinquere.* Sen. nat. qu. 3, 27, 13 *poetarum ingeniosissimus, . . . nisi tantum impetum ingenii et materiae ad pueriles ineptias reduxisset.* Quint. 10, 1, 88 *lascivus quidem in herois quoque Ovidius et nimium amator ingenii sui, laudandus tamen in partibus.* Cf. ib. 93 (*Ovidius utroque*—Tibullus and Propertius—*lascivior*). 98 *Ovidii Medea videtur mihi ostendere quantum ille vir praestare potuerit, si ingenio suo imperare quam indulgere maluisset.* Among Ovid's own expressions the following are most significant: trist. 4, 10, 26 *quidquid tentabam dicere* (in prose) *versus erat;* ib. 40 *otia iudicio semper amata meo.* He feels himself to be the child of his time: (a. a. 3, 121 *prisca iuvent alios, ego me nunc denique natum gratulor; haec aetas moribus apta meis . . . quia cultus adest, nec nostros mansit in annos rusticitas*). His ideas on the gods are very free: *expedit esse deos, et ut expedit esse putemus . . . innocue vivite, numen adest* (a. a. 1, 637; cf. 3, 654. am. 3, 3, 23). Kruse, de Ov. moribus et operibus, Strals. 1856. AJReichart, die sittliche Lebensanschauung des Ovid, Potsd. 1867.

7. As his proper domain and chief performance Ovid himself considers (erotic) elegy (am. 2, 18, 13. 3, 1. 3, 15, 13. a. a. 3, 343. rem. am. 389. 395. trist. 4, 10, 54. Pont. 3, 3, 29), in the peculiar metre of which he also treated subjects properly belonging to epic (the Fasti) or iambic poetry (Ibis). Among his predecessors he thought most of Tibullus (cf. am. 3, 9), from whom he frequently borrowed subjects, thoughts, illustrations, expressions and phrases (AZingerle 1, especially 54), though he often turns them to frivolous use (cf. a. a. 2, 669 with Tib. 1, 1), next of Propertius (cf. § 246, 2). There are also reminiscences of the other literature of the time (Vergil, Horace, Lygdamus etc.) and of Lucretius, as indeed may easily be supposed of a poet gifted with such a prodigious memory; he is fond of dressing up citations of this kind mythologically (fast. 3, 465 = Catull. 64, 132; met. 14, 812 and fast. 2, 487 = Enn. ann. 1, 47 Vahl.). Reminiscences of the epigrammatist Philodemos of Gadara: see below p. 497, l. 5. The comparisons and metaphors so frequent in Ovid are also almost all the result of reading. JAWashietl, de similitudinibus imaginibusque Ovidianis, Vienna 1883. He also repeats himself very frequently, and sometimes, it may be supposed, quite intentionally (e.g. a. a. 2, 77 = met. 8, 217). Cf. Sen. suas. 3, 7. Cf. AZingerle, Ovid u. s. Verhältnis zu den Vorgängern u. gleichzeitigen römischen Dichtern (I Cat. Tib. Prop., II Enn. Lucr. Verg., III Hor.), Innsbr. 1869–71 III. ALüneburg, de Ovidio sui imitatore, Königsberg 1888. All this, and his treatment of his materials, show that Ovid's principal strength lies in his formal style. His wonderful gift of adaptation and his sensibility enable him to deal with every kind of idea, to transform it with ever-varying modifications, and to illuminate it with all the brilliancy of his skilful rhetoric. After the fashion of an improvisatore, Ovid delights his readers with a display which, like a fine show of fireworks, burns out and leaves no lasting impression. Ovid has a masterly command of the mythological jargon of his time, though he is just as lax in regard to the particulars as he is in all matters of detail (e.g. am. 3, 6, 31. 12, 21. rem. am. 783).

8. His diction is simple, clear and full of natural grace; his verse is smooth, fluent and elegant: no Roman has shown greater mastery of the elegiac metre than Ovid; yet his verse, as applied to all subjects alike, gives a certain impression of monotony.—GVBucht, de usu infinitivi ap. Ov., Upsala 1875. ETrillhaas, d. Inf. bei Ov., Erlangen 1877. StSobieski (see § 225, 7). RvKittlitz, Phil. 11, 283 (part. fut. act. in Ov.). PHau, de casuum usu Ovid., Münst. 1887. Löwe, Lexikalisches zu Ov., Strehlen 1888. See further under the various poems.—MSchmidt, de Ovidii hexametris, Cleves 1856. LMüller, de re metr. 91. 408. ThBirt, hist. hexam. lat. 52. JDraheim, Herm. 14, 253. Cf. above § 19, 2. 32, 4 and 5. On the same or similar verse-endings: EGeibel, Hadersleben 1872. HStSedlmayer, Wien. Stud. 2, 293.

9. On Ovid and his writings see EvLeutsch in Ersch. and Gruber's Enc. 3, 8, 54. Teuffel, PRE. 5, 1028. MHaupt pref. to his ed. of the met. p. iii. WABHertzberg in the ausgew. Gedd. d. röm. Elegiker (Stuttg. 1855) 227. Cavallin, ad libros Ov. prolegg., Lund 1859. ARiese pref. to his ed. 1, v. MSappa, Ovidio umorista, Riv. di filol. 11, 347.

248. The most faithful image of Ovid's peculiar character may be gained from his erotic poems, with which he commenced his literary career: the Amores, three books of elegies, lascivious scenes connected with the name of Corinna, the rhetorical Epistulae (Heroides), fictitious love-letters addressed by ladies of the heroic age to their lovers, with the addition of some spurious compositions; then also the Ars amatoria, a humorous didactic poem in three books, wanton in tone and contents though displaying great knowledge of the subject and much psychological refinement—and its companion, the Remedia amoris, also the poem on female toilet (libellus de medicamine faciei). In the same period Ovid wrote his tragedy of Medea and other works which have not come down to us.

1. Lines from the Amores and Ars were found on the walls of Pompeii; see CIL. 4, p. 260. The MSS. of all the carmina amatoria of Ovid are derived from an archetype, where they seem to have been in the following order: ars. am., remedia, amores, epistulae, medicamina (see n. 7). The best MSS. are two Parisini, 8242 P(utanus) s. XI and 7311 R(egius) s. X, and Sangallens. 864 s. XI, Etonensis s. XI (see Sedlmayer, proleg. crit. ad Ov. her. p. 4) etc. See further under the various works.—Editions: Ovidii amatoria c. var. lect. ed. CGWernsdorf, Helmstedt[2] 1802; recogn. (without epist. and medic.) LMüller, Berl. 1861. Cf. LMüller, zur Kritik des ersten Teils der ovid. Dichtungen, RhM. 17, 522. 18, 71. 20, 256; de re metr. 43. Ovid's erotic works translated by ABerg, Stuttg. 1867.

2. Early poems, trist. 4, 10, 57 *carmina cum primum populo iuvenilia legi, barba resecta mihi bisve semelve fuit. moverat ingenium totam cantata per urbem nomine non vero dicta Corinna mihi* (cf. am. 2, 13. a. a. 3, 538. Mart. 5, 10, 10. 8, 73, 10 and other passages). Ap. Sidon. carm. 23, 159 calls her (manifestly by an error) *Caesarea puella*. Much of the subject-matter of the amores was no doubt fur-

nished by the poet's own life (cf. am. 3, 1, 16. 22, 53. 3, 12); but the whole work is nevertheless a creation of poetic fancy fed on well-known themes, situations and literary models, not a poetic idealisation of actual facts, such as Tibullus' and Propertius' songs on Delia and Cynthia. The name Corinna is only chosen as a collective title for the elegies (cf. besides a. 2, 17. 29. a. a. 3, 538). The work breathes the refined dissoluteness of the Roman aristocracy. The obscenity of these poems is sometimes quite distressing (e.g. esp. 2, 13 sq. 3, 7). But they also contain such beautiful compositions as the elegy on the death of Tibullus (3, 9). Ovid (according to the epigram prefixed) himself brought out two editions of his Amores: the first in five books probably published in his early youth about 740/14 (e.g. 3, 9 shortly after the death of Tibullus 735/19), the second (now extant) had been revised, what was immature being rejected. The Amores appeared (the second edition as well) before the a. a., therefore before 752/2; see am. 2, 18, 19. a. a. 3, 343 *deve tribus* (?) *libris titulus quos signat amorum elige quod docili molliter ore leges*. 3, 538. The epilogue (am. 3, 15, 18) announces an important work (perhaps tragedies; cf. n. 8).—Gruppe, röm. El. 1, 374. 2, 205. LMüller, de Ov. amorum libris, Phil. 11, 60. 192. ERautenberg, de arte compositionis in Ov. am., Bresl. 1868. JHeuwes, de tempore quo Ov. amores, heroides, ars am. conscripta et edita sint, Münster 1883. His use of the epigrams of Philodemos of Gadara (a friend of L. Calpurnius Piso cos. 696/58 § 179, 37): GKaibel, Philod. Gad. epigr., Greifsw. 1885.—Translated by WHertzberg (Stuttg. 1854; a selection in the röm. Elegiker, Cl. d. Alt. p. 225), HLindemann (Lpz. 1859), ABerg (see n. 1) and HOelschläger, Lpz.[2] 1881.

3. Ars. am. 3, 345 (after mentioning the Amores) *vel tibi composita cantetur epistula voce; ignotum hoc aliis ille* (Ovid) *novavit opus*. It is a special kind of the poetic epistle first introduced by Ovid (§ 25), which may have been suggested by Propertius' letter of Arethusa (5, 3) to Lycotas (EReisch, Wien. Stud. 9, 143) or by Greek models (KDilthey, obss. in Ov. her. I, Gött. 1884, 1). The poet is not very careful as to the exact character of time and situation, but even here the fluctuating moods are finely represented. Prisc. Gl. 2, 544, 4 *Ovidius in heroidibus*. In the MSS. they are generally entitled *epistulae*. The letters of a) Penelope, b) Phyllis, c) Oenone, d) Canace, e) Hypsipyle, f) Ariadne, g) Phaedra, h) Dido, and i) Sappho are mentioned as finished or planned by Ovid am. 2, 18, 21–26, also answers by their respective lovers to a. g. h. b. e. i. composed by his friend Sabinus ib. 27–38 (§ 252, 4).—The present collection consists of the following letters (those which are also mentioned in the amor. l.l. are spaced): by 1) Penelope, 2) Phyllis, 3) Briseis, 4) Phaedra, 5) Oenone, 6) Hypsipyle, 7) Dido, 8) Hermione, 9) Deianira, 10) Ariadne, 11) Canace, 12) Medea, 13) Laodamia, 14) Hypermnestra, 15) Sappho, 16) Paris, 17) Helena, 18) Leander, 19) Hero, 20) Acontius, 21) Cydippe.—Among these no. 15 Sappho occupies a special position, as it either does not appear at all in the MSS. of the Heroides at present known to us (this applies to the majority of them and to the best), or it is not to be found included among the Heroides and hardly ever (only in the Vindob. 3111 s. XV) bears the name of Ovid. But that there did exist an early MS. version which gave Sappho as no. 15 of the Heroides (perhaps this was also known to NHeinsius when he placed Sappho after no. 14) is shown not only by the excerpts in Vincent of Beauvais, but especially by the Paris MS. excerpts 7647 and 17903 (see § 245, 7), in which excerpts from no. 15 are placed between those from 14 and 16. Allusions to the Sappho in the Epicedion Drusi (§ 251, 5) also prove that it belonged to the best period: at a subsequent time we find such allusions in Sacerdos GL. 6, 482, 1 (from this Probus GL. 4, 30, 19) and in Ausonius, while its author himself made

use of Lucan (cf. v. 139 with Lucan. 6, 508 sqq.). On the very exaggerated use of the poems of Ovid in the Sappho epistle see FXWerfer, acta sem. Monac. phil. 1, 4 and Loers in his ed.—FWSchneidewin, RhM. 2, 138. 3, 144 (for the contrary view VLoers, RhM. 4, 40). JMähly, ib. 9, 624. FGWelcker, RhM. 11, 241; kl. Schr. 2, 116. DComparetti, sulla epistola Ovidiana di Saffo (Publicaz. dell' Inst. di studi superiori), Florence 1876. EBährens, de ep. Sapphus, Riv. di filol. 13 (1884), 49. ThBirt, RhM. 32, 388. 399. HStSedlmayer, prolegg. p. 32; Wien. Stud. 10, 167. MHaupt, op. 1, 339. SdeVries, ep. Sapph. ad Phaonem, Leid. 1885. NBarbu, de Sapph. ep., Berl. 1887.—ILuniak, quaestt. Sapphicae (p. 2 de Ovid. Sapphus ep. fontt.; p. 97 critt. et exeget.), Kasan 1888. ABilger, de Ovid. her. appendice. Paridis et Helenae epp. sintne Ovidi quaeritur, Marb. 1888.—Of 21 (Cydippe), the last number, the majority and the best of the MSS. give only vs. 1–12, the rest occurs only in old editions and in very few and quite late MSS., e.g. vs. 13–144 Par. 7997, Guelferb. Gud. 279, Cremifanensis 329, and on the other hand vs. 13–248 Laur. 36, 27 (here however these lines are only added by some writer of s. XVI; Sedlmayer, Wien. Stud. 3, 158), and Lips. 47, all s. XV. These lines are nevertheless most certainly genuine, i.e. they are the original continuation of the commencement extant in the MSS. In the old editions we find *heroidum Ovidii ultima recens reperta* (cf. § 251, 5). CDilthey, de Cydippe Callimachea, Lps. 1863 (where also p. 133 is the text of no. 20 and 21, together with Maximus Planudes' Greek translation of 20 and 21, 1–12; on the latter see WStudemund, Phil. 34, 370. AGudeman, Berl. Studd. 8, 1)—Lastly, it is only in old copies (e.g. Parm. 1477) that we find preserved lines 16, 39–142, which are indeed very weak (see also ARiese, Lit. Centr.-Bl. 1879, 776), but which probably formed part of the original; the gaps are to be accounted for by the loss of some leaves, Peters l.l. ThBirt, Gött. GA. 1882, 831. —The best of the MSS. now extant is the P (§ 248, 1), next Eton. (ib.), Bern. 478 s. XII (a collation by GWartenberg, WschrfklPh. 1887, 1272. 1366. 1464; cf. Dilthey, obss. in her. 1, 11), the G(uelferbytanus 260 s. XIII), but the later MSS. are valuable by way of check and supplement, especially where the P is wanting. An enumeration and critique of the MSS. in Sedlmayer, prolegg. 1, 32. 85 and also Dilthey's obss. in her. 1, 10. WPeters l.l. cap. 1.

The last six epistulae differ even externally from 1–14, both by their being in pairs, and by their greater volume and peculiarities of metre and prosody. Lachmann, kl. Schriften 2, 61. LMüller, de re metr. 46; RhM. 17, 192. 18, 87. BEschenburg, metr. Untersuchungen üb. die Echtheit der Heroiden des Ovid, Lübeck 1874; wie hat Ov. einzelne Ww. u. Wortklassen verwandt? e. Beitr. z. Echtheitsfrage der Her., Lüb. 1886. But they too follow throughout the metrical construction of the first century. It remains a question how these differences are to be accounted for. Apparently (and this view seems the most obvious and probable) some clever imitator composed these last pieces as a continuation of the Ovidian style of composition (see e.g. Haupt, op. 1, 125. NMadvig, adv. 2, 77. ThBirt, RhM. 32, 386), and they were afterwards, together with the Sappho (15) which is certainly not by Ovid, incorporated with the Ovidian collection: or did Ovid himself in later years (perhaps in order to amuse himself during the dreary period of his banishment) return with less freshness, but with all the more abundant phraseology to the kind of composition which he had originated in his youth? ARiese, JJ. 109, 569; JB. 1874/75 1, 234. 1877 2, 20. 1878 2, 243.—WZingerle, Unterss. zur Echtheitsfrage der Heroiden Ovids, Innsbr. 1878. HStSedlmayer, ZföG. 30, 816. JVahlen, d. Anfänge der Her. d. Ov. (on missing parts at the beginning of the Her.), Abhh. d. Berl. Akad. 1881. RBodenstein, Studd. zu. Ov. Her., Merseb. 1882. HJurenka, Beittr. z. Krit. d. Ov. Her., Vienna 1881; quaestt. crit., Vienna 1885, 6. 12.

WPeters, obss. ad Ov. her., Gött. 1882. CDilthey, obss. in Ov. epp. her. I, Gött. 1884. AStJezierski, de universis Ov. epist. her. et singillatim de Sapph. ep., Tarnow 1886. Gilbert, Meissen 1887. JTolkiehn, Königsb. 1888.—On the sources of the Heroides (principally Hellenistic, but with occasional use of the tragedians) see CDilthey Cyd. 41 and elsewhere. ERohde, gr. Roman 129. Welcker, gr. Trag. 495 and elsewhere. ThBirt, RhM. 32, 398; antikes Buchwesen 378. AKalkmann (§ 249, 1). MMayer, de Eur. mythopoeia, Berl. 1883; Herm. 20, 101. —In general cf. besides Gruppe, Minos 495. KLehrs in his Horatius (1869) ccxxii–ccliv. Separate editions by GBachet de Meziriac, la Haye [2]1716 II, DJv Lennep, Amst.[2] 1812, WTerpstra (Leid. 1829), VLoers (Cologne 1829 sq. II), APalmer, Lond. 1874. Ovidii epp. XIII, ESShuckburgh, Lond. 1879. Ov. heroides appar. crit. instr. HStSedlmayer, Vienna 1878 and a small ed., Prague 1886 (cf. the same writer, proleg. crit. ad her. Ov., Vienna 1878; krit. Commentar zu Ov. Her., Vienna 1881).—Translated by JHenning, EFMetzger (Stuttg. 1855), HLindemann (Lpz. 1867).

4. A. Sabini epistolae tres (cf. n. 3 l. 12), printed in editions of Ovid (first Vicent. 1480, Venet. 1486), were composed by the Italian Angelus Quirinus Sabinus about a. 1467 (Sabini poetae opp., Rome 1474, as a supplement to his Ammianus). OJahn, ZfAW. 1837, 631. CEGläser, RhM. 1, 437.

5. Ars amatoria is the title in the MSS., against which there is no very weighty argument in 1, 1 *si quis . . . artem non novit amandi me legat*, and am. 2, 18, 19 *artes teneri profitemur amoris* (cf. Sen. controv. 3, 7 *est eius qui hoc saeculum amatoriis non artibus tantum sed sententiis implevit*). Ovid generally calls it only ars (e.g. trist. 2, 303). The first two books contain rules for men how to gain (b. 1) and to retain (b. 2) the love of young girls (libertinae); b. 3 contains similar rules for girls. It is in vain that the poet now and then talks gravely (2, 599. 3, 483. 615) or plays the moral man (3, 494. 613) and pretends to have written his poem *solis meretricibus* (tr. 2, 303 cf. ib. 244. Pont. 3, 3, 50), as love is here taken as mere sensual pastime. The poem, didactic in form, becomes ironical from the lively enjoyment which the poet derives from dressing up his wanton subject-matter. He is well acquainted with ordinary feminine nature, e.g. 1, 99 *spectatum veniunt, veniunt spectentur ut ipse*; 705 . . . *ut pudor est quondam coepisse priorem, sic alio gratumst incipiente pati*. The work was probably published a. 752/2 or 753/1. Allusions to contemporary history 1, 177 e.g. *Parthe, dabis poenas; . . . ultor adest . . . bellaque non puero tractat agenda puer. parcite natales, timidi, numerare deorum* etc.—Collation of a MS. Oxon. s. IX for b. 1: REllis, Herm. 15, 425.—Translated by ChrFAdler (Lpz. 1843) and esp. by WABHertzberg (with introd. and notes, Stuttg. 1854), and by HCriepen (= Pernice), Lpz. 1856. Edited (with the Amores) by JHWilliams, Lond. 1884.

6. Remedia amoris, in one book, probably written a. 754/1 or 755/2, advice how to free oneself from troublesome passion (v. 15, 41), rather a weak performance when compared with the Ars, but not without psychological refinement and masterly technique. rem. 385, *Thais in arte mea. lascivia libera nostrast . . . si mea materiae respondet Musa iocosae, vicimus* etc.—A. Zingerle, Notes from MSS. on Ov. R. A. (from an Innsbruck MS. saec. XV), in his kl. philol. Abhh., I (Innsbruck 1871) p. 31–34.—Transl. by Strombeck (Brunswick [2]1829). WHertzberg, (Stuttg. 1855).

7. Ovid. a. a. 3, 205 *est mihi quo dixi vestrae* (ladies) *medicamina formae parvus, sed cura grande libellus opus*. It was, therefore, written before the close of the a. a.; the lively introduction was transferred as a whole (part of it without

the slightest change) into the a. a. 3, 101. 2, 97. V. 39 is quoted as Ovidian in Charis. GL. 1, 90, 16; Pliny NH. 30, 33 *huius medicinae auctor est Ovidius poeta* is an allusion to this work. Cf. ThBirt, de Halieuticis (1878), 41. On the MSS. see Kunz l.l. In the 100 lines which are extant (the heading in the Laur. Marc. 223 s. XI/XII, the best MS., is *libellus de medicamine faciei femineae*, in the other MSS. *de medicamine faciei*) we have only the smaller part (perhaps a fifth) of the whole, which was based on Greek medical authorities. LMüller, de re metr. p. 43; RhM. 20, 256 accounts for the lost portions by supposing the poem to have stood at the end of the archetype (see n. 1); cf. also MSchanz, RhM. 39, 313. REhwald, JB. 1882 2, 179. 1885 2, 184.—Ov. de medic. faciei ed., Ovidio vindicavit AKunz, Vienna 1881. Translated by WHertzberg (Stuttg. 1855).

8. Tac. dial. 12 *nec ullus Asinii aut Messalae liber* (speech) *tam illustris est quam Medea Ovidii aut Varii Thyestes.* Quint. 10, 1, 98 (above § 247, 6). Cf. Ovid. am. 2, 18, 13. 3, 1, 11. 67. trist. 2, 553, above n. 2 l. 20. Also cited in the epistola Valerii ad Rufinum (see however § 477, 7). LMüller, JJ. 95, 496. Only two lines from it are preserved in Quint. 8, 5, 6 and Sen. suas. 3, 7. Cf. ORibbeck, RhM. 30, 626. It may perhaps have been used in Seneca's Medea. FLeo, Sen. trag. 1, 166.

9. A poem on the nuptials of Fabius Maximus (cos. 743/11) Pont. 1, 2, 133.

10. Quint. 6, 3, 96 *Ovidius ex tetrastichon Macri* (§ 223, 4) *carmine librum* (an entire book) *in malos poetas composuit.*—Prisc. GL. 2. 149 *Ovidius in epigrammatis* (a pentameter follows). From the same source is perhaps derived the satirical pentameter in Quint. 9, 3, 70 and the two phalaecic lines ib. 12, 10, 75.—Lactant. inst. div. 2, 3 *Naso . . . eum librum quo Φαινόμενα breviter comprehendit, his tribus versibus terminavit* (3 hex. follow). Prob. ad Verg. ge. 1, 138 *Ovidius in phaenomenis* (2 hex.). See also FPR. 349. Cf. ThBirt, de Halieut. Ovid. (Berl. 1878) 40.

249. The Metamorphoses, in fifteen books, contain a version of the Greek legends concerning transformations, beginning with Chaos: with these are connected in the two last books a few Italo-Roman ones. The whole work closes—somewhat abruptly—with an act of homage to the reigning princely house, i.e. Caesar's transformation into a star, and a reference to the future deification of Augustus himself. The poet cleverly arranges his chronology and the sequence of the various legends so as to mystify the reader, and derives one transformation from another, or knits them together. The subject-matter, which is borrowed almost entirely from the Greeks, but treated freely throughout, offers an abundant opportunity for the display of Ovid's brilliant talent for narrative, the flowing eloquence of his diction, the ease and elegance of his verse. He unweariedly invents fresh alternations in order to avoid monotony and to gain the reader's sympathy for the varied and almost bewildering succession of pictures in this book of magic and marvels. The Fasti (six books in elegiac metre) explain and interpret the calendar

(astronomical, civil and religious) of the Romans according to the months. The work was begun before Ovid's banishment and was planned to extend to twelve books. It was first intended to be dedicated to Augustus and after his death to Germanicus, but it was never completed and was published only after the death of the author.

1. On the subject-matter see e.g. IGLMellmann, de causis et auctoribus narrationum de mutatis formis, Lps. 1786. Among the Greeks it had been treated by Ps. Boios (Ὀρνιθογονία Athen. 9, 393 ad fin. Anton. Liber. 3, 7, 11, and elsewhere; GKnaack, anall. 1) and especially the Alexandrine poet Nikandros of Colophon (Ἑτεροιούμενα, 5 bb. in hex.), as well as Parthenios of Nicaea (Μεταμορφώσεις, and likewise Theodoros and Didymarchos), and Antigonos (Ἀλλοιώσεις). It is not possible to refer to Ovid's sources in detail, as the Greek originals are not extant, and besides Ovid evidently dealt very freely with the fantastic materials which his incomparable memory culled from his reading both of earlier and later literature. Nikandros and Parthenios are rightly mentioned among his sources (for Theodoros see Probus on Verg. ge. 1. 399); also other Alexandrines (e.g. Euphorion, Phanokles etc.), then Homer, the Greek tragedians (esp. Euripides), Theokritos and others. But Ovid assuredly did not trouble himself with arduous researches; he drew his materials from works lying ready to his hand, therefore also from manuals, epitomes, summaries (e.g. the hypothesis to Eur. Med.; KRobert, Bild und Lied, in Kiessl.-Wilamow. philol. Unterss. 5, 231) and so forth. Cf. ARiese, praef. ad metam. p. iv. ERhode, gr. Rom. 124. 127. ASurber, die Meleagersage . . . zur Bestimmung der Quellen von Ov. met. 8, 170 sqq., Zür. 1880. RFörster, Raub. d. Perseph. (Stuttg. 1874) 84. GKnaack, anall. alexandrino-rom., Greifsw. 1880, 53; quaestt. Phaethonteae, in Kiessl.-Wilamow. philol. Unterss. 8, 22. UvWilamowitz, Herm. 18, 396; ind. lect. Gott. 1884; Isyllos v. Epid. 60. AKalkmann, de Hippolytis Eurip. quaestt., Bonn 1882. GPlaehn, de Nicandro aliisque poetis gr. ab Ov. in met. adhibitis, Halle 1882.—ASchmekel, de Ovidiana Pythagorae doctrinae (esp. met. 15, 75) adumbratione Greifsw. 1884.—The attempt of WPetersen, quaestt. Ov., Kiel 1877, to prove that Parthenios' work was Ovid's only original has entirely failed. GNick, phil. Anz. 9, 554.—Quint. 4, 1, 77 *illa vero frigida et puerilis est in scholis affectatio, ut ipse transitus efficiat aliquam utique sententiam, . . . ut Ovidius lascivire in Μεταμορφώσεσιν solet, quem tamen excusare necessitas potest.* Sen. nat. quaest. 3, 27, 31 (cf. above § 247, 6).

2. Ovid. trist. 1, 7, 13 *carmina mutatas hominum dicentia formas, infelix domini quod fuga rupit opus. haec ego discedens, sicut bene multa meorum, ipse mea posui maestus in igne manu.* . . . (23) *quae quoniam non sunt penitus sublata, sed exstant, pluribus exemplis scripta fuisse reor* (cf. trist. 4, 10, 62 sqq.; supposing Ovid to have actually burnt them, still he knew that they were preserved elsewhere) . . . (26) *nec tamen illa legi poterunt patienter ab ullo, nesciet his summam si quis abesse manum. ablatum mediis opus est incudibus illud, defuit et scriptis ultima lima meis.* . . . (39) *quidquid in his igitur vitii rude carmen habebit emendaturus, si licuisset, eram.* See trist. 2, 255 *dictaque sunt nobis* (*quamvis manus ultima coepto defuit*) *in facies corpora versa novas.* 559 *pauca quibus prima surgens ab origine mundi in tua deduxi tempora, Caesar, opus.* trist. 3, 14, 19 *sunt quoque mutatae ter quinque volumina formae.* Sen. nat. quaest. 3, 27, 12. Quint. 4, 1, 77. The length of the Metam. according to an epigram in the MSS. was 11985 lines

(our vulgate numbers 11996): Birt, antikes Buchwesen 507.—'Narrationes fabularum quae in Ov. Metam. occurrunt' (in 15 books), in the Marcianus (see n. 3) without the name of the author; in a later Laur. entitled 'Donati breviatio fabularum Ovidii'; in the editions it is for some unexplained reason attributed to Lactantius Placidus (§ 321, 10 e.g. in the ed. of the Met., Antverp. 1591, in the Mythographi lat. by Muncker 2, p. 189; cf. 2, praef. p. vii). Cf. RFörster, Raub d. Perseph. 289.—In 1210 Albrecht von Halberstadt composed in rhyme a translation of the Met., which was remodelled by Jörg Wickram (Mayence 1545), see § 251, 2. Ὀβιδίου μεταμορφώσεις (a Greek translation by Maximus Planudes) ed. FBoissonade, Par. 1822.—On a (worthless) mediaeval commentary on the Met. s. XI/XII (in the Monac. 4610) see KMeiser, Münch. SBer. 1885 1, 47; on another s. XV MBHauréau, acad. des inscript. 30, 2 (1883), 45. Cf. also HStSedlmayr, Wien. Stud., 6, 142.

3. Manuscripts: Laur. Marc. 225 s. XI, Harl. 2610 s. XI (for b. I–III; cf. REllis, journ. of phil. 12, 62; collation by Ellis in the anecd. Oxon. 1 — 1885 —, 5; cf. REhwald, JB. 1885 2, 181). Laur. 36, 12 s. XI, fragments in Bern. 363 s. VIII, London (Brit. 11967 s. XI), Leipzig s. X (on these and on some in Munich ClHelmuth, Münch. SBer. 1883 1, 221). The numerous late MSS. are often much interpolated. Ov. MSS. in Paris Ellis, journ. of phil. 15, 241.—ARiese, praef. metam. p. vi.—Critical and explanatory editions of the Met. by GEGierig ([2]Lps. 1821–23 II by JChrJahn), ECChrBach (Hanover 1831–36 II), DCGBaumgarten-Crusius (Lps. 1834), VLoers (Lpz. 1843).—Recensuit OKorn, Berl. 1880. Explained by MHaupt, OKorn and HJMüller (Berl. I[7] 1885, II[2] 1881). Ed. AZingerle, Prague 1884 (cf. the same Wien. Stud. 6, 59). Explained by HMagnus, Gotha 1885 (and the same writer in JJ. 135, 129; Studd. z. Ov. Met., Berl. 1887).

Recent selections for schools e.g. by OEichert (Bresl.[3] 1866), JSiebelis and FPolle (Lpz.[13] 1887 II), LEnglmann (Munich[2] 1878). JMeuser, Paderb.[3]1886. B. 13 by CHKeene, Lond. 1884. B. 13 and 14 by ChSimmons, Lond. 1887.—Lexicons for the Metamorphoses by OEichert (Hanov.[9] 1886) and JSiebelis (Lpz.[4] 1885 by FPolle).

4. Liebau, de consilio Ov. in comp. met., Elberf. 1846. GBréton, metam. Ov quo consilio susceperit, qua arte perfecerit, Par. 1882. Henneberger, Ov. met. contin. seriesque, Hildburgh. 1846. Lüdke, Lautmaleri in Ov. Met., Strals. 1871; rhythmische Malerei in Ov. Met., Strals. 1878. 79 II. HLoewe, de nonnullis figuris in met. I–VII, Grimma 1863. LScheibe, de sermonis Ov. proprietatibus . . . in metam., Halberst. 1880. FUrban, d. Alliteration in Ov. Met., Braunau 1882. JFavre, de Ovidio novatore vocabulorum in metam., Par. 1885.—IBekker, variae lectt. cod. Berol. Ov. Met., Berl. SBer. 1853. MHaupt, op. 2, 195. JRappold, z. Krit. u. Erkl. d. Met., Leoben 1870 (cf. § 251, 7 ad fin.). PSchönfeld, Ov.s Met. in ihrem Verhältn. zur antiken Kunst, Lpz. 1877. LLange, Leipz. Studien 1, 381. HKöstlin, Phil. 39, 175. ClHellmuth, zu Ov. Met., Kaiserslautern 1880. EGnesotto, in Ov. met., Padua 1881. REllis, journ. of phil. 12, 62. FPolle, JJ. 131, 889. Ebert, d. Anachronismus in Ov. Met., Ansb. 1888.

5. Translations by AvRode (Berl. 1816), JHVoss (Brunswick[2] 1829; a selection, newly revised by FLeo, Stuttg. 1883), HChrPfitz (Stuttg.), HLindemann (Lpz. 1853–56), RSuchier (Stuttg. 1858), WvTippelskirch (Berl. 1873).

6. Trist. 2, 549 *sex ego fastorum scripsi totidemque libellos* (*sex . . . totidemque* = 12 bb., see fast. 6, 725; *scripsi* refers to his labour upon the work, not to its completion), *cumque suo finem mense volumen habet. idque tuo nuper scriptum sub nomine, Caesar* (Augustus), *et tibi sacratum sors mea rupit opus.* The extant

work is, however, dedicated to Germanicus (§ 275, 4); see 1, 3 sqq. 63. 285. After the death of Augustus Ovid probably commenced at Tomi a revision of bb. 1–6 in order to dedicate them to Germanicus, but (except in a few passages; e.g. 4, 81 sqq.) he did not get beyond the first book. Merkel, quaest. Ov. critt., Halle 1835 and pref. to his ed. p. cclvii. ARiese in his ed. of Ovid 3, vi; JJ. 109, 563; JB. 1874/75 1, 243. 1877 2, 26. HPeter in his ed. 1, p. 11; JJ. 111, 499. PGoldscheider, de retractione fastorum Ov., Halle 1877. WKnoegel, de retractione fastorum ab Ovid. Tomis instituta, Montabaur 1885 (and HWinther, WschrfklPh. 1886, 326). On the subject-matter see fast. 1, 1 *tempora cum causis* (αἰτίαις) *Latium digesta per annum lapsaque sub terras ortaque signa canam.* 1, 7 *sacra recognosces annalibus eruta priscis et quo sit merito quaeque notata dies.* 4, 11 *tempora cum causis annalibus eruta priscis lapsaque . . . cano* (same as 1, 2). The chief source whence Ovid took the whole framework of his poem was the Fasti of Verrius Flaccus which, at that time, had not long been published (§ 74, 3. 261, 1): the fragments of these Fasti extant in inscriptions coincide in a remarkable degree with Ovid's statements, and the calendar of Verrius in book form probably supplied other matter. HWinther, de fastis Verrii Flacci ab Ovidio adhibitis, Berl. 1885. As in the Metamorphoses, Ovid here no doubt preferred to transfer into verse the materials thus ready to his hand rather than to work them out for himself. In the astronomical portion we meet with numerous errors (LIdeler, Abh. d. Berl. Ak. a. 1882, 137; Hoffmann, die Auf- und Niedergänge etc., Trieste 1879), which existed only in part in his authorities. Elsewhere too in this poet, who cared more for the form than for the subject, we meet with numerous blunders, cf. e.g. GNick, Phil. 41, 450. Perhaps Ovid may have made use of Eratosthenes' καταστερισμοί for the legends connected with the celestial bodies. See CRobert on Eratosth. catast. 29. Against ChrHülsen, Varronianae doctrinae (from the antiquitt. div. et hum.) quaenam in Ovidii fast. extent vestigia, Berl. 1880, see GNick, phil. Anz. 11, 182; Phil. 40, 380. ARiese, JB. 1881 2, 89. Ovid besides probably turned to account (especially in some poetical artifices) Kallimachos' Αἴτια (HPeters ed. 1, p. 15. RFörster, Raub d. Perseph. 76. ERhode, gr. Rom. 87). Are there traces of Livy being used? see KSchenkl, ZföG. 11, 401. It is possible that the choice of this subject may have been suggested by the unfinished fifth book of Propertius (Merkel l.l. p. ccxlviii). Cf. § 246, 2. The elegiac form shows itself to be in many ways less appropriate to the descriptive subject.—On calendars drawn up in accordance with Ovid's Fasti (extant in MSS.) see Merkel pref. to his ed. p. liii and GBoissier, rev. de phil. 8, 55.

7. Manuscripts: Vatic.-Regin. 1709 (Petavianus) s. X, also Vatic. 3262 (Ursinianus) s. XI, Monac. 8122 (Mallerstorfiensis) s. XII/XIII; besides these, later manuscripts, often much interpolated. Merkel p. cclxxi. HPeter, disp. crit. de Ov. fastis, Meissen 1877. VLoers, de tribus Ov. fast. codd. MSS. (with var. lect. of the cod. Trevir.), Trèves 1857. CMFrancken, cod. Fonteinii ap. Merkelium in fast., Mnemos. 12, 292.—FKrüger, de Ov. fast. recensendis, Rostock 1887.

8. More recent editions of the Fasti by GEGierig (Lps. 1812–14 II) and especially by RMerkel (ed. et interpr., Berlin 1841). Explained by HPeter, Lpz.[2] 1879 II.—Text by OGüthling, Prague 1883. With notes by TKeightley, Lond. 1848, FAPaley, Lond.[3] 1888, GHHallam, Lond. 1881. Criticism and explanation: OKreussler (Bautzen 1872). HPeter, Lps. 1874. EHoffmann, JJ. 115, 396. GNick, Phil. 36, 428. 41, 445. ARiese, JJ. 117, 398. WGilbert, ib. 117, 771.—Translations by EFMetzger (Stuttg.) and EKlussmann (Stuttg. 1859). WvTippelskirch, Berl. 1873.

9. In the time immediately preceding his exile Ovid composed an elegy on the death of Messalla (§ 222, 1); Pont. 1, 7, 30 *cui nos . . dedimus medio scripta canenda foro.*

250. During his exile Ovid wrote in 762/9–765/12 his five books of Tristia, and the continuation of them in the four books of Epistles ex Ponto, composed with failing powers and hopes and with less care, from 765/12 nearly until the death of the poet; then Ibis, an abusive poem in elegiac metre, in imitation of Kallimachos, against an anonymous person at Rome who endeavoured to injure the interests of the exile. The panegyric poems on Augustus and Tiberius (one on the former in the native Getic dialect) composed also at Tomi, have not come down to us; the didactic poem on fish (Halieutica), in imitation of Greek originals, was left incomplete by the author.

1. Chronology of the trist. and epp. ex Ponto, recipients of the letters (whose names, though disguised in the tristia, are mentioned in ex Ponto, n. 2): HBrandes, JJ. 115, 350. CSchrader, JJ. 115, 846; 131, 487. EMeyer, ZfGW. 32, 449. ThMatthias, JJ. 129, 206. HSchulz, quaestt. Ovid., Greifsw. 1883. GGräber, quaestt. Ovid., Elberf. 1881; Unterss. üb. Ov. Briefe aus d. Verbann., Elberf. 1884. BLorentz, de amicorum in Ov. trist. personis, Lpz. 1881. GWartenberg, quaestt. Ovid. de trist. Ibid. epp. ex Ponto temporibus, Berl. 1884. The separate tristia are arranged chronologically, the books were published separately: I during the journey, in the spring of 762/9 A.D., II consisting of a letter to Augustus in self-defence, elaborated with much care and skill, and closing with the petition that a more endurable place of banishment may be assigned to him, written at Tomi in the end of 762/9; III 763/10; IV commencement of 764/11 (cf. 4, 7, 1); V commencement of 765/12 (cf. 5, 10, 1) describes Ovid's departure from Rome. The poet's letters to his wife are especially touching (1, 6. 3, 3. 4, 3. 5, 5. 11. 14).

For trist. 1, 5, 11–3, 7, 1 and 4, 1, 12–4, 7, 5 the most important MS. is the Laurentianus olim S. Marci 223 s. XI, for the rest of the work especially the Guelferbyt. Gud. 192 s. XIII and Vatic. 1606 s. XIII. FTank, de tristibus Ov. recensendis, Greifsw. 1879.—Separate editions by RMerkel (Berl. 1837), VLoers (Trèves 1839). B. I by SGOwen, Lond. 1885. Libri V rec. SGOwen, Lond. 1889. —Contributions to research and criticism on the manuscripts: JPBinsfeld, qu. Ov. crit. I Bonn 1853. II Cologne 1855. III RhM. 14, 39; obss. Ov., Bonn 1860. REhwald, ad. hist. carmm. Ovid. recensionemque symbb., Gotha 1889.—Translation by HWölffel (Stuttg. 1858) and ABerg (with Pont., Ibis and Halieut., Stuttg. 1865).

2. The epistles ex Ponto, mostly of 765/12, at first published separately, were afterwards brought out collectively in three books 766/13. Pont. 3, 9, 51 *nec liber ut fieret, sed uti sua cuique daretur littera, propositum curaque nostra fuit. post modo collectas, utcumque sine ordine, iunxi: hoc opus electum ne mihi forte putes.* The later epistles (down to 769/16) were added as b. 4 (perhaps only after the death of Ovid). On the relation of this work to the Tristia see Pont. 1, 1, 16 *non minus hoc illo triste quod ante dedi. rebus idem titulo differt, et epistola cui sit non occultato*

nomine missa docet. Ovid's store of words is quite inexhaustible, and he has done his best in point of variation, yet the nature of the subject does not admit of much variety. Repetitions and slight mistakes of all kinds, in thought, diction, and metre, are not rare in these productions of melancholy. His flattery and adulation surpass all bounds.

Manuscripts (besides the Wolfenbüttel fragment s. VI/VII) Hamburg. s. XII, Monac. 384 ('Bavaricus') s. XII/XIII and Monac. 19476, concerning them see OKorn, Strehlen 1874.—Ov. ex Ponto l. IV, ad codd. fidem apparatu crit. instr. OKorn, Lps. 1868 (cf. OKorn, zur Hss.-Kunde der Br. ex P., Wesel 1866; de codd. duobus carmm. Ov. ex Ponto Monac., Strehlen 1874; de carm. Ov. ex P. compos. strophica, RhM. 22, 201). B. I by CHKeene, Lond. 1887.—BDinter, de Ov. ex P. libris, Grimma 1858. 65 II.—Translated by HWölffel (with introduction and notes, Stuttg. 1858) and ABerg (see n. 1).—OEJacobi, de syntaxi in Ov. trist. et epp. ex P., Lyck 1870. ARothmaler, emend. Ov. (on Tr. and ex P.), Nordhausen 1871.

3. The title of Ibis was taken from a similar poem of Kallimachos against Apollonios of Rhodes (v. 55). It was written after the 50th year of the poet (v. 1 *lustris bis iam mihi quinque peractis*) in Tomi (v. 6. 11 et al.) during the lifetime of Augustus (v. 23) and before the composition of Pont. 4, 14; cf. 44 *exstat adhuc nemo saucius ore meo.* Riese's ed. 3, vii. GWartenberg, quaestt. Ov. 112. ThMatthias, JJ. 129, 212. The name of the person attacked is at first withheld (v. 9. 51. 61. 637), though there are threats of subsequent iambic poems with mention of the name (v. 53. 641). From v. 19 (*debuerat*) we might infer him to have been a relation or former friend of Ovid. The incongruity between the elegiac metre (which was used also by Kallimachos in his Ibis) and the subject is admitted by Ovid himself (v. 46), as well as the fact that Kallimachos' *ambages* and obscure (*caecae*) subjects (especially those taken from mythology) were not in general his business (v. 57–60). Against OSchneider, Callimach. 2, 273 ARiese, JJ. 109, 377 argues pertinently. In general see Ellis pref. to his ed.

Manuscripts: Turon., Cantabrig., both s. XII, Vindob. s. XII/XIII, AMaag, de Ibidis Ov. codd., Berne 1887.—On the confused and almost useless scholia to the Ibis (in Merkel p. 460, of saec. VI/VII) see REhwald, de schol. qui est ad Ov. Ibin, Gotha 1876. JGeffcken, die Kallimachuscitate der Ibis-Scholien, Herm. 25, 91. Editions with the Tristia; especially by RMerkel (with a prolusio ad Ibin, p. 333). Separate edition: ex novis codd. ed., scholia vet., commentarium add. REllis, Oxf. 1881 (supplementary notes: journ. of phil. 1885, 93). Criticism: MSchmidt, RhM. 20, 457. KSchenkl, ZföG. 34, 259.—Translated (with Halieut. and Nux) by HWölffel (Stuttg. 1867) and others.

4. The fragment (130 hexam.) on fishes, in the Vienna MS. entitled *versus Ovidi de piscibus et feris* (this addition on account of animals being mentioned vs. 49–81), was known to Pliny as *Ovidi Halieutica*, and only as a fragment. Ovid has treated drily and without much success the thankless subject-matter, which is not, as Pliny (see below) asserts, peculiar to the author and based on personal observation of the fish, but is derived simply from Greek books. Notwithstanding this, and in spite of much that is strange in diction and metrical construction, the genuineness of the poem is undoubted.—Plin. NH. 32, 11 *mihi videntur mira et quae Ovidius prodidit piscium ingenia in eo volumine quod Halieuticon inscribitur;* ib. 152 *his adiciemus ab Ovidio posita nomina* (*animalia* Birt) *quae apud neminem alium reperiuntur, sed fortassis in Ponto nascentia, ubi id volumen supremis suis temporibus incohavit.* In the list of his authorities for b. 31 *ex . . . Ovidio* and for b. 32 *ex . . . Ovidio poeta.* In the face of these passages to allow as

we must, that Pliny was acquainted with the identical poem of which a fragment is preserved to us, and yet to assert on the other hand that this was a forgery deliberately written under the name of Ovid about the middle of the 1st cent., is an inadmissible evasion which is not made more plausible by a reference to the supposed Vergilian Culex.—The best MSS. Vindob. 277 (Sannazarianus) s. IX and Paris. 8071 (Thuaneus) s. IX/X: an edition (with Grattius and others; see § 253, 1) by MHaupt, Lpz. 1838. Already Muretus and others doubted Ovid's authorship. See also WHartel, ZföG. 17, 334 and esp. ThBirt, de Halieuticis Ovidio poetae falso adscriptis, Berl. 1877; cf. the same writer's antikes Buchwesen 298. The genuineness was defended by AZingerle, kl. philol. Abhandl. (Innsbr. 1877) 2, 1; cf. ib. 114; and ZföG. 30, 178.

5. A poem on Tiberius' triumph (16 Jan. 766/13, HSchulz l.l. 15), accompanied by Pont. 3, 4 (to Rufinus). Cf. ib. 2, 5, 27. KSchrader, JJ. 139, 213.

6. In point of linguistic interest we may regret the loss of the Getic poem in honour of Augustus, his successor, and his family, on which see ex Pont. 4, 13, 19; cf. 3, 2, 40; see also trist. 3, 14, 48.

7. For another poem on the death of Augustus see Pont. 4, 6, 17; cf. 4, 9, 131.

251. The authority enjoyed by Ovid during the first century of the Christian era in the schools of the rhetoricians and still longer with the poets, as well as the smoothness and ease of his verse, were the reason that at an early time and also in the Middle Ages many productions, especially in elegiacs, were ascribed to his name. Such productions of ancient date, and belonging to a good period, are the elegy entitled Nux and the Consolatio ad Liviam; in the Middle Ages jocular poems such as the Elegia de pulice, de vetula, the verses de philomela and others.

1. The philosopher Seneca shows his intellectual affinity with Ovid in his predilection for quoting him, e.g. benef. 4, 14, 1. 5, 15, 3. nat. quaest. 2, 44, 1. 3, 1, 1. 3, 20, 3. 3, 26, 4. The frequent quotations from Ovid in Quintilian show his great authority in the schools of the rhetoricians of the period. The later poets imitated Ovid industriously (trist. 4, 10, 55 *utque ego maiores, sic me coluere minores*), e.g. the Priapea, Manilius, Seneca, Lucanus, Calpurnius (paneg. ad Pisonem), Silius Italicus (Homerus latinus), Statius, Martialis and many others. Cf. also LMüller, de re metr. 136.—The (perhaps incomplete) inscription *Ovidianus poeta hic quiescit* CIL. 10, 6271 Wilm. 2480 refers to an imitator of Ovid (cf. § 231, 3).

2. In the Middle Ages especially the Metamorphoses (see § 249, 2), the Ars and the Heroides were much read, employed and imitated: see KBartsch, Albrecht von Halberstadt und Ovid im Mittelalter, Quedlinb. 1861. HDunger, die Sage vom trojanischen Kriege (Dresd. 1869) p. 49. 53 and elsewhere. See also below n. 6. ad fin.

3. No. 3 of the Priapea (§ 254, 5) is attributed by Sen. controv. 1. 2, 22 (p. 92 K.) to Ovid (*Ovidianum illud 'inepta loci'*, a passage found Priap. 3, 8). It is pos-

sible that other pieces of that collection are by Ovid (cf. Wernicke, Priapei. p. 120–124. 126–131), though it is impossible to identify them with certainty.

4. The elegy of Nux (in 182 lines, *P. Ovidii Nasonis liber nucis* in the Laur.) somewhat diffuse and rhetorically ornate (e. g. v. 108. 175), but pure and fluent in metrical construction and in parts of graceful style. The subject is a development of a Greek theme (anth. Pal. 9, 3), being the complaint of a nut-tree concerning ill-treatment, with mournful reflections on better times and manners (e. g. v. 23). *Caesar . . deus* v. 142. Nothing prevents us from assigning the composition of this poem to a time soon after Ovid. LMüller, de re metr. 49; ARiese JJ. 101, 282. According to Wilamowitz l.l. 400 it is a *manifestum indicium* against Ovid's authorship that *miserum illud 'forsitan,' quod . . . Ovidius constanter vitavit* should occur in the poem: it is unfortunate that Ovid uses the proscribed *forsitan* more than eighty times (AKunz, Ov. de medic. fac. p. 54). WFröhner, Phil. Suppl. 5, 46 takes it to be a youthful work of Ovid. The earliest MS. is a Laur. s. XI (§ 250, 1). Printed e. g. with a commentary by FLindemann, Zittau 1844. New critical revision by UvWilamowitz, commentt. Mommsen. 390 and EBährens PLM. 1. 90. Supplements to the collation of the Laur. ARiese, JB. 1878, 2, 160. GGoetz, quaestt. misc. III, Jena 1889, p. vii.—Translated by HWölffel see § 250, 3 ad fin.).

5. *P. Ovidii Nasonis consolatio ad Liviam Augustam de morte Drusi Neronis, filii eius, qui in Germania morbo periit:* this poem is extant in a few quite late MSS. (Dresd., Laur. 36, 2, Urbinas 353, Brit. 11973, Ottobon. 1469, all s. XV; see on this subject KSchenkl, Wien. Stud. 2, 56. 7, 339, where are also the complete collations), and is printed in the ed. Romana of Ovid's works, a. 1471 (not however in the contemporary Bononiensis), in the Veneta of 1472 and subsequently: most recently in MHaupt's op. 1, 315 and EBährens' PLM. 1, 104. In the Laur. 36, 2 there is a vita Ovidii, in which we read concerning the consolatio as a poem by Ovid: *quae nuper inventa est* (see Hübner l.l. 427). This is a rhetorical exercise by a petty imitator of Ovid and Propertius, and also of Tibullus and Vergil, who had before him Seneca's consolationes (§ 289, 4, 6. 11. 12); it is very similar to the first elegy on Maecenas (§ 229, 3), and probably also dates from the first century. EWagner, de Martiale imitatore, Königsb. 1880. 44 supposes that the author of this elegy on Maecenas intends by its opening words *Defleram iuvenis tristi modo carmine fata* to designate himself as the author of the consolatio. Haupt (Epicedion Drusi, Lps. 1849 = op. 1, 315) held the poem to have been composed by some Italian scholar of the 15th cent., because up to the present time no early MSS. of it have been discovered and the poem shows an absence of all positive information which might not be derived from well-known writers (see however *Isargus* 386 and *Dacius Appulus* 388), etc. See for the contrary view FThAdler, de Ovidii consolat. etc., Anclam 1851 and esp. EHübner, Herm. 13, 145. 427; cf. besides FBücheler, phil. Kritik (Bonn 1878) 21. EBährens, PLM. 1, 97. KSchenkl l.l. See in addition Gruppe, Aeacus 157, JMähly, de Drusi atq. Maecen. epicediis etc., Bas. 1873. HNettleship, the latinity of epic. Dr., Transact. of Oxf. phil. soc. 1885/86, 16. OHirschfeld, Berl. SBer. 1886, 1164. WWilding, de aetate consolationis ad Liv. deque carmm. consolatoriorum ap. Gr. et Rom. hist., Marb. 1889.

6. A collection of most of the spurious Ovidiana in Goldast, Catalecta Ovidii, Francof. 1610. Of mediaeval origin are the lines de philomela (§ 23, 3), de pediculo, de medicamine aurium (MS. in Berne, Sinner 1, 543. Hagen 429), de pulice (by Ofilius Sergianus) and the three books de vetula (HCochéris, la Vielle, ou les derniers amours d'Ovide, poème français du XIV siécle etc., précédé de recherches

sur l'auteur de Vetula, Paris, 1861). De anulo and Somnium are in Ovid. am. 2, 15 and 3, 5 though they have frequently been copied with spurious pieces in MSS. Cf. KBartsch, Albr. v. Halberst p. iv.—Tables of contents for the Vergilian poems wrongly attributed to Ovid: § 231, 8. Cf. ROpitz, Lpz. Stud, 6, 298. Various works on Ovid during the Middle Ages in HStSedlmayer, Wien. Stud. 6, 142; also JHuemer, ZföG. 32, 415.

7. Collective editions e.g. by GBersmann (Lps. 1582 sqq. cum notis varr., Frankf. 1601), by DHeinsius (Leid. 1629 III), but esp. by Nicolaus Heinsius (Amstelod. 1652. 1658, the best in 1661 III; cum Heinsii notis integris (these have also appeared separately) cur. JFFischer, Lps. 1758 II (with ind. verbb.), illustr. DCrispinus in us. Delphini, Lyons 1689 IV (vol. 4 ind. verbb.), ed. PBurman (cum notis variorum, Amstelod. 1727 IV [with ind. verbb.]; praefatio, ib. 1756); cum notis variorum, Oxf. 1827 V (in it are RBentley's MS. notes). First methodical revision with praefationes criticae by RMerkel (and REhwald, Lps.[4] 1888 sqq. III).—Ed. AReise, Lpz.[2] 1889 sqq. III. Ed. OGüthling, HStSedlmayer, AZingerle, Prague 1883 sqq.—Criticism (besides what is cited above) Madvig, adv. 2, 66. Bergk, op. 1, 655. AZingerle, kl. phil. Abhh. 3 (Innsbr. 1882), 35. JRappold, ZföG. 32, 401. 801 and many other treatises. Literary reviews of Ovid by ARiese and REhwald, JB. 1873, 137. 1874/75 1, 229. 1876 2, 97. 1877 2, 20. 1878 2, 241. 1881 2, 72. 1882 2, 157. 1885 2, 125.

252. Among those friends of Ovid, who attempted poetical composition, the oldest are the epic poet Ponticus, who was also on friendly terms with Propertius, the translator Tuticanus, Macer, who was somewhat younger, and wrote an epic poem on the Trojan legends, and Sabinus, the author of answers to the heroic Epistles of Ovid and of a work resembling his Fasti; then also Cornelius Severus, an epic poet who chose his subject from the history of the time (bellum siculum); Albinovanus Pedo, the author both of a Theseis and of an epic poem on a subject derived from contemporary history, as well as of epigrams; and others. Outside of this circle, Rabirius and Sextilius Ena of Corduba chose their material from the recent Civil Wars. Most of the epic poets, however, followed the track of the Alexandrines, and besides Homer the Cyclic poets were also made use of. Epic poems of this kind on mythological subjects were written by Iullus Antonius and Largus, Camerinus, Lupus, Abronius Silo, and others.

1. The principal source of information on the poets contemporary with Ovid is ex Ponto 4, 16, a poem which, however, gives only indirect allusions and is obscure and corrupt in parts (on its construction see Ehwald l.l.). In general see the treatises (cited § 250, 1) by GGräber, GWartenberg, BLorentz and by OHennig (§ 247, 2 ad fin.) and also REhwald, JB. 1885 2, 140.—Trist. 4, 10, 47 *Ponticus heroo, Bassus quoque clarus iambo, dulcia convictus membra fuere mei.* An allusion to the latter occurs probably ex Pont. 4, 16, 21 *velivolique maris vates, cui credere possis carmina caeruleos composuisse deos* (this is disputed by OHaube, carm. ep. p.

19). That he wrote a Thebaid appears from Prop. 1, 7, 1 *dum tibi Cadmeae dicuntur, Pontice, Thebae armaque fraternae tristia militiae, atque, ita sim felix, primo contendis Homero* etc. cf. ib. 9, 9 *quid tibi nunc misero prodest grave dicere carmen aut Amphioniae moenia flere lyrae?* It may be inferred that he imitated Antimachos. He seems to have been still living when Ovid wrote Pont. 4, 16.

2. Tuticanus is mentioned as a friend in youth and a contemporary of Ovid, ex Pont. 4, 12, 20. Besides this letter, 4, 14 is also addressed to him, both with the observation that the trochaic measure of the name did not agree with dactylic metre. Hence his name is avoided ib. 4, 16, 27 *et qui Maeoniam Phaeacida vertit* (the translator of the story of Nausikaa). But that he is meant appears from ib. 4, 12, 27 *dignam Maeoniis Phaeacida condere chartis cum te Pierides perdocuere deae.* Ib. v. 25 shows that he was very strict in point of form.

3. Macer (who should be distinguished from the earlier didactic poet of the same name, § 223, 4) was Ovid's companion in his travels in Asia and Sicily (Pont. 2, 10, 21. 31). He calls him *Iliacus*, Pont. 4, 16, 6, and he seems to have treated the legends antecedent to the Iliad, i.e. Antehomerica (am. 2, 18, 1 *carmen ad iratum dum tu perducis Achillen primaque iuratis induis arma viris, nos, Macer, . . . cessamus*), cf. Pont. 2, 10, 13 *tu canis aeterno quidquid restabat Homero, ne careant summa troica bella manu*), no doubt in imitation of the Cyclic poets; cf. Hennig l.l. (see n. 1) 22. REhwald, JB. 1885 2, 142. He is perhaps identical with the Macer mentioned by Quint. 6, 3, 96 (see above § 223, 4 ad fin.). The opinion (of Wernsdorf and others) is probable that he is identical with (the grandson of the Pompeian Theophanes of Mytilene) Pompeius Macer, to whom Augustus *ordinandas bybliothecas delegaverat* (Suet. Iul. 56 extr.). Perhaps he may also have been a grammarian; Prisc. GL. 2, 13, 9 *auctoritas quoque tam Varronis quam Macri teste Censorino nec* K *nec* Q *nec* H *in numero adhibet litterarum.* The son of this Macer was probably the praetor of 768/15 A.D. (Tac. ann. 1, 72, cf. 6, 18 *praetorius*), who together with his father (*illustris eques rom.*, Tac. ann. 6, 18) died a voluntary death, a. 786/33 A.D.

4. Ovid. am. 1, 18, 27 *meus Sabinus.* Pont. 4, 16, 13 *et qui Penelopae rescribere iussit Ulixen* (cf. am. 2, 18, 27), . . . *quique suam † trisemem imperfectumque dierum* (Gläser, RhM. 1, 437) *deseruit celeri morte Sabinus opus.* Hence it appears that the epic poem, the title of which is corrupt, was actually finished. In point of chronology he might be the Sabinus mentioned by Hor. ep. 1, 5, 27. His gentile name is not known. Cf. § 248, 3 (l. 12) and 4.

5. Quint. 10, 1, 89 *Cornelius Severus, etiamsi versificator quam poeta melior, si tamen ad exemplar primi libri bellum Siculum* (with Sex. Pompeius, a. 716/38 sqq.) *perscripsisset, vindicaret sibi iure secundum locum* (among the Roman epic poets). Valer. Prob. GL. 4, 208, 16 *Cornelius Severus rerum romanarum lib. I dicit 'pelagum pontumque moveri.'* As Ovid. Pont. 4, 16, 9 alludes only to a *carmen regale* which Severus *Latio dedit* (cf. Pont. 4, 2, 1; see below), the b. sic. probably formed part of these res romanae. GWartenberg, quaestt. Ovid., Berl. 1884, 100 takes a different view. From this epic may be the quotation in Sen. suas. 2, 12, the σπονδειάζων in Schol. Pers. 1, 95, the quotations in Charis. GL. 1, 80, 7. 81, 16 (= GL. 7, 291, 8). 86, 7. 100, 24. 107, 29 (= GL. 5, 590, 23). Diomed. GL. 1, 378, 2. schol. Bern. ad Luc. 9, 402, as well as the description of Aetna mentioned by Sen. ep. 79, 5 (cf. App. b. c. 5, 117). From the same also the 25 eloquent and elegant hexameters on the death of Cicero in Sen. suas. 6, 26 (with the introductory observation: *nemo ex tot disertissimis viris melius Ciceronis mortem deflevit quam Severus Cornelius*). A

line given without special mention of the author in an incomplete passage of Charis. GL. 1, 105, 19, by collation with gramm. de dub. nom. GL. 5, 588, 2, has been proved to belong to Cornelius (Severus; cf. ib. 588, 26. 590, 1). This line is in Charisius followed by the words: *cuius* (Corn. Sev.) *moveremur, inquit Plinius, auctoritate, si quidquam eo carmine puerilius dixisset.* Diomed. GL. 1, 375, 22 is doubtful, where after Severus the quotation given by Priscian. GL. 2, 546, 21 but corruptly, (*in VIII de statu suo ad quem* etc.) seems to have been lost; this quotation has not yet been put into any metrical form such as would agree with the well-known elegance of Corn. Sev., whence we may perhaps ascribe it to Cassius Sev. (§ 267, 11); lastly Severus' claim to two anonymous hexameters in Charis. GL. 1, 287, 4 is quite uncertain. Ovid. ex Pont. 4, 2 is addressed to Corn. Sev. (v. 1 *o vates magnorum maxime regum*; 11 *fertile pectus habes interque Helicona colentes uberius nulli provenit ista seges*, i.e. *carmina*), and so perhaps is 1, 8 (v. 2 *pars animae magna, Severe, meae.* 25 *o iucunde sodalis*), though 4, 2 Ovid apologises *eius adhuc nomen nostros tacuisse libellos* (v. 3). In general see Wernsdorf, PLM. 4, 25; the fragments ib. 217 and FPR. 352.—JBecker, ZfAW. 1848, 587. OHaube, de carm. ep. (Bresl. 1870) p. 10.

6. Albinovanus Pedo; the correct sequence of names—for Albinovanus is the gentile name, see EHübner, ephem. epigr. 2, 32—occurs in Sen. contr. 2, 2, 12 p. 180 and 233 K; it is inverted *Pedo Albin.* in Sen. ep. 122, 15; both names occur separately in Ovid. ex Ponto 4, 10, 4. 65; elsewhere the poet is only named as Pedo, his praenomen is unknown. He is probably the praef. eqq. Pedo mentioned in Tac. ann. 1, 60. Cf. also above § 242, 5. The philosopher Seneca knew him personally, calls him *fabulator elegantissimus* and gives a specimen of this gift of his for stories (ep. 122, 15). Another of his good stories is given by Sen. controv. 2, 10, 12 (p. 180 K.). A witty saying of his in Quint. 6, 3, 61. Martial, who in one instance calls him *doctus* (see § 243, 2), mentions him repeatedly as one of his forerunners and a master of epigram. Cf. also Sidon. Apoll. 1, 256.—He is enumerated among the epic writers by Quint. 10, 1, 90. *Rabirius ac Pedo non indigni cognitione, si vacet.* He wrote a Theseis; see Ovid in the epistle ex Ponto 4, 10, 71. 75 addressed to Pedo (*carissime* v. 3). Concerning an epic poem on a Roman subject see Sen. suas. 14 *latini declamatores in descriptione Oceani non nimis viguerunt. . . . nemo illorum potuit tanto spiritu dicere quanto Pedo, qui navigante Germanico dicit 'iam pridem*, etc.' Here follow 23 hexameters of sonorous cadence and rhetorical descriptive style (commented on by Wernsdorf, PLM. 4, 229; cf. MHaupt, op. 3, 412. ThBergk, mon. Anc. 97. 124. OHaube, Albin. Pedo 12). The description refers to the storm which the fleet of Germanicus encountered in the North-sea 769/16 a.d., see Tac. ann. 2, 23; not to the expedition of Drusus to the North-sea 742/12 a.d., as Haube Alb. Pedo 21 and others suppose. PHöfer, d. Feldz. des Germanicus im J. 16, Festschr. z. Begrüss. d. Dessauer Phil.-Vers., Bernb. 1884, attempts unsuccessfully to prove that Tacitus made use of this epic. Haube, de carm. ep. (1870) 14 and Albin. Pedo 22 refers also to Albinovanus Prisc. GL. 2, 304, 20 *Albinus rerum romanarum I* (followed by three hexameters), which is not borne out by the twice repeated use of *cui* as an iambic. Cf. § 383, 8. To conclude (with Weichert, rell. poett. 382, Haube, Albin. Pedo 9 and others) from the epithet *sidereus* (Ov. Pont. 4, 16, 6 *Iliacusque Macer* [above n. 3] *sidereusque Pedo*) that Pedo wrote de sideribus is so much the less admissible as Ovid Pont. 4, 10—where the description of the freezing of the Pontus should have been set down to Pedo's interest in natural phenomena—expressly gives a personal reason for the insertion of this description (v. 65), and in this poem mention is made (not of the supposed phenomena but) only of the Theseis (v. 71) of Pedo. Concerning *sidereus* cf. the

passage quoted from SEN. suas. 1, 14 and Ov. Pont. 4, 10, 76, also COLUM. 10, 434. In gen. see OHAUBE, zur Kenntn. des Alb. Pedo, Fraustadt 1880.

7. Carus (the gentile name unknown), the tutor of the sons of Germanicus (Pont. 4, 13, 47), *non dubios inter sodales, vere carus* (ib. v. 2; cf. trist. 3, 5, 17). On their joint studies in poetry see Pont. 4, 13, 43,. An allusion to his epic poem on Hercules ib. v. 11 and 4, 16, 7 *et qui Iunonem laesisset in Hercule* (by composing poetry on him) *Carus, Iunonis si non iam gener* (as the husband of Hebe) *ille foret.* Cf. SEN. Herc. Oet. 1441, and Octavia 216.—Possibly it is from a Heracleis of this period that was derived the hexameter *Barbarus aere cavo tubicen dedit . . . signa* (CIL. 4, 1069[a]), which occurs under a Pompeian wall-painting (Hesione set free by Herakles and Telamon, WHELBIG, campan. Wandgem. 1132 pl. XIV). REHWALD, Phil. 46, 640.

8. A list of epic poets who wrote on mythological subjects is given in OVID. ex Pont. 4, 16, 17 *ingeniique sui dictus cognomine Largus, gallica qui phrygium duxit in arva senem. quique canit domito Camerinus ab Hercule Troiam.* ib. v. 25 *Trinacriusque suae Perseidos auctor, et auctor Tantalidae reducis Tyndaridosque Lupus.* Largus, who appears to have written on the legendary settlement of Antenor in Cisalpine Gaul, is supposed to be the faithless friend and accuser of Cornelius Gallus (§ 232, 2), called Valerius Largus (DIO 53, 23). Camerinus, whose subject was the capture of Troy, might be identical with Q. Sulpicius Camerinus, consul 762/9 A.D. Lupus (who wrote an epic poem on the return of Menelaos and Helena) is generally identified with the rhetorician Rutilius Lupus (§ 270). Trinacrius (=Siculus?) does not look like a proper name; a Perseid had been written among the Greeks by Choirilos and Musaios. See MERKEL's edition of the Tristia etc. p. 376.—The words of OVID Pont. 4, 16, 20 concerning Tuscus, who is mentioned in a list of exclusively epic poets, *quique sua nomen Phyllide Tuscus habet* may mean: 'Tuscus, who is named after his epyllion on the story of Damophon and Phyllis' (see Ov. Her. 2) i.e. who has been surnamed Damophon as though he were the admirer of the Phyllis celebrated in his poem. In that case Tuscus should be identified with Damophoon, the pseudonymous friend of Propertius (3, 22). Cf. AKIESSLING, coniecturae Prop., Greifsw. 1875. MERKEL l.l. 373 suggested that he might be the grammarian Clodius Tuscus (§ 263, 3). On Iullus Antonius see § 242, 6.

9. VELL. 2, 36, 3 *inter quae (ingenia) maxime nostri aevi eminent princeps carminum Vergilius Rabiriusque* (while Horace is not mentioned!). QUINT. judges more sensibly 10, 1, 90 (above n. 6). OVID. Pont. 4, 16, 5 *magnique Rabirius oris.* An hexameter by Rabirius ap. Charis. GL. 1, 65, 9. Other notices in the gramm. de dub. rom. GL. 5, 578, 7. 13. 590, 19. Cf. FPR. 356 and MHAUPT, op. 1, 158. On the subject of his poem see SEN. benef. 6, 3, 1 *egregie mihi videtur M. Antonius apud Rabirium poetam . . . exclamare 'hoc habeo quodcumque dedi.'* From this indication of the subject-matter, he is supposed by Ciampitti and others to be the author of the fragment discovered in the papyrus no. 817 of Herculaneum (specimen in ZANGEMEISTER-WATTENBACH's exempl. codd. pl. 3; Hayter's copy is facsimiled in WSCOTT's fragm. Herculanensia, Oxf. 1885) on the battle of Actium and the death of Kleopatra; see Volumina Herculan. (Naples 1809) 2, 7 sqq. JTHKREYSSIG, carminis latini de bello actiaco sive alexandrino fragmenta, Lps. 1814, and esp. after his comm. de Sall. hist. fragm. (Meissen 1835) p. 117. AL. 482, cf. 2, VI. PLM. 1, 214. Cf. AWEICHERT, de L. Vario 157, 163. RELLIS, Journ. of phil. 16, 81. Those fragments actually exhibit a preference for the same

caesura which is noticed in the citation in Sen. l.l. The mention of Atropos points to a treatment of the subject similar to that in the Aeneid (cf. § 228, n. 5).

10. Sen. suas. 6, 27 *Sextilius Ena* (?) *fuit homo ingeniosus magis quam eruditus, inaequalis poeta et plane quibusdam locis talis quales esse Cicero* (pArch. 26) *Cordubenses poetas ait, pingue quiddam sonantes atque peregrinum. is hanc ipsam proscriptionem* (of Cicero) *recitaturus in domo Messalae Corvini . . . in principio hunc versum . . . recitavit 'deflendus Cicero est'* etc. From this and the preceding expression *municipem nostrum* it appears that he was a native of Corduba.

11. Ovid. ex Pont. 4, 16, 10 *et cum subtili Priscus uterque Numa.* The connection of the passage justifies the inference that both Priscus and Numa were also epic poets. They are, however, completely unknown, unless Priscus is the Clutorius Priscus mentioned by Tacitus and Dio. Tac. ann. 3. 49 *fine anni* (21 A.D.) *Clutorium Priscum eq. rom. post celebre carmen quo Germanici suprema defleverat pecunia donatum a Caesare corripuit delator obiectans aegro Druso composuisse quod, si extinctus esset, maiore praemio volgaretur.* Priscus was immediately put to death. Cf. Dio 57, 20. OHennig, de Ovidii sodalibus.

12. Equally obscure is the allusion in Ovid. ex Pont. 4, 16, 23 *quique acies libycas romanaque proelia dixit, et Marius scripti dexter in omne genus.* The first would from this appear to have written a bellum punicum. OHaube, de carm. ep. (1870) 18 understands it of the wars in Africa with Juba and the partisans of Pompey. Pont. 4, 16, 33 is quite corrupt and not yet set right *Tityron antiquas passerque rediret ad herbas* (so cod. Bavar.).

13. Ovid. Pont. 4, 16, 11 *quique vel imparibus numeris, Montane, vel aequis sufficis et gemino carmine nomen habes.* This Montanus, a person equally celebrated in elegy and in epic poetry, is probably the same as Iulius Montanus in Sen. contr. 7, 16, 27 *Montanus Iulius, qui comis fuit quique egregius poeta;* cf. the judgment of Seneca's son (ep. 122, 11) *tolerabilis poeta et amicitia Tiberii notus et frigore* (Teuffel on Hor. sat. 2, p. 28). *ortus et occasus libentissime inserebat* (cf. Apocoloc. 2). He then gives (11-13) specimens of his verse. Donat. vita Vergil. 29 (44) *Seneca tradidit Iulium Montanum poetam solitum dicere* etc.

14. Sen. suas. 2, 19 *memini auditorem* (Porcii) *Latronis Arbronium* (or *Abronium*) *Silonem, patrem huius Silonis qui pantomimis fabulas scripsit et ingenium grande non tantum deseruit sed polluit* (see § 8, 13 ad fin.), *recitare carmen,* of which the subject-matter was derived from the Iliad, and from which Seneca quotes two rhetorical hexameters.

15. We are not aware what department of poetry the younger son of the orator Messalla, Cotta, attempted (see § 267, 6). Cf. Ovid. ex Pont. 4, 16, 42 (*Pieridum lumen praesidiumque fori*) and 3, 5, 39 (*recitas factum modo carmen amicis,* cf. 1, 5, 57).

253. Didactic poetry was in the Augustan period cultivated by Grattius, of whose dull poem on the chase (Cynegetica) we possess a part. It was not until the reign of Tiberius that the so-called Manilius published his Astronomica (now five books), a work which treats less of astronomy than of astrology, and though he fails to win our sympathy by his superstitious treat-

ment of this worthless subject, we are yet attracted by the versatility of his knowledge, the independence of his views and especially by his originality and power of giving shape to his dry and stubborn subject-matter, and his seriousness and depth of thought. Both by the latter qualities and by the unevenness and heaviness of his style, Manilius reminds us of Lucretius, though he differs from him in his mastery of all technical forms.

1. Ovid. ex Pont. 4, 16, 34 (*cum*) *aptaque venanti Gratius arma daret*, an allusion to Grat. cyneg. 23 *carmine et arma dabo venanti et persequar artes armorum.* He is not mentioned elsewhere. It has been supposed, without sufficient reason, from v. 40 (*nostris—Faliscis*) that he came from Falerii. We can only tell that he was an Italian from the passage in question (in contrast with the *lina Hispanae Saetabis* mentioned above). 536 lines are extant (together with 5 fragments of lines) in Vindob. 277 (Sannazarianus) s. IX; the Paris. 8071 (Thuaneus) s. IX/X consists only of v. 1–159. Cf. § 250, 4. The work is incomplete at the end: the heading in both MSS. *gratti cynegeticon libî* (*libri*) shows that there were originally several books; see ARiese, anth. lat. 1, xxxvi.—The poet is generally called *Gratius* and he appears to be mentioned under this name in the MSS. of Ovid. l.l., but in the two MSS. of the Cynegetica the name is *Grattius* (see above) and this form is to be preferred as it occurs in the inscriptions and elsewhere (e.g. Cic. pArch. 8. 12 in the MSS.) almost exclusively (see the indices nominum in CIL. vol 2. 3. 5. 8. 10. 12. 14 and CIL. 6, 19117–19125), FBücheler, RhM. 35, 407.—The style of the work is technical, dry, and heavy, and but very rarely rises somewhat higher, e.g. v. 812 in the rhetorical excursus on the disadvantages of luxury. The metrical construction is careful. The episodes 427, 479 contain many reminiscences of Vergil. V. 348 (*Fatum . . . nigris circumvolat alis*) reminds the reader of Hor. s. 2, 1, 58.—Ed. princeps (with Halieut., Nemes. and Calpurnius) cura GLogi, Ven. 1534. Then in the Auctt. rei venaticae ed. IUlitius (Leid. 1645. 1655) and SHavercamp (Leid. 1728); in vol. 1 of the PLM. by PBurman (Leid. 1731), by JCWernsdorf (Altenb. 1780) and by EBährens (Lps. 1879). Cum comm. varior. ed. RStern, Halle 1832 (with Nemesianus). Ex rec. MHauptii, Lps. 1838 (with Ov. Halieut., Nemes. etc.)—Cf. ThBirt, hist. hex. lat. 57.

2. The name of the poet of the Astronomica is uncertain. It is just the earliest and best MSS. which furnish us with no useful data (in the Gembl. the heading is scratched out, in the Lips., Voss. 1, Brux. 2, we read: *Arati philosophi astronomicon liber primus* etc.); in the late MSS. also the headings are evidently very corrupt: Voss. 2 and 3 *M. Mallii eqvom* (*eq. rom.*? —for this in the Voss. 3 *Antiochi* [from Plin. NH. 35, 199? cf. § 212, 3] *Poeni*) *astronomicon divo oct.* (*octavio* Voss. 3) *quirino aug.*, similarly also Vat. 3099; *M. Manlii* Laur. 30, 15; *M. Manilii* Vatic.-Urbin. 667; *M. Manilii Boeci* Urbin. 668; *C. Manilii* cod. Cassin. Gerbert († 1003) ep. 78 p. 45 Olleris entreats a friend for a copy of *M. Man(i)lius de astrologia.*—The author is entirely unknown, and is not mentioned by any other writer. The inscription (Orelli 4804) which contains Manil. 4, 16 is spurious; see Ritschl, op. 4, 251. Possibly Germanicus in his Aratea (§ 275, 6) already imitated Manilius; cf. Freier l.l. 63. Cramer l.l. 58. There are distinct traces of his having been used in Nemesianus (§ 386, 1) 1, 39, 40=Manil. 1, 760. 761. 1, 800 has been imitated by Dracont. 5, 326, see Rossberg, JJ. 119, 476.—The non-Italian origin of the author (Bentley took him to be a Greek from Asia Minor, Jacob, an African, cf.

besides the spurious heading in the Voss. 3, above l. 6) was formerly assumed, without sufficient reason, from the nature of the language (see n. 5). There are also certain passages which tell the other way, e.g. 2, 888 *censum sic proxima Graiae nostra subit linguae.* 3, 40 *et si qua externa referentur nomina lingua, hoc operis, non vatis erit.* 4, 41. His geographical horizon is uncommonly large; cf. e.g. 4, 715. 749. The choice of such a subject necessitated an exact acquaintance with Greek literature, see however esp. e.g. 2, 1 sqq., 3, 5 sqq., 5, 461 sqq. Allusions to the poems of Aemilius Macer (§ 223, 4), of Grattius (above n. 1)? see 2, 43 sqq. (cf. 5, 197 sqq.).

3. Chronological hints. The first book must have been written after the battle in the Teutoburg Wood (a. 762/9 A.D.); 1, 898 *ut foedere rupto cum fera ductorem rapuit Germania Varum infecitque trium legionum sanguine campos.* Tiberius had however already been at least recognised as Augustus' successor. 4, 764 *est Rhodos hospitium recturi principis orbem.* Opinions differ as to whether the first books were composed after the death of Augustus; it is certain that book 5 was not written until the reign of Tiberius. Cf. 5, 513 *hinc Pompeia manent veteris monumenta triumphi, non exstincta acie semperque recentia flammis*; this may be understood of the theatre of Pompey, which was burnt down a. 775/22 A.D. (TAC. ann. 3, 72, cf. SUET. Tib. 47). FJACOB p. XVI. LACHMANN, kl. Schrr. 2, 42. There is evidence that even the first book was written under Tiberius, particularly 1, 800 *caelum . . . . quod regit* (presumably after his deification!) *Augustus socio per signa Tonante.* Other passages are more doubtful 1, 7 *tu, Caesar, patriae princepsque paterque, qui regis augustis parentem legibus orbem concessumque patri mundum deus ipse mereris.* 1, 384 *cetera (sidera) non cedunt; uno vincuntur in astro Augusto, sidus nostro quod contigit orbi; Caesar nunc terris, post caelo maximus auctor.* LACHMANN l.l. BFREIER, de Manilii astronomicon aetate, Gött. 1880. The fifth book is incomplete at the end; the work must have contained 6 books (MBECHERT, Lpz. Studd. 1, 17. WOLTJER l.l. 80).

4. Manilius takes astronomy in the sense usually attached to it in antiquity as also embracing astrology, and the latter even preponderates with him, see at the very commencement 1, 1 *Carmine divinas artes et conscia fati sidera, diversos hominum variantia casus deducere mundo aggredior.* On the difficulty of putting the subject in verse see 1, 20. 3, 26. He apologises for using foreign i.e. Greek (technical) expressions: 2, 693. 830. 897. 3, 41. He is proud of being the first poetic writer on this subject in Latin literature: 1, 4. 113. 2, 57. 136. 3, 1. 5, 1. He disdains the old beaten track of legendary and historical epic poetry: 3, 5. He unfolds his arrangement of the subject-matter: 1, 120. 2, 750. 4, 119. A review of the contents of the work in WOLTJER l.l. 41. He voluntarily resigns all claims to elegance: *ne dulcia carmina quaeras. ornari res ipsa negat, contenta doceri* (3, 38). But in his excursuses (especially his introductions, also 1, 884, and particularly in the fifth book in various descriptions) he furnishes ornament, and whenever he comes to speak of the dignity of man and of his reason (2, 106. 4, 883) or of human greed (4, 1), he is eloquent, earnest, and pleasing. Fatalism is implied 4, 14; on the relation of this to free will and human responsibility see 4, 108 (e.g. 117 *non refert scelus unde cadit; scelus esse fatendumst*). On the sway of ratio in the world: 1, 483 (against the atomists). 2, 60 cf. 4, 920 (932 *ratio omnia vincit*). Over-finished rhetorical colouring may be noticed in the account of Andromeda and Perseus 5, 540. OGRUPPE, Herm. 11, 235 tried to prove that book 6 of Varro's disciplinae (§ 166, 6, a.) was M's chief authority: cf. however HDIELS, doxogr. gr. and RhM. 34, 490.

5. Manilius' style is remarkable in many ways, especially for its violent contrasts e.g. between dry or dull and elevated, inspired or rhetorically ornate language, which is sometimes so intricate and pompous as to be almost unintelligible, and crowded with metaphors and figures and miscellaneous ingredients drawn from legend or real life. The poet has not succeeded in equalising and smoothing down these contrasts in tone which irritate and perplex the reader; but the later books, especially the fifth, show decided improvements. The diction too is not without peculiarities, e.g. in the use of the prepositions and moods, but they do not nearly suffice to establish the assumption of former times that Manilius was not of Italian origin; in particular no graecisms are adduced as evidence to corroborate the theory of his Greek extraction. He rarely employs new words or antique phraseology (only *itiner* 1, 88; *clepsisset* 1, 27, *diu=die* 4, 823), but he abounds in alliteration. Of the early poets Manilius imitates especially Vergil and Lucretius in their diction, also Ovid and others, see Jacob's index p. 199, Freier l.l. 44. Woltjer l.l. 30 and esp. ACramer, de Manilii elocutione, Strassb. 1882 (diss. Argentor. 7, 57). Cf. also MBechert, JJ. 119, 798.—Manilius' metrical and prosodiacal treatment is strict and elegant, e.g. he is careful in the employment of elision. LMüller, Phil. 15, 481. 492; de re metr. 52. 329. 333. ThBirt, hist. hex. lat. 52. ACramer l.l. 7. By the same writer, d. Inf. bei Manil., comm. in honor. Studemundi, Strassb. 1889, 60.

6. All our MSS. of Manilius are derived from an archetype itself very corrupt. Most of them are of s. XV and greatly interpolated, as is also the Leidensis 3 (Voss. 2) s. XV erroneously preferred by Jacob. By far the best MS. is the Bruxellensis 10012 (Gemblacensis) s. X/XI, then the Lipsiensis 1465 s. XI, the less important Leidensis 18 (Voss. 1) s. XII and Bruxell. 10699 (Cusanus) s. XII. Cf. Jacob's praefatio p. v. CTBreiter, de emendatione Manilii, Hamm 1854 and esp. MBechert, de Manili emendandi ratione, Leipz. Stud. z. Phil. 1, 3. PThomas, lucubratt. Manil. (cont. a new collation of the Gemblac.), Ghent 1888.

7. Ed. princeps at Nürnberg about 1472 (see CGSchwarz, de prima Manilii astr. editione, Altorf 1764). Principal editions by JScaliger (Par. 1579. Heidelb. 1590. Leid. 1600), RBentley (Lond. 1739; see on this MHaupt, op. 3, 43) and FJacob (rec., Berl. 1846).—Explanatory: by FJacob, Posen 1830 (spec. ed.). Lübeck 1832 (I de Manilio poeta). 1833 sqq. (II de versibus a Bentleio abiudicatis libr. 1–5).—JWoltjer, de Manilio poeta, Groningen, 1881. GLanson, de Manilio poeta eiusque ingenio, Par. 1887. AKraemer, de Man. astronomicis, Marb. 1890. Critical: HHaupt, op. 3, 473. 583.—Book I with a German translation by JMerkel (Manilius' celestial globe etc.), Aschaffenb. 1844. 1857. THBreiter, JJ. 139, 193. 693. 845. KRossberg, JJ. 139, 705.

8. Isid. or. 18, 69 *pila . . . quod sit pilis plena. haec antea et sphaera dicta, de quarum genere et pondere Dorcatius* (concerning the name cf. CIL. 5, 2793) *sic tradit.* Here follow two hexameters, probably therefore from a didactic poem, which is perhaps alluded to by Ovid trist. 2, 485 *ecce canit formas alius iactusque pilarum.* MHaupt, op. 3, 571.—On Plotius Crispinus, who versified the Stoic doctrine, see § 266, 3.

254. In other departments of poetry the declining age of Augustus produced only mediocrities. Such were the erotic elegiac poets Proculus and perhaps Alfius Flavus, the iambic poet Bassus, the lyric poet Rufus, the tragic poets Turranius and

Gracchus. On the other hand the collection of the Priapea, which as far as most of the pieces are concerned certainly belongs to the period of Augustus and is chiefly derived from the circles of aristocratic dilettantism, shows perfection of metrical construction, and sparkling though strongly flavoured humour.

1. Ovid. Pont. 4, 16, 32 (*cum*) *Callimachi Proculus molle teneret iter* (which REhwald, JB. 1885 2, 141 insists on taking in reference to an imitation of the σατυρικὰ δράματα, τραγῳδίαι, κωμῳδίαι of Kallimachos!).—On Tuscus see § 252, 8 in fin.—On Alfius Flavus, the author of trifling erotic poems, see § 268, 9.—Ovid. Pont. 4, 16, 36 (*cum*) *Naidas a Satyris caneret* (in idylls?) *Fontanus amatas, clauderet imparibus verba Capella modis.* Cf. ib. 11 (§ 252, 13). Perhaps therefore Capella composed epigrams, or rather elegies.

2. The iambographer Bassus, a friend of Ovid, (see § 252, 1) is probably the person addressed by Propertius 1, 4, 1. 12, and perhaps identical with a rhetorician of this period, Julius Bassus, *homo disertus, cui demptam velles quam consectabatur amaritudinem et simulationem actionis oratoriae* (Sen. contr. 10, praef. 12), and who *consectari solebat res sordidas et inveniebat qui illas unice suspicerent* (ib. 10, 30, 13. p. 475, 7 K.). Lengthy specimens of his lectures ib. 1, 6, 2–6. 7, 8.

3. Ovid. Pont. 4, 16, 28 *Pindaricae fidicen tu quoque, Rufe, lyrae.* It is not very probable that he is the same Rufus who is addressed ib. 2, 11 and who had an estate at Fundi, considering that the latter is not complimented on any poetical productions; nor is he the same as Valgius Rufus (§ 241) or Antonius Rufus, for Glandorp's statement that he *teste Acrone vertit Homerum et Pindarum* rests only on an erroneous combination (cf. Wernsdorf PLM. 3, xxx). Acro on Hor. AP. 288 says only: *praetextas et togatas scripserunt Aelius Lamia* (a certain ⟨*Aelius*⟩ *Lamia* is quoted by Fest. 131[b], 5. 6 in a fragmentary passage), *Antonius Rufus, Cn. Melissus* etc. On the other hand this poet of togatae may well be identical with the grammarian Antonius Rufus in Quint. 1, 5, 43 and Vel. Long. GL. 7, 79, 13. AReifferscheid, coniectanea nova (Bresl. 1880) 7 attempts to connect this Pindaric Rufus with the Pindaric Titius in Horace (§ 242, 4) as Titius Rufus, and takes him to be the son of C. Titius L. f. Rufus praetor 704/50.—Ov. Pont. 4, 16, 29 *Musaque Turrani tragicis innixa cothurnis.* Cf. § 132, 6. The pseudo-Apuleius (de orthogr., see § 367, 10) pretends to know that he had written a tragedy on the subject of Helena!

4. Ovid. Pont. 4, 16, 31 *cum Varus Gracchusque darent fera dicta tyrannis.* The name is generally written Varius on the assumption that he is the author of the Thyestes (§ 223, 2), though the latter died as early as 740/14! In this case the association would be caused by the fact that Gracchus also wrote a Thyestes. Prisc. GL. 2, 269, 8 *Gracchus in Thyeste* (a well constructed senarius follows). So likewise is the one quoted from *Gracchus in Atalanta* (ib. 206, 11). An anapaestic dimeter from *Graius in Peliadibus* ap. Non. p. 202, 17. Welcker, griech. Trag. p. 1431. Trag. lat. (ed. Ribb.)[2] p. 230. He is probably identical with *Sempronius Gracchus familia nobili, solers ingenio et prave facundas* whom Tiberius had killed a. 767/14 a.d. on the island of Cercina, where he had already spent 14 years in exile, on account of his former connection with Julia (the daughter of Augustus), see Tac. ann. 1, 53, cf. Vell. 2, 100, 5. If so, Ovid would seem to have mentioned two deceased poets together.

5. Priapea (*diversorum auctorum Priapeia incipit* in the Laur.) is the name

given in late MSS. (the earliest is Laur. 33, 31 s. XIV), in which they are preserved, to a collection of 80 jocular and obscene poems on Priapus in various metrical forms (hendecasyllabics, distichs, choliambics), which the editor (who himself prefaced them by 1 and 2) had gleaned from literature (3 is from Ovid, see § 251, 3) and especially from the walls of the shrines of Priapus (probably about the middle of the first Christian century) and himself revised. Hor. s. 1, 8 is also a kind of enlarged Priapus poem, and has evidently been influenced by the fashion then prevailing.—To this collection, which had been transmitted as a whole, the editors add five Priapea, which were extant elsewhere: of these two (81 *Vilicus*, 82 *Quid hoc*) bear the name of Tibullus (§ 245, 5), though they are certainly not by him. The first of these (81) was discovered in an inscription at Padua, and by chance got inserted in the Tibullus MSS. See Mommsen, CIL. 5, 2803. EHiller, Herm. 18, 343. EBährens, JJ. 127, 860. The second (82) was in the Cuiacianus of Tibullus (§ 245, 7) and is frequently to be found in MSS. of the Pseudovergiliana (§ 229, 1; cf. Bährens' ed. of Tib. p. xx), and in the same way the three others (83–85) have been transmitted among Vergil's Catalepton, see § 230, 5, 2.—The Priapea are printed in the Latt. Antholl. by Burmann (l. VI) and HMeyer (no. 1616 sqq.), especially in FBücheler's small ed. of Petronius (Berl.[3] 1882; cf. his vindiciae libri Priapeorum, RhM. 18, 381), in LMüller's Catullus (Lps. 1870) and in EBährens' PLM. 1, 58. A treatise by JEWernicke, I Thorn 1853. On Vatic. 2876 s. XV of the Priapea REllis, RhM. 43, 258.

6. Hieron. on Eus. chron. ad a. Abr. 2023 (in the cod. Petav. on 2022) = 760/7 a.d.: *Philistio mimographus natione Magnes Asianus* (according to Suidas from Nicaea or Prusa) *Romae clarus habetur*. He wrote in Greek and is perhaps that author who was served by Crassicius (§ 263, 2) as an interpreter and assistant (*circa scenam versatus est dum mimographos adiuvat*, Suet. gr. 18); he may also be identical with the jocular *Filistus, Augusto familiaris, orator et poesin mediocriter doctus*, who is mentioned in a passage of Donatus' vita Vergilii (18, 77; in Reifferscheid's Suetonius p. 67). On the other hand it seems that the Aesopus mentioned together with Philistion in Amm. Marc. 30, 4, 21 (*ex Philistionis aut Aesopi cavillationibus*) must have composed Latin mimi, as Aristides and Cato are compared l.l. with these two authors.

III. PROSE-WRITERS.

255. Among the prose-writers of the Augustan age the historians occupy the first place. At first a great number devoted their attention to defending or eulogising the celebrities of the times immediately preceding their own. Thus Volumnius and Bibulus wrote on M. Brutus, Q. Dellius on M. Antony, Tiro on Cicero; and also the authors of Memoirs on their own share in politics, such as Augustus, Agrippa, and M. Messalla, followed in the same path. Asinius Pollio started a large work on the whole period of the Civil Wars, but soon found that the time was not favourable to candid relations of recent events.

1. Plut. M. Brut. 48 Πόπλιος Βολούμνιος, ἀνὴρ φιλόσοφος καὶ συνεστρατευμένος ἀπ' ἀρχῆς Βρούτῳ, . . . λέγει. ib. 51 δύο στίχους, ὧν τὸν ἕτερον Βολούμνιος ἀνέγραψε

etc. Appian's account (b. c. 4, 112–135) seems also to be derived in parts from this source (and from Messalla, see § 222, 3), see HPeter, die Quellen Plutarchs 137. A certain Volumnius Flaccus is mentioned as a friend of D. Brutus in Cic. ad fam. 11, 12. 18.

2. L. Calpurnius Bibulus, the son of Porcia (§ 215, 3) and of M. Bibulus cos. 695/59. He served with his step-father at Philippi, was taken prisoner by M. Antony, entered his service and fell as his lieutenant in Syria c. 723/31 (Drumann, GR. 2, 105); *καί τι βιβλίδιον μικρὸν ἀπομνημονευμάτων Βρούτου, γεγραμμένον ὑπ' αὐτοῦ, διασώζεται*, Plut. Brut. 13; cf. ib. 23 *ταῦτα ὁ τῆς Πορκίας υἱὸς ἱστόρηκε Βύβλος*. HPeter, l.l. 139. Hor. sat. 1, 10, 86 (*Bibule*).

3. Strab. 11, 13, 3. p. 523 C *ὥς φησιν ὁ Δέλλιος ὁ τοῦ 'Αντωνίου φίλος, συγγράψας* (probably in Latin; see WSieglin, phil. Wschr. 1883, 1454) *τὴν ἐπὶ Παρθυαίους αὐτοῦ στρατείαν, ἐν ᾗ παρῆν καὶ αὐτὸς ἡγεμονίαν ἔχων*. Plut. Anton. 59 *πολλοὺς καὶ τῶν ἄλλων φίλων οἱ Κλεοπάτρας κόλακες ἐξέβαλον, . . . ὧν καὶ Μάρκος ἦν Σιλανὸς καὶ Δέλλιος ὁ ἱστορικός. οὗτος δὲ . . . φησὶν* etc. CWichmann, de Plut. in vitis Bruti et Antonii fontibus, Bonn 1874. ABürcklein, Quellen d. röm. parth. Feldzüge, Berl. 1879, 7. Sen. suas. 1 *bellissimam rem Dellius dixit quem Messala Corvinus desultorem bellorum civilium vocat, quia ab Dolabella ad Cassium transiturus salutem sibi pactus est si Dolabellam occidisset, a Cassio deinde transiit ad Antonium, novissime ab Antonio transfugit ad Caesarem. hic est Dellius cuius epistolae ad Cleopatram lascivae feruntur.* Cf. Hor. c. 2, 3. WFabricius, Theophanes v. Mitylene u. Q. Dellius als Quellen des Strabo, Strassb. 1888.

4. Tiro on Cicero see § 191, 2; Munatius Rufus the younger on Cato § 215, 2. —The autobiographies of Augustus (see § 220, 3), Agrippa (§ 220, 14), M. Messalla (§ 222, 3).—On Asinius Pollio's history of the Civil Wars see § 221, 3. On the historical work of Q. Tubero see § 208, 1; on that of the rhetorician Seneca see § 269, 3.

5. Ps.-Vergil. catal. 11, 1 *quis deus, Octavi, te nobis abstulit? 5 scripta quidem tua nos multum mirabimur et te raptum et romanam flebimus historiam.* He is probably identical with *Musa* Vergil. cat. 4 (cf. v. 10 *Clio nam per te candida nunc loquitur*) and with the Octavius mentioned Hor. s. 1, 10, 82, therefore the *Octavius Musa, civis Mantuanus idemque magistratus* in Serv. Verg. ecl. 9, 7 and Schol. Bern. ecl. 8, 6 (an historian, M. Octavius, is quoted in the origo gentis rom. 12, 19, see § 414, 5). But it is doubtful whether he is the same as the *Octavius venerandus* (*sanctus*) *puer* who is addressed (§ 230, 1) in the Culex (l. 25. 26. 37). ORibbeck, app. Verg. p. 8. Bährens, tib. Bl. 54; JJ. 117, 119; PLM. 2, 34.—Of the Ruso mentioned in Hor. s. 1, 3, 86, who compelled his debtor to listen to his *historiae amarae*, Porph. ad loc. says *Octavius Ruso . . . scriptor historiarum* (the same name is borne by a quaestor of Marius, Sall. Iug. 104, 3).—Perhaps to the Augustan or Tiberian period belong a few authors otherwise unknown, whom Suetonius in his v. Aug. quotes as authorities for details of the life of Augustus: Aquilius Niger (Aug. 11), C. Drusus (94), Julius Saturninus (27) and Baebius Macer, who is quoted for the same purpose by Servius ecl. 9, 47. Aen. 5, 556.

6. Nothing is certain concerning the Annales of the younger Cincius (see § 117, 4. Plüss, de Cinciis 38; NSchweiz. Mus. 6 [1866], 45).

256. The most important prose-writer of the Augustan period is T. Livius of Patavium a. 695/59 b.c.–770/17 a.d. He spent

the greater part of his life at Rome, far from political life, though on friendly terms with Augustus. Having studied rhetoric he wrote several philosophical works of popular tendency, in the shape of dialogues, a work on rhetorical training addressed to his son, in epistolary form, but especially a comprehensive account of the whole history of Rome from the foundation of the City until the death of Drusus (a. 745/9) in 142 books, of which, however, only 35 have come down to us, being the first decade and books 21–45. The outlines (periochae) which we possess of almost all the books are but an unsatisfactory compensation for the loss of the rest.

1. Recent general literature on Livy: WWeissenborn (-HJMüller) introduction to the Berlin ed. and prolegg. before the second Leipzig ed. (1860). MHertz (prolusio) before his ed. of the text (Lpz. 1857). AFrigell, Liv. som historieskrifvare, Stockholm 1881. HTaine, essai sur Tite-Live, Par.[5] 1888. LEKöhler, de T. L. vita ac moribus, Berl. 1851. MWeingärtner, de T. L. vita, I. Berl. 1852.

2. Hieron. on Eus. chron. a. Abr. 1958=695/59 *Messala Corvinus orator nascitur* (this is incorrect: see § 222, 1) *et T. Livius Patavinus scriptor historicus;* and a. Abr. 2033=770/17 a.d. *Livius historiographus Patavi moritur.* His birth at Padua is confirmed by the charge of *patavinitas* (see § 257, 14), and by Mart. 1, 61, 3 (*censetur Apona Livio suo tellus*) and Stat. Silv. 4, 7, 55 (*Timavi alumnum*), also Plut. Caes. 47 (ἐν Παταβίῳ Γάϊος Κορνήλιος, . . . Λιβίου τοῦ συγγραφέως πολίτης καὶ γνώριμος).—On the supposed grave of Livy and the inscription which it bears (that of a freedman *T. Livius Halys*) see Mommsen in CIL. 5, 2865. Portraits: RBecker, Görlitzer Philol.-Vers. 1890.

3. Liv. 4, 20, 7 *hoc ego cum Augustum Caesarem* (see n. 5) . . . *se ipsum* . . . *legisse audissem.* Tac. ann. 4, 34 *T. Livius* . . . *Cn. Pompeium tantis laudibus tulit ut Pompeianum eum Augustus appellaret; neque id amicitiae eorum offecit. Scipionem, Afranium, hunc ipsum Cassium, hunc Brutum nusquam latrones et parricidas, quae nunc vocabula imponuntur, saepe ut insignes viros nominat.* Cf. Sen. nat. quaest. 5, 18, 4 *quod de Caesare maiore volgo dictitatum est et a T. Livio positum, in incerto esse utrum illum nasci magis reip. profuerit an non nasci.* Suet. Claud. 41 *historiam in adulescentia hortante T. Livio* . . . *scribere adgressus est* (Claudius, born c. 744/10). GSchwab, de Livio et Timagene hist. script. aemulis, Stuttg. 1834.

4. Sen. ep. 100, 9 *nomina adhuc* (as a philosophical writer) *T. Livium. scripsit enim et dialogos, quos non magis philosophiae adnumerare possis quam historiae, et ex professo philosophiam continentes libros.* In the sequel he is associated with Cicero and Asinius Pollio (*tribus eloquentissimis*). Liv. is also named as a philosophical writer in Sen. ep. 46, 1 (see § 307, 2). Quint. 10, 1, 39 *apud Livium in epistola ad filium scripta, legendos Demosthenen atque Ciceronem, tum ita ut quisque Demostheni et Ciceroni simillimus.* Cf. ib. 2, 5, 20 (*quemadmodum Livius praecipit*). Hence probably also ib. 8, 2, 18 (*cum iam apud T. Livium inveniam fuisse praeceptorem aliquem qui discipulos obscurare quae dicerent iuberet*), and the quotations of Seneca contr. 9, 24, 14 p. 399 K. (on Sallust), and 9, 25, 26 (cf. § 221, 6 in fin.). This son of the historian was also an author: Plin. NH. ind. auct. to b. 5, 6 (geography) *ex* . . *T. Livio filio.*—Strange statements by Aelian (fragm. 83 Herch.) in

Suidas v. Κορνοῦτος: *δύω συγγραφέε Ῥωμαίων ἤστην, Τῖτος Λίβιος, οὗ διαρρεῖ πολὺ καὶ κλεινὸν ὄνομα, καὶ* Κορνοῦτος, the latter of whom, being childless and rich, attracted a great crowd *τῶν ἀκροωμένων. ὁ χρόνος δὲ . . . καὶ ἡ ἀλήθεια . . . τὸν μὲν ἀνέφηναν . . . ὥσπερ κεκρυμμένον θησαυρόν . . τοῦτον τὸν Λίβιον* etc.

5. His plan: praef. 1 *a primordio urbis res populi Rom.* (=*principis terrarum populi*) *perscribere.* The author takes refuge *a conspectu malorum* of the present in the ancient splendour of Rome, he intends that his reader should feel *per quos viros quibusque artibus domi militiaeque et partum et auctum imperium sit* and how Rome has fallen *ad haec tempora quibus nec vitia nostra nec remedia pati possumus.*—Livy commenced his history between a. 727/27 and 729/25, as 1, 19, 3 (see n. 3) Octavian is already entitled Augustus (since 727/27), and though he knows of the first (a. 725/29) he is unaware of the second closing of the temple of Janus by him (729/25). B. 9 was written before 734/20, b. 28 after 735/19 (28, 12, 12), b. 59 after 736/18. The latest event which can be shown to have been mentioned by Livy is Drusus' death and burial in the winter of 745/9 sq.; it is an idle conjecture that Livy intended continuing his work down to the death of Augustus (767/14) and completing the number of 150 books, as Livy (who was only 4 years younger than Augustus) could not know beforehand the time of Augustus' death, neither if and for how long he would outlive him, hence he could have formed that plan only after the death of Augustus. But Livy himself was at that time 72 years old, and had at the most finished book 120 down to 711/43 (see below). He had already devoted nearly 40 years of his life to the work, and yet we are to suppose that like a thoughtless boy, ignorant of the uncertainty of human life, he would set himself the task of chronicling down to the end the whole of Augustus' over-eventful reign of fifty-six years! The single portions (§ 257, 11) were, as it seems, separately published by the author under special titles, hence supplementary corrections could not be added. Cf. above p. 229 l. 9. Books 109–116 in the cod. Nazar. of the periochae bear the title *belli civilis libri VIII.* The periocha libri CXXI in the cod. Nazar. is headed: *ex lib. CXXI, qui editus post excessum Augusti dicitur.* The passages quoted in n. 8, and the opinion of Augustus (n. 3) and Asinius Pollio presuppose that large portions of the work were then known; so also the introductions to several books (§ 257, 11). See besides Plin. NH. praef. 16 *T. Livium . . . quodam volumine sic orsum, satis iam sibi gloriae quaesitum et potuisse se desidere, ni animus inquies pasceretur opere.*

6. The work was divided into books, decades etc. see § 257, 11.

7. The title of the history: Liv. 43, 13, 2 *ea pro indignis habere quae in meos annales referam.* Plin. NH. praef. 13 *T. Livium . . . in historiarum suarum, quas repetit ab origine urbis, quodam volumine.* According to the Verona palimpsest and other old MSS. of Livy and the periochae and citations in the grammarians, the real title is *ab urbe condita libri;* cf. Liv. 6, 1, 1 *quae ab condita urbe Roma ad captam . . . Romani . . . gessere* etc. Cf. the similar title of Pliny (§ 312, 2. 5), Tacitus (§ 338, 1) and Herodian (*τῆς μετὰ Μάρκον βασιλείας ἱστοριῶν βίβλοι*).

8. Estimation by the writer's contemporaries. Sen. controv. 10, praef. 2 (p. 459 K) *L. Magius, gener T. Livi . . . cum illum homines non in ipsius honorem laudarent, sed in soceri ferrent.* Plin. ep. 2, 3, 8 *nunquamne legisti Gaditanum quendam Titi Livi nomine gloriaque commotum ad visendum eum ab ultimo terrarum orbe venisse statimque ut viderat abisse?* Cf. Hieron. ep. 53. In the later Imperial period Livy's work was used almost without criticism, and it was also copied and epitomised. UKöhler, qua ratione T. Livii annalibus usi sint historici latini

atque graeci, Gött. 1861.—Self-confidence of the author: PLIN. NH. praef. 16 (above n. 5 ad fin.).

9. The extant books treat of Roman history (b. 1–10 first decade) from the foundation of the City to the third Samnite war 461/293, then b. 21–45 (the third, fourth and half of the fifth decade), from the beginning of the second Punic war (a. 536/218) to the triumph of Aemilius Paulus over Macedonia (a. 587/167). The scanty fragments of the other books may be seen in the editions, e.g. MHERTZ and WEISSENBORN-MÜLLER 1881. Cf. MHERTZ, de fragmentis T. Livii, Bresl. 1864 II. The loss of the largest part was no doubt caused by the great extent of the whole work (see n. 10 init.). Cf. VANHEUSDE, Verslagen etc. 5, 4, 374.

10. An abridgment of Livy is mentioned already in MART. 14, 190 *Pellibus exiguis artatur Livius ingens, quem mea non totum bibliotheca capit* (cf. AKIESSLING, coniectt. II, Greifsw. 1884, VI). The extant periochae (*T. Livi periochae omnium librorum* in Nazar.) give a dry enumeration of the most important facts together with a few hints for the use of the rhetorical schools. Those of book 136 and 137 have been accidentally lost, but two of b. 1 are extant. They are commonly found in the MSS. of Florus, the best example being in the Palat. 894 (Nazarianus) s. IX in Heidelberg (see § 348, 5); their author is unknown. These periochae were compiled perhaps in the 4th cent. A.D. from a fuller abridgment of Livy (now lost), the same which was used by Orosius (§ 455, 4); see KZANGEMEISTER on Oros. p. XXV; on the periochae of Liv. in the Festschr. of the Karlsruh. Philol.-Vers., Freib. 1882, p. 87. An edition of the same by OJAHN, Lps. 1853. Proposed emendations by CHALM, JJ. 81, 507. EVLEUTSCH, exercitt. critt., Gött. 1859. Cf. EWÖLFFLIN, die Periochae des Liv. (especially on interpolations), comment. Mommsen. 337. In general HNISSEN, RhM. 27, 558. FHEYER, JJ. 111, 645 and AEUSSNER ib. 881. OROSSBACH, RhM. 45, 65 (with new collations).—A collation of the prodigies noted in Livy by Julius Obsequens, see § 416, 4; of Livy's fasti in Cassiodorus' chronicle, see § 483, 4.

11. The MSS. of the first decade bear various subscriptions. At the end of all the books therein we read: *Victorianus v. c. emendabam domnis Symmachis;* together with this we find at the end of b. 6. 7 and 8: *Nicomachus Flavianus* (§ 428, 2) *v. c. III praefect. urbis emendavi apud Hennam;* after b. 3. 4 and 5: *Nicomachus Dexter v. c. emendavi ad exemplum parentis mei Clementiani.* It would seem to result from this that Victorianus emended the whole decade, but the two Nicomachi only several books each. OJAHN, Lpz. SBer. 1851, 335.—Specimens of the writing in the four earliest MSS. (the Veron. and Vatican. palimpsests, the Putean. and Vindob.) in MOMMSEN, analecta Liv., Lps. 1873. WHERAEUS, quaestt. crit. et palaeogr. de vetustiss. codd. Liv., Berl. 1885. Vindiciae Liv. I, Hanau 1889.

12. For the first decade we possess about thirty MSS., which are divided into two equally important classes. One of these is represented only by the palimpsest in the chapter-library at Verona, containing b. 3–6, first published by FBLUME, RhM. 2 (1828), 336. Cf. AWZUMPT, de Liv. libr. inscriptione et cod. antiquiss. Veron., Berl. 1859. MOMMSEN, T. Livii ab u. c. libr. III–VI quae supersunt in codice rescripto Veronensi descr. et ed., Abh. d. Berl. Ak. 1868. AWODRIG, anall. Liv. de cod. veron., Greifsw. 1873. WJUNG, de fide cod. Veron. cum recensione Victoriana comparati, Gött. 1881.—The other class is the Nicomachean recension (see n. 11), which is best represented by the (now lost) cod. Vormaciensis and its equal, the important Mediceus s. XI (in Florence Laur. 62, 19). Next to this comes the Parisinus 5725 (formerly Colbertinus), s. X, Florent. Marc. 326 s. XII, Upsaliensis s. XI/XII and Helmstad. I (on these two MSS., which are very nearly related to

each other, see EWHäggström excerpta Liv., Ups. univers. arsskrift 1874), Vatican. 3329 s. XI, Paris. 5724 s. X (Floriacensis) Paris. 5726 (on this see LDuvau, rev. de phil. 1886, 148) and others. AFrigell, Livianorum librorum primae decadis emendandae ratio, Ups. 1875; collatio codicum Liv. atque editt. antiquiss. I (b. 1–3), Upsala 1878 (from the Nordisk Tidskr. f. Filol. NF. 5); epilegomena ad Liv. l. I, Ups. Univers. arsskr. 1881. Supplements to this by ORiemann, rev. de phil. 4, 100. 159. JCornelissen, Mnem. 17, 175.

13. For the third decade also we have a double version: the chief representative of the one class is the excellent Paris. 5730 (Puteanus) s. V. (specimens of the writing in Mommsen, anall. (see n. 12) and Zangem.-Wattenbach, exempla codd. Latt. t. 19) in uncial writing, which has however unfortunately gaps at beginning and end. Cf. EWölfflin, Herm. 8, 361. PdeNolhac, biblioth. de FOrsini, Par. 1887, 89. The results of a new collation are given by ALuchs, Herm. 14, 141; cf. especially his ed. (n. 16). Copies of this are Vat. Regin. 762 s. IX (EWölfflin, Phil. 33, 186), also Laur. 63, 20, Paris. 5731 (Colbert.) s. XI and XII (Wölfflin, Herm. 8, 364), and Bamberg. s. XI (JMeyer, Nürnb. 1847 sq. Progr.).—The second version, contemporaneous with that of the Puteanus, comes to us through seven leaves of a Turin palimpsest (s. V) for b. 27 and 29; also through the cod. Spirensis s. XI, which was used by BRhenanus in his annotationes before the ed. Frobeniana, Bas. 1535, and by SGelenius, who brought out this edition; it is however lost all but one leaf (containing 28, 39–41), which was discovered in Munich by KHalm (see Münch. SBer. 1869 2, 580); finally through MSS. nearly related to the Spirensis, especially Harl. 2684, Vatic.-Palat. 876, Londin. (Burn.) 198 and others. HWHeerwagen, comment. crit. de Liv. 26, 41, 18–44, 1, Nürnb. 1869. Mommsen and Studemund, anal. Liv. p. 6. 32 (collation of single passages from 82 MSS. of the third decade) and esp. the prolegg. of ALuchs in his ed. of b. 26-30 (see n. 16). —Cf. also HPerthes, quaest. Liv., Bonn 1863. JHasenmüller, RhM. 19, 313. EWölfflin, Antioch. und Antip. (1872) 87. 95; Herm. 8. 366; JB. 1874/75 1, 740. HNohl, Herm. 9, 243. FLeo, RhM. 35, 236. ORiemann, rev. de phil. 6, 193.

14. The fourth decade rests on Bamberg. s. XI (which contains b. 31–38, 46) and the now lost Moguntinus, the readings of which are given in the Mayence ed. of 1518 and the Basle ed. of 1535 (see n. 16). LUrlichs, Eos 1 (1864), 84. W Weissenborn, de codice Livii Moguntino, Eisenach 1865; de ratione qua Gelenius IV Liv. decadem emendaverit, commentat. Mommsen. 302. On a late MS. (of no value) at Liegnitz see HKraffert, JJ. 103, 69 and RPeiper, ib. 211.

15. What we possess of the fifth decade (b. 41–45) rests on cod. Laurishamiensis (found 1527 in the Benedictine monastry at Lorsch by SGrynaeus, see his letter to Melanchthon in Haupt's op. 2, 117), now Vindobonensis 15, in uncial writing s. V. On the subscriptio s. VIII *Iste codex est theuberti* (*theatberti* according to Gitlbauer) *epi de dorostat* (=Wijk bij Duurstede, near Utrecht) see esp. Gitlbauer l.l. Cf. Kreyssig, annott. ad Liv. XLI–XLV ex cod. Vindob. I, 1849. Madvig, de Liv. libr. xliii initio e cod. Vindob. emendando, Copenh. 1852. JVahlen, ZföG. 5, 249. 17, 307. WHartel, ib. 17, 1 and esp. MGitlbauer, de cod. Liv. vetust. Vindobon., Vienna 1876; ZföG, 29, 341. Anall. Bollandiana 6, 1 (1887), no. 5. Specimen of writing in Zangemeister-Wattenbach's exempla cod. latt. pl. 18. WHartel, Krit-Vers. 3. 5. Dek. des Liv., Wien. SBer. 116, 1888.

16. Collective editions (cf. Drakenborch 15, 1, 628. Schweiger, class. Bibliographie 2, 1, 524. Engelmann-Preuss 2, 368 and others). Ed. princeps Rome about 1469 cura Jo. Aleriensis (without b. 33 and 41–45), supplemented (by 26, 41, 18 ff.) ed. Ven. 1498 (by Barthol. de Zanis), also (from cod. Mogunt. see n. 14) in the

Mayence ed. of 1518 and still more (from the cod. Laurish., see n. 15) by SGrynaeus (Basel bei Froben 1531); lastly (from cod. Bamberg. see n. 14) a. 1616 sq. especially by JHorrio. On account of the use of the cod. Spirensis (see n. 13) and the Moguntinus (see n. 14) the ed. by BRhenanus and SGelenius (Basel bei Froben 1535) is important. Cum scholiis CSigonii, Ven. 1555.—First critical ed. ex rec. IFGronovii, Leid. 1645. 1679 III. Most copious collection of materials by A Drakenborch (cum comm. Dukeri et variorum, cum supplementis JFreinshemii), Amsterd. 1738–46 VII; Stuttg. 1820–28 XV. Ed. IBekker and ERaschig (Berl. 1829 sq. III). Critical editions: by CFSAlschefski, Berl. 1841–46 (only down to b. 23) III. JNMadvig and JLUssing (Copenh. 1861 sqq; [4] 1886 sqq.), appar. crit. adi. ed. ALuchs, Berl. 1888 (up to the present b. 21–25). Critical editions of portions: Livi libri xxvi–xxx, recensuit ALuchs, Berl. 1879 (compare AWodrig, JJ. 123, 193).—Liber xxx ad. codd. fid. emend. ed. CFSAlschefski, Berl. 1839.—Liber xxxiii ad cod. Bamb. denuo ed. JGKreyssig; acced. var. lect. in libris xxx–xxxviii ex cod. Bamberg., Meissen 1839. Texts with critical prefaces by WWeissenborn and MMüller, Lps.[2] 1860. 1881 sqq., by MHertz (Lps. 1857–64 IV). AZingerle (still incomplete) Prague 1883 sqq.—With explanatory German notes by WWeissenborn and HJMüller, Berl. [2–8] 1867–88 X; by MMüller, FLuterbacher, EWölfflin, HJMüller, FFriedersdorff (incomplete), Lpz. 1875 sqq.; by MHeynacher, FLuterbacher, ThKlett, GEgelhaaf (incomplete), Gotha 1883 sqq. —Recent edd. of texts (still incomplete) by HJMüller, Berl. 1881 sqq. AFrigell, Gotha 1882 sqq. (the text with prolegg. ad. Liv. XXII, Gotha 1883, ad Liv. XXIII, Gotha 1885). AZingerle, Prague 1883 sqq.: see also n. 17.

17. A large number of school editions of separate portions: e.g.; B. 1 by JRSeeley, Oxf.[2] 1876. LPurser, Dublin 1881. ECocchia, Turin 1887. B. 2 HBelcher, Lond. 1881. AFrigell, Stockholm 1882. B. 2, 3 HMStephenson, Lond.[2] 1886. B. 4 HMStephenson, Lond. 1890. B. 5 ChSimmons, Lond. 1881. LWhibley, Lond. 1890. JPrendeville, Lond.[13] 1890. B. 5–7 ARCluer and PEMatheson, Lond. 1881. B. 7, 8 FLuterbacher, Lpz. 1889–90. B. 21. 22 AFrigell, Ups. 1871, Stockh. 1880 (with epilegomena, Ups. 1881). EWFabri and HWHeerwagen, Nürnb.[2] 1852. LDDowdall, Lond. 1885. WWCapes, Lond.[8] 1889. MSDimsdale, Lond. 1888–9. B. 21–23 MTTatham, Lond.[2] 1889. B. 23 AFrigell, Stockh. 1888.—B. 21–25 AHarant, Par.[2] 1886 II. ORiemann et EBenoist, Par.[4] 1836 II.—B. 23 and 24 by EWFabri, Nürnb. 1840. GCMacaulay, Lond.[2] 1888. B. 27 HMStephenson (forthcoming). B. 26–30 ORiemann and THomolle, Par. 1889.

18. Contributions to the criticism of the text: e.g.: JFGronov, observationum libri IV, Leid. 1642 and subs. Emendationes Livianae by GLWalch (Berl. 1815), EWFabri (Nürnb. 1842), HAKoch (Brandenb. 1860 f), ALuchs, Erl. 1881–87 III and especially (the leading work) by JNMadvig (Copenh. 1860. [2] 1877). Emendatiunculae by SWesenberg in the Tidskr. f. Filol. IX and X. 1870 sqq. EWölfflin, livianische Kritik und liv. Sprachgebrauch, Berl. 1864 (esp. on b. 22) and Antioch. u. Antip. (1872) 84; Boot, Verslagen en mededeel. IX, Amsterd. 1865 (on B. 21); MMüller, z. Krit. u. Erklär., Stendal 1866. 1871. 1888; JJ. 99, 339. 129, 185. 133, 855. LVielhaber (Liv. Studien, Vienna 1873 II), AWodrig (see n. 12), Mommsen and Studemund (analecta Liv., Lps. 1873). JVahlen, Berl. ind. lect. 1876/77. ADederich, emendatt. Liv. I, Emmerich 1876; JJ. 119, 481. AHarant, rev. de philol. 1, 36; emendatt. et adnott. ad T. Liv., Par. 1880. ORiemann (B. 23–25), rev. de phil. 6, 193. 12, 97. CGCobet, Mnemos. 9. 400. 10, 97. 113. AMayerhöfer, crit. studd. Liv., Bamb. 1881. AZingerle (3. Decade), Wien. SBer. 101, 555. EGrunauer, zum Text des Liv., Winterth. 1882. CHachtmann, symb. critt. ad Liv. decadem III,

Dessau 1884 and others. JCGBoot, Mnemos. 17, 1. JVahlen, Berl. SBer. 1889, 1049; Berl. ind. lect. 1890.

19. Translations by EHeusinger (Brunswick 1821 V; Lpz. 1884 Reclam.), Örtel (Munich 1822 sqq. IX), CFKlaiber and WTeuffel (Stuttg. [2]1854–56 VI). FDGerlach (Stuttg. 1856 sqq.). Philemon Holland, Lond. 1600. B. 21–25, AJChurch and WJBrodripp, Lond.[2] 1890.

257. If we examine Livy's work from the point of view of the modern historian, we meet with many shortcomings. The author has not troubled himself with laborious investigation of the sources nor visited the scenes of the events related by him, but has generally contented himself with rendering the narratives of his predecessors, especially Polybios and the later Roman Annalists, in an improved and elegant style. He also lacks adequate knowledge of political law and most of all of military art and discipline, and he even writes without a settled system of chronology. But these numerous faults are compensated by one great virtue, his unquestionable intention of stating the truth, which he never violates or withholds against his better knowledge; and even where his trifling with history is worst, it is veiled and excused by the writer's irresistible charm. His mild nature recoils from harshness and sympathises with the oppressed and vanquished; the stalwart characters of the ancient days of Rome are worshipped by him with enthusiastic fondness. This warm sympathy and his versatile talent for description make him as great an historical writer as he is insignificant as an historical critic. His strength lies in the representation of events, moods and characters. He is fond of giving descriptive sketches of his actors by attributing speeches to them, in which the writer's rhetorical training appears to the greatest advantage. On the whole, like almost all Roman historians, he interests his readers by his rhetorical power and style and by his entertaining and instructive presentation of the past, more than by the endeavour to ascertain historical fact. Livy's diction lacks severe classicality and even polish in details, but is lively, elegant and adapted to every situation with unerring tact. Both his contemporaries and posterity justly celebrated Livy as the greatest Roman historian. His influence extended over the whole of antiquity, and of all the severe losses suffered by Roman historical literature, none is sadder than the disappearance of the greater part of this work, the product of a rare combination of happy gifts and fortunate circumstances.

1. Personal avowals of Livy. Praef. 5 *ego hoc quoque laboris praemium petam ut me a conspectu malorum quae nostra tot per annos vidit aetas tantisper certe, dum prisca illa tota mente repeto, avertam, omnis expers curae quae scribentis animum etsi non flectere a vero, sollicitum tamen efficere posset.* 43, 13, 2 *et mihi vetustas res scribenti nescio quo pacto anticus fit animus et quaedam religio tenet quae illi prudentissimi viri publice suscipienda censuerint* (omens), *ea pro indignis habere quae in meos annales referam.*

2. Judgments of antiquity. Sen. suas. 6, 21 *quotiens magni alicuius viri mors ab historicis narrata est, toties fere consummatio totius vitae et quasi funebris laudatio redditur. hoc . . . T. Livius benignius omnibus magnis viris praestitit. . . . ut est natura candidissimus omnium magnorum ingeniorum aestimator T. Livius.* Sen. de ira 1, 20, 6 *apud disertissimum virum Livium.* Plin. NH. praef. 16 *T. Livium, auctorem celeberrimum.* Tac. Agr. 10 *Livius veterum, Fabius Rusticus recentium eloquentissimi auctores.* ann. 4, 34 *T. Livius, eloquentiae ac fidei praeclarus imprimis.* Quint. 8, 1, 3 *in T. Livio, mirae facundiae viro.* A very happy criticism ib. 10, 1, 101 *neque indignetur sibi Herodotus aequari T. Livium, cum in narrando mirae iucunditatis clarissimique candoris tum in contionibus supra quam enarrari potest eloquentem; ita quae dicuntur omnia cum rebus tum personis accommodata sunt. affectus quidem praecipueque eos qui sunt dulciores, ut parcissime dicam, nemo historicorum commendavit magis;* ib. 32 *neque illa Sallustiana brevitas . . . neque illa Livii lactea ubertas.* 2, 5, 19 *ego candidissimum quemque* (writer) *et maxime expositum velim, ut Livium a pueris magis quam Sallustium.* But Caligula (Suet. Cal. 34) *ut verbosum in historia neglegentemque carpebat* (*T. Livium*).

3. Modern opinions on Livy as an historian: Niebuhr, röm. Geschichte 1, 3. 2, 609; Vorträge über RG. 1, 45; and other writers on (early) Roman history, e.g. Schwegler (1, 103. 2, 10) and GCLewis (on the credibility of early Roman history etc. 1, 51. ch. 7, § 3. 4.); cf. also the introductions to recent editions (n. 16) e.g. by Weissenborn, Hertz and others. HUlrici, antike Historiographie 120. FDGerlach, Geschichtschr. d. Römer 133. Mommsen, Herm. 5, 270. HNissen, RhM. 27, 539; ital. Landeskunde, Berl. 1833, 21 and many others. Cf. also § 256, 1.

4. Political views of Livy (see FXFrühe, Constance 1851). Livy is no political partisan; this would not agree with his romantic, idealistic and sympathetic nature. Nor does his mild temper admit of party-hatred. But he has his strong antipathies. All violence, rant, and harshness are disagreeable to him, wherever he may meet with them; hence he dislikes App. Claudius as much as C. Terentius Varro, C. Flaminius or the impatient tribunes of the people; even Scipio the Elder is not quite orderly enough for him. His admiration is most sincere for Romans of the old style, such as Cincinnatus, Papirius Cursor, Camillus, Sex. Tempanius, P. Decius, Fabius Cunctator; in a case of party-strife he is always on the side of moderation, reasonableness and conciliation. He is most averse to the mob, which he frequently lashes for its want of sense and honour, and for its licentiousness (e.g. 23, 2. 24, 25, 8. 31, 34. 44). His aversion to it leads to his unfairly placing on a par the plebs of the Civil War with the mob of his own time; this is at once an evidence of his want of penetration in regard to the political development of Rome. EHeydenreich, Liv. u. die röm. Plebs, Berl. 1882. But in ancient Rome he sees his ideal realised, and *romanus* accordingly signifies in his language all that is noble (e.g. 1, 53, 4. 5, 28, 3. 5, 36, 1. 5, 38, 5. 22, 57, 6. 25, 36 extr. Cf. § 1, 2). He thus involuntarily appears partial in favour of Rome, and unjust to her enemies; see Weissenborn's introd. p. 749. Compared with those palmy days, his own period appears to him depraved, and many times he mourns the loss of ancient *pudor*,

simplicitas, modestia, aequitas, altitudo animi and especially of *pietas.* On the other hand, *neglegentia deum, omnis divini humanique moris* characterises the time in his eyes. This sentimental mode of viewing things renders him not only eloquent, but also courageous; cf. 7, 40, 2 *nondum erant tam fortes ad sanguinem civilem, nec praeter externa noverant bella, ultimaque rabies secessio ab suis habebatur.*

5. Livy's piety is altogether of a pantheistic colour. Man, conscious of his littleness and weakness, must be meek, watch the manifestations of divine sway, honour the deity and beware of ever sinning against it. Hence arises also Livy's fatalism, which is chiefly conspicuous in the first decade, in the absence of a clear perception of a reasonable co-ordination of things, e.g. 1, 42, 2 *nec rupit tamen fati necessitatem humanis consiliis.* 5, 37, 1 *adeo obcaecat animos fortuna, ubi vim suam ingruentem refringi non volt.* 8, 24, 4 *ut ferme fugiendo in media fata ruitur.* 25, 6, 4 *nulla providentia fatum imminens moveri potuit.* Another passage is somewhat rationalistic, 8, 7, 8 *movet ferocem animum iuvenis seu ira seu . . . pudor seu inexsuperabilis vis fati.* Cf. 3, 8, 1. Here we should also mention his belief in miracles (which from a. 536/218 he chronicles regularly); cf. 27, 23, 6 *in capita consulum rep. incolumi exitiabilis prodigiorum eventus vertit.* 43, 13, 1 *non sum nescius ab eadem neglegentia qua nihil deos portendere volgo nunc credant neque nuntiari admodum ulla prodigia iu publicum neque in annales referri.* Some limitations 3, 5, 14. 5, 21, 9. 24, 10, 6. 27, 23, 2.—Queck, Beitr. z. Charakt. des Liv., 1 Sondersh. 1847. OFabricius, zur religiösen Anschauungsweise des Liv., Königsb. 1865.

6. Limitation of his historical subject-matter. 33, 20 extr. *non operae est persequi ut quaeque acta in his locis sint, cum ad ea quae propria romani belli sunt vix sufficiam.* In nearly the same words he says 41, 25 extr. 39, 48, 6 *cuius belli et causas et ordinem si expromere velim immemor sim propositi, quo statui non ultra attingere externa nisi qua romanis cohaerent rebus.* Cf. 8, 24, 18. 29, 29, 5 (*excedere paululum*). 35, 40, 1. The chronology he adopts is the pontifical, according to which the foundation of Rome took place in Ol. 7, 2=750 B.C.

7. The aesthetical view which Livy takes of his subject-matter is characterised by his repeated expressions *piget scribere, enumerare* etc. (e.g. 10, 18, 7. 10, 31, 15. 26, 49), also by such expressions as 27, 37 (§ 94, 7). Of the two motives distinguished by him praef. 2 (*dum novi semper scriptores aut in rebus certius aliquid allaturos se aut scribendi arte rudem vetustatem superaturos credunt*) he has certainly been influenced by the second.

8. Authorities. Livy with his imaginative temperament and rhetorical training could not bring to bear on the historical work of his predecessors a thorough methodical criticism, nor could it ever have been his intention to do so, considering the plan of his work, which was calculated for a wide circle of readers. He was therefore not very particular in the choice of his authorities, contented himself for the period concerned with a few (and not always the best) sources, and only incidentally recognised others. He did not attempt to avail himself of original historical documents (inscriptions, public records, etc.), and does not appear to have used even the *annales pontificum* (§ 76, 5). He does not seem to have had regular recourse to any one of the early historians, not even to Fabius Pictor (see § 116, 2) nor Piso (§ 132, 4), but contents himself with comparing authors of a later period, such as Valerius Antias (§ 155, 3), Licinius Macer (§ 156, 6), Claudius Quadrigarius (§ 155, 1), Coelius Antipater (§ 137, 6), his chief authority for the war with Hannibal, and Aelius Tubero (§ 208, 1). Only at a later time did he begin to estimate Antias more justly, see § 155, 3. Livy did not turn to account Cato's

origines until the fourth decade, for the description of Cato's own career. He neither used Dionysios of Halicarnassus, nor was he used by the latter, but both probably drew from the same sources. Cf. CPeter, Phil. 33, 572; RhM. 29, 513; zur Krit. d. Quellen der älteren röm. Gesch. (Halle, 1879) 82. On the other hand Polybios is one of his principal authorities. From his cold expression (*haud spernendus auctor*, P. is here first mentioned) it might indeed be supposed that Livy undervalued Polybios: but it is obvious that in the fourth and fifth decade, in the narrative of the wars of the Romans in the East, he translates him almost word for word, now abridging, now amplifying him (33, 10, 10 *nos Polybium secuti sumus, non incertum auctorem cum omnium romanarum rerum tum praecipue in Graecia gestarum*). But he shrank from openly confessing himself to be indebted chiefly to a Greek. Besides it is even now a moot point from what epoch Livy begins to use him: it is most likely however that from the Hannibalian war (beg. b. 21) Livy compared Polybios, whose work begins with an account of that war, together with Coelius and others (perhaps at first only in an abridgment? See OHirschfeld, ZföG. 28, 801; cf. above § 210, 3).—It is hardly likely that Livy made use of Ennius himself, but more probable that in his account of the earliest period much of Ennius' work has been introduced through the medium of the annalists whom he consulted. Cf. § 101, 3 ad fin. EZarncke, commentatt. Ribbeck. 274.—In regard to his use of the authorities the details must, for the most part, remain uncertain, inasmuch as those authorities have been almost entirely lost. Comparatively little evidence of any value has been brought to light by the over-zealous research of the last ten years in this field.

FLachmann, de fontibus historiarum T. Livii, Gött. 1821 sq. II. CPeter, d. Verh. d. Liv. u. Dion. Hal. zu einander u. zu d. älteren Annalisten, Anclam 1853 (cf. above). LKieserling (§ 37, 6). HPeter, hist. rell. 1, lxxxix. cxcviii. ccxxv. cccxiii. cccxlvii. EWölfflin, Antioch. u. Antip. (1872) 22; cf. his ed. of b. 21, p. xiv.—KWNitzsch, Quellenanalyse von Liv. 2, 1–4, 8 and Dion. Hal. 5, 1–11, 63 in his Röm. Annalistik (1873) 11. HVirck, d. Quellen d. Liv. (2, 1–33) u. Dionys. für d. älteste Gesch. der röm. Rep., Strassb. 1877. ELübbert, de Liv. libri IV fontt., Giessen 1872. EHeydenreich, Fabius Pictor u. Liv., Freiberg 1878. GKlinger, de Liv. l. X fontt., Lpz. 1884.—JNeuling, de belli punici primi scriptorum fontibus, Gött. 1873.—ThLucas, qua ratione Liv. usus est opere Polybiano, I Glogau 1854. Michael, in wie weit hat L. den Pol. als Hauptquelle benützt, Torgau 1859. LTillmanns, qua rat. L. (in b. 31–45) Polybio usus sit, I Bonn 1860; quo libro Liv. Polybio uti coeperit. JJ. 83, 844. CPeter, Liv. u. Pol., üb. d. Quellen des 21. u. 22. B. des Liv., Halle 1863. WMichael, qua ratione L. in decade III Polybio usus sit, Bonn 1867. CFöhlisch, d. Benutzung des Pol. in B. 21 u. 22 des Liv., Pforzh. 1884. MPosner, quibus auctoribus in bello Hannibalico enarrando usus sit Dio Cassius, symbola ad cognoscendam rationem quae inter Liv. et Pol. intercedat, Bonn 1874. FFriedersdorff, Liv. et Pol. Scipionis rerum scriptores, Gött. 1869; das 26. B. des Liv., Marienb. 1874. KKessler, secundum quos auctores Liv. res a Scipione maiore in Africa gestas narraverit, Marb. 1877. CBöttcher, de Liv. l. XXI et XXII fontibus, Königsb. 1867; d. Quellen d. Liv. im 21. u. 22. B., JJ. Suppl. 5, 353. OHirschfeld, ZföG. 28, 801. FLuterbacher, de fontt. l. XXI et XXII, Strassb. 1875. AVollmer, unde belli punici secundi scriptores sua hauserint (Gött. 1872) 44; d. Quellen der 3. Dekade des Liv., Düren 1881. LKeller, der 2. pun. Krieg u. s. Quellen, Marb. 1875; RhM. 29, 88. OGilbert, Rom u. Karthago (Lpz. 1876) 10. WPirogow, Forschungen z. 3. Dekade des Liv., Petersb. 1878 (Russ.). WSieglin, Chronologie der Belagerung von Sagunt, Lpz. 1878; RhM. 38, 348. GEgelhaaf, Pol. u. Liv. über den Krieg der J. 218–217, JJ.

Suppl. 10, 471. OSeeck, Herm. 8, 152. HJMüller, die Schlacht an der Trebia, Berl. 1867. EMüller, noch einmal die Schlacht an der Trebia, Conitz 1876. HHesselbarth, de pugna Cannensi, Gött. 1874; hist.-krit. Unterss. im Bereiche der 3. Dekade des Liv., Lippstadt 1882. JBSturm, quae ratio inter Liv. decadem III et Coelii Antip. historias intercedat, Würzb. 1883 (compare LBauer, phil. Rundsch. 1884, 1578). ThZielinski, d. letzten Jahre des 2. pun. Kriegs, Lpz. 1880.—HNissen, krit. Unterss. über die Quellen der 4. und 5. Dekade des L., Berl. 1863. GFUnger, die röm. Quellen des L. in der 4. u. 5. Dekade, Phil. Suppl. 3, 2, 3.—WHeimbach, quid et quantum Cassius Dio libro XL and l. XLVII (a. 700/54–712/42) e Livio desumpserit, Bonn 1878. HHesselbarth, Unterss.² z. 3. Dek. des Liv., Halle 1889. AvBreska, Quellenunterss, im 21.–23. B., Berl. 1889.

9. Livy's standard of historical criticism. Whenever his predecessors agree, a matter must be very improbable in itself (cf. 5, 21, 8 sq. 6, 12, 2 sqq.) if Livy is to doubt it. Things agreed upon by his authorities he generally considers true, and thus only renders the ordinary tradition. If his predecessors disagree, he frequently abstains from deciding himself, or he combines their views (Wölfflin, Antioch. 55. 57. 74), or pronounces for the majority or the earliest and least suspected witness, sometimes also for the more intrinsically probable account, but often for the one more favourable to the Romans (e.g. 7, 27, 9. 10, 39) or the most charitable (e.g. 4, 29, 6. 6, 38, 10. 8, 18, 2) or the most impressive (e.g. 7, 39 sqq. 10, 37. 21, 46, 10. 26, 15), or merely adopts a mediating account (e.g. 26, 49, 6). Especially in the earlier period his judgment frequently wavers; cf. 5, 21, 9, *in rebus tam antiquis si quae similia veri sint pro veris accipiantur satis habeam.* In this part he frequently declares himself incompetent to decide. But elsewhere also he is fond of choosing this solution, partly from defective study of his authorities or owing to his shallow estimation of the controverted points, partly from his natural diffidence and trustfulness. This is carried so far that he does not even profit by some very disagreeable lessons. Though his experience with Valerius Antias ought to have taught him to beware of high numbers in the accounts of battles, he still does not hesitate (37, 44) in stating about 54,000 killed and even (27, 49) 56,000. Such instances show his want of practical discernment. As concerns his modesty, we may refer e.g. to 29, 14, 9, *id . . . sicut proditum a proximis memoriae temporum illorum scriptoribus libens posteris traderem, ita meas opiniones coniectando rem vetustate obrutam non interponam.* He frequently lets his own preferences decide whether a thing is true or has not taken place (FLachmann l.l. 2, 69). But he tries to exclude some of the more flagrant inventions of Roman national vanity (Wölfflin, Antioch. 22. 36. 39. 80).

10. His dependence on his authorities and a certain inadvertence—which may be easily explained in so extensive a work,—partly also the successive elaboration and publication of detached pieces, have caused many errors in details, repetitions, contradictions, omissions, mistakes, erroneous translations etc. Instances are given in Weissenborn's introduction ⁷42. Cf. besides JSchmidt, Herm. 16, 155. In consequence of all this, Livy as a historical authority should be used, especially on the earliest time, only with much caution, though his personal intention to state the truth cannot be questioned. Treatises de fide Livii (omitting those which are antiquated) by CKruse (Lps. 1812. II) and Bäumker (Liv. antiquiss. rerum rom. hist. etc., Paderborn 1863). ThStade, die Schlachtenschilderungen in L. erster Dekade, Jena 1873. JMaissiat, Annibal en Gaule (Par. 1874) 308.

11. Division and plan of the work: Livy divided his work first into books; 10, 31, 10 *Samnitium bella quae continua per quartum iam volumen* (=b. 7–10) *agimus.*

6, 1, 1 *quinque libris exposui.* 21, 1, 1 *cum in mentem venit LXIII annos . . . aeque multa volumina* (that is 15 books) *occupasse mihi quam* etc. The gigantic subject next fell into large sections (cf. 21, 1, 1 *partes singulae tanti operis*), e.g. the earliest period down to the Punic wars (b. 1–15 with the sub-divisions: Rome down to the capture by the Gauls b. 1–5, the remainder 6–15; b. 6 has a separate preface); the Punic wars (b. 16–30, with the sub-division: first Punic war b. 16–20, second Punic war b. 21–30; b. 21 with a preface); the Macedonian wars (b. 31–45; b. 31 with a preface, in three sub-divisions of 5 books each; war with Philippos; Syro-Aetolian war, war with Perseus) etc. There was also, as may be seen from the examples quoted and others (b. 17 opens with the plans of Livius Drusus and the Social war; in b. 80 we have the death of Marius, in b. 90 that of Sulla), a systematical internal arrangement by decades or half-decades, or rather decades-and-a-half. At the close of antiquity, the division in decades was taken by the copyists as the basis of the work. The earliest mention of this known to us occurs in Pope Gelasius' epist. ad Andromachum (Mansi, concil. 7, 197) *Lupercalia propter quid instituta sunt . . . Livius secunda decade loquitur.* But the recension of Victorianus (§ 256, 11) proves this arrangement to be of earlier date.—Livy himself in the progress of his work and especially in the description of his own life-time (from b. 109; cf. Serv. Aen. 1, 373 *Livius ex annalibus et historia constat*; cf. § 37, 3) did not carry out this arrangement by decades: in b. 100. 110. 120. 130. 140 there is evidently no division (nor does any, according to HNissen l.l., occur in b. 10. 50. 60. 80). On the other hand cf. b. 109–116 = *belli civilis libri VIII* above § 256, 5. EWölfflin, Phil. 33, 139. HNissen, RhM. 27, 539. In detail Livy's work resembles that of the annalists not only because in describing events it follows in the main a chronological order, but also because it devotes a comparatively short space to the most remote past, and gradually expands as it approaches the better known periods (§ 37 and 116). B. 1–30 comprises 550 years, b. 31–68 100 years, b. 69–108 50 years, lastly b. 109–142 (beginning with 701/53) 42 years.

12. A means of portraying character frequently and successfully employed by Livy is that of speeches, which he interposes in order to give a *simulacrum* of a certain person (45, 25, 3) or to indicate the motives of the actors (e.g. 8, 7, cf. 3, 47, 5), and which for this reason have so little pretension to historical truth (*in hanc sententiam locutum accipio* 3, 67, 1) as not even to shun anachronisms (e.g. 5, 4, 12) or to attempt to imitate the style of the time. But they are generally a very faithful reflection of the character or position of the speaker; cf. e.g. 7, 34. In some instances we are still able to trace in what manner Livy rhetorically enlarges upon the brief hints of a predecessor, cf. Polyb. 3, 64 with Liv. 21, 40 sq. OKohl, Zweck u. Bedeutung der liv. Reden, Barmen 1872. FFriedersdorff, de oratt. operi Liv. insertarum origine et natura I, Tilsit 1886. Livy's speeches were (like those of Sallust § 205, 4) disseminated in separate editions (see § 319, 6). On the rhetorical character of the history of Livy see HTaine, essai sur Tite-Live, Paris [5] 1888.

13. Livy's relation is characterised by a certain rotundity and easy fulness, like that of Herodotos (cf. Quintilian above n. 2), so as to become really prolix in some parts. Quint. 8, 3, 53 *vitanda μακρολογία*, i.e. *longior quam oportet sermo, ut apud T. Livium.* Cf. Charis. Gl. 1, 271 with the parallel passages there indicated and MHertz, prolusio (§ 256, 1) not. 77. This quality also reminds us of the manner of Cicero, whom Livy imitated (see § 256, 4) and approached more closely than any other Roman prose-writer. Though his (rhetorical) art is conspicuous throughout his work, it never becomes artifice or want of naturalness. Livy's remarkable power of realising the motives of a certain situation lends also to his descriptions

the colouring suitable to the occasion. Only the description of the earliest period (the first third of b. 1) is meagre: here (and at the beginning of b. 2) Livy attempts with very little success to establish internal connections and proofs. In dealing with such obscure times and personages, little effect could be produced with the psychological colouring which elsewhere constitutes one of Livy's strong points. Otherwise he succeeds in describing public feeling (e.g. 8, 7, 20 sq. 9, 2, 10 sq. 5 sq. 33, 32) as well as external events (e.g. 5, 39 sqq. 21, 58. 23, 27, 6 sq. 24, 26) with the utmost vividness. The most brilliant description in the extant books is that of the war with Hannibal. We are unfortunately precluded from forming an opinion of just those portions of the narrative where the writer's increased interest in his subject-matter led him into greater detail (n. 11). Here Livy's talent for skilful and vivid narrative and description must have found a specially congenial field.

14. Livy's diction is intentionally (§ 256, 4) classical, and it certainly approaches the standard of classicality far more closely than Quintilian or Tacitus in his youthful Ciceronian work. But even in Livy numerous poetical phrases betray the approach of the silver age (*haec ubi dicta dedit* after Vergil; *ubi Mars est atrocissimus; ad arma consternatum esse; cogitationibus animum volutare; adversa montium; stupens animi; laeta pascua* etc.), as does also a certain fondness for strong expressions (e.g. *attonitus, ingens* etc.). He uses by preference Vergilian phraseology. It may have been his employment of words which sometimes appeared strange to those who were accustomed to the sermo urbanus. QUINT. 1, 5, 55 *peregrina (verba) ex omnibus, prope dixerim, gentibus . . . venerunt; . . . quemadmodum Pollio* (see § 221, 6) *deprehendit in Livio patavinitatem.* Cf. ib. 8, 1. 2 *ut sint (verba) quam minime peregrina et externa.* (3) *et in T. Livio, mirae facunuiae viro, putat inesse Pollio Asinius quandam patavinitatem.* DGMORHOF. de patavinitate Liviana, Kil. 1685 (also in DRAKENBORCH's Livy 15, 1, 50). CGWIEDEMANN, de patavinitate Livii, Görlitz 1848–54 III. Cf. MHAUPT, op. 2, 69. HJMÜLLER, ZfGW. 41, Jahresber. 25.—In point of diction it is noticeable that the style, which in the first book is still fluctuating, becomes more settled and conformable to rule as the work progresses. EWÖLFFLIN, livianische Kritik und livianischer Sprachgebrauch (Berl. 1864) 29, cf. Antioch. u. Antip. (1872) 84.

15. Literature on the language of Livy: AWERNESTI, glossarium Livianum, edd. GHSCHÄFER et ITHKREYSSIG, Lpz. 1827. Chief work: ORIEMANN, études sur la langue et la grammaire de Tite-Live, Par. [2]1884 (epitomised in RIEMANN's edd. of b. 21 and 22; see § 256, 17). LKÜHNAST, d. Hauptpunkte der livian. Syntax, Berl. [2]1872. EWÖLFFLIN (see n. 14). EBALLAS, d. Phraseologie des Liv., Posen 1885. WEISSENBORN's introduction to his Berlin edition [7]68. GQUECK, Beiträge z. Charakt. des Liv. II: Die Darstellung des L., Sondersh. 1853. GHILDEBRAND, über einige Abweichungen im Sprachgebr. des Cic. Caes. Liv. usw., Dortm. 1854; specimina lexici Liviani, Dortmund 1857. 68 II; Beitr. z. Sprachgebr. des L., Dortm. 1865. FFÜGNER (who intends to publish a lex. Liv. founded on Hildebrand's work), specimen lex. Liv., Nienburg 1888.—EKRAH, spec. grammaticae Liv., Insterb. 1859. CEGÜTHLING, de T. Livii oratione, I de usu verborum simplicium, Lauban 1867, II de participiis, Liegnitz 1872. LADRIAN, das Part. Praes. Pass. (in Liv.), Grossglogau 1875. MWENGER, zum Gebr. der Partizipien bei Liv., Seitenstetten 1882. MMÜLLER, zum Sprachgebr. d. L., I haud, haudquaquam, Stendal 1877. GRICHTER, Beitr. z. Gebr. des Zahlworts im Lat., I Livius, Oldenb. 1880. JEELLENDT, de praepos. A cum nominibus urbium iunctae ap. Liv. maxime usu, Königsb. 1843. HLÖWE, de praepos. DE usu ap. Liv., Grimma 1847. GWULSCH, de praepos. PER usu Liv., Halle 1880. PGLYTH, de usu praepos. PER ap. Liv. eiusque

aliquot synonymarum, Visboae 1883. KLEINE, de genetivi usu Liv., I Cleves 1865. LORENZ, der Dativ. d. Bestimmung bei L., bes. der Dativ. Gerundivi, Meldorf 1871. 74 II. RJONAS, de Gebr. der vv. frequentativa u. intensiva bei Liv., Posen 1884. ALEHMANN, de vv. compositis ap. Sall. Caes. Liv. Tac. I, Leobschütz 1884. EWESENER, de quibusd. Liv. orationis proprietatibus, Coblenz 1854; de periodorum Liv. proprietatibus, Fulda 1860. WKRIEBEL, see § 177, 3. WIGNATIUS, see § 198, 12. KREIZNER, de propria orationis Liv. indole proprio maxime adiectivorum usu, Hadamar 1844. ENGLERT, d. attributive Gebrauch adverbialer Bestimmungen bei L., Aschaffenb. 1866. GÜNTHER, die Formen der Hypothesis aus Liv., Bromb. 1871. SCHMIDT, de temporum historicorum ap. L. usu, Demmin 1874. JNMADVIG, die syntaktischen Mittel der Sprache, . . . bei Liv., kl. philol. Schr. (Lpz. 1875) 356. FWHOLTZE, de syntaxi Liv. dispertienda et ordinanda, Naumb. 1881. HJMÜLLER, -ĔQUE bei Livius, RhM. 43, 637. AMASCHMIDT, zur liv. Lexicographie, Baden b/Wien 1888. Waidhofen a. Th. 1889 II. AFÜGNER, Liv. b. 21–23, grammatisch untersucht, Berl. 1888; Lexicon Livianum, Lps. 1889 sq. GWULSCH, de verbis cum praepos. PER compos. ap. Liv. I, Barmen 1889. AKÖBERLIN, de participiorum usu Liv., Erl. 1890.

258. About the same time as Livy and as it were to supplement his history, Pompeius Trogus wrote his Universal History, Historiae Philippicae, in 44 books, beginning with Ninus and extending to the writer's own time, from a Greek source (probably Timagenes); it was composed in a lively style and classical diction and was also more rich in material and less rhetorical than Livy. We know the work chiefly through the abridgment of Justinus. Besides his historical work, Trogus wrote also on zoology and botany, after the best authorities, Aristotle and Theophrastos.

1. IUSTIN. 43, 5, 11 *in postremo libro Trogus maiores suos a Vocontiis originem ducere, avum suum Trogum Pompeium Sertoriano bello civitatem a Cn. Pompeio percepisse dicit, patruum Mithridatico bello turmas sub eodem Pompeio duxisse, patrem quoque sub C. Caesare militasse epistularumque et legationum, simul et anuli curam habuisse.* His grandfather's name may, therefore, have been Cn. Pomp. Tr.; the inference drawn from an inscription from Vaison (CIL. 12, 1371) that his patruus was called Q. is very doubtful; his father was probably the Cn. Pompeius whom Caesar b. g. 5, 36 mentions as an interpreter employed by himself a. 700/54; whence it becomes probable that the historian had also the praenomen of Cn. JBECKER, Phil. 7, 389. Cf. KNIPPERDEY, op. 411.—LEHALLBERG, de Trogo Pompeio, Par. 1869.

2. CHARIS. GL. 1, 102, 10 *Valgius et Verrius et Trogus de animalibus.* ib. 137, 9 *Trogum de animalibus libro X.* A longer quotation from this (*Trogus, et ipse auctor e severissimis*) in PLIN. NH. 11, 275. All the fragments are literally translated—not without errors—from Aristotle's hist. anim. PLINY mentions Trogus in his ind. auct. to b. 7–11 (mankind and animals). 12–18 (trees and agriculture). 31 (medicinae ex aquatilibus) and quotes him repeatedly in his work. According to this Trogus would appear to have also written a treatise de plantis, and it was probably (as is shown by the quotation in PLIN. NH. 17, 58) based on Theophrastos. AGUTSCHMID, JJ. Suppl. 2, 180; RhM. 37, 548. THBIRT, de halieut. Ovid. 136.

3. His principal work is the 44 books historiarum philippicarum, a universal history with special reference to geography (hence the MSS. are entitled *Historiae Philippicae et totius mundi origines et terrae situs*), written in the digressive manner of Theopompos, and skilfully planned, so that the history of Macedonia and the successors of Alexander the Great furnished the theme for the narrative, while Roman history, with the exception of the regal period, which in Trogus' opinion was best to be derived from Greek sources (it is added in b. 43), was systematically excluded (cf. praef. 1). B. 1–6 gives as an introduction the history of Asia and Hellas. The latest fact mentioned in the work is the recovery of the standards taken by the Parthians a. 734/20 (42, 5, 11). AvGutschmid conjectures that 42, 4, 16 (*Parthiae, in qua iam quasi sollemne est reges parricidas haberi*) was meant in reference to the murder of Phraates IV by his son Phraatakes (Oct. 3 B.C. at latest). The lively style of the work is frequently conspicuous even in Justinus' abridgment. Justinus praef. 1 calls him *vir priscae eloquentiae;* cf. Vopisc. Prob. 2, 7 *ut non Sallustios, Livios, Tacitos, Trogos atque omnes disertissimos imitarer viros.* Sober judgment and strict principle seem to be indicated in Iustin. 38, 3, 11 *quam (orationem) obliquam Pompeius Trogus exposuit* (cf. Iust. 28, 2. 38, 4–7), *quoniam in Livio et in Sallustio reprehendit quod contiones directas pro sua ratione* (thus Wölfflin reads: the MSS. have *pro sua oratione*; Gutschmid reads *perversa ratione*) *operi suo inserendo historiae modum excesserint.* He referred to his contemporary Vergil; see Serv. ad Aen. 6, 783 *de hoc loco et Trogus et Probus quaerunt.* Trogus' diction also appears to be considerably influenced by Vergil. ASonny, RhM. 41, 473. He imitated Sallust. JSellge, symb. ad hist. libr. Sall. I: de studiis in Sallustio a Trogo et Iustino collocatis, Bresl. 1882.—Hugo de Fleury (Ecclesiastical History; abbot of Canterbury from 1091?) and from him the chronicler Roger Wendover and from him again Matthew of Westminster, Flores Histor. (ed. 1570) 1, 81 (see AvGutschmid [n. 5] p. 260, Reifferscheid's Suetonius p. 382 and especially FRühl, die Verbreitung Justins p. 25): *anno divinae incarnationis nono, Caesare Augusto imperii sui LIum agente annum* (762/9 A.D.), *Trogus Pompeius chronica sua terminavit . . . Romanorum remp. . . . ab initio usque ad praesens tempus prosequitur.* Radulfus de Diceto, de viris illustr. (of a. 1210, from unknown but good sources): *Trogus Pompeius a tempore Nini regis Assyriorum usque ad annum XXIXum Hyrcani principis Iudaeorum chronica sua digessit* (Rühl, l.l. p. 32).

4. AvGutschmid in the lit. Centrabl. 1872, 659 has conjectured with much probability and developed the theory in RhM. 37, 548 that Trogus' historiae Philippicae is a version of a Greek historical work (by Timagenes). He considers that a Roman is not to be credited with having originated such a unique piece of literary mosaic, carried out with such constant recourse to original sources, and such conscientious accuracy. Cf. also Mommsen, Herm. 16, 619. Among the sources of the Greek original are Theopompos' Φιλλιππικά (on which Trogus founded himself also for the title of his work), Ephoros, Timaios, Kleitarchos, Polybios (HNissen, krit. Unters. 305), Poseidonios, Deinon and others. AHLHeeren, de Trogi fontibus, in the commentt. soc. Gotting. 15 (1804), 185 (repeated in Frotscher's ed.). CRaun, de Clitarcho Diodori Curtii Iustini auctore, Bonn 1868. HWolffgarten, de Ephori et Dinonis historiis a Tr. expressis, Bonn 1868. WFricke, d. Quellen des Plut. im Alkib. (Lpz. 1869) 71. GRichter, de fontibus ad Gelonis hist., Gött. 1873. PNatorp, see § 198, 11. LGeschwandtner, quibus fontt. Tr. in rebus successorum Alex. M. usus sit, Halle 1878. LHolzapfel (see § 198, 11) 47. JHeinz, Justin als Quelle zur Gesch. des Cyrus, Sigmar. 1879. RKöhler, see § 292, 3. AEnmann, d. Quellen des Tr. für die Griech. and sicilische Gesch., Dorpat 1880. ONeuhaus, die Quellen d. Tr. in d. pers. Gesch., Hohenstein 1882–86 IV. ABibeljé, Quellen des Tr. im 3.

Perserzug, Rost. 1888.—HCrohn, de Trogi ap. antiquos auctoritate, Strassb. 1882 (diss. Argentor. 7, 1).

5. Our knowledge of Trogus' historical work is derived partly from the *prologi* (tables of contents) of all the books, partly from the abridgment of Justinus, who in his praefatio says: *Trogus Pompeius graecas et totius historias orbis latino sermone composuit. . . . cuius libris omnium saeculorum, regum, nationum populorumque res gestae continentur. . . . ea omnia Pompeius divisa temporibus et serie rerum digesta composuit. horum igitur XLIV voluminum (nam totidem edidit) per otium quo in urbe versabamur cognitione quaeque dignissima excerpsi.* Justinus gives us very little of the work word for word, e.g. Mithridates' address to his soldiers 34, 4–7; cf. Iust. 38, 3, 11 *quam orationem dignam duxi cuius exemplum brevitati huius operis insererem.* Some passages are also quoted by Priscian, Cassiodorus (Jordanis), Servius and Junius Philargyrius, see AvGutschmid l.l. 186. All other writers know only Justinus, though they may mention Trogus. The fragments which Bielowski (n. 6) pretended to have taken from Polish chronicles have been shown to be fictions by AvGutschmid, die Fragmente des P. Tr., JJ. Suppl. 2. 202. Cf. duRieu, Mnemos. 3 (1854), 177. JBernays, op. 3, 211.

6. Pompei Trogi fragmenta . . . una cum prologis historiarum Philipp. et criticis annotationibus edidit ABielowski, Lemberg 1853 (see n. 5). The fragments of the Hist. are also collected in the ed. of Justinus by Frotscher 1, xcviii and elsewhere. Trogi prologi ed. GHGrauert, Münster 1827; the same rec. AvGutschmid, see n. 10.—On the alleged new fragments of Trogus (from b. 12) in the Vatic. 1869 s. 12 see § 292, 5 ad fin.

7. The time of M. Junian(i)us Justinus (so named only in the Laur. 66, 21, see n. 9) is not positively known, though probably he lived in the age of the Antonines (FRühl, d. Verbreitung, p. 36). Considering his old-school way of thinking and the style of his preface as well as his reference to Cato the Elder, we should not like to put him much later than Florus who epitomised Livy. (Cf. however CLachmann, kl. Schr. 2, 193.) Radulfus de Diceto (see n. 3 ad fin.) says indeed (Rühl p. 32): *Iustinus philosophus Trogi Pompei abbreviator, scripsit eodem anno* (with which Josephus concluded his Antiquities), but probably confounds him with Justus of Tiberias, just as in the Middle Ages he was confounded with Justinus Martyr (Rühl l.l. 36, 46). The first writer who mentions Justinus is Hieronymus 5, 621 Vall. *praecipue nostri Livii et Pompei Trogi atque Justini.* Orosius made great use of him, cf. n. 9.

8. On Justinus' treatment see praef. 4 *omissis his quae nec cognoscendi voluptate iucunda nec exemplo erant necessaria breve veluti florum corpusculum* (nosegay, anthology) *feci.* Cf. n. 5. Augustin. de civ. d. 4, 6 *Iustinus qui graecam vel potius peregrinam, Trogum Pompeium secutus, non latine tantum . . . verum etiam breviter scripsit historiam.* Oros. 1, 8 *Pompeius historicus eiusque breviator Justinus;* ib. 10 *Pompeius sive Justinus.* Justinus seems to have made but few changes in the diction of Trogus and to have merely alloyed it with several new additions. Justinus' individual talents were but very small. Even the text of Trogus used by J. must have been corrupt. Aethicus Ister employed probably a different abridgment of Pomp. Tr. (perhaps in Cassiodorus' Gothic History); see Rühl p. 6. It is uncertain whence are derived those portions which are in agreement with J. in the Anecdoton to the Gothic History in Rühl, JJ. 121, 549.

9. In the Middle Ages the abridgment of Justinus was much read and copied, though it never found a place among the school-books. FRühl, die Verbreitung

des Iustinus im MAlter, Lpz. 1871. The extant MSS. of Justinus divide into two groups. The first is represented only by Laur. 66, 21 s. XI. This alone fills up a large gap at 24, 6, 6, but at the same time is itself inaccurate and imperfect, and interpolated by various hands. The other group falls into three classes: J (under this e.g. Eusebianus s. X, Laur. 66, 20 s. XI, Sessorianus s. XI, Voss. Q. 101 s. XI), T (under which Paris. 4950 s. IX, SGallensis s. IX, Gissensis s. IX, Ashburnham. s. IX etc.). II (under which Petropolit. 422 s. IX, Palat-Vatic. 927, s. XII). Besides the MSS. Orosius is also specially important for criticism. See FRühl l.l. and his treatise on the sources of Justinus' text, JJ. supplementary vol. 6, 1 and pref. to his ed.; cf. the same author JJ. 105, 853.—Cf. also JJeep in his praefatio and in the Wolfenbüttler Progr. 1855. JARozsek, über fünf Iustinus-Hss., Graz 1871. ILHeiberg, nye fragmenter af et Iustinushdskr., Nord. Tidskr. f. Fil. 3, 275. AHarant, variantes d'un ms. de Justin (in Laon) s. XII, rev. de phil. 2 (1878), 78.

10. Editions of Justinus. Ed. princ. Venet. 1470 and Rom. 1470 (cf. Rühl, d. Verbreitung, p. 51). From good MSS. JBongarsius (cum notis), Par. 1581; with additions by FModius (Frankf. 1587). Cum notis IsVossii, Leid. 1640. Cum notis variorum ed. IGGraevius, Utr. 1668. Leid. 1683. 1701. A variorum edition by Abr. Gronov, Leid. 1719. 1760; revised and added to by CHFrotscher, Lps. 1827–30 III. CBenecke, with notes, Lpz. 1830, FDübner (adnot. crit. instr., Lps. 1831), WFittbogen (with notes, Halle 1835), Johanneau et Dübner (Par. 1838 II), rec. JJeep (Lps. 1859, with comm. criticus p. 1–188) and especially ex recensione FRühl, acc. prologi in Pomp. Trog. ab AdeGutschmid recensiti, Lpz. 1886.

11. OEichert, Wörterbuch zu Iust., Hanover 1881. JFRecke, d. Spracheigentümlichkeiten Justins, Mühlhausen 1855. FSeck, de Trogi sermone, Constance 1881. 82 II. JFMüller, de casuum ap. Iust. usu, Budissin 1859. JARozsek, de natura latinitatis Iustin., Hermannst. 1865. FFischer, de eloc. Iustini, Halle 1868. HDomke, d. Gebr. d. Präposs. ab ex u. de bei Just., Bresl. 1877.—CPaucker, über justinische Syntax, ZföG. 34, 321. JBenesch, de casibus obl. ap. Just., Vienna 1889.—Criticism: UKöhler, JJ. 91, 427. FRühl, ib. 101, 21. 133, 365. Madvig, adv. 2, 616. FBorchardt, quaestt. Iustin., Greifsw. 1875.—Translated by Ostertag (Frankf. 1781 II), Kolbe (1824) and ChrSchwarz (Stuttg. 1834–37).

259. At the close of the Augustan period and perhaps under Tiberius wrote the exact scholar Fenestella, whose pattern was Varro. He composed Annales and, in these or in a separate work, devoted minute attention to the history of Roman manners and to the political condition of Rome. L. Arruntius on the other hand imitated and rather exaggerated Sallust's manner in his History of the Punic war. The early history of Rome was, perhaps in this period, related by Annius Fetialis, and somewhat later A. Cremutius Cordus composed a narrative of the times immediately preceding his own.

1. Hieronym. on Eus. Chron. ad a. Abr. 2035 = 772/19 a.d. *Fenestella historiarum scriptor et carminum septuagenarius moritur sepeliturque Cumis.* He would, therefore, seem to have been born 702/52; this agrees with Plut. Crass. 5 τούτων φησὶ τὴν ἑτέραν (who was about 18 years old a. 668/86 and therefore born c. 650/104) ἤδη

πρεσβῦτιν οὖσαν ὁ Φαινεστέλλας ἰδεῖν αὐτὸς καὶ πολλάκις ἀκοῦσαι (perhaps in Spain). Not much probability attaches, therefore, to the statement of PLINY NH. 33, 146 *sua memoria coeptum Fenestella tradit, qui obiit novissimo Tiberii Caesaris principatu.* As Tiberius died 790/37 A.D. this statement would oblige us to place Fenestella's life c. 719/35 B.C.–789/36 A.D. (MERCKLIN l.l. 3). That he wrote the work in question in the reign of Tiberius, does not appear from PLINY NH. 8, 195 *togas rasas . . . divi Augusti* (words of Pliny?) *novissimis temporibus coepisse scribit Fenestella.* It is certain that he wrote before Asconius, who frequently mentions and argues against him. The statement of LYD. magistr. 3, 75 is certainly wrong ὡς Φενεστέλλας καὶ Σισένας οἱ Ῥωμαῖοί φασιν, ὧν τὰς χρήσεις ὁ Βάρρων ἐπὶ τῶν ἀνθρωπίνων πραγμάτων ἀνήγαγεν. ἐγὼ δὲ τὰς βίβλους οὔπω τεθέαμαι. Probably Fenestella quoted Sisenna and Varro, and Lydus' authority seems to have mixed up the three names. Praenomen and nomen of Fenestella are unknown (the cognomen *Fenestella* CIL. 5, 469? 12, 259); the same applies to his *carmina*, mentioned only by Hieronym. l.l. (SCALIGER's conjecture in Hieron. is *historiarum scriptor et annalium*; cf. § 37, 3. 257, 11.)

2. Annales. ASCON. in Cic. Corn. 66 p. 59 *neque apud Sallustium neque apud Livium neque apud Fenestellam* etc. Exact quotations from the annales of F. occur only in NONIUS, viz. 221, 35 (v. *reticulum*, perhaps from a description of customs): *Fen. annalium (III)*, 154, 16 (v. *praesente*): *Fenestella annalium lib. II* (of unknown date), and 385, 7 (v. *rumor*): *F. annali lib. XXII* (a. 698/56). No doubt the statements in PLUT. Sull. 28 and Crass. 4 sq. are derived from that work. Even if the details concerning Roman life are taken from the annales (n. 3), they do not prove that these reached back into the regal period, as they (e.g. PLIN. NH. 15, 1) may have formed part of digressions. The mistakes which ASCONIUS, PLINIUS (NH. 9, 123 *Fenestella . . . manifesto errore*), and GELLIUS adduce against Fenestella are partly unimportant, and partly based on difference of opinion, hence they do not disprove the estimate of LACTANT. (inst. div. 1, 6, 14): *Fenestella diligentissimus scriptor*, which is rather borne out by passages such as SUETON. vit. Terent. 1 and MACR. 1, 10, 5 f. Cf. besides LACTANT. de ira dei 22, 5 *plurimi et maximi auctores tradiderunt, . . . nostrorum Varro et Fenestella.* The few connected passages which we know (esp. in NON. 385, 7, also PRISC. GL. 2, 386, 13) prove his style to have been discursive and circumstantial. Hence the abridgment mentioned in DIOM. GL. 1, 365, 7 *apud Fenestellam in libro epitomarum secundo: quemadmodum Caesar a piratis captus sit* etc., such as were also made of Fannius (§ 137, 4 ad fin.), Coelius (§ 137, 6 ad fin.), Livius (§ 256, 10), Trogus (§ 258, 5), Valerius Maximus (§ 279, 9), and of several works of Varro and others (§ 165, 1 ad fin.). The quotation *ut Fenestella in Achaicis* (or *Arch.*) *scribit* is based only on Fulgentius (mythol. 3, 2) and is therefore worthless.

3. Fenestella is quoted as an authority for numerous statements concerning the Roman constitution and ritual, e.g. on provocatio, the quaestors, the XVviri, the leges Aureliae, the dies festi and profesti, the Roman year, the ludi circenses, libri sibyllini, also on the expense of the aqua Marcia; concerning costume (togae rasae, uniones, anuli aurei, calcei), silver vessels, money, domestic life (fish, introduction of olea, rise of luxury) and literary history (on Terence and Cicero). But we never find his annales quoted as the source of any of these statements (except in the very uncertain passage in NON. 154, 16). The definite quotations from the Annals actually bear the stamp of a historical relation, but those other statements have something of a philosophical character, though connected with numerical dates (MERCKLIN p. 10). SEN. ep. 108, 31 also says: *aeque notat* (Cic. in Rep.) . . . *provocationem ad populum etiam a regibus fuisse; id ita in ponti-*

ficalibus libris, et alii putant et Fenestella. The manner in which Fenestella is here associated with the pontificales libri agrees with the combination of his name with those of Gracchanus (§ 138, 2) and Trebatius (who wrote de religionibus, § 207, 3) in Ulpian, dig. 1, 13, 1, 1 *et Junius et Trebatius et Fenestella scribunt.* We can scarcely connect with this the designation of him as *annalium commentator* (rather='author') in Tertull. adv. Valent. 34. Pliny mentions and uses him as an authority in b. 8 (de elephantis etc.), 9 (de aquatilium natura), 14, 15 (frugiferae arbores), 33 (metals), 35 (painting).

4. The fragments of Fenestella were last collected by HPeter, hist. fragm 272, and in Frotscher's edition of Corte's Sallust (Lpz. 1825) 1, 489 (additions by LMercklin, de Fen. p. 12, and by JPoeth, de Fen. p. 21).—LMercklin, de Fenestella historico et poeta, Dorpat 1844. JPoeth, de Fen. historiarum scriptore et carminum, Bonn 1849.

5. The work de magistratibus et sacerdotiis Romanorum published under the name of LFenestella (e.g. Vindob. 1510. Paris 1530. 1535) is the composition of the Canon ADFiocchi († 1452), and was also edited under his name (Floccus) by Aegid. Witsius 1561. The fact that the author (fol. 6[b] of the Vienna ed.) compares the different ranks of the Roman flamines with the Christian bishops, archbishops, cardinals etc. proves that he did not intend an absolute forgery. OMeinertz, d. Hss. und alten Drucke zu Braunsberg, 1882, 11.

6. Suet. gr. 20 *fuit (Hyginus) familiarissimus Ovidio poetae et Clodio Licino consulari historico, qui eum . . . tradit liberalitate sua quoad vixerit sustentatum.* He is no doubt the cos. suff. of a. 757/4 a.d. (ex Kal. Iul.) C. Clodius Licinus (Orelli 644. 3260. CIL. 1, p. 473 sq. p. 180), and perhaps also identical with *Clodius Licinus in libro III rerum romanarum* quoted by Livy (29, 22, 10) (for a. 561/194) with rather astonishing accuracy. To the same writer we should probably refer Nonius 535, 20 (*Claudius rerum romanarum libro XII*) and 221, 13 (*Licinius rerum romanarum libro XXI*). Cf. § 156, 6 and HPeter, hist. fragm. p. xxiii. It would therefore, seem that he began his history with the Punic wars and carried it down to the time of Augustus. MHertz, de historic. 1871 p. 4.

7. Sen. ep. 114, 17 *L. Arruntius, vir rarae frugalitatis* (Vell. 2, 86, 2 of a. 723/31 *L. Arruntii, prisca gravitate celeberrimi, fides*), *qui historias belli punici scripsit, fuit Sallustianus et in illud genus nitens.* 18 *quae apud Sallustium rara fuerunt apud hunc crebra sunt et paene continua.* 19 *Arruntius in primo libro belli punici.* He is no doubt the same Arruntius who is mentioned by Plin. NH. in his list of authorities in b. 3. 5. 6 (Spain, Africa, Asia). This historian was probably L. Arruntius L. f. L. n. cos. 732/22, the father of the consul of the same name a. 759/6 a.d. † 790/37. To the latter refer Tac. ann. 11, 6 *meminissent . . . recentiorum Arruntii et Aeservini* (§ 267, 8): *ad summa provectos incorrupta vita et facundia* and Sen. contr. 7, praef. 7 (a diligent pleader before the court of the centumviri). KNipperdey, op. 409. GZippel, d. Losung der Proconsuln, Königsb. 1883, 16.

8. Annius Fetialis, mentioned by Pliny among his authorities in b. 16, 33 and 36, and quoted 34, 29 as an authority for the statement that the statue of Cloelia rather represented a Valeria. Conjectures on this in Schwegler, RG. 2, 8, HPeter, hist. rell. 1, cccxviii. LUrlichs, d. Quellenregister zu Plin. letzten BB. (Würzb. 1878) 5.

9. Suet. Aug. 79 *Iulius Marathus, libertus et a memoria eius* (Augustus), . . . *tradit;* cf. ib. 94 *auctor est I. M.* (of a legend in praise of Augustus).

10. SUET. Vitell. 1 *extatque elogi* (cf. § 81, 2) *ad Q. Vitellium divi Augusti quaestorem* (the uncle of the emperor Vitellius, cf. SUET. Vitell. 2. Tac. a. 2, 48. DIO 51, 22) *libellus* on the history of the gens Vitellia, evidently a party pamphlet in eulogy of the family, which was then becoming powerful (§ 80).—On Cremutius Cordus see § 277, 1.—On T. Labienus see § 267, 10. On the historical works of Hyginus and Verrius Flaccus, see § 261, 1. 262, 2.

260. As concerns the grammarians, Sinnius Capito followed the example of earlier writers in composing both grammatical works and such as treated of the history of literature. Varro's influence on Sinnius appears in the national tendency of his investigations and in the epistolary form adopted by him.

1. GELL. 5, 20, 1 *soloecismus, . . . a Sinnio Capitone eiusdemque aetatis aliis imparilitas appellatus, vetustioribus Latinis stribiligo dicebatur.* 5, 21, 9–11 *Sinni Capitonis, doctissimi viri* (cf. HIERON. in n. 2), *epistulae sunt uno in libro multae positae . . . in templo Pacis* (§ 219, 21 l. 5). *prima epistula scripta est ad Pacuvium Labeonem* (§ 207, 6). . . . *in ea rationes grammaticas posuit per quas docet 'pluria' latinum esse, 'plura' barbarum.* 5, 20, 2 *Sinnius Capito in litteris quas ad Clodium Tuscum dedit.* Cf. FEST. 162 (*si diligentius inspiciatur, ut fecit Sinnius Capito*). 170. To the same class we should probably add the *liber de syllabis . . . Sinni Capitonis* mentioned by POMPEIUS GL. 5, 110, 2. Cf. JBECKER, ZfAW. 1847, no. 133. In his etymologies (FEST. 138. 230. 340) Capito, like Nigidius (§ 170, 4) appears to rely on mere empirical analysis of the Latin.

2. LACTANT. inst. 6, 20, 35, *Sinnius Capito in libris spectaculorum docet.* Cf. FEST. 326. 364. MHERTZ l.l. 20. His explanations of proverbial phrases (FEST. 145. 261. 282. 322. 325. 334) were probably contained in a work specially devoted to this subject. HERTZ l.l. p. 22. 32; Phil. 1, 610. Geographical and ethnographical investigations? HIERON. in Gen. 3, p. 319 Vall. *legamus Varronis de antiquitatibus libros et Sinnii Capitonis et Graecum Phlegonta ceterosque eruditissimos viros, et videbimus omnes paene insulas* etc. HERTZ l.l. 23. 30, who uses this passage in support of his assumption that Sinnius Capito, like Varro, wrote a comprehensive work, Antiquitates or De antiquitatibus, in which he stored up his investigations on subjects of Roman religion, polity, and law. CWACHSMUTH, in his ed. of Lydus de ostent. p. xx, understands also LYD. ost. 3 (p. 6, 16) and de magistr. prooem. (ὅ τε Καπίτων καὶ Φοντήϊος) as referring to this.—MHERTZ, Sinnius Capito, Berl. 1845 (with a collection of the fragments). Cf. EGGER, vet. serm. lat. reliqq. p. 63.

261. Fenestella's and Sinnius Capito's tendency in the investigation of antiquarian lore and their Varronian direction were shared by the learned freedman M. Verrius Flaccus, chiefly known by his Fasti and his comprehensive lexicon entitled de verborum significatu, a rich store-house of the most important information concerning Roman antiquities and old Latin. We possess part of the copious abridgment made of this work by Pompeius Festus, which is unfortunately incomplete: only the

second half, and this badly mutilated, is now extant. On the other hand the abridgment of Festus by Paulus Diaconus, which is preserved intact, offers only a dry skeleton of the original work.

1. SUETON. gr. 17 *M.* (so in the ind. gramm. p. 98 R) *Verrius Flaccus libertinus docendi genere maxime inclaruit. . . . quare ab Augusto quoque nepotibus eius* (born 734/20 and 737/17) *praeceptor electus transiit in Palatium cum tota schola* (probably about 744/10 B.C.) . . . *decessit aetatis exactae sub Tiberio.* On his renown as a teacher see also § 263, 2. HIERON. ad a. Abr. 2024 = 761/8 A.D. . . . *et M. Verrius Flaccus grammaticus insignes habentur* fixes his floruit too late. The Praenestine Fasti of Verrius (see below) are brought down in the original work to about 760/7, the additions (perhaps made by Verrius himself) inscribed on the stone to shortly before 775/22. MOMMSEN, CIL. 1, p. 295ª. SUET. l.l. adds: *statuam habet Praeneste* (his birthplace?? OHIRSCHFELD, Herm. 9, 105. AREIFFERSCHEID, ind. schol. Vratisl. 1877/78 p. 5) *in inferiore* (*superiore*) *fori parte, circa* (not *contra* with JVAHLEN, ind. schol. Berol. 1877/78 p. 4: see AREIFFERSCHEID l.l. p. 4) *hemicyclium in quo fastos a se ordinatos et marmoreo parieti incisos publicarat.* The Fasti are still partly extant: § 74, 3. On their employment in Ovid's Fasti: § 249, 6.—The inscription M. VERRIO T. F. FAL. FLACCO CELSVS FRATER (CWKING, BerlphWschr. 1887, 158) now in Cambridge has as little to do with the grammarian, who was a freedman, as the spurious one CIL. 14, 278* ORELLI 1167. 4009, which used formerly to be taken in reference to him. *Verrius Flaccus, iuris pontificii peritissimus* in MACR. 1, 15, 21 might perhaps be the manumitter of the grammarian; it is however more likely that Veranius was meant. Cf. § 199, 4.

2. The fragments of Verrius are collected in OMÜLLER's edition of Festus (praef. p. XIII). GELL. 4, 5, 6 *in Verri Flacci libro 1 rerum memoria dignarum.* From the same source may be derived the information borrowed by PLINIUS NH. b. 3. 7. 8. 9. 14. 15. 18. 28. 29. 33–35 *ex Verrio* (*Flacco*). GELL. 17, 6, 2 *libri . . . Verrii Flacci de obscuris Catonis* (§ 122, 4). *in libro II scriptum est* etc. 5, 17, 1 (and 18, 2) *Verrius Flaccus in quarto de verborum significatu.* SCHOL. VERON. ad Aen. 10, 183 and 200 (p. 103 K.) *Flaccus primo Etruscarum.* MACR. 1, 4, 7 (cf. ib. 1, 8, 5) *Verrius Flaccus in eo libello qui Saturnus inscribitur.* Vague quotations concerning Roman ritual ib. 1, 6, 15. 1, 10, 7. 1, 12, 15. LACTANT. inst. 1, 20. SERV. Aen. 8, 203. 11, 143 (*alii, sicut Varro et Verrius Flaccus, dicunt*). Concerning his (questionable) studies on Vergil see RIBBECK, prolegg. Verg. p. 175. SUET. gr. 19 *Scribonius Aphrodisius . . . docuit quo Verrius tempore, cuius etiam libris de orthographia rescripsit, non sine insectatione studiorum morumque eius.* From this work are probably derived the statements on the orthographical views of Verrius Flaccus in Charisius, Diomede, Velius Longus and others. HNETTLESHIP, journ. of phil. 15, 189. If the disquisitions given there with regard to gender, accidence, and etymology be derived from the same work, it would appear that Verrius took orthography in the sense of spelling in conformity with linguistic rules. Like Varro, he used the epistolary form in his grammatical disquisitions; SERV. Aen. 8, 423 *antea* HOC *adverbium loci fuit; . . . nam crebro in antiquis lectionibus invenitur, sicut in epistolis probat Verrius Flaccus exemplis, auctoritate, ratione.* The origo gentis romanae (§ 414, 5) is attributed by BSEPP, p. 45 of his ed. of the work, to Verrius Flaccus!

3. The work de verborum significatu was alphabetically arranged by Verrius, so that each letter extended over a number of books, e.g. *P* over at least

five (FEST. 326 b, 2 *causam Verrius in libro V quorum prima est P litera reddidit*), *A* over at least four (see GELL. in n. 2), and *S* over several books in the same way (FEST. 309 a, 5). Within each separate letter two distinct portions may be discerned: in the 'first (and larger) portion' the lemmata are arranged alphabetically according to the first and second and often according to the three first letters, in the 'second portion' no attention is paid to the second and third letter, but on the contrary we find connected groups of glossae, e.g. for each author, Cato, Plautus and so forth, and numerous quotations from authors who are not cited in the 'first portions' (Antistius Labeo § 265, 2, Veranius § 199, 4, Messalla augur § 199, 2). Cf. on this OMÜLLER pref. to his ed. p. XVI. OGRUPPE, commentatt. Mommsen. 547. HNETTLESHIP, Americ. journ. of phil. 1 (1880), 253. 2 (1881), 1. FHOFFMANN, de Festo quaestt. 21. RREITZENSTEIN, Verrianische Forsch., Bresl. 1887. This fact is difficult to account for: the most plausible explanation is that of REITZENSTEIN, that the 'second portions' also belong to Verrius (not to Festus) and are part of the collection of materials from which by a revision and recasting in strict alphabetical order Verrius attempted to restore the 'first portions.' He would appear to have been unable to carry out this attempt, and the work to have been hastily got ready for publication after his death.—Of the later poets only Lucretius and Vergil (all his poems) are mentioned by Verrius with any frequency; others are never quoted, e.g. Horace (§ 219, 17). The date of the composition of the work may be inferred from 154 b, 7 *cum mansisset ab urbe condita ad principatum Augusti Caesaris inviolatum*, and 347, 25 *ubi nunc est aedis Concordiae inter Capitolium et forum*, this temple having been consecrated a. 763/10 A.D. Hence the work would appear to be one of the latest of Verrius. See MERKEL on Ovid's Fasti p. XCIV.

4. Festus probably explained his treatment of Verrius' work in the preface, which is lost together with the first half of his work. Verrius is frequently mentioned by name in Festus (and Paulus). Festus tries rather obtrusively to assert his independence with regard to the author on whom he has founded his work: he often applies to Verrius cheap criticism, and makes various trivial additions. Cf. 218 b, 1 *cuius* (i.e. Verrius) *opinionem neque in hoc neque in aliis compluribus refutare minime necesse est, cum propositum habeam ex tanto librorum eius numero intermortua iam et sepulta verba atque ipso saepe confitente nullius usus aut auctoritatis praeterire, et reliqua quam brevissime redigere in libros admodum paucos* (fortunately he is not consistent in the execution of this plan). *ea autem de quibus dissentio et aperte et breviter, ut sciero, scripta in iis* (*his* in the MS.) *libris meis invenientur* ⟨*qui*⟩ *inscribuntur 'priscorum verborum cum exemplis.'* Thus in the first place Festus gives an abridgment of Verrius, in the second place he is preparing a work in which he proposes to justify his contradiction of V. Of the latter nothing is otherwise known.—Cf. also 209 a, 12 *cur hoc loco relatum sit a Verrio, cum de significatu verborum scribere propositum habuerit, equidem non video;* also 360, 34 *quod ad significationem verborum non magis pertinet quam plurima alia et praeterita iam et deinceps quae referentur.* 326 b, 30 *quam inconstantiam Verrii nostri non sine rubore rettuli.* 329 a, 23 SPONDERE *Verrius putat dictum quod . . ., deinde oblitus inferiore capite . . . ait quod* etc. (v. *monstrum* 138 *inde dici apparet id quartum quod mihi visum est adiciendum, praesertim cum ex eadem significatione pendeat et in promptu sit omnibus*). 309 a, 5 SUBURAM *Verrius alio libro*—that is 302 a, 15—*a pago Succusano dictam ait, hoc vero maxime probat eorum auctoritatem qui aiunt* etc. 206 b, 19 *sed, ut mihi videtur.* 209 a, 26 . . . *Verrius ait: mihi non satis persuadet.* 214 b, 11 . . . *ait Verrius: mihi id falsum videtur, nam* etc. 261 a, 14 *non, ut V. putat.* 294 a, 29 ⟨SUDUM *Verrius ait sig*⟩*nificare sub*⟨*udum. sed*

auctor⟩um omnium fere ⟨exempla poscunt ut sud⟩us siccum significet. 340 b, 30 *quod totum Verrius ἀπιθάνως introduxit.* 347b, 23 *inquit Verrius . . . absurde, ut mihi videtur.* 351 b, 14 *quod quam aniliter rela⟨tum sit cui⟩vis manifestum est* and other passages. The quotations from Lucan (34, 11) and Martial (369, 2) were added by Festus.

5. The age in which Sex. Pompeius Festus lived is not known, but he quotes Lucan and Martial (n. 4 ad fin.) and is himself quoted by CHARISIUS (i.e. Julius Romanus) GL. 1, 220, 28 (*Porphyrio ex Verrio et Festo*), also by MACROBIUS (sat. 3, 3, 10 and 3, 5, 7 *Pompeius Festus*, 3, 8, 9 *Iulius Festus de verborum significationibus libro XIII*), also in the gl. Philox. p. 6[d], 27 Labb. '*Adoriosus* ἔνδοξος, ὡς Πομπήϊος. *Ador* νίκη, ὡς Πομπήϊος' (cf. Paul. p. 3. 12). Porphyrio (see § 374, 3) quotes him, hence Festus must have lived before the 3rd cent. A.D. He divided his abridgment into 20 books of nearly equal size, without arranging that each book should begin a new letter (OMÜLLER p. XXXI).—We possess the work in only one MS. (see RhM. 17, 310), cod. Farnesinus s. XI (now at Naples), which was no doubt complete in that century. Of the 16 quaternios (each of 16 double columns) of which the MS. originally consisted, the quaternios VIII–XVI (commencing with the second half of *M*) were before 1477 brought by Manilios Ralles Kabakes from Illyria to Rome (to Pomponius Laetus), and even these were badly injured by fire in the outer column. Of these nine three have long since been lost again (q. VIII, X, XVI) and are known to us only in the copies made of them in the 15th cent., e.g. by Pomponius Laetus (the so-called schedae Pomponii Laeti). The copy made by Politian (important for q. XV) is preserved in the Vatic. 3368. PDENOLHAC, rev. de phil. 10, 145; biblioth. de FOrsini. Par. 1887, 212; also a collation of the same with the ed. Ald. 1513 by PVICTORIUS, now in Munich. Other editions of importance for the text are those of Milan 1500 and of FURSINUS 1581, and also the much interpolated copies Vatic. 1549. 2731. Voss. O 9. Cf. OMÜLLER pref. to his ed. p. II. REITZENSTEIN l.l. 97. Additions to the collation of the Farnesinus in Müller's ed. are given by HKEIL, RhM. 6, 618. Cf. also MOMMSEN, Festi codicis quaternionem XVI[um] denuo edidit, Abh. d. Berl. Ak. 1864, p. 57. Important extracts from Festus in the glossaries (§ 42): cf. HKETTNER, Bemerkk. zu Varro u. lat. Glossaren (Halle 1868) 85. GLOEWE, in the commentatt. philol. (Lpz. 1874) 243; prodrom. gloss. 193. 234 and esp. GGOETZ, RhM. 40, 324; melet. Festina, Jena 1885. 87 II.

6. Just as Festus' abridgment may originally have contributed to the loss of the original work, Festus himself was in his turn superseded by his epitomiser, whom BETHMANN in Pertz' Arch. 10, 320 erroneously considered not to be identical with Paulus Diaconus (§ 500, 6): both the date of the epitomiser and his attitude towards Charlemagne are appropriate to Paulus Diaconus, while the style of the preface, except for a few phrases, agrees with that of the works of Paul. Diac. and Festus is often quoted in this writer's historia romana. GWAITZ, Gött. gel. Anz. 1876, 1520 and pref. to his scriptores rer. Langob. et Ital. s. VI–IX (Hanover 1878) p. 19. In the missive to Charlemagne which serves as a preface we read: *Sextus Pompeius . . . opus suum ad XX usque prolixa volumina extendit. ex qua ego prolixitate superflua quaeque et minus necessaria praetergrediens et quaedam abstrusa penitus stilo proprio enucleans, nonnulla ita ut erant posita relinquens, haec vestrae celsitudini legendum compendium obtuli.* Paulus ruthlessly adapted the abridgment of Festus to the very moderate demands of his own period. But the original work was so rich and extensive that even this repeated abridging, diluting and bungling could not efface all its original wealth. Paulus deserves praise for his almost complete abstinence from additions of his own (cf. 36, 3 the quotation from

Roman customs 1, 14). As he copies even the orthographical mistakes of the cod. Farnes. of Festus or avoids them by omitting the words in question, it seems that he used the same MS. of Festus as the copyist of the Farnesinus. See OMüller's praef. p. xxxii. viii. GGoetz, nova melet. Fest., Jen. 1887, vi. vii. The abridgment of Paulus exists in a great many MSS.: among the most important are Monac. 14734 s. X/XI, Leid. Voss. 116, Trecensis 2291 s. X/XI (cf. EThewrewk de Ponor, mélanges Graux, Par. 1884, 659), Escorialens. O III 31 etc. Cf. EThewrewk, Ungarische Revue 1, 80.

7. Editions of Festus and Paulus: cf. Müller's praef, p. xxxv. Festus and Paulus were separated and a critical treatment inaugurated by AAugustinus, Ven. 1559 and elsewhere. Excellent contributions to the criticism of the whole are found in JScaliger's castigationes, first ed. 1565. With supplements by Fulvius Ursinus, Rome 1581. Cum nott. varr., Par. 1584. Notis illustr. ADacier, Paris 1681 and Amst. 1700. In Lindemann's Corp. gramm. II, and separately Lpz. 1832. Edidit AEEgger, Par. 1838. Principal edition; emendata et annotata a COMüller, Lpz. 1839; a new unaltered edition of this, Lpz. 1880. Ed. EThewrewk de Ponor I, Pesth 1889.

8. HNettleship, lectures and essays 201. FHoffmann, de Festi de verbb. signif. quaestt., Königsb. 1886.—ELeidolph, de Festi et Pauli locis Plautinis in the commentt. Jenens. 2 (1883), 199. HEDirksen, d. röm. rechtl. Quellen des Verr. Fl. u. Fest., hinterlass. Schrr. 1, 64. SBugge, Altlatein bei Fest. u. Paul., JJ. 105, 91. GKettner, Beobachtungen über d. Benutzung des Verr. Fl. (in the Festprogramm f. Meissen), Pforta 1879.—Criticism e.g. LMercklin, obss. ad etc., Dorpat 1860, WCorssen (Phil. 20, 730), Mommsen, Berl. Akad. 1864, p. 66, MVoigt, RhM. 31, 149 and others.

262. Augustus' freedman and librarian C. Julius Hyginus (c. 690/64 B.C.–770/17 A.D.?) combined the studies of Varro with those of Nigidius Figulus. He imitated Varro in the variety and in the national direction of his literary activity and attained respect. He wrote de situ urbium italicarum and on celebrated men of Roman history; but he also wrote commentaries on one of Cinna's poems and on Vergil's works and composed original treatises on agriculture and the treatment of bees. In imitation of Nigidius, Hyginus composed works on theology and astrology, which seem, however, to have been more sober than those of Nigidius.—We possess under the name of Hyginus two school-treatises on mythology; the so-called Fabulae, which are especially valuable on account of the extensive use made of the tragic literature of the Greeks, but which we have in an abridged form and unclassical diction; and four books de astrologia from Alexandrine sources, in a better text, but also abridged. Both works are no doubt by the same writer; but it is doubtful whether this Hyginus is identical with the Augustan writer Julius Hyginus.

1. Suet. gr. 20 *C. Iulius Hyginus, Augusti libertus, natione Hispanus—nonnulli*

Alexandrinum putant et a Caesare puerum Romam adductum Alexandria capta (a. 707/47). On account of his apprenticeship to Alexander Polyhistor (see below), who as an adult received from Sulla (therefore 676/78 at latest) the rights of Roman citizenship, we can hardly suppose Hyginus to have been born later than 690/64, as *familiarissimus Ovidio* (see below) would otherwise suggest. He is erroneously supposed to have been even earlier than Vergil (born 684/70) by RReitzenstein de scriptor. R.R., Berlin 1884, 18, who draws this conclusion from Colum. 1, 1, 13 (see n. 3). Suet. l.l.: *studiose et audiit et imitatus est Cornelium Alexandrum grammaticum graecum, quem propter antiquitatis notitiam Polyhistorem multi . . . vocabant* (hence perhaps Hyginus is styled Alexandrinus). *praefuit palatinae bybliothecae* (founded a. 726/28), *nec eo secius plurimos docuit; fuitque familiarissimus Ovidio poetae* (who addressed trist. 3, 14 perhaps to him) *et Clodio Licino* (§ 259, 6), . . . *qui eum admodum pauperem decessisse tradit. . . . huius libertus fuit Iulius Modestus, in studiis vestigia patroni secutus.* This is carelessly excerpted by Jerome on Euseb. chron. ad a. Abr. 2008=745/9: *C. Iulius Hyginus, cognomento Polyhistor* (!), *grammaticus habetur inlustris.* When Columella (1, 1, 13) wrote, Hyginus had long been dead (n. 3). As early as in Fest. 182a, 16 *Yginus* is quoted together with Aelius Gallus and Cornificius.—ChrBBunte, de C. Iulii Hygini . . . vita et scriptis I, Marb. 1846; also in his edition of the Fabulae p. 1. Cf. also GFUnger, Abh. d. Münch. Akad. 16, 196. 205. 209. 217 sqq.

2. Gell. 1, 14, 1 *Iulius Hyginus dicit in libro de vita rebusque inlustrium virorum sexto.* Ascon. ad Cic. Pis. p. 13 Or. 12 K.-S. *Varronem tradere . . . Iulius Hyginus dicit in libro priore de viris claris.* Does this indicate two divisions, or, as is more probable (see § 259, 2 in fin.), two versions, a shorter and a longer? Unger l.l. takes the two books *de viris claris* (i.e. *de imperatoribus Rom.* and *de Romanis in toga claris*) to be the distinctive title of part of the viri illustres, which is however refuted by the wording in Asconius. Cf. also Gell. 6, 1, 2 (and 6) *et C. Oppius* (§ 197, 3) *et Iulius Hyginus aliique qui de vita et rebus Africani scripserunt* and Hieronymus above § 211, 2. On the sources of Hygin. de vir. ill. see HHildesheimer, de libro de vir. ill. Urb. Rom., Berl. 1880, p. 63. On the conjectures of GFUnger, who attributes to Hyginus the book on the generals usually ascribed to Cornelius Nepos, see § 198, 7 (cf. also Unger, Phil. 43, 431).—Gell. 10, 18, 7 *Hyginus in exemplis refert* (cf. § 198, n. 4, 3). Serv. Aen. 5, 389 *secundum Hyginum, qui de familiis troianis scripsit* (with Varro, above p. 259, e). Macr. 3, 4, 13 *Hyginus in libro quem de dis penatibus scripsit.* 3, 2, 13 *Hyginus* (so Mommsen CIL. 1, p. 26: the MSS. read *Hyllus*) *libro quem de dis composuit.* 3, 8, 4 *Hyginus de proprietatibus deorum, cum de astris ac de stellis loqueretur, ait* etc. Cf. Non. 518, 35. From this (or from the Genealogiae, see n. 6) may be derived what Paulin. Nol. carm. 36, 131–143 states as Hyginus' view on Vesta.—Serv. Aen. 3, 553 *secundum Hyginum, qui scripsit de situ urbium italicarum;* cf. ib. 1, 277. 530. 7, 412 (*H. in ital. urb.*). 8, 597 (*in urb. it.*). 600. 7, 678 (*de urb. it.*). 8, 638 (*de origine urbium it.*). Macr. 5, 18, 16 (*Iulius Hyg. in libro II urbium*); cf. ib. 1, 7, 19 (*ut Hyginus Protarchum Trallianum secutus tradit*). HPeter, hist. fragm. 280.

3. Charis. GL. 1, 142 *Hyginus de agricultura II.* Cf. Colum. 1, 1, 13 *nec postremo quasi paedagogi eius* (of Vergil in the georg.; cf. GFUnger l.l.) *meminisse dedignemur, Iulii Hygini . . . non minorem tamen laudem meruerunt nostrorum temporum viri, Cornelius Celsus* etc.; according to this Hyginus' work was published before Vergil's georg. (which came out 724/30), and, as Varro de RR. (published 717/37) does not mention it, it must have appeared after the latter work; cf. RReitzenstein, de scriptt. RR. 19. GFUnger l.l. 220 takes a different view. 3, 11, 8 *Hyginus, secutus Tremellium* (§ 160, 2). 11, 2, 83. 11, 3, 62. Pliny who cites him (always

as *Hyg.*) in his list of sources for the NH. b. 3–6 (geography, see n. 2 in fin.) 10–22 (zoology and botany) mentions him NH. 13, 134. 16, 230. 18, 232. 19, 88. 20, 116. 21, 53. He also wrote separately on bees, or this may have formed part of his work de agricultura; cf. against this view RReitzenstein l.l. 191. Colum. 9, 13, 8 *Hyginus in eo libro quem de apibus scripsit;* cf. ib. 9, 13, 6. 9, 11, 5 (*H. auctoritatem Graecorum sequens*). 9, 13, 3. 9, 14, 1–18. Plin. NH. 20, 116. On the character of this work see Colum. 9, 2, 1 *de quibus* (bee-hives) *neque diligentius quidquam praecipi potest quam ab Hygino iam dictum est nec ornatius quam Vergilio . . . Hyginus veterum auctorum placita secretis dispersa monimentis industrie collegit . . . ea quae Hyginus fabulose tradita de originibus apum non intermisit poeticae magis licentiae quam nostrae fidei concesserim.* PRusch, on Hygin. de apibus (used in Plin. NH. b. 11, 21) in the commentatt. sodal. philol. Gryphisw. 1887, 42.—Gloss. Labb. p. 128c *Paleta* (read *Pala*)*: σφενδόνη δακτυλίου, ὡς Ὑγῖνος ἐν τῷ* (the name of the work is missing).

4. Charis. GL. 1, 134 *Iulius Hyginus in Cinnae propemptico* (cf. § 213, 3). Gellius 16, 6, 14 (on Aen. 4, 57) *Hyginus Iulius, qui ius pontificum non videtur ignorasse, in quarto librorum quos de Vergilio fecit.* Hence also Macr. 6, 9, 7 *Hyginus, qui ius pontificium non ignoravit, in quinto librorum quos de Vergilio fecit.* Gellius 1, 21, 2 *Hyginus, non hercle ignobilis grammaticus, in commentariis quae in Vergilium fecit*, states that *in libro qui fuerit ex domo atque ex familia Vergilii* he found *amaror* georg. 2, 247. 7, 6, 2 sqq. Gellius defends Vergil against the censure of Julius Hyginus (concerning *praepes*), and 10, 15 notices a number of objections made to the Aeneid by Hyginus in order to show that it had never been completed. (1 *reprehendit Hyginus Vergilium correcturumque eum fuisse existimat.* 11 *item hoc quoque in eodem libro reprehendit et correcturum fuisse Vergilium putat nisi mori occupasset.* 14 *item in his versibus errasse Vergilium dicit.* 18 *versus . . . quem Vergilius procul dubio exempturus fuit*). See also Serv. on Aen. 2, 15. 7, 47. 12, 120. Bunte p. 22. Ribbeck, prolegg. Vergil. p. 117. The doubt expressed concerning the identity of the commentator on Vergil and C. Julius Hyginus by FBorgius, de tempp. quibus Verg. georg. scripta sint 27 is unfounded.

5. De astrologia or astronomia, de ratione sphaerae and so forth are the headings which the work generally entitled Poetica astronomica bears in the MSS.; see Bursian JJ. 93, 761. The work is cited only by Isidorus de nat. deorum 17, 1. 19, 1. 48, 1, and simply as *Hyginus* without any mention of the title (see Bursian, Münch. SBer. 1876 1, 1). It is dedicated to an otherwise unknown person, M. Fabius, who is thus addressed in the preface: *etsi te studio grammaticae artis inductum non solum versuum moderatione . . . sed historiarum quoque varietate . . . praestare video, . . . tamen . . . ne nihil in adolescentia laborasse dicerer et imperitorum iudicio desidiae subirem crimen, hoc velut rudimento scientiae scripsi ad te.* Then follows the table of contents. After this we read: *in his igitur tam multis et variis rebus non erit mirum aut pertimescendum quod tantum numerum versuum scripserimus; . . . quodsi longiōr in sermone visus fuero, non mea facunditate, sed rei necessitate factum existimato, . . . etenim praeter nostram scriptionem sphaerae quae fuerunt ab Arato obscurius dicta persecuti planius ostendimus. . . . quodsi vel optimis usus auctoribus effeci ut neque brevius neque verius diceret quispiam* etc. *ideoque maioribus etiam niti laboribus cogitamus. . . . etenim necessariis nostris hominibus scientissimis maximas res scripsimus, non levibus occupati rebus populi captamus existimationem.* The sources he used are especially the *καταστερισμοί* of Eratosthenes, with which Hyginus in b. 2 and 3 is in complete accord (see the comparison in Robert l.l.), and other Alexandrine writers (Parmeniskos, Asklepiades,

Istros, Euhemeros, Aratos, Kallimachos etc.), see Robert l.l. 221. Cicero's translation of Aratos is quoted 3, 29 and 4, 3. The end is defective. Of the MSS. Vatic. (Reginensis) 1260 s. IX, Montepessul. 334 s. X, Voss. s. IX–X, SGall. s. IX, Dresd. s. IX–X are specially important; later, much interpolated MSS. are very numerous. On the history of MSS. see ECHHeydenreich, die Freiberger Hyginh., Lpz. 1878. On a MS. in tachygraphic notes which Pope Julius II received *e Dacia* see RFörster, JJ. 121, 56.—In the editions this work is generally joined to the Fabulae, especially in the Mythographi of Commelinus, Muncker and van Staveren n. 6 ad fin.; rec. BBunte, Dresd. 1875 (on this esp. CBursian, Münch. SBer. 1876, 1, 1). Book 2 and in fragments also in CRobert's ed. of the catasterism. of Eratosth., Berl. 1878. Cf. also Kiehl, Mnemosyne 2, 88 sqq. LWHasper, Hyginus philosophus de imaginibus coeli (=Hyg. de astr. b. 3). Lpz. 1861. Cf. Bursian, Lit. Centralbl. 1861, 854 and JJ. 93, 785, n. 46.—BBunte, eine französ. Bearbeitung der Astron., Herrig's Archiv 56, 155.

6. 'Fabulae'. Hygin. astr. 2, 12 *de quo in primo libro genealogiarum scripsimus* (cf. 2, 17 *nos* [*nostri* in the MSS.] *in progenie deorum*). The first part of the fabulae consists in genealogies of the gods (see below). Dosith. Ἑρμηνεύματα libr. III p. 65 *Maximo et Apro coss.* (a.d. 207) *a. d. III id. Sept. Hygini genealogiam omnibus notam descripsi, in qua erunt* (*erant* emended by Bursian p. 769) *plures historiae interpretatae in hoc libro* = Μαξίμῳ καὶ Ἄπρῳ ὑπάτοις πρὸ γ' εἰδῶν Σεπτεμβρίων Ὑγίνου γενεαλογίαν πᾶσιν γνωστὴν μετέγραψα, ἐν ᾗ ἔσονται πλείονες ἱστορίαι διηρμηνευμέναι ἐν τούτῳ τῷ βιβλίῳ (copied also in MSchmidt Hyg. p. liv). A comparison of what Dositheus gives with the extant fabulae of Hyginus (Bunte, Hyg. fab. p. 18. Lange l.l. p. 6) proves the identity. The extant work begins with a scanty genealogy of the gods and heroes resembling a catalogue; it is followed by the main subject, a recital of the whole mythological subject-matter specially requisite for understanding the poets, according to the different cycles of legend (the title Fabulae was given by Mycillus to the whole work with special reference to this main subject); the conclusion consists of indices, which divide the subject-matter and collate it according to topics. Cf. MSchmidt p. xxvii. CBursian, JJ. 93, 773. Owing to long use in the schools and corrupt transmission the work, in comparison with its original condition, has been greatly damaged (by erasures, additions, inversions etc.). The greater part of the work as it stands is evidently translated from one or more Greek sources. The original of the middle portion especially drew upon the dramatic literature of the Greeks and the epic poets. But little recourse was had to Roman sources (Vergil, Ovid; see n. 7. RFörster, Raub d. Perseph. 68. 87. 89. 289; cf. the heading fab. 8 *Eadem* [*Antiope*] *Euripidis, quam scribit Ennius.* At the end of the fabb. before the indices is now to be found a Latin fable concerning Care (220), in which the trochaic septenarii are still recognisable (§ 103, 1 ad fin.). There are many mistakes as to mythological names, Lange p. 19; cf. Bursian l.l. 784. The third part (the indices) is also based on very good ancient authorities. They contain short mythological collections of examples (also for the use of schools) in catch-words, e.g. *qui facti sunt ex mortalibus immortales, qui filias suas occiderunt, matres quae filios interfecerunt, quis quid invenerit, oppida qui quae condiderunt* etc. Besides the two palimpsest leaves saec. V or VI (discovered by Niebuhr in the Vatican library and edited Rome 1820, see § 180, 2; in Schmidt, Hyg. p. xlix), which appear to be derived from a still shorter version, the work has been preserved in only one MS. (Bursian's program, 1868, p. vii) the Frisingensis (saec. IX) of Micyllus (Bursian ib. p. iv) now lost except for a few fragments. On the fragments of this MS. see CHalm, Münch. SBer. 1870 1, 317. MSchmidt p. xlvii sq. On abstracts of Hyginus in the cod. Strozzianus of the

Germanicus-scholia s. XIV, which are based on a more correct tradition than that of the Frisengensis, see CRobert, Erätosth. catasterism. p. 210.—Editions by JMycillus, Bas. 1535 and 1549, HCommelinus, Heidelb. 1599, JScheffer, Hamb. 1674, ThMuncker, Mythographi latini, Amsterd. 1681, AvanStaveren, Auctores mythogr. lat., Leid. 1742, BBunte, Lps. 1857, MSchmidt, Jena 1872.—CLange, de nexu inter C.Iulii Hygini opera mythologica et fabularum qui nomen eius prae se fert librum; acc. fabb. transmutationum selectae, Mayence 1865. CBursian, JJ. 93, 761 and Ex Hygini Genealogiis excerpta . . . restituta, Zür. 1868; emendatt. Hygin., Jena 1874. EWölfflin, zur Kritik von H. Fabeln, Phil. 10, 303. MSchmidt, ib. 23, 47. 25, 416; RhM. 20, 459. RUnger, Phil. 35, 279. 46, 210. RSchöne, Herm. 6, 125. AOtto, JJ. 133, 281. GKnaack, Herm. 16, 585. MTschiassny, stud. Hyg., Vienna 1888 (compare BBunte, WschrfklPh. 1889, 59. 102. 123). LDietze, quaestt. Hyg., Kiel 1890. GKauffmann, de Hygini memoria, and see addenda to § 177a, 1.

7. The identity of the author of the Genealogy (fabulae) and of the Astrology cannot be doubted; see n. 6 init. But the question is: is he the Augustan writer? In confirmation of this we have only the name Hyginus (not Julius [or C. Julius] Hyginus) under which these works are transmitted and quoted (in Dosith. see n. 6 init. Isid. de rer. nat. 17. 19. 48): all the other data are contrary to this view, e.g. the fact that the author in the Astrology, which he—according to the fabulae—composed *in adolescentia* (see n. 5. 6), clearly betrays his use of the Metam. and Ibis of Ovid (cf. fab. 123 p. 106, 1. 2 Schm. = Ov. Ib. 301. 302; fab. 107 p. 97, 20 = Ov. met. 13, 391), and therefore wrote after 761/8 (§ 250, 3), at which date C. Julius Hyginus was over 70 years of age (see above). MSchmidt, Hygin. fab. p. xxxi. GFUnger, Abh. d. Münch. Ak. 16, 213. The awkward boastful style of the preface to the Astrologia (see n. 5), and the tiro-like mistakes in both works, and especially in the translations from the Greek, do not harmonise with the idea we should be inclined to form of the *grammaticus non hercle ignobilis* (see above, n. 4, l. 5). No quotations are found from any works of this kind by the latter (notwithstanding n. 2 l. 15). Lastly the latinity of both these works points to a later date. But the question becomes involved because we have neither of the books in their original form (this applies specially to the fabulae), see n. 5. 6: we have, for instance, of portions of the genealogiae (fabulae) three redactions of different tenor in Dositheus, in Niebuhr's leaves, and in the text of the Frisingensis. The gromatic writer Hyginus (§ 344, 1) is at all events not the author of these works (Bursian, JJ. 93, 767). The opinion (of CBursian, JJ. 93, 773) that the original work was composed in the second half of the second cent. A.D. is very probable (the reference in Dositheus, n. 6 l. 4 gives the terminus ante quem): but Bursian's attempt at the same time to explain the name of Hyginus from the use of a complete theogony by the Augustan writer is dubious, as nothing is known of any such work, and this conjecture would not equally account for the fact that the astrol. has also come down to us under the name of Hyginus.—It is therefore better to sever all connection with the Augustan writer and to attribute both works to some author unknown, who either adopted the disguise of the Augustan writer, or whose name was actually Hyginus. The latter is most probably the fact: for although the name of Hyginus was not of specially frequent occurrence among the Greeks (see however the indd. to CIG. and CIA.), yet in the Imperial period it was not at all unusual among Romans, as is proved by the inscriptions. This Hyginus III (if we designate the Augustan as I, the gromatic writer as II) wrote a) genealogiae in at least three books (see the quotation n. 6 l. 1), b) de astrologia (n. 5), c) he made preparations for a work on the legends of the gods

and heroes, cf. astr. 2, 12 p. 46, 22 B. *de qua* (Gorgo) *alio tempore plura dicemus;* 2, 20 p. 59, 25 *de qua* (the golden fleece) *alibi plura dicemus;* 2, 34 p. 73, 21 *sed quae post mortem eius* (Orion) *Diana fecerit in eius historiis dicemus.* Hyginus must actually have published this book of legends. This being presupposed, we may (following CRobert's apposite conjecture Eratosth. p. 236) conclude that the school text-book 'fabulae' before us was compiled from a) the genealogies and c) the book of legends of Hyginus III. It remains uncertain whether Hyginus or only the compiler added the indices (n. 6).

263. Besides this writer, the Augustan period possessed a considerable number of less important grammarians and professors, most of whom were also busied with literature. Such were Cloatius Verus, Caecilius Epirota, L. Crassicius, Scribonius Aphrodisius, and others. Clodius Tuscus wrote on subjects connected with worship. An astronomical calendar by this author is extant in the Greek translation of Laurentius Lydus. The works bearing the name of the physician Antonius Musa are of later origin.

1. Gell. 16, 12 Lemma: *quae Cloatius Verus aut satis commode aut nimis absurde et inlepide ad origines linguae graecae redigit.* 1 *Cloatius Verus in libris quos inscripsit verborum a Graecis tractorum non pauca hercle dicit curiose et sagaciter conquisita neque non tamen quaedam futtilia et frivola* . . . (5) *commode haec sane et conducenter. sed in libro III 'faenerator' inquit 'appellatus est quasi φαινεράτωρ, ἀπὸ τοῦ φαίνεσθαι ἐπὶ τὸ χρηστότερον'* etc. (6) *idque dixisse ait Hypsicraten quempiam grammaticum* (§ 159, 12) etc. Macrobius also quotes this work 3, 18, 4 (*in libro a Graecis tractorum*) and likewise *Cloatius Verus Ordinatorum Graecorum libri*, the heading perhaps=Graeca ex ordine tractata, arranged and discussed systematically and technically, in contrast to such titles as quaestiones confusae, silvae and so forth. The work probably dealt with technical matters rather than mere nomenclature. B. 2 of this is cited by Macr. 3, 6, 2 (the altar of Apollo at Delos), b. 4 by the same author 3, 18, 8 (*nux*) and 3, 19, 2 (enumeration of varieties of apples in alphabetical order). It is probably the same grammarian whom Verrius quotes six times as Cloatius (without Verus), each time as a commentator on the Roman liturgical formulae: cf. Fest. 141a, 25. 189a, 25. 193a, 4. 213a, 29. 309a, 26. 318a, 24. As the attempt to derive the Roman terms from the Greek is not traceable in any of these passages, a third work by Cloatius must here have been used.

Suet. Gr. 16 *Q. Caecilius Epirota, Tusculi natus, libertus Attici* (§ 172, 1), . . . *cum filiam patroni nuptam M. Agrippae* (§ 220, 10) *doceret, suspectus in ea et ob hoc remotus ad Cornelium Gallum* (§ 232) *se contulit vixitque una familiarissime, quod ipsi Gallo inter gravissima crimina ab Augusto obicitur. post deinde damnationem mortemque Galli scholam aperuit, sed ita ut paucis et tantum adolescentibus praeciperet, praetextato nemini.* . . . *primus dicitur latine ex tempore disputasse primusque Vergilium et alios poetas novos praelegere coepisse.*

2. Suet. gr. 18 *L. Crassicius, genere Tarentinus ordinis libertini, cognomine Pasicles, mox Pansam se transnominavit. hic initio circa scenam versatus est dum mimographos adiuvat* (cf. § 254, 6), *deinde in pergula docuit, donec commentario Zmyrnae* (§ 213, 3) . . . *inclaruit*; (here follows a eulogistic epigram on this com-

mentary) . . . *sed cum . . . doceret iam multos ac nobiles, in his Iullum Antonium* (§ 242, 6), . . *ut Verrio quoque Flacco compararetur, dimissa repente schola transit ad Q. Sexti* (§ 266, 5) *philosophi sectam.*

3. SUET. gr. 19 *Scribonius Aphrodisius, Orbili* (§ 200, 3) *servus atque discipulus, mox a Scribonia, . . . quae prior Augusti uxor fuerat, redemptus et manumissus docuit quo Verrius tempore, cuius etiam libris de orthographia rescripsit* etc. (§ 261, 2).

4. FEST. 352 b, 5 TOPPER *significare ait Artorius cito, fortasse* etc. Cf. ib. 225, 12. 364 b, 16. QUINT. 9, 1, 2 *nec desunt qui tropis figurarum nomen imponant, quorum est C. Artorius Proculus.*—FEST. 170 b, 5 *at Panurgus Antonius haec ait* etc. Is the same author referred to 274a, 21 ⟨*meminit etiam trientis*⟩*ratiti Antonius* etc. or Antonius Gnipho (§ 159, 5)?—*Porcellus grammaticus* also, who cut down a line of Cornelius Severus (§ 252, 5), for which he was censured by SENECA suas. 2, 13, belongs perhaps to this period. A fragment of the same writer occurs in (SUET.) diff. p. 310, 28 Roth *Procellus ait: 'quae L. littera finiuntur in declinatione* etc.'

5. SERV. Aen. 1, 176 *Clodius scribit commentariorum quarto.* Cf. ib. 1, 52 *Clodius commentariorum.* 2, 229 *Clodius scriba commentariorum.* 12, 657 *Clodius Tuscus: mussare est ex graeco* etc. This Clodius Tuscus composed an astronomical calendar, which we possess in the Greek translation of LAURENTIUS LYDUS (de ostentis p. 114 Wachsm.). The heading is: ἐφημερὶς τοῦ παντὸς ἐνιαυτοῦ, ἤγουν σημείωσις ἐπιτολῶν τε καὶ δυσμῶν τῶν ἐν οὐρανῷ φαινομένων, ἐκ τῶν Κλαυδίου τοῦ Θούσκου καθ' ἑρμηνείαν πρὸς λέξιν; cf. p. 155 καὶ ταῦτα μὲν ὁ Κλώδιος ἐκ τῶν παρὰ Θούσκοις ἱερῶν πρὸς λέξιν.—GELL. 5, 20, 2 *Sinnius Capito in litteris* (on points of grammar) *quas ad Clodium Tuscum dedit.* It is quite uncertain whether he is the same Tuscus whom Ovid (ex Pont. 4, 16, 20. cf. § 252, 8) mentions as a poet. On the *historicus Tuscus* see § 277, 4. A certain *Fabricius Tuscus* is mentioned by PLINY NH. ind. auct. to b. 3. 4 and 6 (geography).

6. In the time of Augustus grammatical works were also written by M. Messalla (§ 222, 3), Antonius Rufus (§ 254, 3), Cornificius (§ 209, 2 in fin.); works on antiquities were produced by Cincius (§ 117, 4) and Fenestella (§ 259, 3); on natural history by Pompeius Trogus (§ 258, 2) and Sabinus Tiro (§ 54, 4. 266, 11 ad fin.).

7. Of the physician Antonius Musa (PRE. 1^2, 1188, 65) we often hear what remedies he employed (e.g. PLIN. NH. 30, 117 and in Galen), but in a manner which does not justify the inference of extant works by him; see EMEYER, Gesch. d. Botanik 2, 48, who pronounces the writer on remedies in Greek mentioned in GALEN. 12 p. 989 to be identical with Petronius Musa († c. 50 A.D.) Under the name of Antonius Musa we possess a treatise 'de herba betonica' introduced by a letter to M. Agrippa (*Antonius Musa M. Agrippae s.*) with prescriptions (cf. § 367, 7, b; there is also a fragment 'de tuenda valitudine ad Maecenatem'; see Antonii Musae fragmenta quae extant, collegit FCALDANI, Bassano 1800). Manuscripts of this work de herba betonica in Leyden s. VI (see LMÜLLER, RhM. 23, 189), Breslau s. XI (see CECHRSCHNEIDER, ind. lect. Vratisl. 1839/40), Florence Laur. s. XI and XIII (see EBÄHRENS, miscell. crit. 107). In these MSS. are included two agreeable poems in senarii freely modelled after the archaic method (see WSTUDEMUND, Phil. Anz. 7, 40) 'Precatio terrae matris' and 'Precatio omnium herbarum' (in the Laur. s. XI *herbarum precatio Antonii Musae*). Printed e.g. AL. 5. 6 PLM. 1, 138. Cf. on these MSCHMIDT, Jena Vorles.-Verz. 1874. EBÄHRENS, misc. crit. l.l., who with slight probability takes Antonius Musa to be the author; see also ARIESE, lit. centr.-Bl. 1879, 1671.

264. The architect and technologist Vitruvius Pollio dedicated in his later years to Augustus his ten books de architectura, in which this subject-matter is treated in its widest sense. The author appears to possess varied education and learning and a reflecting mind; yet he had not acquired refined culture and taste. In point of its subject, this work (the only one of its kind which we possess) is very important, but its form is repulsive and crotchety, and disfigured by debased Latin. Besides the original work we possess also an abridgment made by M. Cetius Faventinus.

1. Personal circumstances. The work itself gives us only the name of Vitruvius, his cognomen has the authority of the epitome (see n. 5). The praenomen has not been transmitted and can only be inferred from the inscription at Verona, CIL. 5, 3464 *L. Vitruvius L. l. Cerdo architectus*, if this Cerdo, who was formerly wrongly supposed to be the author, was a disciple and freedman of the latter. Only the statements of Vitruvius himself are trustworthy, especially those in the preface to b. 1, which looks like a paraphrase of the beginning of Hor. ep. 2, 1 in the peculiar taste of Vitruvius: *cum divina tua mens et numen, imperator Caesar* (Augustus), *imperio potiretur orbis terrarum invictaque virtute cunctis hostibus stratis, triumpho* (August 725/29) *victoriaque tua cives gloriarentur . . . populusque rom. et senatus liberatus timore amplissimis tuis cogitationibus consiliisque gubernaretur, non audebam tantis occupationibus de architectura scripta . . . edere, metuens ne non apto tempore interpellans subirem tui animi offensionem* (cf. Hor. s. 2, 1, 20. ep. 1, 13, 4. 2, 1, 220). *cum vero attenderem te* etc. . . . *ut civitas per te non solum provinciis esset aucta* (Egypt 724/30, Galatia 729/25) *verum etiam* etc., *non putavi praetermittendum quin . . . ea tibi ederem, ideo quod primum parenti tuo* (Caesar) *de eo fueram notus et eius virtutis studiosus. cum autem . . . imperium parentis in tuam potestatem transtulisset, idem studium meum in eius memoria permanens in te contulit favorem. itaque cum M. Aurelio et P. Minidio et Cn. Cornelio ad apparationem ballistarum et scorpionum reliquorumque tormentorum refectionem fui praesto et cum eis commoda accepi. quae cum primo mihi tribuisti, recognitionem per sororis* (Octavia, † 743/11) *commendationem servasti. cum ergo eo beneficio essem obligatus ut ad exitum vitae non haberem inopiae timorem, haec tibi scribere coepi, quod animadverti multa te aedificasse et nunc aedificare.* He mentions the *pronaus aedis Augusti* 5, 1, 7 (p. 107, 3 R). Reference to Caesar is made 2, 9, 15 sq. (p. 59, 18 R) *divus Caesar cum exercitum habuisset circa Alpes* etc. with a detailed description such as an eyewitness would give; 8, 3, 25 (p. 203, 11 R) *C. Iulius, Masinissae filius, . . . cum patre Caesari militavit* (a. 708/46). *is hospitio meo est usus.* He always addresses Augustus as Imperator or Caesar, but knows also the title of Augustus, which had been awarded to him a. 727/27. The mention he makes of the numerous buildings of Augustus also leads us beyond a. 727/27 and even beyond 738/16, at which time the temple of Quirinus was built at Rome, Vitr. 3, 2, 7 (p. 70, 4) *dipteros . . . est aedis Quirini dorica.* On the other hand, Vitruv. 3, 2, 2 speaks only of a single stone theatre at Rome, whereas two more were built a. 741/13. Hence the work appears to have been composed about a. 740/14. AHirt, in Wolf's Mus. der Alt.-Wiss. (1806), 228. Pliny mentions Vitruvius NH. ind. auct. b. 16. 35. 36 (*ex Vitruvio*), and there is evidence of the extant work having been used in the above-named books of the NH. (and also in b. 31 and 33), HBrunn, de indic. Plin. (Bonn 1856) 57. DDetlefsen, Phil. 31, 385. GOehmichen, plinian. Studd., Munich 1880,

211. Serv. Aen. 6, 43 *Vitruvius qui de architectonica scripsit, ostium dicit* etc. (but the passage cited does not occur in Vitruvius). Sidon. ep. 4, 2 (p. 228, 5 Sav.) *quaeque si fors attigit, tenere non abnuit cum Orpheo plectrum, . . . cum Vitruvio perpendiculum* etc.

2. On the character of the work. Vitr. 2, prooem. 5 *mihi autem, Imperator, staturam non tribuit natura, faciem deformavit aetas, valetudo detraxit vires. itaque quoniam ab his praesidiis sum desertus per auxilia scientiae scriptaque, ut spero, perveniam ad commendationem.* 6, prooem. 4 *cum et parentium cura et praeceptorum doctrinis auctas haberem copias disciplinarum, philologis et philotechnis rebus commentariorumque scripturis me delectans eas possessiones animo paravi e quibus haec est fructuum summa, . . . nihil desiderare. . . . ego, Caesar, non ad pecuniam parandam ex arte dedi studium. . . . ideo notities parum est adsecuta, sed tamen his voluminibus editis, ut spero, etiam posteris ero notus. neque est mirandum quid ita pluribus sim ignotus. ceteri architecti rogant et ambiunt ut architectentur, mihi autem a praeceptoribus est traditum rogatum, non rogantem, oportere suscipere curam.* 1, 1, 17 *peto, Caesar, et a te et ab is qui ea volumina sunt lecturi ut si quid parum ad regulam artis grammaticae fuerit explicatum ignoscatur. namque non uti summus philosophus nec rhetor disertus nec grammaticus . . ., sed ut architectus his litteris imbutus haec nisus sum scribere.* But he is fond, especially in the garrulous introductions he prefixes to each book (Schneider's ed. 1, p. liii), of displaying his knowledge in philosophy (cf. § 266, 2) and history, though frequently with small success, e.g. 6, prooem. 3 *non minus poetae qui antiquas comoedias graece scripserunt easdem sententias verbis in scena pronuntiaverunt, ut Eucrates, Chionides, Aristophanes, maxime etiam cum his Alexis.* He declares his purpose to be brief: 5, prooem. 3 *cum animadvertissem distentam occupationibus civitatem publicis et privatis negotiis, paucis iudicavi scribendum, uti angusto spatio vacuitatis ea legentes breviter percipere possent*, and again ib. 5 *cum ergo . . . animo advertam inusitatas et obscuras multis res esse mihi scribendas, quo facilius ad sensus legentium pervenire possint, brevibus voluminibus iudicavi scribere.*

3. Vitruvius himself states at great length and repeatedly the contents of the single books (volumina) at the beginning and close of each. The first seven books treat of architecture proper (consecrated and private buildings). The eighth book treats of water and aqueducts, the ninth of instruments for measuring time (sun-dials), the tenth of machines, *uti totum corpus omnia architecturae membra in decem voluminibus habeat explicata* (10, 22, 12). Vitruvius' principal sources were Greek writers (cf. also MCantor, röm. Agrimensoren 87), whom he chiefly enumerates 7, prooem. 11–14, with the declaration: *quorum ex commentariis quae utilia esse . . . animadverti collecta in unum coegi corpus.* But his knowledge of Greek is deficient, in spite of such bold formations as ἀνιατρολόγητος. He frequently does not succeed in expressing himself intelligibly; he lacks literary talent and facility. His style is sometimes immoderately diffuse, sometimes unduly brief, now oddly affected and distorted, now plebeian. EWölfflin, Phil. 34, 148. HUlrich, de Vitr. copia verborum, Frankenthal 1883, Schwabach 1885 II. JPraun Bemm. z. Synt. des V. mit eingehender Darst. der Subst.-Sätze, Bamb. 1885. PhEberhard, Vitruvianae obss. gramm., Pforzh. 1887. 88 II. Cf. n. 6. MStock, de Vitr. sermone: de formis enuntiatorum tempp., Berl. 1888.

4. Of the two existing MSS. the most important are Harlei. 2767 s. IX and Gud. 69 s. XI (see Rose pref. to his ed.). Both, however, are derived from the same original, as they have the same gaps and errors, and the same transposition of leaves at 7, 6. On a Schlettstadt MS. s. X. see AGiry, rev. de philol. 3, 16. On the Spanish Vitruvius MSS. see GLoewe, Wiener Studd. 9, 327.

5. The abridgment bears in a Vienna MS. (suppl. 2867 s. IX/X see JHaupt, Wien. SBer. 69, 31) and in the Schlettstadt MS. (see n. 4) the heading *M. Ceti Faventini artis architectonicae privatis usibus adbreviatus liber*, in the others the name of the author of the epitome is wanting and it bears the title: *De diversis fabricis architectonicae*, and begins: *De artis architectonicae peritia multa oratione Vitruvius Polio aliique auctores scientissime scripsere. verum ne longa eorum disertaque facundia humilioribus ingeniis alienum faceret studium, pauca ex his mediocri licet sermone privatis usibus ornare fuit consilium.* The arrangement of Vitruvius has been kept unchanged, but the subject limited to private buildings. At the end (c. 29) an explanation of horologium pelecinum and hemicyclium is added from another source; c. 30 also (on maltae, which is missing e.g. in the Schlettstadt MS.) is taken from some other source and is of later origin. The whole composition has been edited from three MSS. s. X by Rose p. 285. Cf. ib. p. xii. This epitome was used by Palladius (§ 410, 2) and Isidorus (§ 496, 7). Cf. HNohl, commentat. Mommsen. 64.

6. Editions of Vitruvius (cf. Schneider's edition 1, xi) e.g. by Io. de Laet, Amsterd. 1649 (c. nott. varr. and with BBaldi's Lex. Vitruv., see n. 7). BGaliani, Naples 1758. ARode, Berl. 1800 II. Rec. em. ill. IGSchneider, Lps. 1807 sq. III. Collective editions by Stratico, Udine 1825–30 IV and AMarini, Rome 1836 IV. Rec. atque emend. et in germ. serm. vertit CLorentzen, 1, 1 (not completed), Gotha 1856.—Ad antiquiss. codd. nunc primum ediderunt VRose et HMüller-Strübing, Lps. 1867; to this an index Vitruvianus by HNohl, Lpz. 1876.—Criticism: CLorentzen, observatt. crit. ad Vitr., Gotha 1858. FHultsch, JJ. 113, 251. AWilmanns, commentatt. Mommsen. 254. FEyssenhardt, epistula urbica ad IClassenum, Hamb. 1879. HNohl, anall. Vitruv., Berl. 1882.

7. Translations: By ARode, Lpz. 1796 II; plates and notes, Berl. 1801. Translated and explained in notes and woodcuts by FReber, Stuttg. 1864 sq.—French translations by ClPerrault (Par. 1673. 1684).—With text and atlas, by Tardieu and Cousin (Paris 1839); by Maufras (Par. 1847 sqq. II).—English translations by WNewton, Lond. 1771-91 II. Wilkins, Lond. 1813 II. etc.—Explanatory works: BBaldus, de verborum Vitruv. significatione, Augsb. 1614. (CPromis, vocabuli latini di architettura posteriori a Vitruvio, oppure a lui sconosciuti, complemento del lessico Vitruv. di Baldi, Turin 1876.) JPolenus, exercitatt. Vitruvianae, Padua 1739. 1741. HCGenelli, Briefe über Vitr., Brunswick 1801. Berl. 1804 II. JFRösch, Erläuterungen über Vitr., Stuttg. 1802. CGHaubold, exercitatt. Vitr., Lps. 1821 III. Vitr. 10, 13–15 in Köchly und Rüstow's griechischen Kriegsschriftst. 1 (Lpz. 1853), 347. EHFMeyer, Gesch. d. Botanik 1 (Königsb. 1854), 382. FReber, Phil. 27, 185. ATerquen, la science rom. à l'époque d'Auguste; étude hist. d'après Vitr., Par. 1885. GOehmichen, d. gr. Theaterbau nach Vitr. etc., Berl. 1886; RhM. 43, 524 and other technical treatises.

265. Among the jurists of the Augustan age the two most important are Labeo and Capito. M. Antistius Labeo's (c. 700/54–c. 770/17 a.d.) legal knowledge was based on comprehensive culture and supported by a character of unconquerable firmness, which no less than his numerous legal works contributed to maintain his name in respectful and honourable remembrance. His opposite was the monarchist C. Ateius Capito (a. 720/34–

775/22 A.D.), who ranked far below Labeo in scientific importance and literary activity. To the same period belong Blaesus, a pupil of Trebatius, and probably also the jurist Fabius Mela.

1. POMPON. dig. 1, 2, 2, 47: *post hunc* (Aelius Tubero, § 208, 1) *maximae auctoritatis fuerunt Ateius Capito, qui Ofilium secutus est, et Antistius Labeo, qui omnes hos* (all professors of law of that period, see § 207 and 208) *audivit, institutus est autem a Trebatio* (§ 207, 3). *ex his Ateius consul fuit* (a. 758/5 A.D.); *Labeo noluit, cum offerretur et ab Augusto consulatus, quo suffectus fieret, honorem suscipere* (for he had been previously passed over by Augustus, his junior Capito obtaining the preference; see the passage from TAC. below l. 20), *sed plurimis studiis operam dedit et totum annum ita diviserat ut Romae sex mensibus cum studiosis esset* (and *consulentibus de iure publice responsitaret*, GELL. 13, 10, 1), *sex mensibus secederet* (probably to his fundus Gallianus, see GELL. 13, 12, 4) *et conscribendis libris operam daret. itaque reliquit quadringenta volumina, ex quibus plurima inter manus versantur. hi duo primum veluti diversas sectas fecerunt* (see above p. 406); *nam . . . Labeo ingenii qualitate et fiducia doctrinae, qui et ceteris operis sapientiae operam dederat, plurima innovare instituit* (§ 49, 5). GELL. 13, 10, 1 *Labeo Antistius iuris quidem civilis disciplinam principali studio exercuit, . . . sed ceterarum quoque bonarum artium non expers fuit et in grammaticam sese atque dialecticam literasque antiquiores altioresque penetraverat latinarumque vocum origines rationesque percalluerat eaque praecipue scientia ad enodandos plerosque iuris laqueos utebatur.* The example given ib. 3 (*soror* from *seorsum*) prove him to have been a purist (above p. 57). TAC. ann. 3, 75 *Capitoni consulatum adceleraverat Augustus, ut Labeonem Antistium, isdem artibus praecellentem, dignatione eius magistratus anteiret. namque illa aetas duo pacis decora simul tulit. sed Labeo incorrupta libertate et ob id fama celebratior, Capitonis obsequium dominantibus magis probabatur. illi quod praeturam intra stetit commendatio ex iniuria, huic quod consulatum adeptus est odium ex invidia oriebatur.* GELL. 13, 12, 1 *in quadam epistula Atei Capitonis scriptum legimus Labeonem Antistium legum atque morum populi rom. iurisque civilis doctum adprime fuisse. 'sed agitabat* (hence it was written after Labeo's death),' *inquit, 'hominem libertas quaedam nimia atque vecors, tamquam eorum divo Augusto iam principe et remp. obtinente ratum tamen pensumque nihil haberet nisi quod iustum sanctumque esse in romanis antiquitatibus legisset.*' PORPHYRIO on HOR. s. 1, 3, 82 *Marcus Antistius Labeo praetorius, iuris etiam peritus, memor libertatis in qua natus erat multa contumaciter adversus Caesarem dixisse et fecisse dicitur, propter quod nunc Horatius adulans Augusto insanum eum dicit.* Cf. ACRO ib. (p. 58 H.). Horace l.l. (*Labeone insanior inter sanos dicatur*, written a. 716/38 or 717/37) certainly does not refer to the jurist, though it may perhaps to his father (§ 207, 6). Cf. PERNICE, Labeo 1, 12. KIESSLING ad loc. TEUFFEL, PRE. 1², 1163, 26.

2. Labeo's works included 400 books (see n. 1). The fragments from the Digest in HOMMEL, Palingenesia 1, 321; OLENEL, Palingenesia 502; those from other authors in HUSCHKE, iurispr. anteiust. ⁵110. GELL. 13, 10, 2 *sunt libri post mortem eius editi, qui Posteriores inscribuntur, quorum librorum tres continui, XXXVIII et XXXIX et XL, pleni sunt id genus* (see n. 1) *rerum ad enarrandam et inlustrandam linguam latinam conducentium.* In other respects the work was a system of civil law, arranged according to the design (variously modified) of Q. Mucius (§ 154, 2), and its plan was also the standard for the ius civile of Sabinus (§ 281, 1); cf. KRÜGER l.l. MVOIGT (§ 154, 2 l. 6) 348. Notes on Labeo were written by Proculus, Aristo and Paulus (dig. 29, 2, 60. Mommsen conjectures *Aulus*). Two epitomes were made by Javolenus, which were employed in the Digest, just as the eight books

Probabilium (πιθανῶν) are there quoted from the epitome of Paulus. The two works are quoted 63 times in all in the Digest. *Labeo libris epistolarum* (dig. 41, 3, 30, 1); *libri responsorum*, at least 15 books (Collat. 12, 7, 3). Gell. 13, 10, 3 *in libris quos ad praetoris edictum scripsit multa posuit partim lepide atque argute reperta. sicuti hoc est quod in quarto ad edictum libro scriptum legimus* etc. dig. 50, 16, 19 *Labeo libro primo praetoris urbani* (notes on this were written by Quintus, dig. 4, 3, 7, 2 = Q. Saturninus § 360, 6 ad fin. or Q. Cervidius Scaevola § 369, 1?) 4, 3, 9, 4: *Labeo libro trigesimo praetoris peregrini.* Gell. 1, 12, 18 *in commentariis Labeonis quae ad XII tabulas composuit*; cf. ib. 20, 1, 13 and 6, 15, 1 *Labeo in libro de XII tabulis secundo.* Fest. 253a, 7 *Labeo de iure pontificio l. XI;* then ib. 9 and 13 *Labeo Antistius*, and *Antistius de iure pontificali l. IX*; 348, where he is also quoted for other purposes: *Labeo Antistius l. X commentari iuris pontifici*; 351[a] *Antistius Labeo in commentario XV iuris pontifici.* Perhaps also ⟨*de*⟩ *officio augu⟨rum⟩*, ib. p. 290[a]. Gell. 1, 12, 1 *qui de virgine capienda scripserunt, quorum diligentissime scripsit Labeo Antistius.* Macr. 3, 9, 4 (after a previous citation of Ateius Capito *ex libro I de iure sacrificiorum*) *Labeo vero sexagesimo et octavo libro intulit* etc. Pernice, Labeo 1, 46 without cogent reason refers this passage to Cornelius Labeo (§ 389, 8). But the large number of books causes difficulty. CThomasius, comparatio Labeonis et Capitonis, Lps. 1683. CvEck, de vita . . . Labeonis et . . . Capitonis, Franeker 1692 (and in Oelrich's thes. nov. 1, 2, 825). FABiener, op. (1830) 1, 196. SWZimmern, Gesch. d. PRechts 1, 1, 306. AFRudorff, röm. RGesch, 1, 178. 236. DeGeer, Versl. en Med. d. k. Akad. v. Wetensch. XI. 1868. LBorchert, num A. L. stoicae philosophiae fuerit addictus, Berl. 1869. APernice, M. Ant. Labeo, d. Privatrecht im 1. Jahrh. d. Kaiserzeit, Halle 1873–1878 II. PKrüger, Gesch. d. Quellen u. Lit. d. röm. Rechts, Lpz. 1888, 141. MSchanz, Phil. 42, 309 (compare Bekker, ZdSavigny-Stift. 6, 75. Krüger l.l. 142, 9).

3. C. Ateius (CIL. 1 p. 198, nr. 750 sq. Fasti praenest. ib. p. 474, XIII) Capito, *principem in civitate locum studiis civilibus adsecutus, sed avo centurione Sullano, patre praetorio. consulatum ei adceleraverat Augustus* etc. (n. 1), Tac. a. 3, 75. If this was said of the consulship of a. 758/5, Capito would appear to have been born c. a. 720/34. He was curator aquarum from a. 766/13 a.d. to his death, a. 775/22 a.d. (Tac. l.l.), Frontin. aq. 102. As a jurist he was a pupil of Ofilius (§ 207, 2). Gell. 10, 20, 2 *Ateius Capito, publici privatique iuris peritissimus.* Macr. 7, 13, 11 *apud Ateium Capitonem, pontificii iuris inter primos peritum.* Tac. a. 3, 70 *Capito insignitior infamia fuit* (on account of his servility, cf. Suet. gr. 22. Dio 57, 17), *quod humani divinique iuris sciens egregium publicum et bonas domi artes dehonestavisset.*

4. The works of Capito. Coniectanea (Gell. 2, 24, 2. 15. 20, 2, 3; ib. 4, 14, 1 *cum librum VIII Atei Capitonis coniectaneorum legeremus, qui inscriptus est De iudiciis publicis*; 10, 6, 4); liber de officio senatorio (Gell. 4, 10, 7 sq.; perhaps b. 9 of the Coniectanea, see ib. 14, 7, 12 *quod Ateius Capito in coniectaneis scriptum reliquit; nam in libro IX . . . ait nullum senatusconsultum fieri posse* etc. ib. 14, 8, 2 *Ateius Capito in coniectaneorum IX ius esse praefecto senatus habendi dicit*); de pontificio iure (b. 5 ap. Gell. 4, 6, 10; Fest. 154 b *Capito Ateius in l. VII pontificali*, cf. Macr. 7, 13, 11); Macr. 3, 10, 3 *Ateius Capito . . . libro primo de iure sacrificiorum.* Epistulae (Gell. 13, 12, 1 sqq. cf. note 1). Cf. Huschke, iurisprud. anteiust. [5]115. This work is repeatedly quoted by Festus, and by Plin. NH. ind. auct. to b. 3. 4. 14. 15. 18, probably from the Coniectanea. In the later jurists he is quite neglected, as he *in his quae ei tradita fuerant perseverabat* (Pompon. dig. 1, 2, 2, 47) i.e. was unproductive. There are very few quotations from him, e.g. in

Proculus dig. 8, 2, 13, 1. OLenel, Palingenesia 106. Zimmern, Gesch. d. PRechts 1, 1, 307. ThFrederking (and LMercklin), Phil. 19, 650. PRE. 1², 1955, 4. PKrüger, l.l. 145.

5. Labeo dig. 33, 2, 31 *Blaesus ait Trebatium respondisse*, etc. Majansius, comm. 2, 162.

6. Fabius Mela (dig. 43, 23, 1, 12) is in the Digest frequently quoted together with Labeo and Trebatius (15, 3, 7, 2 sq. 19, 2, 13, 8. 19, 5, 20. 27, 3, 1, 5 sq. 47, 10, 17, 2), being probably a contemporary of theirs, especially as he himself quotes Aquilius Gallus (§ 174, 1) and Servius Sulpicius (§ 174, 2): (dig. 19, 1, 17, 6 *Gallus Aquilius, cuius Mela refert opinionem.* 33, 9, 3, 10 *Servius apud Melam.* Cf. dig. 46, 3, 39 pr. *Mela libro X*). HEDirksen, de Fabio Mela, Königsb. 1808.

7. Vitellius, on whom Massurius Sabinus and Cassius Longinus (see § 281, 1 and 298, 3) wrote notes under Tiberius (and perhaps Paulus at a later time? § 377, 4), appears to belong to the Augustan period, but is otherwise unknown, unless he be the *rerum Augusti procurator Vitellius* mentioned by Suet. Vitell. 2 (§ 259, 10).

8. On Veranius see § 199, 4.—To the Augustan period we should perhaps attribute the pactum fiduciae, found in Spain, which was concluded between Dama L. Titi ser(vos) and L. Baianius; see CIL. lat. 2, 5042, p. 700. Bruns, font.⁵ 251; cf. EHübner, Herm. 3, 283 and HDegenkolb, ZfRGesch. 9, 117.

266. Interest in philosophy was generally evinced in the Augustan age, all writers of eminence, e.g. especially Vergil, Horace, and Livy, manifesting it, and in common with them also Labeo, Vitruvius, Varus, Lynceus, and others. Owing to the influence of the favourite system of Epicurus, this interest was now extended to the physical side, though ethics retained always the upper hand. Yet it never exceeded the limits of dilettantism, even with those who professed to write on philosophy, e.g. Augustus and Livy, and perhaps even with the Stoics Crispinus and Stertinius. A certain importance attaches only to Q. Sextius, both father and son, whose zealous adherents were Crassicius, Papirius Fabianus, and others: they, however, wrote in Greek. The father, a man of austere morality, and an independent thinker, aimed at realising his conception of moral worth in individual life. The so-called Sextus-maxims have no direct connection with the Sextii.

1. Cf. above p. 411. On Vergil's philosophical bent see § 224, 3; on Horace § 235, 5; T. Livius § 256, 4; Augustus § 220, 3; Alfenus Varus § 208, 3; on the author of the Ciris § 230, 2, n. 1; on Lynceus § 244, 3; P. Volumnius § 255, 1; Labeo § 265, 1. Seneca's mother Helvia would have liked to study philosophy, if her husband had allowed her; see § 269, 1.

2. Vitruv. 1, 1, 7 *philosophia perficit architectum animo magno et uti non sit adrogans, sed potius facilis, aequus et fidelis sine avaritia* etc. . . . *praeterea de rerum natura* . . . *philosophia explicat, quam necesse est studiosius novisse, quod*

habet multas et varias naturales quaestiones, ut etiam in aquarum ductionibus. . . . quorum (i.e. *spiritus naturales*) *offensionibus mederi nemo poterit nisi qui ex philosophia principia rerum naturae noverit.* But even without a practical interest of this kind natural philosophy was much studied in this period together with ethics by Iccius (Hor. c. 1, 29, 13. ep. 1, 12, 15), the author of the Ciris (Cir. 5. 11. 39), Lynceus (Prop. 3, 34, 27. 51), and Manilius (astr. 1, 96. 118. 4, 866). In the same way, the elder Sextius Niger (n. 5–7) and Papirius Fabianus (below n. 10 sq.), Celsus (§ 280), Seneca, Pliny the Elder and Suetonius exemplify a connection of philosophical and physical studies.

3. Porphyrio on Hor. s. 1, 1, 13 *Fabius Maximus Narbonensis, equestri loco natus, Pompeianas partes secutus aliquot libros ad Stoicam philosophiam pertinentes conscripsit;* the same on Hor. s. 1, 1, 120 *Plotius Crispinus philosophiae studiosus fuit. idem et carmina scripsit, sed tam garrule ut aretalogus diceretur* (Acro ib.: *hic Crispinus poeta fuit, qui sectam stoicam versibus scripsit*).

4. Acro on Hor. ep. 1, 12, 20 *Stertinius philosophus, qui CCXX libros Stoicorum latine scripsit. hos notat quod versibus suis obscuriorem philosophiam fecerint.* The first statement, which is in itself not very probable, is not found in Porphyrio, who says merely: *hunc et alibi tangit ut Stoicum qui de paradoxis loquitur*, and on p. 2, 3, 33 *Stertinius unus e Stoicis fuit.*

5. Sen. ep. 98, 13 *honores reppulit pater Sextius, qui ita natus ut remp. deberet capessere latum clavum divo Iulio dante non recepit:* according to this Sextius must have been born not later than 684/70. Plut. prof. in virt. 5 p. 77 ad fin. . . . φασὶ Σέξτιον τὸν Ῥωμαῖον ἀφεικότα τὰς ἐν τῇ πόλει τιμὰς καὶ ἀρχὰς διὰ φιλοσοφίαν, ἐν δὲ τῷ φιλοσοφεῖν αὖ πάλιν δυσπαθοῦντα καὶ χρώμενον τῷ λόγῳ χαλεπῷ τὸ πρῶτον, ὀλίγου δεῆσαι καταβαλεῖν ἑαυτὸν ἔκ τινος διήρους. Sen. ep. 59, 7 *Sextium . . . lego, virum acrem, graecis verbis, romanis moribus philosophantem.* 64, 2 *lectus est liber Quinti Sextii patris, magni . . . viri et, licet neget, Stoici. quantus in illo . . . vigor est, quantum animi! . . . cum legeris Sextium dices: vivit, viget, liber est, supra hominem est, dimittit me plenum ingentis fiduciae. in qua positione mentis sim cum hunc lego fatebor tibi: libet omnes casus provocare, libet exclamare 'quid cessas, fortuna? congredere. paratum vides.' . . . hoc quoque egregium Sextius habet quod et ostendet tibi beatae vitae magnitudinem et desperationem eius non faciet.* 73, 12 *solebat Sextius dicere Iovem plus non posse quam bonum virum.* 73, 15 *credamus itaque Sextio . . . clamanti 'hac itur ad astra, hac secundum frugalitatem, hac secundum temperantiam, hac secundum fortitudinem.'* de ira 3, 36, 1 *faciebat hoc Sextius ut consummato die . . . interrogaret animum suum 'quod hodie malum tuum sanasti?'* ib. 2, 36, 1. ep. 108, 17 *dicebat quare Pythagoras animalibus abstinuisset, quare postea Sextius.* The latter looked upon animal food as an incentive to cruelty and to luxury, and as unwholesome. Plin. NH. 18, 274 *hoc* (EZeller, Gesch. d. gr. Phil. 3 [3], 1, 676) *postea Sextius e Romanis sapientiae adsectatoribus Athenis fecit eadem ratione.*

6. Under the name of Sextus a collection of maxims has been transmitted to us, which we can trace back to the middle of the third Christian century (see below the passages from Origen). This was originally written in Greek: an abridgment of the Greek original collection, which is not extant in a complete and independent form, is to be found in FBoissonade's anecd. 1, 127 (γνῶμαι σοφῶν from the cod. Paris. 1630): numerous Greek Sextus-maxims also occur in Porphyrios' epist. ad Marcellam, in Stobaios and elsewhere, some of which we do not meet with in the translators. Gildemeister, ed. p. xxxviii. xlix, and Herm. 4, 81. JCOrelli, op. sent. 1, 244; Mullach's fragm. philos. gr. 1, 522. 2, 116.

Origen already quotes from the Greek collection c. Cels. 8 p. 397 (*ἐν ταῖς Σέκστου γνώμαις*) and in Matth. 19, 3 (*Σέξστος ἐν ταῖς γνώμαις, βιβλίῳ φερομένῳ παρὰ πολλοῖς ὡς δοκίμῳ*) the maxims 13. 109. 273 Gildem.—The Greek collection was translated into Latin by Rufinus (§ 435, 1); in his preface he says: . . . *Sextum in Latinum verti, quem Sextum ipsum esse tradunt qui apud vos, id est in urbe romana, Xystus vocatur, episcopi et martyris gloria decoratus* (this refers to Sixtus II. a. 256–258 bishop of Rome: Jerome already controverts this repeatedly, below, l. 7 from end of page . . . *omne autem opus ita breve est ut de manu eius* (the reader's) *numquam possit recedere totus liber, unius pristini alicuius pretiosi anuli obtinens locum. . . . nunc ergo interim habeatur pro anulo liber. . . . addidi praeterea electa quaedam religiosi parentis ad filium, sed breve totum, ut merito omne opusculum vel 'enchiridion,' si graece, vel 'anulus' si latine appelletur.* The appendix to the Sextus-maxims indicated by Rufinus in these last words (*electa religiosi parentis ad filium*) is not extant: Jerome was however acquainted with it, as he repeatedly alludes to Rufinus having divided the maxims: *in duas partes divisit* (5, 206 Vall. cf. 4, 993). Rufinus' version is preserved in numerous MSS.: unfortunately however the two best, Paris 10318 s. VII/VIII (Salmasianus, cf. § 476) and Paris. 2676 s. X (§ 211, 5) do not give the whole collection; the latter gives only no. 1–84, the former only a selection of 173 maxims out of the whole number of 451. On the MSS. see Gildemeister l.l. p. xiv.—Lastly the collection was translated from the Greek into Syriac and is extant in two versions; the first under the title 'Selected maxims of S. Xystus, bishop of Rome,' gives only a selection of 131 maxims (with a few additions), but the second gives the whole collection (with a few unimportant omissions): both were edited from 7 London MSS. (two of them s. VI) by PdeLagarde, analecta Syriaca (Lps. 1858), p. 1, translated into Latin in Gildemeister in the principal edition (the older ones are useless): Sexti sententiarum recensiones latinam graecam syriacas coniunctim exhibuit IGildemeister, Bonn 1873.

The collection, as we now have it, is not the personal confession of faith of an individual philosopher set forth in the form of maxims, but rather a would-be formal, but essentially unmethodical, combination of various philosophical and religious thoughts put together from reading; this accounts for the very large number of variants of maxims identical or nearly related, which are given side by side, and for the colouring which is alternately Stoical, Pythagorean, and Christian. As regards the Christian maxims we notice however that the peculiarly Christian doctrines and the name of Christ do not occur, and this much is certain, that, as compared with the extant Greek maxims, the Christianising of the collection is carried much further in the hands of the Christian editors, Rufinus and the Syrians (the attempt of ORibbeck, comic. lat.[2] p. c, to detect traces of metrical maxims in Rufinus is unsuccessful). It must remain an open question whether the original Greek collection was absolutely free from Christian matter (cf. Zeller l.l. 679) or whether the first collator already attempted to harmonise the old and new faiths by cautiously adopting Christian maxims: Origen and Porphyry took the collection for the work of a Greek philosopher, and Jerome repeatedly lays stress on its Pagan character (1, 1030. 4, 993. 5, 206 Vall.). See also Augustine (after his previous error de nat. et gratia 64) retract. 2, 42 and Gelasius (§ 469, 5) decr. 7, 24; cf. also Isidorus de vir. illustr. 7, 139 Arev.

The composition of the extant collection makes it evident that it cannot be the work of one of the Roman Sextii, but even should we decide to assume the existence of a purer original collection (i.e. free from Christian matter), the authorship of the Sextii would still be equally impossible. The conjecture that all the subsequent matter may have gradually gathered round a small nucleus of proverbial maxims of the Sextii leads to nothing, as we have no evidence for the existence of any such nucleus from which the collection might have derived its name; though we do not wish to deny that maxims of the Sextii were actually incorporated in his work by the collector. It would be more plausible to suppose that the extant collection with its neutral attitude towards Greek philosophy and Christianity was brought out (perhaps in the second century) under the name of Sextius the grave Roman, and that at a later period, e.g. from the genitive *Sexti* (=*Sextii*), *Sextus* was wrongly supposed to be the author. For the Roman philosopher is throughout called 'Sextius,' the collector of the maxims 'Sextus.' But this presumption is traversed by the fact that Jerome several times mentions *Sextus Pythagoreus* as the author of the collection of maxims, and under this name no doubt refers to the writer of whom he read in Euseb. Chron. for Ol. 195, 1 (=754/1 A.D.): Σέξτος Πυθαγορικὸς φιλόσοφος ἤκμαζε (*Sextus Pythagoricus philosophus agnoscitur:* Jerome himself gives this as the translation, and so does the Armenian version, see ASchöne ad loc.). Iamblichos in Simplicius on Aristot. p. 64 b, 12 and p. 327 b, 10 ed. Berol. also mentions this Pythagorean Sextus: παρὰ δὲ τοῖς Πυθαγορείοις (τὸν τετραγωνισμὸν τοῦ κύκλου) ηὑρῆσθαί φησιν Ἰάμβλιχος, ὡς δῆλόν ἐστιν ἀπὸ τῶν Σέξτου τοῦ Πυθαγορείου ἀποδείξεων, ὃς ἄνωθεν κατὰ διαδοχὴν παρέλαβε τὴν μέθοδον τῆς ἀποδείξεως. But (quite apart from the difference in name) there are many obstacles to our identifying this Pythagorean Sextus with the Roman Sextius. Q. Sextius could hardly (in spite of Sen. ep. 108, 17; see n. 5 in fin.) bear the regular title of a Pythagorean; rather if we had to assign him to a particular school—he himself avoided this (see n. 5)—he could only be called a Stoic. Just as little appropriate to him is the solution of the problem of squaring the circle which has been fathered on him, in support of which the work περὶ ὕλης can hardly be appealed to (see n. 7). Lastly Eusebios-Hieronymus would place his floruit at least 40 years too late (see n. 5 init.). Moreover the opinion of Jerome, which again involves us in serious difficulties, with regard to the authorship of the Pythagorean Sextus, is doubtless founded on a mere supposition. On the other hand it seems that Sextius is really referred to by Himerios (in Photii bibl. p. 366 a, 41 Bk.) in the enumeration in inverted chronological order: θρηνῶ νῦν ὃν (his son) δεινότερον ἤλπισα Μινουκιανοῦ φθέγξασθαι, σεμνότερον δὲ Νικαγόρου, Πλουτάρχου δὲ εὐγλωττότερον, Μουσωνίου δὲ (see § 299, 3) φιλοσοφώτερον, Σέξτου (read Σεξτίου) δὲ καρτερικώτερον.—Cf. EZeller, Gesch. d. gr. Philos. 3, 1^3, 675. MOtt, Charakter u. Ursprung der Sprüche des Sextius, Rottweil 1861; die syrischen auserlesenen Sprüche des Xistus, Bischofs von Rom, eine überarbeitete Sextiusschrift, Rottweil 1862 sq. II. Criticism: AEberhard, JB. 1873, 1302.

7. It was probably the same Sextius (though he does not elsewhere bear the cognomen Niger) who wrote on natural sciences, likewise in Greek. A work περὶ ὕλης (materia medica) is mentioned by Erotian. Lex. p. 94 Kl. v. λείριον. *Sextius Niger, qui graece (de medicina) scripsit,* is mentioned by Pliny NH. ind. auct. 6. 12–16. 20–30. 32–34 (medicinal use of plants, animals and minerals) who quotes him eight times in the work and at 32, 26 as *diligentissimus medicina.* MWellmann, Herm. 24, 530. Dioscorides also made frequent use of Sextius. OJahn, Lps. SBer. 1850, 277. CMayhoff, novae lucubr. Plin. (1874) p. 7.—A bust at Florence (engraved in the Archäel. Ztg. 35, pl. 9) was erroneously taken for a portrait of this Sextius, see KRobert, Herm. 17, 135.

8. The son (cf. n. 5) continued his father's work; cf. Sen. nat. quaest. 7, 32, 2

Sextiorum nova et romani roboris secta inter initia sua, cum magno impetu coepisset, extincta est. On L. Crassicius see § 263, 2; on Papirius Fabianus below n. 10 sq. Subsequently *scripsit non parum multa Cornelius Celsus, Sextios secutus* (see below § 280). Seneca's master Sotion (§ 287, 1) appears also to have been amongst the pupils of Sextius. The Sextii are also alluded to in CLAUDIAN. MAMERT. de statu animae 2, 8 (*Sextius pater Sextiusque filius*).

9. QUINT. 10, 1, 124 *Plautus in Stoicis rerum cognitioni utilis.* 2, 14, 2 *haec interpretatio non minus dura est quam illa Plauti 'essentia' et 'queentia.'* Cf. 3, 6, 23 οὐσίαν, *quam Plautus 'essentiam' vocat.* 8, 3, 33 *multa ex graeco formata nova ac plurima a Sergio † flavio* (thus in the best MSS.), *quorum dura quaedam admodum videntur, ut 'queens' et 'essentia'; quae cur tantopere aspernemur nihil video.* SEN. ep. 58, 6 says on *essentia: Ciceronem auctorem huius verbi habeo, puto locupletem. si recentiorem quaeris, Fabianum, disertum et elegantem, orationis etiam ad nostrum fastidium nitidae* (cf. also SIDON. ep. praef. carm. 14): this does not however raise any serious difficulty, as Seneca mentions only two authors of different periods who both used *essentia.* The passages in Quintilian can be made to agree by means of the very slight alteration *Sergio Plauto* for *Sergio Flauio.* The author whose name is thus obtained may perhaps be identified with the *Sergius Plautus* mentioned in PLIN. NH. ind. auct. b. 2, 18 (although with the variant *Paulus;* § 54, 4). Cf. CIL. 2, 1406 *L. Sergio Regis f. Arn. Plauto Q(uaestori) Salio Palatino.* DDETLEFSEN, üb. einige Quellenschriftsteller d. Plin., Glückst. 1881, 5.—Is the same Sergius referred to in (APUL.) περὶ ἑρμην. p. 262 Hild.? *vocat Sergius 'effatum,' Varro 'proloquium', Cicero 'enuntiatum', Graeci [tum] 'protasin', tum 'axioma', ego verbum ex verbo tum 'protensionem', tum 'rogamentum'.*

10. Papirius Fabianus, called philosophus by SEN. suas. 1, 9. contr. 2, 9, 25. 2, 13, 18. 7, praef. 4. SEN. ep. 40, 12. *Fabianus, vir egregius et vita et scientia et . . . eloquentia quoque.* de brev. vitae 10, 1 *Fabianus, non ex his cathedrariis philosophis, sed ex veris et antiquis.* He commenced with the study of rhetoric. SEN. contr. 2, praef. 1 *Fabianus philosophus, qui adolescens admodum tantae opinionis in declamando quantae postea in disputando fuit. exercebatur apud Arellium Fuscum* etc. *ab hac* (i.e. the *oratio lasciva* of Ar. F.) *cito se Fabianus separavit et luxuriam quidem cum voluit abiecit, obscuritatem non potuit evadere; haec illum in philosophiam persecuta est.* (2) *deerat illi* (i.e. Fab.) *oratorium robur . . .; splendor vero . . . orationi aderat. voltus dicentis lenis et pro tranquillitate morum* (cf. SEN. ep. 11, 4) *remissus.* (4) *cum aliquando Sextium audiret* (cf. n. 8) *nihilominus declamitabat. . . .* (5) *habuit et Blandum rhetorem* (§ 268, 1) *praeceptorem . . . apud Blandum diutius quam apud Fuscum Arellium studuit, sed cum iam transfugisset* (to philosophy). . . . *nec ille declamationibus vacabat et ego tanto minorem natu quam ipse eram* (hence Fabianus would appear to have been born 715/39–720/34. cf. SEN. contr. 2, 12, 12) *audiebam quotiens inciderat, non quotiens volueram.* An extensive specimen of his declamations ib. 2, 9, 10–13; others ib. 2, 12, 3. 10. 2, 13, 6. 2, 14, 4. Hence in all probability his habit of giving public lectures (on philosophy); cf. SEN. ep. 52, 11 *disserebat populo Fabianus, sed audiebatur modeste. erumpebat interdum magnus clamor laudantium, sed quem rerum magnitudo* (cf. ep. 100, 10) *evocaverat.* Among his pupils were Albucius Silus (see § 268, 4) and Seneca the philosopher (ep. 100, 3. 12).

11. On the diction of Fabianus see SEN. ep. 58, 6 (n. 9) and especially ep. 100, where he says 1: *Fabiani Papirii libros qui inscribuntur (artium) civilium legisse te scribis et non respondisse expectationi tuae; deinde oblitus de philosopho agi composi-*

tionem eius accusas; upon which Seneca elaborately defends and characterises Fabianus and states (9) that in his philosophical works (with regard to style) only Cicero (*cuius libri ad philosophiam pertinentes paene totidem sunt quot Fabiani*), Asinius Pollio and Livy surpassed him. He differed from Cicero in writing chiefly on subjects of natural history: *Fabianus causarum naturalium II* in Charis. GL. 4, 106, 14; less accurately *causarum libro II et III* ib. 146, 28; *causarum tertio* in Diomed. GL. 1, 375, 22. See also Val. Prob. GL. 4, 209, 21 and Serg. ib. 542, 16. Charis. GL. 1, 105, 14 *Fabianus de animalibus primo;* cf. ib. 142, 14. Cf. Plin. NH. 9, 25. He seems to have treated both of zoology and botany (pharmacology), according to the quotations in Plin. NH. 12, 20. 15, 4. 18, 276 (*a Fabiano graecisque auctoribus*) 23, 62. 28, 54 (*Aristoteles et Fabianus*). But he appears to have been somewhat uncritical, to conclude from the statement ib. 36, 125 *inter plurima alia Italiae miracula ipsa marmora in lapicidinis crescere auctor est Papirius Fabianus, naturae rerum peritissimus.* Likewise ib. 2, 121. 224. Pliny quotes Fabianus NH. ind. auct. b. 2. 7. 9. 11–15. 17. 23. 25. 28 and 36. His full name may perhaps also be restored in Plin. NH. ind. auct. 6. 18 *ex . . . Sabino Fabiano* (Detlefsen, ind. Plin. s.v.). But elsewhere in the lists of authorities he is mentioned only as Fabianus, and as in the ind. auct. b. 19 (in the continuation of the naturae frugum) Sabinus Tiro (§ 54, 1; more correctly Sabinius, see DDetlefsen, üb. einige Quellenschriftsteller d. Plin., Glückst. 1881, 5) is mentioned, we should rather in ind. auct. 18 write: *ex . . . Sabino ⟨Tirone⟩, Fabiano.*—HGHöfig, de Papirii Fabiani philosophi vita scriptisque, Bresl. 1852.

267. Oratory, so far as it still throve in the Republican time, was represented by Asinius Pollio and M. Messalla, besides whom we may mention Furnius, Atratinus, L. Arruntius, Q. Haterius (a. 690/64 B.C.–779/26 A.D.) and others. The younger generation adapted their talents to the narrow sphere allowed by the Monarchy; *e.g.* the sons of Messalla, Messalinus and Cotta, Fabius Maximus, and others. Greater importance attaches to T. Labienus and Cassius Severus, whose candour of expression brought them into trouble, Labienus becoming obnoxious through his historical work. Cassius Severus, a writer hated and feared on account of his poignant humour, may still be considered an orator and only against his will engaged in scholastic declamation, yet in the manner of his eloquence he betrayed his affinity to the prevailing style of the period.

1. On Asinius Pollio and Messalla as orators see above § 221, 4 and 222, 2. Pedius is mentioned, in conjunction with Messalla, as a renowed orator who like the latter (§ 222, 2 l. 11) carefully cultivated a pure Latin style avoiding the use of foreign words, by Hor. s. 1, 10, 28 *cum Pedius exudet causas Poplicola atque Corvinus.* It is doubtful whether Horace here calls him *Pedius Poplicola* (in proof of which we can no longer quote the inscription CIA. 3, 866, as the stone reads Λευκίου Γελλίου [not Πεδίου, as in the bull. arch. 1855, xxx] Ποπλικόλα) or whether *Poplicola* does not rather belong to *Corvinus;* cf. Verg. catal. 9, 40 *praemia Messallis maxima Poplicolis* and PRE. 6, 2352**. He might be a natural son of Q. Pedius cos. 711/43, and would thus be connected on the mother's side with Messalla (Plin. NH. 35, 21).

It is usual to identify him (following Ps.-ACRON) with the author mentioned in HORACE s. 1, 10, 85 (*te Messala, tuo cum fratre*) and to take him for an adopted son of Q. Pedius. But this opinion of Ps.-Acron probably rests only on a hasty inference drawn from a comparison of the two passages in Horace, and it will therefore be more correct (with KNIPPERDEY, op. 494. 540) to identify this brother of Messalla with his half-brother L. Gellius L. f. Poplicola (cos. 718/36; PRE. 3, 664. LSCHWABE, quaest. Catull. 111). We might also think of Valerius Messalla Potitus cos. suff. 725/29, if it were quite certain that he was a brother of Messalla the orator (for this view see BORGHESI, oeuvr. 1, 412). It is probably this Potitus who is quoted by PLIN. ind. auct. to b. 19 as the author of κηπουρικά (§ 54, 4). Cf. PLIN. NH. 14, 69 and DDETLEFSEN, üb. einige Quellen des Plin., Glückst. 1881, 6.—On Furnius § 209, 9; Sempronius Atratinus § 209, 10. On the rhetorical training and the oratory of Augustus § 220, 2; of Maecenas § 220, 7; of Agrippa § 220, 11.

2. HOR. ep. 1, 5, 9 (perhaps a. 735/19 to Torquatus) *mitte . . . Moschi causam;* on this PORPHYRIO: *Moschus hic Pergamenus fuit rhetor notissimus. reus veneficii fuit, cuius causam ex primis tunc oratores egerunt, Torquatus hic, de quo nunc dicit, cuius exstat oratio, et Asinius Pollio.* Of the same Torquatus, HOR. c. 4, 7, 23 praises the *genus, facundia et pietas.* As Suetonius' narrative allows us to infer that the Manlii Torquati had become extinct in the Civil Wars, this Torquatus is probably (see WEICHERT de Cass. Parm. p. 304) the person mentioned by SUET. Aug. 43: *in hoc (Troiae) ludicro Nonium Asprenatem lapsu debilitatum aureo torque donavit passusque est ipsum posterosque Torquati ferre cognomen.* Cf. ib. 56 *cum Asprenas Nonius artius ei* (i.e. Augustus) *iunctus causam veneficii accusante Cassio Severo diceret* etc. He may, therefore, be one of the two Asprenates whose declamations are mentioned by the rhetorician Seneca, frequently in the case of Publius, e.g. suas. 7, 4. contr. 1, 1, 5. 1, 2, 9. 1, 8, 4–6 and 12. 2, 10, 4. 7, 23, 6. 10, 33, 25 (*P. Asprenates dixit*), once in the case of Lucius, ib. 10, praef. 2 (*pertinere ad rem non puto quomodo . . . L. Asprenates aut Quintilianus senex declamaverit; transeo istos quorum fama cum ipsis extincta est*). L. Nonius Asprenas was cos. 759/6 A.D., another a. 782/29 A.D.; a P. Nonius Asprenas (son of the declaimer?) cos. 791/38 A.D. in the reign of Caligula.

3. On L. Arruntius (n. 8) see above § 259, 7.

4. Q. Lucretius Vespillo, cos. 735/19; PRE. 4, 1195. A funeral speech on his wife Turia, who died after a married life of 41 years, about 746/8–752/2, a fervid outpouring of feeling, is preserved in an inscription, CIL. 6, 1527. ORELLI 4859. BRUNS, font. [5] 303. MOMMSEN, zwei Sepulcralreden aus der Zeit Augusts u. Hadr., Abh. der Berl. Akad. 1863, 455. 464. 477. GBDEROSSI, in the studi di storia e diritto 1 (1880), 1. Cf. § 356, 5.

5. HIERON. on Eus. chr. a. Abr. 2040 = 777/24 A.D. *Q. Haterius promptus et popularis orator usque ad XC prope annum cum summo honore consenescit.* TAC. a. 4, 61 *fine anni* (779/26 A.D.) *excessere insignes viri, Asinius Agrippa . . . et Q. Haterius, familia senatoria, eloquentiae quoad vixit celebratae. monimenta ingeni eius haud perinde retinentur. scilicet impetu magis quam cura vigebat. . . . Haterii canorum illud et profluens cum ipso simul extinctum est.* SEN. contr. 4, praef. 6–11 *Q. Haterium scio . . . imbecillo animo mortes sex filiorum* (*mortem Sex. filii* KIESSLING) *tulisse. . . . declamabat Haterius admisso populo ex tempore. solus omnium Romanorum quos modo ipse cognovi in latinam linguam transtulerat graecam facultatem. tanta erat illi velocitas orationis ut vitium fieret. . . . nec verborum illi tantum copia sed etiam rerum erat. . . . quaedam antiqua et a Cicerone dicta, a ceteris deinde deserta dicebat. . . . multa erant quae reprehenderes, multa quae suspiceres* etc. SEN.

ep. 40, 10. Specimens of his declamations are frequently given by Seneca the Elder, see p. 541 Kiessl. Cf. also Tac. a. 2, 33 (*consularis*). Suet. Tib. 27. 29. ACima, de Q. Haterio Oratore, in his Saggj di studj lat., Flor. 1889, 105.

6. M. Valerius Corvinus Messalla or Messalinus, the orator's eldest son, cos. 751/3; PRE. 6, 2355, 100. GGräber, quaestt. Ovid. 1 (Elberf. 1881), 17. Tac. a. 3, 34 *Valerius Messalinus, cui parens Messala ineratque imago paternae facundiae.* Ov. Pont. 2, 2, 51 *vivit enim in vobis* (this Messallinus and Cotta who is just about to be mentioned) *facundi lingua parentis.* Cf. § 230, 2, n. 1. His appointment as XVvir sacr. is celebrated in Tib. 2, 5 (of a. 735/19 ?) Letters addressed to him by Ovid ex Pont. 1, 7. 2, 2 and trist. 4, 4 (cf. v. 5 *cuius in ingeniost patriae facundia linguae*); cf. Gräber l.l. 1, 20.—His younger brother was called M. Aurelius Cotta Maximus, from the time (after a. 762/9 A.D.) when he was adopted into the family of his mother, the gens Aurelia, but after the death of his brother (who may have died childless) he assumed his cognomen of Messalinus. He took little part in politics (cos. 773/20) and shifting his position with the utmost servility led the life of a voluptuary (*egens ob luxum, per flagitia infamis*, Tac. a. 6, 7), adding to the pleasures of the table (Plin. NH. 10, 52) the pastime of verse-making (§ 252, 15) and repartee (Tac. a. 6, 5). He was on very friendly terms with Ovid though much his junior; ex Ponto 1, 5. 9. 2, 3. 8. 3, 2. 5, probably also trist. 4, 5 (see esp. v. 29 sqq.). 9. Ovid read at Tomi a speech which he had made before the tribunal of the Centumvirs, Pont. 3, 5, 7 (*legimus, o iuvenis patrii non degener oris, dicta tibi pleno verba diserta foro*). He is also mentioned as a patron of poets in Juv. 5, 108. 7, 94. Cf. also the epigram in exaggerated praise of him by a certain Zosimus, his freedman, in WHenzen, ann. arch. 37, 5.—On him see PRE. 6, 2356, 101. Henzen, l.l.; act. fratr. Arv. p. 179. Gräber l.l. 1, 19. BLorentz, de Ovidii in trist. amicis, Lps. 1881, 3.

7. Paulus Fabius Q. f. Maximus, cos. 743/11 † 767/14. Ovid addressed to him ex Ponto 1, 2. 3, 3. 8. On him ib. 4, 6, 9 (*Fabiae laus, Maxime, gentis*). 1, 2, 69 (*romanae facundia, Maxime, linguae*). 117 *vox . . . tua . . . auxilio trepidis quae solet esse reis . . . doctae dulcedine linguae*) and 137 (*tua nonnumquam . . . scripta legebas*). Hor. c. 4, 1, 9 (*pro sollicitis non tacitus reis et centum puer artium*). Quint. 6, 3, 52. He (his brother cos. 744/10 *Q. Fabius Q. f. Maximus Africanus* is not otherwise known as an orator) is probably the same person who is several times mentioned in Sen. contr.: 2, 4, 9 (*Fabius Maximus*). 10, praef. 13 (*Fabius*). 2, 4, 11 *sed ut aliquid iocemur, Fabius* (*Fabianus* in the MSS.) *Maximus nobilissimus vir fuit qui primus foro romano hunc novicium morbum quo nunc laborat intulit, de quo Severus Cassius, antequam ab illo reus ageretur, dixerat: 'quasi disertus es, quasi formosus es, quasi dives es: unum tantum non es quasi—vappa.'* PRE. 6, 2919, 67. Gräber l.l. 1, 10. Lorentz l.l. 19.

8. Tac. a. 11, 6 (in the time of Claudius, A.D. 47) *meminissent Gai Asinii, M. Messalae ac recentiorum Arruntii* (n. 3) *et Aesernini: ad summa provectos incorrupta vita et facundia.* Aeserninus is probably the son of the cos. of 732/22 M. Claudius Marcellus Aeserninus, and grandson to Asinius Pollio (Suet. Aug. 43), born perhaps 725/29–730/24, initiated into oratory by his grandfather; see Sen. contr. 4, praef. 3 sq., where we read e.g.: *Marcellus, quamvis puer, iam tantae indolis erat ut Pollio ad illum pertinere successionem eloquentiae suae crederet.* Specimens (though generally short ones) of his declamations are given by Sen. suas. and contr. (see Kiessling's ind. p. 544). Cf. also Tac. a. 3, 11 and above § 259, 7.

9. Plin. NH. 34, 47 *duo pocula . . . quae Cassio Salano . . . praeceptori suo Germanicus Caesar . . . donaverat.* This is the Salanus to whom Ovid addressed

ex Pont. 2, 5, in which he is called *doctissimus* (v. 15), and his *eloquium* (40) and *facundia* (69) are praised, and also poetical compositions by him are indicated (63–68), his relations to Germanicus (41–56) being mentioned.

10. On T. Labienus see especially SEN. contr. 10, praef. 4 sqq. e.g.: *declamavit non quidem populo, sed egregie. . . . magnus orator, qui multa impedimenta eluctatus ad famam ingeni confitentibus magis hominibus pervenerat quam volentibus. summa egestas erat, summa infamia, summum odium. . . .* (5) *color orationis antiquaè, vigor novae, cultus inter nostrum ac prius saeculum medius. libertas tanta ut libertatis nomen excederet et, quia passim ordines hominesque laniabat, 'Rabie⟨nu⟩s' vocaretur. . . . in hoc primum excogitata est nova poena: effectum est enim per inimicos eius ut omnes eius libri* (ex senatus consulto) *comburerentur. . . .* (7) *non tulit hanc Labienus contumeliam nec superstes esse ingenio suo voluit, sed in monimenta se maiorum suorum ferri iussit atque ita includi* (c. 765/12 A.D.?) . . . (8) *memini aliquando cum recitaret historiam, magnam partem illum libri convolvisse et dixisse 'haec quae transeo post mortem meam legentur.'* SUET. Calig. 16 *Titi Labieni, Cordi Cremuti, Cassi Severi scripta, senatus consultis abolita, requiri et esse in manibus lectitarique permisit.* SEN. contr. 4, praef. 2 *homo mentis quam linguae amarioris.* Specimens of his declamations are found p. 483. 485 sq. 489. 498. 501 K. In the law-suit about the inheritance of Urbinia, Labienus conducted the case of Figulus and was opposed to Asinius Pollio; cf. QUINT. 1, 5, 8. 4, 1, 11. 9, 3, 13. CHARIS. GL. 1, 77, 14. 376, 8. A speech of Lab. against Bathyllus is alluded to by SEN. contr. 10 praef. 8. Cf. WEICHERT de L. Vario p. 319.

11. TAC. a. 1, 72 *primus Augustus cognitionem de famosis libellis . . . tractavit, commotus Cassii Severi libidine, qua viros feminasque inlustres procacibus scriptis diffamaverat.* The aristocratic historian's indignation at this presumption appears also ib. 4, 21 *relatum de Cassio Severo exule, qui sordidae originis, maleficae vitae, sed orandi validus, per immodicas inimicitias ut . . . Cretam amoveretur effecerat; atque illic eadem actitando recentia veteraque odia advertit, bonisque exutus . . . saxo Seripho consenuit.* HIERON. ad a. Abr. 2048=785/32 A.D.: *Cassius Severus, orator egregius, qui Quintianum illud proverbium luserat, XXV exilii sui anno in summa inopia moritur vix panno verenda contectus.* He may, therefore, have been born c. 710/44 B.C., and for this very reason, even if there were no others, HOR. epod. 6 cannot relate to him; see TEUFFEL, ZfAW. 1845, 596. His character is delineated by SEN. contr. 3, praef. 2 *oratio eius erat valens, culta, ingentibus plena sententiis. . . .* (3) *non est quod illum ex his quae edidit aestimetis; . . . auditus longe maior erat quam lectus . . . corporis magnitudo conspicua* (cf. PLIN. NH. 7, 55 *Cassio Severo celebri oratori armentarii mirmillonis obiecta similitudo est*), *suavitas valentissimae vocis. . . .* (4) *gravitas, quae deerat vitae, actioni supererat. . . .* (5) *uno die privatas plures agebat, . . . publicam vero numquam amplius quam unam uno die. nec tamen scio quem reum illi defendere nisi se* (against the accusation of Fabius Maximus, ib. 2, 12, 11) *contigerit. . . .* (7) *omnia habebat quae illum ut bene declamaret instruerent: phrasin . . . lectam, genus dicendi . . . ardens et concitatum . . . explicationes plus sensuum quam verborum habentes. . . . tamen non tantum infra se, cum declamaret, sed infra multos erat. itaque raro declamabat et non nisi ab amicis coactus.* He himself instructively explains this ib. 12 (c. a. 744/10; JBRZOSKA, comm. phil. in honor. Reifferscheidii, Bresl. 1884, 40) by saying that he was able only *causas agere, in foro dicere*, but not to pursue this idle occupation seriously. Cf. suasor. 6, 11. Specimens of his witticisms in SEN. contr. 2, 12, 11. 4, praef. 11. 9, 26, 14. 10, praef. 8. 10, 34, 20. QUINT. 6, 3, 27 cf. 78 sq. 6, 1, 43. 8, 2, 2. 8, 3, 89. 11, 3, 133. SUET. gr. 22.

Specimens of his declamations are given by SEN. contr. 7, 18, 10. 9, 25, 12 and especially 10, 33, 2. The exaggeration of details in the latter confirms the judgment of TAC. dial. 19 : *antiquorum admiratores . . . Cassium Severum . . . primum affirmant flexisse ab ista vetere atque directa dicendi via*, and ib. 26: *equidem non negaverim Cassium Severum, . . . si iis comparetur qui postea fuerunt, posse oratorem vocari, quamquam in magna parte librorum suorum plus viri habet quam sanguinis; primus enim contempto ordine rerum, omissa modestia ac pudore verborum . . . non pugnat, sed rixatur. ceterum et varietate eruditionis et lepore urbanitatis et ipsarum virium robore multum ceteros superat.* QUINT. 10, 1, 116 *multa, si cum iudicio legatur, dabit imitatione digna Cassius Severus, qui, si ceteris virtutibus colorem et gravitatem orationis adiecisset, ponendus inter praecipuos foret.* (117) *nam et ingenii plurimum est in eo et acerbitas mira et urbanitas et fervor; sed plus stomacho quam consilio dedit.* According to DIO 55, 4, he prosecuted (a. 745/9) Augustus' friend, Nonius Asprenas, (see n. 2) on a charge of poisoning, Asinius Pollio being the defendant's counsel QUINT. 10, 1, 22. One of his speeches is quoted by DIOM. 1, 371, 19. *Cassius Severus ad Maecenatem* (a letter ?) in CHARIS. GL. 1, 104, 11 = PRISC. GL. 2, 333, 11 : *Cassius ad Tiberium secundo* in DIOM. GL. 1, 373, 20 = PRISC. 2, 489, 3. Cf. also HERTZ on Prisc. 2, 380, 1. TERTULL. apol. 10. adv. nat. 2, 12 mentions him among historians, but he confounds him with Cassius Hemina (§ 132, 1. 368, 1). The assumption that he was a native of Longula has lost its foundation since the punctuation has been changed in the ind. auct. in PLIN. NH. 35, in the following manner: *ex . . . Cassio Severo, Longulano.* This Longulanus, however, (see a conjecture in LURLICHS, die Quellenregister zu Plin. letzten BB. [Würzb. 1878] 14), is as completely unknown to us as *Fabius Vestalis qui de pictura scripsit*, who is mentioned directly afterwards and also quoted (without mention of this work) in the ind. auct. to b. 7. 34 and 36. Cf. URLICHS l.l.—THFROMENT, un orateur républicain sous Auguste, Cass. Sev., Annal. de la fac. d. lettr. de Bordeaux 1 (1879), 121.

12. *Varius Geminus, sublimis orator* (L. Seneca ap. HIERON. adv. Iovin. 1 p. 170), *apud Caesarem dixit: Caesar, qui apud te audent dicere magnitudinem tuam ignorant, qui non audent, humanitatem* (SEN. contr. 6, 8, 6). Specimens of his declamations are given by SEN. suas. 6, 11–14. contr. 7, 16, 18 and 23. 7, 19, 5. 7, 21, 10 and 15–17. 7, 22, 11.

268. Among the rhetoricians of the Augustan age the most aristocratic of the older generation was the Roman knight Blandus, but among the most famous was M. Porcius Latro, the compatriot and early friend of Seneca the Elder; Arellius Fuscus, who followed the prevailing taste of Asia, his native country; C. Albucius Silus of Novara : Passienus the Elder; the vain Cestius Pius of Smyrna; L. Junius Gallio, also a friend of the elder Seneca. In the younger generation we may mention among the, relatively speaking, most eminent rhetoricians Papirius Fabianus, a man of philosophical training, and Alfius Flavus, who wrote also in verse. We meet with a great number of other school-rhetoricians in the pages of Seneca the Elder.

1. SEN. contr. 2, pr. 5 *Blandum rhetorem qui ⟨primus⟩ eques Rom. Romae docuit* (rhetoric § 45, 1). From Tibur according to TAC. a. 6, 27 *in domum Rubellii Blandi, cuius avum Tibertem eq. Rom. plerique meminerant* (BORGHESI, op. 4, 486). Cf. besides SEN. contr. 1, 7, 13. 2, 5, 14. 15. 7, 5, 13. Did this writer also compose historical works? SERV. ge. 1, 103 *Rubellius Blandus et Quadrigarius historici dicunt* etc.—SEN. contr. 10, praef. 13 *primum tetradeum quod faciam quaeritis? Latronis, Fusci, Albuci, Gallionis.* As a proof of the prevalent bad taste he mentions ib. 3, praef. 14: *et Pollionem Asinium et Messalam Corvinum et Passienum . . minus bene videri quam Cestium aut Latronem.* In general see ASCHOTT, de claris apud Senecam rhetoribus, in his ed. of Seneca (§ 269, 8) and the indices to the edd of Seneca by KIESSLING and HJMÜLLER.

2. HIERON. chron. a. Abr. 2013 = 750/4 B.C. *M. Porcius Latro* (cf. SUET. ind. rhet. p. 99 Rffsch.) *latinus declamator taedio duplicis quartanae semet ipsum interficit.* His character is delineated by SEN. contr. 1, praef. 13–18. 20–24, e.g. *Latronis Porcii, carissimi mihi sodalis, memoriam . . . et a prima pueritia usque ad ultimum eius diem perductam familiarem amicitiam . . . nihil illo viro gravius, nihil suavius, . . . nemo plus ingenio suo imperavit, nemo plus indulsit. in utraque parte vehementi viro modus deerat. . . .* (16) *corpus illi erat natura solidum et multa exercitatione duratum. . . . vox robusta sed sordida, lucubrationibus et neglegentia . . . infuscata. . . . nulla umquam illi cura vocis exercendae fuit: illum fortem et agrestem et hispanae consuetudinis morem non poterat dediscere.* (17) . . . *memoria ei natura quidem felix, plurimum tamen arte adiuta.* (20) . . . *cum in illo, si qua alia virtus fuit, et subtilitas fuerit. . . .* (22) *cum condiscipuli essemus* (at Rome) *apud Marullum rhetorem, hominem satis aridum* (see n. 10) . . . (24) *controversia . . . quam primam Latronem meum declamasse memini admodum iuvenem in Marulli schola.* 9, praef. 3 *Latronem Porcium, declamatoriae virtutis unicum exemplum, cum pro reo in Hispania Rustico Porcio propinquo suo diceret* etc. (= QUINT. 10, 5, 18 *P. L., qui primus clari nominis professor fuit*). 10, praef. 15 *Latro numquam solebat disputare in convivio aut alio quam quo declamare poterat tempore. . . . negabat itaque ulli se placere posse nisi totum.* Numerous specimens of his declamations are given by Seneca the Elder (e.g. contr. 7, 16, 16 sqq.), which show him to have been a relatively natural and moderate rhetorician. Cf. LINDNER l.l. p. 25. Messalla thought his style not purely Roman (SEN. contr. 2, 12, 8). From a declamatio de raptore (SEN. contr. 2, 11) by Latro a passage is quoted by QUINT. 9, 2, 91. His pupils were greatly attached to him: see SEN. contr. 9, 25, 23 *nec ulli alii contigisse scio quam apud Graecos Niceti, apud Romanos Latroni ut discipuli non audiri desiderarent, sed contenti essent audire.* They would even drink cuminum silvestre to look pale like their master (PLIN. NH. 20, 160). Among these pupils were Ovid (§ 247, 1), Florus (SEN. contr. 9, 25, 23), Fulvius Sparsus (n. 10) and Abronius Silo (§ 252, 14). FGLINDNER, de M. Porcio Latrone, Bresl. 1855. THFROMENT, Porc. Latro ou la déclamation sous Auguste, Ann. de la fac. de lettr. de Bordeaux 4 (1882), 335.

3. SEN. contr. 9, 29, 16 *Fuscus Arellius cum esset ex Asia* etc. was closely allied to his compatriots Addaios (ib. 9, 24, 12) and Hybreas (ib. 9, 29, 16). suas. 4, 5 *quia soletis mihi molesti esse de Fusco, quid fuerit quare nemo videretur dixisse cultius, ingeram vobis Fuscinas explicationes. dicebat autem suasorias libentissime et frequentius graecas quam latinas.* His manner is repeatedly characterised by Seneca the Elder; e.g. suas. 2, 10 *ut sciretis quam nitide Fuscus dixisset vel quam licenter. . . . nihil fuisse me iuvene* (which shows that Fuscus was somewhat older than Seneca) *tam notum quam has explicationes Fusci* etc. Cf. ib. 3, 7 *descrip-*

tionibus Fusci vos satiem? contr. 2, praef. 1 *erat explicatio Fusci Arelli splendida quidem sed operosa et implicata, cultus nimis adquisitus, compositio verborum mollior . . .; summa inaequalitas orationis, quae modo exilis erat, modo nimia licentia vaga et effusa; principia, argumenta, narrationes aride dicebantur; in descriptionibus extra legem omnibus verbis, dummodo niterent, permissa libertas; nihil acre, nihil solidum, nihil horridum; splendida oratio et magis lasciva quam laeta.* To this should be added suas. 3, 5 *solebat Fuscus ex Vergilio multa trahere, ut Maecenati imputaret;* cf. ib. 4, 5. Seneca the Elder's work contains numerous specimens of the oratory of Fuscus, the longest of which stand suas. 2, 1 sqq. and contr. 2, 9, 4–8. 7, 21, 7 sq. Cf. LINDNER l.l. p. 11. As Seneca in some of these passages calls him *Arellius Fuscus* (or *Fuscus Arellius*) *pater*, we infer that, like Clodius Turrinus (SEN. contr. 10, praef. 14 sqq. contr. 10, praef, 16 *Apollodoreos sequitur* and elsewhere, see p. 536 Kiessl.), he had, at the time when Seneca wrote his work, a son who in his turn pursued rhetorical studies, though it does not entitle us to explain those passages, in which *pater* is omitted and we read only Arellius Fuscus or Fuscus Arellius, of the son, the designation of *filius* never being added. On the contrary it appears from the numerous instances in which in one and the same sentence *pater* is now added and then again omitted, that all the passages of Seneca should be understood of the father, he being the famous rhetorician of the name; see TEUFFEL, PRE. 1², 1496, 6. LINDNER l.l. p. 4–6. Among his pupils were Ovid (§ 247, 1) and Papirius Fabianus (§ 266, 10). Certainly not of him, but perhaps of his son, PLINY says NH. 33, 152: *vidimus et ipsi Arellium Fuscum motum equestri ordine ob insignem calumniam, cum celebritatem assectarentur adolescentium scholae, argenteos anulos habentem.* FGLINDNER, de Arellio Fusco, Bres. 1862.

4. SUET. rhet. 6 (=gr. 30) *C. Albucius Silus Novariensis cum aedilitate in patria fungeretur . . . contendit . . . inde Romam, receptusque in Planci oratoris* (§ 209, 8) *contubernium . . . ex eo clarus propria auditoria instituit, solitus declamare genere vario: modo splendide atque adornate, tum . . . circumcise ac sordide et tantum non trivialibus verbis. egit et causas, verum rarius, dum amplissimam quamque sectatur nec alium in ulla locum quam perorandi. postea renuntiavit foro, partim pudore partim metu* (especially after in a suit pleaded before the Centumviri L. Arruntius had made him feel the difference between rhetorical figures and legal deductions, SEN. contr. 7, praef. 7. SUET. l.l. QUINT. 9, 2, 95). *et rursus in cognitione caedis Mediolani apud L. Pisonem proconsulem* (cos. 739/15) *defendens reum . . . paene poenas luit. iam autem senior ob vitium vomicae Novariam rediit convocataque plebe causis propter quas mori destinasset diu ac more contionantis redditis abstinuit cibo.* HIERON. ad a. Abr. 2011 = 748/6 B.C. *Albucius Silo Novariensis clarus rhetor agnoscitur.* Everything proves him to have been a contemporary of Seneca the Elder (LINDNER l.l. p. 7). QUINT. 2, 15, 36 *Albucius, non obscurus professor atque auctor*, a passage which also shows that he wrote on the theory of oratory. Cf. ib. 3, 3, 4. 3, 6, 62 (in VERGIL. catal. 7, 3 the reference to Albucius is based on a false conjecture). His oratorical style is described by SEN. contr. 7, praef., e.g.: (1) *instatis mihi quotidie de Albucio. non ultra vos differam, quamvis non audierim frequenter, cum per totum annum quinquiens sexiensve populo diceret* (declaimed publicly) . . . *alius erat cum turbae se committebat, alius cum paucitate contentus erat. . . . illa intempestiva in declamationibus eius philosophia sine modo tunc . . . evagabatur. cum populo diceret omnes vires suas advocabat et ideo non desinebat. . . . argumentabatur moleste magis quam subtiliter. . . .* (2) . . . *splendor orationis quantus nescio an in nullo alio fuerit. . . . dicebat citato et effuso cursu, sed praeparatus. . . . sententiae . . . simplices, apertae. . .* (3) . . . *non posses de inopia sermonis latini queri cum illum audires:*

tantum orationis cultae fluebat . . . (4) *timebat ne scholasticus videretur.* . . . *quem proxime dicentem commode audierat imitari volebat. memini illum* . . . *apud Fabianum philosophum tanto iuveniorem quam ipse erat cum codicibus sedere;* (5) *memini admiratione Hermagorae stupentem ad imitationem eius ardescere. nulla erat fiducia ingenii sui et ideo adsidua mutatio.* . . . (6) *raro Albucio respondebat fortuna, semper opinio.* . . . (7) *erat homo summae probitatis, qui nec facere iniuriam nec pati sciret.* Cf. also ib. 1, 4, 14 (*Albucius, qui Graecos praeminet*). Numerous specimens of his declamations are given by Seneca the Elder, e.g. contr. 7, 16, 1–3. 9, 25, 6–8. FGLindner, de C. Albucio Silo, Bresl. 1861.

5. Hieron. ad a. Abr. 2008=745/9 b.c. *Passienus pater, declamator insignis diem obit.* Sen. contr. 2, 13, 17 *Passienus, vir eloquentissimus et temporis sui primus orator.* 3, praef. 14 *Passienum, qui nunc primo loco stat.* 10, praef. 11 *Passieno* . . . *declamatori subtili, sed arido.* 3, praef. 10 *Passienus noster* (Cassius Severus being the speaker) *cum coepit dicere, secundum principium statim fuga fit, ad epilogum omnes revertimur, media tantum quibus necesse est audiunt.* He was esteemed by Augustus (*tantus vir*), ib. 10, 34, 21. Cf. also ib. 7, 16, 20. His son was *Passienus Crispus bis consul* (iterum 799/44 a.d.), *orator, Agrippinae matrimonio et Nerone privigno clarior postea* (Plin. NH. 16, 242). Cf. Schol. Iuv. 4, 81 (though there he appears to be confounded with Vibius Crispus § 297, 2) *plurimas sponte causas apud centumviros egit.* . . . *consulatus duos gessit. uxores habuit duas, primam Domitiam, deinde Agrippinam.* . . . *omnium principum gratiam adpetivit, sed praecipue C. Caesaris.* . . . *periit per fraudem Agrippinae* etc. Tac. a. 6, 20 *scitum Passieni oratoris dictum.* Quint. 6, 1, 50. 10, 1, 24 *nobis pueris insignes pro Voluseno Catulo Domitii Afri, Crispi Passieni, D. Laelii orationes ferebantur.* To him is addressed the epigram (perhaps by Seneca) AL. 405 PLM. 4, 60, in which v. 2 *Crispe, vel antiquo conspiciende foro.* v. 8 *cuius cecropio pectora melle madent, maxima facundo vel avo vel gloria patri.* Cf. AL. 445 PLM. 4, 78.

6. Hieron. ad a. Abr. 2004=741/13 b.c. *L. Cestius Pius* (Suet. ind. rhett., p. 99 Rffsch.) *Smyrnaeus rhetor latine Romae docuit.* Sen. suas. 7. 13 *erat Cestius* . . . *Ciceroni etiam infestus, quod illi non inpune cessit. nam cum M. Tullius, filius Ciceronis, Asiam obtineret* (a. 725/29) . . . *cenabat apud eum Cestius* . . . *servus* . . . *interroganti domino quis ille esset qui in imo recumberet ait 'hic est Cestius qui patrem tuum negabat litteras scisse'; adferri ocius flagra iussit et Ciceroni* . . . *de corio Cestii satisfecit.* contr. 3, praef. 16 *pueri fere aut iuvenes scholas frequentant; hi non tantum disertissimis viris* (contemporaries) *Cestium suum praeferunt sed etiam Ciceroni praeferrent ni lapides timerent.* . . . *huius declamationes ediscunt, illius orationes non legunt nisi eas quibus Cestius rescripsit.* (16) *memini* (says Cassius Severus) *me intrare scholam eius cum recitaturus esset in Milonem* (cf. Quint. 10, 5, 20 *rescribere veteribus orationibus, ut fecit Cestius contra Ciceronis actionem habitam pro Milone*). . . . *Cestius Ciceroni responsurus mihi quod responderet non invenit.* . . . (17) *deinde libuit* (*mihi*) *Ciceroni de Cestio in foro satisfacere.* . . . *dixi molestum me amplius non futurum si iurasset disertiorem esse Ciceronem quam se. nec hoc ut faceret vel ioco vel serio effici potuit.* contr. 7, praef. 8 *Cestii, mordacissimi hominis.* 7, 16, 27 *Cestium latinorum verborum inopia hominem graecum laborasse, sensibus abundasse.* Many specimens of his declamations occur in the pages of Seneca. Of his pupils we may mention Surdinus (§ 15, 3), Aietius Pastor (Sen. contr. 1, 3, 11), Quintilius Varus (the son of the general known for his defeat and son-in-law to Germanicus, ib. 1, 3, 10), and especially Argentarius, see Sen. contr. 9, 26, 12 *Cestius* . . . *quid putatis, aiebat, Argen-*

tarium esse? Cesti simius est. . . . fuerat enim Argentarius Cesti auditor et erat imitator. (13) . . . *aeque ex tempore dicebat, aeque contumeliose multa interponebat; illud tamen optima fide praestitit, cum uterque Graecus esset, ut numquam graece declamaret.* Cf. PRE. 1², 1518, 1. FGLindner, de L. Cestio Pio, Züllichau 1856.

7. (L.) Junius Gallio, friend to Seneca the Elder (*Gallio noster*, Sen. suas. 3, 6. contr. 2, 1, 33. 2, 5, 11. 13. 7, praef. 5), and Ovid (*Nasoni suo*, Sen. suas. 3, 7), probably the same Gallio whom Ovid endeavours to console on the death of his wife, ex Pont. 4, 11. He seems to have been nearer in age to Ovid than to Seneca the Elder; Sen. contr. 7, praef. 5 sq. He wrote a rhetorical work (Quint. 3, 1, 21 *pater Gallio*) and declamations (ib. 9, 2, 91 *remissius et pro suo ingenio pater Gallio*; cf. Tac. dial. 26 *tinnitus Gallionis*), which were still extant in the age of Hieronymus, (comm. in Esaiam, praef. *qui . . . concinnas declamationes desiderant legant Tullium, Quintilianum, Gallionem, Gabinianum*). Specimens which lead us to infer relative sobriety of style (e.g. Schmidt l.l. 22) are frequent in Seneca; the longer ones occur suas. 5, 8. contr. 1, 1, 8 and 14. 1, 2, 11 sq. 1, 7, 12. 1, 8, 9. 2, 11, 6 sq. and 14. 7, 16, 12 sq. 7, 22, 3–5. 7, 23, 4. 7, 24, 8 and 10. 9, 26, 2 sq. and 6. 9, 27, 12 sq. 9, 28, 1. 7 sq. 11. 21. 10, 31, 1–3. 10, 34, 13–17. See also 10, praef. 8 *monstrabo bellum vobis libellum, quem a Gallione vestro petatis. recitavit rescriptum Labieno pro Bathyllo Maecenatis.* Tac. a. 6, 3. Dio 60, 35. 62, 25. BSchmidt, de L. Iunio Gallione rhetore, Marb. 1866. FGLindner, de I. G. comm. Hirschb. 1868. He adopted the eldest son of his friend Seneca, M. Annaeus Novatus, who was subsequently called L. Junius Gallio (Dio 60, 35); the latter obtained a consulship (cf. JAsbach, anall. hist. et. epigr. 22) and then governed Achaia (A.D. 52). Stat. silv. 2, 7, 32 calls him *dulcis.* His brother Seneca addressed to him (under the name of Novatus) his treatises de ira and (ad Gallionem) de vita beata. According to Tac. a. 15, 73, he survived Seneca († 65), but was soon forced to follow his example; Hieron. a. Abr. 2080=64 A.D. (instead of 65) *Iunius Gallio, frater Senecae, egregius declamator* (perhaps a confusion with his adoptive father) *propria se manu interficit.* PRE. 1², 1025, 13ª.

8. Sen. contr. 2, 9, 33 *Iunius Otho pater . . . edidit IV libros colorum, quos belle Gallio noster Antiphontis libros vocabat; tantum in illis somniorum est.* Cf. 1, 3, 11 *Othonem Iunium patrem memini colorem stultum inducere, quod minus ferendum est quod libros colorum edidit.* Seneca gives specimens of his declamations also. He was praetor a. 775/22 A.D. Of him Tac. a. 3, 66 *Iunio Othoni litterarium ludum exercere vetus ars fuit; mox Seiani potentia senator obscura initia impudentibus ausis propolluebat.*

9. Sen. contr. 1, 1, 22 *hanc partem memini apud Cestium declamari ab Alfio Flavo, ad quem audiendum me fama perduxerat; qui cum praetextatus esset tantae opinionis fuit ut populo rom. pure eloquentia notus esset. . . . tanto concursu hominum audiebatur ut raro auderet post illum Cestius dicere. ipse omnia mala faciebat ingenio suo. naturalis tamen illa vis eminebat quae post multos annos, tam et desidia obruta et carminibus* (perhaps erotic poems) *enervata, vigorem tamen suum tenuit.* Cf. 2, 14, 8 *Flavum Alfium, auditorem suum, qui eandem rem lascivius dixerat, obiurgavit (Cestius).* 3, 7, 3 *Alfius Flavus hanc sententiam dixit: . . . hunc Cestius quasi corrupte dixisset obiurgans 'apparet,' inquit, 'te poetas studiose legere: iste sensus eius est qui hoc saeculum amatoriis non artibus tantum sed sententiis implevit'* (of Ovid). Specimens of the declamations of Alfius ib. 1, 1, 23. 1, 7, 7. 2, 10, 3. He is probably the same as Alfius Flavus whom Plin. NH. 9, 25, (*ni res Maecenatis et Fabiani et Flavi Alfii multorumque esset litteris mandata*, cf. ind. auct. b. 9), quotes as his authority for an anecdote of the age of Augustus.

10. Among the other rhetoricians from whom Seneca the Elder quotes extracts and who partly belonged to the period of Tiberius, those who are most frequently mentioned are Argentarius (above n. 6), P. (Nonius) Asprenas (§ 267, 2), Bruttedius Brutus, (Fabius?) Buteo, Capito (Sen. contr. 10, praef. 12), Clodius Sabinus (cf. § 211, 5) and Turrinus (see n. 3), Cornelius Hispanus, Fulvius Sparsus (an imitator of Latro, Sen. contr. 10, praef. 11; *homo inter scholasticos sanus, inter sanos scholasticus*, ib. 1, 7, 15), Gavius Sabinus and Silo (10 praef. 14), Julius Bassus (cf. § 254, 2), Licinius Nepos, Marullus (*praeceptor noster*, Sen. contr. 7, 17, 11; cf. above n. 2), Murredius (very slightingly treated by Seneca, see Körber p. 64), Musa (Sen. contr. 10, praef. 9), Pompeius Silo (*sedens et facundus et litteratus est et haberetur disertus si a praelocutione dimitteret; declamat male*, ib. 3, praef. 11; *homo qui iudicio censebatur*, ib. 9, 25, 22; a contemporary of Porcius Latro, see ib. 7, 23, 10. 9, 28, 10. Extensive specimens are given suas. 7, 5 and 10 sq. contr. 1, 2, 20. 1, 5, 3. 1, 7, 13. 2, 9, 16 and 20 sq. 9, 25, 17 sq. 9, 29, 14 sq. 10, 32, 11; cf. also § 276, 7); the delator Romanius Hispo (*erat natura qui asperiorem dicendi viam sequeretur*, ib. 9, 26, 11; cf. 7, 17, 13. Tac. a. 1, 74. 14, 65. Quint. 6, 3, 100), Sepullius Bassus, Triarius (*compositione verborum belle cadentium multos scholasticos delectabat*, Sen. contr. 7, 19, 10; a contemporary of Asinius Pollio, Latro and Cestius, ib. 2, 11, 19. 7, 19, 10. 9, 29, 11; long specimens suas. 7, 6. contr. 1, 2, 21. 2, 12, 8. 7, 20, 1 sq. 9, 25, 20 sq. 9, 29, 9 and 11. 10, 33, 4. 10, 34, 5); Vallius Syriacus, Vibius Gallus (*fuit tam magnae olim eloquentiae quam postea insaniae*, a contemporary of Papirius Fabianus Sen. contr. 2, 9, 25 sq.; specimens ib. 2, 9, 9. 7, 20, 3. 7, 23, 5. 9, 24, 4. 9, 29, 2) and Vibius Rufus (*erat qui antiquo genere diceret*, ib. 9, 25, 25. Specimens ib. 2, 9, 2. 2, 11, 8. 2, 14, 10. 7, 18, 4; but the one quoted by Plin. NH. ind. auct. on b. 14. 15. 19. 21. 22 is called *Vibius Rufinus* and is otherwise unknown), L. Vinicius (*quo nemo civis rom. in agendis causis praesentius habuit ingenium*, Sen. contr. 2, 13, 20; IIIvir monetalis a. 738/16 [Cohen 1², no. 541] and in reference to this *eleganter dixit divus Augustus: L. Vinicius ingenium in numerato habet*, ib.; a specimen ib. 19), and his cousin (ib. 19), son of the cos. suff. 735/19 (OGruppe, quaest. Ann. p. 27, not. 23), P. Vinicius (*exactissimi vir ingenii, qui nec dicere res ineptas nec ferre poterat*, ib. 7, 20, 11 *summus amator Ovidii*, ib. 10, 33, 25; a specimen ib. 1, 2, 3; against him see Sen. ep. 40, 9. Consul 755/2 a.d. PRE. 6, 2627, 4 and 5): Votienus Montanus (see § 276, 1).

11. A certain Popilius Lenas is mentioned as a rhetorician and the author of rhetorical works by Quint. 10, 7, 32; cf. 3, 1, 21. 11, 3, 183. He probably lived as late as Tiberius; cf. § 280, 1.

12. On the rhetoricians of this period who were both Greek by birth and taught in Greek, such as Artemon, Damas, Diokles, Euktemon, Glykon Spyridion (Quint. 6, 1, 41), Hybreas, Moschos (§ 267, 2; Bursian, JB. 1880 2, 142), Niketes Potamon and others, see HBuschmann, Charakteristik der griech. Rhetoren beim Rhetor Sen., Parchim 1878; die enfants terribles unter den Rhett. b. Sen., in the Festschr. f. GCHRaspe, Parch. 1883, 25. Baumm, de rhetoribus graecis a Sen. in suas. et contr. adhibitis, Kreuzb. 1885.

269. Nearly the whole of the 8th century u.c. was embraced by the life of L. Annaeus Seneca of Corduba. A man of genuine Roman severity, which is, however, frequently tempered with pleasant humour, of sober and refined judgment, and in

point of style an admirer of Cicero, he himself does not appear to have figured among the florid orators of his time. But, besides an historical work, he composed in his later years a survey of the themes commonly treated in the schools, 10 books of controversiae and one book of suasoriae, under the title: oratorum et rhetorum sententiae, divisiones, colores, which bears witness to his wonderful memory, and is a rich store-house for the history of rhetoric under Augustus and Tiberius. We possess this work with considerable gaps. Some of them are filled up by a still extant abridgment (Excerpta) made in the 4th or 5th century of the Christian era.

1. The praenomen in part of the MSS. (especially the Antverp. and Bruxell.) is *Lucius*, which may be owing to confusion with the son, but may also be right. Since the time of RVolaterranus the initial *M.* has been arbitrarily assumed. The family were of equestrian rank (Tac. a. 14, 53) and well-off (Sen. ad. Helv. 14, 3). Their home was Corduba, see Mart. 1, 61, 7 *duosque Senecas . . . facunda loquitur Corduba.* His personal character: Sen. ad Helv. matr. 17, 3 *patris mei antiquus rigor. . . . utinam . . . pater meus, minus maiorum consuetudini deditus, voluisset te praeceptis sapientiae erudiri potius quam inbui! . . . propter istas quae litteris non ad sapientiam utuntur, sed ad luxuriam instruuntur, minus te indulgere studiis passus est.* This agrees with such expressions of his father as contr. 1, praef. 6 (*insolens Graecia*) and 8 sq. (*cantandi saltandique obcena studia* etc.). 1, 6, 12 (*valde levis et graeca sententia*). 10, 33, 23 (*latinam linguam facultatis non minus habere, licentiae minus* than the Greek). Nothing proves Seneca to have himself been a rhetorician; there is not in his works a single example from a declamation composed by himself.

2. His life. Contr. 1, praef. 11 *omnes magni in eloquentia nominis excepto Cicerone videor audisse; ne Ciceronem quidem aetas mihi eripuerat, sed bellorum civilium furor, qui tunc orbem totum pervagabatur, intra coloniam meam me continuit; alioqui in illo atriolo in quo duos grandes praetextatos ait secum declamasse, potui adesse illudque ingenium . . . cognoscere et . . . potui vivam vocem audire.* He appears, therefore, to have been born a. 700/54 at the very latest. He died c. 792/39 A.D.; see note 5. He certainly was not living when his son was exiled (a. 796/43); see LSen. ad Helv. 2, 4 sq. He twice stayed at Rome; contr. 4, praef. 3 *audivi illum* (Asinius Pollio, a. 678/76–758/5) *et viridem et postea iam senem.* His accurate knowledge of the Roman rhetoricians of that period shows that his sojourn in the city lasted for some time. His masters (see § 268, 2 and 10) and friends (§ 268, 2 and 7) lived there. At a mature age he married at Corduba *Helviam, bene in antiqua et severa institutam domo,* Sen. ad Helv. 16, 3; cf. ib. 2, 4 *carissimum virum, ex quo mater trium liberorum eras, extulisti.* The eldest of them was (cf. n. 4) Novatus (see § 268, 7); the second the philosopher L. Seneca (§ 287, 1); for the third, Mela, the father of Lucan (§ 303), see Tac. a. 16, 17; cf. Polyaen. 8, 62. Cf. § 303, 2.

3. His works. L. Seneca de vita patris (vol. 3, 436 ed. Haase) *si quaecumque composuit pater meus et edi voluit iam in manus populi emisissem, ad claritatem nominis sui satis ipse prospexerat; nam nisi me decipit pietas, . . . inter eos*

haberetur qui ingenio meruerunt ut puris scriptorum titulis nobiles essent. quisquis legisset eius historias ab initio bellorum civilium . . . paene usque ad mortis suae diem, magni aestimaret scire quibus natus esset parentibus ille qui (so excellently described) *res romanas.* This historical work appears not to have been edited at that time. From this work may be taken the statement on the death of Tiberius, SUET. Tib. 73 (*Seneca eum scribit*, etc., unless his son be meant), and LACTANT. instit. 7, 15, 14 (*non inscite Seneca romanae urbis tempora distribuit in aetates*), unless LACT. has confused Sen. with 'Annaeus' Florus (SALMASIUS); see § 348. The reference in QUINT. 9, 2, 98 suits neither the existing work of the father nor any one of the son's works. ORossbach, de sen. libr. recens. et emend. 161 sqq.

4. His extant work. Contr. 1, praef. *Seneca Novato, Senecae, Melae filiis salutem.* (1) *Exigitis rem magis iocundam mihi quam facilem: iubetis enim quid de his declamatoribus sentiam qui in aetatem meam inciderunt indicare et si qua memoriae meae nondum elapsa sunt ab illis dicta colligere. . . . est, fateor, iocundum mihi redire in antiqua studia melioresque ad annos respicere* etc. (2) *sed cum multa iam mihi ex meis desideranda senectus fecerit, oculorum aciem retuderit, aurium sensum hebetaverit, nervorum firmitatem fatigaverit, inter ea quae retinui memoria est. . . . hanc aliquando in me floruisse, ut . . . in miraculum usque procederet, non nego: nam et duo milia nominum recitata quo erant ordine dicta reddebam* etc. (3) . . . *ex parte bene spero* (concerning the account desired); *nam quaecumque apud illam aut puer aut iuvenis deposui quasi recentia aut modo audita sine cunctatione profert.* . . . (4) *ita ex memoria quantum vobis satis sit superest. . . . illud necesse est impetrem, ne me quasi certum aliquem ordinem velitis sequi in contrahendis quae mihi occurrunt.* (5) . . . *necesse est me ad delicias componam memoriae meae.* (10) *quaecumque a celeberrimis viris facunde dicta teneo, ne ad quemquam privatim pertineant, populo dedicabo* (so that it would appear to have been published before his death). (12) *facile est mihi ab incunabulis nosse rem post me natam* (i.e. declamatio). At the close (10 praef. 1) he has the confession: *sinite me ab istis iuvenilibus studiis ad senectutem meam reverti. fatebor vobis, iam res taedio est. primo libenter adsilui, velut optimam vitae meae partem mihi reducturus; deinde me iam pudet, tamquam diu non seriam rem agam.* Yet he added the suasoriae to the controversiae; see contr. 2, 12, 8 *quae dixerit suo loco reddam, cum ad suasorias venero.* He also completed them; suas. 6, 27 *si hic desiero, scio futurum ut vos . . . desinatis legere. . . . ergo ut librum velitis usque ad umbilicum revolvere adiciam suasoriam proximae similem* (n. 7, the last).

5. The work was written in Seneca's senectus (see n. 4), after the fall of Sejanus (a. 784/31 A.D.; suas. 2, 12) and the death of Scaurus (a. 787/34): suas. 2, 22 *Tuscus ille qui Scaurum Mamercum, in quo Scaurorum familia extincta est, maiestatis reum fecerat.* The latest parts contain traces of events posterior to the death of Tiberius († March 790/37): suas. 3, 7 *Tiberius . . . offendebatur Nicetis ingenio*, also the statements on the accuser of Scaurus (suas. 2, 22), on the judicial burning of books (contr. 10, praef. 5 sq.), and the quotation from the work of Cremutius Cordus which was burnt under Tiberius, suas. 7, 19 sq.

6. The controversiae are divided into ten books (*libelli* 2, praef. 5; cf. 4, praef. 1), always marked by prefaces in which one or several rhetoricians are characterised, and which deserve reading both in point of form and subject. The prefaces to books 5, 6 and 8 are lost; that to b. 9 is not complete. In the single themes the writer generally observes the division according to sententiae (the opinions of the rhetoricians concerning the application of a law to a given case), divisio (distribution into single questions), and colores (disguises of a criminal act); yet the

method of the work is free, with numerous digressions. The accounts of the performances of the single rhetoricians are so much alike that they appear to be rendered merely in their general sense (against this see Sander and Karsten ll. ll.). There is a fair sprinkling of anecdotes and witticisms. The criticisms on individuals are sober and severe, sometimes even harsh. The author admires Cicero, see contr. 1, praef. 11. 10, praef. 6. The diction shows in the prefaces but few traces of the silver age, but more in the controversiae and suasoriae themselves.

7. Only one half of the ten books of controversiae, viz., b. 1. 2. 7. 9 and 10 (containing 35 themes), have come down to us, partly with gaps, especially when the utterances of Greek rhetoricians had been quoted in the original. A lost controversia is quoted by Quint. 9, 2, 42. In the 4th or 5th century of the Christian era a rather awkward (see Bursian p. vii) abridgment was made by an unknown author for the use of schools which, including all the 10 books of the controversiae, embraces also almost all the lost works (39 themes) and has preserved the complete prefaces to b. 1. 2. 3 and 4. The suasoriarum liber (the beginning incomplete, 7 themes) is in the MSS. placed before the controversiae, this being the gradation adopted in school-instruction. The MSS. of the unabridged original (the best are Bruxell. 9581, Antverp. 411, and Vatic. 3872, all s. X) are derived from one and the same source, which was, however, itself depraved and incomplete. Of the numerous MSS. in which the Excerpta are preserved, the best is the Montepessulanus 126 s. IX/X; see on it MBonnet, rev. de phil. 8, 78. KHoffmann, über eine Admonter Hs. (s. XII) der Excerpta des älteren Sen., Graz 1875. The writer of the abridgment had before him a copy of the complete work, which differed from the archetype transmitted to us by ABV. Cf. Bursian's, Kiessling's and HJMüller's prefaces. OGruppe (see n. 10), p. 1–24 (de codice archetypo). Its employment in the Gesta Romanorum, LFriedländer, Sittengesch. Roms 3^5, 423. Oesterley in his ed. of the Gesta, Berl. 1872, 714.

8. In the earliest editions the father's work is mixed up with the works of his son; it was not separated before the editions of NFaber (Par. 1587. 1598) and ASchott (Par. 1607. 1613); by JFGronovius (Leid. 1649) and cum notis varior. ex rec. Gronovii, Amsterd. 1672. Critical editions; rec. et emend. CBursian, Lips. 1857. Recogn. AKiessling, Lips. 1872. Ed. HJMüller, Prague 1887.

9. Criticism: HHöfig, de Sen. rhet. IV codd. MSS. Schottianis, Görlitz 1858. JVahlen, RhM. 13, 546. AKiessling, ib. 16, 50; Beitr. z. Krit. lat. Prosaiker (Basle and Geneva 1864) 32; neue Beitr. zur Kr. des Rh. S., Hamb. 1871. HJMüller, RhM. 21, 405; 24, 636. 25, 451; ZfGW. 22, 81. 715; JJ. 107, 525; JB. 1888 2, 175. CFWMüller, JJ. 93, 483; ZfGW. 22, 490. ClKonitzer, ib. 22, 966; quaest. in Sen. crit., Bresl. 1864; Beitr. z. Krit. des Rh. Sen., Bresl. 1866. RWachsmuth, quaest. in Sen., Posen 1867. ORebling, obss. crit. in S. patrem, Gött. 1868. MHaupt, op. 3, 412. 442. 598. CBursian, spicilegium crit. in Sen., Zür. 1869; lit. Centralbl. 1873, 1555; JB. 1880 2, 129. EThomas, schedae crit. in Sen. rhet., Berl. 1880; Herm. 21, 40. CGertz in philol.-hist. samfunds mindeskr. (Kopenh. 1879) 148; JJ. 137, 293. HTKarsten, spicil. crit. (Leid. 1881) 33; elocutio rhetorica Sen. rhet., Rotterd. 1881. AOtto, JJ. 131, 415. ROpitz, JJ. 137, 273; commentatt. Ribb. 35. SLinde, emendatt., Lund 1883, 39; Phil. 46, 760. 47, 173. ROpitz, Phil. 48, 67.

10. JKörber, über den Rhetor Seneca (p. 1–23. 58–66) und die röm. Rhetorik seiner Zeit (p. 23–58), Marb. 1864. OGruppe, quaestiones Annaeanae, Stettin 1873,

p. 24–47 (de declamandi ratione et de claris quibusdam declamatoribus).—MSANDER, quaestt. syntact. in Sen. rhet., Greifsw. 1872; d. Sprachgebrauch des Rhet. Sen., Waren 1877–80 II; JJ. 117, 787. AAHLHEIM, de Sen. rhet. usu dicendi, Giessen 1886.

270. Coincident with the latter part of the life of Seneca was probably the rhetorician P. Rutilius Lupus, the author of two extant books of schemata lexeos, being an abridged translation of one of Gorgias' works on the figures of speech, but which seem to have formed only part of the original work.

1. Though Seneca never mentions Rutilius Lupus, this does not prove that he did not know him, but rather may be explained from the design of his work; see contr. 1, praef. 4 *neque de his me interrogatis quos ipsi audistis, sed de his qui ad vos usque non pervenerunt.* That Rutilius wrote before Celsus, appears from QUINT. 9, 2, 102 *praeter illa quae Cicero inter lumina posuit sententiarum multa alia et Rutilius, Gorgian secutus, non illum Leontinum, sed alium sui temporis* (who at Athens taught young Cicero, ad fam. 16, 21, 6 of a. 710/44) *cuius quattuor libros in unum suum transtulit* (which shows that the division into two books is of later origin; HLAHRENS, ZfAW. 1843, 158 conjectures *usum* instead of *unum*), *et Celsus, videlicet Rutilio accedens, posuerunt schemata.* Cf. also ib. 101. 106 (*Rutilius sive Gorgias*). 9, 3, 36. 84. 89 (*qui proprie libros huic operi*—i.e. rhetorical figures—*dedicaverunt sicut Caecilius, Dionysius, Rutilius, Cornificius, Visellius*, see § 276, 11). 91–94. 99. Lupus was perhaps the son of the partisan of Pompey who bore the same name (PRE. 6, 588, 14). Cf. § 252, 8 l. 9.

2. The extant work fully illustrates the unnecessary and puerile multiplication of oratorical figures of the later rhetoric, in which Gorgias seems to have either been independent or to have availed himself of other sources unknown to us, his lists and terms possessing many peculiarities of their own (DZIALAS, l.l. 15). His small work is valuable chiefly for the numerous and well-translated examples (perhaps from Messalla's translations—§ 222, 3.—see IwMÜLLER, JB. 1879 2, 155), taken from Greek orators now mostly lost. In comparison with these there is a marked inferiority of style in the elucidations of the figures of rhetoric. That the Greek original was abridged in the process of translation appears from 2, 12 *quid intersit . . . cognoscere poteris . . . multo diligentius ex graeco Gorgiae libro, ubi pluribus uniuscuiusque ratio redditur.*

3. That the work in its present shape is incomplete, appears both from the oratorical figures (σχήματα διανοίας) which are quoted by QUINT. 9, 2, 103. 106 (cf. 9, 3, 89. 99) from Rutilius, but are not found in the present work, and from the title of the treatise in the MSS.: *P. Rutilii Lupi schemata dianoeas ex Graeco versa Gorgia*, the extant part relating only to the figures of speech (σχήματα λέξεως). The title may, therefore, originally have been: *schemata dianoeas et lexeos ex graecis Gorgiae versa* (RUHNKEN). Cf. DZIALAS, quaest. 14. 28. Under these circumstances the conjecture of DZIALAS, that only an epitome of Rutilius is extant (ib. p. 36), and that of DRAHEIM (p. 3. 9. 23), that Rutilius only treated of the schemata dianoeas quite incidentally (perhaps in the prooem) and that his work has come down to us almost unabridged, have little foundation. The author of the carmen de figuris

(§ 451, 1) knew only the present extent of the work, even with the gap between 1, 5 and 6: see DZIALAS 15. On the supplement furnished for this gap by CSCHÖPFER (Quedlinb. 1837) see FHAASE, de fragmentis Rutilio Lupo a Schöpfero suppositis, Bresl. 1856.

4. The manuscripts (especially two Laur. s. XIV and XV) are late (see DRAHEIM p. 19).—Editions e.g. in the Rhett. ant. of FPITHOEUS (Par. 1599), CLCAPPERONNIER (Strassb. 1756) and esp. in the Rhetores latini minores of CHALM (Lpz. 1863) p. 3–21. Rec. et annot. adi. DRUHNKEN, Leid. 1768 (Lps. 1831). In us. schol. explanavit FJACOB, Lüb. 1837.—GDZIALAS, quaestt. Rutilianae, Bresl. 1860; rhetorum antiq. de figuris doctrina (Bresl. 1869). CSCHMIDT, de Rutilio Lupo, Bresl. 1865. JDRAHEIM, schedae Rutilianae, Berl. 1874.—Criticism: JMÄHLY, Phil. 14, 764, JGFRÖHLICH, JJ. 89, 202, JSIMON, Phil. 27, 642, MHAUPT, op. 3, 367, MADVIG, adv. crit. 3, 273 and others.

ADDENDA.

(§ 1–214.)

§ 2, l. 7 (the use of Greek by the earliest Roman historians) EZarncke, commentatt. Ribbeck. 267. 4 (general works on Roman lit.) RBurn, Roman literature in relation to Roman art, Lond. 1888. MSchanz, Gesch. d. röm. Litt. I: Republik, Munich 1890 (in IwMüller's Handb. 8). **3,** 1 (Rom. poetry) ORibbeck, Gesch. d. röm. Dicht., vol. 2: Augusteisches Zeitalter, Stuttg. 1889.—LMüller, d. Entstehung der röm. Kunstdichtung, Hamb. 1889. APais, degli epicedii lat., riv. di fil. 18, 142. **5** (Fescenninae) WDeecke, die Falisker, Strasb. 1888, 111. **6,** 2 (satura, meaning) FMarx, Deutsche Lit.-Ztg. 1888, 662.—AFunck, satur, Kiel 1888. **9,** 1 (Atellanae) RMaffei, le favole Atell., Volterra 1886. 3 l. 8 (Dossennus) on the passage from Horace KMacke, JJ. 137, 703. **14,** 2 ad fin. (praetextae) KMeiser, historische Dramen der Römer, an address (Bayr. Akad.), Munich 1887. **19,** 3 (Epos) OHaube, die Epen des silb. Zeitalters II, Fraustadt 1887. **26,** 2 (Tityrus, cento) printed also by CSchenkl in the Corp. script. eccles. lat. Vindob. 16, 609 and cf. there generally on the centones p. 541. **27,** 4 (satire) ThBirt, zwei politische Satiren d. alten Rom., Marb. 1887, 6. IBruns, zur antiken Sat., Preuss. Jahrbb. 61, 509.—MHeitzmann, de substantivi ap. poett. satir. collocatione, Bonn 1887. FLeo, Varro und die Satire, Herm. 24, 67, FMarx, de sat. rom. origine, Rost. 1888; (on the spelling *satura* and *satira*) interpretationum hexas II, Rost. 1889, 13.

30, 2 (hymns) FWERoth, lat. Hymnen d. MAlters, Nachtr. zu Daniel u. a., Augsb. 1888. APasdera, le origini dei canti popolari lat. cristiani, riv. di fil. 17, 455. **32,** 5 (elegy) KHMüller, de similitudinibus et imaginibus ap. vett. poett. eleg., Gött. 1887. **35,** 2 (prose) HSchlottmann. ars dialogorum apud Gr. et Rom., Rost. 1889. **36,** 5 (speeches in the histt.) see addenda to § 196, 8. 6 (historians, descriptions) EZarncke, commentatt. Ribbeck. 274 sqq. **37,** 1 ad fin. (Annalists) BNiese, de ann. rom. obss. alterae, Marb. 1888. 6 AReckzey, gramm. u. rhetor. Stellung des Adjektivums bei d. Annalisten, Cato u. Sall., Berl. 1888. **39,** 3 (historical writers under the Empire) EKlebs, d. dynastische Element in der Gesch.schreibung d. Kaiserzeit, histor. Zeitschr. NF. 25, 213. 7 (Brunichius) HGelzer, Iul. Afric. 1, 229. **40,** 1 (Corp. inscrr. lat.) there have now appeared also vol. XI (1888), XII (1888), XIV (1887). Vol. III: supplem. fasc. 1, 1890. Vol. V.: supplem. Italica ed. HPais, Rome 1888. 3 GBdeRossi, inscr. christianae II, 1, Rome 1888. **41,** p. 57, l. 19 read 585/169. 7 (grammar) HNettleship, Grammar among the Romans in the first cent. A.D., Journ. of phil. 15, 189. **42,** 2 (metrical systems) GSchultz, Herm. 22, 278. FLeo, ib. 24, 180. 6 (glosses) GGötz, Scaliger's glossogr. Studd., Lpz. SBer. 1888, 219. 9 (glossaries) Corpus glossariorum lat. a GLoewe incohatum compos. rec. ed. GGoetz. II: glossae latinograecae et graecolatinae, acc. minora utriusque linguae glossaria; IV: gl. codd. Vat. 3321, SGall. 912, Leid. 67 F., Lps. 1888. 89. **43,** 5 (oratory) ATartara, i precursori di Cicerone, Pisa 1888.

46, 12 (Papal epistles) Cf. § 469, 5. **48,** 2 (jurisprudence) GKrüger, Gesch. d. Quellen u. Lit. des röm. Rechts, Lpz. 1888. PJörs, röm. Rechtswissensch. z. Zeit d. Republik: I bis auf die Catonen, Berl. 1888. **49,** 5 LMai, der Gegensatz der Sabinianer u. Proculianer etc., Heidelb. 1887. **51** (philosophy) PHartlich, exhortationum (προτρεπτικῶν) a Graecis Romanisque scriptarum historia, Lpz. Studd. 11, 209. **52** sqq. SGünther. Mathem. Naturwissensch. u. Erdkunde im Altertum in IwMüller's Handb. d. Alt. W. 5, 1, Nördl. 1888. **53,** 1 (Dessius Mundus) he is identified with the Mundus in Cic. Att. 15, 29, 1 (J. 710/44) DDetlefsen, Quellenschriftsteller des Plin., Glückst. 1881. **54,** 4 (Sabinus Tiro) Detlefsen l.l. reads more correctly Sabinius Tiro. On Sergius Paullus (or Plautus) Detlefsen l.l. 5. Cf. § 266, 9. 11. 5 (Oppius) Mommsen, Münzw. 289.

7 (husbandry) ABaranski, Gesch. d. Tierzucht u. Tiermedizin im Altertum, Vienna 1887. OKeller, Tiere des klassischen Altertums in kulturgeschichtl. Beziehung, Innsbr. 1887. **55,** 2 (oculists) a list of those mentioned on the seals in SReinach, rev. archaeol. 1888 1, 254. 6 ThPuschmann, Gesch. des medicin. Unterrichts von d. ältesten Zeiten bis zur Gegenwart, Lpz. 1889.

61, 2 (Saturnius) FRamorino, mem. dell' istit. Lombardo 16 (1886) 215. LValmaggi, riv. di filol. 14, 228. **64,** 3 (song of the Salii) carm. sal. rell. ed. CMZander, Lund 1888. **65,** 1 (acta Arvalium) additional discoveries: Röm. archäol. Mitteil. 2, 141; Berl. phil. Wschr. 1889, 42.—JWeisweiler, zur Erkl. der Arvalakten, JJ. 139, 37. **75,** 2 (fasti capitolini) ChrHülsen, on the date of their composition, Herm. 24, 185. CCichorius, de fastis coss., Lpz. Studd. 9, 171. JKaerst, Phil. 48, 338. 3 (acta triumphalia) a new fragment: ChrHülsen, BerlphilWschr. 1889, 394. **77,** 1 (augural books) PRegell, JJ. 135, 489. 137, 380. **78,** 1 (commentarii consulum) noticed in Bruns font.[5] 162.

83, 4 (earliest inscriptions, *manios med fhefhaked numasioi*) HDDarbishire, Journ. of phil. 16, 196. COZuretti, riv. di filol. 17, 63. 5 (Dvenos inscription) Elliot, Oxf. phil. soc. 1888/89, 20. RSConway, Americ. journ. of phil. 10, 445. 6 (Caso Cantovios) GEdon, acad. des inscr. 17. Aug. 1888. 8 (column. rostr.) EWölfflin, Münch. SBer. 1890, 293. **86,** 2 (Laws of the Twelve Tables, Greek influence) against this view GSteinhausen, de XII tabb. patria, Greifsw. 1887.—GGoetz, ad leg. XII tabb. adnotatt., Jena 1889. **88** (Cn. Flavius) LTriemel, JJ. 139, 209. **91,** 8 LKoprivšek, die Gegner des Hellenismus in Rom bis z. Z. Cic.'s, Rudolfswert 1887. **94,** 2 (Andronicus) ThZielinski, quaestt. com. 103.

96, 1 (Plautus) Varro LL. 7, 104 *Maccius* (so Flor.) *in Casina a fringuilla 'Quid fringutis'* (Cas. 2, 3, 49). **97,** 3 (Aulul.) rec. PLangen, Paderb. 1889. —LHavet, rev. de phil. 11, 142. 12, 106. 187. 4 (Capt.) uitgegeben door JSSpeijer, Leid. 1887. ed. by WMLindsay, Oxf. 1887.—JSSpeijer (on cod. Voss. Q. 30 s. XII, closely related to Ambros. E), Mnem. 16, 121. 9 (Bacch.) ATartara, de Pl. Bacch., Pisa 1889. AEAnspach (date of composition), JJ. 139, 355. 17 (Rud.) FSchöll, RhM. 43, 298. GLangrehr. Plautina. De Plauti Rudente, Friedl. i. M. 1888. 19 (Trin.) explained by JBrix and MNiemeyer, Lpz.[4] 1888.

98, 7 (diction, see also addenda to § 111, 6) Arlt, servare bei Ter. und Pl., Wohlau 1887. JDorsch, Assimilation in den Compositis bei Pl. u. Ter., Prager phil. Studien (1887), 1. FHansen, die Adjektiva auf -bilis im archaischen Lat., Phil. 47, 274. JBach, de pronomm. demonstr. ap. prisc. scriptores lat. I, Strassb. 1888. APrehn, quaestt. Pl. de pronom. indefinit., Strassb. 1887. EZimmermann, quaestt. Plaut. et Ter. I, de verbi posse formis dissolutis, Lörrach 1882. ABell, de locativo in prisca lat., Breslau 1889. Breytheer, de omissione verbi substantivi ap. Plaut., Lingen 1888. HNeumann, de futuro in priscorum Latt. vulgari et cotidiano sermone, Bresl. 1888. JMReinkens, d. acc. c. inf. bei Pl. u. Ter. I, Düsseldorf 1887. PHinze, de an particula ap. prisc. scriptt., Brandenb. 1887. HCElmer, the copulative conjunctions que et atque in the inscriptions of the Republ., in Ter. and in Cato, Baltimore 1887. JSchneider, de tempp. ap. prisc. scriptt. lat. usu quaestt., Glatz 1888. ERodenbusch, de tempp. usu Plaut., Strassb. 1888. AWirtzfeld, de consecutione tempp. Plaut. et Ter., Münster 1888. EPMorris (interrogative sentences in Pl. and Ter.), Americ. journ. of phil. 10, 397. EBecker, beiordnende und unterordnende Satzverbindung b. d. altlat. Schriftstellern, Metz 1888. WBock, subiecta rei cum actionis verbis coniungendi usus in prisca latinitate usque ad tempp. Cic., Lps. 1889. FGoldmann (see l. 5 from the end), d. poet. Personification II, Halle 1887. WvWyss, d. Sprüchwörter bei d. röm. Komikern, Zür. 1889. EWölfflin, d. Wortspiel im Lat., Münch. SBer. 1887 2, 187 8 (prosody) against WMeyer (l. 4 from the end) PLangen, Phil. 46, 401.

99, 2 (prologues) PTrautwein, de prologis Pl., Berl. 1890. 8 (Beccadelli as emendator of Pl.) GSuster, Phil. 48, 456. 9 (MSS.) Studemund's apographon of Ambros. has now appeared: Pl. fabb. reliq. Ambros. ed. WStudemund, Berl. 1890. 11 (Editions) by Ritschl and others: III, 4 Pseud. 1887. 5 Men. 1889. IV, 1 Cas. 1890. 13 (criticism) FLeo, vindic. Plaut., Rost. 1887. BBaier, in the Abhh. f. MHertz, Berl. 1888, 271.

100 (Ennius), 1 (birth-place) ECocchia, riv. di fil. 15, 489. 6 (portrait) discovered 1884 at Trèves (Ber. Arch. Ges. Sitz. 9. Dec. 1888). **101,** 3 (tradition) EZarncke, commentatt. Ribbeck. 274. ThBirt, zwei polit. Satt., Marb. 1887, 64

102, 1 (Alcumeo) JVahlen, Berl. ind. lect. 1887/88. **104,** 6 (criticism)

JVahlen, Berl. SBer. 1888, 31; ind. lect. Berl. 1888/89. JMähly, BlfbayrGW. 24, 469. LHavet, rev. de phil. 1890, 25. (chronology) FSchöll, RhM. 44, 158. (linguistic) AReichardt, de Enn. ann., JJ. 139, 81. 777. **105,** 2 (Pacuvius) LMüller, de Pacuvii fabulis, Berl. 1889. **106,** 3 (Caecilius Statius, Rastraria) on the title EWölfflin, RhM. 43, 308. **108,** (TERENCE), 1 (life) EAbel, die aus d. Altert. u. MAlter stammenden Terenzbiographien, Budapest 1887 (in Hungarian, abridgment: WschrfklPh. 1888, 1000). 8 (supposed bust of Terence) FMarx, Rostock ind. lect. 1888/89, 10. Gercke, Berl. Archäol. Ges. 1890. March. **109,** 2 (MSS.) on the Bembinus EHauler, Wien. Studd. 11, 268. 6 (prologues) PhFabia, les prologues de Ter., Par. 1889. 7 (edd.) best ind. verbb. in NELemaire's Ausg., Par. 1828, 2, 2. **110,** 3 (Heaut. tim.) HKriege, JJ. 141, 78. 4 (Phorm.) ed. by ASloman, Lond. 1887. 5 (Hec.) publ. par PThomas, Par. 1887. 6 (Ad.) par RAPessonneaux, Par. 1888.—FSchöll, RhM. 44, 280. FNencini, contaminazione in Ter. Ad., Pisa 1888. **111,** 6 (diction, see also addenda to § 98, 7) OBöttger, de DUM particulae usu ap. Ter. et in reliquiis tragg. et comm., Halle 1887. PGutjahr-Probst, d. Gebr. von UT bei Ter. u. Verwandtes, Lpz. 1888. ELalin, de DUM DONEC QUOAD particulis ap. Ter., Norcopiae 1888. AWeninger, de parataxi in Ter. fabb., Erl. 1888. **120** (CATO), 3 (Origines) WSoltau, WschrfklPh. 1888, 373. **122,** 1 (de agri cultura, original form) PWeise, quaestt. Caton. capp. V, Gött. 1886, and also RReitzenstein, WschrfklPh. 1888, 587. 4 (diction) Reckzey, see above on § 37, 6. **134** (Accius), 4 LMüller, de Accii fabulis, Berl. 1890. **141,** 7 (Titius) l. 2 Macr. 3, 13, 13 *Titius in suasione legis Fanniae.*

143, 4 (LUCILIUS, b. 26) ThBirt, zwei politische Satiren, Marb. 1887, 74. 89. 112. 11 (criticism) Bücheler, RhM. 43, 291. CMFrancken, Mnem. 16, 395. JMähly, BlfbayrGW. 24, 474. LHavet, rev. de phil. 1890, 86. 12 (in gen.) PRasi, satira Lucil., Padua 1888. **148,** 2 (Stilo) FMentz, de L. Aelio Stilone, diss. Ienens. 4, 1. **151,** 5 (NOVIUS, Pictores) Wölfflin, RhM. 43, 309. **153,** 5 ad fin. (Cannutius) is he also referred to Tac. dial. 21 (*ganuti* in the MSS.)? Cf. § 209, 9. **159,** 2 (L. Plotius Gallus) FMarx, interpretationum hexas II, Rost. 1889, 9. **160,** 2 (Tremellius Scrofa) RHeinze, commentt. Ribbeck. 433. **162** (Cornific. ad Herenn.), 7 FMarx, studia Corn., RhM. 43, 376. GThiele, de Cornif. et Cic. artibus rhetoricis, Greifsw. 1889. **166** (VARRO), 2 (Logistorici) l. 1. The Logistoricus Pius de pace was composed only after Sallust's death, therefore during Varro's last years. Gell. 17, 18. 4 (Antiqq. div. et hum.) ESchwarz, de M. Varr. ap. sanctos patres vestigiis cap. II, acc. Var. antiquitatt. rer. div. l. XVI, JJ. Suppl. 16, 405. 5 (literary history) CCichorius. Varro's libri de scaenicis originibus, commentatt. Ribbeck., Lps. 1888, 415. FLeo, Varro und die Satire, Herm. 24, 67. **167,** 3 (de ling. lat.) GAntonibon, riv. di fil. 17, 177; Phil. 48, 185 (cod. Mutin.). **168,** 2 (de re rust.) recogn. HKeil, Lps. 1889 (bibl. Teubn.).—RHeinze, commentt. Ribbeck. 431. **169,** 3 (diction) ORössner, de praeposs. AB DE EX usu Varron., Halle 1888. JSitzler, d. Casusgebr. bei Varro I (gen. and dat.), Tauberbischofsh. 1889. **170,** 2 (Nigid. Fig.) HWinther, WschrfklPh. 1889, 376. ASwoboda, Nig. Fig. fragmenta cum quaestt. Nigid., Vienna 1889. **172,** 2 (Atticus, annales) used in the restoration of the fasti Capitolini: CCichorius, de fast. consul. antiq., Lpz. Stud. 9, 249. 7 (Sulpicius Blitho) cf. § 208, 2. **174,** 4 (Sulpicius Rufus) on his latinity JHSchmalz, ZfGW. 35, 90. 5, l. 7 (T. Caesius) cf. § 199, 6.

175 (CICERO), 3 (portrait) discovered a. 1884, in the mosaic representing the Muses, at Trèves (Arch. Ges. Berlin, Sitz. 9. Dec. 1888). **177,** 3 (diction) l. 11 ChrJänicke, d. Verbindung etc. II, Vienna 1887. HLattmann, de coincidentia ap. Cic., Gött. 1888. JLindvall, de coniunctivo fut. periphr. ap. Cic., Lund 1888. AMarchi HUMANITAS, HUMANUS etc. nel Cic., Milano 1889; ORiemann, UNUS avec le *génit.* chez Cic., rev. de phil. 12, 176. 4 (tradition) HKarbaum, de origine exemplorum Ciceronian. ap. grammaticos lat., Werniger. 1889. **177a,** 1 (Aratea) GSieg, de Cicerone, Germanico, Avieno Arati interprett., Halle 1886. JMaybaum, de Cic. et Germanico Arati interprett., Rost. 1889. GKauffmann, de Hygini memoria scholiis in Ciceronem Harleianis servata; acc. scholia apparatu critico et notis instructa, Bresl. 1888 (Bresl. phil. Abh. 3, 4). 3 (de invent.). WHaellingk, Ciceronem libros de inv. inscripsisse rhetoricos, Commentatt. in hon. Studemundi, Strassb. 1889, 337. 7 (de invent., MSS.) WFriedrich, varietas cod. Voss. 70 ad Cic. de inv., Mühlhausen 1889. EStröbel, Phil. 47, 170. Baudouin, rev. de phil. 12, 19. **178,** 1 (jests) ChrHerwig, d. Wortspiel in Cic. Reden,

Attendorn 1889. 6 (selected speeches) 6. Von Nohl's ed. vol. 4 (Mur. Sull. Arch.) 1889. vol. 5 (Mil. Lig. Deiot.) 1888. Oratt. sel. ex edit. CFWMuelleri expr., Lps. 1889 II. 6 (criticism relating to the speeches) ThStangl, Tulliana et Mario-Victoriniana, Munich. 1888, 1–11. **179,** 11 (Verr.) de sign.; de supplic. expl. by KHachtmann, Gotha 1888. 89.—ACClark. excerpts from the Verr. in Harl. 2682, journ. of phil. 18, 69. 19 (pRab. perd. reo) JSchmidt, ZföG. 39, 211. ASchneider, d. Process. d. C. Rab., Zür. 1889. 20–23 (in Catil.) CJohn, Phil. 46, 651. KFüsslein, Cic. erste R. gegen Catil., Merseb. 1889. AChambalu, d. Verh. d. 4. catil. Rede zu der wirklich gehaltenen Rede, Neuwied 1888. 24 (pMur.) AGrumme, Cic. pMur. or. dispositio, Gera 1887. 28 (cum senatui grat. egit) WStock, de recens. Cic. or. c. sen. gr. eg., in the Genethl. Gotting. 1888, 106. 30 (de domo) FSchöll, Interpolatt. etc. in Cic. de domo, RhM. 43, 419. ThMatthias, JJ. 139, 274. LSchaum, de consecratione domus Cic., Mayence 1889. 34 (pCael.) ad optt. codd. recogn. JCVollgraff, Leiden 1887. 37 (in Pis.) EStröbel, BlfbayrG. 25, 381. 38 (pPlancio) on the date AEKörner, de epp. Cic. post red., Lpz. 1885, 49. 40 (pMil.) AThChrist, ZföG. 34, 577. FItzinger, die Metaphern in Cic. pMil., Budweis 1888. 89 II. 41 (pMarc.) SSchmid, die Echtheit der Rede pMarc., Zürich 1888. 42 (pLig.) expl. by JStrenge, Gotha 1888. 43 (pDeiot., MSS.) CFWMüller, JJ. 137, 137. HNohl, ib. 137, 398.

182 (rhetorical works) GThiele, see addenda to § 162, 7. 2 (tradition) RSabbadini, riv. di fil. 16, 97. (de or.) b. I by RStölzle, Gotha 1887. OHarnecker, adnott. ad Cic. de or. l. II, Friedeb. Nm. 1888. 6 (top., MSS., crit.) WFriedrich, JJ. 139, 281. 7 (de opt. gen. orat.) rec. EHedicke, Sorau 1889 (Progr.).

183, 5 (philos. works, tradition) on Vind. 198 PSchwenke, BerlphWschr. 1889, 618. 6 CGiambelli, fonti delle opere filosof. di Cic., Riv. di fil. 17, 116. 222. WKahl, Demokrit in Cic.'s philos. Schrr., Diedenhofen 1889. **184,** 1 (de rep.) CWachsmuth, Lpz. Studd. 11, 197. 5 (Hortensius) HDiels, zu Aristoteles' Protrept. u. Cic.'s Hort., Arch. f. Gesch. d. Philos. 1, 477. PHartlich (above, § 51) 292. HUsener on Dion. Halic. de imitatione, Bonn 1889, 114. 6 (de fin.) PLangen, ad Cic. de fin. adnott., Münst. 1888. 1888/89 II. 8 (Tusc.) ASpengel, die Personenzeichen in den Hss. der Tusc., Phil. 48, 367. EStröbel (on Vatic. 3246 s. IX), Phil. 49, 49. 10 (nat. deor.) PWendland, Arch. f. Philos. 1, 200. LReinhardt, d. Quellen v. Cic. n. d., Bresl. phil. Abhh. 3, 2 1888. PSchwenke, appar. crit., Classical Review Vol. 4. nos. 9 and 10 (1890). 11 and 14 (Cato and Lael.) rec. RNovak, Prague 1889. Cato expl. by HAnz, Gotha 1889.—MSS. of Cato: SGdeVries, exercitatt. palaeogr., Leid. 1890. CHofstede de Groot, Herm. 25, 293. 16 (off.) commentati da RSabbadini, Turin 1888.—PKlohe, de Cic. de off. fontibus, Greifsw. 1889. **186,** 2 (history, ὑπόμνημα) CBuresch, commentt. Ribbeck. 217. 7 (grammar) HSchlag, Cic. als Verfasser einer grammatischen Schrift, Siegen 1888. EZarncke, commentt. in honor. Studemundi, Strassb. 1889, 195.—JWBeck, de synonyma Cic., in the periodical: Coniunctis viribus 1 (1889), 158; BerlphWschr. 1890, 297. GGoetz, ib. 1890, 195.

187, 2 (letters, chronol.) WSternkopff, Cic.'s Korrespondenz aus J. 68–60, Elberfeld 1889. 4 (tradition) LGurlitt, Nonius u. die Cic.-Briefe, Steglitz 1888 (especially on the letters ad Caesarem). 7 (crit.) LHolzapfel, Phil. 46, 644. FMaixner, ZföG. 40, 386. **188,** 1, 2 (ad fam.) on b. 5 genus severum, grave etc. epistularum) and b. 6 (letters of condolence and congratulation) LGurlitt, JJ. 137, 863. 3 (ad Q. fr.), 2: ad Q. fr. epistula prima, avec un comment. par FAntoine, Par. 1888. 4 (ad M. Brut.) OESchmidt, JJ. 141, 109; Phil. 49, 38. **189,** 1 (poems) Lindner, Cic. als Dichter, Prague 1888. **191,** 5 (notae Tiron.) WSchmitz, d. tironischen Noten des Bern. 611, Stenographenzeitung 1888 no. 23; d. tiron. Noten in den Hss. der Kölner Dombibliothek, NArchfädGesch. 11, 109. FRuess, d. tironischen Endungen, Munich 1889.

195, 9 (Caesar, diction) PHellwig, d. Pleonasmus b. C., Berl. 1889. RMenge, d. Relativum b. Caes., Halle 1889; d. Bezeichn. des reciproken Verhältnisses bei C., JJ. 139, 265. **196,** 2 (MSS.) FRamorino, cod. Ricc. (di Caes.) collazionato, riv. di fil. 18, 253. 8 (bell. gall.) HKloevekorn, d. Kämpfe Caes.'s gegen die Helvetier, Lpz. 1889. PhFabia, de oratt. in Caes. b. g., Paris 1889. RRichter, krit. Bem. zu Caes. b. g. b. 7, Stargard 1889. JLange (b. g. 5, 8 sqq.), JJ. 139, 187. 11 (b. civ.) ed. WThPaul, Prague 1889. JJCornelissen (b. civ. and alex., Mnem. 17, 44. (reports of legates) WEhrenfried, qua ratione Caesar legatorum relationes adhibuerit, Würzb. 1888. **197,** 1 (continuator of Caesar) OHirschfeld (on the preface to b. g. VIII), Herm. 24, 101.—EFourer, ephemerides Caesarianae rerum ab ineunte bello afr. usque ad extr. bell. hisp. gestarum, Bonn 1889. 6 (bell. alex.) expl. by RSchneider, Berlin 1888. 7 GLandgraf, Unterss. zu Caes. u. s. Fortsetzern, insbes. über Autorschaft u. Kompos. des b. alex. u. afr., Erl. 1888 (compare AKöhler, BlfbayrGW. 25, 516. RSchneider, ZfGW. 43, Jahresb. 112). GLandgraf, bell. Alex. 48-64 recently published, Erl. 1890. C. Asinii Polionis (!) bellum africum rec. emend. adn. EWölfflin et AMiodonski, Lps. 1889. EWölfflin, Münch. SBer. 1889, 319; ArchfLexikogr. 6, 85.

198, 5 (NEPOS, de vir ill.) abbot Wibald of Stablo (s. XII) in Jaffé's bibl. rer. Germ. 1, 277 *lege Tranquillum, lege Cornelium Nepotem et alios quosdam gentiles de viris illustribus: tanta esse scripta intelleges quae vix a quoquam studiosissimo legi possint*, derived his knowledge of the viri illustres of Nepos solely from Hieronymus, notwithstanding MManitius, Philol. 47, 567. 9 (crit.) GGemss, z. Reform der Textkritik d. Corn. N., Berl. 1888; a new class of MSS. of Corn. Nep., BerlWschrfklPh. 1889, 801. 11 (sources) ELippelt, quaestt. biograph., Bonn 1889, 37-43. GHähnel, d. Quellen d. Nepos im Hann., Jena 1888. 12 (diction) EKöhler, Sprachgebr. d. Nep. in d. Kasussyntax, Gotha 1888. **200,** 2 (Dirae) MRothstein, de diris et Lydia, Herm. 23, 508. GEskuche, de Val. Catone deque diris et Lydia, Marb. 1889. **203,** 2 (LUCRETIUS, models) HPullig, Ennio quid debuerit Lucretius I, Halle 1888. 4 (authorities and system) HSchütte, Theorie der Sinnesempfindd. bei Lucr., Danz. 1888. MLongo, Lucrezio, sagg. critico, Sansevero 1887. Lohmann, Analyse des lucr. Ged. u. philos. Gehalt I, Helmstedt 1889. OWeissenfels, Lucrez u. Epikur, Analyse etc., Lausitz. Magazin 65, 1.—FMarx, d. Venus des Lucrez, Bonner Studien für RKekulé, Bonn 1890, 115. 5 (diction) JWoltjer, Mnemos. 17, 64 (Personalpronomina bei Lucr.). 10 (crit.) ThTohte, Lucr. 1, 483-598, Wilhelmshaven 1889. **205,** 2 (SALLUST, Cat.) rec. GLinker, ed. 2 cur. PhKlimscha, Vienna 1888; avec un commentaire etc. par FAntoine et RLallier, Par. 1888.—CThiaucourt, étude sur la conjuration de Catil. de Sall., Par. 1887. **206,** 7 (Sall. and Thuk.) RSchild, quibus in rebus Sall. Thucydidem respexerit, Nordhausen 1888. 9 (diction) GMüller, Phraseologie des Sall. I, Köthen 1888. EBökman, de particulis copul. ET QUE ATQUE ap. S., Upsala 1887. Reckzey, see addendum to § 37, 6. Wilckens, z. Synt. des S., Lahr 1888. JSorn, cf. § 348, 7. FAntoine, sur l'emploi de quelques particules (SED, CETERUM, EQUIDEM, NE) dans S., Ann. de Bord. 1889, 51. AStitz, das Gerundium bei S., Krems 1889. **209,** 2 (Cornificius) ACima, de Q. Cornificio e numero oratorum eximendo, Riv. di filol. 16, 301. 12 (Ann. Cimber) on the *Tau gallicum*: GKaibel, RhM. 44, 316. **212,** 4 (Publilius, Sentenzen aus s. Mimen gesammelt) Date? Conjecture by ORossbach. de Sen. libr. recens. (Bresl. 1888) 86. **213,** 1 (Ticidas) on Perilla = Metella see FLeo in Kiessl.-Wilam. phil. Unterss. 2, 22. 4 (Quintil. Varus Cremon.) CPascal, de Q. V. Cr. poeta, riv. di filol. 17, 145. Adherents of the Epicurean Philodemos: AKörte, RhM. 45, 174.

214 (CATULLUS), 6 MBüdinger, Catull u. d. Patriziat, Wien. SBer. 1890. ABDrachmann, Catuls digtning etc., Copenh. 1887. 9 (diction) StBednarski, de infinitivo ap. Cat., Tarnow 1886. AReeck, Beitr. z. Synt. des C., Bromb. 1889. 10 (MSS.) PSchulze, der cod. M. (Ven. 107), Herm. 23, 567. Complete photographic reproduction of the cod. Germ. LClédat, collection des reproductions en photolithographie I, avec une étude d'EChatelain, Par. 1890.—KWeyman (survival of Catullus), Phil. 48, 760. 11 REllis, a commentary on Cat., 2 ed., Oxf. 1889. rec. JPostgate, Lond. 1889. 12 (translations) by ThHeyse, 2. ed., Berl. 1889. 14 (critical commentary) AFürst, de Cat. c. LXII, Melk 1887. REllis, Journ. of phil. 17, 128. ATeuber (on Cat. 36), JJ. 137, 777. JVahlen (poem 66), Berl. SBer. 1888, 1361. 1889, 47. JAPostgate, Journ. of phil. 17, 226. 18, 145. FHermes, Beitr. etc. II, Frankf. on/O. 1889. WMeyer, Munich. SBer. 1889 2, 245. ThBirt, de Cat. c. 68, Marb. 1889. WHörschelmann, de Cat. c. 68, Dorp. 1889. HWeber, quaestt. Catull., Gotha 1890.